Regulation of Lawyers: Problems of Law and Ethics

Regulation of Lawyers:
Problems of Law and Ethics

Third Edition

Stephen Gillers

Professor of Law
New York University School of Law

Little, Brown and Company
Boston   Toronto   London

Library of Congress Catalog Card No. 91-76699
ISBN 0-316-31428-5

Third Edition

Second Printing

MV-NY

Published simultaneously in Canada
by Little, Brown & Company (Canada) Limited

Printed in the United States of America

In loving dedication to
Gillian Gillers
and
Heather Gillers

les enfants du paradis

Summary of Contents

Part Four

AVOIDING AND REDRESSING
PROFESSIONAL FAILURE   533

Part Five

FIRST AMENDMENT RIGHTS OF LAWYERS   745

Part Six

ISSUES IN THE WORK LIVES OF LAWYERS   841

Contents

Chapter III   Protecting the Client-Lawyer Relationship Against Outside Interference   **71**

Part Six

ISSUES IN THE WORK LIVES OF LAWYERS   841

Chapter XVII   The Work Lives of Lawyers   843

The Three Perspectives:
A Preface to Students

Titles like "Professional Responsibility" and "Legal Ethics" do not fully describe the subject matter of this book. It is a book about the legal profession and about the practice of law. The book includes laws governing the practice of law, rules contained in ethical codes, court rules, and constitutions and, to a lesser extent, behavior that springs from custom and experience. These laws, ethical rules, and customs can be discussed from three perspectives.

Perhaps most immediate for those about to enter on a legal career are the rules that constrain working lawyers. In such areas as competence, fees, advertising and solicitation, confidentiality, conflicts of interest, negotiation, and the attorney-client relationship: what may you do, how may you behave, with confidence that your conduct will not land you before a disciplinary committee or in a civil lawsuit and, sometimes more important, will not damage your reputation among your peers?

The second perspective of the book is the relationship between the profession and society. The rules lawyers impose on themselves or that are imposed on them, taken together, define the nature and operation of the entire profession, and therefore, to an extent, the behavior of our legal institutions and the quality of our social justice.

For example, a rule that allows lawyers to advertise certain kinds of information will influence the conduct of individual members of the bar. But it may also affect whether, and how, large categories of people use lawyers and the size of legal fees. Similarly, a rule that prohibits or requires a lawyer to reveal certain kinds of information about a client will control the lawyer's individual conduct, but it may also affect which client populations use lawyers and how. In short, nearly every rule, whatever its source, has social and political consequences beyond any single representation, although there is often disagreement both over what these consequences will be and whether they should be avoided or encouraged.

About to go off into law practice, you may be more interested in such questions as: "How do I behave?" and "How can I stay out of trouble?"

than in asking "What are the consequences to society and justice if one or another version of a particular ethical rule is applied to America's more than 800,000 lawyers?" Still, the last question is important and, if not as immediate, will surely arise in the course of your professional life. Both kinds of questions, but more so the second, engender different, and sometimes vehement, responses. Why? In part because to answer them we must call upon political and moral values more fundamental than the "ethics" that inform various codes; and, of course, political and moral values of different people differ substantially, sometimes diametrically.

Furthermore, in addressing these questions, we are likely to make a threshold determination, conscious or not, of the extent to which we want the answers to further our self-interest. However we couch our responses, in truth whose best interests do we mean to protect? Those of society generally? The legal profession's? The interests of lawyers in practices like the one we have or expect to have? Those of the particular client population we serve? Our firm's? Our own? Law school and law practice, it is sometimes said, encourage more rather than less self-interestedness in addressing the kinds of questions that will be raised here. In transition as you are, your answers to many of the questions raised in this book will likely vary from what they would have been before you entered law school and may change again when you become a practicing lawyer.

At the outset I wrote that rules governing the practice of law can be discussed from three perspectives, and I have so far listed two. The third is the effect of lawyers' work on the people who do the work, that is, the effect of role on self. For example, a rule that requires silence though it means that another will suffer injustice may cause great discomfort to those who must obey it. As men and women, we consider it laudable to speak up to prevent injustice to others. As lawyers, we may be forbidden to do so. Can we reconcile these two positions, not intellectually or theoretically but personally, within ourselves? A similar point can be made with regard to the rule that requires lawyers zealously to pursue the lawful goals of their clients, even if these goals (or the legal strategies to achieve them) offend the lawyer's values.

Conflict between work life and private life also arises in another way. It concerns not the particular deeds that a lawyer may be called on to perform for a client and that he or she might find morally repugnant if performed outside the professional role, but the way that professional service (and the culture of law practice) affect other aspects of a lawyer's life. Most obvious is the clash between job and family. For example, does the profession allow people to reach its higher rungs and also be conscientious and responsible parents? A second issue is the possible discrepancy between the qualities of personality that law office culture tends to reward and the ones encouraged elsewhere. Do you have to learn behavior to survive in professional environments that will make you downright unpleasant in social and familial ones — unless you also learn to "leave it at the office"? (One thinks of the common criticism from a lawyer's lay relatives: "Oh, stop talking like a lawyer!").

When the first edition of this book appeared seven years ago, little had been written about these conflicts. Now there is much more, though not perhaps as much as appears about Rule 10b-5, Rule 11, or the rule against hearsay. But they are important matters, and we shall speak of them again.

Stephen Gillers

January 1992

Acknowledgments

This third edition of Regulation of Lawyers: Problems of Law and Ethics is the fortunate beneficiary of conscientious research assistance from Mary E. McDonald, NYU Law School Class of 1993. As with the first and second editions of the book, I also gratefully acknowledge invaluable help from Shirley Gray, who provided essential support in the organization and preparation of the manuscript and in shepherding the entire project through to conclusion.

Laura Gilbert, NYU Law School Class of 1990, and Barbara Quackenbos, NYU Law School Class of 1988, made important contributions to the second edition of this book, and these live on in the third. Students whose work advanced the first edition of this book are Patricia C. Hayashi, NYU Law School Class of 1983; Virginia L. Richards, NYU Law School Class of 1986; and Susan A. Waxenberg, NYU Law School Class of 1982. I continue to be grateful to each of them.

I thank Professor Vanessa H. Merton of the Pace University School of Law for expanding her bibliography of sources in legal ethics. Professor Merton's bibliography is a valuable resource that I am pleased to include as an appendix.

My debt to members of the professional staff of the NYU Law School Library continues. Exceptionally useful assistance was repeatedly available from Carol Alpert, Ronald Brown, Elizabeth Evans, Gretchen Feltes, Leslie Rich, and Jay Shuman.

Barbara Gillers provided critical aid and analysis at every stage of each edition. David A. Kaplan has been a reliable contributor of information about the profession since this enterprise began nearly a decade ago.

I wish to acknowledge the invaluable work of my colleague Norman Dorsen on the first two editions of this casebook. Other demands on his time have prevented Professor Dorsen from working on this edition. Nevertheless, in countless ways it benefits from his contributions to its predecessors.

I would like to thank the following for permission to reprint the identified material:

American Bar Association, Model Rules 3.1, 4.2, and 4.3 and Formal Opinions 87-353 and 87-355; Model Rules of Professional Conduct, copyright © the American Bar Association. All rights reserved. Reprinted by permission.

Association of the Bar of the City of New York, Ethics Opinion 80-23. Republished by permission of the Committee on Professional and Judicial Ethics of the Association of the Bar of the City of New York and Oceana Publications, Inc.

Association of the Bar of the City of New York, Report of Sixth Annual Retreat, Presentations by H. Richard Uviller and Anthony Amsterdam. Reprinted by permission of the Council on Criminal Justice of the Association of the Bar of the City of New York.

Ball, Milner S., Wrong Experiment, Wrong Result: An Appreciatively Critical Response to Schwartz, 1983 Am. B. Found. Res. J. 565, 569-571. Reprinted by permission.

Belkin, Lisa, Bare-Knuckles Litigation Jars Many in Dallas, The New York Times, May 13, 1988. Copyright © 1988 by The New York Times Company. Reprinted by permission.

Cox, Meg, Friendlier Endings: Some Divorcing Couples Find Mediation Cheaper and More Humane Than Battles in Courtroom, The Wall Street Journal, Nov. 15, 1983, p.60. Reprinted by permission of The Wall Street Journal, copyright © 1983 Dow Jones & Company, Inc. All Rights Reserved Worldwide.

Frankel, Marvin E., Partisan Justice 11-19 (Hill & Wang 1980). Excerpt adapted from Partisan Justice by Marvin E. Frankel. Copyright © 1978, 1980 by Marvin E. Frankel. Reprinted by permission of Hill & Wang, a division of Farrar, Straus & Giroux, Inc.

Johnson, Kirk, Slashed Model Cross-Examined in Attack Trial, The New York Times, Mar. 27, 1987. Copyright © 1987 by The New York Times Company. Reprinted by permission.

Kolata, Gina, Being Thorough Can Be Costly — To the Doctor, The New York Times, Mar. 20, 1986. Copyright © 1986 by The New York Times Company. Reprinted by permission.

Kornstein, Daniel J., A Tragic Fire — A Great Cross-Examination, New York Law Journal, Mar. 28, 1986, p.2. Reprinted by permission.

Luban, David, Lawyers and Justice: An Ethical Study 282-287 (Princeton University Press, 1988). Reprinted by permission.

Margolick, David, At the Bar, The New York Times, Jan. 22, 1988. Copyright © 1988 by The New York Times Company. Reprinted by permission.

Mintz, Morton, At Any Cost: Corporate Greed, Women and the Dalkon Shield. Copyright © 1985 by Morton Mintz. Reprinted by permission of Pantheon Books, a division of Random House, Inc.

Mitchell, John B., Reasonable Doubts Are Where You Find Them: A Response to Professor Subin's Position on the Criminal Lawyer's "Different Mission," 1 Geo. J. Legal Ethics 339 (1987). Reprinted by permission.

New York State Bar Association, Committee on Professional Ethics, Ethics Opinion 479. Reprinted by permission.

Note, Legal Ethics and the Destruction of Evidence, 88 Yale L.J. 1665 (1979). Reprinted by permission of The Yale Law Journal.

Post, Robert C., On the Popular Image of the Lawyer: Reflections in a Dark Glass, 75 Calif. L. Rev. 379, 379-380, 387-389 (1987). Reprinted by permission.

Rifkind, Simon H., The Lawyer's Role and Responsibility in Modern Society, 30 The Record of the Assoc. of the Bar of the City of N.Y. 534 (1975). Copyright © 1975 by Simon H. Rifkind.

Ruben, Emily and Ruben, Ann, Letter to the Editor, New York Law Journal, Apr. 14, 1986, p.2. Reprinted by permission.

Rubin, Alvin B., A Causerie on Lawyers' Ethics in Negotiation, 35 La. L. Rev. 577 (1975). Copyright © 1975 by Louisiana Law Review. Reprinted by permission.

Schwartz, Murray L., The Zeal of the Civil Advocate, 1983 Am. B. Found. Res. J. 543, 553-554. Reprinted by permission.

Spiegel, Mark, Lawyering and Client Decisionmaking: Informed Consent and the Legal Profession, 128 U. Pa. L. Rev. 41, 67-68 (1979).

State Bar of Michigan Professional and Judicial Ethics Committee, Ethics Opinion CI-1164.

Subin, Harry I., Is This Lie Necessary? Further Reflections on the Right to Present a False Defense, 1 Geo. J. Legal Ethics 689, 690-691 (1988). Reprinted by permission.

Waldman, Peter, Pre-Paid Legal Plans Offer Consultations, Follow-up Calls and Referrals at Low Cost, The Wall Street Journal, Feb. 25, 1986. Reprinted by permission of The Wall Street Journal, copyright © 1986 Dow Jones & Company, Inc. All Rights Reserved Worldwide.

White, James J., Machiavelli and the Bar: Ethical Limitations on Lying in Negotiation, 1980 Am. B. Found. Res. J. 926. Reprinted by permission.

Finally, I am grateful to the Filomen D'Agostino and Max E. Greenberg Research Fund of New York University Law School for its financial assistance.

A Word About Case Editing

No case is reprinted unedited. Omissions are identified with ellipses or the presence of bracketed material except that no ellipsis is used when authority alone is deleted. Cases and other authorities are freely omitted, including those following brief quotes, for considerations of space and ease of reading. However, as a rule case citations are retained if the court's discussion of the case bears on its legal analysis or if the case is substantially addressed elsewhere in the book.

Regulation of Lawyers:
Problems of Law and Ethics

I

Where Do "Ethics" Rules Come From?

As was emphasized in the Preface, "legal ethics" is something of a misnomer for the subject of this book and the courses in which it is likely to be used. The term is fine as a shorthand — it's used here often — but the subject is considerably broader (some would say "narrower") than that simple label implies. Rules that govern how members of the legal profession may or must behave — and that includes judges as well as lawyers — come from many sources. Here I introduce some of the traditional sources and also a new source of indefinite scope: the idea(l) of professionalism.

WHO MAKES THE RULES?

The Constitution intrudes here as elsewhere. Most obvious will be the First and Sixth Amendments. The First Amendment appears in the material on lawyer advertising and solicitation (Chapter 16), lay participation in legal delivery systems (Chapter 14), and the rights of lawyers to criticize judges or to comment on pending cases (Chapter 15). The Sixth Amendment guarantee of the effective assistance of counsel in criminal cases will appear in Chapter 13, where our concern is the quality of legal services, and in Chapter 8, which deals with criminal litigation. Also prominent of late has been the Privileges and Immunities Clause (Article 4, §2), which several times has been cited to invalidate laws impeding the ability of lawyers from one state to practice in another (see Chapter 12). Due process rights restrict the conduct of prosecutors.

1

More prevalent sources of rules regulating lawyers are statutes (including the antitrust laws), procedural and evidentiary (for example, privilege) rules, the common law, court rules, and state constitutions. State high courts often rely on their own constitutions to assume responsibility for promulgating rules governing admission to practice and the conduct of attorneys. Sometimes they cite particular language in their state's constitution, sometimes they rely on separation of powers principles, and sometimes they speak about an "inherent power" to regulate the profession.

The so-called inherent powers doctrine and specific or general constitutional language have been cited not only to support judicial rulemaking but also to invalidate direct legislative efforts to regulate the admission or conduct of lawyers, even when these efforts do not seek to preempt judicial ones. The theory behind such "negative" inherent powers is that the power to regulate the bar belongs to the courts almost exclusively.* One effect of the negative inherent powers doctrine is to inhibit legislative (that is, popular) attempts directly to control the conduct of lawyers. When coupled with judicial deference to professional self-regulation, the negative inherent powers doctrine may result in precious little government oversight. Sometimes, however, courts do uphold the regulatory efforts of legislators while taking pains to stress their own supremacy.

Unauthorized practice of law (Chapter 12) is a prime area in which to find the clash between judges and lawmakers. Lawmakers may attempt to authorize persons who are not admitted to practice to perform a particular "legal" service, an effort that has economic consequences for lawyers and consumers. Do you see why? If the effort is challenged, a court may invalidate it on the ground that the specified service constitutes "the practice of law" (a broad and fluid term), for which the courts insist they alone may license practitioners.

Codes of ethics, under various names, are a (perhaps *the*) central source of rules governing the behavior of lawyers. Without doubt, the

---

*For examples of the application of the inherent powers doctrine, see State ex rel. Fiedler v. Wisconsin Senate, 155 Wis. 2d 94, 454 N.W.2d 770, 774 (1990), which struck down legislation that imposed a continuing legal education requirement on attorneys who wished to be appointed as guardians ad litem. The court held that "once an attorney had been determined to have met the legislative and judicial threshold requirements and is admitted to practice law, he or she is subject to the judiciary's inherent and exclusive authority to regulate the practice of law." See also Matter of Public Law No. 154-1990, — Ind. — , 561 N.E.2d 791, 793 (1990), where the court reviewed legislation, common in American jurisdictions, that required lawyers to put escrowed funds in interest-bearing accounts, with the interest to be used to finance legal services for the indigent. Lawyers who deposited money in these accounts were exempted from discipline for doing so. The court held that the exemption "clearly and literally attempt[s] to exercise by limitation the attorney disciplinary function of the judicial department" and was unconstitutional. But see Aponte v. Raychuk, 160 A.D.2d 636, 559 N.Y.S.2d 255, 256 (1st Dept. 1990), finding "no inconsistency between" the court's authority to regulate attorneys and requirement by city government that lawyer ads comply with local prohibitions against deceptive advertising.

dominant force in articulating such codes has been the American Bar Association. Some may question the wisdom of allowing those who will be regulated to write the regulations. As we shall see, this skepticism has occasionally proved justified. Proponents of the practice argue that self-regulation is the hallmark of a profession. (For the profession's reaffirmation of this position, see the Preamble to the Rules of Professional Conduct.) This loops us into a debate about professionalism: If lawyers are losing professional status because of "creeping commercialism," as some argue, do they also lose the right of self-regulation, assuming they should have it in the first place? Asked another way: What is it about law that makes it a "profession" and thereby justifies allowing lawyers to have so significant a role in their own regulation? Answers to these questions turn on our definition of a profession, a matter to which we shall shortly turn.

The ABA is a private organization with no power to impose its rules on anyone. That is why the Code of Professional Responsibility and the Rules of Professional Conduct are both preceded by the word "Model." Before a rule in either document can be more than a model — that is, before it can actually govern a lawyer's behavior — some institution of government must adopt it. The inherent powers doctrine has left that authority largely to the courts, to the exclusion of executive or legislative government. But courts have traditionally deferred to the ABA's decisions on the subject, often as modified by their own state's bar associations. Until recently, serious judicial scrutiny has been relatively rare. To a modest extent that is changing. The latest ABA promulgation, the Model Rules, has enjoyed (if that's the word) substantial professional and even popular debate. Alerted, perhaps, by this debate, several courts have rejected a "rubber stamp" role and insisted on some oversight before adopting the new Rules for their states, though the extent of that oversight has varied appreciably. In any event, no one should confuse this trend with judicial activism. The bar is still very much a self-governing institution and is likely to remain so indefinitely.

The ABA's first effort at codifying ethical rules saw the adoption of the 1908 Canons of Professional Ethics, which remained in effect — if of diminishing relevance — for 62 years. Effective in 1970, the ABA (and soon thereafter all states, in some form) adopted the Code of Professional Responsibility. Testament to the poverty of this document came less than seven years later when, its several weaknesses apparent, the ABA inaugurated a new commission to prepare a new set of rules. That commission soon became known as the Kutak Commission, after Robert J. Kutak, an energetic and visionary lawyer from Omaha, Nebraska, who chaired the commission until his death in early 1983. Meanwhile, perhaps because so many lawyers were implicated in Watergate and because the absolute number of practicing lawyers was rising so rapidly, professional and popular interest in legal ethics increased dramatically. Consequently, the Kutak Commission's work prompted extensive discussion inside and outside bar associations. After much debate and several drafts, the ABA House of Delegates adopted the Model Rules of Professional Conduct on August 2, 1983.

Whereas state adoption of the predecessor document, the Model Code, was fairly quick, adoption of the Model Rules is still in process nearly a decade later. As of early 1992, 34 states had adopted the Model Rules with some variation. Six other states had incorporated moderate to significant portions of the rules into their ethical codes.

Robert Kutak's commission proposed several drafts of the Model Rules between the time of its creation and August 1983. Occasionally, we will cite to and excerpt sections from one of the publicly released drafts of the proposed Model Rules. These drafts are dated January 30, 1980; May 30, 1981; and June 30, 1982. We will especially refer to them when the substance of a proposed rule differs significantly from the corresponding rule finally adopted by the ABA in 1983, or where there is no corresponding rule adopted by the ABA.*

Different jurisdictions accord the code and rules varying degrees of authority. The New York Court of Appeals, for example, has ruled that the code does not have "the status of decisional or statutory law." But the court has also said that the "courts should not denigrate [the code] by indifference." In re Estate of Weinstock, 40 N.Y.2d 1, 351 N.E.2d 647, 649, 386 N.Y.S.2d 1 (1976). See also New York Criminal and Civil Courts Bar Assn. v. Jacoby, 61 N.Y.2d 130, 136, 460 N.E.2d 1325, 1327, 472 N.Y.S.2d 890, 893 (1984). The Pennsylvania Supreme Court has said the code has the "force of statutory rules of conduct for lawyers." Slater v. Rimar, Inc., 462 Pa. 138, 338 A.2d 584, 587 (1975). Federal courts often rely on code provisions, although it is sometimes said that there is no obligation to do so. See, for example, Rosen v. NLRB, 735 F.2d 564, 575 (D.C. Cir. 1984); Freschi v. Grand Coal Venture, 564 F. Supp. 414, 417 (S.D.N.Y. 1983):

> There exists no statutory obligation upon the federal courts to apply the Code as enacted by the American Bar Association. Although the Code does set guidelines for the professional conduct of attorneys appearing before the federal bar the application of the Code is a part of the court's general

---

*For a discussion of the role and possible motives of the ABA in preparing and adopting ethics codes, see Richard Abel, Why Does the ABA Promulgate Ethical Rules?, 59 Tex. L. Rev. 639 (1981); Deborah Rhode, Why the ABA Bothers: A Functional Perspective on Professional Codes, 59 Tex. L. Rev. 689 (1981); Marvin Frankel, Why Does Professor Abel Work at a Useless Task?, 59 Tex. L. Rev. 723 (1981). For interest-analyses of the Model Code and Model Rules see, respectively, Thomas Morgan, The Evolving Concept of Professional Responsibility, 90 Harv. L. Rev. 702 (1977), and Stephen Gillers, What We Talked About When We Talked About Ethics: A Critical View of the Model Rules, 46 Ohio St. L.J. 243 (1985). Ted Schneyer reviews the six-year debate over the Model Rules from a political perspective in Professionalism as Bar Politics: The Making of the Model Rules of Professional Conduct, 14 J. Am. Bar Found. Res. J. 677 (1989).

supervisory authority to ensure fairness to all who bring their cause to the judiciary for resolution.

These references have treated the code but the rules have received the same reception. See, for example, Culebras Enterprises Corp. v. Rivera-Rios, 846 F.2d 94 (1st Cir. 1988). See also Rand v. Monsanto Co., 926 F.2d 596 (7th Cir. 1991) (refusing to enforce DR 5-103(B) as inconsistent with Rule 23 Fed. R. Civ. P.). The appendix to *Rand* reviews the status of ethics rules in all district courts.

Beyond the code or rules as adopted in particular jurisdictions, the ethics oeuvre includes interpretations of these documents by bar-association ethics committees. Most state and local bar associations have ethics committees, composed of their members, and so does the ABA. A lawyer may write (or in an emergency sometimes telephone) for advice about prospective conduct. For example, a lawyer may be inclined to accept a new client but fear that conflict of interest rules forbid it. He or she can ask an ethics committee for an advisory opinion. Compliance with such opinions demonstrates a lawyer's good faith, although the opinions generally are not binding on a disciplinary committee or court. Important (that is, nonroutine) ethics opinions are published as guidelines for other lawyers and for whatever persuasive force they may have with judges in future cases (ranging from none to considerable). Published opinions do not reveal the inquirer's identity.

In addition to the sources listed here, ethics researchers can consult law review literature, where articles on professional regulation are appearing with greater frequency, and various books, treatises, manuals, and reporters. The Georgetown Journal of Legal Ethics is devoted entirely to the field. A full bibliography for ethics research, compiled by Professor Vanessa Merton at Pace Law School, appears at the end of this book.

Finally, the American Law Institute has undertaken the massive job of producing a Restatement of the Law Governing Lawyers. Beginning in 1986, Charles Wolfram of Cornell Law School, the Reporter, and associate Reporters John Leubsdorf, Rutgers University Law School, Thomas Morgan, George Washington University National Law Center, and (since 1989) Linda Mullenix, University of Texas Law School, have produced many drafts toward creation of a document that proposes to restate in black letter format the legal and ethical rules that govern the American legal profession.

Are we forgetting something? Even as a shorthand, the subject *is* often called legal *ethics*. Does it have anything to do with real ethics — the kind that moral philosophers study in the tradition of Plato, Kant, and Mill? Yes and no. Clearly the profession hopes to trade on the ideal of ethics, but less clearly has it appealed to classical ethical principles in elaborating the rules governing the behavior of lawyers. However, in the last two decades real ethicists have turned to the ethics of lawyers and held them up to the standards of moral philosophy. See Richard Wasserstrom's path-breaking article, Lawyers as Professionals: Some Moral Issues, 5 Hum. Rights 1 (1975). See also David Luban's book, Lawyers and Justice: An Ethical Study (1988).

This attention has influenced legal academics, who have joined in turning the spotlight of moral philosophy on the behavior of practicing lawyers. See, for example, Deborah Rhode's critique in Ethical Perspectives on Legal Practice, 37 Stan. L. Rev. 589 (1985). In Ethical Discretion in Lawyering, 101 Harv. L. Rev. 1083 (1988), Professor William Simon argues that as a "professional duty of reflective judgment" lawyers "should have ethical discretion to refuse to assist in the pursuit of legally permissible courses of action and in the assertion of potentially enforce-able legal claims." Serena Stier criticizes the theory that "the ethical obli-gations one undertakes as a lawyer are distinct from and supersede the ethical obligations one is under in one's nonprofessional everyday life." Instead of such a "role-differentiated" defense, Professor Stier proposes an "integrity thesis [which] reframes the professional perspective and demonstrates its possibilities for integrating one's cherished personal val-ues with one's obligations as an attorney." Serena Stier, Legal Ethics: The Integrity Thesis, 52 Ohio St. L.J. 551 (1991).

So far there has been little cross-fertilization, as a *practical* matter, be-tween the philosophical and the professional enterprises. Undoubtedly, many lawyers would like to keep it that way. Moral philosophers may teach at law schools and influence law teachers, but they have not yet been invited to join the profession's ethics-writing committees. Although the philosophers are not going to go away and are in fact becoming more influential in the academy, the full force of their influence on the practic-ing bar has yet to be determined.

WHAT IS "PROFESSIONALISM"?

In the mid-1980s, the word "professionalism" began to appear with some frequency in bar publications and to be heard increasingly at bar meet-ings large and small. The American Bar Association and some local bar groups formed committees on professionalism (or committees on the profession) to study the topic and write reports about it. In 1986, the ABA's Commission on Professionalism issued its report, which is avail-able in most law libraries. The report offers dozens of solutions to correct the perception "that the Bar might be moving away from the principles of professionalism." In defining "professionalism," the Commission quoted Roscoe Pound's 1953 statement:

> The term refers to a group . . . pursuing a learned art as a common calling in the spirit of public service — no less a public service because it may incidentally be a means of livelihood. Pursuit of the learned art in the spirit of a public service is the primary purpose.*

The Commission also quoted a definition for "profession" framed by Professor Eliot Freidson, a sociologist and Commission member:

1. That its practice requires substantial intellectual training and the use of complex judgments,
2. That since clients cannot adequately evaluate the quality of the service, they must trust those they consult,
3. That the client's trust presupposes that the practitioner's self-interest is overbalanced by devotion to serving both the client's interest and the public good, and
4. That the occupation is self-regulating — that is, organized in such a way as to assure the public and the courts that its members are competent, do not violate their client's trust, and transcend their own self-interest.

These definitions share a theme: A professional subordinates self-interest and private gain to the interests of clients or to the public good generally. Now, obviously, subordination must be a matter of degree or else professionals would be expected to work without regard to a client's or patient's ability to pay. Nothing so radical has been suggested. (Should it be?) Quite the contrary, professionalism committees recognize the economic pressures on lawyers and their need to earn a living. Some acknowledge that the practice of law shares some of the attributes of a business. The search seems to be for the proper balance between professionalism and business. Certain trends are said to take the profession too far in the wrong direction. We are warned against "overcommercialization."**

It is too soon to say what effect the idea of professionalism will have on rules regulating the practice of law. Several possibilities exist. The professionalism theme may be viewed as something of a public relations campaign in which lawyers reaffirm — to themselves and to the nation generally — their special status in American society. This is at least part

---

*Roscoe Pound, The Lawyer from Antiquity to Modern Times 5 (1953).

**For critiques of the Commission's work see Nancy Moore, Professionalism Reconsidered, 1987 Am. B. Found. Res. J. 773; Ronald Rotunda, Lawyers and Professionalism: A Commentary on the Report of the American Bar Association Commission on Professionalism, 18 Loy. U. Chi. L.J. 1149 (1987). For a stimulating and challenging discussion of the meaning of professionalism written in dialogue form, see Jack Sammons, Jr.'s short book, Lawyer Professionalism (1988).

of it, as anyone reading reports of bar association professionalism committees should quickly glean.

More substantively, professionalism may represent an effort to improve the behavior of the bar other than through rules whose violation carries sanctions. We see several indications of this. For example, in August 1988 the ABA House of Delegates adopted a Creed of Professionalism and a Pledge of Professionalism, though the former carried the disclaimer that "nothing in such a creed shall be deemed to supersede or in any way amend the Model Rules of Professional Conduct or other disciplinary codes, alter existing standards of conduct against which lawyer negligence might be judged or become a basis for the imposition of civil liability of any kind." The creed contains 33 numbered paragraphs describing a lawyer's responsibility toward clients, opposing parties and counsel, tribunals, and the system of justice. Much of it duplicates provisions of the Model Rules ("I will refrain from utilizing delaying tactics"). Other provisions are hortatory ("my responsibilities as a lawyer include a devotion to the public good").

Finally, the concept of professionalism may actually come to influence the content of rules regulating the conduct of lawyers and the way judges decide cases. For example, argument about whether law is a business or a profession has been prominent in the debate over whether law firms should be permitted to operate nonlaw businesses and have nonlawyer partners.* See Chapter 14 infra. The same theme appears in Supreme Court decisions on the constitutionality of state rules that limit ways in which lawyers may market their services. See Chapter 16 infra.

The ABA Professionalism Commission concluded, "All segments of the Bar should resist the temptation to make the acquisition of wealth a principal goal of law practice." But exactly what does that mean? And how should this caution influence support or opposition to particular proposals? For example, should lawyer advertising be opposed because it makes lawyers too conscious of the business aspects of practicing law, a reason Justice O'Connor found persuasive in her Shapero v. Kentucky Bar Assn. dissent (page 813 infra)? Or should lawyer advertising be supported because it tends, as the Federal Trade Commission concluded (see page 802 n.13 infra), to reduce the price of routine legal services?

Take another example. The ABA Commission urged "limited licensing of paralegals to perform certain functions" as a way to reduce the cost of legal services. "Possible areas for the provision of such limited services," the Commission wrote, "include certain real estate closings, the drafting of simple wills, and selected tax services now being performed by lawyers." Lawyers would also be able to perform such services, but

---

*I use the word "nonlawyer" with a certain self-consciousness. With some accuracy, it has been labeled a "lawyer chauvinist word." No other profession so describes everyone else in the world. Have you ever heard of a nondentist or a nonarchitect?

"they should have to compete with properly licensed paraprofessionals." Should lawyers support this suggestion because it will reduce the cost of legal services even though it will also reduce the incomes of many lawyers? Or should they oppose it because it will dilute the professional status of the bar, heighten competition, and force lawyers to be more commercial?

Beyond legal advertising and lawyer-owned businesses, a third trend that to many signals professionalism's decline is a supposed increase in lawyer incivility — also labeled "hardball," "Rambo," or "scorched earth" tactics — especially in litigation (see page 380 infra). Even lawyers too young to remember whether the particular Camelot ever existed may yet be heard to invoke that kinder, gentler period when courtesy was king (not queen, mind you) and lawyers treated each other like, well, like professionals. Bar chatter today is spiced with anecdotes of other lawyers' (usually an adversary's) monstrous behavior. Meanwhile, some seek to turn the perceived decline to advantage by proudly (and loudly) proclaiming their readiness to "go right up to the line" for their clients. This presumes, of course, that the line, like the one down the center of the interstate, is always conspicuous. Much of this book is meant to tell you that it is not and what could happen should you cross it, even unwittingly.*

As you work your way through this book, keep the following questions in mind:

1. Is it socially or conceptually useful to have a category called "professions" that we distinguish from all other occupations in which men and women earn their livelihood?
2. If so, do the particular rules studied here honor the reasons for making this distinction?
3. Do the rules of ethics for lawyers purport to serve purposes not already and adequately served by substantive law, including the law of fiduciary duty?
4. If so, do the particular rules studied here facilitate those purposes, or are they neutral, or even hostile, toward them?

---

*Incivility may not be peculiar to the legal profession. Believe it or not, it apparently plagues accountants too. According to the Wall Street Journal, the "staid accounting profession has been transformed into a Darwinian jungle. . . . Accountants are leaving the business in droves. Those who remain are finding that the law of survival of the fittest prevails over generally accepted behavioral principles." One senior partner is quoted as saying "We're at war. We must attack with a vengeance to survive." July 24, 1991, at A1.

Part One

THE CLIENT-LAWYER
RELATIONSHIP

II

Defining the Client-Lawyer Relationship

In the beginning is the client.

Lawyers like to quote Lord Brougham, who said that "an advocate, in the discharge of his duty, knows but one person in all the world, and that person is his client."* Lawyers have obligations to courts, adversaries, partners, and associates too, but responsibilities to clients are the dominant focus of ethical and legal rules governing lawyers and, therefore, will also be ours. Whether these responsibilities, in addition to being more numerous, should also be viewed as more important than the demands of "justice" or the "public interest" is a question fit for debate. Indeed, debate is unavoidable.

We should recognize, however, that the debate is more likely to occur in law schools than in practice. Practicing lawyers would generally agree with a Connecticut trial lawyer's comment that "a lawyer serves justice and the public interest best by serving the private interests of his clients, one at a time." Is he right? Lord Brougham would probably say yes. He argued that "hazards and costs to other persons" are of no concern to the lawyer, who "must not regard the alarm, the torments, the destruction which he may bring upon others. . . . [H]e must go on reckless of the consequences, though it should be his unhappy fate to involve his country in confusion."** Is that what legal ethics rules encourage?

This chapter introduces the main attributes of the attorney-client relationship. What you study here will supply a foundation for much else in the book. We will examine the lawyer's duties of confidentiality, loyalty, and diligence; the lawyer's status as an agent for and fiduciary toward clients; the lawyer's duty to keep a client informed about the client's matter; the allocation between client and lawyer of power to choose the goals the

*2 Trial of Queen Caroline 8 (J. Nightingale ed. 1821).
**Id.

13

lawyer will pursue and the means employed to reach them; and the circumstances under which client and lawyer can end the professional relationship.*

But before we begin that journey, we should recognize a threshold question that will recur: Is there a client-lawyer relationship? That's a recurring question of law on which much will often turn, such as whether a lawyer has a conflict that restricts his or her actions; whether a lawyer is liable in malpractice or subject to discipline; and whether communications are confidential or privileged. Here are some preliminary observations.

"The client is no longer simply the person who walks into a law office," Judge Sprecher wrote in Westinghouse Electric Corp. v. Kerr-McGee Corp., 580 F.2d 1311, 1318 (7th Cir.), cert. denied, 439 U.S. 955 (1978). His meaning is clear. Although many client-lawyer relationships are still formed in the old-fashioned way — with face-to-face meetings followed by a formal written retainer agreement spelling out the responsibilities of each party — they can be formed in other ways too. In Togstad v. Vesely, Otto, Miller & Keefe (page 613 infra), a lawyer was held to have a professional relationship with a client for purposes of malpractice liability although he declined to accept her case. Indeed, the lawyer had a professional relationship with the spouse of the client, too, although he had apparently never met him. Class action lawyers have duties to class members whose names they will never know. And as we shall see in the material on conflicts of interest (pages 227 and 256 infra), companies that are members of trade groups may be deemed clients of lawyers for those groups.

Money need not change hands for a client-lawyer relationship to exist. A lawyer appointed by a court to represent an indigent criminal defendant has a professional relationship with the defendant and will be liable for her errors in malpractice (see Ferri v. Ackerman, page 622 infra). It is of no moment that lawyer and client do not get along (see Morris v. Slappy, page 703 infra) or that they disagree on strategy (see Jones v. Barnes, page 57 infra).

Even though a client-lawyer relationship can arise without a payment, the fact of payment is often pretty good evidence of a professional undertaking. A lawyer would be hard pressed to deny a person's claim that he or she was the lawyer's client in the face of a bill and a cancelled check. But it would not be impossible. As we shall see (page

---

*Roy Anderson and Walter Steele analyze the "professional responsibility required of attorneys in their commercial relations as compared with the professional expectations demanded of other professions and fiduciaries." They find that the "expectations for attorneys are continually said to be much higher than for other professionals," but challenge "whether those expectations are warranted." Ethics and the Law of Contract Juxtaposed: A Jaundiced View of Professional Responsibility Considerations in the Attorney-Client Relationship, 4 Geo. J. Legal Ethics 791 (1991).

181 infra), a lawyer may be paid by one person to represent another, in which case the second person, not the first, is the lawyer's client. See Rules 1.8(f) and 5.4(c). See also In re Grand Jury Subpoena (Reyes-Requena), 926 F.2d 1423 (5th Cir. 1991), holding that the identity of a person who pays a lawyer's fee to represent another is not protected by the attorney-client privilege unless the lawyer can show that the fee-payor was also a client of the lawyer and that the fee information was part of a confidential communication.

Courts are alert to what a person claiming to be a client might reasonably have believed under the circumstances, especially if the client has given the lawyer confidential information on the assumption that the lawyer was performing a legal service for the benefit of the client and possibly others. See Analytica Inc. v. NPD Research, Inc. 708 F.2d 1263 (7th Cir. 1983), at page 247 infra. If a lawyer wants to avoid a claim that a professional relationship was established, he or she would be well advised to make that clear to the other person in writing. In certain situations conducive to misunderstanding, the Model Rules expressly require that lawyers clarify a possible misimpression. See Rules 1.13(d) and 4.3. Similarly, when a lawyer considers a representation to have ended, he or she should inform the client that the relationship is over if there is a reasonable chance that the client may believe otherwise. People v. Bennett, 810 P.2d 661 (Colo. 1991) (relationship is ongoing unless and until the client understands, or reasonably should understand, that he can no longer depend on it). See also page 69 infra.

Duties in the professional relationship are, as we shall see, based in part on the law of agency. Even when a client-lawyer relationship is established, it will almost always have a finite scope. For example, the Brobeck firm was retained to file a certiorari petition for Telex in Brobeck, Phleger & Harrison v. Telex Corp. (page 102 infra). It had no right or duty to hold itself out as Telex's counsel on a tender offer. The Telex retainer agreement was quite specific, but often the contours of the relationship will not be as clear. If a lawyer is retained to bring a personal injury action, he or she has no authority or obligation to negotiate the client's employment contract. But must the lawyer protect the client's no-fault insurance benefits even though that service was never mentioned? The client may look at the matter holistically while the lawyer may define the retainer by reference to a particular service. So the client thinks "the lawyer will help with all the legal problems caused by this accident," while the lawyer thinks "I'm retained to sue the other driver for damages." Once again, courts will probably expect the lawyer to be sensitive to, and to clarify, ambiguity. (That expectation will diminish, but not necessarily disappear, if the client is sophisticated or is dealing with the lawyer through other lawyers, as in the *Telex* case.)

The conventional image of the client-lawyer relationship posits two people who have agreed that one will provide a defined service to the other for a fee. As we have seen, however, no formalism is necessary to create the relationship, nor must the participants be limited to two. There can be several or many lawyers and several or many clients. Joint-defense agreements can create limited client-lawyer relationships (see pages 204 and 230 infra). Nor must the client be a person. Corporations, trade associations, estates, and governments can all be clients. Lawyers must still be people, of course. Even if they practice in a partnership, in a professional corporation, or with a prepaid legal services plan, one rule that has not changed is that flesh-and-blood professionals (as well, perhaps, as their colleagues or employers; see page 628 supra) will be responsible for their failures.

Some ways remain in which client-lawyer relationships cannot be created. For example, in United States v. Weinstein, 511 F.2d 622, 628 (2d Cir.), cert. denied, 422 U.S. 1042 (1975), the district judge, on his own initiative, appointed counsel to represent 23 fugitive defendants who had been indicted under the selective service laws. The judge ordered the government to produce the files of these defendants so that appointed counsel could determine whether motions might be made to dismiss the indictments. The Second Circuit ordered the judge to vacate his order, concluding that he had no power to create a client-lawyer relationship for a fugitive defendant. Any action taken by the lawyer "without the defendant's knowledge or consent could not bind the fugitive defendant." In Lynch v. Deaconess Medical Center, 113 Wash. 2d 162, 776 P.2d 681 (1989), a hospital was deemed not the client of a lawyer simply because it benefitted from the attorney's work for a client who owed the hospital money.

Much of our empirical knowledge of the attorney-client relationship is anecdotal. Empirical studies of the relationship are rare, given its traditional secrecy. But some investigators succeed. An oft-cited study by Douglas Rosenthal reported that personal injury lawyers get better results when they let their clients participate in decisions. Lawyer and Client: Who's In Charge (1974). Lisa Lerman was able to pierce the profession's secrecy by promising lawyers anonymity. Her careful and disturbing study, descriptively entitled Lying to Clients, can be found at 138 U. Pa. L. Rev. 659 (1990). Responses from Carrie Menkel-Meadow, Frederick Miller, and Edmund Spaeth, Jr. begin at page 761. A third empirical report, by Austin Sarat and William Felstiner, entitled Law and Social Relations; Vocabularies of Motive in Lawyer/Client Interaction, 22 Law & Soc. Rev. 737 (1988), analyzes 115 conferences between lawyers and matrimonial clients. The authors grapple with the different orientations of the two and the effect on the exercise of professional authority.

A. ELEMENTS OF THE CLIENT-LAWYER RELATIONSHIP

1. *Confidentiality*

Privileged and Ethically Protected Information

Ethical rules define a category of information about a client, which may or may not have been gained from the client, that the lawyer may not voluntarily use or reveal. The limitation is one the profession has sought to impose on itself through legislative enactment, judicial rule, or otherwise. (Why would it want to do that?) The law of evidence, on the other hand, defines a category of information that a lawyer has gained from his or her client (or agents of the client) and that no court or other body with subpoena power may force the lawyer to reveal. Information protected by the law of evidence is traditionally called "privileged," although the word "privileged" is sometimes loosely and confusingly used to refer to the information protected under the rules of ethics too. The vocabulary in this area is not uniform. We will generally refer to information protected by the rules of ethics as *ethically protected information* (the code calls this information "secrets") and information protected under the rules of evidence as *privileged information* (the code calls this information "confidences"). Compare DR 4-101 with Rule 1.6.

Whatever the labels, it is important to realize that the two bodies of rules have different sources and define overlapping but not congruent categories. Much information that is ethically protected will not be privileged. On the other hand, virtually all information considered privileged under the rules of evidence will also be ethically protected. A lawyer whom a court orders to reveal information that is ethically protected but not privileged under the rules of evidence will be required to reveal the information under pain of contempt. But if that lawyer had *voluntarily* revealed the same information, he or she might be guilty of a disciplinary violation for failure to protect a client's secrets unless revelation was for one of the purposes recognized by DR 4-101 or Rule 1.6. Similarly, a client will not be permitted to refuse to disclose information simply because it is ethically protected. The information must be legally privileged.

Cases recognizing these differences are few. But in Brennan's, Inc. v. Brennan's Restaurants, 590 F.2d 168, 172 (5th Cir. 1979), the court resisted an effort to incorporate an exception to the privilege as an exception to the ethical duty. It wrote:

> But the ethical duty is broader than the evidentiary privilege: "This ethical precept, unlike the evidentiary privilege, exists without regard to the nature or source of information or the fact that others share the knowl-

edge." ABA Code of Professional Responsibility, EC 4-4 (1970). "A lawyer should not use information acquired in the course of the representation of a client to the disadvantage of the client. . . ." Id. EC 4-5. . . . Information so acquired is sheltered from use by the attorney against his client by virtue of the existence of the attorney-client relationship. This is true without regard to whether someone else may be privy to it. The obligation of an attorney not to misuse information acquired in the course of representation serves to vindicate the trust and reliance that clients place in their attorneys.

Compare Kleinfeld v. State, 568 So. 2d 937 (Fla. App. 1990) (client's statement to counsel implicating himself in a past homicide and threatening future violence remained privileged even though counsel had the authority to reveal this statement under Florida ethics rules).

As you've probably gleaned, the ethical prohibition against voluntary use or disclosure generally continues even if persons other than the lawyer know of the information, whether through the client or otherwise. (The Model Rules make an exception here. If a former client's ethically protected information has become "generally known," the lawyer may use or reveal it to the former client's disadvantage. Rule 1.9(c).) The privilege, however, may be lost for any information the client gives the lawyer in the presence of third persons.

The following material is intended to introduce you to the nature of ethically protected information and to the operation of the evidentiary privilege. The privilege, though also part of the course in evidence, is discussed here because of its close relationship to the ethical rules and because of its import for the attorney-client relationship.

Issues involving ethical and evidentiary rules protecting information from or about a client arise in many contexts — litigation and advocacy (discussed in Chapters 7 and 8), conflicts of interest (covered in Chapters 5 and 6), and negotiation and entity representation (discussed in Chapters 10 and 9). This chapter deals with the attributes of the attorney-client relationship. One of those attributes is the duty, as a general matter, to protect client information.

Legislative History

Something of the division of opinion that besets the profession over the proper scope of the ethical duty of confidentiality may be seen by looking at drafts of the Model Rules and by comparing DR 4-101 with Model Rule 1.6 as adopted. Which is more protective of the client's interests? Of the lawyer's interests? (Do they diverge?) Which is the better resolution of the issues they address? Then consider the predecessors to Rule 1.6 in the January 1980 draft and in the May 1981 draft. How might these other standards have led to different results in the cases and problems that follow?

The January 1980 draft provided (in Rule 1.7) in part as follows: *(1ˢᵗ draft)*

SHALL

(b) a lawyer shall disclose information about a client to the extent it appears necessary to prevent the client from committing an act that would result in death or serious bodily harm to another person. . . .

(c) a lawyer may disclose information about a client . . . to the extent it appears necessary to prevent or rectify the consequences of a deliberately wrongful act by the client, except when the lawyer has been employed after the commission of such an act to represent the client concerning the act or its consequences.

By May 1981, the mandatory disclosure provision was deleted and the following relevant portions of Rule 1.6 were substituted:

MAY REVEAL

(b) a lawyer may reveal [confidential] information to the extent the lawyer believes necessary . . . (2) to prevent the client from committing a criminal or fraudulent act that the lawyer believes is likely to result in death or substantial bodily harm, or substantial injury to the financial interest or property of another; (3) to rectify the consequences of a client's criminal or fraudulent act in the commission of which the lawyer's services had been used.

The definition of the word "believes" in the May 1981 draft is the same as in the Model Rules as finally adopted.*

State Variations

Rule 1.6 was much debated as states considered the Model Rules. Something of the division among them can be seen in the following variations. A number of states, including Arizona, Indiana, Kansas, Michigan, Minnesota, North Carolina, and Washington, retained the code's provision allowing a lawyer to reveal "the intention of a client to commit a crime" (or equivalent language) without regard to the nature of the crime. Some states, including Arizona, Connecticut, Illinois, New Jersey, and Texas, require lawyers to disclose information to prevent clients from committing serious violent crimes. A few states retain language (or its equivalent) from the draft version of Rule 1.6 that permits lawyers to reveal confidential information "to rectify the consequences of a client's criminal or fraudulent act in the furtherance of which the lawyer's services had been used." These states include Connecticut, Pennsylvania, Maryland, New Jersey, Texas, and Wisconsin. Also retaining language from a draft of Rule 1.6, Connecticut, Maryland, and Pennsylvania,

---

*Exceptions to the confidentiality duty are discussed at page 32 infra and in the material on advocacy and negotiation (pages 310 and 469 infra).

among other states, permit a lawyer to reveal information necessary to prevent the client from committing a criminal act "likely to result in substantial injury to the financial interests or property of another." Maryland creates this authorization even when the act is fraudulent and not criminal.

New Jersey and Florida may be the states least protective of client confidences. New Jersey requires a lawyer to reveal confidential information "to prevent a client from committing a criminal, illegal, or fraudulent act . . . likely to result in death or substantial bodily harm or substantial injury to the financial interest or property of another." Florida requires lawyers to reveal information the lawyer believes "necessary (1) to prevent a client from committing a crime or (2) to prevent death or substantial bodily harm to another." By contrast, California may be the state most protective of client confidences. Section 6068(e) of the California Business and Professions Code states that it is the duty of an attorney to "maintain inviolate the confidence, and at every peril to himself or herself to preserve the secrets, of his or her client." This statutory language has no exceptions. The California Rules of Professional Conduct do not expressly address confidentiality. The San Diego Bar Association has interpreted the statute to *forbid* lawyers to reveal a client's clear intention to commit a violent crime. San Diego Opinion 1990-1.

What explains the great diversity of views among American jurisdictions with regard to the amount of protection client confidences should enjoy? Who is correct?

Individual Clients

In re JAMES M. POOL
Supreme Judicial Court, Suffolk County, Massachusetts,
No. 83-37 BD (Jan. 17, 1984)

In the course of his representation of a client on a serious Federal charge, at a time in 1974 when he had been in private practice for himself for almost six months, the attorney became concerned about the payment of substantial investigating expenses he was incurring. The client told the attorney that he had a substantial amount of cash in safe deposit boxes, as well as false identifications and a handgun. The only available keys were in the possession of the F.B.I.

The attorney asked an Assistant United States Attorney to return the keys, saying that he needed the keys to the safe deposit boxes in order to obtain funds for his client's defense. The attorney said that, if the Assistant U.S. Attorney would let him have the keys, he would go to the boxes and only remove the money. In exchange, the attorney agreed to disclose the location of the boxes and the alias under which they were listed. The Assistant U.S. Attorney accepted the offer.

The attorney advised the client's sister that he had obtained the keys pursuant to a court order. The two of them went to the bank, where, using a deputy power of access from his client, he opened the boxes and removed $48,600 in cash (and nothing else). The attorney turned the money over to his client's sister. The attorney never told his client or his client's sister of his arrangement with the Assistant U.S. Attorney.

On the next day, based on an affidavit that was at best obscure as to the source of the information set forth in it, the F.B.I. obtained a search warrant, obtained access to the boxes, and "inventoried" the contents. About two weeks later, the attorney and his client executed a retainer agreement, and, at the same time, the attorney agreed to remove certain material from the safe deposit boxes. The next day the attorney met with his client's sister, but said he alone would go to the bank. He returned thirty minutes later (without entering the boxes) and announced that the F.B.I. had seized the material from the boxes.

The client subsequently learned of what the attorney had done, after the attorney told successor counsel of his arrangement with the Assistant U.S. Attorney. . . .

The disclosure of confidential information by a defense attorney to a prosecutor, without the client's consent, is a serious violation of the defense attorney's obligations. The attorney's arrangement with the Assistant U.S. Attorney revealed the path to certain materials that could have been detrimental to his client's interests. On the record, it is not clear what, if any, adverse consequences came to the client. The additional compensation provided for in the retainer agreement was obtained at a time when the attorney agreed to remove materials from the safe deposit boxes which he could not do, as he knew, because of the F.B.I.'s seizure of the contents of the boxes and which was, in any event, inconsistent with his agreement with the Assistant U.S. Attorney.

Sympathetic understanding of the attorney's inexperience and his otherwise good record warrants consideration in determining the period of time that must pass before he may seek readmission to the bar, but it does not warrant imposition of only an order of a suspension rather than an order of disbarment.

Judgment shall be entered disbarring the attorney, with the right, however, to seek readmission to the bar on and after one year from the date of judgment.*

In In re Rhame, 416 N.E.2d 823 (Ind. 1981), the attorney

*Pool was eventually reinstated. 401 Mass. 460, 517 N.E.2d 444 (1988).

had represented Dick and Connie Parker individually and as attorney for one or more corporations in which the Parkers were the principals. For a period of time, Respondent represented Connie Parker, with Dick's consent, in an ensuing divorce. Subsequently, Connie Parker was arrested as the alleged perpetrator of the alleged murder of Dick Parker. Respondent met with a close mutual friend, Lloyd, who was also a member of the local police department, and related to him the Parkers' desperate financial condition and the particulars of their divorce. At the suggestion of Lloyd, Respondent also met with a deputy prosecuting attorney and related to him similar information before Respondent realized that he was revealing privileged communication. Thereafter, Respondent refused to testify and cooperated fully with Connie Parker's defense counsel. He reported these matters to the Disciplinary Commission on a voluntary basis.

The sanction was a public reprimand.

NEW YORK STATE OPINION 479 (1978)

PRELIMINARY STATEMENT

[In the summer of 1973, Robert Garrow was charged with murder in upstate New York. The Court assigned two lawyers, Frank Armani and Francis Belge, to represent him. In discussions with his lawyers, Garrow revealed that he had committed two other unsolved murders and he identified the locations of the bodies on a diagram. Belge located and photographed the bodies but made no attempt to conceal or move them. Belge later presented these events to the ethics committee of the New York State Bar Association. The committee addressed the following ethical issues.]

1. Under the circumstances alleged, would a lawyer be acting improperly in failing to disclose to the authorities his knowledge of the two prior murders and the location of the bodies?

2. Under the circumstances alleged, would a lawyer be acting improperly in withholding and destroying (a) the records of his conversation with the client, (b) the photographs taken by him of the bodies of the victims and (c) the diagram showing the physical location of the bodies? . . .

4. Under the circumstances alleged, would a lawyer be acting improperly, in his attempt to negotiate a plea disposition, in suggesting to the District Attorney that he had information concerning two unsolved murders?

OPINION

The questions raised are complex and difficult. Legal issues, upon which we do not pass, may be inextricably interwoven with ethical considerations. Illegal conduct involving moral turpitude is per se unethical. DR 1-102(A)(3)

1. The lawyer's failure to disclose his knowledge of the two unrelated homicides was not improper, assuming, as the facts given us indicate, that the information came to the lawyer during the course of his employment. Furthermore, the requirements of Canon 4 that "a lawyer should preserve the confidences and secrets of a client," and of EC 4-1 and DR 4-101(B), would have been violated if such disclosure had been made. . . .

Proper representation of a client calls for full disclosure by the client to his lawyer of all possibly relevant facts, even though such facts may reveal the client's commission of prior crimes. To encourage full disclosure, the client must be assured of confidentiality, a requirement embodied by law in the attorney-client privilege and broadly incorporated in Canon 4 of the Code and the EC's and DR's thereunder.

Frequently clients have a disposition to withhold information from lawyers. If the client suspects that his confidences will not be adequately protected or may in some way be used against him, he will be far more likely to withhold information which he believes may be to his detriment or which he does not want generally known. The client who withholds information from his lawyer runs a substantial risk of not being accorded his full legal rights. At the same time, the lawyer from whom such information is withheld may well be required to assert, in complete good faith and with no violation of EC 7-26 or DR 7-102(A), totally meritless or frivolous claims or defenses to which his client has no legal right. Thus, the interests served by the strict rule of confidentiality are far broader than merely those of the client, but include the interests of the public generally and of effective judicial administration.

Narrow and limited exceptions to the rule of confidentiality have been incorporated in DR 4-101(C) and DR 7-102(B)(1), the most important of which relate to information involving the intention of the client to commit a crime in the future or the perpetration of a fraud during the course of the lawyer's representation of the client, or where the client consents following full disclosure. The future crime exception recognizes both the possible preventability of the crime, as well as the total absence of any societal need to encourage criminal clients to make such disclosures to their lawyers. . . .

Thus, the lawyer was under an injunction not to disclose to the authorities his knowledge of the two prior murders, and was dutybound not to reveal to the authorities the location of the bodies. The lawyer's knowledge with respect to the location of the bodies was obtained solely from the client in confidence and in secret. Without the client's revelation in secret and in confidence, he would not have been in a position to assist the authorities in this regard. Thus, his personal knowledge is a link solidly welded to the chain of privileged communications and, without the client's express permission, must not be disclosed. The relationship between lawyer and client is in many respects like that between priest and penitent. Both lawyer and priest are bound by the bond of silence. . . .

2. A lawyer's obligation to hold a client's confidences and secrets inviolate extends beyond information imparted orally and embraces written material from the client "coming into existence merely as a communication to the attorney."

memoralization also privileged

The memorialization by a lawyer of statements, information and documents received from a client, whether by shorthand or longhand notes, dictated and typed memoranda, speedwriting, electronic or magnetic recording, xerox, photostat, photograph or other form of recordation or reproduction does not alter the fact that the communication from the client is privileged. Such memorialization may be useful in facilitating the handling of a matter by the lawyer and is part of the lawyer's work product. When the lawyer's purpose is served, the work product may be destroyed without violation of ethical standards.

Similarly, written material prepared by the client for his lawyer is a form of written communication and falls within the attorney-client privilege. Such documents are not instruments or fruits of the crime, which under certain circumstances the lawyer might be obliged to turn over to authorities. See, e.g., State v. Olwell, [page 415 infra]. Accordingly, neither the lawyer nor his client was obliged to reveal an incriminating diagram, whether prepared by the client for his lawyer or by the lawyer on the basis of information gained by him during the course of the client's representation, under EC 7-27 and DR 7-102. Provided it was not contrary to his client's wishes for him to do so, there was no ethical inhibition against its destruction by the lawyer. . . .

no ethical problem w/ discussion of plea disposition

4. There is no ethical impropriety in the lawyer's discussing with the District Attorney the possibility of an appropriate plea disposition, provided that the lawyer had the express consent of his client before making such disclosure. Plea bargaining is an accepted part of our criminal procedures today. A lawyer engaged or attempting to engage in it with his client's consent would be properly serving his client. Thus, the lawyer's suggestion to the District Attorney that he might be in a position to assist the authorities in resolving open cases during such a discussion would appear to involve no violation of proper professional standards. One can conceive of a variety of circumstances in which such a disclosure might be helpful to a client. For example, the disclosure of the client's commission of prior crimes of violence might very well establish the client's need for confinement for medical treatment rather than imprisonment.

Eventually, the attorneys who were the subject of Opinion 479 revealed the existence of the other bodies as part of an unsuccessful effort to have their client found not guilty by reason of insanity. There was substantial protest at their failure earlier to reveal the location of the bodies. One of the lawyers was indicted for two health law misdemeanors, one of which imposed a duty to provide a decedent with a decent burial and the other of which required disclosure of a death occurring without medical attention. The trial court dismissed the indictment, and the intermediate appellate court, in affirming, wrote:

> We believe that the attorney-client privilege attached insofar as the communications were to advance a client's interests, and that the privilege effectively shielded the defendant attorney from his actions which would otherwise have violated the Public Health Law. In view of the fact that the claim of absolute privilege was proffered, we note that the privilege is not all-encompassing and that in a given case there may be conflicting considerations. We believe that an attorney must protect his client's interests, but also must observe basic human standards of decency, having due regard to the need that the legal system accord justice to the interests of society and its individual members. We write to emphasize our serious concern regarding the consequences which emanate from a claim of an absolute attorney-client privilege. Because the only question presented, briefed and argued on this appeal was a legal one with respect to the sufficiency of the indictments, we limit our determination to that issue and do not reach the ethical questions underlying this case.

People v. Belge, 83 Misc. 2d 186, 372 N.Y.S.2d 798 (Co. Ct. 1975), aff'd, 50 A.D.2d 1088, 376 N.Y.S.2d 771, 771-772 (4th Dept. 1975), aff'd, 41 N.Y.2d 60, 390 N.Y.S.2d 867 (1976).

QUESTIONS

2.1   A lawyer is retained to represent a man who has been arrested for an assault arising out of a barroom fight and who has not yet been released on bail. In a jail interview with the man, in which the lawyer is eliciting information that will help persuade the court to set a modest bail, the man tells the lawyer that he has AIDS. He also tells her that he lives with a woman who is unaware of his condition and with the woman's six-year-old daughter. The man has a job and no criminal record. What should the lawyer do? What may or must she do?

2.2   "My name is Susan Espinoza. I was appointed by the court here in Nevada to represent a man named Ken Hess who was arrested for selling drugs. It was a small quantity. Hess doesn't have a serious record, so I think I can strike a deal for maybe six months or at most a year. I went to visit Hess yesterday, a few days after his arrest, and we talked about the charge. He also told me that when he was arrested the police searched him but they did not discover a small gun that he had hidden in his boot. The police put him in the back of the police car alone and even though he was handcuffed, he was able to reach down into his boot and retrieve the gun and push it down into the seat behind him so it could not be seen. He says it is probably still there. He also says that it has two bullets in it. Now I am worried that the police might arrest someone else who will discover it there and use it. I asked Hess to let me tell the police, even anonymously, that the gun is there, but he told me that he had used the gun in a convenience store robbery in which someone was shot and he is afraid that a ballistics test will identify him as the robber. He figures his fingerprints are on the gun. I checked to see if there really was a convenience store robbery as Hess described it and I found out that not only was there a robbery but also someone was arrested for it and charged with attempted murder. I don't know what to do next."

2.3   "I do estate planning in a small firm in Fairfield. My name's Winston Masuda but people call me Win. The other day a man comes in, well-dressed man in his, I'd say, early sixties, expensive suit, manicure, obviously used to running things. I'll call him Paul. He says he got my name from a lawyer I know, that he needs an estate plan, will, trust, the whole thing. Rather complicated tax problems. And he needs it in a week or ten days. He's got kids from several marriages he wants taken care of, grandchildren too, charities, and a woman I'd call a "significant other" except it's not a term I'd think of using for a man that age. He tells me his third wife died and his first and second marriages ended in divorce. He's got all the papers.

"So we get to talking, as you have to do to learn about the person whose estate you're planning and make suggestions, and I get the distinct impression, one, that Paul is fully competent to execute his estate plan but, two, that soon after he does he plans to kill himself. I pick this up from things he said. Other people in estate planning have over the years told me similar stories but it never happened to me. I probe him on it but he clams up and suggests that I'm worried about getting paid, which I'm not, but he assures me that I have nothing to worry about in the fee area. After a three-hour meeting where I get the details I'll need and arrange to call him if I need anything further, we make an appointment for him to come in to sign the papers next Thursday, five days from now. I'm supposed to call him the day before with the amount of my fee and he's going to bring a check. What do I do next?"

Entity Clients

As Rule 1.13 and its comment make clear, a lawyer has the same confidentiality duties under Rule 1.6 whether the client is a biological person or an entity like a corporation, a labor union, or the government. Special problems do arise with regard to a lawyer's duty or power to reveal confidential information among the various constituents of an entity client — employees, officers, shareholders, directors — and we shall study these in Chapter 9 infra. The *privilege* also protects communications between an entity client and its counsel. Upjohn Co. v. United States, 449 U.S. 383 (1981). This is true whether counsel is an employee of the entity or a retained outside lawyer. Rossi v. Blue Cross & Blue Shield of Greater New York, 73 N.Y.2d 588, 540 N.E.2d 703, 542 N.Y.S.2d 508 (1989). One debated question has been the identity of those persons within an entity client whose communications with entity counsel will be protected as privileged. The Supreme Court resolved this issue for the federal privilege in *Upjohn*, which follows.

UPJOHN CO. v. UNITED STATES
449 U.S. 383 (1981)

[The government was investigating illegal payments by Upjohn to foreign governments. Upjohn instructed its general counsel, Gerard Thomas, and outside counsel to conduct their own investigation, which resulted in interviews with and questionnaires from Upjohn employees throughout the world. The government subpoenaed the files "relative to the investigation conducted under the supervision of Gerard Thomas." The lower court held that communications between counsel and the company's "control group" were privileged, but those with lower level Upjohn employees were not. The Supreme Court reversed. It first reaffirmed that corporations enjoy the attorney-client privilege. It then ruled that the privilege applies to communications between corporate counsel and corporate agents or employees about matters within the scope of their corporate duties. The Court rejected the lower court's use of the "control group test," under which only communications between counsel and a company's senior management are privileged. After emphasizing a lawyer's ethical duty to be fully informed (quoting Ethical Consideration 4-1), Justice Rehnquist wrote:]

In the case of the individual client the provider of information and the person who acts on the lawyer's advice are one and the same. In the corporate context, however, it will frequently be employees beyond the control group as defined by the court below — "officers and agents . . . responsible for directing [the company's] actions in response to legal advice" — who will possess the information needed by the corporation's lawyers. Middle-level — and indeed lower-level — employees can, by actions within the scope of their employment, embroil the corporation in serious legal difficulties, and it is only natural that these employees would have the relevant information needed by corporate counsel if he is adequately to advise the client with respect to such actual or potential difficulties. . . .

The control group test adopted by the court below thus frustrates the very purpose of the privilege by discouraging the communication of relevant information by employees of the client to attorneys seeking to render legal advice to the client corporation. The attorney's advice will also frequently be more significant to noncontrol group members than to those who officially sanction the advice, and the control group test makes it more difficult to convey full and frank legal advice to the employees who will put into effect the client corporation's policy.

The narrow scope given the attorney-client privilege by the court below not only makes it difficult for corporate attorneys to formulate sound advice when their client is faced with a specific legal problem but also threatens to limit the valuable efforts of corporate counsel to ensure their client's compliance with the law. In light of the vast and complicated array of regulatory legislation confronting the modern corporation, corporations, unlike most individuals, "constantly go to lawyers to find out how to obey the law," Burnham, The Attorney-Client Privilege in the Corporate Arena, 24 Bus. Law. 901, 913 (1969), particularly since compliance with the law in this area is hardly an instinctive matter. . . . The test adopted by the court below is difficult to apply in practice, though no abstractly formulated and unvarying "test" will necessarily enable courts to decide questions such as this with mathematical precision. But if the purpose of the attorney-client privilege is to be served, the attorney and client must be able to predict with some degree of certainty whether particular discussions will be protected. An uncertain privilege, or one which purports to be certain but results in widely varying applications by the courts, is little better than no privilege at all. The very terms of the test adopted by the court below suggest the unpredictability of its application. The test restricts the availability of the privilege to those officers who play a "substantial role" in deciding and directing a corporation's legal response. Disparate decisions in cases applying this test illustrate its unpredictability.

The communications at issue were made by Upjohn employees to counsel for Upjohn acting as such, at the direction of corporate superiors in order to secure legal advice from counsel. As the Magistrate found, "Mr. Thomas consulted with the Chairman of the Board and outside counsel and thereafter conducted a factual investigation to determine the nature and extent of the questionable payments *and to be in a position to give legal advice to the company with respect to the payments.*" Information, not available for upper-echelon management, was needed to supply a basis for legal advice concerning compliance with securities and tax laws, foreign laws, currency regulations, duties to shareholders, and potential litigation in each of these areas. The communications concerned matters within the scope of the employees' corporate duties, and the employees themselves were sufficiently aware that they were being questioned in order that the corporation could obtain legal advice. The questionnaire identified Thomas as "the company's General Counsel" and referred in its opening sentence to the possible illegality of payments such as the ones on which information was sought. A statement of policy accompanying the questionnaire clearly indicated the legal implications of the investigation. The policy statement was issued "in order that there be no uncertainty in the future as to the policy with respect to the practices which are the subject of this investigation." It began "Upjohn will comply with all laws and regulations," and stated that commissions or payments "will not be used as a subterfuge for bribes or illegal payments" and that all payments must be "proper and legal." Any future agreements with foreign distributors or agents were to be approved "by a company attorney" and any questions concerning the policy were to be referred "to the company's General Counsel." This statement was issued to Upjohn employees worldwide, so that even those interviewees not receiving a questionnaire were aware of the legal implications of the interviews. Pursuant to explicit instructions from the Chairman of the Board, the communications were considered "highly confidential" when made, and have been kept confidential by the company. Consistent with the underlying purposes of the attorney-client privilege, these communications must be protected against compelled disclosure.

The Court of Appeals declined to extend the attorney-client privilege beyond the limits of the control group test for fear that doing so would entail severe burdens on discovery and create a broad "zone of silence" over corporate affairs. Application of the attorney-client privilege to communications such as those involved here, however, puts the adversary in no worse position than if the communications had never taken place. The privilege only protects disclosure of communications; it does not protect disclosure of the underlying facts by those who communicated with the attorney. . . . Here the Government was free to question the employees who communicated with Thomas and outside counsel. Upjohn has provided the IRS with a list of such employees, and the IRS has already interviewed some 25 of them. While it would probably be more convenient for the Government to secure the results of petitioner's internal investigation by simply subpoenaing the questionnaires and notes taken by petitioner's attorneys, such considerations of convenience do not overcome the policies served by the attorney-client privilege. As Justice Jackson noted in his concurring opinion in Hickman v. Taylor, 329 U.S. [495 (1947)], at 516: "Discovery was hardly intended to enable a learned profession to perform its functions . . . on wits borrowed from the adversary."

Needless to say, we decide only the case before us, and do not undertake to draft a set of rules which should govern challenges to investigatory subpoenas. Any such approach would violate the spirit of Federal Rule of Evidence 501. While such a "case-by-case" basis may to some slight extent undermine desirable certainty in the boundaries of the attorney-client privilege, it obeys the spirit of the Rules. At the same time we conclude that the narrow "control group test" sanctioned by the Court of Appeals in this case cannot, consistent with "the principles of the common law as . . . interpreted . . . in the light of reason and experience," Fed. Rule Evid. 501, govern the development of the law in this area.

[The discussion upholding invocation of the work-product privilege is omitted. The Chief Justice concurred in part and concurred in the judgment.]*

Other courts have adhered to the control group test in construing state privileges. The Illinois Supreme Court rejected *Upjohn*'s approach because it has the "potential to insulate so much material from the truth seeking process." Consolidation Coal Co. v. Bucyrus-Erie Co., 89 Ill. 2d 103, 432 N.E.2d 250, 257 (1982). (In the nature of federalism, then, an Illinois company cannot be confident of the protection *Upjohn* believed necessary.) On the other hand, some lower federal courts have extended *Upjohn*. For example, the Ninth Circuit has held that the privilege applies even to conversations between corporate counsel and a former corporate employee where counsel is seeking "relevant information needed . . . to advise the [corporate] client." In re Coordinated Pre-Trial Proceedings, 658 F.2d 1355, 1361 n.7 (9th Cir. 1981), cert. denied, 455 U.S. 990 (1982). See also Admiral Insurance Co. v. United States District Court, 881 F.2d 1486, 1493 (9th Cir. 1989). *Admiral Insurance* also holds that the privilege may apply notwithstanding that a communication is between corporate counsel and an employee of the corporation's subsidiary.

QUESTIONS ABOUT UPJOHN

1. Justice Rehnquist assumed that the "Government was free to question the employees who communicated with Thomas and outside counsel." Is this true? What about DR 7-104(A)(1) and Rule 4.2, both of which gener-

---

*For a thorough discussion of the *Upjohn* case, see John Sexton, A Post-*Upjohn* Consideration of Corporate Attorney-Client Privilege, 57 N.Y.U. L. Rev. 443 (1982). Additional issues in the representation of corporate (or other entity) clients appears in Chapter 9. — ED.

ally forbid a lawyer to speak with an opposing lawyer's client (including certain agents of a corporate client) without the opposing lawyer's permission? See Chapter 3. Won't these ethics rules prevent the IRS from interviewing the same employees? Or is the IRS exempt from these ethics rules because of its investigative responsibilities? When the rules do apply — and at the very least they apply to lawyers representing private clients — doesn't this magnify the likelihood of excessive corporate secrecy?

2. *Upjohn* says that the control group test "frustrates the very purpose of the privilege by discouraging the communication of relevant information by employees of the client to attorneys seeking to render legal advice to the client corporation." Is this true? Won't the attorneys remain as eager to speak to employees with relevant information as before, and won't those employees be equally forthcoming? In other words, is it correct to assume that information will be lost if the privilege doesn't protect communications with corporate employees? If it is correct to make this assumption, then isn't the Court wrong when it says that the IRS will be able to obtain the same information through its own interviews with Upjohn's employees? If without the privilege those employees would be less forthcoming when speaking to Upjohn's *counsel*, how candid will they be with the IRS?

3. It was not always clear that the attorney-client privilege would protect communications between the agents of an entity client and its lawyers. See Radiant Burners, Inc. v. American Gas Assn., 207 F. Supp. 771 (N.D. Ill. 1962), rev'd, 320 F.2d 314 (7th Cir. 1963), cert. denied, 375 U.S. 929 (1963). The privilege against self-incrimination does not protect corporations. See Hale v. Henkel, 201 U.S. 43 (1906). Was the decision to extend the attorney-client privilege to entities wise as a matter of social policy? In answering this question, consider whether we should treat small family-owned corporations differently from General Motors? What if the client is a government agency? Should the privilege exist for communications between the General Counsel of the Federal Communications Commission and its employees? Between New York City employees and its counsel? Or is it impossible to ask these questions without asking whether the attorney-client privilege is defensible in the first place?

QUESTIONS

2.4 Support or criticize the following position:

> *Upjohn* results in an increase of power for large corporations at the expense of the public interest. Corporations will now be encouraged to use lawyers for all services that could conceivably be called "legal," thereby enjoying the blanket of secrecy they could not assert if they utilized others for the same purposes. The behavior of large and powerful private organizations in society will be even further shielded from public view and control. Furthermore, if a high executive of a corporation suspects illicit

conduct by certain of its employees or subsidiaries, he or she will now use a lawyer to ferret out the facts and, if these prove damaging to the company, invoke the attorney-client privilege. If the corporate client is prepared to rectify the illegality, *Upjohn* will be irrelevant because it will have no need for the privilege. It is the corporation that desires to conceal the illegality and enjoy its fruits that will rely on *Upjohn*. The case is a disaster for an open society and the rule of law.

2.5   GHQ Corp., which manufactures baby food, learns that the Justice Department is investigating whether it has violated certain rules of the Food and Drug Administration. It retains outside counsel Ann Melford to conduct an internal investigation. GHQ's CEO sends out a memorandum explaining why Melford has been retained and instructing all personnel to cooperate with her. Melford speaks with several hundred GHQ employees throughout the United States and then writes a report which she delivers to the GHQ Board. The report states that three employees in the company's Seattle plant had indeed misstated data in their FDA filings. This conclusion is based on Melford's own investigation of the records in the Seattle office and conversations with the employees. In an effort to cooperate with the government and show its good faith, the Board instructs Melford to report her findings to the FDA and the Justice Department. Do the Seattle employees have grounds to object? Does Rule 1.13 address this issue?

Exceptions to the Privilege or the Ethical Duty

Despite the absolute terms with which lawyers sometimes describe the sanctity of client confidences, in fact there are several significant circumstances under which lawyers may reveal, or may be required to reveal, information clients would like to protect. The following examples are among the important exceptions to (or exclusions from) the privilege and the ethical duty to maintain client confidences.

Self-Defense.   Both the rules and code contain this exception to the ethical duty of confidentiality. The code provides that an attorney may reveal confidential information if "necessary . . . to defend himself . . . against an accusation of wrongful conduct." DR 4-101(C)(4). The rules retain this exception, using even broader language. A lawyer "may reveal [confidential] information to the extent the lawyer reasonably believes necessary . . . to establish a defense to a criminal charge or civil claim against the lawyer based upon conduct in which the client was involved, or to respond to allegations in any proceeding concerning the lawyer's representation of the client." Rule 1.6(b)(2).

What do you make of the fact that the rules expanded the circumstances under which lawyers may use or reveal client confidences in their own behalf, and at the same time narrowed the circumstances under which a lawyer may reveal client confidences to protect others? Compare DR 4-101(C)(3) with Rule 1.6(b)(1). As we have seen (page 19 supra), many jurisdictions, while adopting the rules, rejected the language of Rule 1.6(b)(1) and opted instead for various broader authorities.

Rule 1.6 and several cases recognize that a lawyer's right of self-defense applies whether charges against the lawyer are made by the client or third parties. In Meyerhofer v. Empire Fire & Marine Insurance Co., 497 F.2d 1190 (2d Cir.), cert. denied, 419 U.S. 998 (1974), Goldberg had been an associate in a law firm when the firm handled a registration statement for a client. The firm rejected Goldberg's view that certain information omitted from the statement had to be revealed. Goldberg quit and gave the SEC detailed information about the episode in affidavit form, with supporting documents. Three months later, Goldberg was named as one of a number of defendants in a civil action arising out of the registration statement. In a successful effort to extricate himself from the civil action, he gave information, including the SEC affidavit, to the plaintiff's lawyers. In the context of a subsequent motion to disqualify the plaintiff's lawyers for receiving this information, the Second Circuit held Goldberg's conduct proper.

The court emphasized that Goldberg had not provided information to the plaintiff's lawyers in order to enable them to bring the lawsuit in the first place. Goldberg was a victim, not an instigator. It also noted that the complaint against Goldberg alleged violation of civil and criminal statutes and sought damages of more than four million dollars. The court continued: "The cost in money of simply defending such an action might be very substantial. The damage to [Goldberg's] professional reputation which might be occasioned by the mere pendency of such a charge was an even greater cause for concern. Under these circumstances Goldberg had the right to make an appropriate disclosure with respect to his role in the public offering. Concomitantly, he had the right to support his version of the facts with suitable evidence." Id. at 1195. See also In re Robeson, 293 Or. 610, 652 P.2d 336, 344-345 (1982) (lawyer facing charge brought before disciplinary committee by third party may reveal client confidences).

Goldberg did not have to wait until the trial to defend himself against the charge of wrongdoing. He was allowed to reveal the information at an early stage of the action. In fact, had Goldberg known in advance that he was about to be sued, he could ethically have revealed the information even before the action was filed. In In re Friend, 411 F. Supp. 776, 777 (S.D.N.Y. 1975), the court applied *Meyerhofer* to a situation where a lawyer and his former client were under criminal investigation by the United States. The lawyer wanted to provide the grand jury with documents that would tend to exonerate him but which the client claimed were privileged. The court granted the lawyer's motion to be allowed to provide the documents to the grand jury, citing *Meyerhofer* and DR 4-101(C)(4). "Although, as yet, no formal accusation has been made against Mr. Friend, it would be senseless to require the stigma of an indictment to attach prior to allowing Mr. Friend to invoke the exception of DR 4-101(C)(4) in his own defense." Friend's luck eventually ran out. Both he and his corporate client were convicted of criminal charges. United States v. Amrep Corp., 418 F. Supp. 473 (S.D.N.Y. 1976).

United States v. Weger, 709 F.2d 1151, 1156-1157 (7th Cir. 1983), was a case like *Friend*. A law firm gave the government a typewritten letter from a former client which the government then used to convict the client of fraud by proving that the typestyle of the letter was the same as the typestyle on a purloined piece of law firm letterhead which the former client had used to forge a fraudulent title opinion. The court, citing *Friend*, said the law firm could properly give the letter to the government to aid its investigation of the former client. The firm could fear a "reasonable belief on the part of government officials that the law firm had been involved in the preparation of the fraudulent title opinion until such time as the firm could show that its letterhead stationery was used without its permission." While the court did not ultimately reach the *Meyerhofer* issue because it concluded that the firm had not revealed client confidences by providing a former client's letter merely so the government could compare typestyles, it expressed clear approval of the *Meyerhofer* rationale.

Rule 1.6 continues this position. The Comment to it states: The self-defense exception "does not require the lawyer to await the commencement of an action or proceeding that charges . . . complicity [in client wrongdoing], so that the defense may be established by responding directly to a third party who has made such an assertion." One court has suggested that a claim for Rule 11 sanctions (page 360 infra) would be "an accusation of wrongful conduct" within the meaning of the code exception. Brandt v. Schal Associates, Inc., 121 F.R.D. 368, 385 n.48 (N.D. Ill. 1988).

The self-defense exception is circumscribed by a rule of reasonable necessity. DR 4-101(C)(4); Rule 1.6(b)(2). A lawyer must have good reason to believe revelation of the information is necessary to his or her self-protection. In Sullivan v. Chase Investment Services of Boston, Inc., 434 F. Supp. 171, 188-189 (N.D. Cal. 1977), the court cited *Meyerhofer* approvingly but speculated that the "prospect of obtaining potentially damaging and otherwise unavailable evidence will encourage plaintiffs to sue defendants' attorneys routinely as aiders and abettors. In addition to causing attorneys great nuisance and expense, such a development could seriously undermine the willingness of clients to be completely open with their counsel." For a critical analysis of *Meyerhofer's* "unprecedented expansion of the self-defense exception" and proposals designed to prevent abuse of the privilege by overzealous prosecutors and civil plaintiffs," see Note, Eliminating "Backdoor" Access to Client Confidences: Restricting the Self-Defense Exception to the Attorney-Client Privilege, 65 N.Y.U. L. Rev. 992 (1990) (authored by Jennifer Cunningham). See also Eckhaus v. Alfa Laval, Inc., 764 F. Supp. 34 (S.D.N.Y. 1991) (refusing to broaden the self-defense exception to permit a lawyer to reveal client confidences in a defamation action against the client).

Equivalent self-defense exceptions have been recognized for privileged information. In re National Mortgage Equity Corp., 120 F.R.D. 687 (C.D. Cal. 1988); Housler v. First National Bank of East Islip, 484 F. Supp. 1321 (E.D.N.Y. 1980); First Federal Savings & Loan Assn. of Pittsburgh v. Oppenheim, Appel, Dixon & Co., 110 F.R.D. 557 (S.D.N.Y. 1986).

Collection of Fees.   Both the code and rules permit lawyers to reveal confidential information to the extent necessary to collect their fees. Compare DR 4-101(C)(4) with Rule 1.6(b)(2). Can you reconcile this authority with the ABA's refusal to authorize revelation of confidential information to (a) prevent the client from committing a "fraudulent act . . . likely to result in . . . substantial injury to the financial interest or property of another"; or (b) to "rectify the consequences of a client's . . . fraudulent act in the commission of which the lawyer's services had been used"? (See page 18 supra.)

Waiver.   A client may waive the protection of either the privilege or the ethical duty of confidentiality. Waiver may be explicit or implicit. Waiver will be implied when the client puts the confidential communication in issue in a litigation. For example, a defendant charged with transporting fraudulently obtained securities in interstate commerce claimed that his actions were taken in good faith reliance on counsel's advice. Consequently, the government was entitled to cross-examine him about a letter from counsel that might otherwise have been privileged. United States v. Miller, 600 F.2d 498 (5th Cir.), cert. denied, 444 U.S. 955 (1979). Similarly, in United States v. Bilzerian, 926 F.2d 1285 (2d Cir. 1991), the Court upheld the lower court ruling that if a defendant in a securities fraud case were to testify to his "good faith" belief in the "lawfulness" of his conduct, he would thereby waive the privilege for communications from his former counsel on the same subject. By contrast, in United States v. White, 887 F.2d 267, 270 (D.C. Cir. 1989), privilege was not waived when a defendant, charged with conspiring to defraud the United States, simply denied any criminal intent. "To be acquitted for lack of criminal intent, White did not need to introduce any evidence of communications to and from [counsel], and he did not do so." He simply put the government to its proof.

Clients may waive the protection of the attorney-client privilege by revelation of all or part of a confidential communication. In In re Subpoenas Duces Tecum, 738 F.2d 1367 (D.C. Cir. 1984), Tesoro Petroleum provided the SEC with information regarding illegal foreign bribes in order to receive more lenient treatment. Later, Tesoro's shareholders brought a derivative action and sought the same documents in discovery. Tesoro argued unsuccessfully that revelation to the SEC constituted only a "limited waiver" of the privilege. In In re Martin Marietta Corp., 856 F.2d 619, 623 (4th Cir. 1988), cert. denied, 490 U.S. 1011 (1989), Martin Marietta gave the United States attorney a Position Paper describing why it should not be indicted. Later, Pollard, a former employee of Martin Marietta, was indicted for fraud and sought to subpoena this information in his defense. The court held that "the Position Paper as well as the underlying details are no longer within the attorney-client privilege."

Contrast these results with the holding in In re von Bulow, 828 F.2d 94, 96-102 (2d Cir. 1987). Claus von Bulow was convicted of attempting to murder his wife, Martha, but the Rhode Island Supreme Court reversed, and, on retrial, he was acquitted. Alan Dershowitz of Harvard Law School, who had been von Bulow's appellate lawyer, then wrote a book about the case called Reversal of Fortune: Inside the *von Bulow* Case. Thereafter, in a civil action against Claus brought by Martha's children from a prior marriage, the plaintiffs "moved to compel discovery of certain discussions between [Claus] and his attorneys based on the alleged waiver of the attorney-client privilege with respect to those communications related in the book." The court held that publication of the book worked a "waiver by von Bulow as to the particular matters *actually disclosed* in the book," but no waiver of undisclosed conversations on the same or related subjects. The result would be opposite if a client made selective disclosure of privileged information in court. The "fairness doctrine" would then "requir[e] production of the remainder." But the "fairness doctrine" does not apply when "the privilege-holder or his attorney has made extrajudicial disclosures, and those disclosures have not subsequently been placed at issue during litigation."

The Crime-Fraud Exception.   Communications between clients and counsel are not protected when the client has consulted the lawyer to further a crime or fraud, regardless of whether the lawyer is aware of the client's purpose. In re Grand Jury Investigation (Schroeder), 842 F.2d 1223 (11th Cir. 1987); United States v. Laurins, 857 F.2d 529 (9th Cir. 1988). In those circumstances, you might say there was never a professional relationship to begin with because the client's purposes were inconsistent with our reasons for protecting these relationships. The Third Circuit has ruled, in what it said "may be . . . an issue of first impression," that the crime-fraud exception to the privilege will apply when the focus of the investigation is the misconduct of the law firm rather than the client. In re Impounded Case (Law Firm), 879 F.2d 1211, 1214 (3d Cir. 1989). The exception has also been applied where a third person is using an innocent client to further a fraudulent scheme. Duttle v. Bandler & Cass, 127 F.R.D. 46 (S.D.N.Y. 1989).

Assume a litigant asserts the attorney-client privilege and the opponent wants to contest the assertion on the ground of the crime-fraud exception. Must the opponent actually prove a crime or fraud in order to discover the allegedly privileged information? Sometimes the ultimate issue in the case within which the privilege question arises will be the very same alleged crime or fraud. Unless something is done, this can lead to a "chicken and egg" problem where a party has to prove his or her case in order to get the information needed to prove his or her case.

Courts have avoided this problem by establishing a second (lesser) burden of proof to invoke the crime-fraud exception. As the Second Circuit said in In re Grand Jury Subpoena Duces Tecum (Marc Rich & Co.), 731 F.2d 1032 (2d Cir. 1984):

> The crime or fraud need not have occurred for the exception to be applicable; it need only have been the objective of the client's communication. And the fraudulent nature of the objective need not be established definitively; there need only be presented a reasonable basis for believing that the objective was fraudulent. . . . As a practical matter, there is little difference between [the prima facie and the probable cause] tests. Both require that a prudent person have a reasonable basis to suspect perpetration or attempted perpetration of a crime or fraud, and that the communications were in furtherance thereof.

A final question is whether the trial court may review the allegedly privileged information in camera in deciding whether the opponent of the privilege has met the burden of proving the crime-fraud exception. In the federal system, United States v. Zolin, 491 U.S 554, 572 (1989), holds that it may if the opponent of the privilege can meet yet a third (still lesser) burden of proof:

> Before engaging in in camera review to determine the applicability of the crime-fraud exception, "the judge should require a showing of a factual basis adequate to support a good faith belief by a reasonable person" . . . that in camera review of the materials may reveal evidence to establish the claim that the crime-fraud exception applies.

But what evidence may a trial judge consider in determining whether to conduct the in camera review in the first place? (As you can see, this has now become a "chicken and egg and chicken and egg" problem.) The *Zolin* Court said "that the threshold showing to obtain in camera review may be met by using any relevant evidence, lawfully obtained, that has not been adjudicated to be privileged." Id. at 575.

Identity and Fees. Whether a client's identity or fee payments are protected by the attorney-client privilege is an issue that has received a good deal of attention lately, possibly because prosecutors have shown greater willingness to subpoena criminal defense lawyers before grand juries. See page 425 infra. Identity and fee payments are not generally privileged. In re Grand Jury Subpoena Served upon Doe (Slotnick), 781 F.2d 238 (2d Cir.) (en banc), cert. denied, 475 U.S. 1108 (1986). However, relatively rarely, a court will create an exception when "disclosure of [the client's] identity would disclose *other*, privileged communications (e.g., motive or strategy) and when the incriminating nature of the privileged communications has created in the client a reasonable expectation that the information would be kept confidential." Rabin v. United States, 896 F.2d 1267, 1273, vacated as moot, 904 F.2d 1498 (11th Cir. 1990) (collecting cases). In In re Grand Jury Proceedings 88-9 (MIA), 899 F.2d 1039 (11th Cir. 1990), the lawyer unsuccessfully sought to protect the identity of the client who had paid him $30,200 to represent another client. "On this record," the court held, "we are not persuaded that disclosure of this usually nonprivileged information will reveal other privileged information." Id. at 1043. By contrast, in Matter of Grand Jury Proceeding, Cherney, 898 F.2d 565, 568 (7th Cir. 1990), the claim succeeded. Cherney was hired by *X* to represent Hrvatin. The government sought the identity of *X*. The court held that

> the privilege protects an unknown client's identity where its disclosure would reveal a client's motive for seeking legal advice. . . . [Here, *X*] sought legal advice concerning his involvement in the drug conspiracy. Disclosure of [*X*'s] identity would necessarily reveal the client's involvement in that crime and thus reveal his motive for seeking legal advice in the first place. . . . This is not the typical case where the government seeks disclosure of a known client's general fee structure, which is usually to determine whether the attorney was paid with illicit funds. In that scenario, revelation of the fee information would most likely serve to incriminate the fee payer, but would not risk exposure of a confidential communication.

See also In re Grand Jury Subpoena for Attorney Representing Criminal Defendant Reyes-Requena (DeGeurin), 926 F.2d 1423 (5th Cir. 1991) (fee and identity protected when revelation will expose the client's confidential purpose in seeking counsel).

Public Policy? Courts occasionally suggest that the attorney-client privilege may sometimes have to give way to other values. The New Jersey Supreme Court wrote in Matter of Nackson, 114 N.J. 527, 537, 555 A.2d 1101, 1106 (1989), that "the privilege is not absolute. Like other privileges, it must in some circumstances yield to the higher demands of order." See also People v. Osorio, 75 N.Y.2d 80, 549 N.E.2d 1183, 550 N.Y.S.2d 612, 614 (1989): "[E]ven if the technical requirements of the privilege are satisfied, it may, nonetheless, yield in a proper case where strong public policy requires disclosure."

Nonetheless, it is rare to find a case in which public policy is held to require disclosure of privileged information. The much-headlined Stuart case in Massachusetts is an example of judicial reluctance to subordinate the privilege to public policy concerns. Carol DiMaiti Stuart was fatally wounded while sitting in her car in a Boston street with her husband Charles. Carol was pregnant. Her son Christopher was born alive but then died. Charles, who was also wounded but survived, told the police that he and Carol were attacked in a robbery. Charles consulted counsel and shortly thereafter committed suicide. The State, which suspected that Charles and others still alive might have criminal responsibility, wanted to question Charles's counsel about conversations with Charles. It argued that Charles "no longer can be harmed by the disclosure of his communications to his attorney, and therefore . . . the privilege should be 'overridden' because society's interest in ascertaining the truth concerning the deaths of [the victims] and in identifying the parties responsible . . . outweighs the value sought to be promoted by means of the attorney-client privilege." The court disagreed:

> A rule that would permit or require an attorney to disclose information given to him or her by a client in confidence . . . would in many instances . . . so deter the client from "telling all" as to seriously impair the attorney's ability to function effectively. . . . Therefore, except where mandated by constitutional considerations . . . we conclude that the attorney-client privilege should not yield either before or after the client's death to society's interest, as legitimate as we recognize that interest is, in obtaining every man's evidence.

One judge dissented. He argued that the "court should adopt a limited exception to the privilege in those cases where the interests of the client are so insignificant and the interests of justice in obtaining the information so compelling, that the administration of justice is better served through waiver." Matter of John Doe Grand Jury Investigation, 408 Mass. 480, 562 N.E.2d 69, 69-72 (1990). Compare In re Jacqueline F., 47 N.Y.2d 215, 391 N.E.2d 967, 972, 417 N.Y.S.2d 884, 889 (1979), where the New York Court of Appeals required a lawyer to reveal the whereabouts of his client, the guardian of a child, in order to enable the parents of the child to regain custody following a court order requiring the lawyer's client to return the child. The court wrote that on the facts before it the privilege had to "yield to the best interests of the child."

Is There a Professional Relationship? Remember that in order for a communication to be ethically protected or to be privileged, there must be a client-lawyer relationship. The presence of a lawyer is a necessary but not a sufficient condition for that relationship. In In re Grand Jury Investigation (Schroeder), page 36, supra, at 1224, an attorney-accountant prepared a client's tax returns and gave him tax advice. Preparation of the returns was held not to be "legal advice within the scope of [the] privilege," although tax advice was held to be privileged. Consequently, the attorney could be required to answer questions about the tax returns. In another instructive case, a law firm associate's confession, to a firm colleague, of his grand jury perjury was admissible in evidence against him, although other lawyers at the firm were representing the associate on the underlying investigation. The confession was motivated by friendship between the associates and not by a desire to receive legal advice. United States v. Tedder, 801 F.2d 1437 (4th Cir. 1986), cert. denied, 480 U.S. 938 (1987).

Finally, of course, the purported client's communication must be with an attorney or, in some places, someone the client reasonably believes to be an attorney. In United States v. Arthur Young & Co., 465 U.S. 805, 806 (1984), the Court unanimously refused to recognize "a work-product immunity for an independent auditor's tax accrual workpapers." How can we square this result with *Upjohn*? Why should one profession (law) enjoy protection denied to another profession (accounting) when the two sell essentially the same kind of tax advice? After *Arthur Young*, Washington lawyer Lloyd Cutler said: "I think the reason why there are more confidentiality privileges for lawyers is the historic one that lawyers were around long before accountants. In areas where they are doing similar kinds of work, it doesn't make much sense to separate the two." New York Times, April 3, 1984 at D2.

QUESTIONS

2.6   "I'm Anne Sullivan, and for a number of years I've represented the Aristocratic Toy & Novelty Company, a family-owned business run by two brothers and a sister. Basically, they make things for kids — small toys and games, little novelties, stuff you'd put in party bags. One thing they make is bubble bath in various flavors — grape, cherry, and even, if you can believe it, butterscotch. You don't eat the bubble bath — the package says that clearly — but it has the aroma of the particular flavor.

"The three owners — Geoff, Deborah, and Tom — came by to see me last week. 'Anne, we've got a problem,' Geoff said. And he goes on to explain how they discovered that some of the fluid they use to clean the equipment spilled into a batch of soap and wound up in the contents of a bubble bath vat, which was then mixed with diverse flavors. The flavored bubble bath is sold in 12- and 24-ounce bottles and also in little one-ounce capsules so people can use them in party bags or to select a variety pack. It seems the fluid found its way into not more than a hundred or so one-ounce capsules of various flavors, but by the time they discovered what happened, the capsules were already mixed with tens of thousands of other capsules and sent all over the southwest, where the factory is.

"Geoff explained that if a child uses these contaminated capsules that child *may* — depending on the child — get a rash, which could be extensive and painful for two or three days but will then go away. I told them the potential products liability risks; it's a field with which I'm quite familiar. They went out for an hour, and when they returned, Tom told me they didn't want to do anything at all, just wait to see if a claim gets made. If someone makes a claim, they'll settle it out of court in exchange for a secrecy agreement. They say that since the rash won't show up for a day or so and since by then the capsule will probably be in the trash, most people will figure it's something the child ate. Anyway, Deborah said, the negative publicity from this kind of recall — assuming a small business like theirs could even figure out how to recall all those capsules — would hurt them a lot worse than a few claims. They also figure that a recall will encourage false claims, something that I have seen happen before. So they told me to keep quiet about it, which I have — except for telling you. What do I do next?"

2.7   A lawyer for a corporation told a company manager that her contemplated conduct was legal. Relying on this advice, she engaged in the conduct and was indicted in a federal court for giving a federal official an illegal gratuity. At the trial, her defense is that she relied on the advice of counsel (see page 35 supra). However, the company has instructed the lawyer to assert its attorney-client privilege for his conversations with the manager, who has since left the company and is contemplating a civil claim against it. Can he?

FURTHER READING

Issues of confidentiality reappear throughout this book. Students interested in a critique of the fundamental justification for confidentiality rules might begin by looking at Fred Zacharias's two-part study, Rethinking Confidentiality, 74 Iowa L. Rev. 351 (1989), and Rethinking Confidentiality II: Is Confidentiality Constitutional?, 75 Iowa L. Rev. 601 (1990). Nancy Moore has analyzed the values that inform the attorney-client privilege and compared it to the privilege in the physician-patient context. Nancy Moore, Limits to Attorney-Client Confidentiality: A "Philosophically Informed" and Comparative Approach to Legal and Medical Ethics, 36 Case W. Res. L. Rev. 177 (1985). Geoffrey Hazard has examined the attorney-client privilege in its historical context. Geoffrey Hazard, An Historical Perspective on the Attorney-Client Privilege, 66 Calif. L. Rev. 1061 (1978). See also Developments in the Law: Privileged Communications, 98 Harv. L. Rev. 1450 (1985).

2. Agency

Lawyers are their clients' agents. The law of agency therefore applies to the client-lawyer relationship. As attorneys, or agents, before the law (compared to attorneys in *fact*), lawyers have certain authority and certain duties. Because lawyers are also fiduciaries, these duties will sometimes be more demanding than those imposed on other agents. Later we shall discuss some of the duties imposed by the agency and fiduciary status. Here we review the authority agency status affords the lawyer. Not surprisingly, it is an authority to act for the client on the subject matter of the retainer. Acting for the client means that the lawyer's conduct will be attributable to the client, even if the lawyer errs, is careless, or worse. To make sure that the lawyer doesn't exceed his or her retainer, it is important to define so far as is reasonably possible what the lawyer is retained to do. That definition may from time to time require revision as the representation proceeds. A second reason to clearly define the scope of the lawyer's retainer is to protect the lawyer against a charge of neglect or malpractice. An ambiguous retainer might be construed to include services the lawyer never intended to perform. A client may have the opposite impression and accuse the attorney of neglect, as well as seek damages for malpractice, when the anticipated work is not performed. See Jackson v. Pollick, 751 F. Supp. 132 (E.D. Mich. 1990).

TAYLOR v. ILLINOIS
484 U.S. 400 (1988)

[Illinois has a rule that requires criminal defendants to provide a list of their anticipated witnesses in response to prosecutorial demand. Taylor's lawyer was found to have violated this rule willfully. As a sanction, the trial judge refused to let him call one Wormley, whose testimony would arguably have helped establish a defense of self-defense. The defendant was convicted, and the state courts upheld the trial court's preclusion order, rejecting a Compulsory Process Clause claim. The following excerpts from the majority opinion of Justice Stevens and the dissent of Justice Brennan (in which Justices Marshall and Blackmun joined) address the correctness of ordering preclusion in the absence of evidence that the defendant was party to the willful violation of the discovery request.]

The argument that the client should not be held responsible for his lawyer's misconduct strikes at the heart of the attorney-client relationship. Although there are basic rights that the attorney cannot waive without the fully informed and publicly acknowledged consent of the client,[24] the lawyer has — and must have — full authority to manage the conduct of the trial. The adversary process could not function effectively if every tactical decision required client approval. Moreover, given the protections afforded by the attorney-client privilege and the fact that extreme cases may involve unscrupulous conduct by both the client and the lawyer, it would be highly impracticable to require an investigation into their relative responsibilities before applying the sanction of preclusion. In responding to discovery, the client has a duty to be candid and forthcoming with the lawyer, and when the lawyer responds, he or she speaks for the client. Putting to one side the exceptional cases in which counsel is ineffective, the client must accept the consequences of the lawyer's decision to forgo cross-examination, to decide not to put certain witnesses on the stand, or to decide not to disclose the identity of certain witnesses in advance of trial. In this case, petitioner has no greater right to disavow his lawyer's decision to conceal Wormley's identity until after the trial had commenced than he has to disavow the decision to refrain from adducing testimony from the eyewitnesses who were identified in the Answer to Discovery. Whenever a lawyer makes use of the sword provided by the Compulsory Process Clause, there is some risk that he may wound his own client.

JUSTICE BRENNAN dissenting.

Criminal discovery is not a game. It is integral to the quest for truth and the fair adjudication of guilt or innocence. Violations of discovery rules thus cannot go uncorrected or undeterred without undermining the truthseeking process. The question in this case, however, is not whether discovery rules should be enforced but whether the need to correct and deter discovery violations requires a sanction that itself distorts the truthseeking process by excluding material evidence of innocence in a criminal case. I conclude that, at least where a criminal defendant is not personally responsible for the discovery violation, alternative sanctions

24. See, e.g., Brookhart v. Janis, 384 U.S. 1, 7-8 (1966) (defendant's constitutional right to plead not guilty and to have a trial where he could confront and cross-examine adversary witness could not be waived by his counsel without petitioner's consent); Doughty v. State, 470 N.E.2d 69, 70 (Ind. 1984) (record must show "personal communication of the defendant to the court that he chooses to relinquish the right [to a jury trial])"; Cross v. United States, 117 U.S. App. D.C. 56, 325 F.2d 629 (1963) (waiver of right to be present during trial).

are not only adequate to correct and deter discovery violations but are far superior to the arbitrary and disproportionate penalty imposed by the preclusion sanction. Because of this, and because the Court's balancing test creates a conflict of interest in every case involving a discovery violation, I would hold that, absent evidence of the defendant's personal involvement in a discovery violation, the Compulsory Process Clause per se bars discovery sanctions that exclude criminal defense evidence. . . .

In the absence of any evidence that a defendant played any part in an attorney's willful discovery violation, directly sanctioning the attorney is not only fairer but *more* effective in deterring violations than excluding defense evidence. The threat of disciplinary proceedings, fines, or imprisonment will likely influence attorney behavior to a far greater extent than the rather indirect penalty threatened by evidentiary exclusion. Such sanctions were available here. . . .

The situation might be different if the defendant willfully caused the discovery violation because, as the Court points out, some defendants who face the prospect of a lengthy imprisonment are arguably impossible to deter with direct punitive sanctions such as contempt. But that is no explanation for allowing defense witness preclusion where there is no evidence that the defendant bore any responsibility for the discovery violation. . . .

Nor is the issue resolved by analogizing to tactical errors an attorney might make such as failing to put witnesses on the stand that would have aided the defense. Although we have sometimes held a defendant bound by tactical errors his attorney makes that fall short of ineffective assistance of counsel, we have not previously suggested that a client can be punished for an attorney's *misconduct*. There are fundamental differences between attorney misconduct and tactical errors. Tactical errors are products of a legitimate choice among tactical options. Such tactical decisions must be made within the adversary system, and the system requires attorneys to make them, operating under the presumption that the attorney will choose the course most likely to benefit the defendant. Although some of these decisions may later appear erroneous, penalizing attorneys for such miscalculations is generally an exercise in futility because the error is usually visible only in hindsight — at the time the tactical decision was made there was no obvious "incorrect" choice, and no prohibited one. . . .

The rationales for binding defendants to attorneys' routine tactical errors do not apply to attorney misconduct. An attorney is never faced with a legitimate choice that includes misconduct as an option. Although it may be that "[t]he adversary process could not function effectively if every tactical decision required client approval," that concern is irrelevant here because a client has no authority to approve misconduct. Further, misconduct is not visible only with hindsight, as are many tactical errors. Consequently, misconduct is amenable to direct punitive sanctions against attorneys as a deterrent that can prevent attorneys from systemically engaging in misconduct that would disrupt the trial process. There is no need to take steps that will inflict the punishment on the defendant. . . .

The Court's balancing approach [which allowed trial courts to choose among remedies], moreover, has the unfortunate effect of creating a conflict of interest in every case involving a willful discovery violation because the defense counsel is placed in a position where the best argument he can make on behalf of his client is, "Don't preclude the defense witness — punish me personally." In this very case, for example, the defense attorney became noticeably timid once the judge threatened to report his actions to the disciplinary commission. He did not argue, "Sure, bring me before the disciplinary commission; that's a much more appropriate sanction than excluding a witness who might get my client acquitted." I cannot see how we can expect defense counsel in this or any other case to act as vigorous advocates for the interests of their clients when those interests are adverse to their own.

CINE FORTY-SECOND STREET THEATRE
v. ALLIED ARTISTS PICTURES
602 F.2d 1062 (2d Cir. 1979)

[After the antitrust plaintiff repeatedly failed to respond to the defendants' interrogatories, the magistrate recommended that the district judge preclude plaintiff from introducing evidence with respect to damages, a sanction tantamount to dismissal of its damage claim. The district judge, after concluding that if "there were ever a case in which drastic sanctions were justified, this is it," nevertheless assessed costs as the only sanction. In an interlocutory appeal, the court wrote that the "question before us is whether a grossly negligent failure to obey an order compelling discovery may justify the severest disciplinary measures available," namely dismissal. The court agreed that dismissal was inappropriate for an oversight amounting to simple negligence by counsel, and continued]:

. . . But where gross professional negligence has been found — that is, where counsel clearly should have understood his duty to the court — the full range of sanctions may be marshalled. Indeed, in this day of burgeoning, costly and protracted litigation courts should not shrink from imposing harsh sanctions where, as in this case, they are clearly warranted.

A litigant chooses counsel at his peril, Link v. Wabash Railroad Co., 370 U.S. 626 (1962), and here, as in countless other contexts, counsel's disregard of his professional responsibilities can lead to extinction of his client's claim.[10] See, e.g., Anderson v. Air West, Inc., 542 F.2d 522 (9th Cir. 1976) (dismissal for failure to proceed with due diligence); RePass v. Vreeland, 357 F.2d 801 (3d Cir. 1966) (negligent failure to file suit within statute of limitations); Universal Film Exchanges, Inc. v. Lust, 479 F.2d 573 (4th Cir. 1973) (party not relieved under Fed. R. Civ. P. 60(b) from summary judgment where counsel's failure to proffer defenses was grossly, rather than excusably, negligent).

Binding the Client

Generally.   Many are the circumstances in which a lawyer may bind a client. By hiring counsel, a client necessarily delegates authority to speak and act on a range of issues reasonably within the scope of the retainer. If the attorney acts improperly or foolishly, the client may still be bound, but he may be able to sue the lawyer for damages. In litigation, as the previous two cases show, an attorney's default, even if inexcusable, may be laid to the client. As between the client and a third party, isn't this the correct resolution? In criminal cases too?

Sometimes the rights of a third party and the interest of the courts in being expeditious can be vindicated by sanctioning the attorney rather than the client. In M.E.N. Co. v. Control Fluidics, Inc., 834 F.2d 869 (10th Cir. 1987), the lower court had ordered a default judgment against the defendants after they had failed to comply with discovery. On appeal, the Tenth Circuit remanded for a determination of whether the defendants were personally at fault for the discovery failures and suggested that if they weren't, a sanction against the attorneys alone, and possibly discipline, was the appropriate response.

Problems arise if the client wants to disavow a settlement after her lawyer has accepted one. Rule 1.2(a) and case law give the client the right to decide whether to settle a civil matter or enter a plea in a criminal matter. (See page 65 infra.) Clients, however, may delegate authority to settle civil disputes to their lawyers ("get the most you can over two million"). If a lawyer has actual authority to settle (express or implied), there will be no problem. The lawyer will have acted properly and the client will be bound. Hallock v. State, 64 N.Y.2d 224, 474 N.E.2d 1178, 485 N.Y.S.2d 510 (1984). What happens if the lawyer settles without actual authority? The lawyer may still have *apparent* authority to settle, created because the

10. The acts and omissions of counsel are normally wholly attributable to the client. Link v. Wabash Railroad Co., 370 U.S. 626 (1962). This case does not present the extraordinary circumstance of complete disappearance or mental illness of counsel that justified relief in Vindigni v. Meyer, 441 F.2d 376 (2d Cir. 1971) and United States v. Cirami, 563 F.2d 26 (2d Cir. 1977). Indeed, by Magistrate Gershon's finding and counsel's own admission, Clark, Cine's principal officer, was aware of every aspect of discovery and intimately involved with the progress of the case.

client has said or done something that has led the other party to conclude reasonably that the lawyer is authorized to settle. Edwards v. Born, Inc., 792 F.2d 387 (3d Cir. 1986); Hallock v. State, supra. If a lawyer has neither apparent nor actual authority to settle, the client will usually be able to disavow the settlement. See, e.g., Fennell v. TLB Kent, Co., 865 F.2d 498 (2d Cir. 1989); Johnson v. Tesky, 57 Or. App. 133, 643 P.2d 1344 (1982). Some cases, however, bind the client to the settlement, leaving him to seek any remedy in a malpractice action. Glazer v. J.C. Bradford & Co., 616 F.2d 167 (5th Cir. 1980) (Georgia law).

Vicarious Admissions.   A lawyer's statements may be the vicarious admissions of a client. A lawyer, as an agent, is subject to the vicarious admission rules of the law of evidence. See, e.g., Fed. R. Evid. 801(d)(2)(C) and (D). These rules apply in litigation and in negotiations. For statements in negotiation, see United States v. Margiotta, 662 F.2d 131, 142-143 (2d Cir. 1981) (statements by criminal suspect's attorney to persuade attorney general not to indict are vicarious admissions of suspect, but excluded because of immunity agreement); and Brown v. Hebb, 167 Md. 535, 175 A. 602, 606 (1934) (debt to doctor admitted when lawyer responded to doctor's bill by offering a lesser amount "for the service rendered").*

For the operation of this principle in litigation, consider the unusual case of United States v. McKeon, 738 F.2d 26 (2d Cir. 1984), where the government wanted to introduce the opening statement of the defense lawyer in an earlier, aborted trial as a vicarious admission against the defendant on retrial. The opening statement revealed a theory of the case at odds with the theory the defendant was planning to present on retrial. (Do you see the evidentiary value there?) The Second Circuit held that whether a lawyer's prior trial statement may be used vicariously against his client at a new trial would depend on the circumstances. It set out a list of factors to guide district courts, then upheld use of the statement in the case before it. One consequence of this holding was that the lawyer had to be disqualified from retrying the case because the defendant would now need to call him as a witness to explain his earlier statement. (See page 240 infra on the advocate-witness rule.)

McKeon was distinguished, despite dissent, in United States v. Valencia, 826 F.2d 169, 173 (2d Cir. 1987), where, in an effort to win the government's agreement to pretrial release of the defendant, the defense lawyer told a prosecutor that his client had not met a particular person before August 20. In fact, the two were old friends. The government unsuccessfully sought to introduce the lawyer's statement as a "false exculpatory" vicarious admission. (Do you see the evidentiary value?) The

---

*Statements made in the context of settlement discussions are often inadmissible as a matter of policy, whether made by the lawyer or the client. See Fed. R. Evid. 408.

circuit court applied the *McKeon* factors and affirmed. The "defendant's interest in retaining the services of his counsel, assuring uninhibited discussions between his counsel and the prosecutor, and avoiding the risk of impairing his privilege against self-incrimination" supported the trial judge's discretion in refusing to admit the statement.

Vicarious evidentiary admissions can be used against the client, but they don't bind the client. The client can try to disown them or even introduce contrary proof. However, statements a lawyer makes in a case on trial — in court or in pleadings — can indeed bind the client. In McLhinney v. Lansdell Corp. of Maryland, 254 Md. 7, 254 A.2d 177 (1969), the plaintiff's lawyer was relieved of having to introduce proof of the identity of the driver of the truck that hit the plaintiff's car because the defense lawyer's opening statement admitted that the truck was driven by the defendant's employee. Opening statements are not evidence, but assertions in them are established as true for the purpose of trial. See also Oscanyan v. Arms Co., 103 U.S. 261, 263 (1880); United States v. McKeon, supra.

Procedural Defaults.   In criminal cases, an attorney's failure to raise a defendant's constitutional rights in compliance with valid state procedures will generally prevent the defendant from asserting those rights collaterally in federal court unless he or she can prove "actual innocence." Coleman v. Thompson, 111 S. Ct. 2546 (1991); Smith v. Murray, 477 U.S. 527 (1986); Murray v. Carrier, 477 U.S. 478, 496 (1986). If, however, the error is so serious as to amount to the ineffective assistance of counsel, the client will not be bound. See, e.g., Kimmelman v. Morrison, 477 U.S. 365 (1986); Evitts v. Lucey, 469 U.S. 387 (1985). Standards for ineffective assistance claims are discussed at page 689 infra.

3. Fiduciary

A lawyer has a fiduciary relationship with his or her client. Some state courts actually use the word "fiduciary" in describing the nature of the relationship while others describe the lawyer's responsibilities as equivalent to those traditionally associated with fiduciaries. The fiduciary aspect of the relationship is said to arise after the formation of the attorney-client relationship. Kittler & Hedelson v. Sheehan Properties, 295 Minn. 232, 235, 203 N.W.2d 835, 838 (1973). There are at least three reasons for imposing fiduciary obligations on a lawyer. Once the relationship is established, the client will likely have begun to depend on the attorney's integrity, fairness, and judgment. Second, the attorney may have acquired information about the client that gives the attorney an unfair advantage in negotiations between them. Finally, the client will generally not be in a position where he or she is free to change attorneys, but will rather be economically or personally dependent on the attorney's continued representation. The attorney's fiduciary obligation applies to a fee agreement reached after the attorney-client relationship has been entered. See generally, Annot., 13 A.L.R.3d 701 (1967). Several cases will illustrate the contours of the attorney's fiduciary duty.

In Benson v. State Bar of California, 13 Cal. 3d 581, 531 P.2d 1081, 119 Cal. Rptr. 297, 299 (1975), the attorney borrowed money from a current client. He "was heavily in debt, and insolvent, at the time he approached [the client] for these loans." In return for the loans, he gave the client unsecured promissory notes. In disbarring the lawyer, the court said:

> Furthermore, given the fiduciary nature of petitioner's relationship with [the client], it can be fairly inferred that his suggestion of an unsecured promissory note met with her approval because she trusted his judgment. The gravamen of the charge is abuse of that trust, and regardless of petitioner's contention that he never specifically recommended the unsecured loans to [the client], it is undisputed that in soliciting them he failed to reveal the extent of his preexisting indebtedness and financial distress.

James Smith, an attorney, was under investigation for drug use. He offered to cooperate with Colorado police as an undercover informant. He secretly recorded a telephone conversation with a former client in which he asked the former client to sell him cocaine. He then met with the former client wearing a body microphone. The recorded conversations were ultimately used to convict the former client of three felony charges. The Colorado Supreme Court held that although Smith

> no longer represented the [former client], the conduct in all probability would not have occurred had [Smith] not relied upon the trust and confidence placed in him by the [former client] as a result of the recently completed attorney-client relationship between the two. The undisclosed use of a recording device necessarily involves elements of deception and trickery which do not comport with the high standards of candor and fairness to which all attorneys are bound.

For these and other offenses, Smith was suspended for two years. People v. Smith, — Colo. — , 778 P.2d 685, 686-687 (1989).

Lerner, a lawyer, was a member of the board of a cooperative apartment building and its legal committee. Lerner recommended that the co-op retain a particular law firm to challenge its real estate taxes. But he allegedly failed to tell the board that the firm was going to split its fee

with Lerner and his firm. The board sued for Lerner's portion of the fee
plus other damages. The court held that these facts established a claim
for breach of fiduciary duty and fraudulent concealment. "Client knowledge of a joint representation agreement between lawyers is the sine qua
non of its ethical validity. . . . Here, where claims of self-dealing and divided loyalty are presented, a fiduciary may be required to disgorge any
ill-gotten gain even where the plaintiff has sustained no direct economic
loss." Excelsior 57th Corp. v. Lerner, 160 A.D.2d 407, 553 N.Y.S.2d 763,
764-765 (1st Dept. 1990).

Finally, a lawyer who goes into secret competition with his own client,
or assists another of the client's fiduciaries in doing so, may be liable to
the client in a civil action. In Avianca, Inc. v. Correia, 705 F. Supp. 666
(D.D.C. 1989), the lawyer had secretly helped an officer of the lawyer's
corporate client compete with the client in violation of that officer's fiduciary duty. In David Welch Co. v. Erskine & Tulley, 203 Cal. App. 3d
884, 250 Cal. Rptr. 339 (1988), the defendant law firm became the competitor of a client, a collection business, after receiving confidential information from the client about that business. See also Tri-Growth Centre
City Ltd. v. Silldorf, Burdman, Duignan & Eisenberg, 216 Cal. App. 3d
1139, 265 Cal. Rptr. 330 (1990) (allegation that lawyer used confidential
information to usurp client's business opportunity).

4. Loyalty and Diligence

The duties of loyalty and diligence may be considered together since
they overlap somewhat. The duty of loyalty requires that the lawyer pursue, and be free to pursue, the client's objectives unfettered by other,
conflicting responsibilities or interests. The duty of loyalty forms the basis of the conflicts of interest rules discussed in Chapters 5 and 6. As we
shall see, it may survive the termination of the attorney-client relationship. The requirement of diligence imposes on the lawyer an obligation
to pursue the client's interest without undue delay. Generally, divided
loyalties will undermine the lawyer's ability to be diligent in pursuit of the
client's interests as well as threaten the lawyer's fiduciary position. An undivided loyalty will not, however, assure diligence.

The Canons of Professional Ethics provided, in Canon 15 that

> The lawyer owes "entire devotion to the interest of the client, warm zeal in
> the maintenance and defense of his rights and the exertion of his utmost
> learning and ability," to the end that nothing be taken or be withheld from
> him, save by the rules of law, legally applied.

The Code of Professional Responsibility states in Canon 7 that "A lawyer
should represent a client zealously within the bounds of the law." But EC

7-17 makes clear that the duty of loyalty applies only to the lawyer's professional relationship. Similarly, Model Rule 6.4 permits a lawyer to be actively involved in a law reform organization even though the organization's goals "may affect the interests of a client of the lawyer." Rule 1.2(b) emphasizes that a "lawyer's representation of a client . . . does not constitute an endorsement of the client's political, economic, social or moral views or activities."

Close readers may notice that whereas the code gives the duty to "zealously" represent a client the status of a canon (canonization is one notch below getting carved on Mt. Rushmore), the rules relegate the root of the same word ("zeal") to the *comment* to Rule 1.3 (on diligence), qualify it with a prepositional phrase, and immediately temper it with "however," to wit: "A lawyer should act with commitment and dedication to the interests of the client and with zeal in advocacy upon the client's behalf. However, a lawyer is not bound to press for every advantage that might be realized for a client." What do you make of this?

The obligation of diligence appears in both the code and the rules. The code says that "A lawyer shall not neglect a legal matter entrusted to him." DR 6-101(A)(3). It also says that "A lawyer shall not intentionally fail to carry out a contract of employment entered into with a client for professional services," DR 7-101(A)(2), and that "a lawyer shall not intentionally prejudice or damage his client during the course of the professional relationship." DR 7-101(A)(3). The rules say simply that "A lawyer shall act with reasonable diligence and promptness in representing a client." Rule 1.3. Is there a difference between the affirmative command of the rules (be diligent, counselor!) and the prescription against neglect in the code? Does one require more than the other? One of the most frequent grounds for complaints to disciplinary committees is failure to pursue a client's interests. (This failure generally goes hand in hand with the related failure, discussed below, to keep the client informed about the status of a matter.) Sometimes the failure to act diligently will actually prejudice a client's rights, as when a lawyer permits a statute of limitations to expire. If so, the client will likely have a malpractice action against the lawyer.

Sometimes the failure simply has emotional or psychological consequences to the client who, for example, may be eager to have her divorce concluded, his tax dispute with the government resolved, or her will prepared and executed. Although the client is free to change lawyers, that is not always easy. The client will usually have paid the lawyer a fee, have gone through one or more interview sessions, and have "invested" mental and psychological energy in the resolution of the client's problem with the particular lawyer. Of course, if there is no actual prejudice to the client as a result of the delay, there may not be a malpractice action. Or should the emotional consequences of neglect be compensable? In any event, the lawyer may still be subject to discipline.

5.   *The Duty to Inform*

In the course of a representation, a lawyer is likely to learn a great deal of information bearing on the client's matter. How much of it must she tell the client? The answer cannot be "all" because much of the information will be technical or trivial. Time is also a factor. Yet the answer cannot be "none" because the lawyer is the client's agent on the matter. It's the client who will have to live with the result. So where do we draw the line? This issue slides into the autonomy question next discussed, but some introduction is in order.

Rule 1.2(a) says that a "lawyer shall abide by a client's decisions concerning the objectives of representations . . . and shall consult with the client as to the means by which they are to be pursued." The rule also requires lawyers to accept a client's decision on "an offer of settlement." In a criminal case, the rule requires a lawyer to "abide by the client's decision . . . as to a plea to be entered, whether to waive jury trial and whether the client will testify." The comment says that the "client has ultimate authority to determine the purposes to be served by legal representation [and] a right to consult with the lawyer about the means to be used in pursuing those objectives." The comment recognizes that a "clear distinction between objectives and means sometimes cannot be drawn." It gives the lawyer "responsibility for technical and legal tactical issues" but requires the lawyer to "defer to the client regarding such questions as the expense to be incurred and concern for third persons."

Shall we then say that a lawyer has an obligation to keep a client informed on matters within the client's authority or on which the client has a right to consult? Does Rule 1.2(a) and its comment adequately describe those matters? The comment itself recognizes the difficulty of "clear distinction" and adds that "[l]aw defining the lawyer's scope of authority in litigation varies among jurisdictions." The code has no direct counterpart to Rule 1.2(a). Ethical Considerations 7-7 and 7-8 come closest. What do they tell you?

Violation of the duty to communicate with a client can result in discipline even when the client's legal interests are not jeopardized. In re Shaughnessy, 467 N.W.2d 620, 621 (Minn. 1991) (such failures are "intensely frustrating to the client, reflect adversely on the bar, and are destructive of public confidence in the legal profession").

We should also turn to Rule 1.4, which, after all, is titled "Communication." Rule 1.4 has two parts. Subsection (b) requires a lawyer to "explain a matter to the extent reasonably necessary to permit the client to make informed decisions regarding the representation." But what about information on matters that are within the lawyer's domain? Rule 1.4(a) says that lawyers must keep clients "reasonably informed about the status of a matter." (They must also "promptly comply with reasonable requests for information.") That doesn't quite answer the question, does it? Turning to the comment, the first sentence does suggest that the duty to provide information applies to both means *and* ends. It says that "The client should have sufficient information to participate intelligently in decisions concerning the objectives of the representation and the means by which they are to be pursued, to the extent the client is willing and able to do so." However, the balance of the paragraph uses objectives only (i.e., settlement) as an example. The main code references to a lawyer's duty to communicate can be found in Ethical Considerations 7-8 and 9-2.

We have reviewed duties imposed by the code and Rules. How about case law? For that we offer a page from Professor Spiegel's article on the subject.

Mark Spiegel
LAWYERING AND CLIENT DECISIONMAKING: INFORMED CONSENT AND THE LEGAL PROFESSION
128 U. Pa. L. Rev. 41, 67-70 (1979)

Hornbook agency law states that the agent has a duty to disclose all material information to his client. In applying this law to lawyers, courts have faced two problems. The first is similar to the one discussed above: concerning what issues must a lawyer disclose information to his client? The second was faced in the medical cases: assuming a duty to disclose, how is "material" defined? Should the standard of materiality be that of the profession, the lay public, the particular client, or the court?

The issues about which the lawyer must inform his client are the same as those which the lawyer must allow the client to decide — that is, the lawyer must disclose information related to the subject matter of the action and to conflicts of interest. This answer reintroduces the problem of distinguishing subject matter from procedure and tactics. In addition, some courts have confused the question of determining the subject matter of the action with the question of degree of disclosure. If a particular disclosure was not explicitly required by the agreement between the lawyer and client, the courts have imposed on the lawyer no duty of disclosure. For example, one court dismissed the contention that an attorney had any obligation to disclose to his client the right to appeal by finding that the contract between the attorney and client did not require the attorney to appeal the case.[94] The court never asked itself whether a client may reasonably expect an attorney to reveal options for pursuing the case even though the attorney has no intention of continuing representa-

94. Young v. Bridwell, 20 Utah 2d 332, 437 P.2d 686 (1968).

tion. The court's approach puts an affirmative burden on the client to know enough law to require certain disclosures in his contract with the attorney. As discussed later, this is a poor way of approaching the problem.

The second question — the standard of materiality — has not been answered consistently in the cases. In *Spector v. Mermelstein*,[97] the court defined "material facts," which an attorney must reveal to his client, as those "which, if known to the client, might well have caused him, acting as a reasonable man, to alter his proposed course of conduct." This standard is similar to that stated in *Canterbury v. Spence*,[99] the leading medical informed-consent case.

Directly contrary to *Spector* are two cases that require expert testimony to prove that the alleged failure to disclose information to the client fell below the ordinary standards of the profession. In one case, the attorney allegedly failed to disclose a settlement offer;[102] in the other, the lawyer failed to explain the meaning of a clause in a purchase contract.[103] Although one can explain these cases by looking more closely at their facts, acceptance of the standard they adopt would eviscerate any meaningful informed-consent requirement. Certainly, the existence of a settlement offer or the meaning of a proposed agreement is the minimum information a client needs. . . .

This lack of attention to the issue of disclosure raises particularly significant problems with regard to cases involving the lawyer's exercise of judgment. In these, courts generally do not impose an obligation on the attorney to tell a client of the uncertainty of the results of a particular course of action. Rather, as long as the attorney has researched the issue and has found the law uncertain, he has the discretion to weigh the costs and benefits of alternative courses of action. To some extent, these cases are related to the previously discussed problem of who should make a given decision. If the decision belongs to the attorney, one could argue that he need not inform the client. Even in cases of settlement or agreements, however, no clear-cut obligation has emerged to inform the client of any uncertainty in the attorney's recommendations.

A lawyer representing a client in a personal injury action did not relay a $90,000 settlement offer. He considered it too skimpy. The case went to trial. The jury was even more skimpy. It found for the defendant. The client thereafter learned of the settlement offer and sued the lawyer. The client testified that he would have accepted the offer (of course) and

97. 361 F. Supp. 30 (S.D.N.Y. 1972), modified on other grounds, 485 F.2d 474 (2d Cir. 1973).
99. 464 F.2d 772 (D.C. Cir.), cert. denied, 409 U.S. 1064 (1972).
102. Dorf v. Relles, 355 F.2d 488 (7th Cir. 1966).
103. Wright v. Williams, 47 Cal. App. 3d 802, 121 Cal. Rptr. 194 (1975).

the jury believed him. On appeal, the court said it "need not decide . . . whether a lawyer has an obligation to transmit a patently unreasonable offer to his client" because the jury could reasonably have decided that competent counsel would have presented the $90,000 offer. Moores v. Greenberg, 834 F.2d 1105, 1108 (1st Cir. 1987). In Rizzo v. Haines, 520 Pa. 484, 555 A.2d 58 (1989), the court held that a lawyer has a duty to communicate settlement offers to a client, that failure to do so is malpractice, and that expert testimony was not necessary to establish the lawyer's negligence. Compare the criminal analogue, plea bargains. State v. James, 48 Wash. App. 353, 739 P.2d 1161 (1987). A defense lawyer's duties require "not only communicating actual offers, but discussion of tentative plea negotiations and the strengths and weaknesses of defendants' case so that the defendants know what to expect and can make an informed judgment whether or not to plead guilty."

FURTHER READING

The subject of the attorney's duty to inform, and the twin issue of the client's right of informed consent, have received increasing attention of late. In addition to Professor Spiegel's early article, see Susan Martyn, Informed Consent in the Practice of Law, 48 Geo. Wash. L. Rev. 307 (1980); Gary Munneke & Theresa Loscalzo, The Lawyer's Duty to Keep Clients Informed: Establishing a Standard of Care in Professional Liability Actions, 9 Pace L. Rev. 391 (1989); and Cornelius Peck, A New Tort Liability for Lack of Informed Consent in Legal Matters, 44 La. L. Rev. 1289 (1984).

QUESTION

2.8 "My name is Martin Chin. I do general corporate work in Seattle. One of the companies I represent is Endicott Press, a financial printer. My partner Sally Zagott represents Jessie Marsh, an independent investor. Marsh wants to do a joint venture with Endicott and a few others, and Zagott wants to know whether Endicott would agree to use another law firm, as it sometimes does when our firm has a conflict, and let her represent Marsh in negotiating the deal. Marsh is prepared to consent to this too. I checked, and Endicott said no problem. But what I know and Sally does not is that there is an ongoing criminal investigation of Endicott in which the company is cooperating fully, with the understanding that it will be allowed quietly to plead guilty to a misdemeanor that carries a $1,000 fine. Endicott wants to keep all this quiet and won't let me tell Sally or, obviously, Marsh. I'm not sure what my responsibilities are here or what I should do."

B. AUTONOMY OF ATTORNEYS AND CLIENTS

Lawyers as professionals and as agents of their clients exercise judgment and make decisions intended to help achieve their clients' objectives through the law. Clients delegate authority to their lawyers and therewith some of their autonomy. We have seen (page 52 supra) that the ends/means distinction does not distinctly separate those decisions that properly belong to the lawyer from those that belong to the client. Often, though, the distinction works. For example, we now know that criminal clients must decide whether to plead guilty; civil clients must decide whether to settle (although that power can be delegated). On the other hand, a defendant will have no complaint if his lawyer stipulates to the easily provable fact that the banks he allegedly robbed were federally insured. Poole v. United States, 832 F.2d 561 (11th Cir. 1987), cert. denied, 488 U.S. 817 (1988). Between these examples lies an area of uncertainty.

Several questions confront us in deciding how we allocate authority within the professional relationship. Shall we incorporate medicine's informed consent standard? Should clients have the right to insist on more authority than whatever rule we develop might otherwise allow? What will it do to professionalism if lawyers are required to get client approval of too many "means" decisions, or are required to abide by an instruction that the lawyer deems foolhardy? After all, the lawyer was retained because he or she is an expert on means — legal means. The freedom to choose those means is important to the lawyer's professional satisfaction and the quality of his or her work life. If pushed too far, we will turn lawyers into bureaucrats, scribes, or mouthpieces.

Still, some means decisions are not all that complicated, especially if a lawyer is willing to explain a few technical points. Some tactical choices raise important moral or financial issues for the client. Many clients are sophisticated about the subject that forms the basis of the legal representation. In litigation or negotiation, the client may be better able to take the measure of a known opponent. Further, it is the client, not the lawyer, who will have to live with the result. In an oft-told, possibly apocryphal story, a lawyer represented a client in a serious criminal trial that resulted in conviction. "What happens now?" the client asked after the jury announced the verdict. "Now," replied the lawyer with a shrug, "I go back to my office and you go to jail."

These various considerations argue for fluidity in the allocation of authority. Fluidity, however, has its limits. At times, a decision will have to be made although the client and lawyer disagree, in which case we need a rule that tells us whose decision it is. And even before we reach that point, we must recognize that lawyers make dozens of decisions daily (hundreds during a trial). They cannot consult on all of them. They need to know which decisions can safely (that is, without risk of discipline or malpractice liability) be made without consultation.

We have been talking about what standard the legal or ethical rules should adopt. That standard may define the minimum, but it is not the only reference. Can't a lawyer consult with, or defer to, a client more than the rules demand? As mentioned above (page 16 supra), Douglas Rosenthal reported after empirical investigation that personal injury lawyers who consulted with their clients were likely to get higher verdicts or settlements than lawyers who said, in effect, "Thanks for the case. Now go home and I'll call you when I need you." Consultation also makes sense from the perspective of good client relations. It shows the client that the lawyer has been thinking about the case, has concern for the client's point of view, and has respect for the client's intelligence. Many lawyers believe that a client who is consulted is more likely to be satisfied with a result than a client who is suddenly presented with the same result and told to take it or leave it.

In the material that follows, we introduce some of the issues in this still fairly new area of autonomy within the client-lawyer relationship.

1. The Lawyer's Autonomy

JONES v. BARNES
463 U.S. 745 (1983)

CHIEF JUSTICE BURGER delivered the opinion of the Court.

We granted certiorari to consider whether defense counsel assigned to prosecute an appeal from a criminal conviction has a constitutional duty to raise every nonfrivolous issue requested by the defendant.

ISSUE

I

In 1976, Richard Butts was robbed at knifepoint by four men in the lobby of an apartment building; he was badly beaten and his watch and money were taken. Butts informed a Housing Authority Detective that he recognized one of his assailants as a person known to him as "Froggy," and gave a physical description of the person to the detective. The following day the detective arrested respondent David Barnes, who is known as "Froggy."

Respondent was charged with first and second degree robbery, second degree assault, and third degree larceny. The prosecution rested primarily upon Butts' testimony and his identification of respondent. During cross-examination, defense counsel asked Butts whether he had ever undergone psychiatric treatment; however, no offer of proof was made on the substance or relevance of the question after the trial judge sua sponte instructed Butts not to answer. At the close of trial, the trial judge declined to give an instruction on accessorial liability requested by the defense. The jury convicted respondent of first and second degree robbery and second degree assault.

The Appellate Division of the Supreme Court of New York, Second Department, assigned Michael Melinger to represent respondent on appeal. Respondent sent Melinger a letter listing several claims that he felt should be raised. Included were claims that Butts' identification testimony should have been suppressed, that the trial judge improperly excluded psychiatric evidence, and that respondent's trial counsel was ineffective. Respondent also enclosed a copy of a pro se brief he had written.

In a return letter, Melinger accepted some but rejected most of the suggested claims, stating that they would not aid respondent in obtaining a new trial and that they could not be raised on appeal because they were not based on evidence in the record. Melinger then listed seven potential claims of error that he was considering including in his brief, and invited respondent's "reflections and suggestions" with regard to those seven issues. The record does not reveal any response to this letter.

Melinger's brief to the Appellate Division concentrated on three of the seven points he had raised in his letter to respondent: improper exclusion of psychiatric evidence, failure to suppress Butts' identification testimony, and improper cross-examination of respondent by the trial judge. In addition, Melinger submitted respondent's own pro se brief. Thereafter, respondent filed two more pro se briefs, raising three more of the seven issues Melinger had identified.

At oral argument, Melinger argued the three points presented in his own brief, but not the arguments raised in the pro se briefs. On May 22, 1978, the Appellate Division affirmed by summary order....

[Eventually, the Second Circuit, relying on Anders v. California, 386 U.S. 738 (1967), granted Barnes's habeas corpus petition on the ground that he had a Sixth Amendment right to have his lawyer raise all nonfrivolous issues on appeal. The Second Circuit also held that Barnes did not have to demonstrate a likelihood of success on these issues. One judge dissented.]

II

In announcing a new per se rule that appellate counsel must raise every nonfrivolous issue requested by the client, the Court of Appeals relied primarily upon Anders v. California, supra. There is, of course, no constitutional right to an appeal, but in Griffin v. Illinois, 351 U.S. 12, 18 (1956), and Douglas v. California, 372 U.S. 353 (1963), the Court held that if an appeal is open to those who can pay for it, an appeal must be provided for an indigent. It is also recognized that the accused has the ultimate authority to make certain fundamental decisions regarding the case, as to whether to plead guilty, waive a jury, testify in his or her own behalf, or take an appeal. In addition, we have held that, with some limitations, a defendant may elect to act as his or her own advocate, Faretta v. California, 422 U.S. 806 (1975). Neither *Anders* nor any other decision of this Court suggests, however, that the indigent defendant has a constitutional right to compel appointed counsel to press nonfrivolous points requested by the client, if counsel, as a matter of professional judgment, decides not to present those points.

This Court, in holding that a State must provide counsel for an indigent appellant on his first appeal as of right, recognized the superior ability of trained counsel in the "examination into the record, research of the law, and marshalling of arguments on [the appellant's] behalf," Douglas v. California, 372 U.S., at 358. Yet by promulgating a per se rule that the client, not the professional advocate, must be allowed to decide what issues are to be pressed, the Court of Appeals seriously undermines the ability of counsel to present the client's case in accord with counsel's professional evaluation.

Experienced advocates since time beyond memory have emphasized the importance of winnowing out weaker arguments on appeal and focusing on one central issue if possible, or at most on a few key issues. Justice Jackson, after observing appellate advocates for many years, stated:

> One of the first tests of a discriminating advocate is to select the question, or questions, that he will present orally. Legal contentions, like the currency, depreciate through over-issue. The mind of an appellate judge is habitually receptive to the suggestion that a lower court committed an error. But receptiveness declines as the number of assigned errors increases. Multiplicity hints at lack of confidence in any one. . . . [E]xperience on the bench convinces me that multiplying assignments of error will dilute and weaken a good case and will not save a bad one. Jackson, Advocacy Before the Supreme Court, 25 Temple L.Q. 115, 119 (1951).

Justice Jackson's observation echoes the advice of countless advocates before him and since. . . .

There can hardly be any question about the importance of having the appellate advocate examine the record with a view to selecting the most promising issues for review. This has assumed a greater importance in an era when oral argument is strictly limited in most courts — often to as little as 15 minutes — and when page limits on briefs are widely imposed. Even in a court that imposes no time or page limits, however, the new per se rule laid down by the Court of Appeals is contrary to all experience and logic. A brief that raises every colorable issue runs the risk of burying good arguments — those that, in the words of the great advocate John W. Davis, "go for the jugular" — in a verbal mound made up of strong and weak contentions.

This Court's decision in *Anders*, far from giving support to the new per se rule announced by the Court of Appeals, is to the contrary. *Anders* recognized that the role of the advocate "requires that he support his client's appeal to the best of his ability." Here the appointed counsel did just that. For judges to second-guess reasonable professional judgments and impose on appointed counsel a duty to raise every "colorable" claim suggested by a client would disserve the very goal of vigorous and effective advocacy that underlies *Anders*. Nothing in the Constitution or our interpretation of that document requires such a standard.[7] The judgment of the Court of Appeals is accordingly reversed.

[Justice Blackmun, concurring in the judgment, thought that "as an *ethical* matter, an attorney should argue on appeal all nonfrivolous claims upon which his client insists." However, Justice Blackmun did not believe that his view on the "ideal allocation of decisionmaking authority between client and lawyer necessarily assumes constitutional status." The client's "remedy, of course, is a writ of habeas corpus."]

JUSTICE BRENNAN, with whom JUSTICE MARSHALL joins, dissenting. . . .

It is clear that respondent had a right to the assistance of counsel in connection with his appeal. . . .

The Constitution does not on its face define the phrase "assistance of counsel," but surely those words are not empty of content. No one would doubt that counsel must be qualified to practice law in the courts of the State in question, or that the representation afforded must meet minimum standards of effectiveness. To satisfy the Constitution, counsel must function as an advocate for the defendant, as opposed to a friend of the court. Anders v. California, 386 U.S., at 744; Entsminger v. Iowa, 386 U.S., [748 (1967)] at 751. Admittedly, the question in this case requires us to look beyond those clear guarantees. What is at issue here is the relationship between lawyer and client — who has ultimate authority to decide which nonfrivolous issues should be presented on appeal? I believe the right to "the assistance of counsel" carries with it a right, per-

---

7. The only question presented by this case is whether a criminal defendant has a constitutional right to have appellate counsel raise every nonfrivolous issue that the defendant requests. The availability of federal habeas corpus to review claims that counsel declined to raise is not before us, and we have no occasion to decide whether counsel's refusal to raise requested claims would constitute "cause" for a petitioner's default within the meaning of Wainwright v. Sykes, 433 U.S. 72 (1977). See also Engel v. Isaac, 456 U.S. 107 (1982).

sonal to the defendant, to make that decision, against the advice of counsel if he chooses.

If all the Sixth Amendment protected was the State's interest in substantial justice, it would not include such a right. However, in Faretta v. California, 422 U.S. 806 (1975), we decisively rejected that view of the Constitution. . . . *Faretta* establishes that the right to counsel is more than a right to have one's case presented competently and effectively. It is predicated on the view that the function of counsel under the Sixth Amendment is to protect the dignity and autonomy of a person on trial by *assisting* him in making choices that are his to make, not to make choices for him, although counsel may be better able to decide which tactics will be most effective for the defendant. Anders v. California also reflects that view. Even when appointed counsel believes an appeal has no merit, he must furnish his client a brief covering all arguable grounds for appeal so that the client may "raise any points that he chooses." 386 U.S., at 744.

The right to counsel as *Faretta* and *Anders* conceive it is not an all-or-nothing right, under which a defendant must choose between forgoing the assistance of counsel altogether or relinquishing control over every aspect of his case beyond its most basic structure (i.e., how to plead, whether to present a defense, whether to appeal). A defendant's interest in his case clearly extends to other matters. Absent exceptional circumstances, he is bound by the tactics used by his counsel at trial and on appeal. He may want to press the argument that he is innocent, even if other stratagems are more likely to result in the dismissal of charges or in a reduction of punishment. He may want to insist on certain arguments for political reasons. He may want to protect third parties. This is just as true on appeal as at trial, and the proper role of counsel is to *assist* him in these efforts, insofar as that is possible consistent with the lawyer's conscience, the law, and his duties to the court.

I find further support for my position in the legal profession's own conception of its proper role. The American Bar Association has taken the position that

> [W]hen, in the estimate of counsel, the decision of the client to take an appeal, *or the client's decision to press a particular contention on appeal*, is incorrect[, c]ounsel has the professional duty to give to the client fully and forcefully an opinion concerning the case and its probable outcome. *Counsel's role, however, is to advise. The decision is made by the client.* ABA Standards for Criminal Justice, Criminal Appeals, Standard 21-3.2, Comment, at 21-42 (1980) (emphasis added). . . .

ABA

It is no secret that indigent clients often mistrust the lawyers appointed to represent them. There are many reasons for this, some perhaps unavoidable even under perfect conditions — differences in education, disposition, and socio-economic class — and some that should (but may not always) be zealously avoided. A lawyer and his client do not always have the same interests. Even with paying clients, a lawyer may have a strong interest in having judges and prosecutors think well of him, and, if he is working for a flat fee — a common arrangement for criminal defense attorneys — or if his fees for court appointments are lower than he would receive for other work, he has an obvious financial incentive to conclude cases on his criminal docket swiftly. Good lawyers undoubtedly recognize these temptations and resist them, and they endeavor to convince their clients that they will. It would be naive, however, to suggest that they always succeed in either task. A constitutional rule that encourages lawyers to disregard their clients' wishes without compelling need can only exacerbate the clients' suspicion of their lawyers. As in *Faretta*, to force a lawyer's *decisions* on a defendant "can only lead him to believe that the law conspires against him." In the end, what the Court hopes to gain in effectiveness of appellate representation by the rule it imposes today may well be lost to decreased effectiveness in other areas of representation. . . .

Finally, today's ruling denigrates the values of individual autonomy and dignity central to many constitutional rights, especially those Fifth and Sixth Amendment rights that come into play in the criminal process. Certainly a person's life changes when he is charged with a crime and brought to trial. He must, if he harbors any hope of success, defend himself on terms — often technical and hard to understand — that are the State's, not his own. As a practical matter, the assistance of counsel is necessary to that defense. See Johnson v. Zerbst, 304 U.S., [458 (1938)] at 463. Yet, until his conviction becomes final and he has had an opportunity to appeal, any restrictions on individual autonomy and dignity should be limited to the minimum necessary to vindicate the State's interest in a speedy, effective prosecution. The role of the defense lawyer should be above all to function as the instrument and defender of the client's autonomy and dignity in all phases of the criminal process. . . .

The Court subtly but unmistakably adopts a different conception of the defense lawyer's role — he need do nothing beyond what the State, not his client, considers most important. In many ways, having a lawyer becomes one of the many indignities visited upon someone who has the ill fortune to run afoul of the criminal justice system.

I cannot accept the notion that lawyers are one of the punishments a person receives merely for being accused of a crime. Clients, if they wish, are capable of making informed judgments about which issues to appeal, and when they exercise that prerogative their choices should be respected unless they would require lawyers to violate their consciences, the law, or their duties to the court.

The Scope of the Lawyer's Autonomy

Following *Jones*, an indigent defendant submitted his own brief after assigned counsel refused to include certain nonfrivolous arguments on appeal. The intermediate appellate court rejected it. After acknowledging the special plight of indigent criminal defendants, the New York Court of Appeals upheld the rejection. "[R]outine denial of applications to file pro se briefs could support a claim that a court is acting arbitrarily and the failure to accept such a brief in a given case could constitute an abuse of discretion. Accordingly, we believe the better practice would be for the appellate courts to accept timely supplemental pro se briefs. The decision, however, lies within the sound discretion of the court." People v. White, 73 N.Y.2d 468, 479, 539 N.E.2d 577, 541 N.Y.S.2d 749, 755, cert. denied, 493 U.S. 859 (1989).

Jones v. Barnes is a Sixth Amendment case. Justice Blackmun is of the view that the lawyer acted unethically. Do you agree? What if the lawyer thought it clear beyond doubt that inclusion of the client's nonfrivolous claims would undermine the effectiveness of the brief? What if the lawyer would be professionally embarrassed to assert them? In the final paragraph of his dissent, Justice Brennan wrote that a client's choices "should be respected unless they would require lawyers to violate their consciences, the law, or their duties to the court." Would Justice Brennan approve if Melinger were conscientiously opposed to including the client's arguments in the appeal brief?

Jones concerned a matter of strategy. The code and rules allow for lawyer autonomy in several additional ways. DR 7-101(B)(1) says a lawyer may, "where permissible, exercise his professional judgment to waive or fail to assert a right or position of [the] client." That's circular, isn't it? What's "permissible"? DR 7-101(B)(2) permits a lawyer to "[r]efuse to aid or participate in conduct that he believes to be unlawful, even though there is some support for an argument that the conduct is legal." Rule 3.3(c) permits a lawyer to decline to offer evidence that the lawyer "reasonably believes is false"; the code simply forbids a lawyer to offer evidence she "knows" is false. DR 7-102(A)(4). The rules permit a lawyer to "limit the objectives of the representation if the client consents after consultation." Rule 1.2(c). The code has no equivalent provision, but isn't that authority present anyway? Both documents assert, in different ways, that a lawyer's representation of a client on a matter implies nothing about the lawyer's personal belief about the matter nor, according to the rules, does the representation "constitute an endorsement of the client's political, economic, social or moral views or activities." Compare EC 7-17 with Rule 1.2(b). It is odd, isn't it, to find such a disclaimer in an ethics code. It is not a rule that tells lawyers to act or refrain from acting in a particular way. It is not a rule that can be violated. Why is it there?

A lawyer who disagrees with a client, or who feels that professional autonomy is unduly limited, may be able to withdraw from the representation. See page 69 infra. Indeed, the threat of withdrawal gives the lawyer great leverage to get his or her way, doesn't it?

In Ethical Discretion in Lawyering, 101 Harv. L. Rev. 1083 (1988), Professor William Simon argues that "[l]awyers should have ethical discretion to refuse to assist in the pursuit of legally permissible courses of action and in the assertion of potentially enforceable legal claims." In exercising this discretion, he writes, a basic consideration of the lawyer "should be whether assisting the client would further justice." Professor Simon would apparently permit lawyers to exercise this discretion not only in choosing whether to accept a client, as they now may, but also in deciding how to represent the client. What do you think about that? See also Stephen Gillers, Can a Good Lawyer Be a Bad Person?, 84 Mich. L. Rev. 1011 (1986), which posits a series of hypotheticals and asks whether the lawyers who populate them can fairly be subject to moral criticism for their behavior.

2. The Client's Autonomy

OLFE v. GORDON
93 Wis. 2d 173, 286 N.W.2d 573 (1980)

[The plaintiff hired Gordon to handle the sale of her real property to Demman. She instructed Gordon that she was willing to take back a first mortgage but only a first mortgage. Gordon negotiated a contract that provided for a second mortgage. Gordon and his partner led Olfe to believe that it was a first mortgage. It was not, and after the purchaser defaulted, and the first mortgage was foreclosed, Olfe lost more than $25,000. The trial court dismissed the case because of the insufficiency of evidence and "a lack of expert testimony relating to the standard of care required of attorneys in similar circumstances." On this point, the state supreme court wrote:]

Since Olfe did not present expert testimony to establish the standard of care and a departure from that standard, we must determine whether Gordon's actions fall within the exception to the rule requiring expert testimony. Olfe's first two allegations, that Gordon failed to provide in the offer to purchase that Olfe's security interest would be a first mortgage and that he failed to draft or cause to be drafted a mortgage that would be senior to any other Demman would obtain on the premises of sale, are contentions that Gordon is liable for damages caused by his negligent disregard of Olfe's instructions. The legal theory on which these allegations are premised is well established:

It has generally been recognized that an attorney may be liable for all losses caused by his failure to follow with reasonable promptness and care the explicit instructions of his client. Moreover, an attorney's honest belief that the instructions were not in the best interests of his client provides no defense to a suit for malpractice. [Footnotes omitted.] Note, Attorney Malpractice, 63 Colum. L. Rev. 1292, 1302 (1963).

The attorney-client relationship in such contexts is one of agent to principal, and as an agent the attorney "must act in conformity with his authority and instructions and is responsible to his principal if he violates this duty." Ford v. Wisconsin Real Estate Examining Board, 48 Wis. 2d 91, 102, 179 N.W.2d 786, 792 (1970). While actions for disregard of instructions can be based upon fiduciary and contractual principles, the principal's cause of action for an agent's breach of duty may also lie in tort. "[I]f a paid agent does something wrongful, either knowing it to be wrong, or acting negligently, the principal may have either an action of tort or an action of contract." Restatement (Second) of Agency, sec. 401, Comment a, 238 (1958). See also: Estate of Pratt, 221 Wis. 114, 120, 266 N.W. 230, 233 (1936), where this court stated, "It is elementary that a principal has a cause of action sounding in tort against his agent when the latter violates a duty that he owes to the former." Expert testimony is not required to show that the agent (attorney) has violated his duty.

The Scope of the Client's Autonomy

Gordon failed to follow Olfe's instructions. Melinger refused to follow Barnes's instructions too. Barnes lost and Olfe won. Why? Was it simply because one action depended on the Sixth Amendment and the other was in malpractice? Olfe's employment of Gordon did not authorize him to make the decision he did in the face of her contrary instruction. The court finds Gordon's conduct improper as a matter of law. Not only does Olfe not have to present expert evidence on the issue, she need not present any evidence. If Olfe had said nothing about security, could Gordon then have elected to accept a second mortgage without talking to Olfe? Or would he have had to ask for direction? See Rule 1.4.

Courts have designated certain decisions as belonging to clients. Rule 1.2(a), note 24 to Justice Stevens's opinion in *Taylor* (page 43 supra), and numerous cases state that in criminal matters the decision whether to plead guilty, whether to testify, whether to be present during trial, and whether to waive a jury are all for the client to decide. See also United States v. Martinez, 883 F.2d 750 (9th Cir. 1989), cert. denied, 111 S. Ct. 2886 (1991) (in accord, but presuming waiver when a represented defendant fails to testify). The decision whether to appeal also belongs to the defendant. ABA Standard for Criminal Justice 4-8.2(a). A defendant has been held entitled to decide whether lesser included offenses should be submitted to the jury. State v. Boeglin, 105 N.M. 247, 731 P.2d 943 (1987).

In civil matters, the decision to settle belongs to the client (page 54 supra), although a client who refuses to settle in order to force counsel to reduce a contingent fee may violate "the duty of good faith and fair dealing implied in" the fee agreement. Hagans, Brown & Gibbs v. First National Bank of Anchorage, 783 P.2d 1164, 1166 (Alaska 1989). Also in civil matters, the client is entitled to make decisions whether to stipulate to facts or law, when the stipulation will have a significant effect on the client's claim or defense, and whether to forgo or pursue an appeal. See Lawyers Manual on Professional Conduct (ABA/BNA) 31:306 (1989).

Do these cases add up to a theory? Consider one more. In Shehade v. Gerson, 148 Ill. App. 3d 1026, 500 N.E.2d 510, 513 (1986), appeal denied, 113 Ill. 2d 585, 505 N.E.2d 362 (1987), a mother asked her lawyer to prevent unsupervised visitation between her former husband and their child. The lawyer did not seek the appropriate court order. The child was kidnapped to Jordan, the father's native country. The mother sued for malpractice. The lower court dismissed the complaint. The appellate court reversed for a trial. "Because the kidnapping took place during a period of unsupervised visitation, and because unsupervised visitation is precisely what Fryda requested Gerson to prevent . . . we cannot say that a jury would be unable to find a causal connection between Gerson's alleged negligence and Fryda's claimed injury."

The Medical Analogy

In medical malpractice cases, courts have chosen between two standards to describe what a physician must tell a patient when eliciting the patient's consent to treatment. The older, "professional" standard required the physician to tell the patient what a reasonable medical practitioner would have disclosed to his patient. The newer, "prudent patient" standard focuses on the listener, not the speaker, and requires the physician to disclose information that a reasonable patient, in what the physician knows or should know is the patient's position, would want to know. See generally Largey v. Rothman, 110 N.J. 204, 540 A.2d 504 (1988) (replacing the "professional" standard with the "prudent patient" standard). Cleckner v. Dale, 719 S.W.2d 535, 540-541 (Tenn. App. 1986), is a rare case that discusses the principle of informed consent in the context of lawyers:

> When a lawyer is advising a client on a legal matter, he or she is in a position no different from that of a physician advising a client of options for medi-

cal treatment. Under the doctrine of informed consent, a doctor can be found negligent for failing to advise a patient regarding the consequences of medical treatment. In this context, the doctor's liability is based upon the nondisclosure of pertinent information. The doctor's liability is independent of the patient's conduct. This Court has held in informed consent cases that the appropriate standard of care and the conformity of the doctor's conduct to this standard must be proved using expert testimony. The same rules should apply to attorneys who are advising their clients. . . .

The principal issues in this case are whether the advice Dale gave the Cleckners adequately informed them of their potential options and the consequences of these options and whether Dale's conduct met the minimum standards of professional conduct expected of lawyers representing the buyers in a real estate transaction. If the finder of fact determines that the lawyer's conduct complies with the applicable standard of professional conduct, then the lawyer cannot be held liable for the consequences of his client's informed decision. If, however, the finder of fact determines that the lawyer's conduct was deficient and did not meet the applicable professional standards, then the lawyer may be liable for the losses resulting from the client's reliance upon the deficient legal advice.

FURTHER READING

Susan Martyn has proposed a statute to define a right of informed consent and provide damages for its violation. Martyn, Informed Consent in the Practice of Law, 48 Geo. Wash. L. Rev. 307 (1980). A cause of action is established if a client proves that a lawyer "failed to disclose reasonably foreseeable choices of action in a manner permitting the client to make a knowledgeable evaluation of the legal consequences of the choices." The client also has to prove proximate cause and damages. A client can waive the protection of the statute.

QUESTION

2.9 David Luban addresses the issue of client autonomy in his article, Paternalism and the Legal Profession, 1981 Wis. L. Rev. 454, 455-456. Professor Luban poses the following hypotheticals, each of which he answers after a philosophical inquiry into the bases for paternalism. What should the lawyer in each of these situations do?

(1) You are the court-appointed attorney representing the interests of a thirteen-year-old boy in a custody case. You must make a report to the court about who should get custody; such reports usually have a major impact on what is decided. Your client, an inarticulate and unhappy-look-

ing boy in a faded jeans jacket, is sullen and suspicious. He says he would rather live with his father, but falls silent when you try to find out why. The father is a glad-handing, sporadically employed alcoholic; the mother is a hard-working disciplinarian who lives with her mother in a tidy row-house. Both women appear concerned for your client's welfare. In your opinion, the boy prefers his father because his father lets him get away with more; the social worker on the case tells you that the boy is part of a drinking and doping crowd.

(2) You are handling the wife's side in a divorce. She does not appear to be coping well. When you broach the subject of the settlement, she insists that she wants nothing in the way of property or child support, because "my husband will do what's right by me."

(3) Another divorce: this time you discover that the husband's attorney is a bit of a patsy. You press hard, and when the smoke clears you have obtained a lopsided settlement in favor of your client. The husband seems willing to go along with it, but your client objects, insisting that you renegotiate a settlement that is fair. Or: your client is the husband. You inform him that he is not legally liable for alimony but he wants to pay it anyway so that his children will know he is a *mensch*.

(4) Your client is a teen-ager who was involved in a car accident in which his date was killed. He is charged with driving while intoxicated and vehicular homicide, but some of the circumstances are unclear, and the prosecutor offers to let him plead guilty to reckless operation of a vehicle. Client, however, insists that he will plead guilty to the greater charges, and in an emotional scene tells you that he cannot live with himself unless he publicly confesses what he knows to be his crime and expiates the guilt by going to jail.

(5) Your state has a law which provides that if a worker is injured on the job, and the injury is exacerbated by psychosomatic factors (even if they are brought on by problems that have nothing to do with work), he is eligible for worker's compensation. The rub is that psychiatric evidence is required to prove the case. Your client is a proud 55-year-old Slovenian-American machinist who took a metal chip in his eye at work. Although his doctor says there is nothing physically wrong with the eye, he complains of distorted vision. You tell him about the law, but he indignantly refuses to see a psychiatrist, now or ever. "Psychiatrists are for crazy people." You sense that you can coerce him into going to the psychiatrist by casting aspersions on his adequacy as a provider.

(6) You are a *pro bono* movement lawyer defending members of an anti-nuclear group that has just suffered a mass arrest for criminal trespass. The judge tells you that if they plead guilty he will let them off with a fine; it is clear, however, that he will not be pleased if any of them insists on a jury trial. Two of your clients insist that they want their day in court; although you have told them that there is no question but that they will be convicted, your impression is that they believe deep down that the world is waiting to hear them utter the clear voice of reason in court. You have heard someone else refer to them as "airheads," and sense that you could convince other members of the group to put pressure on the two.

C. TERMINATING THE RELATIONSHIP

Both the Code and Rules describe the circumstances under which lawyers may withdraw from a representation. Case law describes the client's authority to discharge a lawyer. The inherent powers doctrine (see page 2 supra) has been used to strike legislation that would intrude in this area. Succession of Wallace, 577 So. 2d 1222 (La. 1991).

1. Termination by the Client

Clients, it is said, may fire their lawyers for any reason or no reason. Carlson v. Nopal Lines, 460 F.2d 1209 (5th Cir. 1972). Of course, this holds true only for clients who retain their lawyers. Indigent criminal defendants may not fire the lawyers who have been appointed to represent them, although they can ask the court to assign them a new lawyer or choose to represent themselves. Even a client with a retained lawyer may not be permitted to fire counsel close to or during trial. By then, the interests of others — the courts and the opponent — in not delaying trial will be given substantial weight. Courts also suspect that efforts to fire counsel close to trial are really indirect efforts to force delay. When a matter is in litigation, a lawyer must comply with the withdrawal requirements of the particular tribunal. DR 2-110(A)(1); Rule 1.16(c).

When a client fires a lawyer, the client may still be liable to the lawyer for fees earned to the time of termination. Much depends on the law of the particular jurisdiction. Whether the client is liable may depend on whether the termination was for cause (did the lawyer do something to justify the client's decision?). The amount of the client's liability will depend on the reason for the termination, the contract between the parties, if there is one, and whether the lawyer was working on a contingency basis.

A lawyer who is fired is ethically required to withdraw from the representation. Rule 1.16(a)(3); DR 2-110(B)(4).

2. Termination by the Lawyer

DR 2-110 and Rule 1.16 describe the circumstances under which lawyers may or must withdraw from a matter. Both code and rules require the lawyer to facilitate the transition to new counsel and to protect the client's interests. Rule 1.16(d); DR 2-110(A)(2) and (A)(3).

Apropos our discussion of lawyer autonomy (page 57 supra), both the code and rules recognize permissive withdrawal for what might be called "professional" reasons. Rule 1.16(b)(1) permits withdrawal if the "client persists in a course of action involving the lawyer's services that the lawyer reasonably believes is criminal or fraudulent." Where a law firm withdrew because it had good reason to believe that its client intended to commit perjury, it did not give up its right to unpaid fees. A Sealed Case, 890 F.2d 15 (7th Cir. 1989). Rule 1.16(b)(3) permits withdrawal if the "client insists upon pursuing an objective that the lawyer considers repugnant or imprudent." See also DR 2-110(C)(1)(e). These authorities not only allow the lawyer to get out of the representation, they allow the lawyer to *threaten* to get out (subject to court approval if the matter is in litigation). Further, a lawyer may withdraw for the reasons cited in this paragraph even if the withdrawal will have a "material adverse effect on the interests of the client." Rule 1.16(b). You can imagine then that the threat to withdraw can work wonders with a recalcitrant client. What does that do to client autonomy?

Recall our discussion of professionalism (see page 6 supra). The critical element of the definition had it that members of a profession do not make wealth a prime goal of their work. Now look at Rule 1.16(b)(5), which has no direct equivalent in the code. Under this rule a lawyer may withdraw if the "representation will result in an unreasonable financial burden on the lawyer" even though the withdrawal will have a "material adverse effect on the interests of the client." Does that mean the lawyer may withdraw if it turns out he or she agreed to work for too low an hourly rate? Because a better offer comes along and the lawyer has to free up some time? Because a new client asks the lawyer to sue a current client, which conflict rules would not permit as long as the current client remained current? (See page 219 infra.) Of course, the ethical right to withdraw does not free the lawyer from a breach of contract action, but that means the client has to pay a new lawyer to sue the old lawyer and has to prove damages. Why did the same organization that produced the report on professionalism decide that a lawyer's "financial burden" justified withdrawal from a professional relationship even when the client's interests would be materially adversely affected?

Finally, also new in the Model Rules, is a provision that entitles a lawyer to withdraw for no reason at all if the withdrawal can be accomplished without "material adverse effect on the interests of the client." Rule 1.16(b). Does that refer to financial interests only? Won't clients always incur costs just to bring a new lawyer up to speed? Does the quoted phrase include emotional interests?

We will see several circumstances in which lawyers have a duty to withdraw, whether from litigation (page 310 infra) or negotiation (page 470), because of the conduct or anticipated conduct of their clients.

III

Protecting the Client-Lawyer Relationship Against Outside Interference

Ethics rules and case law protect the client-lawyer relationship against certain kinds of outside interference. One rule forbids lawyers to communicate with another lawyer's client under certain circumstances. Rule 4.2; DR 7-104(A)(1). This "no contact" rule, examined in part A, has been the subject of much recent debate, both in the civil and criminal arenas. But prohibited contact is not the only way in which an outsider may interfere with or "spy on" a client-lawyer relationship. Some other ways, and responses to them, are discussed in part B.

Before moving to this material, we should identify other rules whose purpose or effect is protecting the client-lawyer relationship. The attorney-client privilege (Chapter 2) prevents the state from discovering communications between client and lawyer. Rule 1.7(b) may forbid a lawyer to represent a client if the representation "may be materially limited by the lawyer's responsibilities to another client or to a third person" (Chapter 5). Rules 1.8(f) and 5.4(c) permit lawyers to accept payment from one person to represent another but caution the lawyer against intrusion on the professional relationship. Rule 1.13 reminds entity lawyers that their client is the entity, not its managers (Chapter 9). Rule 5.4 restricts lay managerial authority and financial interests in law firms (Chapter 14). Finally, Rule 5.6 prohibits certain agreements that limit a lawyer's right to practice as a way of ensuring that clients are not frustrated in their choice of counsel.

A. COMMUNICATING WITH ANOTHER LAWYER'S CLIENTS

Rule 4.2 says that "[i]n representing a client, a lawyer shall not communicate about the subject of the representation with a party the lawyer knows to be represented by another lawyer in the matter, unless the lawyer has the consent of the other lawyer or is authorized by law to do so." DR 7-104(A)(1) is substantially identical. This prohibition applies only if the following conditions are present:

1. The communication must occur while the lawyer is "representing a client." A lawyer who is not acting in a representative capacity is not foreclosed by this rule from talking to another lawyer's client about the matter on which the other lawyer is representing the client. A client who is dissatisfied with a lawyer's performance can therefore shop for a new lawyer without fear that other lawyers will not speak with her. An attorney who is personally a litigant may communicate directly with an opposing litigant without violating Rule 4.2 because the attorney is not acting as a representative of a client. Pinsky v. Statewide Grievance Committee, 216 Conn. 228, 578 A.2d 1075 (1990).

    Given the *Shapero* decision protecting targeted direct mail solicitation (page 808 infra), can lawyer *A* write to lawyer *B*'s client urging the client to fire *B* and hire him? Would that constitute the tort of interfering with contractual relations? Can you "interfere" with a contract that the client is empowered to break for any reason or no reason at all? At least two states, Florida and Montana, forbid a lawyer to write to a prospective client about a matter if the lawyer knows that the client is already represented on the particular matter. Florida Rule 7.3(b)(2); Montana Rule 7.3(d).

2. The communicating lawyer must know (knowledge can be inferred from the circumstances) that the person with whom he or she is communicating is represented by another lawyer on the subject of the communication. (See the definitions of "know" and "knowledge" in the Terminology section of the rules.) However, if she does not know that, then she ought to be conscious of the requirements of Rule 4.3 and DR 7-104(A)(2), whose subject is dealing with unrepresented persons.

3. The communicating lawyer is forbidden to communicate only about the "subject" of the other lawyer's representation. She can communicate about anything else.

4. The prohibition does not apply if the other lawyer consents to the communication or if it is "authorized by law."

5. A violation occurs if a lawyer engages in the forbidden communication through a third party, such as an investigator. Rule 8.4(a) directs lawyers not to "violate or attempt to violate the rules . . . knowingly assist or induce another to do so, or do so through the acts of another." DR 1-102(A)(2) forbids a lawyer to "[c]ircumvent a Disciplinary Rule through actions of another." Even a negligent failure might trip a lawyer up. In In re Industrial Gas Antitrust Litigation, 80 Civ. 3479 (N.D. Ill. Jan. 28, 1986), reported at 2 Lawyers Manual on Professional Conduct (ABA/BNA) 71 (Mar. 19, 1986), a lawyer was sanctioned for negligently failing to instruct an investigator not to speak with managerial employees of the opponent. The court relied on Rule 5.3(a) for its conclusion that a negligent, not merely a knowing, failure to supervise was forbidden.

What values does this rule protect? Here are some that have been discussed. With which do you agree? Which should obtain even when the adverse client is an entity and the proposed contact is with its current or former agents? Are each of these values present in criminal as well as civil matters? It is said that the rule prevents the opposing lawyer from

1. Getting a damaging admission from the opposing client,
2. Learning a fact he or she would not learn if counsel were present to protect the opposing client,
3. Settling or winning a concession in the matter without interference from opposing counsel,
4. Learning information protected by the attorney-client privilege and the work product privilege,
5. Weakening the opposing client's resolve by casting doubt on the strength of his or her position, or
6. Disparaging the opposing lawyer to his or her client.

Of the countervailing values, the most prominent are the interest in informal and inexpensive access to information and (mainly in criminal cases) law enforcement. What weight should these values receive?

The no-contact rule is not applicable when lawyers leave a firm and seek to persuade firm clients to leave with them. However, other ethics rules, as well as fiduciary obligations, may apply in these situations. See the material on solicitation at page 808 infra.

1. Civil Matters

Application of the rule presents no problems in civil cases when the adverse parties are individuals. Then it is straightforward. See Papanicolaou v. Chase Manhattan Bank, 720 F. Supp. 1080 (S.D.N.Y. 1989) (bank's entire law firm disqualified after partner at firm had an unauthorized conversation with plaintiff about the merits of the case); Wagner v. Lehman Bros. Kuhn Loeb, Inc., 646 F. Supp. 643 (N.D. Ill. 1986) (disqualifying the plaintiff's lawyer for offering money to an individual defendant to provide evidence against his former corporate employer, also a defendant, and then meeting with the individual in the absence of his counsel). What if a party is a corporation or the government? Take corporations first. Recall *Upjohn* (page 27 supra). Justice Rehnquist assumed that the government would be able to speak to the same employees as Mr. Thomas, the general counsel. The underlying information was not privileged, the Court said, only the communications to counsel. But would Rule 4.2 prohibit direct contact with Upjohn's current or former employees? *Upjohn* involved a criminal investigation, where policy considerations may differ (see part A2 infra). How would Justice Rehnquist's assumption fare in a civil matter?

NIESIG v. TEAM I
76 N.Y.2d 363, 558 N.E.2d 1030, 559 N.Y.S.2d 493 (1990)

KAYE, JUDGE.

Plaintiff in this personal injury litigation, wishing to have his counsel privately interview a corporate defendant's employees who witnessed the accident, puts before us a question that has generated wide interest: are the employees of a corporate party also considered "parties" under Disciplinary Rule 7-104(A)(1) of the Code of Professional Responsibility, which prohibits a lawyer from communicating directly with a "party" known to have counsel in the matter?[1] . . .

As alleged in the complaint, plaintiff was injured when he fell from scaffolding at a building construction site. At the time of the accident he was employed by DeTrae Enterprises, Inc.; defendant J. M. Frederick was the general contractor, and defendant Team I the property owner. Plaintiff thereafter commenced a damages action against defendants, asserting two causes of action centering on Labor Law §240, and defendants brought a third-party action against DeTrae.

Plaintiff moved for permission to have his counsel conduct ex parte interviews of all DeTrae employees who were on the site at the time of the accident, arguing that these witnesses to the event were neither managerial nor controlling employees and could not therefore be considered

---

1. . . . Employees individually named as parties in the litigation, and employees individually represented by counsel, are not within the ambit of the question presented by this appeal. Nor, obviously, are direct interviews on consent of counsel, or those authorized by law, or communications by the client himself (unless instigated by counsel).

"personal synonyms for DeTrae." DeTrae opposed the application, asserting that the disciplinary rule barred unapproved contact by plaintiff's lawyer with any of its employees. . . .

The Appellate Division concluded, for theoretical as well as practical reasons, that current employees of a corporate defendant in litigation "are presumptively within the scope of the representation afforded by the attorneys who appeared [in the litigation] on behalf of that corporation." . . .

In the main we disagree with the Appellate Division's conclusions. However, because we agree with the holding that DR 7-104(A)(1) applies only to current employees, not to former employees, we modify rather than reverse its order, and grant plaintiff's motion to allow the interviews.

We begin our analysis by noting that what is at issue is a disciplinary rule, not a statute. In interpreting statutes, which are the enactments of a coequal branch of government and an expression of the public policy of this State, we are of course bound to implement the will of the Legislature; statutes are to be applied as they are written or interpreted to effectuate the legislative intention. The disciplinary rules have a different provenance and purpose. Approved by the New York State Bar Association and then enacted by the Appellate Divisions, the Code of Professional Responsibility is essentially the legal profession's document of self-governance, embodying principles of ethical conduct for attorneys as well as rules for professional discipline. While unquestionably important, and respected by the courts, the code does not have the force of law.

That distinction is particularly significant when a disciplinary rule is invoked in litigation, which in addition to matters of professional conduct by attorneys, implicates the interests of nonlawyers. In such instances, we are not constrained to read the rules literally or effectuate the intent of the drafters, but look to the rules as guidelines to be applied with due regard for the broad range of interests at stake.

DR 7-104(A)(1), which can be traced to the American Bar Association Canons of 1908, fundamentally embodies principles of fairness. "The general thrust of the rule is to prevent situations in which a represented party may be taken advantage of by adverse counsel; the presence of the party's attorney theoretically neutralizes the contact." (Wright v. Group Health Hosp., 103 Wash. 2d 192, 197, 691 P.2d 564, 567 [(1984)].) By preventing lawyers from deliberately dodging adversary counsel to reach — and exploit — the client alone, DR 7-104(A)(1) safeguards against clients making improvident settlements, ill-advised disclosures and unwarranted concessions.

There is little problem applying DR 7-104(A)(1) to individuals in civil cases. In that context, the meaning of "party" is ordinarily plain enough: it refers to the individuals, not to their agents and employees. The question, however, becomes more difficult when the parties are corporations — as evidenced by a wealth of commentary, and controversy, on the issue.

The difficulty is not in whether DR 7-104(A)(1) applies to corporations. It unquestionably covers corporate parties, who are as much served by the rule's fundamental principles of fairness as individual parties. But the rule does not define "party," and its reach in this context is unclear. In litigation only the entity, not its employee, is the actual named party; on the other hand, corporations act solely through natural persons, and unless some employees are also considered parties, corporations are effectively read out of the rule. The issue therefore distills to *which* corporate employees should be deemed parties for purposes of DR 7-104(A)(1), and that choice is one of policy. The broader the definition of "party" in the interests of fairness to the corporation, the greater the cost in terms of foreclosing vital informal access to facts.

The many courts, bar associations and commentators that have balanced the competing considerations have evolved various tests, each claiming some adherents, each with some imperfection. At one extreme is the blanket rule adopted by the Appellate Division and urged by defendants, and at the other is the "control group" test — both of which we reject. The first is too broad and the second too narrow.

Defendants' principal argument for the blanket rule — correlating the corporate "party" and all of its employees — rests on Upjohn v. United States [page 27 supra]. As the Supreme Court recognized, a corporation's attorney-client privilege includes communications with low- and mid-level employees; defendants argue that the existence of an attorney-client *privilege* also signifies an attorney-client *relationship* for purposes of DR 7-104(A)(1).

Upjohn, however, addresses an entirely different subject, with policy objectives that have little relation to the question whether a corporate employee should be considered a "party" for purposes of the disciplinary rule. First, the privilege applies only to *confidential communications* with counsel, it does not immunize the underlying factual information — which is in issue here — from disclosure to an adversary. Second, the attorney-client privilege serves the societal objective of encouraging open communication between client and counsel, a benefit not present in denying informal access to factual information. Thus, a corporate employee who may be a "client" for purposes of the attorney-client privilege is not necessarily a "party" for purposes of DR 7-104(A)(1).

The single indisputable advantage of a blanket preclusion — as with every absolute rule — is that it is clear. No lawyer need ever risk disqualification or discipline because of uncertainty as to which employees are covered by the rule and which not. The problem, however, is that a ban of this nature exacts a high price in terms of other values, and is unnecessary to achieve the objectives of DR 7-104(A)(1).

Most significantly, the Appellate Division's blanket rule closes off avenues of informal discovery of information that may serve both the litigants and the entire justice system by uncovering relevant facts, thus promoting the expeditious resolution of disputes. Foreclosing all direct, informal interviews of employees of the corporate party unnecessarily sacrifices the long-recognized potential value of such sessions. "A lawyer talks to a witness to ascertain what, if any, information the witness may have relevant to his theory of the case, and to explore the witness' knowledge, memory and opinion — frequently in light of information counsel may have developed from other sources. This is part of an attorney's so-called work product." Costly formal depositions that may deter litigants with limited resources, or even somewhat less formal and costly interviews attended by adversary counsel, are no substitute for such off-the-record private efforts to learn and assemble, rather than perpetuate, information.

Nor, in our view, is it necessary to shield all employees from informal interviews in order to safeguard the corporation's interest. Informal encounters between a lawyer and an employee-witness are not — as a blanket ban assumes — invariably calculated to elicit unwitting admissions; they serve long-recognized values in the litigation process. Moreover, the corporate party has significant protection at hand. It has possession of its own information and unique access to its documents and employees; the corporation's lawyer thus has the earliest and best opportunity to gather the facts, to elicit information from employees, and to counsel and prepare them so that they will not make the feared improvident disclosures that engendered the rule.

We fully recognize that, as the Appellate Division observed, every rule short of the absolute poses practical difficulties as to where to draw the line, and leaves some uncertainty as to which employees fall on either side of it. Nonetheless, we conclude that the values served by permitting access to relevant information require that an effort be made to strike a balance, and that uncertainty can be minimized if not eliminated by a clear test that will become even clearer in practice.

We are not persuaded, however, that the "control group" test — defining "party" to include only the most senior management exercising substantial control over the corporation — achieves that goal. Unquestionably, that narrow (though still uncertain) definition of corporate "party" better serves the policy of promoting open access to relevant information. But that test gives insufficient regard to the principles motivating DR 7-104(A)(1), and wholly overlooks the fact that corporate employees other than senior management also can bind the corporation. The "control group" test all but "nullifies the benefits of the disciplinary rule to corporations." Given the practical and theoretical problems posed by the "control group" test, it is hardly surprising that few courts or bar associations have ever embraced it.

By the same token, we find unsatisfactory several of the proposed intermediate tests, because they give too little guidance, or otherwise seem unworkable. In this category are the case-by-case balancing test and a test that defines "party" to mean corporate employees only when they are interviewed about matters within the scope of their employment. The latter approach is based on rule 801(d)(2)(D) of the Federal Rules of Evidence, a hearsay exception for statements concerning matters within the scope of employment, which is different from the New York State rule.

The test that best balances the competing interests, and incorporates the most desirable elements of the other approaches, is one that defines "party" to include corporate employees whose acts or omissions in the matter under inquiry are binding on the corporation (in effect, the corporation's "alter egos") or imputed to the corporation for purposes of its liability, or employees implementing the advice of counsel. All other employees may be interviewed informally.

Unlike a blanket ban or a "control group" test, this solution is specifically targeted at the problem addressed by DR 7-104(A)(1). The potential unfair advantage of extracting concessions and admissions from those who will bind the corporation is negated when employees with "speaking authority" for the corporation, and employees who are so closely identified with the interests of the corporate party as to be indistinguishable from it, are deemed "parties" for purposes of DR 7-104(A)(1). Concern for the protection of the attorney-client privilege prompts us also to include in the definition of "party" the corporate employees responsible for actually effectuating the advice of counsel in the matter.

In practical application, the test we adopt thus would prohibit direct communication by adversary counsel "with those officials, but only those, who have the legal power to bind the corporation in the matter or who are responsible for implementing the advice of the corporation's lawyer, or any member of the organization whose own interests are directly at stake in a representation." This test would permit direct access to all other employees, and specifically — as in the present case — it would clearly permit direct access to employees who were merely witnesses to an event for which the corporate employer is sued.

Apart from striking the correct balance, this test should also become relatively clear in application. It is rooted in developed concepts of the law of evidence and the law of agency, thereby minimizing the uncertainty facing lawyers about to embark on employee interviews. A similar test, moreover, is the one overwhelmingly adopted by courts and bar associations throughout the country, whose long practical experience persuades us that — in day-to-day operation — it is workable.[6]

---

6. Given the nationwide experience with the test we now adopt, we find no basis for the assertion made in the concurrence that the test will unnecessarily curtail informal fact-

... Today's decision resolves the present controversy by allowing ex parte interviews with nonmanagerial witnesses employed by a corporate defendant; even in that limited context, we recognize that there are undoubtedly questions not raised by the parties that will yet have to be answered. Defendants' assertions that ex parte interviews should not be permitted because of the dangers of overreaching, moreover, impel us to add the cautionary note that, while we have not been called upon to consider questions relating to the actual conduct of such interviews, it is of course assumed that attorneys would make their identity and interest known to interviewees and comport themselves ethically. ...

BELLACOSA, JUDGE (concurring).

I agree that the Appellate Division blanket test too broadly precluded ex parte interviews by defining the term "parties" as used in Disciplinary Rule 7-104(A)(1) to include all current employees of a corporate defendant. The court instead adopts an "alter ego" definition which, as I see it, will function almost identically with the rejected test. Also, it sacrifices an unnecessarily disproportionate amount of the truth-discovering desideratum of the litigation process. Lastly, circularity in the identification of and application to the "alter ego" test group may occur, which could prolong pretrial discovery and allow the shield of DR 7-104(A)(1) to be fashioned into a sword.

These concerns could be avoided by limiting "parties," for the purposes of this professional responsibility rule, only to those who are in the "control group" of the corporate defendant; that is, only those among "the most senior management who exercise substantial control over the corporation."

To be sure, that test is far from perfect itself. But the "control group" definition better balances the respective interests by allowing the maximum number of informal interviews among persons with potentially relevant information, while safeguarding the attorney protections afforded the men and women whose protection may well be of paramount concern — those at the corporate helm and the fictional entity itself, the corporation. Also, this approach is more consistent with the ordinary understanding and meaning of "party," and more reasonably fits the purpose for which the disciplinary rule exists; a professional responsibility purpose quite distinct from enactments in public law prescribing the rights and protections of parties to litigation.

---

gathering or itself generate litigation. Above all, our test is decidedly different from the Appellate Division's blanket ban; in this very case, for example, we are reversing the Appellate Division's prohibition and permitting interviews of employee-witnesses to an accident, which would not be allowed under a blanket ban. In order to put to rest any possible confusion, we make clear that the definition of "party" we adopt for the purposes of DR 7-104(A)(1) is not derived from the Official Comment to ABA Model rule 4.2.

Discovery of the truth and relevant proofs is the end to which litigation is the means. The fewer parties to whom counsel can informally turn in the quest for facts on behalf of a client's cause, the more cumbersome becomes the realization of this goal. The Appellate Division's blanket definition and the "alter ego" test more severely limit access to parties with relevant information than does the control group test which I urge. One commentator has noted, "any rule that limits the attorney's access to the truth necessarily contravenes a basic aim of our legal system." Therefore, I believe the cost of the new "alter ego" test is too high and an unnecessary price to pay.

The court defines "party" as "corporate employees whose acts or omissions in the matter under inquiry are binding on the corporation . . . or imputed to the corporation for purposes of its liability." Similar language to this definition is found in the Official Comment to ABA Model rule 4.2 and caused one commentator to note that "[t]his language is probably the foggiest of all." One consequence is that the determination of who qualifies for the disciplinary rule's protection under the "alter ego" test may ironically replace a useful and straightforward ex parte interview with a whole new and expensive litigation tier. There is, after all, a begging-the-question twist: the purpose of pretrial discovery — or the ultimate litigation question itself — may well be which employees fit into the protected "party" category under the "alter ego" classification. Who comprises the much narrower and smaller corporate "control group" is a relatively less complicated and conflicted problem. . . .

How Large the Circle of Secrecy?

Does it surprise you to learn that amicus briefs supporting the plaintiff were filed by the Committee on Civil Rights of the New York City Bar Association, the NAACP Legal Defense Fund, a teachers' union, the New York State Attorney General, and a civil service employees' union? What common interest could this diverse group possibly have?

Niesig identifies various tests for determining whether a lawyer may communicate with an employee or agent of a corporate opponent. Three deserve special mention.

Some authorities prohibit communication on any subject within a current employee's scope of employment. See, e.g., New York City Opinion 80-46. This is because certain evidentiary rules, like Fed. R. Evid. 801(d)(2)(D), admit these statements against the company, which therefore is deemed entitled to have a lawyer present. *Niesig* did not adopt this test because New York's vicarious admission rule is considerably narrower. Only statements of agents authorized to speak for a principal are admissible against the principal. Second, *Niesig* holds that the rule does not prohibit contact with former employees. Yet can this be true even under *Niesig*'s own reasoning? For example, *Niesig* forbids contact with "[1] employees whose acts or omissions in the matter under inquiry are . . . imputed to the corporation for purposes of its liability, or [2] employees implementing the advice of counsel." Former employees may still be in the first position and might once have been in the second. Can a lawyer talk to them? Last, footnote 6 in *Niesig* rejects the comment to Rule 4.2. This comment is in the very text of California Rule 2-100. How does New York's rule differ from California's?

Might it make some sense to adopt a bright-line rule prohibiting contact with all of an opposing entity's current or former agents, except through discovery or with the opposing lawyer's consent? One court has done so. Public Service Electric & Gas Co. v. Associated Electric & Gas Insurance Services, 745 F. Supp. 1037 (D.N.J. 1990), reads the language and the comment to Rule 4.2 ("any other person whose act or omission . . . may be imputed to the organization for purposes of civil or criminal liability") to include former as well as current employees. Then, because it would not be possible to know before an interview whether the prospective interviewee was a "person" within the meaning of the comment, the court prohibited ex parte contact with *any* former employee. Contra Curley v. Cumberland Farms, Inc., 134 F.R.D. 77 (D.N.J. 1991) (refusing to apply the rule to all former employees). ABA Formal Opinion 91-359 manages, not quite persuasively, to interpret the word "person" in the comment to Rule 4.2 to exclude "former employees," notwithstanding that their acts or omissions may be imputed to the entity for liability purposes. The opinion also says that (1) Rule 4.4 may prevent a lawyer from seeking to obtain privileged information from a former employee and (2) Rule 4.3 requires the lawyer to "make clear the nature of the lawyer's role . . . including the identity of the lawyer's client and the fact that the witness's former employer is an adverse party." Does the language of Rule 4.3 support this interpretation? See also PPG Industries v. BASF Corp., 134 F.R.D. 118 (W.D. Pa. 1990) (permitting communication with plaintiff's former employee, now employed by defendant, so long as defendant does not receive confidential information).

Exactly whom are we protecting when we apply the no-contact rules to the agents and former agents of an organizational party? The organization, you say? How then explain the comment's statement that if the agent "is represented in the matter by his or her own counsel, the consent by that counsel to a communication will be sufficient for purposes of this Rule?" The organization's interests are suddenly ignored. It need not be notified at all, regardless of what the agent knows, did, or was privy to. So whom are we protecting?

Violation of the no-contact rule may lead to disqualification, Papanicolaou v. Chase Manhattan Bank, 720 F. Supp. 1080 (S.D.N.Y. 1989); Cronin v. Nevada District Court, 781 P.2d 1150 (Nev. 1989), or suppression of the improperly obtained information. University Patents, Inc. v.

Kligman, 737 F. Supp. 325 (E.D. Pa. 1990). But see Stagg v. New York City Health and Hospitals Corp., 162 A.D.2d 595, 556 N.Y.S.2d 779 (2d Dept. 1990) (no suppression). Kitchen v. Aristech Chemical, 769 F. Supp. 254 (S.D. Ohio 1991) (no disqualification).

When the Government Is a Party

Does DR 7-104(A)(1), or Model Rule 4.2, require as broad a definition of "party" when the attorney's adversary is a government body? In Note, DR 7-104 of the Code of Professional Responsibility Applied to the Government "Party," 61 Minn. L. Rev. 1007 (1977), the author discussed the issue at some length and concluded as follows:

> When interpreting DR 7-104 in a government context, two competing considerations must be balanced: (1) the desirability of affording the government, as a party, the same kinds of protection against uncounseled concessions of interest afforded other parties, and (2) the desirability of ensuring largely unrestricted public access to government as a check against mismanagement and malfeasance. . . .
>
> It is submitted that the rule should be narrowly construed when contact with the government is sought. A government "party" under the rule should be defined as any official who has the authority to bind the government in a matter that could be litigated. No restrictions should apply to communication with other government employees, except that the attorney be required to disclose his identity and the nature of his representation. Finally, DR 7-104 should be triggered only when a matter has been turned over to the government agency's legal counsel. This interpretation of the rule best accommodates the conflicting considerations that exist when the interests of the government as a party are adverse to those of a member of the public it is charged to serve.

California has dealt with the problem by adopting a variation on DR 7-104(A)(1). Its version of the rule contains the following sentence: "This rule shall not prohibit [c]ommunications with a public officer, board, committee, or body." Rule 2-100(C)(1). The New York State Bar Association, in its Opinion 404 (1975), concluded that an attorney may speak with dissenting members of a board of education without first obtaining the permission of the attorney for the board:

> The overriding public interest compels that an opportunity be afforded to the public and their authorized representatives to obtain the views of, and pertinent facts from, public officials representing them. Minority members of a public body should not, for purposes of DR 7-104(A)(1), be considered adverse parties to their constituents whom they were selected to represent.

The Comment to Model Rule 4.2 speaks obliquely to the relationship between the rule's prohibition and entity clients, governmental or otherwise. As one example of legal authorization justifying an exception to the rule, the Comment cites "the right of a party to a controversy with a government agency to speak with government officials about the matter." New York City Opinion 1991-4 follows *Niesig* where the inquirer represented a former government employee suing the government, but recognized that communications with "high level agency officials . . . may be ethically permitted as authorized by the legal and constitutional rights of the lawyer and his or her client to petition or otherwise have access to the government."

Several cases refuse to prohibit counsel from speaking with the nonmanagerial employees of a government opponent outside opposing counsel's presence. B.H. v. Johnson, 128 F.R.D. 659 (N.D. Ill. 1989), posits one creative solution to the competing interests. A plaintiff class of children challenged a state agency's foster care policies. Plaintiffs' counsel wanted to conduct ex parte interviews with social workers at the agency. The agency, meanwhile, had instructed its employees not to speak with plaintiffs' counsel. The agency sought a protective order against the contacts and the plaintiffs asked the court to prevent the agency from interfering with the interviews. The court held for the plaintiffs. But it also ruled that statements obtained in those interviews could not be admitted against the defendant. Relying on Frey v. Department of Health & Human Services, 106 F.R.D. 32 (E.D.N.Y. 1985), the court said that if the employees were not deemed "parties" within the meaning of the no-contact rule, then neither would they be deemed parties within the meaning of the vicarious admission rule. See also Vega v. Bloomsburg, 427 F. Supp. 593 (D. Mass. 1977); New York State Assn. for Retarded Children, Inc. v. Carey, 706 F.2d 956, 960-961 (2d Cir.) cert. denied, 464 U.S. 915 (1983); New York City Op. 1988-8.

Criminal cases present the most common example of the situation in which the government is a party. Who is the prosecutor's client? The answer is that the client is the state or "the People," not the prosecutor's witnesses and not even the victim. Defense counsel are free to attempt to speak to witnesses including the victim although they, of course, may refuse the interview. See Stearns v. Clinton, 780 S.W.2d 216 (Tex. Cr. App. 1989) (mandamus issued against trial judge who disqualified appointed counsel after counsel had attempted to interview the state's witnesses without permission of the prosecutor).

FURTHER READING

For further discussion of this issue in a civil context, see Comment, Ex Parte Communications With Corporate Parties: The Scope of the Limitations on Attorney Communications With One of Adverse Interest, 82 Nw. U. L. Rev. 1274 (1988) (authored by Jerome Krulewitch); John Leubsdorf, Communicating with Another Lawyer's Client: The Lawyer's Veto and the Client's Interests, 127 U. Pa. L. Rev. 683 (1979); Samuel Miller & Angelo Calfo, Ex Parte Contact with Employees and Former Employees of a Corporate Adversary: Is It Ethical?, 42 Bus. Law. 1053 (1987); Note, Ex Parte Communication and the Corporate Adversary: A New Approach, 66 N.Y.U. L. Rev. 1456 (1991) (authored by Stephen Sinaiko).

QUESTIONS

3.1   You are representing a corporate plaintiff in an antitrust action against a major corporation. In the midst of fierce and difficult discovery, an officer of the plaintiff calls to tell you the following. She has just been contacted by a friend who is an employee of the defendant. The employee has told her that the defendant's officers are about to destroy certain highly inculpatory documents. The informant has made copies of some of the documents and would like to deliver them to you or anyone you designate. The employee also has some correspondence between the adverse client and its counsel that corroborates the destruction plan. The employee insists that you protect his identity. Can you receive the documents? The correspondence? What can you do?

3.2   Lisa Hobbs is denied a promotion at Equinox, Inc., a Fortune 100 company, and suspects race played a role in the decision. She makes an appointment to see you to ascertain her legal remedies. With her she brings Lesley McCorry, a co-worker, who can relate incidents of racial bias on the part of superiors. She also brings Douglas Trumbull, a vice president, who can tell you about the company's personnel policies with regard to promotion of minorities to publicly visible positions. Can you speak to either or both of them?

3.3   Your client is a fast-food franchiser. It suspects that one of the franchisees is violating the franchise agreement by offering foods prohibited under the franchise. Specifically, the franchisee is suspected of offering a brand of soft drink not manufactured under the supervision of your client. The franchise agreement forbids the franchisee from offering certain food products not purchased from your client and not manufactured or produced under its supervision. You want to send an investigator to the particular franchisee and have her ask for the improper product by name. It is not possible simply to observe the franchisee's operation because the product, a cola drink, looks exactly like the cola drink the franchiser makes available. Your investigator is to go to the counter of the franchisee and ask: "What kind of soft drinks do you have?" If the counterperson fails to mention the competing brand, your investigator is to ask for it by name. If the counterperson says that brand is available and sells a glass of it to your investigator, she is to ask for it "to go," and then bring it to you for use as evidence. May you authorize this conduct?

2. Criminal Matters

On their face, Rule 4.2 and DR 7-104(a) apply in both civil and criminal matters. The comment to Rule 4.2 envisions its application in criminal cases. The Sixth Amendment also applies in criminal cases and prohibits the state from questioning a defendant against whom "judicial proceedings have been initiated" outside the presence of his counsel. Brewer v. Williams, 430 U.S. 387, 398 (1977). What if a person is merely under investigation but nevertheless known to the state to be represented by counsel? In United States v. Dobbs, 711 F.2d 84, 86 (8th Cir. 1983), Dobbs was suspected of extortion. He retained counsel. Nevertheless, an FBI agent interviewed him outside the presence of counsel, allegedly at the direction of the United States Attorney. Dobbs claimed that he was entitled to have admissions made in the interview suppressed, citing DR 7-104(A)(1). The court responded:

> Assuming that this disciplinary rule is applicable in this case, it does not require government investigatory agencies to refrain from any contact with a criminal suspect because he or she previously had retained counsel. Although in some circumstances the conduct of a prosecutor and an investigator acting at the prosecutor's behest may implicate the ethical concerns addressed by DR 7-104(A)(1), in this case [the FBI agent's] noncustodial interview of Dobbs prior to the initiation of judicial proceedings against [him] did not constitute an ethical breach.

Why not? Should the court instead have ruled that even if there was an ethical breach, discipline, not suppression, was the correct remedy?

In United States v. Jamil, 707 F.2d 638, 646 (2d Cir. 1983), the court held that the ethical rule was not violated where the government investigator made contact with a represented suspect without the prosecutor's knowledge. It did not decide whether the rule would have been violated if the investigator had "been acting as the prosecutor's alter ego," nor did it "decide whether suppression would have been warranted *if* the disciplinary rule had been violated." A year later, in United States v. Foley, 735

F.2d 45, 48 (2d Cir. 1984), cert. denied, 469 U.S. 1161 (1985), the same court wrote:

> We think that this practice of routinely conducting pre-arraignment interviews raises serious constitutional questions, as well as ethical ones. The ethical problems surrounding this practice are especially vivid in this case, where the [Assistant United States Attorney], by interviewing Edler in spite of a specific request from Edler's soon-to-be appointed Legal Aid Attorney not to do so, contravened the principles of DR 7-104(A)(1), which prohibits a lawyer from communicating "with a party he knows to be represented by a lawyer" without the consent of the party's lawyer.
>
> Most, if not all, of the practice's claimed advantages would appear to be equally available immediately after arraignment, when a defendant would have the benefit of advice from his attorney and would be less vulnerable to psychological manipulation by the prosecutor. Moreover, we agree with defendant that the interview does have two effects which, more than coincidentally we think, aid the prosecutor and harm the defendant. By interviewing a defendant before he is assigned an attorney, the prosecutor may: (1) obtain admissions from the defendant which would not be forthcoming once an attorney enters the picture, and (2) commit the defendant to a "story" or position that would restrict his options at trial, including his option to testify in his own behalf. Were it necessary to our decision here, we might well be required to hold that any benefits accruing to the prosecutor from the interview are outweighed by the need to protect uncounseled defendants' constitutional and legal rights.
>
> Our concern is enhanced by the fact, acknowledged at oral argument, that when a defendant is known to be represented by private counsel the government does not conduct a pre-arraignment interview. In effect, therefore, the practice is invoked only against a defendant who is poor and unrepresented.

A prosecutor's custodial pre-arraignment interview of an indigent suspect invites application of the no-contact rule and suppression even though, technically, the suspect does not yet have a lawyer. The lawyer's identity is nevertheless known: it will be the public defender, whose appointment awaits only a formal charge, an event within the prosecutor's control. Furthermore, the custodial nature of the interview permits the very tactical advantage the no-contact rule aims to prevent. Nevertheless, until United States v. Hammad, infra, apparently no court had suppressed a suspect's statement obtained in violation of the no-contact rule and before attachment of the right to counsel. Some courts denied that the rule even applied to criminal investigations. Others found no violation.

Ironically, perhaps, Hammad had a retained lawyer, and his statement was made to a former accomplice who had agreed to cooperate. The rest of the story is in the opinion. But the opinion is part of a larger story, which is told following the case.

UNITED STATES v. HAMMAD
858 F.2d 834 (2d Cir. 1988), cert. denied, 111 S. Ct. 192 (1990)

KAUFMAN, J.

On Nov. 30, 1985, the Hammad Department Store in Brooklyn, N.Y., caught fire under circumstances suggesting arson. The Bureau of Alcohol, Tobacco and Firearms was assigned to investigate in conjunction with the U.S. Attorney for the Eastern District of New York.

During the course of his investigation, an Assistant U.S. Attorney (AUSA) discovered that the store's owners, Taiseer and Eid Hammad, had been audited by the New York State Department of Social Services for Medicaid fraud. The audit revealed that the Hammad brothers had bilked Medicaid out of $400,000; they claimed reimbursement for special orthopedic footwear but supplied customers with ordinary, nontherapeutic shoes. Consequently, the department revoked the Hammads' eligibility for Medicaid reimbursement and demanded return of the $400,000 overpayment. The Hammads challenged the department's determination and submitted invoices purporting to document their sales of orthopedic shoes. The invoices were received from Wallace Goldstein of the Crystal Shoe Co., a supplier to the Hammads' store.

On Sept. 22, 1986, however, Goldstein informed the AUSA that he had provided the Hammads with false invoices. Government investigators, therefore, suspected the fire had been intended to destroy actual sales records, thereby concealing the fraudulent Medicaid claims. Goldstein agreed to cooperate with the government's investigation. Accordingly, the prosecutor directed Goldstein to arrange and record a meeting with the Hammads.

Some three weeks later, on Oct. 9, Goldstein telephoned the Hammads. He spoke briefly with Eid, who referred him to Taiseer. Goldstein falsely told Taiseer he had been subpoenaed to appear before the grand jury investigating the Hammads' Medicaid fraud. He added that the grand jury had requested records of Crystal's sales to the Hammad Department Store to compare them with the invoices the Hammads had submitted. Taiseer did not deny defrauding Medicaid, but instead urged Goldstein to conceal the fraud by lying to the grand jury and by refusing to produce Crystal's true sales records. He also questioned Goldstein regarding the contents of his subpoena, which did not actually exist. Goldstein responded that he did not have the subpoena in his possession. He agreed to inquire further. One hour later, presumably after speaking with the AUSA, Goldstein telephoned Taiseer again and described the fictitious subpoena.

Goldstein and Hammad saw each other five days later. The meeting was recorded and videotaped. Goldstein showed Hammad a sham subpoena supplied by the prosecutor. The subpoena instructed Goldstein to appear before the grand jury and to provide any records reflecting shoe sales from Crystal to the Hammad Department Store. Hammad apparently accepted the subpoena as genuine because he spent much of the remainder of the meeting devising strategies for Goldstein to avoid compliance. The two held no further meetings.

On April 15, 1987, after considering the recordings, videotapes and other evidence, the grand jury returned a 45-count indictment against the Hammad brothers, including 38 counts of mail fraud for filing false Medicaid invoices. Eid was also indicted for arson and for fraudulently attempting to collect fire insurance. Taiseer faced the additional charge of obstructing justice for attempting to influence Goldstein's grand jury testimony. The case was assigned to Judge Glasser of the Eastern District of New York.

Before trial, Taiseer Hammad moved to suppress the recordings and videotapes, alleging the prosecutor had violated DR 7-104(A)(1) of the American Bar Association's Code of Professional Responsibility. The rule prohibits a lawyer from communicating with a "party" he knows to be represented by counsel regarding the subject matter of that representation. In short, Taiseer alleged that the prosecutor — through his "alter ego" Goldstein — had violated ethical obligations by communicating directly with him after learning that he had retained counsel. . . .

In an order dated Sept. 21, 1987, Judge Glasser granted Taiseer's motion to suppress the recordings and videotapes. The government, he found, "was clearly aware, by at least as early as Sept. 9, 1986, that [Taiseer] had retained counsel in connection with this case." He also determined that Goldstein was the prosecutor's "alter ego" during his discussions with Hammad. Accordingly, the court held that the prosecutor had violated DR 7-104(A)(1) and suppressed the recordings and videotapes secured as a result of the violation. . . .

We decline to hold, as the government suggests, either that DR 7-104(A)(1) is limited in application to civil disputes or that it is coextensive with the Sixth Amendment. Nor has the government provided an adequate basis for reversing the able district judge's determination, after the suppression hearing, that the prosecutor knew Hammad had legal representation or that Goldstein was his "alter ego." We are mindful, however, that suppression of evidence is an extreme remedy that may impede legitimate investigatory activities. Accordingly, we find, in this case, that suppression of the recordings and videotapes constituted an abuse of the district court's discretion. . . .

This circuit conclusively established the applicability of DR 7-104(A)(1) to criminal prosecutions in United States v. Jamil, 707 F.2d 638 (2d Cir. 1983). In *Jamil*, we held that "DR 7-104(A)(1) may be found to apply in criminal cases . . . to government attorneys . . . [and] to non-attorney government law enforcement officers when they act as the alter ego of government prosecutors." Even those courts restricting the rule's ambit have suggested that, in appropriate circumstances, DR 7-104(A)(1) would apply to criminal prosecutions. Thus, the government's contention that DR 7-104(A)(1) is "inapplicable to criminal investigations" is mistaken.

The applicability of DR 7-104(A)(1) to the investigatory stages of a criminal prosecution presents a closer question. The government asserts the rule is coextensive with the Sixth Amendment, and hence, that it remains inoperative until the onset of adversarial proceedings. The appellee responds that several courts have enforced DR 7-104(A)(1) prior to attachment of Sixth Amendment protections. We find no principled basis in the rule to constrain its reach as the government proposes. . . . Nonetheless, we urge restraint in applying the rule to criminal investigations to avoid handcuffing law enforcement officers in their efforts to develop evidence. . . .

The Constitution defines only the "minimal historic safeguards" that defendants must receive rather than the outer bounds of those we may afford them. McNabb v. United States, 318 U.S. 332, 340 (1943). In other words, the Constitution prescribes a floor below which protections may not fall, rather than a ceiling beyond which they may not rise. The Model Code of Professional Responsibility, on the other hand, encompasses the attorney's duty "to maintain the highest standards of ethical conduct." The code is designed to safeguard the integrity of the profession and preserve public confidence in our system of justice. It not only delineates an attorney's duties to the court but defines his relationship with his client and adverse parties. Hence, the code secures protections not contemplated by the Constitution.

Moreover, we resist binding the code's applicability to the moment of indictment. The timing of an indictment's return lies substantially within the control of the prosecutor. Therefore, were we to construe the rule as dependent upon indictment, a government attorney could manipulate grand jury proceedings to avoid its encumbrances.

The government contends that a broad reading of DR 7-104(A)(1) would impede legitimate investigatory practices. In particular, the government fears career criminals with permanent "house counsel" could immunize themselves from infiltration by informants. We share this concern and would not interpret the disciplinary rule as precluding undercover investigations. Our task, accordingly, is imposing adequate safeguards without crippling law enforcement.

The principal question presented to us herein is: To what extent does DR 7-104(A)(1) restrict the use of informants by government prosecutors prior to indictment, but after a suspect has retained counsel in connection with the subject matter of a criminal investigation? In an attempt to avoid hampering legitimate criminal investigations by government prosecutors, Judge Glasser resolved this dilemma by limiting the rule's applicability "to instances in which a suspect has retained counsel specifically for representation in conjunction with the criminal matter in which he is held suspect, and the government has knowledge of that fact." Thus, he reasoned, the rule exempts the vast majority of cases where suspects are unaware they are being investigated.

While it may be true that this limitation will not unduly hamper the government's ability to conduct effective criminal investigations in a majority of instances, we nevertheless believe that it *is* unduly restrictive in that small but persistent number of cases where a career criminal has retained "house counsel" to represent him in connection with an ongoing fraud or criminal enterprise. This court has recognized that prosecutors have a responsibility to perform investigative as well as courtroom-related duties in criminal matters. . . . As we see it, under DR 7-104(A)(1), a prosecutor is "authorized by law" to employ legitimate investigative techniques in conducting or supervising criminal investigations, and the use of informants to gather evidence against a suspect will frequently fall within the ambit of such authorization.

Notwithstanding this holding, however, we recognize that in some instances a government prosecutor may overstep the already broad powers of his office, and in so doing, violate the ethical precepts of DR 7-104(A)(1). In the present case, the prosecutor issued a subpoena for the informant, not to secure his attendance before the grand jury, but to create a pretense that might help the informant elicit admissions from a represented suspect. Though we have no occasion to consider the use of this technique in relation to unrepresented suspects, we believe that use of the technique under the circumstances of this case contributed to the informant's becoming the alter ego of the prosecutor. Consequently, the informant was engaging in communications proscribed by DR 7-104 (A)(1).[1] Therefore, we agree with Judge Glasser that the prosecution violated the disciplinary rule in this case.

Notwithstanding requests for a bright-line rule, we decline to list all possible situations that may violate DR 7-104(A)(1). This delineation is best accomplished by case-by-case adjudication, particularly when ethical standards are involved. As our holding above makes clear, however, the use of informants by government prosecutors in a pre-indictment, non-custodial situation, absent the type of misconduct that occurred in this case, will generally fall within the "authorized by law" exception to DR 7-104(A)(1) and therefore will not be subject to sanctions.

On appeal, the government also claims that even if there was a violation of the disciplinary rule, exclusion is inappropriate to remedy an ethical breach. We have not heretofore decided whether suppression is warranted for a DR 7-104(A)(1) violation. We now hold that, in light of the underlying purposes of the Professional Responsibility Code and the

---

1. See also ABA Standards Relating to the Administration of Criminal Justice, Standard 3-3.1(d) ("It is unprofessional conduct for a prosecutor to secure the attendance of persons for interviews by use of any communication which has the appearance or color of a subpoena or similar judicial process unless the prosecutor is authorized by law to do so.").

exclusionary rule, suppression may be ordered in the district court's discretion. . . .

For half a century, the Supreme Court has recognized that "civilized conduct of criminal trials" demands federal courts be imbued with sufficient discretion to ensure fair proceedings. Thus, as Justice Frankfurter observed, "[j]udicial supervision of the administration of criminal justice in the federal courts implies the duty of establishing and maintaining civilized standards of procedure and evidence." Such standards constitute an exercise of the courts' supervisory authority.

Specifically, the Supreme Court has expressly authorized federal courts to exercise their "supervisory power in some circumstances to exclude evidence taken from the *defendant* by 'willful disobedience of law,' " or "when the defendant asserts a violation of his own rights." Other circuits have expressly included suppression among the panoply of remedies available to district judges for violations of DR 7-104(A)(1). . . .

Accordingly, we reject the government's effort to remove suppression from the arsenal of remedies available to district judges confronted with ethical violations. We have confidence that district courts will exercise their discretion cautiously and with clear cognizance that suppression imposes a barrier between the finder of fact and the discovery of truth.

Judge Glasser apparently assumed . . . that suppression is a necessary consequence of a DR 7-104(A)(1) violation. Exclusion, however, is not required in every case. Here, the government should not have its case prejudiced by suppression of its evidence when the law was previously unsettled in this area. Therefore, in light of the prior uncertainty regarding the reach of DR 7-104(A)(1), an exclusionary remedy is inappropriate in this case.

Accordingly, we find the district court abused its discretion in suppressing the recordings and videotapes, and its decision is reversed.

Ethics and Crime Fighting

The opinion you just read is actually the fourth *Hammad* opinion. In the first, 846 F.2d 854, 862 (2d Cir. 1988), the court upheld the finding that the government had violated the no-contact rule simply by sending Goldstein to talk to Hammad. The lower court's suppression order was reversed because "the law was previously unsettled in this area." Alarmed by the opinion, all United States Attorneys in the Second Circuit petitioned for rehearing. The court denied one at 855 F.2d 36, 37, but Judge Kaufman issued a brief "clarification" because of "some confusion as to the thrust of our opinion." Thereafter, possibly because a petition for rehearing en banc remained pending, the same panel issued a third opinion, which is substantially the same as the one you just read except for how it treated the fact that Goldstein was given a false grand jury subpoena. It characterized the subpoena as "counterfeit," "specious and contrived," and as "an improper and illegitimate strategem," and it said the prosecutor was guilty of "egregious" misconduct. The final opinion, printed here, deleted the quoted words, declined to rule on the use of sham subpoenas, and held only that the subpoena "under the circumstances of this case contributed to the informant's becoming the alter ego of the prosecutor." (If so, what about the fact that Goldstein was wired?)

Although *Hammad* as finally written seems to contain more bark than bite, it has sparked a heated debate among the Justice Department, criminal defense lawyers, the ABA, and others. In a famous (or infamous) memorandum of June 8, 1989, Attorney General Dick Thornburgh emphatically rejected the notion that state ethics rules could restrict federal prosecutors. Compliance was voluntary only. The sole limits on prosecutorial conduct were the Constitution and statutes. While the attorney general focused on the no-contact rule, in subsequent statements the department rejected application of other state ethics rules to federal prosecutors and even to other federal lawyers. The department has suggested, if gingerly, that the separation of powers doctrine prevents federal judges from using ethical rules to restrict federal criminal investigations.*

Actions beget reactions. Criminal defense lawyers and others have protested the department's effort to "exempt" itself from rules that constrain all other lawyers. In February 1990, the American Bar Association adopted a policy that Justice Department "lawyers may not be given blanket exemption from [the no-contact rule] as adopted in individual jurisdictions." The ABA also voted "to oppose any attempt by the Department of Justice unilaterally to exempt its lawyers from the professional conduct rules that apply to all lawyers under applicable rules of the jurisdiction in which they practice." The attorney general then intimated that the ABA's position was traitorous. In a press release during the 1990 ABA convention, he said that "it is most unfortunate that the ABA has lent *aid and comfort*" to the "tactics" of the "defense bar" in "attempting to use rules of professional conduct to stymie criminal investigations and prosecutions" (emphasis added).

That should give you the flavor. To resolve this debate, we will have to answer the following questions:

a. Who decides? Who has the authority to determine the ethical rules that will control the behavior of federal lawyers, including prosecutors? Courts of the state in which the lawyer is admitted? A federal court? The executive branch of the federal government? All three? Can a state disci-

---

*Exercise of Federal Prosecutorial Authority in a Changing Legal Environment, Before the Subcommittee on Government Information, Justice and Agriculture of the House Committee on Government Operations, 101 Cong., 2d Sess., 241 (1990) (statement of Edward S. Dennis, Jr.).

pline a federal prosecutor who is admitted in that state for violating a no-contact (or other) rule in the course of her federal employment? Can a federal court? In answering these questions, consider three additional facts. Federal courts routinely admit lawyers to practice based on the applicant's state court admission. (See page 569 infra.) Federal trial courts generally adopt the ethics rules of the state in which they sit. Many lawyers employed by the federal government are not even admitted to federal court because they do not litigate. In United States v. Lopez, 765 F. Supp. 1433, 1445-1450 (N.D. Cal. 1991), Judge Patel held that federal prosecutors were subject to the no-contact rule despite the Thornburgh memorandum because the district court's local rules, by incorporating California's no-contact rule, had made the rule "federal law" that bound the Department. She then dismissed an indictment after finding an impermissible postindictment contact.

b. Reaching the merits. Issues of federalism and separation of powers aside, should the no-contact rule apply at the investigative stage of a state or federal criminal proceeding? If so, how broadly should we read the "authorized by law" exception? If we read it quite broadly, as *Hammad* ultimately seems to do, little is left of the rule. If that is so, or if we exempt prosecutors entirely, should we "level the playing field" by exempting defense lawyers from the same rule?

Today, defense lawyers can be disciplined for speaking to a represented witness or codefendant. United States v. Dennis, 843 F.2d 652, 657 (2d Cir. 1988); In re Mahoney, 437 N.E.2d 49 (Ind. 1982). In *Dennis*, decided a month after *Hammad I*, a defense lawyer had apparently questioned a government witness in the absence of counsel. The trial judge prevented the lawyer from cross-examining the witness. The Second Circuit reversed, holding that if the conversation violated the ethical rule, the "sanction, absent some serious prejudice to the witness or taint to the trial, should be disciplinary action, not a limitation of the cross-examination."

Consider a prosecution in which a represented person will be called to testify. Both the prosecutor and the defense lawyer wish to question the witness outside the presence of her lawyer. How shall the no-contact rule apply in that instance? Does it affect your analysis that the prosecutor can always subpoena the witness before the grand jury? United States v. Schwimmer, 882 F.2d 22 (2d Cir. 1989), cert. denied, 493 U.S. 1071 (1990).

c. Other government lawyers. If we relieve prosecutors from full compliance with the no-contact rule, how shall we treat all other government lawyers? Should a government lawyer who negotiates a contract for the purchase of real property be required to obey the rule? How about the government lawyer who civilly prosecutes businesses that discriminate based on race or gender? Or the government lawyer whose job is to enjoin conduct that pollutes the environment?

d. *Hammad* **meets** *Niesig*. To the extent we apply the no-contact rule to the conduct of prosecutors at the investigative stage of criminal proceedings, what shall be the rule when the target of the investigation is a corporation and the prosecutor wants to talk to corporate officers, agents and employees outside the presence of corporate counsel? *Upjohn* assumed that this would be permissible but is it? Does it make a difference whether the prosecutor plans to reveal — or have the investigator reveal — his or her identity or whether instead the contact will be undercover? Without citing *Hammad*, State of New Jersey v. Ciba-Geigy Corp., — N.J. Super. — , — A.2d — (App. Div. 1991), invokes the *Niesig* standard in conjunction with a criminal investigation of a corporation. Notably, New Jersey had adopted Rule 4.2, whose commentary the *Niesig* majority expressly disavowed in n.6, page 78 supra. See also In re Criminal Investigation No. 13, 82 Md. App. 609, 573 A.2d 51 (1990); Triple A Machine Shop, Inc. v. State, 213 Cal. App. 3d 131, 261 Cal. Rptr. 493 (1989).

e. Other rules. Rules 3.3(a)(1) and 4.1(a) forbid lawyers to lie to courts or others. Does this mean prosecutors cannot institute or oversee undercover operations, which are based entirely on lies? Recall Abscam. *Hammad* ultimately turned on the fact that the subpoena was false (a lie) as the basis for finding an ethical violation.

FURTHER READING

For further judicial discussion of the issues raised here, see United States v. Ryans, 903 F.2d 731, 736 (10th Cir.), cert. denied, 111 S. Ct. 152 (1990) (characterizing the Second Circuit as the only court that "purported to apply the [no-contact] rule in a non-custodial, pre-indictment setting"); People v. White, 209 Ill. App. 3d 844, 567 N.E.2d 1368 (1991) (following *Hammad* but finding no prosecutorial instigation of contact with target of investigation). See also the thorough treatment of the issue in Note, Prosecutorial Investigations and DR 7-104(A)(1), 89 Colum. L. Rev. 940 (1989) (authored by Marc A. Schwartz).

QUESTION

3.4   You are an Assistant United States Attorney in Chicago and are in charge of investigating securities crimes in the accounting industry. You get the following letter from a white collar criminal defense lawyer at one of the city's large firms:

Dear Prosecutor:

Our firm represents Ernst & Whinney and Roy Morgan, its CEO, in connection with your investigation of securities fraud in the accounting industry for the period 1985 to date. We call your attention to the Second Circuit's decision in United States v. Hammad and to Rule 4.2 and DR 7-104(A)(1).

Pursuant to these authorities, it will be unethical for you or your agents to speak with either of our clients or any of their agents or employees about a matter within the scope of our representation and as to which such agent or employee is empowered to make a statement that would be admissable against our client under the Federal Rules of Evidence.

We include within this prohibition all communications, whether your agent does or does not correctly identify himself or herself. We call upon you to notify all investigative agencies working under your supervision of their responsibilities under the authorities cited in this letter.

Thank you so much.

What do you do?

B. IMPROPER ACQUISITION OF CONFIDENTIAL INFORMATION

The prohibition on communications with another lawyer's client has, as one of its objectives, protection of attorney-client confidences. A lawyer may try to learn an opposing side's confidential information in other ways too. Courts have been protective here as well. In a case that received much attention in the legal and popular press, a New York appellate court, in two highly critical opinions, disqualified Sullivan & Cromwell in a surrogate's court litigation. The basis for the court's order was its conclusion that the firm had knowingly misused the state's discovery rules to obtain the opposing party's confidential information. In re Beiny 129 A.D.2d 126, 517 N.Y.S.2d 474 (1st Dept. 1987); In re Beiny, 132 A.D.2d 190, 522 N.Y.S.2d 511 (1st Dept. 1987), app. dismissed, 71 N.Y.2d 994, 524 N.E.2d 879, 529 N.Y.S.2d 277 (1988). In MMR/Wallace Power & Industrial, Inc. v. Thames Associates, 764 F. Supp. 712, 718 (D. Conn. 1991), Judge Burns held that the "spirit of the ethical norms . . . if not the letter . . . precludes an attorney from acquiring, inadvertently or otherwise, confidential or privileged information about his adversary's litigation strategy." She disqualified a defense firm that had obtained just such information from a former employee who had been part of the plaintiff's litigation team.

Another kind of invasion occurs when a lawyer for one client tries to debrief an expert retained by the other side. In Campbell Industries v.

M/V Gemini, 619 F.2d 24 (9th Cir. 1980), the defendant apparently managed to persuade one of the plaintiff's experts to "turn" and testify for the defense. The trial court disqualified the expert from testifying. The Ninth Circuit affirmed. Confidentiality issues were not mentioned. The court relied on the fact that the ex parte discussion violated discovery rules. See also County of Los Angeles v. Superior Court, 222 Cal. App. 3d 647, 271 Cal. Rptr. 698 (1990) (lawyer disqualified after obtaining other side's work product from opposing lawyer's expert consultant); Loudon v. Mhyre, 110 Wash. 2d 675, 756 P.2d 138 (1988) (refusing to permit ex parte conversations with the wrongful death plaintiff's treating physician, citing a threat to privileged medical information).

Other courts have been less willing to order disqualification as a remedy for improper acquisition of confidential information. In one dramatic case, Cooke v. Superior Court, 83 Cal. App. 3d 582, 147 Cal. Rptr. 915 (1978), a butler intercepted communications between a husband and his counsel and sent these to the wife, who was the husband's adversary in a dissolution proceeding. The wife's lawyer knowingly used the information. The court declined to disqualify the lawyer as a sanction for the conduct. It noted that disqualification had previously been ordered only in cases involving conflicts of interest (see Chapters 5 and 6). Morin v. Trupin, 728 F. Supp. 952 (S.D.N.Y. 1989) (where an attorney obtained an opposing client's confidences in an interview with the opposing client's former attorney the remedy is suppression and not disqualification). Compare the court's treatment of the acquisition of confidential information in Evans v. Artek Systems, 715 F.2d 788 (2d Cir. 1983), set out at page 448 infra.

In Powers v. Chicago Transit Authority, 890 F.2d 1355, 1362 (7th Cir. 1989), a lawyer who brought a civil rights action against his employer produced an internal memorandum of the defendant's that he claimed proved his case. Unfortunately for plaintiff, the memo appeared to contain information protected by the defendant's attorney-client privilege. The defendant moved for a protective order. The trial judge ordered the plaintiff to reveal the source of the memo; when he failed to do so, the court held him in contempt and later dismissed the case. The Seventh Circuit affirmed. To determine whether a protective order should issue for the memo, the trial judge had to decide whether the privilege had been waived. That determination required the judge to know whether plaintiff's source was authorized to waive the privilege. Plaintiff argued that the district judge should have suppressed the memo rather than dismiss the action. The court disagreed: "[T]he identity of Powers' source could lead to the discovery of important evidence that sheds light on Powers' fitness to hold the senior-level attorney position he sought to secure in his §1983 suit. Since exclusion of the memo was not as likely to coerce Powers to reveal his source as dismissal was, we cannot say that the district court abused its discretion."

In the criminal area, a debate has persisted over what, if any, remedy a defendant might win if he can show that the prosecution has improperly obtained confidential information from the defense. The Supreme Court avoided the question when it denied certiorari in Cutillo v. Cinelli, 485 U.S. 1037 (1988). Justice White dissented from the denial of certiorari in a brief opinion joined by the Chief Justice and Justice O'Connor:

> In Weatherford v. Bursey, 429 U.S. 545, 558 (1977), we held that establishing a violation of a defendant's Sixth Amendment right to counsel requires a showing of "at least a realistic possibility" of prejudice to the defendant or benefit to the prosecution. See also United States v. Morrison, 449 U.S. 361, 365-366 (1981). This case presents the issue of who bears the burden of persuasion for establishing prejudice or lack thereof when the Sixth Amendment violation involves the transmission of confidential defense strategy information. The First Circuit held that where confidential defense strategy information is transmitted to the prosecution and the defendant makes a prima facie showing of prejudice, the burden then shifts to the prosecution to prove that there was no prejudice to the defendant from the disclosure. Cinelli v. City of Revere, 820 F.2d 474, 478, 480 (1987); accord United States v. Mastroianni, 749 F.2d 900, 907-908 (CA1 1984). This position conflicts with the approach of other Circuits of requiring the defendant to prove prejudice. United States v. Steele, 727 F.2d 580, 586-587 (CA6), cert. denied sub nom. Scarborough v. United States, 467 U.S. 1209 (1984); United States v. Irwin, 612 F.2d 1182, 1186-1189 (CA9 1980). It also conflicts with a third position that once a defendant shows that the prosecution has improperly obtained confidential defense strategy information or has intentionally placed an informer in the defense camp then no showing of prejudice is required, for those acts constitute a per se violation of the Sixth Amendment. United States v. Costanzo, 740 F.2d 251, 254-255 (CA3 1984), cert. denied, 472 U.S. 1017 (1985). Because of these conflicting approaches amongst the Circuits, I would grant certiorari.

The Second Circuit also requires prejudice unless the defendant can show that the government's conduct was "corrupt." United States v. Schwimmer, 924 F.2d 443, 446 (2d Cir.), cert. denied, 112 S. Ct. 55 (1991).

United States v. Ofshe, 817 F.2d 1508, 1510-1512 (11th Cir.), cert. denied, 484 U.S. 963 (1987), affirmed a conviction but called the conduct of the prosecutor, author Scott Turow (Presumed Innocent, One L), "reprehensible." When Turow moved to delete this reference, the court declined and referred the matter to the federal prosecutor in Miami to determine whether Turow had obstructed justice. The court had earlier recommended that the district court refer Turow's conduct to the disciplinary authorities in Chicago, where Turow practiced. The Justice Department's inquiry cleared Turow, who had acted with approval of his superiors. See N.Y. Times, Dec. 1, 1987, at A16; April 29, 1988, at 38. Here's how the court described Turow's conduct. What do you think?

In December, 1982, appellant Ofshe was arrested in Miramar, Florida, for possession with intent to distribute cocaine. He retained the services of Mel Black, Esquire, who handled the bond hearing, arraignment, initial discovery review and the preparation of a motion to suppress. Mr. Black still represents Ofshe.

In February, 1983, Ofshe retained Marvin Glass, Esquire, to act as co-counsel, and informed Black of his decision. Glass indicated that he would handle all communications with the government, including plea negotiations, and that Black would prepare the case for trial, and would investigate and file appropriate motions. This breakdown of duties was confirmed in a meeting between Black and Glass in March, although Black remained sole counsel of record until July 1, 1983.

Thereafter, while still acting as counsel for Ofshe, Glass contacted the United States Attorney's Office in Chicago, Illinois, and learned he was a target of the "Greylord" investigation. Being keen to diminish his own criminal responsibility, Glass offered to provide information to and cooperate with the government in identifying and investigating suspected drug traffickers. Therefore, Glass periodically met with Assistant U.S. Attorney (AUSA) Turow to provide useful information about certain alleged criminal activities.

Later, on June 8, 1983, Glass mentioned Ofshe as a possible target during a meeting with Turow. When Glass indicated that he was currently representing Ofshe in Fort Lauderdale, Turow warned him not to reveal any privileged attorney-client conversations but encouraged him to proceed as an informant. Glass then began to detail activities regarding certain individuals, whom he had met through Ofshe, who discussed a money laundering scheme. In addition, Glass told AUSA Turow about Ofshe's request that Glass find a buyer for "a ton of marijuana."

AUSA Turow sought and received permission to place a Nagra body bug on Glass and conduct an electronic surveillance of the conversations between Glass and his client. These conversations included some unplanned discussions about his Florida case including the timing and likelihood of success of the motion to suppress. This electronic surveillance was done with Glass' consent while acting as Ofshe's attorney and as a "cooperating individual" for the government. To guard against improper conduct, AUSA Turow testified that the agents installing and monitoring the body tape were given very strict guidelines to instruct Glass not to violate any attorney-client privilege.[3]

Glass, of course, was not told at the time of the electronic surveillance that he had to withdraw from representation of Ofshe. Indeed, Glass was not told to withdraw for several months. Eventually, however, he was told to withdraw, but the United States Attorney did nothing to confirm his withdrawal or otherwise determine the status of the case. Significantly, the government did not file a motion to disqualify Glass or take any other action to inform the defendant of the conflict of interest, although it was

---

3. The monitored conversation was conducted without approval of the United States Attorney's Office or the United States District Court in Miami, Florida.

aware of the conflict since June 8, 1983. Thus, the government allowed the ineffective representation to continue for over 10 months.

In February, 1984, Judge Gonzalez, who was presiding over Ofshe's case, learned that Glass had been enlisted as an informant against his client and ordered the United States Attorney to disclose this fact to the defendant. Glass appealed Gonzalez's decision and did not move to withdraw until April, 1984. Even then he continued to hide the fact that he was working as an informant, with governmental consent, until February, 1985. Since the court file was sealed, defendant Ofshe could not discover the reasons for Glass' withdrawal or about the appeal taken by Glass. . . .

Black first learned, on February 16, 1985, through a letter from Chief Assistant United States Attorney Joseph McSorley, that Glass was a government informant and had worn a body bug during his conversations with his client, Ronald Ofshe, on June 14, 1983. Naturally, Black was concerned. Ofshe was also concerned.

AUSA Turow testified in detail about the procedures employed to assure there would be no violation of any attorney-client privilege. He stated that he and his superiors discussed the matter fully as soon as they learned that Ofshe's counsel, Glass, was "keen on diminishing his criminal responsibility" and wanted to become a "cooperating individual," and was willing to provide information regarding Ofshe's criminal activities. Turow also testified that by June 10, 1983, the United States Attorney in Illinois had given government agents very strict instructions that Glass was to follow based on the attorney-client privilege. The agents were to transmit these guidelines to Glass.

Apparently, as the agents were wiring Glass for his undercover conversation with Ofshe, Glass said that the case against Ofshe had been dismissed. After June 1983, contact between Glass and the United States Attorney's Office in Illinois was sporadic, but in August of 1983 Glass told the agents that the case had been reinstated and that he still represented the defendant. At this time, Turow felt obliged to inform the United States Attorney in the Southern District of Florida of the situation. However, the United States Attorney for the Southern District of Florida and his chief assistants decided not to reveal these matters to the prosecutor, Hursey.

Scott Turow defended himself in an article in the New York Times Magazine entitled Law School v. Reality. Sept. 18, 1988, at 52. In the course of a general discussion on the gap between law school education and actual practice, Turow wrote:

Indeed, the most dismal — and disappointing — moment I have endured as a lawyer arose last year in a sharp dispute over ethical duties. In June 1987, a Federal appellate court in Georgia rebuked me severely for my role as a United States prosecutor in allowing a defense lawyer who was seeking to cooperate with the Government to secretly tape-record a conversation with one of his clients about a drug-selling scheme that the lawyer admitted he and the client were planning. When I protested, the court responded by suggesting that my conduct regarding the defense lawyer might have constituted obstruction of justice. . . . I believed — and continue to believe — that neither clients nor lawyers have the right to plan crimes secure from government law enforcement efforts.

Does this response satisfy you? On the merits of Ofshe's claim, the court concluded that the conduct was not so outrageous as to violate the Fifth Amendment's due process clause. It also stressed that the episode produced no evidence against Ofshe for the government. In Presumed Guilty: The Court of Appeals vs. Scott Turow, 136 U. Pa. L. Rev. 1879 (1988), Professor H. Richard Uviller is highly critical of the Eleventh Circuit's analysis. After weighing various theories, he concludes that Turow violated neither ethical rules nor criminal law. Compare People v. Smith, at page 49 supra; United States v. Marshank, — F. Supp. — (N.D. Cal. 1991).

QUESTION

3.5   You are a United States district judge. In a multimillion dollar antitrust case still in the pretrial stages, defense counsel makes the following motion. A lawyer at the defense firm happened to be on vacation in another city when he observed a lawyer from the plaintiff's firm, Irene Laufer, having dinner with a former paralegal of the defense firm, Mark Hillerman. Hillerman had worked nearly exclusively on the antitrust case until several months earlier, when he left the firm for a different position. Laufer and Hillerman are approximately the same age. Several times during dinner they appeared to be holding hands. The defense firm wishes to conduct discovery about the nature and origins of Laufer's relationship to Hillerman and the substance of their communications. It is worried that Hillerman may have passed defense secrets to Laufer. What do you do?

IV

Financing Legal Services

Legal services have value. Who pays? How much? What rules, if any, limit the nature and size of fees?

Most lawyers get paid by their clients. Lawyers in firms charge fees. Other lawyers, like those who work for corporations or government, receive salaries. Fees, in turn, can be structured in many ways: a flat fee for a specified service, an hourly fee, a contingent fee, or some combination of the three. Some law firms have even introduced the concept of a "performance fee," an additional payment for highly favorable results.

While it may be most common to see the client as the source of the fee, that is not always so. Sometimes a lawyer will represent a client but be paid by someone else. A common example is an insurance company that retains counsel to represent an insured. Another example is when the state pays a lawyer to represent an indigent criminal defendant in fulfillment of its obligation under Gideon v. Wainwright, 372 U.S. 335 (1963). States may also pay for lawyers in certain civil matters. State-financed lawyers may work for an institutional law office (like legal aid), or they may be independent practitioners.

Sometimes a lawyer will be paid by a client's adversary. This can be by agreement, as when a person who obtains a mortgage pays the lender's lawyer, or by court order, as with statutes that authorize a court to order one litigant to pay the fees of a prevailing party. Fee-shifting statutes can be found in the civil liberties world and also in commercial areas like antitrust, copyright, and patent.

Legal services need not be financed with the payment of money at all. Lawyers sometimes work pro bono publico ("for the public good"). When they do, it is the lawyer himself or herself who finances the arrangement. Many lawyers do pro bono work voluntarily. Lately, there has been debate about whether lawyers should be required to perform pro bono work.

Beyond the various ways of financing legal services are questions about the nature and amount of legal fees. How are they controlled?

Most prominent, perhaps, is the market's law of supply and demand. But ethical and legal rules also constrain the nature and size of fees. It is not a wholly laissez-faire system. Should it be? Should courts or legislatures be able to deny a willing lawyer and a competent client the right to determine the structure and amount of the lawyer's fee?

Once we identify the bounds on proper legal fees, the next task is to identify who can receive the money. What limits are there on the division of fees among lawyers in a single firm? When can fees be divided among lawyers in different firms? And what exactly do we mean by "firm" in the first place? These questions assume that legal fees will go to lawyers. But must they? When, if ever, can nonlawyers or businesses other than law firms receive legal fees? This last question brings up the issue of lay participation in law firms and the delivery of legal services, the subject of Chapter 14.

A.   THE ROLE OF THE MARKETPLACE

It is often no small mystery, and not only to laypeople, how lawyers go about charging clients for their services. There is the story — possibly apocryphal — about the Washington attorney who was retained to guide a client through the treacherous waters of the bureaucracy. The lawyer, after careful consideration of the problem, told the client that his best course of action was to do nothing. He submitted a bill for $20,000. The client paid, but after some weeks, in a moment of anxiety, called for reassurance. The lawyer said, "I told you to do nothing!" — and sent another bill for $5,000.

This, while perhaps an extreme example, does point up the fact that some lawyers command quite high fees. Whether or not the client received fair value is a question that perhaps only those familiar with Washington can answer. In the case that follows, though, the court found that an attorney was entitled to the high fee he demanded. (Remember, the court is talking about 1975 dollars!)

BROBECK, PHLEGER & HARRISON
v. TELEX CORP.
602 F.2d 866 (9th Cir.), cert. denied, 444 U.S. 981 (1979)

PER CURIAM.

This is a diversity action in which the plaintiff, the San Francisco law firm of Brobeck, Phleger & Harrison ("Brobeck"), sued the Telex Corpo-

ration and Telex Computer Products, Inc. ("Telex") to recover
$1,000,000 in attorney's fees. Telex had engaged Brobeck on a contin-
gency fee basis to prepare a petition for certiorari after the Tenth Circuit
reversed a $259.5 million judgment in Telex's favor against Interna-
tional Business Machines Corporation ("IBM") and affirmed an $18.5
million counterclaim judgment for IBM against Telex. Brobeck prepared and filed the petition, and after Telex entered a "wash settlement"
with IBM in which both parties released their claims against the other,
Brobeck sent Telex a bill for $1,000,000, that it claimed Telex owed it
under their written contingency fee agreement. When Telex refused to
pay, Brobeck brought this action. Both parties filed motions for summary judgment. The district court granted Brobeck's motion, awarding
Brobeck $1,000,000 plus interest. Telex now appeals. . . .

Having had reversed one of the largest antitrust judgments in history,
Telex officials decided to press the Tenth Circuit's decision to the United
States Supreme Court. To maximize Telex's chances for having its petition for certiorari granted, they decided to search for the best available
lawyer. They compiled a list of the preeminent antitrust and Supreme
Court lawyers in the country, and Roger Wheeler, Telex's Chairman of
the Board, settled on Moses Lasky of the Brobeck firm as the best
possibility.

Wheeler and his assistant made preliminary phone calls to Lasky on
February 3, 4, and 13, 1975 to determine whether Lasky was willing to
prepare the petition for certiorari. Lasky stated he would be interested if
he was able to rearrange his workload. When asked about a fee, Lasky
stated that, although he would want a retainer, it was the policy of the
Brobeck firm to determine fees after the services were performed.
Wheeler, however, wanted an agreement fixing fees in advance and arranged for Lasky to meet in San Francisco on February 10th to discuss
the matter further with Telex's president, Stephen Jatras, and Floyd
Walker, its attorney in the IBM litigation.

[The following fee agreement with Lasky was eventually signed.]

Memorandum

1. Retainer of $25,000.00 to be paid. If Writ of Certiorari is denied and
no settlement has been effected in excess of the Counterclaim, then the
$25,000.00 retainer shall be the total fee paid; provided however, that

2. If the case should be settled before a Petition for Writ of Certiorari is
actually filed with the Clerk of the Supreme Court, then the Brobeck firm
would bill for its services to the date of settlement at an hourly rate of
$125.00 per hour for the lawyers who have worked on the case; the total
amount of such billing will be limited to not more than $100,000.00,
against which the $25,000.00 retainer will be applied, but no portion of the
retainer will be returned in any event.

3. Once a Petition for Writ of Certiorari has been filed with the Clerk of the United States Supreme Court then Brobeck will be entitled to the payment of an additional fee in the event of a recovery by Telex from IBM by way of settlement or judgment of its claims against IBM; and, such additional fee will be five percent (5%) of the first $100,000,000.00 gross of such recovery, undiminished by any recovery by IBM on its counterclaims or cross-claims. The maximum contingent fee to be paid is $5,000,000.00, provided that if recovery by Telex from IBM is less than $40,000,000.00 gross, the five percent (5%) shall be based on the net recovery, i.e., the recovery after deducting the credit to IBM by virtue of IBM's recovery on counterclaims or cross-claims, but the contingent fee shall not then be less than $1,000,000.00.

4. Once a Writ of Certiorari has been granted, then Brobeck will receive an additional $15,000.00 retainer to cover briefing and arguing in the Supreme Court.

5. Telex will pay, in addition to the fees stated, all of the costs incurred with respect to the prosecution of the case in the United States Supreme Court.

Jatras signed Lasky's proposed agreement, and on February 28 returned it to Lasky with a letter and a check for $25,000 as the agreed retainer. To "clarify" his thinking on the operation of the fee agreement, Jatras attached a set of hypothetical examples to the letter. This "attachment" stated the amount of the fee that would be paid to Brobeck assuming judgment or settlements in eight different amounts. In the first hypothetical, which assumed a settlement of $18.5 million and a counterclaim judgment of $18.5 million, Jatras listed a "net recovery" by Telex of "$0" and a Brobeck contingency fee of "$0."

Lasky received the letter and attachment on March 3. Later that same day he replied: "Your attachment of examples of our compensation in various contingencies is correct, it being understood that the first example is applicable only to a situation where the petition for certiorari has been denied, as stated in paragraph 1 of the memorandum.

No Telex official responded to Lasky's letter. . . .

On October 2 IBM officials became aware that the Supreme Court's decision on the petition was imminent. They contacted Telex and the parties agreed that IBM would release its counterclaim judgment against Telex in exchange for Telex's dismissal of its petition for certiorari. On October 3, at the request of Wheeler and Jatras, Lasky had the petition for certiorari withdrawn. Thereafter, he sent a bill to Telex for $1,000,000. When Telex refused to pay, Brobeck filed its complaint. On the basis of depositions and exhibits, the district court granted Brobeck's motion for summary judgment.

In a somewhat contradictory fashion, Telex contends on appeal that a number of genuine issues of fact exist with respect to Brobeck's motion for summary judgment but that none exists concerning its own motion. . . .

[The court dismissed the contention that Brobeck had been discharged by Telex, holding that no facts supported that view. As to the contract, the court pointed out several inconsistencies in Telex's interpretation, and held that Brobeck's understanding was correct. The court held that the contract was unambiguous on its face, and that extrinsic evidence also tended to confirm Brobeck's interpretation.]

Finally, Telex contends that the $1 million fee was so excessive as to render the contract unenforceable. Alternatively it argues that unconscionability depends on the contract's reasonableness, a question of fact that should be submitted to the jury.

Preliminarily, we note that whether a contract is fair or works an unconscionable hardship is determined with reference to the time when the contract was made and cannot be resolved by hindsight.

There is no dispute about the facts leading to Telex's engagement of the Brobeck firm. Telex was an enterprise threatened with bankruptcy. It had won one of the largest money judgments in history, but that judgment had been reversed in its entirety by the Tenth Circuit. In order to maximize its chances of gaining review by the United States Supreme Court, it sought to hire the most experienced and capable lawyer it could possibly find. After compiling a list of highly qualified lawyers, it settled on Lasky as the most able. Lasky was interested but wanted to bill Telex on hourly basis. After Telex insisted on a contingent fee arrangement, Lasky made it clear that he would consent to such an arrangement only if he would receive a sizable contingent fee in the event of success.

In these circumstances, the contract between Telex and Brobeck was not so unconscionable that "no man in his senses and not under a delusion would make on the one hand, and as no honest and fair man would accept on the other." This is not a case where one party took advantage of another's ignorance, exerted superior bargaining power, or disguised unfair terms in small print. Rather, Telex, a multi-million [dollar] corporation, represented by able counsel, sought to secure the best attorney it could find to prepare its petition for certiorari, insisting on a contingent fee contract. Brobeck fulfilled its obligation to gain a stay of judgment and to prepare and file the petition for certiorari. Although the minimum fee was clearly high, Telex received substantial value from Brobeck's services. For, as Telex acknowledged, Brobeck's petition provided Telex with the leverage to secure a discharge of its counterclaim judgment, thereby saving it from possible bankruptcy in the event the Supreme Court denied its petition for certiorari. We conclude that such a contract was not unconscionable.

The judgment of the district court is affirmed.

Telex was in trouble. Moses Lasky was one of the best antitrust litigators. The client had other lawyers to advise it on the fee negotiation with Lasky's firm. It's hard to imagine how a fee agreement could be more "arm's length" than this one. Of course, Lasky's petition for certiorari did provide "leverage" for a settlement that eliminated the possibility of Telex's bankruptcy. We don't have to weep for Telex. The court refused to save the company from its own business judgment. Yet Telex must have been pretty mad. It hired other lawyers to fight the fee all the way to the Supreme Court.

When the Federal Deposit Insurance Corporation retained Cravath, Swaine & Moore to sue Drexel Burnham Lambert, Inc., Michael Milken, and others whose "junk bonds" allegedly caused bank failures, the parties negotiated a fee arrangement of from $300 hourly for senior partners down to $50 hourly for paralegals. These fees were as much as 25 percent less than Cravath's usual charges. In return, Cravath and the FDIC agreed that the fees would be retroactively increased if it recovered more than $200 million from the defendants. The increase could result in as much as $600 hourly for top partners, $270 hourly for associates, and $85 hourly for paralegals. In no event could Cravath's total fee exceed 25 percent of the amount recovered. New York Times, April 5, 1991, at A1. Given the sophistication of the client, whose general counsel negotiated the fee, is this arrangement immune to disciplinary action or judicial review?

Is There a Double Standard?

In Jones v. Amalgamated Warbasse Houses, 721 F.2d 881, 885 (2d Cir. 1983), cert. denied, 466 U.S. 944 (1984), counsel represented a class of minority persons who alleged a systematic exclusion from a publicly subsidized housing development in violation of federal law. Eventually, the defendant settled by agreeing to injunctive relief that virtually ensured that one out of every 10 future vacancies would be filled by a class member. As part of the settlement, defendant agreed to pay plaintiff's counsel $41,350, or about $129 for each hour of counsel's time. The district court reduced the fee to $25,600 (or $75 hourly) even though the defendant made no application to have the fee reduced and even though there was no evidence of collusion, or that the fee agreement was based on inadequate or erroneous information, or that the fee was a windfall. Since the plaintiff class was entitled only to injunctive relief, the reduction would not result in more money for the class. On appeal, counsel argued that the district court was without power to invalidate the fee agreement. The Second Circuit disagreed. It emphasized that the court has "a special responsibility to supervise the matter of attorneys' fees in class actions and in any litigation involving a fee-shifting statute like §1988," even though the reduction will not benefit the class. The lower court's "downward revision of a fee settlement unacceptable to the court will promote confidence in the integrity of the judicial process and is a proper exercise of authority over officers of the court in litigation pending before the court." The Second Circuit stressed that in exercising its discretion, the district court should accord fee settlements "a presumption of regularity once it finds no impropriety, but . . . the presumption can be overcome for good reason, including . . . the public perception of the appropriateness of the fees, and the range of awards allowed in similar cases."

The *Jones* court was less deferential to the fee agreement than the *Telex* court even though, as in *Telex*, the fee was negotiated between counsel. *Jones* held that greater scrutiny was justified in class actions and in litigation involving fee-shifting statutes. Is that because the negotiation occurred under the shadow of a potential judicial award if the parties could not agree? The *Jones* court accepts a presumption of regularity, but apparently a $129 hourly rate (in New York City in 1983) was high enough to rebut the presumption. Or was there something else that did it? Could the district court have *increased* the size of the fee if it had concluded that it was too low?

B. UNETHICAL FEES

Ethics codes limit the size of attorneys' fees. Compare the standards in Rule 1.5 and DR 2-106. Are they different? A lawyer can be disciplined for charging too much, as the following case proves. (Statutory limits on legal fees are considered at page 113 infra.)

BUSHMAN v. STATE BAR OF CALIFORNIA
11 Cal. 3d 558, 522 P.2d 312, 113 Cal. Rptr. 904 (1974)

BY THE COURT.

This is a proceeding to review a recommendation of the State Bar of California that Ted Bushman be suspended from the practice of law for one year. Bushman was found by the State Bar Disciplinary Board to have charged and attempted to collect an exorbitant and unconscionable fee from clients. . . .

Bushman was born in 1936 and admitted to practice in California in 1962. He practiced in partnership with his wife, Soma Baldwin Bushman, except for a period in 1967 or 1968 when another attorney joined in the partnership for a one- or two-year period.

THE COX MATTER

The findings of the state disciplinary board, which are substantially identical with those of the local administrative committee, are as follows:

On November 7, 1969, Bushman was retained by Barbara Cox, aged 16, her mother and father (Mr. and Mrs. Stroud), and Ralph Hughes (hereinafter referred to as the defendants) in connection with an action filed by Barbara's husband, Neal W. Cox, for divorce and custody of a minor child of the marriage. The only substantial issue in Cox's action was custody. Barbara's parents were named as defendants because it was alleged they might have had physical custody of the child, and Hughes was involved because he allegedly was having sexual relations with Barbara and there was a possibility that he would be charged with statutory rape.

Cox was represented by attorney Gertrude Chern. At Bushman's request, the defendants signed a promissory note for $5,000, payable $300 forthwith and the balance at $50 a month. They also signed a retainer agreement providing for an hourly fee of not less than $60. Barbara was a minor, her parents were on welfare, and there was no community property of the Cox marriage. Bushman advised the defendants it was the policy of his office that, whenever attorney Chern was the opposing counsel in a custody matter, a minimum retainer of $5,000 was required without regard to the time spent by Bushman on the case or to other factors, because Mrs. Chern would generate a "paper war." Subsequently, when Cox visited Bushman's office in connection with a possible reconciliation with Barbara, Bushman unsuccessfully sought to induce him to add his signature to the promissory note.

All the pleadings and negotiations on behalf of Cox were handled by an associate of Mrs. Chern. The action did not involve any juvenile court or criminal matters, and the custody issue was resolved by a stipulation of the parties in favor of Barbara, following the usual custody investigation and report of the county probation department. The fee charged Cox by his attorney was $300, plus costs, representing five and one-half hours of work.

The court ordered that the husband pay Bushman a fee of $300, and $60 in costs; Bushman did not advise the court of the $5,000 note signed by the wife and others or of the sums paid thereon. There was nothing unusual or novel in pleadings or research in the Cox case. Bushman filed on Barbara's behalf a demurrer, cross-complaint, petition for appointment of a guardian-ad-litem, and stipulation to a probation report, as well as an answer to the complaint, and a declaration of points and authorities. He attended two hearings on orders to show cause, and subpoenaed and interviewed a doctor.

Bushman claimed that he spent over 100 hours on the case, which at $60 an hour would call for a fee of $6,000. However, he billed the defendants for only $2,800 plus $60 in costs which, at the $60 an hour rate, would amount to far less than 100 hours of time spent. The reasonable value of Bushman's services in the action was the amount awarded by the court, i.e., $300 and $60 in costs.

The $5,000 note is a negotiable instrument and remains in the possession of Bushman or of Soma Baldwin Bushman. The fees charged, and those which Bushman attempted to collect, were excessive, overreaching, exorbitant, and unconscionable. . . .

We agree that under all the circumstances, the fee charged by Bushman was so exorbitant and wholly disproportionate to the services rendered to the defendants as to shock the conscience. An examination of the file in the Cox matter reveals that only a simple, almost routine series of documents was filed by Bushman on Barbara's behalf. Although he asserts that the case was "quite involved," he is unable to articulate any complex issues which required extensive research or specialized skills. The only documentation in the file indicating any research whatever is a one-page "Points and Authorities" filed in support of an order to show cause, which cites the text of five statutes and one case, without any argument. Aside from interviews with the defendants and a doctor, the only additional services performed by Bushman were two appearances in court for hearings on orders to show cause. He failed to substantiate his claim of 100 hours spent on the Cox case, although he could have utilized the subpoena powers of the local committee for this purpose. It is of some significance in this connection that Cox's attorney spent slightly more than five hours on the case. . . .

It is ordered that petitioner be suspended from the practice of law for a period of one year.

QUESTION

4.1   Do you agree or disagree with the following sentiment:

Bushman was wrongly decided. This was a complicated case. A $5,000 retainer was entirely proper. Bushman got a good result. What if the daughter of an old line San Francisco family, worth tens of millions of dollars, had gotten into the trouble that Barbara Cox found herself in? The family hires Moses Lasky's partner in the Brobeck firm who handles matrimonial matters. He charges $5,000 as a nonrefundable retainer against a $250 per hour rate. He achieves the same result in five and one-half hours. Would his fee be called unconscionable? Not a chance. Then the court would say it was his accumulated expertise that the family was paying for and that made the adversary settle so generously. The fact is that there is a double standard depending on where your office is and who your clients are. If you are Moses Lasky, you can charge nearly anything you want (and if you are his client you can promise to pay it). If you are Ted Bushman, some judge is going to be watching over your shoulder. Laissez-faire for the rich, controls for the struggling lawyer.

Courts May Reduce Unethical Fees

Discipline is not the only risk faced by lawyers who charge too much. Courts claim inherent authority to order disgorgement of excessive fees.

When the fee agreement is reached after the attorney-client relationship is formed, courts are especially strict in reviewing it for fairness. Attorney Grievance Commn. of Maryland v. Korotki, 318 Md. 646, 569 A.2d 1224 (1990) (contingency rate increased from one-third to three-quarters after retainer warrants suspension). A postretainer fee agreement is not unlike any business arrangement between lawyer and client (see Rule 1.8(a) and page 174 infra). After retainer, the client is presumed to be less free to go elsewhere and the attorney is assumed to be in a significantly superior bargaining position. The client may have begun to rely on and confide in the attorney, especially in personal legal matters, with the result that the client is not as independent as he or she may have been before retainer. See, for example, Randolph v. Schuyler, 284 N.C. 496, 201 S.E.2d 833 (1974).

Even if the fee arrangement is reached before retainer, courts have been willing to appraise "the amount of the fee [because of the] inherent right to supervise the members of its bar." Rosquist v. Soo Line R.R., 692 F.2d 1107, 1111 (7th Cir. 1982). The *Rosquist* court further said that judicial power to review an attorney's fee "for conformance with the reasonable standard of the Code of Ethics" is present even "when the validity of the fee contract itself has not been challenged by the parties."

Rosquist was limited by United States v. Vague, 697 F.2d 805, 808 (7th Cir. 1983). In preparing to sentence a defendant who had entered a guilty plea, the trial judge learned from the presentence report that the lawyer's fee was $12,000, all but $1000 of which had been paid. The judge concluded that a reasonable fee would be at most $2500 and ordered the lawyer to return the difference. When the lawyer refused, the judge held him in civil contempt. The Seventh Circuit reversed. The trial judge should have referred the matter to discipline. The client did not ask the judge to intervene. The judge was placing himself in the role of both prosecutor and judge. Here the contempt power was misused because there was no "exigency" requiring the judge to act "immediately to uphold the authority of the courts." *Rosquist* was distinguished (on among other grounds) as involving a complaint by the client and a "controversy between the lawyer and a party, not just . . . between the lawyer and a judge." There was a dissent. Accord Gagnon v. Shoblom, 409 Mass. 63, 565 N.E.2d 775 (1991) (contingent fee).

Vague was in turn distinguished in United States v. Strawser, 800 F.2d 704 (7th Cir. 1986), cert. denied, 480 U.S. 906 (1987). Anderson had been hired to represent one of two cousins, Ronald, after Michael and Ronald were charged with distributing marijuana. When Anderson refused to represent Ronald on appeal without further compensation following Ronald's guilty plea, Ronald wrote a letter to the court requesting appellate counsel, which in turn prompted a hearing. Although the facts were disputed, the trial judge accepted Anderson's position that he had been paid $47,500 (of a fee of $50,000) to represent Ronald. The judge held the $47,500 fee "exorbitant and unreasonable" and ordered the lawyer to refund all sums exceeding $20,000 to the United States Treasury. The Seventh Circuit held *Vague* inapplicable because the district judge there had thrust himself into the issue unnecessarily. In the current matter, by contrast, the trial judge needed to resolve the fee issue in order to decide whether Ronald was entitled to have appointed counsel represent him on appeal or whether Anderson was required to provide representation.

Should a Lawyer Be Required to Put Fee Agreements in Writing?

The Model Code urges lawyers to prepare written retainer agreements "[a]s soon as feasible after [they have] been employed," EC 2-19. The January 1980 draft of the Model Rules provided in Rule 1.6(b):

> The basis or rate of a lawyer's fee shall be put in writing before the lawyer has rendered substantial services in the matter, except when (1) [a]n agreement as to the fees is implied by the fact that the lawyer's services are of the same general kind as previously rendered to and paid for by the client; or (2) [t]he services are rendered in an emergency where a writing is impracticable.

As finally adopted, Rule 1.5(b) simply says that "the fee shall be communicated to the client, preferably in writing, before or within a reasonable time after commencing the representation." A contingent fee, however, "shall be in writing." Rule 1.5(c). Do you think the change from the January 1980 draft to the Model Rules as finally adopted was salutary?

How does it affect your answer to know that fee disputes are among the most common complaints clients have about lawyers? Why would a profession — which, if you recall, is supposed to put service and the public interest above the quest for wealth (see page 6 supra) — refuse to require written fee agreements along the lines contemplated by the

January 1980 draft of the Model Rules? Can you defend this omission? New Jersey retains the draft's view where the lawyer has not regularly represented the client. See also §6148 Calif. Bus. & Prof. Code (writing generally required).

C. CONTINGENT FEES AND STATUTORY LIMITS

In a contingent fee agreement, a lawyer agrees to make his or her fee contingent on the occurrence or nonoccurrence of an event. Usually the event is recovery of a sum of money and the fee is a percentage of the recovery. This fee is most prevalent in personal injury actions, whether based in negligence or strict liability. But there are other possibilities. For example, a lawyer can agree that she will be entitled to a fee only if she achieves a particular result for a client (for example, a mortgage commitment). Or a lawyer may agree to a percentage of the amount of money he *saves* the client (for example, persuading the IRS to settle for $10,000 on a $40,000 claim). A fee with contingent dimensions has even appeared in mergers and acquisitions. One New York law firm charged what it called a "performance fee" for its successful representation of Burroughs Corporation in its effort to acquire Sperry Corporation. The Wall Street Journal, Oct. 24, 1986 at 31. Fees can also be partly contingent ("$10,000 plus one-fourth the recovery"). Contingent fees are conceptually possible in all representations that have a definable objective, but they are forbidden in criminal and matrimonial cases (see page 117 infra).

A contingent fee gives the lawyer an interest in the client's matter and as such is an exception to a general prohibition, based on a danger of conflict of interest, against acquiring such an interest. See Rule 1.8(j), DR 5-103(A), and page 179 infra. The propriety of accepting a contingent fee does not depend on the ability of the client to pay a different kind of fee (hourly, flat amount), even though the most frequent justification for contingent fees is that they enable people who could not otherwise afford to hire lawyers to do so. ABA Informal Opinion 86-1521 says that ordinarily a lawyer should give a client the option of a traditional fee.

From the lawyer's perspective, the contingent fee will sometimes enable her to have a client where otherwise she would not, either because the client cannot afford a traditional fee or because the client is unwilling to invest money in his claim. Another advantage is the prospect of substantially greater remuneration for the lawyer than she would receive through an hourly rate. Whether a contingent fee is more favorable to the lawyer than an hourly fee ordinarily depends on four factors: the likelihood of the occurrence of the contingency, when it is likely to occur, the probable size of the recovery, and the amount of the percentage. The first three factors require predictions, which in turn will determine the fourth factor. (For example, the less likely the contingency is to occur, the greater the percentage the lawyer will ask.) Lawyers are usually better able than clients to make these predictions. This capability puts clients at a disadvantage when negotiating the fourth factor (the amount of the contingency) and in deciding whether to opt for a contingent fee at all (assuming they can pay a regular fee). What does this imbalance require of lawyers? Does it mean a lawyer is well advised to comply with ABA Informal Opinion 86-1521?

The most important factor is the likelihood that the contingency will occur. Usually lawyers will not agree to a contingent fee unless there is a high probability of occurrence. If they are willing to take a greater risk, they'll insist on a high percentage of the recovery. If the contingency does not occur, the lawyer does not get paid, although the client may be responsible for the lawyer's out-of-pocket costs (compare Rule 1.8(e) with DR 5-103(B) and see page 179 infra). To compensate for this risk, a lawyer may receive a contingent fee that would be unconscionably high if it were a guaranteed fee. See McKenzie Construction, Inc. v. Maynard, 823 F.2d 43 (3d Cir. 1987) (contingent fee that yields $790 an hour is not unreasonable, although 13 times the lawyer's usual hourly rate, given the favorable result).

Courts have been willing to exert greater control over contingent fee agreements, at least when they are used in personal injury cases, than over ordinary fee agreements. This can be explained by a series of factors: the perception that personal injury plaintiffs are relatively unsophisticated in the use of lawyers; historical abuses of contingency fees; the fact that a contingency agreement can fortuitously yield a lawyer a windfall; the unequal bargaining positions of attorney and client as a result of the lawyer's greater predictive ability; and, finally, because an interest in the client's recovery creates real possibilities of conflicts of interest between lawyer and client. Florida's version of Rule 1.5 is perhaps unique in the protection it gives contingent fee clients in tort cases. The client must receive a statutorily prescribed client bill of rights that tells her, among other things, that "you . . . have the right . . . to bargain about the rate or percentage as in any other contract," and that "you may cancel the contract without any reason if you notify your lawyer in writing" within three business days, in which case "you do not owe the lawyer a fee."

Statutory Fee Ceilings

We consider three kinds of statutes imposing counsel fee limits. One kind applies in certain contingent fee matters. Two other kinds apply in designated matters without regard to the nature of the fee.

Defendants traditionally sued by lawyers who work on contingencies — doctors and insurance companies, for example — are especially critical of contingency fee arrangements, sometimes seeing them as the worst abuse of the civil law system. Partly as a result of lobbying efforts by such defendants, laws have been passed to reduce the size of contingency fees in particular kinds of cases (usually cases against the lobbying defendants, quite often doctors) and thereby presumably the lawyers' incentive as well. Often these laws contain other "remedies," such as caps on the amount the plaintiff can recover for pain and suffering. One such law is reviewed in the following case. But even before the recent spate of laws, contingency fees (at least in personal injury actions) were generally limited to a sliding scale (the percentage decreases as the recovery increases) or to a flat maximum of about one-third the recovery. Sometimes this ceiling is higher for small cases (to make them economically worthwhile), and certain provisions allow courts to raise the ceiling in especially complex cases. These limitations, remember, impose ceilings, not floors. Clients are free to negotiate lower percentages. Both the code and rules require that contingent fee agreements, but not other fee agreements, be in writing. Why is that?

Roa v. Lodi Medical Group, 37 Cal. 3d 920, 695 P.2d 164, 166-170, 211 Cal. Rptr. 77, appeal dismissed, 474 U.S. 990 (1985), was a challenge to a California statute that, among other things, imposed ceilings on attorney's fees in medical malpractice actions. The maximum a lawyer could receive was 40 percent of the first $50,000; one-third of the next $50,000; one-quarter of the next $100,000; and 10 percent above that. A lawyer who recovered $1 million would therefore get about $141,000 in fees, substantially less than the $300,000 to $400,000 lawyers in other states can earn. Of course, the difference goes to the client.

The court first rejected a due process argument that the statute infringed "on the right of medical malpractice victims to retain counsel." While recognizing a right to retain counsel in civil matters, the court cited many opinions approving statutory fee ceilings, including Calhoun v. Massie, 253 U.S. 170 (1920) (Brandeis, J.), which upheld a 20 percent contingency ceiling in actions against the United States. The court also rejected, as empirically without support, the proposition that the statutory limits were "so low that in practice the statute will make it impossible for injured persons to retain an attorney." The challengers next claimed that the "sliding scale" would promote "a conflict of interest between attorney and client, reducing the attorney's incentive to pursue a higher award." The court responded:

> As a number of commentators have explained, however, potential conflicts of interest are inherent in all contingent fee arrangements. (See generally MacKinnon, Contingent Fees for Legal Services (1964) pp.196-200.) On the one hand, whenever a contingency fee agreement provides for either a

flat percentage rate regardless of the amount of recovery or a declining percentage with an increase in recovery, 4t may be to the lawyer's advantage to settle [the case] quickly, spending as little time as possible on the small claim where the increment in value through rigorous bargaining or trial, while significant to the client, is not significant or perhaps compensatory to the lawyer. . . ." (MacKinnon, supra, at p.198.) On the other hand, "[w]here the rate is graduated according to the stage of litigation at which recovery is attained . . . the increase in the rate of fee may lead the lawyer to bring suit or start trial, for example, solely to increase his rate from 25% to 33⅓%, without actually doing that much additional work and without the likelihood of a comparable increment to the client." (Ibid.) Furthermore, no matter how the particular percentage fee is calculated,

> [t]he difference in the financial position of the lawyer and client may make for a complete disparity in their willingness to take a risk on a large recovery as against no recovery at all. In the same way the use of delay to increase the eventual recovery on a claim may have an entirely different impact on the injured and uncompensated claimant than it does on the lawyer, who is busy with other claims and regards this as one of a series which are ripening on the vine. . . . (Id. at 199.)

Thus, though the sliding scale arrangement embodied in section 6146 may affect the settings in which the attorney's and client's interests diverge, it does not create the basic conflict of interest problem.

Indeed, section 6146's decreasing sliding-scale approach has been recommended as the preferable form of regulation by a number of studies that have examined the question. As a report of an American Bar Association commission explained:

> [I]n order to relate the attorney's fee more to the amount of legal work and expense involved in handling a case and less to the fortuity of the plaintiff's economic status and degree of injury, a decreasing maximum schedule of attorney's fees, reasonably generous in the lower recovery ranges and thus unlikely to deny potential plaintiffs access to legal representation, should be set on a state-by-state basis.

Finally, the court rejected an equal protection challenge to the statute on the ground that the limitations were reasonably related to the legislative goal of reducing medical malpractice costs, preventing frivolous suits, and discouraging lawyers from holding out "for unrealistically high settlements."

For a case upholding limitations on contingent fees in "healing art" malpractice actions — actions against dentists, psychologists, and other "healers" as well as doctors — see Bernier v. Burris, 113 Ill. 2d 219, 497 N.E.2d 763 (1986).

Should a prospective client be entitled to waive the statutory ceiling in order to induce a highly skilled lawyer to accept his or her case? The court in Fineberg v. Harney & Moore, 207 Cal. App. 3d 1049, 255 Cal. Rptr. 299, cert. denied, 493 U.S. 852 (1989), said no. Doesn't that unduly interfere with the client's contractual freedom? Can you reconcile the result with the decision of the Massachusetts court in Gagnon v. Shoblom, page 111 supra, which reversed the trial judge's reduction of a contingent fee "because no one is challenging the fee"?

Beyond statutes that cap contingent fees, two other kinds of laws limit payment to attorneys. One extreme variety is reviewed in Walters v. National Assn. of Radiation Survivors, 473 U.S. 305, 321-372 (1985). By 38 U.S.C. §3404(c) (1986), the fee an attorney may receive to represent a veteran seeking benefits from the Veterans Administration for service-connected death or disability is limited to ten dollars. First passed in 1862, this law is not intended to protect against excessive fees, but rather to keep lawyers out of the process through economic disincentive. Although the law applies to all kinds of fees, its greatest practical impact is on contingent fees because those would most often have been used in the cases covered. Lawyers willing to work without compensation can still represent claimants.

In *Walters*, the Court had to decide whether Congress could erect a benefits system that effectively prevented applicants from retaining counsel to assist them. The case is interesting in part because of the ongoing debate over the value of the adversarial system and the new interest in alternate dispute resolution. See Edward Brunet, Questioning the Quality of Alternate Dispute Resolution, 62 Tul. L. Rev. 1 (1987); Jethro Lieberman & James Henry, Lessons from the Alternate Dispute Resolution Movement, 53 U. Chi. L. Rev. 424 (1986). (See also page 522 infra.)

Justice Rehnquist rejected plaintiffs' due process challenge to the statute, using the test established in Mathews v. Eldridge, 424 U.S. 319 (1976), which "requires a court to consider the private interest that will be affected by the official action, the risk of an erroneous deprivation of such interest through the procedures used, the probable value of additional or substitute procedural safeguards, and the government's interest in adhering to the existing system." The government interest was said to be that the claimant "receive the entirety of the award without having to divide it with a lawyer" and that the "system should be as informal and nonadversarial as possible." The Court rejected arguments that absence of lawyers from the adjudication increased the risk of error in determining benefits. The Court also rejected a First Amendment challenge to the law based on cases finding a constitutional right of access to adjudicatory tribunals (see page 715 infra).

The district judge had preliminarily enjoined enforcement of the law based on her prediction that plaintiffs were likely to prevail in their facial challenge. The Supreme Court remanded the case to determine whether the law was invalid as applied to the plaintiffs' particular cases. In dissent, Justice Stevens, joined by Justices Brennan and Marshall, concluded:

In my view, regardless of the nature of the dispute between the sovereign and the citizen . . . the citizen's right to consult an independent lawyer and to retain that lawyer to speak on his or her behalf is an aspect of liberty that is priceless. It should not be bargained away on the notion that a totalitarian appraisal of the mass of claims processed by the Veterans Administration does not identify an especially high probability of error.

A less extreme fee limitation is described in United States Department of Labor v. Triplett, 494 U.S. 715 (1990). *Triplett* concerned the Black Lung Benefits Act of 1972, which provided federal funds for persons totally disabled by a respiratory disease suffered by coal miners. The act envisions administrative adjudication of claims with court review. Lawyers who represent applicants under the act must seek their fees from the agency or court. A Department of Labor rule conditioned fee awards on success on the underlying claim and required that any fee be "reasonably commensurate with the necessary work done." Triplett violated the act by charging a coal miner 25 percent of his recovery. He was charged with unethical conduct, but the state court dismissed on the ground that the act's limitation on counsel fees was unconstitutional. The Supreme Court reversed, holding that "the evidence relied upon by the West Virginia Supreme Court did not remotely establish *either* that black lung claimants are unable to retain qualified counsel *or* that the cause of such inability is the attorney's fee system administered by the Department. The court therefore had no basis for concluding that that system deprives claimants of property without due process of law."

Prohibitions on Contingent Fees in Criminal and Matrimonial Cases

The Model Code forbids a contingent fee in criminal cases, DR 2-106(C), and says they are "rarely justified" in domestic relations cases. EC 2-20. The January 1980 draft of the Model Rules excluded contingent fees where they were "prohibited by law or the Rules of Professional Conduct." As adopted, the Model Rules forbid a contingent fee in a criminal case and impose substantial limitations on contingent fees in domestic relations matters. Rule 1.5(d). Kansas prohibits contingent fees in custody matters, Washington in annulments. In some jurisdictions, if a lawyer charges an illegal contingent fee, she will be denied even quantum meruit compensation. In re Malec, 205 Ill. App. 3d 273, 562 N.E.2d 1010 (1990).

Why are contingent fees banned in matrimonial matters? Here are some reasons often advanced. (1) The state has an interest in seeing as much money stay with the family as possible (especially for nonworking spouses and children). (2) Since statutes already empower the judge to order a wealthier spouse to pay the other spouse's counsel fees, the less wealthy spouse does not need a contingent fee to be able to attract a lawyer. (3) A contingent fee gives the lawyer a stake in the outcome that could cause recommendation of a course of action that is not in the client's best interests. For example, a fee contingent on divorce might prevent the lawyer from encouraging reconciliation. A fee that is a percentage of alimony awarded might cause the lawyer to litigate a matter — with attendant animosity — when settlement ought to have been urged. Do these reasons persuade you? Is the true reason the unseemliness? Is that a valid reason to interfere with freedom of contract?

The reasons for prohibiting contingent fees in criminal cases are not hard to understand. A fee contingent on acquittal could, for example, prompt a lawyer to encourage the client to reject a favorable plea bargain and go to trial in order to give the lawyer a chance to secure the acquittal. It is also sometimes said that a contingent interest in a particular disposition of a criminal case could lead the lawyer to behave improperly (for example, to introduce false evidence) in order to achieve that disposition. But this argument proves too much, doesn't it?

Every once in a while a convicted person will seek to have his conviction overturned on the ground that his lawyer had been working for a contingent fee. These efforts usually fail. The fact that contingent fees are banned in criminal matters because of the risk of conflicts of interest does not mean counsel succumbed to an actual conflict in the defendant's case. Potential conflicts are not enough to prompt a reversal. See People v. Winkler, 71 N.Y.2d 592, 523 N.E.2d 485, 528 N.Y.S.2d 360 (1988); State v. Labonville, 126 N.H. 451, 492 A.2d 1376 (1985). See also the discussion of conflicts in criminal representation at page 186 infra.

Should Contingent Fees Be Outlawed?

In The Litigation Explosion (1991), Walter Olson compares lawyers paid by contingent fee to "impresarios of the boxing arena, whose productions, in pain and ringside drama, have so much in common with those of the courtroom." He adds: "Entrepreneurs of litigation are middlemen not of commerce but of combat. They search out and sedulously promote chances for their fellow citizens to fight." Unlike boxers, however, the contestants in the contingency-fee lawsuit don't enter "the ring of their own free will." Rather, plaintiffs are enticed or coerced into initiating lawsuits by the manipulation of unscrupulous lawyers who cannot resist the "countless temptations to exploit opponents and clients" to reap the benefits of a contingent fee.

Contingency fees are considered unethical in many professions, Olson writes. "Professional sports forbids athletes to bet on their games. . . .

Likewise doctors have never been allowed to charge contingency fees —
in effect to place bets with their patients on the success of their thera-
pies. . . . Contingency fees tend to be disfavored in professions to whom
the interests of others are helplessly entrusted, where misconduct is hard
to monitor."

The interests entrusted to lawyers are, obviously, those of their clients,
but also those of the general public. Olson continues:

> The case against the contingency fee has always rested on the danger it
> poses not to the one who pays it but to the opponent and more widely to
> justice itself. . . . It can yoke together lawyer and client in a perfectly har-
> monious and efficient assault on the general public. There are things law-
> yers will do when a fortune for themselves is on the line that they won't
> do when it's just a fortune for a client. . . . Taking a share in the spoils sub-
> ject[s lawyers] to a sort of moral vertigo.

Although lawyers have a "duty not to stir up lawsuits," the contingency
fee places a strong incentive on attorneys to "get clients interested in the
merchandise." "Volume, volume and more volume" attitudes have
prompted lawyers to advertise and solicit their services. " 'MY CUSTOM
TV ADS CAN MAKE YOU MILLIONS' promises [an advertisement in]
Trial, the magazine for injury lawyers."

The client should be "master of his suit," Olson contends, providing
the "impetus not only for the initial filing, but for any major escalation of
the battle." Contingency fees, however, provide "powerful incentive" for
lawyers to go for the biggest award possible, even if this is not really what
the client may want. Contingency fees encourage dishonesty as well. Olson reminds us:

> The tradition of the English common law, the French and German civil
> law, and the Roman law all agree that it is unethical for lawyers to accept
> contingency fees. . . . [The British] explained that lawyers would no longer
> make their cases "with scrupulous fairness and integrity" [if contingency
> fees were allowed]. . . . America is the only major country that denies to the
> winner of a lawsuit the right to collect legal fees from the loser. In other
> countries, the promise of a fee recoupment from the opponent gives law-
> yers good reason to take on a solidly meritorious case for even a poor client.

Is Olson right?

FURTHER READING

Lester Brickman has written critically and forcefully of the contingency
fee regime. See Brickman, Contingent Fees Without Contingencies:
Hamlet Without the Prince of Denmark?, 37 UCLA L. Rev. 29 (1989).

For Professor Brickman's criticism of Gagnon v. Shoblom, page 111 supra, see A Massachusetts Debacle: *Gagnon v. Shoblom*, 12 Cardozo L. Rev. 1417 (1991).

D. MINIMUM FEE SCHEDULES

Canon 12 of the Canons of Ethics stated that it was "proper" for a lawyer determining his fee "to consider a schedule of minimum fees adopted by a Bar Association, but no lawyer should permit himself to be controlled thereby or to follow it as his sole guide in determining the amount of his fee." Some disciplinary authorities considered it unprofessional for a lawyer consistently to charge less than the minimum fee schedule. In their view, doing so led to price competition, which was seen as inconsistent with a learned profession. Of course, enforcement of minimum fee schedules through threat of discipline could be viewed less charitably — as a form of price fixing in violation of the antitrust laws. That was the position presented to the Supreme Court in the following case, which dramatically reveals the effect of a fee schedule on the cost of a routine legal service.

GOLDFARB v. VIRGINIA STATE BAR
421 U.S. 773 (1975)

CHIEF JUSTICE BURGER delivered the opinion of the Court. . . .

I

In 1971 petitioners, husband and wife, contracted to buy a home in Fairfax County, Va. The financing agency required them to secure title insurance; this required a title examination, and only a member of the Virginia State Bar could legally perform that service. Petitioners therefore contacted a lawyer who quoted them the precise fee suggested in a minimum-fee schedule published by respondent Fairfax County Bar Association; the lawyer told them that it was his policy to keep his charges in line with the minimum-fee schedule which provided for a fee of 1% of the value of the property involved. Petitioners then tried to find a lawyer who would examine the title for less than the fee fixed by the schedule. They sent letters to 36 other Fairfax County lawyers requesting their fees. Nineteen replied, and none indicated that he would charge less than the rate fixed by the schedule; several stated that they knew of no attorney who would do so.

The fee schedule the lawyers referred to is a list of recommended minimum prices for common legal services. Respondent Fairfax County Bar Association published the fee schedule although, as a purely voluntary association of attorneys, the County Bar has no formal power to enforce it. Enforcement has been provided by respondent Virginia State Bar which is the administrative agency through which the Virginia Supreme Court regulates the practice of law in that State; membership in the State Bar is required in order to practice in Virginia. Although the State Bar has never taken formal disciplinary action to compel adherence to any fee schedule, it has published reports condoning fee schedules, and has issued two ethical opinions indicating that fee schedules cannot be ignored. The most recent opinion states that "evidence that an attorney *habitually* charges less than the suggested minimum fee schedule adopted by his local bar Association, raises a presumption that such lawyer is guilty of misconduct...."

Because petitioners could not find a lawyer willing to charge a fee lower than the schedule dictated, they had their title examined by the lawyer they had first contacted. They then brought this class action against the State Bar and the County Bar alleging that the operation of the minimum-fee schedule, as applied to fees for legal services relating to residential real estate transactions, constitutes price fixing in violation of §1 of the Sherman Act. Petitioners sought both injunctive relief and damages.

After a trial solely on the issue of liability the District Court held that the minimum-fee schedule violated the Sherman Act....

The Court of Appeals reversed as to liability....

II

Our inquiry can be divided into four steps: did respondents engage in price fixing? If so, are their activities in interstate commerce or do they affect interstate commerce? If so, are the activities exempt from the Sherman Act because they involve a "learned profession?" If not, are the activities "state action" ..., and therefore exempt from the Sherman Act?

A ...

A purely advisory fee schedule issued to provide guidelines, or an exchange of price information without a showing of an actual restraint on trade, would present us with a different question. The record here, however, reveals a situation quite different from what would occur under a purely advisory fee schedule. Here a fixed, rigid price floor arose from respondents' activities: every lawyer who responded to petitioners' inquiries adhered to the fee schedule, and no lawyer asked for additional information in order to set an individualized fee. The price information disseminated did not concern past standards, but rather minimum fees to be charged in future transactions, and those minimum rates were increased over time. The fee schedule was enforced through the prospect of professional discipline from the State Bar, and the desire of attorneys to comply with announced professional norms, the motivation to conform was reinforced by the assurance that other lawyers would not compete by underbidding. . . .

Moreover, in terms of restraining competition and harming consumers like petitioners the price-fixing activities found here are unusually damaging. A title examination is indispensable in the process of financing a real estate purchase, and since only an attorney licensed to practice in Virginia may legally examine a title, consumers could not turn to alternative sources for the necessary service. All attorneys, of course, were practicing under the constraint of the fee schedule. . . .

B

[The Court concluded that the services at issue affected interstate commerce and were therefore within the ambit of the antitrust laws.]

C

The County Bar argues that Congress never intended to include the learned professions within the terms "trade or commerce" in §1 of the Sherman Act, and therefore the sale of professional services is exempt from the Act. No explicit exemption or legislative history is provided to support this contention; rather, the existence of state regulation seems to be its primary basis. Also, the County Bar maintains that competition is inconsistent with the practice of a profession because enhancing profit is not the goal of professional activities; the goal is to provide services necessary to the community. That, indeed, is the classic basis traditionally advanced to distinguish professions from trades, businesses, and other occupations, but it loses some of its force when used to support the fee control activities involved here.

In arguing that learned professions are not "trade or commerce" the County Bar seeks a total exclusion from antitrust regulation. Whether state regulation is active or dormant, real or theoretical, lawyers would be able to adopt anticompetitive practices with impunity. We cannot find support for the proposition that Congress intended any such sweeping exclusion. The nature of an occupation, standing alone, does not provide sanctuary from the Sherman Act, nor is the public-service aspect of professional practice controlling in determining whether §1 includes professions. Congress intended to strike as broadly as it could in §1 of the Sherman Act, and to read into it so wide an exemption as that urged on us would be at odds with that purpose.

The language of §1 of the Sherman Act, of course, contains no exception. "Language more comprehensive is difficult to conceive." And our cases have repeatedly established that there is a heavy presumption against implicit exemptions. Indeed, our cases have specifically included the sale of services within §1. Whatever else it may be, the examination of a land title is a service; the exchange of such a service for money is "commerce" in the most common usage of that word. It is no disparagement of the practice of law as a profession to acknowledge that it has this business aspect, and §1 of the Sherman Act "[o]n its face . . . shows a carefully studied attempt to bring within the Act every person engaged in business whose activities might restrain or monopolize commercial intercourse among the states."

In the modern world it cannot be denied that the activities of lawyers play an important part in commercial intercourse, and that anticompetitive activities by lawyers may exert a restraint on commerce.

D

In Parker v. Brown, 317 U.S. 341 (1943), the Court held that an anticompetitive marketing program which "derived its authority and its efficacy from the legislative command of the state" was not a violation of the Sherman Act because the Act was intended to regulate private practices and not to prohibit a State from imposing a restraint as an act of government. Respondent State Bar and respondent County Bar both seek to avail themselves of this so-called state-action exemption.

Through its legislature Virginia has authorized its highest court to regulate the practice of law. That court has adopted ethical codes which deal in part with fees, and far from exercising state power to authorize binding price fixing, explicitly directed lawyers not "to be controlled" by fee schedules. The State Bar, a state agency by law, argues that in issuing fee schedule reports and ethical opinions dealing with fee schedules it was merely implementing the fee provisions of the ethical codes. The County Bar, although it is a voluntary association and not a state agency, claims that the ethical codes and the activities of the State Bar "prompted" it to issue fee schedules and thus its actions, too, are state action for Sherman Act purposes.

The threshold inquiry in determining if an anticompetitive activity is state action of the type the Sherman Act was not meant to proscribe is whether the activity is required by the State acting as sovereign. Here we need not inquire further into the state-action question because it cannot fairly be said that the State of Virginia through its Supreme Court Rules required the anticompetitive activities of either respondent. Respondents have pointed to no Virginia statute requiring their activities; state law simply does not refer to fees, leaving regulation of the profession to the Virginia Supreme Court; although the Supreme Court's ethical codes mention advisory fee schedules they do not direct either respondent to supply them, or require the type of price floor which arose from respondents' activities. Although the State Bar apparently has been granted the power to issue ethical opinions, there is no indication in this record that the Virginia Supreme Court approves the opinions. Respondents' arguments, at most, constitute the contention that their activities complemented the objective of the ethical codes. In our view that is not state action for Sherman Act purposes. It is not enough that, as the County Bar puts it, anticompetitive conduct is "prompted" by state action; rather, anticompetitive activities must be compelled by direction of the State acting as a sovereign. . . .

III

We recognize that the States have a compelling interest in the practice of professions within their boundaries, and that as part of their power to protect the public health, safety, and other valid interests they have broad power to establish standards for licensing practitioners and regulating the practice of professions. We also recognize that in some instances the State may decide that "forms of competition usual in the business world may be demoralizing to the ethical standards of a profession." The interest of the States in regulating lawyers is especially great since lawyers are essential to the primary governmental function of administering justice, and have historically been "officers of the courts." In holding that certain anticompetitive conduct by lawyers is within the reach of the Sherman Act we intend no diminution of the authority of the State to regulate its professions. . . .

Reversed and remanded.

JUSTICE POWELL took no part in the consideration or decision of this case.

Antitrust and Legal Ethics

The *Goldfarb* holding has had modest influence on other regulatory efforts by the bar. *Goldfarb* and the lawyer advertising cases (see Chapter 16 infra), operating in tandem, have introduced the price competition the pre-*Goldfarb* bar feared. Now, not only may lawyers undersell the competition; they can announce their fees to the entire community as long as they do not mislead.

Government has also used the antitrust laws against lawyers and not only against the organized bar. In FTC v. Superior Court Trial Lawyers

Assn., 493 U.S. 411 (1990), lawyers who regularly accepted court appointments to represent indigent defendants in the District of Columbia agreed to refuse new cases until hourly rates were increased to $35. It worked. The District raised its rates. But then the FTC filed a complaint against the lawyers, charging a "conspiracy to fix prices and to conduct a boycott." The Court upheld the charge. It rejected the claim that the First Amendment protected their conduct as "politically motivated." "[A] clear objective of the boycott [was] to economically advantage the participants." Id. at 428.

Attempts to use the antitrust laws to challenge other bar regulatory efforts have been unsuccessful. In Bates v. State Bar of Arizona, 433 U.S. 350, 359-360 (1977), page 785 infra, the Court rejected the claim that Arizona's prohibition on legal advertising violated the Sherman Act. The Court concluded that "the challenged restraint is the affirmative command of the Arizona Supreme Court. . . . That Court is the ultimate body wielding the State's power over the practice of law and, thus, the restraint is 'compelled by direction of the State acting as a sovereign.' " Consequently, the action was shielded from the antitrust laws under Parker v. Brown, 317 U.S. 341 (1943). Of course, the Court went on to hold the restrictions unconstitutional under the First Amendment.

The bar applicant in Hoover v. Ronwin, 466 U.S. 558, 558-573 (1984), after failing the bar examination, brought an action alleging that the bar examiners "had set the grading scale . . . with reference to the number of new attorneys [they] thought desirable, rather than with reference to some 'suitable' level of competence." He charged that this conduct restrained competition among lawyers in violation of the Sherman Act. In a 4-to-3 opinion, the Supreme Court did not reach the Sherman Act charge. The majority concluded that the alleged conduct of the bar examiners was authorized by the state supreme court, which "approved the particular grading formula and retained the sole authority to determine who should be admitted to the practice of law in Arizona. Thus, the conduct that Ronwin challenges was in reality that of the Arizona Supreme Court. It therefore is exempt from Sherman Act liability under the state action doctrine of Parker v. Brown."

E. COURT-AWARDED FEES

1. Determination of Amount

With the advent of fee-shifting statutes in civil rights and environmental cases, and the concomitant growth of class actions, courts have increasingly been called upon to determine the size of the fee that must be paid to a successful plaintiff's counsel by the defendant or from the fund recovered for the class. This trend has engendered a cottage industry of judicial opinions and law review articles that seek to identify how fees should be determined. Obviously, to the extent that courts are more generous in the formula they apply, more lawyers will accept and bring class actions or cases under fee-shifting statutes. The Supreme Court has often been sharply divided on these issues.

CITY OF RIVERSIDE v. RIVERA
477 U.S. 561 (1986)

JUSTICE BRENNAN announced the judgment of the Court and delivered an opinion in which JUSTICE MARSHALL, JUSTICE BLACKMUN, and JUSTICE STEVENS join.

The issue presented in this case is whether an award of attorney's fees under 42 U.S.C. §1988 is per se "unreasonable" within the meaning of the statute if it exceeds the amount of damages recovered by the plaintiff in the underlying civil rights action.

I

Respondents, eight Chicano individuals, attended a party on the evening of August 1, 1975, at the Riverside, California, home of respondents Santos and Jennie Rivera. A large number of unidentified police officers, acting without a warrant, broke up the party using tear gas and, as found by the District Court, "unnecessary physical force." Many of the guests, including four of the respondents, were arrested. The District Court later found that "[t]he party was not creating a disturbance in the community at the time of the break-in." . . . Criminal charges against the arrestees were ultimately dismissed for lack of probable cause.

On June 4, 1976, respondents sued the city of Riverside, its chief of police, and 30 individual police officers under 42 U.S.C. §§1981, 1983, 1985(3), and 1986 for allegedly violating their First, Fourth, and Fourteenth Amendment rights. The complaint, which also alleged numerous state-law claims, sought damages, and declaratory and injunctive relief. On August 5, 1977, 23 of the individual police officers moved for summary judgment; the District Court granted summary judgment in favor of 17 of these officers. The case against the remaining defendants proceeded to trial in September 1980. The jury returned a total of 37 individual verdicts in favor of the respondents and against the city and five individual officers, finding 11 violations of §1983, four instances of false arrest and imprisonment, and 22 instances of negligence. Respondents were awarded $33,350 in compensatory and punitive damages: $13,300 for their federal claims, and $20,050 for their state-law claims.

Respondents also sought attorney's fees and costs under §1988. They requested compensation for 1,946.75 hours expended by their two attorneys at a rate of $125 per hour, and for 84.5 hours expended by law clerks at a rate of $25.00 per hour, a total of $245,456.25. The District Court found both the hours and rates reasonable, and awarded respondents $245,456.25 in attorney's fees. The court rejected respondents' request for certain additional expenses, and for a multiplier sought by respondents to reflect the contingent nature of their success and the high quality of their attorneys' efforts.

[The Ninth Circuit affirmed but the Supreme Court vacated the judgment and remanded for reconsideration in light of Hensley v. Eckerhart, 461 U.S. 424 (1983). On remand, the trial court adhered to its earlier determination. The Ninth Circuit affirmed and the Supreme Court granted review.]

II

A

In Alyeska Pipeline Service Co. v. Wilderness Society, 421 U.S. 240 (1975), the Court reaffirmed the "American Rule" that, at least absent express statutory authorization to the contrary, each party to a lawsuit ordinarily shall bear its own attorney's fees. In response to *Alyeska*, Congress enacted the Civil Rights Attorney's Fees Awards Act of 1976, 42 U.S.C. §1988, which authorized the district courts to award reasonable attorney's fees to prevailing parties in specified civil rights litigation. While the statute itself does not explain what constitutes a reasonable fee, both the House and Senate Reports accompanying §1988 expressly endorse the analysis set forth in Johnson v. Georgia Highway Express, Inc., 488 F.2d 714 (C.A.5 1974). See S. Rep. No. 94-1011, 6 (1976) (hereafter Senate Report); H.R. Rep. No. 94-1558, 8 (1976) (hereafter House Report). *Johnson* identifies 12 factors to be considered in calculating a reasonable attorney's fee.[3]

Hensley v. Eckerhart, 461 U.S. 424 (1983), announced certain guidelines for calculating a reasonable attorney's fee under §1988. *Hensley* stated that "[t]he most useful starting point for determining the amount of a reasonable fee is the number of hours reasonably expended on the litigation multiplied by a reasonable hourly rate." Id., at 433. This figure,

---

3. These factors are: (1) the time and labor required; (2) the novelty and difficulty of the questions; (3) the skill requisite to perform the legal service properly; (4) the preclusion of employment by the attorney due to acceptance of the case; (5) the customary fee; (6) whether the fee is fixed or contingent; (7) time limitations imposed by the client or the circumstances; (8) the amount involved and the results obtained; (9) the experience, reputation, and ability of the attorneys; (10) the "undesirability" of the case; (11) the nature and length of the professional relationship with the client; and (12) awards in similar cases.

commonly referred to as the "lodestar," is presumed to be the reasonable fee contemplated by §1988. The opinion cautioned that "[t]he district court . . . should exclude from this initial fee calculation hours that were not 'reasonably expended' " on the litigation.

Hensley then discussed other considerations that might lead the district court to adjust the lodestar figure upward or downward, including the "important factor of the 'results obtained.' " The opinion noted that where a prevailing plaintiff has succeeded on only some of his claims, an award of fees for time expended on unsuccessful claims may not be appropriate. In these situations, the Court held that the judge should consider whether or not the plaintiff's unsuccessful claims were related to the claims on which he succeeded, and whether the plaintiff achieved a level of success that makes it appropriate to award attorney's fees for hours reasonably expended on unsuccessful claims:

> In [some] cases the plaintiff's claims for relief will involve a common core of facts or will be based on related legal theories. Much of counsel's time will be devoted generally to the litigation as a whole, making it difficult to divide the hours expended on a claim-by-claim basis. Such a lawsuit cannot be viewed as a series of discrete claims. Instead the district court should focus on the significance of the overall relief obtained by the plaintiff in relation to the hours reasonably expended on the litigation.

Accordingly, *Hensley* emphasized that "[w]here a plaintiff has obtained excellent results, his attorney should recover a fully compensatory fee," and that "the fee award should not be reduced simply because the plaintiff failed to prevail on every contention raised in the lawsuit."

B

Petitioners argue that the District Court failed properly to follow *Hensley* in calculating respondents' fee award. We disagree. The District Court carefully considered the results obtained by respondents pursuant to the instructions set forth in *Hensley*, and concluded that respondents were entitled to recover attorney's fees for all hours expended on the litigation. First, the court found that "[t]he amount of time expended by counsel in conducting this litigation was reasonable and reflected sound legal judgment under the circumstances."[4] The court also determined

___

4. *Hensley* stated that a fee applicant should "exercise 'billing judgment' with respect to hours worked." Petitioners maintain that respondents failed to exercise "billing judgment" in this case, since they sought compensation for all time spent litigating this case. We think this argument misreads the mandate of *Hensley*. *Hensley* requires a fee applicant to exercise "billing judgment" not because he should necessarily be compensated for less than the actual number of hours spent litigating a case, but because the hours he does seek compensation for must be *reasonable*. "Counsel for the prevailing party should make a good-faith effort to exclude from a fee request hours that are excessive, redundant, or otherwise unnecessary. . . ." In this case, the District Court found that the number of hours expended by

that counsels' excellent performances in this case entitled them to be compensated at prevailing market rates, even though they were relatively young when this litigation began.

The District Court then concluded that it was inappropriate to adjust respondents' fee award downward to account for the fact that respondents had prevailed only on some of their claims, and against only some of the defendants. The court first determined that "it was never actually clear what officer did what until we had gotten through with the whole trial," so that "[u]nder the circumstances of this case, it was reasonable for plaintiffs initially to name thirty-one individual defendants . . . as well as the City of Riverside as defendants in this action." The court remarked:

> I think every one of the claims that were made were related and if you look at the common core of facts that we had here that you had total success. . . . There was a problem about who was responsible for what and that problem was there all the way through to the time that we concluded the case. Some of the officers couldn't agree about who did what and it is not at all surprising that it would, in my opinion, have been wrong for you not to join all those officers since you yourself did not know precisely who were the officers that were responsible. . . .

III

Petitioners, joined by the Solicitor General as amicus curiae, maintain that *Hensley*'s lodestar approach is inappropriate in civil rights cases where a plaintiff recovers only monetary damages. In these cases, so the argument goes, use of the lodestar may result in fees that exceed the amount of damages recovered and that are therefore unreasonable. Likening such cases to private tort actions, petitioners and the Solicitor General submit that attorney's fees in such cases should be proportionate to the amount of damages a plaintiff recovers. Specifically, they suggest that fee awards in damages cases should be modeled upon the contingent fee arrangements commonly used in personal injury litigation. In this case, assuming a 33% contingency rate, this would entitle respondents to recover approximately $11,000 in attorney's fees.

The amount of damages a plaintiff recovers is certainly relevant to the amount of attorney's fees to be awarded under §1988. It is, however, only one of many factors that a court should consider in calculating an award of attorney's fees. We reject the proposition that fee awards under §1988 should necessarily be proportionate to the amount of damages a civil rights plaintiff actually recovers.

---

respondents' counsel was *reasonable*. Thus, counsel did, in fact, exercise the "billing judgment" recommended in *Hensley*.

A

As an initial matter, we reject the notion that a civil rights action for damages constitutes nothing more than a private tort suit benefiting only the individual plaintiffs whose rights were violated. Unlike most private tort litigants, a civil rights plaintiff seeks to vindicate important civil and constitutional rights that cannot be valued solely in monetary terms. And, Congress has determined that "the public as a whole has an interest in the vindication of the rights conferred by the statutes enumerated in §1988, over and above the value of a civil rights remedy to a particular plaintiff. . . ." *Hensley*, 461 U.S., at 444, n.4 (Brennan, J., concurring in part and dissenting in part). Regardless of the form of relief he actually obtains, a successful civil rights plaintiff often secures important social benefits that are not reflected in nominal or relatively small damages awards. In this case, for example, the District Court found that many of petitioners' unlawful acts were "motivated by a general hostility to the Chicano community," and that this litigation therefore served the public interest:

> The institutional behavior involved here . . . had to be stopped and . . . nothing short of having a lawsuit like this would have stopped it. . . . [T]he improper motivation which appeared as a result of all of this seemed to me to have pervaded a very broad segment of police officers in the department.

In addition, the damages a plaintiff recovers contributes significantly to the deterrence of civil rights violations in the future. This deterrent effect is particularly evident in the area of individual police misconduct, where injunctive relief generally is unavailable.

Congress expressly recognized that a plaintiff who obtains relief in a civil rights lawsuit " 'does so not for himself alone but also as a 'private attorney general,' vindicating a policy that Congress considered of the highest importance.' " House Report, at 2. . . .

Because damages awards do not reflect fully the public benefit advanced by civil rights litigation, Congress did not intend for fees in civil rights cases, unlike most private law cases, to depend on obtaining substantial monetary relief. Rather, Congress made clear that it "intended that the amount of fees awarded under [§1988] be governed by the same standards which prevail in other types of equally complex Federal litigation, such as antitrust cases and *not be reduced because the rights involved may be nonpecuniary in nature.*" Senate Report, at 6 (emphasis added). "[C]ounsel for prevailing parties should be paid, as is traditional with attorneys compensated by a fee-paying client, *'for all time reasonably expended on a matter.*' " Ibid. The Senate report specifically approves of the fee awards made in cases such as Stanford Daily v. Zurcher, 64 F.R.D. 680

(N.D. Cal. 1974); Davis v. County of Los Angeles, [cite]; and Swann v. Charlotte-Mecklenburg Board of Education, 66 F.R.D. 483 (W.D.N.C. 1975). In each of these cases, counsel received substantial attorney's fees despite the fact the plaintiffs sought no monetary damages. Thus, Congress recognized that reasonable attorney's fees under §1988 are not conditioned upon and need not be proportionate to an award of money damages. The lower courts have generally eschewed such a requirement.

B

A rule that limits attorney's fees in civil rights cases to a proportion of the damages awarded would seriously undermine Congress' purpose in enacting §1988. Congress enacted §1988 specifically because it found that the private market for legal services failed to provide many victims of civil rights violations with effective access to the judicial process. See House Report, at 3. These victims ordinarily cannot afford to purchase legal services at the rates set by the private market. See id., at 1 ("[b]ecause a vast majority of the victims of civil rights violations cannot afford legal counsel, they are unable to present their cases to the courts"); Senate Report, at 2 ("[i]n many cases arising under our civil rights laws, the citizen who must sue to enforce the law has little or no money with which to hire a lawyer"); see also 122 Cong. Rec. 35127 (1976) (remarks of Rep. Holtzman) ("[p]laintiffs who suffer discrimination and other infringements of their civil rights are usually not wealthy people"); id., at 35128 (remarks of Rep. Seiberling) ("[m]ost Americans . . . cannot afford to hire a lawyer if their constitutional rights are violated or if they are the victims of illegal discrimination"); id., at 31832 (remarks of Sen. Hathaway) ("right now the vindication of important congressional policies in the vital area of civil rights is made to depend upon the financial resources of those least able to promote them"). Moreover, the contingent fee arrangements that make legal services available to many victims of personal injuries would often not encourage lawyers to accept civil rights cases, which frequently involve substantial expenditures of time and effort but produce only small monetary recoveries. As the House Report states:

> [W]hile damages are theoretically available under the statutes covered by [§1988], it should be observed that, in some cases, immunity doctrines and special defenses, available only to public officials, preclude *or severely limit the damage remedy.* Consequently, awarding counsel fees to prevailing plaintiffs in such litigation is particularly important and necessary if Federal civil and constitutional rights are to be adequately protected. . . .

A rule of proportionality would make it difficult, if not impossible, for individuals with meritorious civil rights claims but relatively small potential damages to obtain redress from the courts. This is totally inconsistent with the Congress' purpose in enacting §1988. Congress recognized that private-sector fee arrangements were inadequate to ensure sufficiently vigorous enforcement of civil rights. In order to ensure that lawyers would be willing to represent persons with legitimate civil rights griev- ances, Congress determined that it would be necessary to compensate lawyers for all time reasonably expended on a case.[9]

This case illustrates why the enforcement of civil rights laws cannot be entrusted to private-sector fee arrangements. The District Court ob- served that "[g]iven the nature of this lawsuit and the type of defense presented, many attorneys in the community would have been reluctant to institute and to continue to prosecute this action." . . . The court con- cluded, moreover, that "[c]ounsel for plaintiffs achieved excellent results for their clients, and their accomplishment in this case was outstanding. The amount of time expended by counsel in conducting this litigation was reasonable and reflected sound legal judgment under the circum- stances." . . . Nevertheless, petitioners suggest that respondents' counsel should be compensated for only a small fraction of the actual time spent litigating the case. In light of the difficult nature of the issues presented by this lawsuit and the low pecuniary value of many of the rights respon- dents sought to vindicate, it is highly unlikely that the prospect of a fee equal to a fraction of the damages respondents might recover would have been sufficient to attract competent counsel.[10] Moreover, since counsel might not have found it economically feasible to expend the amount of time respondents' counsel found necessary to litigate the case properly, it is even less likely that counsel would have achieved the excel- lent results that respondents' counsel obtained here. Thus, had respon- dents had to rely on private-sector fee arrangements, they might well have been unable to obtain redress for their grievances. It is precisely for this reason that Congress enacted §1988.

---

9. Of course we do not mean to suggest that private sector comparisons are irrelevant to fee calculations under §1988. We have suggested that in determining an appropriate hourly rate for a lawyer's services, "the rates charged in private representations may afford relevant comparisons." Blum v. Stenson, 465 U.S. 886, 896 n.11 (1984). We have also indi- cated that "[c]ounsel for a prevailing party should make a good-faith effort to exclude from a fee request hours that are excessive, redundant, or otherwise unnecessary, just as a lawyer in private practice ethically is obligated to exclude such hours from his fee submission." Hensley, 461 U.S. 424, 434 (1983). However, while private market considerations are not irrelevant, Congress clearly rejected the notion that attorney's fees under §1988 should be based on private sector fee arrangements.

10. The Solicitor General suggests that "[t]he prospect of recovering $11,000 for repre- senting [respondents] in a damage suit (assuming a contingency rate of 33%) is likely to at- tract a substantial number of attorneys." However, the District Court found that the 1,946.75 hours respondents' counsel spent litigating the case was reasonable and that "[t]here was not any possible way that you could have avoided putting in that amount of time. . . ." We reject the Solicitor General's suggestion that the prospect of working nearly 2,000 hours at a rate of $5.65 an hour, to be paid more than ten years after the work began, is "likely to attract a substantial number of attorneys."

IV

We agree with petitioners that Congress intended that statutory fee awards be "adequate to attract competent counsel, but . . . not produce windfalls to attorneys." Senate Report, at 6. However, we find no evidence that Congress intended that, in order to avoid "windfalls to attorneys," attorney's fees be proportionate to the amount of damages a civil rights plaintiff might recover. Rather, there already exists a wide range of safeguards designed to protect civil rights defendants against the possibility of excessive fee awards. Both the House and Senate Reports identify standards for courts to follow in awarding and calculating attorney's fees, see id., at 6; House Report, at 8; these standards are designed to insure that attorneys are compensated only for time *reasonably expended* on a case. The district court has the discretion to deny fees to prevailing plaintiffs under special circumstances, see *Hensley*, 461 U.S., at 429 (citing Senate Report, at 4) and to award attorney's fees against plaintiffs who litigate frivolous or vexatious claims. See Christiansburg Garment Co. v. EEOC, 434 U.S. 412, 416-417 (1978), Hughes v. Rowe, 449 U.S. 5, 14-16 (1980) (per curiam); House Report, at 6-7. Furthermore, we have held that a civil rights defendant is not liable for attorney's fees incurred after a pretrial settlement offer, where the judgment recovered by the plaintiff is less than the offer. Marek v. Chesny, 473 U.S. 1 (1985).[11] We believe that these safeguards adequately protect against the possibility that §1988 might produce a "windfall" to civil rights attorneys.

In the absence of any indication that Congress intended to adopt a strict rule that attorney's fees under §1988 be proportionate to damages recovered, we decline to adopt such a rule ourselves.[12] The judgment of the Court of Appeals is hereby affirmed.

JUSTICE POWELL, concurring in the judgment.

I join only the Court's judgment. The plurality opinion reads our decision in Hensley v. Eckerhart, 461 U.S. 424 (1983), more expansively than I would, and more expansively than is necessary to decide this case. For me affirmance — quite simply — is required by the District Court's detailed findings of fact, which were approved by the Court of Appeals. On its face, the fee award seems unreasonable. But I find no basis for this Court to reject the findings made and approved by the Courts below. . . .

11. Thus, petitioners could have avoided liability for the bulk of the attorney's fees for which they now find themselves liable by making a reasonable settlement offer in a timely manner. While petitioners did offer respondent $25,000 in settlement at the time the jury was deliberating the case, this offer was made, as the District Court noted, "well after [respondents' counsel] had spent thousands of dollars on preparation for trial. . . ." "The government cannot litigate tenaciously and then be heard to complain about the time necessarily spent by the plaintiff in response." Copeland v. Marshall, 205 U.S. App. D.C. 390, 414, 641 F.2d 880, 904 (1980) (en banc).

12. We note that Congress has been urged to amend §1988 to prohibit the award of attorney's fees that are disproportionate to monetary damages recovered. These efforts have thus far not been persuasive.

II ...

Petitioners argue for a rule of proportionality between the fee awarded and the damages recovered in a civil rights case. Neither the decisions of this Court nor the legislative history of §1988 support such a "rule." The facts and circumstances of litigation are infinitely variable. Under *Hensley*, of course, "the most critical factor [in the final determination of fee awards] is the degree of success obtained." Where recovery of private damages is the purpose of a civil rights litigation, a district court, in fixing fees, is obligated to give primary consideration to the amount of damages awarded as compared to the amount sought. In some civil rights cases, however, the court may consider the vindication of constitutional rights in addition to the amount of damages recovered. In this case, for example, the District Court made an explicit finding that the "public interest" had been served by the jury's verdict that the warrantless entry was lawless and unconstitutional. Although the finding of a Fourth Amendment violation hardly can be considered a new constitutional ruling, in the special circumstances of this case, the vindication of the asserted Fourth Amendment right may well have served a public interest, supporting the amount of the fees awarded.[3] As the District Court put it, there were allegations that the police misconduct was "motivated by a general hostility to the Chicano community in the area. . . ." The record also contained evidence of racial slurs by some of the police.

Finally, petitioners also contend that in determining a proper fee under §1988 in a suit for damages the court should consider the prevailing contingent fee rate charged by counsel in personal injury cases. The use of contingent fee arrangements in many types of tort cases was customary long before Congress enacted §1988. It is clear from the legislative history that §1988 was enacted because existing fee arrangements were thought not to provide an adequate incentive to lawyers particularly to represent plaintiffs in unpopular civil rights cases. I therefore find petitioners' asserted analogy to personal injury claims unpersuasive in this context.

III

In sum, despite serious doubts as to the fairness of the fees awarded in this case, I cannot conclude that the detailed findings made by the District Court, and accepted by the Court of Appeals, were clearly errone-

---

3. It probably will be the rare case in which an award of *private damages* can be said to benefit the public interest to an extent that would justify the disproportionality between damages and fees reflected in this case.

ous, or that the District Court abused its discretion in making this fee award.[4]

CHIEF JUSTICE BURGER, dissenting.

I join Justice Rehnquist's dissenting opinion. I write only to add that it would be difficult to find a better example of legal nonsense than the fixing of attorney's fees by a judge at $245,456.25 for the recovery of $33,350 damages.

The two attorneys receiving this nearly quarter-million-dollar fee graduated from law school in 1973 and 1974; they brought this action in 1975, which resulted in the $33,350 jury award in 1980. Their total professional experience when this litigation began consisted of Gerald Lopez' 1-year service as a law clerk to a judge and Roy Cazares' two years' experience as a trial attorney in the Defenders' Program of San Diego County. For their services the District Court found that an hourly rate of $125 per hour was reasonable.

Can anyone doubt that no private party would ever have dreamed of paying these two novice attorneys $125 per hour in 1975, which, considering inflation, would represent perhaps something more nearly a $250 per hour rate today? For example, as Justice Rehnquist points out, . . . would any private litigant be willing to pay a total of $17,875 simply for preparation of a pretrial order?

This fee award plainly constitutes a grave abuse of discretion which should be rejected by this Court — particularly when we have already vacated and remanded this *identical* fee award previously — rather than simply affirming the District Court's findings as not being either "clearly erroneous" or an "abuse of discretion." The Court's result will unfortunately only add fuel to the fires of public indignation over the costs of litigation.

JUSTICE REHNQUIST, with whom THE CHIEF JUSTICE, JUSTICE WHITE, and JUSTICE O'CONNOR join, dissenting.

. . . I see no escape from the conclusion that the District Court's finding that respondents' attorneys "reasonably" spent 1,946.75 hours to recover a money judgment of $33,350 is clearly erroneous, and that therefore the District Court's award of $245,456.25 in attorney's fees to respondents should be reversed. The Court's affirmance of the fee

---

4. In Part III-B of its opinion, the plurality emphasizes that a primary purpose of §1988 was to assure the availability of counsel in civil rights cases. This was an expressed and proper purpose of Congress when §1988 was enacted a decade ago. Although the tables in the Annual Report of the Director of the Administrative Office are not explicit in this respect, it is clear that the increased filings of civil rights cases that began following Monroe v. Pape, 365 U.S. 167 (1961), particularly §1983 cases, has continued and even accelerated since 1976. These facts suggest that §1988 is serving well Congress' purpose to assure availability of counsel, and that this purpose does not justify more generous fee awards than otherwise would be viewed as fair and reasonable.

award emasculates the principles laid down in *Hensley*, and turns §1988 into a relief act for lawyers.

A brief look at the history of this case reveals just how "unreasonable" it was for respondents' lawyers to spend so much time on it. Respondents filed their initial complaint in 1976, seeking injunctive and declaratory relief and compensatory and punitive damages from the City of Riverside, its Chief of Police, and 30 police officers, based on 256 separate claims allegedly arising out of the police breakup of a single party. Prior to trial, 17 of the police officers were dismissed from the case on motions for summary judgment, and respondents dropped their requests for injunctive and declaratory relief. More significantly, respondents also dropped their original allegation that the police had acted with discriminatory intent. The action proceeded to trial, and the jury completely exonerated nine additional police officers. Respondents ultimately prevailed against only the City and five police officers on various §1983, false arrest and imprisonment, and common negligence claims. No restraining orders or injunctions were ever issued against petitioners, nor was the City ever compelled to change a single practice or policy as a result of respondents' suit. The jury awarded respondents a total of $33,350 in compensatory and punitive damages. Only about one-third of this total, or $13,300, was awarded to respondents based on violations of their federal constitutional rights.

Respondents then filed a request for $495,713.51 in attorney's fees, representing approximately 15 times the amount of the underlying money judgment. In April 1981, the District Court made its initial fee award of $245,456.25, declining to apply respondents' requested "multiplier," but awarding, to the penny, the entire "lodestar" claimed by respondents and their attorneys. . . .

It is obvious to me that the District Court viewed *Hensley* not as a constraint on its discretion, but instead as a blueprint for justifying, in an after-the-fact fashion, a fee award it had already decided to enter solely on the basis of the "lodestar." In fact, the District Court failed at almost every turn to apply any kind of "billing judgment," or to seriously consider the "results obtained," which we described in *Hensley* as "the important factor" in determining a "reasonable" fee award. A few examples should suffice: (1) The court approved almost 209 hours of "prelitigation time," for a total of $26,118.75. (2) The court approved some 197 hours of time spent in conversations between respondents' two attorneys, for a total of $24,625. (3) The court approved 143 hours for preparation of a pre-trial order, for a total of $17,875.00. (4) Perhaps most egregiously, the court approved 45.50 hours of "stand-by time" or time spent by one of respondents' attorneys, who was then based in San Diego, to wait in a Los Angeles hotel room for a jury verdict to be rendered in Los Angeles, where his co-counsel was then employed by the U.C.L.A. School of Law, less than 40 minutes' driving time from the courthouse. The award for "stand-by time" totaled $5,687.50. I find it hard to understand how any attorney can be said to have exercised "billing judgment" in spending such huge amounts of time on a case ultimately worth only $33,350. . . .

The analysis of whether the extraordinary number of hours put in by respondents' attorneys in this case was "reasonable" must be made in light of both the traditional billing practices in the profession, and the fundamental principle that the award of a "reasonable" attorney's fee under §1988 means a fee that would have been deemed reasonable if billed to affluent plaintiffs by their own attorneys. . . .

Suppose that *A* offers to sell Blackacre to *B* for $10,000. It is commonly known and accepted that Blackacre has a fair market value of $10,000. *B* consults an attorney and requests a determination whether *A* can convey good title to Blackacre. The attorney writes an elaborate memorandum concluding that *A*'s title to Blackacre is defective, and submits a bill to *B* for $25,000. *B* refuses to pay the bill, the attorney sues, and the parties stipulate that the attorney spent 200 hours researching the title issue because of an extraordinarily complex legal and factual situation, and that the prevailing rate at which the attorney billed, which was also a "reasonable" rate, was $125. Does anyone seriously think that a court should award the attorney the full $25,000 which he claims? Surely a court would start from the proposition that, unless special arrangements were made between the client and the attorney, a "reasonable" attorney's fee for researching the title to a piece of property worth $10,000 could not exceed the value of the property. Otherwise the client would have been far better off never going to an attorney in the first place, and simply giving *A* $10,000 for a worthless deed. The client thereby would have saved himself $15,000.

Obviously the billing situation in a typical litigated case is more complex than in this bedrock example of a defective title claim, but some of the same principles are surely applicable. If *A* has a claim for contract damages in the amount of $10,000 against *B*, and retains an attorney to prosecute the claim, it would be both extraordinary and unjustifiable, in the absence of any special arrangement, for the attorney to put in 200 hours on the case and send the client a bill for $25,000. Such a bill would be "unreasonable," regardless of whether *A* obtained a judgment against *B* for $10,000 or obtained a take-nothing judgment. And in such a case, where the prospective recovery is limited, it is exactly this "billing judgment" which enables the parties to achieve a settlement; any competent attorney, whether prosecuting or defending a contract action for $10,000, would realize that the case simply cannot justify a fee in excess of the potential recovery on the part of either the plaintiff's or the defendant's attorney. All of these examples illuminate the point made in *Hensley* that "the important factor" in determining a "reasonable" fee is the "results obtained." 461 U.S., at 434. The very "reasonableness" of the hours expended on a case by a plaintiff's attorney necessarily will depend, to a large extent, on the amount that may reasonably be expected to be recovered if the plaintiff prevails.

The amount of damages which a jury is likely to award in a tort case is of course more difficult to predict than the amount it is likely to award in a contract case. But even in a tort case some measure of the kind of "billing judgment" previously described must be brought to bear in computing a "reasonable" attorney's fee. Again, a hypothetical example will illustrate the point. If, at the time respondents filed their lawsuit in 1976, there had been in the Central District of California a widely publicized survey of jury verdicts in this type of civil rights action which showed that successful plaintiffs recovered between $10,000 and $75,000 in damages, could it possibly be said that it would have been "reasonable" for respondents' attorneys to put in on the case hours which, when multiplied by the attorneys' prevailing hourly rate, would result in an attorney's fee of over $245,000? In the absence of such a survey, it might be more difficult for a plaintiff's attorney to accurately estimate the amount of damages likely to be recovered, but this does not absolve the attorney of the responsibility for making such an estimate and using it as a guide in the exercise of "billing judgment."

In the context of §1988, there would obviously be some exceptions to the general rules of "billing judgment" which I have been discussing, but none of these exceptions are applicable here. If the litigation is unnecessarily prolonged by the bad-faith conduct of the defendants, or if the litigation produces significant, identifiable benefits for persons other than the plaintiffs, then the purpose of Congress in authorizing attorney's fees under §1988 should allow a larger award of attorney's fees than would be "reasonable" where the only relief is the recovery of monetary damages by individual plaintiffs. Nor do we deal here with a case such as Carey v. Piphus, 435 U.S. 247, 266 (1978), in which the deprivation of a constitutional right necessarily results in only nominal pecuniary damages. See S. Rep. No. 94-1011, supra, at 6 (fee awards under §1988 should "not be reduced because the rights involved may be nonpecuniary in nature"). Here, respondents successfully claimed both compensatory and punitive damages for false arrest and imprisonment, negligence, and violations of their constitutional rights under the Fourth and Fourteenth Amendments, and the jury assessed damages as juries do in such cases. In short, this case shares none of the special aspects of certain civil rights litigation which the plurality suggests, in Part III of its opinion, would justify an award of attorney's fees totally divorced from the amount of damages awarded by the jury.

The plurality explains the position advanced by petitioner and the Solicitor General concerning fee awards in a case such as this, and then goes on to "reject the proposition that fee awards under §1988 should necessarily be proportionate to the amount of damages a civil rights plaintiff actually recovers." I agree with the plurality that the importation of the contingent-fee model to govern fee awards under §1988 is not warranted by the terms and legislative history of the statute. But I do not agree with the plurality if it means to reject the kind of "proportionality" that I have previously described. Nearly 2,000 attorney-hours spent on a case in which the total recovery was only $33,000, in which only $13,300 of that amount was recovered for the federal claims, and in which the District Court expressed the view that, in such cases, juries typically were reluctant to award substantial damages against police officers, is simply not a "reasonable" expenditure of time. The snippets of legislative history which the plurality relies upon to dismiss *any* relationship between the amount of time put in on a case and the amount of damages awarded are wholly unconvincing. One may agree with all of the glowing rhetoric contained in the plurality's opinion about Congress' noble purpose in authorizing attorney's fees under §1988 without concluding that Congress intended to turn attorneys loose to spend as many hours as possible to prepare and try a case that could reasonably be expected to result only in a relatively minor award of monetary damages.

Court-Awarded Fees That Far Exceed the Client's Recovery

Justice Brennan emphasizes the structural importance of adequate counsel fees to assure the availability of counsel for plaintiffs in civil rights cases. He also stresses that these fees are not meant merely to compensate for the resolution of a "private tort suit," but are also meant to encourage representation in actions that "secur[e] important social benefits." Justice Brennan cited the same interests in his dissent in Evans v. Jeff D., page 141 infra. Yet they were unpersuasive there. Justice Stevens, who wrote the majority opinion in *Evans*, joined Justice Brennan's plurality opinion in *Riverside*, decided two months later.

Justice Powell was the swing vote in *Riverside*. In light of note 3 to his opinion, how broadly can *Riverside* be read? Could one read Justice Powell's opinion to reflect agreement with the principles of the dissent but an unwillingness to find lower court application of those principles clearly erroneous? What do you suppose the dissent would find to be an appropriate fee in this case? Do you think the dissent's award would undermine the goals identified in the plurality opinion? Would future plaintiffs really have a hard time finding counsel if the counsel fee here were half (or a third) as much? Note that Justice Rehnquist agrees that the "contingent-fee model" urged by the Solicitor General as amicus is inappropriate in fee applications under §1988. Why is it inappropriate?

The potential for §1988 fee awards that exceed the value of a client's recovery increased when the Supreme Court, in Missouri v. Jenkins by

Agyei, 491 U.S. 274 (1989), held that §1988 permitted fees for the time of paralegals, including law clerks and recent law school graduates.

Should Courts Increase Fees When There Is a Risk of Nonrecovery?

As we have seen, lawyers may recover more than would otherwise be conscionable when they face a risk of recovering nothing (page 113 supra). Should courts that determine fees under fee-shifting statutes or in class actions similarly increase the award to successful counsel based on a risk of non-recovery? In Pennsylvania v. Delaware Valley Citizens' Council, 483 U.S. 711, 726-733 (1987), an action under the Clean Air Act, Justice White's plurality opinion said no because it was not clear that Congress so intended. Alternatively, the plurality said, an increase for risk of non-recovery should be allowed only in "exceptional" cases, where there is a finding based on "evidence in the record . . . that without risk-enhancement plaintiff would have faced substantial difficulties in finding counsel in the local or other relevant market." The plurality also concluded that "a contingency enhancement may be superfluous under the lodestar approach to setting a fee." It wrote:

> The reasons a particular lawsuit are considered to be "risky" for an attorney are because of the novelty and difficulty of the issues presented, and because of the potential for protracted litigation. Moreover, when an attorney ultimately prevails in such a lawsuit, this success will be primarily attributable to his legal skills and experience, and to the hours of hard work he devoted to the case. These factors, however, are considered by the court in determining the reasonable number of hours expended and the reasonable hourly rate for the lodestar, and any further increase in this sum based on the risk of not prevailing would result not in a "reasonable" attorney's fee, but in a windfall for an attorney who prevailed in a difficult case.

Justice O'Connor was the swing vote. In a concurring opinion, she agreed with the dissent "that Congress did not intend to foreclose consideration of contingency in setting a reasonable fee under fee-shifting provisions," but she also agreed with the alternative holding of the plurality that no risk enhancement "is appropriate unless the applicant can establish that without an adjustment for risk the prevailing party 'would have faced substantial difficulties in finding counsel. . . .' "

The *Rivera* plurality, in a lengthy opinion by Justice Blackmun, dissented in *Delaware Valley*. The *Delaware Valley* plurality and dissent both cite Samuel Berger, Court Awarded Attorneys' Fees: What Is "Reasonable"?, 126 U. Pa. L. Rev. 281 (1977), and John Leubsdorf, The Contingency Factor in Attorney Fee Awards, 90 Yale L.J. 473 (1981). See also Skelton v. General Motors Corp., 860 F.2d 250 (7th Cir. 1988), cert. denied, 493 U.S.

810 (1989) (enhancement for risk of nonrecovery allowed in "common fund" cases, distinguishing cases involving fee-shifting statutes).

Private Arrangements in §1988 Cases

We have seen (page 113 supra) that legislation may limit the amount lawyers can charge. Does §1988 do that? In two cases, the Supreme Court has kept §1988 distinct from private fee agreements. Blanchard v. Bergeron, 489 U.S. 87 (1989), held that a §1988 fee could exceed the contingent fee the successful plaintiff had contracted to pay his lawyer, although the latter may be a factor in determining the fee award. Venegas v. Mitchell, 495 U.S. 82 (1990), held that because §1988 does not set a ceiling on reasonable counsel fees, it could not be used to invalidate a contingent fee contract that yielded an amount greater than the amount awarded under §1988.

QUESTION

4.2   "If someone ever publishes a Guinness Book of Records for legal absurdities, *Rivera* should win first place. Can you imagine giving these new lawyers nearly a quarter million dollars for recovering $13,300 on their federal claim? And that includes 45 hours for time spent sitting around a hotel room and nearly 200 hours on a single pretrial order. This at a time when cities around the country are starving for funds for desperate social problems. If they can get this kind of money for $13,300, why not for winning $5,000 or $1,000? Where's the limit? Make no mistake about it. This is taxpayer money, money that could otherwise go to making life easier or safer or less costly for the body politic. We don't need awards this large to encourage lawyers to bring civil rights cases. Is there any doubt that if the award were, say, half as large, lawyers would still be willing to bring those cases? The test should be the fee that will motivate private lawyers to take similar cases, not a ridiculous windfall for two wet-behind-the-ears ingenues. Don't you agree?"

2. Settlement Conditioned on Fee Waiver

EVANS v. JEFF D.
475 U.S. 717 (1986)

JUSTICE STEVENS delivered the opinion of the Court.

The Civil Rights Attorney's Fees Awards Act of 1976 (Fees Act), provides that "the court, in its discretion, may allow the prevailing party . . . a reasonable attorney's fee" in enumerated civil rights actions. 90 Stat. 2641, 42 U.S.C. §1988. In Maher v. Gagne, 448 U.S. 122 (1980), we held that fees *may* be assessed against state officials after a case has been settled by the entry of a consent decree. In this case, we consider the question whether attorney's fees *must* be assessed when the case has been settled by a consent decree granting prospective relief to the plaintiff class but providing that the defendants shall not pay any part of the prevailing party's fees or costs. We hold that the District Court has the power, in its sound discretion, to refuse to award fees.

I

Facts

[In August 1980, the Idaho Legal Aid Society filed a class action challenging "the educational programs and the healthcare services" available to "children who suffer from emotional and mental handicaps." In March 1983, a week before trial, the defendants "offered virtually all of the injunctive relief [the class] had sought in their complaint." But the settlement offer "included a provision for a waiver . . . of any claim to fees for costs," including those under §1988. Charles Johnson, the Legal Aid attorney, "determined that his ethical obligations to his clients mandated acceptance of the proposal. The parties conditioned the waiver on approval by the District Court."

The district court denied Johnson's motion for fees, but the Ninth Circuit reversed, holding that "the strong federal policy embodied in the Fees Act normally requires an award of fees to prevailing plaintiffs in civil rights actions, including those who have prevailed through settlement." When "attorney's fees are negotiated as part of a class action settlement, a conflict frequently exists between the class lawyers' interest in compensation and the class members' interest in relief." The Court therefore "disapproved simultaneous negotiation of settlements and attorney's fees" absent "unusual circumstances," which were not present here. The Supreme Court granted review.]

II

The disagreement between the parties and amici as to what exactly is at issue in this case makes it appropriate to put certain aspects of the case to one side in order to state precisely the question that the case does present.

To begin with, the Court of Appeals' decision rested on an erroneous view of the District Court's power to approve settlements in class actions. Rule 23(e) wisely requires court approval of the terms of any settlement of a class action, but the power to approve or reject a settlement negotiated by the parties before trial does not authorize the court to require the parties to accept a settlement to which they have not agreed. Although changed circumstances may justify a court-ordered modification of a consent decree over the objections of a party after the decree has been entered, and the District Court might have advised petitioners and respondents that it would not approve their proposal unless one or more of its provisions was deleted or modified, Rule 23(e) does not give the court the power, in advance of trial, to modify a proposed consent decree and order its acceptance over either party's objection. The options available to the District Court were essentially the same as those available to respondents: it could have accepted the proposed settlement; it could have rejected the proposal and postponed the trial to see if a different settlement could be achieved; or it could have decided to try the case. The District Court could not enforce the settlement on the merits and award attorney's fees any more than it could, in a situation in which the attorney had negotiated a large fee at the expense of the plaintiff class, preserve the fee award and order greater relief on the merits. The question we must decide, therefore, is whether the District Court had a duty to reject the proposed settlement because it included a waiver of statutorily authorized attorney's fees.

That duty, whether it takes the form of a general prophylactic rule or arises out of the special circumstances of this case, derives ultimately from the Fees Act rather than from the strictures of professional ethics. Although respondents contend that Johnson, as counsel for the class, was faced with an "ethical dilemma" when petitioners offered him relief greater than that which he could reasonably have expected to obtain for his clients at trial (if only he would stipulate to a waiver of the statutory fee award), and although we recognize Johnson's conflicting interests between pursuing relief for the class and a fee for the Idaho Legal Aid Society, we do not believe that the "dilemma" was an "ethical" one in the sense that Johnson had to choose between conflicting duties under the prevailing norms of professional conduct. Plainly, Johnson had no *ethical* obligation to seek a statutory fee award. His ethical duty was to serve his clients loyally and competently. Since the proposal to settle the merits was more favorable than the probable outcome of the trial, Johnson's decision to recommend acceptance was consistent with the highest standards of our profession. The District Court, therefore, correctly concluded that approval of the settlement involved no breach of ethics in this case.

The defect, if any, in the negotiated fee waiver must be traced not to the rules of ethics but to the Fees Act. Following this tack, respondents argue that the statute must be construed to forbid a fee waiver that is the product of "coercion." They submit that a "coercive waiver" results when the defendant in a civil rights action (1) offers a settlement on the merits of equal or greater value than that which plaintiffs could reasonably expect to achieve at trial but (2) conditions the offer on a waiver of plain-

tiffs' statutory eligibility for attorney's fees. Such an offer, they claim,
exploits the ethical obligation of plaintiffs' counsel to recommend settlement in order to avoid defendant's statutory liability of its opponents'
fees and costs.[16]

The question this case presents, then, is whether the Fees Act requires
a district court to disapprove a stipulation seeking to settle a civil rights
class action under Rule 23 when the offered relief equals or exceeds the
probable outcome at trial but is expressly conditioned on waiver of statutory eligibility for attorney's fees. For reasons set out below, we are not
persuaded that Congress has commanded that all such settlements must
be rejected by the District Court. Moreover, on the facts of record in this
case, we are satisfied that the District Court did not abuse its discretion by
approving the fee waiver.

III

The text of the Fees Act provides no support for the proposition that
Congress intended to ban all fee waivers offered in connection with substantial relief on the merits.[17] On the contrary, the language of the Act, as
well at its legislative history, indicates that Congress bestowed on the
"prevailing *party*" (generally plaintiffs) a statutory eligibility for a discretionary award of attorney's fees in specified civil rights actions. It did not
prevent the party from waiving this eligibility any more than it legislated
against assignment of this right to an attorney, such as effectively occurred here. Instead, Congress enacted the fee-shifting provision as "an
integral part of the remedies necessary to obtain" compliance with civil
rights laws, to further the same general purpose — promotion of respect
for civil rights — that led it to provide damages and injunctive relief. The
statute and its legislative history nowhere suggest that Congress intended
to forbid *all* waivers of attorney's fees — even those insisted upon by a
civil rights plaintiff in exchange for some other relief to which he is indis-

---

16. See committee on Professional and Judicial Ethics of the New York City Bar Association, Op. No. 80-94, reprinted in 36 Record of NYCBA, at 508 ("Defense counsel thus are
in a uniquely favorable position when they condition settlement on the waiver of the statutory fee: they make a demand for a benefit which the plaintiff's lawyer cannot resist as a
matter of ethics and which the plaintiff will not resist due to lack of interest."). Accord, District of Columbia Bar Legal Ethics Committee, Op. No. 147, reprinted in 113 Daily Wash.
L. Rep. 389, 394 (1985).

17. The operative language of the Fees Act provides, in its entirety:

In any action or proceeding to enforce a provision of sections 1977, 1978, 1979,
1980, and 1981 of the Revised Statutes, title IX of Public Law 92-318, or in any civil
action or proceeding, by or on behalf of the United States of America, to enforce, or
charging a violation of, a provision of the United States Internal Revenue Code, or
title VI of the Civil Rights Act of 1964, the court, in its discretion, may allow the prevailing party, other than the United States, a reasonable attorney's fee as part of the
costs. 90 Stat. 2641, 42 U.S.C. §1988.

putably not entitled[20] — any more than it intended to bar a concession on damages to secure broader injunctive relief. Thus, while it is undoubtedly true that Congress expected fee-shifting to attract competent counsel to represent citizens deprived of their civil rights, it neither bestowed fee awards upon attorneys nor rendered them nonwaivable or nonnegotiable; instead, it added them to the arsenal of remedies available to combat violations of civil rights, a goal not invariably inconsistent with conditioning settlement on the merits on a waiver of statutory attorney's fees.[22]

In fact, we believe that a general proscription against negotiated waiver of attorney's fees in exchange for a settlement on the merits would itself impede vindication of civil rights, at least in some cases, by reducing the attractiveness of settlement. . . .

Most defendants are unlikely to settle unless the cost of the predicted judgment, discounted by its probability, plus the transaction costs of further litigation, are greater than the cost of the settlement package. If fee waivers cannot be negotiated, the settlement package must either contain an attorney's fee component of potentially large and typically uncertain magnitude, or else the parties must agree to have the fee fixed by the court. Although either of these alternatives may well be acceptable in many cases, there surely is a significant number in which neither alternative will be as satisfactory as a decision to try the entire case.[23]

The adverse impact of removing attorney's fees and costs from bargaining might be tolerable if the uncertainty introduced into settlement negotiations were small. But it is not. The defendants' potential liability for fees in this kind of litigation can be as significant as, and sometimes even more significant than, their potential liability on the merits. . . .

It is therefore not implausible to anticipate that parties to a significant number of civil rights cases will refuse to settle if liability for attorney's

20. Judge Wald has described the use of attorney's fees as a "bargaining chip" useful to plaintiffs as well as defendants.

22. Indeed, Congress specifically rejected a mandatory fee-shifting provision, see H.R. Rep. No. 94-1558, supra, at 3, 5, 8; 122 Cong. Rec. 35123 (1976) (remarks of Rep. Drinan), a proposal which the dissent would virtually reinstate under the guise of carrying out the legislative will. Even proponents of nonwaivable fee awards under §1988 concede that "one would have to strain principles of statutory interpretation to conclude that Congress intended to utilize fee non-negotiability to achieve the purposes of section 1988." Calhoun, Attorney-Client Conflicts of Interest and the Concept of Non-Negotiable Fee Awards Under 42 U.S.C. §1988, 55 U. Colo. L. Rev. 341, 385 (1984).

23. It is unrealistic to assume that the defendant's offer on the merits would be unchanged by redaction of the provision waiving fees. If it were, the defendant's incentive to settle would be diminished because of the risk that attorney's fees, when added to the original merits offer, will exceed the discounted value of the expected judgment plus litigation costs. If, as is more likely, the defendant lowered the value of its offer on the merits to provide a cushion against the possibility of a large fee award, the defendant's offer on the merits will in many cases be less than the amount to which the plaintiff feels himself entitled, thereby inclining him to reject the settlement. Of course, to the extent that the merits offer is somewhere between these two extremes the incentive of both sides to settle is dampened, albeit to a lesser degree with respect to each party.

fees remains open, thereby forcing more cases to trial, unnecessarily burdening the judicial system, and disserving civil rights litigants. Respondents' own waiver of attorney's fees and costs to obtain settlement of their educational claims is eloquent testimony to the utility of fee waivers in vindicating civil rights claims.[29] We conclude, therefore, that it is not necessary to construe the Fees Act as embodying a general rule prohibiting settlements conditioned on the waiver of fees in order to be faithful to the purposes of that Act.[30]

IV

The question remains whether the District Court abused its discretion in this case by approving a settlement which included a complete fee waiver. As noted earlier, Rule 23(e) wisely requires court approval of the terms of any settlement of a class action. The potential conflict among members of the class — in this case, for example, the possible conflict between children primarily interested in better educational programs and those primarily interested in improved health care — fully justifies the requirement of court approval.

The Court of Appeals, respondents, and various amici supporting their position, however, suggest that the court's authority to pass on settlements, typically invoked to ensure fair treatment of class members,

---

29. Respondents implicitly acknowledge a defendant's need to fix his total liability when they suggest that the parties to a civil rights action should "exchange information" regarding plaintiff's attorney's fees. See, e.g., Committee on Professional and Judicial Ethics of the New York City Bar Association, Op. No. 82-80, p.2 (1985); Grievance Commission of Board of Overseers of the Bar of Maine, Op. No. 17, Advisory Opinions of the Grievance Commission of the Board of Overseers of the Bar 70 (1983). If this exchange is confined to time records and customary billing rates, the information provides an insufficient basis for forecasting the fee award for the reasons stated above. If the "exchange" is more in the nature of an "assurance" that attorney's fees will not exceed a specified amount, the rule against waiving fees to obtain a favorable settlement on the merits is to that extent breached. . . .

30. The Court is unanimous in concluding that the Fees Act should not be interpreted to prohibit all simultaneous negotiations of a defendant's liability on the merits and his liability for his opponent's attorney's fees. We agree that when the parties find such negotiations conducive to settlement, the public interest, as well as that of the parties, is served by simultaneous negotiations. This reasoning applies not only to individual civil rights actions, but to civil rights class actions as well.

Although the dissent would allow simultaneous negotiations, it would require that "whatever fee the parties agree to" be "found by the court to be a 'reasonable' one under the Fees Act." The dissent's proposal is imaginative, but not very practical. Of the 10,757 "other civil rights" cases filed in federal court last year — most of which were §1983 actions for which §1988 authorizes an award of fees — only 111 sought class relief. Assuming that of the approximately 99% of these civil rights actions that are not class actions, a further 90% would settle rather than go to trial, the dissent's proposal would require district courts to evaluate the reasonableness of fee agreements in several thousand civil rights cases annually while they make that determination in slightly over 100 civil rights class actions now. Moreover, if this novel procedure really is necessary to carry out the purposes of the Fees Act, presumably it should be applied to all cases arising under federal statutes that provide for fee-shifting.

must be exercised in accordance with the Fees Act to promote the availability of attorneys in civil rights cases. Specifically, respondents assert that the State of Idaho could not pass a valid statute precluding the payment of attorney's fees in settlements of civil rights cases to which the Fees Act applies. From this they reason that the Fees Act must equally preclude the adoption of a uniform statewide policy that serves the same end, and accordingly contend that a consistent practice of insisting on a fee waiver as a condition of settlement in civil rights litigation is in conflict with the federal statute authorizing fees for prevailing parties, including those who prevail by way of settlement.[31] Remarkably, there seems little disagreement on these points. Petitioners and the amici who support them never suggest that the district court is obligated to place its stamp of approval on every settlement in which the plaintiffs' attorneys have agreed to a fee waiver. The Solicitor General, for example, has suggested that a fee waiver need not be approved when the defendant had "no realistic defense on the merits," . . . or if the waiver was part of a "vindictive effort . . . to teach counsel that they had better not bring such cases."

We find it unnecessary to evaluate this argument, however, because the record in this case does not indicate that Idaho has adopted such a statute, policy, or practice. Nor does the record support the narrower proposition that petitioners' request to waive fees was a vindictive effort to deter attorneys from representing plaintiffs in civil rights suits against Idaho. It is true that a fee waiver was requested and obtained as a part of the early settlement of the education claims, but we do not understand respondents to be challenging that waiver . . . and they have not offered to prove that the petitioners' tactics in this case merely implemented a routine state policy designed to frustrate the objectives of the Fees Act. Our own examination of the record reveals no such policy.

In light of the record, respondents must — to sustain the judgment in their favor — confront the District Court's finding that the extensive structural relief they obtained constituted an adequate quid pro quo for their waiver of attorney's fees. The Court of Appeals did not overturn this finding. Indeed, even that court did not suggest that the option of rejecting the entire settlement and requiring the parties either to try the case or to attempt to negotiate a different settlement would have served the interests of justice. Only by making the unsupported assumption that the respondent class was entitled to retain the favorable portions of the

---

31. See Committee on Professional and Judicial Ethics of the New York City Bar Association, Op. No. 80-94, reprinted in 36 Record of NYCBA, 507, 510 (1981) ("[T]he long term effect of persistent demands for the waiver of statutory fees is to . . . undermine efforts to make counsel available to those who cannot afford it."). Accord, District of Columbia Bar Legal Ethics Committee, Op. No. 147, reprinted in 113 Daily Wash. L. Rep. 389, 394 (1985). National staff counsel for the ACLU estimates that requests for fee waivers are made in more than half of all civil rights cases litigated. See Winter, Fee Waiver Requests Unethical: Bar Opinion, 68 A.B.A.J. 23 (1982).

settlement while rejecting the fee waiver could the Court of Appeals conclude that the District Court had acted unwisely.

What the outcome of this settlement illustrates is that the Fees Act has given the victims of civil rights violations a powerful weapon that improves their ability to employ counsel, to obtain access to the courts, and thereafter to vindicate their rights by means of settlement or trial. For aught that appears, it was the "coercive" effect of respondents' statutory right to seek a fee award that motivated petitioners' exceptionally generous offer. Whether this weapon might be even more powerful if fee waivers were prohibited in cases like this is another question,[34] but it is in any event a question that Congress is best equipped to answer. Thus far, the Legislature has not commanded that fees be paid whenever a case is settled. Unless it issues such a command, we shall rely primarily on the sound discretion of the district courts to appraise the reasonableness of particular class-action settlements on a case-by-case basis, in the light of all the relevant circumstances. In this case, the District Court did not abuse its discretion in upholding a fee waiver which secured broad injunctive relief, relief greater than that which plaintiffs could reasonably have expected to achieve at trial.

The judgment of the Court of Appeals is reversed.

JUSTICE BRENNAN, with whom JUSTICE MARSHALL and JUSTICE BLACKMUN join, dissenting.

Ultimately, enforcement of the laws is what really counts. It was with this in mind that Congress enacted the Civil Rights Attorney's Fees Awards Act of 1976, 42 U.S.C. §1988 (the Act or Fees Act). Congress authorized fee-shifting to improve enforcement of civil rights legislation by making it easier for victims of civil rights violations to find lawyers willing to take their cases. Because today's decision will make it more difficult for civil rights plaintiffs to obtain legal assistance, a result plainly contrary to Congress' purpose, I dissent.

I

The Court begins its analysis by emphasizing that neither the language nor the legislative history of the Fees Act supports "the proposition that Congress intended to ban all fee waivers offered in connection

---

34. We are cognizant of the possibility that decisions by individual clients to bargain away fee awards may, in the aggregate and in the long run, diminish lawyers' expectations of statutory fees in civil rights cases. If this occurred, the pool of lawyers willing to represent plaintiffs in such cases might shrink, constricting the "effective access to the judicial process" for persons with civil rights grievances which the Fees Act was intended to provide. That the "tyranny of small decisions" may operate in this fashion is not to say that there is any reason or documentation to support such a concern at the present time. Comment on this issue is therefore premature at this juncture. We believe, however, that as a practical matter the likelihood of this circumstance arising is remote.

with substantial relief on the merits." . . . I agree. There is no evidence that Congress gave the question of fee waivers any thought at all. However, the Court mistakenly assumes that this omission somehow supports the conclusion that fee waivers are permissible. On the contrary, that Congress did not specifically consider the issue of fee waivers tells us absolutely nothing about whether such waivers ought to be permitted. . . . Accordingly, the first and most important question to be asked is what Congress' purpose was in enacting the Fees Act. We must then determine whether conditional fee waivers are consistent with this purpose. . . .

III

As this [omitted] review of the legislative history makes clear, then, by awarding attorney's fees Congress sought to attract competent counsel to represent victims of civil rights violations. Congress' primary purpose was to enable "private attorneys general" to protect the public interest by creating economic incentives for lawyers to represent them. The Court's assertion that the Fees Act was intended to do nothing more than give individual victims of civil rights violations another remedy is thus at odds with the whole thrust of the legislation. Congress determined that the public as a whole has an interest in the vindication of the rights conferred by the civil rights statutes over and above the value of a civil rights remedy to a particular plaintiff.

I have gone to great lengths to show how the Court mischaracterizes the purpose of the Fees Act because the Court's error leads it to ask the wrong question. Having concluded that the Fees Act merely creates another remedy to vindicate the rights of individual plaintiffs, the Court asks whether negotiated waivers of statutory attorney's fees are "invariably inconsistent" with the availability of such fees as a remedy for individual plaintiffs. Not surprisingly, the Court has little difficulty knocking down this frail straw man. But the *proper* question is whether permitting negotiated fee waivers is consistent with Congress' goal of attracting competent counsel. It is therefore necessary to consider the effect on *this* goal of allowing individual plaintiffs to negotiate fee waivers. . . .

B

1

It seems obvious that allowing defendants in civil rights cases to condition settlement of the merits on a waiver of statutory attorney's fees will diminish lawyers' expectations of receiving fees and decrease the willingness of lawyers to accept civil rights cases. Even the Court acknowledges "the possibility that decisions by individual clients to bargain away fee awards may, in the aggregate and in the long run, diminish lawyers' expectations of statutory fees in civil rights cases." The Court tells us, however, that "[c]omment on this issue" is "premature at this juncture" because there is not yet supporting "documentation." The Court then goes on anyway to observe that "as a practical matter the likelihood of this circumstance arising is remote."

I must say that I find the Court's assertions somewhat difficult to understand. . . . [Pre-Act] experience surely provides an indication of the immediate hardship suffered by civil rights claimants whenever there is a reduction in the availability of attorney's fee awards.[7] Moreover, numerous courts and commentators have recognized that permitting fee waivers creates disincentives for lawyers to take civil rights cases and thus makes it more difficult for civil rights plaintiffs to obtain legal assistance.

But it does not require a sociological study to see that permitting fee waivers will make it more difficult for civil rights plaintiffs to obtain legal assistance. It requires only common sense. Assume that a civil rights defendant makes a settlement offer that includes a demand for waiver of statutory attorney's fees. The decision whether to accept or reject the offer is the plaintiff's alone, and the lawyer must abide by the plaintiff's decision. See, e.g., ABA, Model Rules of Professional Conduct 1.2(a) (1984); ABA, Model Code of Professional Responsibility EC 7-7 to EC 7-9 (1982).[8] As a formal matter, of course, the statutory fee belongs to the plaintiff and thus technically the decision to waive entails a sacrifice only by the plaintiff. As a practical matter, however, waiver affects only the lawyer. Because "a vast majority of the victims of civil rights violations" have no resources to pay attorney's fees, lawyers cannot hope to recover fees from the plaintiff and must depend entirely on the Fees Act for compensation.[10] The plaintiff thus has no real stake in the statutory fee and is unaffected by its waiver. Consequently, plaintiffs will readily agree to waive fees if this will help them to obtain other relief they desire.[11] As

---

7. It is especially important to keep in mind the fragile nature of the civil rights bar. Even when attorney's fees are awarded, they do not approach the large sums which can be earned in ordinary commercial litigation. It is therefore cost inefficient for private practitioners to devote much time to civil rights cases. Consequently, there are very few civil rights practitioners, and most of these devote only a small part of their time to such cases.

8. The attorney is, in fact, obliged to advise the plaintiff whether to accept or reject the settlement offer based on his independent professional judgment, and the lawyer's duty of undivided loyalty requires that he render such advice free from the influence of his or his organization's interest in a fee. See, e.g., Model Code of Professional Responsibility EC 5-1, EC 5-2, DR 5-101(A); Model Rules of Professional Conduct 1.7(b), 2.1.

10. Nor can attorneys protect themselves by requiring plaintiffs to sign contingency agreements or retainers at the outset of the representation. Amici legal aid societies inform us that they are prohibited by statute, court rule, or Internal Revenue Service regulation from entering into fee agreements with their clients. Moreover, even if such agreements could be negotiated, the possibility of obtaining protection through contingency fee arrangements is unavailable in the very large proportion of civil rights cases which, like this case, seek only injunctive relief.

11. This result is virtually inevitable in class action suits where, even if the class representative feels sympathy for the lawyer's plight, the obligation to represent the interests of ab-

summed up by the Legal Ethics Committee of the District of Columbia Bar:

> Defense counsel . . . are in a uniquely favorable position when they condition settlement on the waiver of the statutory fee: They make a demand for a benefit that the plaintiff's lawyer cannot resist as a matter of ethics and one in which the plaintiff has no interest and therefore will not resist.

Of course, from the lawyer's standpoint, things could scarcely have turned out worse. He or she invested considerable time and effort in the case, won, and has exactly nothing to show for it. Is the Court really serious in suggesting that it takes a study to prove that this lawyer will be reluctant when, the following week, another civil rights plaintiff enters his office and asks for representation? Does it truly require that somebody conduct a test to see that legal aid services, having invested scarce resources on a case, will feel the pinch when they do not recover a statutory fee?

And, of course, once fee waivers are permitted, defendants will seek them as a matter of course, since this is a logical way to minimize liability. Indeed, defense counsel would be remiss *not* to demand that the plaintiff waive statutory attorney's fees. A lawyer who proposes to have his client pay more than is necessary to end litigation has failed to fulfill his fundamental duty zealously to represent the best interests of his client. Because waiver of fees does not affect the plaintiff, a settlement offer is not made less attractive to the plaintiff if it includes a demand that statutory fees be waived. Thus, in the future, we must expect settlement offers routinely to contain demands for waivers of statutory fees.[12]

The cumulative effect this practice will have on the civil rights bar is evident. It does not denigrate the high ideals that motivate many civil rights practitioners to recognize that lawyers are in the business of practicing law, and that, like other business people, they are and must be concerned with earning a living. The conclusion that permitting fee waivers will seriously impair the ability of civil rights plaintiffs to obtain legal assistance is embarrassingly obvious.

Because making it more difficult for civil rights plaintiffs to obtain legal assistance is precisely the opposite of what Congress sought to achieve by enacting the Fees Act, fee waivers should be prohibited. We

---

sent class members precludes altruistic sacrifice. In class action suits on behalf of incompetents, like this one, it is the lawyer himself who must agree to sacrifice his own interests for those of the class he represents. See, e.g., Model Code of Professional Responsibility EC 7-12.

12. The Solicitor General's suggestion that we can prohibit waivers sought as part of a "vindictive effort" to teach lawyers not to bring civil rights cases, a point that the Court finds unnecessary to consider, is thus irrelevant. Defendants will seek such waivers in every case simply as a matter of sound bargaining. Indeed, the Solicitor General's brief suggests that this will be the bargaining posture of the United States in the future.

have on numerous prior occasions held that "a statutory right conferred on a private party, but affecting the public interest, may not be waived or released if such waiver or release contravenes the statutory policy." This is simply straightforward application of the well-established principle that an agreement which is contrary to public policy is void and unenforceable.[14]

2

This all seems so obvious that it is puzzling that the Court reaches a different result. The Court's rationale is that, unless fee waivers are permitted, "parties to a significant number of civil rights cases will refuse to settle. . . ." This is a wholly inadequate justification for the Court's result.

First, the effect of prohibiting fee waivers on settlement offers is just not an important concern in the context of the Fees Act. I agree with the Court that encouraging settlements is desirable policy. But it is *judicially* created policy, applicable to litigation of any kind and having no special force in the context of civil rights cases. The *congressional* policy underlying the Fees Act is, as I have argued throughout, to create incentives for lawyers to devote time to civil rights cases by making it economically feasible for them to do so. As explained above, permitting fee waivers significantly undercuts this policy. Thus, even if prohibiting fee waivers does discourage some settlements, a *judicial* policy favoring settlement cannot possibly take precedence over this express *congressional* policy. We must implement Congress' agenda, not our own.

In an attempt to justify its decision to elevate settlement concerns, the Court argues that settlement "provides benefits for civil rights plaintiffs as well as defendants and is consistent with the purposes of the Fees Act" because " '[s]ome plaintiffs will receive compensation in settlement where, on trial, they might not have recovered, or would have recovered less than what was offered.' " . . .

As previously noted, by framing the purpose of the Fees Act in very general terms, the Court merely obscures the proper focus of discussion. The Fees Act was designed to help civil rights plaintiffs in a particular way — by ensuring that there will be lawyers willing to represent them. The fact that fee waivers may produce some settlement offers that are beneficial to a few individual plaintiffs is hardly "consistent with the purposes of the Fees Act" if permitting fee waivers fundamentally undermines what Congress sought to achieve. Each individual plaintiff who waives his right to statutory fees in order to obtain additional relief for himself makes it that much more difficult for the next victim of a civil rights violation to find a lawyer willing or able to bring *his* case. As ob-

---

14. To be sure, prohibiting fee waivers will require federal courts to make a determination they would not have to make if fees could be waived. However, this additional chore will not impose a significant burden.

taining legal assistance becomes more difficult, the "benefit" the Court so magnanimously preserves for civil rights plaintiffs becomes available to fewer and fewer individuals, exactly the opposite result from that intended by Congress.

Moreover, I find particularly unpersuasive the Court's apparent belief that Congress enacted the Fees Act to help plaintiffs coerce relief to which they are "indisputably not entitled." It may be that, in particular cases, some defendants' fears of incurring liability for plaintiff's attorney's fees will give plaintiffs leverage to coerce relief they do not deserve. If so, this is an unfortunate cost of a statute intended to ensure that plaintiffs can obtain the relief to which they are entitled. And it certainly is not a result we must preserve at the expense of the central purpose of the Fees Act.

Second, even assuming that settlement practices are relevant, the Court greatly exaggerates the effect that prohibiting fee waivers will have on defendants' willingness to make settlement offers. This is largely due to the Court's failure to distinguish the fee waiver issue from the issue of simultaneous negotiation of fees and merits claims. The Court's discussion mixes concerns over a defendant's reluctance to settle because total liability remains uncertain with reluctance to settle because the cost of settling is too high. However, it is a prohibition on simultaneous negotiation, not a prohibition on fee waivers, that makes it difficult for the defendant to ascertain his total liability at the time he agrees to settle the merits. Thus, while prohibiting fee waivers may deter settlement offers simply because requiring the defendant to pay a "reasonable attorney's fee" increases the total cost of settlement, this is a separate issue altogether, and the Court's numerous arguments about why defendants will not settle unless they can determine their total liability at the time of settlement are simply beside the point.[17] With respect to a prohibition on fee waivers (and again merely assuming that effects on settlement are relevant), the sole question to be asked is whether the increased cost of settlement packages will prevent enough settlement offers to be a dispositive factor in this case.

The Court asserts, without factual support, that requiring defendants to pay statutory fee awards will prevent a "significant number" of settlements. . . . I believe that the Court overstates the extent to which prohibiting fee waivers will deter defendants from making settlement offers. Because the parties can negotiate a fee (or a range of fees) that is not unduly high and condition their settlement on the court's approval of this fee, the magnitude of a defendant's liability for fees in the settlement

---

17. For the reasons stated in Part III-C, I would permit simultaneous negotiation of fees and merits. The parties could agree upon a reasonable fee which would be subject to judicial approval under the Fees Act. Any settlement on the merits could be made contingent upon such approval. By permitting defendants to ascertain their total liability prior to settling, this approach fully alleviates the Court's concerns in this regard.

context need be neither uncertain nor particularly great. Against this, the defendant must weigh the risk of a non-negotiated fee to be fixed by the court after a trial; as the Court reminds us, fee awards in *this* context may be very uncertain and, potentially, of very great magnitude. . . .

All of which is not to deny that prohibiting fee waivers will deter some settlements; any increase in the costs of settling will have this effect. However, by exaggerating the size and the importance of fee awards, and by ignoring the options available to the parties in settlement negotiations, the Court makes predictions that are inflated. An actual disincentive to settling exists only where three things are true: (1) the defendant feels he is likely to win if he goes to trial, in which case the plaintiff will recover no fees; (2) the plaintiff will agree to relief on the merits that is less costly to the defendant than litigating the case; and (3) adding the cost of a negotiated attorney's fee makes it less costly for the defendant to litigate. I believe that this describes a very small class of cases — although, like the Court, I cannot "document" the assertion.

C

I would, on the other hand, permit simultaneous negotiation of fees and merits claims [with court review for reasonableness], since this would not contravene the purposes of the Fees Act. Congress determined that awarding prevailing parties a "reasonable" fee would create necessary — and sufficient — incentives for attorneys to work on civil rights cases. Prohibiting plaintiffs from waiving statutory fees ensures that lawyers will receive this "reasonable" statutory fee. Thus, if fee waivers are prohibited, permitting simultaneous fees and merits negotiations will not interfere with the Act; the lawyer will still be entitled to and will still receive a reasonable attorney's fee. Indeed, permitting simultaneous negotiations in such circumstances may even enhance the effectiveness of the Fees Act by making it easier for a lawyer to dispose of his cases more quickly. This frees up the lawyer's time to take other cases and may enhance his reputation as an effective advocate who quickly obtains relief for clients.

IV

Although today's decision will undoubtedly impair the effectiveness of the private enforcement scheme Congress established for civil rights legislation, I do not believe that it will bring about the total disappearance of "private attorneys general." It is to be hoped that Congress will repair this Court's mistake. In the meantime, other avenues of relief are available. The Court's decision in no way limits the power of state and local bar associations to regulate the ethical conduct of lawyers. Indeed, several Bar Associations have already declared it unethical for defense counsel to seek fee waivers. Such efforts are to be commended and, it is to be hoped, will be followed by other state and local organizations concerned with respecting the intent of Congress and with protecting civil rights.

In addition, it may be that civil rights attorneys can obtain agreements from their clients not to waive attorney's fees.[20] Such agreements simply replicate the private market for legal services (in which attorneys are not ordinarily required to contribute to their client's recovery[21]), and thus will enable civil rights practitioners to make it economically feasible — as Congress hoped — to expend time and effort litigating civil rights claims. . . .

QUESTIONS ABOUT EVANS v. JEFF D.

1. Assume the plaintiff's lawyer receives a settlement offer and, in her view, the defendant has "no realistic defense on the merits" or she believes the offer is being used as part of "a vindictive effort to deter attorneys" from suing the particular defendant. Under Justice Stevens's analysis, what options are open to the lawyer? To what extent would the lawyer need the agreement of her client? What options are open to the judge?

2. Do you agree with Justice Stevens's statement in note 34? If a "tyranny of small decisions" were to deplete the "pool" of plaintiffs' lawyers, would the Supreme Court be empowered to respond? Or would the response have to come from Congress?

3. What would you do if after you won a sizeable judgment against a municipality in the highest court in your state, the city's lawyer offered to withdraw his certiorari petition in exchange for a waiver of counsel fees? What if it happened in a case such as City of Riverside v. Rivera, page 126 supra?

4. Would you support an ethical requirement forbidding simultaneous negotiation of the merits and counsel fees in actions in which statutory law allows counsel fees to the prevailing plaintiff? Could such a requirement "overrule" *Evans*? How would you respond to the arguments of the defense bar acknowledged in note 29 of *Evans*? In 1988, the Board of Governors of the California State Bar recommended that the state supreme court adopt the following amendment to the state's ethics code:

20. Since Congress has not sought to regulate ethical concerns either in the Fees Act or elsewhere, the legality of such arguments is purely a matter of local law.

21. One of the more peculiar aspects of the Court's interpretation of the Fees Act is that it permits defendants to require plaintiff's counsel to contribute his compensation to satisfying the plaintiff's claims. In ordinary civil litigation, no defendant would make — or sell to his adversary — a settlement offer conditioned upon the plaintiff's convincing his attorney to contribute to the plaintiff's recovery. Yet today's decision creates a situation in which plaintiff's attorneys in civil rights cases are required to do just that.

A member shall not make or present a settlement offer in any case involving a request by the opposing party for attorneys fees pursuant to private attorney general statutes which is conditioned on opposing counsel waiving all or substantially all fees. This rule does not preclude a member from making or presenting an offer of a lump sum to settle all claims including attorney's fees.

What do you think of this solution? The state supreme court rejected it. Efforts to overturn *Evans* have also been made in Congress. One version, part of an effort to overturn a number of Supreme Court decisions in the civil rights area, would have amended the Civil Rights Act of 1964 to provide as follows:

No consent order or judgment settling a claim under this title shall be entered, and no stipulation of dismissal of a claim under this title shall be effective, unless the parties or their counsel attest to the court that a waiver of all or substantially all attorney's fees was not compelled as a condition of the settlement.

How would this language actually work? Assume a defense lawyer says: "I will give your clients the relief they request, but you have to accept a waiver of substantially all of your fees. However, I will not make this offer if you feel that you are compelled to accept that waiver as a condition of this settlement. Get back to me."

5. After *Evans,* could a plaintiff's lawyer insert in his retainer agreement a provision by which the plaintiff promises not to waive or negotiate counsel fees until a settlement is reached on the merits — i.e., where the client waives recourse to the "powerful weapon" described in the penultimate paragraph of the majority opinion? Could the retainer agreement "assign" the right to seek a fee to the lawyer? Would this provision be ethical if the client were fully informed and agreed voluntarily? See Rule 1.8(j); DR 5-103(A)(1). See also page 112 supra.

6. *Evans* was a class action; settlement required judicial approval. What is its import when an attorney is representing an individual plaintiff in a case subject to a fee-shifting statute? See the post-*Evans* decision in Freeman v. B&B Assoc., 790 F.2d 145 (D.C. Cir. 1986) (following *Evans*).

7. Justice Brennan would allow simultaneous negotiation of the fee and the merits, with the entire package contingent on the judge's approval of the fee. In this way, the defendant knows its full obligation before it signs off on the merits. Justice Brennan would apply his rule in class and nonclass actions. Why does the majority reject this solution? See note 30. Do you agree with Justice Brennan? Think about how the Brennan rule would work in practice. What considerations would inform the trial judge's decision whether to approve the fee? Could the judge reject a fee as too high or too low even if it were acceptable to all parties? Com-

pare Jones v. Amalgamated Warbasse Houses, 721 F.2d 881 (2d Cir. 1983), cert. denied, 466 U.S. 944 (1984) (page 106 supra).

8. Prior to *Evans,* the New York City Bar Association, in Opinion 80-94 (1980), decided that it would be unethical for a defendant to make an offer of settlement in "public interest" cases conditioned on the plaintiff's agreement to waive his or her counsel fee. The opinion relied mainly on the fact that such an offer could create a conflict of interest between attorney and client. Justice Stevens (page 143) rejected this explanation: Because an attorney's duty is to urge whatever is best for her client, regardless of her own interests, there can be no "ethical dilemma." Does that sound right to you? If it is right, can we any longer justify prohibitions on representations on the ground that the lawyer's own interests will tempt the lawyer to undermine his duty to his client? See DR 5-101(A); Rule 1.7(b). The New York City opinion would have required delay in negotiation of the fee until resolution of the merits, but plaintiff's counsel would have been free to give the defense lawyer information (hourly rates, hours spent) that would have enabled the defense to predict the fee. No member of the Court accepted that solution. Why not? (Opinion 80-94 (1980) was refined in Opinion 82-80 (1982). After *Evans,* however, both opinions were withdrawn. Opinion 87-4 (1987).)

3. Who May Receive Court-Ordered Fees?

Lawyers, of course. But many lawyers who are eligible for fee awards are salaried employees of nonprofit organizations such as the ACLU or the Environmental Defense Fund. If a court awards a fee for their work, can their employers get it, assuming the client agrees? The employer may not be authorized to practice law. That raises unauthorized practice and fee-splitting questions and, more broadly, questions about who (or what) can be a law firm. Those questions are addressed in Chapter 14 infra.

FURTHER READING

Note, Fee As the Wind Blows: Waivers of Attorney's Fees in Individual Civil Rights Actions Since *Evans v. Jeff D.*, 102 Harv. L. Rev. 1278 (1989), says that "lower courts have indicated an unwillingness to bridle defendants' use of conditional fee waivers in settlement negotiations in individual civil rights actions," as distinguished from class actions. The author "argues that district courts should be receptive to attorneys' challenges to fee waivers in individual civil rights actions" and suggests a way to reintroduce "a mechanism for judicial oversight of the negotiating process while remaining faithful to *Evans'* construction of the Fees Act."

F. MANDATORY PRO BONO PLANS

In the 1980 Kutak Commission draft, Rule 8.1 provided as follows:

> A lawyer shall render public interest legal service. A lawyer may discharge this responsibility by service in activities for improving the law, the legal system or the legal profession, or by providing professional services to persons of limited means or to public service groups or organizations. A lawyer shall make an annual report concerning such service to appropriate regulatory authority.

As finally adopted by the ABA, Rule 6.1 is aspirational. The word "shall" is changed to "should." Rule 6.1, among other changes, also states that its purpose can be satisfied "by financial support for organizations that provide legal services to persons of limited means."

Adoption of the rule did not end the debate over mandatory pro bono plans. Several jurisdictions have them. See Note, Mandatory Pro Bono: The Path to Equal Justice, 16 Pepperdine L. Rev. 355, 361-362 (1989) (authored by John deSteiguer). It looked for a while as though the Supreme Court might address the constitutional and other issues these plans raise when, in Mallard v. United States District Court for the Southern District of Iowa, 490 U.S. 296, 309-317 (1989), an attorney challenged his assignment to represent an indigent prisoner. But the Court held that the statute under which the lower court had assigned the lawyer, 28 U.S.C. §1915(d), did not authorize the assignment. The Court declined to say whether the lower court had "inherent authority to require lawyers to serve" because the issue had not been considered below. Four Justices dissented in an opinion by Justice Stevens. The lower court's plan for "representation for indigent litigants was in operation when petitioner became a member of that court's bar," Justice Stevens wrote. "When a court has established a fair and detailed procedure for the assignment of counsel to indigent litigants, a formal request to a lawyer by the court pursuant to that procedure is tantamount to a command." Distinguishing *Mallard*, the Eighth Circuit held that Title VII of the 1964 Civil Rights Act empowered a trial court to appoint lawyers to represent poor persons who allege employment discrimination. Scott v. Tyson Foods, Inc., 943 F.2d 17 (8th Circuit 1991).

A mandatory pro bono plan is a way to finance legal services. Lawyers absorb the entire cost of the particular service. Objections to these plans have been both moral and practical. In Lawyers and Justice, Professor David Luban proposes a mandatory pro bono plan that he believes would satisfy the practical objections. It would require 40 hours of free service yearly. Professor Luban then evaluates the moral objections. What do you think of his arguments?

David Luban
LAWYERS AND JUSTICE: AN ETHICAL STUDY
282-287 (1988)

The most vehement moral objection is what may be called the "hard-line libertarian" argument. This says that it violates your moral rights to place any redistributive demands whatever on you. For the hard-line libertarian, making one person give up goods, money, or time for the sake of another or for the sake of the community fails to take seriously the fact that (in Robert Nozick's words) "each individual is a separate person, that his is the only life he has." Taxation, for Nozick, is the equivalent of forced labor, and he describes redistributive demands as "violating" a person, as a "sacrifice" of that person, as treating a distinct individual as "a resource" for others.

The same hyperbolic metaphors are used by Charles Fried to argue that there can be no obligation on the part of lawyers to put their talents to work for the general good:

> Must the lawyer expend his efforts where they will do the most good, rather than where they will draw the largest fee, provide the most excitement, prove most flattering to his vanity, whatever? Why must he? If the answer is that he must because it will produce the most good, then we are saying to the lawyer that he is merely a scarce resource. But a person is not a resource. He is not bound to lead his life as if he were managing a business on behalf of an impersonal body of stockholders called human society. . . .
> If the lawyer is really to be impressed to serve these admitted social needs, then his independence and discretion disappear, and he does indeed become a public resource cut up and disposed of by the public's needs.

The reply to this argument is to notice that it turns on claims that are monstrously false if read literally and irrelevant if they are not. It is literally false that a pro bono obligation allows a lawyer to be "cut up and disposed of by the public's needs": nobody is proposing that we turn lawyers into organ banks. Read figuratively, it is an entertaining rhetorical gesture to liken the demand of forty hours a year to the demand that one give up a kidney; but the unexciting fact that these are actually rather different demands means that the outrage we feel at the notion of cutting someone up has nothing to do with the pro bono obligation.

Fried's argument would be more persuasive if the proposal were to put 100 percent of the lawyer's professional time at the disposal of the community (although even here the surgical metaphor is just a distracting exaggeration); but of course, the pro bono proposal requires nothing like that.

In fact, the hard-line libertarian derives the apparent force of her position only from slippery slope rhetoric like Fried's or Nozick's analogizing of minor redistributive demands to "treating a person as a resource." There is a difference between taxing you and stripmining you that is in danger of getting lost here. As H. L. A. Hart puts it in a critique of Nozick,

> we must, I fear, ask such boring questions as: Is taxing a man's earnings or income . . . not altogether different in terms of the burden it imposes from forcing him to labour? Does it really sacrifice him or make him or his body just a resource for others? . . .

Asking Hart's "boring questions" leads to such boring answers as this: there is an obvious moral difference between mandatory pro bono and slavery, or the physical violation of the person. We would, to put it mildly, find no grounds for moral criticism of a person who did not wish to be shanghaied into durance vile, or to have her kidneys extracted for the benefaction of the deserving poor; but there is something undeniably mean about a person whose "integrity" is threatened by minor redistributive demands.

To this libertarians have a reply. They agree that undoubtedly we would find something to criticize morally about a scrooge who, while honoring all the forbearance rules of libertarianism, never lifted a finger to help another person, no matter how great the need and how slight the effort required. But that is not the same thing as to say that the scrooge violates a moral obligation to do so. To say the latter is to venture a much more specific moral criticism.

I disagree. Philosophers have a tendency to treat the word "obligation" as a technical term in moral theory, marking out a distinct and limited moral phenomenon; but there is no reason to go along with them. Perhaps the word has attained the status of a term of art in Anglo-American moral philosophy over the last few decades; so what? The English language does not subscribe to the Philosophical Review. It is much more plausible to say that whenever harsh moral criticism of any sort is appropriate — calling an action or person "morally indecent," "selfish and mean-spirited," saying that he has "the soul of a banker," or is "a stingy little twit" — we have found a moral obligation violated. . . .

It seems to me that hard-line libertarianism has little to recommend it. But there is a softer-line argument that is more plausible. It goes like this:

It is true that poor people need legal assistance they can't afford. It is true that the community has an obligation to offer all its citizens meaningful access to equal justice. And it is true that the community has the right to obtain from its members the means to do so. (It is this last proposition that distinguishes the present argument from hard-line libertarianism, which is opposed to redistributive taxation.) But if the community wants to meet the legal needs of the poor, it should use tax money to fund legal aid or to compensate private attorneys. That way, the *entire* community bears the cost of meeting a community need. A pro bono obligation, on the other hand, conscripts lawyers to work below their market rate, and it thus constitutes an unfair "conscription tax" in order to supply the poor with legal representation. "No representation without compensation — it's unjust taxation!" is the argument. (Opponents of the military draft argue that the draft is similarly an unfair conscription tax, imposed on eighteen-to-twenty-six-year-old men.) Quoting Fried once again, "It is cheap and hypocritical for society to be unwilling to pay the necessary lawyers from the tax revenues of all, and then to claim that individual lawyers are morally at fault for not choosing to work for free."

This is a powerful argument, and the obvious reply, "The community can't afford the market rate," merely invites the obvious counter, "It has no right to demand from a few people good deeds that it is unwilling to pay for." Wouldn't it be wrong for the community to require grocers to feed the hungry "pro bono," if it is unwilling to tax itself to feed the hungry?

Nor will it suffice to argue (as some courts have) that the lawyer's license is a grant of the state, to which the state may attach a pro bono string (or any other string it desires). For grocers are also licensed, yet it would be morally pernicious to palm off an obligation of the whole community — to feed its hungry — onto the grocers, as a condition of their licensing. Grocers run their businesses to make their livings, and it seems iniquitous to treat the license needed to make one's living as a mere perk granted by the state under whatever conditions it chooses to impose.

Yet this argument from the grocer analogy reveals the analogy's shortcomings. The grocery business could exist without state participation; the state's licensing function is used only for consumer protection. Lawyers, by contrast, retail a commodity manufactured by the state: law. They have, moreover, been granted a monopoly on it, in the several ways we have already examined: through unauthorized practice regulations, through the fashioning of laws and regulations, through the erection of a professionalized system designed in large part around the needs of the law retailers. The adversary system itself is predicated on the monopoly of lawyers.

This is the difference between the lawyer and the grocer: the lawyer's lucrative monopoly would not exist without the community and its state; the monopoly and indeed the product it monopolizes is an artifact of the community. The community has shaped the lawyer's retail product with her in mind; it has made the law to make the lawyer indispensible. The community, as a consequence, has the right to condition its handiwork on the recipients of the monopoly fulfilling the monopoly's legitimate purpose.

The only legitimate purpose of the system of law retailing is expressed in our slogan: Equal Justice Under Law. Without equal justice under law, we have seen, the system has no legitimacy, and the legal profession's lucrative monopoly on retailing law should be broken.

For law practice is not a victimless pastime. It is an adversarial profession, and those who can't afford it are often damaged by those who can. One day spent in housing court, watching landlords' lawyers winning against unrepresented poor people who may have had defenses if only they had had lawyers, can convince anyone of that. Even when the result is defensible, as it sometimes is, the mismatch is a scandal — it is an instance of what Judge [Lois] Forer has denounced as "apartheid justice."

Even an office practice that on the face of it has no adversaries may harm the legally disempowered. . . . [T]he law allows us to do many things we couldn't do otherwise. When lawyers secure these advantages for their clients, safeguarding their interests against a range of potential dangers and adversaries, they change the face of society. They set up a network of social practices from which the poor are, willy-nilly, excluded.

This is a second way in which the grocer analogy breaks down. The grocer does not make the hungry worse off by selling to the cash customer; grocery retailing is not an adversarial profession. But law retailing is.

G.   SYNDICATING LAWSUITS

I have a potential $50 million antitrust claim against Oligop, Inc. My chances of recovery are 70 percent. But Oligop has 500 lawyers on staff and six of the mightiest outside law firms. I have no one and no appreciable funds. That reduces my chances of recovery to near zero. I shop around. Some lawyers are unwilling to take my case on a contingency, given the time required; others would take it on a partial contingency and a reduced hourly rate. The few who will take it on full contingency are inexperienced in antitrust. No one is willing to put up the $2 million in out-of-pocket costs needed to prosecute the claim.

So, I figure, why not syndicate my claim? If I can find 500 people to put up $10,000 each, I will have $5 million to litigate a $50 million claim. If you discount the claim by the risk of nonrecovery (or 30 percent), it's worth $35 million in settlement, but only if Oligop is convinced I can litigate. Investors stand to earn several times what they invest. Actually, this is not all that much different from a class action, is it, except that I'm creating the class and charging an entrance fee for membership? But is this any way to fund a lawsuit?

Courts have divided on whether to permit syndicated lawsuits to proceed. Killian v. Millard, 228 Cal. App. 3d 1601, 279 Cal. Rptr. 877 (1991), overruled a trial court's invalidation of a syndication agreement without reaching the merits of the validity of the agreement. The court held that the opposing party lacked standing to challenge the agreement and that the court could not invalidate it under its supervisory powers.

By contrast, in Refac International v. Lotus Development Corp., 131 F.R.D. 56 (S.D.N.Y. 1990), the court reviewed a licensing agreement under which the plaintiff acquired a 5 percent interest in a patent in exchange for a promise to sue alleged infringers and fund the lawsuit. The court held that plaintiff was not the "real party in interest" and that the agreement violated New York's champerty law, a codification of the common law rule forbidding persons to accept assignments of claims for the purpose of suing on them. See N.Y. Judic. Law §489. While this might have been literally so, the larger question is whether there should be such laws in the first place. Or whether there should be exceptions that permit underfinanced plaintiffs to proceed by selling interests in their action. Champerty and the allied concepts of barratry and maintenance mean to prevent stirring up of litigation on the ground that litigation is an evil to be discouraged. Contrast Justice White's view in Zauderer v. Office of Disciplinary Counsel, page 796 infra. For more on champerty, see page 723 infra.

Syndication of lawsuits is still too new a phenomenon to permit generalization. Cases like *Refac* may ensure that it will not be a growing one. But what is wrong with syndication? We all know that the ability to finance a claim or defense can make a great difference in the fact or size of a victory. In court, as elsewhere, money equals credibility. Why shouldn't willing investors be able to pool their resources? What issues of legal ethics do such syndications or assignments raise? Of public policy? For further reading, see Daniel Cox, Lawsuit Syndication: An Investment Opportunity in Legal Grievances, 35 St. Louis U.L.J. 1 (1990); Roy Simon, Lawsuit Syndication: Buying Stock in Justice, 69 Bus. & Soc. Rev. 10 (1989).

investing in π's??
"stock" market for lawsuits

H.   WHO GETS THE MONEY?

When a sole practitioner gets paid, there's not much trouble deciding who gets the money. Many lawyers, however, practice in firms whose sizes range between two and more than a thousand lawyers. These firms must decide how to divide their profits (see below). Sometimes lawyers affiliate to handle a single case. Or one lawyer may refer a matter to another lawyer. As we shall see below, ethics codes have traditionally restricted fee-sharing among lawyers who are not in the same firm. (Lawyers have been forbidden to share legal fees with lay people under almost all circumstances. See page 711 infra.) The restrictions against splitting fees outside a firm make it important to be able to identify a "firm." That task has not usually been hard, but it may be getting harder.

Dividing Money Within a Firm

The last two decades have seen marked growth in the number of consultants, books, and articles dedicated to the elusive art of "law office management." Among management issues is how to divide a firm's profits fairly and with as little resentment as possible. For our purposes, it is worth noting that virtually no ethical rule guides or limits how profits are divided within a firm. As a practical matter, however, many firms tend to reward the same contributions. Partnership shares are generally divided according to formulas that recognize partners who bring in more clients (or whose clients pay higher fees) and partners who bill more hours. Seniority often carries some indpendent weight. For a partner to benefit from bringing in a client, she need not work on the client's matter. In fact, law firm partners may be handsomely rewarded merely for bringing clients to the firm ("rainmakers"), though they may actually do little legal work.

Partners also make money from associate time. The rule of thumb is that associate time is billed at an hourly rate that, when multiplied by the number of hours the associate is expected to bill yearly, will yield three times the associate's salary. If one assumes that one-third of an associate's billings is spent to support the associate (space, secretary), it leaves one-third of annual billings for the firm. If a firm has a partner-to-associate ratio of 1:2, which is common, each partner on average earns the equivalent of double an associate's salary from associate work, above and beyond what the partner may earn for his or her own work. This is a nice rate of return for investment in labor, one that the private market might be willing to undersell. Since nonlawyers cannot invest in law firms, Rule 5.4(b) and (d), but see page 730 infra, only lawyers can profit from the sale of the work of other lawyers. The result may be an increase in the cost of legal services. Can the increase be justified by a need to protect lawyers' "professional independence of judgment," as the comment to Rule 5.4 suggests?

Generalization beyond this point is risky and not helpful. Firms differ greatly, both from other firms and over time. As partners develop or lose significant practices their bargaining power within their firms will rise or fall, sometimes leading to major readjustments in partnership shares. Sometimes, and increasingly of late, the result may be defection of a valuable partner to another firm that promises more generous rewards and more power to direct the firm or, when a career is going downhill, a request to pack up and leave.

Partnership agreements generally define the firm income to which a departing partner is entitled and the terms for payment. Rule 5.6 and DR 2-108 prevent partnerships from conditioning entitlement to postdeparture payments on a departing lawyer's forbearance from competition with the firm. The purported justification is that such a restriction "not only limits [a lawyer's] professional autonomy, but also limits the freedom of clients to choose a lawyer." Rule 5.6 comment. Both rules would allow partnership agreements to deny departing partners a share in future profits, notwithstanding the autonomy consequences to the lawyer, as long as receipt is not conditioned on noncompetition. An exception permits noncompete conditions for retirement payments. See generally Cohen v. Lord, Day & Lord, 75 N.Y.2d 95, 550 N.E.2d 410, 551 N.Y.S.2d 157 (1989).

Division of Fees Outside Firms

Two or more lawyers who are not formally affiliated in a firm may nevertheless work together on a matter or on many matters. One lawyer may refer a client to another lawyer because the first lawyer is not skilled in the client's problem or has an inadequate support staff, or because the client needs a lawyer in a jurisdiction in which the first lawyer is not admitted. Sometimes the referring lawyer will want to work on the referred matter with the receiving lawyer and sometimes he or she will be happy never to hear about the matter again. Despite the absence of restrictions on fee divisions within firms — even to the point that a lawyer may be generously rewarded for bringing to the firm a client on whose matter the lawyer does no work at all — the ethics codes contain detailed rules about fee division by lawyers who are not in the same firm. How can this difference be explained?

Canon 34 of the Canons of Professional Ethics prohibited a division of fees among lawyers unless "based upon a division of service or responsibility." Notice that Canon 34 used the conjunction "or," so that two lawyers were permitted to divide a legal fee so long as they both worked on the matter or so long as they were both responsible for the matter.

The Code of Professional Responsibility changed this rule to require, among other things, that the fee division be "made in proportion to the services performed and responsibility assumed by each" lawyer. DR 2-107(A)(2). The use of the conjunction "and" has been taken to mean that it is not enough that one lawyer simply gets the client or agrees to be subject to liability for the other lawyer's malpractice. Both lawyers must work on the case and in some way the fee division has to be "in proportion" to their work. See, e.g., Palmer v. Breyfogle, 217 Kan. 128, 535 P.2d 955 (1975); In re Diamond, 72 N.J. 139, 368 A.2d 353 (1976).

The Model Rules partly return to the standard set by the Canons of Professional Ethics. Rule 1.5(e) allows a fee division "in proportion to the services performed by each lawyer." With the "written agreement" of the client, a fee division is also permissible if "each lawyer assumes joint responsibility for the representation." In either event, the client must be advised and not object, and the total fee must be reasonable. Possibly, as well, each lawyer's share of the fee must be "reasonable" within the meaning of Rule 1.5(a). Even before the ABA adopted the Model Rules, some courts, including in California, allowed division of fee based solely on an assumption of responsibility without rendition of services. See Moran v. Harris, 131 Cal. App. 3d 913, 182 Cal. Rptr. 519 (1982). Why do the Model Rules have any requirement before a fee can be divided? Why does the client have to be told?

In Excelsior 57th Corp. v. Lerner, 160 A.D.2d 407, 553 N.Y.S.2d 763, 764-765 (1st Dept. 1990), the board of a residential cooperative sued a board member, who was also a lawyer and a member of the board's legal committee. The defendant had recommended that the cooperative retain a particular law firm to reduce its real estate taxes. The cooperative alleged that the board member did not reveal that his own firm had an arrangement with the referred firm to split the contingent fee. The court upheld a claim for breach of fiduciary duty and fraudulent concealment. Under New York ethics rules, "[c]lient knowledge of a representation agreement between lawyers is the sine qua non of its ethical validity, as well as proof that an attorney who claims part of a legal fee must have shared, to some significant degree, the legal work entailed."*

What Is a Law Firm?

Because law firms can divide the profit pie virtually any way they like without disciplinary or judicial control, it can sometimes be attractive to be able to claim status as a firm, even if only for the passing moment. Rule 7.5(d) permits lawyers to "state or imply that they practice in a partnership or other organization only when that is the fact." DR 2-102(C) is substantially the same. This rule has two ostensible purposes. It prevents lawyers from giving clients the misimpression that they have a formal professional relationship when they do not. It also prevents lawyers from circumventing limitations on fee sharing with an unaffiliated lawyer.

In re "Agent Orange" Product Liability Litigation, 818 F.2d 216, 223-224 (2d Cir.), cert. denied, 484 U.S. 926 (1987), was a rare case in which the court was called upon to determine, among other things, whether a purported law firm was in fact a law firm. David Dean, a lawyer representing a class of Agent Orange plaintiffs, needed cash to continue expensive litigation against well-funded defendants. Six prominent

---

* New York has since amended DR 2-107 to omit this second requirement in accord with Rule 1.5(e).

personal injury lawyers promised to advance up to $200,000 each in return for three times their advance from attorneys' fees awarded to the plaintiff class. Fees remaining after these payments were to be divided according to work performed.

The district court ultimately ordered defendants to pay $4.7 million in fees. If the entire fee were distributed based on work performed, Dean would receive $1.4 million. But after the threefold return on investment, Dean would receive only $542,000. By contrast, one investor whose work would have entitled him to only $42,000 in fees would receive $513,000 under the agreement. Dean attacked the investment as unethical even though he himself had earlier solicited it. The district court rejected Dean's challenge, but the Second Circuit reversed.

The circuit court held that counsel could agree to division of a fee that is different from the court's allocation, but "the distribution of fees must bear some relationship to the services rendered." Disproportionate fee awards create "a conflict of interest between class counsel and those whom they have undertaken to represent." The court focused on the settlement process:

> The conflict obviously lies in the incentive provided to an investor-attorney to settle early and thereby avoid work for which full payment may not be authorized by the district court. Moreover, as soon as an offer of settlement to cover the promised return on investment is made, the investor-attorney will be disinclined to undertake the risks associated with continuing the litigation. The conflict was especially egregious here, since six of the nine [class counsel] were investing parties to the agreement.

The fact that the settlement was adequate did not change the analysis. "The test to be applied is whether, at the time a fee sharing agreement is reached, class counsel are placed in a position that might endanger the fair representation of their clients and whether they will be compensated on some basis other than for legal services performed."

Can you reconcile invalidation of the investment agreement, because of the identified conflict, with Justice Stevens's insistence in *Evans* that class counsel had no "ethical dilemma" because his "ethical duty was to serve his clients loyally and competently"? Can't we say the same about the lawyer-investors here?

QUESTION

4.3 "If these lawyers had been in a preexisting partnership, wealthier partners could have agreed to advance costs in exchange for the same three-fold return. The court's statement that 'the distribution of fees must bear some relationship to the services rendered' would have no bearing in a traditional firm. That means it is permissible to 'invest' in a class-action (or presumably any other) lawsuit, as long as you do it through a preexisting partnership. This is formalism. Why can't lawyers come together on an ad hoc basis to maintain a litigation? In fact, why can't any private investor claim the same right to invest in a lawsuit, as long as only lawyers make the legal decisions? (See Chapter 14.)

"One result of the court's decision is that people like Mr. Dean who run out of money to fund major litigation against deep-pocket defendants will no longer find wealthy lawyers or other investors willing to provide desperately needed help. Without the six investors in the *Agent Orange* case, the action would probably have failed for lack of funds. By rejecting the ad hoc arrangement, the court discriminates in favor of entrenched capital formations and against temporary alignments intended to achieve a single defined goal. If the goal is legal, and possibly laudable, why obstruct it?"

Part Two

CONFLICTS OF
INTEREST

V

Concurrent Conflicts of Interest

A Typology of Conflicts

Conflicts of interest are the subject of this chapter and Chapter 6. Here we review varieties of concurrent conflicts. In Chapter 6, we turn to successive conflicts. As should be apparent, one difference between the two types of conflict is temporal. Ethical rules apprehend different risks to client interests depending on whether a conflict is concurrent or successive. Although each kind of conflict creates risks to both loyalty and confidentiality, ensuring loyalty is often the primary concern of rules that prohibit concurrent conflicts, whereas protection of confidences is the dominant goal of the successive conflicts rules.

Conflict of interest dilemmas may arise in any practice and take many forms. They can confront lawyers with many clients and lawyers with only one client. They arise in private practice, in corporate law departments, in prosecutorial offices, and in government agencies. It would be a rare lawyer who never had need to measure contemplated conduct against the conflict of interest rules.

It is probably safe to say that conflicts issues present some of the most complex problems in the area of legal ethics. What's more, their complexity is increasing. Because conflicts issues are often highly fact-specific, they can rarely be resolved with generalizations. Increasingly sophisticated methods, often relying on specially designed computer programs, are utilized by larger firms (and by smaller firms in smaller communities) wishing to avoid conflict risks.

Avoiding those risks is becoming increasingly important. A lawyer caught in a conflict faces a number of unhappy possibilities. Discipline is one, although disciplinary authorities seem to recognize that the technical nature of many conflicts makes them inappropriate candidates for

171

professional sanctions. Conflicts can also lead to disqualification, with attendant embarrassment and cost, Rule 11 or similiar sanctions, delay of a client's cause, and malpractice liability.

In the introductory pages to Chapter 2 we discussed the issue of client identity. As we saw there and shall see again, whether or not there is an attorney-client relationship is not always clear. It may depend on why the question is being asked. For example, a member of a trade association represented by a law firm may not be a client of the firm for one purpose (liability for a fee) but be deemed a client for another purpose (conflicts of interest). See page 228 infra. In any event, before there can be a conflict, there must be a client or, at the very least, some person or entity that a court is prepared to treat as a client for conflict purposes.

In the following pages, we offer some introductory words on the concepts and themes that will occupy Chapters 5 and 6. We then begin our discussion of concurrent conflicts of interest.

First, let us more fully distinguish between concurrent and successive conflicts of interest. In a concurrent conflict situation, the lawyer may have loyalties divided between two or more clients. For example, a lawyer representing codefendants in a civil or criminal case may find that each wants to point the finger at the other. A lawyer representing two parties wishing to enter into a contract may find that he cannot draft a clause one way or another without disadvantaging one of his two clients. The conflict may also be more generalized. May a lawyer who routinely represents landlords represent a tenant whose case requires the lawyer to argue for a statutory construction financially disadvantageous to landlords? May a lawyer who does products liability defense for a company that manufactures consumer products represent a person who wants to sue the company for breach of an employment contract? May a lawyer who represents the Hilton Hotel in town also represent the Sheraton?

Concurrent conflicts need not be between or among concurrent clients. The lawyer may have personal interests at odds with those of a client. Can a lawyer whose spouse owns a large number of shares in a corporation represent a plaintiff wishing to sue it? Can a lawyer represent a person who wishes to challenge the legality of a tax regulation that benefits the lawyer?

These examples raise issues about the lawyer's loyalty and, to a lesser extent, protection of client confidences. The Code of Professional Responsibility uses the word "loyalty" in describing the lawyer's duty to the client. See EC 5-1. So do the Model Rules. See the comment to Rule 1.7. Canon 5 of the Model Code says that "A lawyer should exercise independent professional judgment on behalf of a client," a direction that would presumably be difficult where the lawyer is influenced by the interests of another client or another person or the lawyer's own interests.

A *second* theme running through the conflict of interest material concerns not concurrent conflicts but successive ones. The term "successive conflicts" may sound self-contradictory. Consider: a lawyer represents client *A* in defending the legality of a patent. The lawyer is successful. Later, the lawyer is retained by client *B* to sue client *A* on the ground that the very same patent is illegal. At the time client *B* enters the picture, what is the lawyer's obligation to his former client *A*? Shall we say that the duty of loyalty continues after the end of the representation? The code does not take an explicit position. The Model Rules expressly contemplate that the duty of loyalty survives the end of the relationship. See Rule 1.9 and the Comment under "Adverse Positions."

However we treat the loyalty issue, there is a further problem. The lawyer will likely have gained confidential information in the course of the representation of client *A*. If the lawyer reveals or uses this information on *B*'s behalf, he may violate DR 4-101 and Rule 1.9(c). May the lawyer represent client *B* without using the information? Or will that undermine the lawyer's duty of loyalty to client *B*? What if the lawyer claims he has discovered the same information independently? Will we have to hold a hearing to determine if indeed there was an independent source?

On the other hand, if client *B* seeks to sue former (patent) client *A* for violation of the provisions of a lease, is there any problem? Mightn't we then say that, because the nature of the representation is wholly different from the patent work that the lawyer did for *A*, the lawyer may proceed to sue his former client? Or should we have a flat prohibition against ever suing persons or entities with whom a lawyer once had a professional relationship?

The code is largely silent on successive conflict problems, although, as we shall see, the courts have interpreted various duties in the code so as to yield a rule. The Model Rules speak to successive conflicts in Rule 1.9.

Both concurrent and successive conflicts generate a *third* issue. If we conclude that a lawyer is disqualified from representing a client because of a concurrent conflict (either with the interest of another client or person or with the lawyer's own interests), shall we nevertheless allow a lawyer with whom the first lawyer is affiliated to accept the representation? In other words, shall we impute the disqualified lawyer's status to his or her partners and associates? The same question can be asked with regard to successive conflict situations. If a lawyer is forbidden to represent client *B* in a lawsuit against her former client *A*, may a partner or associate of that lawyer nevertheless accept the representation of *B*? Would your answer depend on whether the first lawyer had represented client *A* while in a different law office, and had thereafter moved to the second lawyer's firm? Sometimes the subject of "imputed disqualification" is referred to as "vicarious disqualification." Should there be imputed or vicarious disqualification? When? The code provisions dealing with imputed disqualification are DR 5-101(B), 5-102, and 5-105(D). The Model Rules cover the issue at Rules 1.9, 1.10, 1.11, 1.12, and 3.7.

A *fourth* issue is the special case presented by the government lawyer who leaves to join a private firm. Shall he or she personally be treated exactly like the lawyer who leaves one private firm to join another? Shall the new firms in each instance be treated exactly the same with regard to imputed disqualification? Consider a lawyer who works for the Justice Department investigating antitrust violations in the automobile industry. He spends two years looking into QRS Motors. Eventually he joins a firm. At the firm, may he represent a competitor of QRS that wants to sue QRS for antitrust violations? If he may not do so, may the firm do so? Alternatively, if QRS comes to the firm seeking representation when it is charged with antitrust violations (by the government or a competitor), may the former government lawyer defend it? Again, if the answer is no, may the firm do so? One sentence of the code speaks to the issue of whether the former government lawyer may represent either QRS or the competitor once in private practice. See DR 9-101(B). As to whether the firm may do so even if the former government lawyer may not, that depends on how broadly we read DR 5-105(D). Rule 1.11 contains the Model Rules' treatment of these issues.

A *fifth* and final problem is one that arises when a lawyer for a client in a litigation will or should be a witness, called either by the client or the opposing side. DR 5-101(B) and DR 5-102 both speak to this issue and to the related one of imputed disqualification. So does Rule 3.7. This so-called advocate-witness rule seeks to avoid a conflict between the lawyer's interest in being an advocate and the interest of the client or the adversary in having the lawyer testify.

As you think about the conflict issues raised in this and the next chapter, remember that these rules, especially those dealing with client-client conflicts, will have a significant effect on the nature and growth of a lawyer's practice. The broader the rules, the greater the number of matters that a lawyer or the lawyer's firm will be forbidden to accept and the greater the number of clients who will be denied counsel of choice. The narrower the rules, the less protection to those clients who may suffer (or believe they will suffer) in the event of a breach of confidentiality or an act of disloyalty.

A. ATTORNEY-CLIENT CONFLICTS

1. *Business Interests*

GOLDMAN v. KANE
3 Mass. App. Ct. 336, 329 N.E.2d 770 (1975)

[The client, Hill, a law school graduate but not a lawyer, needed funds to purchase a boat on which he had already made a down payment. His lawyer, Kane, offered to lend $30,000, through a company Kane controlled, but required that Hill transfer to Kane certain real and personal property and secure the loan with a mortgage on the boat. Having offered the loan, Kane then urged Hill not to accept it, but Hill insisted. Subsequently, the attorney sold the real and personal property, earning about $50,000 and, after the client was unable to repay the loan, seized the boat. Hill's estate thereafter sued Kane and his company for their profits. Judgment for the plaintiff and the defendants appealed.]

The defendants argue that even if an attorney-client relationship existed the record does not support the conclusion that there was a breach of that relationship. We disagree. The relationship of attorney and client is highly fiduciary in nature. "Unflinching fidelity to their genuine interests is the duty of every attorney to his clients. Public policy hardly can touch matters of more general concern than the maintenance of an untarnished standard of conduct by the attorney at law toward his client."

The law looks with great disfavor upon an attorney who has business dealings with his client which result in gains to the attorney at the expense of the client. "The attorney is not permitted by the law to take any advantage of his client. The principles holding the attorney to a conspicuous degree of faithfulness and forbidding him to take personal advantage of his client are thoroughly established." When an attorney bargains with his client in a business transaction in a manner which is advantageous to himself, and if that transaction is later called into question, the court will subject it to close scrutiny. In such a case, the attorney has the burden of showing that the transaction "was in all respects fairly and equitably conducted; that he fully and faithfully discharged all his duties to his client, not only by refraining from any misrepresentation or concealment of any material fact, but by active diligence to see that his client was fully informed of the nature and effect of the transaction proposed and of his own rights and interests in the subject matter involved, and by seeing to it that his client either has independent advice in the matter or else receives from the attorney such advice as the latter would have been expected to give had the transaction been one between his client and a stranger."

Applying these principles to the case at bar, it is clear that the judge was correct in concluding that Kane, by entering into the transaction, breached his fiduciary duty to Hill. While the defendants contend that Kane's conduct did not constitute a breach of his fiduciary duty because Hill fully understood the nature and effect of the transaction and because Kane advised Hill against it, in the circumstances of this case, Kane's full disclosure and his advice were not sufficient to immunize him from liability. The fundamental unfairness of the transaction and the egregious overreaching by Kane in his dealings with Hill are self-evident. In light of the nature of the transaction, Kane, at a bare minimum, was under a duty not to proceed with the loan until he was satisfied that Hill had obtained independent advice on the matter. The purpose of such requirement is to be certain that in a situation where an attorney deals with a client in a business relationship to the attorney's advantage, the "presumed influence resulting from the relationship has been neutralized.". . .

[Affirmed.]

A Lawyer's Financial Interests

Deals with Clients.   Suspicion of business deals between attorneys and clients, reflected in Rule 1.8(a) and DR 5-104(A), is a product of the same factors that lead courts to scrutinize post-retainer fee agreements (see page 110 supra). After payment of a retainer, the client and attorney have a fiduciary relationship. The client will probably have come to depend on the attorney and to assume that the attorney is protecting the client's interest. The attorney may have had access to client confidences that give the attorney an advantage. In short, clients are not likely to see postretainer deals as being at "arm's length" and neither do the courts.

Court scrutiny generally depends upon the existence of a client-lawyer relationship (see pages 13 and 227). Deals between lawyers and persons who are not their clients are not subject to Rule 1.8(a) or DR 5-104(A), although they might be subject to scrutiny if the two have a fiduciary relationship for other reasons. See Stainton v. Tarantino, 637 F. Supp. 1051 (E.D. Pa. 1986). Further, a lawyer who enters a business deal is bound to observe the general dictates of the ethics code even though he is not acting as a lawyer at the time. In re Imming, 131 Ill. 2d 239, 545 N.E.2d 715 (1989) (even absent attorney-client relationship, lawyer "may be subject to discipline . . . for any act that evidences an absence of professional or personal honesty that renders him unworthy of public confidence"). See the discussion at page 674 infra.

When a client challenges the fairness of a transaction entered into with an attorney after the formation of the attorney-client relationship, courts generally require the attorney to prove that the transaction was just and equitable. Some courts presume that the transaction was the product of undue influence unless the lawyer proves otherwise. See, e.g., Odorizzi v. Bloomfield School District, 246 Cal. App. 2d 123, 54 Cal. Rptr. 533 (1966) (thorough discussion of undue influence); Committee on Professional Ethics v. Mershon, 316 N.W.2d 895, 897-898 (Iowa 1982). In Gerlach v. Donnelly, 98 So. 2d 493 (Fla. 1957), the court held that when a client conveys a property right to an attorney, the attorney has the burden of proving by clear and convincing evidence that the transaction was fair and made for full and adequate consideration.

Rule 1.8(a)(2) prohibits certain transactions between a lawyer and a client unless the client is "given a reasonable opportunity to seek the advice of independent counsel," but does not say that the lawyer must advise the client to seek independent counsel, although the comment says that such review "is often advisable." Can you imagine how Rule 1.8(a)(2) can be satisfied without the lawyer advising the client to seek independent counsel? Compare California Rule 3-300(B), which, unlike the Model Rule, requires the lawyer to advise the client "in writing that the client may seek the advice of an independent lawyer of the client's choice." In Pollock v. Marshall, 391 Mass. 543, 462 N.E.2d 312 (1984), the court recognized the value of independent counsel in rebutting any presumption of undue influence, but declined to create a per se rule requiring a lawyer to suggest independent counsel in every case.

Scrutiny of client-lawyer business deals extends to agreements by which the parties withdraw or settle the differences between them. In K.M.A. Associates v. Meros, 452 So. 2d 580 (Fla. App. 1984), rev. dismissed, 464 So. 2d 555 (Fla. 1985), the client challenged an agreement ending a business relationship with former counsel. Counsel relied on a release contained in the agreement. The court held that the defendant lawyer had to prove the fairness of the entire agreement by clear and convincing evidence. All doubts would be resolved in favor of the client. In Abrams, Kisseloff & Kissin v. 160 Bleecker St. Associates, 67 A.D.2d 629, 412 N.Y.S.2d 19, 21 (1st Dept. 1979), the unrepresented client agreed that if the law firm sued for its fee, the client would not be entitledto assert a set-off or counterclaim. The firm sued. The court held that the client's agreement would not be enforced unless former counsel could "establish absence of fraud . . . and that all the terms were fully understood by the client."

Interests Adverse to Clients. The cases so far have addressed a lawyer's financial arrangements with clients. But there are limits too on a lawyer's financial interests with others if these could compromise the lawyer's loyalty to clients. California Rule 3-300, like Rule 1.8(a), forbids a lawyer to "knowingly acquire an ownership, possessory, security or other pecuniary interest adverse to a client," unless certain preconditions are satisfied. See Hawk v. State Bar of California, 45 Cal. 3d 589, 754 P.2d 1096, 247 Cal. Rptr. 599 (1988). Was this principle violated by the following events? A lawyer, call him Gus, represented a wife in a divorce action. The husband's main asset was an apartment building. Gus obtained a court order preventing the husband from selling or encumbering the building. The husband's lawyer, call her Jill, told Gus that if the building could be sold for at least $3 million, the husband would pay his wife $200,000 of the proceeds as part of the divorce settlement. And if Gus located the purchaser, he would get a finder's fee. Informing the wife of none of this, Gus began to seek a buyer. That's Act One. Any problem so far?

In Act Two, still without the wife's knowledge, Gus found a buyer to take the building for about $3.5 million. He negotiated a finder's fee of

$117,500, which he collected at closing. He made no effort to prevent the closing or to protect the wife's interest in the proceeds. The husband absconded with the proceeds, and although the wife eventually obtained a divorce judgment of $436,000, she collected nothing.

In Act Three, based on his behavior in both Act One and Act Two, the court suspended Gus for three years. Matter of Apostle, 169 A.D.2d 80, 571 N.Y.S.2d 820 (2d Dept. 1991).

2. Media Rights

Rule 1.8(d) and DR 5-104(B) forbid lawyers to acquire publicity rights to a story based on the subject of the representation before its conclusion. Why should acquisition of media or publicity rights in a matter create a potential conflict between client and attorney? Consider a lawyer retained to represent a defendant in a celebrated case, for example the trial of Patty Hearst for bank robbery. The lawyer agrees that all or part of his fee will be exclusive rights to the defendant's story, which the lawyer plans to write about or sell to the movies. What's wrong with that?

Clients who assign rights to their lawyers tend to be criminal defendants, possibly because the media are more interested in the stories behind celebrated criminal trials. If the defendant is convicted, she may seek to vacate the conviction on the ground that the lawyer's possession of the media rights created an impermissible conflict of interest. Why should that be? While courts acknowledge that the lawyer may have had a *potential* conflict of interest, this will be insufficient to bring relief unless the conflict became actual and affected the lawyer's performance. (The lawyer is still subject to discipline.) Clients are usually unable to meet this burden of proof. United States v. Marrera, 768 F.2d 201 (7th Cir. 1985), cert. denied, 475 U.S. 1020 (1986); United States v. Hearst, 638 F.2d 1190 (9th Cir. 1980), cert. denied, 451 U.S. 938 (1981) (Patty Hearst).

Maxwell v. Superior Court, 30 Cal. 3d 606, 639 P.2d 248, 255-257, 180 Cal. Rptr. 177 (1982), held that a criminal defendant has a due process right to promise counsel the media rights to his story if the defendant knowingly waives the consequent potential conflict. The "mere possibility of a conflict does not warrant pretrial removal of competent counsel in a criminal case over defendant's informed objection." The 19-page retainer agreement purported to spell out all potential conflicts. The court concluded that the petitioner "was competent to waive his rights." It cited a "psychiatric evaluation" and a record that "suggests neither mental nor emotional incapacity."

Do you agree with this holding? The defendant in *Maxwell* was charged with the murder of 10 Skid Row residents in Los Angeles in 1978-1979. While in jail awaiting trial, he allegedly "told a fellow inmate he committed the murders to procure souls for Satan." New York Times, Nov. 14, 1983.

The *Maxwell* court did not explicitly rely on the Sixth Amendment, although it did rely on United States Supreme Court cases that construe the federally guaranteed right to counsel. Its analysis might therefore appear undercut by the Supreme Court's subsequent opinion in Wheat v. United States, 486 U.S. 153 (1988) (page 194 infra), except that California law has been held to afford greater protection to a criminal defendant's informed waiver of conflicted counsel. Alcocer v. Superior Court, 206 Cal. App. 3d 951, 254 Cal. Rptr. 72 (1988) (distinguishing *Wheat*).

Nothing prevents a private lawyer from negotiating media rights with a client after the representation has ended. Should the same rule apply to a prosecutor? In New York Opinion 606 (1990), an assistant district attorney prosecuted a homicide case to conviction. A national magazine thereafter wrote about the victim's life, sparking television and movie interest in the case. An agent then sought to purchase "lifetime media rights to [the prosecutor's] life so that [she] can be developed as a major character in the story." The opinion states that the prosecutor could not sell the rights to her life prior to the conclusion of the case because of "possible conflicts of interest" between "the lawyer's economic motivation" and her "undivided loyalty to her client." However, once the criminal case has ended, "the potential conflict . . . disappears." Do you agree? If the case was celebrated, isn't there a risk that the prosecutor's decisions will be influenced by her wish to sell the story later on?

3. *Financial Assistance and Proprietary Interests*

Contingent fees (page 112 supra) give a lawyer a direct interest in the client's cause, yet they are allowed (though regulated), often on the ground that less wealthy clients would not otherwise be able to afford to retain a lawyer. Other provisions of the code and rules, however, place strict limits on the ability of a lawyer to have other kinds of direct or indirect interests in a client's case. Why is that?

Consider court costs and other litigation expenses, which can be high. Can a lawyer advance these? Must the client repay them? DR 5-103(B) permits a lawyer to advance the costs of litigation and related expenses as long as the client remains ultimately liable for these. But Rule 1.8(e) allows the lawyer to make repayment contingent on the outcome of the matter and to do away with repayment entirely if the client is indigent. The rule's changes reflect the realities of practice. An ABA opinion earlier construed DR 5-103(B)'s requirement that the client remain ultimately liable for the costs of litigation not to apply to legal aid practices. ABA Informal Opinion 1361 (1976). Neither the code nor the Model

Rules permit a lawyer to advance more than court costs and the expenses of litigation. Both exclude living or medical expenses. Connecticut Opinion 90-3 declares that there is no "humanitarian exception" to the prohibition against advancing living expenses. Early drafts of the Model Rules would have permitted lawyers to advance "reasonable and necessary medical and living expenses, the repayment of which may be contingent on the outcome of the matter." Rule 1.8(e), May 1981 draft.

In In re Brown, 298 Or. 285, 692 P.2d 107 (1984), a lawyer was suspended from practice. One of the charges upheld against him was that he advanced $361 to a client, an accident victim, for living expenses in violation of DR 5-103(B). By so doing, he allegedly acquired a forbidden interest in the subject matter of the litigation. What risks did Brown's loan create that are not already present when lawyers work on a contingent fee or when they advance the expenses of litigation, both of which are permitted?

Permitting lawyers to advance living costs would enable poorer plaintiffs to endure the procedural (and time-consuming) maneuvers of wealthy defendants, who might use delay to win a favorable settlement. The code and rules, as we shall see (page 378 infra), are half-hearted about discouraging dilatory tactics. How, then, can they properly deny the frequent victims of those tactics the remedy of borrowing from their lawyers in order to withstand the tactics? It must be that the risks of even small loans are large, but what are they?

One answer appears in Maryland Attorney Grievance Commission v. Kandel, 317 Md. 274, 563 A.2d 387, 390 (1989). A lawyer was publicly reprimanded for giving a client money to travel to a medical treatment facility. The court wrote that the rule

> is directed at avoiding the acquisition of an interest in litigation through financial assistance to a client. An important public policy interest is to avoid unfair competition among lawyers on the basis of their expenditures to clients. Clients shoud not be influenced to seek representation based on the ease with which monies can be obtained, in the form of advancements, from certain law firms or attorneys.

What do you think of this policy? California addresses it differently. California Rule 4-210(A)(2) states that a lawyer may not "pay or agree to pay . . . the personal or business expenses of a prospective or existing client, except that this rule shall not prohibit [a lawyer] [a]fter employment, from lending money to the client upon the client's promise in writing to repay such loan."

Does the prohibition against financial interests apply to commercial clients? D.C. Opinion 179 (1987) declared that it was not unethical for a lawyer to acquire a small stock or partnership interest in a company the lawyer represented in an application for a government license. Because the stock interest would have no value unless the government application was approved, the interest was like a contingent fee and proper as long as reasonable. By contrast, a patent attorney asked the same committee if he could accept all rights to a patent as security for his fee in prosecuting a patent application. The rights would be reassigned to the client after payment of the fee. In Opinion 195 (1988), the committee said no. Because the client's liability here was not contingent on the success of the application, the lawyer would be receiving a "proprietary interest" in the patent in violation of DR 5-103(A) and no exception would apply. Do these distinctions make sense?

Class actions under Rule 23 of the Federal Rules of Civil Procedure generally require huge cash investments to prosecute. Very few clients would be willing to serve as a class representative if they were required to accept ultimate responsibility for these expenditures regardless of the outcome of the case. Yet DR 5-103(B), though not Rule 1.8(e), requires the client to remain ultimately liable for the costs of litigation. In Rand v. Monsanto Co., 926 F.2d 596 (7th Cir. 1991), the court labeled the Disciplinary Rule a "relic of the rules against champerty and barratry" that was "inconsistent with Rule 23 and therefore may not be applied to class actions."

4. Fee-Payor Interests

Lawyers may sometimes get paid by one person to represent another person. Rules 1.8(f), 5.4(c), and DR 5-107(A)(1) permit this under certain circumstances. The client must consent to the arrangement; the payor must not interfere with the lawyer's "independence of professional judgment or with the client-lawyer relationship"; and the lawyer must protect the client's confidences. Whether or not the fee payor is considered a client of the lawyer along with the person for whom the lawyer performs the service, the lawyer should be aware, and make the fee payor aware, that the fact and amount of the payment will not likely be privileged. (See page 38 supra.)

Sometimes this "triangular" relationship can create conflicts between the interests of the payor and the person for whom services are being rendered. (See also page 236 infra.) In Wood v. Georgia, 450 U.S. 261, 268-271 (1981), the petitioners were sentenced to jail after failing to pay fines imposed following their conviction for distributing obscene materials. The petitioners' lawyer was hired and paid by their employer. Although certiorari had been granted to review the constitutionality of incarcerating persons unable to pay a fine, the Court declined to pass on this issue after it became apparent that the employer's interest in litigating the question may have conflicted with the defendants' interests in avoiding the huge fines required to preserve the issue. The Court said:

> Courts and commentators have recognized the inherent dangers that arise when a criminal defendant is represented by a lawyer hired and paid by a third party, particularly when the third party is the operator of the alleged criminal enterprise. One risk is that the lawyer will prevent his client from obtaining leniency by preventing the client from offering testimony against his former employer or from taking other actions contrary to the employer's interest. Another kind of risk is present where, as here, the party paying the fees may have had a long-range interest in establishing a legal precedent and could do so only if the interests of the defendants themselves were sacrificed. . . .
>
> Where a constitutional right to counsel exists, our Sixth Amendment cases hold that there is a correlative right to representation that is free from conflicts of interest. Here, petitioners were represented by their employer's lawyer, who may not have pursued their interests single-mindedly. It was his duty originally at sentencing and later at the revocation hearing, to seek to convince the court to be lenient. On the record before us, we cannot be sure whether counsel was influenced in his basic strategic decisions by the interests of the employer who hired him. If this was the case, the due process rights of petitioners were not respected at the revocation hearing, or at earlier stages of the proceedings below.

The court vacated the judgment of conviction and remanded for determination of whether a conflict of interest "actually existed."

5.   Other Lawyer Interests

Three other areas ripe for client-lawyer conflicts deserve mention. One is where the lawyer may have criminal (or civil) exposure on the very matter in which he or she is representing the client. United States v. Cancilla, 725 F.2d 867, 870 (2d Cir. 1984), presents one stark example of professional conflict. There, the court reversed a criminal conviction where, unknown to the defendant, his trial counsel may have himself engaged in criminal activity related to the conduct for which the defendant was on trial. Trial counsel had a conflict of interest because "a vigorous defense might uncover evidence or prompt testimony revealing his own crimes." The court pointed out that in fact this concern might have caused trial counsel to back off from a particular line of questioning.

Government of Virgin Islands v. Zepp, 748 F.2d 125, 136 (3d Cir. 1984), reversed a conviction for possession of cocaine and destruction of evidence where the defense lawyer was alone with the defendant in the premises in which the cocaine was allegedly present and then flushed down a toilet. Defense counsel agreed to stipulate that he had not flushed anything down the toilet. Why would he do that? How did the stipulation, which was read to the jury, harm the client? The court held that because the lawyer was "potentially liable for aiding and abetting or encouraging the destruction of evidence" and, in any event, "could have faced severe disciplinary consequences," he had an actual conflict of interest that denied Zepp her Fifth and Sixth Amendment rights. The stipulation further denied Zepp her right of cross-examination. Why?

For other cases in which a lawyer's legal exposure required disqualification, sometimes over client objection, see United States v. Reeves, 892 F.2d 1223 (5th Cir. 1990); United States v. Arrington, 867 F.2d 122 (2d Cir., cert. denied, 493 U.S. 817 (1989); Matter of Kern, — Ind. — , 555 N.E.2d 479 (1990) (lawyer must withdraw when client is offered immunity to testify against lawyer).

Next are personal conflicts that arise when the lawyers on opposite sides of a matter are related. Can two brothers represent opponents in a civil case? Can Mr. Jones represent a plaintiff while his wife's firm (but not his wife personally) represents the defendant? The Model Code doesn't address the issue. The Model Rules allow lawyers who are related as "parent, child, sibling or spouse" to represent direct adversaries if the clients consent after consultation. Rule 1.8(i). The imputed disqualification rules do not extend this disability to the partners or associates of the conflicted lawyer. See Rule 1.10(a). Client consent is therefore not necessary, although it is wise.

Michigan Opinion R-3 (1989) restates Rule 1.8(i) and extends it to lawyers in a "cohabitant relationship." The opinion also directs lawyers "in a dating relationship" to disclose if the relationship could raise questions in the minds of their clients. Finally, the opinion points out that Rule 1.7 might require disclosure and consent where a lawyer represents a client against a close relative's law firm even if the relative is not representing the opposing client. Do you see why that is so? See also Debolt v. Parker, 234 N.J. Super. 471, 560 A.2d 1323 (1988) (representation of estates of deceased husband and wife by lawyer-spouses at different firms approved with informed consent).

California Rule 3-320 requires a lawyer to reveal if "another party's lawyer" is a close relative of the lawyer, lives with her, or has "an intimate personal relationship with" her. In People v. Jackson, 167 Cal. App. 3d 829, 213 Cal. Rptr. 521 (1985), decided before this rule was adopted, the defense lawyer and prosecutor had been dating for eight months before the start of the trial and continued dating during the trial. Neither the defendant nor the judge was informed. The court reversed the conviction on the ground that the defendant had been denied the effective assistance of counsel under the state constitution. It did not address the ethical issue. In California Opinion 1984-83 the committee concluded that a public defender and a prosecutor who were married to each other could appear on opposite sides of the same case if they made full disclosure, including disclosure of the danger of the representation.

A final lawyer-client conflict situation arises where the lawyer has an intimate personal relationship with a friend or relative of the client's. (The tangential issue of attorney-client sexual relationships is discussed in the material on discipline at page 677 infra.) In Barentine v. United States, 728 F. Supp. 1241 (W.D.N.C.), aff'd, 908 F.2d 968 (1990), the court said that a defense lawyer's intimate relationship with a criminal defendant's fiancee during the representation of the defendant constituted a breach of loyalty to the client and created a potential for conflict of interest. The court imposed sanctions on the lawyer but declined to vacate the conviction. In Matter of Webster, 154 Wis. 110, 452 N.W.2d 374 (1990), a lawyer who had an extramarital affair with the wife of the lawyer's divorce client during the period of the representation was publicly reprimanded. What is the reason to condemn this conduct? Should the client be permitted to consent to the lawyer's relationship?

As we wrote at the outset, it is not possible to anticipate the multiplicity of situations in which a lawyer may have interests that conflict with his or her client's interests. We have reviewed some standard problems. A few others are described under Canon 5 and in Rule 1.8, but many are not. These are left to the general conflict of interest provisions, Rule 1.7(b) and DR 5-101(A), which proscribe representations (at least without informed consent) if the lawyer's judgment "will be or reasonably may be affected" (DR 5-101(A)) or if his "representation . . . may be materially limited" (Rule 1.7(b)).

SIMULATED CASE HISTORY

KAREN HOROWITZ

I'm a thirty-year-old fifth-year litigation associate at a large midwestern law firm. I went to law school at Berkeley, clerked for a Ninth Circuit judge, then started at my current firm. Because it is relevant to what I'm about to raise, you also have to know that I'm Jewish. I'm married and have two kids. My husband's a chemist.

I have learned a lot at my job. I have always been treated with respect and courtesy. I work with all the litigation partners. That is not to say I like everyone here equally, but that's another matter.

Two years ago, I began working on a very complicated civil case, brought by a certain southern state in state court, arising out of an alleged violation of state banking laws. The defendant is a bank holding company that our firm represents on many matters. I worked on the pleadings, discovery, evidentiary issues, motions to dismiss and for partial summary judgment, and on a challenge, on federal preemption grounds, to the constitutionality of the statute under which our client is charged. We won some and we lost some.

The case is about to go to trial in a particular county of the state that is not, to put it mildly, known for its enlightened attitudes, religious, gender, or racial. Some say it's a county that has not yet finished fighting the Civil War. There is some not insubstantial antisemitism and antiblack sentiment among the population.

Last week Blair Thomas, the head of our litigation department, told me that I would not be going down as part of the defense team. The reason: They think a Jewish woman lawyer on the defense team will prejudice the jury against our client. I was told that the client concurred in this judgment. They said it was bad enough that some of the lawyers are northerners — we also have local counsel — we couldn't afford to complicate matters by bringing me into the courtroom. I must say, Blair was quite candid. He could have made some excuse — they needed me elsewhere, for instance. I appreciate that, I guess. He said I was a valuable associate, whose work was appreciated and would be recognized at bonus time and with other important assignments. But the firm had a responsibility to its client, which came first.

Well, I think the firm has a responsibility to me too, and that's a responsibility not to exclude me from an important case — on which I've already been working for two years — because of my gender or religion. If clients don't like it, the firm shouldn't represent them. It used to be that businesses justified discrimination against this group or that by pointing to their customers. "It's not us," they'd say, "we're not prejudiced. But our customers won't work with you-name-it so what can we do?" Or: "We can hire you but we can't let you interact with the clientele."

Well, if you ask me, this is no different. The firm tells me it's not prejudiced, even its clients aren't prejudiced, it says, but someone else is and so my career gets sidetracked.

I don't know what I'm going to do about this. I don't know what I can do. But I don't buy the "our client comes first" explanation.

J. BLAIR THOMAS

I know how Karen feels. It stinks. No question about it. We would never tolerate such treatment here for any other reason but this one — our responsibility to our client. Make no mistake about it. It's not the firm that wants to exclude Karen, or even the client, which has worked with Karen on this matter and other matters for years. But we can't ignore where we're trying this case. The demographics of this county are astonishing. Most of the jurors will be fundamentalist rednecks, and the judge isn't much better. If these people don't belong to some hate group or supremacist organization, they probably have at least one friend who does.

Also, this case can cost our client between $20 million and $30 million if it goes the wrong way. Look what happened to Texaco before a local jury in Texas. They had to settle for $3 billion. I think Karen has to be reasonable. The fact is, there are situations — other cases, other states — where we'd *want* her in the courtroom because we'd expect to do better if we had a woman or a Jewish lawyer on our team. The same goes for members of other groups — racial, religious, you name it. Some cases, I want a minority right up there. Other cases, I want a woman. Other cases, I want a younger lawyer or an older lawyer, depending. Gosh, there are some courtrooms a client would have to be crazy to send in an obvious Yankee WASP like me. This courtroom is a good example. I'm not going either.

A good lawyer structures his or her trial team to appeal to the jury, or at least not to alienate it. You know it's the same thing when a firm hires local counsel. Those guys down there don't do anything but sit around, smile at the jurors, and talk in the local idiom a couple of minutes a day. Why do we — why does anyone — hire them? And we all do. It's not because they know the law. It's to curry favor with the locals.

The judge and jury are going to decide this case. We have to appeal to them whether we like their biases or not. I find those biases repulsive. But I don't count. I'm a lawyer with a client who is at serious risk. My client is my only concern whether it's a bank or a death row inmate. Karen has to understand that. Her day will come in other matters. Her career hasn't been sidetracked at all. No one blames her for not being able to continue on this case, and no decision is going to be made based on her religion or the fact that she's a gal or anything else except the quality of her work.

B.   CLIENT-CLIENT CONFLICTS

1.   Criminal Cases (Defense Lawyers)

Issues of concurrent conflicts between clients in criminal representation arise when a single lawyer represents two or more suspects or defendants. Representation can occur during the investigation of the matter (including before the grand jury), in connection with plea negotiations, at trial, or on appeal. Sometimes two partners will represent each of two defendants. See Burger v. Kemp, 483 U.S. 776 (1987) (partners are one lawyer for conflicts purposes). The conflicts issue may be raised if the defendants (or one of them) are convicted and challenge the lawyer's performance.

The conflicts issue arises in an inverted way when a defendant wants to hire a lawyer and the judge refuses to allow the lawyer to represent the defendant (often in response to an objection from the prosecution) on the ground that the lawyer has a disqualifying conflict. The defendant may assert that there is no conflict, that he is prepared to waive whatever conflict exists, and that denying him the lawyer of his choice violates the Sixth Amendment. In turn, the prosecutor will be arguing that the lawyer cannot ethically or constitutionally represent the defendant. Why is that the prosecutor's business? (Compare the California Supreme Court's decision in *Maxwell* at page 178 supra.)

We explore each of these situations with the aid of the next two cases. At this point, note that in addition to the constitutional and ethical questions that swirl around this problem, Rule 44(c) of the Federal Rules of Criminal Procedure applies in federal criminal trials. Adopted in 1979, it is set out in relevant part in Wheat v. United States (page 194 infra) and in note 10 of the following case.

CUYLER v. SULLIVAN
446 U.S. 335 (1980)

JUSTICE POWELL delivered the opinion of the Court.

The question presented is whether a state prisoner may obtain a federal writ of habeas corpus by showing that his retained defense counsel represented potentially conflicting interests.

I

Respondent John Sullivan was indicted with Gregory Carchidi and Anthony DiPasquale for the first-degree murders of John Gorey and Rita Janda. . . .

Two privately retained lawyers, G. Fred DiBona and A. Charles Peruto, represented all three defendants throughout the state proceedings that followed the indictment. Sullivan had different counsel at the medical examiner's inquest, but he thereafter accepted representation from the two lawyers retained by his codefendants because he could not afford to pay his own lawyer.[1] At no time did Sullivan or his lawyers object to the multiple representation. Sullivan was the first defendant to come to trial. The evidence against him was entirely circumstantial, consisting primarily of [a Mr.] McGrath's testimony. At the close of the Commonwealth's case, the defense rested without presenting any evidence. The jury found Sullivan guilty and fixed his penalty at life imprisonment. Sullivan's post-trial motions failed, and the Pennsylvania Supreme

---

1. DiBona and Peruto were paid in part with funds raised by friends of the three defendants. The record does not disclose the source of the balance of their fee, but no part of the money came from either Sullivan or his family.

Court affirmed his conviction by an equally divided vote. Sullivan's code-fendants, Carchidi and DiPasquale, were acquitted at separate trials. . . .

DiBona and Peruto had different recollections of their roles at the trials of the three defendants. DiBona testified that he and Peruto had been "associate counsel" at each trial. Peruto recalled that he had been chief counsel for Carchidi and DePasquale, but that he merely had assisted DiBona in Sullivan's trial. DiBona and Peruto also gave conflicting accounts of the decision to rest Sullivan's defense. DiBona said he had encouraged Sullivan to testify even though the Commonwealth had presented a very weak case. Peruto remembered that he had not "want[ed] the defense to go on because I thought we would only be exposing the [defense] witnesses for the other two trials that were coming up." Sullivan testified that he had deferred to his lawyers' decision not to present evidence for the defense. But other testimony suggested that Sullivan preferred not to take the stand because cross-examination might have disclosed an extramarital affair. Finally, Carchidi claimed he would have appeared at Sullivan's trial to rebut McGrath's testimony about Carchidi's statement at the time of the murders. . . .

[Sullivan sought release in habeas corpus. The Third Circuit ruled in his favor and the state petitioned for certiorari.]

IV

We come at last to Sullivan's claim that he was denied the effective assistance of counsel guaranteed by the Sixth Amendment because his lawyers had a conflict of interest. The claim raises two issues expressly reserved in Holloway v. Arkansas, [435 U.S. 475, 483-484 (1978)]. The first is whether a state trial judge must inquire into the propriety of multiple representation even though no party lodges an objection. The second is whether the mere possibility of a conflict of interest warrants the conclusion that the defendant was deprived of his right to counsel.

A

In *Holloway,* a single public defender represented three defendants at the same trial. The trial court refused to consider the appointment of separate counsel despite the defense lawyer's timely and repeated assertions that the interests of his clients conflicted. This Court recognized that a lawyer forced to represent codefendants whose interests conflict cannot provide the adequate legal assistance required by the Sixth Amendment. Given the trial court's failure to respond to timely objections, however, the Court did not consider whether the alleged conflict actually existed. It simply held that the trial court's error unconstitutionally endangered the right to counsel.

Holloway requires state trial courts to investigate timely objections to multiple representation. But nothing in our precedents suggests that the Sixth Amendment requires state courts themselves to initiate inquiries into the propriety of multiple representation in every case.[10] Defense counsel have an ethical obligation to avoid conflicting representations and to advise the court promptly when a conflict of interest arises during the course of trial.[11] Absent special circumstances, therefore, trial courts may assume either that multiple representation entails no conflict or that the lawyer and his clients knowingly accept such risk of conflict as may exist. Indeed, as the Court noted in *Holloway,* trial courts necessarily rely in large measure upon the good faith and good judgment of defense counsel. "An 'attorney representing two defendants in a criminal matter is in the best position professionally and ethically to determine when a conflict of interest exists or will probably develop in the course of a trial.' " Unless the trial court knows or reasonably should know that a particular conflict exists, the court need not initiate an inquiry.

Nothing in the circumstances of this case indicates that the trial court had a duty to inquire whether there was a conflict of interest. The provision of separate trials for Sullivan and his codefendants significantly reduced the potential for a divergence in their interests. No participant in Sullivan's trial ever objected to the multiple representation. DiBona's opening argument for Sullivan outlined a defense compatible with the view that none of the defendants was connected with the murders. The opening argument also suggested that counsel was not afraid to call witnesses whose testimony might be needed at the trials of Sullivan's codefendants. Finally, as the Court of Appeals noted, counsel's critical decision to rest Sullivan's defense was on its face a reasonable tactical response to the weakness of the circumstantial evidence presented by the prosecutor. On these facts, we conclude that the Sixth Amendment imposed upon the trial court no affirmative duty to inquire into the propriety of multiple representation.

10. In certain cases, proposed Federal Rule of Criminal Procedure 44(c) provides that the federal district courts "shall promptly inquire with respect to . . . joint representation and shall personally advise each defendant of his right to the effective assistance of counsel, including separate representation." See also ABA Project on Standards for Criminal Justice, Function of the Trial Judge §3.4(b) (App. Draft 1972). . . .

11. ABA Code of Professional Responsibility, DR 5-105, EC 5-15 (1976); ABA Project on Standards for Criminal Justice, Defense Function §3.5(b) (App. Draft 1971).

Seventy percent of the public defender offices responding to a recent survey reported a strong policy against undertaking multiple representation in criminal cases. Forty-nine percent of the offices responding never undertake such representation. Lowenthal, Joint Representation in Criminal Cases: A Critical Appraisal, 64 Va. L. Rev. 939, 950, and n.40 (1978). The private bar may be less alert to the importance of avoiding multiple representation in criminal cases. See Geer, Representation of Multiple Criminal Defendants: Conflicts of Interest and the Professional Responsibilities of the Defense Attorney, 62 Minn. L. Rev. 119, 152-157 (1978); Lowenthal, supra, at 961-963.

B

Holloway reaffirmed that multiple representation does not violate the Sixth Amendment unless it gives rise to a conflict of interest. Since a possible conflict inheres in almost every instance of multiple representation, a defendant who objects to multiple representation must have the opportunity to show that potential conflicts impermissibly imperil his right to a fair trial. But unless the trial court fails to afford such an opportunity, a reviewing court cannot presume that the possibility for conflict has resulted in ineffective assistance of counsel. Such a presumption would preclude multiple representation even in cases where " '[a] common defense . . . gives strength against a common attack.' " Glasser v. United States, 315 U.S. 60, 92 (1942) (Frankfurter, J., dissenting).

In order to establish a violation of the Sixth Amendment, a defendant who raised no objection at trial must demonstrate that an actual conflict of interest adversely affected his lawyer's performance. In Glasser v. United States, for example, the record showed that defense counsel failed to cross-examine a prosecution witness whose testimony linked Glasser with the crime and failed to resist the presentation of arguably inadmissible evidence. The Court found that both omissions resulted from counsel's desire to diminish the jury's perception of a codefendant's guilt. Indeed, the evidence of counsel's "struggle to serve two masters [could not] seriously be doubted." Since this actual conflict of interest impaired Glasser's defense, the Court reversed his conviction.

Dukes v. Warden, 406 U.S. 250 (1972), presented a contrasting situation. Dukes pleaded guilty on the advice of two lawyers, one of whom also represented Dukes' codefendants on an unrelated charge. Dukes later learned that this lawyer had sought leniency for the codefendants by arguing that their cooperation with the police induced Dukes to plead guilty. Dukes argued in this Court that his lawyer's conflict of interest had infected his plea. We found " 'nothing in the record . . . which would indicate that the alleged conflict resulted in ineffective assistance of counsel and did in fact render the plea in question involuntary and unintelligent.' " Since Dukes did not identify an actual lapse in representation, we affirmed the denial of habeas corpus relief.

Glasser established that unconstitutional multiple representation is never harmless error. Once the Court concluded that Glasser's lawyer had an actual conflict of interest, it refused "to indulge in nice calculations as to the amount of prejudice" attributable to the conflict. The conflict itself demonstrated a denial of the "right to have the effective assistance of counsel." 315 U.S., at 76. Thus, a defendant who shows that a conflict of interest actually affected the adequacy of his representation need not demonstrate prejudice in order to obtain relief. But until a defendant shows that his counsel actively represented conflicting interests, he has not established the constitutional predicate for his claim of ineffective assistance.

C

The Court of Appeals granted Sullivan relief because he had shown that the multiple representation in this case involved a possible conflict of interest. We hold that the possibility of conflict is insufficient to impugn a criminal conviction. In order to demonstrate a violation of his Sixth Amendment rights, a defendant must establish that an actual conflict of interest adversely affected his lawyer's performance. Sullivan believes he should prevail even under this standard. He emphasizes Peruto's admission that the decision to rest Sullivan's defense reflected a reluctance to expose witnesses who later might have testified for the other defendants. The petitioner, on the other hand, points to DiBona's contrary testimony and to evidence that Sullivan himself wished to avoid taking the stand. Since the Court of Appeals did not weigh these conflicting contentions under the proper legal standard, its judgment is vacated and the case is remanded for further proceedings consistent with this opinion.

So ordered.

JUSTICE BRENNAN, concurring [in part and in the result]. . . .

"[A] possible conflict inheres in almost every instance of multiple representation." Therefore, upon discovery of joint representation, the duty of the trial court is to ensure that the defendants have not unwittingly given up their constitutional right to effective counsel. This is necessary since it is usually the case that defendants will not know what their rights are or how to raise them. This is surely true of the defendant who may not be receiving the effective assistance of counsel as a result of conflicting duties owed to other defendants. Therefore, the trial court cannot safely assume that silence indicates a knowledgeable choice to proceed jointly. The court must at least affirmatively advise the defendants that joint representation creates potential hazards which the defendants should consider before proceeding with the representation.

Had the trial record in the present case shown that respondent made a knowing and intelligent choice of joint representation, I could accept the Court's standard for a postconviction determination as to whether respondent in fact was denied effective assistance. Where it is clear that a defendant has voluntarily chosen to proceed with joint representation, it is fair, if he later alleges ineffective assistance growing out of a conflict, to require that he demonstrate "that a conflict of interest actually affected the adequacy of his representation." Here, however, where there is no evidence that the court advised respondent about the potential for conflict or that respondent made a knowing and intelligent choice to forgo his right to separate counsel, I believe that respondent, who has shown a significant possibility of conflict, is entitled to a presumption that his representation in fact suffered. Therefore, I would remand the case to allow the petitioners an opportunity to rebut this presumption by demonstrating that respondent's representation was not actually affected by the possibility of conflict.

JUSTICE MARSHALL, concurring in part and dissenting in part. . . .

I believe . . . that whenever two or more defendants are represented by the same attorney the trial judge must make a preliminary determination that the joint representation is the product of the defendants' informed choice. I therefore agree with Mr. Justice Brennan that the trial court has a duty to inquire whether there is multiple representation, to warn defendants of the possible risks of such representation, and to ascertain that the representation is the result of the defendants' informed choice.

I dissent from the Court's formulation of the proper standard for determining whether multiple representation has violated the defendant's right to the effective assistance of counsel. The Court holds that in the absence of an objection at trial, the defendant must show "that an actual conflict of interest adversely affected his lawyer's performance." If the Court's holding would require a defendant to demonstrate that his attorney's trial performance differed from what it would have been if the defendant had been the attorney's only client, I believe it is inconsistent with our previous cases. Such a test is not only unduly harsh, but incurably speculative as well. The appropriate question under the Sixth Amendment is whether an actual, relevant conflict of interests existed during the proceedings. If it did, the conviction must be reversed. Since such a conflict was present in this case, I would affirm the judgment of the Court of Appeals. . . .

In the present case Peruto's testimony, if credited by the court, would be sufficient to make out a case of ineffective assistance by reason of a conflict of interests under even a restrictive reading of the Court's standard. In the usual case, however, we might expect the attorney to be unwilling to give such supportive testimony, thereby impugning his professional efforts. Moreover, in many cases the effects of the conflict on the attorney's performance will not be discernible from the record. It is plain to me, therefore, that in some instances the defendant will be able to show there was an actual, relevant conflict, but be unable to show that it changed his attorney's conduct. . . .

Turning Conflicts into Sixth Amendment Claims
After *Cuyler*

Cuyler was decided before Strickland v. Washington, which stated the test for determining ineffective assistance of counsel (see page 692 infra).

That test asks whether counsel's performance "was reasonable considering all the circumstances." If not, the "defendant [must] show that there is a reasonable probability that, but for counsel's unprofessional errors, the result of the proceeding would have been different." In Burger v. Kemp, 483 U.S. 776, 783 (1987), the Court joined the two cases as follows:

> We have never held that the possibility of prejudice that "inheres in almost every instance of multiple representation," justifies the adoption of an inflexible rule that would presume prejudice in all such cases. [Citing *Cuyler*.] Instead, we presume prejudice "only if the defendant demonstrates that counsel 'actively represented conflicting interests' and that 'an actual conflict of interest adversely affected his lawyer's performance.' " [Citing *Strickland* quoting *Cuyler*.]

Sullivan's travels continued for three more years. Ultimately, the Third Circuit affirmed a judgment finding ineffective assistance of counsel. Counsel's conflict led him to fail to call Carchidi, one of his other clients who was awaiting trial. The court quoted Peruto, who explained the failure to call Carchidi this way:

> Carchidi took the position of, hey, don't hurt me. If it's going to help John, yes, I'm willing to help John; but not if it's going to hurt me. So on the one hand I have to listen to John Sullivan, on the other hand I have to listen to Carchidi.

Sullivan v. Cuyler, 723 F.2d 1077, 1087 (3d Cir. 1983). Pennsylvania made a kind of proximate cause argument: If Carchidi had had separate counsel, that counsel would have advised him to assert his privilege against self-incrimination. Consequently, Sullivan was not prejudiced. The court responded: "But, as we noted earlier, a defendant need not demonstrate actual prejudice to make out a violation of his sixth amendment rights where he has already established an actual conflict of interest adversely affecting counsel's performance." Is that what the *Sullivan* majority had in mind?

Juan Ortiz was also denied the effective assistance of counsel because of a conflict. While Ortiz was awaiting trial on drug charges, his lawyer's former client (Gonzalez) told the lawyer that the drugs were his and that Ortiz was innocent. The lawyer called Gonzalez, whose testimony exonerated both Ortiz *and* Gonzalez. The lawyer did not elicit or reveal Gonzalez's confession. The New York Court of Appeals concluded that counsel had an actual conflict that

> affected the conduct of the defense. . . . On one hand, his duty to defendant required him to make what use he could of Gonzalez's testimony to exculpate defendant, but on the other hand, he was obligated to maintain Gonzalez's confidences and secrets. He therefore put Gonzalez on the stand to exculpate

defendant but in the process he elicited false testimony. An attorney not laboring under the conflict would not have made that choice. . . .

We reject the People's suggestion that defendant actually benefitted by being represented by the same attorney who represented Gonzalez, since a different attorney in all likelihood would not have obtained Gonzalez's testimony corroborating defendant's own version of events. Gonzalez's testimony was partly false, and a premise of our jury system is that jurors can detect false testimony. We are unwilling to conclude that defendant was benefitted by having perjured testimony presented on his behalf.

People v. Ortiz, 76 N.Y.2d 652, 564 N.E.2d 630, 631-634, 563 N.Y.S.2d 20 (1990).

James McConico was charged with killing Ricky Morton, his wife's brother. He hired Fred Pickard to represent him. Morton had a life insurance policy. Brenda McConico, James's wife and Ricky's widow, was a partial beneficiary. Brenda hired Pickard to represent her to recover the insurance proceeds. James' defense was self-defense. This defense required Pickard to argue that Morton was the aggressor. But the insurance policy had an exclusion clause that would have denied coverage if Morton was the aggressor. Brenda testified for the prosecution that her brother had not been the aggressor. The court concluded that Pickard had an actual conflict of interest between his obligation to defend James and his obligation to help Brenda get the insurance money. Further, the conflict "had some adverse affect on counsel's performance," including in his less than vigorous cross-examination of Brenda. James did not have to "show that the result of the trial would have been different without the conflict of interest." McConico v. State, 919 F.2d 1543, 1548 (11th Cir. 1990). Is that the standard *Sullivan* had in mind? See also Hoffman v. Leeke, 903 F.2d 280 (4th Cir. 1990) (conflict where lawyer who represented codefendants secretly negotiated a plea bargain that required one of them to testify against the other); Strouse v. Leonardo, 928 F.2d 548 (2d Cir. 1991) (hearing required to see whether habeas petitioner's counsel rendered ineffective assistance where, after unsuccessfully defending petitioner for murdering his mother, counsel sought to become executor of the mother's estate).

Compare the burden the Court imposed on Sullivan before he could escape from his conviction with the standard used below in *Wheat* to uphold disqualification. Why is the second test so much easier to meet?

WHEAT v. UNITED STATES
486 U.S. 153 (1988)

CHIEF JUSTICE REHNQUIST delivered the opinion of the Court.
The issue in this case is whether the District Court erred in

declining petitioner's waiver of his right to conflict-free counsel and by refusing to permit petitioner's proposed substitution of attorneys.

I

Petitioner Mark Wheat, along with numerous codefendants, was
charged with participating in a far-flung drug distribution conspiracy.
Over a period of several years, many thousands of pounds of marijuana
were transported from Mexico and other locations to southern California. Petitioner acted primarily as an intermediary in the distribution
ring; he received and stored large shipments of marijuana at his home,
then distributed the marijuana to customers in the region.

Also charged in the conspiracy were Juvenal Gomez-Barajas and
Javier Bravo, who were represented in their criminal proceedings by
attorney Eugene Iredale. Gomez-Barajas was tried first and was acquitted on drug charges overlapping with those against petitioner. To
avoid a second trial on other charges, however, Gomez-Barajas offered
to plead guilty to tax evasion and illegal importation of merchandise.
At the commencement of petitioner's trial, the District Court had not
accepted the plea; he was thus free to withdraw his guilty plea and proceed to trial.

Bravo, evidently a lesser player in the conspiracy, decided to forgo
trial and plead guilty to one count of transporting approximately 2400
pounds of marijuana from Los Angeles to a residence controlled by
Victor Vidal. At the conclusion of Bravo's guilty plea proceedings on August 22, 1985, Iredale notified the District Court that he had been contacted by petitioner and had been asked to try petitioner's case as well. In
response, the Government registered substantial concern about the possibility of conflict in the representation. After entertaining some initial
discussion of the substitution of counsel, the District Court instructed the
parties to present more detailed arguments the following Monday, just
one day before the scheduled start of petitioner's trial.

At the Monday hearing, the Government objected to petitioner's proposed substitution on the ground that Iredale's representation of
Gomez-Barajas and Bravo created a serious conflict of interest. The Government's position was premised on two possible conflicts. First, the District Court had not yet accepted the plea and sentencing arrangement
negotiated between Gomez-Barajas and the Government; in the event
that arrangement were rejected by the court, Gomez-Barajas would be
free to withdraw the plea and stand trial. He would then be faced with
the prospect of representation by Iredale, who in the meantime would
have acted as petitioner's attorney. Petitioner, through his participation
in the drug distribution scheme, was familiar with the sources and size of
Gomez-Barajas' income, and was thus likely to be called as a witness for
the Government at any subsequent trial of Gomez-Barajas. This scenario

would pose a conflict of interest for Iredale, who would be prevented from cross-examining petitioner and thereby from effectively representing Gomez-Barajas.

Second, and of more immediate concern, Iredale's representation of Bravo would directly affect his ability to act as counsel for petitioner. The Government believed that a portion of the marijuana delivered by Bravo to Vidal's residence eventually was transferred to petitioner. In this regard, the Government contacted Iredale and asked that Bravo be made available as a witness to testify against petitioner, and agreed in exchange to modify its position at the time of Bravo's sentencing. In the likely event that Bravo were called to testify, Iredale's position in representing both men would become untenable, for ethical proscriptions would forbid him from cross-examining Bravo in any meaningful way. By failing to do so, he would also fail to provide petitioner with effective assistance of counsel. Thus, because of Iredale's prior representation of Gomez-Barajas and Bravo and the potential for serious conflict of interest, the Government urged the District Court to reject the substitution of attorneys.

In response, petitioner emphasized his right to have counsel of his own choosing and the willingness of Gomez-Barajas, Bravo, and petitioner to waive the right to conflict-free counsel. Petitioner argued that the circumstances posited by the Government that would create a conflict for Iredale were highly speculative and bore no connection to the true relationship between the co-conspirators. If called to testify, Bravo would simply say that he did not know petitioner and had no dealings with him; no attempt by Iredale to impeach Bravo would be necessary. Further, in the unlikely event that Gomez-Barajas went to trial on the charges of tax evasion and illegal importation, petitioner's lack of involvement in those alleged crimes made his appearance as a witness highly improbable. Finally, and most importantly, all three defendants agreed to allow Iredale to represent petitioner and to waive any future claims of conflict of interest. In petitioner's view, the Government was manufacturing implausible conflicts in an attempt to disqualify Iredale, who had already proved extremely effective in representing Gomez-Barajas and Bravo.

After hearing argument from each side, the District Court noted that it was unfortunate that petitioner had not suggested the substitution sooner, rather than two court days before the commencement of trial. The Court then ruled:

> [B]ased upon the representation of the Government in [its] memorandum that the Court really has no choice at this point other than to find that an irreconcilable conflict of interest exists. I don't think it can be waived, and accordingly, Mr. Wheat's request to substitute Mr. Iredale in as attorney of record is denied.

Petitioner proceeded to trial with his original counsel and was convicted of conspiracy to possess more than 1000 pounds of marijuana with intent to distribute, in violation of 21 U.S.C. §846, and five counts of possessing marijuana with intent to distribute, in violation of §841(a)(1). . . .

II

The Sixth Amendment to the Constitution guarantees that "[i]n all criminal prosecutions, the accused shall enjoy the right . . . to have the Assistance of Counsel for his defence." . . .

The Sixth Amendment right to choose one's own counsel is circumscribed in several important respects. Regardless of his persuasive powers, an advocate who is not a member of the bar may not represent clients (other than himself) in court.[3] Similarly, a defendant may not insist on representation by an attorney he cannot afford or who for other reasons declines to represent the defendant. Nor may a defendant insist on the counsel of an attorney who has a previous or ongoing relationship with an opposing party, even when the opposing party is the Government. The question raised in this case is the extent to which a criminal defendant's right under the Sixth Amendment to his chosen attorney is qualified by the fact that the attorney has represented other defendants charged in the same criminal conspiracy.

In previous cases, we have recognized that multiple representation of criminal defendants engenders special dangers of which a court must be aware. . . .

Petitioner insists that the provision of waivers by all affected defendants cures any problems created by the multiple representation. But no such flat rule can be deduced from the Sixth Amendment presumption in favor of counsel of choice. Federal courts have an independent interest in ensuring that criminal trials are conducted within the ethical standards of the profession and that legal proceedings appear fair to all who observe them. Both the American Bar Association's Model Code of Professional Responsibility and its Model Rules of Professional Conduct, as well as the rules of the California Bar Association (which governed the attorneys in this case), impose limitations on multiple representation of clients. Not only the interest of a criminal defendant but the institutional interest in the rendition of just verdicts in criminal cases may be jeopardized by unregulated multiple representation.

For this reason, the Federal Rules of Criminal Procedure direct trial judges to investigate specially cases involving joint representation. In pertinent part, Rule 44(c) provides:

3. Our holding in Faretta v. California, 422 U.S. 806 (1975), that a criminal defendant has a Sixth Amendment right to represent *himself* if he voluntarily elects to do so, does not encompass the right to choose any advocate if the defendant wishes to be represented by counsel.

[T]he court shall promptly inquire with respect to such joint representation and shall personally advise each defendant of his right to the effective assistance of counsel, including separate representation. Unless it appears that there is good cause to believe no conflict of interest is likely to arise, the court shall take such measures as may be appropriate to protect each defendant's right to counsel.

Although Rule 44(c) does not specify what particular measures may be taken by a district court, one option suggested by the Notes of the Advisory Committee is an order by the court that the defendants be separately represented in subsequent proceedings in the case. . . .

To be sure, this need to investigate potential conflicts arises in part from the legitimate wish of District Courts that their judgments remain intact on appeal. As the Court of Appeals accurately pointed out, trial courts confronted with multiple representations face the prospect of being "whip-sawed" by assertions of error no matter which way they rule. If a district court agrees to the multiple representation, and the advocacy of counsel is thereafter impaired as a result, the defendant may well claim that he did not receive effective assistance. On the other hand, a district court's refusal to accede to the multiple representation may result in a challenge such as petitioner's in this case. Nor does a waiver by the defendant necessarily solve the problem, for we note, without passing judgment on, the apparent willingness of Courts of Appeals to entertain ineffective assistance claims from defendants who have specifically waived the right to conflict-free counsel.

Thus, where a court justifiably finds an actual conflict of interest, there can be no doubt that it may decline a proffer of waiver, and insist that defendants be separately represented. . . .

Unfortunately for all concerned, a district court must pass on the issue of whether or not to allow a waiver of a conflict of interest by a criminal defendant not with the wisdom of hindsight after the trial has taken place, but in the murkier pretrial context when relationships between parties are seen through a glass, darkly. The likelihood and dimensions of nascent conflicts of interest are notoriously hard to predict, even for those thoroughly familiar with criminal trials. It is a rare attorney who will be fortunate enough to learn the entire truth from his own client, much less be fully apprised before trial of what each of the Government's witnesses will say on the stand. A few bits of unforeseen testimony or a single previously unknown or unnoticed document may significantly shift the relationship between multiple defendants. These imponderables are difficult enough for a lawyer to assess, and even more difficult to convey by way of explanation to a criminal defendant untutored in the niceties of legal ethics. Nor is it amiss to observe that the willingness of an attorney to obtain such waivers from his clients may bear an inverse relation to the care with which he conveys all the necessary information to them.

For these reasons we think the District Court must be allowed substantial latitude in refusing waivers of conflicts of interest not only in those rare cases where an actual conflict may be demonstrated before trial, but in the more common cases where a potential for conflict exists which may or may not burgeon into an actual conflict as the trial progresses. In the circumstances of this case, with the motion for substitution of counsel made so close to the time of trial, the District Court relied on instinct and judgment based on experience in making its decision. We do not think it can be said that the court exceeded the broad latitude which must be accorded it in making this decision. Petitioner of course rightly points out that the government may seek to "manufacture" a conflict in order to prevent a defendant from having a particularly able defense counsel at his side; but trial courts are undoubtedly aware of this possibility, and must take it into consideration along with all of the other factors which inform this sort of a decision.

Here the District Court was confronted not simply with an attorney who wished to represent two coequal defendants in a straightforward criminal prosecution; rather, Iredale proposed to defend three conspirators of varying stature in a complex drug distribution scheme. The Government intended to call Bravo as a witness for the prosecution at petitioner's trial.[4] The Government might readily have tied certain deliveries of marijuana by Bravo to petitioner, necessitating vigorous cross-examination of Bravo by petitioner's counsel. Iredale, because of his prior representation of Bravo, would have been unable ethically to provide that cross-examination.

Iredale had also represented Gomez-Barajas, one of the alleged kingpins of the distribution ring, and had succeeded in obtaining a verdict of acquittal for him. Gomez-Barajas had agreed with the Government to plead guilty to other charges, but the District Court had not yet accepted the plea arrangement. If the agreement were rejected, petitioner's probable testimony at the resulting trial of Gomez-Barajas would create an ethical dilemma for Iredale from which one or the other of his clients would likely suffer.

Viewing the situation as it did before trial, we hold that the District Court's refusal to permit the substitution of counsel in this case was within its discretion and did not violate petitioner's Sixth Amendment rights. Other district courts might have reached differing or opposite conclusions with equal justification, but that does not mean that one conclusion was "right" and the other "wrong." The District Court must recognize a presumption in favor of petitioner's counsel of choice, but that

---

4. Bravo was in fact called as a witness at petitioner's trial. His testimony was elicited to demonstrate the transportation of drugs that the prosecution hoped to link to petitioner.

presumption may be overcome not only by a demonstration of actual conflict but by a showing of a serious potential for conflict. The evaluation of the facts and circumstances of each case under this standard must be left primarily to the informed judgment of the trial court.

The judgment of the Court of Appeals is accordingly affirmed.

JUSTICE MARSHALL, with whom JUSTICE BRENNAN joins, dissenting. . . .

The Court's resolution of the instant case flows from its deferential approach to the District Court's denial of petitioner's motion to add or substitute counsel; absent deference, a decision upholding the District Court's ruling would be inconceivable. Indeed, I believe that even under the Court's deferential standard, reversal is in order. The mere fact of multiple representation, as the Court concedes, will not support an order preventing a criminal defendant from retaining counsel of his choice. As this Court has stated on prior occasions, such representation will not invariably pose a substantial risk of a serious conflict of interest and thus will not invariably imperil the prospect of a fair trial. The propriety of the District Court's order thus depends on whether the Government showed that the particular facts and circumstances of the multiple representation proposed in this case were such as to overcome the presumption in favor of petitioner's choice of counsel. I believe it is clear that the Government failed to make this showing. Neither Eugene Iredale's representation of Juvenal Gomez-Barajas nor Iredale's representation of Javier Bravo posed any threat of causing a conflict of interest.

At the time of petitioner's trial, Iredale's representation of Gomez-Barajas was effectively completed. As the Court notes, Iredale had obtained an acquittal for Gomez-Barajas on charges relating to a conspiracy to distribute marijuana. Iredale also had negotiated an agreement with the Government under which Gomez-Barajas would plead guilty to charges of tax evasion and illegal importation of merchandise, although the trial court had not yet accepted this plea arrangement. Gomez-Barajas was not scheduled to appear as a witness at petitioner's trial; thus, Iredale's conduct of that trial would not require him to question his former client. The only possible conflict this Court can divine from Iredale's representation of both petitioner and Gomez-Barajas rests on the premise that the trial court would reject the negotiated plea agreement and that Gomez-Barajas then would decide to go to trial. In this event, the Court tells us, "petitioner's probable testimony at the resulting trial of Gomez-Barajas would create an ethical dilemma for Iredale."

This argument rests on speculation of the most dubious kind. The Court offers no reason to think that the trial court would have rejected Gomez-Barajas's plea agreement; neither did the Government posit any such reason in its argument or brief before this Court. The most likely occurrence at the time petitioner moved to retain Iredale as his defense counsel was that the trial court would accept Gomez-Barajas's plea agreement, as the court in fact later did. Moreover, even if Gomez-Barajas had gone to trial, petitioner probably would not have testified. The record contains no indication that petitioner had any involvement in or information about crimes for which Gomez-Barajas might yet have stood trial. The only alleged connection between petitioner and Gomez-Barajas sprang from the conspiracy to distribute marijuana, and a jury already had acquitted Gomez-Barajas of that charge. It is therefore disingenuous to say that representation of both petitioner and Gomez-Barajas posed a serious potential for a conflict of interest.

Similarly, Iredale's prior representation of Bravo was not a cause for concern. The Court notes that the prosecution intended to call Bravo to the stand at petitioner's trial and asserts that Bravo's testimony could well have "necessitat[ed] vigorous cross-examination . . . by petitioner's counsel." The facts, however, belie the claim that Bravo's anticipated testimony created a serious potential for conflict. Contrary to the Court's inference, Bravo could not have testified about petitioner's involvement in the alleged marijuana distribution scheme. As all parties were aware at the time, Bravo did not know and could not identify petitioner; indeed, prior to the commencement of legal proceedings, the two men never had heard of each other. Bravo's eventual testimony at petitioner's trial related to a shipment of marijuana in which petitioner was not involved; the testimony contained not a single reference to petitioner. Petitioner's counsel did not cross-examine Bravo, and neither petitioner's counsel nor the prosecutor mentioned Bravo's testimony in closing argument. All of these developments were predictable when the District Court ruled on petitioner's request that Iredale serve as trial counsel; the contours of Bravo's testimony were clear at that time. Given the insignificance of this testimony to any matter that petitioner's counsel would dispute, the proposed joint representation of petitioner and Bravo did not threaten a conflict of interest.[3]

---

3. The very insignificance of Bravo's testimony, combined with the timing of the prosecutor's decision to call Bravo as a witness, raises a serious concern that the prosecutor attempted to manufacture a conflict in this case. The prosecutor's decision to use Bravo as a witness was an 11th-hour development. Throughout the course of plea negotiations with Bravo, the prosecutor never had suggested that Bravo testify at petitioner's trial. At Bravo's guilty-plea proceedings, when Iredale notified the District Court of petitioner's substitution motion, the prosecutor conceded that he had made no plans to call Bravo as a witness. Only after the prosecutor learned of the substitution motion and decided to oppose it did he arrange for Bravo's testimony by agreeing to recommend to the trial court a reduction in Bravo's sentence. Especially in light of the scarce value of Bravo's testimony, this prosecutorial behavior very plausibly may be viewed as a maneuver to prevent Iredale from representing petitioner at trial. Iredale had proved to be a formidable adversary; he previously had gained an acquittal for the alleged kingpin of the marijuana distribution scheme. As the District Court stated in considering petitioner's motion, "Were I in [petitioner's] position I'm sure I would want Mr. Iredale representing me, too. He did a fantastic job in that [Gomez-Barajas] trial. . . ." The prosecutor's decision to call Bravo as a witness may well have stemmed from a concern that Iredale would do an equally fantastic job at petitioner's trial. As the Court notes, governmental maneuvering of this kind is relevant to a trial court's

Moreover, even assuming that Bravo's testimony might have "necessitat[ed] vigorous cross-examination," the District Court could have insured against the possibility of any conflict of interest without wholly depriving petitioner of his constitutional right to the counsel of his choice. Petitioner's motion requested that Iredale either be substituted for petitioner's current counsel or be added to petitioner's defense team. Had the District Court allowed the addition of Iredale and then ordered that he take no part in the cross-examination of Bravo, any possibility of a conflict would have been removed. Especially in light of the availability of this precautionary measure, the notion that Iredale's prior representation of Bravo might well have caused a conflict of interest at petitioner's trial is nothing short of ludicrous. . . .

JUSTICE STEVENS, with whom JUSTICE BLACKMUN joins, dissenting.

This is not the first case in which the Court has demonstrated "its apparent unawareness of the function of the independent lawyer as a guardian of our freedom." Walters v. National Assn. of Radiation Survivors, 473 U.S. 305, 371, (1985) (Stevens, J., dissenting) (footnote omitted) [page 116 supra]. But even under the Court's paternalistic view of the citizen's right to select his or her own lawyer, its analysis of this case is seriously flawed. As Justice Marshall demonstrates, the Court exaggerates the significance of the potential conflict. Of greater importance, the Court gives inadequate weight to the informed and voluntary character of the clients' waiver of their right to conflict-free representation. Particularly, the Court virtually ignores the fact that additional counsel representing petitioner had provided him with sound advice concerning the wisdom of a waiver and would have remained available during the trial to assist in the defense. Thus, this is not a case in which the District Judge faced the question whether one counsel should be substituted for another; rather the question before him was whether petitioner should be permitted to have *additional* counsel of his choice. I agree with Justice Marshall that the answer to that question is perfectly clear.

Accordingly, although I agree with the Court's premise that district judges must be afforded wide latitude in passing on motions of this kind,* in this case it is abundantly clear to me that the District Judge abused his discretion and deprived this petitioner of a constitutional right of such fundamental character that reversal is required.

---

decision as to whether to accept a criminal defendant's chosen counsel. The significant possibility that the prosecutor was engaging in such bad-faith conduct provides yet another reason to dispute the Court's resolution of this case.

*In my view, deference to the trial judge is appropriate in light of his or her greater familiarity with such factors as the ability of the defendant knowingly and voluntarily to waive a potential conflict (including the possibility that a codefendant may be exerting undue influence over the defendant), the character of the lawyers, the particular facts of the case, and the availability of alternative counsel of a like caliber.

Wheat's Harvest

Prosecutors have used *Wheat* as a basis to disqualify defense lawyers, often with success.

In United States v. Moscony, 927 F.2d 742, 749 (3d Cir.), cert. denied, 111 S. Ct. 2812 (1991), a lawyer had represented multiple targets of an investigation, including the defendant and three of his employees. After the defendant was indicted, the government successfully moved to disqualify the lawyer on the ground that the three employees would be prosecution witnesses. The defendant was not allowed to waive cross-examination of the employees because the waiver would have resulted in ineffective assistance of counsel. The trial judge had "an institutional interest in protecting the truth-seeking function of the proceedings," as well as an interest in "protecting a fairly-rendered verdict from trial tactics designed to generate issues on appeal."

Tineo v. Kelly, 870 F.2d 854 (2d Cir. 1989), held a defense lawyer properly disqualified where he had previously represented a prosecution witness. The court suggested that *Wheat* had cast doubt on Circuit caselaw more deferential to representation in this circumstance. In United States v. Arrington, 867 F.2d 122 (2d Cir.), cert. denied, 493 U.S. 817 (1989), the same Circuit cited *Wheat* to uphold disqualification of the defendant's lawyer, despite a purported waiver of cross-examination, where the government planned to call a witness who would implicate the lawyer in obstruction of justice in that very case.

By contrast, In re Grand Jury Proceedings (Doe), 859 F.2d 1021, 1026 (1st Cir. 1988), reviewed a trial judge's disqualification of counsel from the representation of an immunized grand jury witness where counsel also represented an indicted defendant in the underlying probe. The First Circuit used the *Wheat* test even though grand jury witnesses do not enjoy Sixth Amendment protection. It then reversed the disqualification because it could not "say there exists an actual, or even a serious potential for, conflict of interest." As the court read *Wheat*, "generally there must be a direct link between the clients of an attorney– or at least some concrete evidence that one client, such as an immunized witness, has information about another client, such as a target of a grand jury investigation — before the right to counsel of choice is barred by disqualification." The case was remanded for "more specific findings of fact."

Appealability of Criminal Disqualification Orders

In Flanagan v. United States, 465 U.S. 259 (1984), the Court unanimously held that pretrial orders disqualifying criminal defense counsel are not subject to immediate appeal under 28 U.S.C. §1291. If defense counsel is disqualified and review is not otherwise available (as through a certified question or mandamus), the defendant will have to proceed with another lawyer. If the defendant is convicted, he will be able to raise the disqualification order on appeal from the judgment of conviction. If the appellate court finds that the order was in error, should it reverse automatically or should the defendant have to show some actual prejudice? If prejudice is required, should it be less prejudice than would be required to reverse without the erroneous order? If not, the disqualification error doesn't count for anything, does it? The Court did not address the prejudice problem in *Flanagan*. Might it be that district courts are the courts of last resort on the question of disqualification? See Anaya v. People, 764 P.2d 779 (Colo. 1988) (defendant need not show prejudice). Compare Fuller v. Diesslin, 868 F.2d 604 (3d Cir.), cert. denied, 493 U.S. 873 (1989), which held that a state trial judge's arbitrary denial of pro hac vice admission to a criminal defendant's counsel of choice required federal habeas relief without proof of prejudice.

Should the rule differ when a prosecutor is disqualified? The Seventh Circuit said yes in In re Grand Jury Subpoena of Rochon, 873 F.2d 170 (7th Cir. 1989). Whereas the disqualification of defense counsel will be subject to review in the event of conviction, disqualification of a prosecutor will never be subject to review. In event of acquittal, there can be no appeal. If the defendant is convicted, the government will not have been harmed. The decision is therefore a collateral order and an interlocutory appeal appropriate.

The Joint-Defense Privilege

We have seen, and will see again (page 13 supra and page 227 infra), that "client" is a fluid concept. Whether there is a client-lawyer relationship may depend on why you're asking. For purposes of the joint-defense privilege, communications from lawyer A's client can be privileged even though delivered to lawyer B. In fact, the oft-used term "joint-defense privilege" is something of a misnomer. The underlying principle may apply in both civil and criminal matters, on behalf of plaintiffs and defendants, in or out of litigation. United States v. Schwimmer, 892 F.2d 237 (2d Cir. 1989), uses the term "common interest rule." What rationale supports that rule?

As Justice Powell wrote in *Cuyler*, quoting Justice Frankfurter, "a common defense . . . gives strength against a common attack" (page 190 supra). In recognition of this, evidence rules often bestow a privilege on conversations between one of two clients or his lawyer and the lawyer for another client "in a matter of common interest." Proposed Rule 503(b)(3) of the Federal Rules of Evidence. United States v. McPartlin, 595 F.2d 1321, 1336-337 (7th Cir. 1979), cert. denied, 444 U.S. 833 (1979), applies this principle to protect a communication transmitted as part of a joint defense. In United States v. Schwimmer, supra, the common interest rule protected communications between a client and an accountant for a codefendant when the communication was intended to serve the joint interests of both defendants. It was irrelevant that no actual litigation was in progress. When no joint-defense purpose is shown, the privilege won't apply. United States v. Lopez, 777 F.2d 543, 552-553 (10th Cir. 1985) (no privilege where no evidence of joint defense); Government of Virgin Islands v. Joseph, 685 F.2d 857, 862 (3d Cir. 1982) (same).

Joint representation (two or more clients and two or more lawyers) and multiple representation (two or more clients with a single lawyer) also give rise to other problems. Can either client waive the privilege over the protest of another client? What if there is a falling out among the clients? What if a client gives a common lawyer information he or she does not want revealed to a coclient? See page 230 infra.

FURTHER READING

Bruce Green reviews Supreme Court decisions on defense counsel conflicts through *Wheat* and argues that *Wheat* "ignores the more sophisticated aspects of the Court's earlier jurisprudence, including ... the relative importance of client autonomy and the sanctity of the attorney-client relationship." Professor Green says the Court unfairly assumes that defense lawyers will not comply with their professional responsibilities. He concludes that trial judges need "further guidance in cases in which defense counsel has a potential conflict of interest" and he proposes "a framework" for the exercise of judicial discretion in such cases. Green, "Through a Glass, Darkly": How the Court Sees Motions to Disqualify Criminal Defense Lawyers, 89 Colum. L. Rev. 1201 (1989).

The Illinois Supreme Court has sought to impose some order on the variety of labels used in the area of criminal conflicts. See People v. Spreitzer, 123 Ill. 2d 1, 525 N.E.2d 30, cert. denied, 488 U.S. 917 (1988), and People v. Holmes, 141 Ill. 2d 204, 565 N.E.2d 950 (1990), which attempt to come to grips with such terms as "per se conflict," "potential conflict," "possible conflict," "actual conflict," "prejudice," and "actual prejudice."

QUESTIONS

5.1 "There are seven or eight top-flight criminal defense lawyers in Boston and I am one of them, Andy Simon. Recently, I was hired by three individuals whom I will call Dash, Kennedy, and Snyder. They were charged with first-degree murder. Dash and Kennedy were accused of actually committing the murder and Snyder was charged under the felony-murder rule. If convicted, they could each get life in prison without parole. In due course, I broached plea bargaining with the prosecutor, Tina Chambers, who told me that she would accept a plea to murder two, which would make my clients eligible for parole in 20 years. But Tina insisted that they all three had to plead guilty or the deal was off. She figures if she's going to try one she'll try them all, I guess. Well, I told this to my clients. Dash and Kennedy said they wanted to take the deal, but Snyder would not. The fact is that Tina has a better case against Dash and Kennedy than she has against Snyder. I told Tina I thought Snyder better get another lawyer, but Tina said it didn't matter to her because whether there was one defense lawyer or two or three, she still wasn't going to accept a deal unless each defendant pled to murder two. Actually, I think it's a pretty good deal, even for Snyder who, because he wasn't a triggerman, will probably get paroled after 20 years. The others I'm not so sure but at least they'd have a shot. So what do I do now?"

5.2   Harry Wolfman is representing Linda Logan, who is charged with bail jumping. The prosecutor has subpoenaed Gloria Ingram to testify against Logan at trial. Ingram and Logan's mother, both in their sixties, are roommates. The prosecutor has interviewed Ingram, who told her that Logan had come to Ingram's home in disguise and that Ingram had driven Logan to the airport. When Ingram got the subpoena, she got worried and called Wolfman, whom she has known for some time. She told Wolfman about her interview with the prosecutor and about the subpoena. Wolfman told her that she could be subject to prosecution herself for aiding Logan's flight by driving her to the airport. Wolfman suggested that Ingram get a lawyer. Ingram asked Wolfman to represent her, and he agreed. He told her she would have to show up in response to the subpoena but he would inform the judge that she was going to assert her privilege against self-incrimination. Exactly that happens on the second day of trial. The judge and the prosecutor are both incensed at what they consider to be Wolfman's obstructionist tactics. They write separate letters to the disciplinary committee. Has Wolfman done anything wrong?

2. Criminal Cases (Prosecutors)

A prosecutor can have a conflict, concurrent or successive, for the same variety of reasons as any lawyer. We saw one possible conflict in People v. Jackson (page 183 supra), where the prosecutor and the defense lawyer were dating, and in California Opinion 1984-83 (page 183 supra), where they were married. *Jackson* was ultimately decided under the state constitution. The ethics opinion found a conflict, which it concluded could be waived. See also In re Ockrassa, 165 Ariz. 576, 799 P.2d 1350 (1990) (prosecutor suspended for 90 days after using defendant's prior convictions to enhance sentence where prosecutor, as a public defender, had been the defendant's lawyer in the prior cases).

YOUNG v. UNITED STATES EX REL. VUITTON ET FILS S.A.
481 U.S. 787 (1987)

[Vuitton, a leather goods manufacturer, had settled a trademark dispute with the defendants. The settlement enjoined the defendants from further trademark violations. When the defendants violated the injunction, Vuitton's lawyer secured an order to show cause why they should not be held in contempt. Vuitton's counsel were appointed special prosecutors and won a conviction. The Supreme Court upheld the district court's power to appoint private counsel to prosecute a contempt charge. It then considered whether Vuitton's counsel could be appointed. Part III-A of Justice Brennan's opinion for the Court follows.]

In Berger v. United States, 295 U.S. 78, 88 (1935), this Court declared:

> The United States Attorney is the representative not of an ordinary party to a controversy, but of a sovereignty whose obligation to govern impartially is as compelling as its obligation to govern at all; and whose interest, therefore, in a criminal prosecution is not that it shall win a case, but that justice shall be done. As such, he is in a peculiar and very definite sense the servant of the law, the twofold aim of which is that guilt shall not escape nor innocence suffer.

This distinctive role of the prosecutor is expressed in Ethical Consideration (EC) 7-13 of Canon 7 of the American Bar Association (ABA) Model Code of Professional Responsibility (1982): "The responsibility of a public prosecutor differs from that of the usual advocate; his duty is to seek justice, not merely to convict."

Because of this unique responsibility, federal prosecutors are prohibited from representing the government in any matter in which they, their family, or their business associates have any interest. 18 U.S.C. §208(a). Furthermore, the Justice Department has applied to its attorneys the ABA Model Code of Professional Responsibility, 28 CFR §45.735-1(b)

(1986), which contains numerous provisions relating to conflicts of interest. The concern that representation of other clients may compromise the prosecutor's pursuit of the Government's interest rests on recognition that a prosecutor would owe an ethical duty to those other clients. "Indeed, it is the highest claim on the most noble advocate which causes the problem — fidelity, unquestioned, continuing fidelity to the client."

Private attorneys appointed to prosecute a criminal contempt action represent the United States, not the party that is the beneficiary of the court order allegedly violated. . . . The prosecutor is appointed solely to pursue the public interest in vindication of the court's authority. A private attorney appointed to prosecute a criminal contempt therefore certainly should be as disinterested as a public prosecutor who undertakes such a prosecution.

If a Justice Department attorney pursued a contempt prosecution for violation of an injunction benefitting any client of that attorney involved in the underlying civil litigation, that attorney would be open to a charge of committing a felony under §208(a). Furthermore, such conduct would violate the ABA ethical provisions, since the attorney could not discharge the obligation of undivided loyalty to both clients where both have a direct interest. The government's interest is in dispassionate assessment of the propriety of criminal charges for affronts to the judiciary. The private party's interest is in obtaining the benefits of the court's order. While these concerns sometimes may be congruent, sometimes they may not. A prosecutor may be tempted to bring a tenuously supported prosecution if such a course promises financial or legal rewards for the private client. Conversely, a prosecutor may be tempted to abandon a meritorious prosecution if a settlement providing benefits to the private client is conditioned on a recommendation against criminal charges.

Regardless of whether the appointment of private counsel in this case resulted in any prosecutorial impropriety (an issue on which we express no opinion), that appointment illustrates the *potential* for private interest to influence the discharge of public duty. Vuitton's California litigation had culminated in a permanent injunction and consent decree in favor of Vuitton against petitioner Young relating to various trademark infringement activities. This decree contained a liquidated damages provision of $750,000 for violation of the injunction. The prospect of such a damage award had the potential to influence whether Young was selected as a target of investigation, whether he might be offered a plea bargain, or whether he might be offered immunity in return for his testimony. In addition, Bainton [Vuitton's lawyer] was the defendant in a defamation action filed by Klayminc [one of the petitioners] arising out of Bainton's involvement in the litigation resulting in the injunction whose violation was at issue in this case. This created the possibility that the investigation of Klayminc might be shaped in part by a desire to obtain information useful in the defense of the defamation suit. Furthermore, Vuitton had various civil claims pending against some of the petitioners. These claims theoretically could have created temptation to use the criminal investigation to gather information of use in those suits, and could have served as bargaining leverage in obtaining pleas in the criminal prosecution. In short, as will generally be the case, the appointment of counsel for an interested party to bring the contempt prosecution in this case at a minimum created *opportunities* for conflicts to arise, and created at least the *appearance* of impropriety.

As should be apparent, the fact that the judge makes the initial decision that a contempt prosecution should proceed is not sufficient to quell concern that prosecution by an interested party may be influenced by improper motives. A prosecutor exercises considerable discretion in matters such as the determination of which persons should be targets of investigation, what methods of investigation should be used, what information will be sought as evidence, which persons should be charged with what offenses, which persons should be utilized as witnesses, whether to enter into plea bargains and the terms on which they will be established, and whether any individuals should be granted immunity. These decisions, critical to the conduct of a prosecution, are all made outside the supervision of the court. . . .

The use of this Court's supervisory authority has played a prominent role in ensuring that contempt proceedings are conducted in a manner consistent with basic notions of fairness. The exercise of supervisory authority is especially appropriate in the determination of the procedures to be employed by courts to enforce their orders, a subject that directly concerns the functioning of the judiciary. We rely today on that authority to hold that counsel for a party that is the beneficiary of a court order may not be appointed as prosecutor in a contempt action alleging a violation of that order. . . .

The Court was fractured in *Vuitton*. Although the exerpt represents the view of seven Justices, only four (Brennan, Marshall, Blackmun, and Stevens) agreed that "harmless error analysis is inappropriate in reviewing the appointment of an interested prosecutor in a case such as this." Justice Blackmun would also have held that due process forbids appointment of any "interested party's counsel" to prosecute for criminal contempt. Justice Scalia, using a separation of powers analysis, concluded that the appointment of a private prosecutor was not an exercise of the "judicial power of the United States" within the meaning of Art. III, §§1, 2 of the Constitution. "Since this is the only grant of power that has been advanced as authorizing these appointments, they were void."

Justice Powell, joined by the Chief Justice and Justice O'Connor, agreed that where "a private prosecutor . . . also represents an interested party, the possibility that his judgment will be compromised is significant," warranting an "exercise of this Court's supervisory powers to hold [such an appointment] improper." He disagreed, however, with the plurality's harmless error analysis and would have remanded the case to determine whether the error was harmless. Justice White "would prefer" that district judges not appoint interested private prosecutors, but discerned no constitutional or other error in doing so and would have affirmed.

Prosecutors avec Deux Chapeaux

Two years before *Vuitton*, the California Supreme Court faced a similar situation. A city seeking to rid itself of stores selling explicit sexual material passed a nuisance statute aimed at closing such stores. The city then retained Clancy, a private lawyer, to bring civil abatement proceedings. His fee was to be $60 hourly if he was successful in closing an establishment, but $30 hourly if he was not. The court disqualified Clancy. It applied the "heightened ethical requirements" that bind government lawyers despite a claim that Clancy was an independent contractor. It then held that the arrangement was "antithetical to the standard of neutrality" required of government lawyers. "When a government attorney has a personal interest in the litigation, the neutrality so essential to the system is violated." The court did not forbid employment of private counsel on contingent fees in all matters, but it stressed the close relationship between civil abatement proceedings and criminal prosecutions. People ex rel. Clancy v. Superior Court, 39 Cal. 3d 740, 705 P.2d 347, 350-353, 218 Cal. Rptr. 24 (1985), cert. denied, 475 U.S. 1121 (1986).

Clancy had personally drafted the civil abatement ordinance (as well as a previous ordinance that had been declared unconstitutional). He was associated with an organization called Committee for Decency through Law. After the court ruling, could the city properly hire Clancy to handle all civil abatement proceedings for an hourly fee?

Young turned on the Court's supervisory powers. Only Justice Blackmun construed the due process clause to reach the same result. The difference made a difference in Dick v. Scroggy, 882 F.2d 192, 196 (6th Cir. 1989). The petitioner had been convicted in state court of felonious assault. The proof showed that, while intoxicated, he caused a collision that injured a passenger in another vehicle. After the conviction, while the appeal was pending, the victim, represented by the prosecutor, sued Dick for damages. (In many sparsely populated areas, part-time prosecutors practice law privately.) In habeas, Dick alleged that he was denied due process because the prosecutor had a pecuniary interest in convicting him. The Sixth Circuit assumed that the prosecutor had been retained to bring the civil action before the criminal case had ended. Nevertheless, it declined to find a due process violation. "Absent a demonstration of selective prosecution . . . even a clear appearance of impropriety in the participation of the prosecutor is normally insufficient to justify a decision, in collateral proceedings, to administer . . . the 'strong medicine' of setting aside a conviction." Of course, even if the due process clause was not violated, ethics rules may have been. In Lyman v. Grievance Committee, 154 A.D.2d 223, 552 N.Y.S.2d 721 (1990), a part-time prosecutor was censured where he represented clients in civil matters while simultaneously investigating or prosecuting those matters criminally.

In *Young*, an interested party's private counsel was appointed to prosecute a contempt. Can the court appoint a government lawyer whose agency has an interest in the underlying proceeding? The Federal Trade Commission obtained a temporary restraining order against Godfree and others, which Godfree allegedly violated. The court appointed FTC attorneys to act as special prosecutors in the ensuing contempt proceeding. Godfree was convicted and appealed. *Young* was not controlling. The FTC, as an independent agency, was not "the equivalent of a private party." Although the court rejected a "per se bar to the participation of government lawyers in contempt prosecutions, we recognize that under certain circumstances a government attorney may lack the impartiality and appearance of impartiality that our system of justice demands of its prosecutors." In resolving this issue, the court cited two factors that increased the likelihood of disinterested prosecution. These were that the U.S. Attorney's office participated in the contempt prosecution and that the FTC attorneys handling the contempt prosecution were not the same as those who participated in the underlying civil suit. FTC v. American National Cellular, 868 F.2d 315, 319 (9th Cir. 1989).

QUESTION

5.3   A state prosecutor indicted David Champer for felonious sexual assault. The charge appeared in the newspaper, where Champer's friend Rummer saw it. Rummer called the alleged victim, May Dearie, a friend of both Champer and Rummer. Dearie later told the police chief of the Town of Newtown that Rummer had threatened her with harm if she didn't drop the charge. Rummer denied it. The police chief arrested Rummer for tampering with a witness. The state prosecutor agreed to drop the charge against Rummer in exchange for a release of liability running to Newtown, its officials, and Dearie. Rummer agreed. Later, Rummer sued Newtown and its officers anyway. He asserted that the dismissal agreement should have no effect. It violated public policy, he argued, because the prosecutor had a conflict of interest between his obligations as a state prosecutor and his effort to protect Newton and its officers. What result?

3. Civil Cases

Civil concurrent conflicts can arise in litigation or outside it. We set out one case in the former context before proceeding with some intriguing variations.

FIANDACA v. CUNNINGHAM
827 F.2d 825 (1st Cir. 1987)

COFFIN, J.

This opinion discusses . . . a class action brought by twenty-three female prison inmates sentenced to the custody of the warden of the New Hampshire State Prison. The suit challenges the state of New Hampshire's failure to establish a facility for the incarceration of female inmates with programs and services equivalent to those provided to male inmates at the state prison. After a bench trial on the merits, the district court held that the state had violated plaintiffs' right to equal protection of the laws and ordered the construction of a permanent in-state facility for plaintiffs no later than July 1, 1989. It also required the state to provide a temporary facility for plaintiffs on or before November 1, 1987, but prohibited the state from establishing this facility on the grounds of the Laconia State School and Training Center ("Laconia State School" or "LSS"), New Hampshire's lone institution for the care and treatment of mentally retarded citizens. . . .

Michael Cunningham, warden of the New Hampshire State Prison, and various executive branch officials responsible for the operation of the New Hampshire Department of Corrections ("state") . . . challenge the district court's refusal to disqualify plaintiffs' class counsel, New Hampshire Legal Assistance ("NHLA"), due to an unresolvable conflict of interest. See N.H. Rules of Professional Conduct, Rule 1.7(b). They also seek to overturn that portion of the district court's decision barring the establishment of an interim facility for female inmates at LSS, arguing that this prohibition is unsupported either by relevant factual findings, see Fed. R. Civ. P. 52(a), or by evidence contained in the record. . . .

This case began in June, 1983, when plaintiffs' appellate counsel, Bertram Astles, filed a complaint on behalf of several female inmates sentenced to the custody of the state prison warden and incarcerated at the Rockingham County House of Corrections. NHLA subsequently became co-counsel for plaintiffs and filed an amended complaint expanding the plaintiff class to include all female inmates who are or will be incarcerated in the custody of the warden. In the years that followed, NHLA assumed the role of lead counsel for the class, engaging in extensive discovery and performing all other legal tasks through the completion of the trial before the district court. Among other things, NHLA attorneys and their trial expert, Dr. Edyth Flynn, twice toured and examined potential facilities at which to house plaintiffs, including buildings at the Laconia State School, the New Hampshire Hospital in Concord, and the Youth Development Center in Manchester. . . .

The state extended [an] offer of judgment to plaintiffs on October 21, 1986. This offer proposed to establish an in-state facility for the incarceration of female inmates at an existing state building by June 1, 1987. Although the formal offer of judgment did not specify a particular location for this facility, the state informed NHLA that it planned to use the Speare Cottage at the Laconia State School. NHLA, which also represented the plaintiff class in the ongoing *Garrity* litigation, rejected the offer on November 10, stating in part that "plaintiffs do not want to agree to an offer which is against the stated interests of the plaintiffs in the *Garrity* class."* The state countered by moving immediately for the disqualification of NHLA as class counsel in the case at bar due to the unresolvable conflict of interest inherent in NHLA's representation of two classes with directly adverse interests. The court, despite recognizing that a conflict of interest probably existed, denied the state's motion on November 20 because NHLA's disqualification would further delay the trial of an important matter that had been pending for over three years. It began to try the case four days later.

[After trial and before decision, the parties reached a tentative settlement that provided for incarceration of female inmates at the Laconia State School. NHLA then "moved to withdraw as class co-counsel . . . and attorney Astles signed the settlement agreement on plaintiffs' behalf. The state, however, refused to sign the agreement." Thereafter, plaintiffs withdrew their consent in light of the state's refusal to sign. The trial judge then issued a decision which found that "the conditions of confinement, programs, and services available to New Hampshire female prisoners are not on par with the conditions, programs, and services afforded male inmates." He ordered the state to build a permanent facility that "shall not be located at the Laconia State School or its environs."]

As noted above, the state challenges the district court's decision on two independent grounds. First, it claims that the court should have disqualified NHLA as plaintiffs' class counsel prior to the commencement of the trial. Second, it contends that the court's proscription of the use of a site at the Laconia State School is unsupported either by relevant findings of fact or by evidence contained in the record. Because we find in favor of the state on its first claim and remand for a new trial on the issue of an

---

*The plaintiffs in the *Garrity* class were challenging conditions at the Laconia State School. Their counsel was NHLA, which was also co-counsel to the plaintiffs in the present action. The *Garrity* plaintiffs opposed the use of Speare Cottage to incarcerate female inmates. — ED.

appropriate remedy, we confine ourselves to an analysis of the disqualification issue.

A. REFUSAL TO DISQUALIFY
FOR CONFLICT OF INTEREST

The state's first argument is that the district court erred in permitting NHLA to represent the plaintiff class at trial after its conflict of interest had become apparent. As we recognized in Kevlik v. Goldstein, 724 F.2d 844 (1st Cir. 1984), a district court is vested with broad power and responsibility to supervise the professional conduct of the attorneys appearing before it. It follows from this premise that "[w]e will not disturb the district court['s] finding unless there is no reasonable basis for the court's determination." Id. We must determine, therefore, whether the court's denial of the state's disqualification motion amounts to an abuse of discretion in this instance.

The state's theory is that NHLA faced an unresolvable conflict because the interests of two of its clients were directly adverse after the state extended its offer of judgment on October 21, 1986. [The court quoted Rule 1.7 and its comment.] . . . In this case, it is the state's contention that the court should have disqualified NHLA as class counsel pursuant to Rule 1.7 because . . . NHLA's representation of the plaintiff class in this litigation was materially limited by its responsibilities to the *Garrity* class.

We find considerable merit in this argument. The state's offer to establish a facility for the incarceration of female inmates at the Laconia State School, and to use its "best efforts" to make such a facility available for occupancy by June 1, 1987, presented plaintiffs with a legitimate opportunity to settle a protracted legal dispute on highly favorable terms. As class counsel, NHLA owed plaintiffs a duty of undivided loyalty: it was obligated to present the offer to plaintiffs, to explain its costs and benefits, and to ensure that the offer received full and fair consideration by the members of the class. Beyond all else, NHLA had an ethical duty to prevent its loyalties to other clients from coloring its representation of the plaintiffs in this action and from infringing upon the exercise of its professional judgment and responsibilities.[4]

NHLA, however, also represents the residents of the Laconia State School who are members of the plaintiff class in *Garrity*. Quite understandably, this group vehemently opposes the idea of establishing a correctional facility for female inmates anywhere on the grounds of LSS. As counsel for

---

4. The fact that the conflict arose due to the nature of the state's settlement offer, rather than due to the subject matter of the litigation or the parties involved, does not render the ethical implications of NHLA's multiple representation any less troublesome. Among other things, courts have a duty to "ensur[e] that at all stages of litigation . . . counsel are as a general rule available to advise each client as to the particular, individualized benefits or costs of a proposed settlement." Smith v. City of New York, 611 F. Supp. 1080, 1090 (S.D.N.Y. 1985).

the *Garrity* class, NHLA had an ethical duty to advance the interests of the class to the fullest possible extent and to oppose any settlement of the instant case that would compromise those interests. In short, the combination of clients and circumstances placed NHLA in the untenable position of being simultaneously obligated to represent vigorously the interests of two conflicting clients. It is inconceivable that NHLA, or any other counsel, could have properly performed the role of "advocate" for both plaintiffs and the *Garrity* class, regardless of its good faith or high intentions. Indeed, this is precisely the sort of situation that Rule 1.7 is designed to prevent.

Plaintiffs argue on appeal that there really was no conflict of interest for NHLA because the state's second offer of judgment was unlikely to lead to a completed settlement for reasons other than NHLA's loyalties to the *Garrity* class. We acknowledge that the record contains strong indications that settlement would not have occurred even if plaintiffs had been represented by another counsel. . . . The question, however, is not whether the state's second offer of judgment would have resulted in a settlement had plaintiffs' counsel not been encumbered by a conflict of interest. Rather, the inquiry we must make is whether plaintiffs' counsel was able to represent the plaintiff class unaffected by divided loyalties, or as stated in Rule 1.7(b), whether NHLA could have reasonably believed that its representation would not be adversely affected by the conflict. Our review of the record and the history of this litigation — especially NHLA's response to the state's second offer, in which it stated that "plaintiffs do not want to agree to an offer which is against the stated interests of plaintiffs in the *Garrity* case" — persuade us that NHLA's representation of plaintiffs could not escape the adverse effects of NHLA's loyalties to the *Garrity* class.

Both the district court and plaintiffs on appeal have also advanced the belief that "necessity" outweighed the adverse effects of NHLA's conflict of interest in this instance and justified the denial of the state's pretrial disqualification motion. The district court recognized the probable existence of the conflict as early as November 20, 1986, when it took up the matter of the disqualification motion at an in-chambers hearing. At that time, the court noted that the state's motion had "quite a bit of merit to it," but that it would deny the motion because the case had already lingered on its docket for approximately three and a half years. The court later identified this balancing of NHLA's conflict of interest against considerations of delay and time pressure as the application of the "doctrine of necessity." The court apparently believed that further delay engendered by a motion to disqualify on the eve of trial, coupled with its own scheduling dilemma, provided a sound basis for ignoring the conflict and proceeding to trial as quickly as possible. It warned plaintiffs' counsel, however, that they should consider the possibility that the trial would be infected by "built-in reversible error."

While it is surely laudable that the court was anxious to resolve a lingering dispute concerning an unfortunate state of affairs, we fail to see how the doctrine of *necessity* is implicated in a case such as this. As plaintiffs' counsel admitted at oral argument, there was no particular emergency at the time of the court's decision to ignore the conflict of interest and proceed to trial. Plaintiffs simply continued to suffer the effects of the same inequitable treatment that had persisted for many years. While it would have been desirable to avoid delaying the trial for up to a year or more, it certainly was not "necessary" in the sense of limiting the court to but one potential course of action. We realize that other courts occasionally consider the possible effects of delay in ruling on disqualification motions, see, e.g., Laker Airways Ltd. v. Pan American World Airways, 103 F.R.D. 22, 27-28 (D.D.C. 1984) ("Were the motion to disqualify to be granted, the resulting additional delay might well be crippling."), but in this circuit, arguments premised on delay have been less availing. As we held in *Kevlik*, "we cannot, in the face of a breach of professional duty, ignore the wrong because appellees' counsel neglected to discern the conflict earlier, *or even opted to delay litigation by raising the motion.* . . ." (emphasis supplied).

Absent some evidence of *true* necessity, we will not permit a meritorious disqualification motion to be denied in the interest of expediency unless it can be shown that the movant strategically sought disqualification in an effort to advance some improper purpose. Thus, the state's motivation in bringing the motion is not irrelevant; as we recognized in *Kevlik*, "disqualification motions can be tactical in nature, designed to harass opposing counsel." However, the mere fact that the state moved for NHLA's disqualification just prior to the commencement of the trial is not, without more, cause for denying its motion. There is simply no evidence to support plaintiffs' suggestion that the state "created" the conflict by intentionally offering plaintiffs a building at LSS in an effort "to dodge the bullet again" with regard to its "failure to provide instate housing for the plaintiff class." We do not believe, therefore, that the state's second offer of judgment and subsequent disqualification motion were intended to harass plaintiffs. Rather, our reading of the record indicates that a more benign scenario is more probable: the state made a good faith attempt to accommodate plaintiffs by offering to establish a correctional facility in an existing building at the Laconia State School and, once NHLA's conflict of interest with regard to this offer became apparent, the state moved for NHLA's disqualification to preserve this settlement option.

As we are unable to identify a reasoned basis for the district court's denial of the state's pre-trial motion to disqualify NHLA from serving as plaintiffs' class counsel, we hold that its order amounts to an abuse of discretion and must be reversed.

B. PROPER REMEDY

In light of the district court's error in ignoring NHLA's conflict of interest, we believe it necessary to remand the case for further proceedings. We must consider a further question, however: must the district court now start from scratch in resolving this dispute? The state argues that the court's failure to disqualify NHLA is plain reversible error, and therefore requires the court to try the matter anew. We subscribe to the view, however, that merely "conducting [a] trial with counsel that should have been disqualified does not 'indelibl[y] stamp or taint' the proceedings." With this in mind, we look to the actual adverse effects caused by the court's error in refusing to disqualify NHLA as class counsel to determine the nature of the proceedings on remand.

We do not doubt that NHLA's conflict of interest potentially influenced the course of the proceedings in at least one regard: NHLA could not fairly advocate the remedial option — namely, the alternative of settling for a site at the Laconia State School — offered by the state prior to trial. The conflict, therefore, had the potential to ensure that the case would go to trial, a route the state likely wished to avoid by achieving an acceptable settlement. Nevertheless, we do not see how a trial on the merits could have been avoided given the manner in which the case developed below. Judge Loughlin stated on the record that he would not approve a settlement infringing on the rights of LSS residents, and under Rule 23(e), any settlement of this class action required his approval to be effective. It seems to us, therefore, that even if some other counsel had advised plaintiffs to accept the state's offer for a building at LSS, a trial on the merits would have been inevitable.

With respect to the merits of the equal protection issue, the state has been unable to identify any way in which the court's error adversely affected its substantial rights at trial. . . .

The situation is different, however, with respect to the remedy designed by the district court. We believe that it would be inappropriate to permit the court's remedial order — which includes a specific prohibition on the use of LSS — to stand in light of the court's refusal to disqualify NHLA. The ban on the use of buildings located on the grounds of LSS is exactly the sort of remedy preferred by NHLA's *other* clients, the members of the *Garrity* class, and therefore has at least the appearance of having been tainted by NHLA's conflict of interest. Consequently, we hold that the district court's remedial order must be vacated and the case remanded for a new trial on the issue of the proper remedy for this constitutional deprivation. . . .

Imputed Conflicts

Assume NHLA had more than one lawyer on staff. Why couldn't one of them represent the *Garrity* class while the other represented the plaintiffs in *Fiandaca*? Or assume (surely counterfactually) that NHLA had 50 lawyers. Wouldn't it then be plausible to screen the *Garrity* team from professional contact with the *Fiandaca* team? Why didn't the court consider this solution? Why didn't the lawyers suggest it?

With some exceptions, mainly in the area of successive representations (page 269 infra), both the code and the rules impute conflicts among all affiliated lawyers. See DR 5-105(D); Rule 1.10(a). Why is that?

This rule can work special hardship where a client is poor and there is only a single legal services or legal aid organization in the community. In Borden v. Borden, 277 A.2d 89 (D.C. App. 1971), the same legal services program that was representing the plaintiff wife in a divorce proceeding was appointed by the court to represent the defendant husband. The legal services program appealed and the appointment was reversed. The appellate court anticipated that it would be possible for the husband to obtain outside representation, but in any event, it was reluctant to treat the legal services organization differently from a private law firm. Accord: ABA Informal Opinions 1418 (1978), 1233 (1972). For an argument that legal services organizations should not be subject to the same rules as apply to private law firms, see Robert Aronson, Conflict of Interest, 52 Wash. L. Rev. 807, 855-858 (1977).

DR 5-105(D) appears to impute all conflicts without exception, but as we shall see, exceptions have been made. (See page 278 infra.) Rule 1.10(a) is more focused. For example, all of the conflicts listed in Rule 1.8, except Rule 1.8(c), are exempt from imputation. Does this mean that one partner can accept the literary rights to a client's story while another partner represents the client? See Rule 1.8(d). For imputation of conflicts under the advocate-witness rule, see page 240 infra.

Standing

Another interesting thing about *Fiandaca* is that the conflicts issue was raised by the defendants, not either of the NHLA clients. Since conflict rules mean to protect clients, why did the court let the adversary raise the matter? And once the matter was raised, why didn't the court check with NHLA's clients to see if *they* objected to the conflict? Who has standing to raise conflicts issues, anyway?

The answer to this question is not uniform. Some courts permit only clients to allege a concurrent conflict. Original Appalachian Artworks, Inc. v. Marchon, Inc., 2 Lawyers Manual Prof. Conduct 371 (N.D. Ga. 1986). Others allow nonclients to do so on the theory that if a lawyer is violating an ethical rule, the court needs to know about it. *Fiandaca*, page 212 supra. A third group of cases seems to take an inevitable middle position. In In re Appeal of Infotechnology, — Del. — , 582 A.2d 215, 221 (1990), the defendant complained that the firm representing plaintiff would likely need to cross-examine one of its own clients, which, however, was not a party to the litigation. That client did not itself make formal objection. The court ruled that nonclients do not ordinarily have standing to assert an opposing lawyer's conflict. Drawing on the comment to Rule 1.7(a), the court held that a nonclient would have standing only when "he or she can demonstrate that the opposing counsel's conflict somehow prejudiced *his* or *her* rights. The nonclient litigant does not have standing to merely enforce a technical violation of the rules." The burden of proof was on the nonclient to show by clear and convincing evidence that a conflict existed and that it would "prejudice the fairness of the proceedings." See also Chapman Engineers v. Natural Sales Co., 766 F. Supp. 949, 955 (Kan. 1991) (nonclient has standing if conflict "greatly implicates public interest and threatens the fairness of the trial," but client may nonetheless waive the conflict); State Farm Mutual Auto Ins. Co. v. K.A.W., 575 So. 2d 630 (Fla. 1991) (insurer has standing, over insured's objection, to raise insured's counsel's conflict where insurer, not insured, would ultimately be liable for any judgment). See page 260 infra on standing to raise successive conflicts.

May a Lawyer Act Adversely to a Client on an Unrelated Matter?

The conflict in *Fiandaca* lay in the inability of NHLA to make an independent judgment about using the Laconia State School as a site for female prisoners. An independent judgment was impossible because NHLA also represented residents of the Laconia School. The clients' interests were inconsistent on a *related* matter — the use of the school. Does that mean that a lawyer may act adversely to a client on an *unrelated* matter?

The comment to Rule 1.7 says that "ordinarily" the lawyer may not do so. See also EC 5-15. In Cinema 5 v. Cinerama, 528 F.2d 1384, 1387 (2d Cir. 1976), an order disqualifying plaintiff's lawyer was affirmed because his partner was representing the defendant in another litigation. The court wrote:

> Whether such adverse representation, without more, requires disqualification in every case, is a matter we need not now decide. We do hold, however, that the "substantial relationship" test [page 251 infra] does not set a sufficiently high standard by which the necessity for disqualification should be determined. That test may properly be applied only where the representation of a former client has been terminated and the parameters of such relationship have been fixed. Where the relationship is a continuing one, adverse representation is prima facie improper, and the attorney must be prepared to show, at the very least, that there will be no actual or *apparent* conflict in loyalties or diminution in the vigor of his representation. We think that appellants have failed to meet this heavy burden.

In IBM v. Levin, 579 F.2d 271, 279-283 (3d Cir. 1978), the law firm CBM represented Levin in an antitrust action against IBM. Before and during the prosecution of that action, certain partners at CBM, not involved in the antitrust action, were representing IBM on various unrelated matters (labor disputes, a replevin action, and the like). IBM moved to disqualify CBM from representing Levin in the antitrust action. CBM argued that DR 5-105 did not foreclose the representation since "no effect adverse to IBM resulted from CBM's concurrent representation . . . and no adverse effect on CBM's exercise of its independent professional judgment on behalf of IBM was likely to result." The court, rejecting this argument, concluded that it is "likely that some 'adverse effect' on an attorney's exercise of his independent judgment on behalf of a client may result from the attorney's adversary posture toward that client in another legal matter." CBM argued that nevertheless it ought not be disqualified because disqualification was "too harsh a sanction," especially in light of the lower court's finding that "CBM did not obtain any information which would aid it in the prosecution of the antitrust suit against IBM." But the court wrote:

> The plaintiffs' interest in retaining counsel of its choice and the lack of prejudice to IBM resulting from CBM's violation of professional ethics are not the only factors to be considered in this disqualification proceeding. An attorney who fails to observe his obligation of undivided loyalty to his client injures his profession and demeans it in the eyes of the public. The maintenance of the integrity of the legal profession and its high standing in the community are important additional factors to be considered in determining the appropriate sanction for a Code violation. The maintenance of public confidence in the propriety of the conduct of those associated with the administration of justice is so important a consideration that we have held that a court may disqualify an attorney for failing to avoid even the appearance of impropriety.

Can you reconcile *Levin* with Board of Education v. Nyquist, 590 F.2d 1241, 1247 (2d Cir. 1979)? Female members of a teachers' union sought to disqualify the union's lawyer from representing male members of the union in an action that would determine whether there should be separate seniority lists for men and women, an issue on which the female teachers and the male teachers had inconsistent interests. The females were also parties to the action. The court, after noting that there was no charge that the union's lawyer "feels any sense of loyalty to the women that would undermine his representation of the men [and] no claim that the men have gained an unfair advantage through an access to privileged information about the women," wrote:

> We agree that there is at least some possibility that [the lawyer's] representation of [one set of clients] has the appearance of impropriety. . . . But

in any event, we think that disqualification was inappropriate. We believe that when there is no claim that the trial will be tainted, appearance of impropriety is simply too slender a reed on which to rest a disqualification order except in the rarest cases. This is particularly true where, as in this case, the appearance of impropriety is not very clear. . . . Since disqualification entails immediate disruption of the litigation, it is better to relegate any questions about [the lawyer's] conduct to other appropriate proceedings.

What if the firm is not proceeding against a client but against the client's affiliate or subsidiary? Can a lawyer who represents the Pontiac division of General Motors on a lease negotiation bring a products liability action against the Cadillac division on behalf of a third party? The comment to Rule 1.7 suggests that this might be permissible. It states: "[A] lawyer representing an enterprise with diverse operations may accept employment as an advocate against the enterprise in an unrelated matter if doing so will not adversely affect the lawyer's relationship with the enterprise or conduct of the suit and if both clients consent upon consultation." California Opinion 1989-113 declares that a lawyer who represents a parent corporation may nevertheless bring an action against its wholly owned subsidiary, notwithstanding the indirect financial impact the action would have on the parent, but only if the subsidiary is truly independent and not the "alter ego" of the parent and, in addition, the lawyer has not obtained relevant confidential information about the subsidiary through his representation of the parent. Teradyne, Inc. v. Hewlett-Packard Co., 1991 WL 239940 (N.D. Cal. 1991), applies the standard of Opinion 113 but concludes that because of the "identity of interest" between a parent and subsidiary, the two had to be treated as "a single client" for conflicts purposes.

The comment to Rule 1.7 also suggests that government lawyers can represent government employees "in proceedings in which a government agency is the opposing party." Compare Aerojet Properties, Inc. v. State of New York, 138 A.D.2d 39, 530 N.Y.S.2d 624, 626 (3d Dept. 1988), which allowed a private firm that was suing the state on behalf of a claimant seeking unpaid rent to continue the representation even though the state's insurer later hired the same firm to defend the state in an unrelated tort action. The court concluded that the firm "had met its heavy burden of demonstrating the absence of any conflict in loyalties or impediments to a vigorous representation of each client. . . . Given the multitudinous nature of the State's activities, even the appearance of impropriety seems de minimis here."

Appealability of Civil Disqualification Orders

An order granting or denying a motion to disqualify civil counsel is not subject to immediate appeal as of right in federal court. Richardson-

Merrell, Inc. v. Koller, 472 U.S. 424 (1985) (disqualification order); Firestone Tire & Rubber Co. v. Risjord, 449 U.S. 368 (1981) (refusal to disqualify). The Ninth Circuit has refused to entertain an appeal by permission (under 28 U.S.C. §1292(b)) from a refusal to disqualify counsel because to do so "would greatly enhance [the] usefulness [of such motions] as a tactical ploy." Shurance v. Planning Control Intl., 839 F.2d 1347, 1349 (9th Cir. 1988). Mandamus remains a possible route to review a disqualification order. Christensen v. United States District Court, 844 F.2d 694 (9th Cir. 1988).

FURTHER READING

Nathan Crystal analyzes two approaches the courts take in analyzing unrelated matter conflicts and offers a "new framework" which, among other things, evaluates disqualification and damages as alternative remedies. Crystal, Disqualification of Counsel for Unrelated Matter Conflicts of Interest, 4 Geo. J. Legal Ethics 273 (1990).

QUESTIONS

5.4 "As the Rehnquist Court has made it harder to bring Title VII actions for employment discrimination, my colleagues and I have gotten more and more requests for help. We work at the Texas Fair Employment Resource Center. The other day two guys, Miguel Nunez and William Joseph — who are Hispanic and African-American, respectively — came in to see me. They were both passed over for a supervisory promotion. Instead, their employer, Beware Industries, a manufacturer of security devices, gave the job to a white guy with substantially less seniority. Miguel and Bill believe they were the victims of discrimination based on their national origin and race. 'Sheila,' they practically pleaded with me, 'we went to five or six lawyers but we can't afford to pay and the lawyers are afraid they won't get a big enough fee from the court.' So they want us to take the case. I'm not sure we can take on another case right now, but even if we can, I'm not sure whether or how we could represent both of them. Whomever we don't represent will not get a lawyer. What's your advice?"

5.5 A lawyer is arguing for one construction of the securities law in a case pending in the Second Circuit. May another lawyer in the same firm, representing a different client, argue for an opposite construction of the same law in an unrelated case in the Seventh Circuit?

Malpractice Based on Conflicts

Sometimes the remedy for a conflict of interest will be disqualification and remand, as in *Fiandaca*. Sometimes it will be discipline, as in *Apostle* (page 178 supra) and In re Sabato, — Ind. —, 560 N.E.2d 62 (1990) (lawyer suspended for representing multiple parties in real estate transaction). Conflicts can also lead to malpractice liability. These remedies are not mutually exclusive. We discuss malpractice globally at page 611 infra, but here we take a moment to view it through the conflicts prism.

SIMPSON v. JAMES
903 F.2d 372 (5th Cir. 1990)

WISDOM, CIRCUIT JUDGE.

This appeal concerns a malpractice suit brought by the sellers of corporate assets against the partners of a law firm that represented both the buyers and the sellers in the transaction. The plaintiffs alleged two incidents of negligence on the part of the attorneys: the handling of the original sale and the subsequent restructuring of the buyers' note in favor of the plaintiffs. After a jury trial, the court rendered judgment in favor of the plaintiffs, awarding the sellers $100,000 for each act of negligence. We affirm.

STATEMENT OF THE CASE

The plaintiffs, Sheila Simpson and Lovie and Morelle Jones, were the sole stockholders in H.P. Enterprises Corporation. The business of H.P. Enterprises was operating and franchising catfish restaurants. Sheila Simpson's late husband, Buck Simpson, handled most of the business affairs of the corporation until his death. Mrs. Simpson then took over operation of the company, but she later decided to sell the corporation to devote more time to her children.

Mrs. Simpson turned to Ed Oliver for help in selling the corporation. Since 1968, Oliver practiced in Texarkana, Texas, with the firm now known as Keeney, Anderson & James. He had represented Mr. Simpson for many years in matters relating to H.P. Enterprises and in personal matters. In November 1983 a group of investors approached Oliver to inquire into purchasing H.P. Enterprises. Oliver formed a corporation for the investors, Tide Creek, and drew up the legal documents to transfer the assets of H.P. Enterprises to Tide Creek. Oliver was the sole source of legal advice for both parties.

The price agreed upon was $500,000, of which $100,000 was paid at the execution of the sale. As security for the sellers, Oliver provided for a lien on the stock of Tide Creek, personal guarantees of the buyers on the corporation's $400,000 note to the sellers, and certain restrictions on operation of the business. The sale took place on November 18, 1983. After the transaction, Mr. Oliver's firm continued to represent Mrs. Simpson in estate and tax matters. During this time, all of her business records were kept at the firm's office.

Thereafter, two significant events occurred. In April 1984 a fire destroyed Tide Creek's commissary, which contained its inventory. David James, a partner in Oliver's firm, represented Tide Creek in recovering over $200,000 in insurance proceeds. In October 1984, Oliver left the firm to practice in Houston. The firm was renamed Keeney, Anderson, & James. An associate in the firm, Fred Norton, took over tax and estate work for Mrs. Simpson.

Under the original terms of the sale arranged by Oliver, a $200,000 note by Tide Creek in favor of the plaintiffs became due on November 18, 1984. Tide Creek did not meet this obligation. On January 29, 1985, the plaintiffs visited David James at his office. James told them that Tide Creek was having financial difficulties, and that the company could pay them only $50,000 at that time. James restructured the note between the parties. At that meeting, Mrs. Simpson asked James what he would do if her interests and those of Tide Creek diverged. James replied: "We would have to support you."

In the Fall of 1985, Mrs. Simpson became concerned when she heard rumors of Tide Creek's impending bankruptcy. She called Fred Norton, an associate at the firm, and Norton arranged a meeting for her with David James. James advised Mrs. Simpson that her interests were in conflict with those of Tide Creek. He told her that she should find another lawyer to represent her; James was representing Tide Creek.

The plaintiffs received their last payment from Tide Creek on October 1, 1985. Tide Creek then filed for bankruptcy. The plaintiffs filed a claim in bankruptcy court, but received nothing. Their efforts to enforce the personal guarantees proved fruitless; the guarantors filed for personal bankruptcy.

Mrs. Simpson filed suit against the three partners of Keeney, Anderson, and James on January 16, 1987. The suit alleged that acts of negligence by Oliver and James proximately damaged the plaintiffs. The plaintiffs alleged that the defendants had a conflict of interest that prevented them from acting in the plaintiffs' best interests. The jury found that Ed Oliver was negligent in his representation of Mrs. Simpson and the Joneses and awarded them $100,000 damages. It also found David James liable for negligence for his role in restructuring the delinquent note and awarded $100,000 damages to Simpson. . . .

In Texas, an attorney malpractice claim is based on negligence. A plaintiff in a malpractice action must prove four elements to recover: that 1) the defendant owed a duty to the plaintiff; 2) the defendant breached that duty; 3) the breach proximately caused the plaintiff injury; and 4) damages resulted. The defendants challenge the existence of a number of these elements.

A. ATTORNEY-CLIENT RELATIONSHIP: JAMES AND SIMPSON

The defendants argue that no attorney-client relationship existed between David James and Sheila Simpson, and consequently, James owed no duty to her that could form the basis of malpractice liability. . . .

The evidence adduced at trial indicated that Ed Oliver represented the plaintiffs' business interests in H.P. Enterprises before and at the time of the sale of its assets to Tide Creek. After Oliver left, the firm represented Mrs. Simpson in tax and estate matters and continued to maintain all of her business records. Mrs. Simpson testified that on January 29, 1985, at the time the note was restructured, and on a subsequent occasion, James encouraged her about Tide Creek's future economic viability. She added that she relied on those assurances. Significantly, Simpson stated that James advised her that she was entering into a good deal in agreeing to the restructuring. At the same meeting, James assured Simpson that he would stand by her in the event of a conflict of interest between Simpson and Tide Creek. James stated that at no time did Mrs. Simpson specifically ask him to represent her interests against Tide Creek. He testified that he never gave any advice to Mrs. Simpson and never charged her for his time. Nevertheless, the evidence was sufficient for a reasonable jury to conclude that an attorney-client relationship existed, as manifested through the parties' conduct.

B. NEGLIGENCE

Under Texas law, an attorney "is held to the standard of care which would be exercised by a reasonably prudent attorney." This is not a result-oriented analysis; an attorney will not be liable for undesirable effects of a decision that was reasonable at the time it was made.

The plaintiffs alleged negligent acts that arose out of the defendants' conflicts of interest in representing both sides of a transaction. Liability may not be premised solely on the fact that an attorney represented both buyer and seller; after full disclosure by the attorney, it may be proper in some circumstances for an attorney to represent both sides in a real estate transaction.

Both sides in this case presented expert testimony on the propriety of Oliver's representing both the plaintiffs and the investors from Tide Creek. Of course, in case of conflicting expert testimony, the jury is entitled to make credibility determinations and to believe the witness it considers more trustworthy. Although the defense maintains that Oliver merely reduced a settled agreement to writing, the plaintiffs presented evidence suggesting that Oliver negotiated the sale price for the assets of H.P. Enterprises and determined the "mechanics" of the sale. Moreover, the plaintiff's expert witness, John Ament, testified that Oliver did not adequately protect Simpson against the possibility that Tide Creek would fail financially. For example, he stated that instead of a lien on Tide Creek stock, Oliver should have provided for a lien on the assets. Oliver also might have named the plaintiffs as beneficiaries of insurance policies. Ament added that the interests of plaintiffs and buyers varied significantly from the beginning. Although the evidence of Oliver's negligence is not overwhelming, we are not persuaded that the jury's conclusion is unreasonable.

David James prepared the instrument whereby Tide Creek's note in favor of Simpson and Jones was restructured. Simpson argues that James did not disclose Tide Creek's desperate financial condition, did not explain other options to her, and did not pursue over $200,000 insurance money for her benefit. The plaintiff's expert also testified that it was improper for James to represent parties with such divergent interests: a creditor seeking recovery and a debtor in default. We believe that this evidence is sufficient to uphold the jury's finding of negligence. . . .

[The court held that defendants' malpractice was the approximate cause of plaintiffs' loss and affirmed.]

What Did Oliver and James Do Wrong?

What was the basis for Oliver's malpractice? For James' malpractice? If the two had acted differently, Simpson and the Joneses *might* have been protected even after the purchasers declared bankruptcy. Fine. But then what does the alleged conflict of interest have to do with it? Wouldn't any lawyer who failed in the same way, assuming the failure was negligent, be liable, conflict or no conflict? Or perhaps the conflict just made the negligence clearer. After all, Oliver and James did have dual loyalties. Perhaps these prevented them from seeking maximum protection for plaintiffs or giving better advice. In this view, the conflict had forensic value by making it easier for the plaintiffs to persuade the jury that the lawyers should pay. Yet, Oliver, at least, insisted on the buyers' personal guarantees, which suggests that he had no qualms about offending them. Can *they* now sue on the ground that an unconflicted lawyer would have protected them against promises that might ultimately have forced them into bankruptcy? It seems that anything the lawyers might have done to favor one side would necessarily disfavor the other side and be a potential ground for malpractice. A zero-sum game for the clients was a lose-lose situation for the lawyers, wasn't it?

Waiving Conflicts

Could James and Oliver have avoided liability with a proper consent? Both the code and the Model Rules permit a client to waive concurrent conflicts of interest, although each document places limits on such waivers and the code's limits are (at least textually) more stringent. DR 5-105(C) allows a lawyer to represent multiple interests otherwise disallowed by DR 5-105(A) and (B) "if it is obvious that he can adequately represent the interest of each [client] and if each consents to the representation after full disclosure." Ethical Considerations 5-14 through 5-17 expand on this language.

How easy is it to meet the test of obviousness? EC 5-15 says that a lawyer "should never represent in litigation multiple clients with differing interests; and there are few situations in which he would be justified in representing in litigation multiple clients with potentially differing interests." Both in and out of litigation, EC 5-17 states that each case "depends upon an analysis" of its particular facts. By contrast, the rules prohibit a lawyer from representing a client if (1.7(a)) the representation will be "directly adverse to another client" or if (1.7(b)) "the representation of that client may be materially limited by the lawyer's responsibilities to another client." However, in each case, the lawyer may proceed with the representation if he or she "reasonably believes" that no representation will be adversely affected and the client "consents after consultation." In Levine v. Levine, 56 N.Y.2d 42, 436 N.E.2d 476, 479, 451 N.Y.S.2d 26 (1982), the court held that a single lawyer could represent two spouses in the preparation of a separation agreement:

> While the potential conflict of interests inherent in such joint representation suggests that the husband and wife should retain separate counsel, the parties have an absolute right to be represented by the same attorney provided "there has been full disclosure between the parties, not only of all relevant facts but also of their contextual significance, and there has been an absence of inequitable conduct or other infirmity which might vitiate the execution of the agreement."

Would consent have saved Oliver and James? Think about what the lawyers could have asked Simpson to consent to. The multiple representation? The omission of a security interest in the assets? Supervening loyalty to the buyers? Malpractice? See Rule 1.8(h).

Is There a Client-Lawyer Relationship?

Defendant James said he had no professional relationship with Simpson and therefore owed her no duty. This defense is often asserted in malpractice actions. See the *Togstad* case at page 613 infra. As we have seen (see page 13 supra) and will see again (page 256 infra), whether a client-attorney relationship exists may depend on why we are asking. Consider the following cases, in each of which the court found that a law firm had to be disqualified even though none involved a traditional professional relationship.

In Glueck v. Jonathan Logan, Inc., 653 F.2d 746, 749-750 (2d Cir. 1981), the plaintiff, a former executive of the defendant, alleged breach of an employment contract without cause. The firm representing him also conducted collective bargaining for a trade association of which the defendant was a member. The court characterized the case as one in which "an adverse party is only a vicarious client." Consequently, "the risks against which Canon 5 guards will not inevitably arise." It would therefore not be applied to disqualify the law firm unless "the subject matter of [the] suit is sufficiently related to the scope of the matters on which [the] firm represents [the] association as to create a realistic risk either that the plaintiff will not be represented with vigor or that unfair advantage will be taken of the defendant." Here, the trial court could properly have identified such a risk. "[T]he issue of whether Logan had cause to terminate Glueck might well arise in the course of collective bargaining discussions conducted by [Glueck's law firm for the trade association]." Furthermore, the law firm might, "in preparing for collective bargaining sessions . . . learn of Logan's policies or past practices bearing on the subject of Glueck's termination."

In Fund of Funds, Ltd. v. Arthur Andersen & Co., 567 F.2d 225, 234-236 (2d Cir. 1977), Morgan Lewis & Bockius had agreed to represent the plaintiff in connection with possible securities actions against various entities and persons, as might be disclosed by the investigation Morgan Lewis would undertake. Morgan Lewis was aware that the investigation could unearth accusations against its current client, Arthur Andersen & Co., which it subsequently did. Morgan Lewis sued other entities on behalf of the plaintiff. In these cases, co-counsel was Robert Meister of a different firm. When it became clear that Fund of Funds also had a claim against Andersen, Morgan Lewis's client, Meister's firm was selected (it is unclear by whom) to assert it. Nevertheless, Morgan Lewis's files and associates were used to assist Meister. In moving to disqualify Meister, the defendant called him the "understudy" of Morgan Lewis and the court agreed. For disqualification purposes, Meister was limited by the same fiduciary responsibilities that would have prevented Morgan Lewis from suing Andersen directly. Judge Kaufman discussed various precedents, then wrote:

> These cases are illuminating in their teaching and the principle they announce applies with singular potency here. The truism that the firm of Morgan Lewis would have been disqualified from suing Andersen because

it was Andersen's counsel, is of little comfort to Andersen which now finds itself embroiled in litigation resulting from Morgan Lewis's extensive investigation of the natural resource assets scheme. And Robert Meister is the extension of Morgan Lewis's continuing involvement in the underlying action for, as we have earlier stated, Morgan Lewis was instrumental in the choice of Meister and his firm, Milgrim Thomajan, to bring the suit and helpful to Meister in advancing the suit even if, as claimed by Meister, that help was of small significance. Moreover, Meister accepted the retainer from Orr [Fund of Fund's liquidator] to sue Andersen knowing of the Morgan firm's ethical dilemma. Indeed, his retention as counsel was premised on and resulted from the Morgan firm's incapacity to pursue the claim itself. Armed with that knowledge, and aided in some degree by Morgan Lewis, Meister should not have accepted the retainer.

The determination that Meister should be disqualified under Canon 5 is further underpinned by the restraints imposed by Canon 9. We see this in applying the principle clearly set forth in Cinema 5 v. Cinerama Ltd., [page 219 supra] at 1389. . . . While *Cinema 5* relied on the nexus of partnership, we have also held that disqualification extends to individuals associated with a firm in a lesser capacity, for example, a law clerk. Consolidated Theatres v. Warner Bros. Cir. Man. Corp., 216 F.2d 920, 927 (2d Cir. 1954). And we have never believed that labels alone — partner, clerk, co-counsel — should control our decisions in so sensitive an area. Here, where Meister worked closely with Morgan Lewis not only in *King* (a related case) but in SEC v. Vesco, an appearance of impropriety arises from this close association. Further, given the extraordinary, *sui generis* facts underlying this action, the generally stated rule that a "co-counsel" relationship will not alone warrant disqualification is of little relevance to this case.*

The impropriety of Meister's continued representation of the Fund appears with even greater clarity in the context of Canon 4's admonition that an attorney must not disclose the confidences of his client. . . . In undertaking the background investigation, and in segregating the papers which were, in part, ultimately used against Andersen, Morgan Lewis was applying its privileged knowledge with respect to Andersen. For, as Judge Stewart found, Morgan Lewis was privy to Andersen's practices and procedures, and had access to internal papers. It is inevitable that Meister, who dealt closely with Morgan Lewis throughout this entire period, was afforded the opportunity to benefit from this privileged information with regard to Andersen.

Three members of a trade association submitted confidential information to the law firm that represented the trade association in the "reasonable belief" that the firm "was acting in the undivided interest of each company." Later, the firm, Kirkland & Ellis, sued the three trade association members for violations of the antitrust laws. Judge Sprecher wrote that "[t]he client is no longer simply the person who walks into a law office." After listing other nontraditional situations in which professional

---

*The "appearance of impropriety" test is discussed at page 261 infra. — ED.

duties may arise, the judge wrote: "A fiduciary relationship may result because of the nature of the work performed and the circumstances under which confidential information is divulged." Canons 4, 5, and 9 were held to require that the firm be disqualified from the litigation unless the plaintiff was prepared to dismiss the three trade association members. Westinghouse Elec. Corp. v. Kerr-McGee Corp., 580 F.2d 1311, 1318-1321 (7th Cir.), cert. denied, 439 U.S. 955 (1978).

Many prominent private practitioners serve on boards of legal services organizations, which sometimes represent clients who are opposed to clients of the board member's firm. Is that a conflict? The code does not speak directly to this problem, but the ABA, even before the Model Rules were drafted, concluded that board membership in that circumstance does not violate the code so long as the attorney board member does not participate in board decisions in the conflict area. ABA Opinion 345 (1979). Rule 6.3 adopts this approach.

Confidentiality in Multiple Representation

The general rule is that where an "attorney acts for two or more parties having a common interest, neither party may exercise the [attorney-client] privilege in a subsequent controversy with the other. This is true even where the attorney acts jointly for two or more persons having no formalized business arrangement between them." Garner v. Wolfinbarger, 430 F.2d 1093, 1103 (5th Cir. 1970), cert. denied, 401 U.S. 974 (1971). (See also page 204 supra.) In Wortham & Van Liew v. Superior Court, 188 Cal. App. 3d 927, 233 Cal. Rptr. 725 (1987), the court upheld a lower court discovery order requiring an attorney for a general partnership to disclose to the plaintiff, a partner, information about partnership transactions which had been obtained from the general partner defendants. The court relied on the rule (statutory in California) that joint clients do not enjoy the privilege "in a civil proceeding between [them]." While the case arose in the context of the attorney-client privilege, the court also stated that the lawyer's fiduciary obligations required him to reveal to each partner all matters concerning the partnership, apparently even without a court order.

This last point raises a conflict between the duty of confidentiality and the duties of loyalty and keeping a client informed. (See generally Chapter 2.) Even if a communication from one of two joint clients is not privileged as to the second joint client, so that the lawyer would have to reveal it if subpoenaed by the second client, does the lawyer have a duty to volunteer the same information to that second client if it is something he or she would want to know (that is, something that the lawyer would be expected to tell the client if he had learned the same thing from a stranger), but which the source of the information (the first client) wants the lawyer to conceal? In New York State Opinion 555 (1984), a majority of the committee, over a strong dissent, concluded that the confidentiality duty was superior to the duty to inform. Is this correct? In any event, mustn't the lawyer withdraw? See also New York City Opinion 86-2 (1986): A lawyer hired by a general partner to represent a limited partnership should reveal to the limited partners the general partner's misconduct toward the partnership even over the general partner's objection.

How would your analysis differ if A and B are *unrelated* clients and their common lawyer learns from client A information that would be advantageous for client B to know? What if A tells counsel that she plans to open a horse stable across the way from where client B is planning to open an expensive outdoor restaurant? What if A hires a lawyer to negotiate an antenuptial agreement with a man she is about to marry, then B consults the lawyer on an estate problem and reveals that she is already married to the same man? Delaware Opinion 1990-1 concerned a lawyer who represented company A and company B on unrelated matters. The president of company A informed the lawyer that he planned to hire separate counsel to sue company B. The opinion concluded that this information was confidential to company A and that the lawyer could not reveal it to company B.

What happens if after a joint representation one of the multiple clients wishes to reveal privileged information and the others object? In In re Grand Jury Subpoenas, 902 F.2d 244 (4th Cir. 1990), and John Morrell & Co. v. Local Union 304A of United Food & Commercial Workers, 913 F.2d 544 (8th Cir. 1990), cert. denied, 111 S. Ct. 1683 (1991), the courts held that no party to a joint defense privilege (which the Fourth Circuit labeled the "common interest rule") may waive it without the consent of the others. The Fourth Circuit even extends the rule to "communications protected by the work-product doctrine." See also Polycast Technology Corp. v. Uniroyal, Inc., 125 F.R.D. 47 (S.D.N.Y. 1989), which proposes to distinguish between "a joint attorney-client privilege," in which the parties retain their right to waive without the consent of the other parties, and "a joint defense privilege," which may not be waived "without the consent of all co-defendants." The joint-defense privilege "covers conversations between actual or potential co-defendants [and counsel] for any common defense purpose. . . . Actual or potential litigation is a necessary prerequisite for . . . the joint-defense privilege."

How should these rules operate on the following facts: Joe and Jane consulted Attorney Evans, who gave them advice about a matter of common interest. Subsequently, Joe and Jane were indicted. Joe wished to rely on Evans's advice to establish his good faith and lack of criminal intent. Jane, who had a different strategy, wished to assert the privilege. Can Jane object to Joe's decision to reveal what Evans told them? A broad reading of the Fourth and Eighth Circuit cases cited above would suggest that she could. Yet this would be intolerable, wouldn't it? See United

States v. Walters, 913 F.2d 388 (7th Cir. 1990) (assumes without analysis that Joe may invoke the advice of counsel defense but, if he does, Jane will be entitled to a separate trial).

FURTHER READING

Nancy Moore, Conflicts of Interest in the Simultaneous Representation of Multiple Clients: A Proposed Solution to the Current Confusion and Controversy, 61 Tex. L. Rev. 211 (1982); Developments in the Law — Conflicts of Interest in the Legal Profession, 94 Harv. L. Rev. 1244, 1292-1315 (1981).

SIMULATED CASE HISTORY

— make list of potential conflict
— what should be done if a conflict

ANITA ENG *any sanction/malprac ??*

✱✱✱ IMPORTANT

I own a small company in Seattle, which operated what had been a fairly successful Burger Queen franchise for a fast food restaurant. Under my franchise agreement with Burger Queen, I have to maintain certain quality control procedures, offer a certain menu, buy my supplies from certain suppliers, charge certain prices, have my servers dress in a certain way, and spend a certain sum on advertisements monthly. Burger Queen does not allow me to serve beer but state law does. I started losing a lot of money to a new Taco Rico that opened across the boulevard because it served beer and I could not. I asked Burger Queen to allow me to serve beer because of this. Burger Queen's Director of Franchises, a man named Erskine Barth, summarily rejected my request because, he said, it would harm Burger Queen's image as a family restaurant, an image Burger Queen tried to emphasize in all its advertising by showing adults coming into Burger Queen with children and by having special things for kids to do (like a slide) at all Burger Queen locations.

I understand that explanation and for a while just lived with it, but then my sales started to fall precipitously and I worried that I would lose the franchise (I have to maintain a certain dollar volume of sales) or I would have to close simply because I could no longer earn a living. So I approached them again, and again I was flatly turned down. Finally, in desperation, I retained Blackburn, Winston and Karmel, a good small law firm in town with an expertise in franchise law, to try to negotiate a compromise or if it came to it to sue Burger Queen for an injunction or what have you. I worked with a lawyer named Casper Voll.

At first, it seemed like Burger Queen was going to respond more attentively to Voll's entreaties than it responded to mine. After Voll wrote

Barth a letter, Burger Queen hired Spaeth & Wells, one of the biggest firms in town. Vanessa Mitchell was the lawyer there who negotiated with Voll. Pretty quickly, Mitchell proposed the following settlement. Diners could bring their own beer so long as they sat at one of the tables on the outside deck. Great. First off, when people come to a restaurant they expect to be able to get what they want. They don't want to have to stop off at a grocery store on the way. Second, how useful do you think it is to let beer drinkers sit outside in a city like Seattle? It's often too hot in the summer and too wet and cold in the winter and spring.

So we negotiated some more. Meanwhile I was continuing to lose money and I had to pay counsel fees besides. I repeatedly urged Voll to go to court, but he was reluctant to do so because, he said, it would be expensive, the case would take longer than I could afford to stay in business, and Burger Queen had a lot more money than I did to litigate. I understand those points, but I told Voll I had no real options. Besides, if I had a good case, they might back down once we filed suit. And if I had to go out of business during the action because I was losing too much money, Burger Queen had to anticipate that the loss of my profitable business would become part of my damages if I won.

Well, we talked and we negotiated and negotiated. Finally, Mitchell said that Burger Queen would allow me to sell beer (they would choose the brands), but I could only sell it after six P.M. weekdays, eight P.M. Saturdays, never on Sundays, and only draft (no cans). Also, no pitchers (like they have at Taco Rico). Oh, and the beer had to be served in opaque, not transparent, cups. I couldn't advertise it anywhere, including in the window. But inside I could have three signs two inches high listing the brand names and the price. There also had to be a sign that said beer was only available at the particular hours and the particular days I mentioned. Finally, I couldn't reveal my arrangement to any other Burger Queen franchisee.

Voll said it was Mitchell's last offer. Take it or leave it. He said if I wanted to litigate, he assessed my chances of success, based on the franchise agreement and the state franchise law, at between 25 and 35 percent, depending on whether Washington was prepared to follow some favorable decisions in other states. He said his firm would need a retainer of $15,000 to begin the litigation.

I thought I could do better in court. I argued that Burger Queen would not want the publicity and the risk of a large judgment that would encourage other franchisees to sue. But Voll was putting a lot of pressure on me to settle. He seemed real proud of the compromise. He said it was "creative lawyering" at its best. He kept on me. Every time we talked, his projection of the cost of litigation went up another $5,000. In effect, he refused to bring the action without actually saying no. Finally, I gave in and accepted the offer. I tell you, though, that I never felt very happy about it. I think Burger Queen got off easy. This was seven months ago.

My sales have picked up since I started serving beer under the compromise, but they have not regained their former level. I'll survive, though.

However, let me tell you what amazing information I learned last week. First, other lawyers at Voll's firm represent Cal McGuire, a big Seattle businessman. McGuire is a limited partner in the partnership that has the Taco Rico franchise. Second, Voll's firm was started about four years ago by former associates at Spaeth & Wells, who have a pretty cozy relationship with their former colleagues and in fact get a lot of spillover business from Spaeth. Third, Voll and Mitchell each represent a defendant in a big civil securities fraud case in federal court. Voll's firm got the client from a senior partner at Spaeth & Wells.

And as if all that weren't enough, wait until you hear this: Burger Queen's parent corporation, Monarch Foods, is also a client of Blackburn, Winston. Monarch retained the firm *after* I did to do the bank financing work for a shopping center Monarch is planning to build near Tacoma. After I settled, Monarch retained the firm for the construction contracts too. Voll says that's because his firm delivers good service. I say what they delivered was me.

You know what I think? I think I was snookered, and I've written to the disciplinary committee about Voll's and his firm's behavior.

CASPER VOLL

Talk about ungrateful clients! I saved that woman from certain financial disaster. She came in here like she was John D. Rockefeller ready to litigate unto death with a Fortune 500 company. "I'm tough," she told me, "that's how I built the most successful Burger Queen franchise in the northwest and I won't let those bozos back me down." Well, not only could they have backed her down, they would have buried her. Her franchise, by the way, was successful because eight months after she opened it, the state decided to build its new office building a quarter mile away. Anita's a hard worker, to be sure, but more than half her success is dumb luck.

I saved Anita Eng by cooling down the situation. Elihu Root once said that "about half of the practice of a decent lawyer is telling would-be clients that they are damned fools and should stop." I did Eng a great service by not suing Burger Queen. The odds of winning were three to one against her and if she lost she'd be bankrupt. She'd have no business, and she would have spent her entire savings on legal fees. If she didn't like my advice she could have gone elsewhere. Look, you know as well as I that there'll always be lawyers who'll pound the table for a client, feed his aggressions, tell him "they can't do that to you, let's sue the bastards," and go on and on until the client can't wait to write out a retainer check. Then when they lose these lawyers say, "Well, we told you you could lose. You took the risk. No promises. We did our best. Sorry. Goodbye." Well, I don't practice that way.

Eng is just looking around for a reason to blame me for dissuading her from pursuing her own worst instincts. She says my partners and I are "cozy" with the Spaeth people. Hey, I'm cozy with a lot of lawyers. Seattle is a small town. We know each other here. That doesn't stop me from representing my clients and it doesn't stop them. So what if Vanessa and I are on the same side of another case? That's inevitable in a small city, especially when a relatively few lawyers do a particular kind of representation. You think Joe Flom and Marty Lipton are enemies? I'll tell you something else Anita doesn't know yet. My wife, Linda Stark, is a partner at Spaeth & Wells. I have a feeling that Anita will hit the roof when she learns this but she has no basis to. We couldn't know whom Burger Queen was going to retain when Anita hired me. And anyway, my wife is not Burger Queen's lawyer. Vanessa is.

Eng says we get cases from Spaeth. We get cases from half the big firms in town. Why? Because we're good and they know we won't embarrass them. We happen to get more work from Spaeth than anyone else — about a quarter of our business — because some of my partners worked there once and they know us better, but so what? The securities case I did with Vanessa, my partner Dave Blackburn got that case from Mr. Wells. You think that's bad for Eng? Let me tell you, when Eng's negotiation wasn't going anywhere and it looked like she might have to sue, Mr. Wells called me to say that he thought a litigation would be inadvisable for all concerned. He offered to use his good offices to advance the discussion. And he did. It was largely through his intercession that Burger Queen was willing to make the offer it finally made.

About Cal McGuire: we represent him and the McGuire interests on a lot of matters. About $100,000 of his money, maybe one-half of 1 percent of the man's wealth, is invested in a limited partnership that owns the Taco Rico franchise that is Anita's main competitor. And it, of course, sells beer. Cal is probably the largest cash investor among the dozen limited partners. You think that affected me? I didn't even know McGuire had that interest. I don't happen to handle McGuire at the firm. I'm not even sure McGuire himself knows that he's a limited partner in Taco Rico. The man is worth $20 million. And even if I did know, you think I'd care? McGuire has more important things to do than complain because we negotiated to get Burger Queen the right to sell beer. Hell, not only do we represent McGuire, my labor law partner does occasional work for Taco Rico itself. Another thing Eng doesn't know.

Finally, Eng is bitching — I mean complaining — because we handled the bank financing for Monarch Foods, Burger Queen's parent company, on a project near Tacoma. I was not on that case. After Anita hired us, Monarch retained my partner Nina Karmel to do the bank financing. Perfectly reasonable choice because Nina is one of the three or four top banking lawyers in the state. The two matters are entirely unrelated. No one at Monarch so much as mentioned the Burger Queen case to Nina. I just don't understand for the life of me what any of this has to do with the reasonableness of the settlement we won for Eng. A settlement is for a client to accept or reject and she accepted it, not us. Any objective person looking at all the facts and all the risks would have to say it was a fair result. After all, Burger Queen did have a point and probably had the law on its side as well.

All in all, I got Burger Queen to give Eng a lot more than it was prepared to give before I entered the picture. It seems to me that the very factors that Eng now says undercut our representation of her actually enhanced our ability to get a favorable result, a result that has kept her in business.

The Insurance Triangle

PUBLIC SERVICE MUTUAL INSURANCE CO. v. GOLDFARB
53 N.Y.2d 392, 425 N.E.2d 810, 442 N.Y.S.2d 422 (1981)

JASEN, JUDGE.

The question before us is whether a policy of professional liability insurance issued by plaintiff affords coverage to a dentist in a civil suit commenced by a former patient grounded upon an act of sexual abuse alleged to have occurred in the course of dental treatment.

Plaintiff Public Service Mutual Insurance Company, a multi-line insurer, issued a "Dentist's Professional Liability Policy" to the Dental Society of the State of New York. Defendant, Saul Goldfarb, a member of the society, obtained coverage under that policy. Defendant Jacqueline P. Schwartz is a former patient of Dr. Goldfarb who received dental treatment from him on May 23, 1977. She claims that in the course of receiving such treatment, she was sexually abused by Dr. Goldfarb. This claim, which is the subject of a pending civil suit, also formed the basis of professional disciplinary proceedings against Dr. Goldfarb and resulted in a criminal conviction of the crime of sexual abuse in the third degree. In this declaratory judgment action, plaintiff has asked the court to determine whether its policy of insurance provides coverage for the civil claim seeking compensatory and punitive damages. . . .

On this appeal, plaintiff argues that its policy of insurance was not intended by the parties to provide coverage against a claim of sexual abuse. . . . It is further argued that even if, as a contractual matter, coverage exists, it should not be enforced in this case because the public policy of this State does not allow contractual indemnification for civil liability which arises out of the commission of a crime.

Defendant argues that the broad language of the insurance policy in issue specifically provides coverage for a claim of sexual abuse in the course of dental treatment. . . . He further argues that where, as here, the policy explicitly provides coverage, such protection should not be denied upon public policy grounds. . . . [T]he insurance policy in issue was intended by the parties to provide coverage for liability arising out of the acts complained of by defendant Schwartz. The policy specifically states that the insurer will "pay on behalf of the Insured named in this certificate all sums, including punitive damages, which the Named Insured shall become obligated to pay by reason of the liability imposed upon him by law for damages because of injury resulting from professional dental services rendered . . . and resulting from any claim or suit based upon . . . [m]alpractice, error, negligence or mistake, assault, slander, libel [or] undue familiarity." This language clearly indicates an intent on the part of the insurer to pay both compensatory and punitive damages arising out of unlawful or inappropriate physical contact which occurs during the course of dental treatment. Defendant Schwartz claims that such contact occurred. Hence, as a purely contractual matter absent any consideration of public policy, a claim within the stated coverage has been made and the insurer is obligated to defend the suit.

Whether indemnity will ultimately be required, however, cannot be determined at this stage of the proceeding. It is possible, of course, that the trier of fact could find that unlawful contact with defendant Schwartz occurred, but that it did not occur in the course of professional dental services. In this event, defendant Schwartz could recover from defendant Goldfarb, but he, in turn, could not seek contractual indemnity from his insurer because the policy imposes liability upon the insurer only for "injury resulting from professional dental services rendered." This being so, any determination as to whether the insurer must indemnify Dr. Goldfarb must await a trial of defendant Schwartz' claim, at which time a special verdict should be obtained on the issue of whether or not the acts complained of occurred in the course of professional dental treatment.

Having determined that plaintiff has contractually obligated itself at least to defend Dr. Goldfarb against the claim in issue, we must now address the question whether the public policy of this State precludes insurance coverage for a claim of sexual abuse in the course of dental treatment. Plaintiff notes that defendant was convicted of the crime of sexual abuse in the third degree and argues that, as a matter of public policy, he may not be indemnified for any civil liability arising out of this criminal act. We disagree. The mere fact that an act may have penal consequences does not necessarily mean that insurance coverage for civil liability arising from the same act is precluded by public policy. Whether such coverage is permissable depends upon whether the insured, in committing his criminal act, intended to cause injury. One who intentionally injures another may not be indemnified for any civil liability thus incurred. However, one whose intentional act causes an unintended injury may be so indemnified.

In this case, the complaint against Dr. Goldfarb alleges both intentional acts which caused unintended injury, seeking compensatory damages therefor and intentional causation of injury, seeking compensatory and punitive damages therefor. To the extent that defendant Schwartz' complaint can be construed as a claim for injuries unintentionally caused by Dr. Goldfarb, he may seek indemnity from his insurer for that claim. Thus, the insurer would be obligated to pay any judgment against Dr. Goldfarb for compensatory damages only, assuming, of course, that the trier of fact determined, in a special verdict, that such unintended injury occurred in the course of dental treatment.

Under no circumstances, however, can the insurer be compelled to indemnify Dr. Goldfarb for punitive damages. Such damages are, as the name implies, a punishment for intentional wrongdoing. As we have only recently noted, to allow insurance coverage for such damages "is totally to defeat the purpose of punitive damages." . . .

Furthermore, if a finding that defendant Goldfarb *intended to injure* defendant Schwartz is made in a special verdict, he would be precluded from seeking indemnity from his insurer for either compensatory or punitive damages flowing from this intentional causation of *injury*. This is so because to allow such indemnity would be to violate the "fundamental principle that no one shall be permitted to take advantage of his own wrong." . . .

We note also that although the insurer need not indemnify Dr. Goldfarb for any liability for punitive damages, it must, nonetheless, defend him in the pending lawsuit because a claim within the stated coverage has been made. Moreover, inasmuch as the insurer's interest in defending the lawsuit is in conflict with the defendant's interest — the insurer being liable only upon some of the grounds for recovery asserted and not upon others — defendant Goldfarb is entitled to defense by an attorney of his own choosing, whose reasonable fee is to be paid by the insurer.*

---

*That is not to say that a conflict of interest requiring retention of separate counsel will arise in every case where multiple claims are made. Independent counsel is only necessary in cases where the defense attorney's duty to the insured would require that he defeat liability on any ground and his duty to the insurer would require that he defeat liability only upon grounds which would render the insurer liable. When such a conflict is apparent, the insured must be free to choose his own counsel whose reasonable fee is to be paid by the insurer. On the other hand, where multiple claims present no conflict — for example, where the insurance contract provides liability coverage only for personal injuries and the claim against the insured seeks recovery for property damage as well as for personal injuries — no threat of divided loyalty is present and there is no need for the retention of separate counsel. This is so because in such a situation the question of insurance coverage is not intertwined with the question of the insured's liability.

In sum, we hold that plaintiff is obligated to defend Dr. Goldfarb in the lawsuit commenced by defendant Schwartz and to provide independent counsel for the defense, to be chosen by Dr. Goldfarb. At this stage of the litigation, however, it is impossible to determine whether any indemnity for any compensatory damages which ultimately may be assessed against Dr. Goldfarb will be required, for such a determination can only be made after the trier of fact in the Schwartz action has rendered its special verdict. . . .

The Obligation to Defend

The problem described in *Goldfarb* arises because an insurer's obligation to defend its insured is broader than its obligation to indemnify the insured. No conflict problem arises if the complaint against the insured alleges conduct squarely within the policy and seeks damages below the policy limit. Nor does a problem arise if the complaint alleges conduct clearly outside the language of the policy. But where the complaint alleges conduct that may fall within or outside the policy, or when it seeks damages above the policy limits, the interests of the insurer and the insured may begin to diverge. This is so because, as *Goldfarb* puts it, "the question of insurance coverage is [then] intertwined with the question of the insured's liability." We will eventually learn whether the insured is covered because the jury will tell us in its "special verdict." But by then the defense costs will have been expended.

What will happen at the trial of Schwartz v. Goldfarb? Consider the three interests: Goldfarb has an interest in (1) avoiding liability for compensatory or punitive damages or (2) limiting his liability to compensatory damages for nonintentional injuries. Do you see why (2) is the fallback position? Schwartz has an interest in establishing liability for compensatory and punitive damages. Would she prefer that the compensatory damages be based on intentional injuries or nonintentional injuries? That's really a decision of high strategy, isn't it? Schwartz will need to know whether she can get punitive damages for nonintentional injuries and Goldfarb's net worth. Why? The insurance company doesn't much care about punitive damages since it won't have to pay them under any circumstances. With regard to compensatory damages, it prefers that these be based on intentional injuries. Do you see why? This means, doesn't it, that the insurance company must have the right to participate in Schwartz v. Goldfarb through counsel? The leading California case on insurance-related conflicts is San Diego Credit Union v. Cumis, 162 Cal. App. 3d 358, 208 Cal. Rptr. 494 (1984). For a factually complex case illustrating the application of conflict of interest rules to *Cumis* counsel (as they are called in California), see Employers Insurance of Wausau v. Albert D. Seeno Construction Co., 692 F. Supp. 1150 (N.D. Cal. 1988).

QUESTION

5.6   "We have a client I'll call law firm *X*. We are retained by *X*'s malpractice carrier to defend it in an action brought by a former client
of *X*. The action charges that a partner of *X*, whom I will call
Charles Sobol, caused it significant losses in connection with the
representation of the client. The complaint alleges various theories, including negligence and intentional fraud. Sobol is named as
a defendant along with *X*, but obviously he has separate counsel.
Under the malpractice policy, the insurance company will pay any
judgment against *X* based on Sobol's negligence. But it won't pay
any judgment based on Sobol's intentional fraud. However, under
the vicarious liability rules in this jurisdiction, all the partners of *X*
will be liable for Sobol's intentional fraud in the course of his law
practice. So you see the score? If the jury finds negligence, *X* is
covered, but if it finds fraud, the partners of *X* will have to pay any
judgment against the firm. Last week, another firm partner,
Nancy Frankel, made an appointment to see me. She had some information tending to support the view that Sobol's conduct was intentional and fraudulent. I talked the matter over with the firm's
executive committee — Nancy is on it — and they instructed me to
explore the possibility of settlement within the policy limit. The
committee is afraid of a discovery request that will require me to
produce the information and wants to try to settle the case before
that happens. If we do settle, the insurance company will pay because there will be no finding of fraud. But what are my obligations to the insurance company? Furthermore, the plaintiff would
rather win on a negligence theory because then it knows it will collect the judgment whereas if it wins on a fraud theory it is by no
means clear that all the partners will have sufficient assets to pay.
So even if the plaintiff gets this evidence of fraud, it doesn't have
the same interest as the insurance company would have in pursuing it. In that case, what are my obligations?"

C.   THE ADVOCATE-WITNESS RULE

A special conflict confronts attorneys who are or ought to be called as witnesses in a litigation in which they represent one of the parties. It may be
that the attorney ought to be a witness for the party he or she represents.
It may be that the attorney will or ought to be called by an opposing
party. The Code of Professional Responsibility addresses the issue of the

attorney as advocate and witness in DR 5-101(B) and in DR 5-102. DR 5-101(B) speaks to the attorney's responsibility before accepting a representation. It says that the attorney "shall not accept employment in contemplated or pending litigation if he knows or it is obvious that he or a lawyer in his firm ought to be called as a witness." There are four exceptions that you should review. DR 5-102 speaks to the lawyer's responsibility if the issue arises after he or she has already accepted employment. Paragraph (A) of the rule says that if "a lawyer learns or it is obvious that he or a lawyer in his firm ought to be called as a witness on behalf of his client, he shall withdraw from the conduct of the trial and his firm . . . shall not continue representation in the trial." The exceptions contained in DR 5-101(B) are then incorporated by reference. Paragraph (B) of DR 5-102 is concerned with the lawyer's responsibility when, after accepting employment in a contemplated or pending litigation, the "lawyer learns or it is obvious that he or a lawyer in his firm may be called as a witness" by another party. In that case, the rule is less strict. The lawyer "may continue the representation until it is apparent that his testimony is or may be prejudicial to his client." One reason the rule is less insistent at this juncture is to guard against an adversary's improper strategic efforts to call an opposing party's lawyer in order to force disqualification. Freeman v. Kulicke & Soffa Industries, 449 F. Supp. 974 (E.D. Pa. 1978), aff'd, 591 F.2d 1334 (3d Cir. 1979).

Note that the language of the code imputedly disqualifies all other lawyers in the firm of the lawyer who may or ought to be called as a witness.

Model Rule 3.7 is a streamlined version of the code's provisions. It does not distinguish between testimony for or against a client. Unless an exception applies, it simply prohibits lawyers from acting "as advocate at a trial [if] the lawyer is likely to be a necessary witness." Notice the several limitations these words imply. The disqualification runs only to advocacy at trial, not to pretrial work. ABA Informal Opinion 89-1529 is in accord, provided the client consents to the lawyer's abbreviated role and the lawyer reasonably concludes that the client's interests will not be adversely affected by the fact that the lawyer may testify. See also Culebras Enterprises Corp. v. Rivera-Rios, 846 F.2d 94 (1st Cir. 1988); Bottaro v. Hatton Associates, 680 F.2d 895 (2d Cir. 1982). An attorney who is permitted to represent a client only before trial may not be permitted to submit a factual affidavit in support of a motion. Citrus Marketing Board of Israel v. M/V Ecuadorian Reefer, 754 F. Supp. 229 (D. Mass. 1990); McIntosh v. Southwestern Truck Sales, 304 Ark. 224, 800 S.W.2d 431 (1990) (also holding that lawyer-witness cannot represent client on appeal).

Another difference between the rules and the code is in the way they articulate the likelihood of the lawyer's testimony. The code's language envisions that the lawyer "ought to be called as a witness" or, after retention, if it becomes "apparent that [the lawyer's] testimony is or may be prejudicial to [the] client." The rule, by contrast, applies if the lawyer is "likely" to be a "necessary" witness for any side, regardless of when that likelihood first appears. Compare S&S Hotel Ventures L.P. v. 777 S.H. Corp., 69 N.Y.2d 437, 508 N.E.2d 647, 515 N.Y.S.2d 735 (1987) (disqualification not required even if lawyer's testimony would be "highly useful" to client unless it would be "strictly necessary") (construing code).

By far the most dramatic change from the code to the rules is in the deletion of imputed disqualification. Rule 3.7(a) disqualifies the lawyer personally but not his or her firm. Only in the limited circumstance described in Rule 3.7(b) will imputation arise. Rule 3.7(b) allows associates of the disqualified lawyer to act as advocate "unless precluded from doing so by Rule 1.7 or Rule 1.9." In other words, the conflict must run deeper than the reasons underlying the advocate-witness rule (hereafter discussed) in order to trigger imputation. Can you think of an example in which the entire firm of a lawyer-witness should be disqualified? What if in *P* v. *D*, *D* calls *W*, a partner in the firm representing *P*? *W*'s testimony will be highly damaging to *P*'s case. What will *P*'s trial lawyer wish to do if free to do it?

Policies Behind the Advocate-Witness Rule

These are several, somewhat overlapping, somewhat inconsistent.

First, it is said that the jury may accord the lawyer's testimony too much weight because of his or her "special knowledge of [the] case." MacArthur v. Bank of New York, 524 F. Supp. 1205, 1209-1211 (S.D.N.Y. 1981). Of course, this argument is overinclusive. Even if the lawyer-witness is not also an advocate, the jury will learn about his or her "special knowledge" in the course of the testimony.

Second, it is said that professional courtesy may handicap the opposing lawyer on cross-examination. Id. But why is this any more true if the lawyer-witness is also an advocate than if he or she is not?

Third, it is said that "the bar is ill-served when an attorney's veracity becomes an issue in a case; lay observers especially might speculate whether counsel has compromised his integrity on the stand in order to prevail in the litigation." Id. at 1206. If that is true, then we should retain the imputed disqualification rule because the lawyer-witness will have an obvious interest in the outcome if someone else in her firm is representing a party. Compare Cresswell v. Sullivan & Cromwell, 922 F.2d 60 (2d Cir. 1990). A lawyer-witness testified on behalf of a former client in a case that grew out of his former representation. He did not act as advocate. The court said it was unethical for the lawyer to have agreed to accept a fee for testifying contingent on, and a percentage of, the former client's recovery. The court cited the advocate-witness rule and DR 7-109(C), which forbids contingent witness fees.

Fourth, the jury might not distinguish between the lawyer's role as witness and the lawyer's role as advocate. As a result it may "accord testimonial weight to his closing arguments." *MacArthur*, supra. In addition, in summation the lawyer will be in a position to say to the jury, "as I told you when I testified. . . ." Can you reconcile the concern that the jury might give undue weight to the lawyer's testimony with the concern that the lawyer may appear to have "compromised his integrity on the stand in order to prevail in the litigation"?

MacArthur was a jury trial. Do the reasons supporting the advocate-witness rule apply at judge trials? The rule itself makes no distinction.

A client whose lawyer has testimony favorable to the client may wish to keep the lawyer and waive the testimony. That's not allowed. The rule is mandatory. As the *MacArthur* court explained:

> Nor may the client waive the rule's protection by promising not to call the attorney as a witness. The ostensible paternalism of disregarding such waivers is justified by the circumstances in which the problem arises. The client will generally be reluctant to forego the assistance of familiar counsel or to incur the expense and inconvenience of retaining another lawyer. The most serious breaches of the rule, in which an attorney has become intimately involved in the subject matter of the dispute, will often be the very situations in which withdrawal is most burdensome. Moreover, the party will generally be guided in its decision by the very attorney whose continued representation is at issue. At the same time, the attorney will be reluctant to jeopardize good relations with the client and may — against his better judgment — defer to the client's desire for representation.

Because the rule is mandatory, it "requires that the court be able to disqualify counsel sua sponte when the need arises." In *MacArthur*, the judge disqualified an entire law firm in the middle of trial. In Lamborn v. Dittmer, 873 F.2d 522 (2d Cir. 1989), a judgment for $30 million was reversed when the trial judge erroneously used the advocate-witness rule to prevent the defendant from calling the plaintiff's lawyer as a witness. The proper remedy was disqualification.

One objection to imputed disqualification is that it prevents a firm from providing "soup to nuts" service to a client. As the *MacArthur* court wrote:

> Finally, defendant objects that the effect of the court's ruling, if consistently applied, would be to prevent a law firm from maintaining a continuing relationship with a client. That fear is groundless. A lawyer can choose, as McNicol did here, to participate actively in a client's business affairs — not just as an adviser, but also as a negotiator and agent. (McNicol was also a director and a member of the executive committee of the company that plaintiff claims to have rehabilitated.) Such conduct is entirely proper. But if an attorney chooses to become intimately involved in the client's business,

then he or she must be prepared to step aside if the matters involved result in litigation. This may be displeasing to firms that wish to have some members act as businessmen and others as litigators. But when these firms place themselves in the position of having an attorney acquire information that makes his testimony necessary, they must accept the consequences.

Both a law firm and its clients may have good reason to desire a "soup to nuts" practice. Is the court too dismissive? Should it matter that the client in *MacArthur* was a large bank?

The advocate-witness rule has several exceptions. The vaguest is that disqualification "would work substantial hardship on the client." Rule 3.7(a)(3). The code adds "because of the distinctive value of the lawyer or his firm as counsel in the particular case." DR 5-101(B)(4). *MacArthur*, construing the code, said:

> Hardship alone, however substantial, is insufficient to permit continued representation. The deprivation to the client will often be greatest precisely when the attorney was most intimately involved in, and familiar with, the events giving rise to the suit. . . .
>
> The exception expressly qualifies the hardship that must be shown to permit continued representation as one that arises "because of the distinctive value of the lawyer or his firm as counsel in the particular case." Here, defendant failed to demonstrate that his attorney has distinctive value as trial counsel.

Does deletion of the "distinctive value" language change this result?

The Advocate-Witness Rule in Criminal Cases

The rule has been applied to defense counsel notwithstanding the defendant's willingness to waive counsel's testimony. United States v. Arrington, 867 F.2d 122 (2d Cir. 1989); United States v. McKeon, 738 F.2d 26 (2d Cir. 1984).

Does the rule apply to prosecutors? According to an en banc decision of the Seventh Circuit, the rule not only applies to prosecutors, but in an apparent case of first impression, the court held that it applies in a suppression hearing before a judge without a jury. Although the court finds the rule inapplicable in the case before it for other reasons, it cited American Bar Association Standards Relating to the Prosecution Function and the Defense Function (Approved Draft 1971) §3.1(f) as follows:

> The prosecutor should avoid interviewing a prospective witness except in the presence of a third person unless the prosecutor is prepared to forego impeachment of a witness by the prosecutor's own testimony as to what the

witness stated in an interview or to seek leave to withdraw from the case in order to present his impeaching testimony.

United States v. Johnston, 690 F.2d 638, 643-645 (7th Cir. 1982). The *Johnston* court cited United States v. Birdman, 602 F.2d 547, 553-555 (3d Cir. 1979), cert. denied 444 U.S. 1032 (1980), on the reasons for applying the advocate-witness rule to prosecutors:

> First, the rule eliminates the risk that a testifying prosecutor will not be a fully objective witness given his position as an advocate for the government. Second, there is fear that the prestige or prominence of a government prosecutor's office will artificially enhance his credibility as a witness. Third, the performance of dual roles by a prosecutor might create confusion on the part of the trier of fact as to whether the prosecutor is speaking in the capacity of an advocate or of a witness, thus raising the possibility of the trier according testimonial credit to the prosecutor's closing argument. Fourth, the rule reflects a broader concern for public confidence in the administration of justice, and implements the maxim that "justice must satisfy the appearance of justice." This concern is especially significant where the testifying attorney represents the prosecuting arm of the federal government. In addition to the policies articulated in *Birdman*, there is at least one other consequence deserving of consideration, particularly by United States Attorneys. United States Attorneys are expected to adhere to the highest standards of professional behavior and to be worthy of public trust and confidence. Nevertheless, the United States Attorney who becomes both witness and advocate runs the risk of impeachment or otherwise being found not credible by the district judge. That would be an unfortunate situation for government counsel which could impair not only continuation as an effective advocate in the case, but could also produce lingering adverse aftereffects.

One court has gone so far as to disqualify a local district attorney and require appointment of a special prosecutor when two former members of the office were going to testify against the defendant. Pease v. District Court, 708 P.2d 800 (Colo. 1985). Other courts have rejected this approach. See, for example, State v. Johnson, 702 S.W.2d 65 (Mo. 1985).

FURTHER READING

Arnold Enker, The Rationale of the Rule That Forbids a Lawyer to Be Advocate and Witness in the Same Case, 1977 Am. B. Found. Res. J. 455; Note, The Advocate-Witness Rule: If Z, Then X. But Why?, 52 N.Y.U. L. Rev. 1365 (1977); Note, Disqualification of Law Firms Under the Attorney-Witness Rule, 54 Tul. L. Rev. 521 (1980) (authored by D. Veta).

VI

Successive Conflicts of Interest

A. PRIVATE PRACTICE

ANALYTICA, INC. v. NPD RESEARCH, INC.
708 F.2d 1263 (7th Cir. 1983)

POSNER, J.

Two law firms, Schwartz & Freeman and Pressman and Hartunian, appeal from orders disqualifying them from representing Analytica, Inc. in an antitrust suit against NPD, Inc. . . .

[Malec was an employee of NPD between 1972 and 1977. Malec had two shares, or 10 percent, of NPD's stock. During the course of his employment, his two co-owners wished to give him an additional two shares of stock as compensation for his services. They told him to find "a lawyer who would structure the transaction in the least costly way." Malec hired Richard Fine, a partner in Schwartz & Freeman, and Fine devised a plan for the transfer of the stock. Since Malec had to pay income tax on the stock, it was necessary to evaluate it. NPD gave Fine information on its financial condition, sales trends, and management, after which Fine fixed a value for the stock, which the corporation adopted. NPD paid Fine's bill for the services. Eventually Malec and his wife, who was also employed at NPD, left their jobs. Mrs. Malec thereafter incorporated Analytica to compete with NPD in the market-research business. At the time of the decision, Mrs. Malec had left Analytica.

In October 1977, several months after the Malecs had left NPD, Analytica retained Schwartz & Freeman to represent it in connection with its claim of anticompetitive behavior against NPD. After complaints to the FTC proved unavailing, Analytica authorized Schwartz & Free-

247

man to hire Pressman and Hartunian as trial counsel. An antitrust suit was brought against NPD in 1979. The defendant moved to disqualify both of the plaintiff's law firms. The district judge disqualified both firms and ordered Schwartz & Freeman to pay NPD $25,000 for resisting the disqualification motion. Schwartz & Freeman appealed.]

For rather obvious reasons a lawyer is prohibited from using confidential information that he has obtained from a client against that client on behalf of another one. But this prohibition has not seemed enough by itself to make clients feel secure about reposing confidences in lawyers, so a further prohibition has evolved: a lawyer may not represent an adversary of his former client if the subject matter of the two representations is "substantially related," which means: if the lawyer could have obtained confidential information in the first representation that would have been relevant in the second. It is irrelevant whether he actually obtained such information and used it against his former client, or whether — if the lawyer is a firm rather than an individual practitioner — different people in the firm handled the two matters and scrupulously avoided discussing them.

There is an exception for the case where a member or associate of a law firm (or government legal department) changes jobs, and later he or his new firm is retained by an adversary of a client of his former firm. In such a case, even if there is a substantial relationship between the two matters, the lawyer can avoid disqualification by showing that effective measures were taken to prevent confidences from being received by whichever lawyers in the new firm are handling the new matter.* The exception is inapplicable here; the firm itself changed sides.

Schwartz & Freeman's Mr. Fine not only had access to but received confidential financial and operating data of NPD in 1976 and early 1977 when he was putting together the deal to transfer stock to Mr. Malec. Within a few months, Schwartz & Freeman popped up as counsel to an adversary of NPD's before the FTC, and in that proceeding and later in the antitrust lawsuit advanced contentions to which the data Fine received might have been relevant. Those data concerned NPD's profitability, sales prospects, and general market strength — all matters potentially germane to both the liability and damage phases of an antitrust suit charging NPD with monopolization. The two representations are thus substantially related, even though we do not know whether any of the information Fine received would be useful in Analytica's lawsuit (it might just duplicate information in Malec's possession, but we do not know his role in Analytica's suit), or if so whether he conveyed any of it to his partners and associates who were actually handling the suit. If the

*This is a reference to the utility of screening against imputed disqualification in the transient lawyer situation. Authorities are divided on whether screening can prevent imputation. See page 269 infra. Screening would, in any event, be inadequate here because of the next sentence in Judge Posner's opinion. — ED.

"substantial relationship" test applies, however, "it is not appropriate for the court to inquire into whether actual confidences were disclosed," unless the exception noted above for cases where the law firm itself did not switch sides is applicable, as it is not here. . . .

Schwartz & Freeman argues, it is true, that Malec rather than NPD retained it to structure the stock transfer, but this is both erroneous and irrelevant. NPD's three co-owners retained Schwartz & Freeman to work out a deal beneficial to all of them. All agreed that Mr. Malec should be given two more shares of the stock; the only question was the cheapest way of doing it; the right answer would benefit them all. Cf. Coase, The Problem of Social Cost, 3 J. Law & Econ. 1 (1960). The principals saw no need to be represented by separate lawyers, each pushing for a bigger slice of a fixed pie and a fee for getting it. Not only did NPD rather than Malec pay Schwartz & Freeman's bills (and there is no proof that it had a practice of paying its officers' legal expenses), but neither NPD nor the co-owners were represented by counsel other than Schwartz & Freeman. Though Millman, an accountant for NPD, did have a law degree and did do some work on the stock-transfer plan, he was not acting as the co-owners' or NPD's lawyer in a negotiation in which Fine was acting as Malec's lawyer. As is common in closely held corporations, Fine was counsel to the firm, as well as to all of its principals, for the transaction. If the position taken by Schwartz & Freeman prevailed, a corporation that used only one lawyer to counsel it on matters of shareholder compensation would run the risk of the lawyer's later being deemed to have represented a single shareholder rather than the whole firm, and the corporation would lose the protection of the lawyer-client relationship. Schwartz & Freeman's position thus could force up the legal expenses of owners of closely held corporations.

But it does not even matter whether NPD or Malec was the client. In Westinghouse's antitrust suit against Kerr-McGee and other uranium producers, Kerr-McGee moved to disqualify Westinghouse's counsel, Kirkland & Ellis, because of a project that the law firm had done for the American Petroleum Institute, of which Kerr-McGee was a member, on competition in the energy industries. Kirkland & Ellis's client had been the Institute rather than Kerr-McGee but we held that this did not matter; what mattered was that Kerr-McGee had furnished confidential information to Kirkland & Ellis in connection with the law firm's work for the Institute. Westinghouse Elec. Corp. v. Kerr-McGee Corp., [580 F.2d 1311 (7th Cir.), cert. denied, 439 U.S. 955 (1978)]. As in this case, it was not shown that the information had actually been used in the antitrust litigation. The work for the Institute had been done almost entirely by Kirkland & Ellis's Washington office, the antitrust litigation was being handled in the Chicago office, and Kirkland & Ellis is a big firm. The connection between the representation of a trade association of which Kerr-McGee happened to be a member and the representation of its adversary thus was rather tenuous; one may doubt whether Kerr-McGee really thought its confidences had been abused by Kirkland & Ellis. If there is any aspect of the Kerr-McGee decision that is subject to criticism, it is this. The present case is a much stronger one for disqualification. If NPD did not retain Schwartz & Freeman — though we think it did — still it supplied Schwartz & Freeman with just the kind of confidential data that it would have furnished a lawyer that it had retained; and it had a right not to see Schwartz & Freeman reappear within months on the opposite side of a litigation to which that data might be highly pertinent.

We acknowledge the growing dissatisfaction, illustrated by Lindgren, Toward a New Standard of Attorney Disqualification, 1982 Am. Bar Foundation Research J. 419, with the use of disqualification as a remedy for unethical conduct by lawyers. The dissatisfaction is based partly on the effect of disqualification proceedings in delaying the underlying litigation and partly on a sense that current conflict of interest standards, in legal representation as in government employment, are too stringent, particularly as applied to large law firms — though there is no indication that Schwartz & Freeman is a large firm. But we cannot find any authority for withholding the remedy in a case like this, even if we assume contrary to fact that Schwartz & Freeman is as large as Kirkland & Ellis. NPD thought Schwartz & Freeman was its counsel and supplied it without reserve with the sort of data — data about profits and sales and marketing plans — that play a key role in a monopolization suit — and lo and behold, within months Schwartz & Freeman had been hired by a competitor of NPD's to try to get the Federal Trade Commission to sue NPD; and later that competitor, still represented by Schwartz & Freeman, brought its own suit against NPD. We doubt that anyone would argue that Schwartz & Freeman could resist disqualification if it were still representing NPD, even if no confidences were revealed, and we do not think that an interval of a few months ought to make a critical difference.

The "substantial relationship" test has its problems, but conducting a factual inquiry in every case into whether confidences had actually been revealed would not be a satisfactory alternative, particularly in a case such as this where the issue is not just whether they have been revealed but also whether they will be revealed during a pending litigation. Apart from the difficulty of taking evidence on the question without compromising the confidences themselves, the only witnesses would be the very lawyers whose firm was sought to be disqualified (unlike a case where the issue is what confidences a lawyer received while at a former law firm), and their interest not only in retaining a client but in denying a serious breach of professional ethics might outweigh any felt obligation to "come clean." While "appearance of impropriety" as a principle of professional ethics invites and maybe has undergone uncritical expansion because of its vague and open-ended character, in this case it has meaning and weight. For a law firm to represent one client today, and the client's adversary tomorrow in a closely related matter, creates an unsavory appearance of conflict of interest that is difficult to dispel in the eyes of the lay public — or for that matter the bench and bar — by the filing of affidavits, difficult to verify objectively, denying that improper communication has taken place or will take place between the lawyers in the firm handling the two sides. Clients will not repose confidences in lawyers whom they distrust and will not trust firms that switch sides as nimbly as Schwartz & Freeman.

[The court affirmed the dismissal and the $25,000 payment. Judge Coffey dissented on the ground that the presumption of shared confidential information should not be irrebuttable.]

The "Substantial Relationship" Test

The "substantial relationship" test, repeated in Rule 1.9(a) of the Model Rules, is generally credited to Judge Weinfeld's opinion in T.C. Theatre v. Warner Bros. Pictures, 113 F. Supp. 265, 268 (S.D.N.Y. 1953). Judge Weinfeld wrote:

> [W]here any substantial relationship can be shown between the subject matter of a former representation and that of a subsequent adverse representation, the latter will be prohibited. . . .
>
> [T]he former client need show no more than that the matters embraced within the pending suit wherein his former attorney appears on behalf of his adversary are substantially related to the matters or cause of action wherein the attorney previously represented him, the former client. The Court will assume that during the course of the former representation confidences were disclosed to the attorney bearing on the subject matter of the representation.

See also Trone v. Smith, 621 F.2d 994, 998 (9th Cir. 1980).

The "substantial relationship" test has undergone some change since first articulated by Judge Weinfeld in 1953, as this and the next two paragraphs reveal. In *Analytica*, Judge Posner states that the lawyer will be disqualified if the "subject matter of the two representations is 'substantially related,'" and then immediately states this to mean: "if the lawyer could have obtained confidential information in the first representation that would have been relevant in the second." That's the correct inquiry, isn't it? It's not the kind of legal advice the lawyer rendered in the two matters but the information she learned. But is Judge Posner's articulation too broad? Would it apply whatever the amount or importance of "confidential information" the lawyer "could have obtained"? Yes, according to Cornish v. Superior Court, 209 Cal. App. 3d 467, 257 Cal. Rptr. 383, 387 (1989) ("if there was even one confidential communication which relates to the current dispute, a basis for disqualification would exist"). See also Bridge Products, Inc. v. Quantum Chemical Corp., 1990 U.S. Dist. LEXIS 2202 (N.D. Ill. 1990) (a firm that has a preliminary interview with a client may not thereafter represent the client's adversary on the subject of the interview unless it has instructed the prospective client that information received will not be treated as confidential).

For a different variation on the substantial relationship test see Evans v. Artek Systems, 715 F.2d 788, 791 (2d Cir. 1983), where the court set out three conditions for successive disqualification. The first is that the moving party be a former client. The second is that there be a "substantial relationship between the subject matter of the . . . prior representation . . . and the issues in the present lawsuit." And the third requirement is that the "attorney whose disqualification is sought had access to, or was likely to have had access to, relevant privileged information in the course of his prior representation." Didn't Judge Weinfeld's test presume the third requirement from the existence of the second?

A trend toward focusing on facts, sometimes to the exclusion of issues, finds support in Carlson v. Langdon, 751 P.2d 344, 349 (Wyo. 1988). The court identified two "approaches" to the substantial relationship test. Under one approach, "the issues of the two cases are examined to determine whether there are common issues." Under the other, the court determines "whether in the factual context the matters involving the two clients are related in some substantial way." The court adopted the second approach because if "the two matters have common facts, the attorney is in a position to receive confidential information which possibly could be used to the detriment of the former client in the latter proceeding." See also Duncan v. Merrill Lynch, Pierce, Fenner & Smith, Inc., 646 F.2d 1020 (5th Cir.), cert. denied, 454 U.S. 895 (1981) (fact that current and prior matters involved the securities laws insufficient to establish substantial relationship); United States Football League v. National Football League, 605 F. Supp. 1448, 1460 n.26 (S.D.N.Y. 1985) (it "is the congruence of *factual* matters, rather than areas of law, that establishes a substantial relationship") (emphasis in original); INA Underwriters Insurance Co. v. Nalibotsky, 594 F. Supp. 1199 (E.D. Pa. 1984) (fact that prior and subsequent actions both relate to same housing development is insufficient standing alone to establish substantial relationship); H. F. Ahmanson & Co. v. Salomon Bros., 229 Cal. App. 3d 1445, 280 Cal. Rptr. 614, 620 (1991): "[T]he court should 'focus on the similarities between the two factual situations, the legal questions posed, and the nature and extent of the attorney's involvement with the cases. As part of its review, the court should examine the time spent by the attorney on the earlier cases, the type of work performed, and the attorney's possible exposure to formulation of policy or strategy,'" quoting Judge Adams's concurrence in Silver Chrysler Plymouth v. Chrysler Motors, 518 F.2d 751 (2d Cir. 1975).

How would you decide Sirianni v. Tomlinson, 133 A.D.2d 391, 519 N.Y.S.2d 385 (2d Dept. 1987)? A lawyer represented one of two share-holders of a closely held corporation in an action against the other share-holder. The lawyer had previously represented the wife of the defendant shareholder in a matrimonial action (thereafter discontinued) against her husband. The issues in the matters were dissimilar. Should disqualification be ordered?

Concern over such considerations as a client's right to counsel of choice, the loss of time and money incurred when counsel is disqualified, and the fact that disqualification complicates and delays litigation, have resulted in Second Circuit cases strictly interpreting the substantial relationship test. In Government of India v. Cook Industries, 569 F.2d 737, 739-740 (2d Cir. 1978), for example, the court said that disqualification would be granted only when the issues in the present and prior cases were "identical" or "essentially the same." See also Silver Chrysler Plymouth v. Chrysler Motors, supra, at 754 (defining a substantial relationship as where the connection between the cases is "patently clear"); Emle Industries v. Patentex, 478 F.2d 562, 572 (2d Cir. 1973) (emphasizing that "matters in controversy in each case . . . are not merely 'substantially related,' but are in fact identical"). Government of India v. Cook Industries, supra, placed the burden of proving the facts required for disqualification on the movant. See also Evans v. Artek, supra, ("the moving defendants bear the heavy burden of proving facts required for disqualification").

The lesson of the Second Circuit cases is that conduct that may be unethical and grounds for discipline will not necessarily result in disqualification because different considerations apply. Other courts have made the same distinction. Professional Service Industries, Inc. v. Kimbrell, 758 F. Supp. 676 (D. Kan. 1991); Dewey v. R. J. Reynolds Tobacco Co., 109 N.J. 201, 536 A.2d 243 (1988). Does *Analytica* tacitly assume the opposite? Which approach is correct?

Although application of successive disqualification rules virtually always occur in litigation, they are equally applicable to other legal services. See, e.g., United States Football League v. National Football League, 605 F. Supp. 1448 (S.D.N.Y. 1985) (corporate representation followed by litigation); Hannan v. Watt, 147 Ill. App. 3d 456, 497 N.E.2d 1307 (1986) (labor negotiation).

The Successive Duty of Loyalty

The principal case used the substantial relationship test as a proxy or surrogate for determining whether confidences from a prior matter are relevant in a later matter. A proxy or surrogate is used so that the former client need not reveal the very confidences it wishes to protect. But confidentiality is not the only goal of successive conflict rules. Another, less prominent, goal is loyalty to to the former client. In Trone v. Smith, supra, 621 F.2d at 998-999, the court wrote:

> Both the lawyer and the client should expect that the lawyer will use every skill, expend every energy, and tap every legitimate resource in the exercise of independent professional judgment on behalf of the client and in undertaking representation on the client's behalf. That professional commitment is not furthered, but endangered, if the possibility exists that the lawyer will change sides later in a substantially related matter. Both the fact and the appearance of total professional commitment are endangered by adverse representation in related cases. From this standpoint it matters not whether confidences were in fact imparted to the lawyer by the client. The substantial relationship between the two representations is itself sufficient to disqualify.

See also Cord v. Smith, 338 F.2d 516, 524 (9th Cir. 1964).

The notion that loyalty to a former client survives the termination of the relationship is carried over in Model Rule 1.9 and its comment. But what exactly does this loyalty duty demand? Take an easy case. A lawyer negotiates a contract for a client. Thereafter, the lawyer is retained to attack the validity of the contract as against public policy. The lawyer argues that the claim of invalidity will rely solely on legal theories, not facts. So no confidences are at risk. Or perhaps any facts needed to make the argument are already a matter of public record and "generally known." See Rule 1.9(c)(1). Nevertheless, the surviving duty of loyalty will prevent the lawyer from attacking his or her own handiwork. The lawyer cannot produce a product for a client and then turn around and seek to destroy its legal usefulness.

Loyalty to former clients arises in a more complicated way too. Assume attorney Blue jointly represents clients Green and Grey in connection with a business deal between them and others. After a falling out, Green hires Blue to sue Grey. When Grey protests, Green and Blue argue that Grey could have had no expectation that information she gave Blue would be secret from Green. They cite the exception to the attorney-client privilege for multiple representations. See page 230 supra. Should this argument defeat Grey's effort to disqualify Blue?

Courts are divided. Allegaert v. Perot, 565 F.2d 246 (2d Cir. 1977), and Christensen v. United States District Court, 844 F.2d 694 (9th Cir. 1988), are perhaps the leading cases refusing to disqualify attorneys in Blue's position on the theory that Grey could not reasonably have expected that her confidences would be kept from her former coclient. See also Borges v. Our Lady of the Sea Corp., 935 F.2d 436, 440 (lst Cir. 1991) (defendant's former attorney "had all the corporate information he needed for Borges' personal injury case available at his client's fingertips" where Borges was a "one-third owner of the defendant corporation and its treasurer"). Taking the view that a duty of loyalty prevents the successive representation apart from the need to protect confidences are Brennan's, Inc. v. Brennan's Restaurants, Inc., 590 F.2d 168 (5th Cir. 1979); Anchor Packing Co. v. Pro-Seal, Inc., 688 F. Supp. 1215 (E.D. Mich. 1988); Western Continental Operating Co. v. National Gas Corp. of Calif., 212 Cal. App. 3d 752, 261 Cal. Rptr. 100, 105-106 (1989); and Brent v. Smathers, 529 So. 2d 1267 (Fla. App. 1988). *Western Continental* wrote:

> In the first instance, we are not concerned in this case with discovery of allegedly privileged communications. Instead, the pertinent issue is the propriety of an attorney's representation adverse to a former client. Our courts have distinguished the rule against representing conflicting interests from the attorney-client evidentiary privilege noting that the former is broader than the latter. The evidentiary privilege and the ethical duty not to disclose confidences both arise from the need to encourage clients to disclose all possibly pertinent information to their attorneys, and both protect only the confidential information disclosed. The duty not to represent conflicting interests . . . is an outgrowth of the attorney-client relationship itself, which is confidential, or fiduciary, in a broader sense. Not only do clients at times disclose confidential information to their attorneys; they also repose confidence in them. The privilege is bottomed only on the first of these attributes, the conflicting-interests rule, on both.

The Consequences of Disqualification

Analytica, the Model Rules (1.10(a)), and DR 5-105(D) disqualify all lawyers in a law firm from opposing a client when any lawyer in the firm has represented that client on a substantially related matter. Mr. Fine's disqualification in *Analytica* was imputed to his entire firm. It is not knowledge as such, but the disqualified status, that the rule imputes. As *Analytica* stated and as we shall see when we come to imputed disqualification in part B, the presumption of shared knowledge is generally rebuttable (and imputed disqualification on loyalty grounds alone rejected) where the conflict arises not because "the firm itself changed sides," but because "a member or associate of a law firm (or government legal department) has changed jobs, and later he or his new firm is retained by an adversary of a client of his former firm."

How far will the conclusive imputation of a disqualifying conflict travel? One stopping place may be with co-counsel who has worked with the disqualified lawyer but is not in the same firm. Because they are not in the same firm, co-counsel do not present the same *prospective* risk that confidences will be leaked following disqualification of the tainted lawyer. The only concern here should be whether the confidences that required the disqualification of one lawyer have *already* been given to co-counsel. General Electric Co. v. Industra Products, 683 F. Supp. 1254 (N.D. Ind. 1988), presumes they have, but then lets the remaining lawyer rebut the presumption. Smith v. Whatcott, 774 F.2d 1032 (10th Cir. 1985), rejects "double imputation," examines the facts, and concludes that no confidences were transmitted. Brennan's, Inc. v. Brennan's Restaurants, Inc., 590 F.2d 168 (5th Cir. 1979) (same).

When a lawyer or firm is disqualified, the client will have to hire new counsel, who will want to receive the disqualified firm's files. The opposing party might object on the ground that this gives the new firm the benefit of the suspect work. Nevertheless, absent an identifiably tainted item, the courts have been disposed to allow turnover to successor counsel. First Wisconsin Mortgage Trust v. First Wisconsin Corp., 584 F.2d 201 (7th Cir. 1978); IBM v. Levin, 579 F.2d 271 (3d Cir. 1978) (turnover permitted). In Wagner v. Lehman Bros. Kuhn Loeb, Inc., 683 F. Supp. 189 (N.D. Ill. 1987), the prior counsel was disqualified for obtaining evidence improperly (see page 73 supra). Successor counsel was allowed access to prior counsel's files but was denied the right to use improperly acquired information in his case in chief. Also, successor counsel could not communicate with prior counsel except to arrange delivery of the files. In Fund of Funds, Ltd. v. Arthur Andersen & Co., 567 F.2d 225 (2d Cir. 1977), the court declined to follow disqualification with dismissal of the complaint or suppression of facts or documents.

Who Is a Former Client?

We encountered the client identity issue in the prior chapter (see page 227 supra). It is a question that often arises in the conflicts arena because without a client there cannot be a conflict. In the area of successive conflicts, the issue is more complex because not only must we ask whether a person or entity was a client (the subject of this discussion), but if so, whether the relationship is over (the subject of the next discussion).

1. In *Analytica*, the company that provided the information was either the client of the firm or treated as a client-equivalent for successive disqualification purposes because it had provided "just the kind of confidential data that it would have furnished a lawyer that it had retained."

2. In the *Westinghouse* case, cited in *Analytica*, Kerr-McGee was not a formal client of Kirkland & Ellis but it had given the firm confidential information so that the firm could perform certain work for a trade association of which Kerr-McGee was a member. (See also the *Glueck* case at page 228 supra.)

3. In Trinity Ambulance Service, Inc. v. G.&L. Ambulance Services,

Inc., 578 F. Supp. 1280 (D. Conn. 1984), one of two plaintiffs in an anti-trust action realigned as a defendant. While a plaintiff, however, its counsel had participated in joint strategy sessions with the other plaintiff and its counsel. The court disqualified the attorney for the realigned defendant after concluding that he had had a professional relationship with the remaining plaintiff, which had divulged confidences in the belief that it was "approaching the attorney in a professional capacity with the intent to secure legal advice." See also Nemours Foundation v. Gilbane, Aetna, Federal Ins. Co., 632 F. Supp. 418 (D. Del. 1986).

4. A corporate attorney secured a patent. The inventor was a corporate employee. The patent was issued in the name of the corporation, which then assigned it to Medtronic. The attorney later represented a third party in an effort to invalidate the patent. Medtronic and the inventor moved for disqualification. The court rejected the motion. Assignment of the patent did not bring with it assignment of the lawyer's responsibilities to the assignor. The lawyer had no professional relationship with the inventor, but only with his employer. Telectronics Proprietary, Ltd. v. Medtronic, 836 F.2d 1332 (Fed. Cir. 1988). For a similar case, see Quaker Oats Co. v. Uni-Pak Film Systems, 683 F. Supp. 1186 (N.D. Ill. 1987).

5. First Boston retained Fried, Frank to assist it after Dart hired First Boston to advise Dart regarding a financial acquisition. Dart agreed to pay Fried, Frank's bills to First Boston. Dart also had its own legal counsel at the time. Fried, Frank received permission from Dart's counsel to communicate directly with Dart. Thereafter, Fried, Frank represented a plaintiff in an action against Dart. Dart moved to disqualify the firm. Among other things, the court had to decide whether Fried, Frank had had a client-lawyer relationship with Dart. It held that there was a relationship on three grounds: There was a traditional professional relationship by implication arising out of the fact that Dart provided information and Fried, Frank did legal work based on it; First Boston as Dart's agent had created a client-lawyer relationship between Dart and Fried, Frank; and using the *Westinghouse* standard, Dart consulted with Fried, Frank on the assumption that the firm would exercise "the same professional judgment and . . . display the same loyalty as [its] own attorneys." Jack Eckerd Corp. v. Dart Group Corp., 621 F. Supp. 725 (D. Del. 1985).

6. A lawyer represents one party in negotiations with an opposing party. Later, the lawyer is asked to represent a third party against the same former opposing party. The opponent complains because, it says, the lawyer learned its confidential information in the prior negotiation. Perhaps so, but the former opponent was never a client of the lawyer. Consequently, the substantial relationship test would not apply. Dillingham v. Crowley Maritime Corp., 1990 U.S. Dist. Lexis 1472 (D. Alaska 1990). The opponent could have avoided the problem by bargaining for secrecy.

"Like a Hot Potato"

It should be clear to you by now that a client who wishes to disqualify a lawyer would prefer to be characterized as a current client while the lawyer would prefer to say that the client was a former client (if a client at all). Why is that?

Imagine this situation. Smith Knight, a law firm, represents *XYZ* Company on some small matters that will come to completion in the next six months. One day Smith Knight receives a visit from Marie Shelton. Shelton has a claim against *XYZ* for $10 million and wants the firm to take it. Assume Shelton's claim is factually unrelated to the matters the firm currently handles for *XYZ*. If Shelton had come by only six months later, the representation of *XYZ* would have ended and the firm could have accepted the factually unrelated claim. But Shelton wants to file her claim now. She doesn't want to wait.

Smith Knight cannot accept Shelton's case, and sue *XYZ*, while continuing to represent the company on unrelated matters, can it? See page 219 supra. How nice if *XYZ* could be made to disappear a little ahead of time! So Smith Knight "fires" *XYZ*, waits a respectable period, and then accepts Shelton's retainer. *XYZ* moves to disqualify the firm, which defends by arguing that *XYZ*, as a former and not a current client, can only disqualify it on a substantially related adverse matter, which Shelton's claim is not. What should *XYZ* argue?

In Unified Sewerage Agency v. Jelco, Inc., 646 F.2d 1339, 1345 n.4 (9th Cir. 1981), the court wrote that law firms could not escape the stricter current client conflict rules simply by withdrawing from the representation and converting a current client into a former one. Why not? If the second matter is truly unrelated, who is hurt? Certainly the "former" client may encounter some additional expense in bringing new counsel up to speed, but assume the "former" law firm is prepared to absorb that expense.

The *Jelco* footnote, as it has become known, protects a client's interest in uninterrupted representation to the conclusion of a matter. While a law firm may withdraw from a current representation, it can only do so for the reasons listed in DR 2-110 and Rule 1.16. The law firm's own economic interests have not (despite some ambiguity in Rule 1.16(b) and (b)(5)) been deemed an acceptable reason for dropping the client. But see Borges v. Our Lady of the Sea Corp., 935 F.2d 436 (1st Cir. 1991), where the court said that although it did "not condone a lawyer suing his own client," it declined to reverse the lower court's refusal to disqualify. Not only were the matters unrelated, but "the simultaneous representation had ceased by the time the disqualification issue arose." Id. at 440.

The *Jelco* footnote acquired a metaphor in Picker International v. Varian Associates, 670 F. Supp. 1363 (N.D. Ohio 1987), aff'd, 869 F.2d

578 (Fed. Cir. 1989). There, the district judge determined that Jones Day (get it? Smith Knight, Jones Day?) had dropped one client "like a hot potato" in order to be free to continue with the representation of another client. Was this characterization fair? The facts in *Picker* are more subtle than those in the Smith Knight hypothetical. Jones Day, which had been Picker's lawyer since 1911, was representing Picker in an action against Varian. It came to pass that Jones Day had an opportunity to merge with MH&S, a boutique patent law firm in Chicago. Unfortunately, MH&S was representing Varian on patent matters unrelated to Picker v. Varian. If the merger were to come off, Jones Day would find itself litigating against a current client, which is forbidden without consent. MH&S asked Varian to consent. It pointed out that the *Picker* litigation was factually unrelated to the patent matters so there was no threat to Varian's confidences. And MH&S offered to screen the Chicago lawyers working on Varian's patent matters from the Jones Day lawyers in Cleveland working on the *Picker* litigation. Although Varian refused to consent, MH&S and Jones Day consummated the merger anyway. A few days before it did, MH&S purported to withdraw as Varian's counsel.

Varian moved to disqualify Jones Day in *Picker*. Citing the *Jelco* footnote, it claimed protection as a current client despite MH&S's purported withdrawal. The court agreed: "A firm may not drop a client like a hot potato, especially if it is in order to keep happy a far more lucrative client." 670 F. Supp. at 1365. MH&S's effort to "fire" Varian was rejected, Varian was deemed a current client of Jones Day (in its postmerger incarnation), and the rule prohibiting suits against current clients was held to apply.

Should Jones Day's interest in the merger with MH&S have been accorded greater respect than the interest of Smith Knight in the previous hypothetical? Are there any differences? Should the court have weighed the reasonableness of Varian's refusal to consent? In thinking about these questions, consider the following variations on the "hot potato" problem.

1. A law firm represents Client *A* and Client *B* on unrelated matters. Client *A* then asks the firm to sue Client *B* on a matter unrelated to the firm's representation of *B*. The firm seeks to withdraw from representing *B* so that it can bring the lawsuit. See Stratagem Development Corp. v. Heron International N.V., 756 F. Supp. 789 (S.D.N.Y. 1991).

2. A law firm represents *D* in litigation against its insurer to determine the insurer's liability to *D*. The law firm also represented another insurance company, FIGA, in unrelated matters. When *D*'s insurer failed, FIGA became the successor in interest to the failed insurer by operation of state law. The law firm now wants to withdraw from representing FIGA so that it may continue to represent

       D. See Florida Insurance Guaranty Assoc. v. Carey Canada, Inc., 749 F. Supp. 255 (S.D. Fla. 1990).

  3. A firm represents *P* against *D* when either (a) *D* acquires another client of the law firm or (b) another client of the law firm acquires *D*. The firm wants to continue to represent *P*. See Gould, Inc. v. Matsui Mining & Smelting Co., 738 F. Supp. 1121 (N.D. Ohio 1990), and Pennwalt Corp. v. Plough, Inc., 85 F.R.D. 264 (D. Del. 1980).

Do you see how a prospective litigant can exploit the "hot potato" rule to keep an anticipated adversary from using its longstanding counsel? Can a large company use the rule to neutralize powerful law firms? Is there anything a law firm can do to protect itself and other clients that may depend upon it?

In *Picker*, Jones Day was disqualified from representing Picker, not Varian. Assuming the conflict could not continue, who should choose which client remains? In Estates Theatres, Inc. v. Columbia Pictures Indus., 345 F. Supp. 93 (S.D.N.Y. 1972), Judge Weinfeld said it was the court, not the law firm. On appeal in *Picker*, the Federal Circuit agreed: "To allow the merged firm to pick and choose which clients will survive the merger would violate the duty of undivided loyalty that the firms owe each of their clients under DR 5-105." 869 F.2d at 583. The court then affirmed the trial court's determination that Picker, not Varian, should lose its counsel. Jones Day could have anticipated the conflict months before the merger. Had it "withdrawn when it knew that the conflict was unavoidable, new counsel could, by now, have become well acquainted with the case." 670 F. Supp. at 1367.

Both the district and circuit courts recognized that disqualification of either party's counsel would injure that party "through no fault of its own." Why then didn't the court undo the merger instead? That would have imposed the penalty on the two law firms, which both courts concluded were at fault. Alternatively, will Picker now have a malpractice action against Jones Day for entering into a merger that forced it to lose its lawyers "through no fault of its own?"

For a *Jelco* variation, where a law firm seeks to remove a conflict by "firing" a lawyer, see page 272 infra.

Standing and Waiver

As we saw, concurrent conflicts may sometimes be waived (page 227 supra). Successive conflicts may always be waived. Rule 1.9(a). Why the difference? Given this distinction, should nonclients ever have standing to seek disqualification in successive conflict situations? Some courts have said yes because of the court's interest in ethical conduct. See Tessier v. Plastic Surgery Specialists, Inc., 731 F. Supp. 724, 728 n.3 (E.D. Va.

1990) (collecting cases). Others have said no because the rule is meant to protect the former client, not a stranger. In re Yarn Processing Patent Validity Litig., 530 F.2d 83 (5th Cir. 1976). See also *Infotechnology* at page 218 supra.

The Appearance of Impropriety

Neither the Canons of Professional Ethics nor the Code of Professional Responsibility contained a direct equivalent to Rule 1.9(a). Courts fashioned one, relying on the duty of loyalty, the duty of confidentiality, and, under Canon 9 of the Code, the direction to "avoid even the appearance of professional impropriety." Pretty soon the appearance of impropriety standard became overused and the object of criticism, not least of all because of its unpredictability. The Second Circuit in Board of Education v. Nyquist, page 220 supra, deemed it "too slender a reed" on which to base disqualification. The Eighth Circuit rejected it as nothing more than an "eye of the beholder" test. Fred Weber, Inc. v. Shell Oil Co., 566 F.2d 602 (8th Cir. 1977), cert. denied, 436 U.S. 905 (1978). Even the ABA disowned it. Opinion 342 (1975) calls it "too vague a phrase to be useful." The Model Rules omit the appearance standard altogether.

But don't write it off quite yet! First, tens of thousands of lawyers and judges have grown up with "appearance of impropriety" etched in their consciousness. Second, some courts, as in Rosman v. Shapiro, 653 F. Supp. 1441 (S.D.N.Y. 1987), may continue to rely on the "appearance of impropriety" in disqualifying a lawyer. See also Armstrong v. McAlpin, page 278 infra. Third, many states retain the Code of Professional Responsibility and its Canon 9. While that doesn't mean that courts in those states will make judgments about conflicts, or anything else, based on the "appearance" language *alone*, the language may be part of a court's reasoning. See Brennan's, Inc. v. Brennan's Restaurants, Inc., page 255 supra. Finally, even states that have adopted the Model Rules may continue to look to appearances. In First American Carriers, Inc. v. Kroger Co., 302 Ark. 86, 787 S.W.2d 669, 671 (1990), the court wrote: "The fact that Canon 9 is not in the Model Rules does not mean that lawyers no longer have to avoid the appearance of impropriety." New Jersey made a point of retaining the "appearance" language in Rules 1.7 and 1.9 of that state's version of the Model Rules. So it is worth remembering that appearances may still count, depending on where you are.

Conflicts in Class Actions

The application of traditional successive disqualification doctrine to class actions can work great hardship, sometimes for little gain. The Second Circuit had to confront this problem in In re "Agent Orange" Product Liability Litigation, 800 F.2d 14 (2d Cir. 1986), after class counsel switched from representing class members supporting a settlement to those opposing it. See also Bash v. Firstmark Standard Life Ins. Co., 861 F.2d 159 (7th Cir. 1988). Rejecting disqualification in *Agent Orange*, 800 F.2d at 18-19, Judge Kearse wrote:

> Class action litigation presents additional problems that must be considered in determining whether or not to disqualify an attorney who has represented the class and who seeks to represent thereafter only a portion of the class. See generally [In re Corn Derivatives Antitrust Litigation, 748 F.2d 157, 162-165 (3d Cir. 1984)] (Adams, J., concurring). These problems are created by, inter alia, the facts that there are, by definition, numerous class members and that there is often no clear allocation of the decision-making responsibility between the attorney and his clients. Further, though there will be common questions affecting the claims of the class members, it is not unusual for their interests, especially at the relief stage, to diverge. Such a divergence presents special problems because the class attorney's duty does not run just to the plaintiffs named in the caption of the case; it runs to all of the members of the class. . . .
>
> Automatic application of the traditional principles governing disqualification of attorneys on grounds of conflict of interest would seemingly dictate that whenever a rift arises in the class, with one branch favoring a settlement or a course of action that another branch resists, the attorney who has represented the class should withdraw entirely and take no position. Were he to take a position, either favoring or opposing the proposed course of action, he would be opposing the interests of some of his former clients in the very matter in which he has represented them.
>
> Nonetheless, as Judge Adams noted in his concurring opinion in *Corn Derivatives*, although automatic disqualification might "promote the salutary ends of confidentiality and loyalty, it would have a serious adverse effect on class actions." When many individuals have modest claims against a single entity or group of entities, the class action may be the only practical means of vindicating their rights, since otherwise the expenses of litigation could exceed the value of the claim. In such class actions, often only the attorneys who have represented the class, rather than any of the class members themselves, have substantial familiarity with the prior proceedings, the fruits of discovery, the actual potential of the litigation. And when an action has continued over the course of many years, the prospect of having those most familiar with its course and status be automatically disqualified whenever class members have conflicting interests would substantially diminish the efficacy of class actions as a method of dispute resolution. This is so both because the quality of the information available to the court would likely be impaired and because even if a class member were familiar with all the prior proceedings, the amount of his stake in the litigation might well make it unattractive for him to participate actively, either on his own or through new counsel. . . .

Thus, we conclude that the traditional rules that have been developed in the course of attorneys' representation of the interests of clients outside of the class action context should not be mechanically applied to the problems that arise in the settlement of class action litigation. A motion to disqualify an attorney who has represented the entire class and who has thereafter been retained by a faction of the class to represent its interests in opposition to a proposed settlement of the action cannot be automatically granted. Rather, there must be a balancing of the interests of the various groups of class members and of the interest of the public and the court in achieving a just and expeditious resolution of the dispute.

Relevant considerations in determining whether the moving party has shown sufficient ground for disqualification of prior class counsel include "the amount and nature of the information that has been proffered to the attorney, its availability elsewhere, its importance to the question at issue, such as settlement, as well as actual prejudice that may flow from that information." *Corn Derivatives*, 748 F.2d at 165 (Adams, J., concurring). The court must consider as well the costs to the class members of requiring that they obtain new counsel, taking into account such factors as the nature and value of the claim they are presenting, the ease with which they could obtain new counsel, the factual and legal complexity of the litigation, and the time that would be needed for new counsel to familiarize himself with all that has gone before.

For further reading on conflicts in class actions, see Deborah Rhode, Class Conflicts in Class Actions, 34 Stan. L. Rev. 1183 (1982); Developments in the Law — Conflicts of Interest in the Legal Profession, 94 Harv. L. Rev. 1244, 1447-1457 (1981) (hereafter Harvard Conflicts Note).

QUESTIONS

6.1 Victor Henry of Henry & Lee represents Patrick Roth in a criminal tax prosecution. Roth is acquitted. Two years later, Henry's partner, Vivian Lee, is retained by Roth's wife to bring a divorce action and to seek equitable distribution of Roth's assets. May Lee represent Mrs. Roth?

6.2 Jane Parker is retained by Bill Wallace to help him with the legal work in connection with opening a large record store. Parker incorporates the store, negotiates and reviews the terms of the lease, works out credit arrangements with suppliers, and helps Wallace get a registered tradename for the store. Six months after Parker's work is done and she has billed the store for her services and been paid, may Parker:

1. perform the same services for Wendy Noonan, who wants to open a competing record store a block away from Wallace's store? (Could Parker have represented Noonan and Wallace at the same time?)
2. represent a record company suing Wallace for unpaid bills where the defense will be that the merchandise was defective?
3. represent Wallace's landlord in an action to evict him for breach of Wallace's lease? The lease specifies that Wallace will sell only records, CDs, tapes, "and related products." The landlord claims that Wallace has violated the clause by offering to sell videotapes and musical instruments?
4. represent a funeral parlor adjoining Wallace's record store in an action to close the store under a municipal nuisance ordinance that permits such actions when a commercial establishment is responsible for "excessive noise"?

6.3   Winter & Straw is a large multicity firm of 356 lawyers. Tom Hurley is a corporate partner in a branch office. From time to time over the last 10 years Hurley has represented Company *AB*. The assignments are specific and limited, usually lasting six to 12 months. *AB* also has a corporate law department and other outside firms that work for it.

Mariana Guerro is a litigation partner in W&S's home city. As of March 1992, Guerro has represented Company *YZ* for three years in a $500 million antitrust litigation in Denver arising out of *YZ*'s alleged conspiracy with other companies to prevent technological innovations that would significantly reduce the market for *YZ*'s product.

In March 1992, facts come to light that cause lawyers at *AB* (and other companies) to conclude that the alleged antitrust conspiracy might have been broader than originally appeared and that *AB* might also have a claim against *YZ*. *AB* hires Soloway & Crumwell to sue *YZ* on this claim, which it does in Denver in April 1992, moving to consolidate *AB*'s claim with the other antitrust claims against *YZ* because they share common questions of fact and law.

It happens that in February 1992, *AB* had retained Hurley to handle certain regulatory work unrelated to the antitrust claim. When the AB v. YZ complaint and motion to consolidate are served, the general counsel at *YZ* sends it to Guerro as the W&S partner in charge of its antitrust litigation. In a conflicts check, Guerro learns that Hurley is representing *AB*. Hurley tells her that his work will take another six months.

Guerro calls you. She tells you that *YZ* has paid her firm nearly $10 million in the three years of the antitrust litigation and that the team handling it, comprising six lawyers and nine paralegals, has massive amounts of legal and factual information about the case. The firm also has extensive litigation support databases and computer programs developed especially for the litigation at great expense. None of the work Hurley has done for *AB* over the years is related to the antitrust claim against *YZ*.

The Model Rules apply. What advice do you give Guerro about her firm's options and why?

B.   IMPUTED DISQUALIFICATION AND MIGRATORY LAWYERS

In *Analytica*, the "firm itself changed sides." What happens when a conflicted lawyer who is subject to disqualification joins a new firm? To what extent is the lawyer's status "contagious"? When a conflicted lawyer leaves a firm, does the lawyer take the disqualification with him, so that the firm is now free to do what it would not have been permitted to do had the lawyer remained? As we shall see, in each case it may be possible for the new firm to avoid imputation of the conflict.

It is possible to argue that a disqualifying conflict ought not be imputed as a matter of course even where, as in *Analytica*, the firm itself changes sides. For example, if several lawyers in a large firm once represented client *A*, the firm might argue that different lawyers in the firm could subsequently (or, indeed, concurrently) represent client *B* against client *A*, even on a substantially related matter, so long as the two sets of lawyers are kept apart. However, as we have seen, efforts to avoid imputed disqualification within a single firm have not been successful. Rule 1.10(a), in accord, operates from the "premise that a firm of lawyers is essentially one lawyer for purposes of the rules governing loyalty to the client, or from the premise that each lawyer is vicariously bound by the obligation of loyalty owed by each lawyer with whom the lawyer is associated." Rule 1.10, comment. But as we shall see, if a lawyer is imputedly disqualified by operation of Rule 1.10(a), he or she may be able to escape that status by ending the association with the lawyer from whom the disqualification has been imputed.

The following opinion, written by the judge who dissented in *Analytica*, speaks to the situation where *a lawyer has changed firms. Analytica* is distinguished in note 2.

SCHIESSLE v. STEPHENS
717 F.2d 417 (7th Cir. 1983)

COFFEY, J.

The plaintiff, Eleanor Schiessle, appeals from an order of the United States District Court for the Northern District of Illinois, Eastern Division, disqualifying her co-counsel, the law firm of Ross, Hardies, O'Keefe, Babcock & Parsons in this antitrust action. The question presented for review is whether, in light of our recent pronouncements on attorney disqualification, the district court erred in its determination that disqualification was required in this case. . . .

[Schiessle sued 18 defendants including the Swansons, alleging antitrust violations. The plaintiff was represented by Richter, a partner in the Ross firm. Before the Swansons appeared, Michael King, then a partner at Antonow & Fink, contacted Richter on behalf of the Swansons and asked that the case against them be dismissed. Richter declined. Thereafter, Kenneth Lodge, of another firm, appeared on behalf of the Swansons, but subsequently withdrew and Antonow & Fink were substituted as counsel. By this time, however, King had left Antonow & Fink and had joined the Ross firm as a partner. Two years later, Antonow & Fink sought disqualification of the Ross firm. The district court granted the disqualification. It concluded "that because the representation of the Swansons by Attorney King and his former firm . . . and the representation of Schiessle by the Ross firm . . . involved the identical antitrust lawsuit, the court would irrebuttably presume that confidences were shared between King and the other members of the Ross firm." Schiessle appealed.]

Questions of ethical propriety like those presented in this appeal have been addressed by this court within the past year. In those cases we noted two important considerations invoked in motions to disqualify counsel and emphasized the delicacy of the balance that must be maintained between them: the sacrosanct privacy of the attorney-client relationship (and the professional integrity implicated by that relationship) and the prerogative of a party to proceed with counsel of its choice. Accordingly, this court adopted an approach for resolution of disqualification questions which accommodated these important considerations and we have continuously maintained that disqualification is a "drastic measure which courts should hesitate to impose except when absolutely necessary."

The analysis outlined in our prior decisions concerning attorney disqualification comprises three steps. First, we must determine whether a substantial relationship exists between the subject matter of the prior and present representations. If we conclude a substantial relationship does exist, we must next ascertain whether the presumption of shared confidences with respect to the prior representation has been rebutted.[2] If we conclude this presumption has not been rebutted, we must then determine whether the presumption of shared confidences has been rebutted with respect to the present representation. Failure to rebut this presumption would also make disqualification proper.

In the case at bar, there is no dispute that the subject matter of the prior and present representations are substantially related — indeed the subject matter is identical as it concerns the same antitrust litigation. The only factor that has changed is that Attorney King is now a partner of the Ross firm rather than the Antonow & Fink firm. Therefore, we find no difficulty in concluding that the representation involved is substantially related.

The second step in our analysis requires us to ascertain whether the presumption of shared confidences which arises from our determination that the representations are substantially related has been rebutted with respect to the prior representation. In other words, we must determine whether the attorney whose change of employment created the disqualification issue was actually privy to any confidential information his prior law firm received from the party now seeking disqualification of his present firm. The evidence presented to rebut this presumption must "clearly and effectively" demonstrate that the attorney in question has no knowledge of the information, confidences and/or secrets related by the client in the prior representation. In the case at bar, the affidavit of Attorney Goldberg of the Antonow & Fink firm stands uncontradicted in its recital that King, while a partner at Antonow & Fink, was (1) "partner in charge" of representing the Swansons in the *Schiessle* litigation; (2) that King discussed the lawsuit on four occasions with Paul Swanson; and (3) that King had taken part in numerous discussions at Antonow & Fink regarding the antitrust lawsuit. Accordingly, we conclude that Attorney King has not rebutted the presumption of shared confidences with respect to his involvement in the case while he was partner at Antonow & Fink.

2. The existence of a substantial relationship gives rise to a presumption of shared confidences.

The present fact situation should be distinguished from that found in our recent decision in *[Analytica]* where we held that the presumption of shared confidences was irrebuttable. In that case we stated:

There is an exception for the case where a member or associate of a law firm (or government legal department) changes jobs, and later he or his new firm is retained by an adversary of a client of his former firm. In such a case, even if there is a substantial relationship between the two matters, the lawyer can avoid disqualification by showing that effective measures were taken to prevent confidences from being received by whichever lawyers in the new firm are handling the new matter. . . .

Unlike *Analytica*, only one attorney has moved from the law firm now representing some of the defendants to the law firm representing the plaintiff. Since the present fact situation falls within the exception recognized in *Analytica*, our analysis does not conflict with that decision.

Lastly, the district court must determine whether the presumption of shared confidences has been rebutted with respect to the present representation. In other words, the court must determine whether the knowledge of the "confidences and secrets" of the Swansons which King brought with him has been passed on to or is likely to be passed on to the members of the Ross firm. [We have previously] held that the presumption of shared confidences could be rebutted by demonstrating that "specific institutional mechanisms" (e.g., "Chinese Walls") had been implemented to effectively insulate against any flow of confidential information from the "infected" attorney to any other member of his present firm. Such a determination can be based on objective and verifiable evidence presented to the trial court and must be made on a case-by-case basis. Factors appropriate for consideration by the trial court might include, but are not limited to, the size and structural divisions of the law firm involved, the likelihood of contact between the "infected" attorney and the specific attorneys responsible for the present representation, the existence of rules which prevent the "infected" attorney from access to relevant files or other information pertaining to the present litigation or which prevent him from sharing in the fees derived from such litigation.

We hold that the district court erred in relying on an irrebuttable presumption to find that confidences and secrets had been shared between King and other members of the Ross firm because our decisions . . . make it clear that the presumption of shared confidences can be rebutted. However, we reach the same conclusion as the district court that the Ross firm must be disqualified from representing Schiessle because: (1) Attorney King obviously had knowledge of the Swansons' case as he failed to answer the affidavit of the Antonow & Fink firm reciting (a) that he was the "partner in charge" of representing the defendants, (b) that he discussed the lawsuit on four occasions with Paul Swanson, and (c) that he had taken part in numerous discussions at the firm regarding the antitrust litigation; and (2) no evidence exists in the record establishing that the Ross firm had "institutional mechanisms" in effect insulating King "from all participation in and information about [the] case." It should be noted that counsel for the plaintiff informed the court at oral argument that the Ross firm was without "formal institutional[ized] . . . screening" insulating Attorney King from the members of the firm representing Schiessle.

We hold that at the time Attorney King changed firms he had knowledge of the Swansons' case and that there were no "institutional mechanisms" in existence at the Ross firm to protect the sacrosanct privacy of the defendants' attorney-client relationship. [W]hen an attorney with knowledge of a prior client's confidences and secrets changes employment and joins a firm representing an adverse party, specific institutional mechanisms must be in place to ensure that information is not shared with members of the new firm, even if inadvertently. The record in this case shows that the Ross firm at the time of Attorney King's transfer did not have specific institutional mechanisms . . . to ensure that King would have no contact with the Schiessle case. We hold that the Ross firm must be disqualified from the continued representation of Schiessle. . . .

[Affirmed.]

Presumptions in Imputed Disqualification

If firm X wants to represent client A against B, which is represented by firm Y, may it do so if a partner or associate of firm X was formerly affiliated with firm Y during Y's representation of B? No, says the Seventh Circuit, if (1) Y's representation of B was on a matter that has a "substantial relationship" to X's proposed representation of A and (2) the lawyer formerly affiliated with firm Y shared confidences of client B on the matter while at firm Y; and (3) the other lawyers at firm X in turn shared (or are likely to share) those confidences with the lawyer who has moved from firm Y to firm X. The Seventh Circuit creates rebuttable presumptions that the confidences identified in (2) and (3) were, or will be, shared. While there is near universal agreement that the presumption in (2) should be rebuttable, much authority disagrees with the Seventh Circuit's willingness to permit the use of screening mechanisms to rebut the presumption identified in (3). The most notable opposition is in the Model Rules themselves. See Rule 1.9 comment. This note discusses the two presumptions and the relative merits of rebuttability.

First, you should know that there is deep division in the profession and the courts about whether the second presumption should be rebuttable. Whereas the Model Rules reject rebuttability, the Restatement of the Law Governing Lawyers §204 (Tentative Draft No. 4) would allow it if, in addition to screening, the information at risk "is not likely to be significant" in the second matter.* Courts are also divided. Joining the Seventh Circuit in permitting rebuttability are Manning v. Waring, Cox, James, Sklar & Allen, 849 F.2d 222 (6th Cir. 1988) (emphasizing that the greater mobility of lawyers and an increase in mergers and sizes of firms necessitate a more flexible rule); Nemours Foundation v. Gilbane, Aetna, Federal Insurance Co., 632 F. Supp. 418 (D. Del. 1986); and Geisler v. Wyeth Laboratories, 716 F. Supp. 520 (D. Kan. 1989). Illinois, Michigan, and Pennsylvania permit screening in their ethics rules. Decisions that have rejected screening include Cheng v. GAF, 631 F.2d 1052 (2d Cir. 1980), vacated on other grounds, 450 U.S. 903 (1981); Roberts v. Hutchins, 572 So. 2d 1231 (Ala. 1990); Parker v. Volkswagenwerk, 245 Kan. 580, 781

---

* In fact, the Draft goes even further. It would sometimes allow screening in successive conflict situations even when no lawyer has changed firms, but rather the firm itself has changed sides. No primary authority appears to support this position, which has not yet been formally adopted by the ALI.

P.2d 1099 (1989); and State ex rel. Freezer Services, Inc. v. Mullen, 235 Neb. 981, 458 N.W.2d 245 (1990). The District of Columbia, New Jersey, and New York reject screening in their ethics rules. It is sometimes unclear whether courts that have accepted or rejected screening have done so categorically or because the particular facts present a small or great risk of abuse of confidential information.

What is the justification for allowing the first of the *Schiessle* presumptions to be rebutted, but not the second?

It should be possible for the former affiliate in the first instance to establish his or her lack of knowledge of a client's confidential information without the client running the risk of having confidential information revealed at the hearing held to allow the lawyer to rebut the presumption. This is because the lawyer's proof will generally be by way of evidence of nonaccess to the work of other lawyers at the firm, and so distinguishable from the situation in which a single firm wishes to show that none of the client confidences it admittedly has as a result of a prior representation bears on the matter with regard to which it now wants to sue its former client. Further, it is increasingly unlikely that lawyers who are affiliated with large law firms and corporate law offices actually learn all the confidential information possessed by their offices. If a presumption that they do is made irrebuttable, lawyer mobility between firms will be severely constrained, an effect especially damaging to lawyers at the start of their careers.

Silver Chrysler Plymouth v. Chrysler Motors, 518 F.2d 751, 753-754 (2d Cir. 1975), nicely illustrates this point. The plaintiff was represented by a small firm, one of whose partners, Schreiber, formerly worked as an associate at Kelley Drye, a large firm representing defendant Chrysler. Kelley Drye sought to disqualify Schreiber's firm because Schreiber, while an associate at Kelley Drye, had had access to confidential information regarding Chrysler. The Second Circuit rejected this effort.

> It is unquestionably true that in the course of their work at large law firms, associates are entrusted with the confidences of some of their clients. But it would be absurd to conclude that immediately upon their entry on duty they become the recipients of knowledge as to the names of all the firm's clients, the contents of all files relating to such clients, and all confidential disclosures by client officers or employees to any lawyer in the firm. Obviously such legal osmosis does not occur. . . .
>
> Fulfilling the purpose of the disqualification remedy . . . does not require such a blanket approach. . . . Thus, while this Circuit has recognized that an inference may arise that an attorney formerly associated with a firm himself received confidential information transmitted by a client to the firm, that inference is a rebuttable one. . . . The importance of not unnecessarily constricting the careers of lawyers who started their practice of law at large firms simply on the basis of their former association underscores the significance of this language.

The court concluded that Schreiber had rebutted any presumption that he had obtained substantially related confidential information about Chrysler while at Kelley Drye. Under the Model Rules, Schreiber's imputed disqualification under Rule 1.10(a) would end once he left Kelley Drye and he would similarly be entitled to rebut the presumption of shared knowledge. See Rule 1.9(b) and comment.

By contrast, there is said to be a strong argument for an irrebuttable presumption that a lawyer who, in a prior affiliation, has acquired confidential information about a client will share that information with current partners and associates. As a result, the entire firm will be disqualified from representing a client whose interests are materially adverse to those of the former client. One commentator described the justification for irrebuttability in this instance as follows:

> From the moment an attorney has reason to expect that he will represent a client in a matter to which the confidences and secrets of one of his present affiliate's former clients may be relevant, he has a significant incentive, completely absent in the classic former affiliate case, to elicit such information deliberately from his colleague. Although the fellow lawyer need not knowingly cooperate in the sharing of information (seemingly innocuous questioning or casual examination of relevant files will suffice), he may have appreciable incentive and opportunity to do so. The fact of affiliation alone is generally enough to guarantee that there will be economic, sentimental, and hegemonic ties between the associated lawyers sufficient to induce an affiliate's cooperation with his colleague. Although such ties might exist even between former affiliates, the probability that an attorney will feel free to request his affiliate's sub rosa assistance and that the affiliate will oblige is plainly greater when the lawyers are presently affiliated. It is this risk of deliberate sharing, customarily disregarded in the case of former affiliates, that is the distinctive danger of present affiliation.*

Are you persuaded that the second presumption should be irrebuttable? Look at it from the lawyer's point of view. If it is irrebuttable, firms will hesitate to hire lawyers who have worked elsewhere. The danger of imputed disqualification will be especially high in smaller communities and in specialized areas of practice. But look at it from the client's point of view. A client may find itself opposed by a law firm one of whose members has relevant confidential information about the client, gained in a prior affiliation. Can a client be comfortable that a purported screening mechanism is really being honored? How can it know? Should the profession ask clients to "trust us?"

Recall that the successive conflicts rules protect not only the former client's confidences but also its expectation of ongoing loyalty. See page 253 supra. Where a lawyer who has not changed firms is disqualified from

---

* Harvard Conflicts Note, page 263 supra, at 1361-1363.

opposing a former client *solely* because of a surviving duty of loyalty — i.e., no confidences are at risk — then Rule 1.10(a) would impute that disqualification to all lawyers in her firm. But if the lawyer then changed firms, the imputation will not travel with her. The Model Rules say that where a migratory lawyer is disqualified only because of loyalty to a former client, that status will not be imputed to a new firm. Rule 1.9 comment. (The literal language of Rule 1.10(a) when combined with Rule 1.9(a) ignores this distinction. But the commentary preserves it. See Rule 1.9, comment 11.)

The Model Rules also speak to the situation where a lawyer terminates an association with a firm and the firm then wishes to represent a new client whose interests are materially adverse to those of a former client represented by the formerly associated lawyer while at the firm. In such a situation, Rule 1.10(b) permits the firm to represent the new client, even if the matter is the same or substantially related to that in which the formerly associated lawyer represented the former client, so long as no lawyer remaining in the firm has confidentially protected information that could be used to the disadvantage of the former client. Thus, just as a disqualified lawyer who comes to a firm with certain confidential information may "infect" every other lawyer in it, when such a disqualified lawyer departs, the entire firm may be "purged" of the imputed disqualification.

The District of Columbia has opted for a more stringent resolution of the "departing lawyer" issue. D.C. Rule 1.10(c) uses the conjunction "or" in lieu of the conjunction "and" as it appears at the end of Rule 1.10(b)(1). As a result, a firm may not represent a client in opposition to a former client on the same or substantially related matter notwithstanding that all lawyers with any confidential information about that matter have left the firm. D.C. Opinion 212 (1990). Can you defend the D.C. rule? Think about it from a former client's point of view. Think about the difficulty of proving whether lawyers remaining in a 200-lawyer firm have confidential information from the prior matter.

Here is a story to tell the next time someone proclaims that law is a profession, not a business. Client *ABC* asks its longtime firm to represent it in an action against *XYZ*. But it happens that *XYZ* is a client of the firm on an unrelated matter. We know from *Picker*, page 258 supra, that the firm cannot simply drop *XYZ* "like a hot potato" and accept the representation of *ABC*. But it also happens that all of *XYZ*'s matters have been handled by a particular partner at the firm — call him James Polk — who joined the firm laterally a few years earlier, bringing *XYZ* with him. *XYZ* is devoted to Polk and he to it. Can the firm fire Polk, correctly predicting that *XYZ* will choose to leave with him, and thereby free itself to accept *ABC*'s matter? The firm can then argue that it is not dropping *XYZ* "like a hot potato." Rather *XYZ* would be leaving of its own accord after the firm dismissed Polk. You probably find this plan too clever for words. Yet in

Hartford Accident & Indemnity Co. v. R. J. R. Nabisco, Inc., 721 F. Supp. 534 (S.D.N.Y. 1989), it worked. LeBoeuf, Lamb sued R. J. R. on behalf of Hartford while its partner Wood was representing Reynolds, an R. J. R. subsidiary. LeBoeuf then fired Wood and Reynolds left with him. R. J. R., citing *Jelco*, moved to disqualify LeBoeuf from representing Hartford. Judge Walker held that R. J. R. was a LeBoeuf client via Reynolds because the parent controlled the subsidiary's litigation. But he distinguished *Jelco* because here it was the lawyer, not the client, who was fired. The client has not been denied its "longtime counsel."

Is Judge Walker's distinction persuasive? Judge Patel reached a contrary result, despite the departure of the firm lawyer whose presence created a conflict, but in her case a concurrent violation "occurred at the time the complaint was filed and . . . cannot be cured [by the lawyer's] resignation from [the firm]." Teradyne, Inc. v. Hewlett-Packard Co., 1991 WL 239940 (N.D. Cal. 1991).

Rebutting the Presumptions

What kind of evidence will suffice to rebut the first presumption created by the Seventh Circuit? In Freeman v. Chicago Musical Instrument, 689 F.2d 715, 723 (7th Cir. 1982), the court said:

> [I]f an attorney can clearly and effectively show that he had no knowledge of the confidences and secrets of the client, disqualification is unnecessary and a court order of such might reasonably be regarded as an abuse of discretion. A district court, in resolving this issue, may of course rely on any of a number of factors, among them being the size of the law firm, the area of specialization of the attorney, the attorney's position in the firm, and the demeanor and credibility of witnesses at the evidentiary hearing.

See also Gas-A-Tron v. Union Oil, 534 F.2d 1322 (9th Cir.), cert. denied, 429 U.S. 861 (1976); Silver Chrysler Plymouth v. Chrysler Motors, 370 F. Supp. 581 (E.D.N.Y. 1973), aff'd, 518 F.2d 751 (2d Cir. 1975).

Consider the dilemma of the lawyer who wishes to oppose the effort to rebut the first presumption. Can she effectively cross-examine the migratory lawyer's testimony of nonaccess without revealing the very information her client wishes to protect? Will her witnesses be able to rebut the claim of nonaccess without revealing the protected information? These daunting practical problems proved insurmountable in Graham By Graham v. Wyeth Laboratories, 760 F. Supp. 1451 (D. Kan. 1991). *Graham* also held that when a former client challenges a former lawyer's claim of nonaccess, the client can no longer claim privilege for the communications it wishes to protect. Doesn't that ruling defeat the very purpose of the substantial relationship test?

As *Schiessle* demonstrates, the party seeking to rebut the second presumption, where that is allowed, must prove that the firm took effective steps to protect against leaks of confidential information. *Schiessle* uses the term "Chinese Wall" to invoke the requirement. This is the term used in hundreds of court opinions in the area of lawyer conflicts. Some people find it troubling. Does the term have ethnic connotations or only structural ones? This edition of the casebook uses the term "screening" as do the Model Rules. See Rule 1.11. Other terms have also been suggested, including "cone of silence" and "code of silence." Whatever the label, what kind of preventive measures should a law firm be expected to take?

In United States v. Goot, 894 F.2d 231, 235-236 (7th Cir. 1990), Goot, under investigation for certain federal offenses, hired James Richmond to represent him. A little more than a year later, Richmond was appointed United States Attorney in the district investigating Goot. Goot was later indicted and convicted of the offenses. On appeal, he argued that the United States Attorney's Office should have been disqualified despite the effort to screen Richmond from participation in Goot's case. The court disagreed. The U.S. Attorney's Office had to meet a "strict standard of proof" to overcome the presumption of shared confidences. Screening was "timely employed." It "began before Richmond took office." Other attorneys in the office

> were instructed on Richmond's recusal, thus preventing any discussion with him about the case. By his recusal, Richmond was prohibited from having access to the files on this case. "[B]oth the disqualified attorney and others in the office affirmed these facts under oath." . . .
>
> We agree with Goot that more could have been done. During oral arguments the government conceded that the case files conceivably could have been accessed by the United States Attorney at night or on weekends. The practice of maintaining locked case files with keys distributed to a select few has been cited previously by this court as a substantial screening mechanism. Likewise, the codes necessary to access pertinent information on electronic hardware must remain secret. Nevertheless, the absence of one or both of these mechanisms would not render infirm the screening mechanisms employed in this case.

Oregon permits screening but adds a novel precaution to enhance confidence that the screen will be respected. The Oregon rule requires the "personally disqualified lawyer" to give his or her former firm an affidavit attesting that he or she "will not participate in any manner in the matter or the representation and will not discuss the matter or representation with any other firm member." In addition, if requested, the personally disqualified lawyer must submit a further affidavit once the matter is over "describing the lawyer's actual compliance with these undertakings." Finally, a member of the lawyer's new firm must also provide the first affidavit and, if asked, the second as well. Do you think these procedures are adequate to satisfy the former client of the "personally disqualified lawyer"?

FURTHER READING

Steven Goldberg, The Former Client's Disqualification Gambit: A Bad Move in Pursuit of an Ethical Anomaly, 72 Minn. L. Rev. 227 (1987); Howard Liebman, The Changing Law of Disqualification: The Role of Presumption and Policy, 73 Nw. U. L. Rev. 996 (1979); Martin Lipton & Robert Mazur, The Chinese Wall Solution to the Conflict Problems of Securities Firms, 50 N.Y.U. L. Rev. 459 (1975); Comment, The Chinese Wall Defense to Law-Firm Disqualification, 128 U. Pa. L. Rev. 677 (1980).

QUESTIONS

6.4 Kane, Grossman & Rossi handles the products liability defense work for Admiral Industries, a nationwide manufacturer of consumer products. The firm has 309 lawyers, about two-thirds of them associates.

Admiral is the defendant in some three dozen lawsuits nationwide, brought by consumers who have alleged that they suffered injuries as a result of malfunctions in Admiral's products. KGR is handling each of these cases for Admiral, engaging local counsel where the case is brought in a jurisdiction in which the firm has no office.

Stuart Monk graduated from Georgetown Law School in 1990 and has been working as an associate at a firm in Indiana. His wife, a physician, is about to begin her residency in Tucson, where KGR has an office. Monk writes to the firm about employment. He is interviewed, well received, and hired.

Three months later, KGR begins to receive motions to disqualify it in various Admiral matters. The motions fall into four categories:

1. A motion from Monk's former firm alleging that the firm was handling a claim based on an Admiral toaster oven while Monk was there. It seeks to disqualify KGR from continuing to represent Admiral on that claim.

2. A second motion from Monk's former firm alleging that while Monk was there the firm was handling a claim based on an Admiral blender. It seeks to disqualify KGR from continuing to represent Admiral on that claim.

3. A third motion from Monk's former firm alleging that after Monk left, the firm filed a claim for a new client also based on one of Admiral's coffee makers. It seeks to disqualify KGR from appearing for Admiral on that claim.
4. Twenty-one motions from other firms representing plaintiffs in cases based on Admiral toaster ovens. These allege that the other firms, together with Monk's former firm, were part of an "Admiral Toaster Oven Committee" that pooled confidential and tactical information about their claims. Consequently, the other firms assert standing to disqualify KGR.

How should these motions be decided? What if any further information do you need?

6.5 A state legislature is considering passage of a law that will impose strict truth in sales and antifraud requirements on used car dealers. Sara Cole is hired by the Federation of Reliable Used Auto Dealers (FRUAD) to represent it before the state legislature at hearings on the bill. Cole testifies that current case and statutory law is adequate to protect used car purchasers. She also argues that the contemplated law will be in violation of the state's constitution. She submits a brief covering both points. The law is nevertheless passed. Subsequently, Cole changes firms. Her new firm is asked to represent Ariel Lemon in a damage action under the law against Ace Used Cars. Ace is a large used car dealer in the state and one of the organizers of FRUAD. May either Cole or the firm represent Lemon?

6.6 "Our firm has a chance to lure Antonia Zendzian from her current firm, which is great because Toni is one of the best land-use lawyers in the state — in the region, actually. This is no overstatement. She'll be bringing a busload of clients, too. We've done a conflicts check, and it looks okay right now. It does. But we've read *Jelco* and *Picker* and some of those other cases (page 258 supra) and we're worried that something might happen that will knock us out of a future representation that we can't afford not to be in because of a conflict we cannot now predict. We realize there's no insurance policy here, but we'd like to ask certain of our and Toni's current clients, and also new clients in designated industries that are especially conflicts prone, to agree to waive all future successive conflicts on substantially related matters, with provision for screening, and all future concurrent conflicts on unrelated matters, again with screening. We think they'd agree. But I don't know, even if they did, if we can make it stick when the conflict comes up or if it's all right even to ask current or new clients to do that in advance."

C. GOVERNMENT SERVICE

Government lawyers are confronted by many of the same conflict problems that corporate lawyers encounter. Some of these are raised in Chapter 9. The problem of identifying the client is especially acute for government lawyers. Consider an attorney who works in the northeast regional office of a bureau of a federal agency. Does the lawyer owe her loyalty to the head of that regional office, the regional office as an entity, the bureau of the agency, the head of that bureau, the agency as a whole, the head of that agency, or the entire government? These questions and others are addressed in a number of useful articles on ethics of government lawyers. See, for example, Kaufman, The Former Government Attorney and the Canons of Professional Ethics, 70 Harv. L. Rev. 657 (1957); Harvard Conflicts, Note, page 263 supra, at 1413-1428.

Here we study one issue in particular. You have surely heard about the "revolving door," the one that leads in and out of government service. Toil in the vineyards of public service, acquire expertise and know-*who* in a lucrative field, then trade on this knowledge in the private market. The prospect of attractive postgovernment employment makes the official tour of duty appealing to many.

Still, various rules limit the postdeparture conduct of government employees (whether or not they are lawyers). Some of these are in federal and state law. Some of these laws carry criminal sanctions. For lawyers, restrictions also appear in the code and rules, which are written so that it does not matter whether the lawyer's government employment was in a legal capacity. Rule 1.11; DR 9-101(B). You can look at this issue as a type of successive conflict when (as is usually the case) the lawyer's former employer was a government entity. But the revolving door also revolves in the other direction, imposing limits on the conduct of government lawyers based on their prior, private representations. Rule 1.11(c). United States v. Goot, page 274 supra.

If the government were no different from any other former client, successive employment issues would be resolved by the rules already studied in this chapter. Why do we need a special rule for government lawyers who change jobs? What broader or different issues does their postdeparture employment raise? See Rules 1.10, comments 4 and 5; 1.11, comment 3.

ARMSTRONG v. McALPIN
625 F.2d 433 (2d Cir. 1980) (en banc), vacated on other grounds, 449 U.S. 1106 (1981)

[Altman, while a lawyer at the SEC, supervised an investigation and litigation against certain of the defendants including McAlpin. The SEC litigation alleged that McAlpin and others had looted millions of dollars from the Capital Growth companies. McAlpin and other defendants defaulted and the trial judge appointed Armstrong as receiver of the Capital Growth companies.

Armstrong was charged with recovering all misappropriated property. With the trial judge's permission, he retained the law firm of Barrett Smith, of which he was a partner. When it appeared that Barrett Smith had a conflict of interest, the law firm of Gordon Hurwitz was substituted as counsel. Prior to the substitution, Altman ended a nine-year tenure with the SEC and became associated with Gordon Hurwitz. In the last three years of his tenure, Altman was assistant director of the SEC's Enforcement Division with responsibility over numerous cases including the Capital Growth investigation and litigation. Although Altman "was not involved on a daily basis, he was generally aware of the facts of the case and the status of the litigation. . . . Altman's name appeared on the SEC complaint, although he did not sign it."

Gordon Hurwitz and Armstrong concluded that Altman "should not participate in the Gordon firm's representation of the receiver, but that the firm would not be disqualified if Altman was properly screened from the case." Thereafter, Gordon Hurwitz "asked the SEC if it had any objection to the retention, and was advised in writing that it did not, so long as Altman was screened from participation." After Armstrong began this action, McAlpin and others moved to disqualify Gordon Hurwitz. The trial judge (Werker) denied the disqualification but a panel of the Second Circuit reversed. The case was then reargued to the court en banc. Following is a portion of the opinion of Judge Feinberg joined by four of the other eight judges on the court.

Judge Feinberg first held that the denial of disqualification was not immediately appealable but nevertheless concluded that there were "strong reasons in the unusual context of this case to reach the merits of the appeal rather than to dismiss it." Ultimately, the Supreme Court vacated the Second Circuit's decision in *Armstrong* on the ground of nonappealability.]

FEINBERG, J. . . .

[The trial judge] noted that Altman was concededly disqualified from participating in the litigation under Disciplinary Rule 9-101(B) . . . That Rule prohibits an attorney's private employment in any matter in which he has had substantial responsibility during prior public employment. The judge then considered the effect of Disciplinary Rule 5-105(D), which deals with disqualification of an entire law firm if one lawyer in the firm is disqualified. . . . The ABA, in its Formal Opinion No. 342, had recognized that "[p]ast government employment creates an unusual situation in which an inflexible application of D.R. 5-105(D) would actually thwart the policy considerations underlying D.R. 9-101(B)," and concluded that, absent an appearance of significant impropriety, a government agency could waive Rule 5-105(D), if adequate screening procedures effectively isolated the former government lawyer from those members of his firm handling the matter. . . .

Judge Werker then carefully examined the screening of Altman by the Gordon firm, noting that:

> Altman is excluded from participation in the action, has no access to relevant files and derives no remuneration from funds obtained by the firm from prosecuting this action. No one at the firm is permitted to discuss the matter in his presence or allow him to view any document related to this litigation, and Altman has not imparted any information concerning Growth Fund to the firm.
>
> [N]othing before this court indicates that Altman, while employed by the SEC, formed an intent to prosecute a later action involving Growth Fund. Indeed, sworn affidavits reveal that he has never participated in any fashion whatever in the Gordon firm's income derived from prosecution of this action. And . . . Altman and his two partners Velie and Butowsky have attested under penalty of perjury that Altman has never discussed the action with other firm members. These statements are uncontradicted by defendants and provide a basis for *not* imputing Altman's knowledge to other members of the firm.

Under all the circumstances, the district judge concluded that "the proper screening of Altman rather than disqualification of the Gordon firm is the solution to the present dispute." . . . On appeal . . . a panel of this court reversed the order of the district court, apparently on the ground that disqualification was required "as a prophylactic measure to guard against misuse of authority by government lawyers."

On this rehearing en banc, we are favored with briefs not only from the parties but also from the United States, the Securities and Exchange Commission, the Interstate Commerce Commission, the Federal Maritime Commission, the Commodities Futures Trading Commission and twenty-six distinguished former government lawyers now employed as practicing attorneys, corporate officers, or law professors, all attesting to the importance of the issues raised on appeal. Thus, the United States asserts that a "decision to reject screening procedures is certain to have a serious, adverse effect on the ability of Government legal offices to recruit and retain well-qualified attorneys"; this view is seconded by the other government amici. And the former government lawyers, including two former Attorneys General of the United States and two former Solicitors General of the United States, state that they are all "affected at least indirectly, by the panel opinion's underlying assumption that government lawyers cannot be trusted — trusted to discharge their public responsibilities faithfully while in office, or to abide fully by screening procedures afterwards." While the tone of these assertions may be overly apocalyptic, it is true that a decision rejecting the efficacy of screening procedures in this context may have significant adverse consequences. Thus, such disapproval may hamper the government's efforts to hire qualified attorneys; the latter may fear that government service will transform them into legal "typhoid Marys," shunned by prospective private employers because hiring them may result in the disqualification of an entire firm in a possibly wide range of cases. The amici also contend that those already employed by the government may be unwilling to assume positions of greater responsibility within the government that might serve to heighten their undesirability to future private employers. Certainly such trends, if carried to an extreme, may ultimately affect adversely the quality of the services of government attorneys.

Not only is the panel decision possibly of great practical importance, the ethical issues it addresses are also complex and are currently being hotly contested by various groups. . . .

We do not believe that it is necessary or appropriate for this court to enter fully into the fray, as the panel opinion did. Indeed, the current uncertainty over what is "ethical" underscores for us the wisdom, when considering such issues, of adopting a restrained approach that focuses primarily on preserving the integrity of the trial process. We expressed this view in Board of Education v. Nyquist [page 220 supra]. . . .

We believe that this approach is dispositive here and requires our affirmance of the ruling of the district court. It is apparent from a close reading of Judge Werker's opinion that he saw no threat of taint of the trial by the Gordon firm's continued representation of the receiver. Nor did the panel opinion in this case challenge that view. Although appellants assert that the trial will be tainted by the use of information from Altman, we see no basis on the record before us for overruling the district court's rejection of that claim. Using the *Nyquist* analysis, there is certainly no reason to fear any lack of "vigor" by the Gordon firm in representing the receiver; this is not a case where a law firm, by use of a "Chinese wall," is attempting to justify representation of conflicting interests at the same time. Nor is the Gordon firm "potentially in a position to use privileged information" obtained through prior representation of the other side. And finally, the receiver will not be making unfair use of information obtained by Altman as a government official, since the SEC files were turned over to the receiver long before he retained the Gordon firm and Altman has been entirely screened from all participation in the case, to the satisfaction of the district court and the SEC.[24] Nor is there any reason to believe that the receiver retained the Gordon firm because Altman was connected with it or that Altman had anything to do with the retention. If anything, the presence of Altman as an associate at that time was a problem, not a benefit, for the Gordon firm, as the district court, the receiver and the Gordon firm all apparently recognized.

Thus, because the district court justifiably held that the Gordon firm's representation of the receiver posed no threat to the integrity of the trial process, disqualification of the firm can only be based on the possible appearance of impropriety stemming from Altman's association with the firm. However, as previously noted, reasonable minds may and do differ on the ethical propriety of screening in this context. But there can be no doubt that disqualification of the Gordon firm will have serious consequences for this litigation; separating the receiver from his counsel at this late date will seriously delay and impede, and perhaps altogether thwart, his attempt to obtain redress for defendant's alleged frauds. Under the circumstances, the possible "appearance of impropriety is simply too slender a reed on which to rest a disqualification order . . . particularly . . . where . . . the appearance of impropriety is not very clear." *Nyquist*, 590 F.2d at 1247. Thus, we need not resolve the ethical propriety of the screening procedure used here at this time as long as the district court justifiably regarded it as effective in isolating Altman from the litigation.

We recognize that a rule that concentrates on the threat of taint fails to correct all possible ethical conflicts. In adopting this approach, we do not denigrate the importance of ethical conduct by attorneys practicing in this courthouse or elsewhere, and we applaud the efforts of the organized bar to educate its members as to their ethical obligations. However, absent a threat of taint to the trial, we continue to believe that possible ethical conflicts surfacing during a litigation are generally better addressed by the "comprehensive disciplinary machinery" of the state and federal bar, or possibly by legislation.[27] While there may be unusual situations where the "appearance of impropriety" alone is sufficient to warrant disqualification, we are satisfied that this is not such a case. Nor do we believe, as Judge Newman asserts, that a failure to disqualify the Gordon firm based on the possible appearance of impropriety will contribute to the "public skepticism about lawyers." While sensitive to the integrity of the bar, the public is also rightly concerned about the fairness and efficiency of the judicial process. We believe those concerns would be

24. The case therefore is entirely distinguishable from General Motors Corp. v. City of New York, 501 F.2d 639 (2d Cir. 1974), where an attorney who had substantial responsibility over antitrust litigation against General Motors Corporation while he was employed by the Antitrust Division of the Justice Department later accepted employment as plaintiff's attorney in a private antitrust action against the same defendant for substantially the same conduct.

27. Cf. 18 U.S.C. §207.

disserved by an order of disqualification in a case such as this, where no
threat of taint exists and where appellants' motion to disqualify opposing
counsel has successfully crippled the efforts of a receiver, appointed at
the request of a public agency, to obtain redress for alleged serious
frauds on the investing public. Thus, rather than heightened public
skepticism, we believe that the restrained approach this court had
adopted towards attempts to disqualify opposing counsel on ethical
grounds avoids unnecessary and unseemly delay and reinforces public
confidence in the fairness of the judicial process.

Accordingly, we vacate the panel opinion in this case and affirm the
judgment of the district court.

[Two other judges concurred with the majority on the merits, but disagreed on the appealability issue. One judge would have dismissed the
appeal for lack of jurisdiction. One judge agreed with the majority on the
appealability issue, but disagreed on the merits.]

The Revolving Door in the Model Rules

In *Armstrong*, the successive conflict risks were not the traditional ones
that accrue when a lawyer opposes a former client on a substantially related matter. The interest was rather that lawyers not be free to exploit
government service, including confidential information gained during it,
for private gain and the advantage of private clients. Yet we also encourage people to enter government service by emphasizing that they
will acquire knowledge and experience on which they can capitalize in
private life. How do we reconcile these positions? The following discussion tries to identify the line dividing "good" and "bad" exploitation of
government experience.

Could Altman, the former SEC lawyer in *Armstrong*, ethically have represented the receiver? The firm offered to screen him, but did it have to?
In General Motors v. City of New York, 501 F.2d 639, 649-650 (2d Cir.
1974), distinguished in footnote 24 of *Armstrong*, New York City brought
an antitrust action against GM charging monopolization in the manufacture and sale of city buses. The city was represented by private counsel,
George Reycraft, who had previously worked for the antitrust division of
the Department of Justice. In that job, Reycraft had substantial involvement in an action brought by the United States against GM for monop-
olizing the manufacture and sale of city and intercity buses. Resisting
GM's motion to disqualify Reycraft, the city argued that he had not
"switched sides" in his new retainer but was continuing to represent a
government entity, although a different one and as a private practitioner, against the same defendant, GM. The Second Circuit rejected this
argument. After noting that the code did not textually support it, the
court continued:

We believe, moreover, that this is as it should be for there lurks great potential for lucrative returns in following into private practice the course already charted with the aid of governmental resources. And, with such a large contingent fee at stake, we could hardly accept "pro bono publico" as a proper characterization of Reycraft's work, simply because the keeper of the purse is the City of New York. . . .

The court, applying a literal reading of Rule 9-101(B), was concerned that former government lawyers not be allowed to profit from information learned in their government employment. The city's argument that disqualification would "chill the ardor for Government service by rendering worthless the experience gained in Government employ" was not credited.

The Model Rules partly reject the holding of the *General Motors* case. Rule 1.11(a) would allow a lawyer to represent "a private client in connection with a matter in which the lawyer participated personally and substantially as a public officer or employee" so long as the "appropriate government agency consents after consultation." Furthermore, Rule 1.11(a) is not limited to the situation where the former government lawyer remains on the same "side," as the city claimed Reycraft had. Rule 1.11(a) would permit the lawyer to turn around and represent the other "side" on the very issue on which she had worked while in public office — e.g., *for* GM in New York City's case against it. However, it might then be difficult to get agency consent and, depending on the facts, it might even be a crime (see page 284 infra). Is the agency consent provision objectionable on the ground that those responsible for giving the consent are in a conflict situation given their own expectations after leaving government service? Should we fear that government lawyers will identify a work agenda based on their expectations of future private employment and the likelihood of consent? See Note, Ethical Problems for the Law Firm of a Former Government Attorney: Firm or Individual Disqualification?, 1977 Duke L.J. 512, 520-521.

There is one instance in which the Model Rules would not allow the agency to consent to a former government lawyer's successive private representation. That is where the lawyer has "confidential government information" about a person, which could be used in the representation of a client whose interests are adverse to that person. We are here concerned with "confidential *government* information," a term to be distinguished from "confidential information." Compare Rule 1.6 with Rule 1.11(e). Rule 1.11(b) and (e) contemplates that while in government service a lawyer may gain information about individuals to which only the government has access or which is particularly within the power of the government to compel — tax returns, trade secrets, and grand jury testimony are some examples. The rules mean to prevent a private client from hiring a former government lawyer in order to obtain such information about an opponent. The rules also prevent the former government lawyer from being able to attract clients by offering to use this information on their behalf.

If the former government lawyer cannot get the consent contemplated by Rule 1.11(a), or is disqualified because she possesses "confidential government information" under Rule 1.11(b), the rules still permit her firm to continue the representation so long as the lawyer is screened and receives no portion of the fee. No permission need be obtained from the government to use the screening device. *Armstrong* states the policy reasons to tolerate screening in this situation although the rules reject it for migratory private lawyers.

Rule 1.11 is not meant to exclude other rights the government may have as a client, such as the right to have its lawyers avoid successive conflicts under Rule 1.9(a), to the avoidance of concurrent conflicts of interest (Rule 1.7), and to the protection of the government's own confidential information under Rules 1.6 and 1.9(c).

The Model Rules, but not the code, speak to a lawyer's responsibility when moving from private practice to government employment. See Rule 1.11(c). A government lawyer is disqualified under this rule from participating "in a matter in which the lawyer participated personally and substantially while in private practice or nongovernmental employment." Nevertheless, as the comment makes clear, "other lawyers in the agency with which the lawyer in question has become associated" are not disqualified. Reaves v. State, 574 So. 2d 105 (Fla. 1991), reversed a murder conviction and death sentence where the prosecutor had previously represented the defendant in a prosecution involving similar issues. The court said it would allow screening in future cases but that, absent adequate screening, a trial court may be required "to disqualify the entire state attorney's office." In United States v. Caggiano, 660 F.2d 184 (6th Cir. 1981), cert. denied, 455 U.S. 945 (1982), the court refused to disqualify the entire United States Attorney's Office on the retrial of a matter because a new assistant prosecutor had represented the accused during his first trial. See also United States v. Goot, page 274 supra. By contrast, in State v. Tippecanoe County Court, 432 N.E.2d 1377 (Ind. 1982), the entire prosecutorial office was disqualified because the chief prosecutor had represented the accused as a public defender on substantially related matters. Turbin v. Superior Court, 165 Ariz. 195, 797 P.2d 734 (Ct. App. 1990), rejected screening on appearance of impropriety grounds where the charges were severe, the case simple, and the size of the prosecutor's office small.

Many jurisdictions have statutes controlling the postdeparture work of government employees, including lawyers. See Harvard Conflicts Note, page 263 supra, at 1437 n.102. In the federal system, 18 U.S.C. §207 imposes certain postdeparture restrictions on former government employees. These include permanent restrictions, two-year restrictions, and one-year restrictions on a variety of activities before the employee's former department or agency. The duration of the disability depends on the nature of the employee's work and his or her status. Violation of the section is a crime. See also 28 C.F.R. 45.735-7 (1988) for disqualification rules applicable to former Justice Department employees. The New York State Ethics in Government Act, which also imposes certain limits on post-termination work of government employees, was upheld in Forti v. New York State Ethics Commission, 75 N.Y.2d 596, 544 N.E.2d 876, 555 N.Y.S.2d 235 (1990). By contrast, the Pennsylvania act was declared invalid in so far as it purported to control the law practice of a former judge. Wajert v. State Ethics Commission, 491 Pa. 255, 420 A.2d 439 (1980), held that supervision of the conduct of an attorney and former judge "was a matter exclusively for this Court."

What Is the Meaning of "Matter" and "Substantial Responsibility"?

DR 9-101(B) states that: "A lawyer shall not accept private employment in a matter in which he had substantial responsibility while he was a public employee." This provision raises at least two subsidiary questions. What constitutes a "matter"? What constitutes "substantial responsibility"? With regard to the definition of "matter," ABA Formal Opinion 342 (1975) states:

> [T]he term seems to contemplate a discrete and isolatable transaction or set of transactions between identifiable parties. . . . The same lawsuit or litigation is the same matter. The same issue of fact involving the same parties and the same situation or conduct is the same matter. By contrast, work as a government employee in drafting, enforcing or interpreting government or agency procedures, regulations, or laws, or in briefing abstract principles of law, does not disqualify the lawyer under DR 9-101(B) from subsequent private employment involving the same regulations, procedures, or points of law; the same "matter" is not involved because there is lacking the discrete, identifiable transactions or conduct involving a particular situation and specific parties.

D.C. Opinion 187 (1987) is in accord but cautions the lawyer not to accept the representation if the lawyer's independent professional judgment will be compromised by the fact that he or she previously had responsibility for drafting the regulation or rule or if the work will require the use of government confidences.

New York City 889 (1976) agrees with this definition of "matter" except for its exclusion of rulemaking, citing cases "where a lawyer has specifically analyzed and passed upon the validity of a regulation and after leaving government service is faced with the question of accepting employment in a matter which may involve an attack upon the validity of that very regulation." Rule 1.11(d)(1) seems to define "matter" in accord with the ABA exclusion of rulemaking. See also National Bonded Warehouse Assn. v. United States, 718 F. Supp. 967 (C.I.T. 1989) (rulemaking and policy-making activities are not "matters" within the meaning of DR 9-101(B)). Nevertheless, Rule 1.9 applies to government lawyers as well as to private practitioners (see Rule 1.11 comment) and would prohibit the former government lawyer from attacking in private practice the validity of the very rule he had earlier promulgated on behalf of the government. However broadly the word is defined, in deciding whether a subsequent matter is the same as the matter upon which the lawyer worked while with the government, one should probably apply the "substantial relationship" test used for deciding whether there is a successive conflict of interest in the private practice context. General Motors v. City of New York, 501 F.2d 639, 655 n.22 (2d Cir. 1974) (test is not whether the two actions rely on same section of the law, but whether the underlying facts "are sufficiently similar"). See also Harvard Conflicts Note, page 263 supra, at 1435-1436.

What is "substantial responsibility"? In Opinion 342 (1975), the ABA wrote:

> As used in DR 9-101(B), "substantial responsibility" envisages a much closer and more direct relationship than that of a mere perfunctory approval or disapproval of the matter in question. It contemplates a responsibility requiring the official to become personally involved to an important, material degree, in the investigative or deliberative processes regarding the transactions or facts in question. Thus, being the chief official in some vast office or organization does not ipso facto give that government official or employee the "substantial responsibility" contemplated by the rule in regard to all the minutiae of facts lodged within that office. Yet it is not necessary that the public employee or official shall have personally and in a substantial manner investigated or passed upon the particular matter, for it is sufficient that he had such a heavy responsibility for the matter in question that it is unlikely he did not become personally and substantially involved in the investigative or deliberative processes regarding that matter. With a responsibility so strong and compelling that he probably became involved in the investigative or decisional processes, a lawyer upon leaving the government service should not represent another in regard to that matter. To do so would be akin to switching sides, might jeopardize confidential government information, and gives the appearance of professional impropriety in that accepting subsequent employment regarding that same matter creates a suspicion that the lawyer conducted his governmental work in a way to facilitate his own future employment in that matter.

Rule 1.11(a) substitutes the phrase "participated personally and substantially" for the code's "substantial responsibility." For a case whose facts were said to lie "at the outer bounds of the 'substantial responsibility' required to invoke the disciplinary rule," see Kessenich v. Commodity Futures Trading Commn., 684 F.2d 88 (D.C. Cir. 1982). See also Twin Laboratories v. Weider Health & Fitness, 1989-1 Trade Cases ¶68,578 (S.D.N.Y. 1989) (mere perfunctory approval or disapproval of an agency matter does not constitute substantial responsibility).

FURTHER READING

Harvard Conflicts Note, supra page 263 at 1413-1446; Thomas Morgan, Appropriate Limits on Participation by a Former Agency Official in Matters Before an Agency, 1980 Duke L.J. 1; Comment, Conflicts of Interest and the Former Government Attorney, 65 Geo. L.J. 1025 (1977) (authored by G. Bollwerk).

QUESTION

6.7   After the local newspaper reports abuses by landlords in town — charging excessive rents, failure to provide services, and the like — the city council retains Cynthia Andrews to conduct an investigation and recommend legislation. Andrews conducts a six-month investigation, followed by three months of hearings before the appropriate city council committee. All the while, Andrews, a partner in a private firm, continues to represent other clients. After the hearings, Andrews drafts legislation that would give tenants treble damage claims against landlords who violate certain provisions of the new law. The legislation passes. Thereafter, may Andrews or her firm represent (1) a tenant suing under the statute or (2) a landlord sued under the statute? The latter representation would require a challenge to the validity of the law on state constitutional grounds unless that issue had already been resolved in a prior action. Would your answers differ if Andrews was a salaried employee of the city council when she did the work, and joined her law firm only after the legislation passed?

Part Three

SPECIAL LAWYER ROLES

VII

Ethics in Advocacy

The role of the courtroom advocate probably raises more controversial ethical and moral issues, for both the public and the bar, than any other part of a lawyer's work. Why is that? In this chapter we look at problems common to civil and criminal cases. In Chapter 8, we focus on problems particularly likely to arise in criminal prosecutions. Before we proceed, however, here are some preliminary observations.

Many think of the advocate as amoral, and many advocates accept this characterization. An advocate may concede that she means to win all or as much as possible for her client, regardless of who is "right." The advocate may deny that it is possible to talk about "right" in the conventional sense. (This will not, however, prevent the advocate from trying to get as much mileage as possible from conventional notions of "right" and "wrong" or "good" and "bad.") The advocate may see herself as the agent for her client in a highly structured, artificial combat system called litigation, a system the client doesn't fully understand but that can play havoc with the client's life. In this system, as the advocate knows, you are "right" if you win; you don't necessarily win because you are right.

The advocate views her job as to use all available legal and ethical means to achieve her client's goal, subject only to her client's willingness and ability to pay the cost, which includes the advocate's fee, if any. It matters not that a particular strategy might encourage the "wrong" result, because just as there is no "right," there is no "wrong," except by reference to how the system resolves the issue. As Johnson reportedly told Boswell (page 296 infra) "you do not know [a cause] to be good or bad till the judge determines it." So far as the advocate is concerned, the loser is wrong by definition.

The advocate adopts this perspective only after she has been retained by a client. She may, of course, reflect on the rightness of a client's case *before* accepting it and decline cases she finds repugnant. But she may also accept such cases. An advocate thus divides herself into parts. Once she has taken an assignment, she acts as though the client's cause were her own. Many trial lawyers delight in quoting Lord Brougham, who was the lawyer for Queen Caroline in her trial for adultery. Brougham apparently had some evidence that would embarrass the King, but would he use it to defend the Queen? Brougham let it be known not only that he would but that he would consider himself bound to do so. He told the judges: "[A]n advocate in the discharge of his duty, knows but one person in all the world, and that person is his client." He then added, lest there be any doubt, that the "hazards and costs to other persons" are of no concern to the advocate, that the advocate "must not regard the alarm, the torments, the destruction which he may bring upon others. [H]e must go on reckless of the consequences, though it should be his unhappy fate to involve his country in confusion." 2 Trial at Large of Her Majesty Caroline Amelia Elizabeth, Queen of Great Britain 3 (J. Nightengale ed. 1821).

For many people, this behavior is repugnant. How can you be one person at your work and someone completely different outside of work? (For some lawyers, the risk is not that they will be unable to adopt the advocate's mask at work but that they will be unable to remove it at home.) Popular suspicion of this conduct encourages cynicism about lawyers and often leads to that ancient question: "How can you defend a guilty person?" For the advocate, that question is nonsense. Guilt is a legal conclusion. By definition, no one can be guilty until declared so after trial. (If the question is rephrased: "How can you defend someone who 'did it'?" the advocate will have other answers about his or her role in the Anglo-American criminal justice system.) To many members of the public, this sounds like "lawyer talk" or dissembling. The public may conclude that it is also duplicitous once it realizes that despite the advocate's effort to defend her role by appealing to some greater good, her motives are generally financial. ("She wouldn't do it if she weren't getting paid and she'd probably work for the first one to hire her.")

Things get more complicated when the focus shifts from the dubious goals of the advocate's client, goals she is helping him achieve, to the means the advocate might employ to help the client win. Those means, though legal and ethical, may impede a fair result. But just as the words "right" and "wrong" do not have the same meaning in the advocate's world, neither does the word "fair" retain its conventional meaning. The most obvious example is when a well-funded client prolongs a litigation with creative but nonfrivolous procedural motions, thereby forcing a desperate plaintiff to compromise for much less than the value of his claim. Another example is when a lawyer knowingly demeans a truthful witness through vigorous cross-examination.

What rules should govern the behavior of a lawyer when acting as an advocate? The answer to this question will in part depend upon a theory of adversary justice. A theory of adversary justice, in turn, presumes a theory of justice itself. We must also remember that theories are not self-executing. They must accommodate a political and historical tradition. They must take account of human frailty and institutional incompetence. An imperfect system of justice might be as close to the "most perfect" system of justice that a society's traditions and institutions are capable of at the time. In measuring a nation's system of justice, we also take the measure of the nation.

We begin with selections from the vast literature defending and criticizing the adversary system in the United States. It is not possible to provide a representative survey of this literature or even to develop fully the views of the few authors we can include. We can, however, give you a feel for the debate. In turn, you should be able to begin to form your own conclusions as you assess the particular practices described in the succeeding material.

For further background reading at this point, see David Luban's extensive investigation, Lawyers and Justice: An Ethical Study (1988); Stephen Bundy & Einer Elhauge, Do Lawyers Improve the Adversary System? A General Theory of Litigation Advice and Its Regulation, 79 Cal. L. Rev. 313 (1991) (using "rational actor analysis" to examine the "considerations that determine the informational effects and social value of litigation advice"); Charles Fried's classic defense of adversary justice in Fried, The Lawyer as Friend: The Moral Foundations of the Lawyer-Client Relation, 85 Yale L.J. 1060 (1976); Stephen Gillers, Can a Good Lawyer Be a Bad Person?, 84 Mich. L. Rev. 1011 (1986); and Stephen Pepper's challenging discussion in Pepper, The Lawyer's Amoral Ethical Role: A Defense, a Problem, and Some Possibilities, 1986 Am. B. Found. Res. J. 613 (with responses in the same volume from Professors Luban and Andrew Kaufman and a rejoinder from Professor Pepper). For a view of the lawyer's role that goes beyond advocacy, see Richard Wasserstrom's pathbreaking article, Lawyers as Professionals: Some Moral Issues, 5 Hum. Rights 1 (1975).

Should answers to questions raised here differ when a lawyer litigates civil matters for the government? Catherine Lanctot contrasts a lawyer's traditional duty of adversarial zeal with the government lawyer's special duty "to seek justice." EC 7-14. "This double standard," she writes, "furnishes much of the ethical tension inherent in the role of the government lawyer." After framing the issues with three hypotheticals, Professor Lanctot develops and seeks to clarify them in The Duty of Zealous Advocacy and the Ethics of the Federal Government Lawyer: The Three Hardest Questions, 64 S. Cal. L. Rev. 951 (1991).

A.   FIVE VIEWS ON ADVERSARY "TRUTH"

Rifkind and Frankel

Simon H. Rifkind

THE LAWYER'S ROLE AND RESPONSIBILITY IN MODERN SOCIETY

30 The Record 534, 535-545 (1975)

When I was first admitted to the bar, I was formally authorized to act as an attorney-at-law. The concept of attorneyship, of course, includes agency. An agent must have a principal; so must an attorney have a client. The lawyer's role and responsibility as attorney comes into being only when he is a member of a client-attorney, symbiotic team.

Once he becomes a member of such a team then, in the United States and in other countries having a common law tradition, he works in an environment called the adversary system and engages in maneuvers called the adversary process.

Awareness of this fact is crucial to the understanding of the attorney's duty and responsibility. Failure to grasp the significance of the adversary system has given rise to much misunderstanding, both within and without the bar, and has, I suggest, led to some unproductive developments.

In an actual lawsuit, the operation of the adversary process becomes fully visible even to the uninitiated. As a matter of history and habit, we accept unquestioningly the bizarre arrangement by which the State hires one lawyer to prosecute a citizen for an alleged crime, another to defend him and a third to decide between them. A visitor from Mars might inquire, "Why not hire one to ascertain the truth?"

But it is not only for litigated matters that the adversary system constitutes the living ambience. Consensual arrangements may become the subject of litigation; the draftsman must, to the best of his ability, anticipate the vicissitudes his writing will experience during its voyage in the adversary process. Every will prepared in the privacy of a law office may be contested, every advice given may be challenged, every opinion given must be formulated in the light of the possibility of attack upon its validity and its subjection to the adversary process and judicial arbitrament.

Both the prospect of litigation and its actuality impose great restraint upon the attorney and challenge his learning, his wisdom and his capacity to prophesy. It also relieves him of much responsibility. In the course of his advocacy, he may urge propositions of which he is less than certain, because the lawyer is not the final arbiter. The final judgment will emerge out of the contest. In the collision of the two opposing forces, out of the cross-exposure by each of his adversary's weakness and out of the need to discover and articulate one's own virtues and advantages, in the fire of that antagonism a more refined truth is smeltered and a better judgment is filtered.

The adversary process is thus seen as a form of organized and institutionalized confrontation. Because organized confrontations also occur in many forms of sport, some have seized upon the superficial similarity to downgrade the adversary process as socially trivial. This contemnation would be appropriate if the object of the adversary process were to select the more skillful lawyer, as it is, for instance, to select the better boxer or tennis player. In the courtroom contest, the judge does not award prizes for skill. He uses the adversary process for illumination. And it is, I believe, the teaching of experience that the incentives generated by the adversary system do, indeed, tend to bring about a more thorough search for and evaluation of both the facts and the law. . . .

From some of my philosophically oriented brethren I hear murmurs that the Anglo-American reliance on the adversary process may have exceeded the limits of its utility and that re-examination is now in order. Re-examination of a major premise is always in order. Most logical errors are imbedded in major premises uncritically accepted. I have no doubt that to the logician, the adversary process will present many flaws. The inequality of resources between the contestants, the disparity in talent, are but two of many. But I should recall the sage words of the Yankee from Olympus, "The life of the law has not been logic; it has been experience."

Experience tells me that the adversary system has been good for liberty, good for peaceful progress and good enough to have the public accept that system's capacity to resolve controversies and, generally, to acquiesce in the results.

And it has also accomplished something else. It has tended to reward most highly those lawyers who are best suited to the adversary process. In consequence, such lawyers have established the norms of performance. Any one who has worked with lawyers around the globe knows that those brought up in the Anglo-American tradition of the adversary process devote themselves more comprehensively, more passionately, to the solution of their clients' problems than the lawyers reared under any other system.

Recent events surrounding the whole epoch called Watergate have caused an unflattering light to shine upon quite a number of lawyers. Some laymen have suggested that the very function the attorney presumes to discharge involves a conflict of interest between his duty to his client and his duty to society.

Those who have voiced such views have not taken account of the operation of the adversary process. The utility of that process is that it relieves the lawyer of the need, or indeed the right, to be his client's judge and thereby frees him to be the more effective advocate and champion. Since the same is true of his adversary, it should follow that the judge who will decide will be aided by greater illumination than otherwise would be available.

Lord MacMillan in his famous address on the ethics of advocacy delivered in 1916 quotes this exchange:

Boswell: "But what do you think of supporting a cause which you know to be bad?"

Johnson: "Sir, you do not know it to be good or bad till the judge determines it. You are to state facts clearly; so that your *thinking,* or what you call *knowing,* a cause to be bad must be from reasoning, must be from supposing your arguments to be weak and inconclusive. But, sir, that is not enough. An argument which does not convince yourself may convince the judge to whom you urge it; and if it does convince him, why then, sir, you are wrong and he is right. It is his business to judge; and you are not to be confident in your opinion that a cause is bad, but to say all you can for your client, and then hear the judge's opinion."

Of course the process I have described is subject to human frailty. Sometimes the poorer cause prevails. That is a price worth paying for the long-range benefits of the system. It is comparable to the price we are willing to pay for democracy in the acceptance of the mistakes of the majority. We pay a price for the jury system. We pay these in return for values which we believe exceed the costs.

Even when the poorer cause prevails at the end of the adversary process, it is not necessarily a total loss. Sometimes it flags an error in the law. Sometimes it stokes the fires of reform and produces corrective legislative action.

What I have said thus far would have sounded orthodox twenty years ago. Today I think it is radical doctrine. It is radical because it rejects the notion which has gained considerable ground at the bar and very widespread allegiance on the campus that the lawyer should not be client-oriented but cause oriented. . . .

In the Cardozo lecture delivered last December at the Association of the Bar of the City of New York, Judge Marvin Frankel, a superb scholar and unusually gifted judge, spoke of the search for truth in the litigational world which he explored. On innumerable occasions I have heard judges, presiding at a trial, express an impatient desire to get at the truth or pronounce the generalization that the object of a trial was the ascertainment of the truth.

In general terms, truth commands a very high respect in our society. No one can be heard to challenge judges when they pay homage to truth.

With some trepidation I should like to tender the suggestion that in actual practice the ascertainment of the truth is not necessarily the target of the trial, that values other than truth frequently take precedence, and that, indeed, courtroom truth is a unique species of the genus truth, and that it is not necessarily congruent with objective or absolute truth, whatever that may be.

When I once casually expressed this notion to a group of laymen, they expressed shock and dismay as if I were a monk uttering some unutterable heresy to a Tenth Century congregation of bishops. But that reaction has not deterred me. On reflection, I have framed the hypothesis that courtroom truth is one of several varieties of truth and I have discovered that, consciously or unconsciously, the practicing trial lawyer behaves in a way compatible with that hypothesis. I have also formulated the conclusion that the object of a trial is not the ascertainment of truth but the resolution of a controversy by the principled application of the rules of the game. In a civilized society these rules should be designed to favor the just resolution of controversy; and in a progressive society they should change as the perception of justice evolves in response to greater ethical sophistication.

When the author of the Song of Solomon says, "I am the rose of Sharon and the lily of the valleys," no one believes that he is speaking of horticultural specimens. Nor is he suspected of suborning perjury when he causes a maiden to avow to her lover, "I have compared thee, o my love, to a company of horses in Pharaohs chariots." Manifestly, a poet's perception of the truth is different from that of a speaker of prose. So, too, I believe, the courtroom has developed its own version of truth.

The reception of information in most court proceedings is conducted through a complex filtering process. The filtering is designed in large measure to exclude information which is suspect or which experience has adjudged generally untrustworthy. In addition, there are baffles which exclude information, without reference to its truthbearing quality. These exclusions have been established to serve policies and to recognize values totally unrelated to truth.

It seems inescapable to me that the so-called truth which the trier of the facts, judge or jury, will discover at the end of the trial may, likely will, differ materially from the truth it might have found had no such barriers to information been in place. I make no assessment whether, measured by some standard not yet invented, such truth is of higher or lesser quality than courtroom truth. All I assert is that it may very well, and likely will, be different.

A few specific illustrations may help to flesh out the proposition I am asserting.

1. *The burden of proof:* By rule of law, we assign the burden of proof to one or the other of the courtroom contestants on every issue to be resolved. If the bearer of the burden fails to discharge it, the issue goes against him. Certainly, no such rule is observed in

scientific research. Science has the advantage that it may leave issues unresolved in the interest of truth, but trials are primarily concerned with the resolution of controversies, the search for truth being merely one of the tools for the accomplishment of that purpose.

2. *Competence:* Courts have excluded and still exclude vast bodies of information as incompetent. For example, in some jurisdictions a wife may not give testimony against her husband except in limited circumstances, although she is the bearer of information both relevant and material.

3. *Privileged possessors of both relevant and material information:* Clergymen, lawyers, doctors, Congressmen and in some jurisdictions, news reporters, are either forbidden to disclose or permitted to withhold that which they had learned in confidence. This exclusion is not occasioned by the suspect quality of the information. This exclusion serves societal policies which presumably are regarded as superior to truth. They rest upon a pragmatic need for such confidential exchanges. To this category may be added executive privilege, the ambassador's privilege, the Speech or Debate privilege, the informer's privilege, the privilege with respect to offers of compromise, and others.

4. *Exclusions responsive to the commands of the Fifth and Fourth Amendments to the Constitution of the United States:* These have no such pragmatic underpinning. They are nourished by profound philosophical appraisals of man's need for a zone of such deep privacy that no one may penetrate it.

5. *Exclusionary rules founded on so-called experience of lack of trustworthiness:* These include the hearsay rule, the parol evidence rule, the deadman's statute, the statute of frauds.

6. *Exclusionary rules founded on the apprehension that the information will carry more persuasion than is warranted:* An example is the rule prohibiting a prosecutor from offering during his direct case proof of prior convictions.

It seems to me that were trials exposed to information utterly unfiltered by rules of the kind I have mentioned, the truth they would reveal would frequently be different from the truth presently ascertained. If I had to hazard a guess I would assert that the quality of our justice would suffer grievously were trials exposed to such unrestricted information.

Having over the years entertained these reflections, I have freed myself of the necessity of uttering the litany that the object of trials is to ascertain the truth and I have come to embrace the perhaps less exalted but more viable proposition that the office of a trial is to resolve a controversy.

This perception has more than academic significance. It affects the day to day work of the practicing trial lawyer. I have seen lawyers struggling like a butterfly beating its wings against an enveloping net when they find themselves caught in a contest between what they "know" of an event and the version of that event which emerges from the witness stand. Only the latter is the operative scenario. The effective lawyer must learn to deal with it even as an artist accommodates himself to the limitations of his pigments or the playwright to the time frame of one evening on the stage. . . .

Marvin E. Frankel
PARTISAN JUSTICE
11-19 (1980)

Our leading religions may teach about loving our neighbors, about the expectancies of the meek, and about forbearance, gentleness, and other fond virtues. In our arena for secular justice, however, we enthrone combat as a paramount good. The "adversary system," as we call it, is not merely borne as a supposedly necessary evil. It is cherished as an ideal of constitutional proportions, not only because it embodies the fundamental right to be heard, but because it is thought (often) to be the best assurance of truth and sound results. Decisions of the Supreme Court give repeated voice to this concept. We are taught to presume as a vital premise the belief that "partisan advocacy on both sides," according to rules often countenancing partial truths and concealment, will best assure the discovery of truth in the end. We are not so much as slightly rocked in this assumption by the fact that other seekers after truth have not emulated us. Ours is, after all, a special world of special cases. Even we who made and run that world would fear for our lives if physicians, disagreeing about the cause of our chest pains, sought to resolve the issue by our forms of interrogation, badgering, and other forensics. But for the defendant whose life is at stake — and for the public concerned whether the defendant is a homicidal menace — this is thought to be the most perfect form of inquiry. We live, at any rate, as if we believe this.

Like any sweeping proposition, the claim that our adversary process is best for truth seeking has qualifications and limits recognized by its staunchest proponents. While it would not be essential, we have again the high authority of Supreme Court pronouncements noting that lawyers in the process are often expected, with all propriety, to help block or conceal rather than pursue the truth. These endeavors are commonly justified in the service of interests that outweigh truth finding — interests in privacy, personal dignity, security, autonomy, and other cherished values. The problem of how to weigh the competing values is, obviously, at the heart of the concerns to be addressed in these chapters. Nobody doubts that there are ends of diverse kinds, at diverse times and places, more worthy than the accurate discovery or statement of facts; that there are even occasions, not easily defined with unanimity, when a lie is to be preferred. One way to state the thesis of this book is to say, recognizing the complex relativities of life, that the American version of the adversary process places too low a value on truth telling; that we have allowed ourselves too often to sacrifice truth to other values that are inferior, or even illusory. But the elaboration of the position is best postponed until after we have described how the process works and how its actors perform.

The quality of private initiative and private control is, in its degree, the hallmark of the American judicial process. While the administration of justice is designated as the public's business and the decision-makers are public people (whether full-time judges or the lay judges who sit in jury boxes), the process is initiated, shaped, and managed by the private contestants in civil matters and by the government and nongovernment lawyer-contestants in criminal matters. The deciders, though commissioned to discover the truth, are passive recipients, not active explorers. They take what they are given. They consider the questions raised by counsel, rarely any others. Issues not joined are not resolved, though they might have led to wiser, fairer dispositions than those reached. The parties, almost always the lawyers or those under their direction, investigate the facts, interview possible witnesses, consult potential experts to find opinions most agreeable to their causes, decide what will be told and what will not be told. The judges and jurors almost never make inquiries on their own, and are not staffed or otherwise equipped to do so. The reconstructions of the past to be given in the courtroom are likely to be the sharply divergent stories told by partisans, divergent from each other and from the actual events supposed to be portrayed. If history can never reproduce the past with total fidelity, one wonders often whether we could not miss by margins much narrower than those marked in courtrooms. . . .

The system rests, we must always remember, on the assumption that we can accurately re-create the facts so that our rules of law, democratically evolved, will work just results. If the rule is that the signer of the note must pay, it works acceptably only if we correctly identify the signer. If we fail to make the identification, or, worse yet, falsely identify one who really did not sign, the result will be an injustice. It is no answer that some of our laws are no good. Nobody who thinks the society good enough to preserve, and improve, argues seriously that the cure for bad laws is feckless decisions about facts.

The simple point to be stressed, here and throughout, is that many of us trained in the learned profession of the law spend much of our time subverting the law by blocking the way to the truth. The subversion is not for the most part viewed as a pathology; rather, if somewhat paradoxically, it follows from the assigned roles of counsel in the very system of law which thus finds its purposes thwarted.

The games we play about fact finding are, of course, an old story and an old source of professional worry and efforts toward reform. During the last half century or so, much has been done through rules of "discovery" to cut down on concealment and surprises at trial. The idea is to allow demands for information before trial and to require responses from the adverse party. The device has on the whole worked substantial improvements. Predictably, however, it has been turned — and twisted — to adversary uses. Lawyers react characteristically by demanding as much as possible and giving as little as possible. What is not demanded is not given. It remains as true as ever that if a lawyer fails to ask the right question, the adversary will cheerfully refrain from disclosing what might be vital or decisive information. The discovery process itself, with rules that frequently are (or are made to be) intricate and abstruse, becomes the occasion for expensive contests, producing libraries full of opinions. Where the object always is to beat every plowshare into a sword, the discovery procedure is employed variously as weaponry. A powerful litigant in a complex case may impose costly, even crushing, burdens by demands for files, pretrial testimony of witnesses, and other forms of discovery. An approximately converse ploy has also been evolved to make the procedure a morass rather than the revelatory blessing it was meant to be. A litigant may contrive to dump truckloads of unassorted files on the party demanding discovery, hoping, often not in vain, that the searcher will be so exhausted that the damaging items will be overlooked or never reached.

The key point at every stage, which will bear recalling from time to time, is that the single uniformity is always adversariness. There are other goods, but the greatest is winning. There are other evils, but scarcely any worse than losing. Every step of the process, and any attempt to reform it, must be viewed in this light until or unless the adversary ethic comes to be changed or subordinated. The lawyer's response to a tax is how to avoid or minimize its impact on the client. Every law is probed for its loopholes — unless the lawyer has done the job in advance by being placed strategically to sew them in during the legislative process. Every idea for improved procedures must be imaginatively pretested to foresee its evolving shapes under the fires of adversary zeal.

Because the route of a lawsuit is marked by a running battle all the way, the outcome is nothing like the assuredly right result imagined in our dream that "justice will out." In that dream, neither eloquence nor lawyers' techniques nor cunning has much place. The person who is "right" should win. But that is very far from assured in the kind of contest we've been considering. When skill and trickery are so much involved, it must inevitably happen that the respective qualities of the professional champions will make a decisive difference. Where sheer power and endurance may count, the relative resources of clients become vital. Describing the tendency of the enterprise as the major forces propel it, two students of the American legal system were led to conclude: "In an ideal adversary system, the less skillful antagonist is expected to lose, which under the laissez-faire notion is the proper outcome."

If that is, fortunately, an exaggeration, it describes a probability high and uncertain enough to be harrowing. One of the nation's greatest judges, Learned Hand, paid grim tribute to the uncertainty in a famous utterance: "I must say that, as a litigant, I should dread a lawsuit beyond almost anything else short of sickness and of death." Hand's distinguished colleague for a number of years, Jerome Frank [once] focused . . . on the utter chanciness of factual determinations as the main reason why lawsuits are gambles too often and routes to justice more seldom than they should be.

Schwartz and Ball

Murray L. Schwartz
THE ZEAL OF THE CIVIL ADVOCATE
1983 Am. B. Found. Res. J. 543, 553-554

[A]rriving at as accurate a reconstruction of the past event as is possible is a paramount goal of the civil adjudicatory system. The rules should be constructed with this goal in mind — that is, on the assumption that their basic purpose is to arrive at the truth rather than, as in the criminal proceeding, to avoid one type of error.

1. THE CORRECT RESULT

A good start in that direction would be to adopt a set of rules such as those proposed by Marvin Frankel. Those rules would require a lawyer to report to the court and opposing counsel the existence of relevant evidence or witnesses the lawyer does not intend to offer; prevent or, when prevention has proved unsuccessful, report to the court and opposing counsel the making of any untrue statement by client or witness or any material omissions; and question witnesses with purpose and design to elicit the whole truth.

Much of the opposition to those proposals is based on the same arguments that were used in the fight against expanded civil discovery. In a real sense, the question is whether expanded civil discovery rules should be converted into professional ones. To do so would be to take one step further in the attempt to make real the Postulates of Equal Competence and Equal Adversariness. That is, it would provide all parties, regardless of their personal resources, with both the favorable and the unfavorable relevant materials for the adjudication.

2. VINDICATION OF LEGAL RIGHTS

Such rules would also maximize that justification of the adversary system concerned with vindicating legal rights. First, a judgment based on a determination of a legal right that is itself predicated on an erroneous factual finding should have no higher standing than the erroneous factual determination itself. Second, misconceptions of the tribunal about what the law is should be eliminated; there is no reason in the civil case to maintain that a party is entitled to a judgment on an erroneous conception of the law. Indeed, professional rules themselves require attorneys to advise the tribunal of material adverse decisions that have not been cited by their opponents.[20]

3. PROTECTION OF HUMAN DIGNITY

Implicit — and sometimes explicit — in the discussions of the adversary system is its function in protecting human dignity. In the criminal context, it is undoubtedly caught up in the possible outcome — conviction, with its harsh, degrading, and stigmatizing consequences. In part, it signifies that persons on trial should not be constrained in their efforts to avoid conviction: as previously stated, the full realization of the self depends on untrammeled freedom to challenge the power and resources of the state.

In a civil contest between two civilians, however, the ability to ensure that the state does not become a juggernaut is most often not needed. Cross-examination of truthful witnesses to give the impression that they are telling falsehoods may be justified as a way of keeping the state from overreaching. When neither contestant is the behemoth state, the human dignity argument takes on a different — and lesser — significance.[21]

Subsequently, I shall discuss the extent to which professional representation is an independent value of the adversary system. At this point, it is sufficient to say that if there is such a value, its vindication does not require the kind of tactics apparently deemed appropriate for criminal cases. In the criminal case, the recognized loss of human dignity appears

20. E.g., Model Code of Professional Responsibility DR 7-106(B)(1) (Aug. 1980).

21. Of course the fact that the ultimate outcome in both civil and criminal proceedings is a judicial decree does not mean that there is no difference between a criminal and a civil proceeding in the ways in which human dignity is to be preserved. The role of the state as civil judgment enforcer is significantly different from its roles of prosecutor, adjudicator, sentencer, and punisher.

limited to that suffered by the defendant. In the civil case, one party's gain of human dignity may well be outweighed by another's loss. Moreover, a party who is forced to use means he or she deems immoral in order to counter similar means used by the other party who is not so circumspect suffers a loss of human dignity. The net balance of human dignity preserved in a civil trial conducted according to criminal defense lawyer rules may well be negative. Protection of human dignity in civil litigation requires high standards of candor.

4. Ameliorating Impact of the Rules

If the rules for the behavior of lawyers in civil litigation are drawn with the primary objective of ascertaining truth, the consequences of gross differences in lawyer competence will be ameliorated by greater availability of information to all — one of the intended consequences of discovery. Lawyers will not misleadingly cross-examine truthful witnesses, exploit incorrect testimony adduced by the opposition, or fail to reveal material evidence helpful to the other side. Lawyers may continue to be equally adversary in their partisanship; what will be changed are the kinds of behavior permitted under the partisan banner.

Although all moral challenges to lawyers' behavior will not disappear, at least the aspect of alleged lawyer immorality concerned with procedural and evidentiary tactics will be removed. To the extent that moral problems of procedural or tactical behavior remain, the relationship of the lawyer's zeal to immoral ends must be examined.

Milner S. Ball
WRONG EXPERIMENT, WRONG RESULT: AN APPRECIATIVELY CRITICAL RESPONSE TO SCHWARTZ
1983 Am. B. Found. Res. J. 565, 569-571

Schwartz nominates truth ascertainment as the paramount goal of civil litigation and therefore as the ruling concern for the behavior and accountability of advocates. This certainly connotes a higher stage of moral evolution than the view that trials are battles that attorneys enter to gain victory for their clients, defeat for their opponents, and money, power, and fame for themselves. If the image of the lower form of judicial process is a battlefield, then the image of Schwartz's more advanced form is a laboratory. In this laboratory, the parties — who may be zealous, but in the way that scientists are — try to reconstruct a past event as accurately as possible.

Schwartz holds to a correspondence theory of truth. For him, truth is a matter of accuracy, a matter of reflecting an objective, external reality (in this case a past event); the measure of truth in a civil trial is the measure of correspondence between what is reconstructed and what happened. Our understanding of litigation and the role of advocates would be enhanced by a more generous view of truth. There are alternatives to correspondence theory.

A developing literature across several fronts — science, philosophy, artificial intelligence, art — has challenged the axiom of an objective reality, of things-in-themselves. This literature has not posed subjectivity as an alternative to objectivity but has proposed that there are ways of thinking and experiencing other than those revolving around the subject-object dichotomy. Science — even that hardest of hard sciences, physics — may be understood as a creative undertaking. Science does not unlock the secrets of nature; it helps to make them. When the study of subatomic patterns yields quarks and strange particles and the study of the universe yields black holes and big bangs, we know that the creative imagination has been at work making metaphors, the stuff of poetry. We realize that science (and philosophy) is not merely reflecting realities external to the brain. The mind is not a passive mirror of an external reality. Knowing, like seeing, is a complex creative act. This may be radical but it is not new. For example, when the author of Genesis wished to say that Adam had sexual intercourse with Eve, he put down "Adam knew Eve." Knowledge is relational.

A new metaphor has been tried as a replacement for the old metaphors of knowledge as passive seeing and of the mind as a passive mirror of objective reality. According to this experimental metaphor, "the mind and the world jointly make up the mind and the world." This metaphor, too, leaves much out of account, but I shall defer until another time comment on its limitations, which are, in any event, less constricting than those of the Cartesian dualism favored by Schwartz. According to the version of truth contained in the new metaphor, there is neither external reality nor detached observer. Quarks, strange particles, black holes, and big bangs are joint ventures undertaken by us and our universe. All of this does not mean that we lose the notion of truth. Rather, truth becomes a creative relational act, an adventure.

Such a conception of truth has fruitful implications for our understanding of judicial process and participation in it. For example, it invites us to explore the possibility that the truth of the judicial process is the truth of art and right action, of aesthetics and ethics. Truth in litigation is not to be ascertained; it is to be performed, created, achieved, generated, done, practiced. Immediate consequences do constitute a difference between litigation and the new physics or painting or poetry or theater. After the performance of an experiment or a play, everyone goes home, and that is that. Well, not exactly. Art has an effect, but it is subtle and long term. While a play does ask a judgment of us, no member of the cast has to go to jail or pay money as a result of what we decide. After the performance of a case in court, on the other hand, there is a judgment that must be complied with. This distinction does not disqualify adjudication as an art form. It only means that the judicial process has instant as well as subtle and long-range effects. Attorneys have more immediate factors to reckon with than do playwrights, actors, and astronomers.

If to litigate is to participate in the creation or performance of truth, then the role of the advocate is multidimensional. There is responsibility for facts — the advocate is not discharging a commission for fiction. She is a historian, not a myth maker. But as Ernst Bloch observed, "fact is a clod-material alien to history." What constitute facts, which facts are relevant, and what story they are made to tell, all depend on the advocate and what she brings to the task. Simply assembling the facts is only a start; they must be worked into judicially cognizable shape. Were a past event subject to accurate reconstruction, that would not end the advocate's responsibility, for she would also have to render the reconstruction persuasive.

Further, there is not only the responsibility of the attorney to represent (take the part of) the client, but also the responsibility to perform as a member of an ensemble comprising counsel, judge, and jury. That is, the attorney both produces a play for her client and acts in the larger play of the case as a whole, played to the audience of the public. The advocate has responsibilities to her fellow actor-advocate and to the audience of society. Schwartz's truth-ascertaining trial model does not affect the basic nature of the advocate as partisan and adversary. Litigation understood as truth performing would introduce an altogether different category of behavior, requiring more of the advocate. For example, if the courtroom is neither battleground nor laboratory but theater, then opposing counsel would be engaged in a joint enterprise, a performance, requiring fundamental mutuality or affection rather than fundamental antagonism.

I have said that we are not bound by the correspondence theory of truth to which Schwartz subscribes. There are other possibilities. I have offered a sketch of such a possibility. I have not attempted to make a convincing argument in behalf of its validity because that has not been my purpose, and it would be impossible here. It has been my purpose to show that there is another view of truth and that this view would produce another, more comprehensive understanding of litigation and advocates' roles in litigation than that accessible to Schwartz.

The Advocate as Performance Artist

Both Judge Rifkind and Professor Ball use artistic imagery to explain the role of the advocate and the meaning of truth in the adversary system. Professor Robert Post has attempted to explain popular ambivalence toward lawyers, especially advocates, by a reference to their status as performers, to the fact that they learn to present a "self" that is not their actual self. An excerpt from Professor Post's article follows.

Robert C. Post
ON THE POPULAR IMAGE OF THE LAWYER: REFLECTIONS IN A DARK GLASS
75 Calif. L. Rev. 379, 387-389 (1987)

We owe especially to the sociologist Erving Goffman the insight that the self in modern society can be understood not as something of substance that actually exists, but rather as a series of performances. The character attributed by others to an individual is the result of these performances. Goffman tells us:

> In our society the character one performs and one's self are somewhat equated, and this self-as-character is usually seen as something housed within the body of its possessor. . . . I suggest that this view is . . . a bad analysis of the presentation. In this [book] the performed self was seen as some kind of image, usually creditable, which the individual on stage and in character effectively attempts to induce others to hold in regard to him. While this image is entertained *concerning* the individual, so that a self is imputed to him, this self does not derive from its possessor, but from the whole scene of his action, being generated by that attribute of local events which renders them interpretable by witnesses.[29]

It is of immense importance for us as a society, however, to deny this insight. We get queasy when we view the personality of others to be constituted merely by a series of staged performances.[30] Sartre makes a similar point in his famous analysis in Being and Nothingness:

> A grocer who dreams is offensive to the buyer, because such a grocer is not wholly a grocer. Society demands that he limit himself to his function as a grocer, just as the soldier at attention makes himself into a soldier-thing with a direct regard which does not see at all. . . . There are indeed many precautions to imprison a man in what he is, as if we lived in perpetual fear that he might escape from it, that he might break away and suddenly elude his condition.[31]

29. E. Goffman, The Presentation of Self in Everyday Life 252 (1959).
30. For a criticism of "the 'dramaturgic approach' to social experience," see Messinger, Life as Theater: Some Notes on the Dramaturgic Approach to Social Reality, 25 Sociometry 98 (1962).
31. J. Sartre, Being and Nothingness 59 (H. Barnes trans. 1956).

This perpetual fear of the self escaping its concrete and given substance is in some measure behind the centuries of abuse and loathing that the premodern era poured onto actors,[32] for actors are the living embodiment of the performing, protean self. Jean-Jacques Rousseau, for example, thought actors "dishonorable" because the talent of the actor lies in "the art of counterfeiting himself, of putting on another character than his own, of appearing different than he is, . . . of forgetting his own place by dint of taking another's."[33] Rousseau contrasted the actor to the orator:

> When the orator appears in public, it is to speak and not to show himself off; he represents only himself; he fills only his own role, speaks only in his own name, says, or ought to say, only what he thinks; the man and the role being the same, he is in his place; he is in the situation of any citizen who fulfils the functions of his estate. But an actor on the stage, displaying other sentiments than his own, saying only what he is made to say, often representing a chimerical being, annihilates himself, as it were, and is lost in his hero.[34]

Actors, however, lie directly: we all know that Olivier is only pretending to be King Lear, and that it is just a performance. But consider, in this light, the trial lawyer making a summary to the jury. In that case we know both (1) that the lawyer must be representing the interests of his client, so that his speech does not sincerely represent his "personal" views; and (2) that if the lawyer distinguishes between his personal views and those of his client, his client will suffer, so that the lawyer can perform his job only if he "appears" to be and in fact convinces us that he is sincere. Unlike the actor, then, the lawyer's job requires that he totally conceal his performance. And he must do this about issues of public importance, where the integrity of the self as a constituted member of the community is most at stake. To paraphrase Rousseau, the lawyer must convince us that he is an orator, exercising his highest function as a citizen, when in reality he is simply a secret actor, "lost" in the identity of his client.

---

32. "[I]n every country their profession is one that dishonors, . . . [t]hose who exercise it, excommunicated or not, are everywhere despised. . . ." J. Rousseau, Politics and the Arts: Letter to M. D'Alembert on the Theatre 76 (A. Bloom trans. 1960) (1758). . . .

33. J. Rousseau, supra note 32, at 79. In language that is often today applied directly to lawyers, Rousseau condemned the actor's profession as

> a trade in which he performs for money, submits himself to the disgrace and the affronts that others buy the right to give him, and puts his person publicly on sale. I beg every sincere man to tell if he does not feel in the depths of his soul that there is something servile and base in this traffic of oneself.

Id. . . .

34. J. Rousseau, supra note 32, at 80-81.

This is extraordinarily disturbing. And so in popular culture we say of the lawyer, as the old adage goes, "A good lawyer must be a great liar."[35] Or we say, with Jonathan Swift, that lawyers are a "society of men . . . bred up from their youth in the art of proving by words multiplied for the purpose, that white is black and black is white, according as they are paid."[36]

QUESTIONS

7.1   Assume that you can choose one of two societies in which to live. They are identical except in one regard. One society has an adversarial justice system and the other has a cooperative justice system. Under the adversarial system, it is a lawyer's responsibility to win (or get the best possible settlement) regardless of the merits of his client's case, so long as the lawyer does not do anything illegal. A client's chance of winning is improved if the client has more information than the adversary. Information may be factual or legal. Factual information is obtained by hiring investigators and experts (economists, scientists, and the like). Legal information is secured by hiring smart lawyers able to engage in extensive research and capable of making novel arguments. If the factual or legal investigations produce information that is damaging to the client's matter, the client will generally have no obligation to reveal this information to the adversary or the judge. Hiring investigators, experts, and smart lawyers costs money, sometimes huge amounts of money. Therefore, the more money a client has, the greater the likelihood that he will be able to win, or at least force a settlement more generous than he would have been able to obtain if he did not have all the information.

In the cooperative legal system, on the other hand, lawyers for both sides are responsible for pooling all information about a dispute in an effort to determine what really happened. All reports from investigators and experts must be shared. Lawyers are also responsible for sharing their legal research, favorable or unfavorable. While no client is obligated to search for facts or find cases useful to his opponent, if in preparing his case he happens to come upon such facts or cases, he must reveal them.

In making the choice about the society in which you prefer to live, you do not know if in fact you will ever be a litigant or have a legal claim in either society, nor the kind of litigation or claim it

35. The Facts on File Dictionary of Proverbs (R. Ferguson ed. 1983), at 139.
36. J. Swift, Gulliver's Travels 295 (P. Dixon & J. Chalker eds. 1967) (1726).

might be. You also do not know how much money you will have in the society you are about to enter. How do you choose?

7.2   "You know, we make an awful mistake if we divert the attention of lawyers from zeal on behalf of their clients to a general concern for the public interest or the social good. I think a lawyer should be commended, not ostracized or punished, for putting his or her client's objectives ahead of all other considerations, as long as those objectives are legal and the lawyer uses no unlawful or unethical means to achieve them. The fact is that a lawyer serves justice best precisely by serving his or her clients well and one at a time. Lawyers cannot do that if they must weigh the consequences of particular decisions for some notion of justice. I doubt that lawyers will agree on a definition of justice. I also doubt that lawyers have enough information to foresee those consequences accurately. For example, even if a lawyer is convinced that justice requires her to temper her zeal on behalf of a client in a particular matter, how can she know the long-range structural consequences when clients realize that lawyers routinely make those kinds of decisions? No one can know.

"Perhaps most important is that utopian rules of ethics will simply not work if they require people to behave contrary to their own ethical codes, as, for example, by betraying clients. Rules of ethics cannot be used as a tool of social engineering or in an effort to create a new society. That's for the political theorists and divinity students. Justice is the job of the entire system."

"Let me see if I understand your position. If a lawyer's investigation reveals that the lawyer's client committed a murder for which an innocent person is about to be executed, you're saying that the lawyer should remain silent because she can't know whether justice is or is not better served by revealing the information and saving the life of the condemned prisoner?"

Does the first speaker have an acceptable response?

B.   TRUTH AND CONFIDENCES

What should a lawyer do if she learns, through a confidential communication, that a client has committed or is in the process of committing a criminal or fraudulent act? Perhaps the lawyer has actually been used as the unwitting instrument of this fraud or crime. Of course, if the crime or fraud is still prospective, the lawyer cannot ethically aid it, Rule 1.2(d), and may be guilty as an accessory if she does. A lawyer may even have the authority, or an obligation, to reveal a future crime or fraud (see page 19 supra). But what if all or part of the criminal or fraudulent act is concluded? May or must the lawyer blow the whistle on the client's wrongdoing?

These issues have won much notice. The attention we pay them is probably disproportionate to the frequency of the underlying conduct. They appear to raise not only practical problems but also fundamental questions about what it means to be an American lawyer.

Several variables should be noted. The issue may arise in negotiation, discussed at page 469 infra, or litigation, discussed here. A litigation may be civil or criminal. The fraud may come in the form of client perjury or the perjury of a witness who lies with or without the client's connivance. Where the perjurer is the client, the lie may come on direct or cross-examination. If the case is civil, the client may have been called by his or her own lawyer or the adversary. If the perjurer is not the client, he may have been called by any party whether the case is civil or criminal. Where the client is an entity, obviously it can commit fraud on a court only through its agents, who are not literally the entity lawyer's clients.

Despite these variables, the paradigmatic example has been the perjury of a criminal defendant. This is seen to present the hardest case. Given the stakes, if we resolve the criminal defendant's perjury in favor of revelation, we thereby solve all the "easier" cases, don't we? Or are there "harder" cases?

What should a defense lawyer do when she concludes that the defendant plans to lie on the witness stand? Or when after the client testifies the defense lawyer learns, perhaps from the client, that he lied? (Should it matter whether the trial is still in progress? The appeal?) Or where the defense lawyer has called the defendant to testify and the defendant lies without warning, whether on direct or cross? Should these three situations — anticipated perjury, completed perjury, and surprise perjury — be treated alike?

The specter of the perjurious criminal defendant requires us to address not only the ethical issue, but also the Sixth Amendment right to the effective assistance of counsel. Does this right impose separate duties on defense counsel *not* to reveal client perjury? If it does, a state ethics rule could not purport to impose inconsistent obligations.

Stated most broadly, then, the debate is over whether a lawyer's duties of confidentiality and loyalty shall be superior to any duty the lawyer would otherwise have to correct a fraud on the court; or whether instead the lawyer as an officer of the court has a duty to correct such frauds notwithstanding that doing so will reveal a client's confidences and perhaps lead to evidence that will subject the client to further prosecution and longer incarceration.

Legislative History of the Code

The Canons of Ethics and the Code of Professional Responsibility both opted for confidentiality and loyalty over correction of the client's perjury. The Model Rules have reversed that election, at least in part, including in criminal cases. While most of this history is described in the following selections, we add some further background, including one piece of code legerdemain and a brief history of the Model Rules provision.

Take a look at DR 7-102(B)(1). As originally adopted, it did not have the "except" clause at its end. This clause was added in 1974 to make it clear that the lawyer's duty under (B)(1) was subordinate to the lawyer's Canon 4 duty to maintain the confidences and secrets of a client. Recall that the code defines "confidences" as information protected by the attorney-client privilege while "secrets" includes all other information gained in the professional relationship (i.e., not from the client or its agents). DR 4-101(A). See page 17 supra. Unfortunately, the 1974 Amendment refers only to "privileged" communications. This would seem to suggest that the lawyer's duty under DR 7-102(B)(1) is not "excepted" if the lawyer knows of the client's fraud through a "secret" as opposed to a "confidence." (Compare the New York version of the same "except" clause. New York lawyers were not taking any chances. The New York Code eliminates the lawyer's duty to correct client fraud if the lawyer's knowledge is *either* a secret *or* a confidence.)

To the rescue, ABA Opinion 341 (1975) interpreted the words "privileged communication" in DR 7-102(B)(1) to include both secrets and confidences. In reaching this odd construction, the opinion said that its "interpretation does not wipe out DR 7-102(B)." Really? Can you imagine a realistic situation in which a lawyer might acquire information that a client has committed a fraud on a person or tribunal "in the course of the representation" where the information would *not* be a secret or confidence? A majority of jurisdictions refused to subscribe to the reversed priorities of the 1974 amendment. Only 18 states eventually adopted the exception as part of their rules and several more adopted it through interpretation.

Three more things worth noting about the Code: DR 7-102(B)(1) adopts the same rule whether a client's fraud is on a tribunal or a person. By contrast, Rule 3.3(a) and (b) speaks to the obligations of a lawyer whose client defrauds a tribunal, while Rule 4.1 (discussed at page 470 infra) and Rule 1.2(d) are concerned with fraud on persons. Next, the exception to the duty stated in DR 7-102(B)(1) only applies where the fraud is completed. If the fraud is prospective and a crime, as perjury would be, then the lawyer may but need not warn. DR 4-101(C)(3). Finally, take a look at DR 7-102(B)(2). When a lawyer discovers that a person "other than his client has perpetrated a fraud on a tribunal," the lawyer must "promptly reveal the fraud to the tribunal." But what if the fraud of the "other person" was suborned by the client, so that revelation would also subject the client to sanction? Read literally, the rule makes no exception. The 1974 "except" language was added only to (B)(1) and not (B)(2). Could that have been intentional?

Legislative History of the Rules

Rule 3.3 was intensely debated on its way to ABA adoption. Earlier versions were significantly broader. The January 1980 draft (where it appeared as Rule 3.1) said in part:

RULE 3.1   Candor Toward Tribunal

A lawyer shall be candid toward a tribunal . . .

> (b) except as provided in paragraph (f), if a lawyer discovers that evidence or testimony presented by the lawyer is false, the lawyer shall disclose that fact and take suitable measures to rectify the consequences, even if doing so requires disclosure of a confidence of the client or disclosure that the client is implicated in the falsification. . . .
> (d) except as provided in paragraph (f), a lawyer shall disclose a fact known to the lawyer even if the fact is adverse, when disclosure: . . .
> > (2)   is necessary to correct a manifest misapprehension resulting from a previous representation the lawyer has made to the tribunal.
> (e) except as provided in paragraph (f), a lawyer may apprise another party of evidence favorable to that party and may refuse to offer evidence that the lawyer believes with substantial reason to be false.
> [Subparagraph (f) concerns lawyers for defendants in criminal cases. The issues it raises will be discussed at page 331 infra.]

The May 1981 draft eliminated these obligations. It substituted the following provision, among others: "A lawyer shall not knowingly fail to make a disclosure of fact necessary to prevent a fraud on the tribunal." Rule 3.3(a)(2). This sentence was deleted in the June 1982 draft, which contains the rule as finally adopted. How does Rule 3.3(a)(2) differ from the proposal in the May 1981 draft?

The ABA had occasion to construe Rule 3.3 in its Opinion 353 (1987). That opinion also reviews the treatment of the underlying issue in the canons and the code. Further, it speaks to the duties of both civil lawyers and criminal defense lawyers. When the rules were adopted in 1983, uncertainty prevailed over the constitutional (and therefore the ethical) obligations of criminal defense lawyers whose clients committed perjury. That uncertainty, reflected in Rule 3.3, comment ¶¶[7]-[10], was resolved in 1986 when the Supreme Court decided Nix v. Whiteside. We first set out the portions of Opinion 353 construing Rule 3.3 generally. We follow with Nix v. Whiteside. We conclude with the portion of Opinion 353 that relies on *Nix* to construe a criminal defense lawyer's ethical obligations.

ABA OPINION 353 (1987)

The professional obligations of a lawyer relating to client perjury as now defined by the Model Rules of Professional Conduct (1983), particularly in Model Rule 3.3(a) and (b), require a reconsideration of ABA Formal Opinion 287 (1953), which was based upon an interpretation of the earlier ABA Canons of Professional Ethics (1908), and Informal Opinion 1314 (1975), which interpreted the predecessor Model Code of Professional Responsibility (1969, revised 1980). Formal Opinion 287 discussed in part the lawyer's responsibility with regard to false statements the lawyer knows that the client has made to the tribunal. Informal Opinion 1314 dealt with the lawyer's duty when the lawyer knows of the client's intention to commit perjury.

FORMAL OPINION 287

Formal Opinion 287 addressed two situations: one, a civil divorce case; the other, the sentencing procedure in a criminal case. In the civil matter, the client informs his lawyer three months after the court has entered a decree for divorce in his favor that he had testified falsely about the date of his wife's desertion. A truthful statement of the date would not have established under local law any ground for divorce and would have resulted in the dismissal of the action as prematurely brought. Formal Opinion 287 states that under these circumstances, the lawyer must advise the client to inform the court of his false testimony, and that if the client refuses to do so, the lawyer must cease representing the client.[2] However, Formal Opinion 287 concluded that Canon 37 of the ABA Canons of Professional Ethics (dealing with the lawyer's duty to not reveal the client's confidences) prohibits the lawyer from disclosing the client's perjury to the court.

In this factual situation, Model Rule 3.3 also does not permit the lawyer to disclose the client's perjury to the court, but for a significantly different reason. Contrary to Formal Opinion 287, Rule 3.3(a) and (b) require a lawyer to disclose the client's perjury to the court if other reme-

---

2. This requirement of withdrawal from the representation stated in Opinion 287 is inconsistent with Model Rule 1.16, which, under the facts posited in the Opinion, provides only for discretionary withdrawal.

dial measures are ineffective, even if the information is otherwise protected under Rule 1.6, which prohibits a lawyer from revealing information relating to representation of a client. However, under Rule 3.3(b), the duty to disclose continues only "to the conclusion of the proceeding. . . ." From the Comment to Rule 3.3, it would appear that the Rule's disclosure requirement was meant to apply only in those situations where the lawyer's knowledge of the client's fraud or perjury occurs prior to final judgment and disclosure is necessary to prevent the judgment from being corrupted by the client's unlawful conduct.[3] Therefore, on the facts considered by Formal Opinion 287, where the lawyer learns of the perjury after the conclusion of the proceedings — three months after the entry of the divorce decree[4] — the mandatory disclosure requirement of Rule 3.3 does not apply and Rule 1.6, therefore, precludes disclosure.

In the criminal fact setting, Formal Opinion 287 is directly contrary to the Model Rules with regard to one part of its guidance to lawyers. Briefly, the criminal defense lawyer is presented with the following three situations prior to the sentencing of the lawyer's client: (1) the judge is told by the custodian of criminal records that the defendant has no criminal record and the lawyer knows this information is incorrect based on his own investigation or from his client's disclosure to him: (2) the judge asks the defendant whether he has a criminal record and he falsely answers that he has none; (3) the judge asks the defendant's lawyer whether his client has a criminal record.

Formal Opinion 287 concluded that in none of the above situations is the lawyer permitted to disclose to the court the information he has concerning the client's actual criminal record. The opinion stated that such a disclosure would be prohibited by Canon 37, which imposed a paramount duty on the lawyer to preserve the client's confidences. In situations (1) and (3) Opinion 287 is still valid under the Model Rules, since there has been no client fraud or perjury, and, therefore, the lawyer is prohibited, under Rule 1.6, from disclosing information relating to the representation.[5] However, in situation (2), where the client has lied to the

---

3. This explanation, at least, is consistent with the distinction between information relating to continuing crime, which is not protected by the attorney-client privilege, and information relating to past crime, which is protected. See, e.g., In re Grand Jury Proceeding, 680 F.2d 1026 (5th Cir. 1982) (discussing crime/fraud exception to attorney-client privilege).

4. The Committee assumes that there were no further proceedings and that this was a final decree. This is not to say, however, that the judgment could not be set aside by the court if the court subsequently learns of the fraudulent representations of the client.

5. Although in situation (3), where the court puts a direct question to the lawyer, the lawyer may not reveal the client's confidences, the lawyer, also, must not make any false statements of fact to the court. Formal Opinion 287 advised lawyers facing this dilemma to ask the court to excuse the lawyer from answering the question. The Committee can offer no better guidance under the Model Rules, despite the fact that such a request by the lawyer most likely will put the court on further inquiry, as Opinion 287 recognized.

court about the client's criminal record, the conclusion of Opinion 287 that the lawyer is prohibited from disclosing the client's false statement to the court is contrary to the requirement of Model Rule 3.3.[6] This rule imposes a duty on the lawyer, when the lawyer cannot persuade the client to rectify the perjury, to disclose the client's false statement to the tribunal for the reasons stated in the discussion of Rule 3.3 below.[7]

CHANGE IN POLICY IN MODEL RULE 3.3

Model Rule 3.3(a) and (b) represent a major policy change with regard to the lawyer's duty as stated in Formal Opinions 287 and 341 when the client testifies falsely. It is now mandatory, under these Model Rule provisions, for a lawyer, who knows the client has committed perjury, to disclose this knowledge to the tribunal if the lawyer cannot persuade the client to rectify the perjury.

The relevant provisions of Rule 3.3(a) are: "(a) A lawyer shall not knowingly: . . . (2) fail to disclose a material fact to a tribunal when disclosure is necessary to avoid assisting a criminal or fraudulent act by the client; . . . (4) offer evidence that the lawyer knows to be false. If a lawyer has offered material evidence and comes to know of its falsity, the lawyer shall take reasonable remedial measures." Rule 3.3(a)(2) and (4) complement each other. While (a)(4), itself, does not expressly require disclosure by the lawyer to the tribunal of the client's false testimony after the lawyer has offered it and learns of its falsity, such disclosure will be the only "reasonable remedial [measure]" the lawyer will be able to take if the client is unwilling to rectify the perjury. The Comment to Rule 3.3 states that disclosure of the client's perjury to the tribunal would be required of the lawyer by (a)(4) in this situation.

Although Rule 3.3(a)(2), unlike 3.3(a)(4), does not specifically refer to perjury or false evidence, it would require an irrational reading of the language: "a criminal or fraudulent act by the client," to exclude false testimony by the client. While broadly written to cover all crimes or frauds a client may commit during the course of the proceeding, Rule 3.3(a)(2), in the context of the whole of Rule 3.3, certainly includes perjury.

---

6. The validity of Formal Opinion 287 in this regard was initially put in question in 1969 when the ABA adopted DR 7-102(B)(1). This provision required a lawyer to reveal to an affected person or tribunal any fraud perpetrated by the client in the course of the representation discovered by the lawyer. Because of its apparent inconsistency with DR 4-101, prohibiting a lawyer from revealing a confidence or secret of the client, DR 7-102(B)(1) was amended in 1974 to provide an exception to the duty to reveal the client's fraud when the information is protected as a privileged communication. Formal Opinion 341 (1975) interpreted the words "privileged communication" to encompass confidences and secrets under DR 4-101, thereby making the amendment consistent with Formal Opinion 287.

7. The Comment to Rule 3.3 suggests that the lawyer may be able to avoid disclosure to the court if the lawyer can effectively withdraw. But the Committee concludes that withdrawal can rarely serve as a remedy for the client's perjury.

Since 3.3(a)(2) requires disclosure to the tribunal only when it is necessary to "avoid assisting" client perjury, the important question is what conduct of the lawyer would constitute such assistance. Certainly, the conduct proscribed in Rule 3.3(a)(4) — offering evidence the lawyer knows to be false — is included. Also, a lawyer's failure to take remedial measures, including disclosure to the court, when the lawyer knows the client has given false testimony, is included. It is apparent to the Committee that as used in Rule 3.3(a)(2), the language "assisting a criminal or fraudulent act by the client" is not limited to the criminal law concepts of aiding and abetting or subornation. Rather, it seems clear that this language is intended to guide the conduct of the lawyer as an officer of the court as a prophylactic measure to protect against client perjury contaminating the judicial process. Thus, when the lawyer knows the client has committed perjury, disclosure to the tribunal is necessary under Rule 3.3(a)(2) to avoid assisting the client's criminal act.

Furthermore, as previously indicated, contrary to Formal Opinions 287 and 341 and the exception provided in DR 7-102(B)(1) of the Model Code, the disclosure requirement of Model Rule 3.3(a)(2) and (4) is not excused because of client confidences. Rule 3.3(b) provides in pertinent part: "The duties stated in paragraph (a) . . . apply even if compliance requires disclosure of information otherwise protected by Rule 1.6." Thus, the lawyer's responsibility to disclose client perjury to the tribunal under Rule 3.3(a)(2) and (4) supersedes the lawyer's responsibility to the client under Rule 1.6.

The Duty to Withdraw

Whether or not the lawyer is authorized or obligated to reveal a client's fraud, a separate issue is whether the lawyer can continue to represent the client. Opinion 287, construing the canons, stated that the lawyer "should have nothing further to do" with a client who refuses to correct a fraud on a tribunal. Opinion 341, although it agreed with Opinion 287 about the superiority of the confidentiality duty, said nothing about an obligation to withdraw. Consequently, whether or not the lawyer could or had to withdraw would be determined by reference to DR 2-110. See A Sealed Case, 890 F.2d 15 (7th Cir. 1989). Some state courts, however, continued to require lawyers in this situation to withdraw. See In re A, 276 Or. 225, 554 P.2d 479 (1976). The Model Rules do not require withdrawal when a client has committed a fraud on a tribunal (see page 314 n.2 supra); but unlike the canons and the code, the Model Rules will often require revelation of the fraud, an event that will usually make it impossible for the lawyer to continue to represent the client in any event.

NIX v. WHITESIDE
475 U.S. 157 (1986)

CHIEF JUSTICE BURGER delivered the opinion of the Court.

We granted certiorari to decide whether the Sixth Amendment right of a criminal defendant to assistance of counsel is violated when an attorney refuses to cooperate with the defendant in presenting perjured testimony at his trial.[1]

I

A

Whiteside was convicted of second degree murder by a jury verdict which was affirmed by the Iowa courts. The killing took place on February 8, 1977 in Cedar Rapids, Iowa. Whiteside and two others went to one Calvin Love's apartment late that night, seeking marihuana. Love was in bed when Whiteside and his companions arrived; an argument between Whiteside and Love over the marihuana ensued. At one point, Love directed his girlfriend to get his "piece," and at another point got up, then returned to his bed. According to Whiteside's testimony, Love then started to reach under his pillow and moved toward Whiteside. Whiteside stabbed Love in the chest, inflicting a fatal wound.

Whiteside was charged with murder, and when counsel was appointed he objected to the lawyer initially appointed, claiming that he felt uncomfortable with a lawyer who had formerly been a prosecutor. Gary L. Robinson was then appointed and immediately began investigation. Whiteside gave him a statement that he had stabbed Love as the latter "was pulling a pistol from underneath the pillow on the bed." Upon questioning by Robinson, however, Whiteside indicated that he had not actually seen a gun, but that he was convinced that Love had a gun. No pistol was found on the premises; shortly after the police search following the stabbing, which had revealed no weapon, the victim's family had removed all of the victim's possessions from the apartment. Robinson interviewed Whiteside's companions who were present during the stabbing

---

1. Although courts universally condemn an attorney's assisting in presenting perjury, Courts of Appeals have taken varying approaches on how to deal with a client's insistence on presenting perjured testimony. The Seventh Circuit, for example, has held that an attorney's refusal to call the defendant as a witness did not render the conviction constitutionally infirm where the refusal to call the defendant was based on the attorney's belief that the defendant would commit perjury. United States v. Curtis, 742 F.2d 1070 (CA7 1984). The Third Circuit found a violation of the Sixth Amendment where the attorney could not state any basis for her belief that defendant's proposed alibi testimony was perjured. United States ex rel. Wilcox v. Johnson, 555 F.2d 115 (CA3 1977). See also Lowery v. Cardwell, 575 F.2d 727 (CA9 1978) (withdrawal request in the middle of a bench trial, immediately following defendant's testimony).

and none had seen a gun during the incident. Robinson advised Whiteside that the existence of a gun was not necessary to establish the claim of self defense, and that only a reasonable belief that the victim had a gun nearby was necessary even though no gun was actually present.

Until shortly before trial, Whiteside consistently stated to Robinson that he had not actually seen a gun, but that he was convinced that Love had a gun in his hand. About a week before trial, during preparation for direct examination, Whiteside for the first time told Robinson and his associate Donna Paulsen that he had seen something "metallic" in Love's hand. When asked about this, Whiteside responded that "in Howard Cook's case there was a gun. If I don't say I saw a gun, I'm dead." Robinson told Whiteside that such testimony would be perjury and repeated that it was not necessary to prove that a gun was available but only that Whiteside reasonably believed that he was in danger. On Whiteside's insisting that he would testify that he saw "something metallic" Robinson told him, according to Robinson's testimony,

> we could not allow him to [testify falsely] because that would be perjury, and as officers of the court we would be suborning perjury if we allowed him to do it . . . I advised him that if he did do that it would be my duty to advise the Court of what he was doing and that I felt he was committing perjury; also, that I probably would be allowed to attempt to impeach that particular testimony.

Robinson also indicated he would seek to withdraw from the representation if Whiteside insisted on committing perjury.[2]

Whiteside testified in his own defense at trial and stated that he "knew" that Love had a gun and that he believed Love was reaching for a gun and he had acted swiftly in self defense. On cross examination, he admitted that he had not actually seen a gun in Love's hand. Robinson presented evidence that Love had been seen with a sawed-off shotgun on other occasions, that the police search of the apartment may have been careless, and that the victim's family had removed everything from the apartment shortly after the crime. Robinson presented this evidence to show a basis for Whiteside's asserted fear that Love had a gun.

The jury returned a verdict of second-degree murder and Whiteside moved for a new trial, claiming that he had been deprived of a fair trial by Robinson's admonitions not to state that he saw a gun or "something metallic." The trial court held a hearing, heard testimony by Whiteside

---

2. Whiteside's version of the events at this pretrial meeting is considerably more cryptic:

Q. And as you went over the questions, did the two of you come into conflict with regard to whether or not there was a weapon?
A. I couldn't — I couldn't say a conflict. But I got the impression at one time that maybe if I didn't go along with — with what was happening, that it was no gun being involved, maybe that he will pull out of my trial. . . .

and Robinson, and denied the motion. The trial court made specific findings that the facts were as related by Robinson.

[The Iowa Supreme Court affirmed, holding that Robinson's actions were not only "permissible, but were required." The Eighth Circuit directed that Whiteside be granted a writ of habeas corpus.]

II

A

The right of an accused to testify in his defense is of relatively recent origin. Until the latter part of the preceding century, criminal defendants in this country, as at common law, were considered to be disqualified from giving sworn testimony at their own trial by reason of their interest as a party to the case. . . .

By the end of the nineteenth century, however, the disqualification was finally abolished by statute in most states and in the federal courts. Although this Court has never explicitly held that a criminal defendant has a due process right to testify in his own behalf, cases in several Circuits have so held and the right has long been assumed. We have also suggested that such a right exists as a corollary to the Fifth Amendment privilege against compelled testimony.

B

In Strickland v. Washington, [466 U.S. 668 (1984)], we held that to obtain relief by way of federal habeas corpus on a claim of a deprivation of effective assistance of counsel under the Sixth Amendment, the movant must establish both serious attorney error and prejudice. To show such error, it must be established that the assistance rendered by counsel was constitutionally deficient in that "counsel made errors so serious that counsel was not functioning as 'counsel' guaranteed the defendant by the Sixth Amendment." To show prejudice, it must be established that the claimed lapses in counsel's performance rendered the trial unfair so as to "undermine confidence in the outcome" of the trial.

In *Strickland*, we acknowledged that the Sixth Amendment does not require any particular response by counsel to a problem that may arise. Rather, the Sixth Amendment inquiry is into whether the attorney's conduct was "reasonably effective." To counteract the natural tendency to fault an unsuccessful defense, a court reviewing a claim of ineffective assistance must "indulge a strong presumption that counsel's conduct falls within the wide range of reasonable professional assistance." Id., at 689. In giving shape to the perimeters of this range of reasonable professional assistance, *Strickland* mandates that

Prevailing norms of practice as reflected in American Bar Association Standards and the like, . . . are guides to determining what is reasonable, but they are only guides.

Under the *Strickland* standard, breach of an ethical standard does not necessarily make out a denial of the Sixth Amendment guarantee of assistance of counsel. When examining attorney conduct, a court must be careful not to narrow the wide range of conduct acceptable under the Sixth Amendment so restrictively as to constitutionalize particular standards of professional conduct and thereby intrude into the State's proper authority to define and apply the standards of professional conduct applicable to those it admits to practice in its courts. In some future case challenging attorney conduct in the course of a state court trial, we may need to define with greater precision the weight to be given to recognized canons of ethics, the standards established by the State in statutes or professional codes, and the Sixth Amendment, in defining the proper scope and limits on that conduct. Here we need not face that question, since virtually all of the sources speak with one voice.

C

We turn next to the question presented: the definition of the range of "reasonable professional" responses to a criminal defendant client who informs counsel that he will perjure himself on the stand. We must determine whether, in this setting, Robinson's conduct fell within the wide range of professional responses to threatened client perjury acceptable under the Sixth Amendment.

In *Strickland*, we recognized counsel's duty of loyalty and his "overarching duty to advocate the defendant's cause." Plainly, that duty is limited to legitimate, lawful conduct compatible with the very nature of a trial as a search for truth. Although counsel must take all reasonable lawful means to attain the objectives of the client, counsel is precluded from taking steps or in any way assisting the client in presenting false evidence or otherwise violating the law. This principle has consistently been recognized in most unequivocal terms by expositors of the norms of professional conduct since the first Canons of Professional Ethics were adopted by the American Bar Association in 1908. The 1908 Canon 32 provided that

No client, corporate or individual, however powerful, nor any cause, civil or political, however important, is entitled to receive nor should any lawyer render any service or advice involving disloyalty to the law whose ministers we are, or disrespect of the judicial office, which we are bound to uphold, or corruption of any person or persons exercising a public office or private trust, or deception or betrayal of the public. . . . He must . . . observe and advise his client to observe the statute law. . . .

Of course, this Canon did no more than articulate centuries of accepted standards of conduct. Similarly, Canon 37, adopted in 1928, explicitly acknowledges as an exception to the attorney's duty of confidentiality a client's announced intention to commit a crime:

> The announced intention of a client to commit a crime is not included within the confidences which [the attorney] is bound to respect.

These principles have been carried through to contemporary codifications of an attorney's professional responsibility. . . . Both the Model Code of Professional [Responsibility] and the Model Rules of Professional Conduct also adopt the specific exception from the attorney-client privilege for disclosure of perjury that his client intends to commit or has committed. DR 4-101(C)(3) (intention of client to commit a crime); Rule 3.3 (lawyer has duty to disclose falsity of evidence even if disclosure compromises client confidences). Indeed, both the Model Code and the Model Rules do not merely *authorize* disclosure by counsel of client perjury; they *require* such disclosure. See Rule 3.3(a)(4); DR 7-102(B)(1); Committee on Professional Ethics and Conduct of Iowa State Bar Association v. Crary, 245 N.W.2d 298 (Iowa 1976).*. . .

It is universally agreed that at a minimum the attorney's first duty when confronted with a proposal for perjurious testimony is to attempt to dissuade the client from the unlawful course of conduct. Wolfram, Client Perjury, 50 S. Cal. L. Rev. 809, 846 (1977). A statement directly in point is found in the Commentary to [Rule 3.3] under the heading "False Evidence." . . . The Commentary . . . also suggests that an attorney's revelation of his client's perjury to the court is a professionally responsible and acceptable response to the conduct of a client who has actually given perjured testimony. Similarly, the Model Rules and the commentary, as well as the Code of Professional Responsibility adopted in Iowa expressly permit withdrawal from representation as an appropriate response of an attorney when the client threatens to commit perjury. Withdrawal of counsel when this situation arises at trial gives rise to many difficult questions including possible mistrial and claims of double jeopardy.[6]

---

* Has the Chief Justice accurately described the duty imposed by DR 7-102(B)(1) in light of Opinion 341? See page 312 supra. — ED.

6. In the evolution of the contemporary standards promulgated by the American Bar Association, an early draft reflects a compromise suggesting that when the disclosure of intended perjury is made during the course of trial, when withdrawal of counsel would raise difficult questions of a mistrial holding, counsel had the option to let the defendant take the stand but decline to affirmatively assist the presentation of perjury by traditional direct examination. Instead, counsel would stand mute while the defendant undertook to present the false version in narrative form in his own words unaided by any direct examination. This conduct was thought to be a signal at least to the presiding judge that the attorney considered the testimony to be false and was seeking to disassociate himself from that course. Additionally, counsel would not be permitted to discuss the known false testimony in closing arguments. See ABA Standards for Criminal Justice, 4-7.7 (2d ed. 1980). Most

The essence of the brief amicus of the American Bar Association reviewing practices long accepted by ethical lawyers, is that under no circumstance may a lawyer either advocate or passively tolerate a client's giving false testimony. This, of course, is consistent with the governance of trial conduct in what we have long called "a search for truth." The suggestion sometimes made that "a lawyer must believe his client not judge him" in no sense means a lawyer can honorably be a party to or in any way give aid to presenting known perjury.

D

Considering Robinson's representation of respondent in light of these accepted norms of professional conduct, we discern no failure to adhere to reasonable professional standards that would in any sense make out a deprivation of the Sixth Amendment right to counsel. Whether Robinson's conduct is seen as a successful attempt to dissuade his client from committing the crime of perjury, or whether seen as a "threat" to withdraw from representation and disclose the illegal scheme, Robinson's representation of Whiteside falls well within accepted standards of professional conduct and the range of reasonable professional conduct acceptable under *Strickland*. . . .

The Court of Appeals' holding that Robinson's "action deprived [Whiteside] of due process and effective assistance of counsel" is not supported by the record since Robinson's action, at most, deprived Whiteside of his contemplated perjury. Nothing counsel did in any way undermined Whiteside's claim that he believed the victim was reaching for a gun. Similarly, the record gives no support for holding that Robinson's action "also impermissibly compromised [Whiteside's] right to testify in his own defense by conditioning continued representation . . . and confidentiality upon [Whiteside's] *restricted* testimony." The record in fact shows the contrary: (a) that Whiteside did testify, and (b) he was "restricted" or restrained only from testifying falsely and was aided by Robinson in developing the basis for the fear that Love was reaching for a gun. Robinson divulged no client communications until he was compelled to do so in response to Whiteside's post-trial challenge to the quality of his performance. We see this as a case in which the attorney successfully dissuaded the client from committing the crime of perjury.

---

courts treating the subject rejected this approach and insisted on a more rigorous standard, see, e.g., United States v. Curtis, 742 F.2d 1070 (CA7 1984); McKissick v. United States, 379 F.2d 754 (CA5 1967), aff'd after remand, 398 F.2d 342 (CA5 1968); Dodd v. Florida Bar, 118 So. 2d 17, 19 (Fla. 1960). The Eighth Circuit in this case and the Ninth Circuit have expressed approval of the "free narrative" standards. Whiteside v. Scurr, 744 F.2d 1323, 1331 (CA8 1984); Lowery v. Cardwell, 575 F.2d 727 (CA9 1978).

The Rule finally promulgated in the current Model Rules of Professional Conduct rejects any participation or passive role whatever by counsel in allowing perjury to be presented without challenge.

Paradoxically, even while accepting the conclusion of the Iowa trial court that Whiteside's proposed testimony would have been a criminal act, the Court of Appeals held that Robinson's efforts to persuade Whiteside not to commit that crime were improper; *first*, as forcing an impermissible choice between the right to counsel and the right to testify; and *second*, as compromising client confidences because of Robinson's threat to disclose the contemplated perjury.[7]

Whatever the scope of a constitutional right to testify, it is elementary that such a right does not extend to testifying *falsely*. . . .

The paucity of authority on the subject of any such "right" may be explained by the fact that such a notion has never been responsibly advanced; the right to counsel includes no right to have a lawyer who will cooperate with planned perjury. A lawyer who would so cooperate would be at risk of prosecution for suborning perjury, and disciplinary proceedings, including suspension or disbarment.

Robinson's admonitions to his client can in no sense be said to have forced respondent into an *impermissible* choice between his right to counsel and his right to testify as he proposed for there was no *permissible* choice to testify falsely. For defense counsel to take steps to persuade a criminal defendant to testify truthfully, or to withdraw, deprives the defendant of neither his right to counsel nor the right to testify truthfully. . . . When an accused proposes to resort to perjury or to produce false evidence, one consequence is the risk of withdrawal of counsel.

On this record, the accused enjoyed continued representation within the bounds of reasonable professional conduct and did in fact exercise his right to testify; at most he was denied the right to have the assistance of counsel in the presentation of false testimony. Similarly, we can discern no breach of professional duty in Robinson's admonition to respondent that he would disclose respondent's perjury to the court. The crime of perjury in this setting is indistinguishable in substance from the crime of threatening or tampering with a witness or a juror. A defendant who informed his counsel that he was arranging to bribe or threaten witnesses or members of the jury would have no "right" to insist on counsel's assistance or silence. Counsel would not be limited to advising against that conduct. An attorney's duty of confidentiality, which totally covers the client's admission of guilt, does not extend to a client's announced plans to engage in future criminal conduct. In short, the responsibility of an ethical lawyer, as an officer of the court and a key component of a system

7. The Court of Appeals also determined that Robinson's efforts to persuade Whiteside to testify truthfully constituted an impermissible threat to testify against his own client. We find no support for a threat to testify against Whiteside while he was acting as counsel. The record reflects testimony by Robinson that he had admonished Whiteside that if he withdrew he "probably would be allowed to attempt to impeach that particular testimony," if Whiteside testified falsely. The trial court accepted this version of the conversation as true.

of justice, dedicated to a search for truth, is essentially the same whether the client announces an intention to bribe or threaten witnesses or jurors or to commit or procure perjury. No system of justice worthy of the name can tolerate a lesser standard.

The rule adopted by the Court of Appeals, which seemingly would require an attorney to remain silent while his client committed perjury, is wholly incompatible with the established standards of ethical conduct and the laws of Iowa and contrary to professional standards promulgated by that State. The position advocated by petitioner, on the contrary, is wholly consistent with the Iowa standards of professional conduct and law, with the overwhelming majority of courts, and with codes of professional ethics. Since there has been no breach of any recognized professional duty, it follows that there can be no deprivation of the right to assistance of counsel under the *Strickland* standard.

E

We hold that, as a matter of law, counsel's conduct complained of here cannot establish the prejudice required for relief under the second strand of the *Strickland* inquiry. Although a defendant need not establish that the attorney's deficient performance more likely than not altered the outcome in order to establish prejudice under *Strickland*, a defendant must show "that there is a reasonable probability that, but for counsel's unprofessional errors, the result of the proceeding would have been different." According to *Strickland*, "[a] reasonable probability is a probability sufficient to undermine confidence in the outcome." The *Strickland* Court noted that the "benchmark" of an ineffective assistance claim is the fairness of the adversary proceeding, and that in judging prejudice and the likelihood of a different outcome, "[a] defendant has no entitlement to the luck of a lawless decisionmaker."

Whether he was persuaded or compelled to desist from perjury, Whiteside has no valid claim that confidence in the result of his trial has been diminished by his desisting from the contemplated perjury. Even if we were to assume that the jury might have believed his perjury, it does not follow that Whiteside was prejudiced.

In his attempt to evade the prejudice requirement of *Strickland*, Whiteside relies on cases involving conflicting loyalties of counsel. In Cuyler v. Sullivan, 446 U.S. 335 (1980), we held that a defendant could obtain relief without pointing to a specific prejudicial default on the part of his counsel, provided it is established that the attorney was "actively represent[ing] conflicting interests."

Here, there was indeed a "conflict," but of a quite different kind; it was one imposed on the attorney by the client's proposal to commit the crime of fabricating testimony without which, as he put it, "I'm dead."

This is not remotely the kind of conflict of interests dealt with in Cuyler v. Sullivan. Even in that case we did not suggest that all multiple representations necessarily resulted in an active conflict rendering the representation constitutionally infirm. If a "conflict" between a client's proposal and counsel's ethical obligation gives rise to a presumption that counsel's assistance was prejudicially ineffective, every guilty criminal's conviction would be suspect if the defendant had sought to obtain an acquittal by illegal means. Can anyone doubt what practices and problems would be spawned by such a rule and what volumes of litigation it would generate?

Whiteside's attorney treated Whiteside's proposed perjury in accord with professional standards, and since Whiteside's truthful testimony could not have prejudiced the result of his trial, the Court of Appeals was in error to direct the issuance of a writ of habeas corpus and must be reversed.

Reversed.

JUSTICE BRENNAN, concurring in the judgment.

This Court has no constitutional authority to establish rules of ethical conduct for lawyers practicing in the state courts. Nor does the Court enjoy any statutory grant of jurisdiction over legal ethics.

Accordingly, it is not surprising that the Court emphasizes that it "must be careful not to narrow the wide range of professional conduct acceptable under the Sixth Amendment so restrictively as to constitutionalize particular standards of professional conduct and thereby intrude into the State's proper authority to define and apply the standards of professional conduct applicable to those it admits to practice in its courts." I read this as saying in another way that the Court *cannot* tell the states or the lawyers in the states how to behave in their courts, unless and until federal rights are violated.

Unfortunately, the Court seems unable to resist the temptation of sharing with the legal community its vision of ethical conduct. But let there be no mistake: the Court's essay regarding what constitutes the correct response to a criminal client's suggestion that he will perjure himself is pure discourse without force of law. As Justice Blackmun observes, *that* issue is a thorny one, but it is not an issue presented by this case. Lawyers, judges, bar associations, students and others should understand that the problem has not now been "decided."

I join Justice Blackmun's concurrence because I agree that respondent has failed to prove the kind of prejudice necessary to make out a claim under Strickland v. Washington, 466 U.S. 668 (1984).

JUSTICE BLACKMUN, with whom JUSTICE BRENNAN, JUSTICE MARSHALL, and JUSTICE STEVENS join, concurring in the judgment.

How a defense attorney ought to act when faced with a client who intends to commit perjury at trial has long been a controversial issue.[1] But I do not believe that a federal habeas corpus case challenging a state criminal conviction is an appropriate vehicle for attempting to resolve this thorny problem. When a defendant argues that he was denied effective assistance of counsel because his lawyer dissuaded him from committing perjury, the only question properly presented to this Court is whether the lawyer's actions deprived the defendant of the fair trial which the Sixth Amendment is meant to guarantee. Since I believe that the respondent in this case suffered no injury justifying federal habeas relief, I concur in the Court's judgment. . . .

II . . .

B

The Court approaches this case as if the performance and prejudice standard requires us in every case to determine "the perimeters of [the] range of reasonable professional assistance" . . . but Strickland v. Washington explicitly contemplates a different course:

> Although we have discussed the performance component of an ineffectiveness claim prior to the prejudice component, there is no reason for a court deciding an ineffective assistance claim to approach the inquiry in the same order or even to address both components of the inquiry if the defendant makes an insufficient showing on one. In particular, a court need not determine whether counsel's performance was deficient before examining the prejudice suffered by the defendant as a result of the alleged deficiencies. . . . If it is easier to dispose of an ineffectiveness claim on the ground of lack of sufficient prejudice, which we expect will often be so, that course should be followed.

In this case, respondent has failed to show any legally cognizable prejudice. Nor, as is discussed below, is this a case in which prejudice should be presumed.

The touchstone of a claim of prejudice is an allegation that counsel's behavior did something "to deprive the defendant of a fair trial, a trial

---

1. See, e.g., Callan and David, Professional Responsibility and the Duty of Confidentiality: Disclosure of Client Misconduct in an Adversary System, 29 Rutgers L. Rev. 332 (1976); Rieger, Client Perjury: A Proposed Resolution of the Constitutional and Ethical Issues, 70 Minn. L. Rev. 121 (1985); compare, e.g., Freedman, Professional Responsibility of the Criminal Defense Lawyer: The Three Hardest Questions, 64 Mich. L. Rev. 1469 (1966), and ABA Standards for Criminal Justice, Proposed Standard 4-7.7 (2d ed. 1980) (approved by the Standing Committee on Association Standards for Criminal Justice, but not yet submitted to the House of Delegates), with Noonan, The Purposes of Advocacy and the Limits of Confidentiality, 64 Mich. L. Rev. 1485 (1966), and ABA Model Rules of Professional Conduct, Rule 3.3 and comment (1983).

whose result is reliable." The only effect Robinson's threat had on Whiteside's trial is that Whiteside did not testify, falsely, that he saw a gun in
Love's hand.[4] Thus, this Court must ask whether its confidence in the
outcome of Whiteside's trial is in any way undermined by the knowledge
that he refrained from presenting false testimony. . . .

It is no doubt true that juries sometimes have acquitted defendants
who should have been convicted, and sometimes have based their decisions to acquit on the testimony of defendants who lied on the witness
stand. It is also true that the Double Jeopardy Clause bars the reprosecu-
tion of such acquitted defendants, although on occasion they can be prosecuted for perjury. But the privilege every criminal defendant has to
testify in his own defense "cannot be construed to include the right to
commit perjury." Harris v. New York, 401 U.S. [222 (1971)] at 225.[5]
To the extent that Whiteside's claim rests on the assertion that he would
have been acquitted had he been able to testify falsely, Whiteside claims a
right the law simply does not recognize. "A defendant has no entitlement
to the luck of a lawless decisionmaker, even if a lawless decision cannot be
reviewed." Strickland v. Washington, 466 U.S., at 695. Since Whiteside
was deprived of neither a fair trial nor any of the specific constitutional
rights designed to guarantee a fair trial, he has suffered no prejudice.

The Court of Appeals erred in concluding that prejudice should have
been presumed. Strickland v. Washington found such a presumption appropriate in a case where an attorney labored under " 'an actual conflict
of interest [that] adversely affected his . . . performance,' " quoting Cuyler v. Sullivan [page 187 supra]. . . .

In addition, the lawyer's interest in not presenting perjured testimony
was entirely consistent with Whiteside's best interest. If Whiteside had
lied on the stand, he would have risked a future perjury prosecution.
Moreover, his testimony would have been contradicted by the testimony

4. This is not to say that a lawyer's threat to reveal his client's confidences may never
have other effects on a defendant's trial. Cf. United States ex rel. Wilcox v. Johnson, 555
F.2d 115 (CA3 1977) (finding a violation of Sixth Amendment when an attorney's threat to
reveal client's purported perjury caused defendant not to take the stand at all).

5. Whiteside was not deprived of the right to testify in his own defense, since no suggestion has been made that Whiteside's testimony was restricted in any way beyond the fact
that he did not claim, falsely, to have seen a gun in Love's hand.
I must confess that I am somewhat puzzled by the Court's implicit suggestion that
whether a defendant has a constitutional right to testify in his own defense remains an open
question. . . . It is true that in Ferguson v. Georgia, 365 U.S. 570 (1961), the Court expressly
declined to address the question of a defendant's constitutional right to testify, but that was
because the case did not properly raise the issue. Id., at 572, n.1. Since then, the Court repeatedly has referred to the existence of such a right. See, e.g., Jones v. Barnes, 463 U.S.
745, 751 (1983) (the defendant has the "ultimate authority to make certain fundamental
decisions regarding the case, [such as] . . . whether to . . . testify in his or her own behalf");
Brooks v. Tennessee, 406 U.S. 605, 612 (1972) ("Whether the defendant is to testify is an
important tactical decision as well as a matter of constitutional right."); Harris v. New York.
I cannot imagine that if we were presented with a state statute that prohibited a defendant
from testifying at his own trial, we would not rule that it violates both the Sixth and Fourteenth Amendments, as well as, perhaps, the Fifth.

of other eyewitnesses and by the fact that no gun was ever found. In light of that impeachment, the jury might have concluded that Whiteside lied as well about his lack of premeditation and thus might have convicted him of first-degree murder. And if the judge believed that Whiteside had lied, he could have taken Whiteside's perjury into account in setting the sentence. In the face of these dangers, an attorney could reasonably conclude that dissuading his client from committing perjury was in the client's best interest and comported with standards of professional responsibility. In short, Whiteside failed to show the kind of conflict that poses a danger to the values of zealous and loyal representation embodied in the Sixth Amendment. A presumption of prejudice is therefore unwarranted.

C

In light of respondent's failure to show any cognizable prejudice, I see no need to "grade counsel's performance." Strickland v. Washington, 466 U.S., at 697. The only federal issue in this case is whether Robinson's behavior deprived Whiteside of the effective assistance of counsel; it is not whether Robinson's behavior conformed to any particular code of legal ethics.

Whether an attorney's response to what he sees as a client's plan to commit perjury violates a defendant's Sixth Amendment rights may depend on many factors: how certain the attorney is that the proposed testimony is false, the stage of the proceedings at which the attorney discovers the plan, or the ways in which the attorney may be able to dissuade his client, to name just three. The complex interaction of factors, which is likely to vary from case to case, makes inappropriate a blanket rule that defense attorneys must reveal, or threaten to reveal, a client's anticipated perjury to the court. Except in the rarest of cases, attorneys who adopt "the role of the judge or jury to determine the facts," United States ex rel. Wilcox v. Johnson, 555 F.2d 115, 122 (CA3 1977), pose a danger of depriving their clients of the zealous and loyal advocacy required by the Sixth Amendment.[8]

I therefore am troubled by the Court's implicit adoption of a set of standards of professional responsibility for attorneys in state criminal

8. A comparison of this case with *Wilcox* is illustrative. Here, Robinson testified in detail to the factors that led him to conclude that respondent's assertion he had seen a gun was false. The Iowa Supreme Court found "good cause" and "strong support" for Robinson's conclusion. State v. Whiteside, 272 N.W.2d, at 471. Moreover, Robinson gave credence to those parts of Whiteside's account which, although he found them implausible and unsubstantiated, were not clearly false. . . . By contrast, in *Wilcox*, where defense counsel actually informed the judge that she believed her client intended to lie and where her threat to withdraw in the middle of the trial led the defendant not to take the stand at all, the Court of Appeals found "no evidence on the record of this case indicating that Mr. Wilcox intended to perjure himself," and characterized counsel's beliefs as "private conjectures about the guilt or innocence of [her] client." 522 F.2d, at 122.

proceedings. The States, of course, do have a compelling interest in the integrity of their criminal trials that can justify regulating the length to which an attorney may go in seeking his client's acquittal. But the American Bar Association's implicit suggestion in its brief amicus curiae that the Court find that the Association's Model Rules of Professional Conduct should govern an attorney's responsibilities is addressed to the wrong audience. It is for the States to decide how attorneys should conduct themselves in state criminal proceedings, and this Court's responsibility extends only to ensuring that the restrictions a State enacts do not infringe a defendant's federal constitutional rights. Thus, I would follow the suggestion made in the joint brief amici curiae filed by 37 States at the certiorari stage that we allow the States to maintain their "differing approaches" to a complex ethical question. The signal merit of asking first whether a defendant has shown any adverse prejudicial effect before inquiring into his attorney's performance is that it avoids unnecessary federal interference in a State's regulation of its bar. Because I conclude that the respondent in this case failed to show such an effect, I join the Court's judgment that he is not entitled to federal habeas relief.

JUSTICE STEVENS, concurring in the judgment.

Justice Holmes taught us that a word is but the skin of a living thought. A "fact" may also have a life of its own. From the perspective of an appellate judge, after a case has been tried and the evidence has been sifted by another judge, a particular fact may be as clear and certain as a piece of crystal or a small diamond. A trial lawyer, however, must often deal with mixtures of sand and clay. Even a pebble that seems clear enough at first glance may take on a different hue in a handful of gravel.

As we view this case, it appears perfectly clear that respondent intended to commit perjury, that his lawyer knew it, and that the lawyer had a duty — both to the court and to his client, for perjured testimony can ruin an otherwise meritorious case — to take extreme measures to prevent the perjury from occurring. The lawyer was successful and, from our unanimous and remote perspective, it is now pellucidly clear that the client suffered no "legally cognizable prejudice."

Nevertheless, beneath the surface of this case there are areas of uncertainty that cannot be resolved today. A lawyer's certainty that a change in his client's recollection is a harbinger of intended perjury — as well as judicial review of such apparent certainty — should be tempered by the realization that, after reflection, the most honest witness may recall (or sincerely believe he recalls) details that he previously overlooked. Similarly, the post-trial review of a lawyer's pre-trial threat to expose perjury that had not yet been committed — and, indeed, may have been prevented by the threat — is by no means the same as review of the way in which such a threat may actually have been carried out. Thus, one can be convinced — as I am — that this lawyer's actions were a proper way to provide his client with effective representation without confronting the much more difficult questions of what a lawyer must, should, or may do after his client has given testimony that the lawyer does not believe. The answer to such questions may well be colored by the particular circumstances attending the actual event and its aftermath.

Because Justice Blackmun has preserved such questions for another day, and because I do not understand him to imply any adverse criticism of this lawyer's representation of his client, I join his opinion concurring in the judgment.

ABA OPINION 353 (continued)

APPLICATION TO CRIMINAL CASES —
EFFECT OF *NIX V. WHITESIDE*

The Comment to Rule 3.3 makes it clear that this disclosure requirement applies in both civil and criminal cases. However, the Comment states that if such disclosure by a lawyer would constitute a violation of a criminal defendant's constitutional rights to due process and effective assistance of counsel, "[t]he obligation of the advocate under these Rules is subordinate to such a constitutional requirement." Subsequent to the publishing of this Comment, however, the Supreme Court of the United States held in Nix v. Whiteside [475 U.S. 157] (1986), that a criminal defendant is not entitled to the assistance of counsel in giving false testimony and that a lawyer who refuses such assistance, and who even threatens the client with disclosure of the perjury to the court if the client does testify falsely, has not deprived the client of effective assistance of counsel. Some states, nevertheless, may rely on their own applicable constitutional provisions and may interpret them to prohibit such a disclosure to the tribunal by defense counsel. In a jurisdiction where this kind of ruling is made, the lawyer is obligated, of course, to comply with the constitutional requirement rather than the ethical one.

As stated earlier, the obligation of a lawyer to disclose to the tribunal client perjury committed during the proceeding, which the lawyer learns about prior to the conclusion of the proceeding, represents a reversal of prior opinions of this Committee given under earlier rules of professional conduct. However, the Committee has done nothing more in this opinion than apply the ethical rule approved by the American Bar Association when it adopted Rule 3.3(a) and (b) of the Model Rules of Professional Conduct. Even so, a question may be raised whether this application is incompatible with the adversary system and the develop-ment of effective attorney-client relationships.[8]

The Committee believes it is not. Without doubt, the vitality of the ad-versary system, certainly in criminal cases, depends upon the ability of the lawyer to give loyal and zealous service to the client. And this, in turn, requires that the lawyer have the complete confidence of the client and be able to assure the client that the confidence will be protected and honored. However, the ethical rules of the bar which have supported these basic requirements of the adversary system have emphasized from the time they were first reduced to written form that the lawyer's duties to the client in this regard must be performed within the bounds of law.

For example, these ethical rules clearly recognize that a lawyer repre-senting a client who admits guilt in fact, but wants to plead not guilty and put the state to its proof, may assist the client in entering such a plea and vigorously challenge the state's case at trial through cross-examination, legal motions and argument to the jury. However, neither the adversary system nor the ethical rules permit the lawyer to participate in the cor-ruption of the judicial process by assisting the client in the introduction of evidence the lawyer knows is false. A defendant does not have the right, as part of the right to a fair trial and zealous representation by counsel, to commit perjury. And the lawyer owes no duty to the client, in providing the representation to which the client is entitled, to assist the client's perjury.

On the contrary, the lawyer, as an officer of the court, has a duty to prevent the perjury, and if the perjury has already been committed, to prevent its playing any part in the judgment of the court. This duty the lawyer owes the court is not inconsistent with any duty owed to the client. More particularly, it is not inconsistent with the lawyer's duty to preserve the client's confidences. For that duty is based on the lawyer's need for information from the client to obtain for the client all that the law and lawful process provide. Implicit in the promise of confidentiality is its nonapplicability where the client seeks the unlawful end of corrupting the judicial process by false evidence.

It must be emphasized that this opinion does not change the profes-sional relationship the lawyer has with the client and require the lawyer now to judge, rather than represent, the client. The lawyer's obligation to disclose client perjury to the tribunal, discussed in this opinion, is strictly limited by Rule 3.3 to the situation where the lawyer *knows* that the client has committed perjury, ordinarily based on admissions the client has made to the lawyer.[9] The lawyer's suspicions are not enough. U.S. ex rel. Wilcox v. Johnson, 555 F.2d 115, 122 (3d Cir. 1977).

8. See Monroe Freedman, Professional Responsibility of the Criminal Defense Lawyer: The Three Hardest Questions, 64 Mich. L. Rev. 1469 (1966).

9. The Committee notes that some trial lawyers report that they have avoided the ethical dilemma posed by Rule 3.3 because they follow a practice of not questioning the client

INFORMAL OPINION 1314

So far, this opinion has discussed the duty of the lawyer when the lawyer learns that the client has committed perjury. The lawyer is presented with a different dilemma when, prior to trial, the client states an intention to commit perjury at trial. This was the situation addressed in ABA Informal Opinion 1314 (1975). The Committee, in that opinion, stated that the lawyer in that situation must advise the client that the lawyer must take one of two courses of action: withdraw prior to the submission of the false testimony, or, if the client insists on testifying falsely, report to the tribunal the falsity of the testimony.

The Committee distinguished, in Informal Opinion 1314, the situation where the lawyer does not know in advance that the client intends to commit perjury. In that case, the Committee stated that when the client does commit perjury, and the lawyer later learns of it, the lawyer may not disclose the perjury to the tribunal because of the lawyer's primary duty to protect the client's confidential communications. The Committee believes that Model Rule 3.3 calls for a different course of action by the lawyer.

The duty imposed on the lawyer by Informal Opinion 1314 — when the lawyer knows in advance that the client intends to commit perjury, to advise the client that if the client insists on testifying falsely, the lawyer must disclose the client's intended perjury to the tribunal — was based on the Committee's reading of DR 7-102(A)(4), (6) and (7). These provisions prohibit a lawyer from: (1) knowingly using perjured testimony or false evidence; (2) participating in the creation or preservation of evidence the lawyer knows to be false; and (3) counseling or assisting the client in conduct the lawyer knows to be illegal or fraudulent. However, none of these prohibitions *requires* disclosure to the tribunal of any information otherwise protected by DR 4-101. Although DR 4-101(C)(3) permits a lawyer to reveal a client's stated intention to commit perjury, this exception to the lawyer's duty to preserve the client's confidences and secrets is only discretionary on the part of the lawyer.

Informal Opinion 1314 in this regard is more consistent with Model Rule 3.3(a)(2) than with any provision of the Model Code, upon which the opinion was based. However, the Committee does not believe that the mandatory disclosure requirement of this Model Rule provision is necessarily triggered when a client states an intention to testify falsely, but has not yet done so. Ordinarily, after warning the client of the consequences of the client's perjury, including the lawyer's duty to disclose it to the court, the lawyer can reasonably believe that the client will be persuaded

---

about the facts in the case and, therefore, never "know" that a client has given false testimony. Lawyers who engage in such practice may be violating their duties under Rule 3.3 and their obligation to provide competent representation under Rule 1.1. ABA Defense Function Standards 4-3.2(a) and (b) are also applicable.

not to testify falsely at trial. That is exactly what happened in Nix v. Whiteside. Under these circumstances, the lawyer may permit the client to testify and may examine the client in the normal manner. If the client does in fact testify falsely, the lawyer's obligation to make disclosure to the court is covered by Rule 3.3(a)(2) and (4).

In the unusual case, where the lawyer does know, on the basis of the client's clearly stated intention, that the client will testify falsely at trial, and the lawyer is unable to effectively withdraw from the representation, the lawyer cannot examine the client in the usual manner. Under these circumstances, when the client has not yet committed perjury, the Committee believes that the lawyer's conduct should be guided in a way that is consistent, as much as possible, with the confidentiality protections provided in Rule 1.6, and yet not violative of Rule 3.3. This may be accomplished by the lawyer's refraining from calling the client as a witness when the lawyer knows that the only testimony the client would offer is false; or, where there is some testimony, other than the false testimony, the client can offer in the client's defense, by the lawyer's examining the client on only those matters and not on the subject matter which would produce the false testimony. Such conduct on the part of the lawyer would serve as a way for the lawyer to avoid assisting the fraudulent or criminal act of the client without having to disclose the client's confidences to the court. However, if the lawyer does not offer the client's testimony, and, on inquiry by the court into whether the client has been fully advised as to the client's right to testify, the client states a desire to testify, but is being prevented by the lawyer from testifying, the lawyer may have no other choice than to disclose to the court the client's intention to testify falsely.

This approach must be distinguished from the solution offered in the initially ABA-approved Defense Function Standard 7.7 (1971). This proposal, no longer applicable,[10] permitted a lawyer, who could not dissuade the client from committing perjury and who could not withdraw, to call the client solely to give the client's own statement, without being questioned by the lawyer and without the lawyer's arguing to the jury any false testimony presented by the client. This "narrative" solution was offered as a model by the ABA and supported by a number of courts[11] on the assumption that a defense lawyer constitutionally could not prevent the client from testifying falsely on the client's own behalf and, therefore, would not be assisting the perjury if the lawyer did not directly elicit the false testimony and did not use it in argument to the jury.

---

10. This particular Standard was not approved by the ABA House of Delegates during the February, 1979 meeting when the Standards were reconsidered and otherwise approved.

11. See, e.g., United States v. Campbell, 616 F.2d 1151, 1152 (9th Cir.), cert. denied, 447 U.S. 910 (1980); State v. Lowery, 111 Ariz. 26, 28-29, 523 P.2d 54, 56-57 (1974).

The Committee believes that under Model Rule 3.3(a)(2) and the recent Supreme Court decision of Nix v. Whiteside, the lawyer can no longer rely on the narrative approach to insulate the lawyer from a charge of assisting the client's perjury. Despite differences on other issues in Nix v. Whiteside, the Justices were unanimous in concluding that a criminal defendant does not have the constitutional right to testify falsely. More recently, this ruling was made the basis of the holding by the Seventh Circuit in U.S. v. Henkel, 799 F.2d 369 (7th Cir. 1986), that the defendant "had no right to lie" and, therefore, was not deprived of the right to counsel when the defense lawyer refused to present the defendant's testimony, which he knew was false.

After *Nix*, What?

Questions Still Open. *Nix* may have answered some constitutional questions, and Opinion 353 (1987) may have answered some ethical ones, but doubts remain, not excluding doubts about the answers. For one thing, the ABA opinion is only an opinion. Just as a state is not bound to adopt the ABA's Model Code or Model Rules unamended, neither is it bound to follow ABA ethics opinions. Despite rejection of the resolution contained in ABA Standard 4-7.7 (see pages 322 and 334 supra) in both *Nix* and Opinion 353 (1987), a state may still follow its guidance. Why isn't Standard 4-7.7 a good compromise?

Both before and after *Nix*, courts have instructed lawyers who move to withdraw to use Standard 4-7.7 to solve their dilemmas. The courts have then held the lawyers in contempt of court when they refused to do so. See In re Goodwin, 279 S.C. 274, 305 S.E.2d 578 (1983); Rubin v. State, 490 So. 2d 1001 (Fla.), rev. denied, 501 So. 2d 1283 (1986), cert. denied, 483 U.S. 1005 (1987). After *Rubin*, Florida amended its Rule 3.3 to forbid lawyers to offer false testimony in narrative form unless ordered to do so. See also Jackson v. United States, 928 F.2d 245 (8th Cir.), cert. denied, 112 S. Ct. 98 (1991), finding no denial of effective assistance of counsel where a lawyer with a "reasonable factual basis" suggested to the court that the defendant planned to commit perjury and the court then gave defendant the option of testifying in narrative. Shockley v. State, — Del. — , 565 A.2d 1373, 1380 (1989), rejected the ABA's disavowal of the "narrative" solution to client perjury. It held that where counsel knows "beyond a reasonable doubt" that a criminal defendant will commit perjury, she may require narrative testimony, which the court called a "commonly accepted method of dealing with client perjury." *Shockley* cites Norman Lefstein, Client Perjury in Criminal Cases: Still in Search of an Answer, 1 Geo. J. Legal Ethics 521 (1988).

When a defense lawyer does employ Standard 4-7.7, may the prosecutor ask the jury to draw inferences of guilt from the lawyer's failure to argue the defendant's testimony? State v. Long, 148 Ariz. 295, 714 P.2d 465 (Ct. App. 1986), sensibly holds no: "We find this effort to make affirmative evidence of guilt out of defense counsel's ethical behavior to be prejudicial error."

The Epistemology Problem. *Nix* moved the focus of the inquiry back a few squares. While we continue to debate defense counsel's obligations when a defendant testifies falsely or wants to, what has suddenly become of prime importance is how the defense lawyer *knows* that the defendant is lying. All agree that a defense lawyer does not act improperly merely by calling a witness (defendant or not) whom the lawyer merely *believes* is going to lie. (But cf. United States v. Curtis, 742 F.2d 1070 (7th Cir. 1984), cert. denied, 475 U.S. 1064 (defendant has absolute right to testify against counsel's advice, but not where it was "apparent" that defendant would testify falsely).) See also Rule 3.3(c) and comment.

When does a lawyer know that testimony is false? In *Nix* Justice Stevens emphasized that the Court was in the relatively luxurious position of being able to assume that the defendant planned to lie, but that a trial lawyer is usually in a much more ambiguous situation. United States v. Long, 857 F.2d 436 (8th Cir. 1988) ("firm factual basis" required before lawyer concludes client will lie). Harry Subin tackles the knowledge issue in The Criminal Lawyer's "Different Mission": Reflections on the "Right" to Present a False Case, 1 Geo. J. Legal Ethics, 125, 136-143 (1987).

In Doe v. Federal Grievance Committee, 847 F.2d 57, 63 (2d Cir. 1988), a lawyer in a civil case had strong reason to suspect that an agent of the opposing entity client lied at a deposition. The lawyer was operating under DR 7-102(B)(2) of the code. This section applied because the suspected perjurer was not the client of the lawyer. Consequently, there was no apparent exception for information protected by Canon 4. Furthermore, the code speaks about "information clearly establishing . . . a fraud on the tribunal." It does not use the word "know." Nevertheless, the Second Circuit interpreted the quoted phrase to require knowledge. It wrote:

> Our experience indicates that if any standard less than actual knowledge was adopted in this context, serious consequences might follow. If attorneys were bound as part of their ethical duties to report to the court each time they strongly suspected that a witness lied, courts would be inundated with such reports. Court dockets would quickly become overburdened with conducting these collateral proceedings which would necessarily hold up the ultimate disposition of the underlying action. We do not believe that the Code's drafters intended to throw the court system into such a morass. Instead, it seems that the only reasonable con-

clusion is that the drafters intended disclosure of only that information which the attorney reasonably knows to be a fact and which, when combined with other facts in his knowledge, would clearly establish the existence of a fraud on the tribunal.

To interpret the rule to mean otherwise would be to require attorneys to disclose mere suspicions of fraud which are based upon incomplete information or information which may fall short of clearly establishing the existence of a fraud. We do not suggest, however, that by requiring that the attorney have actual knowledge of a fraud before he is bound to disclose it, he must wait until he has proof beyond a moral certainty that fraud has been committed. Rather, we simply conclude that he must clearly know, rather than suspect, that a fraud on the court has been committed before he brings this knowledge to the court's attention.

Can it be said that lawyers never "know" anything or otherwise they'd be witnesses? Even when a client confesses, the lawyer doesn't know that the client is telling the truth. The client may be delusional or covering for someone else. Is this a fair response to the *Nix* problem? Can lawyers rightfully use the concept of knowledge in their ethics code and then claim that knowledge cannot exist?

Accepting that there is such a thing as knowledge, imagine a conversation between a criminal defense lawyer and a client over whether the client will testify. The client wants to testify but the lawyer believes she "knows" that he will lie. Relying on *Nix* and Rule 3.3, the lawyer declines to call the client and threatens reactions like those described in *Nix* if the client insists. The client tells the lawyer she is wrong in her conclusion that his testimony will be false. He insists on the benefit of the doubt, which is the same as saying that the lawyer may strongly believe that the client is going to lie, but does not know it and therefore cannot refuse to call him. (If so, is the client correct? Or can the lawyer refuse anyway? See United States v. Curtis, supra.) How do we get out of this loop? For one creative solution, which envisions a collateral hearing before a judge other than the judge who will try the criminal matter, see Carol Rieger's article, Client Perjury: A Proposed Resolution of the Constitutional and Ethical Issues, 70 Minn. L. Rev. 121 (1985).

Assuming knowledge can exist, is it ethical for a lawyer to avoid getting it? Without knowledge, a lawyer might be able to do certain things (for example, call a witness or introduce a document) helpful to a client that the lawyer could not do if she "knew" that the evidence was false. A lawyer might avoid knowledge by not doing an investigation, by not even asking for her client's story. Then wouldn't the lawyer find it rather difficult to represent the client competently? Is it possible to learn the facts but not "know" them? What do you think of the following solution attributed by the New York Times (August 1, 1981, at 16) to criminal defense lawyer Richard "Racehorse" Haynes (though others also claim credit for it):

I never asked the client what it is that he contends are the facts from his point of view in the initial interview . . . in order to avoid being compromised in deciding whether to put him on the witness stand. The thing to do is to ask him what he suspects the other side might claim.

Pretty clever, isn't it? Is there anything wrong with it? Is there anything wrong with telling a client the elements of a defense before asking the client to relate the facts of the alleged crime? (See page 332 n.9 supra and page 354 infra.)

Giving the Problem to the Judge.   If lawyers are required to take remedial measures when a witness has committed perjury, that may relieve the lawyer of responsibility, but what does the judge do? The Code of Judicial Conduct does not have an analog to Rule 3.3(a)(4). Imagine a lawyer informing a judge that a witness, possibly a criminal defendant, has lied or will lie on the stand. How might the judge respond? What if the client denies the lawyer's allegation? If the judge instructs the jury to ignore the testimony or does not let the defendant testify, isn't there a risk that the lawyer will turn out not to have "known" that it was false (even though the lawyer truly believed he knew)? Compare the *Wilcox* case in note 8 of Justice Blackmun's opinion in *Nix*. One possibility is to have the judge do nothing and to leave the credibility issue to the jury. But if that's the solution, why require defense counsel to reveal the perjury in the first place?

Consider the following segment from "L.A. Law." Michael Kuzak represents a man named Sears who is accused of leaving the scene of an accident. The car belongs to Sears's aunt, whom Kuzak calls as a witness to explain how others may have gained access to it. In the middle of her highly credible testimony and to Kuzak's surprise, the aunt volunteers that she and Sears were at the beach when the accident occurred. Kuzak knows she is lying at the request of her nephew. He asks to speak with the judge in chambers, where he moves to withdraw. The judge denies the motion after a discussion that might have enlightened the Supreme Court's reasoning in Nix v. Whiteside:

Judge: What's to prevent him [the defendant] from playing the same time and money wasting game with his next lawyer and the one after that? No, Mr. Kuzak, withdrawing is not the answer to your dilemma. The answer is to let the system work. You do your job, let the D.A. do her job, and the jury will do their job of sorting out the truth, the falsity, of the testimony.

Kuzak: That's a comforting homily, your Honor. But you know as well as I that Sears will be aquitted. That sweet little old lady had the jury eating out of the palm of her hand. . . .

Judge: Witnesses lie on the stand every day, Mr. Kuzak. You want to debate the ethical conundrum, we'll have dinner after this thing is
over. In the meantime, let's just do our jobs.

Kuzak returns to court, tries to resume questioning, cannot, refuses to
continue, and is jailed for contempt. The judge tells the defendant to get
a new lawyer and return for a new trial. What has been gained? Who was
right? See Stephen Gillers, Taking *L.A. Law* More Seriously, 98 Yale L.J.
1607 (1989).

In one post-*Nix* case, the Eighth Circuit (in which the *Nix* case had
originated) addressed what the trial judge's duties are when a lawyer has
"a firm factual basis" for concluding that a defendant will testify falsely
and so informs the judge. In United States v. Long, 857 F.2d 436, 446-
447 (8th Cir. 1988), the court wrote:

> We note that, once the possibility of client perjury is disclosed to the trial
> court, the trial court should reduce the resulting prejudice. It should limit
> further disclosures of client confidences, inform the attorney of his other
> duties to his client, inform the defendant of her rights, and determine
> whether the defendant desires to waive any of those rights.
>
> The trial judge here acted primarily with these concerns in mind. The
> judge discussed the conflict with only the attorney and his client present.
> He prevented further disclosures of client confidences. He advised Jackson
> of his right to testify and determined that Jackson understood his rights
> and his attorney's ethical obligation not to place false testimony before the
> court. He advised Jackson that if he took the stand, his lawyer would be re-
> quired to refrain from questioning Jackson on issues which the lawyer be-
> lieved Jackson would perjure himself and that Jackson would have to
> testify in narrative form. He then directly asked Jackson if he wished to tes-
> tify. We add that a trial court should also impress upon defense counsel
> and the defendant that counsel must have a firm factual basis before fur-
> ther desisting in the presentation of the testimony in question.[8]

FURTHER READING

The article that forced the bar to confront the ethical dilemma presented
when a criminal defense lawyer's client commits or intends to commit
perjury was Monroe Freedman, Professional Responsibility of the Criminal Defense Lawyer: The Three Hardest Questions, 64 Mich. L. Rev.

---

8. We believe a trial court should also specifically inform a defendant of the possible
consequences of false testimony: (1) the lawyer may reveal to the court what he believes to
be false; (2) the lawyer may refrain from referring to the false testimony in final argument;
and (3) the defendant may be prosecuted for perjury.

1469 (1966). Professor Freedman's analysis of *Nix* can be found in Client Confidences and Client Perjury: Some Unanswered Questions, 136 U. Pa. L. Rev. 1939 (1988). See also Brent R. Appel, The Limited Impact of Nix v. Whiteside on Attorney-Client Relations, 136 U. Pa. L. Rev. 1913 (1988). Mr. Appel argues that *Nix* was a narrower decision than subsequent courts have assumed, that it permits the states "broad leeway to determine their own solutions" to the client perjury problem, and that the decision will "rarely [have] a direct impact on criminal defense attorneys and their clients."

QUESTION

7.3   "I was assigned to represent a man, I'll call him Carl, who is charged with two violent homicides. The evidence against Carl is strong — fingerprints, a confession, eyewitnesses. But the facts of Carl's life and the circumstances of the crimes provide an excellent basis for a claim of insanity. After conferring with my client, we agreed to assert that defense. In our state, that meant that the prosecutor got to have her psychiatrist examine the defendant and I got funds to hire my own psychiatrist. At trial, as you might expect, our shrink said Carl could not appreciate the consequences of his acts and the state shrink said he could. Both relied a good deal on what Carl told them, including about his horrible childhood, abuse by his parents and others, and that sort of thing, all of which came out in their testimony. The doctors just interpreted the stuff differently. You could see, however, that the stories made quite an impression on the jury.

"The trial ended Friday and we get to sum up Monday. I was working on my summation here at the office today, Saturday, when I get a call from a woman who says she's Carl's older sister. She and Carl had been out of contact for 15 years. She had seen a news story about the case and wanted to talk to me. Well, she came in, a nice woman, married with kids, living in Tulsa, works as a nurse at a hospice. She told me that none of the stuff Carl told the shrinks about being an abused child and the like was true. She said Carl has a great imagination and just made it up. She went on to tell me all about their childhood in detail, even taking out a photo album. Frankly, I believe her and realize Carl lied to the doctors and to me. But I'm not sure what I should now do. Carl didn't lie under oath. He didn't testify. The doctors didn't lie either, although I guess if my doctor knew the truth, she'd revise her opinion. As I say, summation is Monday. What should I do?"

C. FOSTERING FALSITY

Here we briefly review a variety of tactics that may be used in civil or criminal cases, often quite properly, to increase the chances of victory at the acknowledged cost of misleading the judge or jury.

1. Cross-Examining the Truthful Witness

Max Steuer was considered an exceptional criminal defense lawyer in New York City in the early 1900s. He represented the defendants in the criminal case arising out of the Triangle Shirtwaist Company Fire. Daniel Kornstein's article praises Steuer's skills in that case. A response to the article follows. We re-encounter Max Steuer at page 405 infra.

Daniel J. Kornstein
A TRAGIC FIRE — A GREAT
CROSS-EXAMINATION
N.Y.L.J., March 28, 1986, at 2

We remember events for different reasons. For example, March 25 was the seventy-fifth anniversary of the terrible Triangle Shirtwaist Fire, which killed 146 sweatshop workers, mostly young immigrant women barred by locked doors from escaping the blaze in their New York City factory. The fire in 1911 stands as a turning point in the history of labor because it led to significant labor reforms in workplace health and safety laws. Important as those reforms are, however, they are not the only reason for lawyers to remember the Triangle Shirtwaist Fire.

Lawyers should remember the fire for another reason, unmentioned in the anniversary accounts. Lawyers should remember it because it was the subject of one of the all-time great cross-examinations in American courtroom history.

The memorable cross-examination grew out of the criminal case that followed the fire. Within a month after the fire, the government indicted the two owners of the Triangle Shirtwaist Company on manslaughter charges. The indictment was based on a New York State law providing that factory doors "shall be so constructed as to open outwardly, where practicable, and shall not be locked, bolted or fastened during working hours." For their defense counsel, the proprietors chose Max D. Steuer.

It was a good choice, for Max D. Steuer is still a courtroom legend. In the early part of this century, he was perhaps the leading trial lawyer in

New York City. Realist and idealist, shrewd and comprehensive of the ways of men, Steuer built a reputation as a superb master of trial tactics. "No one at the New York Bar," wrote Francis L. Wellman, author of The Art of Cross-Examination, "knows more about the way to conduct a trial from an artistic standpoint than Mr. Steuer." Wellman includes Steuer's performance in the Triangle Shirtwaist Fire case in the section of his book called "Cross-Examination of the Perjured Witness."

Steuer had to bring to bear all of his considerable skills in the Triangle Fire criminal case. The tragedy had, understandably, aroused public opinion against his clients. The undisputed facts — locked doors forcing scores of women, clothes and hair ablaze, to leap from windows to their deaths — made the defendants' prospects bleak. Surely this was a case that would result in convictions. But the zealous prosecutor overplayed his hand and did not count on Steuer's ability.

The trial lasted several weeks. Just before it rested, the prosecution called a final witness to supply a missing piece of crucial evidence. This final witness was supposed to testify that Rose Schwartz, one of the fire's victims named in the indictment, was in fact the same person who lost her life in the fire. Up to that point in the trial, the testimony had uniformly been that the bodies discovered in the building were so charred that identification was impossible.

The prosecution had built suspense. It had kept its final witness in Philadelphia, beyond reach of defense counsel who knew neither her identity nor her location. There, the prosecutor and his staff met with her several times in preparation for her testimony. When the government's final witness appeared, everyone in the courtroom felt that something important was about to happen. They were not disappointed.

First, the key witness testified to preliminary details. She said that she had been an employee at the factory and was there when the fire broke out and that she knew Rose Schwartz. Then the prosecutor asked her: "Now tell everything that you saw and did on the ninth floor of those premises from the time the fire broke out." The response was heartrending.

The witness told how she first saw the flames. She described how the girls scattered from one floor and ran to another. She testified that many of them ran to the windows and began to jump out and that she herself had decided to follow their example.

While at the window ready to jump, the witness said she looked around the room in a last-ditch effort to escape. She then saw Rose Schwartz, the witness said, with both hands on the knob of the door desperately turning and pushing, but the door would not give.

Watching Rose, the witness was mesmerized. She saw the flames envelop Rose's hands, saw her fall to the floor and then saw her once more struggle to her feet, again grab the knob of the door and turn it one way and then another, pull and then push, but the door would not give. Once more the flames enveloped Rose and again she had to withdraw her hands from the door knob and she fell to the floor; the flames were now coming very close to the witness; she turned once more toward the door and there for the third time, was Rose Schwartz, on her knees, screaming and praying, with both hands on the door knob, turning it first one way, then the other, and pulling and pushing, but the door would not give, and finally she was completely covered by the flames, and fell to the floor within a foot of the door.

At the end of her direct testimony, tears ran down the cheeks of the jurors.

Steuer began his cross-examination slowly. He spent the first half hour on preliminaries. At the end of the half hour, using the exact words employed by the prosecutor, he asked the witness to state all she did herself and all that she saw done on the ninth floor from the moment she first saw the fire.

There was something odd about the witness's answer. She started her narrative with exactly the same word that she had used when telling her story the first time. She went on in precisely the same words that she had used when answering the same question put to her by the prosecutor.

Steuer changed the subject for a while and asked the witness to describe what happened for the third time. The witness again started with the same word and continued to narrate the story in precisely the same words that she had used twice before. The only difference was that this time she omitted one word. Steuer asked her if she had omitted a word, naming the word.

Her lips began to move and start the narrative to herself all over again, and when she reached the position where that word belonged she said: "Yes, I made a mistake; I left that word out." Q. "But otherwise your answer was correct?" She again began to move her lips, obviously reciting to herself what she had previously said, and then said, "Yes, otherwise my answer is correct."

When Steuer asked her the same question a third time, the prosecutor objected but was overruled. After twenty minutes on other subjects, Steuer asked, for the fourth time: "Will you please tell the jury what you saw and what you did after you first observed any sign of the flames?"

She started with the same word, and continued her narrative, but again left out one word, this time a different word. Asked whether she had not now omitted a word, naming it, she went through the same lip performance and replied that she had, and upon being asked to place the word where it belonged, she proceeded to do so.

Neither Steuer nor the prosecutor had any further questions of that witness. The tears in the jury box had dried. The situation had entirely changed. The witness had not hurt, but had very materially helped, the defense; she had succeeded in casting grave suspicion on the testimony of many of the girls who had previously testified; her carefully prepared story had aroused the suspicion of the jury regarding the entire case of the prosecution.

The jury acquitted the two defendants. Historians say the acquittal was due to the trial judge's narrow charge to the jury. But Steuer's brilliant cross-examination of the People's star witness must have had more than a little to do with the result.

Steuer's performance vividly illustrated an unorthodox style of cross-examination. Normally we are told not to ask an opposing witness to repeat harmful testimony on cross-examination. The usual reason is that such repetition only reinforces the original bad impact of such testimony. But Steuer found a proper occasion for breaking this rule and compelling a witness to repeat on cross-examination every detail of the story given on direct. The constant repetition of the story showed a carefully prepared recital, rather than a spontaneous recollection of actual events.

So let us remember the Triangle Shirtwaist Fire and celebrate the labor reforms it engendered. But let us also recall the cross-examination that exploded perjured testimony about that tragedy. And let us celebrate the importance of cross-examination — what Wigmore once called the "greatest engine ever developed for the discovery of truth."

Ann Ruben & Emily Ruben
LETTER TO THE EDITOR
N.Y.L.J., April 14, 1986, at 2

In 1911, one hundred forty-six sweatshop workers, mostly young immigrant women, were incinerated as a result of the sweatshop's owners' efforts to ensure maximization of profit. When fire broke out at the Triangle Shirtwaist Factory, workers were unable to escape because the owners had bolted exits shut. The men charged with responsibility were acquitted after trial.

Daniel Kornstein's eulogy of Max Steuer's role in this acquittal ("A Tragic Fire — A Great Cross-Examination," N.Y.L.J., March 28, 1986, p. 2, col. 3) underscores the moral vacuum in which many lawyers operate. Kornstein asks us to "celebrate" Max Steuer's cross-examination of Kate Alterman, one of the young immigrant women who managed to survive the fire. We cannot.

Mr. Kornstein's facile assumption that this young woman's testimony was perjured leads him to extol the virtues of Steuer's cross-examination. Mr. Kornstein exhibits all of the narrow-mindedness of the men (judge, jury and lawyers) who exonerated those responsible for the results of this tragic fire. He fails even to consider the very obvious and likely possibility that the testimony was not perjured. To equate Kate Alterman's possibly rehearsed testimony with premeditated dishonesty represents an enormous leap of faith and completely ignores the socio-economic and historic context of that testimony. The women who testified at the trial spoke little English. Approximately half of them spoke no English at all, and many of those who did were illiterate. (A. Steuer, Max D. Steuer Trial Lawyer, Random House, NY [1950], p. 86.) They had barely survived a traumatic fire in which many of their friends and co-workers had burned to death. The notorious conditions under which they had worked in this country provided no basis for them to believe that their own words could sway the power structure the legal system represented. Unfortunately, the judge's narrow jury instructions, Steuer's technique, and the jury results underscored the powerlessness of young immigrant women.

Mr. Kornstein has used the anniversary of the Triangle Shirtwaist Factory Fire to applaud the technique of Max Steuer and to belittle the courage of women like Kate Alterman who came forward to testify. It would be more appropriate for lawyers to remember those who lost their lives in the fire and to explore ways to combat the oppressive working conditions that still exist throughout this country.

In response to the letter from Ann Ruben and Emily Ruben, Daniel Kornstein has written:*

The Rubens movingly make telling points that, in retrospect, I wish I had expressly taken into consideration. First, they are absolutely correct in saying that I neglected to distinguish between outright perjury and overly rehearsed, overly memorized but essentially truthful testimony. I should have drawn that distinction, and I regret not having done so. But even that distinction in no way lessens Steuer's tactical achievement in neutralizing and offsetting the natural sympathy the jury must have had for the witness. For, in light of the obvious coaching, the fact remains that we simply do not know if the witness's testimony was or was not truthful and accurate.

Second, as the Rubens point out, the class struggle aspects of the cross-examination and the whole trial are obvious. But that economic overhang is not the end of the story. Unless we have come to the point where representing unpopular clients (such as sweatshop owners, landlords, large corporations, defendants accused of heinous crimes, or persons with controversial political, social, or moral beliefs) is itself unethical, I do not see how Steuer overstepped his professional responsibility. We have not yet so abandoned the presumption of innocence of the adversary process, so that we know who will win or lose a trial before the evidence is in.

The Rubens rightly press for a closer moral study of Steuer's trial tactics and their impact on the trial outcome. That is quite different from broadside attacks on the "power structure the legal system represented." It may

---

*Letter from Daniel Kornstein to Professor Gillers, dated November 1, 1988.

be that, in some cosmic sense, the wrong side prevailed in the Triangle Shirtwaist factory case; but it was not because Steuer did anything inappropriate. He did precisely what he should have done — and what any good lawyer should have done. I don't think Steuer acted irresponsibly or in a "moral vacuum" by cross-examining the witness as he did. He took advantage of an adversary's blunder, which happens all the time.

2. Arguing for False Inferences

When an advocate is presented with evidence that tends to undermine his case, he has two choices, assuming he cannot persuade the judge to exclude it. First, he may try to discredit the evidence through impeachment devices, which are calculated to encourage the jury to believe that a witness is mistaken or lying or that a document is false. Second, if the evidence is ambiguous, he can ask the jury to draw an inference favorable to his client. These strategies can be used concurrently.

What if the advocate knows that the witness is telling the truth, perhaps because his client has confirmed the accuracy of the testimony or because the lawyer has incontrovertible corroboration? Can he still try to discredit the witness? Can he ask the jury to draw a favorable inference that he knows is false?

The Subin-Mitchell Debate

Professor Harry Subin has envisioned a role for criminal defense lawyers that is sharply less adversarial than the present conception. He would forbid defense lawyers to present "a false case" using the techniques described below. The right to present a defense, he argues, is "not absolute." Witness the prohibition on the use of perjured testimony. Professor Subin criticizes "the utterly arbitrary line we have drawn between" the use of perjured testimony (disallowed) and the presentation of a "false case" (allowed).

After Professor Subin's article appeared, John B. Mitchell, an experienced criminal defense lawyer whose previous work Professor Subin had cited, challenged Subin's conception with a fact pattern and the argument he would make to the jury based on it. Subin then replied to Mitchell's critique. Excerpts from all three articles follow.*

_____

*See Harry Subin, The Criminal Lawyer's "Different Mission"; Reflections on the "Right" to Present a False Case, 1 Geo. J. Legal Ethics 125, 146-150 (1987); John B. Mitchell, Reasonable Doubts Are Where You Find Them: A Response to Professor Subin's Position on the Criminal Lawyer's "Different Mission," 1 Geo. J. Legal Ethics 339, 343-346 (1987); Harry Subin, Is This Lie Necessary? Further Reflections on the Right to Present a False Defense, 1 Geo. J. Legal Ethics 689, 691-692 (1988).

SUBIN

The question is not, however, whether a "guilty" person has a right to a defense, but what kind of defense can be advanced on behalf of anyone, whether known to be guilty or not, or even if known to be innocent. Here what the defense attorney knows should be crucial to what he or she does.

It may help to explain this position by positing the defense function as consisting of two separate roles, usually intertwined but theoretically distinct. One enlists the attorney as the "monitor" of the state's case, whose task it is to assure that a conviction is based on an adequate amount of competent and admissible evidence. The lawyer as monitor is a kind of quality inspector, with no responsibility for developing a different product, if you will, to "sell" to the jury. The other attorney role involves the attorney as the client's "advocate," whose task is to present that different product, by undermining the state's version of the facts or presenting a competing version sufficient at least to establish a reasonable doubt about the defendant's guilt. The monitor's role is to assure that the state has the facts to support a conviction. The advocate attempts to demonstrate that the state's evidence is not fact at all. Where, as in most cases, the facts are in doubt, or where the state's case is believed or known to be based upon mistaken perceptions or lies, the defense attorney quite properly plays both roles. Having monitored the state's case and found it factually and legally sound, however, should he or she be permitted to act as advocate and attempt to undermine it? I submit that the answer to that is no, and that the defendant's rights in cases of this kind extend only as far as the monitoring role takes the attorney. The right in question, to have the state prove guilt beyond a reasonable doubt, can be vindicated if the attorney is limited to good faith challenges to the state's case; to persuading the jury that there are legitimate reasons to doubt the state's evidence. It may on occasion be more effective for the attorney to use his or her imagination to create doubts; but surely there cannot be a right to gain an acquittal whenever the imagination of one's attorney is good enough to produce one. . . .

I propose a system in which the defense attorney would operate not with the right to assert defenses known to be untrue, but under the following rule:

> It shall be improper for an attorney who knows beyond a reasonable doubt the truth of a fact established in the state's case to attempt to refute that fact through the introduction of evidence, impeachment of evidence, or argument.

In the face of this rule, the attorney who knew there were no facts to contest would be limited to the "monitoring" role. Assuming that a defendant . . . wanted to assert his right to contest the evidence against him, the attorney would work to assure that all of the elements of the crime were proven beyond a reasonable doubt, on the basis of competent and admissible evidence. This would include enforcing the defendant's rights to have privileged or illegally obtained evidence excluded: The goal sought here is not the elimination of all rules that result in the suppression of truth, but only those not supported by sound policy. It would also be appropriate for the attorney to argue to the jury that the available evidence is not sufficient to sustain the burden of proof. It would not, however, be proper for the attorney to use any of the presently available devices to refute testimony known to be truthful. I wish to make clear, however, that this rule would not prevent the attorney from challenging *inaccurate* testimony, even though the attorney knew that the defendant was guilty. Again, the truth-seeking goal is not applicable when a valid policy reason exists for ignoring it. Forcing the state to prove its case is such a reason. . . .

Mitchell

[I]magine I am defending a young woman accused of shoplifting a star one places on top of Christmas trees. I interview the store manager and find that he stopped my client when he saw her walk straight through the store, star in hand, and out the door. When he stopped her and asked why she had taken the star without paying, she made no reply and burst into tears. He was then about to take her inside to the security office when an employee called out, "There's a fire!" The manager rushed inside and dealt with a small blaze in the camera section. Five minutes later he came out to find my client sitting where he had left her. He then took her back to the security room and asked if she would be willing to empty her pockets so that he could see if she had taken anything else. Without a word, she complied. She had a few items not belonging to the store and a ten-dollar bill. The star was priced at $1.79.

In an interview with my client, she admitted trying to steal the star: "It was so pretty, and would have looked so nice on the tree. I would have bought it, but I also wanted to make a special Christmas dinner for Mama and didn't have enough money to do both. I've been saving for that dinner and I know it will make her so happy. But that star. . . . I could just see the look in Mama's eyes if she saw that lovely thing on our tree."

At trial, the manager tells the same story he told me, except he *leaves out* the part about her waiting during the fire and having a ten-dollar bill. If I bring out these two facts on cross-examination and argue for an acquittal based upon my client "accidentally" walking out of the store with the star, surely Professor Subin will accuse me of raising a "false defense." I have brought out testimony, not itself false, to accredit a false theory and have argued to the jury based on this act. But I am not really arguing a false theory in Professor Subin's sense.

My defense is not that the defendant accidentally walked out, but rather that the prosecution cannot prove the element of intent to permanently deprive beyond a reasonable doubt. Through this theory, I am raising "doubt" in the prosecution's case, and therefore questioning the legitimacy of the government's lawsuit for control over the defendant. In my effort to carry out this legal theory, I will *not assert* that facts known by me to be true are false or those known to be false are true. As a defense attorney, I do not have to prove what *in fact* happened. That is an advantage in the process I would not willingly give up. Under our constitutional system, I do not need to try to convince the factfinder about the truth of any factual propositions. I need only try to convince the factfinder that the prosecution has not met its burden. Again, I will not argue that particular facts are true or false. Thus, in this case I will not claim that my client walked out of the store with innocent intent (a fact which I know is false); rather, I will argue:

> The prosecution claims my client stole an ornament for a Christmas tree. The prosecution further claims that when my client walked out of that store she intended to keep it without paying. Now, maybe she did. None of us were there. On the other hand, she had $10.00 in her pocket, which was plenty of money with which to pay for the ornament without the risk of getting caught stealing. Also, she didn't try to conceal what she was doing. She walked right out of the store holding it in her hand. Most of us have come close to innocently doing the same thing. So, maybe she didn't. But then she cried the minute she was stopped. She might have been feeling guilty. So, maybe she did. On the other hand, she might just have been scared when she realized what had happened. After all, she didn't run away when she was left alone even though she knew the manager was going to be occupied with a fire inside. So, maybe she didn't. The point is that, looking at all the evidence, you're left with "maybe she intended to steal, maybe she didn't." But, you knew that before the first witness was even sworn. The prosecution has the burden, and he simply can't carry any burden let alone "beyond a reasonable doubt" with a maybe she did, maybe she didn't case. . . .

Is this a "false defense" for Professor Subin? Admittedly, I am trying to raise a doubt by persuading the jury to appreciate "possibilities" other than my client's guilt. Perhaps Professor Subin would say it is "false" because I know the possibilities are untrue. But if that is so, Professor Subin will have taken a leap from defining "false defense" as the assertion that true things are false and false things are true, for I am doing neither of those things here. The fact that one cannot know how Subin would reach this "pure" reasonable doubt case only reinforces my initial statement that Professor Subin's categories are imprecise.

Another perspective from which to look at the function of a defense attorney involves understanding that function in the context of the nature of evidence at trial. Professor Subin speaks of facts and the impropriety of trying to make "true facts" look false and "false facts" look true. But in a trial there are no such things as facts. There is only information, lack of information, and chains of inferences therefrom. In the courtroom there will be no crime, no store, no young girl with a star in her hand. All there will be is a collection of witnesses who are strangers to the jury, giving information which may include physical evidence and documents. For example, most people would acknowledge the existence of eyewitness identifications; however, in an evidentiary sense they do not exist. Rather, a particular person with particular perceptual abilities and motives and biases will recount an observation made under particular circumstances and will utter particular words on the witness stand (e.g., "That's the man"). From this mass of information, the prosecution will argue, in story form, in favor of the inference that the defendant is their man (e.g., "The victim was on her way home, when . . ."). The defense will not then argue that the defendant is the wrong man in a *factual sense,* but instead will attack the persuasiveness of the criminal inference and resulting story (e.g., "The sun was in the witness's eyes; she was on drugs").

In our shoplifting example, the prosecution will elicit that the defendant burst into tears when stopped by the manager. From this information will run a chain of inferences: defendant burst into tears; people without a guilty conscience would explain their innocence, not cry; defendant has a guilty conscience; her guilty conscience is likely motivated by having committed a theft. Conversely, if the defense brings out that the manager was shaking a lead pipe in his hand when he stopped the defendant, defense counsel is *not asserting* that defendant did not have a guilty conscience when stopped. Counsel is merely *weakening* the persuasiveness of the prosecution's inference by raising the "possibility" that she was crying not from guilt, but from fear. By raising such "possibilities," the defense is making arguments against the ability of the prosecution's inferences to meet their burden of "beyond a reasonable doubt." The defense is not arguing what are true or false facts (i.e., that the tears were from fear as opposed to guilt). Whatever Professor Subin cares to call it, this commentary on the prosecution's case, complete with raising possibilities which weaken the persuasiveness of central inferences in that case, is in no ethical sense a "false case." "False case" is plainly a misnomer. In a system where factual guilt is not at issue, Professor Subin's "falsehoods" are, in fact, "reasonable doubts."

SUBIN

[Subin notes that Mitchell states that he will not "claim that my client walked out of the store with innocent intent (a fact which I know is false)," but will instead make what Mitchell calls a "pure" reasonable doubt argument. Subin then continues:]

I applaud this apparent concession that presenting a false defense might be ethically wrong. (Why else would Mitchell go to the trouble of making the argument?) I believe, moreover, that if defense attorneys were required to give this kind of closing argument in "reasonable doubt" cases, it would help to reconcile the goals of assuring a truthful verdict and putting the state to its proof. Mitchell's presentation is, however, flawed in two respects. In the first place, the closing argument which he offers, with its intimations that the defense theory is not dependent upon the facts, is much more forthright than those which most attorneys would give. What they would actually say would be more cryptic with respect to what the jury should conclude about the truth, something like:

> The prosecution claims that my client walked out of the store intending not to pay. I ask you, members of the jury, why would this young lady, with $10.00 in her pocket, steal a $1.79 Christmas tree ornament? Isn't it more likely that in the hustle and bustle of Christmas shopping she saw the ornament, focused for a second on the beautiful Christmas tree she was decorating, picked it up and then forgot she had it when she left the store? At the very least, don't you believe that possibility creates a reasonable doubt about whether she intended to steal the ornament?

Moreover, even if Mitchell's sanitized closing was given, it still is designed to persuade the jury of the existence of facts he knows not to be true: here, that the woman in fact left the store accidentally (i.e., "maybe she did (leave accidentally). None of us was there."). That is not a lie, but it certainly creates a false impression, which amounts to the same thing.

Consider another example of "not arguing what are true or false facts" which Mitchell draws from his hypothetical: the woman bursts into tears after being caught stealing the ornament. The lawyer knows that she did so as a result of her guilty conscience. The store manager, however, was shaking a lead pipe in his hand when he stopped the woman. Mitchell says that if he brings out that fact, he is not "asserting" that the defendant did not have a guilty conscience; he is merely "weakening the persuasiveness of the prosecutor's inferences." It is perfectly clear, however, that he is attempting to do this by suggesting to the jury that this woman was in fact frightened by this lead pipe. Mitchell would, moreover, make this argument even if his client swore to him that she never even *saw* the lead pipe.

QUESTIONS

1. Who wins this debate? Mitchell, you say? Then how do you answer Subin's argument that it is "utterly arbitrary" to draw the line at perjuri-

ous testimony while permitting a "false case"? If the latter is acceptable, why not the former? If the former is unacceptable, why do we permit the latter?

2. Subin predicts that defense lawyers would give a different summation than Mitchell sets out. Is there anything wrong with the summation Subin describes? He seems to think it is self-evidently wrong and that Mitchell concedes as much. Is he right?

3. Does Mitchell concede more than he must? Using Mitchell's hypothetical, could the defense lawyer argue that his client did not knowingly take the ornament? Could he argue that the defendant's tears were caused by the lead pipe? Could he make these arguments even though he knew both were false? If your answer is yes, would you also let the defense lawyer call the defendant to testify that she cried because she feared the lead pipe even if she never saw it? If your answer to this last question is no, how can your answer to the prior questions be yes?

Richard H. Underwood & William H. Fortune
TRIAL ETHICS
365-366 (1988)

Prosecutors have a responsibility to the truth not shared by defense counsel. A prosecutor cannot argue an inference known to be false, even though the record supports the inference.[1] A defense attorney, however, may create false inferences so long as this is not accomplished through false evidence because the prosecution bears the burden of proof and cannot force the defendant to testify.[2] It is the obligation of defense counsel to test the state's witnesses even though they are testifying truthfully.[3] United States v. Latimer[4] provides an excellent example of the different responsibilities of prosecutor and defense counsel. In a trial for bank robbery there was testimony that a surveillance camera was activated, but no reference was made to photos obtained. In closing, defense counsel alluded to the lack of testimony and suggested that the reason no photos were introduced was because the photos would not reveal the defendant as the robber. The truth of the matter was that the surveillance camera had malfunctioned and no photos were obtained. To rebut the false inference, the prosecutor told the jury of the malfunction; the appellate court reversed because the prosecutor had gone outside the rec-

1. Wolfram, Modern Legal Ethics 651 (1986); ABA Standards Relating to the Administration of Criminal Justice, Prosecution Functions 3-1.1(d), 3-5.7.
2. Michigan Op. CI-1164 (1987), ABA/BNA Law. Man. Prof. Con. [Current] 44 (ethical to introduce witnesses to testify truthfully when purpose is to create a false inference).
3. M. Freedman, Lawyers' Ethics in an Adversary System 44-45, 79-80 (1975).
4. 511 F.2d 498 (10th Cir. 1975).

ord. The court, in effect, held that it was improper to refer to facts outside the record to rebut a false inference.

While the peculiar role of the criminal defense attorney may support the use of a false inference, civil attorneys should be discouraged from such arguments.[5] Unfortunately, the Code and Model Rules do not directly proscribe false inferences. Attorneys are told not to make false statements of *fact*[6] but there is nothing in the ethical standards prohibiting counsel from leading the jury to a false finding.

Do you agree that the code and rules permit arguing for false inferences? If so, do you agree that this result is "unfortunat[e]"?

3. Literal Truth

In Bronston v. United States, 409 U.S. 352 (1973), the defendant was convicted of perjury. A company of which he was sole owner had filed a petition under the Bankruptcy Act. At a hearing, Bronston testified under oath as follows:

Q. Do you have any bank accounts in Swiss banks, Mr. Bronston?
A. No, sir.
Q. Have you ever?
A. The company had an account there for about six months, in Zurich.
Q. Have you any nominees who have bank accounts in Swiss banks?
A. No, sir.
Q. Have you ever?
A. No, sir.

At the time of the questioning, Bronston did not have a Swiss bank account in his own name, but he had previously had one. The Supreme Court unanimously reversed the conviction. Bronston's answer (the second one above) was "true and complete on its face." It did not matter that Bronston may have intended to evade and mislead. Protection against misleading answers lay in effective cross-examination: "It is the responsibility of the lawyer to probe; testimonial interrogation, and cross-examination in particular, is a probing, prying, pressing form of inquiry. If a witness evades, it is the lawyer's responsibility to recognize the evasion and to bring the witness back to the mark, to flush out the whole truth with the tools of the adversary examination."

---

5. Wolfram, supra note 1, at 651.
6. DR 7-102(A)(5); Model Rule 3.3(a)(1).

If Bronston's lawyer had coached him to give literally truthful but evasive and misleading answers (but not untruthful ones), would the lawyer have acted unethically even if Bronston would not thereby have committed perjury?

4. Coaching

Lawyers routinely prepare witnesses whom they plan to call to testify. It would be considered poor advocacy to call someone "cold" unless there were no choice. Witness preparation is ethical. See D.C. Opinion 79 (1980); R. Underwood & W. Fortune, Trial Ethics 320-323 (1988). In Partisan Justice (1980) (pp.14-16), Judge Marvin Frankel looked at the underside of witness preparation or coaching.

> That the quoted words, from the witness's oath, are not meant quite literally may be seen from more than one perspective. Consider the lawyer's major work of interviewing and "preparing" witnesses, including the client who plans to take the stand. It might be supposed that if the witness were expected simply to tell the relevant things he knew about the events or things in question, there would be no legitimate occasion for preparing him or her. That supposition would probably oversimplify, at least as any American lawyer sees the matter. In matters of any complexity, memories need to be refreshed, ordered, stimulated, all of which may involve perfectly legitimate forms of preparatory assistance. Papers and diaries may have to be reviewed. The proposed testimony may fairly be organized and tailored to eliminate matters that are irrelevant or inadmissible, and even to arrange that honest recollections are given with sufficient flow and verve to avoid some of the tedium that is at best inevitable in large doses during most trials.
>
> Granting that sort of thing, every lawyer knows that the "preparing" of witnesses may embrace a multitude of other measures, including some ethical lapses believed to be more common than we would wish. The process is labeled archly in lawyer's slang as "horseshedding" the witness, a term that may be traced to utterly respectable origins in circuit-riding and otherwise horsy days but still rings a bit knowingly in today's ear. Whatever word is used to describe it, the process often extends beyond helping organize what the witness knows, and moves in the direction of helping the witness to know new things. At its starkest, the effort is called subornation of perjury, which is a crime, and which we are permitted to hope is rare. Somewhat less stark, short of criminality but still to be condemned, is the device of telling the client "the law" before eliciting the facts — i.e., telling the client what facts would constitute a successful claim or defense, and only then asking the client what the facts happen perchance to be. The most famous recent instance is fictional but apt: Anatomy of a Murder, a 1958 novel by Robert Traver, was an account by a pseudonymous state supreme court justice of a murder defendant educated by his lawyer about a defense of impaired

mental capacity and then, conveniently, but obviously not truthfully, re-
counting "facts" that fit the defense and won an acquittal. It is not unduly
cynical to suspect that this, if not in such egregious forms, happens with
some frequency.

Moving away from palpably unsavory manifestations, we all know that
the preparation of our witnesses is calculated, one way and another, to
mock the solemn promise of the whole truth and nothing but. To be sure,
reputable lawyers admonish their clients and witnesses to be truthful. At
the same time, they often take infinite pains to prepare questions designed
to make certain that the controlled flow of truth does not swell to an embarrassing flood. "Don't volunteer anything," the witnesses are cautioned. The
concern is not that the volunteered contribution may be false. The concern
is to avoid an excess of truth, where the spillover may prove hurtful to the
case. . . .

5. *Exploiting Error*

MICHIGAN OPINION CI-1164 (1987)

Client is charged with armed robbery. He proposes to call some
friends as witnesses at trial; who will give truthful testimony that he was
with them at the time of the crime. At the preliminary examination the
victim had testified that the robbery occurred at the same hour and time
to which the friends will testify. Client has confided to attorney that he
robbed the victim; his theory on the time mix-up is that he stole the victim's watch and rendered him unconscious so that the victim's sense of
time was incorrect when relating the circumstances of the robbery to the
investigating detectives. Months later, at the preliminary examination,
the victim relied on the detectives' notes to help him recall the time. Client and attorney have decided that client will not testify at trial. Would it
be ethical for attorney to subpoena the friends to trial to testify that client
was with them at the alleged time of the crime?

DR 7-101 requires counsel to represent the client zealously. A defense
attorney can present any evidence that is truthful; if the ethical rule were
otherwise it would mean that a defendant who confessed guilt to his
counsel would never be able to have an active defense at trial.

The danger of an opposite approach is that sometimes innocent defendants "confess guilt" to their counsel or put forth a perceived "truthful" set of facts that do not pass independent scrutiny. Many crimes have
degrees of guilt, as in homicide, where the "true facts" go to the accused's
intent; something a jailed defendant may not be in a reflective mood to
assess. Criminal defense counsel are not sent to the jail's interview room
to be their client's one person jury and they certainly are not dispatched
to court to be their client's hangman. Our society has made the decision

to permit a person charged with crime to make full disclosure to his counsel without fear that, absent the threat of some future conduct (such as a threat to kill a witness), the lawyer will not disclose the information so provided.

The role of criminal defense counsel is to zealously defend the client within the boundaries of all legal and ethical rules. Therefore, if the information confidentially disclosed by the client were to prevent counsel from marshaling an otherwise proper defense, the client would, in effect, be penalized for making the disclosure. Such a policy, over a longer run, would tend to cause future defendants to fail to disclose everything to their lawyer; the result would be that they would receive an inadequate defense. Such an approach would be fundamentally inconsistent with the implicit representation made to defendants as a part of procedural due process that they may disclose everything to their lawyer without fear of adverse consequence.

It is the prosecution's responsibility to marshal relevant and accurate testimony of criminal conduct. It is not the obligation of defense counsel to correct inaccurate evidence introduced by the prosecution or to ignore truthful evidence that could exculpate his client. Although the tenor of this opinion may appear to risk an unfortunate result to society in the particular situation posed, such an attitude by defense counsel will serve in the long run to preserve the system of criminal justice envisioned by our constitution.

DR 7-102(4) prohibits counsel from using perjured testimony or "false evidence," but it is perfectly proper to call to the witness stand those witnesses on behalf of the client who will present truthful testimony. The testimony of the friends will not spread any perjured testimony upon the record. Client indeed was with the witnesses at the hour to which they will testify. The victim's mistake concerning the precise time of the crime results in this windfall defense to the client.

In CI-394 (1979) this Committee reviewed a situation where there were tire marks at the scene of the crime. Defendant, after being charged with the crime, altered the tire treads on his car. An expert witness, retained by the defense, was misled when he examined the evidence of the tire tracks. We there opined that the defense attorney could not ethically present evidence through an expert witness when his opinion was based upon a set of circumstances where the client tampered with the evidence. To do so would perpetrate a fraud upon the court. The situation with the friends as alibi witnesses in the instant case does not involve tampering with evidence. One cannot suborn the truth.

We said in CI-634 (1981) that it is axiomatic that the right of a client to effective counsel does not include the right to compel counsel to knowingly assist or participate in the commission of perjury or the creation or presentation of false evidence. Thus, where truthful testimony will be offered, it seems axiomatic that a defendant is entitled to the effective assistance of counsel in presenting evidence, even though the defendant has made inculpatory statements to his counsel. . . .

6. Silence

Is silence permissible when a lawyer knows that another is laboring under a misimpression that the lawyer did not personally create? What if the other person is the judge? Conventional wisdom is that silence is permissible, so long as the lawyer doesn't *assist* another in committing a crime or fraud and subject to the specific constraints of Rule 3.3(a)(4) and (b). This rule will sometimes require a lawyer to take remedial measures when the lawyer "comes to know" that he or she has introduced false evidence. Absent this special circumstance, only Rule 3.3(a)(2) would seem specifically to obligate lawyers to speak up to prevent a fraud on the court. But that rule says that a lawyer "shall not knowingly fail to disclose a material fact . . . when disclosure is necessary to avoid assisting a criminal or fraudulent act by the client." Most lawyers would probably say that the meaning of "assist" incorporates the substantive law concept of accessorial conduct. If the substantive law does not make silence actionable, then the lawyer can remain silent.

Opinion 353 (1987), page 314 supra, seems to have interpreted Rule 3.3(a)(2) more broadly than conventional wisdom would have it. The opinion says that "assisting" is "not limited to the criminal law concepts of aiding and abetting or subornation. Rather, it seems clear that this language is intended to guide the conduct of the lawyer as an officer of the court as a prophylactic measure to protect against client perjury contaminating the judicial process."

Scattered authority supports a "prophylactic" rule. In Matter of Whitmore, 117 N.J. 472, 569 A.2d 252 (1990), a police officer had absented himself from a courtroom in order to help the defendant avoid a conviction for drunken driving. The prosecutor, knowing this, told the judge that the officer was unavailable without revealing why. When the judge asked for an explanation, the prosecutor did not reply. The case was dismissed. Although the prosecutor's statement was literally true, the Supreme Court issued a public reprimand. The court relied, in part, on a rule unique to New Jersey, which says that a "lawyer shall not knowingly fail to disclose to the tribunal a material fact with the knowledge that the tribunal may tend to be misled by such failure." Rule 3.3(a)(5). But the court also relied on Rule 3.3(a)(2), which is the same as the Model Rule. The court wrote:

> Here, while respondent's "client" was the State of New Jersey, the police officer was the State's key witness. The respondent's failure to disclose material information, namely, the officer's motive to aid the defendant in the

DWI case, could be said to have assisted the improper act of the officer —
to abort the prosecution. . . .

We thus determine that when a municipal prosecutor becomes aware
of an improper motive directly affecting the administration of justice on
the part of a police officer . . . which, if undisclosed, could mislead the
court, or could contribute to an improper or illegal result that benefits
the witness, the failure to disclose such information constitutes a violation of the Rules.

See also Office of Disciplinary Counsel v. Heffernan, 58 Ohio St. 3d 260,
569 N.E.2d 1027, cert. denied, 112 S. Ct. 191 (1991) (where criminal defendant misidentified himself to court, lawyer had obligation to correct
fraud on learning of it thereafter); People v. Brown, 31 Ill. 2d 415, 201
N.E.2d 409 (1964) (defense lawyer whose client claims insanity has duty
"to take all proper steps to insure a fair determination of the issue"); People v. Lewis, 75 Ill. App. 3d 560, 393 N.E.2d 1380 (1979) (when defense
lawyer knows that his client is attempting to deceive the trier of fact with
regard to his mental state, "it is [his] ethical responsibility . . . to disclose
to the trial court the facts as he knows them"); New Jersey Opinion 586
(1986) (lawyer who learned from new client fact that demonstrated fraud
by adversary of former client is required to reveal it).

The word "assist" appears elsewhere in the Model Rules (see Rule
1.2(d) and 4.1(b)). In addition, Rule 3.3(a)(2) is incorporated by reference in Rule 3.9. The committee's construction of "assisting" in Rule
3.3(a)(2) as essentially "prophylactic" may require a like construction in
each of these other provisions. That would make the concept of assistance broader in the rules of ethics than it is in the law of torts or crimes.
A broad definition of "assisting" throughout the rules could work a fundamental change in the responsibility of lawyers, couldn't it?

It is still too early to predict the outcome of this part of Opinion 353.
Perhaps the committee intended to limit the expansion of Rule 3.3(a)(2)
to instances of client perjury, however difficult that limitation may be
textually.

The Committee's analysis is further clouded by the fact that although
the opinion refers to client perjury, its hypothetical does not assume that
the client lied under oath. In addition, in most instances of client perjury,
a lawyer would already be under a remedial obligation because of Rule
3.3(a)(4). Thus, if the Committee intended to broaden Rule 3.3(a)(2) only
in the client perjury context, its construction will usually be unnecessary.

Given Opinion 353, what should a lawyer do when she knows that

1. her client has lied under oath in response to the question of an-
    other party, whether on cross-examination or direct?
2. her client has lied under oath in response to a question from the
    court?

3. her client has answered a question from the court falsely but not under oath (what the hypothetical in Opinion 353 actually assumes)?
4. a nonclient has lied under oath in response to a question from the lawyer, another lawyer, or the court?
5. a client or nonclient has given a literally truthful but misleading answer on which the court is about to rely?
6. another lawyer has made a literally true but misleading statement on which the court is about to rely?

Would these questions have different answers under the code?

Legal rules may require revelation of information even when ethics rules do not. Rule 26(e)(2) Fed. R. Civ. P., like many discovery rules, requires a party to amend a discovery response if the party learns that the response was "incorrect when made" or, though once correct, is "no longer true and . . . a failure to amend the response is in substance a knowing concealment."

What happens when a lawyer learns information that would require a client to amend a discovery response but the information is confidential? DR 4-101(C)(2) permits revelation of client confidences "when required . . . by law or court order." (Rule 1.6 has no such exception. How can that be? Can the rules authorize lawyers to conceal information that the law requires them to reveal?) New York City Opinion 1990-2 concluded that Rule 26(e)(2) was "law" within the meaning of DR 4-101(C)(2). As a result, a lawyer may comply with the federal duty without violating DR 4-101. But the code provision is permissive, while the discovery rule is mandatory. If the lawyer chooses not to reveal — e.g., because revelation would implicate the client in fraud on the court — he or she might have to withdraw to avoid violation of the discovery provision.

QUESTION

7.4 "I do personal injury. Plaintiffs. Small stuff, no big deal, but I make a living, okay? Mostly car crashes. I get my share of whiplash, sprained backs, pain and suffering. It's all contingency, okay? Client hires me, I'll call him Pinocchio. You know what's coming. Intersection accident. Question is who had the right of way. Usually the two insurance companies split the difference, I get my cut, lawyer for other guy gets his. Or hers nowadays.

"We're at the EBT and the lawyer says to my guy 'I see you wear contacts. You were wearing them at the accident?' His license says he's got to. My guy says 'no, glasses.' What he told me too. Okay? Lawyer says 'prescription?' Clever dude, right? Client says yes. Lawyer's still suspicious. Asks if he brought them to the EBT like the notice said. Pinocchio produces them. Lawyer puts them up to the light. He says 'deemed defendant's four for identification' — 'deemed' so we don't actually have to attach a sticker to them — then gives them back. Later, I tell Pinocchio I'd better hold onto them, they're being deemed and all, if he doesn't mind. He says, get this, he's got to give them back to his son.

"What it turns out is these were the glasses Pinocchio was wearing, like he said. And they're prescription too, like he said. But they're not Pinocchio's. Okay? They're his son's. Day of the accident, Pinocchio picked them up by mistake on the way to his car. By the time he realizes they're not his, being a mile too weak, he's pulling out of the garage and thinks what the hell, he's just running down to the video store to get *Terminator II*. On the way to which the accident happens. I mean, Jeez, okay? This is only a four, five thou case I'm lucky. I don't need the trouble. So what do I do now, you're so smart?"

D.   FRIVOLOUS POSITIONS AND ABUSIVE TACTICS

Like malpractice actions and actions for attorney liability to third parties (pages 611 and 649 infra), court-imposed sanctions for frivolous claims or defenses and abusive tactics have increased dramatically in the last decade. Judges and commentators disagree on the wisdom of these sanctions in both general and particular cases; they also disagree on the many subissues that a sanctions regime must resolve.

Between its amendment in 1983 and the spring of 1988, Rule 11 of the Federal Rules of Civil Procedure, by far the most prominent of the sanction vehicles, was cited in more than 1000 federal opinions. Note, A Uniform Approach to Rule 11 Sanctions, 97 Yale L.J. 901 (1988) (authorized by Alan Untereiner). By 1991, one report identified "more than 3000 Rule 11 opinions . . . since August 1983." Comments on Federal Rule of Civil Procedure 11 and Related Rules, 46 The Record 267 (April 1991) (Report of Committee on Federal Courts of Association of the Bar of the City of New York). Between 1938 and 1976, by contrast, the unamended rule produced only 19 cases. Michael Risinger, Honesty in Pleading and Its Enforcement: Some "Striking" Problems with Federal Rule of Civil Procedure 11, 61 Minn. L. Rev. 1, 34-37 (1976).

Rule 11 imposes the following duties on lawyers who sign a "pleading, motion, [or] other paper." The lawyer's signature certifies

1.   that the lawyer "has read the pleading, motion or other paper";

2. "that to the best of the [lawyer's] knowledge, information and belief" the document "is well grounded in fact and is warranted by existing law or a good faith argument for the extension, modification, or reversal of existing law";

3. that this conclusion was reached "after reasonable inquiry"; and

4. that the paper "is not interposed for any improper purpose, such as to harass or to cause unnecessary delay or needless increase in the cost of litigation."

While it is universally agreed that the duty to make "reasonable inquiry" is evaluated by an objective standard, courts disagree on the standard to be used to evaluate the separate prohibition on "improper purpose." The Seventh Circuit has employed a subjective standard. Tabrizi v. Village of Glen Ellyn, 883 F.2d 587 (7th Cir. 1989). Other circuits have used an objective standard to determine whether a lawyer had an improper purpose. See, e.g., Sheets v. Yamaha Motors Corp., 891 F.2d 533 (5th Cir. 1990).

You should know that although Rule 11 gets most of the attention, it is not the only source of judicial sanctioning power at the federal level. (Furthermore, many states have their own sanctioning provisions.) Other provisions in a federal judge's arsenal include 28 U.S.C. §1927, which says that any "attorney or other person . . . who so multiplies the proceeding in any case unreasonably and vexatiously may be required" to pay costs and attorneys' fees "reasonably incurred because of such conduct"; Rules 16, 26, and 37 of the Federal Rules of Civil Procedure, which permit sanctions for discovery abuse and other misconduct in civil litigation; Rule 38 of the Federal Rules of Appellate Procedure, which permits "damages and single or double costs to the appellee" if "an appeal is frivolous." Courts also have inherent power to award counsel fees and expenses if an opposing lawyer has acted in bad faith, vexatiously, wantonly, or for oppressive reasons. This power is not displaced by Rule 11 or other provisions of the federal rules. Chambers v. Nasco, Inc., 111 S. Ct. 2123 (1991), affirmed a district judge's award of nearly $1 million against a plaintiff for bad-faith litigation. The sum represented the entire amount of the defendant's litigation costs over a three-year period.

The scope of these various rules and authorities varies. Some require subjective bad faith while others use an objective standard; some are only available on appeal, while others are for the trial court. There is also much overlap. By far, however, it is Rule 11 that has received the most attention, much of it highly critical, even caustic.

Academic comment on Rule 11 and its cousins has been nonstop. Law professors have disagreed on the wisdom and direction of the enterprise. Compare Melissa Nelken's study, Sanctions Under Amended Federal Rule 11 — Some "Chilling" Problems in the Struggle Between Compensation and Punishment, 74 Geo. L.J. 1313 (1986), with Jeffrey Parness's response, More Stringent Sanctions Under Federal Civil Rule 11: A Reply to Professor Nelken, 75 Geo. L.J. 1937 (1987). Other worthy excursions into the interstices of Rule 11 include Georgene Vairo, Rule 11 Sanctions: Case Law Perspectives and Preventive Measures (1991); American Judicature Society, Rule 11 in Transition (Stephen Burbank, reporter); Lawrence Grosberg, Illusion and Reality in Regulating Lawyer Performance: Rethinking Rule 11, 32 Vill. L. Rev. 575 (1987) (which includes treatment of other sanctioning authority); Judith Maute's use of game theory and sports analogies, together with analysis of Second, Seventh, and Ninth Circuit cases, in an effort to bring rationality to the enterprise, Sporting Theory of Justice: Taming Adversary Zeal with a Logical Sanctions Doctrine, 20 Conn. L. Rev. 7 (1987); and Note, The Dynamics of Rule 11: Preventing Frivolous Litigation by Demanding Professional Responsibility, 61 N.Y.U. L. Rev. 300 (1986) (authored by Neal Klausner). Further academic commentary appears below.

Important studies have also come from the ABA, whose Federal Procedure Committee of its Section on Litigation has published Sanctions — Rule 11 and Other Powers (2d ed. 1988), and the Federal Judicial Center, which has given us Saul Kassin, An Empirical Study of Rule 11 Sanctions (1985).

One preliminary but startling discovery was that only a few judges accounted for a disproportionate number of Rule 11 sanctions. According to Professor Grosberg (and other investigators), supra at 587 n.42, in the first two years of the rule's operation, three federal judges (out of 684) "wrote 14.2 percent of the opinions in which the rule was cited and 12.2 percent of the opinions in which sanctions were imposed."

Rule 11 and related sanctions alarm lawyers for several reasons. For most, having a judge find that they engaged in frivolous or vexatious conduct, no matter how modest the sanction, is disturbing. The court's opinion may appear in the case reports or in the popular or legal press. Client relations may suffer if sanctions are jointly imposed on the lawyer and client, if the sanction undermines the client's cause, or if it requires additional legal expense beyond the sanction itself. In addition, a sanction may be sizeable. Avirgan v. Hull, 932 F.2d 1572 (11th Cir. 1991) (Rule 11 sanctions of more than $1 million); Unioil, Inc. v. E. F. Hutton & Co., 809 F.2d 548 (9th Cir. 1986), cert. denied, 484 U.S. 822 (1987) (Rule 11 sanctions of $294,000, plus counsel fees and expenses of $166,000 as a condition of voluntary dismissal); Brandt v. Schal Associates, 131 F.R.D. 512 (N.D. Ill. 1990) (sanction of $351,000 where unsuccessful RICO claim required the defendant to pay for 3,000 hours of lawyer and paralegal time in a four-year period). Despite these exceptional cases, one study found that the median award level was only about $5,100. Thomas Willging, The Rule 11 Sanctioning Process (1988).

Once a Rule 11 violation is found, a sanction is mandatory. It need not be monetary, though it usually is. In Gaiardo v. Ethyl Corp., 835 F.2d

479 (3d Cir. 1987), the court wrote that sanctions may include warnings, oral reprimands in open court, or written admonition. The court cited one case that ordered the offending lawyers to attend a seminar on federal practice. It also listed dismissal of the case as an additional, if extreme, remedy. See also Pony Express Courier Corp. of America v. Pony Express Delivery Service, 872 F.2d 317 (9th Cir. 1989) (public reprimand a permissible sanction). The fact that an opposing party may not move for sanctions will not prevent the court from imposing them. The rule says that the court "shall" impose sanctions "upon motion or upon its own initiative" if the rule is violated. This eliminates Rule 11 sanctions as a "bargaining chip," doesn't it? Do you see why?

The sanctioning industry assumes that it is possible, with some consistency and fairness, to determine when a case is frivolous. Sanford Levinson, versed not only in law but also in literary theory and hermeneutics, questions the assumption in a tantalizing article that should give prevailing dogma some pause. Sanford Levinson, Frivolous Cases: Do Lawyers Really Know Anything At All?, 24 Osgoode Hall L.J. 353 (1987). Some support for Professor Levinson's skepticism comes from the Ninth Circuit, where the Rule 11 pendulum seems of late to be swinging away from "open season" and toward greater caution. In Operating Engineers Pension Trust v. A-C Co., 859 F.2d 1336 (9th Cir. 1988), the district court imposed a sanction of $10,000. In reversing, Judge Reinhardt cautioned trial judges to "use more restraint" and to avoid inhibiting creative lawyering. He described Rule 11 as an "extraordinary" remedy. He then held that the sanctioned attorney's claims were not only *not* frivolous, they were meritorious! The court noted that this was not the first time that the merits of a sanctioned lawyer's claim eventually prevailed on appeal. In International Shipping Co., S.A. v. Hydra Offshore, Inc., 875 F.2d 388 (2d Cir. 1989), the district court imposed sanctions because the plaintiff had asserted a frivolous theory of jurisdiction. The Second Circuit affirmed the sanctions, even though one judge thought the jurisdictional theory valid.

The first edition of this book, prepared during Rule 11's birth and infancy, contained four pages on the subject under discussion. This edition could contain one hundred pages. But don't worry, it won't. We mean here only to provide an introduction to court-imposed sanctions, which we do mainly through the Supreme Court's opinion in *Cooter & Gell.*

COOTER & GELL v. HARTMARX CORP.
— U.S. —, 110 S. Ct. 2447 (1990)

JUSTICE O'CONNOR delivered the opinion of the Court.

This case presents three issues related to the application of Rule 11 of the Federal Rules of Civil Procedure: whether a district court may impose Rule 11 sanctions on a plaintiff who has voluntarily dismissed his complaint pursuant to Rule 41(a)(1)(i) of the Federal Rules of Civil Procedure; what constitutes the appropriate standard of appellate review of a court's imposition of Rule 11 sanctions; and whether Rule 11 authorizes awards of attorney's fees incurred on appeal of a Rule 11 sanction.*

I

In 1983, Danik, Inc., owned and operated a number of discount men's clothing stores in the Washington, D.C., area. In June 1983, Intercontinental Apparel, a subsidiary of respondent Hartmarx Corp., brought a breach-of-contract action against Danik in the United States District Court for the District of Columbia. Danik, represented by the law firm of Cooter & Gell (petitioner), responded to the suit by filing a counterclaim against Intercontinental, alleging violations of the Robinson-Patman Act. In March 1984, the District Court granted summary judgment for Intercontinental in its suit against Danik, and, in February 1985, a jury returned a verdict for Intercontinental on Danik's counterclaim. Both judgments were affirmed on appeal.

While this litigation was proceeding, petitioner prepared two additional antitrust complaints against Hartmarx and its two subsidiaries, respondents Hart, Schaffner & Marx and Hickey-Freeman Co. One of the complaints, the one giving rise to the Rule 11 sanction at issue in this case, alleged a nationwide conspiracy to fix prices and to eliminate competition through an exclusive retail agent policy and uniform pricing scheme, as well as other unfair competition practices such as resale price maintenance and territorial restrictions.

Petitioner filed the two complaints in November 1983. Respondents moved to dismiss the antitrust complaint at issue, alleging, among other things, that Danik's allegations had no basis in fact. Respondents also moved for sanctions under Rule 11. In opposition to the Rule 11 motion, petitioner filed three affidavits setting forth the prefiling research that supported the allegations in the complaint. In essence, petitioner's research consisted of telephone calls to salespersons in a number of men's clothing stores in New York City, Philadelphia, Baltimore, and Washington, D.C. Petitioner inferred from this research that only one store in each major metropolitan area nationwide sold Hart, Schaffner & Marx suits.

In April 1984, petitioner filed a notice of voluntary dismissal of the complaint, pursuant to Rule 41(a)(1)(i). The dismissal became effective in July 1984, when the District Court granted petitioner's motion to dis-

---

*Because petitioners did not raise the argument that Rule 11 sanctions could only be imposed against the two attorneys who signed the complaint, see Pavelic & LeFlore v. Marvel Entertainment Group, 493 U.S. 120 (1990), either in the courts below or in their petition for certiorari here, we decline to consider it.

pense with notice of dismissal to putative class members. In June 1984, before the dismissal became effective, the District Court heard oral argument on the Rule 11 motion. The District Court took the Rule 11 motion under advisement.

In December 1987, 3½ years after its hearing on the motion and after dismissal of the complaint, the District Court ordered respondents to submit a statement of costs and attorney's fees. Respondents filed a statement requesting $61,917.99 in attorney's fees. Two months later, the District Court granted respondent's motion for Rule 11 sanctions, holding that petitioner's prefiling inquiry was grossly inadequate. Specifically, the District Court found that the allegations in the complaint regarding exclusive retail agency arrangements for Hickey-Freeman clothing were completely baseless because petitioner researched only the availability of Hart, Schaffner & Marx menswear. In addition, the District Court found that petitioner's limited survey of only four Eastern cities did not support the allegation that respondents had exclusive retailer agreements in every major city in the United States. Accordingly, the District Court determined that petitioner violated Rule 11 and imposed a sanction of $21,452.52 against petitioner and $10,701.26 against Danik.

The Court of Appeals for the District of Columbia Circuit affirmed the imposition of Rule 11 sanctions. . . .

II . . .

An interpretation of the current Rule 11 must be guided, in part, by an understanding of the deficiencies in the original version of Rule 11 that led to its revision. The 1938 version of Rule 11 required an attorney to certify by signing the pleading "that to the best of his knowledge, information, and belief there is good ground to support [the pleading]; and that it is not interposed for delay . . . or is signed with intent to defeat the purpose of this rule." An attorney who willfully violated the rule could be "subjected to appropriate disciplinary action." Moreover, the pleading could "be stricken as sham and false and the action [could] proceed as though the pleading had not been served." In operation, the rule did not have the deterrent effect expected by its drafters. The Advisory Committee identified two problems with the old Rule. First, the Rule engendered confusion regarding when a pleading should be struck, what standard of conduct would make an attorney liable to sanctions, and what sanctions were available. Second, courts were reluctant to impose disciplinary measures on attorneys and attorneys were slow to invoke the rule. Vairo, Rule 11: A Critical Analysis, 118 F.R.D. 189, 191 (1988).

To ameliorate these problems, and in response to concerns that abusive litigation practice abounded in the federal courts, the rule was amended in 1983. See Schwarzer, Sanctions Under the New Federal Rule 11 — A Closer Look, 104 F.R.D. 181 (1985). It is now clear that the central purpose of Rule 11 is to deter baseless filings in District Court and thus, consistent with the Rule Enabling Act's grant of authority, streamline the administration and procedure of the federal courts. Rule 11 imposes a duty on attorneys to certify that they have conducted a reasonable inquiry and have determined that any papers filed with the court are well-grounded in fact, legally tenable, and "not interposed for any improper purpose." An attorney who signs the paper without such a substantiated belief "shall" be penalized by "an appropriate sanction." Such a sanction may, but need not, include payment of the other parties' expenses. Although the rule must be read in light of concerns that it will spawn satellite litigation and chill vigorous advocacy, any interpretation must give effect to the rule's central goal of deterrence.

III

We first address the question whether petitioner's dismissal of its antitrust complaint pursuant to Rule 41(a)(1)(i) deprived the District Court of the jurisdiction to award attorney's fees. . . .

Rule 41(a) permits a plaintiff to dismiss an action without prejudice only when he files a notice of dismissal before the defendant files an answer or motion for summary judgment and only if the plaintiff has never previously dismissed an action "based on or including the same claim." Once the defendant has filed a summary judgment motion or answer, the plaintiff may dismiss the action only by stipulation, Rule 41(a)(1)(ii), or by order of the court, "upon such terms and conditions as the court deems proper." Rule 41(a)(2). If the plaintiff invokes Rule 41(a)(1) a second time for an "action based on or including the same claim," the action must be dismissed with prejudice.

Petitioner contends that filing a notice of voluntary dismissal pursuant to this rule automatically deprives a court of jurisdiction over the action, rendering the court powerless to impose sanctions thereafter. Of the Circuit Courts to consider this issue, only the Court of Appeals for the Second Circuit has held that a voluntary dismissal acts as a jurisdictional bar to further Rule 11 proceedings.

The view more consistent with Rule 11's language and purposes, and the one supported by the weight of Circuit authority, is that district courts may enforce Rule 11 even after the plaintiff has filed a notice of dismissal under Rule 41(a)(1). The district court's jurisdiction, invoked by the filing of the underlying complaint, supports consideration of both the merits of the action and the motion for Rule 11 sanctions arising from that filing. As the "violation of Rule 11 is complete when the paper is filed," a voluntary dismissal does not expunge the Rule 11 violation. In order to comply with Rule 11's requirement that a court "shall" impose sanctions "[i]f a pleading, motion, or other paper is signed in violation of this rule," a court must have the authority to consider whether there has been a violation of the signing requirement regardless of the dismissal of the underlying action. In our view, nothing in the language of Rule 41(a)(1)(i), Rule 11, or other statute or Federal Rule terminates a district court's authority to impose sanctions after such a dismissal. . . .

Because a Rule 11 sanction does not signify a District Court's assessment of the legal merits of the complaint, the imposition of such a sanction after a voluntary dismissal does not deprive the plaintiff of his right under Rule 41(a) to dismiss an action without prejudice. "Dismissal without prejudice" is a dismissal that does not "operat[e] as an adjudication upon the merits," and thus does not have a res judicata effect. Even if a district court indicated that a complaint was not legally tenable or factually well founded for Rule 11 purposes, the resulting Rule 11 sanction would nevertheless not preclude the refiling of a complaint. Indeed, even if the Rule 11 sanction imposed by the court were a prohibition against refiling the complaint (assuming that would be an "appropriate sanction" for Rule 11 purposes), the preclusion of refiling would be neither a consequence of the dismissal (which was without prejudice) nor a "term or condition" placed upon the dismissal (which was unconditional), see Rule 41(a)(2). . . .

Both Rule 41(a)(1) and Rule 11 are aimed at curbing abuses of the judicial system, and thus their policies, like their language, are completely compatible. Rule 41(a)(1) limits a litigant's power to dismiss actions, but allows one dismissal without prejudice. Rule 41(a)(1) does not codify any policy that the plaintiff's right to one free dismissal also secures the right to file baseless papers. The filing of complaints, papers, or other motions without taking the necessary care in their preparation is a separate abuse of the judicial system, subject to separate sanction. As noted above, a voluntary dismissal does not eliminate the Rule 11 violation. Baseless filing puts the machinery of justice in motion, burdening courts and individuals alike with needless expense and delay. Even if the careless litigant quickly dismisses the action, the harm triggering Rule 11's concerns has already occurred. Therefore, a litigant who violates Rule 11 merits sanctions even after a dismissal. Moreover, the imposition of such sanctions on abusive litigants is useful to deter such misconduct. If a litigant could purge his violation of Rule 11 merely by taking a dismissal, he would lose all incentive to "stop, think and investigate more carefully before serving and filing papers." . . .

IV

Petitioner further contends that the Court of Appeals did not apply a sufficiently rigorous standard in viewing the District Court's imposition of Rule 11 sanctions. Determining whether an attorney has violated Rule 11 involves a consideration of three types of issues. The court must consider factual questions regarding the nature of the attorney's prefiling inquiry and the factual basis of the pleading or other paper. Legal issues are raised in considering whether a pleading is "warranted by existing law or a good faith argument" for changing the law and whether the attorney's conduct violated Rule 11. Finally, the district court must exercise its discretion to tailor an "appropriate sanction." . . .

Although the Courts of Appeal use different verbal formulas to characterize their standards of review, the scope of actual disagreement is narrow. No dispute exists that the appellate courts should review the district court's selection of a sanction under a deferential standard. In directing the district court to impose an "appropriate" sanction, Rule 11 itself indicates that the district court is empowered to exercise its discretion.

The Circuits also agree that, in the absence of any language to the contrary in Rule 11, courts should adhere to their usual practice of reviewing the district court's finding of facts under a deferential standard. In practice, the "clearly erroneous" standard requires the appellate court to uphold any district court determination that falls within a broad range of permissible conclusions. When an appellate court reviews a district court's factual findings, the abuse of discretion and clearly erroneous standards are indistinguishable: A court of appeals would be justified in concluding that a district court had abused its discretion in making a factual finding only if the finding were clearly erroneous.

The scope of disagreement over the appropriate standard of review can thus be confined to a narrow issue: whether the court of appeals must defer to the district court's legal conclusions in Rule 11 proceedings. A number of factors have led the majority of Circuits, as well as a number of commentators, to conclude that appellate courts should review all aspects of a district court's imposition of Rule 11 sanctions under a deferential standard.

The Court has long noted the difficulty of distinguishing between legal and factual issues. Making such distinctions is particularly difficult in the Rule 11 context. Rather than mandating an inquiry into purely legal questions, such as whether the attorney's legal argument was correct, the rule requires a court to consider issues rooted in factual determinations. For example, to determine whether an attorney's prefiling inquiry was reasonable, a court must consider all the circumstances of a case. An inquiry that is unreasonable when an attorney has months to prepare a complaint may be reasonable when he has only a few days before the statute of limitations runs. In considering whether a complaint was supported by fact and law "to the best of the signer's knowledge, information, and belief," a court must make some assessment of the signer's credibility. Issues involving credibility are normally considered factual matters. The considerations involved in the Rule 11 context are similar to those involved in determining negligence, which is generally reviewed deferentially. Familiar with the issues and litigants, the district court is better situated than the court of appeals to marshall the pertinent facts and apply the fact-dependent legal standard mandated by Rule 11. Of course, this standard would not preclude the appellate court's correction of a district court's legal errors, e.g., determining that Rule 11 sanctions could be imposed upon the signing attorney's law firm, see Pavelic & LeFlore v. Marvel Entertainment Group, 493 U.S. 120 (1989), or relying on a materially incorrect view of the relevant law in determining that a pleading was not "warranted by existing law or a good faith argument" for changing the law. An appellate court would be justified in concluding that, in making such errors, the district court abused its discretion. "[I]f a district court's findings rest on an erroneous view of the law, they may be set aside on that basis."

Pierce v. Underwood, 487 U.S. 552 (1988), strongly supports applying a unitary abuse of discretion standard to all aspects of a Rule 11 proceeding. In *Pierce,* the Court held a District Court's determination under the Equal Access to Justice Act (EAJA), 28 U.S.C. §2412(d) (1982 ed.), that "the position of the United States was substantially justified" should be reviewed for an abuse of discretion. As a position is "substantially justified" if it "has a reasonable basis in law and fact," EAJA requires an inquiry similar to the Rule 11 inquiry as to whether a pleading is "well grounded in fact" and legally tenable. Although the EAJA and Rule 11 are not completely analogous, the reasoning in *Pierce* is relevant for determining the Rule 11 standard of review.

Two factors the Court found significant in *Pierce* are equally pertinent here. First, the Court indicated that " 'as a matter of the sound administration of justice,' " deference was owed to the " 'judicial actor ... better positioned than another to decide the issue in question.' " Because a determination whether a legal position is "substantially justified" depends greatly on factual determinations, the Court reasoned that the district court was "better positioned" to make such factual determinations. A district court's ruling that a litigant's position is factually well grounded and legally tenable for Rule 11 purposes is similarly fact-specific. *Pierce* also concluded that district court's rulings on legal issues should be reviewed deferentially. According to the Court, review of legal issues under a de novo standard would require the courts of appeals to invest time and energy in the unproductive task of determining "not what the law now is, but what the Government was substantially justified in believing it to have been." Likewise, an appellate court reviewing legal issues in the Rule 11 context would be required to determine whether, at the time the attorney filed the pleading or other paper, his legal argument would have appeared plausible. Such determinations "will either fail to produce the normal law-clarifying benefits that come from an appellate decision on a question of law, or else will strangely distort the appellate process" by establishing circuit law in "a most peculiar, secondhanded fashion."

Second, *Pierce* noted that only deferential review gave the district court the necessary flexibility to resolve questions involving " 'multifarious, fleeting, special, narrow facts that utterly resist generalization.' " The question whether the government has taken a "substantially justified" position under all the circumstances involves the consideration of unique factors that are "little susceptible . . . of useful generalization." The issues involved in determining whether an attorney has violated Rule 11 likewise involve "fact-intensive, close calls." Contrary to petitioner's contentions, Pierce v. Underwood is not distinguishable on the ground that sanctions under Rule 11 are mandatory: that sanctions "shall" be imposed when a violation is found does not have any bearing on how to review the question whether the attorney's conduct violated Rule 11.

Rule 11's policy goals also support adopting an abuse-of-discretion standard. The district court is best acquainted with the local bar's litigation practices and thus best situated to determine when a sanction is warranted to serve Rule 11's goal of specific and general deterrence. Deference to the determination of courts on the front lines of litigation will enhance these courts' ability to control the litigants before them. Such deference will streamline the litigation process by freeing appellate courts from the duty of reweighing evidence and reconsidering facts already weighed and considered by the district court; it will also discourage litigants from pursuing marginal appeals, thus reducing the amount of satellite litigation.

Although district courts' identification of what conduct violates Rule 11 may vary, see Schwarzer, Rule 11 Revisited, 101 Harv. L. Rev. 1013, 1015-1017 (1988); Note, A Uniform Approach to Rule 11 Sanctions, 97 Yale L.J. 901 (1988), some variation in the application of a standard based on reasonableness is inevitable. "Fact-bound resolutions cannot be made uniform through appellate review, de novo or otherwise." An appellate court's review of whether a legal position was reasonable or plausible enough under the circumstances is unlikely to establish clear guidelines for lower courts; nor will it clarify the underlying principles of law. . . .

V

Finally, the Court of Appeals held that respondents were entitled to be reimbursed for attorney's fees they had incurred in defending their award on appeal. . . .

Respondents interpret the last sentence of Rule 11 as extending the scope of the sanction to cover any expenses, including fees on appeal, incurred "because of the filing." In this case, respondents argue, they would have incurred none of their appellate expenses had petitioner's lawsuit not been filed. This line of reasoning would lead to the conclusion that expenses incurred "because of" a baseless filing extend indefinitely. Such an interpretation of the rule is overbroad. We believe Rule 11 is more sensibly understood as permitting an award only of those expenses directly caused by the filing, logically, those at the trial level. A plaintiff's filing requires the defendant to take the necessary steps to defend against the suit in district court; if the filing was baseless, attorneys' fees incurred in that defense were triggered by the Rule 11 violation. If the district court imposes Rule 11 sanctions on the plaintiff, and the plaintiff appeals, the expenses incurred in defending the award on appeal are directly caused by the district court's sanction and the appeal of that sanction, not by the plaintiff's initial filing in district court.

The Federal Rules of Apellate Procedure place a natural limit on Rule 11's scope. On appeal, the litigants' conduct is governed by Federal Rule of Appellate Procedure 38, which provides: "If a court of appeals shall determine that an appeal is frivolous, it may award just damages and single or double costs to the appellee." If the appeal of a Rule 11 sanction is itself frivolous, Rule 38 gives appellate courts ample authority to award expenses. Indeed, because the district court has broad discretion to impose Rule 11 sanctions, appeals of such sanctions may frequently be frivolous. If the appeal is not frivolous under this standard, Rule 38 does not require the appellee to pay the appellant's attorney's fees. Respondent's interpretation of Rule 11 would give a district court the authority to award attorney's fees to the appellee even when the appeal would not be sanctioned under the appellate rules. To avoid this somewhat anomalous result, Rules 11 and 38 are better read together as allowing expenses incurred on appeal to be shifted onto appellants only when those expenses are caused by a frivolous appeal, and not merely because a Rule 11 sanction upheld on appeal can ultimately be traced to a baseless filing in district court.

Limiting Rule 11's scope in this manner accords with the policy of not discouraging meritorious appeals. If appellants were routinely compelled to shoulder the appellees' attorney's fees, valid challenges to district court decisions would be discouraged. The knowledge that, after an unsuccessful appeal of a Rule 11 sanction, the district court that originally imposed the sanction would also decide whether the appellant should pay his opponent's attorney's fee would be likely to chill all but the bravest litigants from taking an appeal. Moreover, including appellate attorney's fees in a Rule 11 sanction might have the undesirable effect of encouraging additional satellite litigation. For example, if a district court included appellate attorney's fees in the Rule 11 sanction on remand, the losing party might again appeal the amount of the award.

It is possible that disallowing an award of appellate attorney's fees under Rule 11 would discourage litigants from defending the award on appeal when appellate expenses are likely to exceed the amount of the sanction. There is some doubt whether this proposition is empirically correct. The courts of appeals have ample authority to protect the beneficiaries of Rule 11 sanctions by awarding damages and single or double costs under Rule 38 — which they may do, as we have noted, when the appellant had no reasonable prospect of meeting the difficult standard of abuse of discretion. Beyond that protection, however, the risk of expending the value of one's award in the course of defending it is a natural concomitant of the American Rule, i.e., that "the prevailing litigant is ordinarily not entitled to collect a reasonable attorneys' fee from the loser." *Alyeska Pipeline Service Co. v. Wilderness Society,* 421 U.S. 240, 247 (1975). Whenever damages awards at the trial level are small, a successful plaintiff will have less incentive to defend the award on appeal. As Rule 11 is not a fee-shifting statute, the policies for allowing district courts to require the losing party to pay appellate, as well as district court attorneys' fees, are not applicable. "A movant under Rule 11 has no entitlement to fees or any other sanction, and the contrary view can only breed appellate litigation." American Judicature Society [page 362 supra] at 49. . . .

JUSTICE STEVENS, concurring in part and dissenting in part. . . .

In theory, Rule 11 and Rule 41(a)(1) should work in tandem. When a complaint is withdrawn under Rule 41(a)(1), the merits of that complaint are not an appropriate area of further inquiry for the federal court. . . .

The Court holds, however, that a voluntary dismissal does not eliminate the predicate for a Rule 11 violation because a frivolous complaint that is withdrawn burdens "courts and individuals alike with needless expense and delay." That assumption is manifestly incorrect with respect to courts. The filing of a frivolous complaint which is voluntarily withdrawn imposes a burden on the court only if the notation of an additional civil proceeding on the court's docket sheet can be said to constitute a burden. By definition, a voluntary dismissal under Rule 41(a)(1) means that the court has not had to consider the factual allegations of the complaint or ruled on a motion to dismiss its legal claims.

The Court's observation that individuals are burdened, even if correct, is irrelevant. Rule 11 is designed to deter parties from abusing judicial resources, not from filing complaints. Whatever additional costs in reputation or legal expenses the defendant might incur, on top of those that are the product of being in a dispute,[1] are likely to be either minimal or non-compensable.[2] More fundamentally, the fact that the filing of a complaint imposes costs on a defendant should be of no concern to the rulemakers if the complaint does not impose any costs on the judiciary:

---

1. It is telling that the primary injury that the respondent points to is the injury to its reputation caused by the public attention that lawsuit attracted.

2. In those rare cases in which the defendant properly incurs great costs in preparing a motion to dismiss a frivolous complaint, he can lock in the right to file a Rule 11 motion by answering the complaint and making his motion to dismiss in the form of a Rule 12(c) motion for judgment on the pleadings.

the Rules Enabling Act does not give us authority to create a generalized federal common law of malicious prosecution divorced from concerns with the efficient and just processing of cases in federal court. The only result of the Court's interpretation will be to increase the frequency of Rule 11 motions and decrease that of voluntary dismissals. . . .

Despite the changes that have taken place at the bar since I left the active practice 20 years ago, I still believe that most lawyers are wise enough to know that their most precious asset is their professional reputation. Filing unmeritorious pleadings inevitably tarnishes that asset. Those who do not understand this simple truth can be dealt with in appropriate disciplinary proceedings, state law actions for malicious prosecution or abuse of process, or, in extreme cases, contempt proceedings. It is an unnecessary waste of judicial resources and an unwarranted perversion of the Federal Rules to hold such lawyers liable for Rule 11 sanctions in actions in federal court.

I respectfully dissent.

You Are Entering Sanction City, Population Growing

Robert Frost tells of a walk he took in an open field. When he stepped on the upright teeth of an unseen hoe, its handle flew up and hit him in the forehead. The moral he drew: "The first tool I stepped on turned into a weapon."

Is Rule 11 a tool or a weapon? Critics argue that the rule has created a mini-industry of costly satellite litigation, detracting from the main event, and that it encourages the very abuses it was designed to stop. Rule 11 motions to sanction lawyers for filing frivolous Rule 11 motions are not uncommon. Efforts to dilute or even repeal Rule 11 seem constantly under way. The rule is a favorite topic at bar meetings; many believe it will be modified but not significantly.

The rule has spawned thousands of contested applications and appeals. The Supreme Court has so far resolved five Rule 11 questions. Three appear in *Cooter & Gell*. A fourth question was whether all firm lawyers, or only the one who signed an offending paper, could be sanctioned. Pavelic & LeFlore v. Marvel Entertainment Group, 493 U.S. 120 (1990), held that only a signator may be sanctioned. The Court relied on the language of the rule, which literally authorizes sanctions only against "the person who signed" the paper. Is this the right result as a policy matter? Will a firm take greater care if all lawyers (or all partners) are potentially liable? The issue of vicarious liability for another lawyer's defaults arises again in the material on malpractice (page 628 infra).

The fifth Rule 11 issue so far addressed by the Supreme Court arose in Business Guides, Inc. v. Chromatic Communications Enterprises, Inc.,

111 S. Ct. 922, 927-933 (1991). Resolving an ambiguity in the rule and a split among the circuits, a bare majority of the Court held that Rule 11 permits sanctions against a represented party who signs an offending paper and that, as with lawyers, the standard for party liability should be objective. The Court purported to interpret the "plain language of the Rule," while acknowledging that "the legal inquiry that can reasonably be expected from a party may vary from case to case." Quoting the lower court, the Court said that "what is objectively reasonable for a client may differ from what is objectionably reasonable for an attorney."

One consequence of *Business Guides* is potentially enormous. If counsel and client can be subjected to sanction, what will a motion against both do to their relationship? It may lead to finger-pointing and recrimination. It may lead to revelation of client confidences in self-defense. Brandt v. Schal Assocs., 131 F.R.D. 512 (N.D. Ill. 1990). It may even create a conflict of interest that defeats continued representation. Might these disruptions inspire a movant's very strategy?

In *Business Guides*, the client was required to sign an application for a restraining order later found to violate Rule 11. The Court said that "[e]ven if Business Guides had not been required to sign the TRO application but did so voluntarily, the language of Rule 11 would still require that the signature satisfy the certification requirement." 111 S. Ct. at 929. A lawyer, then, gets a kind of "insurance" if he has a client cosign a paper, doesn't he? Yet it would seem that lawyers have an ethical obligation to prevent clients from signing a paper whenever the client's signature is not required. That lessens the client's exposure. In any event, must a lawyer advise a client on the potential Rule 11 liability each time the client is asked to sign a paper that will be filed in court? What else should the lawyer do to protect the client from risk? What should the lawyer do to protect the lawyer against liability for the client's errors? Are these precautions consistent?

Whether a paper violates Rule 11 will be a highly fact-based inquiry. In Thomas v. Capital Securities Services, Inc., 836 F.2d 866, 875-876 (5th Cir. 1988), the en banc court tried to account for the factual variations this way:

> The determination of whether a reasonable inquiry into the facts has been made in a case will, of course, be dependent upon the particular facts; however, the district court may consider such factors as the time available to the signer for investigation; the extent of the attorney's reliance upon his client for the factual support for the document; the feasibility of a prefiling investigation; whether the signing attorney accepted the case from another member of the bar or forwarding attorney; the complexity of the factual and legal issues; and the extent to which development of the factual circumstances underlying the claim requires discovery. As to the determination of whether a reasonable inquiry into the law has been made, a district court may consider the time available to the attorney to prepare the document; the plausibility of

the legal view contained in the document; the pro se status of a litigant; and the complexity of the legal and factual issues raised.

See also Kraemer v. Grant County, 892 F.2d 686 (7th Cir. 1990).

Rule 11 is not a fee-shifting statute. As the Court wrote in *Business Guides,* 111 S. Ct. at 934:

> Rule 11 sanctions are not tied to the outcome of litigation; the relevant inquiry is whether a specific filing was, if not successful, at least well founded. Nor do sanctions shift the entire cost of litigation; they shift only the cost of a discrete event. Finally, the Rule calls only for "an appropriate sanction" — attorneys' fees are not mandated.

The party moving for Rule 11 sanctions has a duty to mitigate its damages and may lose the motion entirely if it does not. *Thomas,* supra; Brooks v. Allison Division of General Motors Corp., 874 F.2d 489 (7th Cir. 1989). The Fifth Circuit said in *Thomas* that "the district court should utilize the sanction that furthers the purposes of Rule 11 and is the least severe sanction adequate to such purpose." One mitigating factor is the sanctioned party's ability to pay. Jackson v. Law Firm of O'Hara, Ruberg, Osborne & Taylor, 875 F.2d 1224 (6th Cir. 1989).

Assume a lawyer files a paper that does not violate Rule 11. Later she learns facts or discovers legal principles that, had she known them earlier, would have prevented her from filing the particular paper. Does Rule 11 now require the lawyer to withdraw or change the paper? In *Thomas,* the Fifth Circuit said it did not, although other sanctioning rules may. Rule 11 was like "a snapshot," not a motion picture. See also Samuels v. Wilder, 906 F.2d 272 (7th Cir. 1990) (same). Other courts have disagreed. See Herron v. Jupiter Transportation Co., 858 F.2d 332 (6th Cir. 1988) (continuing duty). How will the Supreme Court decide this issue?

One question the Court will soon decide is whether a district judge can impose Rule 11 sanctions in a case in which she lacks subject matter jurisdiction. Willy v. Coastal Corp., 915 F.2d 965 (5th Cir. 1990), cert. granted, 111 S. Ct. 2824 (1991). *Willy* was brought in state court. The defendant erroneously removed it to federal court. It had to be remanded because the district court lacked jurisdiction. Sanctions, however, were imposed not against the removing defendant but against the plaintiff for conduct occurring before remand.

Does Rule 11 Unduly Inhibit Civil Rights Lawyers?

The Advisory Committee's note to amended Rule 11 warned that the rule "is not intended to chill an attorney's enthusiasm or creativity in pursuing factual or legal theories." But "[t]he reality of large fee-shifting awards under the amended rule and the routine resort to attorney's fees as the sanction of choice seriously undermine that goal," writes Melissa Nelken, "particularly in the area of civil rights." Has the Chancellor Shot Himself in the Foot? Looking for a Middle Ground on Rule 11 Sanctions, 41 Hastings L.J. 383 (1990). In Chilling Problems in Rule 11 Sanctions, 74 Geo. L.J. 1313 (1986), Nelken notes that "[a]lthough civil rights cases accounted for only 7.6% of the civil filings between 1983 and 1985, 22.3% of the rule 11 cases involved civil rights claims." Stephen Burbank reports that in one year in the Third Circuit "civil rights plaintiffs, their lawyers, or both were sanctioned at a rate (47.1%) far higher than the rate for plaintiffs as a whole (15.9%), and higher still than the rate for plaintiffs in non-civil rights cases (8.45%)." These numbers are for all plaintiffs, counselled and pro se. For counselled plaintiffs only, the corresponding numbers are 45.5 percent, 13.75 percent, and 8.7 percent. Burbank, The Underlying Assumptions of the Federal Rules of Civil Procedure, 137 U. Pa. L. Rev. 1925 (1989).

Carl Tobias, in Rule 11 and Civil Rights Litigation, 37 Buffalo L. Rev. 485 (1988-1989), writes that "the resource constraints of civil rights lawyers make them peculiarly susceptible to the rule's potential chilling effect." He adds that "one dissenting circuit judge aptly captured the disturbing implications of this [situation] by proclaiming 'no information until litigation, but no litigation without information.'" Johnson v. United States, 788 F.2d 845, 856 (2d Cir.) (Pratt, J., dissenting), cert. denied, 479 U.S. 914 (1986). Professor Tobias contends that the very nature of civil rights claims makes them vulnerable to sanctions:

> Certain characteristics intrinsic to many civil rights actions can leave impressions that the legal inquiries which preceded their filing were insufficient. Instructive illustrations are afforded by the substantial number of civil rights suits that attempt to assert new or comparatively untested theories of law. These concepts are at the cutting edge of legal development, which means that they are difficult to conceptualize and substantiate, that discovery can be essential to drafting a very specific complaint or to articulating a precise theory of the case, and that the concepts, once formulated, look nontraditional and even implausible — all of which can contribute to appearances of inadequacy.

Proposed Amendments to Rule 11

Rule 11 is currently under review by the various groups charged with studying and making recommendations for changes in the Federal Rules of Civil Procedure. No change is likely to be effective before December 1993 at the earliest. Among the proposals of the Standing Committee on

Rules of Practice and Procedure of the Judicial Conference of the United States are the following, 7 Lawyers Manual on Prof. Conduct 309 (Oct. 9, 1991):

1. creation of a continuing duty to withdraw papers or abandon positions on learning of their lack of merit;
2. provision for lawyers to make factual allegations on information and belief when appropriate without risking sanction;
3. overruling *Pavelic & LeFlore* so that sanctions may be imposed on a firm, lawyers at a firm other than a signator, or co-counsel;
4. limiting *Business Guides,* a restriction on monetary awards against a represented party to those situations in which the party acts for an improper purpose, such as to harass or cause needless delay or expense;
5. creation of a "safe harbor" provision that requires an adversary to give notice of a Rule 11 violation, thereby allowing the alleged violator to withdraw the offending allegation or paper before a Rule 11 motion may be filed;
6. retention of a court's power, on notice, to impose sanctions on its own initiative, with no "safe harbor" protection. But, partly overruling *Cooter & Gell,* monetary sanctions would not be allowed where notice follows settlement or voluntary discontinuance;
7. authority in the court to award a successful party expenses and counsel fees for a Rule 11 motion; and
8. a requirement that sanctions imposed after motion be accompanied, if requested, by recitation of the conduct or circumstances justifying them.

Concluding Words from Archilochus

Speaking 2600 years before Rule 11, the lyric poet said: "The fox knows many things, but the hedgehog knows one great thing." How shall we criticize Rule 11, as a fox or a hedgehog? Should we, like the fox, concentrate on the details in an effort to determine which ones will produce the best sanctioning regime or best express the drafters' intent? Or should we ask the hedgehog's question: Do we, in the long run, fundamentally damage advocacy and the attorney-client relationship — without commensurate gain — by giving judges any authority objectively to grade a lawyer's performance on pain of embarrassment and financial loss? Archilochus was obviously biased in favor of the hedgehog; but then he also said that "old women should not seek to be perfumed." So what did he know, anyway?

E.   DILATORY TACTICS

THE WASHINGTON MONTHLY
Sept. 1979, at 10

[A lawyer who once practiced with a large Washington firm told the editor-in-chief of the Washington Monthly that] a major corporate client came to his firm with an antitrust problem. The firm's advice was that the problem was hopeless in the sense that the client was ultimately doomed to lose. But the case could be stretched out for as long as ten years. Would the client be prepared to pay the $500,000 to $1,000,000 in annual legal fees that delay would require? Of course. Here is a client who knows he's wrong and whose law firm knows he's wrong. Yet they are both willing to make the government spend millions over ten years to win a case that they know it deserves to win now.

It is often charged that lawyers use delay as a pressure tactic to win or favorably settle lawsuits. In this section we consider the ethics of delay and other "indirect" strategies for gaining legal advantage. By "indirect" strategies, we refer to conduct whose primary purpose is to avoid a contest on "the merits" of a dispute through concentration on collateral issues.

Let us consider an often-cited example. Marian Small is injured in a car accident. She sues the driver, who is defended by a lawyer retained by the driver's insurer. Small is in need of a quick recovery. She has no real savings and sick leave will only cover three weeks' pay. Her medical bills, only a portion of which are insured, are mounting as are other incidental expenses. She asks her lawyer for a loan. Although he is willing to make one because he anticipates a recovery from which she will be able to repay him, the Model Code and Model Rules forbid such loans. See DR 5-103(B) and Model Rule 1.8(e). (See page 179 supra.)

Small senses a subtle pressure from her lawyer to be receptive to a settlement. Her lawyer, after all, is working on a contingent fee arrangement. Delay in settlement increases his uncompensated time in the case. On the other hand, quick settlement, even for less than the case may be "worth," will yield the lawyer a fee and free up time for other cases.

Small's lawyer tells her that if the matter goes to trial, and she wins, she will be entitled to prejudgment interest on the amount of the recovery, but that the interest rate allowed in Small's state is only 6 percent, at a time when the prime rate is 9 percent. Consequently, the lawyer explains, from the insurance company's point of view, it may literally "pay" to delay settlement as long as possible since the company will be able to invest the money at a substantially greater return than it will have to pay in prejudgment interest. Small asks whether the company has any pressure to settle because of the legal costs it incurs in continuing to litigate. Small's lawyer explains that the company is handling the litigation in-house, through a salaried lawyer, and so its costs are comparatively low and are, in any event, tax deductible.

Small's lawyer also tells her that the state court in which her case is pending has a lengthy civil trial calendar so that even when the case is ready for trial, it may take a couple of years to be called.

The insurance company lawyer is aware of all these pressures on Small and of the ways in which pretrial maneuvers in discovery will, along with the systemic delay, postpone Small's recovery. She does her best to put off judgment day as long as possible by, among other things, taking advantage of every procedural right the state's rules offer a litigant.

Is any of this conduct by the insurance company's lawyer unethical? Is it the insurance company's fault that the system is backed up? Doesn't the insurance company have a right to take advantage of all of the procedural and discovery devices that may increase its chances at trial, even though these take a lot of time and time works to the disadvantage of the plaintiff? After all, the insurance company is not a charitable organization. It has a responsibility to conserve its assets. In making a settlement offer early in a litigation, isn't it well within propriety for the insurer to factor in the plaintiff's need for funds and the effect of the prospect of delay on the plaintiff's willingness and need to settle? If so, isn't the insurance company's lawyer entitled to assist it in using all such available leverage? Are there any limits?

Close on the heels of Rule 11 is the issue of improper delay. Dilatory tactics may not only violate Rule 11 or other rules, they may also be unethical. Indeed, some of the language of Rules 3.1 and 4.4 echoes language in Rule 11. Rule 3.2 appears at first blush to go beyond Rule 11. It says that "A lawyer shall make reasonable efforts to expedite litigation consistent with the interests of the client."

Do the last seven words make the rule meaningless? If delay is in the client's interest, the lawyer has no duty to expedite. If delay is not in the client's interest, the lawyer has a duty to expedite because of the duty of diligence (Rule 1.3). The comment to Rule 3.2 seems beside the point. Where the rule speaks about efforts to expedite litigation, the comment talks about the impropriety of tactics that delay it. But can't a lawyer refrain from the latter without pursuing the former? How is your interpretation of the rule influenced by the fact that a draft referred to the client's "legitimate interests?"

It's clear, isn't it, that the texts of and comments to Rules 3.1, 3.2, and 4.4 are ambivalent about the propriety of delay? They appear to require expedition and abjure delay, but they contain loopholes. Adjectives and adverbs ("primarily," "merely," "substantial purpose") allow room for dilatory tactics so long as delay is not the actor's sole purpose. By contrast,

Rule 11 says that a lawyer's signature on a paper certifies that the paper is "not interposed for *any* improper purpose, such as . . . to cause *unnecessary* delay or *needless* increase in the cost of litigation." (Emphasis added.) Is this language more demanding? Recall the division over whether Rule 11's "improper purpose" language employs an objective or subjective test (page 361 supra). The former would reach more conduct but also punish lawyers who resort to unreasonable tactics in good faith. Can you square the use of an objective standard with the word "improper?" If so, would that be the interpretation you would choose as a matter of policy?

Legislative History

As with other rules, Rules 3.1 and 3.2 went through several changes during the debate over the Model Rules. Here is the text of Rule 3.3 in the January 1980 draft (the precursor to Rules 3.1 and 3.2 in the final document). How does it differ from the provisions that succeeded it?

RULE 3.3   Expediting Litigation

(a) A lawyer shall make every effort consistent with the legitimate interests of the client to expedite litigation. Realizing financial or other benefit from otherwise improper delay in litigation is not a legitimate interest of the client. A lawyer shall not engage in any procedure or tactic having no substantial purpose other than delay or increasing the cost of litigation to another party.

(b) Except as stated in paragraph (c), a lawyer shall bring or defend a proceeding, or assert or controvert an issue therein, only when a lawyer acting in good faith would conclude that there is a reasonable basis for doing so.

(c) A lawyer for a criminal accused may so defend the proceeding that the prosecution is required to establish every element of a charge according to the governing standard of proof.

Why do you suppose the ABA deleted the words "legitimate," "good faith," and "reasonable"?

F. HARDBALL

"Hardball" is a recent addition to the bar's lexicon and the debate about its behavior. Along with ancillary businesses (page 740 infra) and marketing (page 785 infra), the use of "hardball" tactics in litigation and elsewhere is seen to betoken a decline in professionalism. The opposite of "hardball," apparently, is "civility." Committees and commissions nation-wide have called for a "return" to civility, the assumption being that it was a place lawyers once made their home. See the report of the Committee on Civility of the Seventh Federal Judicial Circuit, summarized at 7 Lawyers Manual on Prof. Conduct 127 (May 8, 1991).

Lisa Belkin
BARE-KNUCKLES LITIGATION JARS MANY IN DALLAS
N.Y. Times, May 13, 1988, at B6, col. 3

There is a story making the rounds here of the businessman seeking a lawyer to handle his multimillion-dollar lawsuit. He went from one plush office suite to the next, giving written psychological tests to the city's best lawyers.

His goal: to find the most aggressive, most persistent, most take-no-prisoners law firm in town. He is now a client of Bickel & Brewer.

John Bickel, 39 years old, and William Brewer, 36, opened their firm four years ago and quickly developed quite a reputation. Asked to describe themselves, they use words like "hard working," "committed" and "intense." Their critics use "obnoxious" and "dirty players."

The credo of lawyers as gentlemen began to fade across the country years ago, but lingers strongly in Southern cities like Dallas. Firms like Thompson & Knight, which celebrated its centennial last year, and Strasburger & Price wear their manners with pride.

'JUST ISN'T DONE IN DALLAS'

"Being purposefully disagreeable, that just isn't done in Dallas," said Michael Joplin, the Dallas Bar Association's president, who is a Strasburger partner. "This has never been a town where lawyers were mean to each other."

But there are signs of change, he said. For the first time, the bar last year published a code of professional courtesy. "Dallas lawyers conduct themselves as gentlemen," Mr. Joplin said. "But maybe younger people don't know that."

The most common complaint about Bickel is that its 25 lawyers prolong proceedings, making the opposition's ordeal as expensive and tiring as possible. Such accusations resulted in a $15,000 sanction last month against a Bickel & Brewer client. It was the second sanction levied in a year.

"The reputation they're developing, whether deserved or not, is that they're behaving in a fashion that is not the Dallas way," said Charles L. Babcock, of Jackson, Walker, Winstead, Cantwell & Miller. "Dallas lawyers are gentlemen to each other. These two act like New York lawyers."

SNEER TAKEN AS COMPLIMENT

Although said with a sneer, that description is taken as a compliment over on Ross Avenue at the mauve and gray offices of Bickel & Brewer. "New York lawyers are the sharpest in the country," Mr. Brewer said. "We want to play in that league."

In fact, Bickel & Brewer opened a New York office last year, at Park Avenue and 57th Street and raised starting salaries to $75,000 — equal to top New York firms and $20,000 higher than a Dallas starting salary.

"We're going to build the best firm on the backs of the best people," said Mr. Brewer. "But first we have to get their attention."

Attention is something they are getting. Mr. Bickel grew up in Houston, studied at West Point and S.M.U. Law School, then spent three years as head prosecutor and one as head defense counsel for the Army.

Mr. Brewer was reared in Baldwin, L.I., and graduated from St. John's University, the Albany Law School and New York University. He joined the New York Telephone company in the period of deregulation.

MOCK COURTROOM IN OFFICES

In 1984 they formed their own firm, specializing in large-scale litigation. Their clients include the M Bank of Dallas, the Texas city of Garland, MCI Telecommunications Corporation, NYNEX and the New York Republican State Committee. They average healthy billings of $300,000 per attorney, Mr. Brewer said. Their fees are considered steep by many, at up to $250,000 for one-shot clients.

At the center of the firm's philosophy and its offices is a fully equipped mock courtroom. Here, the firm's lawyers test cases and prepare witnesses with a run-through of every major trial. A mock jury is selected from the Dallas telephone book. The jury's posttrial analysis is videotaped for partners' analysis.

The firm's witness preparations have become an issue in actual trials with opponents saying they are too well rehearsed.

Even more controversial is the firm's approach to pretrial depositions. The $15,000 sanction was levied in response to transcript testimony presented to a state judge by Michael Lynn, a partner for Akin Gump Strauss Hauer & Feld. In an accompanying memorandum, Mr. Lynn charged that Bickel & Brewer "witnesses have been coached in a technique to attempt to evade questions, feign ignorance and, in general, to obstruct the deposition process."

In testimony quoted in the complaint and reprinted by The Texas Lawyer was an exchange between an Akin Gump associate and a Bickel & Brewer client:

Attorney: When did you review those documents?
Witness: What do you mean by "when"?
Attorney: The documents that were reviewed, where were they located?
Witness: They were located . . . what do you mean by "where"?

Mr. Brewer says he encourages witnesses to challenge deposition questions. "We tell them to interrogate the interrogator," he said. "The question 'Did you review the document?'" Mr. Bickel said "could mean anything from acknowledging the existence of the document to memorizing it."

Litigation lawyers say it is common for attorneys to urge clients to say as little as possible at a trial. But several took issue with Bickel & Brewer's decision. "People draw their lines different places," said Rod Phelan, a partner with Baker & Botts. "Based on what I read in that transcript, I darn sure wouldn't have drawn it where they did."

Bickel & Brewer appealed the sanctions and filed a cross-motion for sanctions against Akin Gump. "This is round one of 15 rounds," said Mr. Bickel.

Bickel & Brewer recently won a temporary injunction against a software manufacturer accused of theft of trade secrets. The hearing lasted 11 weeks. The average temporary injunction hearing lasts three to 10 days.

Shortly after the injunction was granted, the defendant, Incepts Inc. of Dallas, filed for bankruptcy protection. Chuck Anglin, Incepts' president, said his company's legal fees were $1.8 million and this year's profits were expected to be $2 million. Jones, Day, Reavis & Pogue, Incepts' attorneys, have withdrawn from the case because of the company's inability to pay its bills.

Mr. Bickel and Mr. Brewer deny they intended to drive Incepts to bankruptcy. They also deny they have a manual detailing such tricks as spilling coffee on the paper-laden table at a deposition or arriving late to aggravate opposing counsel. Mr. Brewer said his most prodigious attorneys rarely bill more than 180 hours a month, not the 300 that many rivals suggest.

The partners attribute the attacks to professional jealousy. They say their aggressiveness wins cases and attracts clients. In four years, Mr. Brewer said, his firm has not lost "a major case."

"We were looking for intelligent, aggressive pursuit of a lawsuit," said Francis S. Webster 3d, chief financial officer for the Continuum Company, Inc., the Dallas concern that defeated Incepts. "And we got it."

Some say Bickel & Brewer's approach may backfire. "We all live in a community of lawyers," Mr. Phelan said. "We get our business from other lawyers. They've got to learn to tone things down."

What do you think of Mr. Phelan's point? For another example of hardball we turn to the litigation over the Dalkon Shield.*

Beginning in 1971, the A. H. Robins Company sold 4.5 million Dalkon Shields as intrauterine birth control devices. Sales were halted in the mid-1970s, although Robins did not begin a recall campaign until 1984. Sales were made in 80 countries. About 2.2 million Shields were implanted in the United States alone.

Thousands of wearers of the Dalkon Shield have reported stillbirths, babies with major congenital defects, punctured uteri, forced hysterectomies, and sterilization from infection. The term pelvic inflammatory disease (PID) is used to describe the effect of the Shield on many wearers. PID is caused by the Shield's multifilament tail, which tends to "wick," a phenomenon that can place deadly bacteria in the uterus. About 20 women who wore the Shield died as a result of PID. Robins was aware of the wicking tendency before marketing the Shield but didn't reveal its knowledge. After the Shield was marketed, information from some physicians and others confirmed the wicking tendency and the risk of infection but physicians were not generally notified.

About 5 percent of Shield wearers became pregnant, although the device was advertised as creating only a 1.1 percent risk of pregnancy.

As of mid-1985 more than 14,000 lawsuits had been filed against the A. H. Robins Company arising out of the use of the Shield. New ones were being filed at the rate of about 15 a day. As of mid-1985, Robins and Aetna Life, its insurer, had paid out $378.3 million in settlements, $107.3 million in legal expenses, and $24.8 million in jury verdicts. As is well known, Robins eventually declared bankruptcy. Here is how Mr. Mintz describes Robins's discovery:

Morton Mintz
AT ANY COST: CORPORATE GREED, WOMEN
AND THE DALKON SHIELD
194-195 (1985)

No one disputes that certain sexual activities or unhygienic habits can enhance the environment for pelvic inflammatory disease, even

---

*The following information is drawn from Morton Mintz's book, At Any Cost: Corporate Greed, Women and the Dalkon Shield (1985).

if they do not *cause* PID. This is why A. H. Robins had a right to make inquiries into highly private aspects of the lives of women who filed lawsuits blaming the Dalkon Shield for PID-related injuries. But it did not have a right to make *unreasonable and irrelevant* inquiries.

The record shows that Robins attorneys took depositions from Shield victims in which they asked not only intimate, but also demeaning and even intimidating questions. Although certain judges required defense-counsel to show a connection between the questions and women's injuries, others did not do so and allowed Robins to ask at public trials what plaintiffs' lawyers call "dirty questions."

The following case is from the Shield suit of an Iowa mother of two children who had suffered PID and the consequent loss of her ovaries and womb. Robins's counsel took depositions from her and her husband, each in the presence of the other. To her, the company attorney put queries about her sexual relations before their marriage in 1963, *ten years before she was fitted with a Shield, and fifteen years before she was stricken with PID.* Her lawyer, Kenneth W. Green of Minneapolis, objected, calling such questions "disgusting as well as irrelevant."

Robins then submitted written questions, to her and also to her husband. These, Green said in an affidavit, were "even worse," partly because they returned to the premarital period. Two written questions to the wife were: "Prior to your marriage in 1963, did you have sexual relations with anybody else other than [your husband]?" and "Who were these sexual partners?"

Green's own daughter had worn a Shield and suffered two episodes of PID, one of which almost killed her. But knowing of the invasions of privacy, he advised her not to sue Robins, and she didn't.

Pantyhose can't cause PID; not even defense experts suggested they could. But in a case involving another Shield litigant, a Robins attorney made pantyhose an issue. Among his questions was whether she wore them and what fabric was used in the crotch. To the latter query she replied, "I'll answer that, but this sounds more like an obscene phone call than anything else."

During a deposition in Minnesota in May 1982, lawyers for a Boston woman directed her not to answer questions by Robins counsel about which way she wiped, and whether, and how often she engaged in oral and anal intercourse and used so-called marital aids. Five months later, however, a judge compelled her to return to the Twin Cities to answer the questions. As late as January 1984, a Midwestern woman was asked if before she was fitted with a Shield she had had any sexual partners in addition to her husband. By then the couple had adopted two children, her ability to bear a child of her own having been ruined by Shield-related PID.

Is It Possible to Require or Encourage "Softball"?

The Lawyer's Creed of Professionalism, adopted by the ABA House of Delegates in August 1988 (see page 6 supra), is partly a response to the perception of an increase in "hardball" or "scorched earth" litigation tactics. The Creed is not binding. It explicitly disclaims any wish to allow its text to be used in civil or disciplinary actions against lawyers. Similar exhortations have come from the Committee on Federal Courts of the New York City Bar Association. See A Proposed Code of Litigation Conduct, 43 The Record 738 (1988). Remember we are talking about conduct that while very often unpleasant, even mean-spirited, is legal and generally ethical. Moreover, as the City Bar report states, "hardball" sometimes works. "Many clients do crumble in the face of an opposing counsel's campaign of harassment, and those lawyers who set out to make life unremittingly unpleasant for their adversaries often do succeed in wearing those adversaries down." If that's true, is "hardball" inevitable? Inevitable in high stakes litigation? Does a client have a right to have his or her counsel engage in such tactics? Short of creating new sanctions for this new kind of conduct, can the bar realistically expect to reverse the "race to the cellar"? Can the courts? For a rare case in which the "outrageous" and "pervasive" "misconduct" of a lawyer for a personal injury plaintiff resulted in reversal of a $325,000 verdict (and referral to disciplinary authorities) even though defense counsel had not objected, see Igo v. Coachmen Industries, 938 F.2d 650 (6th Cir. 1991).

G. MISSTATING FACTS, PRECEDENT, OR THE RECORD

In re Curl, 803 F.2d 1004, 1006 (9th Cir. 1986), ordered a lawyer to show cause why he should not be disciplined. In an earlier appeal, the lawyer had mischaracterized a Mexican court's judgment, resulting in a meritless appeal, double costs, and attorney's fees against the lawyer's client. The court accepted the lawyer's claim that his mischaracterization was negligent, not intentional. Nevertheless, it publicly admonished him and cautioned that it would be prepared "to sanction future negligence with substantial monetary fines, suspensions, or disbarment."* In the course of his opinion, Judge Noonan quoted the following passage from Chief Justice Vanderbilt's decision in In re Greenberg, 15 N.J. 132, 104 A.2d 46 (1954), with regard to a lawyer's duty when he or she tries to persuade the court of inferences:

---

*Curl has been overruled insofar as it recognized imposition of Rule 11 sanctions on appeal. Partington v. Gedan, 923 F.2d 686 (9th Cir. 1991) (en banc) (citing Cooter & Gell).

[A lawyer] may assert any inferences from the facts of the case that seem to him arguable, but he cannot present his inferences from the facts as if they were the very facts themselves. When he is indulging, as he has every right to do, in inferences or reasoning from the facts, he must say so — there are many words in the English language fitted to express this process of inference — and to be effective he should state the facts in the record from which he is making his inferences. A fortiori, if, as here, there are no facts on which to predicate a statement or from which he may reason or argue, he makes such false statement of facts or false inferences from such nonexisting facts at his peril. The failure of his adversary to discover his mistake here or below is no excuse for what may turn out to be an imposition on the court, even if it can be attributed merely to carelessness and lack of thoroughness in the preparation of the appeal.

See also Montgomery v. City of Chicago, 763 F. Supp. 301, 307 (N.D. Ill. 1991): "We are gravely concerned with . . . counsel's failure to point out this plainly relevant fact, one that would appear to directly contradict [the client's] implicit assertion. Selective omission of such relevant and apparently contradictory information exceeds the bounds of zealous advocacy."

Several provisions of the code and rules forbid lawyers to make false statements of fact or law. For example, DR 7-102(A)(5) states that a lawyer "shall not knowingly make a false statement of law or fact." The Model Rules state the obligation somewhat differently. Rule 3.3(a)(1) provides that a lawyer "shall not knowingly make a false statement of material fact or law to a tribunal." Rule 4.1(a) contains a parallel prohibition on misstating "material fact or law to a third person." And Rule 8.4(c) forbids a lawyer to "engage in conduct involving dishonesty, fraud, deceit or misrepresentation." Does the addition of the word "material" mean the Model Rules impose a lesser standard of honesty than does the code? The January 1980 Discussion Draft of the Model Rules did not contain the word "material." Shouldn't any knowing falsehood be unethical?

The lawyer's duty not to knowingly misstate fact or law can have consequences in addition to discipline. In Wyle v. R. J. Reynolds Industries, 709 F.2d 585, 590 (9th Cir. 1983), Pacific Far East Line (PFEL) charged one of the defendants, Sea-Land, with paying illegal rebates in violation of the antitrust law. Sea-Land defended in part by alleging that PFEL had also paid illegal rebates, which PFEL denied through its officers and counsel, Alioto & Alioto. Subsequently, PFEL was adjudicated a bankrupt and Wyle was appointed trustee. Wyle admitted the illegal rebating. The district judge thereafter concluded that PFEL had falsely denied the illegal rebating and dismissed its claims. The Ninth Circuit affirmed.

[Plaintiff] challenges also the finding that the Alioto law firm deliberately deceived the court about PFEL's rebating. The court concluded that

Alioto & Alioto's failure to investigate PFEL's denials of pre-October 1976 rebating, even after learning in December 1976 that the company had been fined for rebating, was "the equivalent of knowledge of the truth." PFEL argues that the record does not support such a conclusion.

The record shows, however, that besides the December 1976 fine, the firm met with PFEL in 1977 to discuss rebates paid during that year and, in July 1978, the firm learned that PFEL's agents had paid rebates before October 1976. The district court did not err in concluding that the law firm's deliberate ignorance constituted the equivalent of knowledge of the truth. See United States v. Nicholson, 677 F.2d 706, 710-711 (9th Cir. 1982) (one who is aware of a high probability of the existence of a fact, but deliberately ignores the fact, is deemed to have knowledge of the fact).

H. THE OBLIGATION TO REVEAL ADVERSE LEGAL AUTHORITY

Read DR 7-106(B)(1) and Model Rule 3.3(a)(3). The January 1980 draft of the Model Rules contained the following provision (3.1(c)), which was eventually deleted:

> If a lawyer discovers that the tribunal has not been apprised of legal authority known to the lawyer that would probably have a substantial effect on the determination of a material issue, the lawyer shall advise the tribunal of that authority.

The difference in the obligation imposed by the code and the Model Rules as ultimately adopted, on the one hand, and the January 1980 draft proposal, on the other, is clear, isn't it? What is the justification for the narrow policy adopted by the code and Model Rules? A lawyer's silence is sometimes defended by reference to the client's superior interest in confidentiality. But where we are talking about a lawyer's knowledge of legal authority, can there be a claim that the information is a client confidence? What then is the countervailing consideration?

JORGENSON v. COUNTY OF VOLUSIA
846 F.2d 1350 (11th Cir. 1988)

PER CURIAM:

The appellants, attorneys Eric Latinsky and Fred Fendt, were sanctioned by the district court pursuant to Fed. R. Civ. P. 11 for failing to cite adverse, controlling precedent in a memorandum filed in support of an application for a temporary restraining order and a preliminary injunction. In the appellants' initial appeal to this court, the case was remanded to the district court because the court had failed to notify the attorneys in advance that it was considering sanctions, and did not give them an opportunity to respond. On remand, the district court reaffirmed the imposition of sanctions, and the attorneys appeal. We affirm.

Appellants filed an application in the district court for a temporary restraining order and a preliminary injunction on behalf of their clients, who own and operate a lounge known as "Porky's." In support of the application, appellants filed a memorandum of law which challenged the validity of a Volusia County ordinance prohibiting nude or semi-nude entertainment in commercial establishments at which alcoholic beverages are offered for sale or consumption. The memorandum failed to discuss or cite two clearly relevant cases. We find that this failure supports the imposition of Rule 11 sanctions in the circumstances of this case. . . .

The appellants purported to describe the law to the district court in the hope that the description would guide and inform the court's decision. With apparently studied care, however, they withheld the fact that [a] long-awaited decision by the Supreme Court of Florida had been handed down. This will not do. The appellants are not redeemed by the fact that opposing counsel *subsequently* cited the controlling precedent. The appellants had a duty to refrain from affirmatively misleading the court as to the state of the law. They were not relieved of this duty by the possibility that opposing counsel might find and cite the controlling precedent, particularly where, as here, a temporary restraining order might have been issued ex parte.

In this court, appellants argue that the cases were not cited because they are not controlling. We certainly acknowledge that attorneys are legitimately entitled to press their own interpretations which render particular cases inapplicable. It is clear, however, that appellants' attempts to show that [the cases] are not controlling are simply post hoc efforts to evade the imposition of sanctions. Neither the original complaint nor the memorandum of law filed by appellants in the district court reflect or support the arguments they now raise. Indeed, it is likely that arguments were not raised previously because they are completely without merit. In the circumstances of this case, the imposition of Rule 11 sanctions by the district court was warranted. The judgment of the district court is affirmed.

Under Rule 11, a legal position must be "warranted by [1] existing law or [2] a good faith argument for the extension, modification, or reversal of existing law." Rule 3.1 is in accord. Where precedent is against a legal argument, but a lawyer believes that the precedent should be modified or reversed, must she alert the court that her argument falls within category

2 and not category 1? The Eleventh Circuit has said yes. A lawyer has "a duty to acknowledge at some point, not necessarily [in the pleading], but certainly in [a memorandum] or in a similar document, that the binding precedent of [the] Circuit disfavored [her client's] position." DeSisto College, Inc. v. Line, 888 F.2d 755, 766 (11th Cir. 1989), cert. denied, 110 S. Ct. 2219 (1990). Failure to do so in *DeSisto* resulted in Rule 11 sanctions. Two other circuits have refused to find an "argument identification" duty in Rule 11. Mary Ann Pensiero, Inc. v. Lingle, 847 F.2d 90 (3d Cir. 1988); Golden Eagle Distrib. Corp. v. Burroughs Corp., 801 F.2d 1531 (9th Cir. 1986). Would not Rule 3.3(a)(3) in any event require the lawyer to reveal the adverse circuit precedent?

Is There an Obligation to Reveal That Your Client Has No Case?

The question posed here may sound foolish. After all, if a client has no case, the lawyer shouldn't have accepted it. Furthermore, if the lawyer discovers the client has no case after accepting it, he or she must withdraw. Rules 1.16(a), 3.1. What if the lawyer is court-appointed to represent a criminal defendant? At trial, the lawyer can rightfully put the government to its burden of proving guilt beyond a reasonable doubt. Rule 3.1. How about on appeal? Aren't appeals different because they require some affirmative steps by the appellant's lawyer, some claim of error in or before the trial? If there is no error, the lawyer can't make one up. Yet if the lawyer has been appointed to handle the appeal, neither can he ignore the case. He must tell the appellate court something.

In Anders v. California, 386 U.S. 738, 743 (1967), the Court held that a court-appointed lawyer who moved to withdraw after concluding that an indigent defendant had no grounds for appeal had to accompany his motion with a "brief referring to anything in the record that might arguably support the appeal." Wisconsin, in addition to this, requires the lawyer to include a "discussion of why the issue lacks merit." In McCoy v. Court of Appeals of Wisconsin, 486 U.S. 429, 440-443 (1988), the Court interpreted this duty to mean that lawyers must not only "cite the principal cases and statutes and the facts in the record that support the conclusion that the appeal is meritless," but must also include "a brief statement of why these citations lead the attorney to believe the appeal lacks merit." The Court saw the former duty as consistent with Rule 3.3(a). But it was the second duty — requiring counsel to "assert the basis for [the] conclusion" that the appeal is frivolous — that the defendant especially contested. Upholding it, the Court wrote:

> To satisfy federal constitutional concerns, an appellate court faces two interrelated tasks as it rules on counsel's motion to withdraw. First, it must

satisfy itself that the attorney has provided the client with a diligent and thorough search of the record for any arguable claim that might support the client's appeal. Second, it must determine whether counsel has correctly concluded that the appeal is frivolous. Because the mere statement of such a conclusion by counsel in *Anders* was insufficient to allow the court to make the required determinations, we held that the attorney was required to submit for the court's consideration references to anything in the record that might arguably support the appeal. Wisconsin's rule merely requires that the attorney go one step further. Instead of relying on an unexplained assumption that the attorney has discovered law or facts that completely refute the arguments identified in the brief, the Wisconsin court requires additional evidence of counsel's diligence. This requirement furthers the same interests that are served by the minimum requirements of *Anders*. Because counsel may discover previously unrecognized aspects of the law in the process of preparing a written explanation for his or her conclusion, the discussion requirement provides an additional safeguard against mistaken conclusions by counsel that the strongest arguments he or she can find are frivolous. Just like the references to favorable aspects of the record required by *Anders*, the discussion requirement may forestall some motions to withdraw and will assist the court in passing on the soundness of the lawyer's conclusion that the appeal is frivolous.

The rule does not place counsel in the role of *amicus curiae*. In *Anders* petitioner argued that California's rule allowing counsel to withdraw on the basis of a conclusory statement that the appeal was meritless posed the danger that some counsel might seek to withdraw not because they thought the appeal frivolous but because, seeing themselves as friends of the court, they thought after weighing the probability of success against the time burdens on the court and the attorney if full arguments were presented that it would be best not to pursue the appeal. We agreed that the California rule might improperly encourage counsel to consider the burden on the court in determining whether to prosecute an appeal. Wisconsin's rule requiring the attorney to outline why the appeal is frivolous obviously does not pose this danger.

Justice Brennan's dissent was joined by Justices Marshall and Blackmun. While agreeing with *Anders*, the dissenters could find no "state interest that demands so drastic a departure from defense counsel's 'overarching duty' to advocate 'the undivided interests of his client.'" The dissenters stressed that only indigent clients with appointed counsel suffer the consequences of the state rule. Justice Kennedy did not participate.

VIII

Special Issues in Criminal Advocacy

A. PROSECUTION AND DEFENSE: CRITIQUING EACH OTHER

Prosecutors and criminal defense lawyers are different from civil litigators and from each other. Our rules recognize as much. For example, Rule 3.1, which forbids lawyers to defend a proceeding "unless there is a basis for doing so that is not frivolous," exempts defense lawyers. Why is that? True, defense lawyers are explicitly recognized in the Constitution, but does the Sixth Amendment right to counsel entitle a criminal accused to a different level of lawyering?

For their part, prosecutors seem to be more, rather than less, encumbered by legal and ethical restraints. Rule 3.8 imposes "special" responsibilities on prosecutors. Prosecutors may not argue for false inferences (page 352 supra). And the famous *Brady* rule constitutionally mandates that prosecutors share certain potentially exculpatory information with an accused, although there is no mirror obligation. Brady v. Maryland, 373 U.S. 83 (1963). Is this heightened responsibility justified because, as trial judges sometimes tell juries, "The issue is not whether the government wins or loses. The government always wins when justice is done"?

In this chapter we look at advocacy issues especially common to criminal representation, although they may also arise in civil cases. Issues confronting prosecutors and defense lawyers appear elsewhere in the book too — for example, the perjurious witnesses problem (page 318 supra), and conflicts of interest (pages 186 and 206 supra).

The Association of the Bar of the City of New York held a retreat in December 1986 to explore whether the roles of prosecutors and defense lawyers serve justice. Professor Richard Uviller of Columbia Law School, a former prosecutor, and Professor Anthony Amsterdam of New York University Law School, whose career has included work as prosecutor and defense lawyer, gave introductory talks. Professor Uviller critiqued defense lawyers, Professor Amsterdam prosecutors. Below are portions of the remarks of each as summarized in the report of the Retreat.*

RICHARD UVILLER: CRITIQUING THE DEFENSE BAR

Professor Uviller stated his object as "a friendly one: to hold the mirror up to you in the defense bar to let you take a fresh look at your somewhat tarnished image . . . to echo for you what you say about what you do and why you do it . . . and (with considerable hesitation) to propose a partial remedy for at least one of your perceived excesses and shortcomings."

Within the "adversary mode that sometimes seems to be the proudest boast of our system of criminal justice," Professor Uviller attempted to identify the motives of prosecution and defense. He passed lightly over the first — leaving "this topic to the able hands of my colleague, Professor Amsterdam" — but did acknowledge that in "a liberal democracy such as ours, most lawabiding people consider the government a force for the preservation of peace." Consequently, "lawyers for the state . . . are assigned the white helmets. And along with the psychic benefits accruing to that position, they are prey to the character disorder of arrogance. It is far too easy for these very young lawyers to develop the sense that they are exclusively in charge of justice, the courts being mere instruments to their ends, and defense counsel obstacles."

But the bulk of Professor Uviller's talk addressed the motives of the defense bar. The speaker had taken a poll among friends and associates in that bar, asking: "Why do you do what you do?" No one, he reported, replied that he or she did it "for the money." Answers fell within four other categories.

Category one contained a single response, but a response that Professor Uviller considered sufficiently representative to be genuine. The respondent, a former prosecutor who had gone to work for the Legal Aid Society, was asked by former colleagues "how he could work for that clientele. . . . [He] confessed that all his life he had wanted to sass cops and get away with it." Professor Uviller expressed his strong suspicion "that many of those who thrive on the defense side take their reward from their anti-government stance, expressing a rebel's instinctive suspicion, if not outright aggression, toward those who would presume to speak for the 'decent folk' of the established social order."

---

*Stephen Gillers, The Prosecution and Defense Functions: Do They Promote Justice?, 42 The Record 626, 630-639 (1987).

In Professor Uviller's second category went those "who pursue the sweet exaltation of a victory, heightened by long odds, for its own sake." Acquittals and reversals might be rare, but it was that "very elusiveness" that "fires the drive for its achievement." The game is all, and in it "the gratification" of victory "can overshadow any concern with the worthiness of the recipient of the lawyer's talents."

No one gave an answer within Professor Uviller's third category, so its existence was "largely a matter of conjecture." Still, the speaker was confident that there were lawyers to populate it. If so, their "line must go something like this." First, some who are factually innocent are accused of crime; their conviction and punishment "would be an unspeakable horror." Second, sometimes even "the most conscientious prosecutor will fail to detect that true innocent among the masses of guilty defendants." And so, finally, "the most effective way to discover that innocent trapped by the system is to hammer on every prosecution case as though it was founded on fabrication and brought by malice." Defense lawyers in this category opt to treat every accused as innocent. If it weren't for the defense counsel's dedicated efforts, "the arresting officer would be judge and jury and the innocent would be swept in with the guilty."

Professor Uviller described the fourth and last category, the most common, this way: "It is not the guilty and dangerous defendant that the lawyer defends, but the precious rights of us all . . . virtuous and honorable citizens are rarely charged with serious crime, [so] the promises of the Bill of Rights must be constantly tested and strengthened by means of the cases at hand." The lawyer who works for the acquittal of any accused person "serves the interests of the community at large, and thereby feels entitled to wear the same white helmet as his or her opposite number."

In Professor Uviller's mind, the "product of any one or combination of these job descriptions is an intensification of the adversary position of the defense bar." Further, the views encourage defense lawyers to ignore the "larger picture" — that is, a "just outcome in substantial accord with the historical facts" — and instead concentrate on "the incidental opportunities to attack targets of opportunities presented in the course of the prosecution, from the earliest omissions in the arresting officer's memo book to the last chance to assail the faulty memory or character of the victim." The larger picture, meanwhile, "is left to the prosecutor and to the court."

One result of this "exaggerated adversary frame of mind" is "a world of multiple motions." Professor Uviller cataloged the "motions ex ante [that] have sprung up at every turn. Almost every sort of evidence contemplated by the prosecution is subject to some form of pretrial scrutiny, often complete with testimony and argument." Arrays of motions may be limited by greater use of sanctions for those that are frivolous. But what is frivolous? Lack of factual support? Yet some motions are statutorily authorized to be made without factual support. Further, motions are routinely used to learn facts that the lack of traditional discovery devices makes unavailable. "If such motions are a sham for the discovery of facts relating to the issue, it is more the fault of a system in which the defense is kept in the dark than it is an example of devious tactics by the defense."

And so Professor Uviller endorsed "a generous expansion of early pretrial discovery, at least up to the point of potential harassment of a witness or danger to physical evidence." In the event that we arrive at such a sensible system, or to the extent that voluntary disclosure provides necessary information, "I would require supporting affidavits of fact before granting hearings" on the many available pretrial motions. Professor Uviller would also "require that lawyers attest to the accuracy of the allegations so far as they are known or reasonably knowable to them."

Expanded pretrial discovery, and a concomitant reduction in the extent of factually unsupported pretrial motion practice, would in the speaker's view restore the importance of professional judgment to the adversary system. Professor Uviller emphasized that he did not believe that "the adversary system . . . require[s] a lawyer to lose the professional attribute of judgment." He urged his listeners "not to allow mistaken or exaggerated notions of the role requirements imposed upon us by the adversary model to deprive us of the central feature of our professional identity: the capacity for and the sound exercise of judgment."

ANTHONY AMSTERDAM: CRITIQUING
THE PROSECUTION

Professor Amsterdam then presented a critique of the prosecution function. His thesis was this: "Many of the problems which afflict the prosecution function arise from tensions between the adversary model and aspects of the prosecutor's role which do not fit that model." While the adversary model suggests "two prize-fighters" each trying to knock the other out, in fact "the prosecutor is not simply the antagonistic mirror image of defense counsel." The cliche that "the Government wins when justice is done" bespeaks "the tensions which two potentially inconsistent and largely unreconciled concepts of the prosecutor's role create for day-to-day performance of the ordinary prosecuting attorney."

Professor Amsterdam gave two examples.

First, the prosecutor has no client, where the defense counsel "is not merely permitted but obliged, with great single-mindedness, to pursue a course of action dictated by" his or her client, so long as it is ethical and legal. While the defense counsel is charged with maximizing the likelihood of achieving the client's goals, and may not decide what those goals should be, the prosecutor "is realistically both lawyer and client." The prosecutor chooses the government's goals. The government "has no mind to make up . . . other than the prosecutor's own mind."

Defense lawyer and prosecutor differ in a second way. The defense lawyer will ordinarily try to get the lightest conviction and sentence. However, "the interests of the prosecution do not invariably lie in obtaining the heaviest conviction and sentence . . . they do not even presumptively call for visiting upon a defendant the harshest possible consequences that the law allows." What this means is that "the role of defense counsel comes very close to that of the prize-fighter who symbolizes the 'adversary' process: it is to knock the prosecution out if possible." Meanwhile, the prosecutor's role is "to do justice. Yet consider how very difficult it is for any human being to stand in the ring getting pummeled by left jabs and right hooks from an adversary whose avowed, legitimate and obvious purpose is to knock the hell out of you . . . and in that atmosphere to remember that your goal is not to strike back . . . but rather to do justice . . . The plain fact is that, when any human creature is being slugged left and right by an adversary with blood in its eye, every instinct cries out powerfully to hit back first and worry about doing justice later."

Beyond these two differences between the prosecutorial and defense functions — one lawyer has a client who defines the goals while the other does not; one lawyer must pursue a goal regardless of the "justice of the goal while the other must pursue only goals that are just" — Professor Amsterdam identified four associated problems that afflict the prosecutor's role.

Because "penology is an inexact science . . . the prosecutor has almost no useful guidance or enlightenment" in deciding what the public interest requires by way of sanction. So the prosecutor will be greatly tempted to seek the heaviest conviction in response to the defense lawyer's effort to seek the lightest one. "Rectitude is hard to achieve when there are no standards for what is right."

Next, because whatever the prosecutor does will be "woefully ineffectual in getting at the complicated wellsprings of crime in our complicated society . . . the thoughtful prosecutor's fate . . . is complete frustration." He or she cannot succeed in achieving his or her primary goal — making society safer. "It is therefore all too easy and too human to substitute for this unachievable goal a more achievable one, like winning cases in court or 'beating' the defense at the bargaining table." Furthermore, Professor Amsterdam noted, the risks of leniency can come back to haunt the prosecutor whereas severity is rarely criticized.

A third dilemma prosecutors confront is public fear and restiveness toward "the crime problem." Prosecutors are elected, or they are appointed by persons who are elected. As such, they have a need for "public approbation." This requires "an appearance of winning the war on crime," including "by achieving a high body count for lack of any other indicator or possibility of victory."

Finally, because prosecutors have "unbearably heavy" caseloads, it is too easy for them to concentrate more on getting the work "out" than on getting the work "done right." As a result, "conscientious attention to the supposed values and objectives of the prosecutorial function, including the promotion of justice, is a luxury that most prosecutors have no time or energy left to indulge in."

Drawing on these observations, Professor Amsterdam emphasized that prosecutors were "in an unenviable position of role conflict and role confusion," that they were "people asked to do a job that is partly unclear, partly impossible, and wholly frustrating." He stressed that most of their "major faults and shortcomings" were not "personal sins or even the deficiencies of individuals, so much as failures to perform a miracle of surmounting human limitations." He then proceeded to identify overlapping aspects of prosecutorial behavior he believed "inappropriate or questionable."

The first was the prosecutor's failure to conceive of his or her role "as anything but that of the legal technician or the power-broker waging adversarial combat." Professor Amsterdam acknowledged that most prosecutors may be fully conversant with the criminal codes, sentencing options and alternatives, and the rules and court decisions governing criminal procedure and evidence. Some may also know a good deal about investigative techniques, police organization and methods, crime statistics, legislative and commission reports, and the general law-enforcement literature. "But you can bet that they will not be familiar with the criminological, psychological and corrections literature regarding the etiology of criminal behavior, the characteristics and histories of offender types, recidivism and rehabilitation, and other empirical material pertinent to an assessment of the utility of alternative punishment or treatment modes in the case of particular offenses or offenders. . . . In addition, they are seldom systematically informed about the resources available in the community — or even through public agencies — to help to deal with specific behavior problems. . . . Without information of these sorts, charging and bargaining decisions are pure crap-shooting."

This ignorance is emblematic of a second problem: "Too many prosecutors think of their function as being exclusively to advocate for the heaviest possible convictions and the stiffest possible sentences . . . rather than to decide advisedly what disposition of this particular criminal defendant or potential criminal defendant best serves the interests of [the government]. The whole ethic in most prosecutor's offices supports this gangbusters conception. . . . The most admired deputies are those who win big . . . the office prizes go to those who rack up convictions, not to those who exercise wise judgment in concluding that, for many if not most defendants, the public interest is better served by pre-trial diversion strategies and non-adversary, non-incarcerative dispositions."

The "gangbuster ethic" in turn manifests itself in several dimensions that Professor Amsterdam highlighted as being among "the most pervasive and serious faults of the ordinary prosecutor's office." Overcharging is one: "The persistent, thoughtless, undiscriminating papering of cases with the heaviest charge or charges available under the most extreme conceivable view of the facts as they might turn out to be." Multiplication of charges reveals another fault: "Cumulative counts under overlapping statutes that penalize different details of the same criminal offense; recidivist and habitual-offender charges; the addition of attempt charges, conspiracy charges, criminal-instrument-possession charges, and stolen-goods-possession charges to the underlying substantive offenses."

Professor Amsterdam cited a "knee-jerk" advocacy of incarcerative dispositions, and of longer sentences rather than shorter ones, as an additional manifestation of the same ethic.

All of these tactics have the effect of "upping the ante in the plea-bargaining game, increasing the prosecution's leverage and thereby its power to obtain a moderately severe sentence without the trouble of a trial." Another effect of these tactics is to pass "responsibility to the court to decide within the widest possible range of outcomes what the actual outcome will be, either on the basis of the court's examination of pertinent sentencing considerations or on the basis of the court's splitting the baby between the positions of the contending parties."

While the prosecutor is entitled, in making charging decisions, to take into account the fact that charges are likely to be cut back by bargaining or at trial, and the fact that the judge will mediate between the parties and will assume ultimate sentencing responsibility, nevertheless "this entire process is skewed when the prosecutor inflates the defendant's exposure to sanctions beyond all reason. . . . Prosecutors have, I think, the obligation to make a responsible exercise of professional judgment in setting a cap on defendants' sentencing exposure which relates in some reasonable fashion to the gravity of the individual offenses of which there is substantial proof. . . . All too many prosecutors act instead like wishful civil pleaders, tossing multi-million dollar pain-and-suffering claims like grass seeds, apparently in the hope that some of them will take root and grow."

Finally, Professor Amsterdam criticized "the undiscriminating use of various sorts of highly unreliable evidence in criminal trials," including "jail and prison snitches; addict informers, 'sting' operators and other spies and provocateurs retained on what amount to contingent-fee contracts which reward entrapment successfully covered up or supplemented by perjury; and accomplice testimony bought by promises of leniency often subtly phrased and executed. . . . No sophisticated and intelligent prosecutor I know would spank a puppy with newspaper in reliance on the testimony of any of these characters corroborated by a puddle on the livingroom rug." While it is true that judges and juries can choose to reject the credibility of the testimony so presented, that fact "has never been thought sufficient to absolve prosecutors of the responsibility not to present known perjured testimony." Professor Amsterdam reasoned that even where testimony was not knowingly perjured and could constitutionally be offered, "the professional responsibility of the prosecutors forbids their presentation of the latter evidence as well as the former."

In conclusion, Professor Amsterdam again stressed that the "faults of the prosecution are by no means largely the products of personal perversity on the part of prosecuting attorneys, and to treat them as though they were is to misunderstand them badly. They are the failings of people called upon to do a difficult and at least partly impossible job, under oppressive and intolerable conditions, and often under gross provocation by defense attorneys whose role is rightly far more pugilistic than the prosecution's should be. When ... defense lawyers trash overworked and underpaid prosecutors as a class of evil spirits hell-bent on oppression, that is not merely unfair and unproductive, but untrue."

JUSTICE WHITE'S VIEW

United States v. Wade, 388 U.S. 218 (1967), held that a criminal defendant was entitled to have counsel present at a postindictment lineup. The following excerpt is from the opinion of Justice White, concurring in part and dissenting in part, in which Justices Harlan and Stewart joined:

> Law enforcement officers have the obligation to convict the guilty and to make sure they do not convict the innocent. They must be dedicated to making the criminal trial a procedure for the ascertainment of the true facts surrounding the commission of the crime. To this extent, our so-called adversary system is not adversary at all; nor should it be. But defense counsel has no comparable obligation to ascertain or present the truth. Our system assigns him a different mission. He must be and is interested in preventing the conviction of the innocent, but, absent a voluntary plea of guilty, we also insist that he defend his client whether he is innocent or guilty. The State has the obligation to present the evidence. Defense counsel need present nothing, even if he knows what the truth is. He need not furnish any witnesses to the police, or reveal any confidences of his client, or furnish any other information to help the prosecution's case. If he can confuse a witness, even a truthful one, or make him appear at a disadvantage, unsure or indecisive, that will be his normal course. Our interest in not convicting the innocent permits counsel to put the State to its proof, to put the State's case in the worst possible light, regardless of what he thinks or knows to be the truth. Undoubtedly there are some limits which defense counsel must observe but more often than not, defense counsel will cross-examine a prosecution witness, and impeach him if he can, even if he thinks the witness is telling the truth, just as he will attempt to destroy a witness who he thinks is lying. In this respect, as part of our modified adversary system and as part of the duty imposed on the most honorable defense

counsel, we countenance or require conduct which in many instances has little, if any, relation to the search for truth.

FURTHER READING

The prosecutorial and defense functions have been subject to extensive analysis. We list five authors here. Steven Reiss "attempts a systematic examination of the way constitutional principles are utilized to constrain prosecutorial activities," focusing especially on the role of prosecutorial intent. Steven Reiss, Prosecutorial Intent in Constitutional Criminal Procedure, 135 U. Pa. L. Rev. 1365 (1987). Stanley Fisher, drawing on his and his students' experience, concludes that "we have created a vacuum in which prosecutorial overzealousness and misconduct can flourish." His solution is to encourage prosecutors to appreciate their "quasi-judicial" role as a way to displace what he sees as a "conviction mentality." Stanley Fisher, In Search of the Virtuous Prosecutor: A Conceptual Framework, 15 Am. J. Crim. L. 197 (1988). For the defense side, reflections from the front lines can be found in John Mitchell's thoughtful article, The Ethics of the Criminal Defense Attorney: New Answers to Old Questions, 32 Stan. L. Rev. 293 (1980). Fred Zacharias identifies a failure in ethics codes to define prosecutor's ethical obligations at trial. Using the concept of "doing justice," Professor Zacharias articulates "precise ethical directives" for prosecutors, "either through formal rules or, when flexibility is desirable, rebuttable presumptions." Fred Zacharias, Structuring the Ethics of Prosecutorial Practice: Can Prosecutors Do Justice?, 44 Vand. L. Rev. 45 (1991). Bruce Green finds an inconsistency between a defense lawyer's duty to represent a client "zealously" and the duty to do so "within the bounds of the law." He concludes that "the ethical codes inappropriately rely on the ambiguous criminal laws to set the bounds of zealous advocacy." Like Professor Zacharias, but focusing on defense lawyers, he also argues for greater clarity. Bruce Green, Zealous Representation Bound: The Intersection of the Ethical Codes and the Criminal Law, 69 N.C.L. Rev. 687 (1991).

B. BLAMING THE VICTIM

Not infrequently, a defense lawyer's strategy will be to put the alleged victim of the crime on trial. This strategy is often invoked in cases of violent crime, and perhaps most often when the victim is a woman. Is it zealous advocacy? Is it wrong? Is it — can it be — both of these?

The "blame the victim" defense can occur in several ways. One of
them, quite traditional, is to try to create an inference that the victim be-
haved in a way that justified the defendant's conduct. For example, a defendant charged with assault may introduce evidence tending to prove
that the victim hit first. Until the advent of rape-shield statutes, defense
lawyers in rape cases would try to create a reasonable doubt about
whether the victim consented by introducing evidence of her sexual activity with others. A variation on this strategy, although it is not usually
thought of as such, is to cross-examine a crime victim in a way that seeks
to destroy his credibility by creating the impression that he is a liar or unstable. Recall the material on Max Steuer at page 341 supra.

Another "blame the victim" strategy is more problematic. It entails
creating a negative public image of the character of the victim without
regard to whether the particular personality traits establish a criminal defense as a matter of law. The goal is to diminish the worth of the victim in
the eyes of the jury so that the jury will be reluctant to punish the defendant. This strategy has been described by Dr. Willard Gaylin in his book,
The Killing of Bonnie Garland: A Question of Justice (1983). (P.S. The
defense lawyer in the Bonnie Garland murder case was Jack Litman, who
is quoted in David Margolick's article at page 404 infra.)

Because the trial judge might not let the defense lawyer pursue this
strategy before the jury — the rules of evidence might exclude the information the defense lawyer would like the jury to hear — the lawyer
might raise questions about the victim through pretrial publicity in the
hope that the members of the jury eventually chosen will already have
been exposed to the information. This alternative can work only if the
media find the case newsworthy. What risk does the defense lawyer take
that he or she will be charged with a violation of prohibitions against pretrial publicity? See Chapter 15 infra.

The following material reports on two well-publicized trials in New
York City in 1987 and 1988. In each trial, defense lawyer tactics were
criticized and defended.

Kirk Johnson
SLASHED MODEL CROSS-EXAMINED
IN ATTACK TRIAL
N.Y. Times, March 27, 1987, at 2, col. 1

A Manhattan model whose face was slashed with a razor blade last
summer was portrayed by a defense lawyer yesterday as an ambitious
woman who used men, and she was reminded on the stand of a graphic
sexual vulgarity used to describe her minutes before the attack.

The lawyer, Alton H. Maddox Jr., asked repeatedly why the model, Marla Hanson, 25 years old, had been called a vulgar name by the man convicted of arranging the attack. Mr. Maddox, who represents one of the two men being tried on a charge of attacking Miss Hanson, asked her to define the vulgarity for the jury and suggested that it might be applicable to her personality.

Mr. Maddox's questioning, which came on the third day of Miss Hanson's testimony in State Supreme Court in Manhattan, was repeatedly interrupted by objections from the assistant District Attorney, Consuelo Fernandez, and was later angrily condemned by Miss Hanson's attorney outside the courtroom.

"I find his antics a little bit despicable," said Miss Hanson's attorney, Michael G. Shannon. He said that Mr. Maddox was attempting to "try this case with his wild words and ignore the evidence."

"I don't view this trial as a circus," he added.

Ms. Fernandez later told reporters that she had urged the judge, Justice Jeffrey M. Atlas, to curb Mr. Maddox's questioning, calling his line of questions about the vulgarity in particular, "disgusting and filthy."

Justice Atlas allowed the question to be posed as to how Miss Hanson would define the vulgarity in terms of a personality trait, which she responded was "the same as a bitch." But the line of questioning was then dropped.

'ALL I NEED IS THE WHIP'

Earlier, Miss Hanson broke into tears moments before she took the witness stand after Mr. Maddox, standing a few feet away from her, said that he would be the "ringmaster" when she took the stand and then added, "all I need is the whip."

He made the comment to reporters in a voice audible throughout the courtroom, but before the jury had been brought back in to hear Mr. Maddox's cross-examination.

Miss Hanson, whose wounds required about 150 stitches, testified under direct examination on Tuesday that she had been set upon by two men outside a bar on Manhattan's West Side last June 5.

She identified the two defendants, Steven Bowman, 27, and Darren Norman, 20, as the men who performed the slashing, which she said was carried out at the request of another man, Steven Roth, in a dispute over money owed her by Mr. Roth and her refusal to date him. It was Mr. Roth, Miss Hanson said, who used the vulgarism. Mr. Bowman is represented by Mr. Maddox, and Mr. Norman is represented by Plummer Lott.

Mr. Roth, 28, was convicted in December of arranging the attack and faces up to 15 years in prison when he is sentenced next month. Mr. Bowman and Mr. Norman, who are charged with first-degree assault, also face up to 15 years if they are convicted.

Mr. Maddox, who was questioned outside the courtroom about his tactics in cross-examining Miss Hanson, said his "job is to walk Mr. Bowman out of this courthouse."

David Margolick
AT THE BAR
N.Y. Times, Jan. 22, 1988, at 4, col. 1

Most people, accepting the maxim that everyone is entitled to his day in court, are willing to forgive a lawyer for his clients. Attorneys spend legal lifetimes representing drug dealers or Mafia kingpins or murderers, and remain invulnerable. Not so Jack T. Litman, the man representing Robert Chambers in the death of Jennifer Levin in Central Park.

The Guardian Angels are picketing his office. One television commentator called him "a vulture preying on the dead." The American Lawyer named him the "hands down" winner of its annual "Now You Know Why People Hate Lawyers Award." And, according to his friends, he's been the target of dirty tricks of the sort normally directed at child molesters rather than lawyers.

Why Mr. Litman? The reason seems to be simple. First, his case simultaneously involves the most unpopular of defendants and defenses: a man who admits to killing a young woman, but offers the explanation that he was provoked by her sexual conduct. And second, at least in the public mind, Mr. Litman pulled the same sort of thing in another celebrated case 10 years ago.

That time, his client was Richard Herrin, accused of hammering to death his ex-girlfriend, a fellow Yale student named Bonnie Garland. There, Mr. Litman argued that Mr. Herrin, distraught after learning that Miss Garland was involved with another man, could not be held fully accountable. The defense worked, to a point — Mr. Herrin was ultimately convicted of manslaughter.

Afterwards, Mr. Litman (who has refused all interview requests) was asked by a psychiatrist, Willard Gaylin, whether legal attacks on crime victims were inevitable, and Mr. Litman said they probably were. There were those, he said, who held that defense lawyers must resuscitate the deceased so that the jury can kill them one more time. He'd stopped far short of that in the Garland case, he insisted, but confessed it was necessary "to taint her a little bit" so that the jury would understand the nature of her relationship with her killer.

The remark has come back to haunt Mr. Litman, particularly after he sought Jennifer Levin's diary, which Mr. Litman called "a chronicle" of the 18-year-old girl's "kinky and aggressive" sex life. As a result, his very presence has come to inflame an already explosive case.

As a general rule, the more notorious a case, the more a lawyer covets it. Mr. Litman is already among the city's top defense lawyers. He is particularly expert with medical testimony of the sort that could prove crucial in the Levin case. But should he overcome the implausibility inherent in Mr. Chambers's story — that he was just defending himself during rough sex — Mr. Litman could end up the homicide lawyer of choice in New York.

This may account in part for his accepting a case that, at least in the short run, is economic suicide. With lawyers like Mr. Litman charging around $300 an hour, the Chambers defense could be worth over a million dollars. No one thinks the family could pay even a fraction of that, nor is anyone else offering to.

But in the process, Mr. Litman has become what no good lawyer wants to be: a lightning rod. With clients, juries, and judges alike it is crushing to become known as a Peck's Bad Boy of the bar, synonymous with an unpopular cause. Similarly, even in an age of specialization it's no better to be a Johnny One-Note. "If someone shot a man in the subway tomorrow, I wouldn't take his case," said Barry Slotnick, who represented Bernhard Goetz.

Thus, Mr. Litman faces two challenges in the Chambers case. He must not only vindicate his client but also, at least to some extent, himself.

That he finds himself the target of such obloquy is replete with paradox. For one thing, he handles relatively few homicide cases — only a dozen or so in 14 years of practice. His clients, including Rabbi Bernard Bergman, the nursing home owner convicted of fraud, may not always be savory, but they have been varied.

And, as a morning in court reveals, Mr. Litman is the unlikeliest of ogres. His demeanor is subdued and his style stolid, perhaps as a matter of habit, perhaps because, after the raft of bad publicity, he's on his best behavior. In the promiscuous puppy love world of the Levin case, a world populated with characters like "Larissa" and "Alexandra" and "Brock," where you half expect to hear advertisements for Ivory Liquid during recesses, the lawyer seems incongruous, almost ill-at-ease.

Furthermore, the kinds of aggressive tactics Mr. Litman is accused of inventing are as old as the adversary system itself — a system, defense lawyers and ethics experts agree, that not only condones what he does but requires it. Seventy years ago, the legendary Max Steuer won acquittals for the Triangle Shirtwaist Company owners, in part by badgering the surviving workers, mostly immigrant women, who testified against him.

"There are no synagogues named for him, but Steuer did what a good defense lawyer should do," said Leon Stein, who has written about the trial. "He won his case."

QUESTION

8.1   "These guys Maddox and Litman are disgusting pigs. They ought to be ostracized and morally condemned. They're sleazebags numbers one and two. I haven't yet decided which is worse. Dumping on the victims made no sense legally or logically in any of their cases. Marla Hanson didn't ask to have her face slashed. The stuff Maddox was throwing at her had zero to do with the issues in the case. Litman didn't even wait for trial to dump on Jennifer Levin. He started a barrage of publicity intimating that Levin liked rough sex and implying that Chambers killed her in self-defense, an argument he then didn't pursue at trial. But of course the smear was in. Jennifer Levin and Bonnie Garland didn't ask to get killed no matter what their sex lives might have been like. Both lawyers were trying to cheapen the victims just so the jury would care less about punishing the defendants. That's got nothing to do with being a lawyer. Whatever you think of Max Steuer, he at least used a legitimate legal tool — cross-examination — to cast doubt on a witness's credibility as a witness. Steuer was in a whole different league from these two mudslingers. In your heart, you know I'm right."

C.   DESTRUCTION OR CONCEALMENT OF PHYSICAL EVIDENCE

This material is in Chapter 8 because the problem it describes — a lawyer's responsibility on coming into possession of adverse, probative real evidence (guns, documents, stolen property) — usually arises in criminal cases, but it could also arise in civil cases, as some of the discussion will illustrate.

Let us distinguish among at least four different situations. First, generally applicable in civil cases, is the situation in which the client comes to the lawyer because there is a possible lawsuit against it. Or perhaps the lawsuit has already started. The lawyer realizes that there are documents in the client's file that can be used against it. But either the lawsuit has not yet begun or, if it has begun, no discovery request for those documents has been served. Can the lawyer tell the client to destroy the documents? Can the lawyer say nothing, even though she knows the client is intending to destroy the documents? Must the lawyer tell the client not to destroy the documents? Can the lawyer tell the client the legal implications of the documents, expecting that this information will result in their destruction? Of course, there are many reasons why the lawyer may choose not to want to have the documents destroyed. They may not be so harmful. Destruction, once the fact of it is revealed in discovery and at trial, may raise an inference that the documents were even more damaging than they truly are. Our questions are not of strategy. They are questions of ethics and law.

The second situation generally concerns evidence in criminal cases. In this situation the criminal defendant gives the lawyer physical evidence of the crime. For example, the defendant may show up at the lawyer's office with the unlicensed gun used to kill the victim, with the heroin that was smuggled into the country, with the plates that were used to make counterfeit bills, and so on. The gun, the heroin, the plates are all in themselves contraband, illegal to possess. What is the lawyer's responsibility? Does your answer change if the client shows up with evidence of a crime that is not in itself illegal to possess? For example, in a forgery prosecution, the client brings the lawyer the fountain pen used to create the forged instrument. The pen itself is lawfully owned but it was used in connection with a crime. Or the client delivers a written plan for the crime. The plan, in the client's handwriting, proves his guilt but, like the pen, its possession is not illegal.

A third situation, somewhat blending into the second, is where the client reveals the existence of physical evidence of a crime. The client doesn't bring the evidence with him, but tells the lawyer where it can be found. May the lawyer remove the evidence? Must the lawyer do so? If the lawyer does so, must the lawyer turn the evidence over to the authorities?

Yet a fourth possibility is where evidence of the crime comes into the possession of the lawyer through the conduct of a third person who is not the lawyer's client.

NOTE, LEGAL ETHICS AND THE DESTRUCTION OF EVIDENCE
88 Yale L.J. 1665, 1665-1673 (1979)

What if Richard Nixon had burned the tapes? During the period before the recordings were subpoenaed when the President could have destroyed the tapes without direct legal consequences, it is not clear what

ethical considerations would have guided presidential counsel in suggesting such action. The legal or practical consequences of pre-subpoena
destruction often may be insignificant, as illustrated by the recent case of
Berkey Photo, Inc. v. Eastman Kodak Co.* In that case, Kodak lawyers
initially claimed that certain documents had been destroyed before trial.
The statement produced little reaction from opposing lawyers or the
court. Only when it later appeared that the documents had not been destroyed and that a Kodak lawyer had lied under oath did the attorneys'
conduct draw public criticism.

These two examples illustrate the dilemma facing an attorney whose
client may be aided by destroying potentially damaging or embarrassing
documents. A lawyer's duty to aid his client may conflict with his duty not
to undermine the work of the court. Yet the Code of Professional Responsibility — the primary professional source of ethical guidance for a
lawyer — fails to resolve the problems that arise when it appears that a
client's position can be improved by destroying evidence. This Note argues that the Code should confront this situation, and suggests an
amendment to the Code to cover such cases.

I. CURRENT CONSTRAINTS ON THE DESTRUCTION OF EVIDENCE

The Code of Professional Responsibility does not directly preclude an
attorney from advising his client to destroy possible evidence; provisions
of the Code refer only to situations in which destruction of evidence is
illegal. It is therefore essential to examine relevant state and federal statutes. Because these laws do not cover every situation in which the possibility of destroying evidence arises, the attorney's role may not be
governed by current ethical standards. Thus the lawyer is free to base his
advice on competing practical considerations.

A. CURRENT ETHICAL DUTIES

The Code of Professional Responsibility addresses the ethical questions raised by the destruction of evidence most directly in the provision
that a lawyer should not "[c]onceal or knowingly fail to disclose that
which he is required by law to reveal." This provision is simply a specific
instance of the general rule that an attorney should not counsel or assist
his client in conduct the lawyer knows to be illegal.**

---

* 457 F. Supp. 404 (S.D.N.Y. 1978), rev'd in part & remanded in part, 603 F.2d 263 (2d
Cir. 1979). — ED.
** DR 7-102(A)(3) and (7). See also Model Rules 1.2(d) and 3.4(a). — ED.

Other provisions of the Code might appear to prohibit a lawyer from advising his client to destroy possible evidence before its production is required by law. These provisions have not been so interpreted, however. For example, although an attorney should not assist his client in conduct the attorney knows to be fraudulent, "fraud" almost always means acts of affirmative misrepresentation rather than failure to disclose material facts. Moreover, the rule that a lawyer should report attempts by his client to perpetrate a fraud has been weakened considerably by American Bar Association opinions on ethical issues. In requiring certain kinds of disclosure, some courts have emphasized the lawyer's duty of candor as an "officer of the court," but the required disclosures primarily concern such matters as fraudulent conveyances of clients' assets, legal proceedings elsewhere, and special fee arrangements. The principle of requiring disclosure has been applied to cases in which an attorney tampered with evidence or witnesses, but only in the most egregious circumstances.

Prosecutors have a special duty not to destroy evidence that may be helpful to the defense in a criminal action. Recently, courts also have announced that a defense attorney has a duty to reveal to the prosecution any incriminating evidence received from a client. This rule rests on a balancing between the attorney-client privilege and the societal interest in controlling crime and thus does not apply in civil actions. Even in the criminal context, the rule has been severely criticized.

Thus, while attorneys have both ethical and legal duties not to tolerate perjury or fabricate evidence, in most cases they have no duty to volunteer material facts. The Code of Professional Responsibility's provision on the retention of evidence depends entirely upon the legal duty to preserve it, suggesting that it is not unethical for an attorney to recommend destroying documents or other evidence when it is not illegal for the client to do so. It is therefore necessary to examine the laws which establish the illegality of destruction before turning to the problems created by this ethical rule.

B. STATUTORY PROVISIONS

There is no federal statute that explicitly makes destruction of evidence a crime. Nevertheless, once documents or other evidence have been subpoenaed, intentional destruction is clearly criminal contempt or obstruction of justice under federal law. Even before the issuance of a subpoena, the destruction of documents has been held to be a criminal offense provided two conditions are met. First, the documents must be relevant to a pending grand jury or criminal investigation, and second, the intent of the actor must be "corrupt." To justify these holdings, however, judges have had to struggle to show that the proscribed conduct fell within the narrow wording of the federal obstruction-of-justice statutes.

Under federal law it is not illegal to destroy a document, no matter how relevant to future litigation, provided no subpoena has been issued and no grand jury or criminal investigation has yet begun.

Roughly half the states have enacted statutes proscribing the destruction of evidence that have a broader scope than current federal law. These state provisions, which generally are similar to the relevant provision of the Model Penal Code, prohibit destroying documents or other real evidence with intent to impair their availability in a prospective proceeding when the evidence is "about to be produced." In other states, however, statutes apply only to the destruction of evidence that may be pertinent to criminal proceedings, or parallel the federal obstruction-of-justice statutes and apply only to pending proceedings. In some states, destruction of evidence while a grand jury or criminal investigation is pending is a common-law offense.

A final category of statutes, currently adopted by six states, extends the prohibition against destroying evidence even further than the Model Penal Code provision by making destruction of real evidence a criminal offense if done with intent to prevent its production in a trial or other legal proceeding regardless of the time of the act. Similarly, the proposed Criminal Justice Improvement Act of 1978 included a section that proscribed destruction of documents or other real evidence at any time if the actor intended to prevent their availability in any future civil or criminal proceeding.

Statutes concerning the retention of evidence are thus of two kinds: those that focus both on the time of the destruction and the intent of the actor, and those that simply focus on the intent to suppress evidence. The latter seem preferable, since the legality of an act that is intended to obstruct justice should not depend on such fortuities as whether a subpoena has been served or whether a judicial proceeding has begun. The great majority of jurisdictions, however, rely on the first kind of statute.

The author of the Yale Note goes on to recommend a new disciplinary rule as follows:

> In his representation of a client, the lawyer shall not advise or assist in the destruction of documents, records or other real evidence when he knows or reasonably should know that they are relevant to any foreseeable, planned or pending action.

The author recognizes that "enforcement may be difficult," but believes that such a rule is necessary to clarify ambiguities and protect the legal rights of others. The author would also create a "rebuttable presumption that all documents are relevant after an action has begun."

Legislative History

The history of the Model Rules reveals a narrowing of the duty to preserve evidence. Compare Rule 3.4(a) with the following provisions from the 1980 draft. What is the most significant difference?

RULE 2.5   Alteration or Destruction of Evidence

A lawyer shall not advise a client to alter or destroy a document or other material when the lawyer reasonably should know that the material is relevant to a pending proceeding or one that is clearly foreseeable.

RULE 3.2   Fairness to an Opposing Party and Counsel

(b) A lawyer shall not:
(1) improperly obstruct another party's access to evidence, destroy, falsify or conceal evidence, or use illegal methods of obtaining evidence. . . .

PEOPLE v. MEREDITH
29 Cal. 3d 682, 631 P.2d 46, 175 Cal. Rptr. 612 (1981)

TOBRINER, J.

Defendants Frank Earl Scott and Michael Meredith appeal from convictions for the first degree murder and first degree robbery of David Wade. Meredith's conviction rests on eyewitness testimony that he shot and killed Wade. Scott's conviction, however, depends on the theory that Scott conspired with Meredith and a third defendant, Jacqueline Otis, to bring about the killing and robbery. To support the theory of conspiracy the prosecution sought to show the place where the victim's wallet was found, and, in the course of the case this piece of evidence became crucial. The admissibility of that evidence comprises the principal issue on this appeal.

At trial the prosecution called Stephen Frick, who testified that he observed the victim's partially burnt wallet in a trash can behind Scott's residence. Scott's trial counsel then adduced that Frick served as a defense investigator. Scott himself had told his former counsel that he had taken the victim's wallet, divided the money with Meredith, attempted to burn the wallet, and finally put it in the trash can. At counsel's request, Frick then retrieved the wallet from the trash can. Counsel examined the wallet and then turned it over to the police.

The defense acknowledges that the wallet itself was properly admitted into evidence. The prosecution in turn acknowledges that the attorney-client privilege protected the conversations between Scott, his former counsel, and counsel's investigator. Indeed the prosecution did not attempt to introduce those conversations at trial. The issue before us, consequently, focuses upon a narrow point: whether under the circumstances of this case Frick's observation of the *location* of the wallet, the product of a privileged communication, finds protection under the attorney-client privilege.

This issue, one of first impression in California, presents the court with competing policy considerations. On the one hand, to deny protection to observations arising from confidential communications might chill free and open communication between attorney and client and might also inhibit counsel's investigation of his client's case. On the other hand, we cannot extend the attorney-client privilege so far that it renders evidence immune from discovery and admission merely because the defense seizes it first. . . .

On the night of April 3, 1976, Wade (the victim) and Jacqueline Otis, a friend of the defendants, entered a club known as Rich Jimmy's. Defendant Scott remained outside by a shoeshine stand. A few minutes later codefendant Meredith arrived outside the club. He told Scott he planned to rob Wade, and asked Scott to go into the club, find Jacqueline Otis, and ask her to get Wade to go out to Wade's car parked outside the club.

In the meantime, Wade and Otis had left the club and walked to a liquor store to get some beer. Returning from the store, they left the beer in a bag by Wade's car and reentered the club. Scott then entered the club also and, according to the testimony of Laurie Ann Sam (a friend of Scott's who was already in the club), Scott asked Otis to get Wade to go back out to his car so Meredith could "knock him in the head."

When Wade and Otis did go out to the car, Meredith attacked Wade from behind. After a brief struggle, two shots were fired; Wade fell, and Meredith, witnessed by Scott and Sam, ran from the scene.

Scott went over to the body and, assuming Wade was dead, picked up the bag containing the beer and hid it behind a fence. Scott later returned, retrieved the bag, and took it home where Otis and Meredith joined him.

We now recount the evidence relating to Wade's wallet, basing our account primarily on the testimony of James Schenk, Scott's first appointed attorney. Schenk visited Scott in jail more than a month after the crime occurred and solicited information about the murder, stressing that he had to be fully acquainted with the facts to avoid being "sandbagged" by the prosecution during the trial. In response, Scott gave Schenk the same information that he had related earlier to the police. In addition, however, Scott told Schenk something Scott had not revealed to the police: that he had seen a wallet, as well as the paper bag, on the ground near Wade. Scott said that he picked up the wallet, put it in the paper bag, and placed both behind a parking lot fence. He also said that he later retrieved the bag, took it home, found $100 in the wallet and divided it with Meredith, and then tried to burn the wallet in his kitchen sink. He took the partially burned wallet, Scott told Schenk, placed it in a plastic bag, and threw it in a burn barrel behind his house.

Schenk, without further consulting Scott, retained Investigator Stephen Frick and sent Frick to find the wallet. Frick found it in the location described by Scott and brought it to Schenk. After examining the wallet and determining that it contained credit cards with Wade's name, Schenk turned the wallet and its contents over to Detective Payne, investigating officer in the case. Schenk told Payne only that, to the best of his knowledge, the wallet had belonged to Wade.

The prosecution subpoenaed Attorney Schenk and Investigator Frick to testify at the preliminary hearing. When questioned at that hearing, Schenk said that he received the wallet from Frick but refused to answer further questions on the ground that he learned about the wallet through a privileged communication. Eventually, however, the magistrate threatened Schenk with contempt if he did not respond "yes" or "no" when asked whether his contact with his client led to disclosure of the wallet's location. Schenk then replied "yes," and revealed on further questioning that this contact was the sole source of his information as to the wallet's location.

At the preliminary hearing Frick, the investigator who found the wallet, was then questioned by the district attorney. Over objections by counsel, Frick testified that he found the wallet in a garbage can behind Scott's residence.

Prior to trial, a third attorney, Hamilton Hintz, was appointed for Scott. Hintz unsuccessfully sought an in limine ruling that the wallet of the murder victim was inadmissible and that the attorney-client privilege precluded the admission of testimony concerning the wallet by Schenk or Frick.

At trial Frick, called by the prosecution, identified the wallet and testified that he found it in a garbage can behind Scott's residence. On cross-examination by Hintz, Scott's counsel, Frick further testified that he was an investigator hired by Scott's first attorney, Schenk, and that he had searched the garbage can at Schenk's request. Hintz later called Schenk as a witness: Schenk testified that he told Frick to search for the wallet immediately after Schenk finished talking to Scott. Schenk also stated that Frick brought him the wallet on the following day; after examining its contents Schenk delivered the wallet to the police. Scott then took the stand and testified to the information about the wallet that he had disclosed to Schenk.

The jury found both Scott and Meredith guilty of first degree murder and first degree robbery. It further found that Meredith, but not Scott, was armed with a deadly weapon. Both defendants appeal from their convictions.

Defendant Scott concedes, and we agree, that the wallet itself was admissible in evidence. Scott maintains, however, that Evidence Code section 954 bars the testimony of the investigator concerning the location of the wallet. We consider, first, whether the California attorney-client privilege codified in that section extends to observations which are the product of privileged communications.

[The court concluded that California law protected as privileged the defendant's statements to his lawyer regarding the location of the wallet. Furthermore, the information retained its protection even though the lawyer disclosed the substance of the communication to the investigator, since the purpose of this disclosure was to aid in the representation.]

The statutes codifying the attorney-client privilege do not, however, indicate whether that privilege protects facts viewed and observed as a direct result of confidential communication. To resolve that issue, we turn first to the policies which underlie the attorney-client privilege, and then to the cases which apply those policies to observations arising from a protected communication.

The fundamental purpose of the attorney-client privilege is, of course, to encourage full and open communication between client and attorney. "Adequate legal representation in the ascertainment and enforcement of rights or the prosecution or defense of litigation compels a full disclosure of the facts by the client to his attorney. . . . Given the privilege, a client may make such a disclosure without fear that his attorney may be forced to reveal the information confided to him."

In the criminal context, as we have recently observed, these policies assume particular significance: " 'As a practical matter, if the client knows that damaging information could more readily be obtained from the attorney following disclosure than from himself in the absence of disclosure, the client would be reluctant to confide in his lawyer and it would be difficult to obtain fully informed legal advice.' . . . Thus, if an accused is to derive the full benefits of his right to counsel, he must have the assurance of confidentiality and privacy of communication with his attorney."

Judicial decisions have recognized that the implementation of these important policies may require that the privilege extend not only to the initial communication between client and attorney but also to any information which the attorney or his investigator may subsequently acquire as a direct result of that communication. In a venerable decision involving facts analogous to those in the instant case, the Supreme Court of West Virginia held that the trial court erred in admitting an attorney's testimony as to the location of a pistol which he had discovered as the result of a privileged communication from his client. That the attorney had observed the pistol, the court pointed out, did not nullify the privilege: "All that the said attorney knew about this pistol, or where it was to be found, he knew only from the communications which had been made to him by his client confidentially and professionally, as counsel in this case.

And it ought therefore, to have been entirely excluded from the jury. It may be, that in this particular case this evidence tended to the promotion of right and justice, but as was well said in Pearce v. Pearce, 11 Jar. 52, in page 55, and 2 De Gex & Smale 25-27: 'Truth like all other good things may be loved unwisely, may be pursued too keenly, may cost too much.'" State of West Virginia v. Douglass, 20 W. Va. 770, 783 (1882). . . .

More recent decisions reach similar conclusions. In State v. Olwell, 64 Wash. 2d 828, 394 P.2d 681 (1964), the court reviewed contempt charges against an attorney who refused to produce a knife he obtained from his client. The court first observed that "[t]o be protected as a privileged communication . . . the securing of the knife . . . must have been *the direct result of information* given to Mr. Olwell by his client." (Emphasis added.) The court concluded that defense counsel, after examining the physical evidence, should deliver it to the prosecution, but should not reveal the source of the evidence; "[b]y thus allowing the prosecution to recover such evidence, the public interest is served, and by refusing the prosecution an opportunity to disclose the source of the evidence, the client's privilege is preserved and a balance reached between these conflicting interests." (See also Anderson v. State (Fla. Dist. Ct. App.) 297 So. 2d 871.)

Finally, we note the decisions of the New York courts in People v. Belge (N.Y. Sup. Ct. 1975) 83 Misc. 2d 186, 372 N.Y.S.2d 798, affirmed in People v. Belge (N.Y. App. Div. 1975) 50 A.D.2d 1088, 376 N.Y.S.2d 771. [*Belge* is discussed at pages 22-25 supra.] Defendant, charged with one murder, revealed to counsel that he had committed three others. Counsel, following defendant's directions, located one of the bodies. Counsel did not reveal the location of the body until trial, 10 months later, when he exposed the other murders to support an insanity defense.

Counsel was then indicted for violating two sections of the New York Public Health Law for failing to report the existence of the body to proper authorities in order that they could give it a decent burial. The trial court dismissed the indictment; the appellate division affirmed, holding that the attorney-client privilege shielded counsel from prosecution for actions which would otherwise violate the Public Health Law.[5]

The foregoing decisions demonstrate that the attorney-client privilege is not strictly limited to communications, but extends to protect observations made as a consequence of protected communications. We turn therefore to the question whether that privilege encompasses a case in

---

5. In each of the cases discussed in text, a crucial element in the court's analysis is that the attorney's observations were the direct product of information communicated to him by his client. Two decisions, People v. Lee, 3 Cal. App. 3d 514, 83 Cal. Rptr. 715 (1970), and Morrell v. State, 575 P.2d 1200 (Alaska 1978), held that an attorney must not only turn over evidence given him by *third parties*, but also testify as to the source of that evidence. Both decisions emphasized that the attorney-client privilege was inapplicable because the third party was not acting as an agent of the attorney or the client.

which the defense, by removing or altering evidence, interferes with the prosecution's opportunity to discover that evidence.[7]

In some of the cases extending the privilege to observations arising from protected communications the defense counsel had obtained the evidence from his client or in some other fashion removed it from its original location (State v. Olwell, supra, 394 P.2d 681; Anderson v. State, supra, 297 So. 2d 871); in others the attorney did not remove or alter the evidence (People v. Belge, supra.) None of the decisions, however, confronts directly the question whether such removal or alteration should affect the defendant's right to assert the attorney-client privilege as a bar to testimony concerning the original location or condition of the evidence.

When defense counsel alters or removes physical evidence, he necessarily deprives the prosecution of the opportunity to observe that evidence in its original condition or location. As the amicus Appellate Committee of the California District Attorneys Association points out, to bar admission of testimony concerning the original condition and location of the evidence in such a case permits the defense in effect to "destroy" critical information; it is as if, he explains, the wallet in this case bore a tag bearing the words "located in the trash can by Scott's residence," and the defense, by taking the wallet, destroyed this tag. To extend the attorney-client privilege to a case in which the defense removed evidence might encourage defense counsel to race the police to seize critical evidence. (See In re Ryder, 263 F. Supp. 360, 369 (E.D. Va. 1967); Comment, The Right of a Criminal Defense Attorney to Withhold Physical Evidence Received From His Client, 38 U. Chi. L. Rev. 211, 227-228 (1970).)

We therefore conclude that courts must craft an exception to the protection extended by the attorney-client privilege in cases in which counsel has removed or altered evidence. Indeed, at oral argument defense counsel acknowledged that such an exception might be necessary in a case in which the police would have inevitably discovered the evidence in its original location if counsel had not removed it. Counsel argued, however, that the attorney-client privilege should protect observations of evidence, despite subsequent defense removal, unless the prosecution could

---

7. We agree with the parties' suggestion that an attorney in Schenk's position often may best fulfill conflicting obligations to preserve the confidentiality of client confidences, investigate his case, and act as an officer of the court if he does not remove evidence located as the result of a privileged communication. We must recognize, however, that in some cases an examination of evidence may reveal information critical to the defense of a client accused of crime. If the usefulness of the evidence cannot be gauged without taking possession of it, as, for example, when a ballistics or fingerprint test is required, the attorney may properly take it for a reasonable time before turning it over to the prosecution. (Olwell, supra, 394 P.2d, pp. 684-685.) Similarly, in the present case the defense counsel could not be certain the burnt wallet belonged in fact to the victim: in taking the wallet to examine it for identification, he violated no ethical duty to his client or to the prosecution. (See generally Legal Ethics and the Destruction of Evidence, 88 Yale L.J. 1665 (1979).)

prove that the police probably would have eventually discovered the evidence in the original site.

We have seriously considered counsel's proposal, but have concluded that a test based upon the probability of eventual discovery is unworkably speculative. Evidence turns up not only because the police deliberately search for it, but also because it comes to the attention of policemen or bystanders engaged in other business. In the present case, for example, the wallet might have been found by the trash collector. Moreover, [once] physical evidence (the wallet) is turned over to the police, they will obviously stop looking for it; to ask where, how long, and how carefully they would have looked is obviously to compel speculation as to theoretical future conduct of the police.

We therefore conclude that whenever defense counsel removes or alters evidence, the statutory privilege does not bar revelation of the original location or condition of the evidence in question.[8] We thus view the defense decision to remove evidence as a tactical choice. If defense counsel leaves the evidence where he discovers it, his observations derived from privileged communications are insulated from revelation. If, however, counsel chooses to remove evidence to examine or test it, the original location and condition of that evidence lose the protection of the privilege. Applying this analysis to the present case, we hold that the trial court did not err in admitting the investigator's testimony concerning the location of the wallet. . . .

Does the Source Matter?

In *Meredith*, would Scott's lawyer have had to reveal the source of the wallet if the source had been Scott himself, not his garbage can? Analytically, the answer would seem to be yes. By removing the wallet from Scott, as in *Meredith*, the lawyer would have made it impossible for the authorities to seize it from the defendant first. On the other hand, *Meredith* cited *Olwell*, which on these facts would not allow the prosecutor to elicit the source of the incriminating evidence. In People v. Nash, 418 Mich.

---

8. In offering the evidence, the prosecution should present the information in a manner which avoids revealing the content of attorney-client communications or the original source of the information. In the present case, for example, the prosecutor simply asked Frick where he found the wallet; he did not identify Frick as a defense investigator or trace the discovery of the wallet to an attorney-client communication.

In other circumstances, when it is not possible to elicit such testimony without identifying the witness as the defendant's attorney or investigator, the defendant may be willing to enter a stipulation which will simply inform the jury as to the relevant location or condition of the evidence in question. When such a stipulation is proffered, the prosecution should not be permitted to reject the stipulation in the hope that by requiring defense counsel personally to testify to such facts, the jury might infer that counsel learned those facts from defendant. (Cf. People v. Hall, 28 Cal. 3d 143, 152, 167 Cal. Rptr. 844, 616 (1980).)

196, 341 N.W.2d 439 (1983), a divided court concluded that *Olwell* was correct, but a minority read *Meredith* to require revelation of the source of the incriminating evidence even when the source is the client directly. Which solution better serves the ends of justice? In a jurisdiction that subscribed to the *Nash* minority view, what should a lawyer do when a client brings incriminating evidence to the lawyer's office?

Could Nixon Have Destroyed the Tapes? (and Other Intriguing Questions)

He thinks so. He told the New York Times (April 6, 1984, at A17) that one reason for his failure to destroy the tapes was bad advice "from well-intentioned lawyers who had sort of the cockeyed notion that I would be destroying evidence," even though no subpoena had been served. The source of that advice became clearer in an Op-Ed article in the Times on August 18, 1988, at 27. The article, written by journalist Henry Brandon shortly after the death of noted criminal defense lawyer Edward Bennett Williams, quoted Williams as saying in 1985: "Nixon had no obligation to make or keep the tapes and could have argued that his motive in destroying them was to prevent secret exchanges with other heads of government from being compromised." (Could Williams have ethically given Nixon this advice? What if protecting secrets was *not* Nixon's motive? Can a lawyer advise a client to lie when the client is not under oath? Isn't Williams inventing a defense?)

Leonard Garment, the President's legal counsel in 1973, had advised the President not to destroy the tapes. Although a subpoena had not been served, all knew it would be. Destroying the tapes in the face of that knowledge would then constitute obstruction of justice, in Garment's view. In 1985, Brandon related Williams' different perspective to Garment, who defended himself by citing a "1956 decision by the Federal District Court in New York City" to the effect that the crime of obstruction of justice can occur even though no subpoena had been served on the defendant. Later, according to Brandon, even Garment conceded that Williams "was probably right and that Nixon could have got away with the destruction of the tapes."

The 1956 decision Garment referred to was United States v. Solow, 138 F. Supp. 812 (S.D.N.Y. 1956), in which Judge Weinfeld did in fact refuse to dismiss an indictment charging obstruction of justice after the defendant allegedly destroyed four letters in the files of The Nation magazine that the grand jury wanted in connection with a perjury investigation. The defendant was charged with knowing that the letters were relevant to a grand jury investigation and that he would be ordered to produce them. Solow testified before the grand jury on March 16 pursuant to a telephonic request (not a subpoena) received the previous day.

The indictment charged that he had destroyed the letters sometime between February 8 and March 16. The author of the Yale Note (page 407 supra) cites *Solow* in support of the proposition that destruction of *un*subpoenaed documents can be obstruction of justice, but the "documents must be relevant to a pending grand jury or criminal investigation, and . . . the intent of the actor must be 'corrupt.'" Could Nixon have avoided prosecution on the ground that the House Judiciary Committee was not conducting a "criminal investigation" and that his intent was not corrupt (but only, following Williams' advice, to protect the secrets of other governments)? Would the same arguments have avoided impeachment?

Brandon also attributes to Alexander Haig, Nixon's chief of staff, the recollection that Nixon chose not to destroy the tapes because "the tapes were the only true safeguard he had, since he did not know what he would be accused of." There is a lesson here. Destruction is a two-edged sword. As a case unfolds, evidence that might have appeared damaging can take on a different hue. Furthermore, destruction of a document can give rise to an inference about its content that is more damaging than the document actually was.

The ABA's Solution

ABA Criminal Justice Standard 4-4.6 says that a lawyer "who receives a physical item under circumstances implicating a client in criminal conduct should disclose the location of or should deliver the item to law enforcement authorities" if law or court order require. If they don't, the lawyer can return the item to the source but should "advise the source of the legal consequences pertaining to possession or destruction of the item." The lawyer can also keep the item for a reasonable time if the lawyer fears that return will lead to the item's destruction or to physical harm or if the lawyer plans to test or examine the item for defense purposes. A lawyer must hold the item "in his or her law office in a manner that does not impede the lawful ability of law enforcement authorities to obtain the item."

These rules are altered if an item is contraband or poses an unreasonable risk of physical harm. If the item is contraband, the lawyer may suggest that the client destroy it where "there is no pending case or investigation" and where destruction would not "clearly" violate criminal law. Otherwise the lawyer should disclose or deliver the item to the authorities. A lawyer should also give an item to authorities if it presents a physical danger. Whenever a lawyer discloses or delivers an inculpatory item to authorities or to a third party, he or she is directed to "do so in the way best designed to protect the client's interests." Does that mean anonymously?

QUESTION

8.2   "My name is Jon Cline and I have an urgent ethical problem. I'm a
public defender in Alaska. I was appointed to represent a guy
named Morrell who was charged with kidnapping. While Morrell
was inside awaiting trial, he let a friend, Wagner, use his place and
his car. Wagner cleaned the car and found a pad on which, in Morrell's handwriting, is the outline of a plan for the kidnapping. This
is 'throw away the key' stuff. Wagner brought me the pad. After I
read the plan, I asked Wagner to take it back. Maybe I shouldn't
have done that, but I sure as hell didn't want it. Wagner picked up
on my anxiety and said no way was he going to take it back. This
was this morning. Now I've got it, and I don't even know where to
begin to go for quick advice. So I came to you."

Spoliation of Evidence

In some jurisdictions, destruction of evidence may not only have evidentiary consequences, it may also be a tort. In Smith v. Superior Court,
151 Cal. App. 3d 491, 198 Cal. Rptr. 829 (1984), an intermediate appellate court recognized the new tort of "intentional spoliation of evidence,"
where the plaintiff alleged that the defendant lost or destroyed physical
evidence from an automobile accident after her counsel had alerted the
defendant to the fact that the evidence could be material to plaintiff's legal claims. The court rejected arguments that the tort ought not be recognized because a state penal law already punished the intentional
concealment or destruction of physical evidence, or because the plaintiff
might not be able to prove her damages with certainty. *Smith* was distinguished in Koplin v. Rosel Well Perforators, Inc., 734 P.2d 1177, 1181
(Kan. 1987), on the ground that the defendant in *Smith* had agreed to
"safeguard and preserve the automotive parts," whereas there was no
such agreement in *Koplin*. The court also stressed that in *Smith* the "evidence was destroyed by the adverse party in pending litigation to the direct benefit of such party," whereas in *Koplin* the plaintiff was suing his
employer for spoliation of evidence that may have been useful in a claim
against third parties. See also Hazen v. Municipality of Anchorage, 718
P.2d 456 (Alaska 1986) (following *Smith*). California has recognized the
tort of negligent spoliation. Velasco v. Commercial Building Maintenance Co., 169 Cal. App. 3d 874, 215 Cal. Rptr. 504 (1985). Other jurisdictions, while not foreclosing spoliation claims, have insisted on proof
that but for the destruction of the evidence, the plaintiff would have prevailed in the underlying matter. See, e.g., Federated Mutual Ins. Co. v.
Litchfield Precisions Components, Inc., 456 N.W.2d 434 (Minn. 1990).

ADDITIONAL AUTHORITIES AND FURTHER READING

In Commonwealth v. Stenhach, 356 Pa. Super. 5, 514 A.2d 114, 125 (1986), appeal denied, 517 Pa. 589, 534 A.2d 769 (1987), two public defenders took possession of the murder defendant's rifle but did not deliver it to the prosecutor until the court ordered them to do so. Later they were convicted of hindering prosecution and tampering with evidence. The conviction was reversed. The court reviewed the same history recounted in *Meredith*. It held that the defendant's conduct could be subject to criminal sanction, but it concluded that the state statutes under which the defendants were prosecuted were unconstitutionally vague and overbroad "when applied to attorneys representing criminal defendants." The court wrote that these statutes, which are no different from other such statutes, would literally require a lawyer to turn over "a handwritten account of involvement in the crime" given to him by a client. Yet to do so "would be an egregious violation of the attorney's duties to his client." Thereafter, the Supreme Court Disciplinary Board dismissed a petition seeking discipline. It ruled that the lawyers could reasonably have concluded that they did not have an obligation to turn over the rifle until a court ordered them to do so. Office of Disciplinary Counsel v. Stenhach, 5 Lawyers Manual Prof. Conduct 340 (Oct. 25, 1989).

The Supreme Court has held that an attorney may assert the attorney-client privilege in resisting a summons to produce documents delivered to him by his client if the documents would have been privileged while in the client's possession. In Fisher v. United States, 425 U.S. 391 (1976), the issue was whether an attorney had to produce certain tax work papers delivered by the client. The client claimed that the papers would have enjoyed Fifth Amendment immunity from subpoena while in the client's possession. The Court agreed with the general proposition but concluded that the papers on the facts before it would not have enjoyed Fifth Amendment protection while the client had them.

For further commentary see John Fedders & Lauryn Guttenplan, Document Retention and Destruction: Practical, Legal and Ethical Considerations, 56 Notre Dame L. Rev. 5 (1980); Note, Ethics, Law, and Loyalty: The Attorney's Duty to Turn Over Incriminating Physical Evidence, 32 Stan. L. Rev. 977 (1980) (authored by Jane Graffeo); and Note, *People v. Meredith*: The Attorney-Client Privilege and the Criminal Defendant's Constitutional Rights, 70 Calif. L. Rev. 1048 (1982) (authored by Michael Dashjian).

SIMULATED CASE HISTORY

Mary Cahn

I am the elected prosecutor here in Fullerton and have been for nine years. I filed a complaint with the local disciplinary authorities against

Edgar Danforth, one of the big white-collar criminal defense lawyers over in Chicago. I think the man should be disbarred. He is unfit to practice.

Our office charged Hamilton Magruder with first-degree murder in the killing of his brother Maxwell. The Magruders are the wealthiest family in this town. The state was prepared to prove, and did prove, that Hamilton killed Maxwell in a dispute about control of the trucking business that their late father had started and that is now the biggest employer in the county. Hamilton and Maxwell never got along well, even when they were growing up, and maybe this was just the culmination of a lot of festering anger and resentment.

Hamilton was acquitted. Guilty people get acquitted all the time, I realize, and there's not much we can do about it. Sometimes the proof doesn't mount up. Sometimes evidence is suppressed. Sometimes the jury just doesn't trust the word of a government witness. That's our system. Technically, you're not guilty until the jury says so, no matter what you did or didn't do. But the way Hamilton was acquitted broke the rules of the game, and that's why I think Danforth should be disciplined.

Danforth called a witness, Phoebe Bannister, who works at Miller & Vale, the big department store in town, and who knew the brothers casually because she had once done some interior design work for their mother. She testified that she saw Hamilton shopping at M&V in the afternoon of December 19, which is when Maxwell was killed. She said she saw him just before taking her coffee break, at 3:00 P.M., waved to him and he waved back. If Hamilton was in the store at 3:00 P.M., he could not have shot Maxwell Magruder 31 miles away just before 3:15, which is when the witnesses who heard the shot phoned the emergency number.

We checked with Bannister's co-workers. None recalled seeing Hamilton (whom they all knew by sight) in the store that day. Some did confirm that they took their coffee break with Phoebe at 3:00 on the 19th as they always do.

The fact is Phoebe was either lying or wrong. I don't know why she would lie and I'm not saying she did. Maybe she just misremembered or saw someone else whom she mistook for Hamilton. Danforth knows Phoebe is wrong because from the time we arrested Hamilton until the time Danforth delivered the notice of his intention to rely on an alibi defense, no one mentioned this story about Hamilton being at Miller & Vale. If that story had checked out, Hamilton would have saved a lot of people, including especially himself, a lot of trouble. Why didn't he mention it before? Why didn't his lawyer?

But there's more. A week before Maxwell was killed, Hamilton wrote him a letter setting forth his demands with regard to the trucking business and some other things. The letter contained some language that could be construed to threaten dire consequences if Hamilton didn't get his way. I would certainly have liked to have introduced that letter in evidence. I think it would have made a significant impression on the jury. And it would have undercut Danforth's repeated argument in summation that the state had failed to show a motive. The trouble is I didn't have it or even know about the letter.

For reasons I can't reveal because of our ongoing investigation, my office was recently told about the existence of the letter and its general contents, although we still haven't seen it. We have reason to believe that the letter was removed from Maxwell's house or office before the murder was discovered. (It couldn't have been removed afterwards because the house and office were sealed until each could be searched.) And we know for a fact that it wound up in Danforth's office safe.

Finally, my office has recently learned (after the verdict to be sure) that Danforth may have encouraged the disappearance of a witness who might have testified for the government. There were no eyewitnesses to the event, or so we thought. It now appears that a Mr. Krebs, a handyman for Magruder Trucking, was working at a guest house on Maxwell's estate when Maxwell was killed. Although the guest house was some 200 yards from the main house, where the crime occurred, the handyman might have seen something that we could have connected with Hamilton. The color or style of the murderer's clothing, or his means of transportation.

got rid of him —

But we never knew Krebs was there. Shortly after the murder, the company transferred him out of state, to its St. Paul office, where he was given a promotion and a higher salary. Krebs never tried to contact us. He must have known about the murder, the investigation and the trial. My question is how is it that a possibly useful witness — or if not a witness, then a person who may have had important leads — suddenly decided to disappear from the jurisdiction and did not see it as in his interest to help us solve a homicide? I don't know, but I have my strong suspicions and I plan to find out.

We might even have found Krebs on our own because we checked the work assignments of all Magruder employees as part of our general investigation. We know now that the work assignment sheet for Krebs had been removed before our subpoena was served on Magruder Trucking and so we never saw it. If we had, we would have learned that Krebs had been working on the estate and we would certainly have found him and questioned him.

EDGAR DANFORTH

I have nothing to hide.

The case is over and jeopardy has attached. So there's no danger to my client, who did not testify. Also, in a disciplinary proceeding, I'm permitted to reveal even confidential information in my defense.

First, the issue of Phoebe. Phoebe showed up in my office a couple of months after Ham retained me. She said she had been reading about the case in the papers, following it closely, and that she was generally aware that the day Ham was supposed to have shot Maxwell was the day she saw him in the store. But that didn't seem all that important to her. Why would Ham's being in the store exonerate him? But then she read that the murder was supposed to have occurred at the Magruder estate just before 3:15. That's when she realized, she said, that Ham could not have done it. She had seen him in the store just before her three o'clock coffee break and had waved to him. He had waved back. She knew him because she had done some design work for Mrs. Magruder.

I asked Phoebe how she happened to recall it was just before her coffee break that she saw Ham. She always takes her coffee break at 3:00, she told me, but when she saw Ham, she decided that if he was looking for something in her department she would postpone her break to help him. When he didn't stop, she went off for her break. Her colleagues corroborated that she took her break with them that day at 3:00. Since they did this every Saturday — this was a Saturday — quite religiously, they said they would have recalled if Phoebe had not joined them.

Now the fact is that Ham was not in M&V that day. He was elsewhere, or so he told me when he retained me. Establishing his true alibi would have been harder than establishing a false one because he was alone at the critical time and I would have had to call him to testify. Then the prosecutor could have cross-examined him and, frankly, Hamilton would not make a good witness. Even if he did, a defendant's own testimony is always suspect since it is easy to get juries to believe that a defendant will lie to avoid conviction. Meanwhile, Phoebe Bannister appeared to be a highly credible witness. She seemed to have nothing to gain by testifying for Ham. Her credibility could not easily be impeached. Sure it was a gamble to use her, but it worked. She was honest even though she was wrong, and her honesty impressed the jury. She recalled seeing and waving to Ham and I believe she did see and wave to someone, someone who looked like Ham. I haven't the vaguest idea who that might have been. I don't care. I was within my rights to call Phoebe and I'd do it again.

I realize the prosecutor thinks Phoebe is lying to protect Ham and that she's doing it for money. As long as I don't know that that's true, which I don't, I can call Phoebe. My only legitimate and mandated consideration is whether Phoebe will be a credible witness under cross-examination. If I think the prosecutor will be able to persuade the jury she's lying, the whole effort could backfire and I won't call Phoebe. My responsibility is to win, not to tell the truth. What will get my client the best result. So I made a tactical decision that Phoebe was highly credible and that her explanation for not coming forward sooner was also credible. It was a risk that worked.

About the so-called threatening letter. What happened was this. Ham told me that about a week before Maxwell died, Ham had given his brother a handwritten letter at the trucking company offices, keeping a photocopy for himself. The letter contained Ham's position on some disputed points regarding the business and its profits. Yes, it could also be construed as threatening or certainly angry. Ham told me about this the day he retained me, which was the same day Maxwell died. Ham knew that because of enmity between them and because he stood to gain financially from his brother's death, the authorities would immediately suspect him and that the letter could be used against him.

The day Maxwell got the letter, he stormed into Ham's office with it, told Ham that under no circumstances would he agree to the demands in the letter, then dramatically tore it in two and dropped it in Ham's trash can from where, we assume, it was eventually collected and carted away. No one else was in the room. Ham brought the photocopy of the letter to my office. He asked me if he had the right to hide it. I told him I would research the question and held the copy in my office safe until I concluded, about two weeks later, that Ham was within his rights to destroy it. He had no obligation to turn it in or leave it about and risk having it discovered in a search or otherwise. If the prosecutor learned that Ham had destroyed the copy, she might seek to use it as proof of guilt. But she was not likely to learn about it. I told Ham he could destroy the copy, which he elected to do and, since I already had it, he asked if I would burn it for him. I did.

The same is true with regard to Krebs. Ham did nothing wrong in transferring him to St. Paul, nor did I in advising Ham that he could do so. No one said anything to Krebs about Maxwell's death or about not cooperating with the prosecutor. He was free to do his civic duty as he saw it. If Krebs had been subpoenaed to testify before the grand jury, why then he would have had to appear. Furthermore, interstate compacts would have enabled the prosecutor to bring Krebs back from St. Paul. I learned much later, just before the trial, that Ham had destroyed Kreb's work assignment sheet before the office was searched, and frankly I don't know what I would have said if Ham had asked me in advance whether he could do so (that's a nice question). But he did it on his own. I had no obligation to stop representing him because of this possibly questionable conduct.

D. SUBPOENAS TO CRIMINAL
DEFENSE LAWYERS

In the 1980s, criminal defense lawyers had to grapple with three new prosecutorial tools (or weapons, depending on your perspective). The first, discussed here, was the prosecutorial practice of calling defense counsel before grand juries to provide information about their clients. The second, discussed in section E, was a federal statute that enabled prosecutors to attach or seize a defendant's allegedly ill-gotten funds, either before or after those funds were used to pay counsel. The final challenge (section F) was an Internal Revenue Service rule requiring all recipients of cash payments in excess of $10,000, including lawyers, to report the payment and identify the payor.

Assume that a prosecutor who is investigating an individual subpoenas the lawyer who represents that individual to appear before the grand jury. The lawyer may be representing the target of the investigation in connection with that very investigation or on another matter. The prosecutor disclaims any wish to learn privileged information, but believes that the witness has unprivileged information that will be useful in the investigation of the client and others. The defense lawyer complains that the mere requirement to appear before a grand jury that is investigating the lawyer's client undermines the professional relationship. If the lawyer must also answer questions seeking unprivileged information potentially harmful to the client, it will be practically (and possibly ethically) impossible to continue the representation. Thus, the government may be able to force the disqualification of effective counsel — on the immediate matter and on other matters — merely by calling the lawyer before the grand jury.

In In re Grand Jury Subpoena Served upon Doe (Slotnick), 781 F.2d 238 (2d Cir.) (en banc), cert. denied 475 U.S. 1108 (1986), attorney Barry Slotnick was served with a subpoena to testify before a grand jury with regard to "benefactor payments," or fees, he had allegedly received from Anthony Colombo, a reputed organized crime boss, to represent members of Colombo's "crew." Such payments would tend to prove the existence of a criminal enterprise that violated RICO. While Slotnick was challenging the subpoena, Colombo was indicted for various non-RICO offenses. Colombo charged that because the effect of the subpoena would be to disqualify Slotnick from representing him, it violated the Sixth Amendment and was "an abuse of the grand jury process" unless the government could show a "need for the information and that [Slotnick was] the only source of that information." Id. at 243. The court rejected this argument, finding "no constitutional basis for imposing additional requirements for the government to meet before the grand jury subpoena can be enforced in this case." Id. at 243-244.

When the subpoena was served, Colombo had not yet been indicted, so Sixth Amendment rights had not attached. The possibility that Slotnick would eventually be disqualified from representing Colombo because of his grand jury testimony, which the court deemed "speculat[ive]," id. at 245, did not require the government to make a preliminary showing of need for the testimony. Disqualification was an issue for the pretrial, not the grand jury, stage of proceedings. No privilege attached to the information the government sought because the privilege does not generally protect identity or fee information.

The court then considered whether Colombo's indictment changed the analysis because Sixth Amendment rights had now attached. The Amendment "assures [Colombo] of the right to be free of unduly burdensome interruption of his counsel's trial preparation and protects him from any unnecessary or arbitrary disqualification of his counsel." Id. at 250. Slotnick's testimony had "probative value" on whether Colombo was "head of" a criminal enterprise within the meaning of RICO. "Colombo's Sixth Amendment's interests [did] not outweigh the grand jury's need for this information." Id. at 251. Again, disqualification issues would be left to the pretrial stage. Two judges dissented.

Preliminary Showings: The Minority View

The defense bar has been generally unsuccessful in its effort to persuade courts that a preliminary showing of relevance and need should precede subpoenas to criminal defense lawyers. In addition to the previous case, see In re Klein, 776 F.2d 628 (7th Cir. 1985); In re Grand Jury Subpoena (Garber), 774 F.2d 624 (4th Cir. 1985), cert. denied, 475 U.S. 1108 (1986); In re Grand Jury Investigation (Harvey), 769 F.2d 1485 (11th Cir. 1985); In re Grand Jury Proceedings (Doe), 754 F.2d 154 (6th Cir. 1985). There are exceptions. See Williams v. District Court, 700 P.2d 549 (Colo. 1985) (admissibility, relevancy, and need must be shown). The Pennsylvania Rules of Professional Conduct require prosecutors to obtain "prior judicial approval" before seeking to compel a criminal defense lawyer to provide evidence against a client. Rule 3.10. However, in Baylson v. Pennsylvania Supreme Court Disciplinary Board, 764 F. Supp. 328 (E.D. Pa. 1991), the district courts in Pennsylvania declined to enforce that rule against federal prosecutors on the ground that it was in conflict with the Federal Rules of Criminal Procedure.

The Massachusetts Supreme Judicial Court adopted a rule that makes it "unprofessional" for a "prosecutor to subpoena an attorney to a grand jury without prior judicial approval" where the prosecutor "seeks to compel" testimony about a client. The federal district court in Massachusetts then adopted a local court rule that incorporated the state rule by reference. The United States challenged the local rule. In United States v. Klubock, 832 F.2d 664 (1st Cir. 1987) (en banc), the equally divided court affirmed the district court's decision upholding the validity of its rule. The dissent believed that the district court lacked authority to adopt its rule.

In 1990, the ABA amended Rule 3.8 to add a subparagraph (f), which requires "prior judicial approval after an opportunity for an adversarial proceeding" before a prosecutor may "subpoena a lawyer in a grand jury or other criminal proceeding to present evidence about a past or present client." The prosecutor must also reasonably believe that the information is unprivileged, that it is "essential" to an investigation or prosecution, and that no other "feasible alternative" for obtaining the information exists. It remains to be seen how many state courts will adopt this new provision.

FURTHER READING

Max Stern & David Hoffman, Privileged Informers: The Attorney Subpoena Problem and a Proposal for Reform, 136 U. Pa. L. Rev. 1783 (1988).

E.   FEE FORFEITURES

In 1984, Congress amended the criminal forfeiture provisions in federal law. See 18 U.S.C.A. §1963; 21 U.S.C.A. §853. Forfeiture laws empower the government to force persons convicted of identified offenses to forfeit the fruits of those offenses and property used to commit them. In the 1984 amendments, Congress made it easier to use the forfeiture laws and made them applicable to more crimes, including drug offenses and prosecutions under the Racketeer Influenced and Corrupt Organizations (RICO) statute. An excellent history of criminal forfeiture and of the 1984 amendments appears in Judge Tacha's opinion in United States v. Nichols, 841 F.2d 1485 (10th Cir. 1988), which upholds the congressional scheme. Kathleen Brickey studiously analyzes the 1984 amendments in Forfeiture of Attorneys' Fees: The Impact of RICO and CCE Forfeitures on the Right to Counsel, 72 Va. L. Rev. 493 (1986).

The 1984 amendments create pretrial procedures to freeze a defendant's allegedly ill-gotten (or ill-used) property, so it cannot be dissipated before trial, and post-trial procedures to forfeit that property (and any similar property not frozen) to the government in the event of conviction. If the property has been transferred to a third party in the meantime, it can still be forfeited, unless the third party can prove that he or she is a bona fide recipient of the property for value and reasonably without cause to believe that it was subject to forfeiture.

The amendments say nothing about money used to pay a defense lawyer. They neither specifically subject such money to pretrial restraint or post-conviction forfeiture, nor do they explicitly exclude it. The Justice

Department took the position that money used to hire counsel was subject to both procedures, just like any other property.

As you can imagine, this position caused some alarm in the defense bar. With their money frozen, many clients would no longer be able to hire counsel. Or counsel, once hired and paid, could see their fees retroactively forfeited to the government unless they could meet the bona fide purchaser test described above. (How probable is that?) The government's position has also alarmed defendants who, after their assets were frozen, might lack funds to retain a lawyer and would have to accept appointed counsel.

In its 1988 Term, the Supreme Court adjudicated the statutory and constitutional issues raised by application of forfeiture and seizure provisions to counsel fees. Caplin & Drysdale v. United States addressed the postconviction forfeiture provisions. United States v. Monsanto concerned the pretrial restraint provisions of the law. You will find it useful to have the critical language of the statute before you. In footnote 1 of *Monsanto*, the Court described and quoted the forfeiture provisions of the law as follows:

> The Comprehensive Forfeiture Act of 1984 (CFA) added or amended forfeiture provisions for two classes of violations under federal law, racketeering (RICO) offenses and continuing criminal enterprise (CCE) offenses. The CCE forfeiture statute at issue here, now provides:
>
> *§853   Criminal Forfeitures*
>
> (a) Property subject to criminal forfeiture
> Any person convicted of a violation of this subchapter or subchapter II of this chapter punishable by imprisonment for more than one year shall forfeit to the United States, irrespective of any provision of State law —
>
> > (1) any property constituting, or derived from, any proceeds the person obtained, directly or indirectly, as the result of such violation;
> >
> > (2) any of the person's property used, or intended to be used, in any manner or part, to commit, or to facilitate the commission of, such violation; and
> >
> > (3) in the case of a person convicted of engaging in a continuing criminal enterprise in violation of section 848 of this title, the person shall forfeit in addition to any property described in paragraph (1) or (2), any of his interest in, claims against, and property or contractual rights affording a source of control over, the continuing criminal enterprise.

In footnote 2, the *Monsanto* Court quoted the pretrial restraint provision of the law:

> Upon application of the United States, the court may enter a restraining order or injunction . . . or take any other action to preserve the

availability of property described in subsection (a) of [§853] for forfeiture under this section —

(A) upon the filing of an indictment or information charging a violation . . . for which criminal forfeiture may be ordered under [§853] and alleging that the property with respect to which the order is sought would, in the event of conviction, be subject to forfeiture under this section.

Finally, *Monsanto*'s footnote 3 quoted the provision of the law dealing with the rights of third parties who have received property subject to restraint or forfeiture:

Section 853(c), the third-party transfer provision, states that:

All right, title, and interest in property described in [§853] vests in the United States upon the commission of the act giving rise to forfeiture under this section. Any such property that is subsequently transferred to a person other than the defendant may be the subject of a special verdict of forfeiture and thereafter shall be ordered forfeited to the United States, unless the transferee [establishes his entitlement to such property pursuant to §853(n).]

As noted in the quotation of §853(c), a person making a claim for forfeited assets must file a petition with the court pursuant to §853(n):

If, after [a] hearing [on the petition], the court determines that the petitioner has established . . . that —
(A) the petitioner has a legal right, title, or interest in the property . . . [that predates] commission of the acts which gave rise to the forfeiture of the property under [§853]; or
(B) the petitioner is a bona fide purchaser for value of the . . . property and was at the time of purchase reasonably without cause to believe that the property was subject to forfeiture under this section; the court shall amend the order of forfeiture in accordance with its determination.

An attorney seeking a payment of fees from forfeited assets under §853(n)(6) would presumably rest his petition on subsection (B) quoted above, though it is highly doubtful that one who defends a client in a criminal case that results in forfeiture could prove that he was "without cause to believe that the property was subject to forfeiture."

Other provisions of the law are addressed below. We omit those portions of the opinions that discuss whether the forfeiture amendments apply to counsel fees. The Court concluded that Congress did not intend to exempt counsel fees.

CAPLIN & DRYSDALE v. UNITED STATES
491 U.S. 617 (1989)

JUSTICE WHITE delivered the opinion of the Court.

We are called on to determine whether the federal drug forfeiture statute includes an exemption for assets that a defendant wishes to use to pay an attorney who conducted his defense in the criminal case where forfeiture was sought. Because we determine that no such exemption exists, we must decide whether that statute, so interpreted, is consistent with the Fifth and Sixth Amendments. We hold that it is.

I

In January, 1985, Christopher Reckmeyer was charged in a multicount indictment with running a massive drug importation and distribution scheme. The scheme was alleged to be a continuing criminal enterprise (CCE), in violation of 84 Stat. 1265, as amended, 21 U.S.C. §848 (1982 ed., Supp. V). Relying on a portion of the CCE statute that authorizes forfeiture to the government of "property constituting, or derived from . . . proceeds . . . obtained" from drug-law violations, the indictment sought forfeiture of specified assets in Reckmeyer's possession. At this time, the District Court entered a restraining order forbidding Reckmeyer to transfer any of the listed assets that were potentially forfeitable.

Sometime earlier, Reckmeyer had retained petitioner, a law firm, to represent him in the ongoing grand jury investigation which resulted in the January 1985 indictments. Notwithstanding the restraining order, Reckmeyer paid the firm $25,000 for preindictment legal services a few days after the indictment was handed down; this sum was placed by petitioner in an escrow account. Petitioner continued to represent Reckmeyer following the indictment.

On March 7, 1985, Reckmeyer moved to modify the District Court's earlier restraining order to permit him to use some of the restrained assets to pay petitioner's fees; Reckmeyer also sought to exempt from any postconviction forfeiture order the assets that he intended to use to pay petitioner. However, one week later, before the District Court could conduct a hearing on this motion, Reckmeyer entered a plea agreement with the Government. Under the agreement, Reckmeyer pleaded guilty to the drug-related CCE charge, and agreed to forfeit all of the specified assets listed in the indictment. The day after Reckmeyer's plea was entered, the District Court denied his earlier motion to modify the restraining order, concluding that the plea and forfeiture agreement rendered irrelevant any further consideration of the propriety of the court's pretrial restraints. Subsequently, an order forfeiting virtually all of the assets in

Reckmeyer's possession was entered by the District Court in conjunction with his sentencing.

After this order was entered, petitioner filed a petition under 21 U.S.C. §853(n), which permits third parties with an interest in forfeited property to ask the sentencing court for an adjudication of their rights to that property; specifically, §853(n)(6)(B) gives a third party who entered into a bona fide transaction with a defendant a right to make claims against forfeited property, if that third party was "at the time of [the transaction] reasonably without cause to believe that the [defendant's assets were] subject to forfeiture." Petitioner claimed an interest in $170,000 of Reckmeyer's assets, for services it had provided Reckmeyer in conducting his defense; petitioner also sought the $25,000 being held in the escrow account, as payment for preindictment legal services. Petitioner argued alternatively that assets used to pay an attorney were exempt from forfeiture under §853, and if not, the failure of the statute to provide such an exemption rendered it unconstitutional. . . .

III . . .

A

Petitioner's first claim is that the forfeiture law makes impossible, or at least impermissibly burdens, a defendant's right "to select and be represented by one's preferred attorney." Wheat v. United States, 486 U.S. 153 (1988). Petitioner does not, nor could it defensibly do so, assert that impecunious defendants have a Sixth Amendment right to choose their counsel. The amendment guarantees defendants in criminal cases the right to adequate representation, but those who do not have the means to hire their own lawyers have no cognizable complaint so long as they are adequately represented by attorneys appointed by the courts. "[A] defendant may not insist on representation by an attorney he cannot afford." Wheat, supra, at 159. Petitioner does not dispute these propositions. Nor does the Government deny that the Sixth Amendment guarantees a defendant the right to be represented by an otherwise qualified attorney whom that defendant can afford to hire, or who is willing to represent the defendant even though he is without funds. Applying these principles to the statute in question here, we observe that nothing in §853 prevents a defendant from hiring the attorney of his choice, or disqualifies any attorney from serving as a defendant's counsel. Thus, unlike Wheat, this case does not involve a situation where the Government has asked a court to prevent a defendant's chosen counsel from representing the accused. Instead, petitioner urges that a violation of the Sixth Amendment arises here because of the forfeiture, at the instance of the Government, of assets that defendants intend to use to pay their attorneys.

Even in this sense, of course, the burden the forfeiture law imposes on a criminal defendant is limited. The forfeiture statute does not prevent a defendant who has nonforfeitable assets from retaining any attorney of his choosing. Nor is it necessarily the case that a defendant who possesses nothing but assets the Government seeks to have forfeited will be prevented from retaining counsel of choice. Defendants like Reckmeyer may be able to find lawyers willing to represent them, hoping that their fees will be paid in the event of acquittal, or via some other means that a defendant might come by in the future. The burden placed on defendants by the forfeiture law is therefore a limited one.

Nonetheless, there will be cases where a defendant will be unable to retain the attorney of his choice, when that defendant would have been able to hire that lawyer if he had access to forfeitable assets, and if there was no risk that fees paid by the defendant to his counsel would later be recouped under §853(c). It is in these cases, petitioner argues, that the Sixth Amendment puts limits on the forfeiture statute.

This submission is untenable. Whatever the full extent of the Sixth Amendment's protection of one's right to retain counsel of his choosing, that protection does not go beyond "the individual's right to spend his own money to obtain the advice and assistance of . . . counsel." Cf. Walters' v. National Ass'n. of Radiation Survivors, 473 U.S. 305, 370 (1985) (Stevens, J., dissenting). A defendant has no Sixth Amendment right to spend another person's money for services rendered by an attorney, even if those funds are the only way that that defendant will be able to retain the attorney of his choice. A robbery suspect, for example, has no Sixth Amendment right to use funds he has stolen from a bank to retain an attorney to defend him if he is apprehended. The money, though in his possession, is not rightfully his; the government does not violate the Sixth Amendment if it seizes the robbery proceeds, and refuses to permit the defendant to use them to pay for his defense. "[N]o lawyer, in any case, . . . has the right to accept stolen property, or . . . ransom money, in payment of a fee. . . . The privilege to practice law is not a license to steal." Petitioner appears to concede as much, as respondent in *Monsanto* clearly does.

Petitioner seeks to distinguish such cases for Sixth Amendment purposes by arguing that the bank's claim to robbery proceeds rests on "preexisting property rights," while the Government's claim to forfeitable assets rests on a "penal statute" which embodies the "fictive property-law concept of . . . relation-back" and is merely "a mechanism for preventing fraudulent conveyances of the defendant's assets, not . . . a device for determining true title to property." In light of this, petitioner contends, the burden placed on defendant's Sixth Amendment rights by the forfeiture statute outweighs the Government's interest in forfeiture.

The premises of petitioner's constitutional analysis are unsound in several respects. First, the property rights given the Government by virtue of the forfeiture statute are more substantial than petitioner acknowledges. In §853(c), the so-called "relation-back" provision, Congress dictated that "[a]ll right, title and interest in property" obtained by criminals via the illicit means described in the statute "vests in the United States upon the commission of the act giving rise to forfeiture." As Congress observed when the provision was adopted, this approach, known as the "taint theory," is one that "has long been recognized in forfeiture cases," including the decision in United States v. Stowell, 133 U.S. 1 (1890). In *Stowell*, the Court explained the operation of a similar forfeiture provision (for violations of the Internal Revenue Code) as follows:

> As soon [as the possessor of the forfeitable asset committed the violation] of the internal revenue laws, the forfeiture under those laws took effect, and (though needing judicial condemnation to perfect it) operated from that time as a statutory conveyance to the United States of all the right, title, and interest then remaining in the [possessor]; and was as valid and effectual, against all the world, as a recorded deed. The right so vested in the United States could not be defeated or impaired by any subsequent dealings of the . . . [possessor].

In sum, §853(c) reflects the application of the long-recognized and lawful practice of vesting title to any forfeitable assets, in the United States, at the time of the criminal act giving rise to forfeiture. Concluding that Reckmeyer cannot give good title to such property to petitioner because he did not hold good title is neither extraordinary or novel. Nor does petitioner claim, as a general proposition that the relation-back provision is unconstitutional, or that Congress cannot, as a general matter, vest title to assets derived from the crime in the Government, as of the date of the criminal act in question. Petitioner's claim is that whatever part of the assets that is necessary to pay attorney's fees cannot be subjected to forfeiture. But given the Government's title to Reckmeyer's assets upon conviction, to hold that the Sixth Amendment creates some right in Reckmeyer to alienate such assets, or creates a right on petitioner's part to receive these assets, would be peculiar.

There is no constitutional principle that gives one person the right to give another's property to a third party, even where the person seeking to complete the exchange wishes to do so in order to exercise a constitutionally protected right. While petitioner and its supporting amici attempt to distinguish between the expenditure of forfeitable assets to exercise one's Sixth Amendment rights, and expenditures in the pursuit of other constitutionally protected freedoms, there is no such distinction between, or hierarchy among, constitutional rights. If defendants have a right to spend forfeitable assets on attorney's fees, why not on exercises of the right to speak, practice one's religion, or travel? The full exercise of these rights, too, depends in part on one's financial wherewithal; and forfeiture, or even the threat of forfeiture, may similarly prevent a defendant from enjoying these rights as fully as he might otherwise. Nonetheless, we are not about to recognize an antiforfeiture exception for the exercise of each such right; nor does one exist for the exercise of Sixth Amendment rights, either.[5]

Petitioner's "balancing analysis" to the contrary rests substantially on the view that the Government has only a modest interest in forfeitable assets that may be used to retain an attorney. Petitioner takes the position that, in large part, once assets have been paid over from client to attorney, the principal ends of forfeiture have been achieved: dispossessing a drug dealer or racketeer of the proceeds of his wrong-doing. We think that this view misses the mark for three reasons.

First, the Government has a pecuniary interest in forfeiture that goes beyond merely separating a criminal from his ill-gotten gains; that legitimate interest extends to recovering *all* forfeitable assets, for such assets are deposited in a Fund that supports law-enforcement efforts in a variety of important and useful ways. The sums of money that can be raised for law-enforcement activities this way are substantial,[6] and the Government's interest in using the profits of crime to fund these activities should not be discounted.

Second, the statute permits "rightful owners" of forfeited assets to make claims for forfeited assets before they are retained by the government. The Government's interest in winning undiminished forfeiture thus includes the objective of returning property, in full, to those wrongfully deprived or defrauded of it. Where the Government pursues this restitutionary end, the Government's interest in forfeiture is virtually indistinguishable from its interest in returning to a bank the proceeds of a bank robbery; and a forfeiture-defendant's claim of right to use such assets to hire an attorney, instead of having them returned to their rightful owners, is no more persuasive than a bank robber's similar claim.

Finally, as we have recognized previously, a major purpose motivating congressional adoption and continued refinement of the RICO and CCE forfeiture provisions has been the desire to lessen the economic power of organized crime and drug enterprises. This includes the use of such economic power to retain private counsel. As the Court of Appeals put it: "Congress has already underscored the compelling public interest in

5. It would be particularly odd to recognize the Sixth Amendment as a defense to forfeiture, because forfeiture is a substantive charge in the indictment against a defendant. Thus, petitioner asks us to take the Sixth Amendment's guarantee of counsel "for his defense," and make that guarantee *petitioner's defense* to the indictment. We doubt that the Amendment's guarantees, which are procedural in nature, provide such a substantive defense to charges against an accused.

6. For example, just one of the assets which Reckmeyer agreed to forfeit, a parcel of land known as "Shelburne Glebe," was recently sold by federal authorities for $5.3 million. The proceeds of the sale will fund federal, state, and local law enforcement activities.

stripping criminals such as Reckmeyer of their undeserved economic power, and part of that undeserved power may be the ability to command high-priced legal talent." The notion that the government has a legitimate interest in depriving criminals of economic power, even in so far as that power is used to retain counsel of choice, may be somewhat unsettling. But when a defendant claims that he has suffered some substantial impairment of his Sixth Amendment rights by virtue of the seizure or forfeiture of assets in his possession, such a complaint is no more than the reflection of "the harsh reality that the quality of a criminal defendant's representation frequently may turn on his ability to retain the best counsel money can buy." Morris v. Slappy, 461 U.S. 1, 23 (1983) (Brennan, J., concurring in result). Again, the Court of Appeals put it aptly: "The modern day Jean Valjean must be satisfied with appointed counsel. Yet the drug merchant claims that his possession of huge sums of money . . . entitles him to something more. We reject this contention, and any notion of a constitutional right to use the proceeds of crime to finance an expensive defense."[7] . . .

We therefore reject petitioner's claim of a Sixth Amendment right of criminal defendants to use assets that are the government's — assets adjudged forfeitable, as Reckmeyer's were — to pay attorneys' fees, merely because those assets are in their possession.[10]

---

7. We also reject the contention, advanced by amici, see, e.g., Brief the American Bar Association as Amicus Curiae, and accepted by some courts considering claims like petitioner's, that a type of "per se" ineffective assistance of counsel results — due to the particular complexity of RICO or drug-enterprise cases — when a defendant is not permitted to use assets in his possession to retain counsel of choice, and instead must rely on appointed counsel. If such an argument were accepted, it would bar the trial of indigents charged with such offenses, because those persons would have to rely on appointed counsel — which this view considers *per se* ineffective.

If appointed counsel is ineffective in a particular case, a defendant has resort to the remedies discussed in Strickland v. Washington, 466 U.S. 668 (1984). But we cannot say that the Sixth Amendment's guarantee of effective assistance of counsel is a guarantee of a privately-retained counsel in every complex case, irrespective of a defendant's ability to pay.

10. Petitioner advances three additional reasons for invalidating the forfeiture statute, all of which concern possible ethical conflicts created for lawyers defending persons facing forfeiture of assets in their possession.

Petitioner first notes the statute's exemption from forfeiture of property transferred to a bona fide purchaser who was "reasonably without cause to believe that the property was subject to forfeiture." 21 U.S.C. §853(n)(6)(B). This provision, it is said, might give an attorney an incentive not to investigate a defendant's case as fully as possible, so that the lawyer can invoke it to protect from forfeiture any fees he has received. Yet given the requirement that any assets which the Government wishes to have forfeited must be specified in the indictment, see Fed. Rule Crim. Proc. 7(c)(2), the only way a lawyer could be a beneficiary of §853(n)(6)(B) would be to fail to read the indictment of his client. In this light, the prospect that a lawyer might find himself in conflict with his client, by seeking to take advantage of §853(n)(6)(B), amounts to very little. Petitioner itself concedes that such a conflict will, as a practical matter, never arise: a defendant's "lawyer . . . could not demonstrate that he was 'reasonably without cause to believe that the property was subject to forfeiture,' " petitioner concludes at one point.

The second possible conflict arises in plea bargaining: petitioner posits that a lawyer may advise a client to accept an agreement entailing a more harsh prison sentence but no

B

Petitioner's second constitutional claim is that the forfeiture statute is invalid under the Due Process Clause of the Fifth Amendment because it permits the Government to upset the "balance of forces between the accused and his accuser." We are not sure that this contention adds anything to petitioner's Sixth Amendment claim, because, while "[t]he Constitution guarantees a fair trial through the Due Process Clauses . . . it defines the basic elements of a fair trail largely through the several provisions of the Sixth Amendment," Strickland v. Washington, 466 U.S. 668, 684-685 (1984). We have concluded above that the Sixth Amendment is not offended by the forfeiture provisions at issue here. Even if, however, the Fifth Amendment provides some added protection not encompassed in the Sixth Amendment's more specific provisions, we find petitioner's claim based on the Fifth Amendment unavailing.

Forfeiture provisions are powerful weapons in the war on crime; like any such weapons, their impact can be devastating when used unjustly. But due process claims alleging such abuses are cognizable only in specific cases of prosecutorial misconduct (and petitioner has made no such allegation here) or when directed to a rule that is inherently unconstitutional. "The fact that the . . . Act might operate unconstitutionally under some conceivable set of circumstances is insufficient to render it . . . invalid." Petitioner's claim — that the power available to prosecutors under the statute *could* be abused — proves too much, for many tools available to prosecutors can be misused in a way that violates the rights of innocent persons. As the Court of Appeals put it, in rejecting this claim when advanced below: "Every criminal law carries with it the potential for abuse, but a potential for abuse does not require a finding of facial invalidity."

We rejected a claim similar to petitioner's last Term, in Wheat v. United States, 486 U.S. 153 (1988). In *Wheat*, the petitioner argued that

---

forfeiture — even where contrary to the client's interests — in an effort to preserve the lawyer's fee. Following such a strategy, however, would surely constitute ineffective assistance of counsel. We see no reason why our cases such as Strickland v. Washington, 466 U.S. 668 (1984), are inadequate to deal with any such ineffectiveness where it arises. In any event, there is no claim that such conduct occurred here, nor could there be, as Reckmeyer's plea agreement included forfeiture of virtually every asset in his possession. Moreover, we rejected a claim similar to this one in Evans v. Jeff D., 475 U.S. 717, 727-728 (1986).

Finally, petitioner argues that the forfeiture statute, in operation, will create a system akin to "contingency fees" for defense lawyers; only a defense lawyer who wins acquittal for his client will be able to collect his fees, and contingent fees in criminal cases are generally considered unethical. But there is no indication here that petitioner, or any other firm, has actually sought to charge a defendant on a contingency basis; rather the claim is that a law firm's prospect of collecting its fee may turn on the outcome at trial. This, however, may often be the case in criminal defense work. Nor is it clear why permitting contingent fees in criminal cases — if that is what the forfeiture statute does — violates a criminal defendant's Sixth Amendment rights. The fact that a federal statutory scheme authorizing contingency fees — again, if that is what Congress has created in §853 (a premise we doubt) — is at odds with model disciplinary rules or state disciplinary codes hardly renders the federal statute invalid.

permitting a court to disqualify a defendant's chosen counsel because of conflicts of interest — over that defendant's objection to the disqualification — would encourage the government to "manufacture" such conflicts to deprive a defendant of his chosen attorney. While acknowledging that this was possible, we declined to fashion the per se constitutional rule petitioner sought in *Wheat*, instead observing that "trial courts are undoubtedly aware of [the] possibility" of abuse, and would have to "take it into consideration," when dealing with disqualification motions.

A similar approach should be taken here. The Constitution does not forbid the imposition of an otherwise permissible criminal sanction, such as forfeiture, merely because in some cases prosecutors may abuse the processes available to them, e.g., by attempting to impose them on persons who should not be subjected to that punishment. Cases involving particular abuses can be dealt with individually by the lower courts, when (and if) any such cases arise.

IV

For the reasons given above, we find that petitioner's statutory and constitutional challenges to the forfeiture imposed here are without merit. The judgment of the Court of Appeals is therefore affirmed.*

UNITED STATES v. MONSANTO
491 U.S. 600 (1989)

[Funds Monsanto had planned to use to pay his lawyer were frozen before trial. He went to trial with appointed counsel and was convicted. The following portion of Justice White's opinion responds to Monsanto's constitutional attack on the pretrial seizure.]

In addition to the constitutional issues raised in *Caplin & Drysdale*, respondent contends that freezing the assets in question before he is convicted — and before they are finally adjudged to be forfeitable — raises distinct constitutional concerns. We conclude, however, that assets in a defendant's possession may be restrained in the way they were here based on a finding of probable cause to believe that the assets are forfeitable.[10]

---

*The dissent for this case and the next appears at page 439. — ED.

10. We do not consider today, however, whether the Due Process Clause requires a hearing before a pretrial restraining order can be imposed. As noted above, in its initial consideration of this case, a panel of the Second Circuit ordered that such a hearing be held before permitting the entry of a restraining order; on remand, the District Court held an extensive, 4-day hearing on the question of probable cause.

We have previously permitted the Government to seize property based on a finding of probable cause to believe that the property will ultimately be proven forfeitable. Here, where respondent was not ousted from his property, but merely restrained from disposing of it, the governmental intrusion was even less severe than those permitted by our prior decisions.

Indeed, it would be odd to conclude that the Government may not restrain property, such as the home and apartment in respondent's possession, based on a finding of probable cause, when we have held that (under appropriate circumstances), the Government may restrain *persons* where there is a finding of probable cause to believe that the accused has committed a serious offense. Given the gravity of the offenses charged in the indictment, respondent himself could have been subjected to pretrial restraint if deemed necessary to "reasonably assure [his] appearance [at trial] and the safety of . . . the community"; we find no constitutional infirmity in §853(e)'s authorization of a similar restraint on respondent's property to protect its "appearance" at trial, and protect the community's interest in full recovery of any ill-gotten gains.

Respondent contends that both the nature of the Government's property right in forfeitable assets, and the nature of the use to which he would have put these assets (i.e., retaining an attorney), require some departure from our established rule of permitting pretrail restraint of assets based on probable cause. We disagree. In *Caplin & Drysdale,* we conclude that a weighing of these very interests suggests that the Government may — without offending the Fifth or Sixth Amendments — obtain forfeiture of property that a defendant might have wished to use to pay his attorney. Given this holding, we find that a pretrial restraining order does not "arbitrarily" interfere with a defendant's "fair opportunity" to retain counsel. Put another way: if the Government may, posttrial, forbid the use of forfeited assets to pay an attorney, then surely no constitutional violation occurs when, after probable cause is adequately established, the Government obtains an order barring a defendant from frustrating that end by dissipating his assets prior to trial. . . .

DISSENTING OPINIONS IN *CAPLIN & DRYSDALE* AND *MONSANTO*

[Justice Blackmun dissented in both *Monsanto* and *Caplin & Drysdale* in a single opinion in which Justices Brennan, Marshall, and Stevens joined. Justice Blackmun first disputed the majority's conclusion that Congress intended the forfeiture amendments to encompass counsel fees. Reaching the constitutional question, Justice Blackmun discussed the historical and practical importance of the right to retain private counsel. He then continued:]

Had it been Congress' express aim to undermine the adversary system as we know it, it could hardly have found a better engine of destruction than attorney's-fee forfeiture. The main effect of forfeitures under the Act, of course, will be to deny the defendant the right to retain counsel, and therefore the right to have his defense designed and presented by an attorney he has chosen and trusts. If the Government restrains the defendant's assets before trial, private counsel will be unwilling to continue or to take on the defense. Even if no restraining order is entered, the possibility of forfeiture after conviction will itself substantially diminish the likelihood that private counsel will agree to take the case. The "message [to private counsel] is 'Do not represent this defendant or you will lose your fee.' That being the kind of message lawyers are likely to take seriously, the defendant will find it difficult or impossible to secure representation."

The resulting relationship between the defendant and his court-appointed counsel will likely begin in distrust, and be exacerbated to the extent that the defendant perceives his new-found "indigency" as a form of punishment imposed by the Government in order to weaken his defense. If the defendant had been represented by private counsel earlier in the proceedings, the defendant's sense that the Government has stripped him of his defenses will be sharpened by the concreteness of his loss. Appointed counsel may be inexperienced and undercompensated and, for that reason, may not have adequate opportunity or resources to deal with the special problems presented by what is likely to be a complex trial. The already scarce resources of a public defender's office will be stretched to the limit. Facing a lengthy trial against a better-armed adversary, the temptation to recommend a guilty plea will be great. The result, if the defendant is convicted, will be a sense, often well grounded, that justice was not done.

Even if the defendant finds a private attorney who is "so foolish, ignorant, beholden or idealistic as to take the business," the attorney-client relationship will be undermined by the forfeiture statute. Perhaps the attorney will be willing to violate ethical norms by working on a contingent fee basis in a criminal case. But if he is not — and we should question the integrity of any criminal-defense attorney who would violate the ethical norms of the profession by doing so — the attorney's own interests will dictate that he remain ignorant of the source of the assets from which he is paid. Under §853(c), a third-party transferee may keep assets if "the transferee establishes . . . that he is a bona fide purchaser for value of such property who at the time of purchase was reasonably without cause to believe that the property was subject to forfeiture under this section." The less an attorney knows, the greater the likelihood that he can claim to have been an "innocent" third party. The attorney's interest in knowing nothing is directly adverse to his client's interest in full disclosure. The result of the conflict may be a less vigorous investigation of the defendant's circumstances, leading in turn to a failure to recognize or pursue avenues of inquiry necessary to the defense. Other conflicts of interest are also likely to develop. The attorney who fears for his fee will be tempted to make the Government's waiver of fee-forfeiture the sine qua non for any plea agreement, a position which conflicts with his client's best interests.

Perhaps most troubling is the fact that forfeiture statutes place the Government in the position to exercise an intolerable degree of power over any private attorney who takes on the task of representing a defendant in a forfeiture case. The decision whether to seek a restraining order rests with the prosecution, as does the decision whether to waive forfeiture upon a plea of guilty or a conviction at trial. The Government will be ever tempted to use the forfeiture weapon against a defense attorney who is particularly talented or aggressive on the client's behalf — the attorney who is better than what, in the Government's view, the defendant deserves. The spectre of the Government's selectively excluding only the most talented defense counsel is a serious threat to the equality of forces necessary for the adversarial system to perform at its best. An attorney whose fees are potentially subject to forfeiture will be forced to operate in an environment in which the Government is not only the defendant's adversary, but also his own.

The long-term effects of the fee-forfeiture practice will be to decimate the private criminal-defense bar. As the use of the forfeiture mechanism expands to new categories of federal crimes and spreads to the States, only one class of defendants will be free routinely to retain private counsel: the affluent defendant accused of a crime that generates no economic gain. As the number of private clients diminishes, only the most idealistic and the least skilled of young lawyers will be attracted to the field, while the remainder seek greener pastures elsewhere.

In short, attorney's-fee forfeiture substantially undermines every interest served by the Sixth Amendment right to chosen counsel, on the individual and institutional levels, over the short term and the long haul.

We have recognized that although there is a "presumption in favor of [the defendant's] counsel of choice," Wheat v. United States, 486 U.S., at 158, 162, the right to counsel of choice is not absolute. Some substantial and legitimate governmental interests may require the courts to disturb the defedant's choice of counsel, as "[w]hen a defendant's selection of counsel, under the particular facts and circumstances of a case, gravely imperils the prospect of a fair trial," id., at 166, (Marshall, J., dissenting), or threatens to undermine the orderly disposition of the case, see Ungar v. Sarafite, 376 U.S. 575, 589 (1964). But never before today has the Court suggested that the Government's naked desire to deprive a defendant of "the best counsel money can buy," Caplin & Drysdale, quoting Morris v. Slappy, 461 U.S. 1, 23 (1983) (Brennan, J., opinion concurring in result), is itself a legitimate government interest that can justify the Government's interference with the defendant's right to chosen counsel — and for good reason. "[W]eakening the ability of an accused to defend himself at trial is an advantage for the government. But it is not a legitimate government interest that can be used to justify invasion of a constitutional right." And the *legitimate* interests the Government asserts are extremely weak, far too weak to justify the Act's substantial erosion of the defendant's Sixth Amendment rights.

The Government claims a property interest in forfeitable assets, predicated on the relation-back provision, §853(c), which employs a legal fiction to grant the Government title in all forfeitable property as of the date of the crime. The majority states: "Permitting a defendant to use assets for his private purpose that, under this provision, will become the property of the United States if conviction occurs, cannot be sanctioned." But the Government's insistence that it has a paramount interest in the defendant's resources "simply begs the constitutional question rather than answering it. Indeed, the ultimate constitutional issue might well be framed precisely as whether Congress may use this wholly fictive device of property law to cut off this fundamental right of the accused in a criminal case. If the right must yield here to countervailing governmental interests, the relation-back device undoubtedly could be used to implement the governmental interests, but surely it cannot serve as a substitute for them." . . .

Finally, even if the Government's asserted interests were entitled to some weight, the manner in which the Government has chosen to protect them undercuts its position. Under §853(c), a third-party transferee may keep assets if he was "reasonably without cause to believe that the property was subject to forfeiture." Most legitimate providers of services will meet the requirements for this statutory exemption. The exception is the defendant's attorney, who cannot do his job (or at least cannot do his job well) without asking questions that will reveal the source of the defendant's assets. It is difficult to put great weight on the Government's interest in increasing the amount of property available for forfeiture when the means chosen are so starkly underinclusive, and the burdens fall almost exclusively upon the exercise of a constitutional right.

Interests as ephemeral as these should not be permitted to defeat the defendant's right to the assistance of his chosen counsel.

The Due Process Angle

Left undecided in *Monsanto* (see footnote 10) was whether a defendant whose assets the government seeks to restrain between indictment and verdict is entitled to an adversarial hearing at which he or she can challenge the government's contention that the assets are potentially subject to forfeiture. On remand in *Monsanto*, the Second Circuit en banc held that

> the fifth and sixth amendments, considered in combination, require an adversary, post-restraint, pretrial hearing as to probable cause that (a) the de-

fendant committed crimes that provide a basis for forfeiture and (b) the properties specified as forfeitable in the indictment are properly forfeitable. . . .

However, the defendant is entitled to this hearing only as to assets "needed to retain counsel of choice." That interest was pivotal to the court's analysis:

> The private interest at stake is not merely a defendant's wish to use his property in whatever manner he sees fit. Here, that interest is augmented by an important liberty interest: the qualified right, under the sixth amendment, to counsel of choice. The restraining order severely affects that right by putting beyond the defendant's reach assets which are demonstrably necessary to obtain the legal counsel he desires. The temporary, nonfinal deprivation is, in that respect, effectively a permanent one.

Judge Mahoney's majority opinion was joined by six other judges. Five judges agreed with the majority's constitutional analysis but concluded that the majority had "crossed the line between interpreting a statute and wholly rewriting it." They would have declared the law unconstitutional. One judge dissented. United States v. Monsanto, 924 F.2d 1186, 1193-1203 (2d Cir. 1991) (en banc), cert. denied, 112 S. Ct. 382 (1991). Nearly all courts to address the issue are in accord. For a contrary view, see United States v. Bissell, 866 F.2d 1343 (11th Cir.), cert. denied, 493 U.S. 849 (1989).

FURTHER READING

For lower court analysis of the ethical issues presented by the forfeiture law, see Judge Tacha's discussion in *Nichols*, page 428 supra, and Judge Wilkinson's discussion in the Fourth Circuit's *Caplin & Drysdale* opinion, reported at 837 F.2d 637 (4th Cir. 1988).

Bruce Winick, in advance of the Supreme Court's opinions, described how the constitutional problems could be circumvented. See Bruce Winick, Forfeiture of Attorneys' Fees Under RICO and CCE and the Right to Counsel of Choice: The Constitutional Dilemma and How to Avoid It, 43 U. Miami L. Rev. 765 (1989).

F. REPORTING CASH RECEIPTS

Section 6050I of the Internal Revenue Code requires persons who receive cash in excess of $10,000 in connection with a trade or business to report the receipt in an informational return. The statute applies whether the money is received in one or more transactions. The return must include the name, address, and taxpayer identification number of the payor, the amount of cash received, and the date and nature of the transaction.

Lawyers are included in this requirement, so that if a lawyer receives more than $10,000 in cash from a client, he or she must report it. Does this duty clash with the duty of confidentiality? If so, which prevails?

Lawyers have asked ethics committees for advice with regard to their duties under Section 6050I. Arizona Opinion 3 (1987) holds that revelation as required by law does not offend the lawyer's confidentiality obligation under the Model Rules. How can this be? Model Rule 1.6 contains no exception for obligations imposed by law.

DR 4-101(C)(2) does contain such an exception. A lawyer in Illinois, a code state, asked the Chicago Bar Association what to do after a client paid him $100,000 in cash. The client had been charged with violating drug laws. The Association concluded that because the IRS did not intend to exempt lawyers from the cash reporting requirement, the lawyer could reveal the payment without violating the confidentiality duty. Because it was unclear, however, whether the IRS had authority to include lawyers in the reporting requirement, the Association recommended that the lawyer instead file the required form without revealing the client's name, thereby placing the government on notice that the information has been withheld. The government could then seek judicial enforcement and its authority could be tested. Should the lawyer first warn the client and give him a chance to alter the method of payment?

Other bar associations have reached similar conclusions. New Mexico Opinion 1989-2 says that a lawyer should advise a client of the potential consequences of paying with cash and then, if retained anyway, make a good faith challenge to the federal law. Ohio Opinion 90-4 says that lawyers should reveal cash receipts voluntarily but advise their clients of the risk. Michigan Opinion RI-54 (1990) says that lawyers may comply with the requirement but should assert the privilege wherever appropriate.

Such an assertion is not likely to prevail. In United States v. Goldberger & Dubin, 935 F.2d 501 (2d Cir. 1991), the court held that a client's name and the amount of his or her cash payment are not protected by the attorney-client privilege. The court wrote that the "clear and unmistakable intent of Congress in enacting the currency reporting statutes was to enable the IRS to identify tax payers with large cash incomes." Clients who wanted to avoid disclosure by their lawyers "need only pay counsel in some other manner than with cash. The choice is theirs." What will happen if the client uses the cash to get a bank check with which to pay the lawyer?

Daniel Capra takes the measure of these recent trends and the effects they threaten in Deterring the Formation of the Attorney-Client Relationship: Disclosure of Client Identity, Payment of Fees and Communication by Fiduciaries, 4 Geo. J. Legal Ethics 235 (1990).

IX

Lawyers for Entities

A lawyer for an organization — e.g., a corporation, government, a union, or a limited partnership — may face especially thorny professional problems. (The material on confidentiality introduced some of them. See page 27 supra.) These problems often flow from the fact that while the lawyer's client is the organization, the lawyer must represent it through officers and agents who (with rare exception) are not clients. The resulting triangular arrangement is different from the one confronting lawyers employed by an insurer to represent an insured. (Do you see how?)

In a single sentence, Rule 1.13(a) attempts to define the relationship among the parties to this triangle. Does it succeed? Drafts of this sentence put it differently. They said that a lawyer represents an organization "as distinct from its" constituents. What is the difference between representing an entity "as distinct from" its constituents and representing it "acting through" its constituents, as Rule 1.13(a) puts it? How might this difference affect resolution of the issues you are about to study? (Some states, like New Jersey, retained the draft language.)

Generically, the problems that arise when a lawyer represents an entity acting through its constituents are the same as those that confront all lawyers — problems of loyalty, conflicts, client identity, and confidentiality and the duty not to aid a client's crimes and frauds. It seems, however, that when a client is represented "through" others, these problems can become exponentially more complex. The situation is further complicated when a lawyer is employed, rather than retained, by an organization. A single-client lawyer is in an especially vulnerable position, isn't she? If the single client is a corporation, its officers will have almost total control over the lawyer's professional life — her title, income, assignments, office space, and support staff. Put her in a small city with two children in college and a hefty mortgage, and the plot does begin to thicken.

While such facts are supposed to be irrelevant to the lawyer's professional conduct, realistically it may strongly influence how she reacts when faced with a duty to her client that the CEO suggests she ignore. ("Don't be such a goody two-shoes. Learn how to play ball.") We further engage this dilemma in the discussion of corporate whistleblowing and retaliatory discharge below.

Ask yourself what you believe house counsel of a large corporation ought to do if a high ranking officer tells her that

1. He is about to implement a business decision that the lawyer believes unwise but defensible;
2. He is about to implement a business decision that the lawyer believes unwise and certain to result in a substantial loss for the corporation;
3. He is about to implement a business decision that counsel recognizes could be profitable but which she also believes may subject the company to antitrust liability;
4. He is about to implement a business decision that counsel recognizes may be profitable but which is clearly in violation of the antitrust laws;
5. He is about to take action that will personally benefit the officer and that, the lawyer concludes, will violate a fiduciary obligation to the corporation?

In responding to each of these situations, how well guided are you by the code (EC 5-18) or by the Model Rules (Rule 1.13)? How, if at all, would your answers change if instead of an official of the corporation, the board of directors engaged in (or tolerated) the above conduct? Would your responses differ if the conduct was already concluded? For each prospect, may or must the lawyer tell anyone else about the communication and, if so, whom?

These questions are not idle. In 1980, Fortune magazine studied the incidence of corporate crime during the prior decade. It focused on bribery, criminal fraud, illegal political contributions, tax evasion, and criminal antitrust violations (that is, price-fixing and bid-rigging). Only domestic crime was included. Of the 1,043 major corporations in the study, 117 (11 percent) were involved "in at least one major delinquency. . . . Some companies have been multiple offenders. In all, 188 citations are listed covering 163 separate offenses — 98 antitrust violations; 28 cases of kickbacks, bribery, or illegal rebates; 21 instances of illegal political contributions; 11 cases of fraud; and five cases of tax evasion." Irwin Ross, How Lawless Are Big Companies?, Fortune, Dec. 1, 1980, at 56. This kind of thing didn't stop in 1980 either. More recent headlines have told of fraud against customers by the Hertz Corporation, check-kiting by E. F. Hutton, and Beech-Nut's effort to pass sugar water off as children's apple juice.*

And perhaps the largest scandal of all is the failure of so many of America's savings and loan institutions in the 1980s and early 1990s. Martin Mayer, The Greatest-Ever Bank Robbery (1990). Were lawyers privy to, even participants in, some of these shenanigans, as some have charged? Law firms were named, along with others, in civil actions arising out of the S&L crisis. See Steve France, Savings & Loan Lawyers, ABA J. 52 (May 1991). In Lincoln Savings & Loan Assn. v. Wall, 743 F. Supp. 901, 919-920 (D.D.C. 1990), Judge Stanley Sporkin upheld the decision of the federal Office of Thrift Supervision to assume control of Lincoln Savings and Loan, run by Charles Keating. Lincoln's collapse, which alone is estimated to have cost the government billions of dollars in federal deposit insurance, led Judge Sporkin to end his opinion with some rhetorical questions:

> Keating testified that he was so bent on doing the "right thing" that he surrounded himself with literally scores of accountants and lawyers to make sure all the transactions were legal. The questions that must be asked are:
>
> [1.] Where were these professionals, a number of whom are now asserting their rights under the Fifth Amendment, when these clearly improper transactions were consummated?
> [2.] Why didn't any of them speak up or disassociate themselves from the transactions?
> [3.] Where also were the outside accountants and attorneys when these transactions were effectuated?
>
> What is difficult to understand is that with all the professional talent involved (both accounting and legal), why at least one professional would not have blown the whistle to stop the overreaching that took place in this case.

We can let the accountants worry about themselves. But what were the responsibilities of Lincoln's lawyers, some of whom were later sued by the government, as successor in interest to Lincoln, and by bondholders of Lincoln's parent company? Several law firms settled these claims for tens of millions of dollars.

To begin to answer these questions, we turn to Evans v. Artek Systems Corp., which manages to contain issues of client identity, confidentiality, conflicts, and loyalty in a single opinion.

---

*See, respectively, the N.Y. Times, Jan. 26, 1988, at 1, col. 2; N.Y. Times, May 3, 1985, at 1, col. 2; N.Y. Times, Feb. 18, 1988, at 1, col. 6.

EVANS v. ARTEK SYSTEMS
715 F.2d 788 (2d Cir. 1983)

MANSFIELD, J.

[Evans was a shareholder of Artek, a manufacturer of scientific measurement devices. Until March 31, 1976, Artek had been represented by outside counsel, Rabin & Silverman (R&S). In November 1977, Dynatech Corporation acquired a majority of Artek common stock. In July 1980, Leonhardt, then Artek's president, "consulted briefly with R&S about possible legal action that might be taken against Dynatech based on alleged wrongful conduct causing injury to Artek and its minority public stockholders." Leonhardt gave R&S a memorandum outlining what he believed Dynatech had done to drive down the market price of Artek so that Dynatech could then purchase the stock of Artek's minority shareholders "and effectuate a merger at a bargain rate on the basis of the depressed value of Artek stock."

Leonhardt gave R&S a copy of a June 27, 1979, opinion letter from Dynatech's law firm, Crowell & Moring, which supported Leonhardt's theory and had been sent to him by Welsh, a Dynatech vice president and Artek's chair. Welsh's cover memorandum reminded Leonhardt that he was an officer of Dynatech and that the opinion letter was confidential. No other person at Artek or Dynatech was aware that Leonhardt was seeking legal advice from R&S. R&S received no fee for Leonhardt's consultation. Subsequently, Leonhardt "may have consulted R&S not on behalf of Dynatech or Artek but in his individual capacity, seeking to protect the interests of Artek's minority public stockholders."

In August 1982, Artek became a wholly owned subsidiary of Dynatech. Artek's shareholders were given "about $1.75 in market value of Dynatech's stock for each share of Artek's stock." Leonhardt contended that before Dynatech had begun to depress Artek stock's value, it sold as high as $7.00 per share. In August 1982, Evans, a minority shareholder in Artek, brought a class action against Dynatech, Artek, and the Artek directors, charging stock fraud and the use of a false and misleading proxy statement. The complaint also contained a derivative claim charging Dynatech with waste of Artek's corporate assets. Leonhardt and Artek were named as nominal defendants. Evans was represented by R&S. All defendants except Leonhardt moved to disqualify R&S, "primarily on the ground of the July 1980 consultation by Leonhardt with R&S." The district court granted the motion. The Second Circuit first reviewed the cases on disqualification for successive conflicts of interest. (See Chapter 6.) Judge Mansfield then continued]:

The crucial issue, therefore, is whether R&S was consulted by Leonhardt in 1980 on behalf of Artek or Dynatech, as the defendants (except Leonhardt) contend, or on behalf of Leonhardt individually and the minority stockholders, as plaintiff argues. If a confidential attorney-client relationship existed in 1980 between R&S and Dynatech or Artek, R&S must be disqualified from acting as plaintiff's counsel in the present case [because of a successive conflict of interests]. If, on the other hand, R&S was consulted on behalf of Leonhardt individually or the minority public stockholders, no such disqualification is required.

A "corporate attorney" — whether an in-house lawyer or a law firm that serves as counsel to the company — owes a duty to act in accordance with the interests of the corporate entity itself. His client is the corporation. He may not serve the corporation in a particular matter and then represent a plaintiff in a suit against it or its officers in a substantially related matter.

However, when conflicts arise among factions within a corporation and its counsel is unable to represent all factions, since to do so would be to represent "differing interests," an individual member of management or of the board of directors has the right to seek the advice of an attorney who does *not* represent the corporation as an entity but who can instead represent the plaintiff in an individual capacity, or the faction of which the plaintiff is a member. In doing so, such individual member of management or of the board does not necessarily create an attorney-client relationship between the consulted attorney and the corporate entity itself. To so hold would be to penalize unnecessarily the intracorporate dissident, or "whistleblower," since [he] would then be forced, if [he] were advised by [his] independent counsel that corporate management was violating the rights of stockholders and [he] then wished to take action, to hire a second attorney to bring suit.

The existence of an attorney-client relationship calling for disqualification must therefore turn on whether the dissident was acting for himself or a separate group rather than for the corporation in consulting outside counsel. Evidence that the corporate insider was seeking counsel on behalf of a minority faction and that the corporation itself was represented by separate counsel would militate against the conclusion that the attorney's client was the corporation itself. In such event there would be no conflict in an attorney's first advising a dissident member of management who supports a particular minority shareholder faction, and later representing the minority faction itself.

Plaintiff contends that it is the latter situation with which we are confronted here and that the July 1980 consultation was one in which Leonhardt, an individual dissident member of Artek's management, was concerned about misconduct on the part of Dynatech, the 60% majority stockholder of Artek, and its management, in violation of the rights of its minority public stockholders. He therefore sought independent counsel to protect those interests rather than be a party to the wrongdoing. In doing so he may also have wished to protect himself against liability for the alleged wrongful conduct which he sought to prevent. R&S, plaintiff argues, has thus never "switched sides" as counsel but has labored solely on the side of the minority public stockholders.

Appellees, on the other hand, argue that in consulting R&S Leonhardt was acting in his capacity as President of Artek, a subsidiary of Dynatech. In support of their position they point to the fact that his July 1980 letters to R&S enclosing the Crowell and Moring opinion and his own memorandum to R&S were on Artek letterhead, signed by him as "President," and that he suggested that R&S consider the possibility of legal actions that could be taken by Artek against Dynatech. Moreover, the Crowell and Moring opinion was expressly designated by Welsh, Dynatech's Vice-President and Artek's Chairman, as a "privileged and confidential attorney-client communication." However, the mere fact that Leonhardt was President of Artek would not automatically convert his consultation of R&S into a corporate one or bar R&S from representing the plaintiff if Leonhardt was in fact acting in the plaintiff's interests. Nor would Leonhardt's disclosure to R&S of confidential corporate documents, such as the Crowell & Moring letter, establish the existence of an attorney-client relationship between Dynatech or Artek and R&S. There is no suggestion that R&S induced Leonhardt as a corporate officer to furnish them with the documents. On the contrary, it would appear that Leonhardt acted voluntarily and unilaterally in doing so. If R&S was acting as Leonhardt's independent counsel, his decision to disclose the documents to it, whatever the consequences for him would be as a corporate dissident, would not convert R&S into counsel for Artek or Dynatech.

The situation here is similar to that faced in R-T Leasing Corp. v. Ethyl Corp., 484 F. Supp. 950 (S.D.N.Y. 1979), aff'd mem., 633 F.2d 206 (2d Cir. 1980), where the plaintiff moved to disqualify the defendant's attorneys on the ground that they had had access to confidential information in plaintiff's files, both during the acquisition of two of plaintiff's subsidiaries by another client of the attorneys, and during unsuccessful merger negotiations between that client and the plaintiff. We affirmed the denial of the motion after the district court had found that, since an attorney might come into possession of a party's confidential documents through means other than serving as that party's attorney, no attorney-client relationship could be inferred from mere access to documents. Similarly, although Leonhardt's disclosure to a third party of the confidential opinion letter addressed to Dynatech may have been a breach of confidence on his part, this may not be used to change his relationship with R&S. On the contrary, his apparent motive and intent in consulting R&S was not to gain legal help for Dynatech but to secure assistance *against* it.

Thus the record so far supports an inference that Leonhardt may have believed that he could not speak freely about his concerns to the general counsel of Artek and accordingly sought advice from independent attorneys about the proper course of action to be pursued by the minority shareholders. If this is what occurred, and if, as it appears, Leonhardt in fact consents to the representation by R&S of the plaintiff here, then absent proof of further relevant facts Leonhardt's status as President of Artek at the time of the consultation with R&S would not bar R&S from representing the plaintiff here.

Since the disqualification of R&S turns on whether that firm was acting in an attorney-client relationship with Leonhardt and minority Artek stockholders or with the corporate defendants when it was consulted in 1980 and no finding of fact was made by the district court on this crucial issue, we must remand the case to it for a finding on the issue, which will control the question of whether the order disqualifying R&S should be vacated. Since the parties sharply disagree on the factual issue, the court will probably find it necessary to hold an evidentiary hearing with respect to relevant facts, guided by the rule that the moving defendants bear the heavy burden of proving facts required for disqualification. . . .

QUESTIONS ABOUT EVANS

1. Recall the material on improper acquisition of confidential information (page 95 supra). Leonhardt gave R&S a privileged memorandum from Dynatech's counsel. Why didn't the court chastise R&S for accepting this confidential document?

2. If, as the court writes, Leonhardt's "disclosure to a third party of confidential information . . . may have been a breach of confidence on his part," did R&S act improperly by participating in the breach? Or is that just Leonhardt's problem?

3. R&S sued Artek, which had been its client through March 1976. Was that a successive conflict of interest regardless of the capacity in which Leonhardt had consulted R&S in 1980? Why did the parties and the court focus exclusively on the 1980 consultation?

Who Is the Client?

Evans turned on a problem of client identity. The multiple interests in organizational representation make client identity issues inevitable. To reduce confusion, Rule 1.13(d) directs a lawyer to "explain the identity of the client when it is apparent that the organization's interests are adverse to those of the constituents with whom the lawyer is dealing." Compare Rule 4.3 ("Dealing with Unrepresented Person"). Rule 1.13(e) permits joint representation of an organization and its constituents subject to the concurrent conflict provisions of Rule 1.7.

Corporations.   Unless the facts suggest otherwise, corporate lawyers will be deemed to represent the entity and not its officers, directors, employees, or shareholders. In Commodity Futures Trading Commission v. Weintraub, 471 U.S. 343, 349-352 (1985), a trustee for a bankrupt corporation waived attorney-client privilege for all communications between the company's former counsel and its former officers, directors, and employees. Former management objected, but the Supreme Court upheld the waiver: [W]hen control of a corporation passes to new management, the authority to assert and waive the corporation's attorney-client privilege passes as well." In bankruptcy, the Court wrote, "the actor whose duties most closely resemble those of management should control the privilege." That actor was the trustee. The Court could find no "policies underlying the bankruptcy laws" inconsistent with this conclusion.

A corporate officer or employee will enjoy a privilege along with the company if he can establish that his communications with entity counsel were part of a joint representation. Such efforts usually fail. See, e.g., In re Bevill, Bresler & Schulman Asset Management Corp., 805 F.2d 120 (3d Cir. 1986). The Seventh Circuit has said that whether a professional relationship exists with a corporate constituent "hinges upon the client's belief that he is consulting a lawyer in that capacity and his manifested intention to seek professional legal advice." United States v. Walters, 913 F.2d 388 (7th Cir. 1990). *Walters* found an attorney-client relationship where a shareholder revealed personal information to a lawyer in an effort to learn whether the company's contemplated acts were criminal.

Corporate counsel often represent corporate officers in their personal legal matters unrelated to the company. This practice — a corporate "perk" — means that for certain purposes, at least, the company's lawyer was also the officer's lawyer (and may still be). Courts may then be more willing to credit the officer's belief that he had a professional relationship with the company's counsel on corporate matters, too. Wylie v. Marley Co., 891 F.2d 1463 (10th Cir. 1989).

Whether constituents of an organization are clients of the entity's lawyer is an issue that also arises in government agencies. In the criminal prosecution of a U.S. Air Force reserve officer, a conversation between the officer and air force lawyers was privileged because the officer could reasonably have believed it would be and because the lawyers gave the officer legal advice. The court was not impressed by the fact that the lawyers prefaced the conversation by saying that they were not acting as attorneys for the officer. United States v. Schaltenbrand, 930 F.2d 1554 (11th Cir.), cert. denied, 112 S. Ct. — (1991). Compare Humphrey v. McLaren, 402 N.W.2d 535 (Minn. 1987) (no privilege for agency head); D.C. Opinion 148-1985 (no privilege for agency employees). Would it be fair to say that the policies against finding a professional relationship in public agencies are stronger than in the case of a private company?

A finding that a company lawyer also represented a company constituent on a common matter can create grave problems for the company and the lawyer. First, it may present a conflict that will keep the lawyer from representing the company against the constituent. Second, the conflict may vicariously taint other lawyers in the office. Third, it may give the constituent, as coclient, authority to use or waive confidential corporate information. Consequently, corporate lawyers have strong incentive to prevent a successful claim of a professional relationship with a corporate constituent where that is not intended. How can they do that? One remedy is to give "*Miranda* warnings" to all corporate employees whenever a lawyer has any reason to believe that a conversation may produce information that the company may later wish to use, possibly adversely to the employee. (Does Rule 1.13(d) go this far?) Consider, for example, the interviews conducted by the lawyers in Upjohn v. United States (page 27 supra). They talked to corporate employees in connection with an investigation of possible federal criminal law violations, including by the employees themselves. How should the lawyers have prefaced the interviews?

"*Miranda* warnings" carry a price, don't they? If entity constituents realize that interviews with corporate counsel may return to haunt them, they will be circumspect about what they say, frustrating the company's efforts to get information and good advice. What should a corporate lawyer do if a midlevel officer with whom she has frequently worked walks into her office and says: "I've got a little problem, Anne, and I need your help."? Or: "Blanche, can we have a discussion, just between us?" Kathryn Tate focuses on one arena in which these problems arise — the pre-indictment phase of a criminal investigation. She makes "several proposals for clarifying and strengthening the Model Rules and their comments" with a view toward more clearly defining "an attorney's responsibilities to identify conflict of interest situations" and take appropriate action. Kathryn Tate, Lawyer Ethics and the Corporate Employee: Is the Employee Owed More Protection Than the Model Rules Provide?, 23 Indiana L. Rev. 1 (1990).

Partnerships.   Client-identity issues also arise when lawyers represent partnerships. Does the lawyer represent the partnership entity or the partners? Wortham & Van Liew v. Superior Court (Clubb), 188 Cal. App. 3d 927, 233 Cal. Rptr. 725 (1987), held that an attorney for a partnership represents each partner, limited or general. See also Pucci v. Santi, 711 F. Supp. 916 (N.D. Ill. 1989). But Quintel Corp. v. Citibank, N.A., 589 F. Supp. 1235 (S.D.N.Y. 1984), analogized limited partnerships to corporations and held that a lawyer represented the entity only.

Should resolution of this issue partly depend on whether we're talking about loyalty or confidentiality? In *Wortham & Van Liew*, for example, the question was whether a partner was entitled to information in possession of the partnership lawyer in an action charging other partners with fraud and breach of fiduciary duty. But what if a partnership hires a lawyer to sue a partner, say for violating his fiduciary duties to it? Should the defendant have the right to disqualify the lawyer on the ground that she, by virtue of representing the partnership, also represents the defendant and is therefore suing her own client? What's wrong with that argument? Compare Skarbrevik v. Cohen, England & Whitfield, 231 Cal. App. 3d 692, 282 Cal. Rptr. 627 (1991) (rejecting a shareholder's claim of a "confidential relationship" with a lawyer for a small corporation where the lawyer was retained to represent the company in a dispute with the shareholder). See also ABA Formal Opinion 91-361, which concludes that under Rule 1.13 a partnership's lawyer represents the entity but that information the lawyer receives may not "normally be withheld from the individual partners." Would the defendant have a stronger claim to loyalty if the partnership were represented by its long time counsel? Or if a partnership's lawyer represented a third person against a partner on a matter unrelated to the lawyer's work for the partnership? Margulies by Margulies v. Upchurch, 696 P.2d 1195 (Utah 1985) (attorney-client relationship with limited partners inferred if their "individual interests . . . are directly involved" in, and not merely "incidental" to, the partnership representation).*

Privilege and Conflicts in Shareholder Actions

The neat distinction between the corporate client and its constituents suffers a bit when one set of constituents challenges another set. In a shareholder's derivative action, a group of shareholders may sue officers and directors or third parties, on the theory that the company has an unasserted claim against the defendants. The corporation is named as a nominal defendant. May corporate counsel represent both the corporation and any officers and directors of the corporation who are named as defendants? See Harvard Conflicts Note, page 263 supra, 1339-1341:

> The possibility for conflict of interest here is universally recognized. Although early cases found joint representation permissible where no conflict of interest was obvious, the emerging rule is against dual representation in all derivative actions. Outside counsel must thus be retained to represent one of the defendants. The cases and ethics opinions differ on whether there must be separate representation from the outset or merely from the time the corporation seeks to take an active role. Furthermore, this restriction on dual representation should not be waivable by consent in the usual way; the corporation should be presumptively incapable of giving valid consent.

*For resolution of client identity issues in the case of affiliated corporations, see page 221 supra.

It has been suggested that the outside lawyer should represent the individual defendants, perhaps as an indirect means of ensuring that their legal fees are not borne by the corporation. The better rule is to require that outside counsel represent the corporation, while the corporate attorney represents the insider defendant; the question of expenses would be decided separately. This rule recognizes that while the inhouse attorney is nominally the representative of the corporation, his personal loyalties will inevitably be to the individual executives who hired him.

In Messing v. FDI, Inc., 439 F. Supp. 776, 781-782 (D.N.J. 1977), the court identified the "division of authority" on whether there can be joint representation of a corporation and its directors in a derivative action. The court also reviewed arguments that there may not be joint representation at least where the director is charged with fraud on the corporation or where the corporation elects to take an active role in the litigation. Finally, the court noted the view of "commentators . . . that the corporation should always be separately represented in a derivative action." The court sided with the "commentators":

> Irrespective of the nature of the charges against the directors — whether it be fraud or negligence — the interests of the two groups will always be diverse. Nor can we readily perceive the need for independent counsel turning upon the question whether the corporation has already elected to pursue an active or passive stance in the litigation, for that very election may have already been tainted by conflict.

For a case raising a similar problem in the context of union representation, see Yablonski v. United Mine Workers of America, 448 F.2d 1175 (D.C. Cir. 1971). Dissident mine workers, seeking an accounting from union officers, sued the officers and (nominally) the union itself under federal labor laws. The issues were whether the union's outside counsel, Williams & Connolly, could represent both it *and* the officers (no) and whether, after the firm withdrew from representing the officers (whom the firm had represented on other matters), it could continue to represent the union (no again).

Another issue that arises in stockholder derivative actions is whether the plaintiffs can require the corporation's lawyer to give them privileged information on the theory that the plaintiffs are suing to enforce a right of the corporation. The leading case, Garner v. Wolfinbarger, 430 F.2d 1093, 1104 (5th Cir. 1970), cert. denied, 401 U.S. 974 (1971), held that in such an action the stockholders should be permitted "to show cause" why the privilege "should not be invoked in the particular instance." Among the factors to consider, said the court, were the "number of shareholders and the percentage of stock they represent; the nature of the shareholders' claim and whether it is obviously colorable; the apparent necessity or desirability of the shareholders' having the information and the availability of it from other sources; whether the shareholders' claim is of wrongful action by the corporation . . . ; whether the communication is of advice concerning the litigation itself; [and] the risk of revelation of trade secrets or other information in whose confidentiality the corporation has an interest for independent reasons." The *Garner* rationale has been extended to nonderivative shareholder actions against corporate directors and officers, Panter v. Marshall Field & Co., 80 F.R.D. 718 (N.D. Ill. 1978), and to actions in which plaintiffs charge the defendant with breach of a fiduciary duty. See Helt v. Metropolitan District Commn., 113 F.R.D. 7 (D. Conn. 1986) (rejecting defendant's claim of privilege in a beneficiary's action against a pension fund trustee).

Dean Sexton has argued that the rule in *Garner* is inconsistent with "one of the basic assumptions of the *Upjohn* Court . . . that the corporate attorney-client privilege induces communication with the corporation's attorney that would not otherwise occur. To the extent that information-holders communicate only because their statements are protected by the privilege, the *Garner* rule may undercut their willingness to speak, especially since information disclosed in shareholder litigation can be used by non-shareholders in subsequent litigations." John Sexton, A Post-*Upjohn* Consideration of the Corporate Attorney-Client Privilege, 57 N.Y.U. L. Rev. 443 (1982).

Could not the use of the information be limited? In any event, if corporate counsel has information that establishes that an officer has violated a fiduciary duty to the corporation, shouldn't the plaintiff stockholders be entitled to that information in their effort to assert that corporation's claim against the errant official? Or is the interest in controlling information flow paramount?

CFTC strengthens *Garner*, doesn't it? However, at least one district court criticized *Garner* after *CFTC* and asserted that the crime-fraud exception to the attorney-client privilege (see page 36 supra) was sufficient to protect shareholders. Shirvani v. Capital Investing Corp., 112 F.R.D. 389 (D. Conn. 1986).

Closely Held Entities

Rule 1.13(a)'s distinctions work less well when the entity is small. Does it make sense to say that counsel to a corporation whose officers, directors, and shareholders total only three people "represents the organization acting through its duly authorized constituents"? If one of the three is found stealing from the company, will we have much trouble if the corporate lawyer sues him? On the other hand, if three owners disagree about their respective authority within the company and there is a battle for control, can the company's lawyer agree to represent two against the third?

Courts and ethics committees generally purport to make no distinction between large and small corporations — at least, no formal distinction. In Pelletier v. Zweifel, 921 F.2d 1465, 1491 n.60 (11th Cir.), cert. denied, 112 S. Ct. 167 (1991), the court said that a corporation's lawyer owes no fiduciary duty to its shareholders whether the company is closely held or publicly traded. Skarbrevik v. Cohen, England & Whitfield, 231 Cal. App. 3d 692, 282 Cal. Rptr. 627 (1991) (a lawyer for a small corporation may represent the company in an action against a 25 percent shareholder). See also Felty v. Hartweg, 169 Ill. App. 3d 406, 523 N.E. 2d 555 (1988) (a minority shareholder in a close corporation cannot hold the company's lawyer liable for failure to disclose official misconduct). D.C. Opinion 216 (1991) (a corporate lawyer can represent the entity against one of two 50 percent shareholders). But see In re Brownstein, 288 Or. 83, 602 P.2d 655 (1979) (lawyer represents company and shareholders). See if you can reconcile the following three cases.

In Bobbitt v. Victorian House, Inc., 545 F. Supp. 1124, 1126 (N.D. Ill. 1982), the plaintiff, a 50 percent owner of a corporation, sued the company and its president, the other owner, for dissolution and an accounting. The company's counsel defended and the plaintiff sought to disqualify him. The court wrote that "representing such a corporation does not inherently mean also acting as counsel to the individual director-shareholders. Rather the question must be determined on the individual facts of each case." The court then reviewed those matters on which the plaintiff alleged that counsel had represented him personally and concluded that the matters were not "relevant to the current action." The court did not discuss whether the representation of the company as an entity created any duty to Bobbitt personally.

Compare Rosman v. Shapiro, 653 F. Supp. 1441 (S.D.N.Y. 1987), in which corporate counsel represented one of two shareholders against the other, who was seeking to dissolve the corporation. Citing *Bobbitt*, the court wrote that although "corporate counsel does not necessarily become counsel for the corporation's shareholders and directors, where, as here, the corporation is a close corporation consisting of only two shareholders with equal interests in the corporation, it is indeed reasonable for each shareholder to believe that the corporate counsel is in effect his own individual attorney." This was especially true on the facts before the court because both parties treated the company "as if it were a partnership rather than a corporation. In short, it would exalt form over substance to conclude that [the law firm] only represented [the company]." In disqualifying counsel, the court relied on the "appearance of impropriety" test of Canon 9. Does that mean that the court would reach a different result under the Model Rules, which have no such test?

One influential case has skirted the issue of client identity by holding that the attorney for a closely held company might have a fiduciary duty to the individual shareholders even if he or she does not have an attorney-client relationship with them. Fassihi v. Sommers, Schwartz, Silver, Schwartz & Tyler, P.C., 107 Mich. App. 509, 309 N.W.2d 645 (1981) (professional corporation of two physicians). Does this solution use a legal conclusion (fiduciary relationship) as a substitute for the factual inquiry that would otherwise be required? Or does it just substitute one factual inquiry for another?

FURTHER READING

Lawrence Mitchell has grappled with the special problems of lawyers for closely held corporations in Lawrence Mitchell, Professional Responsibility and the Close Corporation: Toward a Realistic Ethic, 74 Cornell L. Rev. 466 (1989).

Whistleblowing and Retaliatory Discharge

BALLA v. GAMBRO, INC.
145 Ill. 2d 492, 584 N.E.2d 104 (1991)

JUSTICE CLARK delivered the opinion of the court:

The issue in this case is whether in-house counsel should be allowed the remedy of an action for retaliatory discharge.

Appellee, Roger Balla, formerly in-house counsel for Gambro, Inc. (Gambro), filed a retaliatory discharge action against Gambro, its affiliate Gambro Dialysatoren, KG (Gambro Germany), [and others]. Appellee alleged that he was fired in contravention of Illinois public policy and sought damages for the discharge. The trial court dismissed the action on appellants' motion for summary judgment. The appellate court reversed. . . .

Gambro is a distributor of kidney dialysis equipment manufactured by Gambro Germany. . . .

Appellee, Roger J. Balla, is and was at all times throughout this controversy an attorney licensed to practice law in the State of Illinois. On March 17, 1980, appellee executed an employment agreement with Gambro which contained the terms of appellee's employment. Generally, the employment agreement provided that appellee would "be responsible for all legal matters within the company and for personnel within the company's sales office." Appellee held the title of director of administration at Gambro. . . .

In August 1983, the manager of regulatory affairs for Gambro left the company and appellee assumed the manager's specific duties. . . . The individual in the position prior to appellee was not an attorney.

In July 1985 Gambro Germany informed Gambro in a letter that certain dialyzers it had manufactured, the clearances of which varied from the package insert, were about to be shipped to Gambro. Referring to these dialyzers, Gambro Germany advised Gambro:

> For acute patients risk is that the acute uremic situation will not be improved in spite of the treatment giving continuous high levels of potassium, phosphate and urea creatine. The chronic patient may note the effect as a slow progression of the uremic situation and depending on the interval between medical check-ups the medical risk may not be overlooked.

Appellee told the president of Gambro to reject the shipment because the dialyzers did not comply with FDA regulations. The president notified Gambro Germany of its decision to reject the shipment on July 12, 1985.

However, one week later the president informed Gambro Germany that Gambro would accept the dialyzers and "sell [them] to a unit that is not currently our customer but who buys only on price." Appellee contends that he was not informed by the president of the decision to accept the dialyzers but became aware of it through other Gambro employees. Appellee maintains that he spoke with the president in August regarding the company's decision to accept the dialyzers and told the president that he would do whatever necessary to stop the sale of the dialyzers.

On September 4, 1985, appellee was discharged from Gambro's employment by its president. The following day, appellee reported the shipment of the dialyzers to the FDA. The FDA seized the shipment and determined the product to be "adulterated" [under federal law].

We agree with the trial court that appellee does not have a cause of action against Gambro for retaliatory discharge under the facts of the case at bar. Generally, this court adheres to the proposition that " 'an employer may discharge an employee-at-will for any reason or for no reason [at all].' " However, in Kelsay v. Motorola, Inc. (1978), 74 Ill. 2d 172, [384 N.E.2d 353,] this court first recognized the limited and narrow tort of retaliatory discharge. In *Kelsay*, an at-will employee was fired for filing a worker's compensation claim against her employer.... This court stressed that if employers could fire employees for filing workers' compensation claims, the public policy behind the enactment of the Workers' Compensation Act would be frustrated.

Subsequently, in Palmateer v. International Harvester Co. (1981), 85 Ill. 2d 124, [421 N.E.2d 876,] this court again examined the tort of retaliatory discharge. In *Palmateer*, an employee was discharged for informing the police of suspected criminal activities of a co-employee, and because he agreed to provide assistance in any investigation and trial of the matter. Based on the public policy favoring the investigation and prosecution of crime, this court held that the employee had a cause of action for retaliatory discharge. Further, we stated:

> All that is required [to bring a cause of action for retaliatory discharge] is that the employer discharge the employee in retaliation for the employee's activities, and that the discharge be in contravention of a clearly mandated public policy.

In this case it appears that Gambro discharged appellee, an employee of Gambro, in retaliation for his activities, and this discharge was in contravention of a clearly mandated public policy. . . .

[In] Herbster v. North American Co. for Life & Health Insurance (1986), 150 Ill. App. 3d 21, [501 N.E.2d 343,] our appellate court held that the plaintiff, an employee and chief legal counsel for the defendant company, did not have a claim for retaliatory discharge against the company due to the presence of the attorney-client relationship. Under the facts of that case, the defendant company allegedly requested the plaintiff to destroy or remove discovery information which had been requested in lawsuits pending against the company. The plaintiff refused arguing that such conduct would constitute fraud and violate several provisions of the Illinois Code of Professional Responsibility. Subsequently, the defendant company discharged the plaintiff. . . .

We agree with the conclusion reached in *Herbster* that, generally, in-house counsel do not have a claim under the tort of retaliatory discharge. However, we base our decision as much on the nature and purpose of the tort of retaliatory discharge, as on the effect on the attorney-client relationship that extending the tort would have. In addition, at this time, we caution that our holding is confined by the fact that appellee is and was at all times throughout this controversy an attorney licensed to practice law in the State of Illinois. . . .

In this case, the public policy to be protected, that of protecting the lives and property of citizens, is adequately safeguarded without extending the tort of retaliatory discharge to in-house counsel. Appellee was required under the Rules of Professional Conduct to report Gambro's intention to sell the "misbranded and/or adulterated" dialyzers. Rule 1.6(b) of the Rules of Professional Conduct reads:

> A lawyer *shall* reveal information about a client to the extent it appears necessary to prevent the client from committing an act that would result in death or serious bodily injury. (Emphasis added.)

Appellee alleges, and the FDA's seizure of the dialyzers indicates, that the use of the dialyzers would cause death or serious bodily injury. Thus, under the above-cited rule, appellee was under the mandate of this court to report the sale of these dialyzers.

In his brief to this court, appellee argues that not extending the tort of retaliatory discharge to in-house counsel would present attorneys with a "Hobson's choice." According to appellee, in-house counsel would face two alternatives: either comply with the client/employer's wishes and risk both the loss of a professional license and exposure to criminal sanctions, or decline to comply with client/employer's wishes and risk the loss of a full-time job and the attendant benefits. We disagree. Unlike the employees in *Kelsay* which this court recognized would be left with the difficult decision of choosing between whether to file a workers' compensation claim and risk being fired, or retaining their jobs and losing their right to a remedy, in-house counsel plainly are not confronted with such a dilemma. In-house counsel do not have a choice of whether to follow their ethical obligations as attorneys licensed to practice law, or follow the illegal and unethical demands of their clients. In-house counsel must abide by the Rules of Professional Conduct. Appellee had no choice but to report to the FDA Gambro's intention to sell or distribute these dialyzers, and consequently protect the aforementioned public policy.

In addition, we believe that extending the tort of retaliatory discharge to in-house counsel would have an undesirable effect on the attorney-client relationship that exists betwen these employers and their in-house counsel. Generally, a client may discharge his attorney at any time, with or without cause. This rule applies equally to in-house counsel as it does to outside counsel. Further, this rule "recognizes that the relationship between an attorney and client is based on trust and that the client must have confidence in his attorney in order to ensure that the relationship will function properly." ... We believe that if in-house counsel are granted the right to sue their employers for retaliatory discharge, employers might be less willing to be forthright and candid with their in-house counsel. Employers might be hesitant to turn to their in-house counsel for advice regarding potentially questionable corporate conduct knowing that their in-house counsel could use this information in a retaliatory discharge suit.

We recognize that under the Illinois Rules of Professional Conduct, attorneys shall reveal client confidences or secrets in certain situations, and thus one might expect employers/clients to be naturally hesitant to rely on in-house counsel for advice regarding this potentially questionable conduct. However, the danger exists that if in-house counsel are granted a right to sue their employers in tort for retaliatory discharge, employers might further limit their communication with their in-house counsel. . . .

Our decision not to extend the tort of retaliatory discharge to in-house counsel also is based on other ethical considerations. Under the Rules of Professional Conduct, appellee was required to withdraw from representing Gambro if continued representation would result in the violation of the Rules of Professional Conduct by which appellee was bound, or if Gambro discharged the appellee. In this case, Gambro did discharge appellee, and according to appellee's claims herein, his continued representation of Gambro would have resulted in a violation of the Rules of Professional Conduct. Appellee argues that such a choice of withdrawal is "simplistic and uncompassionate, and is completely at odds with contemporary realities facing in-house attorneys." These contemporary realities apparently are the economic ramifications of losing his position as in-house counsel. However difficult economically and perhaps emotionally it is for in-house counsel to discontinue representing an employer/client, we refuse to allow in-house counsel to sue their employer/client for damages because they obeyed their ethical obligations. In this case, appellee, in addition to being an employee at Gambro, is first and foremost an attorney bound by the Rules of Professional Conduct. These Rules of Professional Conduct hope to articulate in a concrete fashion certain values and goals such as defending the integrity of the judicial system, promoting the administration of justice and protecting the integrity of the legal profession. An attorney's obligation to follow these Rules of Professional Conduct should not be the foundation for a claim of retaliatory discharge.

We also believe that it would be inappropriate for the employer/client to bear the economic costs and burdens of their in-house counsel's adhering to their ethical obligations under the Rules of Professional Conduct. Presumably, in situations where an in-house counsel obeys his or her ethical obligations and reveals certain information regarding the employer/client, the attorney-client relationship will be irreversibly strained and the client will more than likely discharge its in-house counsel. In this scenario, if we were to grant the in-house counsel the right to sue the client for retaliatory discharge, we would be shifting the burden and costs of obeying the Rules of Professional Conduct from the attorney to the employer/client. The employer/client would be forced to pay damages to its former in-house counsel to essentially mitigate the financial harm the attorney suffered for having to abide by Rules of Professional Conduct. This, we believe, is impermissible for all attorneys know or should know that at certain times in their professional career, they will have to forgo economic gains in order to protect the integrity of the legal profession.

Our review of cases from other jurisdictions dealing with this issue does not persuade us to hold otherwise. In Willy v. Coastal Corp. (S.D. Tex. 1986), 647 F. Supp. 116, the district court declined to extend the tort of retaliatory discharge to the wrongful termination of in-house counsel. . . .

Also, in Nordling v. Northern States Power Co. (Minn. App. 1991), 465 N.W.2d 81, the appellate court of Minnesota, relying exclusively on our appellate court's decision in *Herbster*, held that the plaintiff's status as in-house counsel precluded not only a breach-of-contract claim against the defendant company, but also the plaintiff's retaliatory discharge claim. . . .

In contrast to the two cases discussed above which specifically held that in-house counsel do not have a right to sue for retaliatory discharge, two other cases have allowed in-house counsel to sue their employer for wrongful termination. However, both cases are distinguishable from our holding. In Parker v. M & T Chemicals, Inc. (1989), 236 N.J. Super. 451, 566 A.2d 215, the superior court of New Jersey construed that State's "Whistleblowers Act" as compelling "a retaliating employer to pay damages to an employee-attorney who is wrongfully discharged or mistreated . . . for any reason which is violative of law, fraudulent, criminal, or incompatible with a clear mandate of New Jersey's public policy concerning public health, safety or welfare." . . .

In Mourad v. Automobile Club Insurance Association (1991), 186 Mich. App. 715, 465 N.W.2d 395, the plaintiff, as in-house counsel for the defendant company, sued the defendant for, inter alia, breach of employment contract and retaliatory demotion. The appellate court of Michigan determined that the plaintiff had a cause of action for breach of a just-cause contract, but not for retaliatory demotion. . . .

JUSTICE FREEMAN, dissenting:

I respectfully dissent from the decision of my colleagues. In concluding that the plaintiff attorney, serving as corporate in-house counsel, should not be allowed a claim for retaliatory discharge, the majority first reasons that the public policy implicated in this case, i.e., protecting the lives and property of Illinois citizens, is adequately safeguarded by the lawyer's ethical obligation to reveal information about a client as necessary to prevent acts that would result in death or serious bodily harm. I find this reasoning fatally flawed.

The majority so reasons because, as a matter of law, an attorney cannot even contemplate ignoring his ethical obligations in favor of continuing in his employment. I agree with this conclusion "as a matter of law." However, to say that the categorical nature of ethical obligations is sufficient to ensure that the ethical obligations will be satisfied simply ignores reality. Specifically, it ignores that, as unfortunate for society as it may be, attorneys are no less human than nonattorneys and, thus, no less given to the temptation to either ignore or rationalize away their ethical obligations when complying therewith may render them unable to feed and support their families.

I would like to believe, as my colleagues apparently conclude, that attorneys will always "do the right thing" because the law says that they must. However, my knowledge of human nature, which is not much greater than the average layman's, and, sadly, the recent scandals involving the bench and bar of Illinois are more than sufficient to dispel such a belief. . . .

As reluctant as I am to concede it, the fact is that this court must take whatever steps it can, within the bounds of the law, to give lawyers incentives to abide by their ethical obligations, beyond the satisfaction inherent in their doing so. We cannot continue to delude ourselves and the people of the State of Illinois that attorneys' ethical duties, alone, are always sufficient to guarantee that lawyers will "do the right thing." In the context of this case, where doing " the right thing" will often result in termination by an employer bent on doing the "wrong thing," I believe that the incentive needed is recognition of a cause of action for retaliatory discharge, in the appropriate case. . . .

One of the basic purposes of the attorney-client relationship, especially in the corporate client-in-house counsel setting, is for the attorney to advise the client as to, exactly, what conduct the law requires so that the client can then comply with that advice. Given that purpose, allowing in-house counsel a cause of action for retaliatory discharge would chill the attorney-client relationship and discourage a corporate client from communicating freely with the attorney only where, as here, the employer decides to go forward with particular conduct, regardless of advice that it is contrary to law. I believe that, just as in-house counsel might reasonably so assume, this court is entitled to assume that corporate clients will rarely so decide. As such, to allow a corporate employer to discharge its in-house counsel under such circumstances, without fear of any sanction, is truly to give the assistance and protection of the courts to scoundrels. . . .

In holding as it does, the majority also reasons that an attorney's obligation to follow the Rules of Professional Conduct should not be the basis for a claim of retaliatory discharge.

Preliminarily, I would note that were an employee's desire to obey and follow the law an insufficient basis for a retaliatory discharge claim, *Palmateer* would have been decided differently. In this regard, I do not believe any useful purpose is served by distinguishing attorneys from ordinary citizens. . . . An attorney should not be punished simply because he has ethical obligations imposed upon him over and above the general obligation to obey the law which all men have. Nor should a corporate employer be protected simply because the employee it has discharged for "blowing the whistle" happens to be an attorney.

I find the majority's reasoning that an attorney's ethical obligations should not be the basis of a retaliatory discharge claim faulty for another reason. In so concluding, the majority ignores the employer's decision to persist in the questionable conduct which its in-house counsel advised was illegal. It is that conduct, not the attorney's ethical obligations, which is the predicate of the retaliatory discharge claim. . . .

Additionally, I cannot share the majority's solicitude for employers who discharge in-house counsel, who comply with their ethical obligations, by agreeing that they should not bear the economic burden which that compliance imposes upon the attorney. Unlike the majority, I do not believe that it is the attorney's compliance with his ethical obligations which imposes economic burdens upon him. Rather, those burdens are imposed upon him by the employer's persistence in conduct the attorney has advised is illegal and by the employer's wrongful termination of the attorney once he advises the employer that he must comply with those obligations. . . .

Nordling, on which *Balla* relied, was reversed nine days after the *Balla* decision. The Minnesota Supreme Court allowed an employed lawyer's contract claim to proceed to trial provided "the essentials of the attorney-client relationship are not compromised." Nordling v. Northern States Power Co., 478 N.W.2d 498 (Minn. 1991).

Questions About Balla v. Gambro, Inc.

1. The court says the public is protected because Rule 1.6 (unlike the Model Rule) *required* Balla to report. The dissent disagrees. Who's right? Under the court's theory, would the result change if Balla were merely *permitted* to notify the FDA?

2. The court fears that if lawyers have retaliatory discharge claims, corporate officers will not be "forthright and candid" with them. Explain that argument.

3. The American Corporate Counsel Association (ACCA), whose members are in-house lawyers like Balla, filed an amicus brief. Guess whom ACCA supported? Gambro. Can you explain that choice?

4. The court did not distinguish between retained lawyers and employed lawyers, although it did cite "contemporary realities." What does that mean? Should the two sets of lawyers have different rights? What about law firm associates?

5. Exactly how do the court and the dissent differently view the origin and allocation of "the economic costs and burdens" of a lawyer's compliance with his or her ethical obligations?

6. If Balla had been a scientist or even the CEO, not a lawyer, he would have won. Can it be argued that courts should (if anything) be more, rather than less, protective of lawyers in Balla's position?

FURTHER READING

Stephen Gillers, Protecting Lawyers Who Just Say No, 5 Georgia St. U. L. Rev. 1 (1988); Daniel Reynolds, Wrongful Discharge of Employed Counsel, 1 Geo. J. Leg. Ethics 553 (1988).

The Ethics of Whistleblowing

Retaliatory discharge and similar claims seek to invoke the protection of a jurisdiction's tort or contract law. Whistleblowing is a closely related but distinct area. (It sounds like an oxymoron, doesn't it? Who could be more tightlipped than a corporate lawyer?) A whistleblowing lawyer reveals corporate secrets to outsiders, or threatens to, in order to protect the client or others from the misconduct of insiders, and without regard to whether the lawyer has been instructed to act improperly or is suffering retaliation. Yet the concepts are related in this way: If ethics rules forbid whistleblowing, a lawyer who is fired after revealing corporate wrongdoing is going to have a harder time establishing a retaliatory discharge claim. Do you see why? May a lawyer go outside the organization if its employees, officers, or directors are violating their obligations to it or causing it to act fraudulently or criminally? They may, at the least, if the client's prospective conduct is a violent criminal act within the meaning of Rule 1.6(b)(1), but of course corporate wrongdoing is not likely to fall in that category. DR 4-101(C)(3) permits revelation of *any* future crime, but many financial frauds will not even be criminal.

Drafts of Rule 1.13 proposed to give corporate lawyers greater authority than Rule 1.6 and DR 4-101 tolerate. The January 1980 draft provided that a lawyer "shall use reasonable efforts to prevent [significant] harm" to the organization on learning that one of its employees is acting in a way that both violates the law and is likely to result in such harm. The May 1981 draft softened this language. Now the lawyer was directed to "proceed as is reasonably necessary in the best interest of the organization" when an employee is engaged in unlawful conduct "which reasonably might be imputed to the organization, and is likely to result in material injury" to it. Substantially the same language appears in the June 1982 draft and in Rule 1.13(b) as adopted.

The lawyer's authority to reveal confidential information of the organizational client to outsiders underwent a more dramatic metamorphosis. The January 1980 draft said that a lawyer "may [disclose] client confidences to the extent necessary if the lawyer reasonably believes such action to be in the best interest of the organization." By May 1981, the authority to disclose client confidences was limited to those situations in which the lawyer "reasonably believes that . . . the highest authority in the organization has acted to further the personal or financial interests of members of that authority which are in conflict with the interests of the organization and . . . revealing the information is necessary in the best interest of the organization." This resolution was continued in the June 1982 draft, but Rule 1.13(c) as finally adopted gives the lawyer no authority to reveal organizational confidences even when necessary to prevent self-dealing by the organization's highest authority. Instead, the lawyer is told that he or she "may resign in accordance with Rule 1.16."

Is the final text of Model Rule 1.13(b) and (c) consistent with the assertion in Rule 1.13(a) that the organization, not those who control or run it, is the client? How do you reconcile Rule 1.13's toleration of lay interference with the lawyer's duty to protect the client with Rule 5.4's refusal, because of the fear of lay interference, to permit nonlawyers to own or manage law firms? See page 709 infra.

The Model Rules make an important if tacit assumption: *whenever* internal remedies for unlawful insider conduct prove unavailing, it is *always* preferable to require the client to suffer in silence rather than grant its lawyer the option of alerting persons outside the corporation. In terms of the triangular relationship among counsel, the client, and the client's agents, the first must always accept the final decision of the third unless an exception to confidentiality applies. Is that the correct resolution?

QUESTION

9.1 "Point number one is I don't want any trouble. I don't want to be a hero. I can't afford it. My name is Daphne Berger. I'm a single parent. I have two teenagers, bright kids headed for college. I've got a mortgage. One thing and another. I get no help from their father, but that's another story. For nearly 12 years I've been an assistant general counsel at P&G. Twelve years from now I'll still be an AGC. That's fine with me. There are 83 AGCs. I do work in my own little area, which is monitoring compliance with state regulations of beauty products applied to the skin. I do the Eastern U.S. There are four other people who do what I do for other parts of the country. It is a boring job and that's fine with me too. I'm not saving the world. I'm just keeping P&G out of trouble. That's how I get by.

"I have a good friend, Gloria Tobachnik, a chemist in the New Products Division of the Feminine Hygiene Department of the Personal Hygiene Section, people I have had nothing to do with in 12 years. I don't even know where they are in the building. Gloria has some modest position in testing, barely higher than a technician. She's been here longer than me. She once wanted to be a doctor. I once wanted to be a judge. I call her Dr. T and she calls me Your Honor.

"The other day Gloria and I are having coffee, our kids off together heaven knows where; they don't tell us anymore. Gloria springs it on me. One thing and another — she was asked to run a test on a new tampon P&G has already announced. She's supposed to look for something I don't understand; Gloria doesn't even understand how it all fits together. She does her test and gives her boss, a bastard who's been trying to get Gloria into bed for years, her report and he turns white, says, "Thank-you, go away."

"Now Gloria is curious, her biggest problem actually, so she keeps her ears open, notices things, asks a question here, a question there. She's like the wallpaper, she's worked there so long. Turns out with this new tampon on the way to market, someone discovered that it may cause some kind of shock or toxic reaction in some users. But they're not sure. After a while, they decided to go ahead with the product. Gloria thinks it's a real gamble from what she's learned. ('That's why they call it Percort & Gamble,' she tells me. 'Should be Profit & Gamble, right?') She showed me a memo, which does sound like the mucky-mucks told the lab people to bury it.

"So what am I supposed to do? There's a new GC here and a new chief associate GC. Two hotshots. They'd love to get rid of people like me. To them we're clerks. They want to remake the staff. I'm afraid if I create trouble, they'll find a reason. Insubordination. I can't fight this place. Me going to them is like a GI going to the Joint Chiefs after the President has given an order. What am I supposed to do with this information? People could get hurt. I thought of sending it to the papers anonymously, but I don't know. I'm asking you first."

FURTHER READING

Stephen Gillers, Model Rule 1.13(c) Gives the Wrong Answer to the Question of Corporate Counsel Disclosure, 1 Geo. J. Legal Ethics 289 (1987); F. Michael Higginbotham, "See No Evil, Hear No Evil, Speak No Evil": Developing a Policy for Disclosure by Counsel to Public Corporations, 7 J. Corp. L. 285 (1982); Stanley Kaplan, Some Ruminations on the Role of Counsel for a Corporation, 56 Notre Dame L. Rev. 873 (1980); Jeffrey Slovak, The Ethics of Corporate Lawyers: A Sociological Approach, 1981 Am. B. Found. Res. J. 753.

X

Negotiation

Negotiating is not an intrinsically legal service. Persons who are not members of the bar frequently negotiate for clients without fear that they are engaging in the unauthorized practice of law. Agents of various kinds — for example, real estate, literary, business, theatrical — negotiate large deals for assortments of clients. Most are not lawyers and do not have to be, unless they also want to draft the client's contract.

Although not every negotiator is a lawyer, virtually every lawyer is, at one time or another, a negotiator. It is practically impossible to have a legal career without some need to negotiate. Some lawyers negotiate rarely, others do so daily. How is it that lawyers have so dominated this service even though it is not necessarily a legal service? In part, the answer must be circumstantial. Many clients who need services that only lawyers can provide — such as litigation, contract preparation, legal advice — also need negotiation assistance directly incident to their need for the legal service. So a lawyer who has developed an expertise in copyright law will likely be asked to assist in the negotiation of the book contract. And a lawyer who has developed a specialty in the legal issues surrounding franchising will likely be asked to negotiate the terms of the franchise agreement.

What rules constrain a lawyer in conducting negotiations for a client? Certainly, the status of being a lawyer representing a client will not shield the lawyer from personal liability if the lawyer assists the client in committing a criminal or tortious act. See Slotkin v. Citizens Casualty of New York, 614 F.2d 301 (2d Cir. 1979), cert. denied, 449 U.S. 981 (1980). Further, DR 1-102(A)(4) forbids a lawyer to "[e]ngage in conduct involving dishonesty, fraud, deceit, or misrepresentation." DR 7-102(A) contains various prohibitions on lawyer conduct in the representation of clients, three of which are particularly applicable to negotiation. DR 7-102(A)(3) says that a lawyer shall not "[c]onceal or knowingly fail to disclose that which he is required by law to reveal"; (A)(5) says that a lawyer shall not "[k]nowingly make a false statement of law or fact"; and (A)(7) says that a lawyer shall not "[c]ounsel or assist his client in conduct that the lawyer knows to be illegal or fraudulent." See also EC 1-5 and EC 7-9.

The Model Rules have parallel provisions. See Rules 1.2(d), 1.6, 4.1, and 4.4 and accompanying commentary, especially the commentary on "Withdrawal" under Rule 1.6.

Compare Rule 4.1(b) with Rule 3.3(b). A lawyer must correct fraud on a tribunal under the circumstances described in Rule 3.3(a) even if it means revealing confidences protected by Rule 1.6. However, if a client has engaged in a criminal or fraudulent act against a third person, the lawyer's duty to take corrective action "to avoid assisting" the client is subordinate to Rule 1.6. This is true even though the client's crime or fraud may be devastating to third parties, even if revelation can stop the crime or fraud before it is concluded, and even though the lawyer may have been the unwitting conduit of false information. How do you explain this difference between Rule 3.3 and 4.1?

Of course, a lawyer who discovers that his or her client is perpetrating a fraud or a crime on another will probably have to withdraw from the representation. Rules 1.2(d), 1.16(a)(1). But if the lawyer withdraws without alerting the former client's intended victim before it is too late, isn't there a risk that the victim will later sue the lawyer? While the lawyer may defend by pointing to his ethical responsibilities, the courts may interpret the tort law more expansively and find liability. (See page 649 infra.)

Perhaps for these reasons, the comment to Rule 1.6 appears to back away from the limitation in Rule 4.1(b). Comment 15 states that after withdrawal a lawyer "is required to refrain from making disclosure of the clients' confidences, except as otherwise provided in Rule 1.6." However, the comment then goes on to say that neither Rule 1.6 "nor Rule 1.8(b) nor Rule 1.16(d) prevents the lawyer from giving notice of the fact of withdrawal, and the lawyer may also withdraw or disaffirm any opinion, document, affirmation, or the like." Does this mean that a lawyer who withdraws upon learning of a client's fraud is free to call the other party's lawyer and say something like this: "Listen, Clara, I will no longer be representing Bill for reasons I am not free to disclose, but I just wanted to let you know of my withdrawal. And I also wanted to tell you that I disaffirm the letter I sent last February 2 and the documents enclosed with it"?

New York has raised the language of comment 15 to the text of DR 4-101(C)(5), as an explicit exception to the confidentiality duty. Why didn't the ABA do the same? What does all this add up to? Little more than that lawyers must refrain from violating the substantive law? Stated another way, can a lawyer representing a client in negotiation do on behalf of the client anything the client might legally be entitled to do in its own behalf? Or are there ethical, though not legal, limitations on the conduct of a lawyer as a negotiator that do not constrain the conduct of others who sell negotiating services? If so, how can these be justified? Because the lawyer carries the imprimatur of bar membership? Because the lawyer, in addition to negotiating a deal, also has the power, which nonlawyers do not, to put the agreement into binding form?

Remember, in considering the material that follows, that lawyers can participate in negotiation in various degrees. At one extreme, a lawyer may be the alter ego of a client who is prepared to accept the best deal the lawyer can get. If so, the lawyer is as close as possible to being the principal. At the other extreme, the client may assume virtually all of the responsibility for negotiation and rely on the lawyer simply to put the final deal into legally binding form. In practice, nearly all representations fall between these extremes.

Negotiation issues tend to arise in one of two contexts. The first concerns the lawyer's possession of confidential information that may reveal a client's illegal or unconscionable conduct. When may or must the negotiating lawyer reveal such information? When is he forbidden to do so? How may the possession of such information constrain the lawyer? The second issue concerns fairness and legality. Has the lawyer any obligation to the opposing side in a negotiation to assure that the result is fair? That it is legally enforceable? Lurking in the background of each of these issues is whether the lawyer may sometimes be required to withdraw from the representation in the event of lies or unfairness.

The first of the two excerpted articles that follow is by the late Judge Alvin B. Rubin of the United States Court of Appeals for the Fifth Circuit, in which the author recommends that negotiating lawyers be subject to two new obligations. The second article, by Professor James J. White of the University of Michigan Law School, addresses proposed ethical limitations on lawyers as negotiators that were contained in Rule 4.2(a) and (b) of the January 1980 draft of the Model Rules and that have since been deleted.*

Alvin B. Rubin
A CAUSERIE ON LAWYERS' ETHICS IN NEGOTIATION
35 La. L. Rev. 577, 582-592 (1975)

Let us consider the proper role for a lawyer engaged in negotiations when he knows that the opposing side, whether as a result of poor legal

---

*The text of Rule 4.2(a) and (b) of the 1980 draft is set out at page 475 infra. Beyond the ethical dimension, success in negotiation is important to lawyers because it is often the only (or the least expensive) route to a client's goals. A vast literature examines the nature and structure of negotiation; a number of books and articles promise to teach the reader how to succeed at it. For a thorough recent study of the subject, with cites to many of the other studies, both scholarly and popular, see Carrie Menkel-Meadow, Toward Another View of Legal Negotiation: The Structure of Problem Solving, 31 U.C.L.A. L. Rev. 754 (1984).

representation or otherwise, is assuming a state of affairs that is incorrect. Hypothesize: *L*, a lawyer, is negotiating the sale of his client's business to another businessman, who is likewise represented by counsel. Balance sheets and profit and loss statements prepared one month ago have been supplied. In the last month, sales have fallen dramatically. Counsel for the potential buyer has made no inquiry about current sales. Does *L* have a duty to disclose the change in sales volume?

Some lawyers say, "I would notify my client and advise him that *he* has a duty to disclose," not because of ethical considerations but because the client's failure to do so might render the transaction voidable if completed. If the client refused to sanction disclosure, some of these lawyers would withdraw from representing him *in this matter* on ethical grounds. As a practical matter (i.e., to induce the client to accept their advice), they say, in consulting with the client, the lawyer is obliged to present the problem as one of possible fraud in the transaction rather than of lawyers' ethics.

In typical law school fashion, let us consider another hypothetical. *L*, the lawyer, is representing *C*, a client, in a suit for personal injuries. There have been active settlement negotiations with *LD*, the defendant's lawyer. The physician who has been treating *C* rendered a written report, containing a prognosis stating that it is unlikely that *C* can return to work at his former occupation. This has been furnished to *LD*. *L* learns from *C* that he has consulted another doctor, who has given him a new medication. *C* states that he is now feeling fine and thinks he can return to work, but he is reluctant to do so until the case is settled or tried. The next day *L* and *LD* again discuss settlement. Does *L* have a duty either to guard his client's secret or to make a full disclosure? Does he satisfy or violate either duty if, instead of mentioning *C*'s revelation he suggests that *LD* require a new medical examination?

Some lawyers avoid this problem by saying that it is inconceivable that a competent *LD* would not ask again about *C*'s health. But if the question as to whether *L* should be frank is persistently presented, few lawyers can assure that they would disclose the true facts. . . .

None would apparently deny that honesty and good faith in the sale of a house or a security implies telling the truth and not withholding information. But the Code does not exact that sort of integrity from lawyers who engage in negotiating the compromise of a law suit or other negotiations. . . .

The professional literature contains many instances indicating that, in the general opinion of the bar, there is no requirement that the lawyer disclose unfavorable evidence in the usual litigious situation. The *racontes* of lawyers and judges with their peers are full of tales of how the other side failed to ask the one key question that would have revealed the truth and changed the result, or how one side cleverly avoided producing the critical document or the key witness whom the adversary had not discovered. The feeling that, in an adversary encounter, each side should develop its own case helps to insulate counsel from considering it a duty to disclose information unknown to the other side. Judge Marvin Frankel, an experienced and perceptive observer of the profession, comments, "Within these unconfining limits [of the Code] advocates freely employ time-honored tricks and stratagems to block or distort the truth." . . .

Do the lawyer's ethics protest more strongly against giving false information? DR 7-102(A)(5) forbids the lawyer to "knowingly make" a false statement of law or fact. Most lawyers say it would be improper to prepare a false document to deceive an adversary or to make a factual statement known to be untrue with the intention of deceiving him. But almost every lawyer can recount repeated instances where an adversary of reasonable repute dealt with facts in such an imaginative or hyperbolic way as to make them appear to be different from what he knew they were.

Interesting answers are obtained if lawyers are asked whether it is proper to make false statements that concern negotiating strategy rather than the facts in litigation. Counsel for a plaintiff appears quite comfortable in stating, when representing a plaintiff, "My client won't take a penny less than $25,000," when in fact he knows that the client will happily settle for less; counsel for the defendant appears to have no qualms in representing that he has no authority to settle, or that a given figure exceeds his authority, when these are untrue statements. Many say that, as a matter of strategy, when they attend a pre-trial conference with a judge known to press settlements, they disclaim any settlement authority both to the judge and adversary although in fact they do have settlement instructions; estimable members of the bar support the thesis that a lawyer may not misrepresent a fact in controversy but may misrepresent matters that pertain to his authority or negotiating strategy because this is expected by the adversary.

To most practitioners it appears that anything sanctioned by the rules of the game is appropriate. From this point of view, negotiations are merely, as the social scientists have viewed it, a form of game; observance of the expected rules, not professional ethics, is the guiding precept. But gamesmanship is not ethics. . . .

The courts have seldom had occasion to consider these ethical problems, for disciplinary proceedings have rarely been invoked on any charge of misconduct in the area. But where settlements have in fact been made when one party acted on the basis of a factual error known to the other and this error induced the compromise, courts have set releases aside on the basis of mistake, or, in some cases, fraud.

The monopoly on the practice of law does not arise from the presumed advantages of an attorney's education or social status: it stems from the concept that, as professionals, lawyers serve society's interests by participating in the process of achieving the just termination of disputes. That an adversary system is the basic means to this end does not crown it with supreme value. It is means, not end.

If he is a professional and not merely a hired, albeit skilled hand, the lawyer is not free to do anything his client might do in the same circumstances. The corollary of that proposition does set a minimum standard: the lawyer must be at least as candid and honest as his client would be required to be. The agent of the client, that is, his attorney-at-law, must not perpetrate the kind of fraud or deception that would vitiate a bargain if practiced by his principal. Beyond that, the profession should embrace an affirmative ethical standard for attorneys' professional relationships with courts, other lawyers and the public: *The lawyer must act honestly and in good faith.* Another lawyer, or a layman, who deals with a lawyer should not need to exercise the same degree of caution that he would if trading for reputedly antique copper jugs in an oriental bazaar. It is inherent in the concept of an ethic, as a principle of good conduct, that it is morally binding on the conscience of the professional, and not merely a rule of the game adopted because other players observe (or fail to adopt) the same rule. Good conduct exacts more than mere convenience. It is not sufficient to call on personal self-interest; this is the standard created by the thesis that the same adversary met today may be faced again tomorrow, and one had best not prejudice that future engagement. . . .

While it might strain present concepts of the role of the lawyer in an adversary system, surely the professional standards must ultimately impose upon him a duty not to accept an unconscionable deal. While some difficulty in line-drawing is inevitable when such a distinction is sought to be made, there must be a point at which the lawyer cannot ethically accept an arrangement that is completely unfair to the other side, be that opponent a patsy or a tax collector. So I posit a second precept: *The lawyer may not accept a result that is unconscionably unfair to the other party.*

A settlement that is unconscionable may result from a variety of circumstances. There may be a vast difference in the bargaining power of the principals so that, regardless of the adequacy of representation by counsel, one party may simply not be able to withstand the expense and bear the delay and uncertainty inherent in a protracted suit. There may be a vast difference in the bargaining skill of counsel so that one is able to manipulate the other virtually at will despite the fact that their framed certificates of admission to the bar contain the same words.

The unconscionable result in these circumstances is in part created by the relative power, knowledge and skill of the principals and their negotiators. While it is the unconscionable result that is to be avoided, the question of whether the result is indeed intolerable depends in part on examination of the relative status of the parties. The imposition of a duty to tell the truth and to bargain in good faith would reduce their relative inequality, and tend to produce negotiation results that are within relatively tolerable bounds. . . .

The lawyer should not be free to negotiate an unconscionable result, however pleasing to his client, merely because it is possible, any more than he is free to do other reprobated acts. He is not to commit perjury or pay a bribe or give advice about how to commit embezzlement. These examples refer to advice concerning illegal conduct, but we do already, in at least some instances, accept the principle that some acts are proscribed though not criminal: the lawyer is forbidden to testify as a witness in his client's cause, or to assert a defense merely to harass his opponent; he is enjoined to point out to his client "those factors that may lead to a decision that is morally just." Whether a mode of conduct available to the lawyer is illegal or merely unconscionably unfair, the attorney must refuse to participate. This duty of fairness is one owed to the profession and to society; it must supersede any duty owed to the client. . . .*

Legislative History

The January 1980 draft of the Model Rules contained the following two provisions. Proposed Rule 4.2(a) was close to Judge Rubin's first precept. Proposed Rule 4.3 encompassed the import of his second precept. Both rules were ultimately rejected, although that part of Rule 4.3 that forbids a lawyer to help a client conclude a fraudulent agreement is preserved in Rule 1.2(d). Professor White's article, which follows, addresses Rule 4.2 as it appeared in the January 1980 draft.

RULE 4.2   Fairness to Other Participants

(a) In conducting negotiations a lawyer shall be fair in dealing with other participants.

(b) A lawyer shall not make a knowing misrepresentation of fact or law, or fail to disclose a material fact known to the lawyer, even if adverse, when disclosure is:

(1) required by law or the rules of professional conduct; or

(2) necessary to correct a manifest misrepresentation of fact or law resulting from a previous representation made by the lawyer or known by the lawyer to have been made by the client, except that counsel for an accused in a criminal case is not required to make such a correction when it would require disclosing a misrepresentation made by the accused. . . .

*Lee Pizzimenti, drawing on the UCC and ethics principles, pursues the proposition that "the best and most overt way to minimize the occurrence of unconscionable contracts is to forbid a lawyer from drafting them." Professor Pizzimenti proposes a new disciplinary rule in Prohibiting Lawyers from Assisting in Unconscionable Transactions: Using An Overt Tool, 72 Marq. L. Rev. 153 (1989).

RULE 4.3   Illegal, Fraudulent, or Unconscionable Transactions

A lawyer shall not conclude an agreement, or assist a client in concluding an agreement, that the lawyer knows or reasonably should know is illegal, contains legally prohibited terms, would work a fraud, or would be held to be unconscionable as a matter of law.

James J. White
MACHIAVELLI AND THE BAR: ETHICAL LIMITATIONS ON LYING IN NEGOTIATION
1980 Am. B. Found. Res. J. 926, 926-934

The difficulty of proposing acceptable rules concerning truthfulness in negotiation is presented by several circumstances. First, negotiation is nonpublic behavior. If one negotiator lies to another, only by happenstance will the other discover the lie. If the settlement is concluded by negotiation, there will be no trial, no public testimony by conflicting witnesses, and thus no opportunity to examine the truthfulness of assertions made during the negotiation. Consequently, in negotiation, more than in other contexts, ethical norms can probably be violated with greater confidence that there will be no discovery and punishment. Whether one is likely to be caught for violating an ethical standard says nothing about the merit of the standard. However, if the low probability of punishment means that many lawyers will violate the standard, the standard becomes even more difficult for the honest lawyer to follow, for by doing so he may be forfeiting a significant advantage for his client to others who do not follow the rules.

The drafters appreciated, but perhaps not fully, a second difficulty in drafting ethical norms for negotiators. That is the almost galactic scope of disputes that are subject to resolution by negotiation. One who conceives of negotiation as an alternative to a lawsuit has only scratched the surface. Negotiation is also the process by which one deals with the opposing side in war, with terrorists, with labor or management in a labor agreement, with buyers and sellers of goods, services, and real estate, with lessors, with governmental agencies, and with one's clients, acquaintances, and family. By limiting his consideration to negotiations in which a lawyer is involved in his professional role, one eliminates some of the most difficult cases but is left with a rather large and irregular universe of disputes. Surely society would tolerate and indeed expect different forms of behavior on the one hand from one assigned to negotiate with terrorists and on the other from one who is negotiating with the citizens on behalf of a governmental agency. The difference between those two cases illustrates the less drastic distinctions that may be called for by differences between other negotiating situations. Performance that is standard in one negotiating arena may be gauche, conceivably unethical, in another. More than almost any other form of lawyer behavior, the process of negotiation is varied: it differs from place to place and from subject matter to subject matter. It calls, therefore, either for quite different rules in different contexts or for rules stated only at a very high level of generality.

A final complication in drafting rules about truthfulness arises out of the paradoxical nature of the negotiator's responsibility. On the one hand the negotiator must be fair and truthful; on the other he must mislead his opponent. Like the poker player, a negotiator hopes that his opponent will overestimate the value of his hand. Like the poker player, in a variety of ways he must facilitate his opponent's inaccurate assessment. The critical difference between those who are successful negotiators and those who are not lies in this capacity both to mislead and not to be misled. . . .

TRUTHTELLING IN GENERAL

The obligation to behave truthfully in negotiation is embodied in the requirement of Rule 4.2(a) that directs the lawyer to "be fair in dealing with other participants."* . . .

The comment on fairness under Rule 4.2 makes explicit what is implicit in the rule itself by the following sentence: "Fairness in negotiation implies that representations by or on behalf of one party to the other party be truthful." Standing alone that statement is too broad. Even the Comments contemplate activities such as puffing which, in the broadest sense, are untruthful. It seems quite unlikely that the drafters intend or can realistically hope to outlaw a variety of other nontruthful behavior in negotiations. Below we will consider some examples, but for the time being we will consider the complexity of the task.

Pious and generalized assertions that the negotiator must be "honest" or that the lawyer must use "candor" are not helpful. They are at too high a level of generality, and they fail to appreciate the fact that truth and truthful behavior at one time in one set of circumstances with one set of negotiators may be untruthful in another circumstance with other negotiators. There is no general principle waiting somewhere to be discovered as Judge Alvin B. Rubin seems to suggest in his article on lawyers' ethics. Rather, mostly we are doing what he says we are not doing, namely, hunting for the rules of the game as the game is played in that particular circumstance.

The definition of truth is in part a function of the substance of the negotiation. Because of the policies that lie behind the securities and ex-

---

*This rule was deleted in subsequent drafts of the Model Rules. — ED.

change laws and the demands that Congress has made that information be provided to those who buy and sell, one suspects that lawyers engaged in SEC work have a higher standard of truthfulness than do those whose agreements and negotiations will not affect public buying and selling of assets. Conversely, where the thing to be bought and sold is in fact a lawsuit in which two professional traders conclude the deal, truth means something else. Here truth and candor call for a smaller amount of disclosure, permit greater distortion, and allow the other professional to suffer from his own ignorance and sloth in a way that would not be acceptable in the SEC case. In his article Rubin recognizes that there are such different perceptions among members of the bar engaged in different kinds of practice, and he suggests that there should not be such differences. Why not? Why is it so clear that one's responsibility for truth ought not be a function of the policy, the consequences, and the skill and expectations of the opponent?

Apart from the kinds of differences in truthfulness and candor which arise from the subject matter of the negotiation, one suspects that there are other differences attributable to regional and ethnic differences among negotiators. Although I have only anecdotal data to support this idea, it seems plausible that one's expectation concerning truth and candor might be different in a small, homogeneous community from what it would be in a large, heterogeneous community of lawyers. For one thing, all of the lawyers in the small and homogeneous community will share a common ethnic and environmental background. Each will have been subjected to the same kind of training about what kinds of lies are appropriate and what are not appropriate. . . .

If the Comments or the body of the Model Rules are to refer to truthfulness, they should be understood to mean not an absolute but a relative truth as it is defined in context. That context in turn should be determined by the subject matter of the negotiation and, to a lesser extent, by the region and the background of the negotiators. Of course, such a flexible standard does not resolve the difficulties that arise when negotiators of different experience meet one another. I despair of solving that problem by the promulgation of rules, for to do so would require the drafters of these rules to do something that they obviously could not wish to do. That is, unless they wish to rely on the norms in the various subcultures in the bar to flesh out the rules, they will have to draft an extensive and complex body of rules.

FIVE CASES

Although it is not necessary to draft such a set of rules, it is probably important to give more than the simple disclaimer about the impossibility of defining the appropriate limits of puffing that the drafters have given in the current Comments. To test these limits, consider five cases. Easiest

is the question that arises when one misrepresents his true opinion about
the meaning of a case or a statute. Presumably such a misrepresentation
is accepted lawyer behavior both in and out of court and is not intended
to be precluded by the requirement that the lawyer be "truthful." In writing his briefs, arguing his case, and attempting to persuade the opposing
party in negotiation, it is the lawyer's right and probably his responsibility
to argue for plausible interpretations of cases and statutes which favor
his client's interest, even in circumstances where privately he has advised
his client that those are not his true interpretations of the cases and
statutes.

A second form of distortion that the Comments plainly envision as
permissible is distortion concerning the value of one's case or of the other
subject matter involved in the negotiation. Thus the Comments make explicit reference to "puffery." Presumably they are attempting to draw the
same line that one draws in commercial law between express warranties
and "mere puffing" under section 2-313 of the Uniform Commercial
Code. While this line is not easy to draw, it generally means that the seller
of a product has the right to make general statements concerning the
value of his product without having the law treat those statements as warranties and without having liability if they turn out to be inaccurate estimates of the value. As the statements descend toward greater and greater
particularity, as the ignorance of the person receiving the statements increases, the courts are likely to find them to be not puffing but express
warranties. By the same token a lawyer could make assertions about his
case or about the subject matter of his negotiation in general terms, and if
those proved to be inaccurate, they would not be a violation of the ethical
standards. Presumably such statements are not violations of the ethical
standards even when they conflict with the lawyer's dispassionate analysis
of the value of his case.

A third case is related to puffing but different from it. This is the
use of the so-called false demand. It is a standard negotiating technique in collective bargaining negotiation and in some other multiple-
issue negotiations for one side to include a series of demands about
which it cares little or not at all. The purpose of including these demands is to increase one's supply of negotiating currency. One hopes
to convince the other party that one or more of these false demands is
important and thus successfully to trade it for some significant concession. The assertion of and argument for a false demand involves
the same kind of distortion that is involved in puffing or in arguing
the merits of cases or statutes that are not really controlling. The pro-
ponent of a false demand implicitly or explicitly states his interest in
the demand and his estimation of it. Such behavior is untruthful in
the broadest sense; yet at least in collective bargaining negotiation its
use is a standard part of the process and is not thought to be inappropriate by any experienced bargainer.

Two final examples may be more troublesome. The first involves the response of a lawyer to a question from the other side. Assume that the defendant has instructed his lawyer to accept any settlement offer under $100,000. Having received that instruction, how does the defendant's lawyer respond to the plaintiff's question, "I think $90,000 will settle this case. Will your client give $90,000?" Do you see the dilemma that question poses for the defense lawyer? It calls for information that would not have to be disclosed. A truthful answer to it concludes the negotiation and dashes any possibility of negotiating a lower settlement even in circumstances in which the plaintiff might be willing to accept half of $90,000. Even a moment's hesitation in response to the question may be a nonverbal communication to a clever plaintiff's lawyer that the defendant has given such authority. Yet a negative response is a lie.

It is no answer that a clever lawyer will answer all such questions about authority by refusing to answer them, nor is it an answer that some lawyers will be clever enough to tell their clients not to grant them authority to accept a given sum until the final stages in negotiation. Most of us are not that careful or that clever. Few will routinely refuse to answer such questions in cases in which the client has granted a much lower limit than that discussed by the other party, for in that case an honest answer about the absence of authority is a quick and effective method of changing the opponent's settling point, and it is one that few of us will forego when our authority is far below that requested by the other party. Thus despite the fact that a clever negotiator can avoid having to lie or to reveal his settling point, many lawyers, perhaps most, will sometime be forced by such a question either to lie or to reveal that they have been granted such authority by saying so or by their silence in response to a direct question. Is it fair to lie in such a case?

Before one examines the possible justifications for a lie in that circumstance, consider a final example recently suggested to me by a lawyer in practice. There the lawyer represented three persons who had been charged with shoplifting. Having satisfied himself that there was no significant conflict of interest, the defense lawyer told the prosecutor that two of the three would plead guilty only if the case was dismissed against the third. Previously those two had told the defense counsel that they would plead guilty irrespective of what the third did, and the third had said that he wished to go to trial unless the charges were dropped. Thus the defense lawyer lied to the prosecutor by stating that the two would plead only if the third were allowed to go free. Can the lie be justified in this case?

How does one distinguish the cases where truthfulness is not required and those where it is required? Why do the first three cases seem easy? I suggest they are easy cases because the rules of the game are explicit and well developed in those areas. Everyone expects a lawyer to distort the value of his own case, of his own facts and arguments, and to deprecate those of his opponent. No one is surprised by that, and the system accepts and expects that behavior. To a lesser extent the same is true of the false demand procedure in labor-management negotiations where the ploy is sufficiently widely used to be explicitly identified in the literature. A layman might say that this behavior falls within the ambit of "exaggeration," a form of behavior that while not necessarily respected is not regarded as morally reprehensible in our society.

The last two cases are more difficult. In one the lawyer lies about his authority; in the other he lies about the intention of his clients. It would be more difficult to justify the lies in those cases by arguing that the rules of the game explicitly permit that sort of behavior. Some might say that the rules of the game provide for such distortion, but I suspect that many lawyers would say that such lies are out of bounds and are not part of the rules of the game. . . .

What Is "Fraudulent"?

Both the code and the Model Rules use the words "fraud" and "fraudulent." The code does not define "fraud," but state versions do. For example, the New York version defines "fraud" as follows: " 'Fraud' does not include conduct, although characterized as fraudulent by statute or administrative rule, which lacks an element of scienter, deceit, intent to mislead, or knowing failure to correct misrepresentations which can be expected to induce detrimental reliance by another." ABA Opinion 341 (1975) is in accord. The Model Rules define "fraud" or "fraudulent" as denoting "conduct having a purpose to deceive and not merely negligent misrepresentation or failure to apprise another of relevant information."

Should "fraud" be interpreted as narrowly as the Model Rules and Opinion 341 interpret it? Should, for example, conduct that is negligent but nevertheless characterized as fraudulent by substantive law be treated as ethically improper? In the securities area, especially, the negligent failure to inform may be considered fraudulent under substantive law. One commentator has suggested that this conflict between the substantive standard and the ethical standard subjects lawyers to a risk. They may reveal a client's negligent failure to inform but then find themselves disciplined for disclosing a client confidence. Or they may conceal the client's negligent failure to inform but then find themselves liable as accessories to fraud under securities law. Frederick Lipman, The SEC's Reluctant Police Force: A New Role for Lawyers, 49 N.Y.U. L. Rev. 437, 461-462 (1974).

In Fellerman v. Bradley, 99 N.J. 493, 493 A.2d 1239 (1985), the court, in evaluating the "crime or fraud" exception to the attorney-client privilege (page 36 supra), insisted on a definition of "fraud" broader than the one found in the tort or criminal law. Among the acts constituting fraud was "confederating with clients to allow a court and counsel to labor under a misapprehension."

What Is "Assisting"?

Recall ABA Opinion 353 (1987) (page 314 supra) and the discussion of its definition of the word "assisting" in Rule 3.3(a)(2) (page 357 supra). It defined the word to mean more than the "criminal law concepts of aiding and abetting or subornation. Rather, it seems clear that this language is intended to guide the conduct of the lawyer as an officer of the court as a prophylactic measure to protect against client perjury contaminating the judicial process." "Assist" or "assisting" also appears in Rules 1.2(d) and 4.1(b). Does the committee's expansive definition apply to these provisions as well? Assuming it does, what does that imply? Rule 4.1(b) does not, in any event, allow revelation of information protected by Rule 1.6, which correction would usually require. Consider also Rule 1.2(d), which forbids lawyers to "assist" a client's fraud. If "assist" is defined broadly here too, withdrawal would be mandatory under the broader circumstances, wouldn't it? Is there a reason not to give "assist" the same meaning in Rule 4.1(b) or Rule 1.2(d) that the ABA committee accepted for Rule 3.3(a)(2) in Opinion 353?

If we combine the broad definition of "fraud" adopted by the New Jersey Supreme Court in Fellerman v. Bradley and the broad definition of "assisting" adopted by the ABA in Opinion 353, won't we come quite close to Judge Rubin's two precepts? Is that what the court in the following case did? Was it right?

VIRZI v. GRAND TRUNK WAREHOUSE & COLD STORAGE CO.
571 F. Supp. 507 (E.D. Mich. 1983)

GILMORE, DISTRICT JUDGE.

This case raises an important issue relating to the ethical obligation of an attorney to inform opposing counsel and the Court, prior to concluding a settlement, of the death of his client. For the reasons set forth in this opinion, the Court holds the attorney has an absolute ethical obligation to do so, and sets aside the settlement ordered in this matter.

I

This is a personal injury diversity action. Pursuant to the authority contained in Rule 32 of the Rules of the United States District Court for the Eastern District of Michigan, the case was referred to a mediation panel for mediation prior to the final pretrial conference.

On June 2, 1983, plaintiff's attorney prepared and filed a mediation statement for plaintiff with the mediation panel. Three days later, plaintiff died unexpectedly from causes unrelated to the lawsuit. On June 14, 1983, the case was mediated, and the mediation panel placed an evaluation of $35,000 on the case. At the time of the mediation hearing, plaintiff's attorney did not know that his client had died.[2]

Several days after the mediation hearing of June 14, plaintiff's attorney learned of his client's death. A personal representative was appointed by the probate court on June 24, 1983 to administer plaintiff's estate, although no suggestion of death was made in this Court, and the representative was not substituted as plaintiff.

On July 5, 1983, counsel for plaintiff and defendants appeared before this Court at a pretrial conference and, after negotiations, entered into a settlement of the lawsuit for the amount of the mediation award — $35,000. At no time, from the time plaintiff's attorney learned of the plaintiff's death until the agreement to settle the case for $35,000 at the pretrial conference, did plaintiff's attorney notify defendants' attorney or the Court of the death of the plaintiff.

After the settlement was agreed upon in chambers and placed upon the record, as both attorneys were walking out of chambers to the elevator together, plaintiff's attorney, for the first time, informed defendants' attorney that plaintiff had died. The facts also show that defendants had learned of plaintiff's death shortly before the settlement was agreed upon, but were unable to convey this information to their attorney before the settlement order was entered. At no time did defendants' attorney ask plaintiff's attorney if plaintiff was still alive and available for trial.

Defendants' counsel claims that his sole reason for recommending acceptance of the mediation award was that plaintiff would have made an excellent witness on his own behalf if the case had gone to trial.

Defendants contend that because their lawyer did not know of plaintiff's death at the time of the settlement, and because plaintiff's attorney failed to disclose that fact, the settlement is void. Defendants also argue that the settlement should be void because, although an administrator had been appointed for plaintiff's estate, there was no proper substitution of that party at the time the Court entered its settlement offer, and, therefore, there was no party with whom a settlement could properly be made.

Plaintiff's attorney, on the other hand, contests defendants' motion, claiming that his actions were not unethical or improper. He states that

2. It should be noted that attendance of clients is not generally required in mediation hearings.

plaintiff was alive at the time the mediation statement was filed and that there was nothing in the statement that was false and misleading. He also points out that he was not aware at the time of the mediation hearing that his client was dead, and did not become aware of that until three days after the award of the mediation panel.

In oral argument, plaintiff's attorney indicated that, had defendants' attorney asked him if his client was still alive at the time of the pretrial hearing before this Court, or had the Court asked the same question, he would have revealed the fact that he was dead. He says, however, that he had no duty to volunteer that information and that the settlement entered into is a fair and reasonable settlement.

Finally, plaintiff's counsel argues that the Court had the authority to enter the settlement order in this matter, even though plaintiff was deceased, because a personal representative had been properly appointed by the probate court. He argues that the settlement is binding even though a formal motion to substitute the representative for the deceased plaintiff was never made.

II

The sole issue in the case is whether plaintiff's attorney had an ethical duty to advise this Court and defendant's attorney, who was unaware of the death of plaintiff, that plaintiff had died a few weeks prior to the settlement agreement. . . .

[The court quoted from EC 7-27, DR 7-102(A)(3) and (5), and Michigan's version of Rules 1.6, 3.3(a)(1), (2), (4), and (6), and 4.1.]

The Court also cannot rely on case law to define the parameters of these Rules as there is a paucity of case law on the subject. Nonetheless, the following decisions are helpful. In Spaulding v. Zimmerman, 263 Minn. 346, 116 N.W.2d 704 (1962), plaintiff was injured in an automobile accident. In addition to plaintiff's physician and two specialists, a fourth physician examined plaintiff at the request of defendants. The defendants' physician found an aneurysm of the aorta, which escaped the notice of the other physicians, and he reported this condition to defendants' lawyers.

Without disclosing this condition to plaintiff or plaintiff's counsel, defendants settled the case. Two years later, plaintiff, at a subsequent physical examination, learned of the aneurysm and brought an action for additional damages against the same defendants. The trial judge vacated the earlier settlement, and his order vacating the settlement was affirmed on appeal.

The Minnesota Court found that there was no duty on defendants to voluntarily disclose this knowledge during the course of negotiations, when the parties were in an adversary relationship, but that a duty to disclose arose once the parties reached a settlement and sought the court's approval. It quoted with approval the language of the trial court:

> To hold that the concealment was not of such character as to result in a nonconscionable advantage over plaintiff's ignorance or mistake, would be to penalize innocence and incompetence and reward less than full performance of an officer of the Court's duty to make full disclosure to the Court when applying for approval in minor settlement proceedings.

The Minnesota Court held that defendants' knowing failure to disclose this condition opened the way for the court to later exercise its discretion in vacating the settlement.

In Toledo Bar Association v. Fell, 51 Ohio St. 2d 33, 364 N.E.2d 872 (1977), an attorney specializing in workman's compensation law, with knowledge of the long-established practice of the Ohio Industrial Commission to deny any claim for permanent total disability benefits upon notice of death of a claimant, deliberately withheld information concerning his client's death prior to a hearing on a motion concerning the claim in order to collect a fee. The Supreme Court of Ohio held that this action violated the Code of Professional Responsibility and justified an indefinite suspension from the practice of law. . . .

Here, plaintiff's attorney did not make a false statement regarding the death of plaintiff. He was never placed in a position to do so because during the two weeks of settlement negotiations defendants' attorney never thought to ask if plaintiff was still alive. Instead, in hopes of inducing settlement, plaintiff's attorney chose to not disclose plaintiff's death, as he was well aware that defendants believed that plaintiff would make an excellent witness on his own behalf if the case were to proceed to trial by jury. Here, unlike the factual information withheld in *Spaulding*, above, plaintiff's death was not caused by injuries related to the lawsuit, and did not have any effect on the fairness of the $35,000 mediation award. But the fact of plaintiff's death nevertheless would have had a significant bearing on defendants' willingness to settle.

Also, while a personal representative was appointed by the probate court for the deceased, plaintiff's attorney failed prior to settlement to make a suggestion of death in the record before this Court, or to move for substitution of parties in accordance with Rule 25 of the Federal Rules of Civil Procedure. By not informing the Court of plaintiff's death, or filing a motion to substitute parties, plaintiff's attorney led this Court to enter an order of settlement for a non-existent party. Arguably, this settlement order may be rendered void by Rule 25 [which concerns substitution of parties, including in case of death]. . . .

There is no question that plaintiff's attorney owed a duty of candor to this Court, and such duty required a disclosure of the fact of the death of the client. Although it presents a more difficult judgment call, this Court is of the opinion that the same duty of candor and fairness required a disclosure to opposing counsel, even though counsel did not ask whether the client was still alive. Although each lawyer has a duty to contend, with zeal, for the rights of his client, he also owes an affirmative duty of candor and frankness to the Court and to opposing counsel when such a major event as the death of the plaintiff has taken place.

This Court's position on the ethical duty of a lawyer dealing with an opposing party is well summarized by a passage from Judge Rubin's article entitled "A Causerie on Lawyer's Ethics in Negotiations," 35 La. L. Rev. 577 (1975).

[The court quoted the material at page 471 supra.]

This Court feels that candor and honesty necessarily require disclosure of such a significant fact as the death of one's client. Opposing counsel does not have to deal with his adversary as he would deal in the marketplace. Standards of ethics require greater honesty, greater candor, and greater disclosure, even though it might not be in the interest of the client or his estate.

The handling of a lawsuit and its progress is not a game. There is an absolute duty of candor and fairness on the part of counsel to both the Court and opposing counsel. At the same time, counsel has a duty to zealously represent his client's interests. That zealous representation of interest, however, does not justify a withholding of essential information, such as the death of the client, when the settlement of the case is based largely upon the defense attorney's assessment of the impact the plaintiff would make upon a jury, because of his appearance at depositions. Plaintiff's attorney clearly had a duty to disclose the death of his client both to the Court and to opposing counsel prior to negotiating the final agreement.

For the foregoing reasons, the settlement will be set aside and the case reinstated on the docket for trial. Counsel may present an order.

What Does *Virzi* Stand For?

Does it stand for the proposition that a lawyer must always reveal the death of a client? The death of a client who is a party to the settlement of a litigation? All facts that may be important to the other side in a negotiation? How would you resolve the following actual cases? Should the settlement be invalidated? Should the lawyer be disciplined?

1. A pedestrian, injured when two cars collided, hired Addison to represent him. The client incurred hospital expenses of about $112,000. One driver had a policy of $100,000 and a second policy of $1 million. The other driver had a $50,000 policy. When Addison approached the hospital about releasing its lien on his client's claim, he became aware that the hospital was ignorant of the million dollar policy. He negotiated a re-

lease without revealing the information. Later, the hospital learned of the policy and tried to withdraw its release.

2. A lawyer represented a husband in the negotiation of a separation agreement. There was a dispute over the valuation of certain community property. The wife's lawyer submitted an offer that evaluated the property at a high sum but made an arithmetical error in deducting the amount of an encumbrance. As a result, the proposal stated the wife's interest at about $70,000 when, without the arithmetical error, it would have been $120,000. The husband's lawyer discovered the error. He then accepted the $70,000 figure in a response prepared in a way designed to minimize the danger that the wife or her attorney would discover the mistake. After the separation agreement was signed and a divorce obtained, the former wife learned of the error. She brought an action against the former husband for the additional $50,000.

3. Plaintiff alleged that the county failed to hire her in violation of law protecting handicapped individuals. Eventually plaintiff was hired and the case was tentatively settled for lost pay. Plaintiff's lawyer demanded the pay that plaintiff would have received had she been properly hired in the first place. Plaintiff submitted a written settlement offer designating the pay at step C. The county accepted the offer. Plaintiff's lawyer then learned that plaintiff's starting salary would have been step D, which is higher. When accepting the settlement, the county's lawyer did not know but thought it likely that plaintiff's counsel had mistakenly assumed that step C was the highest pay step possible. Plaintiff moved to vacate the consent judgment entered on the settlement.

4. A prosecutor negotiates a plea bargain with a defense lawyer although, as the prosecutor knows but the defense lawyer does not, the victim of the defendant's crime had died of unrelated causes. After the defendant is sentenced, he learns of the victim's death and his lawyer moves to vacate the conviction, claiming that with the victim dead the state could not have proved its case.

Threatening Criminal Prosecution

The code, but not the rules, forbids a lawyer to threaten criminal prosecution in order to gain an advantage in a civil matter. DR 7-105(A). Do you think the rules erred in omitting this provision? Will the law of extortion fill the gap in any event? Some states, although adopting the rules, have retained the provision. The District of Columbia, expanding it, forbids a lawyer to "seek or threaten to seek criminal charges or disciplinary charges solely to obtain an advantage in a civil matter." Rule 8.4(g). Although the Florida rules are silent on the matter, Florida Opinion 89-3 reads them to continue the prohibition. Michigan Opinion RI-78 (1991), by contrast, concludes that elimination of DR 7-105(A) was intentional. As a result, in negotiating a claim a Michigan lawyer may in good faith refer to possible criminal liability, advise a client to pursue criminal prosecution in order to advance a civil claim, and have a client agree not to report criminal conduct as a condition of settling a civil claim. The opinion concludes that abusive or harassing conduct can still be addressed by the rules.

FURTHER READING

Eleanor Holmes Norton identifies truthfulness and fairness as "two core ethical norms" that can be used to understand the operation of ethics in "bargaining." The author offers "an analytical model called functionalism for evaluating negotiation ethics" and identifies "the doctrines of misrepresentation and unconscionability as proxies for deception and unfairness." She applies her "functionalist assumptions concerning truthfulness and fairness in bargaining in two areas, divorce law and labor law." Professor Norton's article is the first part of a two-part study that will eventually be published as a book. Eleanor Norton, Bargaining and the Ethic of Process, 64 N.Y.U. L. Rev. 493 (1989).

SIMULATED CASE HISTORY

FELICIA CARLYSLE

Ray and I got married in 1978. We met when Ray was in his third year at medical school and I had just started in advertising. Now Ray is a successful psychiatrist and I'm about to become president of a small ad agency. We have three children: Gina, 8; Lewis, 6; and Miranda, 3.

Our marriage began to have problems two years ago. Ray thinks it's because of an affair he suspects I started with a co-worker about then. I've told him his charge is outrageous and I refuse to even discuss it. The truth is, however, that Jim and I did begin to see each other about two years ago but Jim is simply the product of a breakdown that had been in progress for some time. Jim's a symptom, not the cause. The cause — oh, there are many causes of course, but what did it for me is Ray's inability to accept my professional success. He's jealous of what I've achieved and he's unhappy in psychiatry. Probably he never should have been a doctor to begin with, but he doesn't have the courage to try something different. The fact is, he's a paper success but he's disappointed with his life and he blames me for it.

We tried family therapy, but since I was not about to tell about Jim, and I'm sure there were things Ray wasn't about to say, it was all a lie and couldn't work. It took us nearly two years until our life together became so unbearable we both recognized divorce was the only possible solution to our misery.

Once we recognized this, I thought things would proceed quickly. We are both organized people who are accustomed to getting things done and we chose lawyers who are the same way. I hired Ben Butler, whom my friend Lois had used with such success. Ray hired Samantha Kelsey. I think he purposely set out to find a woman lawyer just to make me look unreasonable when I told Ben, as Ray inevitably knew I would, about Ray's professional jealousy and resentment.

Things didn't work out as I expected. Almost immediately, the whole negotiation turned bitter and confrontational. Ray thinks our initial offer was outrageous and responded viciously. Our offer may have been a touch high, but it was an initial offer, not an ultimatum. I told Ben I wanted to be fair, but he said I had to come in high in order to come out at a reasonable result. And remember, I had supported Ray in his last year of medical school and when he earned relatively little as a resident. Anyway, after Ray's response to our offer, things just escalated. I had heard divorces were supposed to be awful, but I never expected this. We have children together, so I must deal with Ray on many things, but I don't expect I'll ever get over this experience.

Samantha Kelsey

I've dealt with Ben Butler many times. He's tough. That's why people hire him and I assume that's why Felicia Carlysle hired him. She wanted the best bottom line she could get. She's not some unworldly housewife, ignorant about money and business. She's rather more sophisticated than her husband about these things, although he earns more.

Lest there be any doubt about Felicia's goal, one need only look at her first offer, or should I more aptly call it a demand? She wanted the house, the country house, both cars, custody with rather restricted visitation, and half of Ray's gross income yearly with a floor (but no ceiling), escalators (but no de-escalators), and guarantees of all health and extracurricular costs, plus all education expenses through graduate or professional school. After the children's emancipation, Felicia wanted one-quarter of Ray's gross income to her for life, regardless of whether she remarried, representing, she said, her investment in his professional license. What about his investment in her career? Piggy, piggy, piggy.

Now, when a first offer looks like that, even the most reasonable soon-to-be-former spouse loses control. Ray declared war and frankly I don't blame him. When my client wants peace, I go out there with the white flag. But when my client declares war, it's my job to gather the ammunition. Sometimes, of course, it's obvious that my client is not in a position to fight a war and I say so. But Ray was.

Our counteroffer was an equal division of the property. No support in either direction. Ray keeps the house and pays Felicia one-half its fair market value. The country house is sold and the proceeds split. Ray gets custody of all three children with visitation for Felicia. On this point, we let it be known that if Felicia sought custody Ray was prepared to testify to Felicia's suicide attempt three years earlier, to her confession to Ray that she found it hard to love Lewis because he reminded her of her father whom she loathed, and to the fact that in her final year of college she had had a brief but intense affair with a woman. We would also be prepared to call Jim to testify and we would ask him about his affair with Felicia.

I apologize for none of it. I take my clients as I find them. I'm not a therapist and if you ask me, lawyers make mistakes when they decide to become therapists. It ultimately disserves the client and it's patronizing. In any event, in this case, Butler and Felicia decided how to pitch the negotiation. Not to mix metaphors, but if they were unable to take the heat, they should have been more reasonable at the outset.

Ben says Ray did not really want custody, that it was just a false demand to gain leverage on other issues because he knew Felicia would not sign any agreement unless it gave her custody. What does "really want" mean? The agreement was a package and Ray really wanted one package over another. He was prepared to accept a package that gave Felicia custody if its other components were acceptable. But if they weren't, then a package that gave him certain property and financial advantages, and included custody, might be preferable. Ben says his first offer was meant to give him something to bargain over. Well, that's how it was with our custody position. It gave us something to trade for a different package. In the end it would have been highly unlikely, but not actually impossible, that Ray would have insisted on custody. We used it to get the best deal we could on the money side. And it worked.

Ben is complaining that Ray hid assets. The fact is that Ray had $100,000 in bearer bonds that Felicia didn't know about. Some of his patients paid in cash. The bonds were kept in a safe deposit box. Ray had no choice but to conceal their existence. If he or I had revealed them, we would have provided evidence of tax evasion. As it turned out, when Butler learned about the bonds, he had Felicia threaten to report Ray to the IRS unless Ray caved in on some important issues. I consider that unethical. And of course, I couldn't reveal the existence of the bonds, which I learned about only as a result of a professional confidence made to me after Ben and I exchanged the standard financial disclosure affidavits of our clients.

Ben has something else to answer for. He knew, but we couldn't, that Felicia had been offered a job heading a small agency at a substantially higher salary plus bonus, altogether about a 30 percent increase in gross income. Ben rushed our negotiation so that the papers would be signed before Felicia took the job. If we had known about that job offer in advance, the final package would have looked rather different. This is no different to my mind from not revealing the $100,000. If one is wrong, so is the other. Ben had a duty to tell us about the new job. Instead, he argued that Felicia's salary would remain relatively constant as against inflation, while Ray, as a principal in an HMO, would earn increasingly more each year. He and Felicia emphasized several times that, given the couple's income disparity, Felicia's offer was "generous."

In the end, Felicia did all right. Not as well as she would have liked. She'd be happy if Ray were walking around in a barrel. If he's got anything left, she feels she lost. But my job isn't to roll over and play dead.

BEN BUTLER

Yes, I play tough, but I play by the rules. Hardball is not foul ball. There's no rule that says your first offer can't be high. If it's not high, there's no place to go, you have nothing to compromise. A friend of mine once tried a negotiating strategy where he objectively tried to identify a fair resolution. In effect, and in all good faith, he tried to be the judge. Then he made his offer, more or less take it or leave it. No bargaining. People just don't go for that, whatever sense it might make in theory. People want to feel they've negotiated something for themselves. The point is that there is no objective fairness. Fairness is largely the product of a process in which the principals participate. So when I make a high first offer, it gives the other side the opportunity to bargain some advantage in those areas important to it. That's how the game is played.

Sam's demand for custody was outrageous. Ray wouldn't know what to do with custody. He'd have to hire Dr. Spock, Selma Fraiberg, Bruno Bettellheim, Robert Coles, and Erik Erikson to help him raise his kids. His relationship with them is nearly as bad as his relationship with Felicia. You know why he asked for custody? Because he knows it's Felicia's single non-negotiable demand and he, or more accurately Samantha, figured it would be a good way to squeeze Felicia.

Then his threat to reveal what was really an ineffectual suicide gesture (pills) three years ago, when Felicia was depressed following the birth of Miranda, and Ray was entirely unsupportive, is nothing but blackmail intended to embarrass Felicia and make her fear that some unpredictable judge might actually give Ray custody. The same with regard to that comment about Lewis, which was a private, intimate statement spoken in anguish about Felicia's estranged father, and about the two affairs (Ray isn't even sure about the one with Jim). There are some things that you don't use, and certainly not because you think the other side's first offer is too high. There are other ways to respond to an offer you think is too high. It's blackmail and intended to be intimidating.

At the last moment, I learned about the bearer bonds — ethically and legally, but never mind how — and I told Felicia, which it was my duty to do. She asked if she had a right to reveal that information to the IRS. Well, of course she does and I told her so. She let Ray know she knew about the bonds and perhaps she intimated that she was not beyond revealing them. How Samantha can say that that was wrong after the threats she herself made on behalf of Ray is beyond me. Felicia had a right to part of that money.

Nor can I be blamed for instructing Felicia not to accept her new job until the agreement was signed. We don't have to tell the other side about our expectations. Sure I argued that Ray had the prospect of much higher income because he was a shareholder in an H.M.O. while Felicia was only a salaried employee. Because I knew about Felicia's job offer at the time, I was careful how I put it. I said "Ray *has no reason to expect* Felicia to have potential for increases in her income equivalent to his or much beyond inflation." That was true. And I said that Felicia's final offer was "generous in light of their income disparities." That was also true for the income they then had. Samantha must have agreed because she accepted. I didn't say anything about what Felicia expected to earn shortly thereafter.

One thing Samantha failed to remember is her willingness to take advantage of a drafting oversight. One of the minor, but still significant, items we had negotiated was Felicia's right to $20,000 in cash representing a percentage of Ray's interest in a tax shelter that couldn't be liquidated. When my associate drafted the final agreement, she failed to include that obligation and I did not notice its absence. After the agreement was signed, Ray couldn't resist telling Felicia about the mistake and gloating. He also told Felicia that Samantha became aware of it before the agreement was signed and had, in fact, pointed it out to Ray. I think Samantha had an obligation to say something. Samantha says her only obligation was to Ray and not to me or Felicia. Now I've got to go to court to get the agreement modified and if I win, as I expect to, my next stop is to go to the disciplinary committee.

XI

Judges, Special Masters, and Mediators

A. JUDGES

As it does for lawyers, the American Bar Association also promulgates a model code of conduct for judges. The ABA adopted the Canons of Judicial Ethics in 1924, which was replaced in 1972 with the Code of Judicial Conduct. The code itself was substantially amended in 1990. Nearly every state, the District of Columbia, and the Judicial Conference of the United States have adopted judicial conduct codes based on the ABA model. All jurisdictions also have a mechanism for judicial discipline. Sanctions for code violations can range from private discipline to removal. Discipline cannot, however, be used to remove federal judges appointed under Article III. Impeachment by Congress is constitutionally required. Nevertheless, discipline short of removal is statutorily contemplated. 28 U.S.C. §372(c).

As with legal ethics, judicial ethics are also enforced outside the disciplinary process through motions for disqualification, or recusal, of a judge based on an alleged conflict of interest. The standards for disqualification appear in §3(C) of the 1972 Code and §3(E) of the 1990 Code.* Standards for disqualification may also appear in statutory law. In the federal system, the statutes are 28 U.S.C. §§144 and 455. The latter is more detailed and more important. Its language is similar to the language of the ABA Codes because Congress relied on the 1972 Code in writing §455.

---

*The nomenclature here is uneven. We use the term "Canon" to refer to the broad principles of the judicial codes (e.g., Canon 1, 2, 3), but "section" to identify particular provisions (e.g., section 3(E)(1)(a) is part of Canon 3).

Beyond codes and statutes, the due process clause of the Constitution offers a third basis for judicial disqualification. Its standards are, however, harder to meet than those in the codes and legislation. Due process challenges to a presiding judge most frequently occur in criminal cases. See, e.g., Tumey v. Ohio, 273 U.S. 510 (1927) (judicial income may not depend on fines from convicted persons). But sometimes, as in *Aetna*, below, the clause applies in a civil matter too.

One interesting distinction between ethics codes for lawyers and those for judges is worth noting here. Whereas lawyer codes have come to disfavor the "appearance of impropriety" as a standard for evaluating a lawyer's conduct (see page 261 supra), judicial codes continue to be sensitive to appearances. One test for disqualifying a judge, as discussed, is that the judge's "impartiality might reasonably be questioned." Why has the profession adhered to an appearance standard for judges but not lawyers?

Part A of this chapter will focus on two broad ethical issues in the behavior of judges. The first, as you've probably guessed, is conflicts of interest. What kind of conflict will prevent a judge from sitting in a matter? We will ask this question initially as a matter of due process, but we will spend most of our time on the conflicts standards in the ethics codes and federal law.

The second issue of judicial ethics we cover deals with racism, sexism, homophobia, and similar bias issues. This is an area in which we have seen much development in the last decade. The 1990 ABA Code speaks to it more clearly than its predecessor. The Senate Judiciary Committee has several times debated whether it would any longer confirm judicial nominees who failed adequately to explain their membership in discriminatory private clubs. See, e.g., Neil Lewis, Committee Rejects Bush Nominee to Key Appellate Court in South, N.Y. Times, Apr. 12, 1991, at 1. State commissions have charged racism in state court systems. Report of the New York State Judicial Commission on Minorities (1991).

The issues here are both more complex and more subtle than whether biased attitudes can be allowed to influence judicial decisions (easy, no) or whether judges should be permitted to refer to women lawyers as "girls" or comment suggestively on their appearance (easy again). But should it be unethical for a judge to tell a mildly racist or homophobic joke at a private dinner party? To attend the nightclub act of a blatantly sexist performer? To belong to a local beach club restricted to persons of the judge's faith? Obviously, this brings up issues of freedom of speech, association, and religion as well as ethical ones.

What Judicial Conflicts Violate the Due Process Clause?

In Aetna Life Insurance Co. v. Lavoie, 475 U.S. 813 (1986), the Supreme Court invoked the due process clause to invalidate a state appellate judgment in a civil matter where one of the participating state judges had a direct financial interest in the outcome. The Alabama Supreme Court had affirmed a $3.5 million punitive damage award against Aetna. Justice Embry wrote the five-to-four per curiam opinion. At the time, as Aetna later discovered, Justice Embry was a plaintiff in a state action against other insurance companies, which, like the claim in the *Aetna* action, alleged a bad-faith failure to pay. After the *Aetna* decision, Justice Embry settled his own case for $30,000. The Supreme Court noted probable jurisdiction of Aetna's appeal and unanimously reversed. After concluding that "Justice Embry's opinion for the Alabama Supreme Court [in the *Aetna* case] had the clear and immediate effect of enhancing both the legal status and the settlement value of his own case," Chief Justice Burger continued:

> We conclude that Justice Embry's participation in this case violated appellants' due process rights. . . . We make clear that we are not required to decide whether in fact Justice Embry was influenced, but only whether sitting on the case then before the Supreme Court of Alabama " 'would offer a possible temptation to the average . . . judge to . . . lead him not to hold the balance nice, clear and true.' " The Due Process Clause "may sometimes bar trial by judges who have no actual bias and who would do their very best to weigh the scales of justice equally between contending parties. But to perform its high function in the best way, 'justice must satisfy the appearance of justice.' "

The Court stressed that Justice Embry had cast the deciding vote. Justice Brennan concurred and Justice Blackmun (joined by Justice Marshall) concurred in the judgment. Both concurring opinions argued that the result should be the same even if Justice Embry had not cast the deciding vote. Justice Brennan wrote: "The participation of a judge who has a substantial interest in the outcome of a case of which he knows at the time he participates *necessarily* imparts a bias into the deliberative process. This deprives litigants of the assurance of impartiality that is the fundamental requirement of due process."

Aetna has its limits, as several subsequent lower court opinions reveal. In one, a state appellate judge who participated in a decision affirming a conviction had been the local prosecuting attorney at the time of the conviction, and his name appeared on the state's appeal brief. The Fifth Circuit initially granted habeas corpus. The petitioner's due process rights were violated, it ruled, whether or not the judge had actually participated in the prosecution personally. The petitioner did not have to show prejudice. Why not? Bradshaw v. McCotter, 785 F.2d 1327 (5th Cir. 1986). On rehearing, the court denied relief. It reiterated its view that the former prosecutor should not have heard the appeal, but upheld the conviction, citing *Aetna*, because the judge's vote was not critical to the result. 796

F.2d 100 (5th Cir. 1986). What about the possibility that the other judges might have been influenced by their colleague's name on the state's appellate brief? Compare Barry v. United States, 528 F.2d 1094 (7th Cir.), cert. denied, 429 U.S. 826 (1976), where a judge's decision to preside at trial in prosecution of an alleged police extortion ring did not violate due process despite a contention, which was disputed, that the judge as United States Attorney had made the initial decision to combat the extortion ring. Was it influential that in neither of these cases was the judge's interest financial?

Consider United States v. Couch, 896 F.2d 78, 79 (5th Cir. 1990). Couch was convicted before Judge Brown and a jury of defrauding a federally insured bank. Judge Brown gave him 20 years. The conviction was affirmed. Couch thereafter brought a collateral attack alleging "that Judge Brown had invested approximately $19,000 in an unsuccessful oil drilling venture with him, that Judge Brown shared leasehold rights with Couch's children in an oil and gas lease, that Judge Brown had not disclosed these contacts, and that in presiding over the trial under these circumstances Judge Brown had created an appearance of partiality in violation of 28 U.S.C. §455 and the Due Process Clause." The court rejected Couch's due process argument and declined to apply §455 on a collateral attack. It said that the two standards were "not coterminous":

> As this and several other circuits have recognized, section 455 establishes a statutory disqualification standard more demanding than that required by the Due Process Clause. Accordingly, conduct violative of section 455 may not constitute a due process deficiency. The conundrum is in blazing the parameters of each.

After discussing *Aetna,* the court continued:

> The Due Process Clause requires a judge to step aside when a reasonable judge would find it necessary to do so. Section 455 requires disqualification when others would have reasonable cause to question the judge's impartiality. It is this additional, systemic concern for avoiding the appearance of impropriety that makes the section 455 standard for disqualification more demanding than that imposed by the Due Process Clause. At some point the two tests overlap. We conclude that it is this area of overlap that the *Liljeberg* court [page 497 infra] was referring to when it noted that the concern for public perceptions of judicial integrity has "constitutional dimensions."

Id. at 81-82. How's that again? Is the court saying that under the due process clause "a reasonable judge" may not find it "necessary" to step aside even when observers "would have reasonable cause to question the judge's impartiality"?

Ethical and Statutory Disqualification

LILJEBERG v. HEALTH SERVICES ACQUISITION CORP.
486 U.S. 847 (1988)

JUSTICE STEVENS delivered the opinion of the Court.

In 1974 Congress amended the Judicial Code "to broaden and clarify the grounds for judicial disqualification." The first sentence of the amendment provides:

> Any justice, judge, or magistrate of the United States shall disqualify himself in any proceeding in which his impartiality might reasonably be questioned....

I

In November 1981, respondent Health Services Acquisition Corp. brought an action against petitioner John Liljeberg, Jr., seeking a declaration of ownership of a corporation known as St. Jude Hospital of Kenner, Louisiana (St. Jude). The case was tried by Judge Robert Collins, sitting without a jury. Judge Collins found for Liljeberg and, over a strong dissent, the Court of Appeals affirmed. Approximately 10 months later, respondent learned that Judge Collins had been a member of the Board of Trustees of Loyola University while Liljeberg was negotiating with Loyola to purchase a parcel of land on which to construct a hospital. The success and benefit to Loyola of these negotiations turned, in large part, on Liljeberg prevailing in the litigation before Judge Collins.

Based on this information, respondent moved pursuant to Federal Rule of Civil Procedure 60(b)(6) to vacate the judgment on the ground that Judge Collins was disqualified under §455 at the time he heard the action and entered judgment in favor of Liljeberg. Judge Collins denied the motion and respondent appealed. The Court of Appeals determined that resolution of the motion required factual findings concerning the extent and timing of Judge Collins' knowledge of Loyola's interest in the declaratory relief litigation. Accordingly, the panel reversed and remanded the matter to a different judge for such findings. On remand, the District Court found that based on his attendance at Board meetings Judge Collins had actual knowledge of Loyola's interest in St. Jude in 1980 and 1981. The court further concluded, however, that Judge Collins had forgotten about Loyola's interest by the time the declaratory judgment suit came to trial in January 1982. On March 24, 1982, Judge Collins reviewed materials sent to him by the Board to prepare for an upcoming meeting. At that time — just a few days after he had filed his opinion finding for Liljeberg and still within the 10-day period allowed for filing a motion for a new trial — Judge Collins once again obtained actual knowledge of Loyola's interest in St. Jude. Finally, the District Court found that although Judge Collins thus lacked actual knowledge during trial and prior to the filing of his opinion, the evidence nonetheless gave rise to an appearance of impropriety. However, reading the Court of Appeals' mandate as limited to the issue of actual knowledge, the District Court concluded that it was compelled to deny respondent's Rule 60(b) motion.

The Court of Appeals again reversed. The court first noted that Judge Collins should have immediately disqualified himself when his actual knowledge of Loyola's interest was renewed. The court also found that regardless of Judge Collins' actual knowledge, "a reasonable observer would expect that Judge Collins would remember that Loyola had some dealings with Liljeberg and St. Jude and seek to ascertain the nature of these dealings." Such an appearance of impropriety, in the view of the Court of Appeals, was sufficient ground for disqualification under §455(a). Although recognizing that caution is required in determining whether a judgment should be vacated after becoming final, the court concluded that since the appearance of partiality was convincingly established and since the motion to vacate was filed as promptly as possible, the appropriate remedy was to vacate the declaratory relief judgment. Because the issues presented largely turn on the facts as they give rise to an appearance of impropriety, it is necessary to relate the sequence and substance of these events in some detail.

II

Petitioner, John Liljeberg, Jr., is a pharmacist, a promoter, and a half-owner of Axel Realty, Inc., a real estate brokerage firm. In 1976, he became interested in a project to construct and operate a hospital in Kenner, Louisiana, a suburb of New Orleans. In addition to providing the community with needed health care facilities, he hoped to obtain a real estate commission for Axel Realty and the exclusive right to provide pharmaceutical services at the new hospital. The successful operation of such a hospital depended upon the acquisition of a "certificate of need" from the State of Louisiana; without such a certificate the hospital would not qualify for health care reimbursement payments under the federal medicare and medicaid programs. Accordingly, in October 1979, Liljeberg formed St. Jude, intending to have the corporation apply for the certificate of need at an appropriate time.

During the next two years Liljeberg engaged in serious negotiations with at least two major parties. One set of negotiations involved a proposal to purchase a large tract of land from Loyola University for use as a hospital site, coupled with a plan to rezone adjoining University property. The proposed benefits to the University included not only the proceeds of the real estate sale itself, amounting to several million dollars, but also a substantial increase in the value to the University of the rezoned adjoining property. The progress of these negotiations was regularly reported to the University's Board of Trustees by its Real Estate Committee and discussed at Board meetings. The minutes of those meetings indicated that the University's interest in the project was dependent on the issuance of the certificate of need.

[Liljeberg was conducting separate negotiations with HAI, predecessor to respondent Health Services Acquisition Corp. Eventually, Liljeberg and HAI entered a contract whose construction became the subject of the instant action. In essence, the question before Judge Collins was whether, under the contract, Liljeberg or HAI owned St. Jude. This was important because in the interim St. Jude had received a certificate of need for the hospital. Only if Liljeberg controlled the certificate would he be able to proceed with his arrangement with Loyola, and would Loyola enjoy the benefits identified in the Court's opinion.]

Respondent filed its complaint for declaratory judgment on November 30, 1981. The case was tried by Judge Collins, sitting without a jury, on January 21 and January 22, 1982. At the close of the evidence, he announced his intended ruling, and on March 16, 1982, he filed a judgment (dated Mar. 12, 1982) and his findings of fact and conclusions of law. He credited Liljeberg's version of oral conversations that were disputed and of critical importance in his ruling.

During the period between November 30, 1981, and March 16, 1982, Judge Collins was a trustee of Loyola University, but was not conscious of the fact that the University and Liljeberg were then engaged in serious negotiations concerning the Kenner hospital project, or of the further fact that the success of those negotiations depended upon his conclusion that Liljeberg controlled the certificate of need. To determine whether Judge Collins' impartiality in the Liljeberg litigation "might reasonably be questioned," it is appropriate to consider the state of his knowledge immediately before the lawsuit was filed, what happened while the case was pending before him, and what he did when he learned of the University's interest in the litigation.

After the certificate of need was issued, and Liljeberg and HAI became embroiled in their dispute, Liljeberg reopened his negotiations with the University. On October 29, 1981, the Real Estate Committee sent a written report to each of the trustees, including Judge Collins, advising them of "a significant change" concerning the proposed hospital in Kenner and stating specifically that Loyola's property had "again become a prime location." The Committee submitted a draft of a resolution authorizing a University vice-president "to continue negotiations with the developers of the St. Jude Hospital." At the Board meeting on November 12, 1981, which Judge Collins attended, the trustees discussed the connection between the rezoning of Loyola's land in Kenner and the St. Jude project and adopted the Real Estate Committee's proposed resolution. Thus, Judge Collins had actual knowledge of the University's potential interest in the St. Jude hospital project in Kenner just a few days before the complaint was filed.

While the case was pending before Judge Collins, the University agreed to sell 80 acres of its land in Kenner to Liljeberg for $6,694,000. The progress of negotiations was discussed at a Board meeting on January 28, 1982. Judge Collins did not attend that meeting, but the Real Estate Committee advised the trustees that "the federal courts have determined that the certificate of need will be awarded to the St. Jude Corporation." Presumably this advice was based on Judge Collins' comment at the close of the hearing a week earlier, when he announced his intended ruling because he thought "it would be unfair to keep the parties in doubt as to how I feel about the case."

The formal agreement between Liljeberg and the University was apparently executed on March 19th. The agreement stated that it was not in any way conditioned on Liljeberg's prevailing in the litigation "pending in the U.S. District Court for the Eastern District of Louisiana . . . involving the obtaining by [Liljeberg] of a Certificate of Need," but it also gave the University the right to repurchase the property for the contract price if Liljeberg had not executed a satisfactory construction contract within one year and further provided for nullification of the contract in the event the rezoning of the University's adjoining land was not accomplished. Thus, the University continued to have an active interest in the outcome of the litigation because it was unlikely that Liljeberg could build the hospital if he lost control of the certificate of need; moreover, the rezoning was in turn dependent on the hospital project.

The details of the transaction were discussed in three letters to the trustees dated March 12, March 15, and March 19, 1982, but Judge Collins did not examine any of those letters until shortly before the Board meeting on March 25, 1982. Thus, he acquired actual knowledge of Loyola's interest in the litigation on March 24, 1982. As the Court of Appeals correctly held, "Judge Collins should have recused himself when he obtained actual knowledge of that interest on March 24."

In considering whether the Court of Appeals properly vacated the declaratory relief judgment, we are required to address two questions. We must first determine whether §455(a) can be violated based on an appearance of partiality, even though the judge was not conscious of the circumstances creating the appearance of impropriety, and second, whether relief is available under Rule 60(b) when such a violation is not discovered until after the judgment has become final.

III

Title 28 U.S.C. §455 provides in relevant part:

(a) Any justice, judge, or magistrate of the United States shall disqualify himself in any proceeding in which his impartiality might reasonably be questioned.

(b) he shall also disqualify himself in the following circumstances: . . .

(4) He knows that he, individually or as a fiduciary, or his spouse or minor child residing in his household, has a financial interest in the subject matter in controversy or in a party to the proceeding, or any other interest that could be substantially affected by the outcome of the proceeding. . . .

(c) A judge should inform himself about his personal and fiduciary financial interests, and make a reasonable effort to inform himself about the personal financial interests of his spouse and minor children residing in his household.

Scienter is not an element of a violation of §455(a). The judge's lack of knowledge of a disqualifying circumstance may bear on the question of remedy, but it does not eliminate the risk that "his impartiality might reasonably be questioned" by other persons. To read §455(a) to provide that the judge must know of the disqualifying facts, requires not simply ignoring the language of the provision — which makes no mention of knowledge — but further requires concluding that the language in subsection (b)(4) — which expressly provides that the judge must *know* of his or her interest — is extraneous. A careful reading of the respective subsections makes clear that Congress intended to require knowledge under subsection (b)(4) and not to require knowledge under subsection (a).[8] Moreover, advancement of the purpose of the provision — to promote public

---

8. Petitioner contends that §455(a) must be construed in light of §455(b)(4). He argues that the reference to knowledge in §455(b)(4) indicates that Congress must have intended that scienter be an element under §455(a) as well. Petitioner reasons that §455(a) is a catch-all provision, encompassing all of the specifically enumerated grounds for disqualification under §455(b), as well as other grounds not specified. Not requiring knowledge under §455(a), in petitioner's view, would thus render meaningless the knowledge requirement under §455(b)(4). The requirement could always be circumvented by simply moving for disqualification under §455(a), rather than §455(b).

Petitioner's argument ignores important differences between subsections (a) and (b)(4). Most importantly, §455(b)(4) requires disqualification no matter how insubstantial the financial interest and regardless of whether or not the interest actually creates an appearance of impropriety. See §455(d)(4); In re Cement and Concrete Litigation, 515 F. Supp. 1076 (Ariz. 1981), mandamus denied, 688 F.2d 1297 (CA9 1982), aff'd by the absence of quorum, 459 U.S. 1191 (1983). In addition, §455(e) specifies that a judge may not accept a waiver of any ground for disqualification under §455(b), but may accept such a waiver under §455(a) after "a full disclosure on the record of the basis for disqualification." Section 455(b) is therefore a somewhat stricter provision, and thus is not simply redundant with the broader coverage of §455(a) as petitioner's argument posits.

confidence in the integrity of the judicial process — does not depend upon whether or not the judge actually knew facts creating an appearance of impropriety, so long as the public might reasonably believe that he or she knew. . . .

Contrary to petitioner's contentions, this reading of the statute does not call upon judges to perform the impossible — to disqualify themselves based on facts they do not know. If, as petitioner argues, §455(a) should only be applied prospectively, then requiring disqualification based on facts the judge does not know would of course be absurd; a judge could never be expected to disqualify himself based on some fact he does not know, even though the fact is one that perhaps he should know or one that people might reasonably suspect that he does know. But to the extent the provision can also, in proper cases, be applied retroactively, the judge is not called upon to perform an impossible feat. Rather, he is called upon to rectify an oversight and to take the steps necessary to maintain public confidence in the impartiality of the judiciary. If he concludes that "his impartiality might reasonably be questioned," then he should also find that the statute has been violated. This is certainly not an impossible task. No one questions that Judge Collins could have disqualified himself and vacated his judgment when he finally realized that Loyola had an interest in the litigation. The initial appeal was taken from his failure to disqualify himself and vacate the judgment *after* he became aware of the appearance of impropriety, not from his failure to disqualify himself when he first became involved in the litigation and lacked the requisite knowledge.

In this case both the District Court and the Court of Appeals found an ample basis in the record for concluding that an objective observer would have questioned Judge Collins' impartiality. Accordingly, even though his failure to disqualify himself was the product of a temporary lapse of memory, it was nevertheless a plain violation of the terms of the statute.

A conclusion that a statutory violation occurred does not, however, end our inquiry. As in other areas of the law, there is surely room for harmless error committed by busy judges who inadvertently overlook a disqualifying circumstance.[9] There need not be a draconian remedy for every violation of §455(a). It would be equally wrong, however, to adopt

---

9. Large, multidistrict class actions, for example, often present judges with unique difficulties in monitoring any potential interest they may have in the litigation. In such cases, the judge is required to familiarize him or herself with the named parties and all the members of the class, which in an extreme case may number in the hundreds or even thousands. This already difficult task is confounded by the fact that the precise contours of the class are often not defined until well into the litigation.

Of course, notwithstanding the size and complexity of the litigation, judges remain under a duty to stay informed of any personal or fiduciary financial interest they may have in cases over which they preside. See 28 U.S.C. §455(c). The complexity of determining the conflict, however, may have a bearing on the Rule 60(b)(6) extraordinary circumstance analysis.

an absolute prohibition against any relief in cases involving forgetful judges.

IV

Although §455 defines the circumstances that mandate disqualification of federal judges, it neither prescribes nor prohibits any particular remedy for a violation of that duty. Congress has wisely delegated to the judiciary the task of fashioning the remedies that will best serve the purpose of the legislation. In considering whether a remedy is appropriate, we do well to bear in mind that in many cases — and this is such an example — the Court of Appeals is in a better position to evaluate the significance of a violation than is this Court. Its judgment as to the proper remedy should thus be afforded our due consideration. A review of the facts demonstrates that the Court of Appeals' determination that a new trial is in order is well supported.

Section 455 does not, on its own, authorize the reopening of closed litigation. However, as respondent and the Court of Appeals recognized, Federal Rules of Civil Procedure 60(b) provides a procedure whereby, in appropriate cases, a party may be relieved of a final judgment. In particular, Rule 60(b)(6), upon which respondent relies, grants federal courts broad authority to relieve a party from a final judgment "upon such terms as are just," provided that the motion is made within a reasonable time and is not premised on one of the grounds for relief enumerated in clauses (b)(1) through (b)(5). The rule does not particularize the factors that justify relief, but we have previously noted that it provides courts with authority "adequate to enable them to vacate judgments whenever such action is appropriate to accomplish justice," while also cautioning that it should only be applied in "extraordinary circumstances." Rule 60(b)(6) relief is accordingly neither categorically available nor categorically unavailable for all §455 violations. We conclude that in determining whether a judgment should be vacated for a violation of §455, it is appropriate to consider the risk of injustice to the parties in the particular case, the risk that the denial of relief will produce injustice in other cases, and the risk of undermining the public's confidence in the judicial process. We must continuously bear in mind that "to perform its high function in the best way 'justice must satisfy the appearance of justice.' " In re Murchison, 349 U.S. 133, 136 (1955) (citation omitted).

Like the Court of Appeals, we accept the District Court's finding that while the case was actually being tried Judge Collins did not have actual knowledge of Loyola's interest in the dispute over the ownership of St. Jude and its precious certificate of need. When a busy federal judge concentrates his or her full attention on a pending case, personal concerns are easily forgotten. The problem, however, is that people who have not served on the bench are often all too willing to indulge suspicions and doubts concerning the integrity of judges.[12] The very purpose of §455(a) is to promote confidence in the judiciary by avoiding even the appearance of impropriety whenever possible. Thus, it is critically important in a case of this kind to identify the facts that might reasonably cause an objective observer to question Judge Collins' impartiality. There are at least four such facts.

First, it is remarkable that the judge, who had regularly attended the meetings of the Board of Trustees since 1977, completely forgot about the University's interest in having a hospital constructed on its property in Kenner. The importance of the project to the University is indicated by the fact that the 80-acre parcel, which represented only about 40% of the entire tract owned by the University, was sold for $6,694,000 and that the rezoning would substantially increase the value of the remaining 60%. The "negotiations with the developers of the St. Jude Hospital" were the subject of discussion and formal action by the trustees at a meeting attended by Judge Collins only a few days before the lawsuit was filed.

Second, it is an unfortunate coincidence that although the judge regularly attended the meetings of the Board of Trustees, he was not present at the January 28, 1982, meeting, a week after the 2-day trial and while the case was still under advisement. The minutes of that meeting record that representatives of the University monitored the progress of the trial, but did not see fit to call to the judge's attention the obvious conflict of interest that resulted from having a University trustee preside over that trial. These minutes were mailed to Judge Collins on March 12, 1982. If the Judge had opened that envelope when he received it on March 14th or 15th, he would have been under a duty to recuse himself *before* he entered judgment on March 16.[13]

---

12. As we held in Aetna Life Ins. Co. v. Lavoie, 475 U.S. 813 (1986), this concern has constitutional dimensions. In that case we wrote:

> We conclude that Justice Embry's participation in this case violated appellant's due process rights as explicated in *Tumey* [v. Ohio, 273 U.S. 510 (1927)], *Murchison*, and *Ward* [v. Village of Monroeville, 409 U.S. 57 (1972)]. We make clear that we are not required to decide whether in fact Justice Embry was influenced, but only whether sitting on the case then before the Supreme Court of Alabama "would offer a possible temptation to the average [judge] . . . [to] lead him not to hold the balance nice, clear and true." . . .

A finding by another judge — faced with the difficult task of passing upon the integrity of a fellow member of the bench — that his or her colleague merely possessed *constructive* knowledge, and not *actual* knowledge, is unlikely to significantly quell the concerns of the skeptic.

13. One of the provisions of the contract between Loyola and Liljeberg is also remarkable. Despite the fact that earlier minutes of the Board make it clear that the University's interest in serious negotiations with Liljeberg was conditioned upon the certificate of need, the contract expressly recites that control of the certificate was the subject of pending litigation and then provides "that this sale shall not be in any way conditioned upon" the outcome of that litigation. The University, however, retained the right to repurchase the property if Liljeberg was unable to go forward with the hospital project. If Liljeberg was

Third, it is remarkable — and quite inexcusable — that Judge Collins failed to recuse himself on March 24, 1982. A full disclosure at that time would have completely removed any basis for questioning the Judge's impartiality and would have made it possible for a different judge to decide whether the interests — and appearance — of justice would have been served by a retrial. Another 2-day evidentiary hearing would surely have been less burdensome and less embarrassing than the protracted proceedings that resulted from Judge Collins' nonrecusal and nondisclosure. Moreover, as the Court of Appeals correctly noted, Judge Collins' failure to disqualify himself on March 24, 1982, also constituted a violation of §455(b)(4), which disqualifies a judge if he "knows that he, individually or as a fiduciary, . . . has a financial interest in the subject matter in controversy or in a party to the proceeding, or any other interest that could be substantially affected by the outcome of the proceeding." This separate violation of §455 further compels the conclusion that vacatur was an appropriate remedy; by his silence, Judge Collins deprived respondent of a basis for making a timely motion for a new trial and also deprived it of an issue on direct appeal.

Fourth, when respondent filed its motion to vacate, Judge Collins gave three reasons for denying the motion,[15] but still did not acknowledge that he had known about the University's interest both shortly before and shortly after the trial. Nor did he indicate any awareness of a duty to recuse himself in March of 1982.

These facts create precisely the kind of appearance of impropriety that §455(a) was intended to prevent. The violation is neither insubstantial nor excusable. Although Judge Collins did not know of his fiduciary interest in the litigation, he certainly should have known. In fact, his failure to stay informed of this fiduciary interest, may well constitute a separate violation of §455. See §455(c). Moreover, providing relief in cases such as this will not produce injustice in other cases; to the contrary, the Court of Appeals' willingness to enforce §455 may prevent a substantive injustice in some future case by encouraging a judge or litigant to more carefully examine possible grounds for disqualification and to promptly

---

found not to control the certificate of need, he, at least arguably, would have been precluded from going forward with the hospital. Moreover, if the parties simply wanted to make the transaction unconditional, they could have omitted any reference to the litigation. An objective observer might reasonably question why the parties felt a need to include this clause.

15. These were his three reasons:

First, Loyola University was not and is not a party to this litigation, nor was any of its real estate the subject matter of this controversy. Second, Loyola University is a nonprofit, educational institution, and any benefits inuring to that institution would not benefit any individual personally. Finally, and most significantly, this Judge never served on either the Real Estate or Executive Committees of the Loyola University Board of Trustees. Thus, this Judge had no participation of any kind in negotiating Loyola University's real estate transactions and, in fact, had no knowledge of such transactions.

disclose them when discovered. It is therefore appropriate to vacate the judgment unless it can be said that respondent did not make a timely request for relief, or that it would otherwise be unfair to deprive the prevailing party of its judgment.

If we focus on fairness to the particular litigants, a careful study of [Circuit] Judge Rubin's analysis of the merits of the underlying litigation suggests that there is a greater risk of unfairness of upholding the judgment in favor of Liljeberg than there is in allowing a new judge to take a fresh look at the issues. Moreover, neither Liljeberg nor Loyola University has made a showing of special hardship by reason of their reliance on the original judgment. Finally, although a delay of 10 months after the affirmance by the Court of Appeals would normally foreclose relief based on a violation of §455(a), in this case the entire delay is attributable to Judge Collins' inexcusable failure to disqualify himself on March 24, 1982; had he recused himself on March 24, or even disclosed Loyola's interest in the case at that time, the motion could have been made less than 10 days after the entry of judgment. . . .

The judgment of the Court of Appeals is accordingly affirmed.

CHIEF JUSTICE REHNQUIST, with whom JUSTICE WHITE and JUSTICE SCALIA join, dissenting.

The Court's decision in this case is long on ethics in the abstract, but short on workable rules of law. The Court first finds that 28 U.S.C. §455(a) can be used to disqualify a judge on the basis of facts not known to the judge himself. It then broadens the standard for overturning final judgments under Federal Rule of Civil Procedure 60(b). Because these results are at odds with the intended scope of §455 and Rule 60(b), and are likely to cause considerable mischief when courts attempt to apply them, I dissent.

I

As detailed in the Court's opinion, §455(a) provides that "[a]ny justice, judge, or magistrate of the United States shall disqualify himself in any proceeding in which his impartiality might reasonably be questioned." . . .

Subsection (b) of §455 sets forth more particularized situations in which a judge must disqualify himself. Congress intended the provisions of §455(b) to remove any doubt about recusal in cases where a judge's interest is too closely connected with the litigation to allow his participation. Subsection (b)(4), for example, disqualifies a jurist if he knows that he, his spouse, or his minor children have a financial interest in the subject matter in controversy. Unlike the more open-ended provision adopted in subsection (a), the language of subsection (b) requires recusal only in

specific circumstances, and is phrased in such a way as to suggest a requirement of actual knowledge of the disqualifying circumstances.

The purpose of §455 is obviously to inform judges of what matters
they must consider in deciding whether to recuse themselves in a given
case. The Court here holds, as did the Court of Appeals below, that a
judge must recuse himself under §455(a) if he *should have known of* the
circumstances requiring disqualification, even though in fact he did not
know of them. I do not believe this is a tenable construction of subsection
(a). A judge considering whether or not to recuse himself is necessarily
limited to those facts bearing on the question of which he has knowledge.
To hold that disqualification is required by reason of facts which the
judge does *not* know, even though he should have known of them, is to
posit a conundrum which is not decipherable by ordinary mortals. While
the concept of "constructive knowledge" is useful in other areas of the
law, I do not think it should be imported into §455(a).

At the direction of the Court of Appeals, Judge Schwartz of the District Court for the Eastern District of Louisiana made factual findings
concerning the extent and timing of Judge Collins' knowledge of
Loyola's interest in the underlying lawsuit. Judge Schwartz determined
that Judge Collins had no actual knowledge of Loyola's involvement
when he tried the case. Not until March 24, 1982, when he reviewed materials in preparation for a Board meeting, did Judge Collins obtain actual knowledge of the negotiations between petitioners and Loyola.

Despite this factual determination, reached after a public hearing on
the subject, the Court nevertheless concludes that "public confidence in
the impartiality of the judiciary" compels retroactive disqualification of
Judge Collins under §455(a). This conclusion interprets §455(a) in a
manner which Congress never intended. As the Court of Appeals noted,
in drafting §455(a) Congress was concerned with the "appearance" of impropriety, and to that end changed the previous subjective standard for
disqualification to an objective one; no longer was disqualification to be
decided on the basis of the opinion of the judge in question, but by the
standard of what a reasonable person would think. But the facts and circumstances which this reasonable person would consider must be the
facts and circumstances *known* to the judge at the time. In short, as is unquestionably the case with subsection (b), I would adhere to a standard of
actual knowledge in §455(a), and not slide off into the very speculative
ground of "constructive" knowledge.

II

The Court then compounds its error by allowing Federal Rule of Civil
Procedure 60(b)(6) to be used to set aside a final judgment in this case.
Rule 60(b) authorizes a district court, on motion and upon such terms as
are just, to relieve a party from a final judgment, order, or proceeding

for any "reason justifying relief from the operation of the judgment." However, we have repeatedly instructed that only truly "extraordinary circumstances" will permit a party successfully to invoke the "any other reason" clause of 60(b).

For even if one accepts the Court's proposition that §455(a) permits disqualification on the basis of a judge's constructive knowledge, Rule 60(b)(6) should not be used in this case to apply §455(a) retroactively to Judge Collins' participation in the lawsuit. In the first place, it is beyond cavil that Judge Collins stood to receive no *personal* financial gain from the transactions involving petitioner, respondent, and Loyola. Judge Collins' only prior tie to the dealings was as a member of Loyola's rather large Board of Trustees and, although Judge Collins was a member of at least two of the Board's subcommittees, he had no connection with the Real Estate subcommittees, the entity responsible for negotiating the sale of the Monroe Tract. In addition, the motion to set aside the judgment was made by respondent almost 10 months after judgment was entered in March 1982; although relief under Rule 60(b)(6) is subject to no absolute time limitation, there can be no serious argument that the time elapsed since the entry of judgment must weigh heavily in considering the motion. Finally, and most important, Judge Schwartz determined that Judge Collins did not have actual knowledge of his conflict of interest during trial and that he made no rulings after he acquired actual knowledge.[4] . . .

JUSTICE O'CONNOR, dissenting.

For the reasons given by Chief Justice Rehnquist, I agree that "constructive knowledge" cannot be a basis for a violation of 28 U.S.C. §455(a). The question then remains whether respondent is entitled to a new trial because there are other "extraordinary circumstances," apart from the §455(a) violation found by the Fifth Circuit, that justify "relief from operation of the judgment." Although the Court collects an impressive array of arguments that might support the granting of such relief, I believe the issue should be addressed in the first instance by the courts below. I would therefore remand this case with appropriate instructions.

---

4. The majority's opinion suggests a number of troubling hypothetical situations, only one of which will demonstrate the difficulties inherent in its decision. Suppose Judge Doe sits on a bench trial involving *X* Corp. and *Y* Corp. The judge rules for *X* Corp., and judgment is affirmed on appeal. Ten years later, officials at *Y* Corp. learn that, unbeknownst to him, Judge Doe owned several shares of stock in *X* Corp. Even in the face of an independent factual finding that Judge Doe had no knowledge of this ownership, the Court's construction of §455(a) and Rule 60(b) would permit the final judgment in *X* Corp.'s favor to be set aside if the "appearance of impartiality" were not deemed wholly satisfied. Such a result will adversely affect the reliance placed on final judgments and will inhibit developments premised on their finality.

the firm that had not definitively rejected his employment. This result is consistent with Model Rule 1.12(b).

A trial judge was negotiating for a job with the United States Justice Department while the Justice Department was trying a criminal case before the judge. The defendant was convicted. The appellate court vacated the conviction and ordered a new trial even though the defendant could show no prejudice. Scott v. United States, 559 A.2d 745 (D.C. Ct. App. 1989).

Consider what the bankruptcy judge did in In re Continental Airlines Corp., 901 F.2d 1259 (5th Cir. 1990). The judge made several important rulings in favor of Continental. Shortly thereafter, he granted Continental's law firm a $700,000 fee. A day later, he accepted employment with the firm. The bankruptcy judge asserted that he was unaware that he would receive an employment offer at the time he made his rulings and granted the fee award. The Fifth Circuit held that when the offer came in, the bankruptcy judge should have rejected it outright or, if he preferred to consider the offer, he should have recused himself and vacated his rulings. Nevertheless, citing *Liljeberg*, the court concludes that the error was harmless and did not require reversal of the judge's rulings. For a discussion of the standards to be used in determining whether violation of section 455 requires an appellate court to vacate a lower court's decisions, see Polaroid Corp. v. Eastman Kodak Co., 867 F.2d 1415 (Fed. Cir.), cert. denied, 490 U.S. 1047 (1989).

A Duty to Sit? In his memorandum refusing to recuse himself in Laird v. Tatum, 409 U.S. 824, 837 (1972), Justice Rehnquist observed that "federal courts of appeals that have considered the matter have unanimously concluded that a federal judge has a duty to *sit* where *not disqualified* which is equally as strong as the duty to *not sit* where *disqualified*" (emphasis in original). Justice Rehnquist went on to say that the policy in favor of the "equal duty" concept is stronger in the case of the Supreme Court, for whose members, unlike lower court judges, no substitute is possible and where there is no higher court to review an equally divided bench.

Justice Rehnquist wrote before adoption of §455. In United States v. Kelly, 888 F.2d 732 (11th Cir. 1989), the court held that §455 did away with the "duty to sit" doctrine and instead requires judges "to resolve any doubts they may have in favor of disqualification." Chief Justice Rehnquist acknowledged the same effect in a portion of his *Liljeberg* dissent omitted here. 486 U.S. at 871. In *Kelly*, the judge presided at a bench trial of a criminal case. The wife of a defense witness was a friend of the judge's wife. The judge acknowledged that the witness's testimony "created the risk that he might bend over backwards to prove that he lacked favoritism." Conversely, he said, if he found the defendant guilty he might jeopardize his wife's relationship with the witness's wife. Nevertheless, the judge did not recuse himself. The Eleventh Circuit reversed.

Was Justice Frankfurter justified in recusing himself in Public Utilities Commission v. Pollak, 343 U.S. 451, 467 (1952), a case challenging the Commission's practice of continuously broadcasting radio programs on its buses and streetcars to the discomfort of some riders? Justice Frankfurter said that his "feelings are so strongly engaged as a victim of the practice in controversy that I had better not participate in judicial judgment upon it."

What happens if any judge in a position to hear a case would be disqualified? In United States v. Will, 449 U.S. 200 (1980), several district judges sued the government to recover additional compensation on the ground that inflation had worked a reduction in their salary in violation of Article III, which provides that the compensation of federal judges "shall not be diminished during their continuance in office." If the plaintiffs were successful, all federal judges would benefit from the victory. Nevertheless, the Supreme Court rejected a claim that 28 U.S.C. §455 and §3(C) of the ABA Code of Judicial Conduct required all United States judges to disqualify themselves, holding that under the "Rule of Necessity, a well-settled principle at common law," a judge having a personal interest in a case not only may but must take part in the decision if the case could not otherwise be heard. Further, Congress, in enacting §455, did not intend to alter this Rule. Accord: Atkins v. United States, 556 F.2d 1028 (Ct. Cl.), cert. denied, 434 U.S. 1009 (1977). See also Evans v. Gore, 253 U.S. 245 (1920).

Financial Interests.   A judge must recuse himself under §455(b)(4) if the judge, his or her spouse, or minor child residing in the household has a financial interest as defined in §455(d)(4). See, for example, Headwaters, Inc. v. Bureau of Land Management, 665 F. Supp. 873 (D. Or. 1987). To enable judges to determine whether they have financial interests in corporate litigants, procedural rules often require corporate parties to list their affiliates, parents, and subsidiaries. See Rule 26.1, Fed. R. App. P.

In re Cement & Concrete Antitrust Litigation (cited in n.8 of *Liljeberg*) was a multidistrict class action charging a price-fixing conspiracy in the cement industry. The plaintiff class consisted of 210,000 individuals and corporate entities, all of whom were alleged to be users of cement. Judge Muecke of the United States District Court for the District of Arizona had spent five years presiding over the litigation when certain of the defendants moved to disqualify him on the ground that it appeared that his wife owned shares of stock in seven of the class plaintiffs. Judge Muecke concluded that the class members in which his wife held stock were "parties" within the meaning of §455(b)(4) even though they were not named parties. He further concluded that his wife's stock interest was a "financial interest" within the meaning of that subsection, according to the definition in §455(d)(4). Judge Muecke computed the total value of his wife's financial interest in the event that the plaintiff class was entirely successful. Before corporate taxes, that interest amounted to $29.70. Nevertheless, Judge Muecke concluded that he had to disqualify himself under the mandatory language of §455 because the definition of "financial interest" included "a legal or equitable interest, however small." (Where a ground for disqualification is one of the provisions under §455(b), as in this case, the parties may not waive the disqualification.) Judge Muecke expressed surprise that "Congress did not consider the effect of §455 on the administration of class action litigation," especially since with the "number of participants in a large class action, it is not an easy matter to determine whether a per se conflict exists. In normal litigation, a judge can simply compare his families' holdings with the names on the caption to the complaint. In a complex multidistrict class action, the litigation may be well under way before a comprehensive class list can be compiled. To switch judges in mid-stream not only wastes judicial time and energy, but can constitute a substantial administrative burden." 515 F. Supp. at 1080.

Section 455(f), added in 1988, now permits a judge with a "financial interest" to remain on a matter if "appearance or discovery" of the interest occurred after the matter was assigned to the judge, the judge devoted "substantial judicial time . . . to the matter" and the interest could not "be substantially affected by the outcome." For an example of the operation of §455(f) in which quick disinvestment enabled a judge to continue with a matter, see Kidder, Peabody & Co. v. Maxus Energy Corp., 925 F.2d 556 (2d Cir.), cert. denied, 111 S. Ct. 2829 (1991).

Disqualification was rejected in Christiansen v. National Savings & Trust, 683 F.2d 520 (D.C. Cir. 1982), a class action involving a government-wide health insurance plan, even though the judges were subscribers to the plan. The plaintiffs merely sought to require the defendants to restore to the fund interest that was lost because the fund was kept in noninterest bearing accounts. They did not seek payments for individual class members. See also In re City of Houston, 745 F.2d 925 (5th Cir. 1984) (per se disqualification rule does not apply to judge who was a class member in voting rights case because no monetary damages sought by plaintiffs).

Lawyer Relatives.   Advisory Opinion No. 58 (1978), issued by a committee of the U.S. Judicial Conference, concerns judicial disqualification in a case in which a relative is employed by a participating law firm. It provides in part:

> We believe the following conclusions find support in the Code [of Judicial Conduct]. A judge is disqualified and should recuse if a relative

within the third degree of relationship to the judge or his spouse (a) is a partner in a law firm appearing in the case; or (b) will profit or lose from the judge's action in the case either financially or otherwise, for example, the reputation of the firm would be significantly affected by the litigation.

The court in Potashnick v. Port City Construction Co., 609 F.2d 1101 (5th Cir.), cert. denied, 449 U.S. 820 (1980), relied in part on Advisory Opinion No. 58 in disqualifying a judge whose father was a partner of a lawyer acting in the case. But see United States ex rel. Weinberger v. Equifax, 557 F.2d 456 (5th Cir. 1977), cert. denied, 434 U.S. 1035 (1978) (in decision rendered prior to Advisory Opinion No. 58, trial judge not required to recuse himself where the defendant was represented by a firm that employed the trial judge's son as an associate). In re Aetna Casualty & Surety Co., 919 F.2d 1136 (6th Cir. 1990) (en banc), issued mandamus disqualifying a judge and vacating certain of his orders where the judge's daughter had briefly participated in the matter as a lawyer with a firm representing one of the parties. It did not matter that the daughter had since left the firm.

Law Clerks.   A law clerk's career can also lead to disqualification. In Hall v. Small Business Administration, 695 F.2d 175, 176-177 (5th Cir. 1983), the court (citing §455(a)) reversed a judgment for the plaintiffs in a Title VII sex discrimination case tried before a magistrate because his "sole law clerk was initially a member of the plaintiff class in this suit, had before her employment with the magistrate expressed herself as convinced of the correctness of its contentions, and accepted employment with its counsel before judgment was rendered." It was "irrelevant" that the magistrate asserted that he had made up his mind "immediately after the hearing" and before the law clerk worked on the case. Accord: Miller Indus. v. Caterpillar Tractor Co., 516 F. Supp. 84, 89 (S.D. Ala. 1980).

But in Hunt v. American Bank & Trust Co. of Baton Rouge, 783 F.2d 1011 (11th Cir. 1986), there was no disqualification ordered where a law clerk did not work on a case in which his prospective employer was counsel, nor did he "even tal[k] with the judge about it to any significant extent." In In re Allied-Signal, Inc., 891 F.2d 967 (1st Cir. 1989), cert. denied, 110 S. Ct. 2561 (1990), disqualification was rejected where parties before the judge were represented by lawyers who were siblings of two of the judge's law clerks. The proper remedy, said the court, was not disqualification but exclusion of the clerks from the matter. Accord: Reddy v. Jones, 419 F. Supp. 1391 (N.D.N.C.) (1976). See also report of the Committee on Recruitment of Lawyers of the New York City Bar Association on Law Firm Recruitment, Judicial Clerks and Avoidance of Any Appearance of Impropriety, 36 The Record 53 (1981).

Judge's Prior Affiliation. Section 455(b)(2) and (3) disqualify a judge based on work the judge (or the judge's law firm) may have done while the judge was in private practice or in government employment. Preston v. United States, 923 F.2d 731 (9th Cir. 1991), presents a variation on this issue. *Preston* was a wrongful death action against the United States, tried before Judge Letts. Preston's estate had also filed a claim against Hughes Aircraft in state court based on the same events. Before his appointment, Judge Letts had been of counsel to Latham & Watkins while Latham represented Hughes in the state court action. After Judge Letts's appointment, Latham represented Hughes in connection with discovery issues in the federal action, but Hughes was not itself a party to the federal action. Hughes had an indemnity agreement that required it to pay any judgment against the United States in the federal case.

After a bench trial, judgment went for the United States and plaintiffs argued on appeal that Judge Letts should have recused himself. The Ninth Circuit agreed. The fact that Hughes was not a party to the federal action was irrelevant. "Rather, the focus has consistently been on the question whether the relationship between the judge and an interested party was such as to present a risk that the judge's impartiality in the case at bar might reasonably be questioned by the public," within the meaning of §455(a). Here the answer to that question was yes. A client of the trial judge's former law firm, whom the firm had represented on the same underlying facts, "would have faced a potential claim for indemnification by the government" if plaintiffs prevailed. 923 F.2d at 735. The remedy was a new trial. The court also cited §455(b)(2). Judge Letts had nothing to do with Hughes while he was of counsel to Latham. Why then should he be disqualified?

Manipulation of Disqualification. Where a litigant selects a lawyer to represent him, knowing that the lawyer is a relative of the trial judge and intending the presence of the lawyer to force the trial judge to recuse himself, the result will instead be that the lawyer will be found disqualified to represent the litigant. So ruled the Fifth Circuit in McCuin v. Texas Power & Light, 714 F.2d 1255, 1261-1265 (5th Cir. 1983). The court acknowledged that "forum shopping is sanctioned by our judicial system [and] is as American as the Constitution." Further, the court recognized "that a litigant's motives for selecting a lawyer are not ordinarily subject to judicial scrutiny." Nevertheless, there are limits.

> A lawyer's acceptance of employment solely or primarily for the purpose of disqualifying a judge creates the impression that, for a fee, the lawyer is available for sheer manipulation of the justice system. It thus creates the appearance of professional impropriety. Moreover, sanctioning such conduct brings the judicial system itself in disrepute. To tolerate such gamesmanship would tarnish the concept of impartial justice. To permit a

litigant to blackball a judge merely by invoking a talismanic "right to counsel of my choice" would contribute to skepticism about and mistrust of our judicial system.

Judge's Duty to Reveal.   How can a lawyer know facts of a judge's life that might support a disqualification motion? Some facts may be a matter of public record. Examples are the judge's prior professional affiliations and the information contained in her financial disclosure forms. But other facts — like the financial or other interests of close relatives — may not be. The comment to §3(E) of the 1990 ABA Code requires judges to "disclose on the record information that the judge believes the parties or their lawyers might consider relevant to the question of disqualification even if the judge believes there is no real basis for disqualification." This obligation is essential, isn't it, to ensure that a judge's decision to sit is reviewable? Recall the Court's criticism of Judge Collins for failure to disclose Loyola's interest in the litigation before him even after he learned of it following trial and before expiration of the deadline for a new trial motion (page 505 supra). See also United States v. Bosch, — F.2d — , — (1991) (O'Scannlain, J., dissenting) (relationship between disclosure and waiver).

Waiver.   Confusion reigns here. Section 455 and the two ABA Codes differ on waiver of judicial conflicts. Section 455 permits waiver of conflicts falling under paragraph (a) ("impartiality might reasonably be questioned") but not of those falling under paragraph (b) — e.g., if the judge's spouse owns ten shares of stock in a litigant. The 1972 Code forbids waiver where the judge's impartiality might reasonably be questioned, but permits waiver of other conflicts the statute makes nonwaivable. Section 3(D). The 1990 Code permits waiver of any conflict except those based on "personal bias." Section 4(F). All three require that waiver follow full disclosure on the record. Waiver provisions have been criticized on two grounds: they give insufficient consideration to the public's interest in the appearance of justice; and even though the trial judge may not be told which of several parties declined to waive, he or she will usually be able to infer the answer, which in turn may harm relationships between that party or its counsel and the judge in other matters. That prospect casts doubt on whether a waiver is really voluntary.

FURTHER READING

John Leubsdorf has analyzed judicial disqualification law by examining theories of judging. John Leubsdorf, Theories of Judging and Judge Disqualification, 62 N.Y.U. L. Rev. 237 (1987). See also Jeffrey Stempel's critical evaluation of Justice Rehnquist's refusal to recuse himself in Laird v. Tatum, Rehnquist, Recusal, and Reform, 53 Brook. L. Rev. 589

(1987). Note, Disqualifying Elected Judges from Cases Involving Campaign Contributors, 40 Stan. L. Rev. 449 (1988) (authored by Stuart Banner), examines the nearly impossible problems that arise when judges must run for election and raise money to do so.

Judicial and Courtroom Bias

In 1990, the ABA amended the Code of Judicial Conduct and dramatically rewrote or introduced sections intended to address judicial and courtroom bias. It is worth taking a look at these provisions.

Exclusionary Organizations.   Section 2(C) states: "A judge shall not hold membership in any organization that practices invidious discrimination on the basis of race, sex, religion or national origin." The commentary to §2(C) says that "an organization is generally said to discriminate invidiously if it arbitrarily excludes from membership on the basis of race, religion, sex or national origin persons who would otherwise be admitted to membership." Does this language do anything other than substitute one word ("arbitrarily") for another ("invidiously")?

Notice that disability, age, socioeconomic status, and sexual preference are not included on the list of the attributes. Should they be? Why do you suppose each was omitted? They are included in the provisions discussed below.

Would it violate §2(C) for a judge to belong to a social club limited to persons of Irish ancestry? Irish Catholics? Irish Catholic men? Should it? The commentary states that an organization does not invidiously discriminate if it is "dedicated to the preservation of religious, ethnic or cultural values of legitimate common interest to its members," or if it is "in fact and effect an intimate, purely private organization whose membership limitations could not be constitutionally prohibited." (Native Americans? Persons of Anglo-Saxon ancestry?) Assume this states the test for determining whether a club's membership rules can constitutionally be regulated under civil rights laws. See New York State Club Assn. v. City of New York, 487 U.S. 1 (1988). Should, then, the answer to whether a judge may ethically belong to an exclusionary organization turn on whether its exclusionary policies could be prohibited consistent with the First Amendment right of association? The commentary to Canon 2 does say that a "judge must . . . accept restrictions on the judge's conduct that might be viewed as burdensome by the ordinary citizen and should do so freely and willingly." Does this mean that a judge may ethically be forbidden to belong to an exclusionary organization although the judge would otherwise have a First Amendment right to belong? Compare the code's limitation on speech, which is broader than the First Amendment would tolerate for others. Section 3(B)(9).

The commentary to §2(C) also says that it would violate Canon 2 and §2(A) "for a judge to arrange a meeting at a club that the judge knows practices invidious discrimination on the basis of race, sex, religion or national origin in its membership or other policies, or for the judge to regularly use such a club."

In the 1972 Code, restrictions on membership in clubs that "invidiously" discriminated were advisory only. See §2(B) commentary.

Courtroom Bias.   The 1990 code introduces obligations of a judge to prevent bias in the courtroom. Section 3(B)(6) says that a judge shall "require lawyers in proceedings before the judge to refrain from manifesting, by words or conduct, bias or prejudice based upon race, sex, religion, national origin, disability, age, sexual orientation or socio-economic status, against parties, witnesses, counsel or others." Why is this list so much longer than the list in §2(C)? The section also states that it does not "preclude legitimate advocacy" when any of the attributes on the list "or other similar factors are issues in the proceeding." What can that mean? That a lawyer can refer to race if it is an issue? Or that a lawyer can "manifes[t] . . . bias or prejudice based upon race" when "legitimate"?

Section 3(B)(5) requires a judge to "perform judicial duties without bias or prejudice." A judge is forbidden, in the performance of those duties, "by words or conduct [to] manifest bias or prejudice, including but not limited to bias or prejudice based upon" the same set of attributes identified in the prior paragraph. Further, the judge "shall not permit staff, court officials and others subject to the judge's direction and control to do so." Again, why is the list longer than the one in §2(C)?

The commentary to §3(B)(5) requires a judge to "refrain from speech, gestures or other conduct that could reasonably be perceived as sexual harassment and must require the same standard of conduct of others subject to the judge's direction and control. . . . Facial expression and body language, in addition to oral communication, can give to parties or lawyers in the proceeding, jurors, the media and others, an appearance of judicial bias." Marina Angel has analyzed this provision in an article that reviews the empirical evidence of judicial sexual harassment and compares remedial efforts with those in the private sector. She calls for "vigorous enforcement" of the Judicial Code commentary. Marina Angel, Sexual Harassment by Judges, 45 U. Miami L. Rev. 817 (1991).

Other institutions have also focused on judicial bias. The Senate Judiciary Committee reviews all nominees to the federal bench pursuant to the Senate's constitutional advise and consent powers. In 1990, the Committee adopted the following resolution. Does it go too far? Not far enough? Remember, we are talking about people who may have belonged to exclusionary organizations while lawyers in private practice.

Assume that the clubs to which they belonged violated no state or local antidiscrimination law. Assume the nominees are prepared, after confirmation, to resign their club memberships. Why should the fact of those memberships count against them? The resolution is not binding on members of the committee or any other Senator. Should it be?

SENATE JUDICIARY COMMITTEE RESOLUTION*

Expressing the sense of the Committee on the Judiciary concerning membership in clubs that engage in discrimination.

Resolved by the Committee on the Judiciary, That it is the sense of the Committee on the Judiciary of the Senate that —

(1) clubs where business is conducted that by policy or practice intentionally discriminate on the basis of race, color, religion, sex, disability or national origin operate to exclude persons, including women and minorities, from business and professional opportunities;

(2) in recent years, awareness has grown that such discrimination is invidious and that membership in such discriminatory clubs may be viewed as a tacit endorsement of the discriminatory practices;

(3) membership in such discriminatory clubs conflicts with the appearance of impartiality required of persons who may serve in positions in the Federal judiciary or the Department of Justice;

(4) it is inappropriate for persons who may be nominated in the future to serve in the Federal judiciary or the Department of Justice to belong to such discriminatory clubs, unless such persons are actively engaged in bona fide efforts to eliminate the discriminatory practices;

(5) such membership is an important factor which Senators should consider in evaluating such persons, in conjunction with other factors which may reflect upon their fitness and ability;

(6) so as to promote a consistent policy on this issue in the legislative branch as well, any Senator belonging to such a club should resign his or her membership in light of this resolution;

(7) to be considered a club where business is conducted, a club must have one of the following characteristics —

---

*This resolution was submitted to the Senate Judiciary Committee by Senator Kennedy and adopted August 2, 1990.

(A) club members bring business clients or professional associates to the club for conferences, meetings, meals, or use of the facilities;

(B) club members or their employers deduct dues, fees or payments as business expenses on tax returns;

(C) the club is one where contacts valuable for business purposes, employment and professional advancement are formed; or

(D) the club receives payments from nonmembers for meals or services provided by the club;

except that country clubs and clubs where meals are served shall be presumed to be clubs where business is conducted;

(8) paragraphs (1) through (7) do not apply to fraternal, sororal, religious or ethnic heritage organizations;

(9) this resolution shall take effect January 1, 1991; and

(10) the Chairman of the Committee on the Judiciary of the Senate is requested to transmit a copy of this resolution to the President and the Attorney General of the United States and all members of the Senate, for such use as they deem appropriate in considering future nominations to the Federal bench and the Department of Justice.

Judicial bias can lead to discipline. Here are some examples. In Matter of Esworthy, 77 N.Y.2d 280, 568 N.E.2d 1195, 567 N.Y.S.2d 390 (1991), a judge was removed from office in part because of his use on two occasions of "racially charged language that was highly insulting to certain ethnic groups." In Matter of Pearson, 299 S.C. 499, 386 S.E.2d 249 (1989), a judge, while off the bench and after a hearing, had a conversation in the Town Hall in which he referred to an individual who was not present by using a derogatory racial epithet. The statement was overheard by a member of the particular racial group. The court held that the judge had violated Canon 1 and §2(A). He was censured.

Judge Greene was presiding over a criminal case in which a man had been charged with assaulting his estranged wife. The judge "made derogatory remarks about Interact, the battered women's assistance group whose representative was present in court in support of the victim, including the comment that they were 'a one-sided man-hating bunch of females ... and a pack of she-dogs.'" After the trial, the judge approached the victim in the hall and told her "in the presence of the Interact representative that once his wife had slapped him and that he had 'laid her on the floor and did not have any more problems from her.'" In In re Greene, 328 N.C. 639, 403 S.E.2d 257, 258-263 (1991), the court held that these comments violated §2(A) and §3(A)(3) of the Judicial Conduct Code. The court held that a further allegation that Judge

Greene had told the victim that "she deserved to be hit and had not been hit that much [was] not supported by clear and convincing evidence." Judge Greene was censured. Is that sanction too harsh under the circumstances? All of these events occurred after the judge had already found the victim's estranged husband guilty.

During a discovery conference in a federal case challenging the military's exclusion of gays and lesbians, the trial judge three times referred to the plaintiff group as "homos." Washington Post, March 7, 1991, at B1. Did this reference violate the Code of Judicial Conduct? Should it be a basis for recusal? Does it affect your judgment to learn that the trial judge was 85 years old?

Return now to the questions posed at the start of this chapter (page 494 supra). Should it be unethical for a judge to tell a mildly racist or homophobic joke at a private dinner party? To attend the nightclub act of a blatantly sexist performer? To belong to a local beach club restricted to persons of the judge's faith?

QUESTION

11.1 Federal District Judge Lowell Grant is presiding over the pretrial stages of a civil action brought by the Securities and Exchange Commission against Durham Bennett Lardon, a major brokerage house and underwriter, and certain of Durham Bennett's officers. Judge Grant's wife, Nina, is the major shareholder of a closely held family corporation, Tres Ritzy, which owns a chain of women's clothing shops. The chain has been generally successful. Judge Grant owns no shares of Tres Ritzy.

While the litigation was in progress, Nina and other shareholders were exploring a sale of the corporation and had engaged a financial consultant, who in turn identified a buyer, the Simpson Venture Capital Group (SVCG). Tres Ritzy and SVCG signed a contract for the sale of the corporation for $85 million, contingent on SVCG's ability to secure financing. After a series of negotiations with various possible financiers, only Durham Bennett remained interested. Durham Bennett agreed to provide financing of $50 million. The balance of the necessary funds was to come from banks with which SVCG had a relationship but which would not provide financing without the Durham cushion. Durham planned to underwrite the financing in the form of high yield bonds, reserving the right to put $8 million of its own money in the purchase as an equity investment. According to industry custom, Durham and SVCG did not sign a contract, and did not plan to do so until Durham actually secured the financing, which it immediately proceeded to try to raise. Once the financing was complete, Nina Grant would receive $30 million from the sale and members of her family would receive another $55 million.

After SVCG and Durham reached their understanding, and while Durham was trying to raise the money in the capital markets, Durham learned that Nina Grant was Judge Grant's wife. So did the SEC. If either moves to recuse Judge Grant, what should be the result? What additional information would you like to have, if any?

B. MEDIATORS, MASTERS, AND MORE

Many people who judge are not judges. That is, they are not members of the federal or state judiciary. Some, like arbitrators, have power to issue decisions that a court will enforce. Others, let's call them mediators, use discussion and persuasion to help parties reach agreement. The relatively recent interest in alternate dispute resolution has won renewed attention for mediation and arbitration, but, of course, certain fields, like labor relations, have made use of these methods for decades. Private judging is a form of arbitration. Two parties may choose a third, often a former judge, to adjudicate their dispute. A private judge may be chosen after a dispute arises or in contemplation of the possibility of one. The parties may prefer a private judge to avoid the acrimony, cost, and delay of formal litigation. This will be true, for example, when the parties have an interest in harmony because of an ongoing relationship.

Mediation takes several forms. A lawyer may try to mediate a dispute between two of her clients. Model Rule 2.2, called "Intermediary," describes the lawyer's obligations when so acting. Read the rule. How does it deal with the inevitable problems of conflict and confidentiality? Rule 2.2 would also apply to a lawyer who enters a dispute to mediate it.

Distinguish the situation where a lawyer represents two clients whose interests are sufficiently alike to satisfy the tests of Rule 1.7(a) and DR 5-105(C). Imagine two people who want to start a business together and need, among other things, a partnership or shareholder agreement. It would not be accurate to say that the lawyer is mediating a dispute — there is none, everyone is friendly — yet the parties may not have congruent interests. One may be putting up the money and the other the know-how. This situation is best analyzed as a potential concurrent conflict, not a mediation, yet it poses some of the same issues.

In yet a third variant, a mediator need not have (nor have had) a lawyer-client relationship with either of the parties. Indeed, mediators and arbitrators need not be lawyers at all. Divorce mediation is in this category. Divorce mediation promises to reduce bitterness and save money. But some have questioned whether its informality will disadvantage the less sophisticated spouse, usually the wife. We look at divorce mediation further below.

Judges — real judges — may appoint special masters and referees to help them with complicated cases that would otherwise demand too much judicial time. The master or referee may take evidence and make a recommendation to the judge. Procedural rules authorize these appointments. See Fed. R. Civ. P. 53.

Masters, mediators, and the like are guided by various ethical documents. When a court appoints a lawyer as a master or referee, the lawyer will be subject to the Code of Judicial Conduct. Belfiore v. New York Times Co., 826 F.2d 177 (2d Cir. 1987), cert. denied, 484 U.S. 1067 (1988); Denkins v. Sterlacci, 849 F.2d 627 (D.C. Cir. 1988). The American Arbitration Association has promulgated an ethical code for its arbitrators. See Stephen Gillers & Roy Simon, Regulation of Lawyers: Statutes and Standards at 519 (3d ed. 1991). The ABA has issued Standards of Practice for Lawyer Mediators in Family Disputes. Id. at 511. And an organization with the unforgettable acronym SPIDR — Society of Professionals in Dispute Resolution — also has Ethical Standards of Professional Conduct. Id. at 530. Rule 1.12 describes the ethical responsibilities of lawyers who have been judges, arbitrators, or other adjudicative officers when they thereafter engage in law practice.

Ethical rules for mediators have assumed greater importance with the increased utilization of a potpourri of alternative dispute resolution (or ADR) mechanisms, especially by businesses. General Mills reportedly requires that all its contracts provide for mediation, minitrials, or other ADR techniques. Wall St. J., July 22, 1991, at A8. A study by the Center for Public Resources, which promotes nonlitigation alternatives to dispute resolution, "showed that 142 companies saved more than $100 million in legal costs by resolving major disputes through ADR." The Center's president, James Henry, described a nine-year battle, costing $60 million, between Texas Utilities and Santa Fe Industries. With ADR, the parties are said to have settled in two days, "saving an estimated $140 million in resolution costs." Id.

Here we address issues that arise when a lawyer or firm proposes to conduct divorce mediation, perhaps in conjunction with a psychologist or other kind of professional. We begin with an article from the Wall Street Journal that describes divorce mediation and then move to an opinion of the Association of the Bar of the City of New York that addresses the ethical questions.

Meg Cox
FRIENDLIER ENDINGS: SOME DIVORCING COUPLES FIND MEDIATION CHEAPER AND MORE HUMANE THAN BATTLES IN COURTROOM
Wall St. J., Nov. 15, 1983, at 60

Stephen Erickson's career as a divorce lawyer ended with a crisis of conscience in 1976, when a client died from bullet wounds inflicted by her estranged husband.

The shooting occurred just four days after a venomous custody hearing, whose intensity "may have pushed him over the brink," Mr. Erickson says. "It makes me think, 'What am I doing?' "

After some soul-searching, Mr. Erickson decided he was through battling in courtrooms as one party's "hired gladiator." So he became a divorce mediator, helping both sides reach a divorce settlement.

Since Mr. Erickson's first case in 1977, divorce mediation has swept the country. Its many advocates say mediation is a more humane alternative to rancorous courtroom proceedings, which often worsen the tension and strain of divorce. Hundreds of lawyers and psychologists have hung out shingles, and law schools and other institutions are offering courses in divorce mediation. California courts assign mediators to work with couples who can't agree on custody questions and divorce courts in Chicago and Miami have adopted similar procedures. Legislatures in a dozen more states are considering measures to require mediation of child custody disputes.

A FEEL-GOOD ALTERNATIVE

Critics think that divorce mediation is becoming overused and that people tend to overlook its drawbacks, such as inexperienced mediators. However, the practice continues to gain devotees, who see it as a preferred alternative to wrenching encounters in a divorce court. In addition to mediation of custody questions, couples say out-of-court negotiating is useful in resolving disputes on property division and child support.

Leaders in the mediation movement are sometimes evangelical about its benefits. "I have always felt that mediation says, 'There's a bit of God in every person,' while traditional divorce assumes there's a bit of rottenness in everyone," says John Haynes, a New York professor of social work and one of the founders of the movement.

On a dollars-and-cents level, mediation is much cheaper than hiring divorce lawyers. Some people gain satisfaction just knowing that they bypassed high-priced attorneys in working out a settlement. Naturally, a few divorce lawyers are grumbling. "It's as difficult right now to be against mediation as it once was to be against motherhood," says Richard Crouch, former head of the American Bar Association's family law ethics committee. Some couples are even made to feel guilty if they choose traditional divorce proceedings over mediation.

FOUNDING A MOVEMENT

Mr. Haynes says he entered the mediation business in the mid-1970s after counseling some friends in "a very bloody divorce." Around the same time, O. J. Coogler, a Georgia attorney, began exploring the prospect of mediating divorces after suffering through a nasty break-up of his own marriage. Both men concluded that if mediators helped couples resolve the major questions of property division and custody, lawyers would be needed only to draw up the legal documents and walk them through the courts.

No-fault divorce laws that first appeared in the early 1970s, which emphasize a fair division of property above any assignment of blame, helped the movement catch on.

Mark Farber, a Miami scientist who used mediation in his divorce, says the process is more constructive and less adversarial than conventional proceedings. "Lawyers want to win for you," he says, "and we just wanted to straighten out our lives." Although an attorney later told Mr. Farber he had been overly generous in the settlement, he remains pleased. "I have to face myself in the mirror every morning," he says.

Mediation isn't without pitfalls, however. Because licensing requirements are nonexistent and training programs meager, there is little way of screening out inept practitioners or charlatans. Mental health specialists, who dominate the field, sometimes lack expertise in complex issues such as the legal valuation of assets. (Only 20 percent of all mediators are trained as lawyers.) And except for a two-year, postgraduate program just begun at Catholic University of America, mediation courses typically run about a week.

"HORRENDOUS MISTAKES"

Jeffrey Greenblatt, a Rockville, Md., divorce lawyer, says he sees "horrendous mistakes just in language" in mediated divorce agreements he reviews. "They might specify support maintenance when they mean alimony," he says. "Alimony is modifiable, but support maintenance isn't. That means the woman is stuck with the same amount of money forevermore, even if her husband becomes a millionaire, or she becomes a paraplegic."

Feminist groups contend that mediation often leaves women with the short end, since their husbands frequently possess greater financial acu-

men and more forceful negotiating styles. A California woman says she
tried mediation because "I wanted us both to be winners and friends,"
but backed out after several months and $3,000 in fees. "I had little
knowledge of our financial situation and my husband was an expert," she
says. "Nobody was looking after my interests, and I was scared."

Badly mediated settlements can be irreversible. Ann Diamond, a
Corte Madera, Calif., lawyer, recalls a client who "gave up lots of property because her husband intimidated her outside the mediator's office,"
by threatening a custody fight if she didn't accept a scaled-down offer on
property division. Later, a judge refused to reopen the agreement unless
the woman could show "out-and-out fraud," Mrs. Diamond says.

Mediation clearly doesn't always succeed in smoothing over animosi-
ties within dissolving marriages. "I've had parents spit on each other and
try to strangle each other in my office," says Robin Drapkin, a California
mediator. A colleague, Leslie Aranoff, says he has met with one couple
15 times without producing an agreement.

By all accounts, the biggest beneficiaries of successful custody mediation are the children of divorcing parents. Concern for kids, along with a
need to thin bulging court dockets, is prompting courts around the country to provide for mediation, either on a voluntary or a mandatory basis.
In California, which began requiring custody mediation in 1981, court
psychologists and social workers usually conduct the sessions. They are
paid out of marriage-license and divorce-court fees.

Hugh McIsaac, coordinator of the mediation program at the Los Angeles County courthouse, says that of 5,073 families that entered mediation there last year, 64 percent reached agreements and stayed out of
court. "Judges hate deciding cases when both people are good parents
and those are the best cases for mediation," he says. "Cases where you
can't mediate, like when one parent is psychotic, are much easier for a
judge to decide."

In Chicago's Cook County, where mediation became mandatory in
January, divorcing parents are required to sit through three two-hour
mediation sessions. Each couple first meets with a judge, who is unlikely
to mince words on the importance of reaching agreement. Recently,
Judge Monica Reynolds told a quarreling couple: "Psychologists say a
custody fight is harder on a child than the loss of each of you through
death. We'd like you to agree on custody, for your son's sake."

Warren Weiss, who runs court mediation services in San Jose, Calif.,
says mediators "can be creative sometimes in solutions because we can
spend hours focusing on a single issue, which a judge can't." In one case,
he recalls, a woman dropped previous objections to visits by her alcoholic
husband with their daughter. The standoff ended when a mediator arranged for the father to use a drug that would make him ill if he drank.
Under the pact, the father agreed to take the drug whenever he was going to spend time with his daughter.

Often court mediators interview the children and let parents know how they have been traumatized by the turmoil. Haile Mackey, a mediator in Los Angeles, included a 14-year-old daughter in custody negotiations with her parents. At the time, the father was making threats toward the mother, who had taken to bringing a bodyguard to the negotiating sessions.

One problem arose from the daughter's refusal to visit with her father. After Mr. Mackey encouraged the girl to talk about her emotions, she faced her father in the mediator's small, nearly bare office, and told him, "I'm afraid of you." The father replied, "I love you; you are very important to me." Eventually, after talking quietly, the girl kissed him and agreed to see him every other weekend.

When mediation succeeds, it makes a painful process less painful. Virgal and Ann Duffell of Oakton, Va., sought mediation after deciding to end their 17-year marriage. Mr. Duffell says the sessions "helped me see her position more clearly," and led to a settlement that eased the financial pressures on his wife as she completed a master's degree and obtained a job. The divorce ended up costing the Duffells $2,500, including mediation and lawyers' fees, about half what they would have paid in a traditional divorce.

Mr. Duffell says he was further convinced of the merits of mediation when his 12-year-old son asked, "Why do they make divorce sound so bad in the movies? It isn't great, but it isn't so bad."

NEW YORK CITY OPINION 80-23
(1980)

We have been asked whether lawyers may ethically participate in a divorce mediation program organized by a non-profit organization. The organization has a staff of licensed mental health professionals who provide marital and family therapy. It now proposes to offer what is known as "structured mediation" in marital cases. Such mediation involves a trained therapist consulting with separating or divorcing couples to aid them in working out various aspects of the separation or divorce, including issues of property division, and child custody, visitation and support. We have been asked whether a lawyer could (a) become part of the mediating team, (b) give impartial legal advice to the parties, such as advice on the tax consequences of proposed separation or divorce agreements, or (c) draft a divorce or settlement agreement after the terms of such agreement have been approved by the parties. . . .

This inquiry raises important and difficult questions concerning the participation of lawyers in non-adversarial roles in dispute resolution. The Code of Professional Responsibility provides comparatively detailed guides for the lawyer representing clients in the adversarial role of zealous advocate or confidential adviser. The Code also recognizes that lawyers may serve as "impartial arbitrators or mediators" (EC 5-20). However, the Code nowhere defines these latter roles and their responsibilities or expressly considers the role of lawyers asked to provide impartial legal assistance to parties with differing interests, in an effort to compose their differences without resort to adversary negotiation or litigation. The Committee nevertheless believes that the principles of the Code permit the extrapolation of certain guidelines for lawyers asked to participate in such non-adversarial activities. . . .

I

The issues raised here require the harmonization of differing policies reflected in the Code of Professional Responsibility. On the one hand, the Code provides that a lawyer may represent multiple clients only "if it is *obvious* that he can adequately represent the interest of each and if each consents to the representation after full disclosure of the possible effect of such representation on the exercise of his independent professional judgment on behalf of each." DR 5-105(C). (Emphasis supplied.) Applying this principle, it has been repeatedly held that the conflicts inherent in a matrimonial proceeding are such, that it is never appropriate to represent both spouses. Thus, New York State Opinion 258 (1972) states:

> It would be improper for a lawyer to represent both husband and wife at any stage of a marital problem, even with full disclosure and informed consent of both parties. The likelihood of prejudice is so great in this type of matter as to make impossible adequate representation of both spouses, even where the separation is "friendly" and the divorce uncontested.

This opinion further cites with approval the view that such representation is improper even if the parties consent and merely are seeking to have the lawyer reduce to writing an agreement that the parties independently arrived at.

On the other hand, EC 5-20 states that a lawyer may serve in the capacity of an "impartial arbitrator or mediator" even for present or former clients provided the lawyer makes appropriate disclosures and thereafter declines to represent any of the parties in the dispute. Accordingly, New York State Opinion 258 also acknowledges that a lawyer can serve as a "mediator" in a matrimonial dispute.

The difficulty arises because the Code nowhere explains what activities constitute "mediation," what responsibilities a lawyer has when acting as a mediator, when a lawyer is "representing" parties or whether it is possible for a lawyer to give legal guidance to all parties to a dispute — to "represent the situation" — without representing any of them or being involved in the conflicts which representing them would involve. . . .

II

This Committee recognizes that there are circumstances where it is desirable that parties to a matrimonial dispute be afforded an alternative to the adversarial process, with its legal and emotional costs. The Code's recognition that lawyers may serve as mediators (EC 5-20), as well as ethical aspirations which recognize a lawyer's duty to assist the public in recognizing legal problems and aiding those who cannot afford the usual costs of legal assistance (EC 2-1; EC 2-25), make it inconceivable to us that the Code would deny the public the availability of non-adversary legal assistance in the resolution of divorce disputes.

At the same time, the Committee also recognizes that in some circumstances, the complex and conflicting interests involved in a particular matrimonial dispute, the difficult legal issues involved, the subtle legal ramifications of particular resolutions, and the inequality in bargaining power resulting from differences in the personalities or sophistication of the parties make it virtually impossible to achieve a just result free from later recriminations of bias or malpractice, unless both parties are represented by separate counsel. In the latter circumstances, informing the parties that the lawyer "represents" neither party and obtaining their consent, even after a full explanation of the risks, may not be meaningful; the distinction between representing both parties and not representing either, in such circumstances, may be illusory. Whether characterized as a mediator or impartial advisor, the lawyer asked to exercise his or her professional judgment will be relied upon by parties who may lack sophistication to recognize the significance of the legal issues involved and the impact they have on their individual interests. Further, the "impartial" lawyer may in fact be making difficult choices between the interests of the parties in giving legal advice or in drafting provisions of a written agreement which purports merely to embody the parties' prior agreement. Although the parties may consent to the procedure, one or both may not be capable of giving truly informed consent due to the difficulty of the issues involved. In such circumstances, a party who is later advised that its interests were prejudiced in mediation or that the impartial advice offered or written agreement drawn, by the lawyer-mediator, favored the other spouse is likely to believe that it was misled into reliance on the impartiality of the lawyer-mediator. In short, we believe there are some activities and some circumstances in which a lawyer cannot undertake to compose the differences of parties to a divorce proceeding, without running afoul of the strictures and policies of DR 5-105 — even if the lawyer disclaims representing the interests of any party, purports to be acting impartially and obtains the consent of the parties to the arrangement.

On the other hand, there are clearly circumstances where these difficulties are not involved and where the parties can truly understand, and the lawyer can plainly carry out, a representation that the lawyer represents neither party.

This seems likely, for example, where the lawyer is not being asked to exercise any professional legal judgment — for example where the lawyer is seeking to bring about a compromise or find a common ground for the division of articles of personal property. Such typical mediation activities can be performed by non-lawyers and we cannot conclude that the Code (which permits lawyers to serve as mediators) intended to bar lawyers from performing the same activities.

It also seems true that the lawyer can meaningfully state that he or she represents neither of the parties where the parties simply ask the lawyer to describe the legal consequences of a particular agreement they have reached. Performing such activities would not involve the lawyer in making choices between the interests of the parties.

Nevertheless, even with regard to such activities, there are likely to be situations of such complexity and difficulty that the lawyer must make the judgment that one or both of the parties' consent cannot be considered fully informed. This may be true even where the lawyer merely is asked to provide services that lay mediators may perform or where the legal question he is asked does not require him to choose between the parties' interests. For example, what may appear to be simply a resolution of a dispute about the division of property, may in fact have complicated and subtle tax consequences about which the parties are unaware. The divorce process has always been considered of special concern to the state and as such, an integral part of the administration of justice. Where the lawyer recognizes that the issues raised by a particular divorce dispute are so difficult or complex that they cannot be fairly or justly resolved unless each party is guided by its own separate counsel, the lawyer's participation in a mediation of the dispute may be prejudicial to the administration of justice. See DR 1-102(A)(5).

Accordingly, to harmonize these various considerations, we have concluded that lawyers may participate in the divorce mediation procedure proposed in the inquiry here, only on the following conditions.

To begin with, the lawyer may *not* participate in the divorce mediation process where it appears that the issues between the parties are of such complexity or difficulty that the parties cannot prudently reach a resolution without the advice of separate and independent legal counsel.

If the lawyer is satisfied that the situation is one in which the parties can intelligently and prudently consent to mediation and the use of an impartial legal adviser, then the lawyer may undertake these roles provided the lawyer observes the following rules:

First, the lawyer must clearly and fully advise the parties of the limitations on his or her role and specifically, of the fact that the lawyer represents neither party and that accordingly, they should not look to the lawyer to protect their individual interests or to keep confidences of one party from the other.

Second, the lawyer must fully and clearly explain the risks of proceeding without separate legal counsel and thereafter proceed only with the consent of the parties and only if the lawyer is satisfied that the parties understand the risks and understand the significance of the fact that the lawyer represents neither party.

Third, a lawyer may participate with mental health professionals in those aspects of mediation which do not require the exercise of professional legal judgment and involve the same kind of mediation activities permissible to lay mediators.

Fourth, lawyers may provide impartial legal advice and assist in reducing the parties' agreement to writing only where the lawyer fully explains all pertinent considerations and alternatives and the consequences to each party of choosing the resolution agreed upon.

Fifth, the lawyer may give legal advice only to both parties in the presence of the other.

Sixth, the lawyer must advise the parties of the advantages of seeking independent legal counsel before executing any agreement drafted by the lawyer.

Seventh, the lawyer may not represent either of the parties in any subsequent legal proceedings relating to the divorce.

Underlying these guidelines is the requirement that the lawyers' participation in the mediation process be conditioned on *informed* consent by the parties. . . .

Are Lawyer Mediators Square Circles?

The committee struggles, doesn't it, to reconcile what it sees as the lawyer's customary adversarial, or at least representational, role with an arrangement in which the lawyer is simply a provider of information and advice? In some situations, the committee says, a lawyer cannot ethically provide advice to two parties (to a divorce or presumably otherwise) no matter how much the parties may wish to buy the advice. Why is that? At those times, the parties will have to accept the profession's traditional adversarial model as a condition of getting the information they need. Of course, this does not mean they have to *behave* adversarially. The structure need not dictate the tone. Right? Or is that not so clear? Does an adversary structure, with lawyers in their traditional role, encourage contentiousness?

Whom does the committee's limitation protect? Lawyers? The participants? Both? Its resolution denies "clients" full autonomy to order their lives as they may wish, even when fully informed, on the apparent theory that no rational person would choose a mediation model under certain circumstances. Is this paternalistic? Would it have been better to identify the risks for the lawyers and the participants and then let each choose whether or not to participate in the contemplated mediation? After all, the question before the committee was not whether lawyers must accept requests to be mediators but whether they could.

FURTHER READING

Professor Edward Brunet is skeptical about the efficacy of alternate dispute resolution in Questioning the Quality of Alternate Dispute Resolution, 62 Tul. L. Rev. 1 (1987). See also Richard Crouch, Divorce Mediation and Legal Ethics, 16 Fam. L.Q. 219 (1982); Note, Is Divorce Mediation the Practice of Law? A Matter of Perspective, 75 Calif. L. Rev. 1093 (1987) (authored by Andrew Morrison); Leonard Riskin, Toward New Standards for the Neutral Lawyer in Mediation, 26 Ariz. L. Rev. 329 (1984); Linda Silberman, Professional Responsibility Problems of Divorce Mediation, 16 Fam. L.Q. 107 (1982).

Judith Maute argues that "when mediated settlement supplants public adjudication, the mediator is accountable for procedurally fair process and minimally fair substantive outcome." She proposes a new Rule 2.4 that "would apply when a lawyer undertakes to mediate a dispute between parties not previously represented by the lawyer." Judith Maute, Public Values and Private Justice: A Case for Mediator Accountability, 4 Geo. J. Legal Ethics 503 (1991).

Part Four

AVOIDING AND REDRESSING PROFESSIONAL FAILURE

XII

Control of Quality: Reducing the Likelihood of Professional Failure

A state may try to prevent professional failures, such as malpractice or neglect of client matters, in many ways. When a professional failure nevertheless occurs, various remedies are possible. In this chapter we look at ways in which a state may try to reduce the incidence of professional failure. In Chapter 13 we address remedial measures. This division is slightly arbitrary. A remedial measure — for example, discipline or a civil action against the lawyer — has a preventive dimension as well as a curative one.

One issue that will arise with regard to the preventive measures discussed in this chapter is the relationship between a particular rule and the reduction of risk of professional failure that the rule is meant to accomplish. For example, do residency requirements, bar examinations, or educational prerequisites to bar membership reduce the likelihood of professional error? If so, by how much is the likelihood of error reduced in relation to the cost of the requirement? A requirement that bar applicants graduate from accredited law schools has an enormous cost — in time and money. Is the cost justified by the higher quality of work that the requirement produces when compared with the quality of work we would have without it? Parallel policy questions can be asked about residency requirements and character tests.

A related issue is epistemological. How can we know the answers to these questions? Do we simply accept some things on faith? In the material that follows, courts and other rulemakers must weigh the costs of a particular requirement, including claimed burdens on constitutional rights, against the interests of the jurisdiction that wishes to impose the requirement. How do they conduct this evaluation? What level of constitutional scrutiny do the courts apply?

Nor should we ignore the selfish side of human nature. A subtext to any discussion of rules that influence the supply of and demand for lawyers is the economic consequence of the particular rule at issue. A rule prohibiting nonresidents from admission to a state's bar protects in-state lawyers from competition. Is that the motive for the prohibition, or is it an interest in assuring quality legal work by reliable lawyers? Or is it both? To what extent should the courts be cognizant of economic motives in analyzing barriers to bar admission? To what extent should such motives be impermissible? Similar questions can and should be asked about restrictions on pro hac vice admission (Chapter 12B), on unauthorized law practice (Chapter 12E), on lay investment in or management of law firms (Chapter 14), and on ways in which lawyers may market their services (Chapter 16).

A. ADMISSION TO THE BAR

1. Geographical Exclusion

May a state prohibit a lawyer who lives outside its borders from gaining admission to its bar? That's the question answered in the following case. A distinct but related question (deferred until part A2) is whether a state may impose restrictions (short of exclusion) on lawyers who live outside the state that are not imposed on in-state lawyers.

SUPREME COURT OF NEW HAMPSHIRE v. PIPER
470 U.S. 274 (1985)

JUSTICE POWELL delivered the opinion of the Court.

The Rules of the Supreme Court of New Hampshire limit bar admission to state residents. We here consider whether this restriction violates the Privileges and Immunities Clause of the United States Constitution, Art. IV, §2.

I

A

Kathryn Piper lives in Lower Waterford, Vermont, about 400 yards from the New Hampshire border. In 1979, she applied to take the February 1980 New Hampshire bar examination. Piper submitted with her application a statement of intent to become a New Hampshire resident. Following an investigation, the Board of Bar Examiners found that Piper was of good moral character and met the other requirements for admission. She was allowed to take, and passed, the examination. Piper was informed by the Board that she would have to establish a home address in New Hampshire prior to being sworn in.

On May 7, 1980, Piper requested from the Clerk of the New Hampshire Supreme Court a dispensation from the residency requirement. Although she had a "possible job" with a lawyer in Littleton, New Hampshire, Piper stated that becoming a resident of New Hampshire would be inconvenient. Her house in Vermont was secured by a mortgage with a favorable interest rate, and she and her husband recently had become parents. According to Piper, these "problems peculiar to [her] situation . . . warrant[ed] that an exception be made." . . .

On May 13, 1980, the Clerk informed Piper that her request had been denied. She then formally petitioned the New Hampshire Supreme Court for permission to become a member of the bar. She asserted that she was well qualified and that her "situation [was] sufficiently unique that the granting of an exception . . . [would] not result in the setting of any undesired precedent." . . . The Supreme Court denied Piper's formal request on December 31, 1980.[2] . . .

II

A

Article IV, §2 of the Constitution provides that the "citizens of each State shall be entitled to all Privileges and Immunities of Citizens in the several States."[6] This clause was intended to "fuse into one Nation a collection of independent, sovereign States." Toomer v. Witsell, 334 U.S. 385, 395 (1948). Recognizing this purpose, we have held that it is "[o]nly with respect to those 'privileges' and 'immunities' bearing on the vitality of the nation as a single entity" that a State must accord residents and nonresidents equal treatment. Baldwin v. Fish & Game Commn. [436 U.S. 371, 383 (1978)]. In *Baldwin*, for example, we concluded that a State

---

2. Piper was not excluded totally from the practice of law in New Hampshire. Out-of-state lawyers may appear pro hac vice in state court. This alternative, however, does not allow the nonresident to practice in New Hampshire on the same terms as a resident member of the bar. The lawyer appearing pro hac vice must be associated with a local lawyer who is present for trial or argument. Furthermore, the decision on whether to grant pro hac vice status to an out-of-state lawyer is purely discretionary. See Leis v. Flynt, 439 U.S. 438, 442 (1979) (per curiam).

6. Under this Clause, the terms "citizen" and "resident" are used interchangeably. See Austin v. New Hampshire, 420 U.S. 656, 662, n.8 (1975). Under the Fourteenth Amendment, of course, "[a]ll persons born or naturalized in the United States . . . are citizens . . . of the State wherein they reside."

may charge a nonresident more than it charges a resident for the same elk-hunting license. Because elk-hunting is "recreation" rather than a "means of a livelihood," we found that the right to a hunting license was not "fundamental" to the promotion of interstate harmony.

Derived, like the Commerce Clause, from the fourth of the Articles of Confederation, the Privileges and Immunities Clause was intended to create a national economic union. It is therefore not surprising that this Court repeatedly has found that "one of the privileges which the Clause guarantees to citizens of State A is that of doing business in State B on terms of substantial equality with the citizens of that State." In Ward v. Maryland, 12 Wall. 418 (1871), the Court invalidated a statute under which nonresidents were required to pay $300 per year for a license to trade in goods not manufactured in Maryland, while resident traders paid a fee varying from $12 to $150. Similarly, in *Toomer*, supra, the Court held that nonresident fishermen could not be required to pay a license fee of $2,500 for each shrimp boat owned when residents were charged only $25 per boat. Finally, in Hicklin v. Orbeck, 437 U.S. 518 (1978), we found violative of the Privileges and Immunities Clause a statute containing a resident hiring preference for all employment related to the development of the State's oil and gas resources.

There is nothing in *Ward, Toomer,* or *Hicklin* suggesting that the practice of law should not be viewed as a "privilege" under Article IV, §2. Like the occupations considered in our earlier cases, the practice of law is important to the national economy. As the Court noted in *Goldfarb*, the "activities of lawyers play an important part in commercial intercourse." Goldfarb v. Virginia State Bar, 421 U.S. 773, 788.

The lawyer's role in the national economy is not the only reason that the opportunity to practice law should be considered a "fundamental right." We believe that the legal profession has a noncommercial role and duty that reinforce the view that the practice of law falls within the ambit of the Privileges and Immunities Clause. Out-of-state lawyers may — and often do — represent persons who raise unpopular federal claims. In some cases, representation by nonresident counsel may be the only means available for the vindication of federal rights. See Leis v. Flynt, 439 U.S. at 450 (Stevens, J., dissenting). The lawyer who champions unpopular causes surely is as important to the "maintenance or well-being of the Union," *Baldwin*, as was the shrimp fisherman in *Toomer*, supra, or the pipeline worker in *Hicklin*.

B

The State asserts that the Privileges and Immunities Clause should be held inapplicable to the practice of law because a lawyer's activities are "bound up with the exercise of judicial power and the administration of justice." Its contention is based on the premise that the lawyer is an "officer of the court," who "exercises state power on a daily basis." The State concludes that if it cannot exclude nonresidents from the bar, its ability to function as a sovereign political body will be threatened.

Lawyers do enjoy a "broad monopoly . . . to do things other citizens may not lawfully do." In re Griffiths, 413 U.S. 717, 731 (1973). We do not believe, however, that the practice of law involves an "exercise of state power" justifying New Hampshire's residency requirement. In In re Griffiths, supra, we held that the State could not exclude an alien from the bar on the ground that a lawyer is an " 'officer of the Court who' . . . is entrusted with the 'exercise of actual governmental power.' " We concluded that a lawyer is not an "officer" within the ordinary meaning of that word. 413 U.S. at 728. He " 'makes his own decisions, follows his own best judgment, collects his own fees and runs his own business.' " Moreover, we held that the state powers entrusted to lawyers do not "involve matters of state policy or acts of such unique responsibility that they should be entrusted only to citizens."

Because, under *Griffiths*, a lawyer is not an "officer" of the State in any political sense, there is no reason for New Hampshire to exclude from its bar nonresidents. We therefore conclude that the right to practice law is protected by the Privileges and Immunities Clause.

III

The conclusion that Rule 42 deprives nonresidents of a protected privilege does not end our inquiry. The Court has stated that "[l]ike many other constitutional provisions, the privileges and immunities clause is not an absolute." Toomer v. Witsell, 334 U.S. at 396. . . . The Clause does not preclude discrimination against nonresidents where: (i) there is a substantial reason for the difference in treatment; and (ii) the discrimination practiced against nonresidents bears a substantial relationship to the State's objective. . . . In deciding whether the discrimination bears a close or substantial relationship to the State's objective, the Court has considered the availability of less restrictive means.

The Supreme Court of New Hampshire offers several justifications for its refusal to admit nonresidents to the bar. It asserts that nonresident members would be less likely: (i) to become, and remain, familiar with local rules and procedures; (ii) to behave ethically; (iii) to be available for court proceedings; and (iv) to do pro bono and other volunteer work in the State.[18] We find that none of these reasons meets the test of "substan-

---

18. A former president of the American Bar Association has suggested another possible reason for the rule: "Many of the states that have erected fences against out-of-state lawyers have done so primarily to protect their own lawyers from professional competition." Smith, Time for a National Practice of Law Act, 64 A.B.A.J. 557 (1978). This reason is not "substantial." The Privileges and Immunities Clause was designed primarily to prevent such economic protectionism.

tiality," and that the means chosen do not bear the necessary relationship to the State's objectives.

There is no evidence to support the State's claim that nonresidents might be less likely to keep abreast of local rules and procedures. Nor may we assume that a nonresident lawyer — any more than a resident — would disserve his clients by failing to familiarize himself with the rules. As a practical matter, we think that unless a lawyer has, or anticipates, a considerable practice in the New Hampshire courts, he would be unlikely to take the bar examination and pay the annual dues of $125.[19]

We also find the State's second justification to be without merit, for there is no reason to believe that a nonresident lawyer will conduct his practice in a dishonest manner. The nonresident lawyer's professional duty and interest in his reputation should provide the same incentive to maintain high ethical standards as they do for resident lawyers. A lawyer will be concerned with his reputation in any community where he practices, regardless of where he may live. Furthermore, a nonresident lawyer may be disciplined for unethical conduct. The Supreme Court of New Hampshire has the authority to discipline all members of the bar, regardless of where they reside. . . .

There is more merit to the State's assertion that a nonresident member of the bar at times would be unavailable for court proceedings. In the course of litigation, pretrial hearings on various matters often are held on short notice. At times a court will need to confer immediately with counsel. Even the most conscientious lawyer residing in a distant State may find himself unable to appear in court for an unscheduled hearing or proceeding. Nevertheless, we do not believe that this type of problem justifies the exclusion of nonresidents from the state bar. One may assume that a high percentage of nonresident lawyers willing to take the state bar examination and pay the annual dues will reside in places reasonably convenient to New Hampshire. Furthermore, in those cases where the nonresident counsel will be unavailable on short notice, the State can protect its interests through less restrictive means. The trial court, by rule or as an exercise of discretion, may require any lawyer who resides at a great distance to retain a local attorney who will be available for unscheduled meetings and hearings.

---

19. Because it is markedly overinclusive, the residency requirement does not bear a substantial relationship to the State's objective. A less restrictive alternative would be to require mandatory attendance at periodic seminars on state practice. There already is a rule requiring all new admittees to complete a "practical skills course" within one year of their admission.

New Hampshire's "simple residency" requirement is underinclusive as well, because it permits lawyers who move away from the State to retain their membership in the bar. There is no reason to believe that a former resident would maintain a more active practice in the New Hampshire courts than would a nonresident lawyer who had never lived in the State.

The final reason advanced by the State is that nonresident members of its bar would be disinclined to do their share of pro bono and volunteer work. Perhaps this is true to a limited extent, particularly where the member resides in a distant location. We think it is reasonable to believe, however, that most lawyers who become members of a state bar will endeavor to perform their share of these services. This sort of participation, of course, would serve the professional interest of a lawyer who practices in the State. Furthermore, the nonresident bar member, like the resident member, could be required to represent indigents and perhaps to participate in formal legal-aid work.

In summary, the State neither advances a "substantial reason" for its discrimination against nonresident applicants to the bar, nor demonstrates that the discrimination practiced bears a close relationship to its proffered objectives. . . .

JUSTICE WHITE, concurring in the result. . . .

I concur in the judgment invalidating the New Hampshire residency requirement as applied to respondent Piper.

JUSTICE REHNQUIST, dissenting.

Today the Court holds that New Hampshire cannot decide that a New Hampshire lawyer should live in New Hampshire. This may not be surprising to those who view law as just another form of business frequently practiced across state lines by interchangeable actors; the Privileges and Immunities Clause of Art. IV, §2 has long been held to apply to States' attempts to discriminate against nonresidents who seek to ply their trade interstate. The decision will be surprising to many, however, because it so clearly disregards the fact that the practice of law is — almost by definition — fundamentally different from those other occupations that are practiced across state lines without significant deviation from State to State. . . .

My belief that the practice of law differs from other trades and businesses for Art. IV, §2 purposes is not based on some notion that law is for some reason a superior profession. The reason that the practice of law should be treated differently is that law is one occupation that does not readily translate across state lines. Certain aspects of legal practice are distinctly and intentionally *nonnational;* in this regard one might view this country's legal system as the antithesis of the norms embodied in the Art. IV Privileges and Immunities Clause. Put simply, the State has a substantial interest in creating its own set of laws responsive to its own local interests, and it is reasonable for a State to decide that those people who have been trained to analyze law and policy are better equipped to write those state laws and adjudicate cases arising under them. The State therefore may decide that it has an interest in maximizing the number of resident lawyers, so as to increase the quality of the pool from which its lawmakers can be drawn. A residency law such as the one at issue is the obvious way to accomplish these goals. Since at any given time within a State there is only enough legal work to support a certain number of lawyers, each out-of-state lawyer who is allowed to practice necessarily takes legal work that could support an in-state lawyer, who would otherwise be available to perform various functions that a State has an interest in promoting.[3]

Nor does the State's interest end with enlarging the pool of qualified lawmakers. A State similarly might determine that because lawyers play an important role in the formulation of State policy through their adversary representation, they should be intimately conversant with the local concerns that should inform such policies. And the State likewise might conclude that those citizens trained in the law are likely to bring their useful expertise to other important functions that benefit from such expertise and are of interest to state governments — such as trusteeships, or directorships of corporations or charitable organizations, or school board positions, or merely the role of the interested citizen at a town meeting. Thus, although the Court suggests that state bars can require out-of-state members to "represent indigents and perhaps to participate in formal legal-aid work," . . . the Court ignores a host of other important functions that a State could find would likely be performed only by in-state bar members. States may find a substantial interest in members of their bar being residents, and this insular interest — as with the opposing interest in interstate harmony represented by Art. IV, §2 — itself has its genesis in the language and structure of the Constitution. . . .

There is yet another interest asserted by the State that I believe would justify a decision to limit membership in the state bar to state residents. The State argues that out-of-state bar members pose a problem in situations where counsel must be available on short notice to represent clients on unscheduled matters. The Court brushes this argument aside, speculating that "a high percentage of nonresident lawyers willing to take the state bar examination and pay the annual dues will reside in places reasonably convenient to New Hampshire," and suggesting that in any event the trial court could alleviate this problem by requiring the lawyer to retain local counsel. . . . Assuming that the latter suggestion does not itself constitute unlawful discrimination under the Court's test, there nevertheless may be good reasons why a State or a trial court would rather not get into structuring attorney-client relationships by requiring the retention of local counsel for emergency matters. The situation would have to be explained to the client, and the allocation of responsibility between resident and nonresident counsel could cause as many problems as the Court's suggestion might cure.

3. In New Hampshire's case, lawyers living 40 miles from the state border in Boston could easily devote part of their practice to New Hampshire clients. If this occurred a significant amount of New Hampshire legal work might wind up in Boston, along with lawyers who might otherwise reside in New Hampshire.

Nor do I believe that the problem can be confined to emergency matters. The Court admits that even in the ordinary course of litigation a trial judge will want trial lawyers to be available on short notice; the uncertainties of managing a trial docket are such that lawyers rarely are given a single date on which a trial will begin; they may be required to "stand by" — or whatever the local terminology is — for days at a time, and then be expected to be ready in a matter of hours, with witnesses, when the case in front of them suddenly settles. A State reasonably can decide that a trial court should not have added to its present scheduling difficulties the uncertainties and added delays fostered by counsel who might reside one thousand miles from New Hampshire. If there is any single problem with state legal systems that this Court might consider "substantial," it is the problem of delay in litigation — a subject that has been profusely explored in the literature over the past several years. . . . Surely the State has a substantial interest in taking steps to minimize this problem.

Federal Court Exclusions

Piper was the first of three Supreme Court cases to overturn limitations on practice by out-of-state lawyers. The other two concerned limits imposed by federal courts. In Frazier v. Heebe, 482 U.S. 641 (1987), the Court reviewed local rules of the Federal District Court for the Eastern District of Louisiana that required members of its bar either to reside or have an office in Louisiana. Frazier was a resident of Mississippi, where he had his law office, but he was also a member of the Louisiana bar and practiced in that state's courts. The challenged rules prevented him from practicing in federal court in Louisiana except by special permission (called pro hac vice admission, see page 571 infra). The rules were defended on the ground that nonresident lawyers without offices in the state were "less competent and less available."

The Supreme Court invalidated the local rules under its "supervisory authority" without addressing the "constitutional questions presented," but its language suggested that the rules would also be constitutionally infirm. In an opinion by Justice Brennan, the Court characterized the rules as "irrational." It said that "no empirical evidence was introduced" to support the claim that lawyers with homes and offices outside the state were less competent than members of the Louisiana bar who lived or had offices in the state. The Court refused to accept this claim on faith. The contention that nonresident lawyers were less available had been undermined by *Piper*. In any event, interest in availability was not furthered by the rules. A lawyer could satisfy the rules by living or practicing within Louisiana but at a greater distance from the federal courthouse than Frazier's Mississippi situs. The availability of pro hac vice admission on a case by case basis was not an acceptable substitute for regular admission.

Chief Justice Rehnquist, joined by Justices O'Connor and Scalia, dissented. The dissent did not believe that the Court had supervisory authority to invalidate the rules and, reaching the constitutional challenge, concluded that the rules did "not classify so arbitrarily or irrationally as to run afoul of the Fifth Amendment Due Process Clause."

In Thorstenn v. Barnard, 842 F.2d 1393 (3d Cir. 1988), the Third Circuit, relying on *Frazier* and its supervisory powers, voided a Virgin Islands District Court rule that required a year's residency before a person could apply for bar admission. The Supreme Court granted certiorari to decide whether the Third Circuit had the same supervisory authority over the Virgin Islands District Court as the Supreme Court has over federal district courts. But the Court then ruled that the Privileges and Immunities Clause of the United States Constitution, made applicable to the Virgin Islands by federal statute, prohibited the territory from adopting any residency requirements. 489 U.S. 546 (1989).

The "New Jersey" Problem

After *Piper*, lawyers living anywhere in the country can choose to take bar examinations in any state. The majority did not adopt Justice White's view that the case should be decided on the narrow ground that Piper lived so close to New Hampshire. Footnote 3 of the dissent speculates that if out-of-state lawyers can easily gain admission to the New Hampshire bar, lawyers in Boston might devote part of their practice to New Hampshire legal work. If that response were significant, the resident New Hampshire ·bar would shrink because there would be less work to support it and because New Hampshire lawyers would follow the work to Boston. The implication is that Boston lawyers might be more attractive to a sufficient number of New Hampshire clients than New Hampshire lawyers would be. So the contest, in this scenario, appears to be between the presumed competitive advantage of Boston lawyers in a free market and the state's wish to curtail the operation of that market to protect its resident bar and to ensure that New Hampshire clients are represented by lawyers with a permanent stake in the life of the state. Are those valid interests?

Several states have reason to fear "client flight," and consequent harm to the economic health of their bars, as geographical limitations on bar admission are eliminated and national or regional firms come looking for work. (Law firm marketing, see Chapter 16, may facilitate this trend.) New Jersey is often used as an example because it is sandwiched between the legal and media markets of Philadelphia and New York. New Jersey cannot, after *Piper*, exclude out-of-state lawyers from taking its bar examination, but it can and does condition admission to its bar on passage of the same examination its own lawyers must pass. New Jersey does not grant reciprocity to out-of-state lawyers, which means it does not allow lawyers admitted in another state to be admitted without examination (i.e., on motion) in New Jersey.

Many states do grant reciprocity, at least for experienced out-of-state lawyers. (According to the Chief Justice Rehnquist's dissent in Supreme Court of Virginia v. Friedman (see page 550 infra), 28 states do not recognize reciprocity.) New York has a reciprocity law. But because New York lawyers were required to take the New Jersey bar examination while New Jersey lawyers gained comparatively painless admission to the New York bar, New York retaliated with a law (present in other states too) that denies reciprocity admissions to out-of-state lawyers whose home states (read New Jersey) do not grant reciprocity to New York lawyers. 22 N.Y.C.R.R. §520.9(a)(1). So far, New Jersey has maintained its position.

As the bar becomes more national, as there are more lawyers and firms with some kind of presence in more jurisdictions, threats to states like New Jersey and New Hampshire will increase. Is that just too bad? Or will the small states lose something valuable and deserving of constitutional respect, as Justice Rehnquist argues in his *Piper* dissent? New Jersey also has strict limits on television advertisements for legal services. See page 824 infra. Can this be competitively explained? It is noteworthy that the "profession or business" dichotomy highlighted in the dissent resurfaces, among other places, in the material on law firm marketing.

2. Geographical Restriction

SUPREME COURT OF VIRGINIA v. FRIEDMAN
487 U.S. 59 (1988)

JUSTICE KENNEDY delivered the opinion of the Court.

Qualified lawyers admitted to practice in other States may be admitted to the Virginia bar "on motion," that is, without taking the bar examination which Virginia otherwise requires. The State conditions such admission on a showing, among other matters, that the applicant is a permanent resident of Virginia. The question for decision is whether this residency requirement violates the Privileges and Immunities Clause of the United States Constitution, Art. IV, §2. We hold that it does.

I

Myrna E. Friedman was admitted to the Illinois bar by examination in 1977 and to the District of Columbia bar by reciprocity in 1980. From 1977 to 1981, she was employed by the Department of the Navy in Arlington, Virginia, as a civilian attorney, and from 1982 until 1986, she was an attorney in private practice in Washington, D.C. In January 1986, she became associate general counsel for ERC International, Inc., a Delaware corporation. Friedman practices and maintains her offices at the company's principal place of business in Vienna, Virginia. Her duties at ERC International include drafting contracts and advising her employer and its subsidiaries on matters of Virginia law.

From 1977 to early 1986, Friedman lived in Virginia. In February 1986, however, she married and moved to her husband's home in Cheverly, Maryland. In June 1986, Friedman applied for admission to the Virginia bar on motion.

The applicable rule, promulgated by the Supreme Court of Virginia pursuant to statute, is Rule 1A:1. The Rule permits admission on motion of attorneys who are licensed to practice in another jurisdiction, provided the other jurisdiction admits Virginia attorneys without examination. The applicant must have been licensed for at least five years and the Virginia Supreme Court must determine that the applicant:

(a)   Is a proper person to practice law.
(b)   Has made such progress in the practice of law that it would be unreasonable to require him to take an examination.
(c)   Has become a permanent resident of the Commonwealth.
(d)   Intends to practice full time as a member of the Virginia bar. . . .

The Clerk wrote Friedman that her request had been denied. He explained that because Friedman was no longer a permanent resident of the Commonwealth of Virginia, she was not eligible for admission to the Virginia bar pursuant to Rule 1A:1. He added that the court had concluded that our decision in *Piper*, which invalidated a residency requirement imposed on lawyers who had passed a State's bar examination, was "not applicable" to the "discretionary requirement in Rule 1A:1 of residence as a condition of admission by reciprocity." . . .

II . . .

A

Appellants concede, as they must, that our decision in *Piper* establishes that a nonresident who takes and passes an examination prescribed by the State, and who otherwise is qualified for the practice of law, has an interest in practicing law that is protected by the Privileges and Immunities Clause. Appellants contend, however, that the discretionary admission provided for by Rule 1A:1 is not a privilege protected by the Clause for two reasons. First, appellants argue that the bar examination "serves as an adequate, alternative means of gaining admission to the bar." In appellants' view, "[s]o long as any applicant may gain admission to a State's bar, without regard to residence, by passing the bar examination," the State cannot be said to have discriminated against nonresidents "as a matter of fundamental concern." Second, appellants argue that the right to admission on motion is not within the purview of the Clause because, without offense to the Constitution, the State could require all bar applicants to pass an examination. Neither argument is persuasive.

We cannot accept appellants' first theory because it is quite inconsistent with our precedents. We reaffirmed in *Piper* the well-settled principle that " 'one of the privileges which the Clause guarantees to citizens of State A is that of doing business in State B on terms of substantial equality with the citizens of that State.' " After reviewing our precedents, we explicitly held that the practice of law, like other occupations considered in those cases, is sufficiently basic to the national economy to be deemed a privilege protected by the Clause. The clear import of *Piper* is that the Clause is implicated whenever, as is the case here, a State does not permit qualified nonresidents to practice law within its borders on terms of substantial equality with its own residents.

Nothing in our precedents, moreover, supports the contention that the Privileges and Immunities Clause does not reach a State's discrimination against nonresidents when such discrimination does not result in their total exclusion from the State. In Ward v. Maryland, 12 Wall. 418 (1871), for example, the Court invalidated a statute under which residents paid an annual fee of $12 to $150 for a license to trade foreign goods, while nonresidents were required to pay $300. Similarly, in *Toomer,* supra, the Court held that nonresident fishermen could not be required to pay a license fee one hundred times the fee charged to residents. In Hicklin v. Orbeck, 437 U.S. 518 (1978), the Court invalidated a statute requiring that residents be hired in preference to nonresidents for all positions related to the development of the State's oil and gas resources. Indeed, as the Court of Appeals correctly noted, the New Hampshire rule struck down in *Piper* did not result in the total exclusion of nonresidents from the practice of law in that State. [See *Piper* at n.2.]

Further, we find appellants' second theory — that Virginia could constitutionally require that all applicants to its bar take and pass an examination — quite irrelevant to the question whether the Clause is applicable in the circumstances of this case. A State's abstract authority to require from resident and nonresident alike that which it has chosen to demand from the nonresident alone has never been held to shield the discriminatory distinction from the reach of the Privileges and Immunities Clause. Thus, the applicability of the Clause to the present case no more turns on the legality *vel non* of an examination requirement than it turned on the inherent reasonableness of the fees charged to nonresidents in *Toomer* and *Ward.* The issue instead is whether the State has burdened the right to practice law, a privilege protected by the Privileges

and Immunities Clause, by discriminating among otherwise equally qualified applicants solely on the basis of citizenship or residency. We conclude it has.

B

Our conclusion that the residence requirement burdens a privilege
protected by the Privileges and Immunities Clause does not conclude the
matter, of course; for we repeatedly have recognized that the Clause, like
other constitutional provisions, is not an absolute. The Clause does not
preclude disparity in treatment where substantial reasons exist for the
discrimination and the degree of discrimination bears a close relation to
such reasons. In deciding whether the degree of discrimination bears a
sufficiently close relation to the reasons proffered by the State, the Court
has considered whether, within the full panoply of legislative choices otherwise available to the State, there exist alternative means of furthering
the State's purpose without implicating constitutional concerns.

Appellants offer two principal justifications for the Rule's requirement that applicants seeking admission on motion reside within the
Commonwealth of Virginia. First, they contend that the residence requirement assures, in tandem with the full-time practice requirement,
that attorneys admitted on motion will have the same commitment to service and familiarity with Virginia law that is possessed by applicants securing admission upon examination. Attorneys admitted on motion,
appellants argue, have "no personal investment" in the jurisdiction; consequently, they "are entitled to no presumption that they will willingly
and actively participate in bar activities and obligations, or fulfill their
public service responsibilities to the State's client community." Second,
appellants argue that the residency requirement facilitates enforcement
of the full-time practice requirement of Rule 1A:1. We find each of these
justifications insufficient to meet the State's burden of showing that the
discrimination is warranted by a substantial State objective and closely
drawn to its achievement.

We acknowledge that a bar examination is one method of assuring
that the admitted attorney has a stake in her professional licensure and a
concomitant interest in the integrity and standards of the bar. A bar examination, as we know judicially and from our own experience, is not a
casual or lighthearted exercise. The question, however, is whether lawyers who are admitted in other States and seek admission in Virginia are
less likely to respect the bar and further its interests solely because they
are nonresidents. We cannot say this is the case. While *Piper* relied on an
examination requirement as an indicium of the nonresident's commitment to the bar and to the State's legal profession, it does not follow that
when the State waives the examination it may make a distinction between
residents and nonresidents.

Friedman's case proves the point. She earns her living working as an attorney in Virginia, and it is of scant relevance that her residence is located in the neighboring State of Maryland. It is indisputable that she has a substantial stake in the practice of law in Virginia. Indeed, despite appellants' suggestion at oral argument that Friedman's case is "atypical," the same will likely be true of all nonresident attorneys who are admitted on motion to the Virginia bar, in light of the State's requirement that attorneys so admitted show their intention to maintain an office and a regular practice in the State. This requirement goes a long way toward ensuring that such attorneys will have an interest in the practice of law in Virginia that is at least comparable to the interest we ascribed in *Piper* to applicants admitted upon examination. Accordingly, we see no reason to assume that nonresident attorneys who, like Friedman, seek admission to the Virginia bar on motion will lack adequate incentives to remain abreast of changes in the law or to fulfill their civic duties.

Further, to the extent that the State is justifiably concerned with ensuring that its attorneys keep abreast of legal developments, it can protect these interests through other equally or more effective means that do not themselves infringe constitutional protections. While this Court is not well-positioned to dictate specific legislative choices to the State, it is sufficient to note that such alternatives exist and that the State, in the exercise of its legislative prerogatives, is free to implement them. The Supreme Court of Virginia could, for example, require mandatory attendance at periodic continuing legal education courses. The same is true with respect to the State's interest that the nonresident bar member does her share of volunteer and pro bono work. A "nonresident bar member, like the resident member, could be required to represent indigents and perhaps to participate in formal legal-aid work."

We also reject appellants' attempt to justify the residency restriction as a necessary aid to the enforcement of the full-time practice requirement of Rule 1A:1. Virginia already requires, pursuant to the full-time practice restriction of Rule 1A:1, that attorneys admitted on motion maintain an office for the practice of law in Virginia. As the Court of Appeals noted, the requirement that applicants maintain an office in Virginia facilitates compliance with the full-time practice requirement in nearly the identical manner that the residency restriction does, rendering the latter restriction largely redundant. The office requirement furnishes an alternative to the residency requirement that is not only less restrictive, but also is fully adequate to protect whatever interest the State might have in the full-time practice restriction. . . .

CHIEF JUSTICE REHNQUIST, with whom JUSTICE SCALIA joins, dissenting. . . .

I think the effect of today's decision is unfortunate even apart from what I believe is its mistaken view of the Privileges and Immunities Clause. Virginia's rule allowing admission on motion is an ameliorative provision, recognizing the fact that previous practice in another State may qualify a new resident of Virginia to practice there without the necessity of taking another bar examination. The Court's ruling penalizes Virginia, which has at least gone part way towards accommodating the present mobility of our population, but of course leaves untouched the rules of those States which allow no reciprocal admission on motion.* Virginia may of course retain the privilege of admission on motion without enforcing a residency requirement even after today's decision, but it might also decide to eliminate admission on motion altogether.

After *Piper, Frazier,* and *Friedman,* What Can a State Do to Discourage Out-of-State Lawyers?

By now you may be wondering whether the effort to make life harder for out-of-state lawyers is motivated by considerations of quality or money. The Supreme Court's decisions in this area echo its multiple rejections of rules limiting legal advertising and solicitation (see Chapter 16). As with those cases, opponents of easier admission standards invoke the theme that law is a profession, not a business, thereby justifying greater state controls, at least over licensure matters. It seems that within both the Court and the profession, Justices and lawyers are operating from markedly different perspectives about what it means to be a lawyer.

Putting aside the issue of motivation, what restraints may a state continue to impose? Certainly no case has required (or is likely to require) a state to do away with its bar examination for attorneys admitted elsewhere. As the *Friedman* dissent emphasizes, 28 states did not permit reciprocal admission on motion.

Piper won because she had passed the New Hampshire bar examination. The Court did not rely on her "possible job" there. Friedman won because her full-time job in Virginia entitled her to the same reciprocity as resident Virginia lawyers with full-time Virginia jobs. A third permutation is revealed in Goldfarb v. Supreme Court of Virginia, 766 F.2d 859 (4th Cir.), cert. denied, 474 U.S. 1986 (1985), decided before *Friedman.* Whereas Friedman lived in Maryland and worked in Virginia, Goldfarb lived in Virginia and practiced law in Washington, D.C. In *Goldfarb,* the Fourth Circuit upheld the work requirement as a condition

---

* At present, 28 states do not allow reciprocal admission on motion: Alabama, Arizona, Arkansas, California, Delaware, Florida, Georgia, Hawaii, Idaho, Kansas, Louisiana, Maine, Maryland, Massachusetts, Mississippi, Montana, Nevada, North Carolina, North Dakota, New Hampshire, New Jersey, New Mexico, Oregon, Rhode Island, South Carolina, South Dakota, Utah, and Washington.

of reciprocal admission when applied to a Virginia resident. Does this decision survive *Friedman?*

Do We Need Another System of Bar Admission?

One group notably disadvantaged by localized admission are lawyers whose clients are multistate companies. Especially disadvantaged are house counsel for such companies. These lawyers have a strong interest in being able to represent their clients in many states and, not surprisingly, they are not eager to take multiple bar examinations. If their representation is in court, the lawyers can at least seek admission pro hac vice, although success in that effort is unpredictable and often requires the added expense of local counsel (see page 570 infra). No equivalent to pro hac vice admission exists for out-of-court work. Lawyers who give legal advice in a jurisdiction in which they are not admitted may be guilty of unauthorized law practice (see page 597 infra). It should come as no surprise that organizations like the American Corporate Counsel Association have urged easier admission without examination.

One solution is a national bar examination. You take one nationally administered test once and (assuming you pass) you qualify for admission everywhere, subject only to each state's character inquiry. A variation would allow each state to set its own passing score on the test.

A second possibility is to create two tiers of bar admission: regular and limited. Lawyers with limited admission might be called "multistate practitioners." They could perform certain tasks especially needed by national clients, such as negotiation, drafting, and advice on federal law. They would not be allowed to perform services such as transfer of real property where a special knowledge of local law is critical. (If we're being cynical, we might identify the excluded services as those in which local practitioners make most of their money.)

What do you think of these alternatives? Do the Supreme Court's opinions provide the constitutional leverage to achieve (if not compel) them? Do you think state legislatures are likely to be receptive to national bar admissions or to the status of multistate practitioner? If not, is it because of concern over quality or to protect the local bar? If protectionism is influential, has Justice Rehnquist's *Piper* dissent convinced you that that is not such a bad thing?

The idea of "multistate practitioner" admissions finds support in separate admissions systems for lawyers from other nations. For example, New York admits foreign lawyers, without examination, as "legal consultants," to give legal advice on the law of the jurisdiction in which they are admitted. A licensed legal consultant is subject to the same disciplinary authority as a lawyer. See Judiciary Law §53(6); 22 N.Y.C.R.R. §§521.1 et seq.

3. Education and Examination

If there is one institution that has resisted all litigation efforts to attack it, it is the bar examination. It is doubtful that anyone seriously believes that bar examinations are a perfect or infallible way to test knowledge or ability to practice law. Even those charged with examining bar applicants probably recognize the rough justice the examination delivers. The trouble is, no one has advanced a persuasive substitute or been able to convince state courts and legislatures that no examination would be better. A few states will admit graduates of law schools in those states without examination. The practice has been upheld. Huffman v. Montana Supreme Court, 372 F. Supp. 1175 (D. Mont.), aff'd, 419 U.S. 955 (1974). The fact that these graduates appear to enter the profession and practice law as uneventfully as their much-examined colleagues would seem to provide a "control group" that could be used to study the predictive value of the bar examination. However, no matter how conclusively such a study might prove that the examination does not predict competence, it would be unlikely to lead to repeal of the examination or to persuade a court to declare it unconstitutional.

One racial group's generally doing better on a bar examination than another will not invalidate the examination, absent a showing of an intent to discriminate. Richardson v. McFadden, 563 F.2d 1130 (4th Cir. 1977), cert. denied, 435 U.S. 968 (1978); Tyler v. Vickery, 517 F.2d 1089 (5th Cir. 1975), cert. denied, 426 U.S. 940 (1976); Pettit v. Gingerich, 427 F. Supp. 282 (D. Md. 1977), aff'd, 582 F.2d 869 (4th Cir. 1978).

Bar examinations have been challenged on nearly every ground imaginable. Plaintiffs have charged that methods of grading were improper, that particular questions were improper, that the format of the examination was improper, that they had a constitutional right to a postexamination hearing, or that they had a constitutional right to see their examination paper and receive model answers. The annotation at 30 A.L.R. Fed. 934 (1976) collects the cases rejecting these and other varieties of challenge. See also Giannini v. Real, 911 F.2d 354 (9th Cir.), cert. denied, 111 S. Ct. 580 (1990). One court has held that an applicant has a constitutional right to see an examination paper and a model answer. In re Peterson, 459 P.2d 703 (Alaska 1969). Of course, a state may choose to allow applicants to review their examination papers and some do. See, e.g., 22 N.Y.C.R.R. §6006.8 (1990); New Mexico Rules Governing Bar Examiners, etc. 15-207 (1986). See also Sutton v. Lionel, 585 F.2d 400 (9th Cir. 1978).

Twenty-five states place a limit on the number of times an applicant may take the bar examination. These range from five times (Illinois, Texas, and Virginia) down to two times (Alabama, Iowa, and New Hampshire). ABA, Comprehensive Guide to Bar Admission Requirements 1991-1992 at 6-7. In some of these states, the limit may be waived with special permission. The Seventh Circuit upheld Indiana's four-time limit in Poats v. Givan, 651 F.2d 495 (7th Cir. 1981). It relied in part on a Tenth Circuit decision rejecting the plaintiff's claim that he had a right to take the Colorado bar examination a fourth time. Younger v. Colorado State Bd. of Law Examiners, 625 F.2d 372 (10th Cir. 1980). See also Jones v. Board of Commissioners of the Alabama State Bar, 737 F.2d 996 (11th Cir. 1984), which, over a dissent, rejected the minority applicants' challenge to an Alabama rule that limited to five the number of times a person could then sit for the bar examination. The *Jones* court also discussed the relationship between limitations on reexamination and the right to review one's paper, citing Lucero v. Ogden, 718 F.2d 355 (10th Cir. 1983), cert. denied, 465 U.S. 1035 (1984).

Rules requiring applicants for admission to be graduates of accredited law schools have also been upheld. Lombardi v. Tauro, 470 F.2d 798 (1st Cir. 1972), cert. denied, 412 U.S. 919 (1973); Cline v. Supreme Court of Georgia, 781 F.2d 1541 (11th Cir. 1986) (upholding such a rule despite a "grandparent" clause that exempted students who attended or were then attending nonaccredited schools).

In Hoover v. Ronwin, 466 U.S. 558 (1984), an unsuccessful bar applicant charged that the bar examiners had set the grading scale "with reference to the number of new attorneys [they] thought desirable, rather than with reference to some 'suitable' level of competence," in violation of the antitrust laws. In a 4-to-3 opinion, the Supreme Court did not reach this allegation, concluding instead that the passing score was set pursuant to state authorization and therefore "immune from antitrust liability under Parker v. Brown, 317 U.S. 341 (1943)." See page 124 infra for further discussion of the antitrust laws as a limit on rules that regulate lawyers.

4. Character Inquiries

In addition to testing for knowledge, jurisdictions also subject bar applicants to a test of what may loosely be called their "character." Character committees have tended to consider it within their domain to inspect at least four aspects of the lives of bar applicants. First, there is an inquiry into the applicant's mental health. Second, there is a check on the applicant's honesty and integrity. Third, there may be some effort to question an applicant about matters in his or her personal life. Finally, character committees have asked about an applicant's loyalty to the American system of government.

Criticism of the work of character committees has taken many forms. Some agree that one or more of the inquiries just listed are appropriate if their focus is sufficiently narrow. Others question the underlying premise of character inquiries, namely that it is possible, based on past conduct, to predict future behavior. See generally Deborah Rhode, Moral Character as a Professional Credential, 94 Yale L.J. 491 (1985). Is the only reason to conduct a character inquiry to determine how the applicant will perform as a lawyer? Or are there other purposes as well? For example, may the state validly exclude persons with "checkered pasts" on the ground that admission of these people would undermine confidence in the bar? Alternatively, might it be argued that when a state licenses a person to be a lawyer, it is implicitly representing that person to the public as a man or woman of honesty and integrity? If so, doesn't it then have a duty to assure itself that he or she fits that description?

Character tests have also been criticized on the ground that they invade the privacy rights of those tested and because, it is said, they were once used to exclude applicants who were "different from," or not members of the same religious or ethnic groups as, those who dominated the bar. See generally Jerold Auerbach, Unequal Justice 94-101 (1976).

The following two cases concern inquiries into a candidate's personal life and inquiries about a candidate's political beliefs. These cases represent a small sample of the varieties of conduct that a character committee might wish to ask about. The subsequent commentary reviews some other conduct that character committees may, or may not, find pertinent to professional performance. How close a "fit" must there be between a particular trait or event and likely performance as a lawyer before a court will permit exclusion?

CORD v. GIBB
219 Va. 1019, 254 S.E.2d 71 (1979)

PER CURIAM.

This is an appeal by Bonnie C. Cord (Cord or petitioner) from an order denying her the certificate of honest demeanor or good moral character required by Code §54-60 as a prerequisite to her right to take the bar examination conducted by the Virginia Board of Bar Examiners. While a number of issues were briefed and argued, we need decide only one of those issues: whether the trial court, on the record before it, erred in refusing to issue to Cord the requested certificate of honest demeanor or good moral character.

Cord, a 1975 law school graduate, was admitted by examination to practice law in the District of Columbia that same year. After engaging in private practice for a period of 13 months, Cord accepted a position as an Attorney-Advisor with an agency of the federal government. She was still employed in that capacity on the date she petitioned for the required certificate. At that time Cord was a member, in good standing, of The District of Columbia Bar, The Bar Association of the District of Columbia, and the American Bar Association.

The court below, as required by the second paragraph of Code §54-60, appointed three practicing attorneys to make an investigation of the moral character and fitness of Cord and to report their findings to the court.

In their written report, the attorneys disclosed that they had completed their investigation, which included a personal interview with Cord and contacts with her former employers. The report also related that petitioner, in her interview, stated that she had jointly purchased a home in a rural area of Warren County with Jeffrey Blue, and that she and Blue jointly resided there. Two of the investigating attorneys reported that they were of the opinion that from the standpoint of "moral character and fitness," Cord was qualified to take the bar examination. One of the investigating attorneys, believing that Cord's living arrangement affected her character and fitness, recommended that the required certificate not be issued.

After reviewing this report, the trial court convened an ore tenus hearing to allow Cord to present further evidence in support of her petition. At this hearing four of Cord's neighbors, all of whom were aware of her living arrangement, vouched for her good moral character, integrity and acceptance in the community. All these witnesses testified that Cord's living arrangement, while generally known in the community, was not a "matter of discussion within the community" and that her admission to practice law would not reflect adversely on the organized bar.

In addition to this testimony, the court received and considered a letter written by Cord's nearest neighbor attesting to her "high character" and acceptance in the community. The court also received and considered letters from three practicing attorneys in the District of Columbia with whom Cord had been associated while in private law practice. Each of these letters vouched for Cord's professional competence, integrity and good moral character in such terms as "she is of the highest moral character both professionally and personally" and "Bonnie, during the thirteen months that she was associated with this firm, always demonstrated the highest possible morals, both professionally and personally."

In its order the trial court, while finding that Cord met the statutory requirements for taking the bar examination in all other respects, refused to issue the certificate of honest demeanor or good moral character "on the grounds that the living arrangement of Applicant would lower the public's opinion of the Bar as a whole." In applying this standard in lieu of the statutory standard, the trial court erred.

Whether a person meets the "honest demeanor, or good moral character" standard of Code §54-60 is, of course, dependent upon the construction placed on those terms. The United States Supreme Court, recognizing that a state may require "high standards of qualification, such as good moral character or proficiency in its law, before it admits an applicant to the bar," has held that such qualifications, to pass constitutional muster, must have a "rational connection with the applicant's fitness or capacity to practice law." . . .

Except for Cord's statement that she and a male to whom she was not married jointly owned and resided in the same dwelling, the record is devoid of any evidence which would otherwise reflect unfavorably on Cord's professional competence, honest demeanor and good moral character. In fact, the evidence of a number of responsible citizens in the community where Cord resides establishes that she is of good character and honest demeanor. Likewise the letters received from Cord's former employers vouch for her good moral character, as well as her professional competence.

While Cord's living arrangement may be unorthodox and unacceptable to some segments of society, this conduct bears no rational connection to her fitness to practice law. It can not, therefore, serve to deny her the certificate required by Code §54-60.

Accordingly, we hold the trial court erred in refusing to issue to petitioner a certificate of honest demeanor or good moral character. The order below will be reversed and the case will be remanded with direction that the trial court forthwith issue the certificate requested by petitioner.

Reversed and remanded.

LAW STUDENTS CIVIL RIGHTS RESEARCH
COUNCIL v. WADMOND
401 U.S. 154 (1971)

JUSTICE STEWART delivered the opinion of the Court.

An applicant for admission to the Bar of New York must be a citizen of the United States* . . . and pass a written examination conducted by the State Board of Law Examiners. In addition, New York requires that the Appellate Division of the State Supreme Court in the judicial department where an applicant resides must "be satisfied that such person possesses the character and general fitness requisite for an attorney and counsellor-at-law." To carry out this provision, the New York Civil Practice Law and Rules require the appointment, in each of the four Judicial Departments into which the Supreme Court is divided, of a Committee or Committees on Character and Fitness. . . .

---

* This requirement is no longer constitutional. In re Griffiths, 413 U.S. 717 (1973). — ED.

This case involves a broad attack, primarily on First Amendment vagueness and overbreadth grounds, upon this system for screening applicants for admission to the New York Bar. The appellants, plaintiffs in the trial court, are organizations and individuals claiming to represent a class of law students and law graduates similarly situated, seeking or planning to seek admission to practice law in New York. They commenced two separate actions for declaratory and injunctive relief in the United States District Court for the Southern District of New York, naming as defendants two Committees on Character and Fitness and their members and two Appellate Divisions and their judges. The complaints attacked the statutes, rules, and screening procedures as invalid on their face or as applied in the First and Second Departments. A three-judge court was convened and consolidated the two suits.

In a thorough opinion, the court considered the appellants' claims and found certain items on the questionnaires as they then stood to be so vague, overbroad, and intrusive upon applicants' private lives as to be of doubtful constitutional validity. It granted the partial relief indicated by these findings, approving or further amending the revised questions submitted by the appellees to conform to its opinion. It upheld the statutes and rules as valid on their face and, with the exceptions noted, sustained the validity of New York's system. This appeal followed, and we noted probable jurisdiction.

We note at the outset that no person involved in this case has been refused admission to the New York Bar. Indeed, the appellants point to no case in which they claim any applicant has ever been unjustifiably denied permission to practice law in New York State under these or earlier statutes, rules, or procedures. The basic thrust of the appellants' attack is, rather, that New York's system by its very existence works a "chilling effect" upon the free exercise of the rights of speech and association of students who must anticipate having to meet its requirements.

I

The three-judge District Court, although divided on other questions, was unanimous in finding no constitutional infirmity in New York's statutory requirement that applicants for admission to its Bar must possess "the character and general fitness requisite for an attorney and counsellor-at-law." We have no difficulty in affirming this holding. Long usage in New York and elsewhere has given well-defined contours to this requirement, which the appellees have construed narrowly as encompassing no more than "dishonorable conduct relevant to the legal profession." The few reported cases in which bar admission has been denied on character grounds in New York all appear to have involved instances of misconduct clearly inconsistent with the standards of a lawyer's calling.

This Court itself requires of applicants for admission to practice before it that "their private and professional characters shall appear to be good." Every State, plus the District of Columbia, Puerto Rico, and the Virgin Islands, requires some similar qualification. . . .

II . . .

We do not understand the appellants to question the constitutionality of the actual oath an applicant must take before admission to practice. In any event, there can be no doubt of its validity. It merely requires an applicant to swear or affirm that he will "support the constitution of the United States" as well as that of the State of New York.

If all we had before us were the language of Rule 9406, which seems to require an applicant to furnish proof of his belief in the form of the Government of the United States and of his loyalty to the Government, this would be a different case. For the language of the Rule lends itself to a construction that could raise substantial constitutional questions, both as to the burden of proof permissible in such a context under the Due Process Clause of the Fourteenth Amendment, and as to the permissible scope of inquiry into an applicant's political beliefs under the First and Fourteenth Amendments. But this case comes before us in a significant and unusual posture: the appellees are the very state authorities entrusted with the definitive interpretation of the language of the Rule. We therefore accept their interpretation, however we might construe that language were it left for us to do so. If the appellees be regarded as state courts, we are of course bound by their construction. If they are viewed as state administrative agencies charged with enforcement and construction of the Rule, their view is at least entitled to "respectful consideration," and we see no reason not to accept their interpretation in this case.

The appellees have made it abundantly clear that their construction of the Rule is both extremely narrow and fully cognizant of protected constitutional freedoms. There are three key elements to this construction. First, the Rule places upon applicants no burden of proof. Second, "the form of the government of the United States" and the "government" refer solely to the Constitution, which is all that the oath mentions. Third, "belief" and "loyalty" mean no more than willingness to take the constitutional oath and ability to do so in good faith.

Accepting this construction, we find no constitutional invalidity in Rule 9406. There is "no showing of an intent to penalize political beliefs." At the most, the Rule as authoritatively interpreted by the appellees performs only the function of ascertaining that an applicant is not one who "swears to an oath pro forma while declaring or manifesting his disagreement with or indifference to the oath." . . .

III

As this case comes to us from the three-judge panel, the questionnaire applicants are asked to complete contains only two numbered questions reflecting the disputed provision of Rule 9406.[18] They are as follows:

26. (a) Have you ever organized or helped to organize or become a member of any organization or group of persons which, during the period of your membership or association, you knew was advocating or teaching that the government of the United States or any state or any political subdivision thereof should be overthrown or overturned by force, violence or any unlawful means? If your answer is in the affirmative, state the facts below.

(b) If your answer to (a) is in the affirmative, did you, during the period of such membership or association, have the specific intent to further the aims of such organization or group of persons to overthrow or overturn the government of the United States or any state or any political subdivision thereof by force, violence or any unlawful means?

27. (a) Is there any reason why you cannot take and subscribe to an oath or affirmation that you will support the constitutions of the United States and of the State of New York? If there is, please explain.

(b) Can you conscientiously, and do you, affirm that you are, without any mental reservation, loyal to and ready to support the Constitution of the United States?

In dealing with these questions, we emphasize again that there has been no showing that any applicant for admission to the New York Bar has been denied admission either because of his answers to these or any similar questions, or because of his refusal to answer them. Necessarily, therefore, we must consider the validity of the questions only on their face, in light of Rule 9406 as construed by the agencies entrusted with its administration.

Question 26 is precisely tailored to conform to the relevant decisions of this Court. Our cases establish that inquiry into associations of the kind

---

18. The District Court ordered the elimination or revision of the following questions contained in the questionnaires at the time this litigation was commenced:

26. Have you ever organized or helped to organize or become a member of or participated in any way whatsoever in the activities of any organization or group of persons which teaches (or taught) or advocates (or advocated) that the Government of the United States or any State or any political subdivision thereof should be overthrown or overturned by force, violence or any unlawful means? If your answer is in the affirmative, state the facts below.

27(a). Do you believe in the principles underlying the form of government of the United States of America?

31. Is there any incident in your life not called for by the foregoing questions which has any favorable or detrimental bearing on your character or fitness? If the answer is "Yes" state the facts. [In the Second Department the words "favorable or" did not appear.]

None of the above questions is in issue here.

referred to is permissible under the limitations carefully observed here. We have held that knowing membership in an organization advocating the overthrow of the Government by force or violence, on the part of one sharing the specific intent to further the organization's illegal goals, may be made criminally punishable. It is also well settled that Bar examiners may ask about Communist affiliations as a preliminary to further inquiry into the nature of the association and may exclude an applicant for refusal to answer. Surely a State is constitutionally entitled to make such an inquiry of an applicant for admission to a profession dedicated to the peaceful and reasoned settlement of disputes between men, and between a man and his government. The very Constitution that the appellants invoke stands as a living embodiment of that ideal.

As to Question 27, there can hardly be doubt of its constitutional validity in light of our earlier discussion of Rule 9406 and the appellees' construction of that Rule. The question is simply supportive of the appellees' task of ascertaining the good faith with which an applicant can take the constitutional oath. Indeed, the "without any mental reservation" language of part (b) is the same phrase that appears in the oath required of all federal uniformed and civil service personnel. New York's question, however, is less demanding than the federal oath. Taking the oath is a requisite for federal employment, but there is no indication that a New York Bar applicant would not be given the opportunity to explain any "mental reservation" and still gain admission to the Bar.

IV

Finally, there emerges from the appellants' briefs and oral argument a more fundamental claim than any to which we have thus far adverted. They suggest that, whatever the facial validity of the various details of a screening system such as New York's, there inheres in such a system so constant a threat to applicants that constitutional deprivations will be inevitable. The implication of this argument is that no screening would be constitutionally permissible beyond academic examination and extremely minimal checking for serious, concrete character deficiencies. The principal means of policing the Bar would then be the deterrent and punitive effects of such post-admission sanctions as contempt, disbarment, malpractice suits, and criminal prosecutions.

Such an approach might be wise policy, but decisions based on policy alone are not for us to make. We have before us a State whose agents have evidently been scrupulous in the use of the powers that the appellants attack, and who have shown every willingness to keep their investigations within constitutionally permissible limits. We are not persuaded that careful administration of such a system as New York's need result in chilling effects upon the exercise of constitutional freedoms. Consequently, the choice between systems like New York's and approaches like that urged by the appellants rests with the legislatures and other policy-making bodies of the individual States. New York has made its choice. To disturb it would be beyond the power of this Court.

The judgment is affirmed.

JUSTICE BLACK, with whom JUSTICE DOUGLAS joins, dissenting.

Of course I agree that a State may require that applicants and members of the Bar possess the good "character and general fitness requisite for an attorney." But it must be remembered that the right of a lawyer or Bar applicant to practice his profession is often more valuable to him than his home, however expensive that home may be. Therefore I think that when a State seeks to deny an applicant admission or to disbar a lawyer, it must proceed according to the most exacting demands of due process of law. This must mean at least that the right of a lawyer or Bar applicant to practice cannot be left to the mercies of his prospective or present competitors. When it seeks to deprive a person of the right to practice law, a State must accord him the same rights as when it seeks to deprive him of any other property. Perhaps almost anyone would be stunned if a State sought to take away a man's house because he failed to prove his loyalty or refused to answer questions about his political beliefs. But it seems to me that New York is attempting to deprive people of the right to practice law for precisely these reasons, and the Court is approving its actions.

Here the Court upholds a New York law which requires that a Bar applicant not be admitted "unless he shall furnish satisfactory proof" that he "believes in the form of the government of the United States and is loyal to such government." It also approves certain questions about political associations and beliefs which New York requires all applicants to answer. From these holdings I dissent.

In my view, the First Amendment absolutely prohibits a State from penalizing a man because of his beliefs. Hence a State cannot require that an applicant's belief in our form of government be established before he can become a lawyer. . . .

Assuming that a New York statute could constitutionally delegate to a committee of lawyers the power to interrogate applicants for the Bar, the specific questions asked in this case are flatly inconsistent with the First Amendment. . . .

I do not think that a State can, consistently with the First Amendment, exclude an applicant because he has belonged to organizations that advocate violent overthrow of the Government, even if his membership was "knowing" and he shared the organization's aims. . . .

Question 27(b) asks: "Can you conscientiously, and do you, affirm that you are, without any mental reservation, loyal to and ready to support the Constitution of the United States?" In my view, this question also invades areas of belief protected by the First Amendment. Here the State seeks to probe an applicant's state of mind to ascertain whether he is "without any mental reservation, loyal to . . . the Constitution." But asking about an applicant's mental attitude toward the Constitution simply probes his beliefs, and these are not the business of the State. For these reasons, I would reverse the judgment of the court below. . . .

JUSTICE MARSHALL, whom JUSTICE BRENNAN joins, dissenting.

This litigation began with a comprehensive constitutional attack by appellants on longstanding state rules and practices for screening applicants for admission to the New York Bar. During the course of the litigation some of these practices were changed by appellees; others were found wanting by the three-judge court below, and changed as a result of that court's opinion and its final order. Now we face the residuum of the appellants' original challenge, and the Court today ratifies everything left standing by the court below. I dissent from that holding because I believe that appellants' basic First Amendment complaint, transcending the particulars of the attack, retains its validity. The underlying complaint, strenuously and consistently urged, is that New York's screening system focuses impermissibly on the political activities and viewpoints of Bar applicants, that the scheme thereby operates to inhibit the exercise of protected expressive and associational freedoms by law students and others, and that this chilling effect is not justified as the necessary impact of a system designed to winnow out those applicants demonstrably unfit to practice law. . . .

QUESTION

12.1   Ought a state bar character committee be able to ask an applicant to list the·name of every organization to which the applicant has belonged since age 18?

Frequently Cited Grounds for Delaying or Denying Admission to the Bar

Criminal Conduct.   Criminal conduct has traditionally served to exclude applicants to the bar, whether or not it has resulted in a conviction. See, for example, In re Goldman, 206 So. 2d 643 (Fla. 1968). Even an acquittal will not prevent the conduct that was the subject of the charge from being weighed in the admission process. The burden of proof in a criminal case is on the state beyond a reasonable doubt, whereas the burden of showing good moral character may be on the applicant. See, for example, Siegel v. Committee of Bar Examiners, 10 Cal. 3d 156, 514 P.2d 967, 110 Cal. Rptr. 15 (1973).

In In re Fine, 303 Or. 314, 736 P.2d 183 (1987), the court denied admission to a man who, while in college and as part of a political protest, set a bomb that accidentally killed someone. The man was then a fugitive for five and half years. In In re DeBartolo, 111 Ill. 2d 1, 488 N.E.2d 947 (1986), an applicant was not admitted partially because he had misrepresented himself as a police officer and also because he had received more than 200 parking tickets in a brief time. Seide v. California State Bar, 49 Cal. 3d 933, 782 P.2d 602, 264 Cal. Rptr. 361 (1989), refused admission to an applicant who had five arrests for drug-related offenses during and after law school and who had also pled guilty to distribution of cocaine.

According to ABA Comprehensive Guide to Bar Admission Requirements 1991-1992, only 12 jurisdictions make a felony conviction an *automatic* disqualification for admission to the bar. Courts elsewhere will examine the nature of the crime, how long ago it occurred, and the applicant's conduct thereafter. In In re Manville, 538 A.2d 1128 (D.C. Ct. App. 1988), the court admitted three applicants who had been convicted, respectively, of manslaughter, attempted armed robbery, and the sale of narcotics. See also In re A. T., 286 Md. 507, 408 A.2d 1023 (1979); In re Davis, 38 Ohio St. 2d 273, 313 N.E.2d 363 (1974).

Lack of Candor in the Application Process. This can be deadly. Preapplication conduct that would not result in exclusion can lead to exclusion if the bar applicant consciously omits it from the application. See In re Greenberg, 126 Ariz. 290, 614 P.2d 832 (1980); In re Farris, 87 Nev. 508, 489 P.2d 1156 (1971). If falsity on an application is discovered after admission, the lawyer can be suspended or disbarred. Carter v. Charos, 536 A.2d 527 (R.I. 1988). The fact that a criminal conviction has been expunged is not generally a ground for omitting it from the application without express permission to do so. In re Watson, 31 Ohio St. 3d 220, 509 N.E.2d 1240 (1987).

Dishonesty or Lack of Integrity in Academic Settings. Cheating on LSAT, bar, or law school examinations can result in delay or denial of admission. In re Knight, 232 Ga. 721, 208 S.E.2d 820 (1974); In re Application of Corrigan, 47 Ohio St. 3d 32, 546 N.E.2d 1315 (1989) (applicant may never reapply); In re Capace, 110 R.I. 254, 291 A.2d 632 (1972).

Mental Health. In In re Ronwin, 113 Ariz. 357, 555 P.2d 315, 316 (1976), cert. denied, 430 U.S. 907 (1977), the court denied admission to an applicant after a special committee concluded that the applicant suffered from a "personality disorder" as a result of which he "would probably be unable to properly represent and serve the interests of his clients [and] will probably . . . bring and prosecute groundless claims and subject clients, parties, the Court and adversary counsel to groundless charges of misconduct and impropriety." Compare In re Schaengold, 83 Nev. 65, 422 P.2d 686 (1967) (rejecting recommendation that admission be denied because of applicant's "long and sustained history of mental illness" and stressing that "[p]sychiatry is far from being an exact science").

Financial Probity.   Admission committees and courts inquire about financial irregularities in the applicant's life. Dishonesty or abuse of trust in business or personal financial matters may predict lack of probity as a lawyer. In In re Gahan, 279 N.W.2d 826 (Minn. 1979), the court denied admission to a lawyer from another jurisdiction who had declared bankruptcy while he still owed some $14,000 in student loans. The court acknowledged that the Supremacy Clause prevented if from denying admission *because* Gahan had declared bankruptcy. It rested its decision on the applicant's failure to satisfy his financial obligations during the prebankruptcy period, when he was employed and able to do so. Matter of Anonymous, 74 N.Y.2d 938, 549 N.E.2d 472, 550 N.Y.S.2d 270 (1989), held that an application may be rejected because of an inability to handle personal finances as long as bankruptcy is not the sole reason for the rejection. Kwasnik v. California State Bar, 50 Cal. 3d 1061, 791 P.2d 319, 269 Cal. Rptr. 749 (1990), admitted an applicant who had declared bankruptcy 16 years earlier to escape a wrongful death judgment where the applicant had no other blemish in his record.

Applicant's Private Life.   In addition to Cord v. Gibb (page 554 supra), consider the following cases, whose focus was gay lawyers.

Kimball, a Florida attorney, had been arrested for "committing an indecent and lewd act in a public place." He was released on bail, which he forfeited. He was then disbarred by the court, State ex rel. Florida Bar v. Kimball, 96 So. 2d 825 (Fla. 1957), after the referee found that he was committing an act of sodomy when apprehended by the police. Sixteen years later, Kimball applied for admission to the New York Bar. In In re Kimball, 33 N.Y.2d 586, 301 N.E.2d 436, 347 N.Y.S.2d 453 (1973), the court reversed an appellate court decision denying admission. The court said, "[w]hile appellant's status and past conduct may be now and has been in the past violative of accepted norms, they are not controlling, albeit relevant, in assessing character bearing on the right to practice." The majority found Kimball "to be of good character and qualified" and affirmed the Character Committee's report, which stated, according to the lower court opinion, that "the applicant possesses the requisite character and fitness for an attorney at law, 'notwithstanding the admission of the applicant to being a homosexual and having engaged in homosexual acts.' "

At the time of Kimball's arrest, sodomy was a felony in both New York and Florida. At the time of application, "consensual sodomy [was] a proscribed act of 'deviate sexual intercourse. ' " The dissenter wrote that "so long as this statute is on our books, it is the law . . . to be observed by all and the court below would have the right to consider violations of the statute as a factor which could militate against the present application. [T]he Appellate Division has full and complete authority to deny admission . . . to one who is an avowed admitted persistent violator of any criminal statute." Id. at 437.

Despite Kimball's disbarment in Florida, that state seems to have subsequently adopted a more liberal view. In In re Florida Board of Bar Examiners, 358 So. 2d 7, 8-10 (Fla. 1978), the court said that "[g]overnmental regulation in the area of private morality is generally considered anachronistic in the absence of a clear and convincing showing there is a substantial connection between the private act regulated and public interests and welfare." Although "[a] [s]tate can require high standards of qualification . . . any qualification must have a rational connection with the applicant's fitness or capacity to practice law." (Emphasis omitted.) The applicant had admitted his homosexual preference. The court emphasized that "[h]e was not questioned about what sexual acts he may have engaged in" and that "no evidence was presented indicating that [he had] acted or plan[ned] to act on his sexual preference." It strictly limited its holding "to situations in which the applicant's sexual orientation or preference is at issue" and held that it could not "believe that the candidate's mere preference for homosexuality threatens . . . societal exigencies," such as lay confidence in the attorney or administration of justice. The court distinguished a preference for homosexuality from the commission of "certain illegal acts in the past," for which an attorney might "represent a future peril to society which would justify denying the applicant admission." Is the court being naive or just politic?

In In re N.R.S., 403 So. 2d 1315, 1317 (Fla. 1981), the Florida Supreme Court went further. The applicant (previously admitted in New York) said he had no intention of engaging in homosexual acts. But he also argued that the statute criminalizing such conduct was unconstitutional. The state supreme court did not reach this issue. It ruled that the Board of Bar Examiners could only make "inquiries which bear a rational relationship to an applicant's fitness to practice law. Private noncommercial sex acts between consenting adults are not relevant to prove fitness to practice law. This might not be true of commercial or nonconsensual sex or sex involving minors." The board was permitted to ask the petitioner to respond to further questions only if "in good faith, it finds a need to assure itself that the petitioner's sexual conduct is other than noncommercial, private, and between consenting adults." The two dissenters pointed out that homosexual conduct was a crime. They would have allowed the board to reject admission if the petitioner were guilty of it.

QUESTIONS

12.2 Should a bar applicant be denied admission under the following circumstances?

    a. The applicant offered two out-of-state law students $5,000 if they would take the bar examination in his name and pass.

    b. The applicant had a history of drunk driving and assaults on his wife and son.

    c. The applicant had held himself out as an attorney when he was not an attorney.

    d. The applicant had failed to register for the draft as required by law.

    e. During law school, the applicant had purchased stock without adequate funds to pay for it.

    f. While the applicant was president of a mortgage company, she expanded the company beyond its financial capabilities, as a result of which the company went bankrupt, causing financial loss to hundreds of individuals.

    g. Prior to law school, the applicant had knowingly entered into a bigamous marriage.

12.3 Louise Burke graduates from the University of Georgia Law School, takes and passes the bar examination, and applies for admission. Her application is denied for the following alternate reasons. What are the arguments that her application should or should not (may or may not) be denied or delayed?

    a. On her application she admits that she is living in a homosexual relationship with another woman. This is a crime in Georgia.

    b. While in college, she was arrested in a sit-in at the school placement office arising out of a protest against on-campus recruitment by employers who refused to promise not to discriminate against homosexuals.

    c. After graduating from college and before going to law school, she applied for a teaching job and wrote on her application that she lived alone although she really lived with a woman roommate.

    d. On her application to the bar, she falsely states that she lives alone.

Disbarment for Preadmission Conduct

Sometimes conduct that would have resulted in delay or denial of admission is discovered after the applicant has been admitted to practice. Courts have acted on such discoveries. In Stratmore v. State Bar of California, 14 Cal. 3d 887, 538 P.2d 229, 230-231, 123 Cal. Rptr. 101 (1975), the court accepted proof that "demonstrated . . . that [Stratmore] obtained money from [11] New York law firms by fraudulent means for . . . personal gain" one year before he was admitted to practice. Under the state statute, the court had power only to "suspend or disbar an attorney for specified causes 'arising after his admission to practice.' " The court, however, held that "a statute cannot limit the inherent power of the court [from also] disbar[ring] him for any additional reason which may satisfy the court he is no longer fit to be one of its officers. . . . Since under our inherent power [to protect "the public's right to representation by attorneys who are worthy of trust"] we may discipline an attorney for conduct 'either in or out of [the] profession' . . . it is irrelevant that Stratmore's misconduct preceded his admission to practice." Stratmore was suspended for nine months.

In Kentucky Bar Assn. v. Signer, 533 S.W.2d 534 (Ky. 1976), the court permanently disbarred a Kentucky attorney for "business dealings" transacted while he was an attorney in Ohio, one year before being admitted to the Kentucky Bar. If the misconduct had come to the attention of the bar association at the time of admission, "consideration of it as a basis for [later] disciplinary action" would have been "precluded" by successful admission. But where the information if known "would have required . . . rejection" and the bar association had not been aware, "public protection against a potential vulture justifies disbarment."

One court has held that since "discipline is properly imposed for acts involving moral turpitude whether or not they relate to [an attorney's] conduct . . . in his professional capacity," "the fact that the act may have been committed prior to any attorney's admission . . . would appear to be irrelevant." In re Bogart, 9 Cal. 3d 743, 511 P.2d 1167, 1171, 108 Cal. Rptr. 815 (1973), appeal dismissed.

In In re Weiner, 31 A.D.2d 603, 297 N.Y.S.2d 617 (2d Dept. 1968), an intermediate appellate court disbarred an attorney for conduct prior to and after admission to the bar. The court found that the respondent "unlawfully practiced law for three months prior to his admission" by acting as an attorney under the name of a friend who was a lawyer and by using that name to endorse checks settling the actions he commenced. For additional cases see Annot., 92 A.L.R.3d 807 (1979).

Procedures Regarding Character Inquiry

Applicants to the bar who are denied admission because of their lack of a good moral character are entitled to a hearing at which they can present evidence in their own behalf and confront the evidence against them. Willner v. Committee on Character & Fitness, 373 U.S. 96 (1963). The hearing may be held before either an administrative body or a reviewing court. Id. If an administrative body makes the determination to exclude the applicant, the scope of court review varies. In In re Willis, 288 N.C. 1, 215 S.E.2d 771, the court said that it would not reverse a determination of its board of law examiners if there was substantial evidence in the record supporting the conclusion. Other courts, however, have stressed that the bar examiners' findings are not controlling, though they may be entitled to great weight with the burden on the applicant to show that the examiners' determination was erroneous. Bernstein v. Committee of Bar Examiners, 69 Cal. 2d 90, 443 P.2d 570, 70 Cal. Rptr. 106 (1968). *Bernstein* also held that reasonable doubts should be resolved in favor of the applicant. The applicant is generally viewed as bearing the burden of showing the presence of good moral character. Siegel v. Committee of Bar Examiners, 10 Cal. 3d 156, 514 P.2d 967, 110 Cal. Rptr. 15 (1973).

5. Experiential Requirements

Former Chief Justice Burger gave a speech at Fordham University Law School in 1973 in which he lamented the poor work of trial counsel in American courts. Warren Burger, The Special Skills of Advocacy: Are Specialized Training and Certification of Advocates Essential to Our System of Justice?, 42 Fordham L. Rev. 227 (1973). A committee thereafter appointed by the Chief Justice surveyed federal trial judges and announced that 41 percent of them would characterize the problem of inadequate advocacy as "severe." The committee's report is reprinted at 79 F.R.D. 187 (1978). Various federal courts then weighed the possibility of imposing experiential requirements on lawyers who wished to try or argue cases before them. Most courts adopted no rule. The Second Circuit adopted a rule that requires lawyers to demonstrate experience in appellate argument as a condition of admission. §46, Rules, U.S. Court of Appeals for the Second Circuit. Of greater moment, perhaps, were rules like the one adopted in the Northern District of Illinois, which demanded certain "trial experience" before an unassisted lawyer could try a criminal case or take testimony in a civil matter. The rule did not apply to other legal services, including making and arguing motions or filing cases.

In Brown v. McGarr, 774 F.2d 777 (7th Cir. 1985), these requirements were upheld in a challenge brought by a lawyer who was a member of the district court's bar but lacked the required trial experience. The court rejected arguments that the rule was implemented without proper notice, that the court lacked authority to adopt the rule, and that the rule effectively "disbarred" the plaintiff without procedural safeguards.

6. Admission in a Federal System

The fact that we have both federal and state court systems raises some interesting problems. One of these deals with discipline and is discussed at page 688 infra. Another concerns admission. As a general rule, federal courts admit applicants who are members of the bar of the highest court of the state in which that federal court is located. Sometimes the federal court may have rules permitting the admission of lawyers not members of the local state bar but who, for example, are employees of the federal government, such as assistant United States Attorneys working in the particular federal district. Admission in these circumstances may last only as long as the lawyer continues in the job. Federal courts are also likely to have their own pro hac vice admission procedures. Federal courts reserve the right to conduct character inquiries and in rare cases decline to admit a lawyer who has been admitted in the state in which the federal court sits. See In re G.L.S., 745 F.2d 856 (4th Cir. 1984).

Should or must a federal court admit an attorney to its bar even if he or she is not a member of the bar of the state in which the federal court sits? What if the attorney is interested only in matters within the exclusive jurisdiction of the federal court and there is no question about the attorney's competence to handle such matters?

In re Roberts, 682 F.2d 105, 108 (3d Cir. 1982), was a challenge to a rule of the Federal District Court in New Jersey that limited membership in the court's bar to members of the New Jersey bar. The Third Circuit found the limitation rational. It wrote that

> tying district court admission to state bar membership tends to protect the interests of the public. For example, when the choice of either a federal or a state forum is available in a particular case, an attorney admitted only to the federal court may choose that forum solely for that reason, possibly disregarding the interests of his client. Moreover, issues of state law are often dispositive in federal tax cases, further supporting the application of the state bar requirement to lawyers specializing in federal taxation.

In Kennedy v. Bar Assn. of Montgomery County, 316 Md. 646, 561 A.2d 200, 208-211 (1989), a lawyer who was admitted in the District of Columbia and before the federal courts of Maryland, but not before the Maryland state courts, wished to open an office in the state without becoming a member of the state bar. He planned to limit his representation to clients with federal court matters. The court held that the state's interest in admission to its bar was to enable it to protect "the public from . . . unethical practitioners" as well as to ensure competence. Even if Kennedy limited himself to clients with federal court claims, he could not know at the outset whether the claims of clients he counseled would fall in that category. The court deemed it "practically impossible" to devise a system that would isolate those clients, but it permitted Kennedy to show how he "could first pinpoint clients whose specific matters actually required counsel before those courts where Kennedy is currently admitted to practice, and thereby could limit his legal representation in Maryland to those specific matters." See also Giannini v. Real, 911 F.2d 354 (9th Cir.), cert. denied, 111 S. Ct. 580 (1990) (upholding rule requiring applicants to the federal bar to be members of the local state bar).

Wouldn't it seem to follow from the reasoning of *Roberts* and *Kennedy* that a trial lawyer admitted to a state's bar should be required to become a member of the local federal bar as well?

B. TRANSIENT LAWYERS AND MULTIJURISDICTIONAL FIRMS: LOCAL INTERESTS CONFRONT A NATIONAL BAR

A client's legal problems do not always stop at a state border. Even when they do, the client may have good reason for seeking the aid of an out-of-state lawyer. Does a lawyer admitted in Oregon have a right to assist a client with legal problems in Nevada if the lawyer is not admitted to practice there? Whether or not the lawyer has that right, does the client have the right to the lawyer's assistance? There are other variables here. For example, will the lawyer perform services in connection with a litigation or simply give advice? In either case, does the litigation or the advice encompass federally protected rights of the client or only rights under the law of the state in which the lawyer is not admitted? Does this matter? If the lawyer is helping the client in connection with a litigation, is the litigation in federal or state court? Does this matter?

Remember, if an out-of-state lawyer serves a client in a jurisdiction in which he is not admitted, he may be guilty of the unauthorized practice of law (see page 597 infra). What does it mean to serve a client "in" a jurisdiction? Does the lawyer actually have to travel to the foreign jurisdiction and give advice there? Or is it a violation for a lawyer admitted in California to advise on Arizona law while present in California? What if a Colorado lawyer gives advice on Colorado law in Kansas? On federal law? What if the client is a Coloradan or a Texan? The problem is obvious. Can the lawyer's geographical location at the time of the advice be the sole test? Modern communication systems would make that look ridiculous, wouldn't they? What, then, should be the test? How can we talk about the authorized practice of law in a multijurisdictional licensing system if we don't know exactly what we want to, and constitutionally are able to, forbid? A further complication — or does it actually simplify things? — are the twin facts that the laws of all jurisdictions are easily accessible to lawyers anywhere and that a good deal of modern law is uniform (or nearly so) nationwide.

This is clearly an area in transition. Not all questions can be answered with certainty, but some can. We are witnessing a delicate balancing between proper, and perhaps sometimes improper, local interests on the one hand, and the reality of a national economy and national interests that need the services of lawyers nationwide. Recall the material on residency requirements (pages 536-551 supra), which in a different context also require a balance between local and national interests.

It can be argued that restrictive rules in this area are an example of economic protectionism for the local bar. Alternatively, is the interest in competence sufficient to justify broad rules of exclusion? Remember, by definition the out-of-state lawyer will not have passed the foreign jurisdiction's bar examination. He or she may be wholly unfamiliar with local court rules. A legal system in any particular geographical and political area has a life and style of its own. Local lawyers and judges have a real interest in assuring its smooth operation. All of these explanations argue in favor of powers of exclusion, but do they argue too much? Could lawyers in a particular county of a state cite them to justify excluding lawyers from other counties from practicing before the courts of their county?

Another state interest is in the probity of lawyers who practice within them. Licensed lawyers are subject to the control of the licensing jurisdiction, including its rules of ethics. What control can a jurisdiction exercise over a lawyer who renders legal advice within its borders — even on the law of her home state — but who does not belong to its bar? This quandry troubled the court in Kennedy v. Bar Assn. of Montgomery County, 316 Md. 646, 561 A.2d 200 (1989). In trying to understand the state interest here, compare medicine. The human body is the same in Iowa as it is in Virginia. Let's assume that Virginia's standards for licensing doctors are at least as stringent as Iowa's standards. What interest does Iowa have in regulating a Virginia doctor's treatment of an Iowan in Iowa?

1. Admissions Pro Hac Vice

Admission pro hac vice, or "for this turn," is a device by which a jurisdiction may admit an out-of-state lawyer for the purpose of participating in a particular trial without requiring that the lawyer pass the jurisdiction's bar examination or go through its character review process. Must a state allow pro hac vice admissions? May it deny them entirely?

LEIS v. FLYNT
439 U.S. 438 (1979)

PER CURIAM.

Petitioners, the judges of the Court of Common Pleas of Hamilton County, Ohio, and the Hamilton County prosecutor, seek relief from a decision of the United States Court of Appeals for the Sixth Circuit. The Court of Appeals upheld a Federal District court injunction that forbids further prosecution of respondents Larry Flynt and Hustler Magazine, Inc., until respondents Herald Fahringer and Paul Cambria are tendered a hearing on their applications to appear pro hac vice in the Court of Common Pleas on behalf of Flynt and Hustler Magazine. Petitioners contend that the asserted right of an out-of-state lawyer to appear pro hac vice in an Ohio court does not fall among those interests protected by the Due Process Clause of the Fourteenth Amendment. Because we agree with this contention, we grant the petition for certiorari and reverse the judgment of the Sixth Circuit.

Flynt and Hustler Magazine were indicted on February 8, 1977, for multiple violations of Ohio Rev. Code Ann. §2907.31 (1975), which prohibits the dissemination of harmful material to minors. At the arraignment on February 25, local counsel for Flynt and Hustler presented an entry of counsel form that listed Fahringer and Cambria as counsel for both defendants. Neither lawyer was admitted to practice law in Ohio. The form was the one used by members of the Ohio Bar, and it neither constituted an application for admission pro hac vice nor alerted the court that Fahringer and Cambria were not admitted to practice in Ohio. The judge presiding at the arraignment routinely endorsed the form but took no other action with respect to the two out-of-state lawyers.

The case was transferred as a matter of course to Judge Morrissey, who had before him another active indictment against Flynt and Hustler Magazine. Fahringer and Cambria made no application for admission pro hac vice to him or any other judge. At a pretrial conference on March 9 Judge Morrissey advised local counsel that neither out-of-state lawyer would be allowed to represent Flynt or Hustler Magazine. Fahringer and Cambria appeared in person before Judge Morrissey for the first time at a motions hearing on April 8, where they expressed their interest in representing the defendants. Judge Morrissey summarily dismissed the request. Respondents then commenced a mandamus action in the Ohio Supreme Court seeking to overturn the denial of admission. They also

filed an affidavit of bias and prejudice seeking to remove Judge Morrissey from the case. The Ohio court dismissed the mandamus action but
did remove Judge Morrissey, stating that while it found no evidence of
bias or prejudice, trial before a different judge would avoid even the appearance of impropriety. The new trial judge ruled that the Ohio
Supreme Court's dismissal of the mandamus action bound him to deny
Fahringer and Cambria permission to represent Flynt and Hustler Magazine, but he did allow both of them to work with in-state counsel in preparing the case.

Respondents next filed this suit in the United States District Court for
the Southern District of Ohio to enjoin further prosecution of the criminal case until the state trial court held a hearing on the contested pro hac
vice application. The court ruled that the lawyers' interest in representing Flynt and Hustler Magazine was a constitutionally protected property right which petitioners had infringed without according the lawyers
procedural due process. Further prosecution of Flynt and Hustler Magazine therefore was enjoined until petitioners tendered Fahringer and
Cambria the requested hearing. The Sixth Circuit affirmed, holding that
the lawyers could not be denied the privilege of appearing pro hac vice
"without a meaningful hearing, the application of a reasonably clear legal
standard and the statement of a rational basis for exclusion."

As this Court has observed on numerous occasions, the Constitution
does not create property interests. Rather it extends various procedural
safeguards to certain interests "that stem from an independent source
such as state law." The Court of Appeals evidently believed that an out-
of-state lawyer's interest in appearing pro hac vice in an Ohio court stems
from some such independent source. It cited no state-law authority for
this proposition, however, and indeed noted that "Ohio has no specific
standards regarding pro hac vice admissions. . . ." Rather the court referred to the prevalence of pro hac vice practice in American courts and
instances in our history where counsel appearing pro hac vice have rendered distinguished service. We do not question that the practice of
courts in most States is to allow an out-of-state lawyer the privilege of appearing upon motion, especially when he is associated with a member of
the local bar. In view of the high mobility of the bar, and also the trend
toward specialization, perhaps this is a practice to be encouraged. But it is
not a right granted either by statute or the Constitution. Since the found-
ing of the Republic, the licensing and regulation of lawyers has been left
exclusively to the States and the District of Columbia within their respective jurisdictions. The States prescribe the qualifications for admission to
practice and the standards of professional conduct. They also are responsible for the discipline of lawyers.[4]

---

4. The dissenting opinion relies heavily on dictum in Spanos v. Skouras Theatres Corp.,
364 F.2d 161 (2d Cir. 1966). The facts of that case were different from those here, and the

A claim of entitlement under state law, to be enforceable, must be derived from statute or legal rule or through a mutually explicit understanding. The record here is devoid of any indication that an out-of-state lawyer may claim such an entitlement in Ohio, where the rules of the Ohio Supreme Court expressly consign the authority to approve a pro hac vice appearance to the discretion of the trial court. Even if, as the Court of Appeals believed, respondents Fahringer and Cambria had "reasonable expectations of professional service," they have not shown the requisite *mutual* understanding that they would be permitted to represent their clients in any particular case in the Ohio courts. The speculative claim that Fahringer's and Cambria's reputation might suffer as the result of the denial of their asserted right cannot by itself make out an injury to a constitutionally protected interest. There simply was no deprivation here of some right previously held under state law.

Nor is there a basis for the argument that the interest in appearing pro hac vice has its source in federal law. There is no right of federal origin that permits such lawyers to appear in state courts without meeting that State's bar admission requirements. This Court, on several occasions, has sustained state bar rules that excluded out-of-state counsel from practice altogether or on a case-by-case basis. These decisions recognize that the Constitution does not require that because a lawyer has been admitted to the bar of one State, he or she must be allowed to practice in another. Accordingly, because Fahringer and Cambria did not possess a cognizable property interest within the terms of the Fourteenth Amendment, the Constitution does not obligate the Ohio courts to accord them procedural due process in passing on their application for permission to appear pro hac vice before the Court of Common Pleas of Hamilton County.[5]

---

precise holding of the court was quite narrow. The court ruled that where a client sought to defend on the ground of illegality against an out-of-state attorney's action for his fee, and where the illegality stemmed entirely from the failure of the client's in-state-attorneys to obtain leave for the out-of-state attorney to appear in Federal District Court, the client would not be allowed to escape from the contract through his own default. Id., at 168-169. The balance of the opinion, which declared that "under the privileges and immunities clause of the Constitution no state can prohibit a citizen with a federal claim or defense from engaging an out-of-state lawyer to collaborate with an in-state lawyer and give legal advice concerning it within the state," id., at 170, must be considered to have been limited, if not rejected entirely, by Norfolk & Western R. Co. v. Beatty, 423 U.S. 1009 (1975).

The dissenting opinion also suggests that a client's interest in having out-of-state counsel is implicated by this decision. The court below, however, "did not reach the issue of whether the constitutional rights of Flynt and Hustler Magazine had also been violated," 574 F.2d 874, 877 (6th Cir. 1978), recognizing as it did that a federal-court injunction enjoining a state criminal proceeding would conflict with this Court's holding in Younger v. Harris, 401 U.S. 37 (1971).

5. The dissenting opinion of Justice Stevens argues that a lawyer's right to "pursu[e] his calling is protected by the Due Process Clause . . . when he crosses the border" of the State that licensed him. Justice Stevens identifies two "protected" interests that "reinforce" each other. These are said to be "the 'nature' of the interest in pro hac vice admissions [and] the 'implicit promise' inhering in Ohio custom."

The petition for writ of certiorari is granted, the judgment of the Sixth Circuit is reversed, and the case is remanded for further proceedings consistent with this opinion.

It is so ordered.

JUSTICE WHITE would grant certiorari and set the case for oral argument.

JUSTICE STEVENS, with whom JUSTICE BRENNAN and JUSTICE MARSHALL join, dissenting.

A lawyer's interest in pursuing his calling is protected by the Due Process Clause of the Fourteenth Amendment. The question presented by this case is whether a lawyer abandons that protection when he crosses the border of the State which issued his license to practice.

The Court holds that a lawyer has no constitutionally protected interest in his out-of-state practice. In its view, the interest of the lawyer is so trivial that a judge has no obligation to give any consideration whatsoever to the merits of a pro hac vice request, or to give the lawyer any opportunity to advance reasons in support of his application. The Court's square holding is that the Due Process Clause of the Fourteenth Amendment simply does not apply to this kind of ruling by a state trial judge.[2]

The first of these lawyer's "interests" is described as that of "discharging [his] responsibility for the fair administration of justice in our adversary system." As important as this interest is, the suggestion that the Constitution assures the right of a lawyer to practice in the court of every State is a novel one, not supported by any authority brought to our attention. Such an asserted right flies in the face of the traditional authority of state courts to control who may be admitted to practice before them. If accepted, the constitutional rule advanced by the dissenting opinion would prevent those States that have chosen to bar all pro hac vice appearances from continuing to do so, and would undermine the policy of those States which do not extend reciprocity to out-of-state lawyers.

The second ground for due process protection identified in the dissenting opinion is the "implicit promise" inherent in Ohio's past practice in "assur[ing] out-of-state practitioners that they are welcome in Ohio's courts. . . ." We recall no other claim that a constitutional right can be created — as if by estoppel — merely because a wholly and *expressly* discretionary state privilege has been granted generously in the past. That some courts, in setting the standards for admission *within their jurisdiction,* have required a showing of cause before denying leave to appear pro hac vice provides no support for the proposition that the Constitution imposes this "cause" requirement on state courts that have chosen to reject it.

2. Although the Court does not address it, this case also presents the question whether a defendant's interest in representation by nonresident counsel is entitled to any constitutional protection. The clients, as well as the lawyers, are parties to this litigation. Moreover, the Ohio trial judge made it perfectly clear that his ruling was directed at the defendants, and not merely their counsel. . . .

A defendant's interest in adequate representation is "perhaps his most important privilege" protected by the Constitution. Powell v. Alabama, 287 U.S. 45, 70. Whatever the scope of a lawyer's interest in practicing in other States may be, Judge Friendly is surely correct in stating that the client's interest in representation by out-of-state counsel is entitled to some measure of constitutional protection:

> We are persuaded, however, that where a right has been conferred on citizens by federal law, the constitutional guarantee against its abridgement must be read to include what is necessary and appropriate for its assertion. In an age of increased spe-

The premises for this holding can be briefly stated. A nonresident lawyer has no right, as a matter of either state or federal law, to appear in an Ohio court. Absent any such enforceable entitlement, based on an explicit rule or mutual understanding, the lawyer's interest in making a pro hac vice appearance is a mere "privilege" that Ohio may grant or withhold in the unrestrained discretion of individual judges. The conclusion that a lawyer has no constitutional protection against a capricious exclusion seems so obvious to the majority that argument of the question is unnecessary. Summary reversal is the order of the day.

A few years ago the Court repudiated a similar syllogism which had long supported the conclusion that a parolee has no constitutionally protected interest in his status. Accepting the premise that the parolee has no "right" to preserve his contingent liberty, the Court nevertheless concluded that the nature of his status, coupled with the State's "implicit promise" that it would not be revoked arbitrarily, was sufficient to require constitutional protection. Morrissey v. Brewer, 408 U.S. 471, 481-482. As the Court observed, it "is hardly useful any longer to try to deal with this problem in terms of whether the parolee's liberty is a 'right' or a 'privilege.'" In my judgment, it is equally futile to try to deal with the problem presented by this case in terms of whether the out-of-state pursuit of a lawyer's calling is based on an "explicit" or an "enforceable" "entitlement" rather than a so-called "privilege." Instead, we should examine the nature of the activity and the implicit promise Ohio has made to these petitioners.

I

The notion that a state trial judge has arbitrary and unlimited power to refuse a nonresident lawyer permission to appear in his courtroom is nothing but a remnant of a bygone era. Like the body of rules that once governed parole, the nature of law practice has undergone a metamorphosis during the past century. Work that was once the exclusive province of the lawyer is now performed by title companies, real estate brokers, corporate trust departments, and accountants. Rules of ethics that once insulated the local lawyer from competition are now forbidden by the Sherman Act[6] and by the First Amendment to the Constitution of

---

cialization and high mobility of the bar, this must comprehend the right to bring to the assistance of an attorney admitted in the resident state a lawyer licensed by "public act" of any other state who is thought best fitted for the task, and to allow him to serve in whatever manner is most effective, subject only to valid rules of courts as to practice before them. Indeed, in instances where the federal claim or defense is unpopular, advice and assistance by an out-of-state lawyer may be the only means available for vindication. Spanos v. Skouras Theatres, 364 F.2d 161, 170 (en banc) (2d Cir. 1966).

6. Because the "transactions which create the need for the particular legal services in question frequently are interstate transactions," the practice of law is now regarded as a

the United States.[7] Interstate law practice and multistate law firms are now commonplace. Federal questions regularly arise in state criminal trials and permeate the typical lawyer's practice. Because the assertion of federal claims or defenses is often unpopular, "advice and assistance by an out-of-state lawyer may be the only means available for vindication." The "increased specialization and high mobility" of today's Bar is a consequence of the dramatic change in the demand for legal services that has occurred during the past century.

History attests to the importance of pro hac vice appearances. As Judge Merritt, writing for the Court of Appeals, explained:

> Nonresident lawyers have appeared in many of our most celebrated cases. For example, Andrew Hamilton, a leader of the Philadelphia bar, defended John Peter Zenger in New York in 1735 in colonial America's most famous freedom-of-speech case. Clarence Darrow appeared in many states to plead the cause of an unpopular client, including the famous *Scopes* trial in Tennessee where he opposed another well-known, out-of-state lawyer, William Jennings Bryan. Great lawyers from Alexander Hamilton and Daniel Webster to Charles Evans Hughes and John W. Davis were specially admitted for the trial of important cases in other states. A small group of lawyers appearing pro hac vice inspired and initiated the civil rights movement in its early stages. In a series of cases brought in courts throughout the South, out-of-state lawyers Thurgood Marshall, Constance Motley and Spottswood Robinson, before their appointments to the federal bench, developed the legal principles which gave rise to the civil rights movement. . . .

The modern examples identified by Judge Merritt, though more illustrious than the typical pro hac vice appearance, are not rare exceptions to a general custom of excluding nonresident lawyers from local practice. On the contrary, appearances by out-of-state counsel have been routine throughout the country for at least a quarter of a century. The custom is so well recognized that, as Judge Friendly observed in 1966, there "is not the slightest reason to suppose" that a qualified lawyer's pro hac vice request will be denied.

This case involves a pro hac vice application by qualified legal specialists; no legitimate reason for denying their request is suggested by the record. They had been retained to defend an unpopular litigant in a trial that might be affected by local prejudices and attitudes. It is the classic situation in which the interests of justice would be served by allowing the defendant to be represented by counsel of his choice.

---

commercial activity subject to the strictures of the Sherman Act. Goldfarb v. Virginia State Bar, 421 U.S. 773, 783-784.

7. Lawyers now have a constitutional right to advertise because "significant societal interests are served by such speech." Bates v. State Bar of Arizona, 433 U.S. 350, 364.

The interest these lawyers seek to vindicate is not merely the pecuniary goal that motivates every individual's attempt to pursue his calling. It is the profession's interest in discharging its responsibility for the fair administration of justice in our adversary system. The nature of that interest is surely worthy of the protection afforded by the Due Process Clause of the Fourteenth Amendment.

II

In the past, Ohio has implicitly assured out-of-state practitioners that they are welcome in Ohio's courts unless there is a valid, articulable reason for excluding them. Although the Ohio Supreme Court dismissed respondents' petition for an extraordinary writ of mandamus in this case, it has not dispelled that assurance because it did not purport to pass on the merits of their claim. In my opinion the State's assurance is adequate to create an interest that qualifies as "property" within the means of the Due Process Clause.

The District Court found as a fact that Ohio trial judges routinely permit out-of-state counsel to appear pro hac vice. This regular practice is conducted pursuant to the Rules of the Supreme Court of Ohio, Ohio's Code of Professional Responsibility, rules of each local court, and a leading opinion of the Ohio Court of Appeals identifying criteria that should inform a trial judge's discretion in acting on pro hac vice applications. While it is unquestionably true that an Ohio trial judge has broad discretion in determining whether or not to allow nonresident lawyers to appear in his court, it is also true that the Ohio rules, precedents, and practice give out-of-state lawyers an unequivocal expectation that the exercise of that discretion will be based on permissible reasons. . . .

III

Either the "nature" of the interest in pro hac vice admissions or the "implicit promise" inhering in Ohio custom with respect to those admissions is sufficient to create an interest protected by the Due Process Clause. Moreover, each of these conclusions reinforces the other.

The mode of analysis employed by the Court in recent years has treated the Fourteenth Amendment concepts of "liberty" and "property" as though they defined mutually exclusive, and closed categories of interests, with neither shedding any light on the meaning of the other. Indeed, in some of the Court's recent opinions it has implied that not only property but liberty itself does not exist apart from specific state authorization or an express guarantee in the Bill of Rights. In my judgment this is not the way the majestic language of the Fourteenth Amendment should be read.

As is demonstrated by cases like Meyer v. Nebraska, 262 U.S. 390, 399; Morrissey v. Brewer, 408 U.S. 471; Bell v. Burson, 402 U.S. 535, 539, and Mr. Justice Frankfurter's classic concurring opinion in Joint Anti-Fascist Refugee Committee v. McGrath, 341 U.S. 123, 162, judicial construction of the words, "life, liberty, or property" is not simply a matter of applying the precepts of logic to accepted premises. Rather, it is experience and judgment that have breathed life into the Court's process of constitutional adjudication. It is not only Ohio's experience with out-of-state practitioners, but that of the entire Nation as well, that compels the judgment that no State may arbitrarily reject a lawyer's legitimate attempt to pursue this aspect of his calling. . . .

Justice Stevens's dissent in Leis v. Flynt explains the interest in allowing a client to hire an out-of-state lawyer. (The constitutional strength of that interest is another matter.) Out-of-state lawyers were especially important in the 1960s, when northern lawyers went south to do civil rights work. For a striking case illustrating the need for those lawyers at the time and efforts by prosecutors and local judges to impede them (including by arrest), see Sobol v. Perez, 289 F. Supp. 392 (E.D. La. 1968) (three judge court).

Recall that Justice Stevens's *Leis* dissent is cited with approval in Justice Powell's majority opinion in *Piper* for the proposition that in "some cases, representation by nonresident counsel may be the only means available for the vindication of federal rights" (page 538 supra). But Justice Powell also distinguished *Leis* in *Piper* on the ground that the nonresident who seeks to join a state's bar, unlike the pro hac vice applicant, "must have the same professional and personal qualifications required of resident lawyers" and "is subject to the full force of [the state's] disciplinary rules." How significant are these distinctions? After *Piper, Leis's* importance shrank somewhat. Was *Piper* a small attempt to atone for *Leis*?

What About the Client's Interests?

Leis v. Flynt addressed the interests of lawyers. The defendants could not seek federal relief because of the *Younger* abstention doctrine (see note 4 of the majority opinion). Would the defendants have had superior interests? Ford v. Israel, 701 F.2d 689 (7th Cir.), cert. denied, 464 U.S. 832 (1983), hovered around this question but did not answer it directly. Ford was charged with murder in a Wisconsin state court. He was indigent but his parents had retained a Chicago lawyer to represent him. Wisconsin, however, had a rule that required all nonresident counsel to appear with local counsel. The public defender (Rosen) offered to serve as local counsel, but the state court ruled that Ford would have to pay for local counsel if he was going to pay for an out-of-state lawyer to try the case. Ford's parents refused to put up the additional money, the Chicago lawyer withdrew, and Rosen was appointed to represent Ford, who was convicted. In habeas, Ford challenged the local rule. Judge Posner, rejecting the challenge, acknowledged that it "has about it the air of a guild restriction and may for all we know be motivated by a desire to increase the fees of Wisconsin lawyers." But it wasn't an arbitrary rule, Judge Posner said, and was in fact "less arbitrary in a criminal than in a civil case." Here is why:

> It is a favorite tactic of an unsuccessful criminal defendant to complain, on appeal or in a habeas corpus proceeding, that he did not have effective assistance of counsel at trial; and if his only trial counsel was from out of state, and made errors of criminal procedure that a local counsel would not have made, a basis is laid for a colorable complaint of ineffective assistance of counsel. If as Ford contends Wisconsin must in every criminal case waive its rule requiring retention of local counsel, criminal defendants will find it easier to draw out the proceedings against them by complaining that they were denied effective assistance of counsel — a complaint that can be raised against retained as well as appointed counsel and is judged under the same standards in both types of case. Cuyler v. Sullivan, 446 U.S. 335, 344-345 (1980). In the present case, it is true, local counsel — Rosen — was willing to serve without fee, and if he had been allowed to do so Ford would have had the counsel of his choice. But Rosen is paid by the state, so it would have meant giving a man who had retained one lawyer another free of charge. The state was not required to do that. The choice was Grant or Rosen; and the state had a reason why it could not be Grant.

Id. at 692-693. One judge dissented.

Fuller had local counsel to represent him in his criminal case in New Jersey but he also wanted help from two nonresident lawyers. The trial judge rejected their pro hac vice admission and Fuller was convicted. In habeas, the Third Circuit held that Fuller had a Sixth Amendment right to out-of-state counsel that could not be arbitrarily denied. The "trial court's wooden approach and its failure to make record-supported findings balancing the right to counsel with the demands of the administration of justice resulted in an arbitrary denial of Fuller's motion." The writ was granted with no requirement that Fuller show harm. Fuller v. Diesslin, 868 F.2d 604 (3d Cir.), cert. denied, 493 U.S. 873 (1989). See also United States v. Bradford, 238 F.2d 395 (2d Cir. 1956), cert. denied, 352 U.S. 1002 (1957). Compare Panzardi-Alvarez v. United States, 879 F.2d 975 (1st Cir. 1989), cert. denied, 493 U.S. 1082 (1990) (using an abuse of discretion standard to determine whether district judge's rejection of pro hac vice application denied defendant his Sixth Amendment right to counsel).

Is Pro Hac Vice the Solution?

Even after the Supreme Court's decisions in *Piper* (page 536 supra), *Frazier* (page 543 supra), and *Friedman* (page 545 supra), the states retain power to condition admission upon passage of a bar examination. Since no lawyer will relish taking many of those, we can expect some disharmony between the fractured admission system and regional or national needs or interests of lawyers and clients. Pro hac vice admission is not a complete solution because it is not recognized for nonlitigation services (page 582 infra). But is pro hac vice a solution for trials and appeals? Maybe. But given the apparent absence of serious federal constraints on pro hac vice admission after *Leis* and *Ford*, enlightened state attitudes are necessary.

What should a model pro hac vice system look like? In Note, Due Process and Pro Hac Vice Appearances by Attorneys: Does Any Protection Remain?, 29 Buffalo L. Rev. 133 (1980) (authored by Timothy Cashmore), the author argues that states should permit pro hac vice admission and suggests that they adopt "more explicit standards so lawyers and clients can know with reasonable certainty whether their professional relationships will remain effective across state boundaries. Explicit standards would also reduce the likelihood that pro hac vice requests will be treated in an arbitrary manner." The author also urges hearings on pro hac vice applications as "appropriate and needed means for revealing the character of a judge's reasons for denying admission." See also Annot., 20 A.L.R.4th 855 (1983); Comment, *Leis v. Flynt*: Retaining a Nonresident Attorney for Litigation, 79 Colum. L. Rev. 572 (1979) (authored by Stephen Madsen); Note, Easing Multistate Practice Restrictions — "Good Cause" Based Limited Admission, 29 Rutgers L. Rev. 1182 (1976).

The New York rule on admission pro hac vice says that an attorney admitted in "another state, territory, district or foreign country may be admitted pro hac vice . . . in the discretion of any court of record, to participate in the trial or argument of any particular cause in which the attorney may be for the time being employed." 22 N.Y.C.R.R. §520.9(e) (1988). By comparison, the New Jersey rule permits out-of-state lawyers to appear pro hac vice but requires that "all pleadings, briefs and other papers filed with the court [shall be] signed by an attorney of record authorized to practice in this State, who shall be held responsible for them and for the conduct of the cause and of the admitted attorney therein." 1 New Jersey Practice, Rule 1:21-2(b)(4) (West 1988).

Once admitted pro hac vice, what rights does the attorney have to stay admitted? In Johnson v. Trueblood, 629 F.2d 302 (3d Cir. 1980), cert. denied, 450 U.S. 999 (1981), the out-of-state attorney had been admitted to represent the plaintiffs in a civil trial. The jury returned a verdict for the defendants. While an appeal was pending, the district judge revoked the attorney's pro hac vice status "retroactively to the date of the verdict. The revocation was based on the attorney's conduct during the trial." The Third Circuit reversed. It held that "some type of notice and an opportunity to respond are necessary when a district court seeks to revoke an attorney's pro hac vice status." The court left

> the form of the notice to the discretion of the district court with the limitation that it adequately inform the attorney of the basis upon which revocation is sought. In short, the attorney should be notified of two things: the conduct of the attorney that is the subject of the inquiry, and the specific reason this conduct may justify revocation. . . .
>
> As to the opportunity to respond, there is the question of whether a full scale hearing is appropriate in every case. We believe that it is not.

Id. at 304. The Third Circuit refused to hold that the revocation proceedings must be heard before a different judge from the trial judge. In Koller v. Richardson-Merrell, 737 F.2d 1038 (D.C. Cir. 1984), vacated on jurisdictional grounds, 472 U.S. 424 (1985), the court held that a lawyer admitted pro hac vice may not be "disqualified more readily than regularly admitted counsel." The court rejected the trial judge's conclusion that conduct falling short of a violation of a disciplinary rule could justify revocation of pro hac vice admission. Accord: United States v. Collins, 920 F.2d 619 (10th Cir. 1990), cert. denied, 111 S. Ct. 2022 (1991) (revocation of pro hac vice status must be evaluated on same standards as though court had disqualified member of its bar); Kirkland v. National Mortgage Network, Inc., 884 F.2d 1367 (11th Cir. 1989). See also Annot., 64 A.L.R.4th 1217 (1988).

In In re Belli, 371 F. Supp. 111 (D.D.C. 1974), the trial judge refused to admit San Francisco attorney Melvin Belli pro hac vice on the retrial of a case because of his behavior following the first trial. In In re Bailey, 57 N.J. 451, 273 A.2d 563 (1971), criminal defense lawyer F. Lee Bailey was prohibited from appearing in the New Jersey courts for a period of one year after it was found that he had acted unethically in previous appearances.

2.   Services Other Than Litigation

The problem of out-of-state practice becomes complex, perhaps intractable, when the lawyer does not go into court for the client and so cannot be admitted pro hac vice. There is no logical reason (but plenty of practical ones) why states could not create a category of pro hac vice admission for nonlitigation services, but no state has done so. To create such a category might require the court to grapple with the multistate admissions problem. Issues of definition would be significant. Pro hac vice admission in court is limited to the pending case. How could we define pro hac vice admission for out-of-court services? Finally, pro hac vice admission in court envisions a judge who will oversee the out-of-state lawyer's behavior, but equivalent oversight is not possible for out-of-court work.

What threats does a lawyer face when she gives legal advice "in" a state in which she is not admitted? (Earlier, we talked about the threshold difficulty of defining the word "in." See page 570 supra.) Prosecution for unauthorized law practice is a theoretical threat (see page 597 infra), but unlikely except in the most egregious cases. What then? Consider the next case.

EL GEMAYEL v. SEAMAN
72 N.Y.2d 701, 533 N.E.2d 245, 536 N.Y.S.2d 406 (1988)

ALEXANDER, JUDGE.

The question presented for our review is whether services rendered by plaintiff to defendant in connection with a Lebanese legal matter constituted the unlawful practice of law in New York such that the contract for such services is illegal and therefore unenforceable. We agree with the courts below that plaintiff's conduct did not constitute the unlawful practice of law in New York within the meaning of Judiciary Law §478 and that, therefore, the contract is not void on this ground.

I

The undisturbed factual determinations of the trial court demonstrate that plaintiff, an attorney admitted to practice in Lebanon but not in any jurisdiction in the United States, resides in Washington, D.C., and maintains an office at Georgetown University where he serves as a Middle Eastern law consultant. In April 1982, defendant's granddaughter Jeneane Aoude was abducted by her natural father from her home in Newton, Massachusetts, in violation of a Massachusetts decree awarding custody to Jeneane's mother, and defendant's daughter, Mary Aoude. Jeneane was subsequently located in Lebanon. Referred by the pastor of Mary's church, defendant and Mary Aoude, then residing together in Phoenix, New York, sought plaintiff's advice on whether Lebanese courts would honor the Massachusetts custody decree. Plaintiff, in a letter addressed to Mary in Massachusetts, rendered his legal opinion that Lebanese courts would honor that Massachusetts decree. He billed Mary $2,000 for this service and was paid in full.

Defendant and Mary Aoude remained in regular contact with plaintiff after he rendered this opinion and, as the trial court found, he subsequently agreed to assist them in getting the child back, while defendant agreed to pay his fee and expenses. The bulk of plaintiff's services were performed in Lebanon, where he confirmed the child's exact location, instituted four separate court actions against Mary's ex-husband, and ultimately assisted Mary in spiriting the child out of Lebanon and back to the United States. Plaintiff's activities in the United States included the commencement of investigations through his Beirut office, accompanying Mary and her Massachusetts attorney to a Massachusetts court to obtain a copy of the judgment awarding Mary custody which would be recognized in Lebanon, authenticating documents so that they might be used in Lebanon, helping Mary complete a power of attorney form, and assisting her in applying for a Lebanese visa. Plaintiff's only contacts with New York during this time, however, were his frequent phone calls to Mary and defendant in Phoenix, New York, to report on and discuss the progress of the case. Additionally, after Mary returned from Lebanon with Jeneane, plaintiff made a single visit to Phoenix to return luggage Mary had left in Lebanon. While in Phoenix, he also discussed his bill with defendant. Plaintiff subsequently mailed a bill for his services to defendant in New York.

When defendant failed to pay the bill, plaintiff commenced this action, asserting causes of action in contract and quantum meruit. . . .

Judiciary Law §478 provides:

> It shall be unlawful for any natural person to practice or appear as an attorney-at-law or as an attorney and counselor-at-law for a person other than himself in a court of record in this state, or to furnish attorneys or counsel or an attorney and counsel to render legal services, or to hold himself out to the public as being entitled to practice law as aforesaid, or in any other manner . . . without having first been duly and regularly licensed and admitted to practice law in the courts of record of this state, and without having taken the constitutional oath.

Its purpose is to protect the public in this State from "the dangers of legal representation and advice given by persons not trained, examined and licensed for such work, whether they be laymen or lawyers from other jurisdictions." As a matter of public policy, a contract to provide services in violation of the statute is unenforceable in our State courts. Moreover, violation of Judiciary Law §478 is a misdemeanor (Judiciary Law §485) and its provisions also may be enforced in civil actions by the Attorney-General or a bar association formed in accordance with the laws of this State (Judiciary Law §476-a).

It is settled that the "law" contemplated by Judiciary Law §478 includes foreign as well as New York law (Matter of New York County Lawyers Assn. *[Roel]*, 3 N.Y.2d 224, 165 N.Y.S.2d 31, 144 N.E.2d 24). In *Roel*, we held that former Penal Law §270, the predecessor of Judiciary Law

§478, prohibited the activities of a Mexican attorney who admittedly practiced foreign law in his New York office by advising members of the public on Mexican law. The practice of Lebanese law likewise falls within the purview of the statute. The issue, however, is whether plaintiff's activities in New York appropriately can be considered the "practice" of Lebanese law.

The "practice" of law reserved to duly licensed New York attorneys includes the rendering of legal advice as well as appearing in court and holding oneself out to be a lawyer. Additionally, such advice or services must be rendered to particular clients and services rendered to a single client can constitute the practice of law (Spivak v. Sachs, 16 N.Y.2d 163, 263 N.Y.S.2d 953, 211 N.E.2d 329 [1965].

Spivak held that a California attorney engaged in the unlawful practice of law by assisting an acquaintance in New York with her divorce. In so doing, the California attorney became substantially involved in the client's New York affairs — spending 14 days in New York attending meetings, reviewing drafts of a separation agreement, discussing the client's financial and custody problems, recommending a change in New York counsel and, based on his knowledge of New York and California law, rendering his opinion as to the proper jurisdiction for the divorce action and related marital and custody issues. While holding that these activities plainly constituted the "practice" of law, we also recognized that the statute should not be construed to prohibit "customary and innocuous practices." We noted that: "recognizing the numerous multi-State transactions and relationships of modern times, we cannot penalize every instance in which an attorney from another State comes into our State for conferences or negotiations relating to a New York client and a transaction somehow tied to New York."

Here, unlike *Spivak*, plaintiff's contacts with New York were, as Supreme Court found, incidental and innocuous. Although plaintiff engaged in substantial litigation in Lebanon, where he was licensed, and even arguably provided legal services while in Washington, D.C., and Massachusetts, his contact with New York consisted entirely of phone calls to defendant and her daughter Mary in New York in which they discussed the progress of the legal proceedings in Lebanon. There was but a single visit to Phoenix, New York, after the successful completion of his legal services. We conclude that, in the circumstances of this case, phone calls to New York by plaintiff, an attorney licensed in a foreign jurisdiction, to advise his client of the progress of legal proceedings in that foreign jurisdiction, did not, without more, constitute the "practice" of law in this State in violation of Judiciary Law §478. To adopt a per se rule such as advanced by defendant would impair the ability of New York residents to obtain legal advice in foreign jurisdictions on matters relating to those jurisdictions since the foreign attorneys would be unable to recover for their services unless they were licensed both in New York as well as in the foreign jurisdiction.

We do not have occasion to decide, however, whether a contract for legal services, rendered in a foreign jurisdiction to a New York client and which constitute the illegal practice of law in that foreign jurisdiction, is enforceable in this State. Although it is undisputed that plaintiff is not a licensed attorney in either Washington, D.C., or Massachusetts, defendant has failed to allege or prove that plaintiff's conduct in either place was unlawful under the law of that jurisdiction.

The "No Payment" Disincentive

The lawyer in Ranta v. McCarney, 391 N.W.2d 161, 164-166 (N.D. 1986), wasn't so lucky. Ranta practiced in Minnesota. For more than a decade he advised McCarney, a North Dakota businessman, on issues of federal tax law. When McCarney died, Ranta was owed about $22,500 but McCarney's estate refused to pay. It alleged that Ranta had been practicing law in North Dakota without a license, even going so far as to open a branch office in Bismarck. The court held that a nonresident attorney "who is not licensed to practice law in this state cannot recover compensation for services rendered" in North Dakota. The court then remanded for a "determination of which fees relate to the practice of law conducted outside of North Dakota." Two judges dissented.

Allowing a former client to avoid paying an out-of-state lawyer on the theory that the lawyer was practicing law without a license is a pretty effective way to stop foreign lawyers from venturing into the state. In *Ranta*, it was of no moment to the court that the lawyer's advice was primarily in the tax area. Can a state forbid an out-of-state lawyer to advise on federal law within the state? Is the North Dakota Supreme Court suggesting that the plaintiff would have won if the advice had been given within the neighboring state of Minnesota? Apparently so, because the court remanded for a determination of where Ranta was located when particular advice was given. What should the lower court do if it concludes that particular advice was given via a computer modem or facsimile machine while Ranta was in Minnesota but the client was in North Dakota?

One justification for excluding laypeople and unlicensed lawyers from giving legal advice to a state's residents is protection of the residents. How is that interest furthered if a Minnesota lawyer is forbidden to advise a North Dakotan on federal law in North Dakota? Does North Dakota have any other legitimate interests?

El Gemayel won because his New York-based work was "incidental and innocuous." The court was concerned, as well it should be, that a "per se rule . . . would impair the ability of New York residents to obtain legal advice in foreign jurisdictions." Spivak v. Sachs, cited in *El Gemayel*, resulted in a loss for the California lawyer who spent 14 days in New York on the client's matter. Is the difference between *Spivak* and *El Gemayel* the number of days? Or is the difference the fact that the lawyer in *Spivak* was advising a New York matrimonial client on New York (and other) law although he was not a member of the New York bar while the lawyer in *El Gemayel* was advising on the law of his home jurisdiction? Similarly, in Lozoff v. Shore Heights, Ltd., 66 Ill. 2d 398, 362 N.E.2d 1047 (1977), a nonresident lawyer was denied compensation for work on a real estate transaction in Illinois.

In Spanos v. Skouras, 364 F.2d 161 (2d Cir.), cert. denied, 385 U.S. 987 (1966), cited in both *Leis* opinions, a California lawyer came to New York at a client's request to assist in a planned antitrust action. The dispute was settled before the lawyer was able to be admitted pro hac vice in the federal court. The client refused to pay for the lawyer's New York work. The Second Circuit held that the client could not take advantage of the fact that the lawyer was not admitted in New York, because he would have been admitted pro hac vice had the client's New York lawyers made the proper motion. The client could not rely on his own failure to make the motion. (An alternate holding, based on the theory that in any event New York could not have forbidden the lawyer to give advice on federal law in New York, was apparently limited or rejected in note 4 of the majority opinion in *Leis*. See page 573 supra.)

QUESTION

12.4 Adams, a New York lawyer, is called by Southern Stories, Inc., a small magazine publishing company in Memphis that issues a monthly magazine with an emphasis on the South. Adams is a copyright expert. Southern Stories wants him to come to Memphis and advise it on the effect of recent changes in the copyright law on its procedures. Adams does so, spending about two weeks in Memphis and another two weeks doing research and preparing a memorandum in New York. He subsequently bills the client for $17,000. In advising the client, Adams had to consider certain aspects of Tennessee unfair competition law and the effect, under the Supremacy Clause, of the federal copyright law. The client refuses to pay on the ground that Adams is not licensed to practice in Tennessee. Adams sues in federal district Court in Memphis. You are the district judge's clerk. What's your advice? Short of getting a retainer in advance, how might Adams have reduced the risk of nonpayment?

3. Multijurisdictional Firms

At the intersection of multijurisdictional practice and advertising lies the firm name. Here the issue is a bit different from the issues previously discussed. No out-of-state lawyer is attempting to give legal advice in a foreign jurisdiction. All advice will come from locally admitted lawyers or lawyers from other jurisdictions working under the supervision of local lawyers. Nevertheless, the firm for which these lawyers work will have a name composed of the names of lawyers who are not admitted to practice in the jurisdiction. Should this matter?

Two kinds of firms might face "the name problem." An old established firm (OEF) might want to set up a branch office in a distant state. The OEF uses its OE name even though none of the name partners has been admitted in the distant state (or is even alive). This practice is quite common and has proceeded without a serious hitch.

Another kind of firm that might want to practice under its own name wherever it opens an office is the national or regional legal clinic. Call such firms Young Upstart Practices (YUPs). YUPs are very much the product of several developments in the last two decades: legal advertising, which permits them to attract many clients; computerization, which permits them to serve many clients efficiently on routine matters; and growth in the number of lawyers and paraprofessionals, which permits them to staff many neighborhood law offices.

A key to a successful mass market legal clinic is name recognition. Would Hyatt Legal Services and Jacoby & Meyers be as successful if they had to practice under a different name wherever they opened shop? Surely not, and the lawyers with whom they compete know it. It should come as no surprise, then, that efforts have been made to deny these firms the right to use their (advertised) names.

Consider In re Review of Opinion 475, 89 N.J. 74, 444 A.2d 1092, appeal dismissed, 459 U.S. 962 (1982). Jacoby & Meyers desired to open an office in New Jersey (see page 544 for The "New Jersey" Problem). A state rule prohibited the use of firm names unless each person whose name was used was or had been a New Jersey lawyer. Neither Mr. Jacoby nor Mr. Meyers was a New Jersey lawyer, and neither planned to practice law in New Jersey. Instead, Jacoby & Meyers would have partners and associates in New Jersey who were members of the state bar. The state supreme court upheld the validity of the state rule on the ground that it served the legitimate purpose of protecting against deception. Is this defensible? The court also concluded that the wisdom of the rule was questionable and ordered hearings on its continued implementation.*

---

*The rule was subsequently changed by amendment to New Jersey's version of DR 2-105(B), and this change was retained when New Jersey adopted the Model Rules. Under the change a firm name may contain the names of lawyers not licensed to practice in New

New Jersey is not the only state in which local lawyers have attempted to prevent Jacoby & Meyers from setting up legal clinics. In New York, a local bar association sought to enjoin the operation of the clinics under the Jacoby & Meyers name on the ground that their presence violated section 478 of the state's judiciary law, which forbids "any natural person to practice or appear as an attorney-at-law . . . without having first been duly . . . licensed and admitted to practice law in the courts of record of this state." A unanimous Court of Appeals affirmed dismissal of the complaint. The court wrote:

> There is no claim that either Jacoby or Meyers or any other partner or associate of the firm not admitted to practice law in New York is actually practicing law in the State of New York. Rather the gravamen of plaintiff's complaint is that use of the firm name is a factual misrepresentation that both of the name partners are available to render legal services in New York. We reject this contention and conclude as a matter of law that use of a firm name comprised of surnames, without more, does not constitute any holding out that there are individual partners bearing those surnames who are admitted to practice in New York, or indeed that there are partners in the firm who bear such surnames, wherever admitted. Plaintiff's attempt to distinguish instances (of which there are many in New York State, particularly in New York City) of the use of firm names made up of surnames of partners one or more of whom are deceased is not persuasive. Its assertion is that the clients, both actual and potential, of such latter firms are sufficiently sophisticated to understand that the use of such firm names constitutes no representation that there is any member of the firm who bears one of the surnames that appear in the firm name. We find no significant difference between the use in a firm name of the surname of a deceased partner and the surname of a partner not practicing in New York. In both instances the firm name is an institutional description and its use constitutes no representation that anyone bearing a surname corresponding to the names in the firm title is available to render professional services. . . .
>
> The firm may use a letterhead disclosing only its firm name and may advertise the availability of its services under the firm name alone provided that it has an active partner who is admitted to practice in New York. If, in either instance, reference is made to the names of individual lawyers who are partners or associates of the firm but not members of the New York bar, there must be a clear indication that each such individual lawyer is not admitted to practice in New York State. [New York Criminal and Civil Courts Bar Assn. v. Jacoby, 61 N.Y.2d 130, 460 N.E.2d 1325, 1327-1328, 472 N.Y.S.2d 890 (1984).]

Jersey, but if it does the letterhead and other communications containing the firm name must also contain the name of at least one New Jersey lawyer responsible for the firm's New Jersey practice or its local office. Where the full names of out-of-state lawyers appear, jurisdictional limitations must be given. New Jersey Rule 7.5.

Hyatt Legal Services surmounted a similar effort to deny it the use of its name. Attorney Grievance Commission of Maryland v. Hyatt, 302 Md. 683, 490 A.2d 1224 (1985) (allegation of improper trade name dismissed; other charges dismissed for lack of jurisdiction).

C.   THE ETHICAL DUTY OF COMPETENCE

Canon 6 of the Model Code states: "A lawyer should represent a client competently." DR 6-101(A)(1) says that a lawyer shall not "[h]andle a legal matter which he knows or should know that he is not competent to handle, without associating with him a lawyer who is competent to handle it." The balance of DR 6-101 forbids a lawyer to handle a legal matter, though competent, "without preparation adequate in the circumstances," and to "[n]eglect a legal matter entrusted to him." DR 6-101(A)(2) and (3).

Similarly, Rule 1.1 of the Model Rules ("Competence") states: "A lawyer shall provide competent representation to a client. Competent representation requires the legal knowledge, skill, thoroughness and preparation reasonably necessary for the representation."

The ethical requirement of competence is not often invoked as a basis for discipline. See generally Susan Martyn, Lawyer Competence and Lawyer Discipline: Beyond the Bar?, 69 Geo. L.J. 705 (1981). Although the courts do say that a single instance of incompetence can justify discipline, State ex rel. Nebraska State Bar Assn. v. Holscher, 193 Neb. 729, 230 N.W.2d 75 (1975), People v. Yoakum, 191 Colo. 269, 552 P.2d 291 (1976), in fact the cases in which these statements are made generally involve significantly more culpable conduct than a single act of incompetence.

Occasionally, however, it does happen that an attorney will be disciplined mainly for incompetence. In Florida Bar v. Gallagher, 366 So. 2d 397 (Fla. 1978), an attorney was publicly reprimanded after he accepted a maritime personal injury claim when he knew that "he was neither qualified nor competent to handle" the claim. But even here, there was the additional fact that the attorney neglected to "timely file suit on the client's behalf, and the claim was barred by the applicable statute of limitations."

In Selznick v. State Bar, 16 Cal. 3d 704, 547 P.2d 1388, 1390-1391, 129 Cal. Rptr. 108 (1976), the lawyer had been retained to prosecute a criminal appeal, but failed to file the appeal on time, and it was dismissed. The court considered a distinction between a willful failure to perform legal services and a negligent failure to do so:

We have repeatedly stated that willful failure to perform legal services for which an attorney has been retained in itself warrants disciplinary action, constituting a breach of the good faith and fiduciary duty owed by the attorney to his clients. Even when such action is grossly negligent or careless rather than willful and dishonest, it is an act of moral turpitude and professional misconduct.

To what extent should incompetence, unaccompanied by willfulness, a pattern of conscious neglect, or failure to prepare, be a basis for discipline? Put aside, for the moment, a pattern of persistent incompetence, which may lead a court to suspend or disbar an attorney not for what he or she may have done in the past, but for what his or her past conduct suggests about the need for protection of the public in the future. See, e.g., In re Williams, 249 Minn. 600, 83 N.W.2d 115 (1957), and In re Rigg, 53 N.J. 601, 252 A.2d 398 (1969). In a case decided under the former Canons of Professional Ethics, which had no express provision governing competence, the court concluded that:

> Mere ignorance of the law in conducting the affairs of his client in good faith is not a cause for discipline. The nearest approach to such conduct is negligence as a ground for discipline when the neglect is so serious as to constitute a violation of his oath as an attorney.

Friday v. State Bar of California, 23 Cal. 2d 501, 505, 144 P.2d 564, 567 (1943). A recent California case is more explicit. Center Foundation v. Chicago Insurance Co., 227 Cal. App. 3d 547, 278 Cal. Rptr. 13 (1991), held that a lawyer may be disciplined for representing a client in a field in which the lawyer has no experience if the lawyer does not associate with an experienced lawyer. For further authorities on neglect and incompetence as a basis for discipline, see Annot., 96 A.L.R.2d 823 (1964).

A competent lawyer may handle matters incompetently not because of the difficulty of the matters but because he or she has too many of them. Competence is a function not only of expertise but also of workload. This especially can be a problem for lawyers employed in high-volume offices who are assigned too much work. The lawyer has a duty to decline more work than he or she can competently handle, but that might not be easy. If the person assigning the work is a lawyer, does that person have an ethical duty not to assign more work than the receiving lawyer can perform well? Yes, according to Wisconsin Opinion E-84-11 (1984), which addressed the situation in a public defender office. See also ABA Informal Opinion 1359 (1976).

Competence is not only an ethical duty. It is also a legal one. Incompetence can serve as the basis for a malpractice action, which in most places may be based in tort or contract or both. Center Foundation supra. (See page 620 infra.) To the extent the market works, incompetence should also lead to fewer clients, while lawyers whose work is more than competent should have more clients. This assumes, however, that prospective clients get complete information about the lawyers they are planning to hire. They don't, of course. Many disciplinary decisions are not public (see page 687 infra), and many malpractice actions are settled out of court, sometimes with a stipulation sealing the record.

For a witty and skeptical look at the debate over competence and the proffered remedies, see Marvin Frankel's article Curing Lawyers' Incompetence: Primum Non Nocere, 10 Creighton L. Rev. 613 (1977). See also Edmund Spaeth, To What Extent Can a Disciplinary Code Assure the Competence of Lawyers?, 61 Temple L. Rev. 1211 (1988).

QUESTION

12.5 With which of the following two positions do you agree? Why?

Position One

The failure of the grievance mechanism to discipline for incompetence is a scandal. The state certifies the competence of lawyers when it admits them to the practice of law. But generally, young lawyers, at the time of their admission, know almost nothing about the actual practice. Their ability to perform as lawyers is largely untested. We all know that that ability demands more than simply being able to research the law and write moot court briefs. The state has an obligation, after admission, to assure itself that the men and women it has certified as competent practitioners are in fact such.

When a grievance body is alerted to the possibility of past incompetence, it should investigate it. I am not speaking about errors in judgment or advice given after adequate research and review, but which turns out not to be the best. I recognize that the line between incompetence and errors of judgment is not crystal clear, but there is a line. We draw it in the malpractice area all the time.

When a grievance body learns of possible incompetence, then investigates and confirms the allegation, it should be obliged to take action to protect the public. The action need not be suspension or disbarment, although in some cases that will be appropriate. The action may be limited to an order to the lawyer not to handle certain categories of matters, at least not without assistance. Or if the incompetence is in an area that pervades all categories of practice — for example, the law of evidence or document drafting — then the disciplinary body may order the attorney to receive continuing legal education.

Position Two

The grievance mechanism cannot police occasional instances of incompetence. We must rely on the market to do that. The market will protect us in at least two ways. First, lawyers who are incompetent will cease to get clients and be forced out of business. Second, lawyers who perform incompetently, to the disadvantage of their clients, will be subject to suit for malpractice. These two ways will suffice to assure the competence of the bar.

Disciplinary action will not work. The disciplinary machinery is simply not capable of reviewing every client allegation of a lawyer's incompetence. The amount of investigation and analysis required in order to determine whether a lawyer acted incompetently in a particular situation can be vast. Disciplinary bodies barely have sufficient time and staff to investigate conscious wrongdoing. Furthermore, charges of incompetence will fall across many areas of the law. The legal staffs of disciplinary bodies are not and cannot be sufficiently conversant with every area of the law to be able to pass judgment on another lawyer's competence.

It is clear to me that while it is fine to have a duty of competent representation as part of the ethics code, we really must rely on mechanisms other than the grievance machinery to enforce that duty.

D. CONTINUING LEGAL EDUCATION

Will a requirement that a lawyer continue law study increase competence and decrease risk of professional failure? Many states think so. According to the ABA's Comprehensive Guide to Bar Admission Requirements 1991-1992 at 46-47, 36 states now have mandatory Continuing Legal Education (CLE) plans. The Florida Supreme Court adopted mandatory CLE in an opinion reported at 510 So. 2d 585 (Fla. 1987). These plans generally require an average of 10 to 15 hours of approved CLE classes yearly. Some states, such as Florida, require a certain number of hours (30 for Florida) every three years. And some, such as Florida, require that some of those hours be in legal ethics(!). Failure to obey CLE requirements can result in discipline. In re Yamagiwa, 97 Wash. 2d 773, 650 P.2d 203 (1982) (suspension).

In Verner v. Colorado, 716 F.2d 1352, 1353 (10th Cir. 1983), cert. denied, 466 U.S. 960 (1984), the plaintiff was a Colorado lawyer suspended from practice for failure to comply with the state's continuing legal education requirements. The plaintiff sought, among other relief, to enjoin the enforcement of those requirements as unconstitutional. In rejecting plaintiff's claim, the Tenth Circuit wrote:

> As the trial court noted, the basic issue presented is a novel one: whether a state supreme court may constitutionally require attorneys to meet continuing legal education requirements. Ample precedent exists supporting the authority to prescribe minimum levels of legal competency, measured by a bar examination, as a prerequisite to admission to a state bar. A fortiori, a state can require an attorney to take reasonable steps to maintain a suitable level of competency, so long as such requirements have a "rational connection with the [attorney's] fitness or capacity to practice law." We cannot say that the CLE requirements in Colorado have no rational connection to a lawyer's suitability to practice law.

Judge Frankel is especially dubious about the value of CLE in his article on lawyer competence (cited at page 592 supra): "Subjecting ourselves to a trivial regimen of fifteen compulsory hours of any old thing will diminish us in our aspiration to be, or to become, a worthy public profession." He lists the kinds of questions administration of these plans has spawned ("How long is an hour?"). See 10 Creighton L. Rev. at 630-631.

E.   SUPERVISORY RESPONSIBILITIES

These are of two kinds. One appears in Model Rule 5.1(a) and 5.1(b). Rule 5.1(a) requires law firm partners to "make reasonable efforts to ensure that the firm has in effect measures giving reasonable assurance that all lawyers in the firm conform to the [Model Rules]." Rule 5.1(b) imposes an equivalent obligation on lawyers with "direct supervisory authority over another lawyer." These "structural" responsibilities do not appear in the Code.

A partner or supervisory lawyer can be disciplined under these provisions even if he or she was unaware of another lawyer's misconduct. Indeed, the way the section reads, the failure to install appropriate preventive measures will warrant discipline even with no additional misconduct.

The rules separately impose a duty to rectify another lawyer's misconduct under certain circumstances. Rule 5.1(c)(2). Parallel preventive and remedial obligations apply in connection with the work of a law office's lay employees. Rule 5.3.

The code is fuzzy about the scope of a lawyer's supervisory obligations, see DR 4-101(D) and EC 3-6, but caselaw is not. If an associate's action is the result of negligent supervision, such carelessness may violate the senior attorney's fiduciary responsibility to his client. Vaughan v. State Bar of California, 6 Cal. 3d 847, 494 P.2d 1257, 100 Cal. Rptr. 713 (1972). The California court in Moore v. State Bar of California, 62 Cal. 2d 74, 396 P.2d 577, 41 Cal. Rptr. 161 (1964), suspended a lawyer who completely failed to supervise his associate's work while assuring the client that his pleadings were being properly filed. The court found that Moore's neglect amounted to a "sustained, deliberate and wilfull dereliction of duty" and came close to moral turpitude.

If the supervising attorney has no reason to suspect misconduct, however, he may not be vicariously liable for discipline. In re Corace, 390 Mich. 419, 213 N.W.2d 124 (1973), involved an associate who signed the name of an opposing party on a stipulation for adjournment, despite the senior partner's earlier explanation that it was firm practice never to sign another's name. The court held that a partner is not vicariously liable in a disciplinary proceeding if he had no reason to suspect or guard against an associate's violation.

A lawyer may also be liable in a disciplinary action for violations of partners or associates whom he does not supervise, if he knew of or reasonably should have suspected the misconduct. In re Fata, 22 A.D.2d 116, 254 N.Y.S.2d 289 (1964), appeal denied, 15 N.Y.2d 487, 208 N.E.2d 790, 260 N.Y.S.2d 1027, (1965); In re Brown, 389 Ill. 516, 59 N.E.2d 855 (1945). Thus, the New York Appellate Division disbarred an attorney whose partner repeatedly submitted false insurance claims, even though

> [i]t is true that the respondent Markowitz did not personally or directly participate in many of the fraudulent and dishonest practices charged here. But he joined and continued in the practice of law with the respondent Gladstone as a partner when he knew or should have known of the fraudulent and unethical practices of the firm and of his partner. . . . He conferred frequently with his partner and participated as a partner in the profits of the firm. It is inconceivable that he did not know that his partner and his firm were repeatedly violating the ethics of his profession. Under the circumstances, he must also assume the responsibility for the unprofessional activities of the firm.

In re Gladstone, 16 A.D.2d 512, 229 N.Y.S.2d 663, 666, appeal denied, 12 N.Y.2d 644, 187 N.E.2d 480, 236 N.Y.S.2d 1026 (1962). See also In re Pollack, 142 A.D.2d 386, 536 N.Y.S.2d 437 (1st Dept. 1989).

Perhaps impelled by the Model Rules' vision of structural precautions against unethical conduct, some courts have lately insisted on greater supervision to guard against misbehavior. In In re Yacavino, 100 N.J. 50, 494 A.2d 801, 803 (1985), the court suspended a lawyer for illegal and grossly negligent acts in connection with the representation of a client. The lawyer, who had recently entered private practice, was assigned to one of his firm's satellite offices, where he claimed he was largely un-supervised. The court did not resolve this claim, but did say: "In the fu-ture . . . this attitude of leaving new lawyers to 'sink or swim' will not be tolerated. Had this young attorney received the collegial support and guidance expected of supervising attorneys, this incident might never have occurred."

In In re Weinberg, 119 Ill. 2d 309, 518 N.E.2d 1037, 1040 (1988), Weinberg was retained to file an appeal for a criminal defendant. He re-tained Triwush, a younger lawyer who shared office space with him, to write the brief. Triwush failed to file the brief in the time allowed and the appeal was dismissed. Weinberg was unaware that Triwush had missed the deadline until it was too late. The client subsequently learned of the dismissal and hired another lawyer, who had the appeal reinstated. The conviction was affirmed. Neither Weinberg nor Triwush had received payment from the client. Triwush was suspended for six months. Wein-berg argued that he should be privately reprimanded. The court im-posed a public censure and wrote:

> "An attorney cannot avoid his professional obligations to a client by the simple device of delegating work to others." Although much of the blame must fall on Triwush, he was a relatively inexperienced attorney, having been admitted to practice . . just shortly before he assumed the brief-writ-ing responsibilities. . . . [Weinberg's] failure to monitor the progress of the appeal more closely is therefore less defensible. Discipline may be appro-priate even though there is no dishonest motive for the misconduct.

A failure to supervise that leads to the client's financial loss will also support malpractice liability. Anderson v. Hall, 755 F. Supp. 2 (D.D.C. 1991) (action against partnership after associate let statute of limitations run on client's claim). Liability for supervisory defaults has its limits. In Pavelic & LeFlore v. Marvel Entertainment Group, 493 U.S. 120 (1990), the Court declined to construe Rule 11 to hold a law firm responsible for the violations of individual lawyers. See page 373 supra and the material on vicarious liability in malpractice at page 628 infra.

QUESTIONS

12.6   You are an associate in a large firm. Since you are also a notary public, other lawyers occasionally ask you to notarize various doc-uments. A younger associate brings you a document and asks you to notarize it and to predate the notarization. When you hesitate, she says "Forget it, I'll find someone else to do it," and leaves. What if any responsibilities do you have under the code? Under the Model Rules?

12.7   "Six months ago, I hired Catherine Sutton. Most of her work is for a major underwriter client. It requires attention to detail and meticulous compliance with numerous regulations. Mistakes can be costly. Since Kitty arrived, I have received a dozen comments about her from other partners and even one from my longtime secretary. A sample: 'She often seems distracted, preoccupied.' 'Her clothing choice is a little provocative.' 'She can be flirtatious, no question about it.' 'I ran into Kitty at a bar. Her friends are, well, freaky.' 'Kitty dropped by the office Saturday morning and she was definitely, totally stoned.'

Yesterday, at Kitty's half-year review, I tried to discuss these things. When she sensed where I was going, she said: 'Look, you just said my work was good,' which I had. 'No client has complained about me,' which is true. 'That's your only legitimate concern. My personal life is not the firm's business as long as I keep it out of the office, which I do.' And she left.

What do I do now?"

F.   UNAUTHORIZED PRACTICE OF LAW

States license lawyers to assure a level of quality and to protect their citizens. One consequence of this barrier to practice is that fewer people are available to provide legal services. As a result, we might expect the cost (as well as the quality) of a particular legal service to be higher than it would be if anyone could offer that service. But what if the service requires little discretion, so the threat to quality is low?

Think about the following questions while reading this section: Shouldn't a consumer of a service be entitled to hire whomever he or she wishes? Should the consumer be entitled to take the risk of hiring a person who has not attended law school to perform a service arguably "legal"? In Alan Morrison, Defining the Unauthorized Practice of Law: Some New Ways of Looking at an Old Question, 4 Nova L.J. 363 (1980), the author wrote:

> [D]riving across the country, you are surely more likely to arrive safely in a 1979 Rolls Royce than you would in a 1940 Studebaker. Yet no one has suggested that everyone has to have a Rolls Royce to drive across country. Even if lawyers are the equivalent of Rolls Royces (and I think most people think they are more equivalent to Studebakers), there are some situations in which society should let people drive Studebakers. In my view, an individual should be able to choose secretaries, real estate brokers, accountants or whatever, instead of having to use lawyers, unless there is a very good rea-

son why free choice and added cost must be imposed for the protection of the individual.

On the other hand, doesn't the state have a right to protect people from their own foolishness? Does your answer to this question vary depending upon whether the client wishes to utilize the services of the attorney in a criminal or civil matter? Does it vary depending on whether the state is prepared to provide free counsel to an indigent client in a civil matter?

The bar's monopoly on the provision of legal services might be diluted in two ways. First, we could create an exception. Even though a particular service is considered "legal," we could allow other professionals to perform the service too. Second, we could adopt a narrow definition of the practice of law. If a service is not defined as legal, a person who is not a lawyer may perform it without being guilty of the unauthorized practice of law.

Traditionally, the definition of the practice of law has been broad. Alan Morrison quotes former ABA President Chesterfield Smith as saying that "[t]he practice of law is anything my client will pay me to do." 4 Nova L.J. at 365. A slightly less comprehensive definition was stated by the New Mexico Supreme Court in State ex rel. Norvell v. Credit Bureau of Albuquerque, 85 N.M. 521, 514 P.2d 40, 45 (1973), as follows.

> [The] indicia of the practice of law, insofar as court proceedings are concerned, include the following: (1) representation of parties before judicial or administrative bodies, (2) preparation of pleadings and other papers incident to actions and special proceedings, (3) management of such action and proceeding, and non-court related activities such as (4) giving legal advice and counsel, (5) rendering a service that requires the use of legal knowledge or skill, (6) preparing instruments and contracts by which legal rights are secured.

An even more expansive definition appears in R. J. Edwards, Inc. v. Hert, 504 P.2d 407, 416 (Okla. 1972), which said the practice of law was "the rendition of services requiring the knowledge and application of legal principles and technique to serve the interests of another with his consent."

Who decides whether to create an exception to unauthorized practice rules? Who decides how to define the practice of law? The answer is the courts, with or without some participation by the legislature, depending on the jurisdiction. Recall the "inherent powers" doctrine (see page 2 supra). It applies in this instance too. Whether or not particular conduct is the practice of law is a question of law, not ethics. The Code and Rules forbid lawyers to engage in unauthorized law practice or help another do so, DR 3-101 and Rule 5.5, but neither document defines law practice.

Remember that not only the rights of laypersons but also the rights of out-of-state lawyers depend on these questions of definition and exception (see page 570 supra). The definitions and exceptions, however, may be differently articulated depending on whether the person who seeks to provide the service is an out-of-state lawyer or a layperson. But why should that be? Remedies may also vary. Out-of-state lawyers are unlikely to be prosecuted, but they do risk losing their fees. (See page 586 supra.)

Unauthorized law practice can occur in two ways. A person who is not admitted to the bar of a jurisdiction may render legal services in that jurisdiction. Alternatively, a person or entity that is not authorized to practice law may hire a licensed lawyer and offer his or her services to another. In the second situation, the client is at least represented by counsel, but restrictions nevertheless apply because of a presumed threat of lay interference with the professional relationship. The second situation is addressed in Chapter 14.

PROFESSIONAL ADJUSTERS, INC. v. TANDON
433 N.E.2d 779 (Ind. 1982)

PIVARNIK, JUSTICE.

Plaintiff-appellant Professional Adjusters, Inc., appeals action of the trial court in dismissing their cause of action for "failure to state a claim upon which relief could be granted." Plaintiff's complaint was based on allegations of a contract obligating defendants Tandon to pay a contingent amount for services by Plaintiff in adjusting the settlement of a claim of Tandon's against their insurance company, United States Fidelity and Guaranty Company. Plaintiff's complaint against USF&G was based on the fact that USF&G settled with the Tandons and paid to them and their attorney a settlement amount without protecting plaintiffs on their alleged contract and assignment of the claim rights.

Defendant's response in its motion to dismiss was that the statutes under which Plaintiff proposed to act as public adjusters in its representation of defendants Tandon, authorized Plaintiffs to practice law in derogation of the Indiana Constitution, specifically, Art. VII §4, which places the exclusive control of regulation and supervision of the practice of law in the Supreme Court of Indiana, and Art. III, §1, which provides for the separation of powers of the legislative, executive and judicial branches, and prohibits any of these branches from exercising any of the functions of another branch except as expressly provided in the Constitution. It was the defendant-appellee's contention that the alleged contract was therefore unenforceable. The trial court granted Defendant-appellee's motion to dismiss, finding that Ind. Code §27-1-24-1 et seq. (Burns 1975) was unconstitutional since it authorized the practice of law by plaintiff corporation. . . .

The facts show that defendants Tandon had a fire loss on their mobile home in Terre Haute, Indiana, on December 22, 1976. They had a policy of insurance to cover such loss with defendant USF&G, and filed a claim with that company. USF&G offered to settle the claim for eight thousand dollars, ($8,000) which figure was unacceptable to the Tandons. The Tandons then hired Professional Adjusters, Inc., to handle their claim against USF&G for them. Plaintiffs prepared estimates of repair cost, temporary electrical costs, depreciation from actual cash value, replacement of outdoor furniture and fixtures, equipment and carpeting, estimates on unscheduled property with dates of purchase and current value and depreciated value, and a claim for additional living expenses, including projections for completion and repair which they claim required the expending of sixty-five hours of time. Professional Adjusters, Inc., then submitted this claim to GAB Service, Inc., which was the adjusting agency of USF&G. In response, Professional Adjusters received from GAB Service, Inc., an offer to settle the claim for substantially more than the original offer of eight-thousand dollars ($8,000). Defendants Tandon, in the meantime contacted a lawyer and subsequently settled the claim with USF&G. Tandons tendered a check in the amount of five-hundred dollars ($500) to Professional Adjusters, Inc., which was offered as payment, which was refused. . . .

[The relevant statute] provides that before anyone can act as a certified public adjuster he must be issued a certificate of authority by the Commissioner of Insurance of the State of Indiana and succeeding sections of the chapter provide for the mechanics to be employed by the Insurance Commissioner. [The statute also] provides for a written examination for the Commissioner to give applicants to determine the trustworthiness and competence of the applicant and provides that such testing shall include but not be limited to the following areas: "1) the Indiana Insurance Code; 2) inventory and appraisal procedures; 3) building construction; 4) standard fire policy; 5) insurance contracts related to claims on real or personal property and 6) insurance coverage questions regarding business interruptions, improvements and betterments, replacement cost coverage, concurrent and nonconcurrent apportionment, co-insurance and contribution."

[The statute] creates a new type of adjuster heretofore unknown in the insurance field. All of the traditional forms and duties of insurance adjusters are excepted from this statute. Adjusters have traditionally been employees or agents of insurance companies hired by them to attempt to ascertain the nature of a loss under one of their policies and to attempt to settle it in behalf of the company. This was true of independent adjusting agencies that were hired by insurance companies to act as their agents in making an adjustment. Those adjusters who were employees of the company were, of course, agents who acted in full authority to bind the company in settling with its insured. Independent adjusting firms were hired by companies to act as independent appraisers to help the company fix and determine the amount of a loss so that the company could then settle the claim with the insured. This statute proposes to create a public adjuster which represents an insured and receives compensation to act on behalf of that assured to negotiate for and effect the settlement of a claim for loss or damages. It does not limit the activity and authority of the adjuster to appraise the loss and report back to the client the fair value of the claim so that the client can then go forward and settle his claim. It authorizes the adjuster to go forward and to negotiate for and effect that settlement as a direct agent and representative of the insured. This is, pure and simple, the practice of law. In acting as the statute authorizes a public adjuster to act, he is acting as an attorney at law.

In the present case, Professional Adjusters, Inc., made a determination of the loss of Tandons and then submitted this claim to the insurance carrier for negotiation of a settlement. The fact that the negotiations did not reach the stage where there was a bargaining process of offers and counter-offers does not make it any less negotiation. Plaintiffs were in all ways acting as attorneys-at-law for Tandons by submitting a figure which they would deem acceptable for their loss and contemplating in return a response from the insurance carrier that would effect the settlement. They expected to receive remuneration in an amount that was contingent upon the amount they recovered. As one of the allegations of their complaint, the plaintiffs alleged: "6. On February 3, 1977, the defendant USF&G formally rejected the proof of loss filed by defendant Tandon on January 10, 1977, and on March 18, 1977, the plaintiff furnished all of the above claim information to GAB Business Service, Inc., the adjusting agent for USF&G pursuant to said contract."

Thus, in their complaint, the plaintiffs state that not only did the contract contemplate that it would be the duty of plaintiffs to take the claim forward to USF&G, but they alleged that is, in fact, what they did. In discussing the subject of the practice of law, this Court stated, in Matter of Perrello, (1979) Ind., 386 N.E.2d 174, 179:

> The core element of practicing law is the giving of legal advice to a client and the placing of oneself in the very sensitive relationship wherein the confidence of the client, and the management of his affairs, is left totally in the hands of the attorney. The undertaking to minister to the legal problems of another, creates an attorney-client relationship without regard to whether the services are actually performed by the one so undertaking the responsibility or are delegated or subcontracted to another. It is the opinion of this Court that merely entering into such relationship constitutes the practice of law.

We further said, in Groninger v. Fletcher Trust Co., (1942) 220 Ind. 202, 207, 41 N.E.2d 140:

> The practice of law is restricted to natural persons who have been licensed upon the basis of established character and competence as a protection to the public against lack of knowledge, skill, integrity, and fidelity. Disbarment procedure is available in the case of those who do not conform to proper practice. The practice of law involves advising or rendering services for another. A natural person may plead his own case in court or do any of the things for himself which if done for another would constitute practicing law. He may discuss the legal aspects of his affairs with other interested parties or with strangers. Either a natural person or a corporation may employ lawyers to do these things.

The very criteria required under Ind. Code §27-1-24-1 et seq. in its creation of Certified Public Adjusters is knowledge and competency in dealing with rights and liabilities of other persons as required in the ethical considerations in case law heretofore relied upon, but does not require admission to the Bar in this State and therefore does not subject those so acting to the disciplinary rules of this Court. Undertaking the determination of rights and liabilities under an insurance contract and the negotiation of settlements requires the interpretation of the terms of that contract. . . .

The trial court is in all things affirmed.

In Cultum v. Heritage House Realtors, Inc., 103 Wash. 2d 623, 694 P.2d 630, 633-635 (1985), the question was whether a real estate salesperson who completed "a form earnest money agreement containing a contingency clause" was engaged in the unauthorized practice of law. The preprinted form was essentially an offer to sell at a stated price contingent on a satisfactory report from an examining engineer. The court held that "although the completion of form earnest money agreements might be commonly understood as the practice of law, we believe it is in the public interest to permit licensed real estate brokers or licensed salespersons to complete such lawyer prepared standard form agreements; provided that in doing so they comply with the standard of care demanded of an attorney." The court continued:

> We no longer believe that the supposed benefits to the public from the lawyers' monopoly on performing legal services justifies limiting the public's freedom of choice. The public has the right to use the full array of services that brokers and salespersons can provide. The fact that brokers and salespersons will complete these forms at no extra charge, whereas attorneys would charge an additional fee, weighs heavily toward allowing this choice.
>
> Another important consideration is the fact that the drafting of form earnest money agreements is incidental to the main business of real estate brokers and salespersons. These individuals are specially trained to pro-

vide buyers and sellers with competent and efficient assistance in purchasing or selling a home. Because the selection and filling in of standard simple forms by brokers and sales persons is an incidental service, it normally must be rendered before such individuals can receive their commissions. Clearly the advantages, if any, to be derived by enjoining brokers and salespersons from completing earnest money agreements are outweighed by the fact that such conveyances are part of the everyday business of the realtor and necessary to the effective completion of such business. . . .

It should be emphasized that the holding in this case is limited in scope. Our decision provides that a real estate broker or salesperson is permitted to complete simple printed standardized real estate forms, which forms must be approved by a lawyer, it being understood that these forms shall not be used for other than simple real estate transactions which arise in the usual course of the broker's business and that such forms will be used only in connection with real estate transactions actually handled by such broker or salesperson as a broker or salesperson and then without charge for the simple service of completing the forms. . . .

In light of the courts' inherent power to regulate the practice of law, we believe it is totally within our power to allow brokers and salespersons to practice law within the narrow confines that our holding allows, irrespective of what [statutory law] might suggest.

The Troubled World of Unauthorized Practice

The Indiana and Washington Supreme Courts agree on one essential fact: *They* decide who can practice law and what "the law" is. The Washington Supreme Court appears marginally more permissive but even it severely limits the authority granted realtors. Exactly which of plaintiffs' services offended the Indiana court?

Few subjects in the area of lawyer regulation are met with as much lay suspicion as unauthorized practice rules. Why is that? First, it is obvious that these rules can be and are used to restrict the "supply side" of legal services and thereby raise fees. Many people are skeptical of the claim that the profession's motive for guarding its borders is selfless concern for clients. See generally Deborah Rhode's examination of the issue in Policing the Professional Monopoly: A Constitutional and Empirical Analysis of Unauthorized Practice Prohibitions, 34 Stan. L. Rev. 1 (1981).

Second, courts occasionally invalidate legislation that means to help consumers by letting laypersons perform fairly routine work at foreseeably lower costs. (These actions may be brought by lawyers or bar groups.) If the court relies on the argument that the definition of law practice is within its inherent power, the public is left with little democratic control (short of a state constitutional amendment) over a major component of their justice systems — the cost and source of advice.

Last, the kinds of "legal" services a layperson may wish to offer will likely be simple, requiring little or no discretion. If a client retains a law firm to provide such a routine service, he may discover that it is mostly performed by a lay employee of the firm, with minimal lawyer supervision. See Florida Opinion 89-5 (nonlawyer law firm employees may handle real estate closings under certain circumstances). The client may then wonder why he cannot hire a nonlawyer directly and save the overhead. Of course, these very simple services form the bulk of many lawyers' practices.

Uncontested Divorces

In many jurisdictions, a person can obtain an uncontested divorce by serving his or her spouse with a summons, completing several forms, and submitting the forms to court. The process is fairly straightforward. Lawyers often have paralegals perform it. Enterprising nonlawyers — sometimes former paralegals or legal secretaries — on occasion seek to begin their own businesses, where they sell or type forms at rates much lower than a lawyer would charge for the same service. Because the forms are foreign to most people, and use some words whose meaning is not self-evident, the nonlawyers who sell or type the forms are often asked to aid in completing them. At this point, lawyers and bar associations step in to charge the nonlawyers with the practice of law. Their challenges have been successful. See, for example, Florida Bar v. Brumbaugh, 355 So. 2d 1186 (Fla. 1978); State Bar v. Cramer, 399 Mich. 116, 249 N.W.2d 1 (1976). Why should behavior become the practice of law simply because one person, who has a constitutional right to sell a form with instructions (see page 608 infra), also helps another person fill it out?

In a move as rare as it is enlightened, the Florida Supreme Court amended its rules regulating the Florida bar to state:

> [I]t shall not constitute the unlicensed practice of law for nonlawyers to engage in limited oral communications to assist individuals in the completion of legal forms approved by the Supreme Court of Florida. Oral communications by nonlawyers are restricted to those communications reasonably necessary to elicit factual information to complete the form(s) and inform the individual how to file such forms. [In re Amendment to Rules Regulating the Florida Bar, 510 So. 2d 596, 597 (Fla. 1987).]

Will Courts Share Power with Legislatures?

May a state legislature authorize nonlawyers to do work that the courts consider the practice of law? The answer seems to turn on construction of state constitutions and assessments of the inherent power of courts.

In Florida Bar v. Moses, 380 So. 2d 412, 418 (Fla. 1980), the respondent, a labor relations specialist, represented a client at an unfair labor practice hearing. The court recognized the power of the state legislature to "convert [the practice of law by nonlawyers] into authorized representation" by qualified persons. This power, coupled with legislative requirements for standards of expertise and qualification, "ousts" the state supreme court's responsibility to protect the public through regulation of the practice of law. In the *Moses* case, the statute validly "authorize[d] agencies to permit [appearances by] 'qualified' lay representatives." But since the agency had set no standards for qualification, "[it] invalidly exercised delegated authority and [the] respondent's conduct constituted the unauthorized practice of law."

Compare Denver Bar Assn. v. Public Utilities Commission, 154 Colo. 273, 391 P.2d 467, 469-471 (1964), which held that "the creature of the legislature, the [Public Utilities] Commission with its rule-making power, does not in any way have the prerogative of superseding the exclusive power of the judiciary . . . to determine what is or is not the practice of law." The court limited the commission, "as an arm of the legislature," to "authoriz[ing] by rule certain things, the doing of which does not constitute the practice of law."

In Hunt v. Maricopa County Employees Merit System Commission, 127 Ariz. 259, 619 P.2d 1036 (1980), the court gave only limited approval to legislation authorizing lay representation on personnel matters in administrative hearings. The court limited authorization to representation at hearings on those matters in which the amount in controversy was so small that hiring an attorney was financially unfeasible. The court also held that a lay representative could not receive compensation for her service.

In Henize v. Giles, 22 Ohio. St. 3d 213, 490 N.E.2d 585 (1986), the Supreme Court of Ohio held that it was not the practice of law to represent parties at hearings of the Ohio Unemployment Compensation Board of Review. Consequently, a Board rule allowing representation by nonlawyers was upheld. The court stressed that claims before the Board are generally less than $3,000, counsel fees are limited to 10 percent of recovery, and the hearings are informal.

Should Paralegals Be Licensed?

Perhaps the mistake here is in thinking of "law" monolithically. In this view, either you are a lawyer and can provide legal services in any area of the law in which you are competent, or you are not a lawyer and can offer to provide no legal services except for the few modest inroads that a few state supreme courts are willing to permit.

Increasingly, reformers have called for legislation or, if need be, a state constitutional amendment, that would permit persons who are not members of a state's bar to provide legal counseling in areas of law for which the traditional educational and examination requirements are unnecessary. Two proposals in California would have created the status of legal technician. Legal technicians would have been regulated not by the courts but by the state Department of Consumer Affairs. Under one scheme, however, the state supreme court would have had ultimate authority. Legal technicians would have been able to render legal services in areas such as family law, housing law, public benefits law, real estate law and estate administration. They would have been licensed and possibly reexamined periodically. See Deborah Rhode, The Delivery of Legal Services by Non-Lawyers, 4 Geo. J. Legal Ethics 209 (1990). The Board of Governors of the California State Bar ultimately rejected the proposals. Wall St. J., Aug. 28, 1991, at B4.

Recall that even the ABA Committee on Professionalism had recommended exploration of paralegal licensing. (See page 8 supra.) But the recommendation went nowhere.

Paralegal licensing holds out the promise of low-cost legal assistance to millions of people who now have no access to lawyers. It would also provide a source of cheaper assistance to people who must now use lawyers. Yet the California proposals inspired instant denunciation. The state bar president labeled them "anti-consumer." Several bankruptcy judges analogized the proposals to licensing "faith healers." A local bar president said the proposals would "flood the market with individuals lacking the requisite knowledge, financial resources, ethical requirements, and proper regulation [to] prey upon the unsuspecting [public]." The president of the Texas (!) State Bar said the proposals would be like allowing "nurses to perform brain surgery." See Rhode, supra, at 223-224.

As you can see, the issue creates much heat and many bad similes. Tens of thousands of lawyers depend on work that might otherwise go to licensed legal technicians. The lawyers would then have to reduce their fees significantly, persuade the public that it ought to pay them more anyway, maintain their customary rates and get less business, or fold.

What about you? You have committed three years of your life to studying law. In tuition, living expenses, and income foregone, your education is going to cost you tens of thousands of dollars. When it is over, you will spend another two grueling months preparing for the bar examination. How will you feel if, after going out into practice, you see out your window a competing office of legal technicians who may have had little or no formal training and passed an easier examination? Their fees are 30 to 50 percent less than yours for the same services. Unfair? Anticonsumer? Are these the same question?

Constitutional Limitations

Despite the claim of inherent judicial power to define law practice, several constraints exist. One is the federal Constitution.

In National Revenue Corp. v. Violet, 807 F.2d 285 (1st Cir. 1986), the court reviewed a state law that prohibited anyone but state-licensed lawyers from engaging in debt collection in Rhode Island. The court held that the law unconstitutionally burdened interstate commerce.

See also Sperry v. State ex rel. Florida Bar, 373 U.S. 379, 385-402 (1963), where the Supreme Court ruled that state power to regulate the practice of law had to yield to incompatible federal legislation that authorized lay representation in cases before the United States Patent Office. By virtue of the Supremacy Clause, Congress could authorize lay agents to provide legal services "reasonably necessary and incident to the preparation and prosecution of patent applications." "The State maintains control over the practice of law within its borders except to the limited extent necessary for the accomplishment of the federal objectives." Furthermore, the Patent Office "safeguards ['citizens from unskilled and unethical practitioners'] by testing applications for registration" and authorizing practice only before the Patent Office. Florida Bar re Advisory Opinion, 571 So. 2d 430 (Fla. 1990) (state court cannot prohibit nonlawyers from preparing and presenting documents to federal agencies that have admitted them to practice). But see Ferguson v. Skrupa, 372 U.S. 726 (1963) (rejecting due process challenge to Kansas law defining "debt adjustment" as the practice of law).

In Johnson v. Avery, 393 U.S. 483, 485-487 (1969), the Supreme Court held that a state could not exercise its power to control the practice of law in a manner that interferes with the federally protected right of a prisoner to file a petition for habeas corpus relief. The Court emphasized the "fundamental importance" of the writ of habeas corpus, which "enable[s] those unlawfully incarcerated to obtain their freedom." The Tennessee regulation prohibited fellow inmates from helping poorly educated prisoners prepare petitions; the Court found "[f]or all practical purposes, if [poorly educated] prisoners cannot have the assistance of a 'jail-house lawyer,' their possibly valid constitutional claims will never be heard in any court." Without reasonable alternatives to help these prisoners, the regulation "effectively" prevented them from filing habeas corpus petitions and was, therefore, invalid.

In a concurrence, Justice Douglas noted "the increasing complexities of our governmental apparatus," and the shortage of lawyers to supervise and manage the filing of legal claims. Since much of the work on these claims requires no legal expertise, he concluded that lay agents should be able to assume the responsibility for their processing, preparation, and filing as a "next friend."

Justice Douglas's view, at least its application outside prison walls, was not followed in Oregon State Bar v. Wright, 280 Or. 693, 573 P.2d 283, 285-292 (1977). The defendant, a nonlawyer, had "draft[ed] pleadings, briefs and demurrers for scores of people," but received no compensation for his services. He argued that this conduct was protected by Justice Douglas's "next friend" doctrine. The Oregon court distinguished Johnson v. Avery. The defendant's clients did "not appear to be prisoners without other alternatives for assistance." Furthermore, the court found no authority to support a federally protected right of nonprisoners to legal assistance from a nonlawyer. In its view, Johnson v. Avery "did not hold that the fellow prisoner had a federally protected right to provide such assistance."

Efforts to stop publication of books or materials that enable purchasers to represent themselves have generally failed, on the theory that the author is offering general advice and is not addressing the reader's or user's legal situation. In New York County Lawyers' Assn. v. Dacey, 21 N.Y.2d 694, 234 N.E.2d 459, 287 N.Y.S.2d 422 (1967), the plaintiff bar association tried to stop Norman Dacey from selling his book How to Avoid Probate. The book purported to instruct readers on how they might go about organizing their assets during their lifetime so that on their death, these assets would pass to others without having to be administered under the supervision of a probate court. Probate is a "bread and butter" area of practice for lawyers, including general practitioners, possibly explaining the motivation for the lawsuit. The New York Court of Appeals ruled that Dacey was not practicing law simply by selling a book containing information about law. See also Oregon State Bar v. Gilchrist, 272 Or. 552, 538 P.2d 913 (1975) (do-it-yourself divorce kits).

These cases recognize a First Amendment interest in the underlying activity. *Dacey* specifically relied on the dissent in the lower court, 28 A.D.2d 161, 283 N.Y.S.2d 984 (1st Dept. 1967), which cited the federal and state constitutional guarantees of freedom of speech and press. *Gilchrist* cited the same dissent.

G. SPECIALIZATION

There are essentially two types of specialization plans: certification and self-designation. In a certification plan, a board tests and certifies applicants as specialists in particular areas of law. Certification may require that the specialists take continuing legal education courses in the area and devote a designated percentage of their practice to the specialty. In a self-designated plan, an attorney is permitted to designate himself or herself as a specialist in a particular area of law if the attorney devotes an identified amount of time to the area. Continuing legal education in the specialty might be required. Some states, including Florida, have both self-designation and certification plans.

Both the Model Code and the Model Rules prohibit the use of certain language that suggests that a lawyer is a specialist in a particular area, unless the lawyer is designated as a specialist by an authority recognized by the state. DR 2-105 forbids a lawyer to "hold himself out publicly as a specialist, as practicing in certain areas of law or as limiting his practice" except under certain circumstances. Some states have adopted this rule in modified form. For example, New York's version of DR 2-105 says: "A lawyer or law firm may publicly identify one or more areas of law in which the lawyer or the law firm practices, or may state that the practice of the lawyer or law firm is limited to one or more areas of law."

The Model Rules have parallel restrictions. Model Rule 7.4 permits a lawyer to communicate "the fact that the lawyer does or does not practice in particular fields of law." But the lawyer is forbidden to "state or imply that the lawyer is a specialist," with certain exceptions.

Prohibition on use of the word "specialist" raises First Amendment issues, doesn't it? Peel v. Attorney Registration & Disciplinary Commn. of Illinois, 110 S. Ct. 2281 (1990), discussed at page 819 infra, invalidated a prohibition against legal advertisements that included the fact of a lawyer's certification as a Civil Trial Specialist by the National Board of Trial Advocacy (NBTA). The NBTA is an organization co-sponsored by a number of private bar groups.

XIII

Control of Quality: Remedies for Professional Failure

A. MALPRACTICE

If the size of our research files is any indication, no subject in this book has seen more change in the last 10 years than a lawyer's liability to clients and third parties, whether based on traditional malpractice rules or on new theories establishing new responsibilities to nonclients (see page 649 infra). Along with legal advertising (see page 785 infra), lay influence on law firms (see Chapter 14), and judicial sanctions for abuse of the adversary process (see page 360 supra), greater professional exposure to civil liability will continue to influence (haunt?) the conduct and nature of professional life.

Here are some questions to keep in mind as we look at the issues:

Is there a "crisis"? That word keeps popping up in discussions about increased professional liability. Indeed, the words "malpractice" and "crisis" have become seemingly inseparable. One half expects to see them hyphenated. Nonetheless, what is a crisis for lawyers may not be all bad, and from the consumer perspective it may even look good. Or have some of the cases gone too far?

How will increased liability change lawyers' behavior? Lawyers argue that greater legal exposure to nonclients will make them timid, that they will begin to think of themselves first and their clients second, that they will no longer be as zealous in pursuit of their clients' goals, and that as a result the legal system will suffer. Some courts have respected these arguments, especially in litigation, perhaps on the theory that in litigation lawyers are most like gladiators and can be least expected to reflect on the interests of anyone but their clients. And of course, other parties to the litigation will usually have their own lawyers to protect them. See Westlake v. Abrams, 565 F. Supp. 1330 (N.D. Ga. 1983).

Is There a Connection Between Professionalism and the "Crisis"? Although perhaps it could never be proved in any but a theoretical way, an increase in civil liability to clients and others may be partly a consequence of the perceived diminution of professionalism (see pages 6-9 supra). This risk is in fact cited by those who favor rules that would prevent law firms from owning ancillary businesses. (See page 740 infra.) Lawyers appear increasingly willing to step over the line that separates advisers from principals, thereby subjecting themselves to greater exposure for their conduct. See Brown v. Donco Enterprises, 783 F.2d 644 (6th Cir. 1986), which draws the adviser-participant distinction in the context of an antitrust claim. See also Westlake v. Abrams, supra, drawing the same distinction with regard to liability under the securities laws. If it appears that lawyers have crossed the line and the deal turns sour — and investors or purchasers who lose money start looking for someone to sue — lawyers, with their deep pockets and large malpractice policies, are going to look mighty tempting. And, complain as they will, lawyers should remember that before they wound up on the defendants' side of the court caption, another lawyer had to put them there.

Is greater exposure the result of a decrease in the sanctity of professions generally?   Here we encounter several trends. First is the sharp increase in medical malpractice actions. By bringing and winning these actions for great sums of money, lawyers made it acceptable to sue professionals and to seek large recoveries or settlements. The idea that it is wrong to sue someone who tried to help you when you were in trouble is no longer influential. Second is the increase in the liability of accountants to persons who are not in privity with them (that is, nonclients). By bringing these actions and persuading courts to adopt doctrines leading to huge recoveries or settlements against accountants, lawyers created the theories that could easily be turned against themselves. After all, lawyers and accountants do very similar things (sometimes, as in the tax area, the same thing).

1. Liability to Clients

Once again we confront the "who is a client?" question. As you know by now, in our new Einsteinian universe of lawyer regulation this question can no longer be answered with good old Newtonian certainty (see pages 13, 227, and 256 supra). Very often, of course, there will be no room to quibble, especially if the purported client has a retainer agreement, monthly statements, and a pile of cancelled checks (generally sufficient but by no means necessary conditions for creation of a professional relationship). Occasionally, however, the issue will be fuzzier, as we see in the somewhat unnerving *Togstad* case that follows.

A lawyer can also be sued by a nonclient on any of a number of theories (which seems to be increasing exponentially). We plumb this trend in part C. But in light of it, why the big deal whether the plaintiff was or was not a client? For two reasons: First, some jurisdictions are less willing than others to recognize liability to nonclients, so it may be that either you were a client or you're out of court. Second, even in places that give nonclients lots of room to sue lawyers, clients will enjoy yet more room. Lawyers always have fiduciary relationships with their clients, but only sometimes with nonclients. And lawyers will always owe clients a duty of care in the performance of legal work, but rarely so with nonclients.

To gain one or both of these advantages of "clienthood," plaintiffs who would not traditionally have been considered clients of a lawyer may attempt, like Cinderella's stepsisters, to squeeze into a client's slippers, to become — we can invent a term here — stepclients? Client-equivalents? We discuss client-equivalents in part A2.

To talk sensibly about the issue of liability to clients, we need to know how to identify a client. Usually, but not always, identifying a client is not a problem.

TOGSTAD v. VESELY, OTTO, MILLER & KEEFE
291 N.W.2d 686 (Minn. 1980)

PER CURIAM.

This is an appeal by the defendants from a judgment of the Hennepin County District Court involving an action for legal malpractice. The jury found that the defendant attorney Jerre Miller was negligent and that, as a direct result of such negligence, plaintiff John Togstad sustained damages in the amount of $610,500 and his wife, plaintiff Joan Togstad, in the amount of $39,000. Defendants (Miller and his law firm) appeal to this court from the denial of their motion for judgment notwithstanding the verdict or, alternatively, for a new trial. We affirm.

In August 1971, John Togstad began to experience severe headaches and on August 16, 1971, was admitted to Methodist Hospital where tests disclosed that the headaches were caused by a large aneurysm on the left internal carotid artery. The attending physician, Dr. Paul Blake, a neurological surgeon, treated the problem by applying a Selverstone clamp to the left common carotid artery. The clamp was surgically implanted on

August 27, 1971, in Togstad's neck to allow the gradual closure of the artery over a period of days. . . .

In the early morning hours of August 29, 1971, a nurse observed that Togstad was unable to speak or move. At the time, the clamp was one-half (50%) closed. Upon discovering Togstad's condition, the nurse called a resident physician, who did not adjust the clamp. Dr. Blake was also immediately informed of Togstad's condition and arrived about an hour later, at which time he opened the clamp. Togstad is now severely paralyzed in his right arm and leg, and is unable to speak.

Plaintiffs' expert, Dr. Ward Woods, testified that Togstad's paralysis and loss of speech was due to a lack of blood supply to his brain. Dr. Woods stated that the inadequate blood flow resulted from the clamp being 50% closed and that the negligence of Dr. Blake and the hospital precluded the clamp's being opened in time to avoid permanent brain damage. Specifically, Dr. Woods claimed that Dr. Blake and the hospital were negligent for (1) failing to place the patient in the intensive care unit or to have a special nurse conduct certain neurological tests every half-hour; (2) failing to write adequate orders; (3) failing to open the clamp immediately upon discovering that the patient was unable to speak; and (4) the absence of personnel capable of opening the clamp. . . .

About 14 months after her husband's hospitalization began, plaintiff Joan Togstad met with attorney Jerre Miller regarding her husband's condition. Neither she nor her husband was personally acquainted with Miller or his law firm prior to that time. John Togstad's former work supervisor, Ted Bucholz, made the appointment and accompanied Mrs. Togstad to Miller's office. Bucholz was present when Mrs. Togstad and Miller discussed the case.[3]

Mrs. Togstad had become suspicious of the circumstances surrounding her husband's tragic condition due to the conduct and statements of the hospital nurses shortly after the paralysis occurred. One nurse told Mrs. Togstad that she had checked Mr. Togstad at 2 A.M. and he was fine; that when she returned at 3 A.M. by mistake, to give him someone else's medication, he was unable to move or speak; and that if she hadn't accidentally entered the room no one would have discovered his condition until morning. Mrs. Togstad also noticed that the other nurses were upset and crying, and that Mr. Togstad's condition was a topic of conversation.

Mrs. Togstad testified that she told Miller "everything that happened at the hospital," including the nurses' statements and conduct which had raised a question in her mind. She stated that she "believed" she had told Miller "about the procedure and what was undertaken, what was done, and what happened." She brought no records with her. Miller took notes

---

3. Bucholz, who knew Miller through a local luncheon club, died prior to the trial of the instant action.

and asked questions during the meeting, which lasted 45 minutes to an hour. At its conclusion, according to Mrs. Togstad, Miller said that "he did not think we had a legal case, however, he was going to discuss this with his partner." She understood that if Miller changed his mind after talking to his partner, he would call her. Mrs. Togstad "gave it" a few days and, since she did not hear from Miller, decided "that they had come to the conclusion that there wasn't a case." No fee arrangements were discussed, no medical authorizations were requested, nor was Mrs. Togstad billed for the interview.

Mrs. Togstad denied that Miller had told her his firm did not have expertise in the medical malpractice field, urged her to see another attorney, or related to her that the statute of limitations for medical malpractice actions was two years. She did not consult another attorney until one year after she talked to Miller. Mrs. Togstad indicated that she did not confer with another attorney earlier because of her reliance on Miller's "legal advice" that they "did not have a case."

On cross-examination, Mrs. Togstad was asked whether she went to Miller's office "to see if he would take the case of [her] husband. . . ." She replied, "Well I guess it was to go for legal advice, what to do, where shall we go from here? That is what we went for." Again in response to defense counsel's questions, Mrs. Togstad testified as follows:

> Q. And it was clear to you, was it not, that what was taking place was a preliminary discussion between a prospective client and lawyer as to whether or not they wanted to enter into an attorney-client relationship?
> A. I am not sure how to answer that. It was for legal advice as to what to do.
> Q. And Mr. Miller was discussing with you your problem and indicating whether he, as a lawyer, wished to take the case, isn't that true?
> A. Yes.

On re-direct examination, Mrs. Togstad acknowledged that when she left Miller's office she understood that she had been given a "qualified, quality legal opinion that [she and her husband] did not have a malpractice case."

Miller's testimony was different in some respects from that of Mrs. Togstad. Like Mrs. Togstad, Miller testified that Mr. Bucholz arranged and was present at the meeting, which lasted about 45 minutes. According to Miller, Mrs. Togstad described the hospital incident, including the conduct of the nurses. He asked her questions, to which she responded. Miller testified that "[t]he only thing I told her [Mrs. Togstad] after we had pretty much finished the conversation was that there was nothing related in her factual circumstances that told me that she had a case that our firm would be interested in undertaking."

Miller also claimed he related to Mrs. Togstad "that because of the grievous nature of the injuries sustained by her husband, that this was only my opinion and she was encouraged to ask another attorney if she wished for another opinion" and "she ought to do so promptly." He testified that he informed Mrs. Togstad that his firm "was not engaged as experts" in the area of medical malpractice, and that they associated with the Charles Hvass firm in cases of that nature. Miller stated that at the end of the conference he told Mrs. Togstad that he would consult with Charles Hvass and if Hvass's opinion differed from his, Miller would so inform her. Miller recollected that he called Hvass a "couple days" later and discussed the case with him. It was Miller's impression that Hvass thought there was no liability for malpractice in the case. Consequently, Miller did not communicate with Mrs. Togstad further.

On cross-examination, Miller testified as follows:

Q.   Now, so there is no misunderstanding, and I am reading from your deposition, you understood that she was consulting with you as a lawyer, isn't that correct?

A.   That's correct.

Q.   That she was seeking legal advice from a professional attorney licensed to practice in this state and in this community?

A.   I think you and I did have another interpretation or use of the term "Advice." She was there to see whether or not she had a case and whether the firm would accept it.

Q.   We have two aspects; number one, your legal opinion concerning liability of a case for malpractice; number two, whether there was or wasn't liability, whether you would accept it, your firm, two separate elements, right?

A.   I would say so.

Q.   Were you asked on page 6 in the deposition, folio 14, "And you understood that she was seeking legal advice at the time that she was in your office, that is correct also, isn't it?" And did you give this answer, "I don't want to engage in semantics with you, but my impression was that she and Mr. Bucholz were asking my opinion after having related the incident that I referred to." The next question, "Your legal opinion?" Your answer, "Yes." Were those questions asked and were they given?

Mr. Collins: Objection to this, Your Honor. It is not impeachment.

The Court: Overruled.

The Witness: Yes, I gave those answers. Certainly, she was seeking my opinion as an attorney in the sense of whether or not there was a case that the firm would be interested in undertaking.

Kenneth Green, a Minneapolis attorney, was called as an expert by plaintiffs. He stated that in rendering legal advice regarding a claim of medical malpractice, the "minimum" an attorney should do would be to request medical authorizations from the client, review the hospital records, and consult with an expert in the field. John McNulty, a Minneapolis attorney, and Charles Hvass testified as experts on behalf of the defendants. McNulty stated that when an attorney is consulted as to whether he will take a case, the lawyer's only responsibility in refusing it is to so inform the party. He testified, however, that when a lawyer is asked his legal opinion on the merits of a medical malpractice claim, community standards require that the attorney check hospital records and consult with an expert before rendering his opinion.

Hvass stated that he had no recollection of Miller's calling him in October 1972 relative to the Togstad matter. He testified that:

A. . . . when a person comes in to me about a medical malpractice action, based upon what the individual has told me, I have to make a decision as to whether or not there probably is or probably is not, based upon that information, medical malpractice. And if, in my judgment, based upon what the client has told me, there is not medical malpractice, I will so inform the client.

Hvass stated, however, that he would never render a "categorical" opinion. In addition, Hvass acknowledged that if he were consulted for a "legal opinion" regarding medical malpractice and 14 months had expired since the incident in question, "ordinary care and diligence" would require him to inform the party of the two-year statute of limitations applicable to that type of action.

This case was submitted to the jury by way of a special verdict form. The jury found that Dr. Blake and the hospital were negligent and that Dr. Blake's negligence (but not the hospital's) was a direct cause of the injuries sustained by John Togstad; that there was an attorney-client contractual relationship between Mrs. Togstad and Miller; that Miller was negligent in rendering advice regarding the possible claims of Mr. and Mrs. Togstad; that, but for Miller's negligence, plaintiffs would have been successful in the prosecution of a legal action against Dr. Blake; and that neither Mr. nor Mrs. Togstad was negligent in pursuing their claims against Dr. Blake. The jury awarded damages to Mr. Togstad of $610,500 and to Mrs. Togstad of $39,000. . . .

In a legal malpractice action of the type involved here, four elements must be shown: (1) that an attorney-client relationship existed; (2) that defendant acted negligently or in breach of contract; (3) that such acts were the proximate cause of the plaintiffs' damages; (4) that but for defendant's conduct the plaintiffs would have been successful in the prosecution of their medical malpractice claim.

This court first dealt with the element of lawyer-client relationship in the decision of Ryan v. Long, 35 Minn. 394, 29 N.W. 51 (1886). The *Ryan* case involved a claim of legal malpractice and on appeal it was argued that no attorney-client relation existed. This court, without stating whether its conclusion was based on contract principles or a tort theory, disagreed:

> [I]t sufficiently appears that plaintiff, for himself, called upon defendant, as an attorney at law, for "legal advice," and that defendant assumed to give him a professional opinion in reference to the matter as to which plaintiff consulted him. Upon this state of facts the defendant must be taken to have acted as plaintiff's legal adviser, at plaintiff's request, and so as to establish between them the relation of attorney and client.

More recent opinions of this court, although not involving a detailed discussion, have analyzed the attorney-client consideration in contractual terms. . . .

We believe it is unnecessary to decide whether a tort or contract theory is preferable for resolving the attorney-client relationship question raised by this appeal. The tort and contract analyses are very similar in a case such as the instant one,[4] and we conclude that under either theory the evidence shows that a lawyer-client relationship is present here. The thrust of Mrs. Togstad's testimony is that she went to Miller for legal advice, was told there wasn't a case, and relied upon this advice in failing to pursue the claim for medical malpractice. In addition, according to Mrs. Togstad, Miller did not qualify this legal opinion by urging her to seek advice from another attorney, nor did Miller inform her that he lacked expertise in the medical malpractice area. Assuming this testimony is true, as this court must do, we believe a jury could properly find that Mrs. Togstad sought and received legal advice from Miller under circumstances which made it reasonably foreseeable to Miller that Mrs. Togstad would be injured if the advice were negligently given. Thus, under either a tort or contract analysis, there is sufficient evidence in the record to support the existence of an attorney-client relationship.

Defendants argue that even if an attorney-client relationship was established the evidence fails to show that Miller acted negligently in assessing the merits of the Togstads' case. They appear to contend that, at most, Miller was guilty of an error in judgment which does not give rise to legal malpractice. However, this case does not involve a mere error of judgment. The gist of plaintiffs' claim is that Miller failed to perform the minimal research that an ordinarily prudent attorney would do before

---

4. Under a negligence approach it must essentially be shown that defendant rendered legal advice (not necessarily at someone's request) under circumstances which made it reasonably foreseeable to the attorney that if such advice was rendered negligently, the individual receiving the advice might be injured thereby. Or stated another way, under a tort theory, "[a]n attorney-client relationship is created whenever an individual seeks and receives legal advice from an attorney in circumstances in which a reasonable person would rely on such advice." 63 Minn. L. Rev. 751, 759 (1979). A contract analysis requires the rendering of legal advice pursuant to another's request and the reliance factor, in this case, where the advice was not paid for, need be shown in the form of promissory estoppel.

rendering legal advice in a case of this nature. The record, through the testimony of Kenneth Green and John McNulty, contains sufficient evidence to support plaintiffs' position.

In a related contention, defendants assert that a new trial should be awarded on the ground that the trial court erred by refusing to instruct the jury that Miller's failure to inform Mrs. Togstad of the two-year statute of limitations for medical malpractice could not constitute negligence. The argument continues that since it is unclear from the record on what theory or theories of negligence the jury based its decision, a new trial must be granted.

The defect in defendants' reasoning is that there is adequate evidence supporting the claim that Miller was also negligent in failing to advise Mrs. Togstad of the two-year medical malpractice limitations period and thus the trial court acted properly in refusing to instruct the jury in the manner urged by defendants. One of defendants' expert witnesses, Charles Hvass, testified:

> Q. Now, Mr. Hvass, where you are consulted for a legal opinion and advice concerning malpractice and 14 months have elapsed [since the incident in question], wouldn't — and you hold yourself out as competent to give a legal opinion and advice to these people concerning their rights, wouldn't ordinary care and diligence require that you inform them that there is a two-year statute of limitations within which they have to act or lose their rights?
>
> A. Yes. I believe I would have advised someone of the two-year period of limitation, yes.

Consequently, based on the testimony of Mrs. Togstad, i.e., that she requested and received legal advice from Miller concerning the malpractice claim, and the above testimony of Hvass, we must reject the defendants' contention, as it was reasonable for a jury to determine that Miller acted negligently in failing to inform Mrs. Togstad of the applicable limitations period.

There is also sufficient evidence in the record establishing that, but for Miller's negligence, plaintiffs would have been successful in prosecuting their medical malpractice claim. Dr. Woods, in no uncertain terms, concluded that Mr. Togstad's injuries were caused by the medical malpractice of Dr. Blake. Defendants' expert testimony to the contrary was obviously not believed by the jury. Thus, the jury reasonably found that had plaintiff's medical malpractice action been properly brought, plaintiffs would have recovered.

Based on the foregoing, we hold that the jury's findings are adequately supported by the record. Accordingly we uphold the trial court's denial of defendants' motion for judgment notwithstanding the jury verdict. . . .

QUESTIONS ABOUT TOGSTAD

1. What is the court's basis for concluding that an attorney-client relationship existed? Who was (were) Miller's client(s)? How did each of the parties try to characterize their conversation so as to encourage the conclusion that there was or was not a professional relationship?

2. Identifying when a statute of limitations will run can sometimes require significant research. Even then, the answer may not be clear. Is there some way a lawyer in Miller's position can shield himself from liability without doing that research or specifying a limitation period?

3. Once Miller interviewed Togstad, could he have rejected the case without getting the hospital records? Or was he then committed to that course?

4. The court seems unconcerned with whether liability is based in contract or in tort. But see Collins v. Reynard, 1991 WL 220561 (Ill. 1991) (generally, only contract claims recognized). Should it much matter which theory is used? How would you articulate the differences? A jurisdiction's limitations period might vary with the basis for liability. McLaughlin v. Herman & Herman, 729 F.2d 331 (5th Cir. 1984) (under Louisiana law, one-year tort period applied to malpractice unless lawyer promised to achieve specific result, in which case 10-year contract period applied.) The theory of liability might also affect the merits, as in Pelham v. Griesheimer, 92 Ill. 2d 13, 440 N.E.2d 96 (1982). See page 627 infra.

What Is the Required Standard of Care?

As the *Togstad* court wrote, a "mere error in judgment" does not constitute malpractice. Instead the court looks at what "an ordinarily prudent attorney would do before rendering legal advice in a case of this nature" and concludes that Miller failed to do the "minimal research" necessary to satisfy that standard. Ordinary prudence is the standard; failure to do the research violated it.

Courts are largely in agreement with *Togstad's* articulation of the generic standard. One court wrote that a lawyer is obligated to exercise "that degree of care, skill, diligence and knowledge commonly possessed and exercised by a reasonable, careful and prudent lawyer in the practice of law in this jurisdiction." Cook, Flanagan & Berst v. Clausing, 73 Wash. 2d 393, 395, 438 P.2d 865, 867 (1968); Cosgrove v. Grimes, 774 S.W.2d 662 (Texas 1989) (attorney's subjective good faith no defense if he failed to act as a reasonably prudent lawyer would have acted under the circumstances). Efforts to extend the geographical range so that the standard is the profession generally and not lawyers in a particular state have been unsuccessful. Kellos v. Sawilowsky, 254 Ga. 4, 325 S.E.2d 757 (1985) (degree of skill, prudence and diligence of Georgia lawyers). See also Russo

v. Griffin, 147 Vt. 20, 510 A.2d 436 (1986). Some states use the lawyer's own locality as the geographical standard. Rorrer v. Cooke, 313 N.C. 338, 329 S.E.2d 355, 366 (1985) ("The standard is that of members of the profession in the same or similar locality under similar circumstances.").

If a lawyer has persuaded a client to use his services by proclaiming some expertise in a particular field, the client will expect him to know more about the field than a lawyer who makes no such claims, and the lawyer will be judged by the standard of the specialty. What kind of statement will suffice to trigger this higher standard? See Neel v. Magana, Olney, Levy, Cathcart & Gelfand, 6 Cal. 3d 176, 491 P.2d 421, 428, 98 Cal. Rptr. 837 (1971) (if a lawyer "further specializes within the profession, he must meet the standards of knowledge and skill of such specialists"); Walker v. Bangs, 92 Wash. 2d 854, 601 P.2d 1279, 1283 (1979) ("Generally, one who holds himself out as specializing and as possessing greater than ordinary knowledge and skill in a particular field, will be held to the standard of performance of those who hold themselves out as specialists in that area").

As *Togstad* shows, the duty of care may include a duty to do research before rendering a legal opinion, even if the lawyer declines to take the case. Compare Procanik v. Cillo, 226 N.J. Super. 132, 543 A.2d 985, 994-995 (1988): A specialist who is asked by an intermediary practitioner whether he is interested in a case does not become the client's lawyer if he turns the case down, which he may do without giving a reason. However, if he gives a reason, he must recognize that others will rely on it, especially because the lawyer specializes in the area. If the lawyer's reason is that the law is settled against the claim, the lawyer "is expected to know what [the law] is and to state it accurately." If the reason is that the law is unsettled, "it is surely enough for him to point out that that is so and why."

In Copeland Lumber Yards, Inc. v. Kincaid, 69 Or. App. 35, 684 P.2d 13, 14 (1984), an attorney argued that his failure to bring a timely foreclosure action for his client was based on his professional judgment that the time for bringing the action had been tolled. He was wrong. It wasn't tolled. The court agreed that "a lawyer should not be held liable for a mistake in the exercise of professional judgment," but it rejected the lawyer's appeal after pointing out that research (which the lawyer failed to do) would have revealed the uncertain state of the law. Given that uncertainty, filing the foreclosure action was the only proper course.

What Is the Scope of the Relationship and When Does It End?

Related to the question of whether an attorney-client relationship exists are questions of its scope and duration. Both questions can have significant consequences.

In Jackson v. Pollick, 751 F. Supp. 132 (E.D. Mich. 1990), aff'd, 941 F.2d 1209 (6th Cir. 1991), the court granted the defendant lawyer summary judgment on a former client's assertion that the lawyer had failed to file an employment discrimination claim within the limitation period. Pollick had in fact accepted the client's workman's compensation claim, and Jackson believed he had accepted his discrimination claim too, but the court found no evidence to support this belief. The two discussed the discrimination claim, but Pollick had not accepted it, though neither had he explicitly rejected it. Why wasn't it his job to clarify any ambiguity?

In Lama Holding Co. v. Shearman & Sterling, 758 F. Supp. 159 (S.D.N.Y. 1991), Lama, a tax client of Shearman & Sterling, claimed to have had to pay $33 million in taxes after S&S failed to advise it of tax law changes that affected the status of an entity S&S had previously created for Lama. S&S claimed that the tax changes occurred after its representation of Lama had ended and that it had no duty to continue to advise Lama. Lama alleged that in fact an S&S partner had told it that the firm would advise Lama of any significant tax law changes. That allegation was sufficient to create an issue of fact and deny summary judgment.

Appointed Lawyers

Appointed lawyers must observe the same level of care as paid ones. In Ferri v. Ackerman, 444 U.S. 193 (1979), the plaintiff brought a malpractice action against his lawyer, who had been appointed to represent the plaintiff in a criminal case in federal court. The malpractice action was brought in state court after the plaintiff had been convicted in the criminal case. The Pennsylvania Supreme Court ruled that the attorney, the defendant in the malpractice case, was absolutely immune from liability for malpractice. The court concluded that a federal rule must control on the subject of immunity, since the lawyer had been appointed to represent the plaintiff in a federal criminal case, and that the federal law would provide the appointed lawyer with absolute immunity.

A unanimous United States Supreme Court disagreed. It found nothing in the Criminal Justice Act of 1964, under which the lawyer had been appointed to represent the plaintiff, to support the state supreme court's conclusion, and the Court refused to read in an immunity. In the course of his opinion, Justice Stevens wrote:

> Although it is true that appointed counsel serves pursuant to statutory authorization and in furtherance of the federal interest in insuring effective representation of criminal defendants, his duty is not to the public at large, except in that general way. His principal responsibility is to serve the undivided interests of his client. Indeed, an indispensable element of the effective performance of his responsibilities is the ability to act indepen-

dently of the Government and to oppose it in adversary litigation. The fear that an unsuccessful defense of a criminal charge will lead to a malpractice claim does not conflict with performance of that function. If anything, it provides the same incentive for appointed and retained counsel to perform that function competently.

Appointed defense lawyers, although subject to malpractice claims, do not act "under color of law" for purposes of federal jurisdiction under 42 U.S.C. §1983 when they are "performing a lawyer's traditional function as counsel to a defendant in a criminal proceeding." Polk County v. Dodson, 454 U.S. 312, 321-325 (1981). Dodson had alleged that the public defender assigned to represent him, and the office that employed her, had denied him his right to counsel and due process of law when the attorney moved to withdraw as counsel on Dodson's appeal on the ground that his claims were frivolous. See Anders v. California, 386 U.S. 738 (1967). Without reaching the merits, the Supreme Court rejected federal jurisdiction, despite the fact that the public defender's office was publicly funded and that the attorneys it employed were considered employees of the county. In rejecting Dodson's jurisdictional claim, the Court stressed the independence of the public defender. She was not "amenable to administrative direction in the same sense as other employees of the State. [A] defense lawyer is not, and by the nature of [her] function cannot be, the servant of an administrative superior." The Court emphasized that a public defender "works under canons of professional responsibility that mandate . . . exercise of independent judgment on behalf of the client." Furthermore, "it is the constitutional obligation of the State to respect the professional independence of the public defenders whom it engages."

In reaching its ruling, the Court acknowledged that it "may be — although the question is not present in this case — that a public defender . . . would act under color of state law while performing certain administrative and possibly investigative functions. And of course we intimate no views as to a public defender's liability for malpractice in an appropriate case under state tort law. See Ferri v. Ackerman, 444 U.S. 193, 198 (1979)." Justice Blackmun was the lone dissenter. Three years later, in Tower v. Glover, 467 U.S. 914 (1984), the Court ruled unanimously that a public defender is not immune from a section 1983 lawsuit where it is charged that he or she conspired with state officials to secure a conviction.

Breach of Fiduciary Duties

Malpractice can be based on conduct other than a failure to exercise the proper standard of care. It can also be based on violation of a duty the lawyer owes the client as a fiduciary. For example, a fiduciary's duty of loyalty requires her to avoid conflicts of interest. (Ethics rules require the same. The relationship between these rules and malpractice is addressed at page 635 infra.) If a client suffers a loss as a result of a lawyer's conflict of interest, the client will be able to recover in malpractice. See Simpson v. James, page 223 supra; Miami Intl. Realty Co. v. Paynter, page 635 infra; Wissore v. Alvey, 204 Ill. App. 3d 931, 562 N.E. 978 (1990).

Similarly, a fiduciary may not use a client's confidential information to the client's disadvantage. (This is an ethical rule too.) Rules 1.8(b), 1.9(c)(1). If a lawyer does that, a malpractice action will lie. See Tri-Growth Centre City, Ltd. v. Silldorf, Burdman, Duignan & Eisenberg, 216 Cal. App. 3d 1139, 265 Cal. Rptr. 330 (1990).

Breach of fiduciary duty can also occur if a lawyer helps another agent of a client violate his or her fiduciary duties to the client. In Avianca, Inc. v. Corriea, 705 F. Supp. 666 (D.D.C. 1989), a lawyer for plaintiff had allegedly helped one of plaintiff's officers secretly compete with it.

As you move through the balance of this material, take note of the theory of malpractice liability and how the plaintiff hoped to prove it in court.

Is Sex with Clients a Breach of Fiduciary Duty?

Of late, debate has centered on when if ever it should be an actionable breach of fiduciary duty for an attorney to initiate an intimate personal relationship with a client. The issue has arisen mostly in divorce cases, when a client is especially vulnerable to imposition. Such cases as there are have been filed by women.

One court has refused to find a breach where the client could show no harm to her legal interests as a result of the intimate relationship. The client's mental anguish, humiliation, and shame were not compensable damages. Among the allegations the court assumed to be true was this one:

> On December 10, 1983, [plaintiff] went to defendant's office, at his request, to discuss her case. On this occasion defendant locked his office door and then unzipped his pants. He then requested that plaintiff have oral sex with him. Plaintiff contended that she was "stunned and confused" but that she complied because she was "fearful that he would not advocate for her and her children's interests in her divorce case were she to refuse."

Suppressed v. Suppressed, 206 Ill. App. 3d 918, 565 N.E.2d 101 (1990). A disciplinary complaint against this lawyer had earlier been dismissed. Id. at 103. A RICO claim arising out of like conduct, and apparently involving the same lawyer but a different plaintiff, has also failed. Doe v. Roe, 756 F. Supp. 353, 357 (N.D. Ill. 1991).

McDaniel v. Gile, 230 Cal. App. 3d 363, 281 Cal. Rptr. 242 (1991), has gone furthest in recognizing an action for breach of fiduciary duty. The former client charged that her lawyer had her fill out a "lengthy and intimate" questionnaire "seeking intimate details of her personal and sexual life." He then repeatedly referred to her answers and made sexual advances toward her. After all were rebuffed, the defendant allegedly did no work on plaintiff's case and ignored her calls. When she complained, he responded that if she "had played the game the right way" she would know how to reach him immediately.

The court upheld claims for intentional infliction of emotional distress and malpractice. As to the first, the court wrote:

> Defendant had a special relationship with plaintiff in that she was a client and plaintiff was her attorney representing her in a dissolution of marriage proceeding. Plaintiff was in a position of actual or apparent power over defendant. Defendant was peculiarly suspectible to emotional distress because of her pending marital dissolution. Plaintiff was aware of defendant's circumstances. The withholding by a retained attorney of legal services when sexual favors are not granted by a client and engaging in sexual harrassment of the client are outrageous conduct under these circumstances.

As to the second, it said:

> The facts before this court show that plaintiff not only delayed rendering legal services, but also withheld them and gave substandard services when defendant did not grant him sexual favors. This conduct necessarily falls below the standard of care and skill of members of the legal profession. We specifically do not address whether sexual relations between an attorney and client constitute a per se violation of the fiduciary relationship.

See also Edwards v. Edwards, 165 A.D.2d 362, 567 N.Y.S.2d 645 (1st Dept. 1991) (reversing sanction against lawyer who failed to withdraw from representation of wife after beginning intimate relationship with her). Discipline as a remedy for intimate sexual relationships with clients is discussed at page 677 infra.

2. Third Parties as "Client-Equivalents"

In section C we will discuss theories of lawyer liability to nonclients that do not depend on viewing the nonclients as essentially like clients (page 649 infra). Some cases have upheld professional liability to third parties, however, by concluding that even though the plaintiff never actually retained or sought to retain the defendant lawyer, nevertheless the plaintiff was entitled to the benefit of the service — and the duty of care

— the lawyer had agreed to provide to his actual client. Remember, a person or entity may be treated as a client for one purpose but not for another. See page 13 supra. Compare Lynch v. Deaconess Medical Center, 113 Wash. 2d 162, 776 P.2d 681 (1989) (hospital that benefitted from attorney's work for client who owed hospital money is not liable to attorney for a legal fee).

The drafting of wills presents the classic fact pattern in which a third party seeks to hold an attorney liable for lack of care in performing a legal service. A testator hires a lawyer to draft a will leaving a sum of money to her friend Jane. The testator dies. It is then discovered that the lawyer had failed to include the bequest or had drafted it inadequately. The testator is no longer around to sue the lawyer. Jane sues. The lawyer claims that Jane was owed no duty.

While some jurisdictions still accept this defense (see Victor v. Goldman, 74 Misc. 2d 685, 344 N.Y.S.2d 672 (Sup. Ct. 1973), aff'd, 43 A.D.2d 1021, 351 N.Y.S.2d 956 (2d Dept. 1974)), many do not. See, for example, Hale v. Groce, 304 Or. 281, 744 P.2d 1289, 1292 (1987), where Justice Linde found the intended beneficiary under the will a "classic . . . third-party beneficiary of the lawyer's promise to his client within the rule of Restatement [of Contracts] section 302(1)(b)." In addition, "[b]ecause under third-party analysis the contract creates a 'duty' not only to the promisee, the client, but also to the intended beneficiary, negligent nonperformance may give rise to a negligence action as well." Illinois has held that a lawyer owes a duty of care to a beneficiary in a will if the testator had retained the lawyer intending to benefit the beneficiary. (When won't this be true?) McLane v. Russell, 131 Ill. 2d 509, 546 N.E.2d 499 (1989).

In Vanguard Production, Inc. v. Martin, 894 F.2d 375, 378 (10th Cir. 1990), Judge Tacha, applying Oklahoma law, held that the lawyer for a mortgage lender was liable to the purchaser of real property for a failure of ordinary care and workmanlike performance. Although the purchaser was not actually the lawyer's client, it was "among the class of nonclients which, as a natural and probable consequence of the attorney's actions in preparing the title opinion [for the lender], could be injured." The case was remanded for trial on the issue of proximate cause. Williams v. Mordkofsky, 901 F.2d 158 (D.C. Cir. 1990), permitted a corporation to sue a lawyer who had been retained by its shareholders and an affiliated company for the purpose of benefitting the plaintiff. See also Nelson v. Nationwide Mortgage Corp., 659 F. Supp. 611 (D.D.C. 1987), and Flaherty v. Weinberg, 303 Md. 116, 492 A.2d 618 (1985). *Flaherty* contains an especially good review of the law.

There are limits. In Fox v. Pollack, 181 Cal. App. 3d 954, 226 Cal. Rptr. 532 (1986), the court refused to impose a duty on a lawyer for one party in a real estate transaction to the opposing unrepresented party, who claimed that the agreement the lawyer prepared did not accurately reflect the parties' oral understanding. The court said that the other party was not the intended beneficiary of the lawyer's service. Nor did the lawyer do anything to encourage an opposite view. The court did, however, advise lawyers "in these circumstances . . . to place a disclaimer in writing" alerting the other side to the fact that he or she is not its lawyer.

In Pelham v. Griesheimer, 92 Ill. 2d 13, 440 N.E.2d 96, 98-100 (1982), the defendant had represented a woman in a divorce proceeding. The decree required the husband to maintain a life insurance policy for his children after he remarried; however, he changed the beneficiary to his second wife, who received the insurance proceeds on his death. The decedent's children then sued their mother's lawyer, alleging that he had breached a duty to them by failing to notify their father's employer or the insurance company of the requirement of the divorce decree and in failing to advise their mother to make such notification. The court rejected the claim.

The court read the complaint to allege negligence but concluded that the defendant had no duty to the plaintiff children. Although "privity is not an indispensable prerequisite to establishing a duty of care between a non-client and an attorney in a suit for a legal malpractice," a nonclient plaintiff "must prove that the primary purpose and intent of the attorney-client relationship" was "to benefit or influence a third party." After noting that courts are more willing to extend an attorney's duty to nonclients in cases in which the attorney's representation of the client has essentially been of a nonadversarial nature, the court continued:

> Where a client's interest is involved in a proceeding that is adversarial in nature, the existence of a duty of the attorney to another person would interfere with the undivided loyalty which the attorney owes his client and would detract from achieving the most advantageous position for his client. . . . In cases of an adversarial nature, in order to create a duty on the part of the attorney to one other than a client, there must be a clear indication that the representation by the attorney is intended to directly confer a benefit upon the third party.

The court stressed that "a different situation would confront us" if the complaint had alleged that the lawyer had in fact "undertaken the duty to notify the insurance company or the husband's employer of the provision in the divorce decree."

Other courts have also shown reluctance to impose duties to third parties on litigators for fear these might compromise the litigators' duties to clients. See, for example, Westlake v. Abrams, 565 F. Supp. 1330, 1350 (N.D. Ga. 1983). What do you think of this distinction? Should it apply in *Pelham*?

3.   Vicarious Liability

Law partners, like other partners, are responsible for each other's professional failures within the scope of the legal partnership. Roach v. Mead, 301 Or. 383, 722 P.2d 1229 (1986). Whether lawyers who are shareholders in a professional corporation are vicariously liable for the defaults of their coshareholders generally depends on the jurisdiction's corporation law. Note, Shareholder Liability in Professional Legal Corporations: A Survey of the States, 47 U. Pitt. L. Rev. 817 (1986) (authored by Karen Maycheck).

When a lawyer borrows money from a client and doesn't pay it back, the lawyer's partners may be sued. The defense might be that borrowing money from a client is not within the scope of a legal partnership so there is no vicarious liability. This defense lost in Roach v. Mead, supra. The court reasoned that the borrowing lawyer was obligated to tell his client to seek independent legal advice and that the loans should be secured. His failures to do so were "failures of Mead as a lawyer advising his client. Because these failures occurred within the scope of the legal partnership, responsibility for Mead's negligence was properly charged to defendant as Mead's law partner."

In a particularly disquieting case, a lawyer overcharged a client more than $3 million. The client sued the lawyer's partners. The court upheld liability on two theories. First, all partners were liable for a partner's wrongful acts within the scope of the partnership business even if the other partners were unaware of those acts. Here, billing clients was within the scope of the law firm's business. Second, and more consequential, the copartners were liable for negligent supervision. The firm had no system in place for identifying the breaches of ethics or dishonest acts of firm lawyers. Dresser Indus., Inc. v. Digges, 1989 WL 139234, and 1989 WL 139240 (D. Md. 1989). See the material on supervisory duties at page 594 supra.

In Federal Deposit Insurance Corp. v. Mmahat, 907 F.2d 546 (5th Cir. 1990), cert. denied, 111 S. Ct. 1387 (1991), a firm partner who was also chair and general counsel of the board of an S&L directed it to make loans that violated federal regulations. After the S&L failed, the FDIC sued the partner and his firm. The court affirmed a jury finding that the partner had acted as a lawyer, not as chairman, in directing the loans and that the firm was vicariously liable.

By contrast, the First Circuit declined to hold a law firm liable for the alleged fraud of one of its partners. The fraud occurred when the partner invited the plaintiff to invest in a real estate venture. The plaintiff was not otherwise a client of the firm and the court found no evidence that the investment itself created an attorney-client relationship with the firm. Nor did the partner act in the ordinary course of the firm's business. The fact that the partner used firm stationery in connection with his business deals was insufficient to create apparent authority from the firm for these activities. Sheinkopf v. Stone, 927 F.2d 1259 (1st Cir. 1991). And in Shelton v. Fairley, 86 N.C. App. 147, 356 S.E.2d 917, 921 (1987), the court found "no precedent for bringing a law partner's activities as executor [of an estate] within the purview of the practice of law." The partner had been charged with negligence and breach of fiduciary duties. The court relied in part on the fact that the firm did not directly share in the executor's fees.

Going perhaps farthest of all is Clients' Security Fund of the State of New York v. Grandeau, 72 N.Y.2d 62, 526 N.E.2d 270, 530 N.Y.S.2d 775 (1988). A state agency that reimburses clients whose lawyers steal from them sued the partner of a lawyer who stole nearly $600,000 from 373 clients. The defendant lawyer had been unaware of the conversions. The court held that partnership law entitled the former clients to seek compensation from the nonconverting partner and that this right had been subrogated to the state agency when it paid the losses.

For the Supreme Court's decision not to create vicarious liability for Rule 11 violations, see page 373 supra.

B. PROVING MALPRACTICE

1. Expert Testimony

Often, but not always, a malpractice plaintiff will need an expert to testify that the defendant's conduct fell below the applicable standard of care or violated a fiduciary duty. But when?

WAGENMANN v. ADAMS
829 F.2d 196 (1st Cir. 1987)*

Selya, J.

It was early in the seventeenth century when George Herbert wrote:

> "Marry your son when you will;
> your daughter when you can."

*Additional excerpts from this case, on the issues of causation and damages, appear at pages 642 and 646 infra.

The sagacity of that advice, suspect in any era, was called into grave doubt some three hundred fifty years later in Worcester, Massachusetts. In the process, bitterly-fought litigation ensued. These lawsuits have now wended their rancorous way to our doorstep. Because the underlying circumstances border on the chimerical, we set out an exegetic account. . . .

[Wagenmann's daughter, Linda, was about to marry a young man, Stephen Anderson, over Wagenmann's forceful objections. A few days before the wedding, to which Wagenmann was not invited, he travelled from New York to Boston. He later claimed he made the trip to reconcile with his daughter. Wagenmann's wife, however, feared his violence and called to warn Linda and the Anderson family. Wagenmann went to his daughter's apartment, but she wasn't there. He told her roommate that he would look for her at the Andersons'. The roommate called the Andersons to warn them. The Andersons called the police.

Wagenmann was arrested as he approached the Anderson home and was charged with disturbing the peace. There was apparently no basis for this charge other than the fears of the Anderson family and Linda. Wagenmann spent the night in jail before arraignment. After the police told the judge about the Andersons' fears, he ordered a psychiatric examination. The psychiatrist (Dr. Myerson) reported that Wagenmann was competent, but the judge insisted that he was dangerous and homicidal. After the judge threatened that the psychiatrist would be responsible if Wagenmann were released and harmed anyone, the psychiatrist "reluctantly agreed to sign a form stating the opinion that [Wagenmann] should be admitted to the hospital for observation."

Healy, a lawyer with 30 years of experience, happened to be in the courthouse that day. The judge appointed him to represent Wagenmann, and Healy appeared on the commitment proceedings and the criminal charges. Healy spoke with Wagenmann for a total of about an hour. He told Wagenmann that he was a friend of Stephen Anderson's father. When Wagenmann asked for another lawyer, Healy refused to get one.

Healy tried to persuade Wagenmann to accept an offer to let him get on a bus for New York. Wagenmann refused. Healy then told Wagenmann that he would have to commit himself to a mental hospital. Wagenmann refused again. Finally, Healy told Wagenmann that he had been committed to a mental hospital (WSH) for a 20-day observation period. Wagenmann spent that night in a state hospital ward. The next day he was released and all charges were dismissed after Dr. Myerson notified the Chief Judge of the events of the previous day.

Wagenmann sued numerous individuals, including Anderson (Stephen's father), Healy, and police officials. The jury awarded approximately $1.6 million in compensatory damages and $85,000 in exemplary damages, which was thereafter reduced to a total of $285,000, plus $125,000 in attorney's fees and costs.

Healy was found guilty of malpractice. His portion of the damages totaled $50,000. Following is the court's treatment of Healy's appeal.]

We turn now to the appeal of Edward Healy, the plaintiff's erstwhile counsel. Healy contends, inter alia, that the district court erred in denying his motions for directed verdict, for judgment notwithstanding the verdict, and for a new trial. He makes several interesting arguments. He urges that, in the absence of expert testimony on the standard of care, the evidence was insufficient to warrant a finding that he failed to exercise a reasonable degree of lawyerly skill. Next, Healy cites what he sees as a paucity of evidence to prove that, but for his negligence, Wagenmann would not have been committed (or would have been released sooner). Third, the appellant questions the plaintiff's right to recover damages for noneconomic loss in this legal malpractice case. We address this trio of claims seriatim.

A. Need for Expert Testimony

In Massachusetts, an attorney owes his or her client a duty to exercise the degree of care and skill of the average qualified practitioner. Glidden v. Terranova, 12 Mass. App. Ct. 597, 598, 427 N.E.2d 1169 (1981). In an action for legal malpractice, expert testimony is generally needed to establish both the level of care owed by the attorney under the particular circumstances and the alleged failure to conform to that benchmark. Nevertheless, the commonwealth's courts have recognized an exception to the expert testimony requirement "where the claimed legal malpractice is so gross or obvious that laymen can rely on their common knowledge or experience to recognize or infer negligence from the facts." It is instructive to rehearse the type of situation in which a finding of legal malpractice without the benefit of expert testimony has been upheld. Glidden v. Terranova, supra, is such a case. There, the attorney, after being hired with respect to a suit in which his clients were named as defendants, assured them that he had removed the action to the state superior court. The lawyer indicated that everything was well in hand; he had the ball and would run with it. Relying on these comforting words, the clients did nothing further. In fact, the attorney — assurances notwithstanding — had not effected the removal and had permitted default judgments to be entered. Thereafter, the lawyer failed to appear at two hearings — one of which was a scheduled contempt hearing that resulted in the arrest and imprisonment of one of the clients (Glidden). When the remaining clients, dumbfounded by the course of events, sought out the attorney, they were told he was in conference and could not be disturbed. His only response to the clients' desperate pleas for help was a call from his secretary suggesting that they raise bail and seek other counsel. On the presentation of evidence suggesting facts such as these, the Supreme

Judicial Court saw no need for expert testimony in order to establish what was obvious to all — that the lawyer had been woefully negligent.

Massachusetts does not stand alone in this wise. Courts in other jurisdictions have also dispensed with any expert testimony requirement in egregious cases, especially those in which an attorney fails to act once he has undertaken to represent a client.

When the events of this litigation are displayed against the backdrop of the foregoing cases, it is clear that, because Healy committed malpractice "so gross or obvious" that expert testimony was not required to prove it, this assignment of error must come to naught. Once Healy undertook to represent Wagenmann, he seems to have done almost nothing to protect his client — either before or after commitment. Virtually from the start, the lawyer paid no heed to the warning signs. He appears to have ignored not only the client's wishes, but the client's protestations of innocence and mental stability. The attorney gave short (if any) shrift to Dr. Myerson's misgivings. Despite Wagenmann's repeated requests to be brought before a judge, Healy did not seek to arrange a hearing. The barrister's lame excuse for not doing so — his self-serving depiction of Wagenmann as uncooperative and as a man who would have "hung himself" — varies markedly from Dr. Myerson's reaction. In light of the verdicts, it is clear that the jury disbelieved Healy's account. We think the record affords a sufficient basis for such a conclusion. We cite but a few examples.

One striking illustration of what the jurors could well have found to be dereliction of duty centered around the psychiatric outlook. Although Healy was aware that Dr. Myerson was in the courthouse and available, he never sought to question him either about the case or about his impressions of the plaintiff. Notwithstanding that he knew of the psychiatrist's generally favorable evaluation, Healy did not deem it important to determine in detail Dr. Myerson's complete opinion or the full extent of his findings. Healy's seeming indifference to Wagenmann's mental state — and to his plight, generally — was little short of appalling.

Another example of the shoddy representation which Wagenmann received involved counsel's failure to interview — or attempt to interview — any of the prosecution witnesses. The lawyer did not try to speak with either Stephen or Linda, two key figures in the psychodrama (both of whom were present in the courthouse). Instead, Healy claims he relied on the police as his sole source of information about the affair. Passing the fact that this amounted to asking the fox if the chickens were secure, Healy did precious little on that front. He was unable to identify from the witness stand even one police officer with whom he had spoken on the infamous day of arraignment and commitment.

The final example — the straw, perhaps, that broke the dromedary's back — relates to Healy's dealmaking. Rather than requesting a formal hearing before Judge Luby, or consulting appropriately with

Wagenmann, or making out a psychiatric case for competency, or interviewing witnesses, the lawyer-appellant avers that he attempted to procure his client's release by striking a bargain with the police. But [the police officers] testified they had no conversations with the lawyer, and Healy failed to produce or to name any police witnesses with whom he attempted to arrange the alleged deal.

Moreover, to the extent there was a possible deal at all, its existence could not excuse the attorney's inattention in other areas. Even Healy concedes that Wagenmann made it clear, early on, that he was not interested in any leave-town-quick proposition. Nor did Healy take any constructive action in the wake of Wagenmann's commitment. He filed no pleadings on behalf of his client. He did nothing anent bail. He neglected even to review the commitment order which had been entered. What is more, there was obviously much which could have been done: after all, a nonlawyer (Dr. Myerson), incensed by what had occurred, was able to effect the plaintiff's release the next day by making a single telephone call to the chief judge of the state district court. . . .

Sometimes an attorney is so grossly ineffective that his lack of professionalism is plain to see. Even the untutored eye can discern blundering of an egregious and uncomplicated sort. For such instances, Massachusetts has recognized a narrow "gross or obvious" malpractice classification in which no expert testimony is needed. This case fits neatly within the contours of that category. Assessing the totality of the evidence both up to the time of commitment and thereafter, we conclude that the record, viewed favorably to the plaintiff, demonstrated a lack of care, skill, and diligence on counsel's part "so gross or obvious" that the jury could reasonably appreciate, without the aid of expert testimony, that malpractice had occurred.

Although a lay jury may need the help of an expert witness in order to decide whether a lawyer's (or a doctor's or an accountant's) work was substandard, no expert is likely to be needed to fault a professional who does (little or) no work at all. Similarly, some fiduciary defaults may be self-evident (using a client's secrets to compete with the client?), while others will require an expert's elucidation, as in *Beattie* below. A plaintiff, again as in *Beattie*, might try to substitute an ethical rule for a live expert, but that can be risky. (We learn more about the relevance of ethical rules in malpractice actions in the following section.)

An example of a case in which a lawyer did do something but not enough is Waldman v. Levine, 544 A.2d 683, 687 (D.C. Ct. App. 1988). The mother of a woman who had died after childbirth hired the defendants to bring a medical malpractice action. The client, on her lawyers' advice, reluctantly settled for about $2,200 six days before trial. Thereafter the client sued the lawyers for legal malpractice, alleging that the lawyers had acted in violation of their duty of care by failing to consult an OB/GYN specialist. Instead, the lawyers had intended to rely on an internist. The client called a legal expert who testified that failure to secure an OB/GYN specialist in a case against obstetricians and gynecologists placed the lawyers' "conduct . . . below the minimum standard of care for attorneys in medical malpractice cases." The legal expert also testified that the defendants should have secured an economic expert to testify to the decedent's lost future earnings. The jury, concluding that with such expert testimony the client would have prevailed in the underlying action, awarded $600,000 against the lawyers. The appellate court affirmed. Compare Houillon v. Powers and Nass, 530 So. 2d 680 (La. App. 1988), where malpractice was not proved because the plaintiff failed to call an expert to testify that the defendant was negligent in failing to call an expert in the underlying matter.

In Beattie v. Firnschild, 152 Mich. App. 785, 394 N.W.2d 107, 110 (1986), plaintiffs brought a malpractice action against their former lawyer, who had concurrently represented plaintiffs and other family members in the purchase and sale of residential real estate. A trial court granted a directed verdict in favor of the defendant on the ground that plaintiffs had failed to provide expert testimony of malpractice. On appeal, plaintiffs argued that "expert testimony is only required where the malpractice claim is not covered by any specific provision in the Disciplinary Rules." Affirming, the appellate court held:

> This reasoning is flawed. This court has rejected the argument that a violation of the Code of Professional Responsibility is negligence per se, in favor of the proposition that a code violation is rebuttable evidence of malpractice. In our view, plaintiffs' allegation that the Disciplinary Rules have been violated, rather than an allegation that the common-law standard of care has been breached, does not relieve them of the obligation to present expert testimony, unless the violation was so obvious that such testimony was not required.
>
> Plaintiffs claim that defendant violated DR 5-105 . . . , which prohibits lawyers from representing multiple clients with conflicting interests. . . .
>
> Expert testimony in this case was required to establish that defendant violated DR 5-105. Defendant was representing members of this family in a simple real estate transaction. It is not obviously apparent that defendant violated the Code of Professional Responsibility. This is especially true if defendant happened to believe his independent judgment would not be adversely affected by representing these multiple clients.

A lawyer's failure to communicate can also be the basis for malpractice, but will an expert be needed to say why or can a jury decide for itself? In Wastvedt v. Vaaler, 430 N.W.2d 561, 566 (N.D. 1988), an expert was needed "to explain whether the failure to explain the ramifications of [a certain clause in a stock purchase agreement] was a deviation from the appropriate standard of care because that conduct is not a matter within the common knowledge of a layperson." But elsewhere a jury needed no expert to help it conclude that a lawyer's failure to communicate a settlement offer to a client was actionable. Rizzo v. Haines, 520 Pa. 484, 555 A.2d 58 (1989).

For more on the use of experts in legal malpractice actions see Michael Ambrosio & Denis McLaughlin, The Use of Expert Witnesses in Establishing Liability in Legal Malpractice Cases, 61 Temple L. Rev. 1351 (1988). See also the next principal case.

2. The Place of Ethical Rules in Actions Against Lawyers

As you saw in Beattie v. Firnschild, malpractice plaintiffs sometimes cite the code or rules in support of their contention that their former lawyers violated a duty. The *Beattie* plaintiff made the mistake of trying to use the code with no expert testimony. The court held that "a code violation is rebuttable evidence of malpractice," but declined to relieve a plaintiff of the "obligation to present expert testimony, unless the violation was so obvious that such testimony was not required."

Often, a plaintiff will call an expert who will rely on the code or rules. What place do these documents have in malpractice (or other) actions against a lawyer? Note that the ABA took pains to emphasize in both the code and the rules that neither should be used to create civil liability. See the code's Preliminary Statement and the rules' Scope. This effort was wishful thinking. As we see below and throughout this book, not only do both documents have a place in actions against lawyers, courts routinely cite them in support of their legal rulings. No court, however, has made code or rules violations per se actionable. (See also the discussion at page 662 infra.)

MIAMI INTERNATIONAL REALTY CO. v. PAYNTER
841 F.2d 348 (10th Cir. 1988)

[This was an action in malpractice against an attorney based on his failure to perform requested services and because of alleged conflicts of interest. The jury awarded more than $2 million in lost profits plaintiff would have earned, but for the defendant's conduct, as promoter of a new time-share project in Mount Crested Butte, Colorado. The Tenth

Circuit affirmed. At trial the plaintiff had called an expert witness, whose testimony was challenged on appeal.]

SETH, J. . . .

Paynter further argues that the trial judge erred when he admitted certain testimony of Miami's legal expert. Specifically, Paynter contends that the legal expert should not have been allowed to testify that Paynter's conduct was contrary to the Colorado Code of Professional Responsibility since the Code sets forth an *ethical* standard rather than a *professional negligence* standard of care. The defendant filed a motion in limine directed to the expected use of the Code which was denied. The testimony of the witness was objected to at trial.

In Colorado, "[a]n attorney owes his client a duty to employ that degree of knowledge, skill, and judgment ordinarily possessed by members of the legal profession." Colorado courts have not decided how its Code of Professional Responsibility is to be treated as an element of proof in a malpractice case.

There is, of course, an underlying issue of the general relevancy of the Code which pretty much falls into place, but here the troublesome aspect of the expert's testimony who testified as to Code provisions is how the conclusion that there was a Code violation was used or how it was presented to the jury. If the acts presented by the witness were concluded to be a violation of the Code and were therefore negligence per se, the Code has been improperly used. The preamble of the Code states:

> The Code makes no attempt to prescribe either disciplinary procedures or penalties . . . nor does it undertake to define standards for civil liability of lawyers for professional conduct.

The expert witness here stated that he was on the state ethics committee for twelve years, on the Colorado Supreme Court Grievance Committee for years, and recited that the Code was a court rule. The witness compared defendant's conduct to particular Code provisions (DR 5-101) and concluded that defendant's action was "substandard" as attorneys in Colorado were guided by the Code. The witness testified that certain specific acts of defendant (and inaction) were "substandard." There was an instruction requested but none was given as to how the Code violation was to be viewed. The plaintiff in its brief describes the expert as having given the "community standard of care." The parties agree that a Code violation does not create a private right of action.

We have examined the transcript and although the expert witness for the plaintiff at the outset of his testimony did refer to the Code as a standard followed by Colorado attorneys, it was not presented as having the force and effect of a law nor that deviations from it constituted negligence per se.

The testimony did not develop any fine distinctions as to the nature of defendant's conduct compared to the Code as the conduct, according to the evidence, was gross under any standard, and it seems reasonable that it made no difference to the jury whether there was a Code or not. We must conclude that the testimony as to the Code of Professional Responsibility as admitted was not error.

Which Court Is Correct?

Courts differ on how precisely to articulate the relationship between unethical conduct and a lawyer's civil liability.

Fishman v. Brooks, 396 Mass. 643, 487 N.E.2d 1377, 1381-1382 (1986): "We add a brief comment about the relationship between the canons of ethics and an attorney's duty of care to his client. A violation of a canon of ethics or a disciplinary rule is not itself an actionable breach of duty to a client. As with statutes and regulations, however, if a plaintiff can demonstrate that a disciplinary rule was intended to protect one in his position, a violation of that rule may be some evidence of the attorney's negligence.

"Expert testimony concerning the fact of an ethical violation is not appropriate, any more than expert testimony is appropriate concerning the violation of, for example, a municipal building code. A judge can instruct the jury (or himself) concerning the requirements of ethical rules. The jurors need no expert on legal ethics to assess whether a disciplinary rule was violated. A jury would not be aided, and their function could be impinged upon, by expert testimony in such a circumstance. Of course, an expert on the duty of care of an attorney properly could base his opinion on an attorney's failure to conform to a disciplinary rule."

Carlson v. Morton, 229 Mont. 234, 745 P.2d 1133, 1137 (Mont. 1987): "While proof of the violation of some disciplinary rules may by itself establish negligence, such is not the case with the rules cited by Carlson. Carlson must prove not that various disciplinary rules were breached in his opinion; rather he must demonstrate that Morton failed in his legal duty. Proof of such a breach requires expert testimony." The rules allegedly violated in *Carlson* prohibited false or dishonest misrepresentations, misuse of client confidences, neglect, and conflicts of interest. If violation of these rules does not "by itself establish negligence," which rules does the court have in mind?

Lazy Seven Coal Sales, Inc. v. Stone & Hinds, 813 S.W.2d 400 (Tenn. 1991): The "Code of Professional Responsibility is not designed to create a private cause of action for infractions of disciplinary rules but is designed to establish a remedy solely disciplinary in nature." But the "standards stated in the Code are not irrelevant in determining the standard of care in certain actions for malpractice. The Code may provide guidance in ascertaining lawyers' obligations to their clients under various circumstances, and conduct which violates the Code may also constitute a breach of the standard of care due a client. However, in a civil action charging malpractice, the standard of care is the particular duty owed the client under the circumstances of the representation, which may or may not be the standard contemplated by the Code."

Lipton v. Boesky, 110 Mich. App. 589, 313 N.W.2d 163, 166-167 (1981): "The Code . . . is a standard of practice for attorneys which expresses in general terms the standards of professional conduct expected of lawyers in their relationships with the public, the legal system, and the legal profession. Holding a specific client unable to rely on the same standards in his professional relations with his own attorney would be patently unfair. We hold that, as with statutes, a violation of the Code is rebuttable evidence of malpractice."

Ethical Violations as a Basis for Reduction or Denial of Fees

An attorney who breaches an ethical duty owed to a client may nevertheless not be liable to the client either because the lawyer's conduct will not have violated the civil law standard, Carlson v. Morton, supra, or because, even if it has, the conduct will not have caused damage to the client. Still, the lawyer may suffer a diminution in his fee, or denial of a fee altogether, as a result of the ethical breach. In re Estate of Halas, 159 Ill. App. 3d 818, 512 N.E.2d 1276 (1987), appeal denied, 119 Ill. 2d 557, 522 N.E.2d 1244 (1988) (breach of fiduciary duties and conflicts of interest); Gilchrist v. Perl, 387 N.W.2d 412 (Minn. 1986) (simultaneous negotiation of multiple personal injury claims); Crawford v. Logan, 656 S.W.2d 360 (Tenn. 1983) (alleged violation of duties upon withdrawal). Fees for untainted work will not be forfeited. Jeffry v. Pounds, 67 Cal. App. 3d 6, 136 Cal. Rptr. 373 (1977). Peck v. Meda-Care Ambulance Corp., 156 Wis. 2d 662, 457 N.W.2d 538 (App. 1990), limited this principle to situations where the violation of an ethical rule breached a duty owed to the client, which was held not to be so for breach of the advocate-witness rule.

What is the theory behind fee forfeiture? Perl v. St. Paul Fire & Marine Ins. Co., 345 N.W.2d 209 (Minn. 1984), said the rule is *not* restitutionary. Goldstein v. Lees, 46 Cal. App. 3d 614, 120 Cal. Rptr. 253 (1975), said the rule was based on "public policy." Kidney Assn. of Oregon, Inc. v. Ferguson, 97 Or. App. 120, 775 P.2d 1383 (1989), modified,

100 Or. App. 523, 786 P.2d 754 (1990), suggests that the aim is deterrence and lists factors to weigh in determining how much of the fee to deny.

FURTHER READING

Robert Dahlquist, The Code of Professional Responsibility and Civil Damage Actions Against Attorneys, 9 Ohio N.U. L. Rev. 1 (1982); Jean Faure & R. Keith Strong, The Model Rules of Professional Conduct: No Standard for Malpractice, 47 Mont. L. Rev. 363 (1986); Note, The Rules of Professional Conduct: Basis for Civil Liability of Attorneys, 39 U. Fla. L. Rev. 777 (1987) (authored by Michael Benjamin); Charles Wolfram, The Code of Professional Responsibility as a Measure of Attorney Liability in Civil Litigation, 30 S.C. L. Rev. 281 (1979).

3. Causation and Defenses

Malpractice plaintiffs, like all tort or contract plaintiffs, must prove that the lawyer's breach of duty caused damages. The next section will take up the issue of damages. Here we discuss causation. When the lawyer's alleged default occurs in connection with litigation, as in *Togstad*, where the lawyer's negligence resulted in a failure to bring the litigation in the first place, the client will usually have to prove that he or she would have won the underlying case had it been brought or properly litigated. This is sometimes called the "case within the case" requirement. The malpractice plaintiff must not only prove the malpractice case against the lawyer (the outer case), but also prove that if not for the lawyer's negligence the underlying (or inner) case would have ended (more) favorably for the former client. We have seen this doctrine at work several times in the preceding materials. See Stewart v. Hall, 770 F.2d 1267 (4th Cir. 1985) ("but for" test on the issue of proximate cause).

In some jurisdictions, however, it is only necessary that the malpractice be a material and substantial cause of loss. In John B. Gunn Law Corp. v. Maynard, 189 Cal. App. 3d 1565, 235 Cal. Rptr. 180 (1987), a widow sued the lawyer who drafted her husband's will, claiming that his negligent work resulted in a challenge to the will. The widow had to retain separate counsel to resist the challenge. She then sought from the first lawyer the money she had to pay the second lawyer. The defendant claimed that the will challenge would have occurred in any event. The trial court gave a "but for" instruction. On appeal, this was held to be error. The client was entitled to a jury instruction allowing her to prevail even if her loss might have occurred absent the alleged malpractice. It was a jury question whether the lawyer's conduct was a "substantial factor" in causing the additional legal expense. Accord: Spickler v. York, 566 A.2d 1385 (Me. 1989). Compare the different articulation of the proximate cause test in *Togstad* at page 617 supra.

Proximate cause is customarily an issue of fact for the jury. It can sometimes be a rather challenging one. In Shehade v. Gerson, 148 Ill. App. 3d 1026, 500 N.E.2d 510 (1986), the unusual jury issue was whether the lawyer's failure to petition for an order prohibiting unsupervised visitation with a child's father was the proximate cause of the father's ability to kidnap the child to his native Jordan. What if the lawyer failed to file a timely appeal, as a result of which the client was denied appellate review? In Daugert v. Pappas, 104 Wash. 2d 254, 704 P.2d 600 (1985), the court held that the proximate cause issue — whether the client would have prevailed on appeal — was one of law for the judge.

Settlements can also raise causation questions. In Fishman v. Brooks, page 637 supra, the plaintiff claimed that he had settled his tort case for less than it was worth because the defendant was not prepared for the imminent trial. The court upheld the judgment for the plaintiff: "[A]n attorney is liable for negligently causing a client to settle a claim for an amount below what a properly represented client would have accepted." Similarly, a lawyer who accepted a settlement on behalf of a client without investigating the opposing party's assets was guilty of gross negligence and liable for compensatory and punitive damages. The settlement, with one of several defendants, also had the effect of extinguishing the client's claim against other defendants. Patrick v. Ronald Williams P.A., 102 N.C. App. 355, 402 S.E.2d 452 (1991). The Pennsylvania Supreme Court has taken a dramatically different view of negligent settlements. In Muhammad v. Strassburger, McKenna, Messer, Shilobod and Gutnick, 526 Pa. 541, 587 A.2d 1346 (1991), the court held that because of the public policy favoring settlements, a former client could not sue for an allegedly inadequate settlement unless the client could prove fraud. If, for example, a lawyer induced a client to settle in order to conceal the lawyer's malpractice, the client would have a claim. But a lawyer who advised a settlement in good faith but with inadequate factual inquiry, or based on a negligent evaluation of the law, will be immune.

Contributory and comparative negligence are both recognized defenses in malpractice. In Pinkham v. Burgess, 933 F.2d 1066 (1st Cir. 1991), a client was held comparatively negligent for failure to fire her attorney when she should reasonably have known, and in fact did know, that the attorney was neglecting her matter. Damages were reduced accordingly. See also Hunt v. Miller, 908 F.2d 1210 (4th Cir, 1990) (contributory negligence, applying North Carolina law). A client who lies at a deposition or a trial on advice of counsel and later sues counsel may meet an unclean hands or in pari delicto defense. Blain v. The Doctor's Co.,

222 Cal. App. 3d 1048, 272 Cal. Rptr. 250 (1990); Evans v. Cameron, 121 Wis.2d 421, 360 N.W.2d 25 (1985).

How do these defenses fare where the malpractice plaintiff is an entity? Successors in interest to a failed company (like the Resolution Trust Corporation for a failed savings and loan) or the company's shareholders may sue the company's lawyers and accountants for aiding the corporate illegality that ultimately resulted in the company's collapse. (Recall Judge Sporkin's rhetorical questions at page 447 supra.) The complaints may charge that the company's officers and directors acted illegally either on behalf of the company or against it. Assuming the lawyers were "in on it," should it matter whether the company was the victim or the victimizer?

The Seventh Circuit has ruled that it should matter. In Cenco, Inc. v. Seidman & Seidman, 686 F.2d 449, 456 (7th Cir.), cert. denied, 459 U.S. 880 (1982), Judge Posner wrote that "[f]raud on behalf of a corporation is not the same thing as fraud against it." When "top management" causes a company to defraud others, the company is a "participant" in and not a "victim" of the fraud. As a result, the auditor defendants had a complete defense in a class action derivative suit. (Compare this holding with Judge Posner's refusal to recognize a contributory negligence defense in Greycas, Inc. v. Proud, page 649 infra.)

A year later the Seventh Circuit decided Schacht v. Brown, 711 F.2d 1343, 1348 (7th Cir.), cert. denied, 464 U.S. 1002 (1983), which was an action by the Illinois Director of Insurance against three accounting firms, two insurance companies, the former officers and directors of Reserve Insurance Company, and Reserve's parent company. Schacht, who was liquidating Reserve following its insolvency, alleged that the defendants fraudulently concealed, or aided in the concealment of, Reserve's true financial situation while Reserve was "systematically looted of its most profitable and least risky business and more than $3,000,000 in income." As a result, Schacht alleged, Reserve, its policyholders and creditors suffered losses exceeding $100 million. The accounting firms and the two insurance companies sought to defend against Schacht's complaint on behalf of Reserve by arguing that management's wrongdoing had to be attributed to Reserve itself. The court distinguished this case from Cenco, emphasizing that "these results cannot be described as beneficial to Reserve." The company was the fatal victim, not the intended beneficiary, of management's unlawful conduct.

When the malpractice plaintiff was not previously represented in connection with a litigation, the plaintiff will still have to prove an "inner" case of sorts. In Miami International, page 635 supra, that inner case required the plaintiff to show that if not for the defendant's defaults, its business venture would have yielded a (greater) profit. See also Wastvedt v. Vaaler, 430 N.W.2d 561 (N.D. 1988) (no recovery where plaintiff failed to introduce expert testimony that attorney's conflict resulted in lower price for plaintiff's stock).

Where the plaintiff was a defendant in the underlying action and lost, allegedly because of the lawyer's malpractice, she will have to show that she would have won the underlying case (or lost less) but for the professional lapse. That was the burden in Wagenmann v. Adams, supra page 629, where you will recall that the plaintiff, the reluctant father of the willing bride, was locked up after he tried to attend his daughter's wedding.

> *B. Causation.* Healy insists that Wagenmann failed to prove he would not have been committed (or would have been released sooner) but for lawyerly negligence. We begin our analysis of this point by acknowledging that the district court, in its instructions to the jury, indubitably placed the burden on the plaintiff to show that Healy's malpractice was a material element and substantial factor in causing Wagenmann's commitment. The court further charged that if Wagenmann would have been committed no matter what action the lawyer took or neglected to take, then in such event, Healy would not be liable. Assaying the evidence as we must, in the light most flattering to the appellee, we conclude that it was sufficient for a rational factfinder to determine that Wagenmann, more likely than not, would have escaped commitment had he been represented with due skill and diligence.
>
> On this issue, the testimony of Dr. Myerson, whose views were not properly voiced due to counsel's boycotting of the physician, was a potent weapon. Furthermore, there was evidence that several other examining psychiatrists apparently agreed in substance with Dr. Myerson's evaluation. On this item alone, the jury could rationally have deduced that, had Healy done his job and brought Dr. Myerson to the forefront, it was unlikely that commitment would have ensued. The jury could likewise have concluded that, had Healy heeded his client's repeated demands for a hearing, Wagenmann's competency would have been as obvious to the magistrate as it was to Dr. Myerson. Finally, the plaintiff's speedy release the next day, facilitated by a paladin with no formal legal training, bore witness to the likelihood that, had the lawyer performed professionally, Wagenmann would have been spared his ordeal at WSH. The district court was of a mind that "the jury was justified in concluding that had Mr. Healy represented his client's case more zealously, Judge Luby might not have committed the plaintiff to the mental hospital." This, we think, understates the matter. The record fully supported a jury finding that, but for the want of reasonably professional representation, Wagenmann would not have been confined to a mental institution. 829 F.2d at 220-221.

QUESTION

13.1   "We've been asked to take a case. We're trying to figure out if the likelihood of recovery justifies accepting it on a contingency. It seems that in 1978, Mrs. Hilda Jones hired Vida Lewis to represent her in a divorce action against her husband, an officer in the California National Guard. California is a community property state, which means that with some exceptions all property acquired during a marriage belongs to both spouses, regardless of source.

"For reasons we don't yet know, Ms. Lewis failed to list General Jones's federal military pension as community property on the list of property to which Mrs. Jones was making a claim. As a result, when the divorce went through in 1979, Mrs. Jones got about $100,000 less than she would probably have received had the pension been listed.

"I say 'probably' because, at the time of the divorce, it was unclear whether a federal military pension could be community property. The answer turned on resolution of ambiguous congressional intent.

"Since then, McCarty v. McCarty, 453 U.S. 210 (1981), construed the applicable statute to hold that federal pensions were exempt from state community property laws. But soon thereafter, Congress passed legislation that overruled *McCarty*. Which is where the law is today.

"I've read how *Togstad* [page 613 supra] and other cases treat the causation issue. But I'll be damned if I know how to apply that kind of straight factual analysis here. Who is going to decide how the courts would have ruled in Mrs. Jones's case back in 1979? How will they know? What evidence should I introduce? And on the issue of liability, does it make a difference why Lewis failed to list the federal pension?"

Causation in Criminal Cases

CARMEL v. LUNNEY
70 N.Y.2d 169, 511 N.E.2d 1126, 518 N.Y.S.2d 605 (1987)

ALEXANDER, J.

In this action for legal malpractice based upon the alleged breach of an attorney's duty to advise his client of potential conflicts of interest and of the possible criminal consequences of incriminating testimony given during a Martin Act hearing, the undisturbed determination of the client's guilt in the subsequent criminal prosecution precludes him, as a matter of law, from recovering for civil damages flowing from the allegedly negligent representation.

Plaintiff, Paul Carmel, worked as a licensed securities salesman with the brokerage firm of Fittin, Cunningham & Lauzon. Among the offerings of that firm was the investment service of Michael Starbuck, Inc. &

Associates. From 1978 to 1980, plaintiff advised various Fittin clients to transfer their securities to the Starbuck operation, promising them guaranteed returns on their investments. In January 1980, the Starbuck enterprise came under investigation for violation of State and Federal securities regulations. Plaintiff and other employees and principals at Fittin were subpoenaed by the Attorney-General to testify at a hearing incident to a Martin Act (General Business Law art. 23-A) investigation of Fittin's role in the promotion and sale of interests in Starbuck. On Fittin's recommendation, plaintiff retained defendant law firm, Lunney & Crocco, to represent him at the Martin Act hearing. Plaintiff claims he was unaware at the time that defendants had already appeared at hearings before the Securities and Exchange Commission on behalf of Fittin principals and coemployees on the Starbuck matter. Plaintiff alleges that defendants counseled him to appear at the Martin Act hearing and to inform the Attorney-General unreservedly about his activities at Fittin. Subsequently, a Grand Jury returned two indictments charging plaintiff with various Martin Act violations, grand larceny, scheming to defraud, and conspiracy.

Defendants never represented plaintiff after the Martin Act hearing. Following his indictment, plaintiff retained the firm of Tabner, Carlson, Farrell & Cholakis, third-party defendants herein, to defend him in the criminal prosecution. Ensuing plea negotiations resulted in plaintiff pleading guilty to a misdemeanor violation of the Martin Act (General Business Law §352-c[1][c]), in full satisfaction of the indictments. Plaintiff then brought this malpractice action against defendants for failing to advise him of the possible criminal implications of testimony given at a Martin Act hearing, of his privilege against self-incrimination, of the possibility of receiving immunity in exchange for cooperating with the Attorney-General in furnishing evidence against actual principals in the fraud scheme, and of potential conflicts of interest stemming from defendants' having already represented other Fittin associates — all in breach of their fiduciary duty, their attorney-client relationship, and the retainer agreement. Plaintiff claims damages in the amount of $2 million resulting from the revocation of his license, his loss of reputation, and his having been called upon to answer civil suits lodged against him by certain of his clients for fraudulent and deceptive practices. He also claims to have been damaged by having to plead to a misdemeanor crime in order to avoid more serious felony charges for which he otherwise might never have been indicted.

Defendants moved for summary judgment contending that plaintiff's guilty plea — not any alleged attorney malpractice — constitutes the proximate cause, as a matter of law, of damages suffered. Supreme Court denied the motion, but the Appellate Division reversed, granted the motion, and dismissed plaintiff's complaint. We now affirm.

To state a cause of action for legal malpractice arising from negligent representation in a criminal proceeding, plaintiff must allege his innocence or a colorable claim of innocence of the underlying offense, for so long as the determination of his guilt of that offense remains undisturbed, no cause of action will lie. Here, because plaintiff's conviction by plea of a misdemeanor violation of the Martin Act has not been successfully challenged, he can neither assert, nor establish, his innocence. He has thus failed to state a cause of action, and his claim was properly dismissed. . . .

As the dissenter at the Appellate Division noted, New York has traditionally applied a "but for" approach to causation when evaluating legal malpractice claims. The test is whether a proper "defense would have altered the result of the prior action". To be sure, a defendant in a criminal proceeding might be able to prove malpractice by establishing that but for the negligent representation he would, for example, have invoked his 5th Amendment rights, or succeeded in suppressing certain evidence conclusive of his guilt. But, because he cannot assert his innocence, public policy prevents maintenance of a malpractice action against his attorney. This is so because criminal prosecutions involve constitutional and procedural safeguards designed to maintain the integrity of the judicial system and to protect criminal defendants from overreaching governmental actions. These aspects of criminal proceedings make criminal malpractice cases unique, and policy considerations require different pleading and substantive rules.

Accordingly, the order of the Appellate Division should be affirmed, with costs.

Acquittal or Innocence?

Glenn v. Aiken, 409 Mass. 699, 569 N.E.2d 783 (1991), reaches the same result. If the defendant would have been convicted of the same crime and received the same sentence in any event, he is not damaged and should not be allowed to collect in malpractice, no matter how serious the lawyer's error. But why should the malpractice plaintiff have to prove more than the likelihood of acquittal, or conviction of a lesser offense, or a lower sentence? Why require him or her to show "innocence or a colorable claim of innocence?" (What is the difference between those two anyway?) Other courts have only required the defendant to show that he would have been acquitted but for the lawyer's negligence. Streeter v. Young, 583 So. 2d 1339 (Ala. 1991).

How would the New York and Massachusetts courts decide the following case? How would you? Krahn is charged with three gambling misdemeanors because she had a gambling device in her bar. She retained Kinney to represent her. Unknown to her, Kinney also represented Shaffer, whose company installed and serviced the device. The prosecutor told Kinney that he would dismiss the charge against Krahn if she testified against Shaffer. Kinney did not communicate this offer to Krahn. He instead recommended that she enter a guilty plea and she did. Krahn cannot establish her actual innocence or a colorable claim of innocence. Should she prevail in her malpractice action against Kinney? How would it affect your answer if Krahn, with new counsel, lost a motion to vacate her conviction on the ground of Kinney's ineffective assistance of counsel? What if she won the motion? See Krahn v. Kinney, 43 Ohio St. 3d 103, 538 N.E.2d 1058 (1989). Glenn v. Aiken, 569 N.E.2d at 785 & n.2, collects cases recognizing the estoppel effect of an unsuccessful ineffective assistance claim in a subsequent malpractice action.

4.   Damages or Injury

The part of a malpractice case concerned with damages or injury draws largely on the law of remedies in tort and contract cases. We have already seen some damage issues in the preceding material. Essentially, the client has to prove that the lawyer's default caused a loss. In *Fishman* (page 637 supra), this meant that the client had to show how much more he would have recovered had the case gone to trial. In *Miami International* (page 635 supra), the plaintiff had to prove the profit it would have earned.

To the extent malpractice plaintiffs may recover only for economic loss, clients who use lawyers for noneconomic problems will have hollow claims if their lawyers act incompetently. Many jurisdictions do decline to recognize noneconomic injuries. See, e.g., Timms v. Rosenblum, 713 F. Supp. 948 (E.D. Va. 1989), aff'd, 900 F.2d 256 (4th Cir. 1990), where the plaintiff charged that the defendants were negligent in a custody matter as a result of which she allegedly lost custody of her children. The court held that the plaintiff could not recover for her emotional distress unless the defendants' behavior was intentional or outrageous or the plaintiff suffered physical injury.

However, significant inroads on the reluctance to allow recovery for noneconomic injury have lately appeared. Let us return for our final segment from Wagenmann v. Adams, page 629 supra, where the client suffered a night's confinement in a mental hospital:

> The lawyer-appellant's attack on damages is based upon the premise that his former client, if entitled to recover at all, was not entitled to receive what Healy characterizes as damages for emotional distress. In the attorney's view, any recovery inuring to the plaintiff's benefit in this legal malpractice case must perforce be limited to economic losses (minimal in this instance). We cannot subscribe to this viewpoint.

As a direct and proximate result of Healy's ineffectiveness, the plaintiff was forcibly deprived of his liberty and dispatched to a mental hospital. The fright and suffering incident to such a wrenching dislocation can hardly be overstated. Subsequent to his release, Wagenmann claimed (credibly) to have undergone continuing anguish and to have felt the weight of the stigma attendant to such confinement. He feared that others would learn of it and question his sanity. The district judge instructed the jurors that if they found liability on this count, they could award reasonable damages to compensate for "any pain, suffering, humiliation and mental anguish" suffered and to be suffered by the plaintiff, caused by Healy's (mis)conduct. We decline the appellant's invitation to relieve him of the foreseeable consequences of his malpractice by the overly simplistic expedient of relabelling the resultant award as damages for "emotional distress.". . .

In Addington v. Texas, 441 U.S. 418 (1979), the Court limned the significance of the personal loss incident to involuntary commitment:

> [C]ivil commitment for any purpose constitutes a significant deprivation of liberty that requires due process protection. . . . Moreover, it is indisputable that involuntary commitment to a mental hospital after a finding of probable dangerousness to self or others can engender adverse social consequences to the individual. Whether we label this phenomen[on] "stigma" or choose to call it something else is less important than that we recognize that it can occur and that it can have a very significant impact on the individual. Id. at 425-26 (citations omitted).

This statement of the stark reality of civil commitment must, in the context of this case, be synchronized with what the Massachusetts Supreme Judicial Court has recently written on the subject of legal malpractice. In Fishman v. Brooks, 396 Mass. at 646, 487 N.E.2d 1377, the court noted that "[a]n attorney who [commits malpractice] is liable to his client for any reasonably foreseeable loss caused by his negligence." Applying *Addington* and *Fishman* in concert, there is little room to doubt that the harm Wagenmann suffered due to Healy's bungling was real and significant, and that the injury was reasonably foreseeable under the circumstances. Any attorney in Healy's position should readily have anticipated the agonies attendant upon involuntary (and inappropriate) commitment to WSH and the subsequent stigma and fear associated with such a traumatic episode. The damages were therefore recoverable under Massachusetts law.

Were we to accept the notion that a client's recovery on the grim facts of a case such as this must be limited to purely economic loss, we would be doubly wrong. The negligent lawyer would receive the benefit of an enormous windfall, and the victimized client would be left without fair recourse in the face of ghastly wrongdoing. Despite having caused his client a substantial loss of liberty and exposed him to a consequent parade of horribles, counsel would effectively be immunized from liability because of the fortuity of the marketplace. That Healy was guilty of malpractice in the defense of commitment procedings, rather than in the prosecution of a civil claim for damages, is no reason artificially to shield him from the condign consequences of his carelessness. We are not required by the law of the common-wealth, as we read it, to reach such an unjust result.

829 F.2d at 221-222.

Other cases that allow damages for emotional distress are Salley v. Childs, 541 A.2d 1297 (Me. 1988) (also allowing damages for injury to reputation), Cummings v. Pinder, 574 A.2d 843 (Del. 1990) (same), and Bowman v. Doherty, 235 Kan. 870, 686 P.2d 112 (1984) (also allowing punitive damages). A client who is incarcerated as a result of a lawyer's negligence or neglect will often have little to show by way of economic loss but a great deal of emotional pain. As in *Wagenmann*, courts have recognized this damage. Holliday v. Jones, 215 Cal. App. 3d 102, 264 Cal. Rptr. 448 (1989) (lawyer's incompetence resulted in manslaughter conviction, later reversed; client acquitted on new trial); Snyder v. Baumecker, 708 F. Supp. 1451 (D.N.J. 1989) (lawyer liable for client's emotional distress caused by incarceration but not for client's resulting suicide because it was not foreseeable).

In one unusual case, a widow did not remarry because her lawyer told her, wrongly, that if she did so she would lose her first husband's pension. Instead, she lived with a man who later left her after striking oil (literally). The court held that she was entitled to the economic and noneconomic losses she suffered as a result of not marrying. The former included the interest state law would have given her in the man's assets had they married. The latter included loss of self-esteem, shame, public ridicule, and moral anguish. Horn v. Croegaert, 187 Ill. App. 3d 53, 542 N.E.2d 1124 (1989).

One question on which courts have divided is whether the client's recovery ought to be reduced by the fee the lawyer would have earned had he not acted negligently. For example, a client retains a lawyer on a one-third contingency basis in a personal injury action. The lawyer forgets to file the complaint on time. The client sues the lawyer and proves that she would have recovered $30,000 at trial of the underlying action. Should the judgment be reduced by the $10,000 the lawyer would have received had he acted properly? Yes: Moores v. Greenberg, 834 F.2d 1105 (1st Cir. 1987); No: Campagnola v. Mulholland, Minion & Roe, 76 N.Y.2d 38, 555 N.E.2d 611, 556 N.Y.S.2d 239 (1990). Should the damages be increased by the amount of money the client will have to pay the second lawyer to recover against the first lawyer? Are these two questions related? On the issue of recovery of legal fees, courts distinguish between the fees paid to sue the former lawyer and fees paid to a new lawyer to avoid or mitigate the harm from the former lawyer's conduct, allowing the second but not the first. Gibralter Savings v. Commonwealth Land Title Insurance Co., 907 F.2d 844 (8th Cir. 1990). If the former client had to pay punitive damages in the case within a case, should the negligent lawyer be liable for those too? Elliott v. Videan, 164 Ariz. App. 113,

791 P.2d 639 (1989) (yes). Is this right? Can you square the answer with Carmel v. Lunney, page 643 supra?

C. BEYOND MALPRACTICE: OTHER GROUNDS FOR ATTORNEY LIABILITY TO CLIENTS AND THIRD PARTIES

GREYCAS, INC. v. PROUD
**826 F.2d 1560 (7th Cir. 1987), cert. denied,
484 U.S. 1043 (1988)**

POSNER, J.

Theodore S. Proud, Jr., a member of the Illinois bar who practices law in a suburb of Chicago, appeals from a judgment against him for $833,760, entered after a bench trial. The tale of malpractice and misrepresentation that led to the judgment begins with Proud's brother-in-law, Wayne Crawford, like Proud a lawyer but one who devoted most of his attention to a large farm that he owned in downstate Illinois. The farm fell on hard times and by 1981 Crawford was in dire financial straits. He had pledged most of his farm machinery to lenders, yet now desperately needed more money. He approached Greycas, Inc., the plaintiff in this case, a large financial company headquartered in Arizona, seeking a large loan that he offered to secure with the farm machinery. He did not tell Greycas about his financial difficulties or that he had pledged the machinery to other lenders, but he did make clear that he needed the loan in a hurry. Greycas obtained several appraisals of Crawford's farm machinery but did not investigate Crawford's financial position or discover that he had pledged the collateral to other lenders, who had perfected their liens in the collateral. Greycas agreed to lend Crawford $1,367,966.50, which was less than the appraised value of the machinery.

The loan was subject, however, to an important condition, which is at the heart of this case: Crawford was required to submit a letter to Greycas, from counsel whom he would retain, assuring Greycas that there were no prior liens on the machinery that was to secure the loan. Crawford asked Proud to prepare the letter, and he did so, and mailed it to Greycas, and within 20 days of the first contact between Crawford and Greycas the loan closed and the money was disbursed. A year later Crawford defaulted on the loan; shortly afterward he committed suicide. Greycas then learned that most of the farm machinery that Crawford had pledged to it had previously been pledged to other lenders.

The machinery was sold at auction. The Illinois state court that determined the creditors' priorities in the proceeds of the sale held that Greycas did not have a first priority on most of the machinery that secured its loan; as a result Greycas has been able to recover only a small part of the loan. The judgment it obtained in the present suit is the district judge's estimate of the value that it would have realized on its collateral had there been no prior liens, as Proud represented in his letter.

That letter is the centerpiece of the litigation. Typed on the stationery of Proud's firm and addressed to Greycas, it identifies Proud as Crawford's lawyer and states that, "in such capacity, I have been asked to render my opinion in connection with" the proposed loan to Crawford. It also states that "this opinion is being delivered in accordance with the requirements of the Loan Agreement" and that

> I have conducted a U.C.C., tax, and judgment search with respect to the Company [i.e., Crawford's farm] as of March 19, 1981, and except as hereinafter noted all units listed on the attached Exhibit A ("Equipment") are free and clear of all liens or encumbrances other than Lender's perfected security interest therein which was recorded March 19, 1981 at the Office of the Recorder of Deeds of Fayette County, Illinois.

The reference to the lender's security interest is to Greycas's interest; Crawford, pursuant to the loan agreement, had filed a notice of that interest with the recorder. The excepted units to which the letter refers are four vehicles. Exhibit A is a long list of farm machinery — the collateral that Greycas thought it was getting to secure the loan, free of any other liens. . . .

Proud never conducted a search for prior liens on the machinery listed in Exhibit A. His brother-in-law gave him the list and told him there were no liens other than the one that Crawford had just filed for Greycas. Proud made no effort to verify Crawford's statement. The theory of the complaint is that Proud was negligent in representing that there were no prior liens, merely on his brother-in-law's say-so. No doubt Proud *was* negligent in failing to conduct a search, but we are not clear why the *misrepresentation* is alleged to be negligent rather than deliberate and hence fraudulent, in which event Greycas's alleged contributory negligence would not be an issue (as it is, we shall see), since there is no defense of contributory or comparative negligence to a deliberate tort, such as fraud. Proud did not merely say, "There are no liens"; he said, "I have conducted a U.C.C., tax, and judgment search"; and not only is this statement, too, a false one, but its falsehood cannot have been inadvertent, for Proud knew he had not conducted such a search. The concealment of his relationship with Crawford might also support a charge of fraud. But Greycas decided, for whatever reason, to argue negligent misrepresentation rather than fraud. It may have feared that Proud's insurance policy for professional malpractice excluded deliberate wrongdoing from its coverage, or may not have wanted to bear the higher burden of proving fraud, or may have feared that an accusation of fraud would make it harder to settle the case — for most cases, of course, are settled, though this one has not been. In any event, Proud does not argue that either he is liable for fraud or he is liable for nothing.

He also does not, and could not, deny or justify the misrepresentation; but he argues that it is not actionable under the tort law of Illinois, because he had no duty of care to Greycas. (This is a diversity case and the parties agree that Illinois tort law governs the substantive issues.) He argues that Greycas had an adversarial relationship with Proud's client, Crawford, and that a lawyer had no duty of straight dealing to an adversary, at least none enforceable by a tort suit. In so arguing, Proud is characterizing Greycas's suit as one for professional malpractice rather than negligent misrepresentation, yet elsewhere in his briefs he insists that the suit was solely for negligent misrepresentation — while Greycas insists that its suit charges both torts. Legal malpractice based on a false representation, and negligent misrepresentation by a lawyer, are such similar legal concepts, however, that we have great difficulty both in holding them apart in our minds and in understanding why the parties are quarreling over the exact characterization; no one suggests, for example, that the statute of limitations might have run on one but not the other tort. So we shall discuss both.

Proud is undoubtedly correct in arguing that a lawyer has no general duty of care toward his adversary's client; it would be a considerable and, as it seems to us, an undesirable novelty to hold that every bit of sharp dealing by a lawyer gives rise to prima facie tort liability to the opposing party in the lawsuit or negotiation. The tort of malpractice normally refers to a lawyer's careless or otherwise wrongful conduct toward his own client. Proud argues that Crawford rather than Greycas was his client, and although this is not so clear as Proud supposes — another characterization of the transaction is that Crawford undertook to obtain a lawyer for Greycas in the loan transaction — we shall assume for purposes of discussion that Greycas was not Proud's client.

Therefore if malpractice just meant carelessness or other misconduct toward one's own client, Proud would not be liable for malpractice to Greycas. But in Pelham v. Griesheimer, 92 Ill. 2d 13, 440 N.E.2d 96 (1982) [page 627 supra], the Supreme Court of Illinois discarded the old common law requirement of privity of contract for professional malpractice; so now it is possible for someone who is not the lawyer's (or other professional's) client to sue him for malpractice. The court in *Pelham* was worried, though, about the possibility of a lawyer's being held liable "to an unlimited and unknown number of potential plaintiffs," so it added that "for a nonclient to succeed in a negligence action against an attorney, he must prove that the primary purpose and intent of the attorney-client relationship itself was to benefit or influence the third party." That, however, describes this case exactly. Crawford hired Proud not only for the primary purpose, but for the sole purpose, of influencing Greycas to make Crawford a loan. The case is much like Brumley v. Touche, Ross & Co., 139 Ill. App. 3d 831, 836, 487 N.E.2d 641, 644-45 (1985), where a complaint that an accounting firm had negligently prepared an audit report that the firm knew would be shown to an investor in the audited corporation and relied on by that investor was held to state a claim for professional malpractice. In Conroy v. Andeck Resources '81 Year-End Ltd., 137 Ill. App. 3d 375, 389-91, 484 N.E.2d 525, 536-37 (1985), in contrast, a law firm that represented an offeror of securities was held not to have any duty of care to investors. The representation was not intended for the benefit of investors. Their reliance on the law firm's using due care in the services it provided in connection with the offer was not invited. Cf. Barker v. Henderson, Franklin, Starnes & Holt, 797 F.2d 490, 497 (7th Cir. 1986).

All this assumes that *Pelham* governs this case, but arguably it does not, for Greycas, as we noted, may have decided to bring this as a suit for negligent misrepresentation rather than professional malpractice. We know of no obstacle to such an election; nothing is more common in American jurisprudence than overlapping torts.

The claim of negligent misrepresentation might seem utterly straightforward. It might seem that by addressing a letter to Greycas intended (as Proud's counsel admitted at argument) to induce reliance on the statements in it, Proud made himself prima facie liable for any material misrepresentations, careless or deliberate, in the letter, whether or not Proud was Crawford's lawyer or for that matter anyone's lawyer. Knowing that Greycas was relying on him to determine whether the collateral for the loan was encumbered and to advise Greycas of the results of his determination, Proud negligently misrepresented the situation, to Greycas's detriment. But merely labeling a suit as one for negligent misrepresentation rather than professional malpractice will not make the problem of indefinite and perhaps excessive liability, which induced the court in *Pelham* to place limitations on the duty of care, go away. So one is not surprised to find that courts have placed similar limitations on suits for negligent misrepresentation — so similar that we are led to question whether, as suggested in HGN Corp. v. Chamberlain, Hrdlicka, White, Johnson & Williams, 642 F. Supp. 1443, 1452-53 (N.D. Ill. 1986), these really are different torts, at least when both grow out of negligent misrepresentations by lawyers. For example, the *Brumley* case, which we cited earlier, is a professional-malpractice case, yet it has essentially the same facts as Ultramares Corp. v. Touche, Niven & Co., 255 N.Y. 170, 174 N.E. 441 (1931), where the New York Court of Appeals, in a famous opinion by Judge Cardozo, held that an accountant's negligent misrepresentation was not actionable at the suit of a lender who had relied on the accountant's certified audit of the borrower.

The absence of a contract between the lender and the accountant defeated the suit in *Ultramares* — yet why should privity of contract have been required for liability just because the negligence lay in disseminating information rather than in designing or manufacturing a product? The privity limitation in products cases had been rejected, in another famous Cardozo opinion, years earlier. See MacPherson v. Buick Motor Co., 217 N.Y. 382, 111 N.E. 1050 (1916). Professor Bishop suggests that courts were worried that imposing heavy liabilities on producers of information might cause socially valuable information to be underproduced. See Negligent Misrepresentation Through Economists' Eyes, 96 L.Q. Rev. 360 (1980). Many producers of information have difficulty appropriating its benefits to society. The property-rights system in information is incomplete; someone who comes up with a new idea that the law of intellectual property does not protect cannot prevent others from using the idea without reimbursing his costs of invention or discovery. So the law must be careful not to weigh these producers down too heavily with tort liabilities. For example, information produced by securities analysts, the news media, academicians, and so forth is socially valuable, but as its producers can't capture the full value of the information in their fees and other remuneration the information may be underproduced. Maybe it is right, therefore — or at least efficient — that none of these producers should have to bear the full costs. At least that was once the view; and while *Ultramares* has now been rejected, in Illinois as elsewhere — maybe because providers of information are deemed more robust today than they once were or maybe because it is now believed that auditors, surveyors, and other providers of professional services were always able to capture the social value of even the information component of those services in the fees they charged their clients — a residuum of concern remains. So when in Rozny v. Marnul, 43 Ill. 2d 54, 250 N.E.2d 656 (1969), the Supreme Court of Illinois, joining the march away from *Utramares*, held for the first time that negligent misrepresentation was actionable despite the absence of a contract, and thus cast aside the same "privity of contract" limitation later overruled with regard to professional malpractice in *Pelham*, the court was careful to emphasize facts in the particular case before it that limited the scope of its holding — facts such as that the defendant, a surveyor, had placed his "absolute guarantee for accuracy" on the plat and that only a few persons would receive and rely on it, thus limiting the potential scope of liability.

Later Illinois cases, however, influenced by section 552 of the Second Restatement of Torts (1977), state the limitation on liability for negligent misrepresentation in more compact terms — as well as in narrower scope — than *Rozny*. These are cases in the intermediate appellate court, but, as we have no reason to think the Supreme Court of Illinois would reject them, we are bound to follow them. They hold that "one who in the course of his business or profession supplies information for the guidance of others in their business transactions" is liable for negligent misrepresentations that induce detrimental reliance. Whether there is a practical as distinct from a merely semantic difference between this formulation of the duty limitation and that of *Pelham* may be doubted but cannot change the outcome of this case. Proud, in the practice of his profession, supplied information (or rather misinformation) to Greycas that was intended to guide Greycas in commercial dealings with Crawford. Proud therefore had a duty to use due care to see that the information was correct. He used no care.

Proud must lose on the issue of liability even if the narrower, ad hoc approach of *Rozny* is used instead of the approach of section 552 of the Restatement. Information about the existence of previous liens on particular items of property is of limited social as distinct from private value, by which we mean simply that the information is not likely to be disseminated widely. There is consequently no reason to give it special encouragement by overlooking carelessness in its collection and expression. Where as in this case the defendant makes the negligent misrepresentation directly to the plaintiff in the course of the defendant's business or profession, the courts have little difficulty in finding a duty of care.

There is no serious doubt about the existence of a causal relationship between the misrepresentation and the loan. Greycas would not have made the loan without Proud's letter. Nor would it have made the loan had Proud advised it that the collateral was so heavily encumbered that the loan was as if unsecured, for then Greycas would have known that the probability of repayment was slight. Merely to charge a higher interest rate would not have been an attractive alternative to security; it would have made default virtually inevitable by saddling Crawford with a huge fixed debt. To understand the astronomical interest rate that is required to make an unsecured loan a paying proposition to the lender when the risk of default is high, notice that even if the riskless interest rate is only 3 percent, the rate of inflation zero, the cost of administering the loan zero, and the lender risk-neutral, he still must charge an annual interest rate of 106 percent if he thinks there is only a 50 percent chance that he will get his principal back.

Proud argues, however, that his damages should be reduced in recognition of Greycas's own contributory negligence, which, though no longer a complete defense in Illinois, is a partial defense, renamed "comparative negligence." It is as much a defense to negligent misrepresentation as to any other tort of negligence. On the issue of comparative negligence the district court said only that "defendant may have proved negligence upon the part of plaintiff but that negligence, if any, had no causal relationship to the malpractice of the defendant or the damages to the plaintiff." This comment is not easy to fathom. If Greycas was careless in deciding whether to make the loan, this implies that a reasonable investigation by Greycas would have shown that the collateral for the loan was already heavily encumbered; knowing this, Greycas would not have made the loan and therefore would not have suffered any damages.

But we think it too clear to require a remand for further proceedings that Proud failed to prove a want of due care by Greycas. Due care is the care that is optimal given that the other party is exercising due care. It is not the higher level of care that would be optimal if potential tort victims were required to assume that the rest of the world was negligent. A pedestrian is not required to exercise a level of care (e.g., wearing a helmet or a shin guard) that would be optimal if there were no sanctions against reckless driving. Otherwise drivers would be encouraged to drive recklessly, and knowing this pedestrians would be encouraged to wear helmets and shin guards. The result would be a shift from a superior method of accident avoidance (not driving recklessly) to an inferior one (pedestrian armor).

So we must ask whether Greycas would have been careless not to conduct its own U.C.C. search had Proud done what he had said he did — conduct his own U.C.C. search. The answer is no. The law normally does not require duplicative precautions unless one is likely to fail or the consequences of failure (slight though the likelihood may be) would be catastrophic. One U.C.C. search is enough to disclose prior liens, and Greycas acted reasonably in relying on Proud to conduct it. Although Greycas had much warning that Crawford was in financial trouble and that the loan might not be repaid, that was a reason for charging a hefty interest rate and insisting that the loan be secured; it was not a reason for duplicating Proud's work. It is not hard to conduct a U.C.C. lien search; it just requires checking the records in the recorder's office for the county where the debtor lives. So the only reason to backstop Proud was if Greycas should have assumed he was careless or dishonest; and we have just said that the duty of care does not require such an assumption. Had Proud disclosed that he was Crawford's brother-in-law this might have been a warning signal that Greycas could ignore only at its peril. To go forward in the face of a known danger is to assume the risk. But Proud did not disclose his relationship to Crawford. . . .

[Portions of the majority opinion addressing evidentiary and damage questions are omitted. The judgment was affirmed.]

BAUER, C.J., concurring.

I am in agreement with the majority opinion. I believe that Proud would be liable without reference to legal malpractice or negligent misrepresentation. The evidence in this case indicates that he is guilty of fraud or intentional misrepresentation. He was lying when he represented that he had made U.C.C., tax and judgment searches on his brother-in-law's farm. He intended the misrepresentation to induce Greycas to make a loan to his brother-in-law; Greycas justifiably relied upon the misrepresentation in making the loan and was injured as a result. Under these facts, Proud's misrepresentation was indefensible.

The Expanding Universe in Professional Liability

The following discussion addresses some of the old, new, and newly applied theories that third parties, and sometimes clients, have asserted in actions against lawyers, or that lawyers have interposed in defense. Clients, of course, also have recourse to traditional professional negligence claims, as do some nonclients (see page 625 supra), although sometimes a nonclient will not be able to claim client status. Courts, in any event, entertain and adopt multiple theories of liability. Judge Posner makes that point in *Greycas* when he contrasts professional negligence with negligent representation and fraud. See also Callahan v. Callahan, 127 A.D.2d 298, 514 N.Y.S.2d 819 (3d Dept. 1987); Nelson v. Nationwide Mortgage Corp., 659 F. Supp. 611 (D.D.C. 1987). Judge Bauer would have affirmed on a theory of intentional wrongdoing. What very good reason do you suppose Greycas had for *not* asserting that theory?

An early case, Biakanja v. Irving, 49 Cal. 2d 647, 320 P.2d 16 (1958), adopted a "balancing of factors" test to decide whether a lawyer has a duty to a nonclient. This test does not offer much in the way of predictability, but perhaps stricter categorization is not easily achieved. California has certainly been the doctrinal leader in this area. It has even influenced states that have adopted other tests in lieu of the "balancing of factors" test. See Flaherty v. Weinberg and Pelham v. Griesheimer (pages 626 and 627 supra).

Consumer Protection Laws. In Guenard v. Burke, 387 Mass. 802, 443 N.E.2d 892, 896 (1982), the plaintiff-client was allowed to invoke the benefit of a state law forbidding "unfair or deceptive acts or practices in the conduct of any trade or commerce" in connection with an action against her former attorney. The court assumed without discussion that the practice of law was a "trade or business" within the meaning of the state statute. Unlike a traditional common law malpractice action, the statute provided for multiple damages, attorney's fees, and costs.

In Rousseau v. Eshleman, 128 N.H. 564, 519 A.2d 243 (1986), the court reversed a judgment against an attorney under a consumer protection act based on its conclusion that the legislature did not intend the act to apply to lawyers. Two justices dissented.

Some states have laws that protect consumers in very specific circumstances. One kind of law provides a right of action against an insurer that does not make a good faith effort to settle a reasonably clear claim. What if the insurer's lawyer aids the avoidance of this statutory responsibility? Doctors' Co. v. Superior Court, 49 Cal. 3d 39, 775 P.2d 508, 260 Cal. Rptr. 183 (1989), refused to impose liability on an insurer's lawyer for aiding the insurer's violation of the statute. The court construed the statute as imposing liability on the insurer only. Compare Gould v. Mutual Life Ins. Co. of N.Y., 37 Wash. App. 756, 683 P.2d 207 (1984), which imposed liability on the lawyers where they had assumed executive responsibility.

Fraud and Negligent Misrepresentation.   Common law or securities fraud claims can be levelled against lawyers as against anyone else, whether by third parties or by their former clients. Also (increasingly), claims of negligent misrepresentation can be made against lawyers, as *Greycas* reveals. In DuPont v. Brady, 828 F.2d 75 (2d Cir. 1987), the former client charged his former counsel with both securities and common law fraud. In Cresswell v. Sullivan & Cromwell, 922 F.2d 60 (2d Cir. 1990), the plaintiffs charged that the defendant firm and its former client had fraudulently and negligently withheld documents during an earlier litigation, as a result of which the plaintiffs alleged that they settled the litigation for less than they would have been able to collect had they received the documents. These facts stated an equitable claim for relief from the settlement, which ultimately failed after the trial judge held that plaintiff's lawyer should have discovered the allegedly withheld information. 771 F. Supp. 580 (S.D.N.Y. 1991). The Tenth Circuit also upheld a claim against an adversary law firm for fraudulent concealment during discovery, as a result of which the plaintiff allegedly was unable to prove his case at trial. Robinson v. Volkswagenwerk, 940 F.2d 1369 (10th Cir. 1991). See also Roberts v. Ball, Hunt, Hart, Brown & Baerwitz, 57 Cal. App. 3d 104, 128 Cal. Rptr. 901 (1976) (negligent misrepresentation); but see Zafiris, Inc. v. Moss, 506 So. 2d 27 (Fla. App. 1987), modified, 524 So. 2d 1010 (Fla. 1988) (privity or third-party beneficiary status required for claim of negligence or misrepresentation but not fraud).

Even jurisdictions that are most ferocious in demanding privity before a lawyer can be held liable to another for a professional error may nonetheless permit negligent misrepresentation claims. New York, for example, has unlatched the privity door less than the width of an eyelash (if that). Nevertheless, Crossland Savings FSB v. Rockwood Ins. Co., 700 F. Supp. 1274, 1281 (S.D.N.Y. 1988), ruled that an attorney could be liable for negligent misrepresentation to third parties when "the lawyer is directed by her client to prepare a document for and on behalf of a third party." Judge Leval closely analyzed New York law and explained why this exception did not threaten the values that the privity requirement was intended to preserve.

Negligent representation claims can also arise in connection with settlement talks. A cautionary tale is found in Slotkin v. Citizens Casualty

Co. of New York, 614 F.2d 301 (2d Cir. 1979), cert. denied, 449 U.S. 981 (1980). A child's parents brought a medical malpractice action against the hospital in which the child was born and others, alleging that the child suffered neurological and brain damage as a result of professional negligence at his birth. While the trial was in progress, but before a verdict, the parties settled for $185,000. Counsel for the hospital made certain representations to counsel for the plaintiff. On one occasion, the hospital's lawyer said that he "knew" that the hospital's insurance coverage was $200,000. On another occasion, he said that this was what he had been informed. In agreeing to the settlement, the plaintiff expressly relied on these statements. It later turned out that the hospital had a separate insurance policy for $1 million in addition to the $200,000 policy to which its counsel was referring. It also turned out that the hospital's counsel had access to documents (of which he claimed to be unaware) revealing the excess coverage. After the settlement and after the plaintiffs learned about the additional insurance coverage, they sued the hospital's counsel, among others, alleging fraud and related claims. The Second Circuit upheld a judgment against the hospital's lawyer because of his representation that he "knew" that the insurance coverage was $200,000. Even if the lawyer truly believed that his "knowledge" was correct, the fact that it turned out false subjected him to personal liability under New York law. How could the lawyer have protected himself?

An especially bizarre case is Cicone v. URS Corp., 183 Cal. App. 3d 194, 227 Cal. Rptr. 887 (1986). See if you can follow this. Attorney C represented L in the sale of his business to URS. URS presented C with a contract that contained a warranty that the business had no liabilities beyond those shown on the balance sheet. L said he would only represent that he *knew* of no other liabilities. At a meeting of all concerned and their counsel, URS's lawyer, Canady, said that the buyers would deem the sellers to be guaranteeing the information only to their best knowledge. The deal then closed with the original warranty language. As it turned out, of course, $200,000 in tax liabilities were not reflected on the balance sheet. URS sued L, who hired new counsel and settled for $125,000, which sum L then sought from C in a malpractice action. C cross-complained against URS and Canady, alleging claims of fraud and negligent misrepresentation. The appellate court upheld both claims. Is this the right result? If URS could have been held to Canady's oral assurance about the meaning of the warranty, wasn't L foolish to settle? Why then should C owe him anything? If URS could not have been held to the oral assurance, so that L did owe URS for the tax liability, then didn't C make a mistake in his representation of L that should not be surcharged to Canady and URS? What if L settled because the law was unclear? In any event, when if ever should one lawyer be liable to an opposing *lawyer* because the first lawyer's client's failure to honor a promise, conveyed by that lawyer, subjected the second lawyer to malpractice liability?

Should a lawyer be liable for negligent misrepresentation to persons of whose reliance the lawyer is unaware? Yes, in Michigan, according to Molecular Technology Corp. v. Valentine, 925 F.2d 910 (6th Cir. 1991) (liability extends to persons whom lawyers "should reasonably foresee will rely on the information"). With so expansive a potential liability, what can a lawyer do to protect himself? Will a disclaimer work? Will rules like these, applied in capital markets, greatly expand potential liability beyond that envisioned by the securities laws?

Errors of Law. Lawyers who negligently misrepresent the *law* may be liable to their clients in malpractice, but they are not likely to be held liable to third parties unless the third parties can persuade the court to treat them as clients (see page 625 supra). Compare the *Roberts* case, page 657 supra, with City National Bank of Detroit v. Rodgers & Morgenstein, 155 Mich. App. 318, 399 N.W.2d 505 (1986). See also Schick v. Bach, 193 Cal. App. 3d 1321, 238 Cal. Rptr. 902 (1987). Why should courts be less willing to impose liability for negligent misrepresentations of law than for negligent misrepresentations of fact?

Helping Fiduciaries Breach Their Duties. Lawyers who purposely or negligently assist fiduciaries in violating their fiduciary duties to beneficiaries may be held liable to the beneficiaries. Albright v. Burns, 206 N.J. Super. 625, 503 A.2d 386, 389 (1986) (lawyer "had reason to foresee the specific harm which occurred"). Compare Angel, Cohen & Rogovin v. Oberon Investment, N.V., 512 So. 2d 192 (Fla. 1987) (negligently helping fiduciary violate trust does not state claim), with Fickett v. Superior Court, 27 Ariz. App. 793, 558 P.2d 988 (1976) (contra).

Government Lawyers. In R. J. Longo Construction Co. v. Schragger, 218 N.J. Super. 206, 527 A.2d 480 (1987), township attorneys negligently failed to obtain easements as required by statute. As a result, a private contractor who had won a bid to construct a sewer facility in the township suffered damages when it began construction in absence of the easements. The contractor sued the government lawyers. The court held that the defendants owed a duty to the plaintiff because of the statutory obligation, despite the absence of an attorney-client relationship. In Barrett v. United States, 798 F.2d 565 (2d Cir. 1986), federal lawyers allegedly conspired to prevent the estate of a decedent from learning the cause of the decedent's death (secret drug experiments conducted by the army). As a result, the estate was unaware of potential federal liability for the death. After the limitations period ran out, the estate sued the lawyers for concealing the truth. The court upheld liability, rejecting a claim of absolute immunity in favor of qualified immunity.

Inducing Breach of Contract.   If X induces Y to breach a contract with Z, Z may be able to sue X for interference with Z's contractual rights or intentional interference with Z's prospective economic advantage. If, however, X had a fiduciary relationship with Y, X might enjoy a privilege that will be a defense to the action. The privilege is based on the agent's duty to protect his principal's interests, a duty that might sometimes require the agent to counsel the principal to break a contract. Attorneys are among the fiduciaries who enjoy this privilege. However, the privilege can be lost if the attorney (or other fiduciary) acts from "improper motives," which includes furthering his own economic interests. The definition of "improper motives" varies with jurisdictions and sometimes with whether the underlying contract was at-will or for a fixed term. Los Angeles Airways v. Davis, 687 F.2d 321 (9th Cir. 1982); Duggin v. Adams, 234 Va. 221, 360 S.E.2d 832 (1987).

Violation of Escrow Agreement.   When a lawyer agrees to act as an escrow agent — to hold property pursuant to an agreement between two parties, one of whom is usually the lawyer's client — the lawyer assumes responsibilities to the parties to the escrow agreement that transcend the responsibilities the lawyer would ordinarily have to his client alone. See New York City Opinion 1986-5 for a thorough discussion. If the lawyer violates those responsibilities, he may be liable even though his violation benefited his client. Escrow agreements usually contemplate holding cash. For example, the lawyer for the seller of a home may hold the buyer's ten percent down-payment in escrow pending the closing on the property. Nonetheless, the subject of the agreement need not be money.

In Wasmann v. Seidenberg, 202 Cal. App. 3d 752, 248 Cal. Rptr. 744, 746-747 (1988), Seidenberg had represented the wife, Barbara, in negotiating a settlement agreement. The husband's lawyer had sent Seidenberg a final draft of the agreement with a deed conveying a piece of realty from Wasmann, the husband, to the wife. The agreement contemplated that in return the wife would pay Wasmann $70,000 for his share of the value of the realty. Wasmann's lawyer instructed Seidenberg that he could record the deed "only upon obtaining" the money for Wasmann. Without getting the money, Seidenberg let the wife get the deed. She recorded it. Wasmann then sued the wife and Seidenberg. The court held that Seidenberg owed Wasmann "no professional duty," but that "his acceptance of [the] deed would give rise to a duty of care. The wellspring of this duty is the fiduciary role of an escrow holder." The court continued:

> As officers of the court, attorneys enjoy both privileges and responsibilities, among which is the duty to deal honestly and fairly with adverse parties and counsel. Wasmann and his attorney Hartman reasonably relied on Seidenberg because of his professional status and role as attorney for Barbara.

If Seidenberg did not want to be responsible for the deed, he should have promptly returned it to Wasmann. We hold a trier of fact could find any failure to do so was an acceptance of Wasmann's entrustment. Thus, the allegations of acceptance are legally sufficient.

Having accepted the deed from Wasmann, Seidenberg was bound to comply strictly with the escrow instructions. Specifically, he was obligated to prevent recordation of the deed until Barbara deposited into escrow the sum due to Wasmann. Violation of an escrow instruction gives rise to an action for breach of contract; similarly, negligent performance by an escrow holder creates liability in tort for breach of duty.

Wasmann foregoes the contract claim and alleges negligence in Seidenberg's handling of the deed. According to the complaint, ". . . Seidenberg breached said duty [by] . . . negligently and carelessly allow[ing] Plaintiff's Grant Deed to be recorded . . . without first obtaining for Plaintiff the sum of $70,000.00, or a note secured by a deed of trust. . . ." The facts pleaded are sufficient to state a cause of action for negligence against Seidenberg.

These allegations of negligence, however, are not the stuff of which legal malpractice claims are made. An attorney's failure to prevent a client's unauthorized seizure and recordation of a document held in escrow is not negligent *lawyering*: "The situation required no professional 'skill, prudence and diligence.' It simply called for the exercise of ordinary care." But Wasmann's erroneous labeling of his cause of action as one for professional negligence is of no consequence. To withstand a general demurrer, a complaint need only state some cause of action from which liability results.

The complaint not only states facts sufficient to support a cause of action for negligence, but for the alleged constructive fraud as well. This tort "arises from a breach of duty by one in a confidential or fiduciary relationship to another which induces a justifiable reliance by the latter to his prejudice." . . . "A form of such fraud is the nondisclosure by the fiduciary of relevant matters arising from the relationship."

Wasmann alleged Seidenberg not only breached his fiduciary duty by allowing recordation of the deed, but compounded his wrongdoing by failing to disclose this fact, despite repeated inquiries from Wasmann's attorney. Clearly, recordation of the deed was a material fact and suppression of this information worked to benefit Seidenberg's client and to prejudice Wasmann.

For a contrary view, in which the court refused to hold an attorney liable to a nonclient even though the attorney allowed his client to withdraw escrow funds without the permission of the nonclient and in violation of the escrow agreement, see Orr v. Shepard, 171 Ill. App. 3d 104, 524 N.E.2d 1105 (1988).

How might a lawyer protect herself from competing claims of escrow beneficiaries?

Abuse of Court Process. A person, lawyers included, can commit a variety of torts by misusing court process. One common tort is malicious prosecution, the definition of which varies from place to place but generally requires the prosecution of an action without probable cause and for an improper purpose. An attorney who does so can be liable to the opposing party notwithstanding that the attorney was acting for a client. See Wilson v. Hayes, 464 N.W.2d 250 (Iowa 1990) (recognizing tort but finding no liability). A lawyer who knowingly garnishes exempt assets of a judgment debtor may also be subject to liability. Penalber v. Blount, 550 So.2d 577 (La. 1989). In one unusual case, a lawyer was charged with conducting discovery in a civil matter in order to obtain information that would benefit his client in a criminal case that arose out of the same events. This allegation stated a claim. Rohda v. Franklin Life Ins. Co., 689 F. Supp. 1034 (D. Colo. 1988).

Ethical Violations. We conclude with a counterpoint to the material on the relationship between ethics and law (see page 635 supra). In Barker v. Henderson, Franklin, Starnes & Holt, 797 F.2d 490, 497 (7th Cir. 1986), purchasers of unpaid bonds and notes issued by the Michigan Baptist Foundation sued a law firm and an accounting firm. The plaintiffs charged that the firms were aiders and abettors of, and conspirators with, the Foundation in violation of section 10b-5 of the Securities Exchange Act of 1934. This section and the SEC's rule 10b-5 provide an implied right of action against persons who intentionally or recklessly engage in deceptive practices in the sale of securities. Judge Easterbrook assumed that the Foundation had itself violated the securities laws and that the law firm was guilty of malpractice in the advice it gave the Foundation. But the plaintiffs could not show the required "scienter and the defendants' commission of a proscribed act." The securities laws "do not impose liability for ordinary malpractice, even though that malpractice may diminish the value of the issuer and thus of the issuer's securities." Id. at 496.

Plaintiffs also argued that "the Firms" were liable because they "must have known" about the Foundation's deception yet did nothing. In rejecting this argument as a basis for liability, the court reflected on the relationship between the securities laws, on the one hand, and a state's malpractice and professional ethics rules on the other. Id. at 497.

> Law firms and accountants may act or remain silent for good reasons as well as bad ones, and allowing scienter or conspiracy to defraud to be inferred from the silence of a professional firm may expand the scope of liability far beyond that authorized in [cases cited]. If the plaintiff does not have direct evidence of scienter, the court should ask whether the fraud (or cover-up) was in the interest of the defendants. Did they gain by bilking the buyers of the securities? In this case the Firms did not gain. They received none of the proceeds from the sales. They did not receive fees for rendering advice in connection with the sales to the plaintiffs. Both Firms billed so little time to the Foundation between 1974 and 1976 (and none after Octo-

ber 1976) that it is inconceivable that they joined a venture to feather their nests by defrauding investors. They had nothing to gain and everything to lose. There is no sound basis, therefore, on which a jury could infer that the Firms joined common cause with other offenders or aided and abetted a scheme with the necessary state of mind.

The district court also held that the Firms had not committed any forbidden act, had not participated in a scheme to defraud by remaining silent when there was a duty to speak. This, too, is a correct conclusion. Neither lawyers nor accountants are required to tattle on their clients in the absence of some duty to disclose. To the contrary, attorneys have privileges not to disclose. See Upjohn Corp. v. United States, 449 U.S. 383 (1981).

The extent to which lawyers and accountants should reveal their clients' wrongdoing — and to whom they should reveal — is a question of great moment. There are proposals to change the rules of legal ethics and the SEC's regulations governing accountants. The professions and the regulatory agencies will debate questions raised by cases such as this one for years to come. We express no opinion on whether the Firms did what they should, whether there was malpractice under state law, or whether the rules of ethics (or other fiduciary doctrines) ought to require lawyers and accountants to blow the whistle in equivalent circumstances. We are satisfied, however, that an award of damages under the securities laws is not the way to blaze the trail toward improved ethical standards in the legal and accounting professions. Liability depends on an *existing* duty to disclose. The securities law therefore must lag behind changes in ethical and fiduciary standards. The plaintiffs have not pointed to any rule imposing on either Firm a duty to blow the whistle.

Affirmed.

Barker is distinguished in Renovitch v. Stewardship Concepts, Inc., 654 F. Supp. 353 (N.D. Ill. 1987), on the ground that the lawyers in that case had knowingly prepared the misleading brochures that were used by the client to accomplish its fraud. Inexplicably, however, the Fourth Circuit relied on *Barker* to uphold dismissal of a complaint charging an adversary law firm with assisting its client in formalizing a contract with the plaintiffs even though the firm allegedly knew that the client had provided the plaintiffs with a false financial statement. The court held that

> a lawyer or law firm cannot be liable for the representations of a client, even if the lawyer incorporates the client's misrepresentations into legal documents or agreements necessary for closing the transaction. In this case, Weinberg & Green merely "papered the deal," that is, put into writing the terms on which the Schatzes and Rosenberg agreed and prepared the documents necessary for closing the transaction. Thus, Weinberg & Green performed the role of a scrivener. Under these circumstances, a law firm cannot be held liable for misrepresentations made by a client in a financial disclosure statement.

Schatz v. Rosenberg, 943 F.2d 485 (4th Cir. 1991). Does the Fourth Circuit really mean to say that a lawyer can knowingly assist a client in the commission of a common law or securities fraud? The Circuit emphasized that it did not "sit as an ethics or other attorney disciplinary committee." Does that explain it?

FURTHER READING

Ronald Mallen & Jeffrey Smith, Legal Malpractice (3d ed. 1989), is a leading textbook on malpractice. Works that specifically address expanding liability to third parties include Nancy Lewis's conceptual vision in Lawyers' Liability to Third Parties: The Ideology of Advocacy Reframed, 66 Or. L. Rev. 801 (1987), and H. Robert Fiebach's critical perspective in A Chilling of the Adversary System: An Attorney's Exposure to Liability from Opposing Parties or Counsel, 61 Temple L. Rev. 1301 (1988). See also Note, Attorneys' Negligence and Third Parties, 57 N.Y.U. L. Rev. 126 (1982) (authored by Ellen Eisenberg). The author proposes a "unified approach in determining the duty of attorneys to third parties." She then applies the proposed test to a variety of factual situations.

D.   DISCIPLINE

1.   Purposes of Discipline

Discipline is a remedy for professional failure, but, unlike malpractice and other remedies previously reviewed, discipline vindicates the public's interest in preventing unethical behavior. Discipline does not have the purpose, although it may have the effect, of providing a remedy to the particular individual injured by a lawyer's improper conduct. An analogy might be to criminal prosecutions. Both civil and criminal actions can derive from the same conduct, but the civil claim belongs to a person or entity, who or which can settle or choose not to pursue it. The criminal case belongs to the sovereign. Indeed, discipline has been called "quasicriminal." In re Ruffalo, 390 U.S. 544 (1968).

Another distinction between discipline and civil liability lies in the nature of the conduct that can serve as a basis for either. An act that violates the rules or the code may bring discipline but, as we have seen (page 635 supra), will not therefore support a civil claim. Similarly, a single negligent act may bring civil liability even though it could not (or as a practical matter would not) support discipline. Of course, there is still a wide area of overlap in which the same conduct will subject a lawyer to both damages and discipline — and sometimes a criminal conviction.

What factors should a court consider in determining the appropriate sanctions? The following quote from State ex rel. Nebraska State Bar Assn. v. Cook, 194 Neb. 364, 384, 232 N.W.2d 120, 130 (1975), is fairly typical:

> Many matters must be considered [in determining appropriate discipline]. These include the nature of the offenses, the need for deterrence of similar future misconduct by others, maintenance of the reputation of the bar as a whole, protection of the public and clients, the expression of condemnation by society on moral grounds of the prohibited conduct, and justice to the respondent, considering all the circumstances and his present or future fitness to continue in the practice of law.

2. Sanctions

While some terms are uniform, there is no national consistency in the labels attached to the escalating types of discipline. "Disbarment" generally refers to indefinite or permanent exclusion from the bar. Jurisdictions use "suspension" to refer to the less harsh sanction of allowing a lawyer to continue as a member of the bar while having the right to practice denied for a period of time. The periods of time generally are in the range of three months to five years. It is also possible for an attorney to be suspended "until further order of the court" without a specified time period given. Even when a time period is specified, resumption of the right to practice might not be automatic on the termination of the time period. The court might suspend the attorney "for two years and until further order of the court," so that the attorney will have to reapply at the end of two years and show that he or she has stayed out of trouble (and out of the practice of law) for that period.

Censure (or public reprimand) is a near universal punishment. Like disbarment and suspension, the fact of censure is public, though some jurisdictions provide for private censures in certain cases. Although the censured lawyer is not removed or suspended from practice, the publicity attached to the censure is seen as significantly foreboding. In addition, the censure (like all prior disciplines) will be considered in determining sanctions should the lawyer again be guilty of a professional transgression.

The nomenclature becomes less uniform at this point. Words like "reprimand," "admonition," "warning," and "caution" are among those used in various jurisdictions. They do not carry a consistent import. But whatever words are used, there are certain gradations of responses that grievance mechanisms seek to have at their disposal.

In New York, for example, the Disciplinary Committee in Manhattan may wish to respond to an attorney's behavior by warning him or her that the behavior, while not technically unethical, nevertheless comes close to the line. The committee will therefore "caution" the lawyer. The caution is confidential. The attorney who is cautioned is not "disciplined," since the underlying conduct violated no rule. One step above caution in New York's hierarchy is an admonition. This is discipline issued after a review of the complainant's and the respondent attorney's position and relevant documents. It is a finding made without a hearing. An attorney dissatisfied with the finding may request a hearing, and if the finding of disciplinary violation is reaffirmed after the hearing, the committee may then issue a reprimand (or recommend a harsher public sanction). Since a reprimand follows a hearing, while an admonition precedes it, the former is seen as a graver sanction.

California has developed a novel way to deal with minor infractions. When appropriate, disciplinary authorities will offer to dismiss a matter provided the attorney attends an eight-hour class on legal ethics. Amy Stevens, What Can a Lawyer Learn in One Day in Downtown L.A.?, Wall St. J., May 1, 1991, p. 1. For example, one participant had "hired four of the most beautiful women he could find to hang out at a singles bar on the beach near San Diego. They were to pick up married men — and hand out business cards for [the lawyer's] divorce practice." Lawyers who take the course must pass a test consisting of 20 true or false questions. The program reports that nobody has ever failed and that recidivism is zero.

Some jurisdictions permit a lawyer under investigation to resign in advance of court imposed discipline. Many times a lawyer will prefer resignation to the virtual certainty of disbarment. In some jurisdictions, the fact of resignation is not made public and this may be an added inducement to resign in advance of disbarment. It is sometimes said that resignation during the pendency of a disciplinary proceeding is tantamount to an admission of the charges against the lawyer. In re Weinsoff v. Committee on Professional Standards, 81 A.D.2d 724, 438 N.Y.S.2d 396 (3d Dept. 1981). Other courts have refused efforts to resign while under investigation, asserting that resignation is not a deterrent to future misconduct and that where discipline is called for, it ought to follow. See, e.g., In re Peck, 302 N.W.2d 356 (Minn. 1981).

In one case receiving substantial public attention, former President Richard M. Nixon was disbarred in New York State for conduct in which he engaged while President. In re Nixon, 53 A.D.2d 178, 385 N.Y.S.2d 305, 308 (1st Dept. 1976). Mr. Nixon had attempted to resign rather than contest the charges made against him. But his resignation was rejected because it did not contain a sworn acknowledgment that "he could not successfully defend himself on the merits against [the] charges," as required by New York law.

As with criminal sentencing, the disparity in sanctions imposed for unethical behavior has long been a criticism of the disciplinary system. This disparity occurs not only among jurisdictions but often within them. The ABA has acknowledged the problem. See ABA, Standards for Imposing Lawyer Sanctions, Preface (1986). The Standards are meant to "formulat[e] standards to be used in imposing sanctions for lawyer misconduct, providing" examples of the range of sanctions that would be appropriate for different ethical lapses and listing the factors to be considered in mitigation and aggravation of sanction. The Standards are reprinted at Lawyers Manual on Prof. Conduct (ABA/BNA) 01:801 (1986).

3. *Acts Justifying Discipline*

Much of this book analyzes conduct that invites professional discipline and other remedies. Here we highlight some of the more frequent reasons why lawyers are sanctioned and, also, some unusual ones.

a. **Dishonest or Unlawful Conduct**

Dishonesty in its many forms, and criminal conduct that may but need not involve dishonesty, are among the two most frequent reasons for discipline (neglect of client matters may be the most frequent). The following case concerns unauthorized withdrawals from an attorney's trust or escrow account. Such withdrawals are the basis for a substantial amount of discipline nationwide. Lawyers are required to place funds that belong to others or to which others have a claim in trust accounts. It is unethical to commingle trust funds with one's own money and even worse actually to make use of trust funds. At this point you should read and memorize the substance of Rule 1.15 and DR 9-102.

IN RE WARHAFTIG
106 N.J. 529, 524 A.2d 398 (1987)

PER CURIAM. . . .

I

The charges filed against respondent were the result of a random compliance audit conducted by the Office of Attorney Ethics pursuant to Rule 1:21-6(c). The audit took place in November and December, 1983, and covered the two-year period ending on October 31st of the same year. The audit findings were summarized in the Board's Decision and Recommendation:

> The audit disclosed that respondent continually issued checks to his own order for fees in pending real estate matters. He would replace the "advance" when the funds were received for the real estate closing.

In one case, a real estate closing occurred on September 19, 1983. Funds totalling $70,722.33 were deposited into respondent's trust account on September 20, 1983. In another case, a real estate closing took place on October 28, 1983. The funds totalling $150,686.27 were deposited into his trust account on October 31, 1983. However, respondent had issued a check to his order for $910 on June 16, 1983 which represented his fee of $455 for each of these two closings. The audit report revealed other instances where respondent similarly took advance fees. . . .

Respondent maintained his own lists of fees taken in advance. This list contained the names of clients and the amounts he anticipated earning from these clients in pending real estate closings. As a closing occurred and the fee was earned, respondent would delete the client's name and fee. When an anticipated closing fell through, respondent would replace the fee he had earlier advanced to himself. . . .

When respondent received notice of the audit, he contacted his accountant who advised him that if his trust account was short he should immediately replace the funds. Respondent borrowed $11,125 from accounts in the names of his two teenage sons and deposited the money into his trust account to cover the withdrawn fees. Respondent made this deposit about five days before the originally scheduled audit date of October 4, 1983.

The auditor was not able to determine which clients' monies respondent had taken because of the size of respondent's real estate practice. Money continually flowed in and out of the trust account. Respondent, at the ethics hearing, maintained that he never failed to make the proper disbursements at the closings and that no one ever lost money as a result of his practice. He discontinued this practice in September 1983 when he received notice of the audit.

At the Ethics Committee hearing, respondent explained that his withdrawal of advance fees from the trust account was necessitated by the "gigantic cash flow burden" he experienced beginning in the early 1980's. Such pressures were the result of a precipitous decline in his real-estate practice. At the same time, an additional strain on respondent's finances was created by his wife's having to undergo treatment for cancer, and by his son's need for extensive psychiatric counseling. According to respondent, only a small portion of these expenses was covered by insurance.

Respondent was also questioned at the hearing as to whether he knew, at the time the advance-fee scheme was implemented, that his conduct constituted an ethical violation. Respondent stated:

> I was aware that what I was doing was wrong, and I was also aware that no one was being hurt by what I was doing. And what I was doing, especially by keeping lists like this, was making sure that nobody would get hurt by what I was doing. . . .
>
> My perspective on the taking of the money was it was wrong, it was a violation of the rules. But I was so certain that no one could possibly be hurt by it that I didn't feel that I was stealing, certainly not stealing. . . .

II

In recommending public discipline, the DRB recognized that In re Wilson which requires the disbarment of an attorney who knowingly misappropriates his clients' funds, controls the outcome of this case. However, the Board emphasized a perceived distinction between respondent's conduct, which it characterized as the "premature withdrawal of . . . monies to which he had a colorable interest[,]" and the knowing misappropriation described in *Wilson,* supra. Apparently, the Board was persuaded by respondent's contention that while he was aware that he was violating a Disciplinary Rule, he "didn't feel that [he] was stealing. . . ."

The distinction drawn by the DRB cannot be sustained under the *Wilson* rule. As we stated in In re Noonan, 102 N.J. 157, 160, 506 A.2d 722 (1986), knowing misappropriation under *Wilson* "consists simply of a lawyer taking a client's money entrusted to him, knowing that it is the client's money and knowing that the client has not authorized the taking." We have consistently maintained that a lawyer's subjective intent, whether it be to "borrow" or to steal, is irrelevant to the determination of the appropriate discipline in a misappropriation case. In *Wilson,* supra, we articulated the reason for this strict approach:

> Lawyers who "borrow" may, it is true, be less culpable than those who had no intent to repay, but the difference is negligible in this connection. Banks do not rehire tellers who "borrow" depositors' funds. Our professional standards, if anything, should be higher. Lawyers are more than fiduciaries: they are representatives of a profession and officers of this Court.

It is clear that respondent's conduct constituted knowing misappropriation as contemplated by *Wilson.* Through the use of the advance-fee mechanisms, he took funds from his trust account before he had any legal right to those monies. These "fees" were taken by respondent before he received any deposits in connection with the relevant real-estate closings. Thus, he was effectively borrowing monies from one group of clients in order to compensate himself, in advance, for matters being handled for other clients. Respondent made these withdrawals with full recognition that his actions had not been authorized by his clients, and that he was therefore violating the rules governing attorney conduct. Respondent's unauthorized misappropriation of clients' trust funds for his personal needs cannot be distinguished from the conduct condemned in *Wilson,* supra.

[The court concluded that various mitigating factors were insufficient to prevent disbarment.]

Taking a client's money without authorization, even if temporarily and with an intent to return it, will almost always result in serious discipline. In some jurisdictions disbarment is nearly automatic. This misconduct has become easier to detect as a result of random audits of attorney trust accounts by authorized state agencies.

IN RE AUSTERN
524 A.2d 680 (D.C. App. 1987)

PRYOR, C.J.

Respondent is charged with violating DR 1-102(A)(4) and DR7-102(A)(7) of the Code of Professional Responsibility by engaging in conduct involving dishonesty and misrepresentation and by counseling or assisting a client in conduct that the lawyer knows to be illegal or fraudulent. Specifically, he is alleged to have assisted in closing a real estate transaction despite being told by his client that the client's escrow account would have insufficient funds to accomplish its stated purpose. The Board on Professional Responsibility finds that respondent's conduct violated both DR 1-102(A)(4) and DR 7-102(A)(7) and recommends a sanction of public censure. Upon review of the record, we are satisfied that the Board's findings of fact are supported by substantial evidence, and accept its conclusion that respondent knowingly assisted his client in conduct involving dishonesty and misrepresentation. Moreover, we conclude that respondent was under a duty to withdraw from representation of his client in this situation. We also adopt the Board's recommended sanction of public censure.

I

The relevant facts in this case are largely uncontested. The Hearing Committee found that respondent represented Milton Viorst and a corporation largely controlled by Viorst known as Harmony House Corporation. Viorst and Harmony House converted several buildings to condominiums. Respondent's clients were anxious to go to closing on the various condominium units as quickly as possible with a number of prospective purchasers. Several of these prospective purchasers had been tenants in the buildings before the conversion and were actually in possession of their units. However, the work necessary to bring the units into compliance with the District of Columbia Housing Code had not yet been completed to the satisfaction of the prospective purchasers.

On January 27, 1981, the parties met to attempt to close on as many of the units as then had committed purchasers. Respondent was not able to be present at the beginning of this closing because of other commitments. He arrived later in the evening as the closing was continuing; before his arrival, Viorst was represented by one of respondent's partners. During this time, Viorst and the purchasers drafted an escrow agreement in order to facilitate closing on that date.

Despite the fact that the purchasers were suspicious of Viorst and entertained doubts concerning his willingness to complete the repairs necessary to the units, they were willing to go to closing on the condition that Viorst deposit $10,000 into the escrow account. The funds in the account were to be available to complete the work on the units if Viorst or Harmony House did not perform. If Viorst did perform, the escrow funds were to be released back to the sellers upon agreement by all parties that the relevant work had indeed been satisfactorily performed.

For their protection, the purchasers insisted that the escrow account be under the control of two co-escrow agents — respondent, who represented the sellers, and Arnold Spevak, who represented the purchasers and who was also acting as the settlement attorney.

Upon respondent's late arrival at the closing, the substance of the escrow agreement had already been agreed upon by the parties. According to respondent, the escrow agreement had been fully drafted, typed, and signed by all the other parties before he arrived. Respondent testified that he was put under considerable pressure to agree to act as the co-escrow agent and that he ultimately yielded and signed the agreement that same evening.

Notwithstanding respondent's testimony,[3] the Hearing Committee found that the escrow agreement, although dated January 27, 1981, had not been finally typed and signed by respondent until the following day. The Hearing Committee's finding was based upon the testimony of Robert Cohen, who acted as the leader of the group of purchasers. The Board concluded that Cohen's testimony was unequivocal and emphatic

3. Respondent maintained that he signed the escrow agreement the evening of January 27, and agreed to act as the co-escrow agent *before* he was informed by Viorst that his check for the escrow account was worthless. The Hearing Committee found that he signed the agreement at the following day's continuation of the closing, on January 28, *after* he was informed that Viorst's check was worthless.

that the escrow agreement was signed by all of the parties, including respondent, on the second day of the settlement, January 28, 1981.[4]

After respondent's arrival at the closing, Viorst wrote a check in the
amount of $10,000, which was intended to fund the escrow account. The
check was exhibited to the purchasers and to their attorney, Spevak. It
was decided that respondent, as one of the two escrow agents, would take
possession of the check and deposit it. Either before or after respondent
gained possession of the check, respondent and Viorst stepped out into
the hall, out of earshot of the other parties to the transaction. Viorst then
informed respondent that there were no funds in the account upon
which the check had been written. Respondent considered the ramifications of this revelation, but took the necessary steps to complete the closing on January 28.

Respondent held the worthless check but did not inform his co-escrow
agent about the situation. Subsequently, on March 23, 1981, Viorst received a $10,000 non-refundable deposit from a purchaser in connection
with the sale of one of the condominium units. He then gave this deposit
check to respondent. Respondent promptly opened an interest-bearing
savings account at a local bank into which this check was deposited on
March 27, 1981. Respondent did not notify his co-escrow agent that the
funds were finally on hand, nor did he ever arrange to have his co-escrow
agent obtain signature authority over the account.

It was not until the beginning of April, after the time the funds were
actually placed in the escrow account, that one of the purchasers made
the first claim against the account. That claim was paid from the account,
and there is no question that the $10,000 was properly administered by
respondent once it was placed into the account. . . .

While a client is entitled to representation by his attorney for any objective within the bounds permitted by law, see Canon 7, District of Columbia Code of Professional Responsibility, he is not entitled to
affirmative assistance by his attorney in conduct that the lawyer knows to
be illegal or fraudulent. DR 7-102(A)(7). Generally, a lawyer should
abide by a client's decisions concerning the objectives of the representation, and the lawyer can determine the means to accomplish these objectives, so long as the lawyer does not knowingly assist the client to engage
in illegal conduct. District of Columbia Ethical Consideration 7-5; see
also ABA Model Rule of Professional Conduct 1.2(a). When the attorney
is presented with a situation where the client's wishes call for conduct that
is illegal or fraudulent, the attorney is under an affirmative duty to withdraw from representation. DR 2-110(B)(2), DR 7-102(A)(7); Model Rule
1.16(a)(1).

4. The Board concluded that the testimony of respondent, however, was ambiguous as
to when he signed the escrow agreement. The Board concluded that Cohen's clear and emphatic testimony, in contrast, provided ample support in the record for the finding that respondent signed the escrow agreement on January 28, 1981.

In the instant case, therefore, respondent was under an affirmative duty to withdraw from his representation of Mr. Viorst once he knew that the escrow account Viorst purported to establish to induce settlement was funded with a worthless check. We do not deem crucial the question of whether respondent signed the escrow agreement before rather than after being informed that the check was worthless. In either event, his conduct in furthering the transaction and acquiescing in its fraudulent purpose is violative of DR 1-102(A)(4) and DR 7-102(A)(7).

III

Turning to the issue of an appropriate sanction, the Board rejected the recommendation of the Hearing Committee that respondent receive a reprimand by the Board and concluded that respondent should receive a sanction of public censure by this court. The Board concluded that this case involved dishonesty and misrepresentation on the part of an attorney, and, in a broad sense, the appropriate sanction should be influenced by our decision in In re Reback, 513 A.2d 226 (D.C. 1986) (en banc) (imposing six-month suspensions against attorneys who neglected a matter and falsified a client's signature, representing it as genuine to both a notary and the court). The Board noted, however, that a similar suspension here would be too severe a penalty because the focus in *Reback* was on subversion of the judicial process, a more serious violation than is involved here.

The Board determined that a public censure by this court would be the most appropriate sanction in this case because the culpability of the conduct at issue here fell short of that in other cases where attorney dishonesty resulted in a brief suspension. Compare, e.g., In re Rosen, 481 A.2d 451 (D.C. 1984) (misrepresentations to court in continuance motions and opposition to motion to set aside attorney's fees warranted 30-day suspension), and In re Kent, 467 A.2d 982 (D.C. 1983) (conviction for shoplifting represented conduct involving dishonesty warranting 30-day suspension).

The Board also considered many mitigating factors in this case. It observed that respondent has no prior disciplinary record, and has indeed made notable contributions in the area of legal ethics. The Board also took into account the fact that respondent's conduct was not motivated by the desire for personal gain, and caused no pecuniary injury to the purchasers of the client's units who relied on the escrow account.[9] The Board further observed that respondent's decision making may have been affected by the extreme animosity which existed between him and

9. The Board noted that since this case is not a civil action for damages, the fact that the purchasers actually suffered no injury is immaterial to the consideration of the ethical obligation of an attorney not to assist in fraud or other conduct involving dishonesty or misrepresentation.

his client, Mr. Viorst. The Board noted that respondent may have been too anxious to overcompensate for this ill will and "may have bent over backwards in the client's favor" by taking part in the fraudulent transaction, concluding that respondent's participation may have been motivated in part by a desire to bring the troubled attorney-client relationship to a speedy close. . . .

To be sure, no monetary harm befell anyone as a result of respondent's failure to disclose that the check funding the escrow account was worthless. But it is important to remember that for a number of weeks the purpose of the escrow account was in fact defeated. The protection the account was supposed to offer did not exist. Respondent, as co-escrow agent, owed a fiduciary duty to the client's purchasers to protect their investment; instead, he aided his client in inducing the buyers to proceed to settlement although there was no escrow protection. Therefore, considering the gravity of respondent's misconduct, the mitigating factors considered by the Board, and viewing respondent's violations "in light of all relevant factors," we conclude that the Board's recommended sanction of public censure is appropriate.*

IN RE COLIN
82 A.D.2d 449, 442 N.Y.S.2d 66 (2d Dept. 1981)

PER CURIAM.

The respondent was admitted to practice by this court on June 23, 1948 under the name Charles R. Colin. In this proceeding to discipline him for professional misconduct, the respondent was charged with having been convicted of a "serious crime" within the meaning of section 691.7 of the rules of this court (22 N.Y.C.R.R. 691.7), in that on September 17, 1979 the respondent was convicted in the United States District Court for the Eastern District of New York of the crime [a felony] of willfully and knowingly attempting to evade and defeat a large part of the income tax due and owing by him and his wife, in violation of section 7201 of title 26 of the United States Code.

The respondent was sentenced to one year imprisonment and fined $10,000. Execution of sentence was suspended and defendent was placed on unsupervised probation for a period of two years.

The referee found that the charge was fully sustained by the evidence. The petitioner has moved, and respondent has cross-moved, to confirm the referee's report.

---

*See the material on the responsibility of lawyers when serving as escrow agents at page 660 supra. — ED.

After reviewing all of the evidence, we are in full agreement with the report of the referee. The respondent is guilty of the afore-mentioned charge of misconduct. The petitioner's motion and the respondent's cross-motion are granted.

In determining an appropriate measure of discipline to be imposed, we are mindful of the fact that the respondent was punished for his crime, as well as the personal problems the respondent was experiencing at the time of his misconduct. Accordingly, the respondent should be, and he hereby is censured for his misconduct.

A lawyer who violates a fiduciary duty owed to a person who is not the lawyer's client may nevertheless be disciplined. Beery v. State Bar of California, 43 Cal. 3d 802, 739 P.2d 1289, 239 Cal. Rptr. 121 (1987). A lawyer may also be disciplined for conduct he or she engages in as a business person. In re Lurie, 113 Ariz. 95, 546 P.2d 1126 (1976). *Lurie* makes the additional point that a lawyer who engages in business continues to be bound by the ethical responsibilities that apply to lawyers.

Deceit and Dishonesty

Can you reconcile *Warhaftig, Austern,* and *Colin?* Whose conduct was most reprehensible? Warhaftig took client money, but no one was likely to be injured thereby. As soon as the closings occurred, the money would be his. Yet it was not his, but in trust, when he took it. Austern did not stand to gain personally by what he did, although he might have enjoyed his client's appreciation. Yet the escrowee in Austern's case was at risk of losing substantial sums as a result of Austern's conduct. And that loss may have been permanent. Colin was prepared to keep money that belonged to the government. He was the only one of the three to suffer a criminal conviction, a felony at that, yet he received a censure only. Tax cheats rarely suffer serious discipline. Why is that? So who is most culpable?

Here are some other cases to weigh in.

Wunschel's wife owned a corporation that owned a motel. Ms. Wunschel wanted to sell the motel. The buyers were proceeding without counsel. The court found that Wunschel, who was representing the seller, had encouraged the buyers to trust him and then took advantage of their trust. Although he had done nothing illegal, Wunschel should have corrected the buyers' misunderstandings. Wunschel was reprimanded. Iowa State Bar Assn. v. Wunschel, 461 N.W.2d 840 (Iowa 1990).

Gunter represented a man who wanted to get divorced. Gunter told the man to place a wiretap on his home phone, which was in the man's name, in the expectation that they would discover conversations re-vealing adultery by the man's wife. They didn't. After the tap was discov-ered, the lawyer was charged with violating state wiretap laws but was acquitted. Nonetheless, the Virginia Supreme Court found the conduct deceitful and suspended Gunter. Gunter v. Virginia State Bar, 238 Va. 617, 385 S.E.2d 597 (1989). See also ABA Opinion 337 (1974) (unethical for lawyer to electronically record conversations in connection with rep-resentation of client); New York City Opinion 80-95 (creating an excep-tion for criminal defense lawyers to put them on par with government investigators).

Pollard was admitted to the bar in 1983. Between June 1984 and the following April, while employed at the Brooklyn D.A.'s office, she sub-mitted fraudulent expense vouchers and received money to which she was not entitled. In the summer of 1985, she worked for a temporary em-ployment agency and submitted false time sheets for which she received funds to which she was not entitled. In suspending Pollard for one year in 1991, the court cited the fact that Pollard had not practiced law since 1985, that she had had "personal problems," and that she had made full restitution. Matter of Pollard, 167 A.D.2d 48, 570 N.Y.S.2d 203 (2d Dept. 1991).

b.   Neglect and Lack of Candor

Neglect of client matters is a recurrent basis for discipline, regardless of the lawyer's motives. (Motives may of course influence the sanction.) The likelihood of discipline increases as the number of neglected matters increases. In Matter of Snow, 142 A.D.2d 835, 530 N.Y.S.2d 886, 889 (3d Dept. 1988), a pattern of neglect of several legal matters resulted in a one-year suspension. The court was especially unimpressed with the law-yer's "attempt to blame his failure to respond to telephone calls or corre-spondence on his secretary's illness." (This is the disciplinary equivalent of "the dog ate my homework.") Neglect should be distinguished from negligence: Sins of omission are more likely to meet with disciplinary committee disapproval than acts of negligence. Why is that?

Neglect in a submission to a court can result in discipline or a sanction directly by the court, bypassing the disciplinary committee. In DCD Pro-grams, Ltd. v. Leighton, 846 F.2d 526, 528 (9th Cir. 1988), a lawyer mis-stated the record from the district court. When ordered to show cause for his misstatement, the lawyer attributed the errors to "neglect in not hav-ing more carefully reviewed the record." He also relied on inexperience, since the appeal was his first in federal court. The court wrote:

> As this court stated in In re Boucher, 837 F.2d 869 (9th Cir. 1988) [mod-ified at 850 F.2d 597 (9th Cir. 1988)], counsel's professional duty requires

scrupulous accuracy in referring to the record. A court should not have to pore over an extensive record as an alternative to relying on counsel's representations. The court relies on counsel to state clearly, candidly, and accurately the record as it in fact exists.

It is not required that the court find intentional conduct in order for an attorney to be disciplined pursuant to Rule 46(c) [of the Federal Rules of Appellate Procedure]. Lack of diligence which impairs the deliberations of the court is sufficient.

The lawyer was suspended for two months. See also Amstar Corp. v. Envirotech Corp., 730 F.2d 1476, 1486 (Fed. Cir.), cert. denied, 469 U.S. 924 (1984), in which a lawyer omitted language when he quoted from the record. The omission was indicated with ellipses, but, as edited, the quote conveyed a meaning opposite to the meaning imparted by the record as a whole. The court said such behavior reflects a "lack of the candor required by . . . Rule 3.3 . . . , wastes the time of the court, and of opposing counsel, and imposes unnecessary costs on the parties and on fellow citizens whose taxes support this court and its staff." The court doubled the costs on appeal as a sanction for this and other conduct.

c. Sexual Relations with a Client

In the film Jagged Edge, the character played by Glenn Close has an affair with a man, charged with murdering his wife, whom Close is defending. Several times during the trial (and the affair), Close's skills as a lawyer are (visibly) hampered because of information about her client's relationships with other women that she learns in the course of the representation and trial. Did Glenn Close act unethically in sleeping with her client during the course of the representation? If you think she did, how if at all would you distinguish the situation of a law firm partner who begins an affair with an officer of the firm's corporate client?

COMMITTEE ON PROFESSIONAL ETHICS & CONDUCT OF IOWA STATE BAR ASSOCIATION v. HILL
436 N.W.2d 57 (Iowa 1989)

ANDREASEN, JUSTICE.

The Committee on Professional Ethics and Conduct of the Iowa Bar Association filed a complaint against attorney William Hill that was heard by a division of the Grievance Commission. It found Hill's conduct violated disciplinary rules DR 1-102(A)(3) and (6), and ethical considerations EC 1-5 and EC 9-6. The commission recommended Hill's license to practice be suspended for three months. . . .

I

In June of 1986, K.C. contacted attorney Hill and requested that he represent her in a domestic matter. This was the first time Hill had met K.C. She advised him of her desire to secure temporary custody of her three children then living with their father and to secure a dissolution of their marriage. She was unemployed and had no money to advance to him as a retainer. Hill agreed to represent her. He prepared a dissolution petition which was filed on June 17 and assisted her in securing a restraining order regarding the children.

On July 1, 1986, K.C. went to Hill's law office and offered to engage in sexual intercourse with him for money. Attorney Hill suggested he would give her money as a personal loan if she did not want to have sex. She told him that she had no means to reimburse him on a personal loan so her payback would be sex. Hill gave her fifty dollars and they then had sexual intercourse in his law office.

During the summer of 1986, K.C. was a drug addict and emotionally unstable. She is now chemically free having undergone chemical dependency treatment. She has reconciled with her husband and the dissolution proceedings commenced by Hill have been dismissed.

II

The commission found that having sex with a client involved in a divorce action involving custody of children constituted unethical conduct on the part of the lawyer, regardless of whether or not the sex was for pay. The commission found Hill's conduct was unethical and unprofessional and in violation of Disciplinary Rules 1-102(A)(3) and (6). . . .

The commission found Hill had failed to conduct himself with the high standards of professional conduct expected of a lawyer and that his conduct did not reflect credit on the legal profession or inspire confidence, respect and trust of his client and the public as required by Ethical Considerations 1-5 and 9-6. . . .

Hill argues that our considerations of his sexual intercourse with K.C. violates his right to privacy. He cites State v. Pilcher, 242 N.W.2d 348, 358 (Iowa 1976), for the proposition that this was a private act between two consenting adults which is protected from public scrutiny.

Constitutional considerations of privacy are not without limits. We must analyze this incident in the context in which it occurred, that of an attorney representing a client in a dissolution action. A lawyer undertaking a divorce action must recognize reconciliation is possible and may be in the best interest of his client. An attorney must be aware that the actions of the client and attorney may affect negotiations in the dissolution case, including determination of custody and visitation of minor children. Sexual intercourse between the lawyer and a client seeking a dissolution of marriage carries a great potential of prejudice both to the client and to the minor children of the marriage. We require lawyers to maintain high standards of ethical conduct and to avoid conduct which would reflect negatively upon the integrity and honor of the profession.

Despite Hill's assertion to the contrary, we cannot ignore the obvious implication of any scheme involving an exchange of sexual favors for money. Hill's characterization of this liaison as a purely romantic one rings hollow in the face of its aura of commercial exploitation.

K.C. had a right to expect Hill to conduct himself in a manner consistent with the tradition of the legal profession; that tradition founded upon service, integrity and vigorous commitment to the client's best interests, as well as an allegiance to the rule of law. Instead of remaining loyal to K.C.'s best interests, Hill chose to exploit the relationship. Sexual contact between an attorney and client in a professional context constitutes professional impropriety.

We, like the commission, find that the actions and conduct of Hill constitute unethical and unprofessional conduct. We hold Hill's license to practice law should be suspended indefinitely with no possibility of reinstatement for three months. This suspension shall apply to all facets of the practice of law. . . .

SNELL, JUSTICE (dissenting).

I respectfully dissent. The majority finds that Hill was representing K.C. in a dissolution of marriage proceeding. K.C. was seeking custody of her three children. Hill assisted her in securing a restraining order regarding her children who were living with their father. She was unemployed and did not have money even for his retainer fee. She was a drug addict and emotionally unstable.

Hill's employment as her attorney gave him the means to exploit the extreme vulnerability of his client. Given the opportunity, he abandoned his professional responsibilities to his client without concern or delay.

Hill's acts constitute grossly unethical and unprofessional conduct. His license to practice law should be suspended for not less than nine months.

HARRIS J., joins this dissent.

Should Lawyers Be Forbidden to Have Sexual Relations with Clients?

Courts and bar association ethics committees have refused blanketly to forbid sexual relationships between lawyers and clients. Several state courts have, however, interpreted their ethical codes to limit such conduct, nearly always in matrimonial or criminal cases. (Why is that?) For example, Office of Disciplinary Counsel v. Ressing, 53 Ohio St. 3d 265, 559 N.E.2d 1359 (1990), publicly reprimanded a lawyer who had a sexual relationship with a divorce client without any showing of specific harm or coercion. For other instances of discipline, see In re Bourdon, 132 N.H. 365, 565 A.2d 1052 (1989) (affair with matrimonial client who had a minor child); In re Ridgeway, 158 Wis. 2d 452, 462 N.W.2d 671 (1990) (public defender had sexual contact with client and gave her beer, which violated terms of her probation); and Dayton Bar Assn. v. Sams, 41 Ohio St. 3d 11, 535 N.E.2d 298 (1989) (acceptance of client's offer to trade sexual favors for legal services, though never consummated, plus purchase of diet pills from client, requires six-month suspension).

On instructions from the legislature, the California Bar has recommended an ethical rule specifically addressing attorney-client sexual relations. Proposed Rule 3-120, which was presented to the State Supreme Court for approval, states:

(A) For the purpose of this rule, "sexual relations," means sexual intercourse or the touching of an intimate part of another person for the purpose of sexual arousal, gratification, or abuse.

(B) A member shall not:

(1) Require or demand sexual relations with a client incident to or as a condition of any professional representation; or

(2) Employ coercion, intimidation, or undue influence in entering into sexual relations with a client; or

(3) Continue representation of a client with whom the member has sexual relations if such sexual relations cause the member to perform legal services incompetently in violation of rule 3-110.

(C) Paragraph (B) shall not apply to sexual relations between members and their spouses or to ongoing consensual lawyer-client sexual relations which predate the initiation of the lawyer-client relationship.

(D) Where a lawyer in a firm has sexual relations with a client but does not participate in the representation of that client, the lawyers in the firm shall not be subject to discipline under this rule solely because of the occurrence of such sexual relations.

(E) A member who engages in sexual relations with his or her client will be presumed to violate rule 3-120, paragraph (B)(3). This presumption shall only be used as a presumption affecting the burden of proof in disciplinary proceedings involving alleged violations of these rules.

Does this rule say anything new? Paragraph (B)(3) presents the only conceivable expansion of a lawyer's ethical duty. But it does not prohibit sex with clients. It is violated only if the lawyer performs "legal services incompetently in violation of" another rule, which provides a separate basis for discipline. So (B)(3) is redundant, isn't it? True, paragraph (E) creates a rebuttable presumption of incompetence but, really now, what will that accomplish? Incredibly, the bar has taken a moral question and reduced it to an evidentiary one. The California Supreme Court remanded the proposal for further comment.

What should the rule be instead? How about this: "A lawyer shall not begin to have sexual relations with a person while that person is his or her client." Would you support that rule? Or does it violate freedom of association of lawyer and client?

Courts have uniformly condemned nonconsensual sexual relationships between lawyers and clients. See Courtney v. Alabama State Bar, 492 So. 2d 1002 (Ala. 1986) (attorney who placed arms around minor client's mother, touched her "buttocks," then kissed her after office meeting, publicly censured); In re Liebowitz, 104 N.J. 175, 516 A.2d 246 (1985); In re Gibson, 124 Wis. 2d 466, 369 N.W.2d 695 (unsolicited physical advances toward client requires 90-day suspension). For further reading on the impropriety of sexual relations with a client in the area of matrimonial law, see Lawrence Dubin, Sex and the Divorce Lawyer: Is the Client Off Limits?, 1 Geo. J. Legal Ethics 585 (1988).

d. The Lawyer's Private Life

To what extent should a lawyer's behavior in his or her private life be a basis for discipline? As we saw above in the *Colin* case, tax crimes can result in discipline even though unconnected to law practice, and so can other crimes. Louisiana State Bar Assn. v. Bensabat, 378 So. 2d 380 (La. 1979) (conspiracy to import cocaine). Some states mandate disbarment for all felony convictions. Mitchell v. Association of Bar of City of New York, 40 N.Y.2d 153, 351 N.E.2d 743, 386 N.Y.S.2d 95 (1976) (disbarment of former Attorney General John Mitchell following conviction of a federal felony). Personal use of drugs has resulted in mild sanctions, In re Anonymous Member of the South Carolina Bar, 293 S.C. 329, 360 S.E.2d 322 (1987) (private reprimand for marijuana use), though even these sanctions are increasingly rare. Private consensual sexual activity between adults almost never leads to discipline any longer, even though it may offend community standards. Compare In re Sprott, 288 S.C. 457, 343 S.E.2d 448 (1986) (indefinite suspension for lawyer who pleaded guilty to sexual conduct with minor boys). In In re Gelfand, 70 N.Y.2d 211, 512 N.E.2d 533, 518 N.Y.S.2d 950, cert. denied, 484 U.S. 977 (1987), a New York trial judge (male) was removed from the bench after exhibiting extreme and obsessive behavior toward a lawyer employed by the court (female). The former dean of a law school was publicly reprimanded after he made unwelcome physical contact and verbal communications of a sexual nature with four female staff members, two of whom were also students of the law school. In re Peters, 428 N.W.2d 375 (Minn. 1988). (See also Cord v. Gibb and the admission cases, pages 554 and 562 supra.)

e.   Racist and Sexist Conduct

Courts have shown increased (if a still rare) willingness to discipline lawyers for racist or sexist conduct in connection with their public roles. In People v. Sharpe, 781 P.2d 659, 660-661 (Colo. 1989), Sharpe, a deputy district attorney, was prosecuting two men named Borrego and Lucero for capital murder. In a hallway conversation, Sharpe told Lucero's attorney, "I don't believe either one of those chili-eating bastards." The court imposed public censure, stressing the need to "emphasize that lawyers, especially those acting as public officials, must scrupulously avoid statements as well as deeds that could be perceived as indicating that their actions are motivated to any extent by racial prejudice." Compare the material on judicial ethics at page 517 supra.

New York, apparently alone among jurisdictions, forbids lawyers to "[u]nlawfully discriminate in the practice of law, including in hiring, promoting or otherwise determining conditions of employment, on the basis of age, race, creed, color, national origin, sex, disability, or marital status." (Why is sexual preference omitted?) A person wishing to complain of any such conduct must first invoke whatever administrative remedies exist. DR 1-102(A)(6).

The 1990 ABA Code of Judicial Conduct, unlike its 1972 predecessor, says that a judge "shall require lawyers in proceedings before the judge to refrain from manifesting, by words or conduct, bias or prejudice based upon race, sex, religion, national origin, disability, age, sexual orientation, or socioeconomic status, against parties, witnesses, counsel or others." However, this directive is not meant to "preclude legitimate advocacy" when these or "similar factors" are "issues in the proceeding." Section 3B(6). When will that be so? See also page 518 supra.

f.   Failure to Report Another Lawyer's Misconduct

Both the code (in DR 1-103(A)) and the rules (Rule 8.3(a)) require lawyers to report misconduct of other lawyers under certain circumstances. Lawyers sometimes call this the "squeal rule," which should tell you something about its popularity. Judges are under a similar obligation. Code of Judicial Conduct (1990) §3(D)(2). The rules require reporting misconduct only if it raises "a substantial question as to [another] lawyer's honesty, trustworthiness or fitness as a lawyer." The code has no such limitation.

The code excuses reporting if a lawyer's knowledge of another lawyer's misconduct is privileged — i.e., a "confidence" within the meaning of DR 4-101, see page 17 supra — but not if the knowledge is merely a "secret." The rules, by contrast, excuse reporting if the basis for a lawyer's knowledge is confidential information as defined in Rule 1.6. It will be unusual, won't it, for a lawyer to have knowledge of another lawyer's unethical conduct that is *not* based on protected information? Yet it will happen, and it will happen even more often under the code, where the category of protected information is narrower.

The duty to report another lawyer's misconduct was honored mostly in the breach, so far as one can tell, until in 1988, the Illinois Supreme Court suspended a lawyer for one year for failure to comply with his code obligation to report another lawyer's misconduct. In re Himmel, 125 Ill. 2d 531, 533 N.E.2d 790, 792 (1988). This opinion roused the profession because of the dearth, if not the complete absence, of public discipline (let alone a suspension) for violation of the reporting obligation theretofore. So far *Himmel* stands alone. It has started no stampede of court decisions publicly punishing lawyers for failures to report.

Further, *Himmel* may have contained extenuating circumstances. Himmel represented a client whose funds (about $23,000) had been converted by a lawyer named Forsberg. Himmel negotiated a deal by which Forsberg would pay the client $75,000 and the client would not report Forsberg for discipline or criminal prosecution. Himmel, who stood to get a third of the negotiated sum, was suspended for not reporting Forsberg. So Himmel did not simply fail to act. He exploited another lawyer's professional exposure as a negotiation tactic that would net him a disproportionate settlement (is there an aroma of extortion there?) and a large fee. So viewed, *Himmel* is not a "plain vanilla" nonreporting case. The opinion might have caused lawyers less anxiety except that the Illinois Court did not specify these added facets in determining the proper discipline.

Himmel argued that his client did not want him to report Forsberg. Obviously, a promise not to report was a valuable bargaining chip for the client. Reporting, indeed, might have made it impossible for the client to get anything. (She eventually got about $10,000. Himmel got nothing.) The court held, however, that a defense based on the client's direction had "no legal support."

Himmel's knowledge of Forsberg's violation was a secret but not a confidence, and therefore not privileged. Under the code, reporting was obligatory. Under the rules, the information would have been confidential information and the lawyer would be obligated *not* to report without the client's permission. So the rules reach the diametrically opposite result.

Which result is correct? Under the rules, can a lawyer use the threat to report misconduct to negotiate a better deal? See page 487 supra.

Subordinate lawyers enjoy a "following orders" defense if directed to do something arguably improper so long as the supervisor's conclusion is "reasonable." Rule 5.2(b). That defense would also seem to relieve the subordinate of the duty to report the supervisor. If, however, a supervisor directs a subordinate lawyer to do something clearly wrong — e.g., to destroy a subpoenaed letter or backdate a document — the subordinate will not be able to rely on a "following orders" defense if she complies. What's more, the subordinate will be obligated to report the supervisor if she "knows" that the supervisor has proceeded with the unethical plan and her knowledge is not confidential or privileged. Bar opinions have confirmed this conclusion. ABA Informal Opinion 1202 (1972); New York City Opinion 82-79. See also In re Connelly, 18 A.D.2d 466, 240 N.Y.S.2d 126 (1st Dept. 1963) (in the pre-*Bates* era, see page 785 infra, law firm associates and partners cooperated with Life magazine on an article complimentary of the firm; the partners were censured; the associates were not disciplined because it was a case of first impression); In re Knight, 129 Vt. 428, 281 A.2d 46 (1971) (associate who participated in partner's plan to entrap divorce client's spouse in adultery suspended for three months; partner is disbarred).

4. Disciplinary Procedures

In broad outline, disciplinary procedures are much alike in all jurisdictions. See ABA, Model Rules for Lawyer Disciplinary Enforcement, reprinted at Lawyers Manual on Prof. Conduct (ABA/BNA) 01:601 (1989). Although many details vary among jurisdictions, the Due Process Clause of the Fourteenth Amendment mandates a certain uniformity. Even when discipline is summarily imposed, as in *DCD Programs*, page 676 supra, the Due Process Clause will entitle the lawyer to certain safeguards, such as notice and (usually) a hearing. The Supreme Court described the notice requirement this way in In re Ruffalo, 390 U.S. 544, 550-551 (1968):

> Disbarment, designed to protect the public, is a punishment or penalty imposed on the lawyer. He is accordingly entitled to procedural due process, which includes fair notice of the charge. See In re Oliver, 333 U.S. 257, 273. It was said in Randall v. Brigham, [75 U.S.] 523, 540, that when proceedings for disbarment are "not taken for matters occurring in open court, in the presence of the judges, notice should be given to the attorney of the charges made and opportunity afforded him for explanation and defence." Therefore, one of the conditions this Court considers in determining whether disbarment by a State should be followed by disbarment

here is whether "the state procedure from want of notice or opportunity to be heard was wanting in due process." Selling v. Radford, 243 U.S. 46, 51.

In the present case petitioner had no notice that his employment of Orlando would be considered a disbarment offense until *after* both he and Orlando had testified at length on all the material facts pertaining to this phase of the case. As Judge Edwards, dissenting below, said, "Such procedural violation of due process would never pass muster in any normal civil or criminal litigation."

These are adversary proceedings of a quasi-criminal nature. Cf. In re Gault, 387 U.S. 1, 33. The charge must be known before the proceedings commence. They become a trap when, after they are underway, the charges are amended on the basis of testimony of the accused. He can then be given no opportunity to expunge the earlier statements and start afresh.

Another Ohio lawyer, named Zauderer, whom we shall meet again when we discuss marketing by lawyers in Chapter 16, placed a newspaper ad to represent persons accused of driving while intoxicated. He also advertised for clients injured by their use of the Dalkon Shield. He was charged with misconduct for both ads.

The first ad said the client would not have to pay a fee if he were convicted of DWI. Disciplinary counsel charged that this was a contingent fee, forbidden in criminal matters. The state court eventually upheld discipline for this ad but on another theory — i.e., it was misleading because rarely did a DWI charge result in a DWI conviction. Zauderer complained that the change in theories denied him notice. The Supreme Court disagreed in Zauderer v. Office of Disciplinary Counsel, 471 U.S. 626, 654-655 (1985):

Finally, we address appellant's argument that he was denied procedural due process by the manner in which discipline was imposed on him in connection with his drunken driving advertisement. Appellant's contention is that the theory relied on by the Ohio Supreme Court and its Board of Commissioners as to how the advertisement was deceptive was different from the theory asserted by the Office of Disciplinary Counsel in its complaint. We cannot agree that this discrepancy violated the constitutional guarantee of due process.

Under the law of Ohio, bar discipline is the responsibility of the Ohio Supreme Court. The Board of Commissioners on Grievances and Discipline formally serves only as a body that recommends discipline to the Supreme Court; it has no authority to impose discipline itself. That the Board of Bar Commissioners chose to make its recommendation of discipline on the basis of reasoning different from that of the Office of Disciplinary Counsel is of little moment: what is important is that the Board's recommendations put appellant on notice of the charges he had to answer to the satisfaction of the Supreme Court of Ohio. Appellant does not contend that he was afforded no opportunity to respond to the Board's recommendation; indeed, the Ohio rules appear to provide ample opportunity for response to Board recommendations, and it appears that appellant availed himself of that opportunity.[17] The notice and opportunity to respond afforded appellant were sufficient to satisfy the demands of due process.

In dissent, Justice Brennan, joined by Justice Marshall, wrote that Zauderer had not had an opportunity to introduce evidence contradicting the theory of liability first adopted by the panel and the court after the case had been heard.

With regard to the Dalkon Shield ad, Zauderer said that the client would have to pay a fee only if there were a recovery. But he failed to say that clients would have to pay *costs* in any event. (See page 179 supra.) The Ohio rule did not explicitly require lawyers to include this disclaimer in contingent fee ads. Even the Ohio Supreme Court's opinion in Zauderer's case left the content of the disclaimer requirement unclear. Zauderer therefore complained that he had not been given notice of what he was required to say in his ad. (Zauderer had presented the advertisement to the disciplinary office for clearance before he ran it, but that office disclaimed authority to advise him.) Justice White characterized the lack of notice as "unfortunate." Citing *Ruffalo*, he wrote that "it may well be that for Ohio actually to disbar an attorney on the basis of its disclosure requirements as they have been worked out to this point would raise significant due process concerns." Nevertheless, the Court saw "no infirmity in a decision to issue a public reprimand." Justices Brennan and Marshall dissented on this point as well.

In addition to a right to notice, other due process rights that must be granted before a state may impose discipline are (1) an opportunity to confront the evidence against the respondent attorney and to cross-examine witnesses, see Willner v. Committee on Character and Fitness, 373 U.S. 96 (1963); (2) the right to present witnesses and argument on one's own behalf, In re Ginger, 372 F.2d 620 (6th Cir.), cert. denied, 387 U.S. 935 (1967); (3) the right to assert the privilege against self-incrimination, Spevack v. Klein, 385 U.S. 511 (1967); and (4) the right to have the facts determined and the sanction imposed by an impartial body, see Morrissey v. Brewer, 408 U.S. 471 (1972), and Gagnon v. Scarpelli, 411 U.S. 778 (1973). All jurisdictions appear to give an accused attorney the right to be represented by retained counsel at the disciplinary proceedings, al-

---

17. Appellant suggests that he was prejudiced by his inability to present evidence relating to the Board's factual conclusion that it was a common practice for persons charged with drunken driving to plead guilty to lesser offenses. If this were in fact the case, appellant's due process objection might be more forceful. But appellant does not — and probably cannot — seriously dispute that guilty pleas to lesser offenses are common in drunken driving cases, nor does he argue that he was precluded from arguing before the Ohio Supreme Court that it was improper for the Board of Commissioners to take judicial notice of the prevalence of such pleas. Under these circumstances, we see no violation of due process in the Ohio Supreme Court's acceptance of the Board's factual conclusions.

though the Supreme Court has never had an opportunity to consider whether this right is constitutionally compelled. Compare In re Gault, 387 U.S. 1 (1967), in which the Court held that a juvenile charged with delinquency has a right to retained or appointed counsel. The Supreme Court has cited *Gault* by analogy in describing the nature of the disciplinary proceeding. *Ruffalo*, 390 U.S. at 551. There is apparently no constitutional right to have a disciplinary decision reviewed by an appellate court. Mildner v. Gulotta, 405 F. Supp. 182 (E.D.N.Y. 1975), aff'd, 425 U.S. 901 (1976); cf. Jones v. Barnes, 463 U.S. 745 (1983) (no constitutional right to appeal in criminal cases). However, all states provide that right at least before serious discipline is imposed.

The majority view is that the disciplining body has the burden of proving the facts justifying discipline by clear and convincing evidence, although the precise articulation of the standard varies. Lawyers Manual on Prof. Conduct (ABA/BNA) 101:2101-2104 (1984). A healthy minority of states requires only a fair preponderance of the evidence. In re Capoccia, 59 N.Y.2d 549, 453 N.E.2d 497, 466 N.Y.S.2d 268 (1983).

Capoccia also holds that an attorney has the right to waive confidentiality and request a public disciplinary hearing. About one-half the states require public hearings whether or not the attorney consents. The disciplinary processes in three states — Oregon, West Virginia, and Florida — are open to public view even if there is no hearing or finding of wrongdoing. Oregon is the most open. The process is public from the time a complaint is received. West Virginia and Florida provide for some secrecy. See Re Amendments to the Rules Regulating the Florida Bar, 558 So. 2d 1008 (Fla. 1990). Florida acted after a federal court invalidated a rule that prohibited a complainant to reveal that a lawyer had been reprimanded. Doe v. Florida Bar, 748 F. Supp. 1520 (S.D. Fla. 1990). See also Baugh v. Judicial Inquiry & Review Commission, 907 F.2d 440 (4th Cir. 1990) (statute prohibiting disclosure of communication to commission must satisfy exacting standard of scrutiny). An ABA commission headed by Dean Robert McKay has recommended the Oregon rule nationwide, along with many other changes in the disciplinary process. Report of the Commission on Evaluation of Disciplinary Enforcement (1991).

As mentioned, the privilege against self-incrimination applies in disciplinary proceedings. See generally Geoffrey Hazard & Cameron Beard, A Lawyer's Privilege Against Self-Incrimination in Professional Disciplinary Proceedings, 96 Yale L.J. 1060 (1987). However, if a lawyer has testified in criminal or other proceedings under a grant of immunity, the immunized testimony may be admitted against the lawyer in a disciplinary proceeding without violating the lawyer's Fifth Amendment rights. In re Daley, 549 F.2d 469 (7th Cir.), cert. denied, 434 U.S. 829 (1977); Anonymous Attorneys v. Bar Assn. of Erie County, 41 N.Y.2d 506, 362 N.E.2d 592, 393 N.Y.S.2d 961 (1977). Does that surprise you? How do you explain it?

5. Readmission

Although we have carefully listed a hierarchical series of responses a state may have to lawyer misconduct, all the way from a caution or a warning to disbarment, it turns out that disbarment itself is not necessarily permanent. The frequent rule is that a disbarred lawyer, after varying periods of years, may apply for readmission. This does not mean that readmission will automatically be granted, no matter how long the period of disbarment, but only that it may be. In considering whether to readmit a disbarred attorney, the courts generally weigh the public interest, the prior character and standing of the attorney, the attorney's mental and moral qualifications, the reason the attorney was disbarred in the first place, his or her conduct while disbarred, the length of time the disbarment lasted, whether, if applicable, restitution has been made, the attorney's overall present fitness to practice law, and evidence that he or she has reformed or been rehabilitated. Although new bar applicants are entitled to a hearing before they can be excluded on character grounds, persons applying for readmission have no right to a hearing. Matter of Rowe, 73 N.Y.2d 336, 537 N.E.2d 616, 540 N.Y.S.2d 231 (1989). *Rowe* held, however, that a lawyer suspended because of a disability is entitled to a hearing if he presents clear and convincing evidence that the disability is over.

One interesting reinstatement case is In re Hiss, 368 Mass. 447, 333 N.E.2d 429 (1975). Alger Hiss had been convicted of perjury before a congressional committee and disbarred in 1952. Former President Nixon was one of his most aggressive public accusers while Nixon was a member of the Committee on Un-American Activities of the House of Representatives. Nixon's accusations, in part, eventually led to Hiss's indictment, conviction, and eventual disbarment. In 1975, the Massachusetts Supreme Judicial Court reinstated Alger Hiss as a lawyer in that state. A year later, a New York court disbarred Richard Nixon for conduct while President. In re Nixon, 53 A.D.2d 178, 385 N.Y.S.2d 305 (1st Dept. 1976).

6. Discipline in a Federal System

The United States Supreme Court has held that "[w]hile a lawyer is admitted into a federal court by way of a state court, he is not automatically sent out of the federal court by the same route." Theard v. United States, 354 U.S. 278, 280-282 (1957). Each judicial system has "autonomous control over the conduct of [its] . . . lawyers." A state court determination of disbarment, therefore, "is not conclusively binding on the federal courts."

Although state courts are not obligated to impose the same discipline another state has imposed, they often do. See In re Kaufman, 81 N.J. 300, 406 A.2d 972 (1979). Occasionally, a state or federal court will opt for a different (often lesser) sanction than a state or federal court previously imposed. In re Weissman, 203 Conn. 380, 524 A.2d 1141 (1987) (federal discipline one year; state imposes one month); In re Evans, 533 A.2d 243 (D.C. App. 1987) (Maryland federal court imposed disbarment; D.C. Court of Appeals imposes public censure).

A rare example of possible conflict between state ethics rules and federal law arose in the discussion of prosecutorial contact with targets of investigations. See page 85 supra. See also Rand v. Monsanto, 926 F.2d 596 (7th Cir. 1991) (Rule 23 superior to state's prohibition against lawyer assuming court costs).

If a federal lawyer is charged with discipline before a state body for conduct "under color" of his federal office, removal to federal court will be available. Kolibash v. Committee on Legal Ethics of West Virginia State Bar, 872 F.2d 571 (4th Cir. 1989). The federal court provides a neutral forum for adjudication of the state ethics complaint. In *Kolibash*, the complainant charged that the respondent, a federal prosecutor, had participated in the prosecution of the complainant after having represented him as a private defense lawyer with regard to the same underlying conduct.

E. CONSTITUTIONAL PROTECTION IN CRIMINAL CASES

The Sixth Amendment guarantees criminal defendants "the assistance of counsel." This guarantee has been interpreted to mean that counsel must be "effective." McMann v. Richardson, 397 U.S. 759, 771, n.14 (1970). The right is enjoyed by defendants who retain counsel or have counsel appointed for them. Cuyler v. Sullivan, 446 U.S. 335 (1980). A convicted defendant whose counsel is proved to be ineffective and whose case was prejudiced thereby will be entitled to have his or her conviction overturned. After Evitts v. Lucey, 469 U.S. 387 (1985), the guarantee of effective assistance of counsel applies to appellate counsel too.

Some overlap must be expected between the level of performance required by the Sixth Amendment, by the law of malpractice, and by the ethical duty of competence, but these are still distinct concepts. The main reason they are distinct is that effective assistance of counsel is a constitutional guarantee and applies uniformly nationwide. Malpractice and ethical rules are determined by each jurisdiction for itself.

A state may insist on a greater level of performance for a lawyer to avoid discipline for incompetence than the Sixth Amendment requires for counsel to be considered effective. The constitutional guarantee applies only in criminal cases, and protects the defendant only, whereas other mechanisms to encourage or remedy professional defaults apply in all kinds of cases.

Looking at the issue institutionally, we might expect judges to be more hesitant to find a lawyer's conduct ineffective when the result is that a conviction must be upset and a new trial held than they will be to allow a jury to award civil damages against a lawyer. Courts might also be expected to be highly deferential toward a criminal defense lawyer's decisions (even, as we shall see, when the decision is to do nothing).

As with malpractice, the ineffectiveness claim, even if proved, will not lead to a remedy unless there is a causal relationship between the professional failure and injury to the client. In malpractice, we have seen that that requirement incorporates the common law proximate cause standard (see page 639 supra). In Sixth Amendment challenges (which usually come in a collateral attack on the judgment but may come in a direct appeal as well), the injury requirement usually obligates the convicted defendant to demonstrate with some degree of likelihood that but for the lawyer's mistakes he or she would have fared better in the criminal trial or appeal. Sometimes, however, we are certain enough of the likelihood of prejudice, either because of experience or for reasons of principle, that we relieve the defendant of this burden. In places such as New York (page 643 supra), which require plaintiffs to establish innocence in order to prevail in a malpractice case against a criminal defense lawyer, will the constitutional test be easier to satisfy because it requires only some demonstration of a different result?

As you can see, a legal system that guarantees the effective assistance of counsel will have a lot of questions to answer. Pretend you are hired to create an enlightened criminal justice system for a new society with a federal system. You mean to guarantee the effective assistance of counsel in criminal cases. How do you answer the following questions:

1.   Who must prove ineffectiveness or its opposite (i.e., the defendant or the state)?
2.   What is the burden of proof? More likely than not? Clear and convincing evidence? Beyond a reasonable doubt?
3.   What is the standard for ineffectiveness? We can't require perfection. Just as a lawyer will not be liable in malpractice for errors of judgment, neither can we make every such error the equivalent of ineffectiveness, even if the error might have made a difference, can we? Nor, as we have seen, can we incorporate the different ethical or malpractice standards of the various states. So what do

we do? In answering this question we must keep in mind (a) why we guarantee counsel in the first place; (b) the cost of making the standard too easy or too hard to satisfy; and (c) the impossibility of anticipating the kinds of acts or failures to act that may later be challenged as inadequate. The fact that categorization is hard counsels a general standard. But the fact that many judges will have to apply the standard in a multiplicity of circumstances requires that it have adequate content to guide them.

4. What is the causation requirement? Or maybe we don't need one. Maybe we should just say that if counsel was ineffective, the defendant should always get a new trial because it is not possible to know how a trial might have gone had counsel not made the mistake that rendered him or her ineffective. Alternatively, we could (rebuttably?) presume prejudice for some kinds of errors and require proof of it for other kinds. But which errors will fall into which categories? For example, what should our system do if a convicted defendant proves that he "paid" his lawyer with the publication rights to the defendant's story? See page 178 supra. Should a defendant who shows that have to show anything else before getting a new trial?

5. If we decide that prejudice will sometimes be required, we must allocate and identify the burden of proof on prejudice too. Who must prove or disprove prejudice and by what quantum? (Will the answers here turn on the reason for the ineffectiveness?) We will also have to define prejudice. Should it be defined as innocence or probable innocence? Or should it suffice that without the ineffectiveness, the verdict might (would probably?) have been different?

6. Have you noticed something interesting about the system we have so far constructed? We have been making a critical and unstated assumption that the way to remedy ineffectiveness in the assistance of counsel in criminal cases is to review the work of counsel *after* the case is over. Is this the best way to do it? Why not take steps in advance of trial to assure that counsel *will be* effective? Of course, to some extent we do this through our system of licensing attorneys. But shouldn't we consider reducing the risk of ineffectiveness in a more focused way, *immediately* before the event, rather than long before it (when the lawyer took the bar examination) or after it is over? By taking preventive measures we may avoid ineffectiveness that would otherwise occur. We also reduce the prospect that we may have to upset a conviction and order a new trial, a result that has high institutional costs and that may discourage judges from finding ineffectiveness despite serious doubts. Are there good reasons to rely nearly exclusively on "autopsies" in lieu of pretrial precautions?

That concludes our questions, but before we attempt answers, consider how the courts of appeals defined the standard of ineffectiveness before the 1970s. In Trapnell v. United States, 725 F.2d 149, 151 (2d Cir. 1983), the Second Circuit was faced with a claim of ineffective assistance. It wrote:

> Before examining appellant's specific contentions, we discuss the appropriate standard of competence for a defendant's attorney in a criminal trial. In the Second Circuit, that standard has been governed for over thirty years by the rule laid down in United States v. Wight, 176 F.2d 376, 379 (2d Cir. 1949), cert. denied, 338 U.S. 950 (1950): "A lack of effective assistance of counsel must be of such a kind as to shock the conscience of the court and make the proceedings a farce and mockery of justice." In *Wight,* this court adopted the standard first formulated by Judge Thurman Arnold for the D.C. Circuit in Diggs v. Welch, 148 F.2d 667, 670 (D.C. Cir.), cert. denied, 325 U.S. 889 (1945).

By 1970, every circuit had adopted the "farce and mockery" standard, but in the next decade, every circuit except the Second abandoned that standard for some form of the "reasonably competent assistance" standard. In *Trapnell,* the Second Circuit joined them. The large majority of state courts also adopted some form of the "reasonably competent assistance" standard. See Note, A Functional Analysis of the Effective Assistance of Counsel, 80 Colum. L. Rev. 1053, 1058 n.41 (1980) (authored by Bruce Green).

The Supreme Court decided Strickland v. Washington and United States v. Cronic in 1984. In *Strickland* the Court answered some of the questions we presented above. In *Cronic* the Court applied the *Strickland* standard to the recurring problem where a defense lawyer is given only a few weeks to prepare a case that the government had been planning for years.

STRICKLAND v. WASHINGTON
466 U.S. 668 (1984)

[The respondent challenged his death sentence on the ground that the lawyer who represented him at the sentencing hearing was constitutionally ineffective. In most states the sentence in a capital case is determined by a jury. Whoever decides, a hearing is held before sentence is imposed and at which evidence in mitigation and aggravation of sentence is elicited. Because, as Justice O'Connor wrote, a capital sentencing hearing is "like a trial in its adversarial format and in the existence of standards for decision," her opinion for the Court applies both to such

hearings and to trials. It expressly does not address the standards of performance at ordinary sentencing hearings.]

III

A convicted defendant's claim that counsel's assistance was so defective as to require reversal of a conviction or death sentence has two components. First, the defendant must show that counsel's performance was
deficient. This requires showing that counsel made errors so serious that
counsel was not functioning as the "counsel" guaranteed the defendant
by the Sixth Amendment. Second, the defendant must show that the deficient performance prejudiced the defense. This requires showing that
counsel's errors were so serious as to deprive the defendant of a fair trial,
a trial whose result is reliable. Unless a defendant makes both showings,
it cannot be said that the conviction or death sentence resulted from a
breakdown in the adversary process that renders the result unreliable.

A

As all the Federal Courts of Appeals have now held, the proper standard for attorney performance is that of reasonably effective assistance.
The Court indirectly recognized as much when it stated in McMann v.
Richardson, [397 U.S. 759 (1970)] at 770, 771, that a guilty plea cannot
be attacked as based on inadequate legal advice unless counsel was not "a
reasonably competent attorney" and the advice was not "within the range
of competence demanded of attorneys in criminal cases." See also Cuyler
v. Sullivan, 446 U.S. 335 (1980), at 344. When a convicted defendant
complains of the ineffectiveness of counsel's assistance, the defendant
must show that counsel's representation fell below an objective standard
of reasonableness.

More specific guidelines are not appropriate. The Sixth Amendment
refers simply to "counsel," not specifying particular requirements of effective assistance. It relies instead on the legal profession's maintenance
of standards sufficient to justify the law's presumption that counsel will
fulfill the role in the adversary process that the Amendment envisions.
The proper measure of attorney performance remains simply reasonableness under prevailing professional norms.

Representation of a criminal defendant entails certain basic duties.
Counsel's function is to assist the defendant, and hence counsel owes the
client a duty of loyalty, a duty to avoid conflicts of interest. See Cuyler v.
Sullivan, supra, at 346. From counsel's function as assistant to the defendant derive the overarching duty to advocate the defendant's cause and
the more particular duties to consult with the defendant on important
decisions and to keep the defendant informed of important developments in the course of the prosecution. Counsel also has a duty to bring

to bear such skill and knowledge as will render the trial a reliable adversarial testing process.

These basic duties neither exhaustively define the obligations of counsel nor form a checklist for judicial evaluation of attorney performance. In any case presenting an ineffectiveness claim, the performance inquiry must be whether counsel's assistance was reasonable considering all the circumstances. Prevailing norms of practice reflected in American Bar Association [Standards for Criminal Justice] and the like are guides to determining what is reasonable, but they are only guides. No particular set of detailed rules for counsel's conduct can satisfactorily take account of the variety of circumstances faced by defense counsel or the range of legitimate decisions regarding how best to represent a criminal defendant. Any such set of rules would interfere with the constitutionally protected independence of counsel and restrict the wide latitude counsel must have in making tactical decisions. See United States v. Decoster, 624 F.2d [196 (D.C. Cir. 1979)], at 208. Indeed, the existence of detailed guidelines for representation could distract counsel from the overriding mission of vigorous advocacy of the defendant's cause. Moreover, the purpose of the effective assistance guarantee of the Sixth Amendment is not to improve the quality of legal representation, although that is a goal of considerable importance to the legal system. The purpose is simply to ensure that criminal defendants receive a fair trial.

Judicial scrutiny of counsel's performance must be highly deferential. It is all too tempting for a defendant to second-guess counsel's assistance after conviction or adverse sentence, and it is all too easy for a court, examining counsel's defense after it has proved unsuccessful, to conclude that a particular act or omission of counsel was unreasonable. A fair assessment of attorney performance requires that every effort be made to eliminate the distorting effects of hindsight, to reconstruct the circumstances of counsel's challenged conduct, and to evaluate the conduct from counsel's perspective at the time. Because of the difficulties inherent in making the evaluation, a court must indulge a strong presumption that counsel's conduct falls within the wide range of reasonable professional assistance; that is, the defendant must overcome the presumption that, under the circumstances, the challenged action "might be considered sound trial strategy." There are countless ways to provide effective assistance in any given case. Even the best criminal defense attorneys would not defend a particular client in the same way. See Goodpaster, The Trial for Life: Effective Assistance of Counsel in Death Penalty Cases, 58 N.Y.U. L. Rev. 299, 343 (1983).

The availability of intrusive post-trial inquiry into attorney performance or of detailed guidelines for its evaluation would encourage the proliferation of ineffectiveness challenges. Criminal trials resolved unfavorably to the defendant would increasingly come to be followed by a second trial, this one of counsel's unsuccessful defense. Counsel's performance and even willingness to serve could be adversely affected. Intensive scrutiny of counsel and rigid requirements for acceptable assistance could dampen the ardor and impair the independence of defense counsel, discourage the acceptance of assigned cases, and undermine the trust between attorney and client.

Thus, a court deciding an actual ineffectiveness claim must judge the reasonableness of counsel's challenged conduct on the facts of the particular case, viewed as of the time of counsel's conduct. A convicted defendant making a claim of ineffective assistance must identify the acts or omissions of counsel that are alleged not to have been the result of reasonable professional judgment. The court must then determine whether, in light of all the circumstances, the identified acts or omissions were outside the wide range of professionally competent assistance. In making that determination, the court should keep in mind that counsel's function, as elaborated in prevailing professional norms, is to make the adversarial testing process work in the particular case. At the same time, the court should recognize that counsel is strongly presumed to have rendered adequate assistance and made all significant decisions in the exercise of reasonable professional judgment.

These standards require no special amplification in order to define counsel's duty to investigate, the duty at issue in this case. As the Court of Appeals concluded, strategic choices made after thorough investigation of law and facts relevant to plausible options are virtually unchallengeable; and strategic choices made after less than complete investigation are reasonable precisely to the extent that reasonable professional judgments support the limitations on investigation. In other words, counsel has a duty to make reasonable investigations or to make a reasonable decision that makes particular investigations unnecessary. In any ineffectiveness case, a particular decision not to investigate must be directly assessed for reasonableness in all the circumstances, applying a heavy measure of deference to counsel's judgments.

The reasonableness of counsel's actions may be determined or substantially influenced by the defendant's own statements or actions. Counsel's actions are usually based, quite properly, on informed strategic choices made by the defendant and on information supplied by the defendant. In particular, what investigation decisions are reasonable depends critically on such information. For example, when the facts that support a certain potential line of defense are generally known to counsel because of what the defendant has said, the need for further investigation may be considerably diminished or eliminated altogether. And when a defendant has given counsel reason to believe that pursuing certain investigations would be fruitless or even harmful, counsel's failure to pursue those investigations may not later be challenged as unreasonable. In short, inquiry into counsel's conversations with the defendant may be critical to a proper assessment of counsel's investigation decisions, just as it may be critical to a proper assessment of counsel's other litigation decisions.

B

An error by counsel, even if professionally unreasonable, does not warrant setting aside the judgment of a criminal proceeding if the error had no effect on the judgment. The purpose of the Sixth Amendment guarantee of counsel is to ensure that a defendant has the assistance necessary to justify reliance on the outcome of the proceeding. Accordingly, any deficiencies in counsel's performance must be prejudicial to the defense in order to constitute ineffective assistance under the Constitution.

In certain Sixth Amendment contexts, prejudice is presumed. Actual or constructive denial of the assistance of counsel altogether is legally presumed to result in prejudice. So are various kinds of state interference with counsel's assistance. Prejudice in these circumstances is so likely that case by case inquiry into prejudice is not worth the cost. Moreover, such circumstances involve impairments of the Sixth Amendment right that are easy to identify and, for that reason and because the prosecution is directly responsible, easy for the government to prevent.

One type of actual ineffectiveness claim warrants a similar, though more limited, presumption of prejudice. In Cuyler v. Sullivan, 446 U.S., at 345-350, the Court held that prejudice is presumed when counsel is burdened by an actual conflict of interest. In those circumstances, counsel breaches the duty of loyalty, perhaps the most basic of counsel's duties. Moreover, it is difficult to measure the precise effect on the defense of representation corrupted by conflicting interests. Given the obligation of counsel to avoid conflicts of interest and the ability of trial courts to make early inquiry in certain situations likely to give rise to conflicts, see, e.g., Fed. Rule Crim. Proc. 44(c), it is reasonable for the criminal justice system to maintain a fairly rigid rule of presumed prejudice for conflicts of interest. Even so, the rule is not quite the per se rule of prejudice that exists for the Sixth Amendment claims mentioned above. Prejudice is presumed only if the defendant demonstrates that counsel "actively represented conflicting interests" and "that an actual conflict of interest adversely affected his lawyer's performance." Cuyler v. Sullivan, supra, at 350, 348 (footnote omitted).

Conflict of interest claims aside, actual ineffectiveness claims alleging a deficiency in attorney performance are subject to a general requirement that the defendant affirmatively prove prejudice. The government is not responsible for, and hence not able to prevent, attorney errors that will result in reversal of a conviction or sentence. Attorney errors come in an infinite variety and are as likely to be utterly harmless in a particular case as they are to be prejudicial. They cannot be classified according to likelihood of causing prejudice. Nor can they be defined with sufficient precision to inform defense attorneys correctly just what conduct to avoid. Representation is an art, and an act or omission that is unprofessional in one case may be sound or even brilliant in another. Even if a defendant shows that particular errors of counsel were unreasonable, therefore, the defendant must show that they actually had an adverse effect on the defense.

It is not enough for the defendant to show that the errors had some conceivable effect on the outcome of the proceeding. Virtually every act or omission of counsel would meet that test, and not every error that conceivably could have influenced the outcome undermines the reliability of the result of the proceeding. Respondent suggests requiring a showing that the errors "impaired the presentation of the defense." That standard, however, provides no workable principle. Since any error, if it is indeed an error, "impairs" the presentation of the defense, the proposed standard is inadequate because it provides no way of deciding what impairments are sufficiently serious to warrant setting aside the outcome of the proceeding.

On the other hand, we believe that a defendant need not show that counsel's deficient conduct more likely than not altered the outcome in the case. This outcome-determinative standard has several strengths. It defines the relevant inquiry in a way familiar to courts, though the inquiry, as is inevitable, is anything but precise. The standard also reflects the profound importance of finality in criminal proceedings. Moreover, it comports with the widely used standard for assessing motions for new trial based on newly discovered evidence. Nevertheless, the standard is not quite appropriate.

Even when the specified attorney error results in the omission of certain evidence, the newly discovered evidence standard is not an apt source from which to draw a prejudice standard for ineffectiveness claims. This high standard for newly discovered evidence claims presupposes that all the essential elements of a presumptively accurate and fair proceeding were present in the proceeding whose result is challenged. An ineffective assistance claim asserts the absence of one of the crucial assurances that the result of the proceeding is reliable, so finality concerns are somewhat weaker and the appropriate standard of prejudice should be somewhat lower. The result of a proceeding can be rendered unreliable, and hence the proceeding itself unfair, even if the errors of counsel cannot be shown by a preponderance of the evidence to have determined the outcome.

Accordingly, the appropriate test for prejudice finds its roots in the test for materiality of exculpatory information not disclosed to the defense by the prosecution, and in the test for materiality of testimony made unavailable to the defense by Government deportation of a witness. The defendant must show that there is a reasonable probability that, but for counsel's unprofessional errors, the result of the proceeding would have been different. A reasonable probability is a probability sufficient to undermine confidence in the outcome.

In making the determination whether the specified errors resulted in the required prejudice, a court should presume, absent challenge to the judgment on grounds of evidentiary insufficiency, that the judge or jury acted according to law. An assessment of the likelihood of a result more favorable to the defendant must exclude the possibility of arbitrariness, whimsy, caprice, "nullification," and the like. A defendant has no entitlement to the luck of a lawless decisionmaker, even if a lawless decision cannot be reviewed. The assessment of prejudice should proceed on the assumption that the decisionmaker is reasonably, conscientiously, and impartially applying the standards that govern the decision. It should not depend on the idiosyncracies of the particular decisionmaker, such as unusual propensities toward harshness or leniency. Although these factors may actually have entered into counsel's selection of strategies and, to that limited extent, may thus affect the performance inquiry, they are irrelevant to the prejudice inquiry. Thus, evidence about the actual process of decision, if not part of the record of the proceeding under review, and evidence about, for example, a particular judge's sentencing practices, should not be considered in the prejudice determination.

The governing legal standard plays a critical role in defining the question to be asked in assessing the prejudice from counsel's errors. When a defendant challenges a conviction, the question is whether there is a reasonable doubt respecting guilt. When a defendant challenges a death sentence such as the one at issue in this case, the question is whether there is a reasonable probability that, absent the errors, the sentencer — including an appellate court, to the extent it independently reweighs the evidence — would have concluded that the balance of aggravating and mitigating circumstances did not warrant death.

In making this determination, a court hearing an ineffectiveness claim must consider the totality of the evidence before the judge or jury. Some of the factual findings will have been unaffected by the errors, and factual findings that were affected will have been affected in different ways. Some errors will have had a pervasive effect on the inferences to be drawn from the evidence, altering the entire evidentiary picture, and some will have had an isolated, trivial effect. Moreover, a verdict or conclusion only weakly supported by the record is more likely to have been affected by errors than one with overwhelming record support. Taking the unaffected findings as a given, and taking due account of the effect of the errors on the remaining findings, a court making the prejudice inquiry must ask if the defendant has met the burden of showing that the decision reached would reasonably likely have been different absent the errors.

[Justice Brennan concurred in the Court's standards. Justice Marshall dissented from both the performance standards and the prejudice standard.]

United States v. Cronic: Inadequate Time to Prepare

Cronic received a 25-year sentence for mail fraud involving the transfer of more than $9 million. The Court of Appeals reversed on the ground that Cronic was denied the effective assistance of counsel. Cronic's lawyer had been appointed on June 12, 1980. A week later, counsel asked for a 30-day continuance of the trial, then scheduled to begin June 30. The trial court granted a 25-day continuance instead. The Supreme Court held that these facts could not alone support a finding of ineffectiveness in the particular case. "This case is not one in which the surrounding circumstances make it unlikely that the defendant could have received the effective assistance of counsel. . . . Respondent can therefore make out a claim of ineffective assistance only by pointing to specific errors made by trial counsel." The case was remanded to give Cronic a chance to demonstrate specific errors. United States v. Cronic, 466 U.S. 648, 649 (1984). (On remand, the Tenth Circuit found such errors, vacated the conviction, and ordered a new trial. United States v. Cronic, 839 F.2d 1401 (10th Cir. 1988).) In the course of his opinion for the Court, Justice Stevens wrote:

> The substance of the Constitution's guarantee of the effective assistance of counsel is illuminated by reference to its underlying purpose. "[T]ruth," Lord Eldon said, "is best discovered by powerful statements on both sides of the question." This dictum describes the unique strength of our system of criminal justice. "The very premise of our adversary system of criminal justice is that partisan advocacy on both sides of a case will best promote the ultimate objective that the guilty be convicted and the innocent go free." It is that "very premise" that underlies and gives meaning to the Sixth Amendment. It "is meant to assure fairness in the adversary criminal process." Unless the accused receives the effective assistance of counsel, "a serious risk of injustice infects the trial itself."
>
> Thus, the adversarial process protected by the Sixth Amendment requires that the accused have "counsel acting in the role of an advocate." The right to the effective assistance of counsel is thus the right of the accused to require the prosecution's case to survive the crucible of meaningful adversarial testing. When a true adversarial criminal trial has been conducted — even if defense counsel may have made demonstrable errors — the kind of testing envisioned by the Sixth Amendment has occurred. But if the process loses its character as a confrontation between adversaries, the constitutional guarantee is violated. . . . 466 U.S. at 655-657.

While the Court of Appeals purported to apply a standard of reasonable competence, it did not indicate that there had been an actual breakdown of the adversarial process during the trial of this case. Instead it concluded that the circumstances surrounding the representation of respondent mandated an inference that counsel was unable to discharge his duties.

In our evaluation of that conclusion, we begin by recognizing that the right to the effective assistance of counsel is recognized not for its own sake, but because of the effect it has on the ability of the accused to receive a fair trial. Absent some effect of challenged conduct on the reliability of the trial process, the Sixth Amendment guarantee is generally not implicated. Moreover, because we presume that the lawyer is competent to provide the guiding hand that the defendant needs, the burden rests on the accused to demonstrate a constitutional violation. There are, however, circumstances that are so likely to prejudice the accused that the cost of litigating their effect in a particular case is unjustified.

Most obvious, of course, is the complete denial of counsel. The presumption that counsel's assistance is essential requires us to conclude that a trial is unfair if the accused is denied counsel at a critical stage of his trial. Similarly, if counsel entirely fails to subject the prosecution's case to meaningful adversarial testing, then there has been a denial of Sixth Amendment rights that makes the adversary process itself presumptively unreliable. No specific showing of prejudice was required in Davis v. Alaska, 415 U.S. 308 (1974), because the petitioner had been "denied the right of effective cross-examination" which " 'would be constitutional error of the first magnitude and no amount of showing of want of prejudice would cure it.' "

Circumstances of that magnitude may be present on some occasions when although counsel is available to assist the accused during trial, the likelihood that any lawyer, even a fully competent one, could provide effective assistance is so small that a presumption of prejudice is appropriate without inquiry into the actual conduct of the trial. Powell v. Alabama, 287 U.S. 45 (1932), was such a case.*

The defendants had been indicted for a highly publicized capital offense. Six days before trial, the trial judge appointed "all the members of the bar" for purposes of arraignment. "Whether they would represent the defendants thereafter if no counsel appeared in their behalf, was a matter of speculation only, or, as the judge indicated, of mere anticipation on the part of the court." On the day of trial, a lawyer from Tennessee appeared on behalf of persons "interested" in the defendants, but stated that he had not had an opportunity to prepare the case or to familiarize himself with local procedure, and therefore was unwilling to represent the defendants on such short notice. The problem was resolved when the court decided that the Tennessee lawyer would represent the defendants, with whatever help the local bar could provide.

"The defendants, young, ignorant, illiterate, surrounded by hostile sentiment, haled back and forth under guard of soldiers, charged with an atrocious crime regarded with especial horror in the community where they

---

*This was the *Scottsboro* case. — ED.

were to be tried, were thus put in peril of their lives within a few moments after counsel for the first time charged with any degree of responsibility began to represent them."

This Court held that "such designation of counsel as was attempted was either so indefinite or so close upon the trial as to amount to a denial of effective and substantial aid in that regard." The Court did not examine the actual performance of counsel at trial, but instead concluded that under these circumstances the likelihood that counsel could have performed as an effective adversary was so remote as to have made the trial inherently unfair. *Powell* was thus a case in which the surrounding circumstances made it so unlikely that any lawyer could provide effective assistance that ineffectiveness was properly presumed without inquiry into actual performance at trial.

But every refusal to postpone a criminal trial will not give rise to such a presumption. In Avery v. Alabama, 308 U.S. 444 (1940), counsel was appointed in a capital case only three days before trial, and the trial court denied counsel's request for additional time to prepare. Nevertheless, the Court held that since evidence and witnesses were easily accessible to defense counsel, the circumstances did not make it unreasonable to expect that counsel could adequately prepare for trial during that period of time. Similarly, in Chambers v. Maroney, 399 U.S. 42 (1970), the Court refused "to fashion a per se rule requiring reversal of every conviction following tardy appointment of counsel." Thus, only when surrounding circumstances justify a presumption of ineffectiveness can a Sixth Amendment claim be sufficient without inquiry into counsel's actual performance at trial.

Some Reasons for Ineffectiveness Claims

The Supreme Court's *Strickland* test means that most ineffectiveness claims will have to be analyzed individually rather than categorically. It should come as no surprise that courts are highly deferential to strategies later attacked as ineffective. If a lawyer chooses to do something and does it, it is exceedingly rare that he or she will be found wanting. For example, a lawyer who interviews the alibi witnesses his client has identified, finds them incredible, and chooses not to call them will not likely be constitutionally deficient even if her decision was tactically misguided. On the other hand, if the lawyer never bothered to interview the alibi witnesses at all, a Sixth Amendment challenge has a fair chance of success. (We saw the same pattern in discipline, where inaction may result in sanction for neglect while errors of commission are usually left to malpractice. See page 676 supra.) Harris v. Reed, 894 F.2d 871 (7th Cir. 1990), draws this omission/commission distinction and then finds a lawyer ineffective where he failed to interview eyewitnesses whose testimony would have exonerated the accused. The court was not impressed by counsel's purported strategy of instead relying on weaknesses in the state's case.

One popular reason for claims of ineffectiveness is that counsel suffered from an actual conflict of interest between the interests of the convicted defendant and the interests of either another client or of the lawyer's own interests. (See page 186 supra.) Applying *Strickland,* United States v. Tatum, 943 F.2d 370 (4th Cir. 1991), overturned a conviction because defense counsel's performance was tainted by his dependence on the defendant's prior lawyer, who had been disqualified on conflict grounds.

Sometimes ineffectiveness is attributed to the fact that the defendant's lawyer was in fact not a lawyer. This can be true for several reasons. First, the "lawyer" may have been suspended or disbarred before or during the trial. Second, the "lawyer," though a law school graduate, may never have been admitted to the bar of any jurisdiction. Third, the "lawyer" may never have gone to law school, much less have been admitted to a bar. Decisions in pre-*Strickland* cases vary, but they generally agreed that if the "lawyer" was never admitted to a bar, then the defendant's Sixth Amendment right would have been violated and prejudice would be presumed. See Solina v. United States, 709 F.2d 160 (2d Cir. 1983) (Friendly, J.) (historical discussion of meaning of "counsel"). Citing *Solina* and reviewing case law in the area, United States v. Novak, 903 F.2d 883 (2d Cir. 1990), vacated a conviction where the defense lawyer, though a member of the bar at the time of trial, was later disbarred after it was discovered that he had gained admission by fraudulently claiming he was entitled to a waiver of the bar examination requirement.

In United States v. Merritt, 528 F.2d 650 (7th Cir. 1976), the lawyer was appointed to represent a defendant in a federal trial in Indiana. The lawyer was a member of the Iowa bar but had failed the Indiana bar examination three times and was ineligible to retake it without an additional year of study. The court concluded that the defendant had been denied the effective assistance of counsel.

By contrast, in United States v. Hoffman, 733 F.2d 596 (9th Cir.), cert. denied, 469 U.S. 1039 (1984), the lawyer's home state (Florida) suspended him during a trial in the Arizona federal court. But the Ninth Circuit rejected the claim of ineffectiveness because the lawyer's pro hac vice admission to the trial court itself was not revoked until the trial ended. A dissent argued that the pro hac vice admission was derivative of the lawyer's Florida admission and ended when Florida suspended the lawyer.

Another kind of claim is that defense counsel, though indeed a lawyer qualified to practice in the jurisdiction, was for some reason not present during a part of the trial. In Javor v. United States, 724 F.2d 831, 832 (9th Cir. 1984), the lawyer was dozing during "a substantial part of [a multidefendant] trial . . . including some occasions when evidence relevant to the prosecution case against defendant . . . was being elicited." The court held that the defendant's right to counsel had been denied and presumed prejudice. In Siverson v. O'Leary, 764 F.2d 1208 (7th Cir. 1985), the lawyer was not present during jury deliberations, nor when the verdict was returned. The court characterized these events as critical stages of the proceedings and relieved the defendant of having to prove prejudice as defined in *Strickland*. The court instead used a harmless error test to decide whether the conviction should be overturned. It concluded that on the facts before it the error was harmless beyond a reasonable doubt.

A final way in which counsel may be "absent" is when he or she is in the courtroom and not asleep but does little or nothing during the trial. Sometimes, a court characterizes this conduct (or lack of conduct) as a "silent strategy" and refuses to second-guess counsel. See Warner v. Ford, 752 F.2d 622 (11th Cir. 1985). Other courts have been less charitable. Martin v. Rose, 744 F.2d 1245 (6th Cir. 1984) (lawyer's lack of participation deprived client of effective assistance; no proof of prejudice required).

Morris v. Slappy: Effectiveness Does Not Include Rapport

In Morris v. Slappy, 461 U.S. 1, 2 (1983), Slappy's court-appointed lawyer was hospitalized for emergency surgery shortly before Slappy's trial for serious felonies was about to begin. The public defender assigned substitute counsel. On the first day of trial and thereafter, Slappy appeared to protest the change in counsel. There was no claim that the new lawyer was constitutionally ineffective. The trial judge made no effort to ascertain how long the first lawyer would be unavailable. After Slappy was convicted, the Ninth Circuit granted his petition for a writ of habeas corpus on the ground that the Sixth Amendment guaranteed Slappy not merely competent counsel but also "the right to a meaningful attorney-client relationship." The Supreme Court unanimously agreed that the issue had not been preserved for review because Slappy had not made a timely motion for a continuance and to be represented by the first lawyer. Five members of the Court, in an opinion by Chief Justice Burger, went on to consider the merits of Slappy's argument, which they rejected in one sentence: "No court could possibly guarantee that a defendant will develop the kind of rapport with his attorney — privately retained or provided by the public — that the Court of Appeals thought part of the Sixth Amendment guarantee of counsel." Justice Brennan, joined by Justice Marshall, dissented on the merits. Justices Blackmun and Stevens concurred in the judgment on the ground that the issue was not preserved.

In *Cronic*, Justice Stevens wrote that in response to a claim of ineffective assistance, "the appropriate inquiry focuses on the adversarial process, not on the accused's relationship with his lawyer as such. If counsel is a reasonably effective advocate, he meets constitutional standards irrespective of his client's evaluation of his performance. [Jones v. Barnes, page 57 supra, Morris v. Slappy.] It is for this reason that we attach no weight to either respondent's expression of satisfaction with counsel's performance at the time of his trial, or to his later expression of dissatisfaction." 466 U.S. at 657 n.21.

The Ineffectiveness Test in a System of Procedural Defaults

Recall that we initially posited an effectiveness standard for a *federal* system. Perhaps our system envisions federal judicial review of state convictions where the state defendant alleges a denial of federal constitutional rights. Call it a petition for a writ of habeas corpus. When we studied the lawyer's status as the client's agent in Chapter 2B, we discovered that a lawyer's decisions, even mistaken ones, will generally bind the client. This is the rule in criminal cases too, where a lawyer's failure to raise a defendant's constitutional claims in state court will generally constitute a procedural default that will prevent the defendant from later raising those claims in a federal collateral attack. This will be true even if counsel's failure was the product of "ignorance or inadvertence," Murray v. Carrier, 477 U.S. 478, 487 (1986), and the defendant was not responsible for it. "[T]he mere fact that counsel failed to recognize the factual or legal basis for a claim, or failed to raise the claim despite recognizing it, does not constitute cause for [excusing] a procedural default." Id. at 486.

A defendant will not, however, be bound by a lawyer's procedural default if the lawyer was constitutionally ineffective. So the harder it is to prove ineffectiveness, the more unforgiving will be the system of procedural defaults. How should that fact affect our articulation of the Sixth Amendment standard? Should it matter if the defense lawyer was retained or assigned? Should it matter if the case is a capital one? Cf. Coleman v. Thompson, 111 S. Ct. 2546 (1991) (federal habeas review foreclosed to death-row inmate where counsel filed state appeal from state collateral attack three days late; ineffective assistance claim rejected because defendant had no constitutional right to counsel on appeal from state collateral attack).

An Ounce of Prevention?

We conclude by returning to our final question posed at page 691: Especially in light of the last note, would it make sense to incorporate some preventive measures that will reduce the incidence of ineffectiveness? In

United States v. Decoster, 624 F.2d 196, 296-297 (D.C. Cir.), cert. denied, 444 U.S. 944 (1979) (en banc), Judge Bazelon, joined by Judge Wright, dissenting, proposed a more active role for the trial judge in criminal cases as a way of guarding against ineffective assistance of counsel. The majority characterized Judge Bazelon's suggestion as constituting a "drastic overhaul" and concluded that he had not "made a case" for it. Following is a portion of Judge Bazelon's lengthy dissent. What do you think of his proposal?

> Because, as this case demonstrates, ineffective representation is often rooted in inadequate preparation, a first step that a trial judge can take is to refuse to allow a trial to begin until he is assured that defense counsel has conducted the necessary factual and legal investigation. The simple question, "Is defense ready?" may be insufficient to provide that assurance. Instead, we should consider formalizing the procedure by which the trial judge is informed about the extent of counsel's preparation. Before the trial begins — or before a guilty plea is accepted — defense counsel could submit an investigative checklist certifying that he has conducted a complete investigation and reviewing the steps he has taken in pretrial preparation, including what records were obtained, which witnesses were interviewed, when the defendant was consulted, and what motions were filed. Although a worksheet alone cannot assure that adequate preparation is undertaken, it may reveal gross violations of counsel's obligations; at a minimum, it should heighten defense counsel's sensitivity to the need for adequate investigation and should provide a record of counsel's asserted actions for appeal.
>
> The trial judge's obligation does not end, however, with a determination that counsel is prepared for trial. Whenever during the course of the trial it appears that defense counsel is not properly fulfilling his obligations, the judge must take appropriate action to prevent the deprivation of the defendant's constitutional rights. "It is the judge, not counsel, who has the ultimate responsibility for the conduct of a fair and lawful trial."
>
> My colleagues fear that judicial "inquiry and standards [may] tear the fabric of [our] adversary system." But for so very many indigent defendants, the adversary system is already in shreds. Indeed, until judges are willing to take the steps necessary to guarantee the indigent defendant "the reasonably competent assistance of an attorney acting as his diligent conscientious advocate," we will have an adversary system in name only. The adversary system can "provide salutary protection for the rights of the accused" only if both sides are equally prepared for the courtroom confrontation.
>
> Some of my colleagues are also concerned that a wide-ranging inquiry into the conduct of defense counsel would transform the role of the trial judge. To emphasize the supposed hazards of such a result, the majority refers to the warning of Judge Prettyman in Mitchell v. United States [259 F.2d 787, cert. denied, 358 U.S. 850 (1958)]: "If the trial judge were required, after a trial has been concluded, to judge the validity of the trial by appraising defense decisions, he would also be under an obligation to pro-

tect those rights of an accused as the trial progressed." Yet this is the very role that the Constitution has assigned the trial judge. His is the ultimate responsibility for ensuring that the accused receives a fair trial, with all the attendant safeguards of the Bill of Rights. It is no answer to say that defense counsel will fulfill the function of protecting the accused's interest; the very essence of the defendant's complaint is that he has been denied effective assistance of counsel. The trial judge simply cannot "stand idly by while the fundamental rights of a criminal defendant are forfeited through the inaction of ill-prepared counsel."

624 F.2d at 296-298.

Judge Bazelon's recommendations have not found support in the Supreme Court. Justice O'Connor (page 694 supra) cites the ABA Standards for Criminal Justice, but eschews adoption of a "set of rules" for defense counsel, in part because they "would interfere with the constitutionally protected independence of counsel and restrict the wide latitude counsel must have in making tactical decisions." Justice O'Connor fears that such rules would also "distract counsel from the overriding mission of vigorous advocacy of the defendant's cause." Justice O'Connor cites the *Decoster* majority opinion. On the other hand, apprehension about intruding upon a defense lawyer's tactical judgments or her professional relationship with the accused disappear if after trial the defendant brings an ineffectiveness claim. Then, obviously, the professional relationship is over and the defendant is inviting the court to review counsel's conduct.

Is Justice O'Connor justified in her concerns? Would Judge Bazelon's inquiry unduly intrude on a defense lawyer's performance? Most criminal defendants are represented by appointed lawyers because they are unable to afford a lawyer. Consequently, they have no choice of counsel. They must accept whomever the state assigns unless they can convince a court that there is good reason for a change. See the dissent to Jones v. Barnes, page 60 supra. How, if at all, should this fact affect the analysis?

Systemic defects in the method of appointing lawyers to represent indigents as a group have, however, occasionally led to prophylactic judicial intervention on the ground that the defects were likely to result in inadequate representation. In an unusual case, State v. Smith, 140 Ariz. 355, 681 P.2d 1374 (1984), an Arizona county fulfilled its obligation to provide counsel to indigent defendants by requesting bids from all attorneys in the county. In 1982-1983, the county accepted the four lowest bidders (ranging from $24,000 to $34,400), each of whom was expected to handle one-quarter of the total caseload, without limit. Bids were accepted without regard to the background or capabilities of the bidding attorney. The costs of investigators, paralegals, secretaries, and the like were expected to be assumed by the bidding attorney. The Arizona Supreme Court held the system in violation of the state and federal Constitutions because it resulted in an attorney being "so overburdened [that he] cannot adequately represent all his clients properly and be reasonably effective." The court faulted the system because it "does not take into account the time that the attorney is expected to spend . . . does not provide for support costs [and] fails to take into account the competency of the attorney [and] the complexity of each case. . . . Even though in the instant case [this court does] not find inadequate representation, so long as the County . . . fails to take into account the items listed above, there will be an inference that the adequacy of representation is adversely affected by the system." See Comment, Quality Control for Indigent Defense Contracts, 76 Calif. L. Rev. 1147 (1980) (authored by Meredith Nelson); Note, (Un)Luckey v. Miller: The Case for a Structural Injunction to Improve Indigent Defense Services, 101 Yale L.J. 481 (1991) (authored by Rodger Citron).

Insofar as this opinion relies on the federal Constitution, does its reasoning survive Strickland v. Washington?

FURTHER READING

Professor Vivian Berger has written a thorough and critical analysis of the Supreme Court's work in this area, reviewing the cases discussed here and others. Vivian Berger, The Supreme Court and Defense Counsel: Old Roads, New Paths — A Dead End?, 86 Colum. L. Rev. 9 (1986). For the pre-*Strickland* views of a federal district judge, see William Schwarzer, Dealing with Incompetent Counsel — The Trial Judge's Role, 93 Harv. L. Rev. 633 (1980). Finally, two investigators, Professors Michael McConville and Chester Mirsky, have published a mammoth empirical study, unprecedented in scope, of the adequacy of representation of indigents in New York City. See Michael McConville & Chester Mirsky, Criminal Defense of the Poor in New York City, 15 N.Y.U. Rev. L. & Soc. Change 581 (1986-1987).

XIV

Control of Quality: Lay Participation in Law Firms and the Delivery of Legal Services*

Peter Waldman
**PRE-PAID LEGAL PLANS OFFER
CONSULTATIONS, FOLLOW-UP CALLS AND
REFERRALS AT LOW COST**
Wall St. J., Feb. 24, 1986, at 37

Suddenly, says I. A. Brown, "I have clout."

For the past three months, the retired merchant marine captain has talked with a lawyer twice a week by telephone, seeking advice on such matters as how to deal with the dry cleaner who shrank his sports jacket and what gives his savings and loan association the right to roll over a certificate of deposit without asking him.

Mr. Brown, who lives in Concord, Calif., is a participant in BankAmerica Corp.'s new "LawAmerica" program, a pre-paid legal-services plan available to the bank's credit-card holders in nine states. For $98 a year, he can make unlimited toll-free calls to attorneys who write letters and make phone calls on his behalf.

"People would have given me the shaft if I didn't have the attorneys," he says. "They always did."

Pre-paid legal plans are growing at an explosive rate. With the recent entry of BankAmerica and such other mass marketers as McKesson Corp. and Montgomery Ward & Co., the plans now cover some 12 mil-

*And a Look at Ancillary Businesses

709

lion people, up from just 1.5 million in 1978, according to Alec M. Schwartz of the Chicago-based American Prepaid Legal Services Institute. He expects the number to double in the next four years.

WORKING MIDDLE CLASS

"We're finally getting legal services to the working middle class," says Michael E. Kilpatrick, senior partner in James & Kilpatrick, the Sacramento, Calif., law firm that serves LawAmerica participants. "There's Legal Aid for the poor (and) private attorneys for the rich, but until now we never had anything for our own."

Typically, pre-paid legal-services plans provide unlimited phone consultations and follow-up letters or calls from attorneys. When more than that is required — as Mr. Kilpatrick says is true of about 12% of the cases handled by his firm — clients are usually referred to outside attorneys who charge an agreed fee of $50 to $70 an hour.

According to a 1977 American Bar Association survey, about 37% of the U.S. population encounters a legal problem in a year, but only 10% consults an attorney. In contrast, usage rates among participants in pre-paid programs are about 20%.

Advocates of the programs insist that pre-paid legal assistance doesn't make people more litigious. By giving participants an opportunity to consult with a lawyer before doing something like signing a contract, they say, the plans can minimize legal wrangles. Says Mr. Kilpatrick: "We're practicing preventive law."

But some lawyers and legal scholars worry that the plans may sacrifice quality for quantity. Murray L. Schwartz, professor of law at the University of California in Los Angeles, says that although telephone advice is suitable for "very, very simple questions," more complex matters could "slip through the cracks."

At the same time, the plans face a variety of state and professional regulatory constraints. In Ohio, for example, a Supreme Court disciplinary rule prohibits attorneys from collecting fees from third-party, profit-making companies, effectively precluding pre-paid legal providers outside the nonprofit sector.

Kentucky doesn't allow plans to specify certain eligible attorneys, and Alaska permits pre-paid programs only as an employee benefit. About half the states allow only casualty insurance companies to offer pre-paid legal plans.

Nonetheless, the plans have become highly popular, especially as an employee benefit. When the Dade County, Fla., school system first offered pre-paid legal services to its teachers in 1983 as part of a flexible benefits package, 52% chose the option; this year 77% signed on. The United Auto Workers, which runs its own pre-paid legal clinics near auto plants, provides the benefit to 870,000 workers.

Employers like the plans because, at less than $100 per employee, they are cheaper than other benefit options. Employees favor the plans not only because they provide access to helpful legal assistance, but also because, until this year at least, the benefit hasn't been taxed as income. (Congress allowed the plans' nontaxable status to expire in December, but is expected to renew it this spring.)

Many people have also signed up on their own. Sacramento-based Caldwell Pre-Paid Legal Ltd., one of the biggest providers in the industry with 300,000 clients, does 60% of its business with individual clients. Another 20% of Caldwell clients are small-business owners and managers who can buy a policy to cover business-related legal problems for $300 a year.

BankAmerica says it mailed out more than a million solicitations for its plan last September and received inquiries from over 3% — a response rate that a bank spokesman characterizes as "overwhelming." Meanwhile, McKesson of San Francisco is pitching its "Lawphone" plan to a mass market through its Pharmaceutical Card System unit, a processor of third-party prescription-drug claims for the insurance industry. And Montgomery Ward is offering pre-paid legal services in a mass-marketing campaign through its Chicago-based Signature Group.

LEARNING COURTESY

The most common customer complaints, according to companies selling the services, are about difficulties in reaching attorneys, delays in getting follow-up calls or letters and brusque responses. Don Caldwell, president of Caldwell Pre-paid Legal Ltd., says his 19-person administrative staff spends a lot of time working with branch firms training employees to be more polite. "Many people have only had adversarial experience with attorneys before," he said. "We have to be pleasant."

Indeed, a major beneficiary of the pre-paid plans may be the legal profession's image. Capt. Brown, who received a new jacket from the dry cleaner after his lawyer sent a stern letter, thinks so. "Those damn attorneys have been making things so difficult, you have to have legal aid just to get along these days," he says. "But I've had nothing but satisfaction."

Blurring the Lines: Nonlawyers in the Law "Business" and Vice Versa

In the mid-1920s, a group of people in Illinois organized the Motorists' Association of Illinois as a not-for-profit corporation. The association hired a staff of lawyers. The only work of the lawyers was to represent the 50,000 members of the association, without charge, in connection with certain court proceedings arising out of the operation of their automobiles. The members of the association paid an annual membership fee. The Chicago Bar Association did not like this arrangement. (Why not?). It petitioned the court to forbid the motorists' group from continuing in business. The bar association contended that the motorists' group was practicing law without a license. True, the lawyers themselves were licensed to practice law, but they were working for the association. The motorists' association, which was providing legal services to its membership, was not licensed to practice law and so allegedly was in violation of the unauthorized practice statute. The Illinois Supreme Court agreed. Not only did it hold that the motorists' association was practicing law without a license, but it went even further. It held that the state legislature was without power to allow the association to do so, since only the court could decide who was, and who was not, fit to engage in the practice of law. People ex rel. Chicago Bar Assn. v. Motorists' Assn. of Illinois, 354 Ill. 595, 188 N.E. 827 (1933). See discussion of the negative inherent powers doctrine, page 2 supra.

From an economic point of view, tolerance for group practice plans will likely affect the cost of legal services. If a hundred consumers interested in purchasing televisions offered to make all purchases from a single retailer, they would be able to command a lower price than if each walked in separately. Group purchasing power should also work where the product is legal services. By hiring a relatively small number of attorneys on salary, the Illinois motorists could have reduced the cost of representation from what each might have had to pay had each been required to retain a private practitioner on his or her own.

Although the material in this chapter is sometimes analyzed as raising "unauthorized practice" issues, in fact these issues are quite different from those present in the material on unauthorized practice at page 597 supra. The earlier material addressed competency risks that arise when persons who are not members of a state's bar perform work labeled the "practice of law." (Whether the work should be so labeled is a separate question.) By contrast, in the following pages we shall discuss legal work performed by lawyers admitted in the particular jurisdiction. There is no competency problem. But the lawyer will be working with, through, or under an entity or person not qualified to practice law. In other words, the *vehicle* through which the legal service is delivered allegedly invites concern about its quality. Why should that be? What difference does it make if it is a traditional law partnership (or, lately, professional corporation or association) furnishing the lawyer in contrast to some other kind of entity?

In reading this chapter, ask yourself whether the prohibitions on lay managerial or ownership authority in the delivery of legal services are justified by the apprehensions of conflict of interest that inform them. How great a risk do such conflicts pose? Why isn't the risk as great when the owners or managers of a law firm are lawyers? Ask whether in other contexts we tolerate equivalent risks of conflict between the interests of lay intermediaries and the interests of clients. Consider, for example, the position of a corporation's house counsel who reports to a vice-president for administration. (See page 458 supra.) Conflicts aside, what risks to the confidentiality of client information does lay management or ownership present?

Efforts to provide legal help through entities that are not themselves law firms, and are dominated by laypeople, take several forms. Variables include whether lawyers are provided from an open panel or a closed panel, as discussed below; whether the lawyers are employed by the entity, as in the Motorists' Association, or retained by it, as when an insurance company retains a firm to defend an insured (see page 239 supra); and whether the entity's motive is political (section A1), cost-sharing (section A2), or profit-making (section B). Conflict risks will vary with the lay intermediary's motives, won't they? So, too, as we shall see, will the degree of constitutional protection.

Lines blur in two directions. Not only may nonlawyers own or run organizations that sell legal services (whether called "firms" or something else), but lawyers may seek to expand into areas that are, strictly speaking, not the practice of law. Blurred lines can disturb one's tranquility and sense of (professional) identity. Lately, some perceive threats to professionalism if law firms are permitted to offer services that are "ancillary" to the practice of law. These threats are said to increase if the services are tendered in association with nonlawyers. For example, a law firm may offer clients and others legislative lobbying or economic forecasting services, either directly or through a separate business that the firm may co-own with lobbyists or economists. Section C examines whether dangers that supposedly inhere when nonlawyers dominate law firms resurface if lawyers market ancillary services, whether or not in affiliation with other professionals.

Legislative History

The Code of Professional Responsibility contains the first effort to deal with the subject of group legal services in a significant way. A draft of the code permitted a lawyer to participate in group legal services sponsored by a "professional association, trade association, labor union, or other bona fide, non-profit organization which, as an incident to its primary activities, furnishes, pays for, or recommends legal services furnished to its members or beneficiaries." In 1969, the ABA House of Delegates rejected the draft as too liberal. The final text permitted lawyers to participate in group legal services sponsored by a "non-profit organization . . . but only in those instances and to the extent that controlling constitutional interpretation at the time of the rendition of the services requires the allowance of such legal service activities, and only if [additional] conditions, unless prohibited by such interpretations, are met."

This conclusion, reached after the decisions in NAACP v. Button, *Trainmen*, and *UMW* (all infra), reveals that the organized bar was prepared to approve group practice only so far as the Constitution protected it.

Efforts were made to liberalize the restriction. In 1974, a more permissive provision was passed and the text of DR 2-103(D)(4) appeared in its present form. Early drafts of this rule had prohibited what have come to be known as "closed panel plans." These are plans under which a small number of lawyers, generally employed on a salary basis by the plan, are available to the beneficiaries of the plan. By contrast, an "open panel plan" is one in which the plan pays all or part of the fees of independent counsel selected by the beneficiary of the plan from a large or the entire pool of practicing lawyers. Closed panel plans, like the one attempted by the Motorists' Association of Illinois, tend to make legal services cheaper than open panel plans. Do you see why? DR 2-103(D)(4)(a) as adopted allows closed panel plans but only if they are not for profit. But subsection (e) requires that such plans provide that a beneficiary be able to hire an outside lawyer if he or she "so desires." The plan must also provide the beneficiary with "appropriate relief" if the beneficiary decides to choose other counsel because representation by the plan's counsel "would be unethical, improper or inadequate under the circumstances." These encumbrances, especially given their ambiguities, made group plans more difficult.

Many believe that the success of group legal services depends on the ability to use closed panel plans. Many lawyers argue against closed panel plans not, they maintain, because of the impact on fees or number of clients, but rather because it is important for a client to be able to select his or her own lawyer, whose allegiance and loyalty is solely to the client and not to the operators of the plan. (Can't a plan member do that anyway?) DR 2-103(D)(4)(e) represents a vague compromise between these opposing views. For an article tracing the history of the development of this disciplinary rule, see Note, Prepaid Legal Plans: A Glimpse of the Future, 47 Tenn. L. Rev. 148 (1979) (authored by Pamela Reeves).

In addition to DR 2-103(D)(4), separate provisions of the Model Code affect group legal practice by forbidding a lawyer to aid in the unauthorized practice of law (including by an organization), to divide a legal fee with a "non-lawyer," or to form a partnership with a "non-lawyer." DR 3-101. Presumably, DR 3-101 will not be violated by a lawyer's affiliation with an organization that meets the requirements of DR 2-103(D)(4).

The Rules of Professional Conduct have a separate history. There is no direct equivalent to DR 2-103(D)(4). For a time, early drafts of the Model Rules lacked any direct equivalent to DR 3-101. Notably, the January 1980 draft of the Model Rules provided as follows:

7.5 A lawyer shall not practice with a firm in which an interest is owned or managerial authority is exercised by a nonlawyer, unless services can be rendered in conformity with the Rules of Professional Conduct. The terms of the relationship shall expressly provide that (a) there is no interference with the lawyer's independence of professional judgment or with the client-lawyer relationship; and (b) the confidences of clients are protected. . . .

The June 1982 draft of the Model Rules continued this language substantially unchanged. But the Model Rules, as finally adopted, dropped it, and while there is still no direct equivalent to DR 2-103(D)(4), most of DR 3-101 is now contained in Model Rules 5.4 and 5.5. See also DR 5-107, incorporated in part in Rule 5.4. What legitimate interest of the bar is served by provisions like Rules 5.4 and 5.5? What are the economic consequences of these rules, whether or not intended?

With regard to the last question, what do you make of the following? Professor Geoffrey C. Hazard, Jr., who was the reporter for the Kutak Commission (see page 3 supra), described how it came to pass that Proposed Rule 7.5 was dropped from the Model Rules pretty much on the eve of their adoption. "During the debate," he reported, "someone asked if your proposal would allow Sears, Roebuck to open a law office. When they found out it would, that was the end of the debate." David Kaplan, Want to Invest in a Law Firm?, Natl. L.J., Jan. 19, 1987, at 28. Yet do the Rules as adopted effectively exclude Sears? Consider this question after reading ABA Opinion 87-355 (page 731 infra). It may indeed be that under the Model Rules lay participation in legal delivery systems, whether or not for profit, is permitted so long as the organizers do not make the strictly formal error of calling their business a law firm or a professional corporation.

The legislative history on lawyer-owned ancillary businesses can be stated in a word: Zero. Neither the code nor rules anticipated the issue as such. Why not? It depends on whom you ask. Some say it's because there's no issue there, that the purported threats are imaginary. Others say it's because large numbers of firms have entered the ancillary market only recently.

A. NONPROFIT ENTITIES AND INTERMEDIARIES

1. Public Interest Organizations

NAACP v. BUTTON
371 U.S. 415 (1963)

[The NAACP sought to enjoin enforcement of certain Virginia laws, including Chapter 33. The NAACP's Virginia chapter had for over 10 years "concentrated upon financing litigation aimed at ending racial segregation in the public schools of the Commonwealth." To this end, the association provided attorneys, whom it paid, to represent litigants challenging segregated schooling. "The actual conduct of assisted litigation is under the control of the attorney, although the NAACP continues to be concerned that the outcome of the lawsuit should be consistent with NAACP's policies. . . . A client is free at any time to withdraw from an action."

In 1956, the Virginia legislature passed certain laws that would have made it more difficult for the NAACP to represent school desegregation plaintiffs. A federal court invalidated three chapters of these laws and ordered the NAACP to go to state court for authoritative interpretations of two remaining chapters. The state courts voided one of these chapters but upheld Chapter 33, which prohibited solicitation by "an agent for an individual or an organization which retains a lawyer in connection with an action to which it is not a party and in which it has no pecuniary right or liability." The Virginia Supreme Court of Appeals held that this amendment prohibited the NAACP's agents from soliciting persons to serve as plaintiffs in challenges to segregated education. The Supreme Court granted review.]

JUSTICE BRENNAN delivered the opinion of the Court. . . .

II . . .

A

We meet at the outset the contention that "solicitation" is wholly outside the area of freedoms protected by the First Amendment. To this contention there are two answers. The first is that a State cannot foreclose the exercise of constitutional rights by mere labels. The second is that abstract discussion is not the only species of communication which the Constitution protects; the First Amendment also protects vigorous advocacy, certainly of lawful ends, against governmental intrusion. In the context of NAACP objectives, litigation is not a technique of resolving private differences; it is a means for achieving the lawful objectives of equality of treatment by all government, federal, state and local, for the members of the Negro community in this country. It is thus a form of political expression. Groups which find themselves unable to achieve their objectives through the ballot frequently turn to the courts. . . . And under the conditions of modern government, litigation may well be the sole practicable avenue open to a minority to petition for redress of grievances.

We need not, in order to find constitutional protection for the kind of cooperative, organizational activity disclosed by this record, whereby Negroes seek through lawful means to achieve legitimate political ends, subsume such activity under a narrow, literal conception of freedom of speech, petition or assembly. For there is no longer any doubt that the First and Fourteenth Amendments protect certain forms of orderly group activity. . . .

The NAACP is not a conventional political party; but the litigation it assists, while serving to vindicate the legal rights of members of the American Negro community, at the same time and perhaps more importantly, makes possible the distinctive contribution of a minority group to the ideas and beliefs of our society. For such a group, association for litigation may be the most effective form of political association.

B . . .

We read the decree of the Virginia Supreme Court of Appeals in the instant case as proscribing any arrangement by which prospective litigants are advised to seek the assistance of particular attorneys. No narrower reading is plausible. We cannot accept the reading suggested on behalf of the Attorney General of Virginia on the second oral argument that the Supreme Court of Appeals construed Chapter 33 as proscribing control only of the actual litigation by the NAACP after it is instituted. . . .

We conclude that under Chapter 33, as authoritatively construed by the Supreme Court of Appeals, a person who advises another that his legal rights have been infringed and refers him to a particular attorney or group of attorneys (for example, to the Virginia Conference's legal staff) for assistance has committed a crime, as has the attorney who knowingly renders assistance under such circumstances. There thus inheres in the statute the gravest danger of smothering all discussion looking to the eventual institution of litigation on behalf of the rights of members of an unpopular minority. . . . We cannot close our eyes to the fact that the militant Negro civil rights movement has engendered the intense resentment and opposition of the politically dominant white community of Virginia; litigation assisted by the NAACP has been bitterly fought. In such circumstances, a statute broadly curtailing group activity leading to litigation may easily become a weapon of oppression, however evenhanded its terms appear. Its mere existence could well freeze out of existence all such activity on behalf of the civil rights of Negro citizens. . . .

We hold that Chapter 33 as construed violates the Fourteenth Amendment by unduly inhibiting protected freedoms of expression and association. In so holding, we reject two further contentions of respondents. The first is that the Virginia Supreme Court of Appeals has guaranteed free expression by expressly confirming petitioner's right to continue its advocacy of civil-rights litigation. But in light of the whole decree of the court, the guarantee is of purely speculative value. As construed by the Court, Chapter 33, at least potentially, prohibits every cooperative activity that would make advocacy of litigation meaningful. If there is an internal tension between proscription and protection in the statute, we cannot assume that, in its subsequent enforcement, ambiguities will be resolved in favor of adequate protection of First Amendment rights. . . .

C

The second contention is that Virginia has a subordinating interest in the regulation of the legal profession, embodied in Chapter 33, which justifies limiting petitioner's First Amendment rights. Specifically, Virginia contends that the NAACP's activities in furtherance of litigation, being "improper solicitation" under the state statute, fall within the traditional purview of state regulation of professional conduct. However, the State's attempt to equate the activities of the NAACP and its lawyers with common-law barratry, maintenance and champerty, and to outlaw them accordingly, cannot obscure the serious encroachment worked by Chapter 33 upon protected freedoms of expression. The decisions of this Court have consistently held that only a compelling state interest in the regulation of a subject within the State's constitutional power to regulate can justify limiting First Amendment freedoms. . . .

However valid may be Virginia's interest in regulating the traditionally illegal practices of barratry, maintenance and champerty, that interest does not justify the prohibition of the NAACP activities disclosed by this record. Malicious intent was of the essence of the common-law offenses of fomenting or stirring up litigation. And whatever may be or may have been true of suits against government in other countries, the exercise in our own, as in this case, of First Amendment rights to enforce constitutional rights through litigation, as a matter of law, cannot be deemed malicious. Even more modern, subtler regulations of unprofessional conduct or interference with professional relations, not involving malice, would not touch the activities at bar; regulations which reflect hostility to stirring up litigation have been aimed chiefly at those who urge recourse to the courts for private gain, serving no public interest. . . .

Objection to the intervention of a lay intermediary, who may control litigation or otherwise interfere with the rendering of legal services in a confidential relationship, also derives from the element of pecuniary gain. Fearful of dangers thought to arise from that element, the courts of several States have sustained regulations aimed at these activities. We intimate no view one way or the other as to the merits of those decisions with respect to the particular arrangements against which they are directed. It is enough that the superficial resemblance in form between those arrangements and that at bar cannot obscure the vital fact that here the entire arrangement employs constitutionally privileged means of expression to secure constitutionally guaranteed civil rights.[26] There has been no showing of a serious danger here of professionally reprehensible conflicts of interest which rules against solicitation frequently seek to prevent. This is so partly because no monetary stakes are involved, and so there is no danger that the attorney will desert or subvert the paramount interests of his client to enrich himself or an outside sponsor. And the aims and interests of NAACP have not been shown to conflict with those of its members and nonmember Negro litigants. . . .

Resort to the courts to seek vindication of constitutional rights is a different matter from the oppressive, malicious, or avaricious use of the legal process for purely private gain. Lawsuits attacking racial discrimination, at least in Virginia, are neither very profitable nor very popular. They are not an object of general competition among Virginia lawyers; the problem is rather one of an apparent dearth of lawyers who are willing to undertake such litigation. There has been neither claim nor proof that any assisted Negro litigants have desired, but have been prevented from retaining, the services of other counsel. We realize that an NAACP lawyer must derive personal satisfaction from participation in litigation on behalf of Negro rights, else he would hardly be inclined to participate at the risk of financial sacrifice. But this would not seem to be the kind of interest or motive which induces criminal conduct.

We conclude that although the petitioner has amply shown that its activities fall within the First Amendment's protections, the State has failed to advance any substantial regulatory interest, in the form of substantive evils flowing from petitioner's activities, which can justify the broad prohibitions which it has imposed. . . .

Reversed.

[JUSTICE DOUGLAS concurred. JUSTICE WHITE concurred in part and dissented in part.]

[JUSTICE HARLAN, joined by JUSTICES CLARK and STEWART, dissented.]

I

At the outset the factual premises on which the Virginia Supreme Court of Appeals upheld the application of Chapter 33 to the activities of the NAACP in the area of litigation, as well as the scope of that court's holding, should be delineated.

---

26. Compare Opinion 148, supra, nn.13, 19, at 312 (1957): "The question presented, with its implications, involves problems of political, social and economic character that have long since assumed the proportions of national issues, on one side or the other [of] which multitudes of patriotic citizens have aligned themselves. These issues transcend the range of professional ethics."

First, the lawyers who participate in litigation sponsored by petitioner are, almost without exception, members of the legal staff of the NAACP Virginia State Conference. (It is, in fact, against Conference policy to give financial support to litigation not handled by a staff lawyer.) As such, they are selected by petitioner, are compensated by it for work in litigation (whether or not petitioner is a party thereto), and so long as they remain on the staff, are necessarily subject to its directions. As the Court recognizes, it is incumbent on staff members to agree to abide by NAACP policies.

Second, it is equally clear that the NAACP's directions, or those of its officers and divisions, to staff lawyers cover many subjects relating to the form and substance of litigation. . . .

In short, as these and other materials in the record show, the form of pleading, the type of relief to be requested, and the proper timing of suits have to a considerable extent, if not entirely, been determined by the Conference in coordination with the national office.

Third, . . . the present record establishes that the petitioner does a great deal more than to advocate litigation and to wait for prospective litigants to come forward. In several instances, especially in litigation touching racial discrimination in public schools, specific directions were given as to the types of prospective plaintiffs to be sought, and staff lawyers brought blank forms to meetings for the purpose of obtaining signatures authorizing the prosecution of litigation in the name of the signer.

Fourth, there is substantial evidence indicating that the normal incidents of the attorney-client relationship were often absent in litigation handled by staff lawyers and financed by petitioner. Forms signed by prospective litigants have on occasion not contained the name of the attorney authorized to act. In many cases, whether or not the form contained specific authorization to that effect, additional counsel have been brought into the action by staff counsel. There were several litigants who testified that at no time did they have any personal dealings with the lawyers handling their cases nor were they aware until long after the event that suits had been filed in their names. This is not to suggest that the petitioner has been shown to have sought plaintiffs under false pretenses or by inaccurate statements. But there is no basis for concluding that these were isolated incidents, or that petitioner's methods of operation have been such as to render these happenings out of the ordinary. . . .

III

The interest which Virginia has here asserted is that of maintaining high professional standards among those who practice law within its borders. This Court has consistently recognized the broad range of judgments that a State may properly make in regulating any profession. But the regulation of professional standards for members of the bar comes to us with even deeper roots in history and policy, since courts for centuries have possessed disciplinary powers incident to the administration of justice.

The regulation before us has its origins in the long-standing common-law prohibitions of champerty, barratry, and maintenance, the closely related prohibitions in the Canons of Ethics against solicitation and intervention by a lay intermediary, and statutory provisions forbidding the unauthorized practice of law. The Court recognizes this formidable history, but puts it aside in the present case on the grounds that there is here no element of malice or of pecuniary gain, that the interests of the NAACP are not to be regarded as substantially different from those of its members, and that we are said to be dealing here with a matter that transcends mere legal ethics — the securing of federally guaranteed rights. But these distinctions are too facile. They do not account for the full scope of the State's legitimate interest in regulating professional conduct. For although these professional standards may have been born in a desire to curb malice and self-aggrandizement by those who would use clients and the courts for their own pecuniary ends, they have acquired a far broader significance during their long development.

First, with regard to the claimed absence of the pecuniary element, it cannot well be suggested that the attorneys here are donating their services, since they are in fact compensated for their work. Nor can it tenably be argued that petitioner's litigating activities fall into the accepted category of aid to indigent litigants. The reference is presumably to the fact that petitioner itself is a nonprofit organization not motivated by desire for financial gain but by public interest and to the fact that no monetary stakes are involved in the litigation.

But a State's felt need for regulation of professional conduct may reasonably extend beyond mere "ambulance chasing." . . .

Underlying this impressive array of relevant precedent is the widely shared conviction that avoidance of improper pecuniary gain is not the only relevant factor in determining standards of professional conduct. Running perhaps even deeper is the desire of the profession, of courts, and of legislatures to prevent any interference with the uniquely personal relationship between lawyer and client and to maintain untrammeled by outside influences the responsibility which the lawyer owes to the courts he serves.

When an attorney is employed by an association or corporation to represent individual litigants, two problems arise, whether or not the association is organized for profit and no matter how unimpeachable its motives. The lawyer becomes subject to the control of a body that is not itself a litigant and that, unlike the lawyers it employs, is not subject to strict professional discipline as an officer of the court. In addition, the lawyer necessarily finds himself with a divided allegiance — to his employer and to his client — which may prevent full compliance with his basic professional obligations. . . .

Second, it is claimed that the interests of petitioner and its members are sufficiently identical to eliminate any "serious danger" of "professionally reprehensible conflicts of interest." Support for this claim is sought in our procedural holding in NAACP v. Alabama ex rel. Patterson, 357 U.S. 449, 458-459. But from recognizing, as in that case, that the NAACP has standing to assert the rights of its members when it is a real party in interest, it is plainly too large a jump to conclude that whenever individuals are engaged in litigation involving claims that the organization promotes, there cannot be any significant difference between the interests of the individual and those of the group.

The NAACP may be no more than the sum of the efforts and views infused in it by its members; but the totality of the separate interests of the members and others whose causes the petitioner champions, even in the field of race relations, may far exceed in scope and variety that body's views of policy, as embodied in litigating strategy and tactics. Thus it may be in the interest of the Association in every case to make a frontal attack on segregation, to press for an immediate breaking down of racial barriers, and to sacrifice minor points that may win a given case for the major points that may win other cases too. But in a particular litigation, it is not impossible that after authorizing action in his behalf, a Negro parent, concerned that a continued frontal attack could result in schools closed for years, might prefer to wait with his fellows a longer time for good-faith efforts by the local school board than is permitted by the centrally determined policy of the NAACP. Or he might see a greater prospect of success through discussions with local school authorities than through the litigation deemed necessary by the Association. The parent, of course, is free to withdraw his authorization, but is his lawyer, retained and paid by petitioner and subject to its directions on matters of policy, able to advise the parent with that undivided allegiance that is the hallmark of the attorney-client relation? I am afraid not. . . .

Third, it is said that the practices involved here must stand on a different footing because the litigation that petitioner supports concerns the vindication of constitutionally guaranteed rights.[12]

But surely state law is still the source of basic regulation of the legal profession, whether an attorney is pressing a federal or a state claim

---

12. It is interesting to note the Court's reliance on Opinion 148, Opinions of the Committee on Professional Ethics and Grievances, American Bar Assn. This opinion, issued in 1935 at the height of the resentment in certain quarters against the New Deal, approved the practice of the National Lawyers Committee of the Liberty League in publicly offering free legal services (without compensation from any source) to anyone who was *unable to afford* to challenge the constitutionality of legislation which he believed was violating his rights. The opinion may well be debatable as a matter of interpretation of the Canons. But in any event I think it wholly untenable to suggest (as the Court does in its holding today) that a contrary opinion regarding *paid* legal services to *nonindigent* litigants would be unconstitutional.

within its borders. The true question is whether the State has taken action which unreasonably obstructs the assertion of federal rights. Here, it cannot be said that the underlying state policy is inevitably inconsistent with federal interests. The State has sought to prohibit the solicitation and sponsoring of litigation by those who have no standing to initiate that litigation themselves and who are not simply coming to the assistance of indigent litigants. Thus the state policy is not unrelated to the federal rules of standing — the insistence that federal court litigants be confined to those who can demonstrate a pressing personal need for relief.

Maintenance, Barratry, Champerty, and Change

Virginia argued that its regulation was a traditional effort to prevent the kinds of evils condemned by the common law offenses of barratry, champerty and maintenance. Maintenance, according to Lord Denning, is "improperly stirring up litigation and strife by giving aid to one party to bring or defend a claim without just cause or excuse." In re Trepca Mines, Ltd. [1962] 3 All E.R. 351 (C.A.). A person lacked just cause, according to the *Button* majority, if he had "malicious intent," which in turn was absent if the maintaining party's motives were charitable. "Champerty is simply a specialized form of maintenance in which the person assisting another's litigation becomes an interested investor because of a promise by the assisted person to repay the investor with a share of the recovery. Barratry is adjudicative cheerleading — urging others, frequently, to quarrels and suits." Charles Wolfram, Modern Legal Ethics 490 (1986). See also page 162 supra on syndicating lawsuits. Much of what we shall see in Chapter 16 and will see in this chapter is constitutional suspicion of these common law offenses when they appear to interfere with interests protected by the First and Fourteenth Amendments. Certainly, maintenance and its cousins can be used to stifle the flow of information. So also can they make it harder for some groups to bring their grievances to court. The question in *Button* and other cases was whether some superior state interest will justify these consequences.

When *Button* reached the Supreme Court, the single remaining issue was whether Virginia could prohibit the NAACP from using agents to solicit plaintiffs whom NAACP staff lawyers would then represent in school desegregation cases. But neither the majority opinion nor the dissent was able to avoid a larger question: May NAACP staff lawyers be stopped from representing plaintiffs in these cases, however the plaintiffs happen to have sought the aid of the organization?

Both opinions identify the state's interest as avoidance of conflicts between the interests of the lawyers' employer (the NAACP) and the interests of their clients. But the majority and dissent disagree about the likelihood of actual conflict. The opinions also disagree about the scope of constitutional protection for the arrangement. Finally, the opinions disagree about motives — Virginia's and the NAACP's. Should motive be a consideration in either event?

The majority believes that Virginia is motivated by hostility to desegregation lawsuits, doesn't it? How does it know that? The dissent, by contrast, accepts Virginia's claim that all it wants to do is maintain "high professional standards among those who practice law within its borders." Chapter 33 was, after all, not unlike antisolicitation provisions in many jurisdictions. As for the NAACP's motives, the fact that they were not pecuniary influenced Justice Brennan to conclude that there was small risk of an actual conflict between the client and the NAACP as sponsor of the action. Justice Harlan was not as impressed by the absence of a pecuniary motive. He is right, isn't he? Doesn't history teach us that political motives can be as strong an influence on actions as financial ones? Even so, can we nevertheless defend *Button* on the ground that the Constitution is more protective of political motives than commercial ones? (This question arises again in the solicitation material at page 785 infra.)

It will not always be possible to distinguish the pecuniary from the political. Fee-shifting statutes like 42 U.S.C. §1988, which came into being after *Button*, raise the prospect that today a politically motivated sponsor of litigation will also hope to be the beneficiary of sizeable court-ordered fees. It may even count on the fee to survive. Does that change the constitutional balance?

At least one recent case has said that it does. ACLU/Eastern Missouri Fund v. Miller, 803 S.W.2d 592 (Mo. 1991), cert. denied, 111 S. Ct. 2239 (1991), was an action between an ACLU chapter and one of its (former) staff lawyers over who would get to keep a legal fee a federal judge had awarded in an action sponsored by the ACLU and handled by the staff lawyer. The plaintiff in the federal case had assigned the fee to the ACLU. When the staff lawyer pocketed the money, the ACLU sued him in state court. The Missouri Supreme Court rejected the Union's First Amendment claim, distinguishing *Button*. It held instead that a state law prohibiting lawyers from sharing legal fees with lay persons prevented the ACLU from receiving the money. *Miller* did not address the Supremacy Clause issue — i.e., whether §1988 superseded state law — but only the constitutional one — i.e., whether the fee-splitting ban violated the First Amendment rights of the ACLU on these facts. Other courts have looked for a middle ground. Jordan v. United States Department of Justice, 691 F.2d 514, 517 n.15 (D.C. Cir. 1982), held that a law school legal clinic could receive attorneys' fees if it placed any recovery beyond its expenses in "a fund exclusively for litigation." National Treasury Employees Union v. United States Department of Treasury, 656 F.2d 848, 855 (D.C. Cir. 1981), held that court-ordered fees could not be paid to a union that sponsored litigation. But it left open the possibility of a different result if the money were paid into a fund for "a legal service program." See generally on these issues Roy Simon's careful sifting of the interests in Fee Sharing Between Lawyers and Public Interest Groups, 98 Yale L.J. 1069 (1989).

This issue could not arise in a state like New York. Section 495(1) of the New York Judiciary Law provides that no corporation or voluntary association shall "practice or appear as an attorney-at-law for any person in any court in this state or before any judicial body, nor . . . furnish attorneys or counsel, nor . . . render legal services of any kind . . . nor . . . assume in any other manner to be entitled to practice law." Before 1979, subsection 5 allowed the four intermediate appellate courts in the state to exempt organizations formed for "benevolent or charitable purposes." In In re Thom (Lambda Legal Defense & Education Fund), 33 N.Y.2d 609, 301 N.E.2d 542, 543, 347 N.Y.S.2d 571 (1973), and Feinstein v. Attorney-General, 36 N.Y.2d 199, 326 N.E.2d 288, 291, 366 N.Y.S.2d 613 (1975), the New York Court of Appeals, interpreting subsection 5 narrowly, limited the discretion of the intermediate appellate courts to deny an exemption. In 1979, the state legislature amended the statute to withdraw all judicial discretion to pass on the kind of plans involved in *Thom* and *Feinstein*. A new subsection 7 provides:

> This section does not apply to organizations which offer prepaid legal services; to non-profit organizations whether incorporated or unincorporated, organized and operating primarily for a purpose other than the provision of legal services and which furnish legal services as an incidental activity in furtherance of their primary purpose; or to organizations which have as their primary purpose the furnishing of legal services to indigent persons.

2. Labor Unions

The second significant "lay intermediary" between lawyers and clients are labor unions. They too had to struggle to earn the constitutional right to assist their members in gaining low-cost legal aid. Several distinctions between unions and organizations such as the NAACP and the ACLU should be noted. First, unions are seeking to provide lawyers for their members whereas the NAACP in *Button* was offering legal help to outsiders. Second, the underlying legal claims of union members have been prosaic — mainly workers' compensation or disability claims — unlike the constitutional rights the NAACP and ACLU try to vindicate. Third, a prime goal of union plans has been to keep down the cost of pursuing a member's claim, not to win judicial recognition for the claim in the first place.

A year after *Button*, the Supreme Court decided Brotherhood of Railroad Trainmen v. Virginia ex rel. Virginia State Bar, 377 U.S. 1, 5

(1964). The Brotherhood's Department of Legal Counsel advised injured members not to settle claims without consulting counsel. The Department also recommended particular counsel whom the union believed were "legally and morally competent to handle injury claims for members." Counsel were recommended based on a plan which divided the country into 16 regions. The union president designated a firm in each region, which the president could also remove from the plan. The Brotherhood would recommend that an injured member retain the firm designated for the particular region. The Virginia court enjoined this practice.

The Supreme Court, in an opinion by Justice Black, held that "the First and Fourteenth Amendments protect the right of the members through their Brotherhood to maintain and carry out their plan for advising workers who are injured to obtain legal advice and for recommending specific lawyers. . . . And, of course, lawyers accepting employment under this constitutionally protected plan have a like protection which the State cannot abridge." Id. at 8. Justice Stewart did not participate. Justice Clark, joined by Justice Harlan, dissented. Justice Clark pointed to the 25 percent kickbacks designated lawyers had been required to give the union until 1959. He doubted that the union had "sincerely reformed," but, even if it had, he anticipated that the Court's opinion would "encourage further departures from the high standards set by canons of ethics . . . and will be a green light to other groups who for years have attempted to engage in similar practices." Distinguishing *Button*, he wrote that "[p]ersonal injury litigation is not a form of political expression." Id. at 10-11.

After the *Trainmen* decision, 48 bar associations joined the ABA in an unsuccessful motion for rehearing. Note, Group Legal Services and the Organized Bar, 10 Colum. J.L. & Soc. Probs. 228, 251 (1974) (authored by Norman Riedmueller).

That was chapter one in this story. Three years later, the Court decided United Mine Workers of America, District 12 v. Illinois State Bar Assn., 389 U.S. 217, 223 (1967). The Mine Workers union had raised the pecuniary stakes substantially. It employed a lawyer on a salary basis to handle members' workers' compensation claims before a state commission. (Union members formerly had retained individual counsel and paid 40 or 50 percent of their recoveries in attorneys' fees.) Again Justice Black reversed a lower court opinion enjoining the practice. Citing the First Amendment, *Button* and *Trainmen*, he wrote: "The litigation in question is, of course, not bound up with political matters of acute social moment . . . but the First Amendment does not protect speech and assembly only to the extent it can be characterized as political." The Court held that it was of no consequence that the rights at issue in *Trainmen* were created by Congress, while those in the present case were created by the state.

Justice Harlan dissented:

> This union plan contains features which, in my opinion, Illinois may reasonably consider to present the danger of lowering the quality of representation furnished by the attorney to union members in the handling of their claims. The union lawyer has little contact with his client. He processes the applications of injured members on a mass basis. Evidently, he negotiates with the employer's counsel about many claims at the same time. The State was entitled to conclude that, removed from ready contact with his client, insulated from interference by his actual employer, paid a salary independent of the results achieved, faced with a heavy caseload, and very possibly with other activities competing for his time, the attorney will be tempted to place undue emphasis upon quick disposition of each case. Conceivably, the desire to process forms rapidly might influence the lawyer not to check with his client regarding ambiguities or omissions in the form, or to miss facts and circumstances which face-to-face consultation with his client would have brought to light. He might be led, so the State might consider, to compromise cases for reasons unrelated to their own intrinsic merits, such as the need to "get on" with negotiations or a promise by the employer's attorney of concessions relating to other cases. The desire for quick disposition also might cause the attorney to forgo appeals in some cases in which the amount awarded seemed unusually low.

Id. at 231-232.

The final chapter (so far) was written in 1971. Justice Black's impatience with state efforts to obstruct the full reach of his earlier opinions is apparent in the following case. (After the three union cases, what do you think of the validity of the *Motorists'* case (page 711 supra)?)

UNITED TRANSPORTATION UNION v. STATE BAR OF MICHIGAN
401 U.S. 576 (1971)

JUSTICE BLACK delivered the opinion of the Court.

The Michigan State Bar brought this action in January 1959 to enjoin the members of the Brotherhood of Railroad Trainmen [later merged into the petitioner] from engaging in activities undertaken for the stated purpose of assisting their fellow workers, their widows and families, to protect themselves from excessive fees at the hands of incompetent attorneys in suits for damages under the Federal Employers' Liability Act. The complaint charged, as factors relevant to the cause of action, that the Union recommended selected attorneys to its members and their families, that it secured a commitment from those attorneys that the maximum fee charged would not exceed 25% of the recovery, and that it recommended Chicago lawyers to represent Michigan claimants. The State Bar's complaint appears to be a plea for court protection of unlimited legal fees. The Union's answers admitted that it had engaged in the practice of protecting members against large fees and incompetent counsel; that since 1930 it had recommended, with respect to FELA claims, that injured member employees, and their families, consult attorneys designated by the Union as "Legal Counsel"; that prior to March 1959, it had informed the injured members and their families that the legal counsel would not charge in excess of 25% of any recovery; and that Union representatives were reimbursed for transporting injured employees, or their families, to the legal counsel offices.

The only evidence introduced in this case was the testimony of one employee of the Association of American Railroads in 1961 that from 1953 through 1960 a large number of Michigan FELA claimants were represented by the Union's designated Chicago legal counsel. Based on this evidence and the Union's admissions set out above, the state trial court in 1962 issued an order enjoining the Union's activities on the ground that they violated the state statute making it a misdemeanor to "solicit" damage suits against railroads. . . .

In affirming the trial court decree, . . . the Michigan Supreme Court gave our holding in *Trainmen* the narrowest possible reading. . . . The Michigan Supreme Court failed to follow our decisions in *Trainmen, United Mine Workers*, and NAACP v. Button, upholding the First Amendment principle that groups can unite to assert their legal rights as effectively and economically as practicable. When applied, as it must be, to the Union's activities reflected in the record of this case, the First Amendment forbids the restraints imposed by the injunction here under review for the following among other reasons.

First. The decree approved by the Michigan Supreme Court enjoins the Union from "giving or furnishing legal advice to its members or their families." Given its broadest meaning, this provision would bar the Union's members, officers, agents, or attorneys from giving any kind of advice or counsel to an injured worker or his family concerning his FELA claim. In *Trainmen* we upheld the commonsense proposition that such activity is protected by the First Amendment. Moreover, the plain meaning of this particular injunctive provision would emphatically deny the right of the Union to employ counsel to represent its members, a right explicitly upheld in *United Mine Workers* and NAACP v. Button. . . .

Second. The decree also enjoins the Union from furnishing to any attorney the names of injured members or information relating to their injuries. The investigation of accidents by Union staff for purposes of gathering evidence to assist the injured worker or his family in asserting FELA claims was part of the Union practice upheld in *Trainmen*. It would seem at least a little strange now to hold that the Union cannot communicate that information to the injured member's attorney.

Third. A provision of the decree enjoins the members of the Union from "accepting or receiving compensation of any kind, directly or indirectly, for the solicitation of legal employment for any lawyer, whether by way of salary, commission or otherwise." The Union conceded that prior to 1959, Union representatives were reimbursed for their actual time spent and out-of-pocket expenses incurred in bringing injured members or their families to the offices of the legal counsel. Since the members of a union have a First Amendment right to help and advise each other in securing effective legal representation, there can be no doubt that transportation of injured members to an attorney's office is within the scope of that protected activity. To the extent that the injunction prohibits this practice, it is invalid under *Trainmen, United Mine Workers,* and NAACP v. Button.

Fourth. . . . Our Brother Harlan appears to concede that the State Bar has neither alleged nor proved that the Union has engaged in the past, is presently engaging, or plans to engage, in the sharing of legal fees. Nonetheless, he suggests that the injunction against such conduct is justified in order to remove any "temptation" for the Union to participate in such activities. We cannot accept this novel concept of equity jurisdiction that would open the courts to claims for injunctions against "temptation," and would deem potential "temptation" to be a sufficient basis for the issuance of an injunction. Indeed, it would appear that jurisdiction over "temptation" has heretofore been reserved to the churches. . . .

Fifth. Finally, the challenged decree bars the Union from controlling, directly or indirectly, the fees charged by any lawyer. The complaint alleged that the Union sought to protect its members from excessive legal fees by securing an agreement from the counsel it recommends that the fee will not exceed 25% of the recovery, and that the percentage will include all expenses incidental to investigation and litigation. The union in its answer admitted that prior to 1959 it secured such agreements for the protection of its members.

United Mine Workers upheld the right of workers to act collectively to obtain affordable and effective legal representation. One of the abuses sought to be remedied by the Mine Workers' plan was the situation pursuant to which members "were required to pay forty or fifty per cent of the amounts recovered in damage suits, for attorney fees." The Mine Workers dealt with the problem by employing an attorney on a salary basis, thereby providing free legal representation for its members in asserting their claims before the state workmen's compensation board. The Union in the instant case sought to protect its members against the same abuse by limiting the fee charged by recommended attorneys. It is hard to believe that a court of justice would deny a cooperative union of workers the right to protect its injured members, and their widows and children, from the injustice of excessive fees at the hands of inadequate counsel. Indeed, the Michigan court was foreclosed from so doing by our decision in *United Mine Workers*.

In the context of this case we deal with a cooperative union of workers seeking to assist its members in effectively asserting claims under the FELA. But the principle here involved cannot be limited to the facts of this case. At issue is the basic right to group legal action, a right first asserted in this Court by an association of Negroes seeking the protection of freedoms guaranteed by the Constitution. The common thread running through our decisions in NAACP v. Button, *Trainmen,* and *United Mine Workers* is that collective activity undertaken to obtain meaningful access to the courts is a fundamental right within the protection of the First Amendment. However, that right would be a hollow promise if courts could deny associations of workers or others the means of enabling their members to meet the costs of legal representation. That was the holding in *United Mine Workers, Trainmen,* and NAACP v. Button. The injunction in the present case cannot stand in the face of these prior decisions.

Reversed.

[Justice Stewart took no part in the decision of this case. Justice Harlan concurred in part and dissented in part. Justice White, with whom Justice Blackmun joined, concurred in part and dissented in part.]

Not all change has come from Supreme Court fiat. On occasion, state high courts have created exceptions to their own rules forbidding lay intermediaries. An enlightened example is In re 1115 Legal Service Care, 110 N.J. 344, 541 A.2d 673, 677 (1988). The petitioner was a prepaid legal service program funded by employers under a collective bargaining agreement with a labor union. In New Jersey, the program employed lawyers to service union members. Elsewhere, it retained law firms. The state supreme court upheld the right of the program to practice this way and to do so in its own name. It emphasized that "individual attorneys providing legal services remain professionally responsible and accountable for their conduct. No control over the rendition of legal services is retained or exerted by non-lawyers. No profits generated by the practice of law enure to the organization itself. The practice of law under the aegis of the plan . . . is in no way inconsistent with or inimical to the regulatory standards governing the legal profession."

B. FOR-PROFIT ENTERPRISES

We have so far discussed lay intermediaries that are not themselves seeking to earn money based on the work a lawyer does for a client. The constitutional protection afforded such arrangements can be seen to depend on the issues they seek to raise (*Button*) or on the right of the intermediary's members to pool their resources to reduce the cost of legal aid (the union cases). If we remove these two characteristics, what constitutional protection remains? Can a state legitimately forbid lay ownership or managerial control of entities that mean to market routine legal services for a profit?

As we saw above (page 713), the code was especially hostile to lay participation in the delivery of legal services for gain. Although this hostility softened over time, it was not because lawyers had become amenable to the idea but because the Supreme Court's decisions in *Button* and the union cases made the earlier broad prohibitions invalid. The ABA's amendments to the code barely went further than the Constitution required. Efforts to make the Model Rules more receptive to lay participation were defeated by the "Sears" question (page 715 supra), which forced the deletion of an express rule authorizing such participation. After ABA Opinion 355 (1987) below, however, isn't that where we end up, so long as the organizers do not make the purely structural error of calling their enterprise a law partnership or a professional corporation?

ABA FORMAL OPINION 355 (1987)

The Committee has received a number of inquiries raising ethical issues concerning for-profit prepaid legal service plans. In view of the widespread interest in this area and the proliferation of diverse plans, and recognizing that prepaid legal service plans can offer increased access to legal services, the Committee in this opinion sets forth guidelines under the ABA Model Rules of Professional Conduct (1983, amended 1987) to aid lawyers in assessing the propriety of their participation in for-profit legal service plans. These guidelines identify criteria for prepaid legal service plans in which it is ethically permissible for a lawyer to participate. The Committee also addresses ethical problems which require special attention.[1]

Most for-profit prepaid legal service plans are owned and operated by plan sponsors which, for a modest monthly charge, offer subscribers certain "covered" legal services for no additional cost and other specified services at reduced fees. The covered legal services are provided by participating lawyers and usually include such services as unlimited tele-

---

1. Similar issues, concerning professional independence and preservation of confidences, were discussed in a different setting, that of government funded legal services offices, in ABA Formal Opinion 334 (1974).

phone consultations and letter writing, and the preparation of simple wills. The reduced fee services usually cover court representation at a fixed hourly rate and contingency fee arrangements, both for less than fees customarily charged by lawyers for similar services. Certain matters are explicitly excluded, such as matters where the interests of two plan members are in direct conflict, suits against the plan's sponsor and complex matters.

The Committee is of the opinion that a lawyer may participate in a for-profit legal service plan under the Model Rules, provided the plan is in compliance with the guidelines in this opinion. The plan must allow the participating lawyer to exercise independent professional judgment on behalf of the client, to maintain client confidences, to avoid conflicts of interest, and to practice competently. The operation of the plan must not involve improper advertising or solicitation or improper fee sharing and must be in compliance with other applicable law. It is incumbent upon the lawyer to investigate and ensure that the arrangement under the plan fully complies with the Rules before the lawyer participates in the plan. Where the plan or the plan sponsor is in violation of the Rules, the lawyer who participates in the plan may violate Rule 8.4(a) by assisting the plan sponsor or by violating the Rules through the acts of the plan sponsor.

I. PROFESSIONAL INDEPENDENCE

At the outset and of primary importance, it is essential that neither the plan nor the participating lawyer permit the sponsoring entity to interfere with the lawyer's exercise of independent professional judgment on behalf of a client or to direct or regulate the lawyer's professional conduct. Model Rule 5.4 deals with the professional independence of a lawyer and contains traditional limitations on nonlawyer involvement in the practice of law, which include the prohibition against division of fees with nonlawyers [Rule 5.4(a)] and the prohibition against lawyer partnerships with nonlawyers [Rule 5.4(b)]. Rule 5.4(c) specifically states that a lawyer is prohibited from permitting "a person who recommends, employs or pays the lawyer to render legal services for another to direct or regulate the lawyer's professional judgment in rendering such legal services." That section states duties implicit in Rules 1.2(a), 1.7(b), and 1.8(f). These rules together undertake to ensure that the lawyer will abide by the client's decisions concerning the objectives of representation and will serve the interests of the client and not those of a third party.[3]

---

3. Rule 5.4(d) contains the only restriction in the Rules specifically placed on a for-profit professional corporation or association authorized to practice law. Although paragraph (d) of Rule 5.4 deals with issues analogous to those considered here, it does not directly apply to prepaid legal service plans which, as the Committee understands, are sponsored by entities not authorized to practice law.

The plan sponsor should have no dealings with plan subscribers on legal issues after their matters have been referred to a lawyer. Once the lawyer-client relationship exists between the plan member and the participating lawyer, that relationship must be no different from the traditional lawyer-client relationship. The plan member becomes a client of the lawyer providing the services, and there should be no interference with that relationship by the plan sponsor. The agreement between the plan and participating lawyer should make clear this basic relationship. This agreement should be in writing.

Although prepaid plans most likely do not involve explicit outside direction or regulation of lawyers' professional judgment in rendering legal services in direct contravention of Rule 5.4(c), there is potential for violation of this Rule inherent in these plans. For example, there is certainly the potential for economic control of a lawyer who is sufficiently involved in a plan to become financially dependent upon it. Therefore, the precise relationship between the participating lawyer and the plan sponsor is an important consideration. To the extent that the participating lawyer or law firm's practice is exclusively or predominantly dependent upon the plan, the issue of assuring the independence of the lawyer's professional judgment becomes more serious. It is, of course, a question of fact as to whether the lawyer's financial dependence upon the plan's sponsor is so extensive that it affects the lawyer's judgment.

Other requirements in the plan also may present a potential for improper control by the plan sponsor of the lawyer's conduct. No provision may interfere with the lawyer's professional judgment. For example, if the plan undertakes to set limits on the amount of time a lawyer may spend with each client's case, or to fix the number of cases which must be handled by a lawyer, or to require the lawyer to commit to the plan that the lawyer will not represent a client beyond the scope of the agreement in the plan, the plan may interfere with the lawyer's independent professional judgment.

Since prepaid plans may have elements of referral services, insurance plans and direct providers of legal services, there may be issues of the unauthorized practice of law, particularly to the extent the plan is deemed to be delivering legal services through its own employees and perhaps even through independent counsel paid by the plan. Whether any aspect of the operation of such plans would constitute the unauthorized practice of law will depend upon the facts of the particular plan and is a matter of state law. The Committee notes that if the plan constitutes the unauthorized practice of law in a particular jurisdiction, Rule 5.5(b) would prohibit a lawyer from participating in the plan in that jurisdiction. See also Rule 8.4(a).

II. CONFIDENTIALITY

Another serious concern about the ethical propriety of a lawyer's participating in a prepaid legal service plan involves the potential detrimental impact on lawyer-client confidentiality. The participating lawyer must ensure that client confidences are preserved in accordance with Model Rule 1.6. For example, plan quality control mechanisms and other features are unacceptable to the extent that they lead to disclosure by the lawyer of information relating to the representation in violation of the Rules. A lawyer should not participate in a plan which requires the lawyer to disclose information relating to the representation except in compliance with Rule 1.6.

III. Conflicts of Interest

The plan must contain no requirement which would interfere with the lawyer's compliance with the conflicts of interest provisions of Model Rules 1.7, 1.8, 1.9 and 1.10. Some plans attempt to prohibit a participating lawyer from bringing certain causes of action against the sponsor or other plan members. Because the lawyer's rejection of a matter in such circumstances may mislead the client into believing that the action has no merit, the lawyer must be able to advise the client to seek other counsel. Care also should be taken that the sponsor does not impose restrictions upon a lawyer's ability to represent a member once the member becomes a client of the lawyer. See, for example, Rule 5.6.

IV. Competence

Regardless of how the plan is structured, a participating lawyer must ensure that the lawyer is competent in the covered areas of law to handle referrals in those areas and has the ability to limit the volume of matters to a volume that the lawyer can competently handle in conformity with the requirements of Model Rule 1.1. A plan must permit the lawyer to reject matters outside the lawyer's area of competence or which overextend the lawyer's existing workload.

V. Advertising and Solicitation

Another concern relates to the manner in which potential subscribers are solicited. For example, it would constitute improper solicitation for a lawyer to participate in a plan in which the plan sponsor engages a sales force that would solicit members by telephone or in person. Model Rule 7.3; see Model Rule 8.4(a), supra note 2, and accompanying text.[4]

4. The Committee notes that it is permissible for a plan sponsor to pay to advertise legal services provided under its auspices as long as the advertisement is truthful. Rule 7.2(c). A lawyer may also contact "representatives of organizations or groups that may be interested in establishing a group or prepaid legal plan for its members. . . . For the purpose of informing such entities of the availability of and details concerning the plan or arrangement which the lawyer or the lawyer's firm is willing to offer." Comment to Model Rule 7.3.

In addition, the plan's advertising must not be false or misleading. Rule 7.1 states that a communication is false or misleading if it contains a material misrepresentation or omits a necessary fact, is likely to create unjustified expectations about the results or compares the lawyer's services with other lawyers' services, unless the comparison can be factually substantiated. A participating lawyer must assure that all advertising is accurate and that it does not mislead or create unjustified expectations. Rules 7.1(a), 7.1(b) and 7.1(c). For example, the advertisement should make it clear that legal services for a plan subscriber will be rendered by a lawyer, not by the plan sponsor.

VI. FEE ARRANGEMENT

An issue remains whether a lawyer's participation in a for-profit prepaid legal service plan constitutes improper fee sharing in violation of Model Rule 5.4 or giving anything of value to a person for recommending the lawyer's services in violation of Rule 7.2(c).[5] Typically, for-profit prepaid legal service plans provide for plan members to pay a monthly fee, part of which is kept by the plan sponsor to cover its overhead and profit and part of which is paid by the plan sponsor to the participating lawyer for those services which the plan offers at no additional cost.[6] The members ordinarily begin the monthly payments before representation by a lawyer commences. The lawyer gives nothing of value to the plan sponsor other than the lawyer's agreement to provide legal services to subscribers in accordance with the plan provisions. Under these circumstances, the plan sponsor is compensating the lawyer; the lawyer is not compensating the plan. . . .

Although the Model Rules do not expressly address the question of whether a lawyer may participate in a prepaid legal service plan where the plan sponsor retains a portion of the subscriber's payment in excess of administrative costs of the plan to provide a profit for the plan sponsor, the legislative history of the Rules and the rationale for the provisions of Rule 5.4 support the conclusion that a lawyer may participate in a for-profit prepaid legal service plan. Significantly, the flat prohibition

---

5. Rule 5.4(a) says "[a] lawyer or law firm shall not share legal fees with a nonlawyer," with exceptions not pertinent here. Rule 5.4(b) prohibits a lawyer forming a partnership with a nonlawyer "if any of the activities of the partnership consist of the practice of law." Rule 7.2(c) states: "A lawyer shall not give anything of value to a person for recommending the lawyer's services, except that a lawyer may pay the reasonable cost of advertising or written communication permitted by this rule and may pay the usual charges of a not-for-profit lawyer referral service or other legal service organization." The Comment to Rule 7.2(c) explains: "This restriction does not prevent an organization or person other than the lawyer from advertising or recommending the lawyer's services. Thus a legal aid agency or prepaid legal services plan may pay to advertise legal services provided under its auspices."

6. The monthly fee is paid in order to insure that the specified legal services will be available for no additional cost or at reduced fees. A subscriber may, however, never need to consult a participating lawyer during the period of the subscriber's membership in the plan.

against a lawyer participating in for-profit plans in DR 2-103(D)(4)(a) of the Model Code was not carried into the Model Rules. In addition, the proponents of amendments now contained in Rule 5.4 explained that the restrictions the Rule imposes on the practice of law specifically "allowed for experimentation in methods of delivering legal services." ABA, The Legislative History of the Model Rules of Professional Conduct: Their Development in the ABA House of Delegates 160 (1987). Furthermore, the fee sharing prohibition, which was in the unauthorized practice Canon of the Model Code, was placed in Model Rule 5.4, which is principally directed towards the maintenance of lawyers' professional independence.

An analysis of the rationale for the prohibition against sharing of fees in Rule 5.4(a) also leads to the conclusion that the participation of a lawyer in a for-profit legal service plan is permissible under the Rules. None of the evils that the prohibition against fee sharing with nonlawyers is meant to prevent are present in a typical for-profit prepaid legal service plan, provided the participating lawyer's independence of professional judgment and freedom of action on behalf of a client is preserved. Two important reasons for the fee-sharing prohibition are: first, to avoid the possibility of a nonlawyer being able to interfere with the exercise of a lawyer's independent professional judgment in representing a client; and second, to ensure that the total fee paid by a client is not unreasonably high. For a lawyer's participation in a legal service plan to be permissible, the independence of the lawyer's professional judgment and client confidentiality must be assured in accordance with the guidelines already outlined in Parts I and II of this opinion. It is likely that the total fee will not be unreasonable in light of the goal of prepaid legal service plans to make legal services more widely available at a lower cost to persons of moderate means. Prepaid legal service plans are seen by many to be a way to deliver legal services in noncomplex matters to an underrepresented client community.

For all of these reasons, the Committee concludes that the retention by the plan sponsor of portions of the monthly payments from plan members to cover a profit as well as its administrative costs does not constitute improper fee sharing in violation of Rule 5.4. Nor does it constitute giving anything of value to a person for recommending the lawyer's services in violation of Rule 7.2(c). . . .

MODEL CODE OF PROFESSIONAL RESPONSIBILITY

Under the predecessor Model Code, a lawyer's participation in a for-profit legal service plan is prohibited. DR 2-103(D)(4)(a). See ABA Informal Opinion 85-1510 (1985). However, the Committee recognizes, as it did in that opinion, that constitutional questions may be involved.[8] Lawyers are again cautioned to review the rules of their jurisdiction, which may differ from the Model Code.

Should Lawyers Be Permitted to Work for Law Firms Owned or Managed by Nonlawyers?

Despite the final paragraph and footnote of Opinion 355, restrictions on for-profit legal service plans are very likely constitutional. See ACLU/Eastern Missouri Fund v. Miller, page 724 supra; Lawline v. American Bar Assn., 738 F. Supp. 288 (1990) (state may prohibit lawyers from working for law firms having nonlawyer partners); Gardner v. North Carolina State Bar, 316 N.C. 285, 341 S.E.2d 517 (1986) (insurer may not use employed lawyer to defend action nominally against insured even if insurer will be solely liable for adverse judgment). Not even in Opinion 355 do we find an unqualified blessing of for-profit legal service plans that employ salaried lawyers. The opinion warns that if a lawyer's "practice is exclusively or predominantly dependent upon the plan, the issue of assuring the lawyer's professional judgment becomes more serious." In the end, whether the lawyer's dependence affects his judgment will be a "question of fact" (page 733 supra).

Washington, D.C., has come closest of any American jurisdiction to permitting lay participation in the ownership or management of traditional law firms. Effective January 1, 1991, Washington D.C. Rule 5.4(b) provides:

> A lawyer may practice law in a partnership or other form of organization in which a financial interest is held or managerial authority is exercised by an individual nonlawyer who performs professional services which assist the organization in providing legal services to clients, but only if:
>
> (1) The partnership or organization has as its sole purpose providing legal services to clients;
>
> (2) All persons having such managerial authority or holding a financial interest undertake to abide by these Rules of Professional Conduct;
>
> (3) The lawyers who have a financial interest or managerial authority in the partnership or organization undertake to be responsible for the non-

8. Commentators have noted that the distinction in DR 2-103(D)(4)(a) between profit and nonprofit plans may be subject to constitutional challenge on First Amendment, equal protection, and right to counsel grounds. See, e.g., Billings, Legal Expense Insurers: Winning the Battle Against Indifferent Insurance Laws and Hostile Ethics Rules, 19 Forum 142, 155-58 (1983-84); Comment, Group Legal Services: From Houston to Chicago, 79 Dickinson L. Rev. 621, 640-41 (1974-75). See also Student Government v. Council, North Carolina State Bar, No. C-C-76-346 (W.D.N.C. Aug. 17, 1977) where a provision restricting all prepaid plans in North Carolina to an open panel format was found to violate the First and Fourteenth Amendment rights of those covered in the plan.

lawyer participants to the same extent as if nonlawyer participants were lawyers under Rule 5.1;

(4) The foregoing conditions are set forth in writing.

Let's be candid. Opinion 355 is hardly forthright. It says that a lawyer who works for a for-profit plan is not splitting legal fees with a lay entity because the entity is giving the lawyer money rather than the other way around. If the money is being paid for legal services, which it is, what difference should it make if it goes to the lawyer, who then gives some of it to the plan, or if it goes to the plan, which then gives some of it to the lawyer? That's a silly distinction, isn't it, just as silly as pretending that the arrangement does not violate Rule 5.4(b) and (d) because the plan is not strictly speaking a law firm or professional corporation. And if the intent of the drafters is a legitimate guide, which the opinion seems to accept, how can we square Opinion 355 with the legislative history, including the "Sears" question (page 715 supra).

All this does not of course mean that the opinion's conclusion is wrong as a matter of policy. So let's ask the question. Should lawyers be able to accept employment with for-profit law firms (call them what you will) that are owned or managed by laypersons? Think of all the jobs that could open up. Think of the new sources of capital for creation and expansion of law firms. Think of the intense competition that the new and expanded firms will offer traditional ones. (Wait. Competition?) So why not let laypersons own even traditional law firms? Indeed, given the transparency of Opinion 355, does not intellectual honesty require as much?

The usual reason to oppose lay ownership or managerial authority is that laypersons might use their power over employed lawyers to cause them to disserve clients in order to maximize profits for the enterprise. This risk arises if the layperson's income depends on the profitability of the enterprise. But wait a minute. Why isn't the same risk present whether the employer is a lawyer or a layperson? Are we assuming that lawyers are more trustworthy than lay people? Or less interested in money? (Compare the professionalism debate, pages 740 and 823 infra.) Is it because lawyers can be disciplined if they cause another person to disserve a client, whereas the bar has no equivalent authority over lay people? (Civil claims would still be possible.) If the need for regulatory control is the answer, why isn't it sufficient that we retain regulatory control over the employed lawyer? What reason do we have to suppose that employed lawyers will risk discipline and allow themselves to be corrupted by the lay profiteer? Think again of the in-house corporate lawyer and the debate over whistleblowing (page 458 supra).

The tone of the preceding paragraphs is decidedly skeptical. Have we perhaps been too dismissive? Not every ethical rule that excludes competition and predictably raises the cost of legal services is necessarily unwise. Even if the motives behind the rule are not wholly selfless, the rule may still serve a valid purpose. Consider the following article, which describes an actual conflict in a health maintenance organization, where lay investment is common. Can't a state legislature or court validly apprehend similar risk in a lay-controlled law firm, at least when it is formed for profit?

Gina Kolata
BEING THOROUGH CAN BE COSTLY —
TO THE DOCTOR
N.Y. Times, March 20, 1986, at E6

Dr. Devra Marcus, a Washington internist, left private practice to work in a prepaid health plan, but felt she had to resign after about a month. The plan, she said, "cast decision-making in terms of finances."

Dr. Marcus decided to join the health maintenance group about three years ago because she knew the doctor who was setting it up and because prepaid plans were receiving favorable publicity at the time. "Everyone was getting all whipped up about them," she said.

But things soured immediately. Her first two patients were diabetics, and so she followed her usual procedure and referred them to an ophthalmologist to check for retinal changes that, if untreated, could lead to blindness. She also referred them to a podiatrist, because diabetics' feet frequently develop nerve damage that could eventually require amputation.

Soon afterwards, another doctor took Dr. Marcus aside and told her that it was all very well for her to send patients to other specialists but that the cost of those specialists would come out of a special fund earmarked for her. The fewer patients she referred, the more money she would receive from this fund at the end of the year.

Dr. Marcus was appalled. "I hadn't read the fine print," she confessed.

"I pulled out. I didn't want to think about whether I would be losing money if I ordered an ophthalmologic consultation. I wanted to think about what was best for the patients."

Dr. Marcus added that patients feel more and more pressure to join prepaid health plans because they cost so much less than traditional fee-for-service plans, such as Blue Cross. She said she loses patients to such plans but has been able to maintain a thriving private practice anyway. And while acknowledging that not all doctors have the option of being uncompromising, Dr. Marcus said that if the prepaid plans ever drew away too many patients, "I would stop practicing."

QUESTION

14.1 "The bank would like to retain you to help us solve a little problem. One of the more lucrative aspects of our business is serving as an or the executor or trustee of the estates of well-to-do individuals. We figure that our chances of getting this business increases if we offer to pay for the testator's lawyer if the testator will name us. Those fees can be rather high for a testator who has tax planning and needs inter vivos or testamentary trusts.

"We can save money here in one of several ways. The best thing for us would be to have a lawyer on staff do the work. We have excellent estates lawyers on staff, really first rate. We'd offer their services free of charge to individuals of a minimum net worth who will name us as the or an executor or trustee.

"Alternatively, we can pick an outside lawyer to do the estate planning and negotiate a lower than market rate for all the work. We can throw volume that individual testators cannot.

"The least desirable route would be for us to let the client pick his or her own lawyer and pay the lawyer's reasonable fee. We probably couldn't get a lower than market rate then, but at least we'd get the business.

"Are any of these plans workable? If not, maybe you can think of some alternatives. Send me your opinion letter and your bill."

C. CAN A LAW FIRM OWN AN ANCILLARY BUSINESS?

Kaye, Scholer has one. Perkins Coie has one. Arnold & Porter has several. They are ancillary businesses. An ancillary business is a certain kind of nonlaw business owned by a law firm, whether operated as a subsidiary of the firm or wholly in-house. Arnold & Porter's ancillary businesses advise on lobbying and management, real estate development, and banking and finance. Kaye, Scholer's business offers international trade consulting. Perkins Coie's subsidiary advises on environmental matters. Clients of the ancillary business may or may not be law clients of the firm.

What makes a business "ancillary" is its logical or functional connection to the firm's legal services. A law firm that owns a clothing store does not have an ancillary business. But a construction law firm that offers architectural or engineering services does.

When a business ancillary to the practice of law is owned or controlled by lawyers, critics point to various dangers: conflicts of interest, domination of lawyers by the lay owners or managers of the business, confusion about whether the customer of the business is also a client of the firm, unethical marketing of legal services by using the business as a "front," and threats to the confidentiality of client information. These threats are supposedly compounded when lawyers ally with laypersons in the operation or control of the business.

Many lawyers vehemently oppose ancillary businesses and support an ethical rule that will prohibit most of them. "What will happen [if they proliferate] is that the profit motive will become the sole motive, not the client's best interest," predicted Dennis Block, of New York's Weil, Gotshal & Manges. Thomas Gibbons, Branching Out, ABA J. 70 (November 1989). However, James Jones of Arnold & Porter in Washington, D.C., said the goal was not profit but client service in a more complex world. "The lawyer's role used to be fairly well defined and one could distinguish . . . between 'legal' matters . . . and 'business' matters. Increasingly, however, the distinction . . . is often quite blurred. Today's lawyer is almost as likely to be focusing on economic, scientific, financial or political questions as on strictly legal issues." Id.

The ABA's Litigation Section has advocated significant curtailment of ancillary businesses, citing threats to independent professional judgment, the quality of legal work, the reputation of the profession, and the profession's obligations to society. This last threat posits that the legal profession is "unique . . . with special obligations different from any other profession or occupation," which ancillary businesses will vitiate.

The Litigation Section would allow law firms to offer clients nonlaw services but only if these are "incidental to, in connection with, and concurrent to, the provision of legal services by the law firm to such clients." Further, the nonlaw services would have to be performed by "employees of the law firm itself and not by a subsidiary or other affiliate of the law firm."

Are the Litigation Section's fears reasonable? Should they lead to a per se rule? Lawrence Fox, a member of the section's governing council, wrote in Restraint Is Good in Trade, Natl. L.J. 17 (Apr. 29, 1991):

> [T]he ancillary business movement introduces non-lawyers into positions of influence and control of the profession. All the safeguards one can imagine do not overcome the reality that those who come to prominence and success in the operations of the ancillary business will end up with real power in the governance of the overall enterprise. Quite simply, money talks, and dependence on money changes perspectives in a way that people of the utmost good will cannot overcome. . . .
>
> Also disquieting is the possibility that, if lawyers enter other fields of endeavor, non-lawyer enterprises such as Household Finance, Coldwell Banker, American Express and WalMart are likely to wish to add legal services to their array of consumer products. As lawyers cloak their drive for financial hegemony in arguments such as "it's a public service to offer the public one-stop shopping," it becomes a very small leap, if a leap at all, to argue that these other non-law-firm, non-lawyer-controlled entities are en-

titled to an equal opportunity to provide this "public service," particularly when law firms seek to offer the services to non-clients of the firm and/or without any relation to the provision of legal services.

Fox anticipates further that ancillary businesses will "expose the profession to levels of liability that have been unheard of until now" and undermine its "entitlement to self-regulation." See also L. Harold Levinson's two articles: Making Society's Legal System Accessible to Society: The Lawyer's Role and Its Implications, 41 Vand. L. Rev. 789 (1988); and Independent Law Firms that Practice Law Only: Society's Need, the Legal Profession's Responsibility, 51 Ohio St. L.J. 229 (1990) (both opposing ancillary businesses); and Thomas Andrews, Non-Lawyers in the Business of Law: Does the One Who Has the Gold Really Make the Rules?, 40 Hastings L. Rev. 577 (1989).

By contrast, the ABA's Standing Committee on Ethics and Professional Responsibility and its Special Coordinating Committee on Professionalism have rejected a per se rule in favor of specific amendments to the Model Rules aimed at protecting customers of these businesses. The Standing Committee reported that its research "has been unable to discover any evidence of actual harm to clients, the public or the profession, arising from lawyers' participation in ancillary business activities." The Litigation Section does not seem to dispute this empirical assertion. Rather, it appears to rely on normative principles, behavioral assumptions, intuition, and considerations of appearance. Should we require empirical support before an ethics rule is used to forbid otherwise lawful conduct? We don't now, do we?

The Standing Committee recommended amendments to the Model Rules that, essentially, would have required

1. disclosure to customers of an "ancillary business entity" of its relationship to the law firm;
2. that the business treat its customers as clients of the law firm unless the customer is not a client of the firm on any matter related to the ancillary service and the lawyer has, in a writing to the customer, informed the customer that it is not deemed a client;
3. adoption of certain preventive and corrective measures intended to ensure that the ancillary business treats customers who are also clients in accordance with the Rules; and
4. that lawyers dissociate from an ancillary business if they reasonably should know that the business is not in compliance with its obligations under the Rules unless the business immediately rectifies the situation.

The Committee's definition of "ancillary business entity" would not have limited ancillary services offered within a law firm. Its limitations would only have applied to freestanding businesses "controlled or operated" by a lawyer or firm. Contrast the Litigation Section's proposal, which would ban ancillary services when offered by outside entities and would permit their availability within a firm only under limited circumstances.

The alternative proposals of the Standing Committee and the Litigation Section were presented to the ABA House of Delegates in August 1991. The House rejected the Standing Committee's proposal and then adopted the Litigation Section's proposal by a vote of 197 to 186. The result is Model Rule 5.7. James Jones of Arnold & Porter, whose comments in support of ancillary business were quoted above, was reported to have "played down the importance of the vote," predicting: "In most states, this proposal will not be adopted."

Read the rule. Do you know what it means by "non-legal services which are ancillary to the practice of law"? The rule does not define this phrase, but the commentary says that the contemplated services will "satisfy all or most" of six "indicia." Does that give you comfort? In a jurisdiction that has adopted the rule, a company asks your law firm to monitor proposed state legislation on toxic waste cleanup. The company wants to know what bills are contemplated as early as possible. Can you do it? What if the request is to lobby against a particular bill? What if the company is a longtime client of the firm on unrelated matters? Remember, violation of the rule can lead to discipline.

Comparing Medicine

Once again we can profit by comparing the ancillary business debate to developments in the medical profession, specifically the increasing incidence of doctors who invest in laboratories and equipment. "Doctors who own or invest in laboratories prescribed 45% more clinical services for Medicare patients than other physicians did," was how the Wall Street Journal of May 1, 1989 reported the results of a government study.

This phenomenon is not confined to Medicare patients. On March 1, 1989, in an article that foreshadowed the ancillary business debate in law, a Journal headline reported the increase of patient referrals to facilities in which the doctor had an interest: "Doctor-Owned Labs Earn Lavish Profits in a Captive Market. Referral of Patients Creates Conflict-of-Interest Issue That Polarizes Profession. March to the Cash Register." Said one Blue Cross researcher: "There is no question that ownership interest leads to more testing." The researcher had just completed "a study showing that physicians have overtested pregnant women with ultrasound imaging devices." The doctors "charge Blue Cross about $100 more than it costs them to rent the devices for a test." Some doctors tested women monthly when, according to the researcher, one or two tests would have sufficed. The article lists other examples of self-interested referrals.

In response to this trend, the United States Department of Health and Human Services issued a ruling aimed at doctors who refer Medicare and Medicaid patients to health care facilities in which the doctors have an interest. Violation can result in prosecution and exclusion from Medicare and Medicaid. The ruling provides that not more than 40 percent of businesses receiving Medicare and Medicaid referrals can be owned by doctors or hospitals in a position to make those referrals. Also, these businesses cannot earn more than forty percent of their income from their own investors. N.Y. Times, July 26, 1991, at A1.

Should this experience inform the ancillary business debate in law?

Part Five

FIRST AMENDMENT RIGHTS OF LAWYERS

XV

Free Speech Rights
of Lawyers

Lawyers enjoy First Amendment protection for two kinds of speech. Like everyone else, though with at least one important exception, lawyers can criticize government, including courts and judges, and speak about public issues, subject only to such narrow limitations as the First Amendment will permit. The exception? A lawyer enjoys less freedom than do others to speak publicly about her own cases. The subject of this chapter is "traditional" free speech issues as they affect lawyers. The First Amendment also protects a lawyer's commercial speech — speech that markets legal services — which is the subject of Chapter 16.

Some crimes in the orbit of the administration of justice are often, though not necessarily, committed through speech. Consider contempt of court or obstruction of justice. Lawyers who commit these crimes can be punished even if they are advocating their clients' interests at the time. See generally Norman Dorsen & Leon Friedman, Disorder in the Court: Report of the Association of the Bar of the City of New York Special Committee on Courtroom Conduct, 131-188 (1973).

Some examples: In In re Dodson, 214 Conn. 344, 572 A.2d 328, 330-331, cert. denied, 111 S. Ct. 247 (1990), summary contempt was affirmed where, immediately after imposition of sentence, the defense lawyer interrupted the court to say that the sentence was "totally outrageous" and had "no basis." Matter of Daniels, 118 N.J. 51, 570 A.2d 416, cert. denied, 111 S. Ct. 371 (1990), affirmed summary contempt where a defense lawyer twice responded to adverse rulings by laughing, rolling his head, and throwing himself back on his seat. In each case, the lawyer's behavior was said to threaten the "dignity" and the "authority" of the court. Contrast Moffatt v. Buano, 391 Pa. Super. 1, 569 A.2d 968 (1990), which reversed summary contempt where counsel was overheard to call a judge an "asshole" in a hallway conversation. There was no evidence that the lawyer intended to, or did in fact, obstruct justice, said the court. Can that lawyer be disciplined? Read on.

Lawyers' free speech issues tend to arise in three contexts: when a lawyer speaks to the press on a case (usually a litigation) with which she is associated; when a lawyer criticizes a judge or the courts; and when a lawyer objects to the fact that an "integrated" bar association is using his dues to promote causes the lawyer opposes. An "integrated" bar, present in some states, is one to which all lawyers in the state must belong.

A. PUBLIC COMMENT ABOUT PENDING CASES

Laurie Cohen had a source. When the United States was investigating Michael Milken for securities law violations, Cohen, a Wall Street Journal reporter, wrote frequent stories, attributed to unidentified sources, revealing bits and pieces of the government's case. Many assumed that Cohen's source was either in the prosecutor's office or, more likely, in a federal agency, like the SEC, and that the source's motive was to pressure Milken to plead guilty, which he eventually did. Milken's lawyers decried the leaks and, with the court's aid, tried but failed to trace them. Milken, not without funds, had his own public relations team, which had mixed success trying to rebut the leaks. Milken's case was one of many in recent years that were pretried, in part at least, in the media. Recall the rape case against William Kennedy Smith.

Some trial judges seek to reduce the incidence of pretrial comment, attributed or not, by issuing "gag" orders that forbid the lawyers, their clients, and persons working with either to talk to the press except perhaps to repeat matters of public record or to state the general nature of a charge or defense. A gag order has double value. Unlike legal ethics rules, a gag order restrains both lawyers and nonlawyers, most notably investigative agencies. And because violation of a gag order can result in a criminal conviction, they get more respect than underenforced ethics rules.

Gag orders have three problems, though: (1) Although violations are easy to detect (there's the news story, after all), violators are hard to catch, especially if the source is in a government agency, where hundreds of people may have access to information; (2) investigation and prosecution may be the job either of the very agency whose personnel are suspect or of an agency that works closely with it; (3) appellate courts differ in their tolerance for gag orders. Compare In re Dow Jones & Co, 842 F.2d 603 (2d Cir. 1988) (upholding gag order in Wedtech trials), with New York Times v. Rothwax, 143 A.D.2d 592, 533 N.Y.S.2d 73 (1st Dept. 1988) (reversing gag order in trial of Joel Steinberg for murder of daughter Lisa).

Some judges have suggested that the First Amendment is more amenable to orders that gag prosecutors. See United States v. Simon, 664 F. Supp. 780 (S.D.N.Y. 1987), aff'd, In re Dow Jones & Co., supra; Levine v. United States District Court, 764 F.2d 590, 602 (9th Cir. 1985), cert. denied, 476 U.S. 1158 (1986) (Sneed, J. concurring); In re Axelrod, 549 A.2d 653 (Vt. 1988). Why should that be?

To understand this subterranean world a little better, consider, in each case and generally, the motives of each side to reveal information to the media. (What were Dominic Gentile's motives in the case following?) Next, which side is likely to have greater media contacts? Last, which side generally has more to gain if a case escapes public attention?

Wait a minute. How many sides are there? If you said two, count again. This play has a third part. Laurie Cohen's. Some cases are big news. The press was going to cover the prosecutions of Claus von Bulow, Michael Milken, Ivan Boesky, Manuel Noriega, Pete Rose, Robert Chambers, Oliver North, Bernhard Goetz, and William Kennedy Smith, come what may. (How else would you know those names?) A lawyer on such cases must conjure with publicity, like it or not. How long will a defense lawyer be able to say "no comment" if, day after day, news stories slant against the defense for lack of the client's side? Unlike Michael Milken, most clients cannot afford a press agent. It's the lawyer or no one.

Rules in every jurisdiction limit what lawyers may say about pending matters. Compare DR 7-107 with its leaner analogue, Rule 3.6. How do they differ? See also Rule 3.8(e), which requires prosecutors to use "reasonable care" to prevent law enforcement personnel from making statements to the press that the prosecutor may not. Further, Rule 5.3 requires a lawyer to supervise nonlegal personnel. Rules 3.8(e) and 5.3 have no Code equivalents.

In *Gentile*, the Supreme Court directly addressed the First Amendment ramifications of ethical rules forbidding comment on pending cases. The Court had avoided the constitutional issue three decades prior. In re Sawyer, 360 U.S. 622 (1959), vacated discipline because the record did not establish a violation of the ethics rule.

GENTILE v. STATE BAR OF NEVADA
111 S. Ct. 2720 (1991)

JUSTICE KENNEDY announced the judgment of the Court and delivered the opinion of the Court with respect to Parts III and VI, and an opinion with respect to Parts I, II, IV, and V in which JUSTICE MARSHALL, JUSTICE BLACKMUN and JUSTICE STEVENS join.

Hours after his client was indicted on criminal charges, petitioner Gentile, who is a member of the Bar of the State of Nevada, held a press conference. He made a prepared statement, which we set forth in Appendix A to this opinion, and then he responded to questions. We refer to most of those questions and responses in the course of our opinion.

Some six months later, the criminal case was tried to a jury and the client was acquitted on all counts. The State Bar of Nevada then filed a complaint against petitioner alleging a violation of Nevada Supreme Court Rule 177, a rule governing pretrial publicity almost identical to ABA Model Rule of Professional Conduct 3.6. Rule 177(1) prohibits an attorney from making "an extrajudicial statement that a reasonable person would expect to be disseminated by means of public communication if the lawyer knows or reasonably should know that it will have a substantial likelihood of materially prejudicing an adjudicative proceeding." Rule 177(2) lists a number of statements that are "ordinarily . . . likely" to result in material prejudice. Rule 177(3) provides a safe harbor for the attorney, listing a number of statements that can be made without fear of discipline notwithstanding the other parts of the rule.

Following a hearing, the Southern Nevada Disciplinary Board of the State Bar found that Gentile had made the statements in question and concluded that he violated Rule 177. The board recommended a private reprimand. Petitioner appealed to the Nevada Supreme Court, waiving the confidentiality of the disciplinary proceeding, and the Nevada court affirmed the decision of the Board.

Nevada's application of Rule 177 in this case violates the First Amendment. Petitioner spoke at a time and in a manner that neither in law nor in fact created any threat of real prejudice to his client's right to a fair trial or to the State's interest in the enforcement of its criminal laws. Furthermore, the Rule's safe harbor provision, Rule 177(3), appears to permit the speech in question, and Nevada's decision to discipline petitioner in spite of that provision raises concerns of vagueness and selective enforcement.

I

The matter before us does not call into question the constitutionality of other States' prohibitions upon an attorney's speech that will have a "substantial likelihood of materially prejudicing an adjudicative proceeding," but is limited to Nevada's interpretation of that standard. On the other hand, one central point must dominate the analysis: this case involves classic political speech. The State Bar of Nevada reprimanded petitioner for his assertion, supported by a brief sketch of his client's defense, that the State sought the indictment and conviction of an innocent man as a "scapegoat," and had not "been honest enough to indict the people who did it; the police department, crooked cops." See infra, Appendix A. At issue here is the constitutionality of a ban on political speech critical of the government and its officials.

A

Unlike other First Amendment cases this Term in which speech is not the direct target of the regulation or statute in question, this case involves punishment of pure speech in the political forum. Petitioner engaged not in solicitation of clients or advertising for his practice, as in our precedents from which some of our colleagues would discern a standard of diminished First Amendment protection. His words were directed at public officials and their conduct in office.

There is no question that speech critical of the exercise of the State's power lies at the very center of the First Amendment. Nevada seeks to punish the dissemination of information relating to alleged governmental misconduct, which only last Term we described as "speech which has traditionally been recognized as lying at the core of the First Amendment."

The judicial system, and in particular our criminal justice courts, play a vital part in a democratic state, and the public has a legitimate interest in their operations. See, e.g., Landmark Communications, Inc. v. Virginia, 435 U.S. 829, 838-839 (1978). Public vigilance serves us well, for "[t]he knowledge that every criminal trial is subject to contemporaneous review in the forum of public opinion is an effective restraint on possible abuse of judicial power. . . . Without publicity, all other checks are insufficient; in comparison of publicity, all other checks are of small account." In re Oliver, 333 U.S. 257, 270-271 (1948). . . . In Sheppard v. Maxwell, 384 U.S. 333, 350 (1966), we reminded that "[t]he press . . . guards against the miscarriage of justice by subjecting the police, prosecutors, and judicial processes to extensive public scrutiny and criticism." . . .

B

We are not called upon to determine the constitutionality of the ABA Model Rule of Professional Conduct 3.6 (1981), but only Rule 177 as it has been interpreted and applied by the State of Nevada. Model Rule 3.6's requirement of substantial likelihood of material prejudice is not necessarily flawed. Interpreted in a proper and narrow manner, for instance, to prevent an attorney of record from releasing information of grave prejudice on the eve of jury selection, the phrase substantial likelihood of material prejudice might punish only speech that creates a danger of imminent and substantial harm. A rule governing speech, even speech entitled to full constitutional protection, need not use the words "clear and present danger" in order to pass constitutional muster. . . .

The drafters of Model Rule 3.6 apparently thought the substantial likelihood of material prejudice formulation approximated the clear and present danger test. See ABA Annotated Model Rules of Professional Conduct 243 (1984) ("formulation in Model Rule 3.6 incorporates a standard approximating clear and present danger by focusing on the likelihood of injury and its substantiality"; citing *Landmark Communications,* supra, at 844).

The difference between the requirement of serious and imminent threat found in the disciplinary rules of some States and the more common formulation of substantial likelihood of material prejudice could prove mere semantics. Each standard requires an assessment of proximity and degree of harm. Each may be capable of valid application. Under those principles, nothing inherent in Nevada's formulation fails First Amendment review; but as this case demonstrates, Rule 177 has not been interpreted in conformance with those principles by the Nevada Supreme Court.

II

Even if one were to accept respondent's argument that lawyers participating in judicial proceedings may be subjected, consistent with the First Amendment, to speech restrictions that could not be imposed on the press or general public, the judgment should not be upheld. The record does not support the conclusion that petitioner knew or reasonably should have known his remarks created a substantial likelihood of material prejudice, if the Rule's terms are given any meaningful content.

We have held that "in cases raising First Amendment issues . . . an appellate court has an obligation to 'make an independent examination of the whole record' in order to make sure that 'the judgment does not constitute a forbidden instrusion on the field of free expression.' "

Neither the disciplinary board nor the reviewing court explain any sense in which petitioner's statements had a substantial likelihood of causing material prejudice. The only evidence against Gentile was the videotape of his statement and his own testimony at the disciplinary hearing. The Bar's whole case rests on the fact of the statement, the time it was made, and petitioner's own justifications. Full deference to these factual findings does not justify abdication of our responsibility to determine whether petitioner's statements can be punished consistent with First Amendment standards. . . . Whether one applies the standard set out in *Landmark Communications* or the lower standard our colleagues find permissible, an examination of the record reveals no basis for the Nevada court's conclusion that the speech presented a substantial likelihood of material prejudice.

Our decision earlier this Term in Mu'Min v. Virginia, 500 U.S. — (1991), provides a pointed contrast to respondent's contention in this case. There, the community had been subjected to a barrage of publicity prior to Mu'Min's trial for capital murder. News stories appeared over a course of several months and included, in addition to details of the crime itself, numerous items of prejudicial information inadmissible at trial. Eight of the twelve individuals seated on Mu'Min's jury admitted some exposure to pretrial publicity. We held that the publicity did not rise even to a level requiring questioning of individual jurors about the content of publicity. In light of that holding, the Nevada court's conclusion that petitioner's abbreviated, general comments six months before trial created a "substantial likelihood of materially prejudicing" the proceeding is, to say the least, most unconvincing.

A. PRE-INDICTMENT PUBLICITY

On January 31, 1987, undercover police officers with the Las Vegas Metropolitan Police Department (Metro) reported large amounts of cocaine (four kilograms) and travelers' checks (almost $300,000) missing from a safety deposit vault at Western Vault Corporation. The drugs and money had been used as part of an undercover operation conducted by Metro's Intelligence Bureau. Petitioner's client, Grady Sanders, owned Western Vault. John Moran, the Las Vegas sheriff, reported the theft at a press conference on February 2, 1987, naming the police and Western Vault employees as suspects.

Although two police officers, Detective Steve Scholl and Sargeant Ed Schaub, enjoyed free access to the deposit box throughout the period of the theft, and no log reported comings and goings at the vault, a series of press reports over the following year indicated that investigators did not consider these officers responsible. Instead, investigators focused upon Western Vault and its owner. Newspaper reports quoted the sheriff and other high police officials as saying that they had not lost confidence in the "elite" Intelligence Bureau. From the beginning, Sheriff Moran had "complete faith and trust" in his officers.

The media reported that, following announcement of the cocaine theft, others with deposit boxes at Western Vault had come forward to claim missing items. One man claimed the theft of his life savings of $90,000. Western Vault suffered heavy losses as customers terminated their box rentals, and the company soon went out of business. The police opened other boxes in search of the missing items, and it was reported they seized $264,900 in U.S. currency from a box listed as unrented.

Initial press reports stated that Sanders and Western Vault were being cooperative; but as time went on, the press noted that the police investigation had failed to identify the culprit and through a process of elimination was beginning to point toward Sanders. Reports quoted the affidavit of a detective that the theft was part of an effort to discredit the undercover operation and that business records suggested the existence of a business relation between Sanders and the targets of a Metro undercover probe.

The Deputy Police Chief announced the two detectives with access to the vault had been "cleared" as possible suspects. According to an unnamed "source close to the investigation," the police shifted from the idea that the thief had planned to discredit the undercover operation to the theory that the thief had unwittingly stolen from the police. The stories noted that Sanders "could not be reached for comment."

The story took a more sensational turn with reports that the two police suspects had been cleared by police investigators after passing lie detector tests. The tests were administered by one Ray Slaughter. But later, the FBI arrested Slaughter for distributing cocaine to an FBI informant, Belinda Antal. It was also reported that the $264,900 seized from the unrented safety deposit box at Western Vault had been stored there in a suitcase owned by one Tammy Sue Markham. Markham was "facing a number of federal drug-related charges" in Tucson, Arizona. Markham reported items missing from three boxes she rented at Western Vault, as did one Beatrice Connick who, according to press reports, was a Columbian national living in San Diego and "not facing any drug related charges." (As it turned out, petitioner impeached Connick's credibility at trial with the existence of a money laundering conviction.) Connick also was reported to have taken and passed a lie detector test to substantiate her charges. Finally, press reports indicated that Sanders had refused to take a police polygraph examination. The press suggested that the FBI suspected Metro officers were responsible for the theft, and reported that the theft had severely damaged relations between the FBI and Metro.

B. THE PRESS CONFERENCE

Petitioner is a Las Vegas criminal defense attorney, an author of articles about criminal law and procedure, and a former Associate Dean of the National College for Criminal Defense Lawyers and Public Defenders. Through leaks from the police department, he had some advance notice of the date an indictment would be returned and the nature of the charges against Sanders. Petitioner had monitored the publicity surrounding the case, and prior to the indictment was personally aware of at least 17 articles in the major local newspapers, the Las Vegas Sun and Las Vegas Review-Journal, and numerous local television news stories which reported on the Western Vault theft and ensuing investigation. Petitioner determined, for the first time in his career, that he would call a formal press conference. He did not blunder into a press conference, but acted with considerable deliberation.

1. Petitioner's motivation

As petitioner explained to the disciplinary board, his primary motivation was the concern that, unless some of the weaknesses in the State's case were made public, a potential jury venire would be poisoned by repetition in the press of information being released by the police and prosecutors, in particular the repeated press reports about polygraph tests and the fact that the two police officers were no longer suspects. Respondent distorts Rule 177 when it suggests this explanation admits a purpose to prejudice the venire and so proves a violation of the Rule. Rule 177 only prohibits the dissemination of information that one knows or reasonably should know has a "substantial likelihood of materially prejudicing an adjudicative proceeding." Petitioner did not indicate he thought he could sway the pool of potential jurors to form an opinion in advance of the trial, nor did he seek to discuss evidence that would be inadmissible at trial. He sought only to counter publicity already deemed prejudicial. The Southern Nevada Disciplinary Board so found. It said petitioner attempted

> (i) to counter public opinion which he perceived as adverse to Mr. Sanders, (ii) . . . to refute certain matters regarding his client which had appeared in the media, (iii) to fight back against the perceived efforts of the prosecution to poison the prospective juror pool, and (iv) to publicly present Sanders' side of the case.

Far from an admission that he sought to "materially prejudic[e] an adjudicative proceeding," petitioner sought only to stop a wave of publicity he perceived as prejudicing potential jurors against his client and injuring his client's reputation in the community.

Petitioner gave a second reason for holding the press conference, which demonstrates the additional value of his speech. Petitioner acted in part because the investigation had taken a serious toll on his client. Sanders was "not a man in good health," having suffered multiple open-heart surgeries prior to these events. And prior to indictment, the mere suspicion of wrongdoing had caused the closure of Western Vault and the loss of Sanders' ground lease on an Atlantic City, New Jersey property.

An attorney's duties do not begin inside the courtroom door. He or she cannot ignore the practical implications of a legal proceeding for the client. Just as an attorney may recommend a plea bargain or civil settlement to avoid the adverse consequences of a possible loss after trial, so too an attorney may take reasonable steps to defend a client's reputation and reduce the adverse consequences of indictment, especially in the face of a prosecution deemed unjust or commenced with improper motives. A defense attorney may pursue lawful strategies to obtain dismissal of an indictment or reduction of charges, including an attempt to demonstrate in the court of public opinion that the client does not deserve to be tried.

2. Petitioner's investigation of rule 177

Rule 177 is phrased in terms of what an attorney "knows or reasonably should know." On the evening before the press conference, petitioner and two colleagues spent several hours researching the extent of an attorney's obligations under Rule 177. He decided, as we have held, see Patton v. Yount, 467 U.S. 1025 (1984), that the timing of a statement was crucial in the assessment of possible prejudice and the Rule's application.

Upon return of the indictment, the court set a trial date for August, 1988, some six months in the future. Petitioner knew, at the time of his statement, that a jury would not be empaneled for six months at the earliest, if ever. He recalled reported cases finding no prejudice resulting from juror exposure to "far worse" information two and four months before trial, and concluded that his proposed statement was not substantially likely to result in material prejudice.

A statement which reaches the attention of the venire on the eve of voir dire might require a continuance or cause difficulties in securing an impartial jury, and at the very least could complicate the jury selection process. As turned out to be the case here, exposure to the same statement six months prior to trial would not result in prejudice, the content fading from memory long before the trial date.

In 1988, Clark County, Nevada had a population in excess of 600,000 persons. Given the size of the community from which any potential jury venire would be drawn and the length of time before trial, only the most damaging of information could give rise to any likelihood of prejudice. The innocuous content of petitioner's statement reinforces my conclusion.

3. The content of petitioner's statement

Petitioner was disciplined for statements to the effect that (1) the evidence demonstrated his client's innocence, (2) the likely thief was a police detective, Steve Scholl, and (3) the other victims were not credible, as most were drug dealers or convicted money launderers, all but one of whom had only accused Sanders in response to police pressure, in the process of "trying to work themselves out of something." He also strongly implied that Steve Scholl could be observed in a videotape suffering from symptoms of cocaine use. Of course, only a small fraction of petitioner's remarks were disseminated to the public, in two newspaper stories and two television news broadcasts.

The stories mentioned not only Gentile's press conference but also a prosecution response and police press conference.[1] The Chief Deputy District Attorney was quoted as saying that this was a legitimate indictment, and that prosecutors cannot bring an indictment to court unless they can prove the charges in it beyond a reasonable doubt. Deputy Police Chief Sullivan stated for the police department, "We in Metro are very satisfied our officers (Scholl and Sgt. Ed Schaub) had nothing to do with this theft or any other. They are both above reproach. Both are veteran police officers who are dedicated to honest law enforcement." In the context of general public awareness, these police and prosecution statements were no more likely to result in prejudice than was petitioner's statement, but given the repetitive publicity from the police investigation, it is difficult to come to any conclusion but that the balance remained in favor of the prosecution.

Much of the information provided by petitioner had been published in one form or another, obviating any potential for prejudice. The remainder, and details petitioner refused to provide, were available to any journalist willing to do a little bit of investigative work.

Petitioner's statement lacks any of the more obvious bases for a finding of prejudice. Unlike the police, he refused to comment on polygraph tests except to confirm earlier reports that Sanders had not submitted to the police polygraph; he mentioned no confessions, and no evidence from searches or test results; he refused to elaborate upon his charge that the other so-called victims were not credible, except to explain his general theory that they were pressured to testify in an attempt to avoid drug-related legal trouble, and that some of them may have asserted claims in an attempt to collect insurance money.

---

1. The sole summary of television reports of the press conference contained in the record is as follows:

2-5-88: GENTILE NEWS CONFERENCE STORY. GENTILE COMPARES THE W. VAULT BURGLARY TO THE FRENCH CONNECTION CASE IN WHICH THE BAD GUYS WERE COPS. GENTILE SAYS THE EVIDENCE IS CIRCUMSTANTIAL AND THAT THE COPS SEEM THE MORE LIKELY CULPRITS, THAT DET. SCHOLL HAS SHOWN SIGNS OF DRUG USE, THAT THE OTHER CUSTOMERS WERE PRESSURED INTO COMPLAINING BY METRO, THAT THOSE CUSTOMERS ARE KNOWN DRUG DEALERS, AND THAT OTHER AGENCIES HAVE OPERATED OUT OF W. VAULT WITHOUT HAVING SIMILAR PROBLEMS.

2-5-88: *METRO NEWS CONFERENCE IN WHICH CHIEF SULLIVAN EXPLAINS THAT THE OFFICERS INVOLVED HAVE BEEN CLEARED BY POLYGRAPH TESTS.* STORY MENTIONS THAT THE POLYGRAPHER WAS RAY SLAUGHTER, UNUSUAL BECAUSE SLAUGHTER IS A PRIVATE EXAMINER, NOT A METRO EXAMINER. REPORTER DETAILS SLAUGHTER'S BACKGROUND, INCLUDING HIS TEST OF JOHN MORAN REGARDING SPILOTRO CONTRIBUTIONS. ALSO MENTIONS SLAUGHTER'S DRUG BUST, SPECULATES ABOUT WHETHER IT WAS A SETUP BY THE FBI. QUOTES GENTILE AS SAYING THE TWO CASES ARE DEFINITELY RELATED.

C. EVENTS FOLLOWING THE PRESS CONFERENCE

Petitioner's judgment that no likelihood of material prejudice would result from his comments was vindicated by events at trial. While it is true that Rule 177's standard for controlling pretrial publicity must be judged at the time a statement is made, ex post evidence can have probative value in some cases. Here, where the Rule purports to demand, and the Constitution requires, consideration of the character of the harm and its heightened likelihood of occurrence, the record is altogether devoid of facts one would expect to follow upon any statement that created a real likelihood of material prejudice to a criminal jury trial.

The trial took place on schedule in August, 1988, with no request by either party for a venue change or continuance. The jury was empaneled with no apparent difficulty. The trial judge questioned the jury venire about publicity. Although many had vague recollections of reports that cocaine stored at Western Vault had been stolen from a police undercover operation, and, as petitioner had feared, one remembered that the police had been cleared of suspicion, not a single juror indicated any recollection of petitioner or his press conference.

At trial, all material information disseminated during petitioner's press conference was admitted in evidence before the jury, including information questioning the motives and credibility of supposed victims who testified against Sanders, and Detective Scholl's ingestion of drugs in the course of undercover operations (in order, he testified, to gain the confidence of suspects). The jury acquitted petitioner's client, and, as petitioner explained before the disciplinary board,

> when the trial was over with and the man was acquitted the next week the foreman of the jury phoned me and said to me that if they would have had a verdict form before them with respect to the guilt of Steve Scholl they would have found the man proven guilty beyond a reasonable doubt.

There is no support for the conclusion that petitioner's statement created a likelihood of material prejudice, or indeed of any harm of sufficient magnitude or imminence to support a punishment for speech.

III

As interpreted by the Nevada Supreme Court, the Rule is void for vagueness, in any event, for its safe harbor provision, Rule 177(3), misled petitioner into thinking that he could give his press conference without fear of discipline. Rule 177(3)(a) provides that a lawyer "may state without elaboration . . . the general nature of the . . . defense." Statements under this provision are protected "[n]otwithstanding subsection 1 and 2(a-f)." By necessary operation of the word "notwithstanding," the Rule contemplates that a lawyer describing the "general nature of the . . . defense." "without elaboration" need fear no discipline, even if he comments on "[t]he character, credibility, reputation or criminal record of a . . . witness," and even if he "knows or reasonably should know that [the statement] will have a substantial likelihood of materially prejudicing an adjudicative proceeding."

Given this grammatical structure, and absent any clarifying interpretation by the state court, the Rule fails to provide " 'fair notice to those to whom [it] is directed.' " Grayned v. City of Rockford, 408 U.S. 104, 112 (1972). A lawyer seeking to avail himself of Rule 177(3)'s protection must guess at its contours. The right to explain the "general" nature of the defense without "elaboration" provides insufficient guidance because "general" and "elaboration" are both classic terms of degree. In the context before us, these terms have no settled usage or tradition of interpretation in law. The lawyer has no principle for determining when his remarks pass from the safe harbor of the general to the forbidden sea of the elaborated.

Petitioner testified he thought his statements were protected by Rule 177(3). A review of the press conference supports that claim. He gave only a brief opening statement, see *infra*, Appendix A, and on numerous occasions declined to answer reporters' questions seeking more detailed comments. One illustrative exchange shows petitioner's attempt to obey the rule:

> *Question from the floor:* Dominick, you mention you question the credibility of some of the witnesses, some of the people named as victims in the government indictment.
>
>   Can we go through it and *elaborate* on their backgrounds, interests —
>
> *Mr. Gentile: I can't because ethics prohibit me from doing so.*
>
>   Last night before I decided I was going to make a statement, I took a close look at the rules of professional responsibility. There are things that I can say and there are things that I can't. Okay?
>
>   I can't name which of the people have the drug backgrounds. I'm sure you guys can find that by doing just a little bit of investigative work. (Emphasis added).

Nevertheless, the disciplinary board said only that petitioner's comments "went beyond the scope of the statements permitted by SCR 177(3)," and the Nevada Supreme Court's rejection of petitioner's defense based on Rule 177(3) was just as terse. The fact Gentile was found in violation of the Rules after studying them and making a conscious effort at compliance demonstrates that Rule 177 creates a trap for the wary as well as the unwary.

The prohibition against vague regulations of speech is based in part on the need to eliminate the impermissible risk of discriminatory enforcement, for history shows that speech is suppressed when either the speaker or the message is critical of those who enforce the law. The question is not whether discriminatory enforcement occurred here, and we assume it did not, but whether the Rule is so imprecise that discriminatory enforcement is a real possibility. The inquiry is of particular relevance when one of the classes most affected by the regulation is the criminal defense bar, which has the professional mission to challenge actions of the State. Petitioner, for instance, succeeded in preventing the conviction of his client, and the speech in issue involved criticism of the government.

IV

The analysis to this point resolves the case, and in the usual order of things the discussion should end here. Five members of the Court, however, endorse an extended discussion which concludes that Nevada may interpret its requirement of substantial likelihood of material prejudice under a standard more deferential than is the usual rule where speech is concerned. It appears necessary, therefore, to set forth my objections to that conclusion and to the reasoning which underlies it.

Respondent argues speech by an attorney is subject to greater regulation than speech by others, and restrictions on an attorney's speech should be assessed under a balancing test that weighs the State's interest in the regulation of a specialized profession against the lawyer's First Amendment interest in the kind of speech that was at issue. The cases cited by our colleagues to support this balancing involved either commercial speech by attorneys or restrictions upon release of information that the attorney could gain only by use of the court's discovery process. Neither of those categories, nor the underlying interests which justified their creation, were implicated here. Petitioner was disciplined because he proclaimed to the community what he thought to be a misuse of the prosecutorial and police powers. Wide-open balancing of interests is not appropriate in this context.

A

Respondent would justify a substantial limitation on speech by attorneys because "lawyers have special access to information, including confidential statements from clients and information obtained through pretrial discovery or plea negotiations" and so lawyers' statements "are likely to be received as especially authoritative." Rule 177, however, does not reflect concern for the attorney's special access to client confidences, material gained through discovery, or other proprietary or confidential information. We have upheld restrictions upon the release of information gained "only by virtue of the trial court's discovery processes." Seattle Times Co. v. Rhinehart, [467 U.S. 20 (1984)], at 32. And *Seattle Times* would prohibit release of discovery information by the attorney as well as the client. Similar rules require an attorney to maintain client confidences. See, e.g., ABA Model Rule of Professional Conduct 1.6 (1981).

This case involves no speech subject to a restriction under the rationale of *Seattle Times*. Much of the information in petitioner's remarks was included by explicit reference or fair inference in earlier press reports. Petitioner could not have learned what he revealed at the press conference through the discovery process or other special access afforded to attorneys, for he spoke to the press on the day of indictment, at the outset of his formal participation in the criminal proceeding. We have before us no complaint from the prosecutors, police or presiding judge that petitioner misused information to which he had special access. And there is no claim that petitioner revealed client confidences, which may be waived in any event. Rule 177, on its face and as applied here, is neither limited to nor even directed at preventing release of information received through court proceedings or special access afforded attorneys. It goes far beyond this. . . .

V

Even if respondent is correct, and as in *Seattle Times* we must balance "whether the 'practice in question [furthers] an important or substantial governmental interest unrelated to the suppression of expression' and whether 'the limitation of First Amendment freedoms [is] no greater than is necessary or essential to the protection of the particular governmental interest involved,'" the Rule as interpreted by Nevada fails the searching inquiry required by those precedents.

A

Only the occasional case presents a danger of prejudice from pretrial publicity. Empirical research suggests that in the few instances when jurors have been exposed to extensive and prejudicial publicity, they are able to disregard it and base their verdict upon the evidence presented in court. See generally Simon, Does the Court's Decision in *Nebraska Press Association* Fit the Research Evidence on the Impact on Jurors of News Coverage?, 29 Stan. L. Rev. 515 (1977); Drechsel, An Alternative View of Media-Judiciary Relations: What the Non-Legal Evidence Suggests About the Fair Trial-Free Press Issue, 18 Hofstra L. Rev. 1 (1989). Voir dire can play an important role in reminding jurors to set aside out-of-court information, and to decide the case upon the evidence presented at trial. All of these factors weigh in favor of affording an attorney's speech about ongoing proceedings our traditional First Amendment protections. Our colleagues' historical survey notwithstanding, respondent has not demonstrated any sufficient state interest in restricting the speech of attorneys to justify a lower standard of First Amendment scrutiny.

Still less justification exists for a lower standard of scrutiny here, as this speech involved not the prosecutor or police, but a criminal defense attorney. Respondent and its amici present not a single example where a defense attorney has managed by public statements to prejudice the prosecution of the state's case. Even discounting the obvious reason for a lack of appellate decisions on the topic — the difficulty of appealing a verdict of acquittal — the absence of anecdotal or survey evidence in a much-studied area of the law is remarkable.

The various bar association and advisory commission reports which resulted in promulgation of ABA Model Rule of Professional Conduct 3.6 (1981), and other regulations of attorney speech, and sources they cite, present no convincing case for restrictions upon the speech of defense attorneys. See Swift, Model Rule 3.6: An Unconstitutional Regulation of Defense Attorney Trial Publicity, 64 Boston U.L. Rev. 1003, 1031-1049 (1984) (summarizing studies and concluding there is no empirical or anecdotal evidence of a need for restrictions on defense publicity); see also Drechsel, supra, at 35 ("data showing the heavy reliance of journalists on law enforcement sources and prosecutors confirms the appropriateness of focusing attention on those sources when attempting to control pre-trial publicity"). The police, the prosecution, other government officials, and the community at large hold innumerable avenues for the dissemination of information adverse to a criminal defendant, many of which are not within the scope of Rule 177 or any other regulation. By contrast, a defendant cannot speak without fear of incriminating himself and prejudicing his defense, and most criminal defendants have insufficient means to retain a public relations team apart from defense counsel for the sole purpose of countering prosecution statements. These factors underscore my conclusion that blanket rules restricting speech of defense attorneys should not be accepted without careful First Amendment scrutiny.

B

Respondent uses the "officer of the court" label to imply that attorney contact with the press somehow is inimical to the attorney's proper role. Rule 177 posits no such inconsistency between an attorney's role and discussions with the press. It permits all comment to the press absent "a substantial likelihood of materially prejudicing an adjudicative proceeding." Respondent does not articulate the principle that contact with the press cannot be reconciled with the attorney's role or explain how this might be so.

Because attorneys participate in the criminal justice system and are trained in its complexities, they hold unique qualifications as a source of information about pending cases. "Since lawyers are considered credible in regard to pending litigation in which they are engaged and are in one of the most knowledgeable positions, they are a crucial source of information and opinion." Chicago Council of Lawyers v. Bauer, 522 F.2d 242, 250 (CA7 1975). To the extent the press and public rely upon attorneys for information because attorneys are well-informed, this may prove the value to the public of speech by members of the bar. If the dangers of their speech arise from its persuasiveness, from their ability to explain judicial proceedings, or from the likelihood the speech will be believed, these are not the sort of dangers that can validate restrictions. The First Amendment does not permit suppression of speech because of its power to command assent.

One may concede the proposition that an attorney's speech about pending cases may present dangers that could not arise from statements by a nonparticipant, and that an attorney's duty to cooperate in the judicial process may prevent him or her from taking actions with an intent to frustrate that process. The role of attorneys in the criminal justice system subjects them to fiduciary obligations to the court and the parties. An attorney's position may result in some added ability to obstruct the proceedings through well-timed statements to the press, though one can debate the extent of an attorney's ability to do so without violating other established duties. A court can require an attorney's cooperation to an extent not possible of nonparticipants. A proper weighing of dangers might consider the harm that occurs when speech about ongoing proceedings forces the court to take burdensome steps such as sequestration, continuance, or change of venue.

If as a regular matter speech by an attorney about pending cases raised real dangers of this kind then a substantial governmental interest might support additional regulation of speech. But this case involves the sanction of speech so innocuous, and an application of Rule 177(3)'s safe harbor provision so begrudging, that it is difficult to determine the force these arguments would carry in a different setting. The instant case is a poor vehicle for defining with precision the outer limits under the Constitution of a court's ability to regulate an attorney's statements about ongoing adjudicative proceedings. At the very least, however, we can say that the Rule which punished petitioner's statement represents a limitation of First Amendment freedoms greater than is necessary or essential to the protection of the particular governmental interest, and does not protect against a danger of the necessary gravity, imminence, or likelihood.

The vigorous advocacy we demand of the legal profession is accepted because it takes place under the neutral, dispassionate control of the judicial system. Though cost and delays undermine it in all too many cases, the American judicial trial remains one of the purest, most rational forums for the lawful determination of disputes. A profession which takes just pride in these traditions may consider them disserved if lawyers use their skills and insight to make untested allegations in the press instead of in the courtroom. But constraints of professional responsibility and societal disapproval will act as sufficient safeguards in most cases. And in some circumstances press comment is necessary to protect the rights of the client and prevent abuse of the courts. It cannot be said that petitioner's conduct demonstrated any real or specific threat to the legal process, and his statements have the full protection of the First Amendment.

VI

The judgment of the Supreme Court of Nevada is reversed.

APPENDIX A — PETITIONER'S OPENING REMARKS AT THE PRESS CONFERENCE OF FEBRUARY 5, 1988.

Mr. Gentile: I want to start this off by saying in clear terms that I think that this indictment is a significant event in the history of the evolution of sophistication of the City of Las Vegas, because things of this nature, of exactly this nature have happened in New York with the French connection case and in Miami with cases — at least two cases there — have happened in Chicago as well, but all three of those cities have been honest enough to indict the people who did it; the police department, crooked cops.

When this case goes to trial, and as it develops, you're going to see that the evidence will prove not only that Grady Sanders is an innocent person and had nothing to do with any of the charges that are being leveled against him, but that the person that was in the most direct position to have stolen the drugs and money, the American Express Travelers' checks, is Detective Steve Scholl.

There is far more evidence that will establish that Detective Scholl took these drugs and took these American Express Travelers' checks than any other living human being.

And I have to say that I feel that Grady Sanders is being used as a scapegoat to try to cover up for what has to be obvious to people at Las Vegas Metropolitan Police Department and at the District Attorney's office.

Now, with respect to these other charges that are contained in this indictment, the so-called other victims, as I sit here today I can tell you that one, two — four of them are known drug dealers and convicted money launderers and drug dealers; three of whom didn't say a word about anything until after they were approached by Metro and after they were already in trouble and are trying to work themselves out of something.

Now, up until the moment, of course, that they started going along with what detectives from Metro wanted them to say, these people were being held out as being incredible and liars by the very same people who are going to say now that you can believe them.

Another problem that you are going to see develop here is the fact that of these other counts, at least four of them said nothing about any of this, about anything being missing until after the Las Vegas Metropolitan Police Department announced publicly last year their claim that drugs and American Express Travelers' c[h]ecks were missing.

Many of the contracts that these people had show on the face of the contract that there is $100,000 in insurance for the contents of the box.

If you look at the indictment very closely, you're going to see that these claims fall under $100,000.

Finally, there were only two claims on the face of the indictment that came to our attention prior to the events of January 31 of '87, that being the date that Metro said that there was something missing from their box.

And both of these claims were dealt with by Mr. Sanders and we're dealing here essentially with people that we're not sure if they ever had anything in the box.

That's about all that I have to say.

[Questions from the floor followed.]

CHIEF JUSTICE REHNQUIST delivered the opinion of the Court with respect to parts I and II, and delivered a dissenting opinion with respect to part III in which JUSTICE WHITE, JUSTICE SCALIA, and JUSTICE SOUTER have joined. . . .

I

[The opinion highlights these additional parts of the press conference in which Gentile responded to questions:

. . . because of the stigma that attaches to merely being accused — okay — I know I represent an innocent man. . . . The last time I had a conference with you, was with a client and I let him talk to you and I told you that that case would be dismissed and it was. Okay?

I don't take cheap shots like this. I represent an innocent guy. All right? . . .

[The police] were playing very fast and loose. . . . We've got some video tapes that if you take a look at them, I'll tell you what, [Detective Scholl] either had a hell of a cold or he should have seen a better doctor.]

II

Petitioner maintains . . . that the First Amendment to the United States Constitution requires a State, such as Nevada in this case, to demonstrate a "clear and present danger" of "actual prejudice or an imminent threat" before any discipline may be imposed on a lawyer who initiates a press conference such as occurred here.[4] He relies on decisions such as Nebraska Press Assn. v. Stuart, 427 U.S. 539 (1976), Bridges v. California, 314 U.S. 252 (1941), Pennekamp v. Florida, 328 U.S. 331 (1946), and Craig v. Harney, 331 U.S. 367 (1947), to support his position. . . .

Respondent State Bar of Nevada points out, on the other hand, that none of these cases involved lawyers who represented parties to a pending proceeding in court. It points to the statement of Holmes, J., in Patterson v. Colorado, 205 U.S. 454, 463 (1907), that "[w]hen a case is finished, courts are subject to the same criticism as other people, but the propriety and necessity of preventing interference with the course of justice by premature statement, argument or intimidation hardly can be denied." Respondent also points to a similar statement in *Bridges*, supra, at 271:

The very word "trial" connotes decisions on the evidence and arguments properly advanced in open court. Legal trials are not like elections, to be won through the use of the meeting-hall, the radio, and the newspaper.

These opposing positions illustrate one of the many dilemmas which arise in the course of constitutional adjudication. The above quotes from *Patterson* and *Bridges* epitomize the theory upon which our criminal justice system is founded: the outcome of a criminal trial is to be decided by impartial jurors, who know as little as possible of the case, based on material admitted into evidence before them in a court proceeding. Extrajudicial comments on, or discussion of, evidence which might never be admitted at trial and ex parte statements by counsel giving their version of the facts obviously threaten to undermine this basic tenet.

4. We disagree with Justice Kennedy's statement that this case "does not call into question the constitutionality of other states' prohibitions upon attorney speech that will have a 'substantial likelihood of materially prejudicing an adjudicative proceeding,' but is limited to Nevada's interpretation of that standard." Petitioner challenged Rule 177 as being unconstitutional on its face in addition to as applied, contending that the "substantial likelihood of material prejudice" test was unconstitutional, and that lawyer speech should be punished only if it violates the standard for clear and present danger set forth in *Nebraska Press*. The validity of the rules in the many states applying the "substantial likelihood of material prejudice" test has, therefore, been called into question in this case.

At the same time, however, the criminal justice system exists in a larger context of a government ultimately of the people, who wish to be informed about happenings in the criminal justice system, and, if sufficiently informed about those happenings might wish to make changes in the system. The way most of them acquire information is from the media. The First Amendment protections of speech and press have been held, in the cases cited above, to require a showing of "clear and present danger" that a malfunction in the criminal justice system will be caused before a State may prohibit media speech or publication about a particular pending trial. The question we must answer in this case is whether a lawyer who represents a defendant involved with the criminal justice system may insist on the same standard before he is disciplined for public pronouncements about the case, or whether the State instead may penalize that sort of speech upon a lesser showing.

It is unquestionable that in the courtroom itself, during a judicial proceeding, whatever right to "free speech" an attorney has is extremely circumscribed. An attorney may not, by speech or other conduct, resist a ruling of the trial court beyond the point necessary to preserve a claim for appeal. Even outside the courtroom, a majority of the Court in two separate opinions in the case of In re Sawyer, 360 U.S. 622 (1959), observed that lawyers in pending cases were subject to ethical restrictions on speech to which an ordinary citizen would not be. There, the Court had before it an order affirming the suspension of an attorney from practice because of her attack on the fairness and impartiality of a judge. The plurality opinion, which found the discipline improper, concluded that the comments had not in fact impugned the judge's integrity. Justice Stewart, who provided the fifth vote for reversal of the sanction, said in his separate opinion that he could not join any possible "intimation that a lawyer can invoke the constitutional right of free speech to immunize himself from evenhanded discipline for proven unethical conduct."

He said that "[o]bedience to ethical precepts may require abstention from what in other circumstances might be constitutionally protected speech." The four dissenting Justices who would have sustained the discipline said:

> Of course, a lawyer is a person and he too has a constitutional freedom of utterance and may exercise it to castigate courts and their administration of justice. But a lawyer actively participating in a trial, particularly an emotionally charged criminal prosecution, is not merely a person and not even merely a lawyer....
>
> He is an intimate and trusted and essential part of the machinery of justice, an "officer of the court" in the most compelling sense.

Likewise, in Sheppard v. Maxwell, where the defendant's conviction was overturned because extensive prejudicial pretrial publicity had denied the defendant a fair trial, we held that a new trial was a remedy for such publicity, but

> we must remember that reversals are but palliatives; the cure lies in those remedial measures that will prevent the prejudice at its inception. The courts must take such steps by rule and regulation that will protect their processes from prejudicial outside interferences. Neither prosecutors, counsel for defense, the accused, witnesses, court staff nor enforcement officers coming under the jurisdiction of the court should be permitted to frustrate its function. *Collaboration between counsel and the press as to information affecting the fairness of a criminal trial is not only subject to regulation, but is highly censurable and worthy of disciplinary measures.* (Emphasis added).

We expressly contemplated that the speech of *those participating before the courts* could be limited.[5] This distinction between participants in the litigation and strangers to it is brought into sharp relief by our holding in Seattle Times Co. v. Rhinehart. There, we unanimously held that a newspaper, which was itself a defendant in a libel action, could be restrained from publishing material about the plaintiffs and their supporters to which it had gained access through court-ordered discovery. In that case we said that "[a]lthough litigants do not 'surrender their First Amendment rights at the courthouse door,' those rights may be subordinated to other interests that arise in this setting," and noted that "on several occasions [we have] approved restriction on the communications of trial participants where necessary to ensure a fair trial for a criminal defendant."

We think that the quoted statements from our opinions in In re Sawyer, and Sheppard v. Maxwell, rather plainly indicate that the speech of lawyers representing clients in pending cases may be regulated under a less demanding standard than that established for regulation of the press in Nebraska Press Assn. v. Stuart and the cases which preceded it. Lawyers representing clients in pending cases are key participants in the criminal justice system, and the State may demand some adherence to the precepts of that system in regulating their speech as well as their conduct. As noted by Justice Brennan in his concurring opinion in *Nebraska Press,* which was joined by Justices Stewart and Marshall, "[a]s officers of the court, court personnel and attorneys have a fiduciary responsibility not to engage in public debate that will redound to the detriment of the accused or that will obstruct the fair administration of justice." Because lawyers have special access to information through discovery and client communications, their extrajudicial statements pose a threat to the fairness of a pending proceeding since lawyers' statements are likely to be

5. The Nevada Supreme Court has consistently read all parts of Rule 177 as applying only to lawyers in pending cases, and not to other lawyers or nonlawyers. We express no opinion on the constitutionality of a rule regulating the statements of a lawyer who is not participating in the pending case about which the statements are made. . . .

received as especially authoritative. See, e.g., In re Hinds, 90 N.J. 604, 627, 449 A.2d 483, 496 (1982) (statements by attorneys of record relating to the case "are likely to be considered knowledgeable, reliable and true" because of attorneys' unique access to information); In re Rachmiel, 90 N.J. 646, 656, 449 A.2d 505, 511 (N.J. 1982) (attorneys' role as advocates gives them "extraordinary power to undermine or destroy the efficacy of the criminal justice system"). We agree with the majority of the States that the "substantial likelihood of material prejudice" standard constitutes a constitutionally permissible balance between the First Amendment rights of attorneys in pending cases and the state's interest in fair trials.

When a state regulation implicates First Amendment rights, the Court must balance those interests against the State's legitimate interest in regulating the activity in question. The "substantial likelihood" test embodied in Rule 177 is constitutional under this analysis, for it is designed to protect the integrity and fairness of a state's judicial system, and it imposes only narrow and necessary limitations on lawyers' speech. The limitations are aimed at two principal evils: (1) comments that are likely to influence the actual outcome of the trial, and (2) comments that are likely to prejudice the jury venire, even if an untainted panel can ultimately be found. Few, if any, interests under the Constitution are more fundamental than the right to a fair trial by "impartial" jurors, and an outcome affected by extrajudicial statements would violate that fundamental right. Even if a fair trial can ultimately be ensured through voir dire, change of venue, or some other device, these measures entail serious costs to the system. Extensive voir dire may not be able to filter out all of the effects of pretrial publicity, and with increasingly widespread media coverage of criminal trials, a change of venue may not suffice to undo the effects of statements such as those made by petitioner. The State has a substantial interest in preventing officers of the court, such as lawyers, from imposing such costs on the judicial system and on the litigants.

The restraint on speech is narrowly tailored to achieve those objectives. The regulation of attorneys' speech is limited — it applies only to speech that is substantially likely to have a materially prejudicial effect; it is neutral as to points of view, applying equally to all attorneys' participating in a pending case; and it merely postpones the attorney's comments until after the trial. While supported by the substantial state interest in preventing prejudice to an adjudicative proceeding by those who have a duty to protect its integrity, the rule is limited on its face to preventing only speech having a substantial likelihood of materially prejudicing that proceeding.

III . . .

Gentile also argues that Rule 177 is void for vagueness because it did not provide adequate notice that his comments were subject to discipline.

The void-for-vagueness doctrine is concerned with a defendant's right to fair notice and adequate warning that his conduct runs afoul of the law. Rule 177 was drafted with the intent to provide "an illustrative compilation that gives fair notice of conduct ordinarily posing unacceptable dangers to the fair administration of justice." The Rule provides sufficient notice of the nature of the prohibited conduct. Under the circumstances of his case, petitioner cannot complain about lack of notice, as he has admitted that his primary objective in holding the press conference was the violation of Rule 177's core prohibition — to prejudice the upcoming trial by influencing potential jurors. Petitioner was clearly given notice that such conduct was forbidden, and the list of conduct likely to cause prejudice, while only advisory, certainly gave notice that the statements made would violate the rule if they had the intended effect.

The majority agrees with petitioner that he was the victim of unconstitutional vagueness in the regulations because of the relationship between §3 and §§1 and 2 of rule 177. Section 3 allows an attorney to state "the general nature of the claim or defense" notwithstanding the prohibition contained in §1 and the examples contained in §2. It is of course true, as the majority points out, that the word "general" and the word "elaboration" are both terms of degree. But combined as they are in the first sentence of §3, they convey the very definite proposition that the authorized statements must not contain the sort of detailed allegations that petitioner made at his press conference. No sensible person could think that the following were "general" statements of a claim or defense made "without elaboration": "the person that was in the most direct position to have stolen the drugs and the money . . . is Detective Steve Scholl"; "there is far more evidence that will establish that Detective Scholl took these drugs and took these American Express travelers' checks than any other living human being"; "[Detective Scholl] either had a hell of a cold, or he should have seen a better doctor"; and "the so-called other victims . . . one, two — four of them are known drug dealers and convicted money launderers." §3, as an exception to the provisions of §§1 and 2, must be read in the light of the prohibitions and examples contained in the first two sections. It was obviously not intended to negate the prohibitions or the examples wholesale, but simply intended to provide a "safe harbor" where there might be doubt as to whether one of the examples covered proposed conduct. These provisions were not vague as to the conduct for which petitioner was disciplined; "[i]n determining the sufficiency of the notice a statute must of necessity be examined in the light of the conduct with which a defendant is charged."

Petitioner's strongest arguments are that the statement was made well in advance of trial, and that the statements did not in fact taint the jury panel. But the Supreme Court of Nevada pointed out that petitioner's statements were not only highly inflammatory — they portrayed prospective government witnesses as drug users and dealers, and as money launderers — but the statements were timed to have maximum impact, when public interest in the case was at its height immediately after Sanders was indicted. Reviewing independently the entire record, we are convinced that petitioner's statements were "substantially likely to cause material prejudice" to the proceedings. While there is evidence pro and con on that point, we find it persuasive that, by his own admission, petitioner called the press conference for the express purpose of influencing the venire. It is difficult to believe that he went to such trouble, and took such a risk, if there was no substantial likelihood that he would succeed.

While in a case such as this we must review the record for ourselves, when the highest court of a state has reached a determination "we give most respectful attention to its reasoning and conclusion." The State Bar of Nevada, which made its own factual findings, and the Supreme Court of Nevada, which upheld those findings, were in a far better position than we are to appreciate the likely effect of petitioner's statements on potential members of a jury panel in a highly publicized case such as this. The Board and Nevada Supreme Court did not apply the list of statements likely to cause material prejudice as presumptions, but specifically found that petitioner had intended to prejudice the trial,[6] and that based upon the nature of the statements and their timing, they were in fact substantially likely to cause material prejudice. We cannot, upon our review of the record, conclude that they were mistaken.

Several amici argue that the First Amendment requires the state to show actual prejudice to a judicial proceeding before an attorney may be disciplined for extrajudicial statements, and since the Board and Nevada Supreme Court found no actual prejudice, petitioner should not have been disciplined. But this is simply another way of stating that the stringent standard of *Nebraska Press* should be applied to the speech of a lawyer in a pending case, and for the reasons heretofore given we decline to adopt it. An added objection to the stricter standard when applied to lawyer participants is that if it were adopted, even comments more flagrant than those made by petitioner could not serve as the basis for disciplinary

6. Justice Kennedy appears to contend that there can be no material prejudice when the lawyer's publicity is in response to publicity favorable to the other side. Justice Kennedy would find that publicity designed to counter prejudicial publicity cannot be itself prejudicial, despite its likelihood of influencing potential jurors, unless it actually would go so far as to cause jurors to be affirmatively biased in favor of the lawyer's client. In the first place, such a test would be difficult, if not impossible, to apply. But more fundamentally, it misconceives the constitutional test for an impartial juror — whether the "juror can lay aside his impression or opinion and render a verdict on the evidence presented in Court." Murphy v. Florida, 421 U.S. 794, 800 (1975). A juror who may have been initially swayed from open-mindedness by publicity favorable to the prosecution is not rendered fit for service by being bombarded by publicity favorable to the defendant. The basic premise of our legal system is that law suits should be tried in court, not in the media. A defendant may be protected from publicity by, or in favor of, the police and prosecution through voir dire, change of venue, jury instructions and, in extreme cases, reversal on due process grounds. The remedy for prosecutorial abuses that violate the rule lies not in self-help in the form of similarly prejudicial comments by defense counsel, but in disciplining the prosecutor.

action if, for wholly independent reasons, they had no effect on the proceedings. An attorney who made prejudicial comments would be insulated from discipline if the government, for reasons unrelated to the comments, decided to dismiss the charges, or if a plea bargain were reached. An equally culpable attorney whose client's case went to trial would be subject to discipline. The United States Constitution does not mandate such a fortuitous difference. . . .

JUSTICE O'CONNOR, concurring.

I agree with much of The Chief Justice's opinion. In particular, I agree that a State may regulate speech by lawyers representing clients in pending cases more readily than it may regulate the press. . . .

For the reasons set out in Part III of Justice Kennedy's opinion, however, I believe that Nevada's rule is void for vagueness. Subsection (3) of Rule 177 is a "safe harbor" provision. . . . Gentile made a conscious effort to stay within the boundaries of this "safe harbor." In his brief press conference, Gentile gave only a rough sketch of the defense that he intended to present at trial — i.e., that Detective Scholl, not Grady Sanders, stole the cocaine and traveler's checks. When asked to provide more details, he declined, stating explicitly that the ethical rules compelled him to do so. Nevertheless, the disciplinary board sanctioned Gentile because, in its view, his remarks went beyond the scope of what was permitted by the rule. Both Gentile and the disciplinary board have valid arguments on their side, but this serves to support the view that the rule provides insufficient guidance. As Justice Kennedy correctly points out, a vague law offends the Constitution because it fails to give fair notice to those it is intended to deter and creates the possibility of discriminatory enforcement. . . .

QUESTIONS ABOUT GENTILE

1. Why, exactly, did Gentile win?

2. How, if at all, should the ABA now amend Rule 3.6? Is it possible to have both a "safe harbor" and constitutionally adequate notice?

3. After *Gentile*, what if any protection against discipline does the First Amendment afford lawyers who speak about their own cases? What protection would Justice Kennedy recognize?

4. After *Gentile*, what if any protection does the First Amendment afford lawyers who speak about some other lawyer's cases? (Rule 3.6(a) and (b), unlike DR 7-107, may be read to apply to all lawyers, not only those associated with a matter.) Do statements by lawyers who are *not* associated with a case present any greater threat to a fair trial (or anything else) than do the statements of others?

5. If we assume that voir dire can discover and eliminate pretrial prejudice — an assumption that courts routinely make in response to de-

fense motions to change venue — what legitimate state interest supports a curb on a lawyer's public statements? Put it another way: If in fact voir dire will remedy prejudice, why do lawyers engage in "spin control" in the first place?

6. In perhaps his most remarkable paragraph, Justice Kennedy wrote (page 755 supra):

> An attorney's duties do not begin inside the courtroom door. . . . [A]n attorney may take reasonable steps to defend a client's reputation and reduce the adverse consequences of indictment . . . including an attempt to demonstrate in the court of public opinion that the client does not deserve to be tried.

Could a "movement" lawyer have put it better? Can it be that four Supreme Court Justices (but only four!) are prepared to vest lawyers with the right, perhaps the duty, to advocate for their clients in public? If they are correct (are they correct?), why have a pretrial publicity rule at all?

QUESTION

15.1   In 1991, William Kennedy Smith was charged with rape in Palm Beach County, Florida. The allegation received worldwide press attention because Smith's mother is the sister of Senator Edward Kennedy and President John F. Kennedy and because Senator Kennedy was staying at the Kennedy's Palm Beach estate when the alleged rape occurred. The court imposed a "gag" order on the prosecution and defense that, essentially, prohibited the lawyers and their agents from speaking with the media about the case.

In the course of her investigation, the prosecutor, Moira Lasch, discovered three other women who were prepared to testify that Smith either raped them or attempted to do so. These three alleged sexual assaults occurred in 1983 and 1988 and were not previously reported to authorities.

Florida law requires a prosecutor to give notice "to the accused" 10 days before trial of the state's intent to offer evidence of prior criminal conduct. Lasch took depositions from the women, in which they described Smith's alleged assaults in some detail, notified Smith's lawyers of her intention to call the women as witnesses, and hours later filed the depositions transcripts in court, where the media would and did obtain them. National headlines followed. Rape Suspect Tied to Prior Incidents, N.Y. Times, July 22, 1991, at A14; Accusation Against Kennedy Nephew Detailed, N.Y. Times, July 23, 1991, at A14.

Smith's lawyers made a number of motions, including to delay the trial and to require that all future court filings be under seal. The trial was delayed until December 1991 following evidence that the revelations prejudiced Smith. The motion to seal was denied, but the judge required that certain court filings first be approved by the court. Thereafter, Smith's lawyer, Roy Black, moved the court for an order allowing the defense to see the medical history and "all relevant records of psychological or psychiatric treatment" of the complainant. The motion alleged that the complainant's "severe pre-existing emotional problems" caused her to invent the accusation against Smith; that there was "strong and compelling evidence [that the complainant] is mentally or emotionally unstable and that due to this instability her allegations are spurious"; that the woman had received counseling "as a result of having been sexually abused when she was 8 years of age"; and that there was a "history of mental disorder" in the woman's family and "traumatic relationships" with her father and stepfather. This motion, too, was publicly filed, and also received media attention, although not as much as the prosecutor's notice. Lawyers in Smith Case Seek Woman's Mental Records, N.Y. Times, Aug. 10, 1991, at 6.

How do you evaluate the conduct of the two lawyers in the Smith case? Did the prosecutor have a higher duty than the defense lawyer? Is the defense lawyer's conduct justified as responsive? Should both lawyers be condemned? Does it affect your judgment that, previously, the New York Times printed a controversial article that named the alleged victim; reported that she had had a child out of wedlock following an affair with the son of a "once-prosperous" Palm Beach family; revealed that she had received 17 tickets for moving violations; and quoted an anonymous source to the effect that she "had a little wild streak"? The article also quoted an acquaintance who said, "She liked to drink and have fun with the ne'er-do-wells in cafe society." Woman in Florida Rape Inquiry Fought Adversity and Sought Acceptance, N.Y. Times, Apr. 17, 1991, at A17.

B.   PUBLIC COMMENT ABOUT JUDGES AND COURTS

1.   Criticizing the Administration of Justice

Robert Snyder, Esquire, (a) wanted to be some kind of hero, (b) held fast on a matter of principle, (c) foolishly hurt his reputation for no transcendent value, (d) all or none of the above, (e)?

Snyder practiced in North Dakota. The district court appointed him to represent a defendant under the Criminal Justice Act (CJA), which authorizes (modest) government compensation to lawyers so appointed. When the case ended, Snyder claimed $1,898 under the meager government rates. The district court approved $1,796. Not bad. But the law required circuit court approval of amounts above $1,000. The chief judge of the circuit returned Snyder's claim with a request for more information. Snyder supplied it, but the chief judge found it wanting. Snyder wrote a letter to the district judge's secretary in which he said:

> In the first place, I am appalled by the amount of money which the federal court pays for indigent criminal defense work. The reason that so few attorneys in Bismarck accept this work is for that exact reason. We have, up to this point, still accepted the indigent appointments, because of a duty to our profession, and the fact that nobody else will do it.
>
> Now, however, not only are we paid an amount of money which does not even cover our overhead, but we have to go through extreme gymnastics even to receive the puny amounts which the federal courts authorize for this work. We have sent you everything we have concerning our representation, and I am not sending you anything else. You can take it or leave it.
>
> Further, I am extremely disgusted by the treatment of us by the Eighth Circuit in this case, and you are instructed to remove my name from the list of attorneys who will accept criminal indigent defense work. I have simply had it.
>
> Thank you for your time and attention.

Now the battle of wills began. The district judge discussed the letter with the chief judge who, irritated by its tone, questioned Snyder's fitness to practice in the federal courts but offered to drop the matter if Snyder would apologize, which Snyder would not. Snyder was ordered to show cause why he should not be suspended, not because of the tone of his letter, mind you, but because of his professed "refusal" to accept further CJA assignments. Snyder responded that many lawyers did not accept CJA assignments and that theretofore his firm had taken 15 percent of the CJA assignments in the district.

A hearing was held. Over Snyder's protest, it focused not on Snyder's refusal to accept future assignments, the subject of the show cause order, but on the tone of Snyder's letter. Snyder was given 10 days to "reconsider" his tone. Instead, he reconsidered CJA assignments. He said he'd accept them if all lawyers in his district were required to do so. The chief judge once again asked Snyder "to apologize for the letter that you wrote." Snyder replied:

> I cannot, and will never, in justice to my conscience, apologize for what I consider to be telling the truth, albeit in harsh terms. . . .

It is unfortunate that the respective positions in the proceeding have so hardened. However, I consider this to be a matter of principle, and if one stands on a principle, one must be willing to accept the consequences.

Citing Snyder's "contumacious conduct," the Eighth Circuit suspended him from practice in all federal courts in the circuit for six months. Readmission was contingent on reapplication (and an apology?). Rehearing en banc was denied, the court writing that the "gravamen of the situation is that [Snyder's letter] became harsh and disrespectful to the Court."

The Supreme Court granted review and, in an opinion by Chief Justice Burger, unanimously reversed the suspension. In re Snyder, 472 U.S. 634 (1985). (Justice Blackmun did not participate.) Avoiding Snyder's First Amendment claim, the Court held that the record did not establish a basis for suspension under Rule 46 of the Federal Rules of Appellate Procedure, which authorizes suspension for conduct "unbecoming a member of the bar." It said that the remedy for Snyder's failure to augment the information in his fee application was denial of a fee, not discipline. The Court continued:

We do not consider a lawyer's criticism of the administration of the Act or criticism of inequities in assignments under the Act as cause for discipline or suspension. The letter was addressed to a court employee charged with administrative responsibilities, and concerned a practical matter in the administration of the Act. The Court of Appeals acknowledged that petitioner brought to light concerns about the administration of the plan that had "merit" and the court instituted a study of the administration of the Criminal Justice Act as a result of petitioner's complaint. Officers of the court may appropriately express criticism on such matters.

The record indicates the Court of Appeals was concerned about the tone of the letter; petitioner concedes that the tone of his letter was "harsh," and, indeed it can be read as ill-mannered. All persons involved in the judicial process — judges, litigants, witnesses, and court officers — owe a duty of courtesy to all other participants. The necessity for civility in the inherently contentious setting of the adversary process suggests that members of the bar cast criticisms of the system in a professional and civil tone. However, even assuming that the letter exhibited an unlawyer-like rudeness, a single incident of rudeness or lack of professional courtesy — in this context — does not support a finding of contemptuous or contumacious conduct, or a finding that a lawyer is "not presently fit to practice law in the federal courts." Nor does it rise to the level of "conduct unbecoming a member of the bar" warranting suspension from practice.

Catch that phrase "single incident." What does it portend? Does any legitimate state interest support a lower level of First Amendment protection for lawyers who criticize the justice system rudely and often?

For the Eighth Circuit's parting shot, in its remand order vacating the suspension, see In re Snyder, 770 F.2d 743 (8th Cir. 1985).

2. *Criticizing Particular Judges*

Judges are public officials. The Supreme Court has held that public officials who sue for defamation must prove falsity and "actual malice" — defined as knowledge of a statement's falsity or reckless (i.e., conscious) disregard for its truth. Harte-Hanks Communications, Inc. v. Connaughton, 491 U.S. 657 (1989); New York Times v. Sullivan, 376 U.S. 254 (1964). Does the same standard apply before a lawyer may be disciplined for public criticism of a judge? *Gentile* gave less protection to lawyers who make pretrial statements about pending cases. Does the same diminished protection apply when a lawyer's criticism of a judge turns out to be false? Ruling under DR 8-102(B), the court in State v. Nelson, 210 Kan. 637, 504 P.2d 211 (1972), rejected a defense based on the *New York Times* standard. Does Rule 8.2(a) overrule that result?

The following case tells the story of Elizabeth Holtzman, Comptroller of New York City, former Brooklyn district attorney, and former member of the House Judiciary Committee during the Watergate investigation. She did not fare as well as Gentile and Snyder.

MATTER OF HOLTZMAN
78 N.Y.2d 184, 577 N.E.2d 30, 573 N.Y.S.2d 39, cert. denied,
112 S. Ct. — (1991)

Per Curiam. . . .

The charge of misconduct that is relevant to this appeal was based on the public release by petitioner, then District Attorney of Kings County, of a letter charging Judge Irving Levine with judicial misconduct in relation to an incident that allegedly occurred in the course of a trial on criminal charges of sexual misconduct (Penal Law §130.20), and was reported to her some six weeks later. Specifically, petitioner's letter stated that:

> Judge Levine asked the Assistant District Attorney, defense counsel, defendant, court officer and court reporter to join him in the robing room, where the judge then asked the victim to get down on the floor and show the position she was in when she was being sexually assaulted. . . . The victim reluctantly got down on her hands and knees as everyone stood and watched. In making the victim assume the position she was forced to take when she was sexually assaulted, Judge Levine profoundly degraded, humiliated and demeaned her.

The letter, addressed to Judge Kathryn McDonald as Chair of the Committee to implement Recommendations of the New York State Task Force on Women in the Courts, was publicly disseminated after petitioner's office issued a "news alert" to the media.

Following a dispute over the truth of the accusations, Robert Keating, as Administrative Judge of the New York City Criminal Court, conducted an investigation into the allegations of judicial misconduct. His report, dated December 22, 1987, concluded that petitioner's accusations were not supported by the evidence. Upon receipt of the report, Albert M. Rosenblatt, then Chief Administrative Judge, referred the matter to the Grievance Committee for inquiry as to whether petitioner had violated the Code of Professional Responsibility.

Some six months later, the Grievance Committee sent petitioner a private Letter of Admonition in which it stated that "the totality of the circumstances presented by this matter require that you be admonished for your conduct." Petitioner's misconduct, the Committee concluded, violated DR 8-102(B), DR 1-102(A)(5),(6) and EC 8-6 of the Code of Professional Responsibility.

In July 1988, after petitioner requested a subcommittee hearing, she was served with three formal charges of misconduct under DR 8-102(B) and DR 1-102(A)(5) and (6). Charge One alleged that petitioner had engaged in conduct that adversely reflected on her fitness to practice law in releasing a false accusation of misconduct against Judge Levine. . . . Only Charge One is in issue on this appeal.

The conduct set forth in Charge One, allegedly demonstrating petitioner's unfitness to practice law, included release of the letter to the media (1) prior to obtaining the minutes of the criminal trial, (2) without making any effort to speak with court officers, the court reporter, defense counsel or any other person present during the alleged misconduct, (3) without meeting with or discussing the incident with the trial assistant who reported it [in memoranda], and (4) with the knowledge that Judge Levine was being transferred out of the Criminal Court, and the matter would be investigated by the Court's Administrative Judge as well as the Commission on Judicial Conduct (to which the petitioner had complained). . . .

Petitioner relies primarily on two arguments. First, she asserts that the allegations concerning Judge Levine's conduct were true or at least not demonstrably false. Second, petitioner asserts that her conduct violates no specific disciplinary rule and further that DR 1-102(A)(6), if applicable, is unconstitutionally vague. These contentions are without merit.

The factual basis of Charge One is that petitioner made false accusations against the Judge. This charge was sustained by the Committee and upheld by the Appellate Division, and the factual finding of falsity (which is supported by the record) is therefore binding on us.

As for the contention that petitioner's conduct did not violate any provision of the Code, DR 1-102(A)(6) provides that a lawyer shall not "[e]ngage in any other conduct that adversely reflects on [the lawyer's] fitness to practice law." As far back as 1856, the Supreme Court acknowledged that "it is difficult if not impossible, to enumerate and define, with legal precision, every offense for which an attorney can be removed" (Ex Parte Secombe, 60 U.S. [19 How] 9, 14). Broad standards governing professional conduct are permissible and indeed often necessary.

Such standards are set forth in Canon 1 and particularly in DR 1-102. An earlier draft of the Code listed "conduct degrading to the legal profession" as a basis for a finding of misconduct under DR 1-102, but this provision was replaced by the "fitness" language of DR 1-102(A)(6) and the "prejudicial to the administration of justice" standard of DR 1-102(A)(5) (see, Annotated Code of Professional Responsibility, Textual and Historical Notes, at 12). The drafters of the Code refined the provisions to provide attorneys with proper ethical guidelines. Were we to find such language impermissibly vague, attempts to promulgate general guidelines such as DR 1-102(A)(6) would be futile.

Rather than an absolute prohibition on broad standards, the guiding principle must be whether a reasonable attorney, familiar with the Code and its ethical strictures, would have notice of what conduct is proscribed.

Applying this standard, petitioner was plainly on notice that her conduct in this case, involving public dissemination of a specific accusation of improper judicial conduct under the circumstances described, could be held to reflect adversely on her fitness to practice law. Indeed, her staff, including the person assigned the task of looking into the ethical implications of release to the press, counseled her to delay publication until the trial minutes were received.

Petitioner's act was not generalized criticism but rather release to the media of a false allegation of specific wrongdoing, made without any support other than the interoffice memoranda of a newly admitted trial assistant, aimed at a named judge who had presided over a number of cases prosecuted by her office. Petitioner knew or should have known that such attacks are unwarranted and unprofessional, serve to bring the bench and bar into disrepute, and tend to undermine public confidence in the judicial system.

Therefore, petitioner's conduct was properly the subject of disciplinary action under DR 1-102(A)(6), and it is of no consequence that she might be charged with violating DR 8-102(B) based on this same course of conduct. Indeed, in the present case there are factors that distinguish petitioner's conduct from that prohibited under DR 8-102(B) — most notably, release of the false charges to the media — and make it particularly relevant to her fitness to practice law.

Petitioner contends that her conduct would not be actionable under the "constitutional malice" standard enunciated by the Supreme Court in New York Times v. Sullivan (376 U.S. 254). Neither this Court nor the Supreme Court has ever extended the *Sullivan* standard to lawyer discipline and we decline to do so here.

Accepting petitioner's argument would immunize all accusations, however reckless or irresponsible, from censure as long as the attorney uttering them did not actually entertain serious doubts as to their truth. Such a standard would be wholly at odds with the policy underlying the rules governing professional responsibility, which seeks to establish a "minimum level of conduct below which no lawyer can fall without being subject to disciplinary action." (Code of Professional Responsibility, Preliminary Statement.)

Unlike defamation cases, "[p]rofessional misconduct, although it may directly affect an individual, is not punished for the benefit of the affected person; the wrong is against society as a whole, the preservation of a fair, impartial judicial system, and the system of justice as it has evolved for generations." It follows that the issue raised when an attorney makes public a false accusation of wrongdoing by a judge is not whether the target of the false attack has been harmed in reputation; the issue is whether that criticism adversely affects the administration of justice and adversely reflects on the attorney's judgment and, consequentially, her ability to practice law.

In order to adequately protect the public interest and maintain the integrity of the judicial system, there must be an objective standard, of what a reasonable attorney would do in similar circumstances. It is the reasonableness of the belief, not the state of mind of the attorney, that is determinative.

Petitioner's course of conduct satisfies any standard other than "constitutional malice," and therefore Charge One must be sustained.*

QUESTIONS ABOUT HOLTZMAN

1. In a public statement issued after the decision, Holtzman said: "The court's decision is a blow to those who value freedom of speech and who care about the treatment of rape victims by the courts." N.Y. Law J., July 2, 1991, at 1. Is she right?

2. Should Holtzman's position as D.A. give her a greater obligation to "get it right" than that imposed on others who criticize judges? (Consider the same court's opinion in *Erdmann* below.)

3. Does the court's standard — "whether a reasonable attorney, familiar with the Code and its ethical strictures, would have notice of what conduct is proscribed" — give adequate notice of the conduct proscribed by DR 1-102(A)(6)? Compare *Gentile. Holtzman* was decided four days after *Gentile.* Why did the court ignore *Gentile's* vagueness analysis?

4. In any event, why wasn't a memorandum from a lawyer on her staff — albeit a "newly admitted" one — a sufficient basis for Holtzman's re-

*Chief Judge Wachtler did not participate. — ED.

sponse? Was it the nature of the response that caused the court to find a violation? Or was it the fact, as the court assumed, that the charge was false? Or both?

Other Examples of Lawyers Criticizing Judges and Justice

Less than two months before *Holtzman,* another prosecutor was reprimanded for a different kind of statement. After losing a case in an intermediate appellate court, the prosecuting attorney of St. Louis County, George Westfall, said this in a television interview of the judge who wrote the opinion: (1) his reasons were "somewhat illogical and I think a little bit less than honest"; (2) he "has distorted the statute and I think convoluted logic to arrive at a decision that he personally likes"; (3) the decision "says to me that [the judge] made up his mind before he wrote the decision, and just reached the conclusion that he wanted to reach."

Missouri has Rule 8.2 and the court agreed that the *New York Times* standard applied. But it held that in applying that standard, the reference should be to what a reasonable attorney would know or believe, not Westfall's own state of mind. The interest in protecting the public, the administration of justice, and the profession made a purely subjective test inappropriate, said the court. Matter of Westfall, — Mo. — , 808 S.W.2d 829, cert. denied, 112 S. Ct. — (1991). Chief Justice Blackmar wrote a lengthy dissent ("We should proceed very carefully when we are asked to censor or censure political speech."). Id. at 839.

Life Magazine published an article about Martin Erdmann, a New York City Legal Aid lawyer, entitled "I Have Nothing to Do with Justice." The article quoted him as follows:

> There are so few trial judges who just judge, who rule on questions of law, and leave guilt or innocence to the jury. And Appellate Division judges aren't any better. They're the whores who became madams.
>
> I would like to [be a judge] just to see if I could be the kind of judge I think a judge should be. But the only way you get it is to be in politics or buy it — and I don't even know the going price.

Erdmann was charged with professional misconduct and censured by an intermediate appellate court other than the one he criticized in the article. He appealed. In In re Erdmann, 33 N.Y.2d 559, 301 N.E.2d 426, 427, 347 N.Y.S.2d 441 (1973), the New York Court of Appeals reversed per curiam:

> Without more, isolated instances of disrespect for the law, Judges and courts expressed by vulgar and insulting words or other incivility, uttered,

written, or committed outside the precincts of a court are not subject to professional discipline. Nor is the matter substantially altered if there is hyperbole expressed in the impoverished vocabulary of the street. . . .

Perhaps persistent or general courses of conduct, even if parading as criticism, which are degrading to the law, the Bar, and the courts, and are irrelevant or grossly excessive, would present a different issue. No such issue is presented now.

Some years later the mayor of New York City appointed Erdmann a criminal court judge.

In State Bar v. Semaan, 508 S.W.2d 429, 431-432 (Tex. Ct. Civ. App. 1974), a newspaper editorially criticized a judicial decision by Judge Benavides. Mr. Semaan then wrote a letter to the newspaper comparing Judge Benavides unfavorably with three other named criminal court judges in the county and concluded: "Standing beside these men, John Benavides is a midget among giants." The letter was printed. Semaan was charged with professional misconduct based on this letter and several others. The court held that the letter did not violate the ethical code. "The criticism related entirely to the writer's opinion of Judge Benavides' qualifications for office. The issue of 'truth and falsity' of the criticism was not involved, nor was the question of improper motive."

C. MANDATORY BAR MEMBERSHIP

Some states require lawyers admitted to their bars to join and pay dues to the state bar association — called an "integrated" bar association because it integrates all lawyers in the state. An integrated bar may, in turn, be given quasi-governmental functions. In California, for example, the state bar aids the State Supreme Court in the admission of new lawyers, in formulating professional conduct rules, with discipline, in preventing unauthorized law practice, and by recommending improvements in procedural law and the administration of justice.

But a state bar may, acting through its governing board, do much more. In California, again, the state bar lobbies, files amicus briefs, and adopts resolutions on public issues. The California State Bar has lobbied against mandatory polygraph testing for private employment, against gun control, and for universal standing to sue for air pollution. It has supported a nuclear weapons freeze and opposed efforts to limit federal jurisdiction in abortion, school prayer, and busing cases. You get the picture.

A California lawyer obliged to belong to the state bar and pay its dues may disagree with these positions and resent supporting them. In fact, at least 21 California lawyers did resent it and, being lawyers, sued for relief in state court. When they lost, being angry lawyers, they made a federal case out of it: Keller v. State Bar of California, 110 S. Ct. 2228 (1990). The issue in *Keller* was not whether the state could require its lawyers to belong to the state bar and pay its dues (it could), or whether the state bar could use those dues to discipline lawyers, advise on the administration of justice, and the like (it could), but whether the state bar's members could keep their own dues from being used to advance ideological positions with which they disagreed. They could. A unanimous Court wrote:

> Precisely where the line falls between those State Bar activities in which the officials and members of the Bar are acting essentially as professional advisors to those ultimately charged with the regulation of the legal profession, on the one hand, and those activities having political or ideological coloration which are not reasonably related to the advancement of such goals, on the other, will not always be easy to discern. But the extreme ends of the spectrum are clear: Compulsory dues may not be expended to endorse or advance a gun control or nuclear weapons freeze initiative; at the other end of the spectrum petitioners have no valid constitutional objection to their compulsory dues being spent for activities connected with disciplining members of the bar or proposing ethical codes for the profession.

What procedures must an integrated state bar adopt to ensure that a member's dues are not used for purposes the member has a constitutional right to oppose? *Keller* didn't say, but Gibson v. Florida Bar, 906 F.2d 624 (11th Cir. 1990), decided shortly after *Keller,* did. The Florida bar's system was challenged because it required a member to object to the use of his or her dues on an issue-by-issue basis; it used an arbitration panel composed of financially interested state bar members to resolve the objection; and it provided for a "refund" with interest if the objection prevailed instead of "advance deduction" of the portion of dues allocated to the opposed use. The Eleventh Circuit rejected each of these challenges. But it held that interest on the refund had to be calculated from the date the dues were paid, not from the date the objection was received. The Supreme Court granted review then dismissed the writ as improvidently granted, 112 S. Ct. — (1991), following restrictions imposed in The Florida Bar, 581 So. 2d 1294 (Fla. 1991). For another post-*Keller* case, see Schneider v. Collegio de Abogados de Puerto Rico, 917 F.2d 620 (1st Cir. 1990) (addressing both refund procedures and the distinction between the purposes for which dues could be used and those for which it could not).

Keller left one intriguing question unresolved because it was not addressed below. Plaintiffs claimed not simply that the state bar could not use their money to advance ideological causes, but that given the mandatory membership, it could not use the state bar's name either. This claim rested on the idea that a person may not be "compelled to associate with an organization that engages in political or ideological activities beyond those for which mandatory support is [constitutionally] justified," even though the person is not required to fund the opposed activities. How should this issue be resolved?

XVI

<hr>

Marketing Legal Services

A. DEFINING THE BORDERS: *BATES* AND *OHRALIK*

For many, success comes too late or not at all. For some lawyers at the New York firm of Olwine Connelly, it came too early.

In 1962, Life magazine published a gushy article about the firm (A Day in the Life of a Wall Street Law Firm) with the help of some Olwine partners and associates. The article, accompanied by photographs, described the firm as "blue chip" and one that enjoys "the cream of corporate business." The participating partners were censured for fostering "self-interest publicity," but the associates were let off because the case was one of first impression. In re Connelly, 18 A.D.2d 466, 240 N.Y.S.2d 126 (1st Dept. 1963).

Vindication, of sorts, came 14 years later. Bates v. State Bar of Arizona, 433 U.S. 350 (1977), said advertising by lawyers was commercial speech entitled to First Amendment protection. *Bates* is usually credited (or discredited) for all those late-night television (and similar) ads for legal services. But *Bates*'s rationale was not limited to traditional advertising. By freeing lawyers to talk to the media, *Bates* invited efforts in self-promotion that were previously off limits. These efforts, in turn, facilitated growth of the "legal press" because lawyers could now freely talk to reporters. (The National Law Journal and the American Lawyer both began after *Bates*.) Today, law firms compete for media attention. Many retain outside public relations experts; some have marketing professionals on their payroll. An article like the one about Olwine Connelly would now be regarded as a great coup.

The point here is that there is more to legal marketing than "PERSONAL BANKRUPTCY/$299." In a stratified and increasingly competitive profession, we should expect many varieties of self-promotion.

Lawyers will aim at the audience that contains their potential client population and do so in commensurate style. So while some resort to the Yellow Pages, billboards, and matchbook covers ("Don't Perish in Jail/Call Murphy for Bail"), others choose more sophisticated venues. For example, Baker & McKenzie, America's largest law firm, profiled itself in a six-page color ad in California Lawyer magazine. One partner reflected that the ad "brought us enormous recognition, which inevitably leads to business." Wall St. J., Sept. 17, 1990, at B1. Squire, Sanders & Dempsey, a 400-lawyer Pittsburgh firm, found another way to generate good will and name recognition. It funded a travelling exhibition of Winslow Homer paintings to celebrate the firm's centennial. Id.

Some large-firm promotional efforts backfire and become news events for unanticipated and unwelcome reasons. One multicity firm sent a letter to potential tax clients boasting of its "direct access to members of congressional tax-writing committees" and to "senior officials in the Treasury and at the [IRS]." The letter also said that the firm provided "more than pure access." Government officials knew the firm's lawyers because of work those lawyers did "when we were with the government." Consequently, "we share a bond of trust" with these officials. While the firm may have thought it was touting its access, the press approached the story differently: "Even for Washington, a city inured to the revolving door between lawmaking and lobbying, the law firm's letter soliciting clients was unusually blunt," read the page one lead. Washington Post, May 27, 1988, at A1.

One excellent form of promotion for elite firms is to have their lawyers quoted in the press, especially the business press. After Iraq invaded Kuwait, the American asset freeze created legal problems for many. A public relations firm contacted reporters covering the story and "strongly" urged them to speak with a particular partner at Washington, D.C.'s Shaw, Pittman. Wall St. J., Aug. 22, 1990, at B5. When new regulations made Mexico a more attractive business environment for American companies, the PR people for New York's Curtis, Mallet-Prevost promoted the firm for its "tradition of Latin-American legal expertise" and organized a firm seminar for possible corporate clients and journalists. Natl. L.J., May 14, 1990, at 13.

But we're getting ahead of the story. Let us begin with the ad at issue in *Bates* (shown on the next page), which was tame, to say the least.

Arizona gave six reasons why it could forbid all legal advertising, including this one. Legal ads (1) would have an "adverse effect on professionalism" and encourage "commercialization," (2) were inherently misleading, (3) would stir up litigation, (4) would increase the cost of legal services, (5) would encourage shoddy work, and (6) were difficult to monitor against abuse. The Court rejected each of these blanket claims, examined the specific ad before it, and held it protected as commercial speech. But the Court also said that a state could prohibit false, deceptive,

787

or misleading ads, might be able to require a warning or disclaimer in legal ads, and could possibly restrict quality claims because they were hard to verify or measure. *Bates* evaluated a print ad. The Court took no position on ads on the "electronic broadcast media." In conclusion, Justice Blackmun wrote:

> The constitutional issue in this case is only whether the State may prevent the publication in a newspaper of appellants' truthful advertisement concerning the availability and terms of routine legal services. We rule simply that the flow of such information may not be restrained, and we therefore hold the present application of the disciplinary rule against appellants to be violative of the First Amendment.

Four Justices dissented.

Bates refused to credit the state's prediction of the harms legal advertising would bring. While some of the evils the state identified were within its power to prevent, there were other, less intrusive ways to prevent them. The status of a legal ad as commercial speech, entitled to limited First Amendment protection, led the Court to require proof of harm more focused than Arizona's general anxiety. By contrast, a year later, the Court was highly deferential to Ohio's reasons for curtailing a different kind of speech promoting a lawyer's services. How would you (how did the Court) explain the difference?

OHRALIK v. OHIO STATE BAR ASSN.
436 U.S. 447 (1978)

JUSTICE POWELL delivered the opinion of the Court.

In Bates v. State Bar of Arizona the Court held that truthful advertising of "routine" legal services is protected by the First and Fourteenth Amendments against blanket prohibition by a State. The Court expressly reserved the question of the permissible scope of regulation of "in-person solicitation of clients — at the hospital room or the accident site, or in any other situation that breeds undue influence — by attorneys or their agents or 'runners.' " Today we answer part of the question so reserved, and hold that the State — or the Bar acting with state authorization — constitutionally may discipline a lawyer for soliciting clients in person, for pecuniary gain, under circumstances likely to pose dangers that the State has a right to prevent.

I

Appellant, a member of the Ohio Bar, lives in Montville, Ohio. . . . On February 13, 1974, . . . appellant learned . . . about an automobile accident that had taken place on February 2 in which Carol McClintock, a young woman with whom appellant was casually acquainted, had been injured. Appellant [visited] Ms. McClintock's parents, [who] explained that their daughter had been driving the family automobile on a local road when she was hit by an uninsured motorist. Both Carol and her passenger, Wanda Lou Holbert, were injured and hospitalized. In response to the McClintocks' expression of apprehension that they might be sued by Holbert, appellant explained that Ohio's guest statute would preclude such a suit. When appellant suggested to the McClintocks that they hire a lawyer, Mrs. McClintock retorted that such a decision would be up to Carol, who was 18 years old and would be the beneficiary of a successful claim.

Appellant proceeded to the hospital, where he found Carol lying in traction in her room. After a brief conversation about her condition,[1] appellant told Carol he would represent her and asked her to sign an agreement. Carol said she would have to discuss the matter with her parents. She did not sign the agreement, but asked appellant to have her parents come to see her.[2] Appellant also attempted to see Wanda Lou Holbert, but learned that she had just been released from the hospital. He then departed for another visit with the McClintocks.

[A]ppellant [first] detoured to the scene of the accident, where he took a set of photographs. He also picked up a tape recorder, which he concealed under his raincoat before arriving at the McClintocks' residence. Once there, [a]ppellant discovered that the McClintocks' insurance policy would provide benefits of up to $12,500 each for Carol and Wanda Lou under an uninsured-motorist clause. . . . The McClintocks . . . told appellant that Carol had phoned to say that appellant could "go ahead" with her representation. Two days later appellant returned to Carol's hospital room to have her sign a contract, which provided that he would receive one-third of her recovery. . . .

[A]ppellant [later] visited Wanda Lou at her home, without having been invited. He again concealed his tape recorder and recorded most of the conversation with Wanda Lou. . . . [A]ppellant told Wanda Lou that he was representing Carol and that he had a "little tip" for Wanda Lou: the McClintocks' insurance policy contained an uninsured-motorist clause which might provide her with a recovery of up to $12,500. The young woman, who was 18 years of age and not a high school graduate at the time, replied to appellant's query about whether she was going to file a claim by stating that she really did not understand what was going on.

1. Carol also mentioned that one of the hospital administrators was urging a lawyer upon her. According to his own testimony, appellant replied: "Yes, this certainly is a case that would entice a lawyer. That would interest him a great deal."

2. Despite the fact that appellant maintains that he did not secure an agreement to represent Carol while he was at the hospital, he waited for an opportunity when no visitors were present and then took photographs of Carol in traction.

Appellant offered to represent her, also, for a contingent fee of one-third of any recovery, and Wanda Lou stated "O.K."[4]

Wanda's mother attempted to repudiate her daughter's oral assent the following day. . . . Appellant insisted that Wanda had entered into a binding agreement. A month later Wanda confirmed in writing that she wanted neither to sue nor to be represented by appellant. She requested that appellant notify the insurance company that he was not her lawyer, as the company would not release a check to her until he did so. Carol also eventually discharged appellant. Although another lawyer represented her in concluding a settlement with the insurance company, she paid appellant one-third of her recovery[6] in settlement of his lawsuit against her for breach of contract.

[After a disciplinary hearing, the Supreme Court of Ohio affirmed the finding that appellant had violated DR 2-103(A) and DR 2-104(A) of the code, and suspended him indefinitely.]

The decision in *Bates* was handed down after the conclusion of proceedings in the Ohio Supreme Court. We noted probable jurisdiction in this case to consider the scope of protection of a form of commercial speech, and an aspect of the State's authority to regulate and discipline members of the bar, not considered in *Bates*. We now affirm the judgment of the Supreme Court of Ohio.

II

The solicitation of business by a lawyer through direct in-person communication with the prospective client has long been viewed as inconsistent with the profession's ideal of the attorney-client relationship and as posing a significant potential for harm to the prospective client. It has been proscribed by the organized Bar for many years. Last Term the Court ruled that the justifications for prohibiting truthful, "restrained" advertising concerning "the availability and terms of routine legal services" are insufficient to override society's interest, safeguarded by the First and Fourteenth Amendments, in assuring the free flow of commercial information. The balance struck in *Bates* does not predetermine the outcome in this case. The entitlement of in-person solicitation of clients to the protection of the First Amendment differs from that of the kind of

4. Appellant told Wanda that she should indicate assent by stating "O.K.," which she did. Appellant later testified: "I would say that most of my clients have essentially that much of a communication. . . . I think most of my clients, that's the way I practice law."

In explaining the contingent-fee agreement, appellant told Wanda Lou that his representation would not "cost [her] anything" because she would receive two-thirds of the recovery if appellant were successful in representing her but would not "have to pay [him] anything" otherwise.

6. Carol recovered the full $12,500 and paid appellant $4,166.66. She testified that she paid the second lawyer $900 as compensation for his services.

advertising approved in *Bates*, as does the strength of the State's countervailing interest in prohibition.

A

Appellant contends that his solicitation of the two young women as clients is indistinguishable, for purposes of constitutional analysis, from the advertisement in *Bates*. Like that advertisement, his meetings with the prospective clients apprised them of their legal rights and of the availability of a lawyer to pursue their claims. According to appellant, such conduct is "presumptively an exercise of his free speech rights" which cannot be curtailed in the absence of proof that it actually caused a specific harm that the State has a compelling interest in preventing. But in-person solicitation of professional employment by a lawyer does not stand on a par with truthful advertising about the availability and terms of routine legal services, let alone with forms of speech more traditionally within the concern of the First Amendment. . . .

To require a parity of constitutional protection for commercial and noncommercial speech alike could invite dilution, simply by a leveling process, of the force of the Amendment's guarantee with respect to the latter kind of speech. Rather than subject the First Amendment to such a devitalization, we instead have afforded commercial speech a limited measure of protection, commensurate with its subordinate position in the scale of First Amendment values, while allowing modes of regulation that might be impermissible in the realm of noncommercial expression. . . .

In-person solicitation by a lawyer of remunerative employment is a business transaction in which speech is an essential but subordinate component. While this does not remove the speech from the protection of the First Amendment, as was held in *Bates* . . . , it lowers the level of appropriate judicial scrutiny.

As applied in this case, the Disciplinary Rules are said to have limited the communication of two kinds of information. First, appellant's solicitation imparted to Carol McClintock and Wanda Lou Holbert certain information about his availability and the terms of his proposed legal services. In this respect, in-person solicitation serves much the same function as the advertisement at issue in *Bates*. But there are significant differences as well. Unlike a public advertisement, which simply provides information and leaves the recipient free to act upon it or not, in-person solicitation may exert pressure and often demands an immediate response, without providing an opportunity for comparison or reflection. The aim and effect of in-person solicitation may be to provide a one-sided presentation and to encourage speedy and perhaps uninformed decisionmaking; there is no opportunity for intervention or countereducation by agencies of the Bar, supervisory authorities, or persons close to the solicited individual. The admonition that "the fitting remedy for evil counsels is good ones" is of little value when the circumstances provide no opportunity for any remedy at all. In-person solicitation is as likely as not to discourage persons needing counsel from engaging in a critical comparison of the "availability, nature, and prices" of legal services; it actually may disserve the individual and societal interest, identified in *Bates*, in facilitating "informed and reliable decisionmaking."

It also is argued that in-person solicitation may provide the solicited individual with information about his or her legal rights and remedies. . . . But neither of the Disciplinary Rules here at issue prohibited appellant from communicating information to these young women about their legal rights and the prospects of obtaining a monetary recovery, or from recommending that they obtain counsel. DR 2-104(A) merely prohibited him from using the information as bait with which to obtain an agreement to represent them for a fee. The Rule does not prohibit a lawyer from giving unsolicited legal advice; it proscribes the acceptance of employment resulting from such advice.[16]

B

The state interests implicated in this case are particularly strong. In addition to its general interest in protecting consumers and regulating commercial transactions, the State bears a special responsibility for maintaining standards among members of the licensed professions. "The interest of the States in regulating lawyers is especially great since lawyers are essential to the primary governmental function of administering justice, and have historically been 'officers of the courts.' " While lawyers act in part as "self-employed businessmen," they also act "as trusted agents of their clients, and as assistants to the court in search of a just solution to disputes." . . .

The substantive evils of solicitation have been stated over the years in sweeping terms: stirring up litigation, assertion of fraudulent claims, debasing the legal profession, and potential harm to the solicited client in the form of overreaching, overcharging, underrepresentation, and misrepresentation. The American Bar Association, as amicus curiae, defends the rule against solicitation primarily on three broad grounds: It is said that the prohibitions embodied in DR 2-103(A) and 2-104(A) serve

16. . . . In recognizing the importance of the State's interest in regulating solicitation of paying clients by lawyers, we are not unmindful of the problem of the related practice, described in *Railroad Trainmen* [page 725 supra], of the solicitation of releases of liability by claims agents or adjusters or prospective defendants or their insurers. Such solicitations frequently occur prior to the employment of counsel by the injured person and during circumstances posing many of the dangers of overreaching we address in this case. Where lay agents or adjusters are involved, these practices for the most part fall outside the scope of regulation by the organized Bar; but releases or settlements so obtained are viewed critically by the courts.

to reduce the likelihood of overreaching and the exertion of undue influence on lay persons, to protect the privacy of individuals, and to avoid situations where the lawyer's exercise of judgment on behalf of the client will be clouded by his own pecuniary self-interest.[19]

[A]ppellant has conceded that the State has a legitimate and indeed "compelling" interest in preventing those aspects of solicitation that involve fraud, undue influence, intimidation, overreaching, and other forms of "vexatious conduct." . . .

III

Appellant's concession that strong state interests justify regulation to prevent the evils he enumerates would end this case but for his insistence that none of those evils was found to be present in his acts of solicitation. He challenges what he characterizes as the "indiscriminate application" of the Rules to him and thus attacks the validity of DR 2-103(A) and DR 2-104(A) not facially, but as applied to his acts of solicitation. And because no allegations or findings were made of the specific wrongs appellant concedes would justify disciplinary action, appellant terms his solicitation "pure," meaning "soliciting and obtaining agreements from Carol McClintock and Wanda Lou Holbert to represent each of them," without more. Appellant therefore argues that we must decide whether a State may discipline him for solicitation per se without offending the First and Fourteenth Amendments.

We agree that the appropriate focus is on appellant's conduct. . . . But appellant errs in assuming that the constitutional validity of the judgment below depends on proof that his conduct constituted actual overreaching or inflicted some specific injury on Wanda Holbert or Carol McClintock. His assumption flows from the premise that nothing less than actual proved harm to the solicited individual would be a sufficiently important state interest to justify disciplining the attorney who solicits employment in person for pecuniary gain.

Appellant's argument misconceives the nature of the State's interest. The Rules prohibiting solicitation are prophylactic measures whose objective is the prevention of harm before it occurs. The rules were applied in this case to discipline a lawyer for soliciting employment for pecuniary gain under circumstances likely to result in the adverse consequences the State seeks to avert. In such a situation, which is inherently conducive to

19. A lawyer who engages in personal solicitation of clients may be inclined to subordinate the best interests of the client to his own pecuniary interests. Even if unintentionally, the lawyer's ability to evaluate the legal merit of his client's claims may falter when the conclusion will affect the lawyer's income. A valid claim might be settled too quickly, or a claim with little merit pursued beyond the point of reason. These lapses of judgment can occur in any legal representation, but we cannot say that the pecuniary motivation of the lawyer who solicits a particular representation does not create special problems of conflict of interest.

overreaching and other forms of misconduct, the State has a strong interest in adopting and enforcing rules of conduct designed to protect the public from harmful solicitation by lawyers whom it has licensed.

The State's perception of the potential for harm in circumstances such as those presented in this case is well founded. The detrimental aspects of face-to-face selling even of ordinary consumer products have been recognized and addressed by the Federal Trade Commission, and it hardly need be said that the potential for overreaching is significantly greater when a lawyer, a professional trained in the art of persuasion, personally solicits an unsophisticated, injured, or distressed lay person.[24] Such an individual may place his trust in a lawyer, regardless of the latter's qualifications or the individual's actual need for legal representation, simply in response to persuasion under circumstances conducive to uninformed acquiescence. Although it is argued that personal solicitation is valuable because it may apprise a victim of misfortune of his legal rights, the very plight of that person not only makes him more vulnerable to influence but also may make advice all the more intrusive. Thus, under these adverse conditions the overtures of an uninvited lawyer may distress the solicited individual simply because of their obtrusiveness and the invasion of the individual's privacy, even when no other harm materializes. Under such circumstances, it is not unreasonable for the State to presume that in-person solicitation by lawyers more often than not will be injurious to the person solicited.

The efficacy of the State's effort to prevent such harm to prospective clients would be substantially diminished if, having proved a solicitation in circumstances like those of this case, the State were required in addition to prove actual injury. Unlike the advertising in *Bates*, in-person solicitation is not visible or otherwise open to public scrutiny. Often there is no witness other than the lawyer and the lay person whom he has solicited, rendering it difficult or impossible to obtain reliable proof of what actually took place. This would be especially true if the lay person were so distressed at the time of the solicitation that he could not recall specific details at a later date. If appellant's view were sustained, in-person solicitation would be virtually immune to effective oversight and regulation by the State or by the legal profession, in contravention of the State's strong interest in regulating members of the Bar in an effective, objective, and self-enforcing manner. It therefore is not unreasonable, or violative of the Constitution, for a State to respond with what in effect is a prophylactic rule.

---

24. Most lay persons are unfamiliar with the law, with how legal services normally are procured, and with typical arrangements between lawyer and client. To be sure, the same might be said about the lay person who seeks out a lawyer for the first time. But the critical distinction is that in the latter situation the prospective client has made an initial choice of a lawyer at least for purposes of a consultation; has chosen the time to seek legal advice; has had a prior opportunity to confer with family, friends, or a public or private referral agency; and has chosen whether to consult with the lawyer alone or accompanied.

On the basis of the undisputed facts of record, we conclude that the Disciplinary Rules constitutionally could be applied to appellant. He approached two young accident victims at a time when they were especially incapable of making informed judgments or of assessing and protecting their own interests. He solicited Carol McClintock in a hospital room where she lay in traction and sought out Wanda Lou Holbert on the day she came home from the hospital, knowing from his prior inquiries that she had just been released. Appellant urged his services upon the young women and used the information he had obtained from the McClintocks, and the fact of his agreement with Carol, to induce Wanda to say "O.K." in response to his solicitation. He employed a concealed tape recorder, seemingly to insure that he would have evidence of Wanda's oral assent to the representation. He emphasized that his fee would come out of the recovery, thereby tempting the young women with what sounded like a cost-free and therefore irresistible offer. He refused to withdraw when Mrs. Holbert requested him to do so only a day after the initial meeting between appellant and Wanda Lou and continued to represent himself to the insurance company as Wanda Holbert's lawyer.

The court below did not hold that these or other facts were proof of actual harm to Wanda Holbert or Carol McClintock but rested on the conclusion that appellant had engaged in the general misconduct proscribed by the Disciplinary Rules. Under our view of the State's interest in averting harm by prohibiting solicitation in circumstances where it is likely to occur, the absence of explicit proof or findings of harm or injury is immaterial. The facts in this case present a striking example of the potential for overreaching that is inherent in a lawyer's in-person solicitation of professional employment. They also demonstrate the need for prophylactic regulation in furtherance of the State's interest in protecting the lay public. We hold that the application of DR 2-103(A) and 2-104(A) to appellant does not offend the Constitution.

Accordingly, the judgment of the Supreme Court of Ohio is affirmed.

[JUSTICE MARSHALL concurred in part and in the judgment. JUSTICE REHNQUIST concurred in the judgment for the reasons contained in his dissent in In re Primus (page 836 infra). JUSTICE BRENNAN did not participate.]

Indirect Solicitation

DR 2-103(C) says that a "lawyer shall not request a person or organization to recommend or promote the use of his services," with certain narrow exceptions. Rule 7.3 generally forbids a lawyer to solicit professional employment in person or by telephone contact. Rule 8.4(a) would forbid a lawyer to do the same "through the acts of another." After *Ohralik*, can a state use rules like these to prevent lawyers from asking intermediaries to refer them to prospective clients? At one extreme is the lawyer who may pay an ambulance driver or a funeral home attendant to give his card to likely clients. But at the other extreme is a lawyer who has a professional relationship with an accountant and asks the accountant "whether you won't think of me if anyone should ask for the name of a lawyer who can handle small business matters." It is not clear where, between these two examples, a state may (or should) draw the line against indirect in-person solicitation. Or is it?

In re Alessi, 60 N.Y.2d 229, 457 N.E.2d 682, 686, 469 N.Y.S.2d 577 (1983), cert. denied, 465 U.S. 1102 (1984), upheld discipline where a law firm sent a letter to 1,000 realtors listing its fees for house closings. The clear implication was that the realtor should consider referring buyers or sellers of homes to the firm. The court stressed that the state could validly forbid such indirect solicitations because referrals from brokers to lawyers could involve the broker "and the attorney in a conflict detrimental to the interests of the client." Do you see how? The court seemed to think that these conflicts were more probable when the lawyer has solicited the broker to be an intermediary than when the broker instigates a pattern of referrals. The court distinguished social contact referrals as "not inherently conducive of conflict." Compare Grievance Committee v. Trantolo, 192 Conn. 27, 470 A.2d 235 (1984), which held that a similar effort to woo brokers was protected by the free speech provisions of the federal and state constitutions.

B. DEFINING THE CENTER: *ZAUDERER, SHAPERO,* AND *PEEL*

1. *Targeted Advertisements*

ZAUDERER v. OFFICE OF DISCIPLINARY COUNSEL
471 U.S. 626 (1985)

JUSTICE WHITE delivered the opinion of the Court.

I . . .

In the spring of 1982, appellant placed an advertisement in 36 Ohio newspapers publicizing his willingness to represent women who had suffered injuries resulting from their use of a contraceptive device known as the Dalkon Shield Intrauterine Device. The advertisement featured a line drawing of the Dalkon Shield accompanied by the question, "DID

YOU USE THIS IUD?" The advertisement then related the following information:

> The Dalkon Shield Interuterine [sic] Device is alleged to have caused serious pelvic infections resulting in hospitalizations, tubal damage, infertility, and hysterectomies. It is also alleged to have caused unplanned pregnancies ending in abortions, miscarriages, septic abortions, tubal or ectopic pregnancies, and full-term deliveries. If you or a friend have had a similar experience do not assume it is too late to take legal action against the Shield's manufacturer. Our law firm is presently representing women on such cases. The cases are handled on a contingent fee basis of the amount recovered. If there is no recovery, no legal fees are owed by our clients.

The ad concluded with the name of appellant's law firm, its address, and a phone number that the reader might call for "free information."

The advertisement was successful in attracting clients: appellant received well over 200 inquiries regarding the advertisement, and he initiated lawsuits on behalf of 106 of the women who contacted him as a result of the advertisement. The ad, however, also aroused the interest of the Office of Disciplinary Counsel. On July 29, 1982, the Office filed a complaint against appellant charging him with a number of disciplinary violations arising out of [the] Dalkon Shield advertisements.

[T]he complaint alleged that in running the ad and accepting employment by women responding to it, appellant had violated the following Disciplinary Rules: DR 2-101(B), which prohibits the use of illustrations in advertisements run by attorneys, requires that ads by attorneys be "dignified," and limits the information that may be included in such ads to a list of 20 items; DR 2-103(A), which prohibits an attorney from "recommend[ing] employment, as a private practitioner, of himself, his partner, or associate to a nonlawyer who has not sought his advice regarding employment of a lawyer"; and DR 2-104(A), which provides (with certain exceptions not applicable here) that "[a] lawyer who has given unsolicited advice to a layman that he should obtain counsel or take legal action shall not accept employment resulting from that advice."

The complaint also alleged that the advertisement violated DR 2-101(B)(15), which provides that any advertisement that mentions contingent-fee rates must "disclos[e] whether percentages are computed before or after deduction of court costs and expenses," and that the ad's failure to inform clients that they would be liable for costs (as opposed to legal fees) even if their claims were unsuccessful rendered the advertisement "deceptive" in violation of DR 2-101(A). The complaint did not allege that the Dalkon Shield advertisement was false or deceptive in any respect other than its omission of information relating to the contingent-fee arrangement; indeed, the Office of Disciplinary Counsel stipulated that the information and advice regarding Dalkon Shield litigation was not false, fraudulent, misleading or deceptive and that the drawing was an accurate representation of the Dalkon Shield. . . .

II

There is no longer any room to doubt that what has come to be known as "commercial speech" is entitled to the protection of the First Amendment, albeit to protection somewhat less extensive than that afforded "noncommercial speech." More subject to doubt, perhaps, are the precise bounds of the category of expression that may be termed commercial speech, but it is clear enough that the speech at issue in this case — advertising pure and simple — falls within those bounds. Our commercial speech doctrine rests heavily on "the 'common-sense' distinction between speech proposing a commercial transaction . . . and other varieties of speech," and appellant's advertisements undeniably propose a commercial transaction. Whatever else the category of commercial speech may encompass, it must include appellant's advertisements.

Our general approach to restrictions on commercial speech is also by now well-settled. The States and the Federal Government are free to prevent the dissemination of commercial speech that is false, deceptive, or misleading or that proposes an illegal transaction. Commercial speech that is not false or deceptive and does not concern unlawful activities, however, may be restricted only in the service of a substantial governmental interest, and only through means that directly advance that interest. Our application of these principles to the commercial speech of attorneys has led us to conclude that blanket bans on price advertising by attorneys and rules preventing attorneys from using nondeceptive terminology to describe their fields of practice are impermissible, but that rules prohibiting in-person solicitation of clients by attorneys are, at least under some circumstances, permissible. To resolve this appeal, we must apply the teachings of these cases to three separate forms of regulation Ohio has imposed on advertising by its attorneys: prohibitions on soliciting legal business through advertisements containing advice and information regarding specific legal problems; restrictions on the use of illustrations in advertising by lawyers; and disclosure requirements relating to the terms of contingent fees.

III

We turn first to the Ohio Supreme Court's finding that appellant's Dalkon Shield advertisement (and his acceptance of employment resulting from it) ran afoul of the rules against self-recommendation and accepting employment resulting from unsolicited legal advice. Because all advertising is at least implicitly a plea for its audience's custom, a broad reading of the rules applied by the Ohio court (and particularly the rule against self-recommendation) might suggest that they forbid all advertising by attorneys — a result obviously not in keeping with our decisions in *Bates* and In re R. M. J. But the Ohio court did not purport to give its rules such a broad reading: it held only that the rules forbade soliciting or accepting legal employment through advertisements containing information or advice regarding a specific legal problem.

The interest served by the application of the Ohio self-recommendation and solicitation rules to appellant's advertisement is not apparent from a reading of the opinions of the Ohio Supreme Court and its Board of Commissioners. The advertisement's information and advice concerning the Dalkon Shield was, as the Office of Disciplinary Counsel stipulated, neither false nor deceptive: in fact, it was entirely accurate. The advertisement did not promise readers that lawsuits alleging injuries caused by the Dalkon Shield would be successful, nor did it suggest that appellant had any special expertise in handling such lawsuits other than his employment in other such litigation.[9] Rather, the advertisement reported the indisputable fact that the Dalkon Shield has spawned an impressive number of lawsuits and advised readers that appellant was currently handling such lawsuits and was willing to represent other women asserting similar claims. In addition, the advertisement advised women that they should not assume that their claims were time-barred — advice that seems completely unobjectionable in light of the trend in many States toward a "discovery rule" for determining when a cause of action for latent injury or disease accrues. The State's power to prohibit advertising that is "inherently misleading," thus cannot justify Ohio's decision to discipline appellant for running advertising geared to persons with a specific legal problem.

Because appellant's statements regarding the Dalkon Shield were not false or deceptive, our decisions impose on the State the burden of establishing that prohibiting the use of such statements to solicit or obtain legal business directly advances a substantial governmental interest. The extensive citations in the opinion of the Board of Commissioners to our opinion in Ohralik v. Ohio State Bar Assn., 436 U.S. 447 (1978), suggest that the Board believed that the application of the rules to appellant's advertising served the same interests that this Court found sufficient to jus-

---

9. The absence from appellant's advertising of any claims of expertise or promises relating to the quality of appellant's services renders the Ohio Supreme Court's statement that "an allowable restriction for lawyer advertising is that of asserted expertise" beside the point. Appellant stated only that he had represented other women in Dalkon Shield litigation — a statement of fact not in itself inaccurate. Although our decisions have left open the possibility that States may prevent attorneys from making nonverifiable claims regarding the quality of their services, they do not permit a State to prevent an attorney from making accurate statements of fact regarding the nature of his practice merely because it is possible that some readers will infer that he has some expertise in those areas. See In re R.M.J., 455 U.S. 191 (1982).

tify the ban on in-person solicitation at issue in *Ohralik*. We cannot agree. Our decision in *Ohralik* was largely grounded on the substantial differences between face-to-face solicitation and the advertising we had held permissible in *Bates*. In-person solicitation by a lawyer, we concluded, was a practice rife with possibilities for overreaching, invasion of privacy, the exercise of undue influence, and outright fraud. In addition, we noted that in-person solicitation presents unique regulatory difficulties because it is "not visible or otherwise open to public scrutiny." These unique features of in-person solicitation by lawyers, we held, justified a prophylactic rule prohibiting lawyers from engaging in such solicitation for pecuniary gain, but we were careful to point out that "in-person solicitation of professional employment by a lawyer does not stand on a par with truthful advertising about the availability and terms of routine legal services."

It is apparent that the concerns that moved the Court in *Ohralik* are not present here. Although some sensitive souls may have found appellant's advertisement in poor taste, it can hardly be said to have invaded the privacy of those who read it. More significantly, appellant's advertisement — and print advertising generally — poses much less risk of overreaching or undue influence. Print advertising may convey information and ideas more or less effectively, but in most cases, it will lack the coercive force of the personal presence of a trained advocate. In addition, a printed advertisement, unlike a personal encounter initiated by an attorney, is not likely to involve pressure on the potential client for an immediate yes-or-no answer to the offer of representation. Thus, a printed advertisement is a means of conveying information about legal services that is more conducive to reflection and the exercise of choice on the part of the consumer than is personal solicitation by an attorney. Accordingly, the substantial interests that justified the ban on in-person solicitation upheld in *Ohralik* cannot justify the discipline imposed on appellant for the content of his advertisement.

Nor does the traditional justification for restraints on solicitation — the fear that lawyers will "stir up litigation" — justify the restriction imposed in this case. In evaluating this proffered justification, it is important to think about what it might mean to say that the State has an interest in preventing lawyers from stirring up litigation. It is possible to describe litigation itself as an evil that the State is entitled to combat: after all, litigation consumes vast quantities of social resources to produce little of tangible value but much discord and unpleasantness. "[A]s a litigant," Judge Learned Hand once observed, "I should dread a lawsuit beyond almost anything else short of sickness and death."

But we cannot endorse the proposition that a lawsuit, as such, is an evil. Over the course of centuries, our society has settled upon civil litigation as a means for redressing grievances, resolving disputes, and vindicating rights when other means fail. There is no cause for consternation when a person who believes in good faith and on the basis of accurate information regarding his legal rights that he has suffered a legally cognizable injury turns to the courts for a remedy: "we cannot accept the notion that it is always better for a person to suffer a wrong silently than to redress it by legal action." [*Bates.*] That our citizens have access to their civil courts is not an evil to be regretted; rather, it is an attribute of our system of justice in which we ought to take pride. The State is not entitled to interfere with that access by denying its citizens accurate information about their legal rights. Accordingly, it is not sufficient justification for the discipline imposed on appellant that his truthful and nondeceptive advertising had a tendency to or did in fact encourage others to file lawsuits.

The State does not, however, argue that the encouragement of litigation is inherently evil, nor does it assert an interest in discouraging the particular form of litigation that appellant's advertising solicited. Rather, the State's position is that although appellant's advertising may itself have been harmless — may even have had the salutary effect of informing some persons of rights of which they would otherwise have been unaware — the State's prohibition on the use of legal advice and information in advertising by attorneys is a prophylactic rule that is needed to ensure that attorneys, in an effort to secure legal business for themselves, do not use false or misleading advertising to stir up meritless litigation against innocent defendants. Advertising by attorneys, the State claims, presents regulatory difficulties that are different in kind from those presented by other forms of advertising. Whereas statements about most consumer products are subject to verification, the indeterminacy of statements about law makes it impractical if not impossible to weed out accurate statements from those that are false or misleading. A prophylactic rule is therefore essential if the State is to vindicate its substantial interest in ensuring that its citizens are not encouraged to engage in litigation by statements that are at best ambiguous and at worst outright false.

The State's argument that it may apply a prophylactic rule to punish appellant notwithstanding that his particular advertisement has none of the vices that allegedly justify the rule is in tension with our insistence that restrictions involving commercial speech that is not itself deceptive be narrowly crafted to serve the State's purposes. Indeed, in In re R.M.J. we went so far as to state that "the States may not place an absolute prohibition on certain types of potentially misleading information . . . if the information also may be presented in a way that is not deceptive." The State's argument, then, must be that this dictum is incorrect — that there are some circumstances in which a prophylactic rule is the least restrictive possible means of achieving a substantial governmental interest.

We need not, however, address the theoretical question whether a prophylactic rule is ever permissible in this area, for we do not believe that the State has presented a convincing case for its argument that the rule before us is necessary to the achievement of a substantial governmental interest. The State's contention that the problem of distinguishing deceptive and nondeceptive legal advertising is different in kind from the problems presented by advertising generally is unpersuasive.

The State's argument proceeds from the premise that it is intrinsically difficult to distinguish advertisements containing legal advice that is false or deceptive from those that are truthful and helpful, much more so than is the case with other goods or services.[12] This notion is belied by the facts before us: appellant's statements regarding Dalkon Shield litigation were in fact easily verifiable and completely accurate. Nor is it true that distinguishing deceptive from nondeceptive claims in advertising involving products other than legal services is a comparatively simple and straightforward process. A brief survey of the body of caselaw that has developed as a result of the Federal Trade Commission's efforts to carry out its mandate under §5 of the Federal Trade Commission Act to eliminate "unfair or deceptive acts or practices in . . . commerce," 15 U.S.C. §45(a)(1), reveals that distinguishing deceptive from nondeceptive advertising in virtually any field of commerce may require resolution of exceedingly complex and technical factual issues and the consideration of nice questions of semantics. In short, assessment of the validity of legal advice and information contained in attorneys' advertising is not necessarily a matter of great complexity; nor is assessing the accuracy or capacity to deceive of other forms of advertising the simple process the State makes it out to be. The qualitative distinction the State has attempted to draw eludes us.[13]

Were we to accept the State's argument in this case, we would have little basis for preventing the government from suppressing other forms of truthful and nondeceptive advertising simply to spare itself the trouble

12. The State's argument may also rest in part on a suggestion that even completely accurate advice regarding the legal rights of the advertiser's audience may lead some members of the audience to initiate meritless litigation against innocent defendants. To the extent that this is the State's contention, it is unavailing. To be sure, some citizens, accurately informed of their legal rights, may file lawsuits that ultimately turn out not to be meritorious. But the State is not entitled to prejudge the merits of its citizens' claims by choking off access to information that may be useful to its citizens in deciding whether to press those claims in court. As we observed in Bates v. Arizona if the State's concern is with abuse of process, it can best achieve its aim by enforcing sanctions against vexatious litigation. In addition, there would be no impediment to a rule forbidding attorneys to use advertisements soliciting clients for nuisance suits — meritless claims filed solely to harass a defendant or coerce a settlement. Because a client has no legal right to file such a claim knowingly, advertisements designed to stir up such litigation may be forbidden because they propose an "illegal transaction."

13. The American Bar Association evidently shares the view that weeding out false or misleading advertising by attorneys from advertising that is accurate and nonmisleading is neither impractical nor unduly burdensome: the ABA's new Model Rules of Professional Conduct eschew all regulation of the content of advertising that is not "false or misleading." ABA, Model Rule of Professional Conduct 7.2 (1983). A recent staff report of the Federal Trade Commission has also concluded that application of a "false or deceptive" standard to attorney advertising would not pose problems distinct from those presented by the regulation of advertising generally. See Federal Trade Commission Staff Report, Improving Consumer Access to Legal Services: The Case for Removing Restrictions on Truthful Advertising 149-155 (1984).

of distinguishing such advertising from false or deceptive advertising. The First Amendment protections afforded commercial speech would mean little indeed if such arguments were allowed to prevail. Our recent decisions involving commercial speech have been grounded in the faith that the free flow of commercial information is valuable enough to justify imposing on would-be regulators the costs of distinguishing the truthful from the false, the helpful from the misleading, and the harmless from the harmful. The value of the information presented in appellant's advertising is no less than that contained in other forms of advertising — indeed, insofar as appellant's advertising tended to acquaint persons with their legal rights who might otherwise be shut off from effective access to the legal system, it was undoubtedly more valuable than many other forms of advertising. Prophylactic restraints that would be unacceptable as applied to commercial advertising generally are therefore equally unacceptable as applied to appellant's advertising. An attorney may not be disciplined for soliciting legal business through printed advertising containing truthful and nondeceptive information and advice regarding the legal rights of potential clients.

IV

The application of DR 2-101(B)'s restriction on illustrations in advertising by lawyers to appellant's advertisement fails for much the same reasons as does the application of the self-recommendation and solicitation rules. The use of illustrations or pictures in advertisements serves important communicative functions: it attracts the attention of the audience to the advertiser's message, and it may also serve to impart information directly. Accordingly, commercial illustrations are entitled to the First Amendment protections afforded verbal commercial speech: restrictions on the use of visual media of expression in advertising must survive scrutiny under the [same] test. Because the illustration for which appellant was disciplined is an accurate representation of the Dalkon Shield and has no features that are likely to deceive, mislead, or confuse the reader, the burden is on the State to present a substantial governmental interest justifying the restriction as applied to appellant and to demonstrate that the restriction vindicates that interest through the least restrictive available means.

The text of DR 2-101(B) strongly suggests that the purpose of the restriction on the use of illustrations is to ensure that attorneys advertise "in a dignified manner." There is, of course, no suggestion that the illustration actually used by appellant was undignified; thus, it is difficult to see how the application of the rule to appellant in this case directly advances the State's interest in preserving the dignity of attorneys. More fundamentally, although the State undoubtedly has a substantial interest in ensuring that its attorneys behave with dignity and decorum in the courtroom, we are unsure that the State's desire that attorneys maintain their dignity in their communications with the public is an interest substantial enough to justify the abridgment of their First Amendment rights. Even if that were the case, we are unpersuaded that undignified behavior would tend to recur so often as to warrant a prophylactic rule. As we held in Carey v. Population Services International, 431 U.S. 678, 701 (1977), the mere possibility that some members of the population might find advertising embarrassing or offensive cannot justify suppressing it. The same must hold true for advertising that some members of the bar might find beneath their dignity.

In its arguments before this Court, the State has asserted that the restriction on illustrations serves a somewhat different purpose, akin to that supposedly served by the prohibition on the offering of legal advice in advertising. The use of illustrations in advertising by attorneys, the State suggests, creates unacceptable risks that the public will be misled, manipulated, or confused. Abuses associated with the visual content of advertising are particularly difficult to police, because the advertiser is skilled in subtle uses of illustrations to play on the emotions of his audience and convey false impressions. Because illustrations may produce their effects by operating on a subconscious level, the State argues, it will be difficult for the State to point to any particular illustration and prove that it is misleading or manipulative. Thus, once again, the State's argument is that its purposes can only be served through a prophylactic rule.

We are not convinced. The State's arguments amount to little more than unsupported assertions: nowhere does the State cite any evidence or authority of any kind for its contention that the potential abuses associated with the use of illustrations in attorneys' advertising cannot be combatted by any means short of a blanket ban. Moreover, none of the State's arguments establish that there are particular evils associated with the use of illustrations in attorneys' advertisements. Indeed, because it is probably rare that decisions regarding consumption of legal services are based on a consumer's assumptions about qualities of the product that can be represented visually, illustrations in lawyer's advertisements will probably be less likely to lend themselves to material misrepresentations than illustrations in other forms of advertising.

Thus, acceptance of the State's argument would be tantamount to adoption of the principle that a State may prohibit the use of pictures or illustrations in connection with advertising of any product or service simply on the strength of the general argument that the visual content of advertisements may, under some circumstances, be deceptive or manipulative. But as we stated above, broad prophylactic rules may not be so lightly justified if the protections afforded commercial speech are to retain their force. We are not persuaded that identifying deceptive or manipulative uses of visual media in advertising is so intrinsically burdensome that the State is entitled to forgo that task in favor of the more convenient but far more restrictive alternative of a blanket ban on the use of illustrations. The experience of the FTC is, again, instructive. Although that agency has not found the elimination of deceptive uses of visual media in advertising to be a simple task, neither has it found the task an impossible one: in many instances, the agency has succeeded in identifying and suppressing visually deceptive advertising. Given the possibility of policing the use of illustrations in advertisements on a case-by-case basis, the prophylactic approach taken by Ohio cannot stand; hence, appellant may not be disciplined for his use of an accurate and nondeceptive illustration.

V

Appellant contends that assessing the validity of the Ohio Supreme Court's decision to discipline him for his failure to include in the Dalkon Shield advertisement the information that clients might be liable for significant litigation costs even if their lawsuits were unsuccessful entails precisely the same inquiry as determining the validity of the restrictions on advertising content discussed above. In other words, he suggests that the State must establish either that the advertisement, absent the required disclosure, would be false or deceptive or that the disclosure requirement serves some substantial governmental interest other than preventing deception; moreover, he contends that the State must establish that the disclosure requirement directly advances the relevant governmental interest and that it constitutes the least restrictive means of doing so. Not surprisingly, appellant claims that the State has failed to muster substantial evidentiary support for any of the findings required to support the restriction.

Appellant, however, overlooks material differences between disclosure requirements and outright prohibitions on speech. In requiring attorneys who advertise their willingness to represent clients on a contingent-fee basis to state that the client may have to bear certain expenses even if he loses, Ohio has not attempted to prevent attorneys from conveying information to the public; it has only required them to provide somewhat more information than they might otherwise be inclined to present. We have, to be sure, held that in some instances, compulsion to speak may be as violative of the First Amendment as prohibitions on speech. . . .

But the interests at stake in this case are not of the same order as those discussed in [prior cases]. Ohio has not attempted to "prescribe what shall be orthodox in politics, nationalism, religion, or other matters of opinion or force citizens to confess by word or act their faith therein." The State has attempted only to prescribe what shall be orthodox in commercial advertising, and its prescription has taken the form of a requirement that appellant include in his advertising purely factual and uncontroversial information about the terms under which his services will be available. Because the extension of First Amendment protection to commercial speech is justified principally by the value to consumers of the information such speech provides, appellant's constitutionally protected interest in *not* providing any particular factual information in his advertising is minimal. Thus, in virtually all our commercial speech decisions to date, we have emphasized that because disclosure requirements trench much more narrowly on an advertiser's interests than do flat prohibitions on speech, "warning[s] or disclaimer[s] might be appropriately required . . . in order to dissipate the possibility of consumer confusion or deception."

We do not suggest that disclosure requirements do not implicate the advertiser's First Amendment rights at all. We recognize that unjustified or unduly burdensome disclosure requirements might offend the First Amendment by chilling protected commercial speech. But we hold that an advertiser's rights are adequately protected as long as disclosure requirements are reasonably related to the State's interest in preventing deception of consumers.[14]

The State's application to appellant of the requirement that an attorney advertising his availability on a contingent-fee basis disclose that clients will have to pay costs even if their lawsuits are unsuccessful (assuming that to be the case) easily passes muster under this standard. Appellant's advertisement informed the public that "if there is no recovery, no legal fees are owed by our clients." The advertisement makes no mention of the distinction between "legal fees" and "costs," and to a layman not aware of the meaning of these terms of art, the advertisement would suggest that employing appellant would be a no-lose proposition in that his representation in a losing cause would come entirely free of charge. The assumption that substantial numbers of potential clients would be so misled is hardly a speculative one: it is a commonplace that members of the public are often unaware of the technical meanings of such terms as "fees" and "costs" — terms that, in ordinary usage, might well be virtually interchangeable. When the possibility of deception is as self-evident as it is in this case, we need not require the State to "conduct a survey of the . . . public before it [may] determine that the [advertisement] had a tendency to mislead." . . . The State's position that it is deceptive to employ advertising that refers to contingent-fee arrangements without mentioning the client's liability for costs is reasonable enough to

---

14. We reject appellant's contention that we should subject disclosure requirements to a strict "least restrictive means" analysis under which they must be struck down if there are other means by which the State's purposes may be served. Although we have subjected outright prohibitions on speech to such analysis, all our discussions of restraints on commercial speech have recommended disclosure requirements as one of the acceptable less restrictive alternatives to actual suppression of speech.

support a requirement that information regarding the client's liability for costs be disclosed.

[The Court reversed Zauderer's reprimand insofar as it was based on his use of an illustration and his offer of legal advice in the advertisement.

JUSTICE POWELL took no part in the consideration or decision of the case. JUSTICES BRENNAN and MARSHALL concurred in part. They generally agreed that a state may require a lawyer to disclose that a client, regardless of the case's outcome, would ultimately be liable for costs, but dissented on procedural grounds from the Court's decision to uphold the discipline here. (See page 684 supra for discussion of procedures in lawyer discipline.) JUSTICE O'CONNOR, joined by the CHIEF JUSTICE and JUSTICE REHNQUIST, concurred with most of Justice White's opinion but dissented from its conclusion in Part III. "In my view," Justice O'Connor wrote, "the use of unsolicited legal advice to entice clients poses enough of a risk of overreaching and undue influence to warrant Ohio's rule." She continued, sounding a theme that would resurface in her 1988 *Shapero* dissent (page 813 infra):]

Merchants in this country commonly offer free samples of their wares. Customers who are pleased by the sample are likely to return to purchase more. This effective marketing technique may be of little concern when applied to many products, but it is troubling when the product being dispensed is professional advice. Almost every State restricts an attorney's ability to accept employment resulting from unsolicited legal advice. At least two persuasive reasons can be advanced for the restrictions. First, there is an enhanced possibility for confusion and deception in marketing professional services. Unlike standardized products, professional services are by their nature complex and diverse. Faced with this complexity, a layperson may often lack the knowledge or experience to gauge the quality of the sample before signing up for a larger purchase. Second, and more significantly, the attorney's personal interest in obtaining business may color the advice offered in soliciting a client. As a result, a potential customer's decision to employ the attorney may be based on advice that is neither complete nor disinterested. . . .

In my view, a State could reasonably determine that the use of unsolicited legal advice "as bait with which to obtain agreement to represent [a client] for a fee," *Ohralik*, 436 U.S. at 458, poses a sufficient threat to substantial state interests to justify a blanket prohibition. As the Court recognized in *Ohralik*, the State has a significant interest in preventing attorneys from using their professional expertise to overpower the will and judgment of laypeople who have not sought their advice. While it is true that a printed advertisement presents a lesser risk of overreaching than a personal encounter, the former is only one step removed from the latter. When legal advice is employed within an advertisement, the layperson may well conclude there is no means to judge its validity or applicability short of consulting the lawyer who placed the advertisement. This is particularly true where, as in appellant's Dalkon Shield advertisement, the legal advice is phrased in uncertain terms. A potential client who read the advertisement would probably be unable to determine whether "it is too late to take legal action against the . . . manufacturer" without directly consulting the appellant. And at the time of that consultation, the same risks of undue influence, fraud, and overreaching that were noted in *Ohralik* are present.

The State also has a substantial interest in requiring that lawyers consistently exercise independent professional judgment on behalf of their clients. Given the exigencies of the marketplace, a rule permitting the use of legal advice in advertisements will encourage lawyers to present that advice most likely to bring potential clients into the office, rather than that advice which it is most in the interest of potential clients to hear. . . . Ohio and other States afford attorneys ample opportunities to inform members of the public of their legal rights. See, e.g., Ohio DR 2-104(A)(4) (permitting attorneys to speak and write publicly on legal topics as long as they do not emphasize their own experience or reputation). Given the availability of alternative means to inform the public of legal rights, Ohio's rule against legal advice in advertisements is an appropriate means to assure the exercise of independent professional judgment by attorneys. A State might rightfully take pride that its citizens have access to its civil courts, while at the same time opposing the use of self-interested legal advice to solicit clients.

In the face of these substantial and legitimate state concerns, I cannot agree with the majority that Ohio DR 2-104(A) is unnecessary to the achievement of those interests. . . .

2.   *Targeted Mail*

SHAPERO v. KENTUCKY BAR ASSN.
486 U.S. 466 (1988)

JUSTICE BRENNAN announced the judgment of the Court and delivered the opinion of the Court as to Parts I and II and an opinion as to Part III in which JUSTICE MARSHALL, JUSTICE BLACKMUN, and JUSTICE KENNEDY join.

This case presents the issue whether a State may, consistent with the First and Fourteenth Amendments, categorically prohibit lawyers from soliciting legal business for pecuniary gain by sending truthful and nondeceptive letters to potential clients known to face particular legal problems.

I

In 1985, petitioner, a member of Kentucky's integrated Bar Association, applied to the Kentucky Attorneys Advertising Commission for approval of a letter that he proposed to send "to potential clients who have had a foreclosure suit filed against them." The proposed letter read as follows:

> It has come to my attention that your home is being foreclosed on. If this is true, you may be about to lose your home. Federal law may allow you to keep your home by *ORDERING* your creditor [sic] to *STOP* and give you more time to pay them.
> You may call my office anytime from 8:30 A.M. to 5:00 P.M. for *FREE* information on how you can keep your home.
> Call *NOW*, don't wait. It may surprise you what I may be able to do for you. Just call and tell me that you got this letter. Remember it is *FREE*, there is *NO* charge for calling.

[Ultimately, the Kentucky Supreme Court held that the letter violated Rule 7.3 of the Model Rules, which, as it *then* read, prohibited mail solicitation that was targeted to persons known to need legal services if a "significant motive for the lawyer's doing so is the lawyer's pecuniary gain."]

II . . .

Our lawyer advertising cases have never distinguished among various modes of written advertising to the general public. Thus, Ohio could no more prevent Zauderer from mass-mailing to a general population his offer to represent women injured by the Dalkon Shield than it could prohibit his publication of the advertisement in local newspapers. Similarly, if petitioner's letter is neither false nor deceptive, Kentucky could not constitutionally prohibit him from sending at large an identical letter opening with the query, "Is your home being foreclosed on?," rather than his observation to the targeted individuals that "It has come to my attention that your home is being foreclosed on." The drafters of Rule 7.3 apparently appreciated as much, for the Rule exempts from the ban "letters addressed or advertising circulars distributed generally to persons . . . who are so situated that they might in general find such services useful."

The court below disapproved petitioner's proposed letter solely because it targeted only persons who were "known to need [the] legal services" offered in his letter, rather than the broader group of persons "so situated that they might in general find such services useful." Generally, unless the advertiser is inept, the latter group would include members of the former. The only reason to disseminate an advertisement of particular legal services among those persons who are "so situated that they might in general find such services useful" is to reach individuals who *actually* "need legal services of the kind provided [and advertised] by the lawyer." But the First Amendment does not permit a ban on certain speech merely because it is more efficient; the State may not constitutionally ban a particular letter on the theory that to mail it only to those whom it would most interest is somehow inherently objectionable.

The court below did not rely on any such theory. Rather, it concluded that the State's blanket ban on all targeted, direct-mail solicitation was permissible because of the "serious potential for abuse inherent in direct solicitation by lawyers of potential clients known to need specific legal services." By analogy to *Ohralik*, the court observed:

> Such solicitation subjects the prospective client to pressure from a trained lawyer in a direct personal way. It is entirely possible that the potential client may feel overwhelmed by the basic situation which caused the need for the specific legal services and may have seriously impaired capacity for good judgment, sound reason and a natural protective self-interest. Such a condition is full of the possibility of undue influence, overreaching and intimidation.

Of course, a particular potential client will feel equally "overwhelmed" by his legal troubles and will have the same "impaired capacity for good judgment" regardless of whether a lawyer mails him an untargeted letter or exposes him to a newspaper advertisement — concededly constitutionally protected activities — or instead mails a targeted letter. The relevant inquiry is not whether there exist potential clients whose "condition" makes them susceptible to undue influence, but whether the mode of communication poses a serious danger that lawyers will exploit any such susceptibility.

Thus, Respondent's facile suggestion that this case is merely "*Ohralik* in writing" misses the mark. In assessing the potential for overreaching and undue influence, the mode of communication makes all the difference. Our decision in *Ohralik* that a State could categorically ban all in-person solicitation turned on two factors. First was our characterization of face-to-face solicitation as "a practice rife with possibilities for overreaching, invasion of privacy, the exercise of undue influence, and outright fraud." [Citing *Zauderer*.] Second, "unique . . . difficulties," [id.] would frustrate any attempt at state regulation of in-person solicitation short of an absolute ban because such solicitation is "not visible or otherwise open to public scrutiny." Targeted, direct-mail solicitation is distinguishable from the in-person solicitation in each respect.

Like print advertising, petitioner's letter — and targeted, direct-mail solicitation generally — "poses much less risk of overreaching or undue influence" than does in-person solicitation. [*Zauderer*.] Neither mode of written communication involves "the coercive force of the personal presence of a trained advocate" or the "pressure on the potential client for an immediate yes-or-no answer to the offer of representation." [Id.] Unlike the potential client with a badgering advocate breathing down his neck, the recipient of a letter and the "reader of an advertisement . . . can 'effectively avoid further bombardment of [his] sensibilities simply by averting [his] eyes.'" A letter, like a printed advertisement (but unlike a lawyer), can readily be put in a drawer to be considered later, ignored, or discarded. In short, both types of written solicitation "conve[y] information about legal services [by means] that [are] more conducive to reflection and the exercise of choice on the part of the consumer than is personal solicitation by an attorney." [Id.] Nor does a targeted letter invade the recipient's privacy any more than does a substantively identical letter mailed at large. The invasion, if any, occurs when the lawyer discovers the recipient's legal affairs, not when he confronts the recipient with the discovery.

Admittedly, a letter that is personalized (not merely targeted) to the recipient presents an increased risk of deception, intentional or inadvertent. It could, in certain circumstances, lead the recipient to overestimate the lawyer's familiarity with the case or could implicitly suggest that the recipient's legal problem is more dire than it really is. Similarly, an inaccurately targeted letter could lead the recipient to believe she has a legal problem that she does not actually have or, worse yet, could offer erroneous legal advice.

But merely because targeted, direct-mail solicitation presents lawyers with opportunities for isolated abuses or mistakes does not justify a total ban on that mode of protected commercial speech. The State can regulate such abuses and minimize mistakes through far less restrictive and more precise means, the most obvious of which is to require the lawyer to file any solicitation letter with a state agency, giving the State ample opportunity to supervise mailings and penalize actual abuses. The "regulatory difficulties" that are "unique" to in-person lawyer solicitation [*Zauderer*] — solicitation that is "not visible or otherwise open to public scrutiny" and for which it is "difficult or impossible to obtain reliable proof of what actually took place" — do not apply to written solicitations. The court below offered no basis for its "belie[f] [that] submission of a blank form letter to the Advertising Commission [does not] provid[e] a suitable protection to the public from overreaching, intimidation or misleading private targeted mail solicitation." Its concerns were presumably those expressed by the ABA House of Delegates in its comment to Rule 7.3:

> State lawyer discipline agencies struggle for resources to investigate specific complaints, much less for those necessary to screen lawyers' mail solicitation material. Even if they could examine such materials, agency staff members are unlikely to know anything about the lawyer or about the pro-

spective client's underlying problem. Without such knowledge they cannot determine whether the lawyer's representations are misleading.

The record before us furnishes no evidence that scrutiny of targeted solicitation letters will be appreciably more burdensome or less reliable than scrutiny of advertisements. As a general matter, evaluating a targeted advertisement does not require specific information about the recipient's identity and legal problems any more than evaluating a newspaper advertisement requires like information about all readers. If the targeted letter specifies facts that relate to particular recipients (e.g., "It has come to my attention that your home is being foreclosed on"), the reviewing agency has innumerable options to minimize mistakes. It might, for example, require the lawyer to prove the truth of the fact stated (by supplying copies of the court documents or material that led the lawyer to the fact); it could require the lawyer to explain briefly how she discovered the fact and verified its accuracy; or it could require the letter to bear a label identifying it as an advertisement; or directing the recipient how to report inaccurate or misleading letters. To be sure, a state agency or bar association that reviews solicitation letters might have more work than one that does not. But "[o]ur recent decisions involving commercial speech have been grounded in the faith that the free flow of commercial information is valuable enough to justify imposing on would-be regulators the costs of distinguishing the truthful from the false, the helpful from the misleading, and the harmless from the harmful." *Zauderer,* supra, at 646.

III

The validity of Rule 7.3 does not turn on whether petitioner's letter itself exhibited any of the evils at which Rule 7.3 was directed. Since, however, the First Amendment overbreadth doctrine does not apply to professional advertising, we address respondent's contentions that petitioner's letter is particularly overreaching, and therefore unworthy of First Amendment protection. In that regard, respondent identifies two features of the letter before us that, in its view, coalesce to convert the proposed letter into "high pressure solicitation, overbearing solicitation." First, respondent asserts that the letter's liberal use of underscored, uppercase letters (e.g., "Call *NOW,* don't wait"; "it is *FREE,* there is *NO* charge for calling") "fairly shouts at the recipient . . . that he should employ Shapero." Second, respondent objects that the letter contains assertions (e.g., "It may surprise you what I may be able to do for you") that "stat[e] no affirmative or objective fact," but constitute "pure salesman puffery, enticement for the unsophisticated, which commits Shapero to nothing."

The pitch or style of a letter's type and its inclusion of subjective predictions of client satisfaction might catch the recipient's attention more than would a bland statement of purely objective facts in small type. But a truthful and nondeceptive letter, no matter how big its type and how much it speculates can never "shou[t] at the recipient" or gras[p] him by the lapels," as can a lawyer engaging in face-to-face solicitation. The letter simply presents no comparable risk of overreaching. And so long as the First Amendment protects the right to solicit legal business, the State may claim no substantial interest in restricting truthful and nondeceptive lawyer solicitations to those least likely to be read by the recipient. Moreover, the First Amendment limits the State's authority to dictate what information an attorney may convey in soliciting legal business. "[T]he States may not place an absolute prohibition on certain types of potentially misleading information ... if the information may also be presented in a way that is not deceptive," unless the State "assert[s] a substantial interest" that such a restriction would directly advance. Nor may a State impose a more particularized restriction without a similar showing. Aside from the interests that we have already rejected, respondent offers none.

To be sure, a letter may be misleading if it unduly emphasizes trivial or "relatively uninformative fact[s]," or offers overblown assurances of client satisfaction. Respondent does not argue before us that petitioner's letter was misleading in those respects. Nor does respondent contend that the letter is false or misleading in any other respect. Of course, respondent is free to raise, and the Kentucky courts are free to consider, any such argument on remand.

The judgment of the Supreme Court of Kentucky is reversed and the case is remanded for further proceedings not inconsistent with this opinion.

JUSTICE WHITE, with whom JUSTICE STEVENS joins, concurring and dissenting in part.

I agree with Parts I and II of the Court's opinion, but am of the view that the matters addressed in Part III should be left to the state courts in the first instance.

JUSTICE O'CONNOR, with whom CHIEF JUSTICE REHNQUIST and JUSTICE SCALIA join, dissenting.

Relying primarily on Zauderer v. Office of Disciplinary Counsel of Supreme Court of Ohio, 471 U.S. 626 (1985), the Court holds that States may not prohibit a form of attorney advertising that is potentially more pernicious than the advertising at issue in that case. I agree with the Court that the reasoning in *Zauderer* supports the conclusion reached today. That decision, however, was itself the culmination of a line of cases built on defective premises and flawed reasoning. As today's decision illustrates, the Court has been unable or unwilling to restrain the logic of the underlying analysis within reasonable bounds. The resulting interference with important and valid public policies is so destructive that I believe the analytical framework itself should now be reexamined.

I . . .

Zauderer dealt specifically with a newspaper advertisement. Today's decision — which invalidates a similar rule against targeted, direct-mail advertising — wraps the protective mantle of the Constitution around practices that have even more potential for abuse. First, a personalized letter is somewhat more likely "to overpower the will and judgment of laypeople who have not sought [the lawyer's] advice." For people whose formal contacts with the legal system are infrequent, the authority of the law itself may tend to cling to attorneys just as it does to police officers. Unsophisticated citizens, understandably intimidated by the courts and its officers, may therefore find it much more difficult to ignore an apparently "personalized" letter from an attorney than to ignore a general advertisement.

Second, "personalized" form letters are designed to suggest that the sender has some significant personal knowledge about, and concern for, the recipient. Such letters are reasonably transparent when they come from somebody selling consumer goods or stock market tips, but they may be much more misleading when the sender belongs to a profession whose members are ethically obliged to put their clients' interests ahead of their own.

Third, targeted mailings are more likely than general advertisements to contain advice that is unduly tailored to serve the pecuniary interests of the lawyer. Even if such mailings are reviewed in advance by a regulator, they will rarely be seen by the bar in general. Thus, the lawyer's professional colleagues will not have the chance to observe how the desire to sell oneself to potential customers has been balanced against the duty to provide objective legal advice. An attorney's concern with maintaining a good reputation in the professional community, which may in part be motivated by long-term pecuniary interests, will therefore provide less discipline in this context than in the case of general advertising. . . .

II . . .

A standardized legal test has been devised for commercial speech cases. Under that test, such speech is entitled to constitutional protection only if it concerns lawful activities and is not misleading; if the speech is protected, government may still ban or regulate it by laws that directly advance a substantial government interest and are appropriately tailored to that purpose. See Central Hudson Gas & Electric Corp. v. Public Service Comm'n of New York, 447 U.S. 557, 566 (1980). Applying that test to attorney advertising, it is clear to me that the States should have considerable latitude to ban advertising that is *"potentially* or demonstrably misleading,"* In re R.M.J., 455 U.S. 191, 202 (1982) (emphasis added), *as well as* truthful advertising that undermines the substantial governmental interest in promoting the high ethical standards that are necessary in the legal profession.

Some forms of advertising by lawyers might be protected under this test. Announcing the price of an initial consultation might qualify, for example, especially if appropriate disclaimers about the costs of other services were included. Even here, the inherent difficulties of policing such advertising suggest that we should hesitate to interfere with state rules designed to ensure that adequate disclaimers are included and that such advertisements are suitably restrained.

As soon as one steps into the realm of prices for "routine" legal services such as uncontested divorces and personal bankruptcies, however, it is quite clear to me that the State may ban such advertising completely. The contrary decision in *Bates* was in my view inconsistent with the standard test that is now applied in commercial speech cases. Until one becomes familiar with a client's particular problems, there is simply no way to know that one is dealing with a "routine" divorce or bankruptcy. Such an advertisement is therefore inherently misleading if it fails to inform potential clients that they are not necessarily qualified to decide whether their own apparently simple problems can be handled by "routine" legal services. Furthermore, such advertising practices will undermine professional standards if the attorney accepts the economic risks of offering fixed rates for solving apparently simple problems that will sometimes prove not to be so simple after all. For a lawyer to promise the world that such matters as uncontested divorces can be handled for a flat fee will inevitably create incentives to ignore (or avoid discovering) the complexities that would lead a conscientious attorney to treat some clients' cases as anything but routine. It may be possible to devise workable rules that would allow something more than the most minimal kinds of price advertising by attorneys. That task, however, is properly left to the States, and it is certainly not a fit subject for constitutional adjudication. Under the *Central Hudson* test, government has more than ample justification for banning or strictly regulating most forms of price advertising. . . .

III

The roots of the error in our attorney advertising cases are a defective analogy between professional services and standardized consumer products and a correspondingly inappropriate skepticism about the States' justifications for their regulations. In *Bates,* for example, the majority appeared to demand conclusive proof that the country would be better off if the States were allowed to retain a rule that served "to inhibit the free flow of commercial information and to keep the public in ignorance." Although the opinion contained extensive discussion of the proffered justifications for restrictions on price advertising, the result was little more than a bare conclusion that "We are not persuaded that price advertising will harm consumers." Dismissing Justice Powell's careful critique of the implicit legislative fact-finding that underlay its analysis, the *Bates* majority simply insisted on concluding that the benefits of advertising outweigh its dangers. In my view, that policy decision was not derived from the First Amendment, and it should not have been used to displace a different and no less reasonable policy decision of the State whose regulation was at issue.

Bates was an early experiment with the doctrine of commercial speech, and it has proved to be problematic in its application. Rather than continuing to work out all the consequences of its approach, we should now return to the States the legislative function that has so inappropriately been taken from them in the context of attorney advertising. The *Central Hudson* test for commercial speech provides an adequate doctrinal basis for doing so, and today's decision confirms the need to reconsider *Bates* in the light of that doctrine.

Even if I agreed that this Court should take upon itself the task of deciding what forms of attorney advertising are in the public interest, I would not agree with what it has done. The best arguments in favor of rules permitting attorneys to advertise are founded in elementary economic principles. Restrictions on truthful advertising, which artificially interfere with the ability of suppliers to transmit price information to consumers, presumably reduce the efficiency of the mechanisms of supply and demand. Other factors being equal, this should cause or enable suppliers (in this case attorneys) to maintain a price/quality ratio in some of their services that is higher than would otherwise prevail. Although one could probably not test this hypothesis empirically, it is inherently plausible. Nor is it implausible to imagine that one effect of restrictions on lawyer advertising, and perhaps sometimes an intended effect, is to enable attorneys to charge their clients more for some services (of a given quality) than they would be able to charge absent the restrictions.

Assuming *arguendo* that the removal of advertising restrictions should lead in the short run to increased efficiency in the provision of legal services, I would not agree that we can safely assume the same effect in the long run. The economic argument against these restrictions ignores the delicate role they may play in preserving the norms of the legal profession. While it may be difficult to defend this role with precise economic logic, I believe there is a powerful argument in favor of restricting lawyer advertising and that this argument is at the very least not easily refuted by economic analysis.

One distinguishing feature of any profession, unlike other occupations that may be equally respectable, is that membership entails an ethical obligation to temper one's selfish pursuit of economic success by adhering to standards of conduct that could not be enforced either by legal fiat or through the discipline of the market. There are sound reasons to continue pursuing the goal that is implicit in the traditional view of professional life. Both the special privileges incident to membership in the profession and the advantages those privileges give in the necessary task of earning a living are means to a goal that transcends the accumulation of wealth. That goal is public service, which in the legal profession can take a variety of familiar forms. This view of the legal profession need not be rooted in romanticism or self-serving sanctimony, though of course it can be. Rather, special ethical standards for lawyers are properly understood as an appropriate means of restraining lawyers in the exercise of the unique power that they inevitably wield in a political system like ours.

It is worth recalling why lawyers are regulated at all, or to a greater degree than most other occupations, and why history is littered with failed attempts to extinguish lawyers as a special class. See generally R. Pound, The Lawyer from Antiquity to Modern Times (1953). Operating a legal system that is both reasonably efficient and tolerably fair cannot be accomplished, at least under modern social conditions, without a trained and specialized body of experts. This training is one element of what we mean when we refer to the law as a "learned profession." Such knowledge by its nature cannot be made generally available and it therefore confers the power and the temptation to manipulate the system of justice for one's own ends. Such manipulation can occur in at least two obvious ways. One results from overly zealous representation of the client's interests; abuse of the discovery process is one example whose causes and effects (if not its cure) is apparent. The second, and for present purposes the more relevant, problem is abuse of the client for the lawyer's benefit. Precisely because lawyers must be provided with expertise that is both esoteric and extremely powerful, it would be unrealistic to demand that clients bargain for their services in the same arms-length manner that may be appropriate when buying an automobile or choosing a dry cleaner. Like physicians, lawyers are subjected to heightened ethical demands on their conduct towards those they serve. These demands are needed because market forces, and the ordinary legal prohibitions against force and fraud, are simply insufficient to protect the consumers of their necessary services from the peculiar power of the specialized knowledge that these professionals possess.

Imbuing the legal profession with the necessary ethical standards is a task that involves a constant struggle with the relentless natural force of economic self-interest. It cannot be accomplished directly by legal rules, and it certainly will not succeed if sermonizing is the strongest tool that may be employed. Tradition and experiment have suggested a number of formal and informal mechanisms, none of which is adequate by itself and many of which may serve to reduce competition (in the narrow economic sense) among members of the profession. A few examples include the great efforts made during this century to improve the quality and breadth of the legal education that is required for admission to the bar; the concomitant attempt to cultivate a sub-class of genuine scholars within the profession; the development of bar associations that aspire to be more than trade groups; strict disciplinary rules about conflicts of interest and client abandonment; and promotion of the expectation that an attorney's history of voluntary public service is a relevant factor in selecting judicial candidates.

Restrictions on advertising and solicitation by lawyers properly and significantly serve the same goal. Such restrictions act as a concrete, day-to-day reminder to the practicing attorney of why it is improper for any member of this profession to regard it as a trade or occupation like any other. There is no guarantee, of course, that the restrictions will always have the desired effect, and they are surely not a sufficient means to their proper goal. Given their inevitable anticompetitive effects, moreover, they should not be thoughtlessly retained or insulated from skeptical criticism. Appropriate modifications have been made in the light of reason and experience, and other changes may be suggested in the future.

In my judgment, however, fairly severe constraints on attorney advertising can continue to play an important role in preserving the legal profession as a genuine profession. Whatever may be the exactly appropriate scope of these restrictions at a given time and place, this Court's recent decisions reflect a myopic belief that "consumers," and thus our nation, will benefit from a constitutional theory that refuses to recognize either the essence of professionalism or its fragile and necessary foundations. In one way or another, time will uncover the folly of this approach. I can only hope that the Court will recognize the danger before it is too late to effect a worthwhile cure.

Reaction to *Shapero*

The ABA responded to *Shapero* by rewriting Rule 7.3 to permit targeted direct mail to potential clients, but to require that where the communication is aimed at a person "known to be in need of legal services in a particular legal matter" the words "Advertising Material" appear "on the outside envelope and at the beginning and ending of any recorded communication," unless the recipient is a member of the lawyer's family or someone with whom the lawyer has a "prior professional relationship."

Some jurisdictions went much further. Consider Florida, where all written communications, whether or not targeted, must have the word "advertisement" written "in red ink" on each page of the communication and the envelope. The written communication can be sent only by regular mail. All targeted communications in personal injury and wrongful death cases are prohibited for 30 days after the incident. Advertisements by facsimile transmission are not allowed. Rule 4-7.4. In Iowa, targeted mail that advises litigation must contain this language: "The filing of a claim or suit solely to coerce a settlement or to harass another could be illegal and could render the person so filing liable for malicious prosecution or abuse of process." DR 2-101(F). Georgia requires the word "Advertisement" on the envelope and the top of each page "of the written communication in typesize no smaller than the largest typesize used in the letter." No targeted direct mail is allowed in a personal injury or wrongful death case. DR 2-101(C). Does this last rule violate *Shapero*?

3. *Claims of Special Expertise*

Gary Peel, an Illinois lawyer, had the following information on his letterhead:

Certified Civil Trial Specialist
By the National Board of Trial Advocacy
Licensed: Illinois, Missouri, Arizona

The NBTA, a private group, established in 1977, had "developed a set of standards and procedures for periodic certification of lawyers with experience and competence in trial work." The standards required "specified experience as lead counsel in both jury and non-jury trials, participation in approved programs of continuing legal education, a demonstration of writing skills, and the successful completion of a day-long examination." A lawyer's certification would expire in five years unless the lawyer demonstrated continuing qualification.

NBTA certification can be seen as privatizing (even usurping?) the states' traditional licensing function. Many lawyers with expertise in a particular area seek to capitalize on their experience with a credential that gives it formal recognition. While some states have certification programs (see page 608 supra), many do not or may not have them in a lawyer's particular field. The NBTA and some other groups have tried to fill this gap.

Illinois charged that Peel had violated its rule prohibiting a lawyer from holding himself out as "a specialist." See Rule 7.4 and DR 2-105(A). While these rules permit lawyers to advertise their areas of practice, they forbid use of the word "specialist" or any of its derivatives on the theory that the public, by analogy to medicine, will mistakenly assume that the lawyer is licensed by the state as having special expertise in the particular area. Illinois also charged that Peel's reference to the NBTA would mislead potential clients about the meaning of the certification.

The Supreme Court held Peel's letterhead protected by the First Amendment. Peel v. Attorney Registration and Disciplinary Commission of Illinois, 110 S. Ct. 2281 (1990). Relying primarily on *Bates* and In re R.M.J., 455 U.S. 191 (1982), a plurality opinion by Justice Stevens closely parsed the letterhead, including its typography, and concluded that it was neither actually nor inherently misleading. Concurring in the judgment, Justices Marshall and Brennan (who also joined the plurality) concluded that the letterhead was potentially misleading because, for example, it could "create the misimpression that the NBTA is an agency of the Federal Government," or because the reference to "certification as a civil trial specialist may cause people to think that [Peel] is necessarily a better trial lawyer than attorneys without the certification." However, Justice Marshall found Illinois' total ban too broad. A state could instead require a lawyer like Peel "to provide additional information in order to prevent [the certification] from being misleading. The state might, for example, require a disclaimer stating that the NBTA is a private organization not affiliated with or sanctioned by the state or Federal Government." Four Justices dissented. It is too soon to know whether *Peel* will give rise to many private accreditation efforts. The potential for private assumption of this historically public function is significant. Unlike public licensure, however, private efforts would be subject to the antitrust laws (page 124 supra).

QUESTION

16.1 A personal-injury lawyer wins $20 million in an important products liability case. The victory makes the front page of the national and local press. The lawyer has won large verdicts before, but nowhere near this amount. She's also lost a few. Can she thereafter (a) send photocopies of the newspaper story to all her clients; (b) send photocopies of the story to 2,000 purchasers of the offending product; (c) put a laminated, framed copy of the story on the wall of her waiting room; (d) take out an ad in the local paper that essentially reproduces the report of the original victory; (e) show the story to all potential clients?

C. DEFINING THE METHODOLOGY

The Court's methodology in legal marketing cases raises some interesting questions about governance and craft. Actually, we find two competing methodologies, nicely captured in the *Shapero* majority and dissent. Both methodologies have to identify how much weight to give the speaker's First Amendment interests. Both have to identify how much respect to give the purported dangers the state wishes to prevent. And both have to identify how much deference to give to the means a state may adopt to promote its goals. The final decision requires empirical assumptions about human motivation and about the causal relationship between the state's means and its goals. How does the Court get this information? Lurking within these issues is a further riddle, eloquently addressed in Justice O'Connor's *Shapero* dissent: the relationship between legal marketing and professionalism. Is there a relationship? Who decides? If there is one, what *constitutional* difference should it make?

How Does the Court Know Things?

In *Ohralik* the Court appeared willing to allow states categorically to forbid in-person solicitation for profit, although it could have stopped short of that holding and rested instead on Ohralik's particular conduct. At one point it seemed the Court might issue a more limited ruling. Justice Powell, distinguishing *Bates*, wrote that the state, "having proved a solicitation in circumstances like those in this case" (page 794 supra), need not also prove actual injury. But elsewhere, Justice Powell made it clear that Ohralik could be disciplined under a "prophylactic" rule for his "general misconduct," regardless of the specific circumstances of the case (page 795 supra).

If *Ohralik* contained an ambiguity, *Shapero* resolved it in favor of state power to adopt a prophylactic rule. Justice Brennan characterized the "decision in *Ohralik*" as holding "that a State could categorically ban all in-person solicitation" (page 810 supra). Even Justice Marshall, who in his *Ohralik* concurrence wrote that the Court's decision was "limited" and depended on the "circumstances" contained in "this record," joined the *Shapero* majority.

Given the result in *Shapero*, the *Ohralik* prophylactic authority is less momentous. Do you see why?

The *Ohralik* opinion contains many "likelys" and "mays." How does the Court know that in-person solicitation is as dangerous as it says it is? How does the Court know that the conduct in *Shapero* is not as dangerous as Kentucky (and many other states) believe it to be? What assumptions is the Court making about motivations and especially about how money influences the behavior of lawyers? Compare Village of Schaumburg v. Citizens for a Better Environment, 444 U.S. 620 (1980), which also reviewed a state law that made certain assumptions about money and behavior. A village ordinance barred door-to-door and on-the-street solicitations of contributions to charities unless the charities used at least 75 percent of their receipts for "charitable purposes," defined to exclude the cost of solicitation. In striking the ordinance, the Court suggested that there were less intrusive methods for protecting privacy interests, such as the ordinance's provision permitting homeowners to bar solicitors from their property by posting signs reading "No Solicitors or Peddlers Invited." Are the decisions in *Schaumburg* and *Ohralik* compatible?

The *Schaumburg* Court cited *Ohralik* in response to the village's contention that the ordinance furthered the goal of preventing fraud. The Court said that that goal could "be better served by measures less intrusive than a direct prohibition on solicitation," such as through a penal law. "Unlike the situation in *Ohralik* . . . charitable solicitation is not so inherently conducive to fraud and overreaching as to justify its prohibition." Is the Court saying that lawyers are more dishonest than people who canvass for charities, justifying greater intrusion on the First Amendment rights of the former? How does the Court know that? Justice O'Connor seems to believe that the Court is not equipped to evaluate the relative risks inherent in legal advertising; accordingly, she counsels deference and would give the states greater (but not unfettered) discretion to fashion rules limiting lawyer advertising.

One big difference between *Ohralik* and *Shapero* is in a state's ability to prove overreaching or fraud. In *Ohralik* the substance of the in-person conversation would not usually be preserved. It would instead be a matter of debate among the participants — a credibility contest. In *Shapero*, at the very least the letter the lawyer sent would be available as evidence in the event of a disciplinary proceeding. Another major difference between the two cases is in the degree of privacy invasion. In-person solicitation is more intrusive than a letter.

Aside from privacy invasion, the other justifications usually advanced to prohibit in-person solicitation by lawyers for profit are the danger of overreaching and the potential conflict between the interests of the lawyer and the interests of the prospective client. Yet aren't these other risks present in all client-lawyer relationships, no matter how the lawyer happens to meet up with the client? What reason is there to believe the risks are greater when a lawyer solicits a client in person? See *Ohralik*, page 793 supra, at n.19 and especially the double negative in the last sentence.

Professionalism and Money

What is the relationship between professionalism and money? Recall Roscoe Pound's definition of a profession as "a group pursuing a learned art as a common calling in the spirit of public service" (page 7 supra). At what point, if any, does the pursuit of money diminish professionalism? Are permissive rules on legal marketing likely to lead us to that point?

Justice O'Connor makes two assumptions in her *Shapero* dissent, a definitional one and a causal one. She writes first that membership in a profession "entails an ethical obligation to temper one's selfish pursuit of economic success" (page 817 supra) and second that "fairly severe constraints on attorney advertising" will "act as a concrete, day-to-day reminder to the practicing attorney of why it is improper for any member of this profession to regard it as a trade or occupation like any other" (page 818). Accordingly, she questions the *Bates* decision.

Justice O'Connor's definitional assumption is in accord with Roscoe Pound's: At some level, pursuit of a profession and pursuit of wealth are inconsistent. Do you accept that definition of professionalism? What are the consequences of rejecting it? One consequence might be to deny lawyers the right of self-regulation — the right, with comparatively modest public control, to write their own code of ethics. The Preamble to the Model Rules, after pointing out that "the legal profession is largely self-governing," stresses the profession's "responsibility to assure that its regulations are conceived in the public interest and not in furtherance of parochial or self-interested concerns of the bar." It then warns that "[t]o the extent that lawyers meet the obligations of their professional calling, the occasion for government regulation is obviated." In her essay criticizing the professionalism report, Professor Nancy Moore questioned, among other things, the accuracy of the equation between professionalism and public service and the wisdom of continued self-regulation. Nancy Moore, Professionalism Reconsidered, 1987 Am. B. Found. Res. J. 773.

What do you think of Justice O'Connor's second assumption about the causal connection between strict rules against legal advertising and the need to remind lawyers that they are not in a "trade or occupation like any other"? Many share her view that as advertising increases, professionalism declines. The cases from *Bates* to *Peel*, and the prominence of lawyer marketing efforts thereby occasioned, have caused something of a professional identity crisis. One result has been the report of the ABA Commission on Professionalism, which cautions lawyers not to make "the acquisition of wealth a principal goal of law practice" and urges "good sense and high standards" in legal ads. Another ABA commission has proposed "aspirational goals" in legal ads intended to assure that they are "dignified" and "tasteful." 4 Lawyers Manual on Prof. Conduct (ABA/BNA) 96 (March 30, 1986).

As Justice O'Connor recognizes, it is not possible to *prove* that an increase in legal advertising comes at the expense of professionalism (or leads to a heightened concern with wealth), though the relationship may have intuitive appeal. The *Shapero* dissenters believe the causality sufficiently probable to render it a legitimate state interest that will in turn support "fairly severe constraints on attorney advertising" despite the First Amendment.

Opponents of this view argue that such restrictions discriminate against those consumers who are unlikely to know that they have a legal problem or which lawyer to see when they do. Wealthy and corporate clients do not need ads to know if they have a legal problem or whom to retain. (Has a lawyer ever been disciplined for in-person solicitation of the corporate VP during a round of golf: "You know, George, we have a fellow in our securities department who . . ."?) Critics also argue that in any event an interest in money is not so bad. It increases the chances that rights will be vindicated. Given the contingency fee (see page 112 supra), a lawyer's economic self-interest may inspire the search for clients who may be unaware of their legitimate claims — claims that, if asserted, will benefit the clients *and* enrich the lawyer. While pursuit of the dollar will sometimes lead to excesses, the argument runs, we can deal with those as they occur and through more tailored rules.

D.   DEFINING THE RULES

Despite the Supreme Court's half-dozen pronouncements about attorney marketing, many questions remain open for the states to answer. American jurisdictions probably vary more in their rules on legal advertising and solicitation than for any other subject in lawyer ethics codes. Tracking the variations would not, to put it mildly, be particularly fascinating. But some recurring questions are worth addressing.

Does the First Amendment Protect Legal Advertising on Radio and Television?

The Supreme Court has not explicitly extended First Amendment protection to legal advertising on radio and television, yet it is routinely allowed. Some states have attempted to limit it beyond the generic restrictions that appear in Rules 7.1 and 7.2. In New Jersey, for example, the state supreme court requires that all ads be "predominantly informational" and specifically forbids "drawings, animations, dramatizations, music or lyrics . . . in connection with televised advertising." Radio advertisements are not similarly encumbered. In re Felmeister & Isaacs, 104 N.J. 515, 518 A.2d 188 (1986). The Iowa Supreme Court bans background sound, visual displays, and more than a single nondramatic voice in legal advertisements on all electronic media. Committee on Professional Ethics v. Humphrey, 377 N.W.2d 643 (Iowa 1985), appeal dismissed, 475 U.S. 1114 (1986). Florida permits use of radio and television, but requires a single voice "with no background sound other than instrumental music. The voice may be a fulltime employee of the firm whose services are advertised; it shall not be that of a celebrity whose voice is recognizable to the public." Rule 4-7.1(b). (Do you suppose there was much debate over the decision to permit "instrumental music"?)

What is the explanation for this effort to exercise greater control over radio and television ads? Perhaps it's the perception that because electronic messages are more likely to be vehicles of manipulation and subtle inducement, they require greater restriction. If legal advertising is permitted, isn't it inevitable that time-tested techniques successfully used to market cereal and automobiles will be employed to market lawyers? Electronic media simply make these techniques more available and effective.

What's wrong with that? One answer is that success in drawing clients is not the proper measure of the value of legal advertising, at least not for society, because success says nothing about either the wisdom of the client's choice of counsel or the information the client used in making the selection. That explains the *Felmeister* court's insistence that all ads be "predominantly informational." We may let people buy cars or soft drinks on the basis of image, but we won't let lawyers sell themselves that way. The Iowa Supreme Court in *Humphrey* wrote that an advertisement on the electronic media "tolerates much less deliberation." Florida cites the "unique characteristics of electronic media . . . the ease with which these media are abused, and the passiveness of the viewer or listener" as reasons why they are "especially subject to regulation in the public interest." Rule 4-7.1 comment.

Can States Require Disclaimers?

Zauderer lost on the disclaimer issue. He failed to state in his ad that a client would be liable for costs — the out-of-pocket expenses of the representation — whether or not the client recovered anything. Costs may include such things as court filing fees, travel expenses, and expert witness fees. Ohio believed that readers or viewers of ads that offered legal services for contingent fees ("no recovery, no fee") might not realize that they would still be liable for costs, so the state court required a disclaimer explaining this fact. The Supreme Court unanimously upheld this requirement, although Justices Brennan and Marshall dissented on procedural grounds. (See page 685 supra.)

Another kind of disclaimer requires lawyers who advertise to state (when true) that they are not certified by the state as specialists in any area of law mentioned in their ads. These disclaimers have been required both in states that do certify specialists in particular areas of legal expertise and in states that do not. The disclaimer is meant to protect the public against wrongly concluding that a lawyer has been recognized as a specialist by a state licensing body. See Justice Marshall's concurrence in *Peel,* page 820 supra.

Certification disclaimers sound harmless enough, but they carry an opposite risk. For example, they may convey the impression that lawyers who declare themselves "not certified as specialists in family law" have in some respects been found wanting. Obviously this would be untrue in states without certification plans. To correct the misimpression, a lawyer would have to add a disclaimer to the disclaimer, saying that the state does not in fact certify people in family law. See Spencer v. Honorable Justices of Supreme Court of Pa., 579 F. Supp. 880 (E.D. Pa. 1984), aff'd, 760 F.2d 261 (3d Cir. 1985) (required disclaimer of certification in states without certification plan held unconstitutional). In states that do have certification plans, the disclaimer's implication may be inappropriately harsh; yet to say nothing is to invite serious consequences. In Texas, for example, where a certification plan exists, a young lawyer not yet certified in family law took a small ad in the Lubbock Avalanche Journal offering his services for fees ranging between $75 and $175 in routine uncontested divorces. Because the ad did not disclaim certification, the lawyer was suspended from practice for six months. The state appellate court upheld the discipline but found the sanction too harsh. The Supreme Court dismissed his appeal. Daves v. State Bar of Texas, 691 S.W.2d 784 (Tex. Ct. App. 1985), appeal dismissed, 474 U.S. 1043 (1986). The result destroys the usefulness of Mr. Daves's little ad, doesn't it?

Can Legal Ads Carry Endorsements?

The California and District of Columbia Bar Associations have found ads with endorsements improper. Oring v. State Bar of California, 4 Lawyers Manual on Prof. Conduct (ABA/BNA) 206 (July 6, 1988). D.C. Op. 142 (1984). The *Oring* case arose after Oring and his partner, Grey, broadcast a radio ad in which a former client made the following statement:

I was rear-ended on the San Diego Freeway and all my medical bills were piling up and the insurance company was giving me a hard time, constantly harassed me, just all in all gave me a hard time. [I was referred to] Grey and Oring. They immediately took the case and we finally ended up in court. I got a nice award of money and all of a sudden I got a phone call from Grey and Oring. They hadn't liked the way the insurance company had treated me and they wanted to take them to trial and suddenly the insurance company offered me a settlement of double the amount of the original trial. If I had any legal problem, car accident or anything, I would definitely go back to Grey and Oring. I certainly do believe that.

Both Grey and Oring were given public reprovals for violating a rule that prohibited testimonials or endorsements in legal advertising. In an unpublished opinion the California Supreme Court refused to review either discipline. The United States Supreme Court declined to review Grey's discipline, 479 U.S. 1034 (1987). A year later it agreed to review Oring's discipline, but then dismissed the appeal for want of a properly presented federal question. Oring v. State Bar of California, 488 U.S. 590 (1989). The issue of endorsements raises some interesting questions. Assume the speaker in the *Oring* ad was a real former client and that everything she said was true. Why forbid the advertisement? In answering that question, think about whether we allow lawyers to give prospective clients the names of former clients as references. Should we ban references?

California has since changed its rule. Testimonials and endorsements are now presumptively misleading unless they "contain an express disclaimer such as 'this testimonial or endorsement does not constitute a guarantee, warranty, or prediction regarding the outcome of your legal matter.' "* The New York State Bar has also upheld the use of client testimonials provided any reference to results are accompanied by appropriate disclaimers. New York Opinion 614 (1990).

Other Lawyers' Clients

Even when the solicitation rules permit written or in-person contact with a prospective client, other law may forbid it. One prominent example is when lawyers plan to leave a firm and start a competing firm. They may wish to take clients with them. At the very least, they will want to inform their clients about their departure. Clients, as we know, have a right to change attorneys. There should be no problem if the departing lawyers act openly. But damage actions, for breach of fiduciary or other duties, have been upheld where former colleagues have attempted to lure clients and effect their own departure in secret. See Meehan v. Shaughnessy, 404 Mass. 419, 535 N.E.2d 1255 (1989); Adler, Barish, Daniels,

*Standard (2), Board of Governors of California State Bar, implementing Rule 1-400 of California Rules.

Levin & Kreskoff v. Epstein, 482 Pa. 416, 393 A.2d 1175 (1978), cert. denied, 442 U.S. 907 (1979). Robert Hillman has studied the legal issues that arise when lawyers separate. Robert Hillman, Law Firm Breakups (1990). See also Vincent Johnson's multiple perspectives in Solicitation of Law Firm Clients by Departing Partners and Associates: Tort, Fiduciary, and Disciplinary Liability, 50 U. Pitt. L. Rev. 1 (1988).

QUESTION

16.2   A firm wants to hire an actor to read the following advertisement on radio:

> My debts were piling up after I was laid off, and it looked certain that I was going to lose my home and car. I didn't know what to do. I called Smith & Jones because I had seen their ads on TV. I made an appointment to see a lawyer who told me about bankruptcy. I didn't think it was for me at first, but I didn't want to lose all I had worked for. The lawyer told me I'd be able to keep my house and some of my savings. I decided to go ahead. I managed to keep my house and most of my savings. The plant began rehiring and I'm now back on my feet. I owe a lot to Smith & Jones.

Then another voice comes on, also an actor, who says:

> Bankruptcy isn't for everyone, but sometimes it's the right choice. At Smith & Jones we show you how it works, answer your questions, and help you decide if it's for you. Give us a call. We might be able to help.

Is this ad protected by the First Amendment? Is it truthful even though the actors are pretending to be what they're not: a real client and a real lawyer describing a real matter? Is it possible to defend this ad while upholding discipline for Grey and Oring (see page 826), who had a real client with a real problem and a real result? If Smith & Jones came to you before broadcasting their ad, which lines, if any, would you advise them to change or delete? Why?

FURTHER READING

Numerous articles and studies on legal advertising have been published since the *Bates* decision. One noteworthy study by the Federal Trade Commission concluded that legal advertising has reduced the cost of legal services and that a "false or deceptive" standard for lawyer advertising would present no greater problems than for other kinds of advertising. FTC Staff Report, Improving Consumer Access to Legal Service: The Case for Removing Restrictions on Truthful Advertising

(1984). Louise Hill argues that "the categorical proscriptions on in-person solicitation . . . lack a firm historical basis and constitute a violation of the first amendment." She attempts to demonstrate that "significantly less restrictive and more precise alternatives exist to safeguard the states' concern that the public be protected from the coercive force of a trained advocate." Louise Hill, Solicitation by Lawyers: Piercing the First Amendment Veil, 42 Maine L. Rev. 369 (1990). Other publications include Frederick Moss's article, The Ethics of Law Practice Marketing, 61 Notre Dame L. Rev. 601 (1986), which addresses nearly every conceivable way in which a lawyer and a firm might seek to make their availability known. For a study of the effects of lawyer advertising on quality and price, see Timothy Muris & Fred McChesney, Advertising and the Price and Quality of Legal Services: The Case for Legal Clinics, 1979 Am. B. Found. Res. J. 179: Fred McChesney & Timothy Muris, The Effect of Advertising on the Quality of Legal Services, 65 A.B.A. J. 1503 (1979). The authors compared the quality and price of routine legal services provided by the Legal Clinic of Jacoby & Meyers, which advertises, with those of traditional firms. See also Geoffrey Hazard, Russell Pearce & Jeffrey Stempel, Why Lawyers Should Be Allowed to Advertise: A Market Analysis of Legal Services, 58 N.Y.U. L. Rev. 1084 (1983).

E. SOLICITATION BY PUBLIC INTEREST AND CLASS ACTION LAWYERS

The precise holding of In re Primus, decided the same day as *Ohralik* (page 788 supra), has now been overshadowed by *Shapero* (page 808 supra), which would protect Primus's letter even if her motive was pecuniary gain. But *Primus* makes a larger and more important point: States have less power to regulate client solicitation when a lawyer's motive is political rather than financial. We encountered the same distinction in NAACP v. Button, page 715 supra, where the factually related question was the constitutionality of a state law that prohibited the NAACP from using lay persons to solicit school desegregation plaintiffs. In *Button,* the focus was on the lay status of the intermediary. In *Primus,* the focus was on the solicitation itself. As in *Button, Primus* assumes that it is possible to determine motives. That assumption gives Justice Rehnquist, the sole dissenter, a rhetorical platform on which to juxtapose *Primus* and *Ohralik.* Rule 7.3, written after *Primus* (and revised after *Shapero*), also uses motive to determine the permissible scope of client solicitation.

IN RE PRIMUS
436 U.S. 412 (1978)

JUSTICE POWELL delivered the opinion of the Court.

We consider on this appeal whether a State may punish a member of its Bar who, seeking to further political and ideological goals through associational activity, including litigation, advises a lay person of her legal rights and discloses in a subsequent letter that free legal assistance is available from a nonprofit organization with which the lawyer and her associates are affiliated. Appellant, a member of the Bar of South Carolina, received a public reprimand for writing such a letter. . . .

I

Appellant, Edna Smith Primus, is a lawyer practicing in Columbia, S.C. During the period in question, she was associated with the "Carolina Community Law Firm," and was an officer of and cooperating lawyer with the Columbia branch of the American Civil Liberties Union (ACLU). She received no compensation for her work on behalf of the ACLU, but was paid a retainer as a legal consultant for the South Carolina Council on Human Relations (Council), a nonprofit organization with offices in Columbia.

During the summer of 1973, local and national newspapers reported that pregnant mothers on public assistance in Aiken County, S.C., were being sterilized or threatened with sterilization as a condition of the continued receipt of medical assistance under the Medicaid program. Concerned by this development, Gary Allen, an Aiken businessman and officer of a local organization serving indigents, called the Council requesting that one of its representatives come to Aiken to address some of the women who had been sterilized. At the Council's behest, appellant, who had not known Allen previously, called him and arranged a meeting in his office in July 1973. Among those attending was Mary Etta Williams, who had been sterilized by Dr. Clovis H. Pierce after the birth of her third child. Williams and her grandmother attended the meeting because Allen, an old family friend, had invited them and because Williams wanted "[t]o see what it was all about. . . ." At the meeting, appellant advised those present, including Williams and the other women who had been sterilized by Dr. Pierce, of their legal rights and suggested the possibility of a lawsuit.

Early in August 1973, the ACLU informed appellant that it was willing to provide representation for Aiken mothers who had been sterilized. Appellant testified that after being advised by Allen that Williams wished to institute suit against Dr. Pierce, she decided to inform Williams of the ACLU's offer of free legal representation. Shortly after receiving appellant's letter, dated August 30, 1973[6] — the centerpiece of this litigation — Williams visited Dr. Pierce to discuss the progress of her third child who was ill. At the doctor's office, she encountered his lawyer and at the latter's request signed a release of liability in the doctor's favor. Williams showed appellant's letter to the doctor and his lawyer, and they retained a copy. She then called appellant from the doctor's office and announced her intention not to sue. There was no further communication between appellant and Williams.

[The Supreme Court of South Carolina issued Primus a public reprimand, holding that she violated DR 2-103(D)(5)(a) and (c) and 2-104(A)(5), and the disciplinary rules of that court. DR 2-103(D)(5)(a) and (c) allow client solicitation by nonprofit organizations only if the primary purpose of the organization is not the rendition of legal services, and if the organization does not derive financial benefit from the offered legal services. DR 2-104(A)(5) prohibits a lawyer from seeking employment from someone to whom she has given unsolicited advice and whom she seeks to join in a class action.]

---

6. Written on the stationery of the Carolina Community Law Firm, the letter stated:

August 30, 1973

Mrs. Marietta Williams
347 Sumter Street
Aiken, South Carolina 29801

Dear Mrs. Williams:

You will probably remember me from talking with you at Mr. Allen's office in July about the sterilization performed on you. The American Civil Liberties Union would like to file a lawsuit on your behalf for money against the doctor who performed the operation. We will be coming to Aiken in the near future and would like to explain what is involved so you can understand what is going on.

Now I have a question to ask of you. Would you object to talking to a women's magazine about the situation in Aiken? The magazine is doing a feature story on the whole sterilization problem and wants to talk to you and others in South Carolina. If you don't mind doing this, call me *collect* at 254-8151 on Friday before 5:00, if you receive this letter in time. Or call me on Tuesday morning (after Labor Day) *collect*.

I want to assure you that this interview is being done to show what is happening to women against their wishes, and is not being done to harm you in any way. But I want you to decide, so call me collect and let me know of your decision. This practice must stop.

About the lawsuit, if you are interested, let me know, and I'll let you know when we will come down to talk to you about it. We will be coming to talk to Mrs. Waters at the same time; she has already asked the American Civil Liberties Union to file a suit on her behalf.

Sincerely,
s/ *Edna Smith*
Edna Smith
Attorney-at-law

II

This appeal concerns the tension between contending values of considerable moment to the legal profession and to society. Relying upon NAACP v. Button, and its progeny, appellant maintains that her activity involved constitutionally protected expression and association. In her view, South Carolina has not shown that the discipline meted out to her advances a subordinating state interest in a manner that avoids unnecessary abridgment of First Amendment freedoms. Appellee counters that appellant's letter to Williams falls outside of the protection of *Button*, and that South Carolina acted lawfully in punishing a member of its Bar for solicitation. . . .

III

In NAACP v. Button the Supreme Court of Appeals of Virginia had held that the activities of members and staff attorneys of the National Association for the Advancement of Colored People (NAACP) and its affiliate, the Virginia State Conference of NAACP Branches (Conference), constituted "solicitation of legal business" in violation of state law. . . .

This Court reversed: "We hold that the activities of the NAACP, its affiliates and legal staff shown on this record are modes of expression and association protected by the First and Fourteenth Amendments which Virginia may not prohibit, under its power to regulate the legal profession, as improper solicitation of legal business violative of [state law] and the Canons of Professional Ethics." The solicitation of prospective litigants, many of whom were not members of the NAACP or the Conference, for the purpose of furthering the civil-rights objectives of the organization and its members was held to come within the right " 'to engage in association for the advancement of beliefs and ideas.' "

Since the Virginia statute sought to regulate expressive and associational conduct at the core of the First Amendment's protective ambit, the *Button* Court insisted that "government may regulate in the area only with narrow specificity." . . . The Court concluded that "although the [NAACP] has amply shown that its activities fall within the First Amendment's protections, the State has failed to advance any substantial regulatory interest, in the form of substantive evils flowing from [the NAACP's] activities, which can justify the broad prohibitions which it has imposed."

Subsequent decisions have interpreted *Button* as establishing the principles that "collective activity undertaken to obtain meaningful access to the courts is a fundamental right within the protection of the First Amendment." . . . Without denying the power of the State to take measures to correct the substantive evils of undue influence, overreaching, misrepresentation, invasion of privacy, conflict of interest, and lay interference that potentially are present in solicitation of prospective clients by lawyers, this Court has required that "broad rules framed to protect the public and to preserve respect for the administration of justice" must not work a significant impairment of "the value of associational freedoms."

IV

We turn now to the question whether appellant's conduct implicates interests of free expression and association sufficient to justify the level of protection recognized in *Button* and subsequent cases. . . .

Although the disciplinary panel did not permit full factual development of the aims and practices of the ACLU, the record does not support the state court's effort to draw a meaningful distinction between the ACLU and the NAACP. From all that appears, the ACLU and its local chapters, much like the NAACP and its local affiliates in *Button*, "[engage] in extensive educational lobbying activities" and "also [devote] much of [their] funds and energies to an extensive program of assisting certain kinds of litigation on behalf of [their] declared purposes." The court below acknowledged that " 'the ACLU has only entered cases in which substantial civil liberties questions are involved. . . .' " It has engaged in the defense of unpopular causes and unpopular defendants and has represented individuals in litigation that has defined the scope of constitutional protection in areas such as political dissent, juvenile rights, prisoners' rights, military law, amnesty, and privacy. For the ACLU, as for the NAACP, "litigation is not a technique of resolving private differences"; it is "a form of political expression" and "political association."

We find equally unpersuasive any suggestion that the level of constitutional scrutiny in the case should be lowered because of a possible benefit to the ACLU. The discipline administered to appellant was premised solely on the possibility of financial benefit to the organization, rather than any possibility of pecuniary gain to herself, her associates, or the lawyers representing the plaintiffs in the Walker v. Pierce litigation,[21] [another sterilization lawsuit against Dr. Pierce]. It is conceded that appellant received no compensation for any of the activities in question. It is also undisputed that neither the ACLU nor any lawyer associated with it would have shared in any monetary recovery by the plaintiffs in Walker v. Pierce. If Williams had elected to bring suit, and had been represented by staff lawyers for the ACLU, the situation would have been similar to that in *Button*, where the lawyers for the NAACP were "organized as a staff and paid by" that organization.

---

21. Appellee conjectures that appellant would have received increased support from private foundations if her reputation was enhanced as a result of her efforts in the cause of the ACLU. The decision below acknowledged, however, that the evidence did not support a finding that appellant solicited Williams on her own behalf. . . .

Contrary to appellee's suggestion, the ACLU's policy of requesting an award of counsel fees does not take the case outside of the protection of *Button*. [I]n a case of this kind there are differences between counsel fees awarded by a court and traditional fee-paying arrangements which militate against a presumption that ACLU sponsorship of litigation is motivated by considerations of pecuniary gain rather than by its widely recognized goal of vindicating civil liberties. Counsel fees are awarded in the discretion of the court; awards are not drawn from the plaintiff's recovery, and are usually premised on a successful outcome; and the amounts awarded often may not correspond to fees generally obtainable in private litigation. . . . And even if there had been an award during the period in question, it would have gone to the central fund of the ACLU. Although such benefit to the organization may increase with the maintenance of successful litigation, the same situation obtains with voluntary contributions and foundation support, which also may rise with ACLU victories in important areas of the law. That possibility, standing alone, offers no basis for equating the work of lawyers associated with the ACLU or the NAACP with that of a group that exists for the primary purpose of financial gain through the recovery of counsel fees.

Appellant's letter of August 30, 1973, to Mrs. Williams thus comes within the generous zone of the First Amendment protection reserved for associational freedoms. The ACLU engages in litigation as a vehicle for effective political expression and association, as well as a means of communicating useful information to the public. As *Button* indicates, and as appellant offered to prove at the disciplinary hearing, the efficacy of litigation as a means of advancing the cause of civil liberties often depends on the ability to make legal assistance available to suitable litigants. . . .

V

South Carolina's action in punishing appellant for soliciting a prospective litigant by mail, on behalf of the ACLU, must withstand the "exacting scrutiny applicable to limitations on core First Amendment rights. . . ." South Carolina must demonstrate "a subordinating interest which is compelling," and that the means employed in furtherance of that interest are "closely drawn to avoid unnecessary abridgment of associational freedoms." . . .

B . . .

Where political expression or association is at issue, this Court has not tolerated the degree of imprecision that often characterizes government regulation of the conduct of commercial affairs. The approach we adopt today in *Ohralik*, that the State may proscribe in-person solicitation for pecuniary gain under circumstances likely to result in adverse consequences, cannot be applied to appellant's activity on behalf of the ACLU. Although a showing of potential danger may suffice in the former context, appellant may not be disciplined unless her activity in fact involved the type of misconduct at which South Carolina's broad prohibition is said to be directed.

The record does not support appellee's contention that undue influence, overreaching, misrepresentation, or invasion of privacy actually occurred in this case. Appellant's letter of August 30, 1973, followed up the earlier meeting — one concededly protected by the First and Fourteenth Amendments — by notifying Williams that the ACLU would be interested in supporting possible litigation. The letter imparted additional information material to making an informed decision about whether to authorize litigation, and permitted Williams an opportunity, which she exercised, for arriving at a deliberate decision. The letter was not facially misleading; indeed, it offered "to explain what is involved so you can understand what is going on." The transmittal of this letter — as contrasted with in-person solicitation — involved no appreciable invasion of privacy; nor did it afford any significant opportunity for overreaching or coercion. Moreover, the fact that there was a written communication lessens substantially the difficulty of policing solicitation practices that do offend valid rules of professional conduct. The manner of solicitation in this case certainly was no more likely to cause harmful consequences than the activity considered in *Button*.

Nor does the record permit a finding of a serious likelihood of conflict of interest or injurious lay interference with the attorney-client relationship. Admittedly, there is some potential for such conflict or interference whenever a lay organization supports any litigation. That potential was present in *Button*, in the NAACP's solicitation of nonmembers and its disavowal of any relief short of full integration. But the Court found that potential insufficient in the absence of proof of a "serious danger" of conflict of interest, or of organizational interference with the actual conduct of the litigation. . . .

The State's interests in preventing the "stirring up" of frivolous or vexatious litigation and minimizing commercialization of the legal profession offer no further justification for the discipline administered in this case. The *Button* Court declined to accept the proffered analogy to the common-law offenses of maintenance, champerty, and barratry, where the record would not support a finding that the litigant was solicited for a malicious purpose or "for private gain, serving no public interest." The same result follows from the facts of this case. And considerations of undue commercialization of the legal profession are of marginal force where, as here, a nonprofit organization offers its services free of charge to individuals who may be in need of legal assistance and may lack the financial means and sophistication necessary to tap alternative sources of such aid.

At bottom, the case against appellant rests on the proposition that a State may regulate in a prophylactic fashion all solicitation activities of lawyers because there may be some potential for overreaching, conflict of interest, or other substantive evils whenever a lawyer gives unsolicited advice and communicates an offer of representation to a layman. Under certain circumstances, that approach is appropriate in the case of speech that simply "propose[s] a commercial transaction." See *Ohralik*. In the context of political expression and association, however, a State must regulate with significantly greater precision.

VI

The State is free to fashion reasonable restrictions with respect to the time, place, and manner of solicitation by members of its Bar. The State's special interest in regulating members of a profession it licenses, and who serve as officers of its courts, amply justifies the application of narrowly drawn rules to proscribe solicitation that in fact is misleading, overbearing, or involves other features of deception or improper influence. As we decide today in *Ohralik*, a State also may forbid in-person solicitation for pecuniary gain under circumstances likely to result in these evils. And a State may insist that lawyers not solicit on behalf of lay organizations that exert control over the actual conduct of any ensuing litigation. Accordingly, nothing in this opinion should be read to foreclose carefully tailored regulation that does not abridge unnecessarily the associational freedom of nonprofit organizations, or their members, having characteristics like those of the NAACP or the ACLU.

We conclude that South Carolina's application of DR 2-103(D)(5)(a) and (c) and 2-104(A)(5) to appellant's solicitation by letter on behalf of the ACLU violated the First and Fourteenth Amendments. The judgment of the Supreme Court of South Carolina is reversed.

JUSTICE REHNQUIST, dissenting.

In this case and the companion case of *Ohralik*, the Court tells its own tale of two lawyers: One tale ends happily for the lawyer and one does not. . . .

If Albert Ohralik, like Edna Primus, viewed litigation " 'not [as] a technique of resolving private differences,' " but as " 'a form of political expression' and 'political association,' " for all that appears he would be restored to his right to practice. And we may be sure that the next lawyer in Ohralik's shoes who is disciplined for similar conduct will come here cloaked in the prescribed mantle of "political association" to assure that insurance companies do not take unfair advantage of policyholders.

This absence of any principled distinction between the two cases is made all the more unfortunate by the radical difference in scrutiny brought to bear upon state regulation in each area. Where solicitation proposes merely a commercial transaction, the Court recognizes "the need for prophylactic regulation in furtherance of the State's interest in protecting the lay public." On the other hand, in some circumstances "[w]here political expression or association is at issue," a member of the Bar "may not be disciplined unless her activity in fact involve[s] the type of misconduct at which South Carolina's broad prohibition is said to be directed."

. . . I believe that constitutional inquiry must focus on the character of the conduct which the State seeks to regulate, and not on the motives of the individual lawyers or the nature of the particular litigation involved. . . .

While *Button* appears to permit such individual solicitation for political purposes by lay members of the organization, it nowhere explicitly permits such activity on the part of lawyers. . . .

A State may reasonably fear that a lawyer's desire to resolve "substantial civil liberties questions," may occasionally take precedence over his duty to advance the interests of his client. It is even more reasonable to fear that a lawyer in such circumstances will be inclined to pursue both culpable and blameless defendants to the last ditch in order to achieve his ideological goals. Although individual litigants, including the ACLU, may be free to use the courts for such purposes, South Carolina is likewise free to restrict the activities of the members of its Bar who attempt to persuade them to do so.

I can only conclude that the discipline imposed upon Primus does not violate the Constitution, and I would affirm the judgment of the Supreme Court of South Carolina.

Communication with Class Members

Before *Shapero* afforded First Amendment protection to direct mail solicitation, there was some question whether a lawyer who brought a class action could seek to communicate with potential class members (before class certification) by targeted mail. Today, after *Shapero*, two questions remain: Despite *Ohralik*, does the First Amendment afford class action lawyers additional protection for in-person solicitation of class members? Despite *Shapero*, can a court order a class action lawyer not to contact potential class members through the mail?

In Gulf Oil Co. v. Bernard, 452 U.S. 89 (1981), the plaintiffs brought a class action charging defendant with employment discrimination based on race. The trial judge, relying on Rule 23(d) Fed. R. Civ. P., granted defendant's motion for an order restraining "all communications concerning the class action between parties or their counsel and any actual or potential class member who was not a formal party, without the prior approval of the court." The Supreme Court held that the trial court had abused its discretion in restraining the communications. It acknowledged that such communications created a "potential for abuse," which provides a trial judge with "both the duty and the broad authority to exercise control over a class action and to enter appropriate orders governing the conduct of counsel and parties." Id. at 100. On the other hand, orders restraining communication with class members may, as in the current case, make it difficult for counsel and the class representatives effectively to represent the class. Justice Powell wrote for a unanimous Court:

> Because of these potential problems, an order limiting communications between parties and potential class members should be based on a clear record and specific findings that reflect a weighing of the need for a limitation and the potential interference with the rights of the parties. Only such a determination can ensure that the court is furthering, rather than hindering, the policies embodied in the Federal Rules of Civil Procedure, especially Rule 23. In addition, such a weighing — identifying the potential abuses being addressed — should result in a carefully drawn order that limits speech as little as possible, consistent with the rights of the parties under the circumstances.

Id. at 101-102.

Consider the converse problem in Kleiner v. First National Bank of Atlanta, 751 F.2d 1193 (11th Cir. 1985), a class action against a bank for interest overcharges. The trial judge instructed defense counsel not to contact plaintiff class members during a period of time within which the members had to decide whether to opt out of the class. After reading *Gulf Oil*, and despite the court order, the bank's counsel concluded that the bank could solicit opt-outs so long as it did so truthfully and without coercion (many of the potential class members were bank customers and dependent on the bank for loans). The bank began a telephone campaign. Its lawyer helped. The campaign identified 2,800 borrowers, with nearly $700 million in loans, who agreed to opt out, although some may have intended to do so in any event.

When the district judge learned of the campaign, she imposed fines and costs totaling more than $100,000 against counsel and the bank, disqualified counsel from continuing to represent the bank, and ruled that the customers who had chosen to opt out would be permitted to rejoin the class after entry of judgment (i.e., after seeing who won). The Eleventh Circuit affirmed (with minor exception on procedural grounds), rejecting the bank's First Amendment claim based on Gulf Oil. v. Bernard:

> *Bernard* was a classic case of noncommercial speech which directly implicated the doctrine of prior restraint. In the domain of commercial speech,

as discussed, the Supreme Court had issued repeated admonitions against the wholesale incorporation of the law of prior restraint. We therefore judge petitioners' prior restraint argument under a relaxed standard of scrutiny better suited to the hardiness of commercial speech. . . .

The trial court's order was narrowly drawn to avoid suppressing utterances worthy of first amendment protection. As a directive addressed to counsel for the Bank, the ambit of the order was restricted to communications regarding the litigation. The order thus did not impinge on the Bank's ability to speak with customers about routine business matters unrelated to the lawsuit. Since defense counsel had an ethical duty to refrain from discussing the litigation with members of the class as of the date of class certification, if not sooner, the order in no way tread on legitimate communications by counsel.

Similarly, we discern no less restrictive alternative to the district judge's order. The purpose of the directive was to filter news of the opportunity for exclusion through the impartial and open medium of court-supervised notice. As such, the order implemented the preview screening which the Supreme Court has commended as a constitutional substitute for a complete ban on communications.

Id. at 1205-1207.

In the pre-*Shapero* era, the Eighth Circuit distinguished *Bernard* and held that a lawyer for a plaintiff in an age discrimination case could not send letters inviting potential class members to join the action. McKenna v. Champion Intl. Corp., 747 F.2d 1211 (8th Cir. 1984). Today, of course, those letters would be constitutionally protected and in accord with Rule 7.3 as revised. But Rule 7.3 would also require that the letters be marked "advertising material." Is that requirement consistent with *Bernard*?

QUESTIONS

16.3 "Thanks for taking the time to talk to me. I'm Max Burkardt. For eight years I worked for a public interest group that protects the rights of people who are profoundly physically disabled. A lot of my work involved benefits law, access rights, and claims of discrimination. I left the job last March to go into private practice, partly because I have two children now and needed a little more money. I want to do some of the same work. Instead of charging fees, I'll rely on fee-shifting statutes to get paid.

"Anyway, a friend of mine who's a social worker told me about conditions at a certain state hospital for disabled adults in long-term care. Neglect. Some brutality. I would like to learn more and maybe represent the residents in a class action if appropriate. I wrote letters to some patients whose names I had, but I haven't heard anything. Sometimes, patients at these hospitals have emotional problems or can't read or never get their mail.

"I need to make contact if I'm going to get retained and bring a case. I'm thinking of asking my social worker friend to help me get in to talk to a few patients. She'd just have to tell them about me and ask if they're willing to see me. Can I do that? I don't want to get into trouble. The hospital will do whatever it can to make my life miserable, including complaints to the grievance panel."

16.4   "I am a quite successful matrimonial lawyer. Gloria Velasquez. Yesterday, I saw in The Standard that a septuagenarian male judge took a four-year-old child away from his mother and put him in foster care because the mother was living in a religious commune with a man who was not her husband. For that reason alone. No evidence of abuse or neglect. As a feminist, I'm incensed. This woman had no lawyer. I wrote to offer my services free of charge — she apparently has no funds anyway — but in this state you have to put the words "Legal Advertisement" on the envelope in big red letters. So I imagine the letter was dumped unopened. I want to call or visit the woman and talk to her. There's no money in it for me although, to be perfectly candid, the publicity won't hurt any. Can I do it?"

Part Six

ISSUES IN THE WORK
LIVES OF LAWYERS

XVII

The Work Lives of Lawyers

Raised here, in dialogue form, are two issues in the work lives of law-yers: conflicts between the demands of professional work and the desire for and needs of family life; and sexual harassment in law offices. Space permitting, we could add other issues, including the problem of lawyer "burnout" and the moral dissonance associated with role-differentiated behavior. The two issues chosen are especially pertinent today because of the large increase in the number of women entering the profession. Har-assment and family conflict issues are not limited to women, of course, nor to law, but the fact is that today, for various reasons, they confront women prominently, including in law offices.

Inquiry into the first of our issues has been especially rich in recent years. A short bibliography includes Nancy Dowd, Work and Family: Restructuring the Workplace, 32 Ariz. L. Rev. 431 (1990), an ambi-tious exploration that concludes: "Nothing less than a restructuring of the workplace is necessary to resolve" the conflict "between work and family responsibilities." David Chambers provides much empiri-cal information in his investigation of the career and family paths of University of Michigan law graduates across more than a decade. David Chambers, Accommodation and Satisfaction: Women and Men Lawyers and the Balance of Work and Family, 14 Law & Social In-quiry 251 (1989). See also a series of articles collected under the title Women in Legal Education: Pedagogy, Law, Theory, and Practice, 38 J. Legal Ed. 1 (1988); and a special issue on Gender and the Law, 40 Stan. L. Rev. 1161 (1988).

Examination of our second issue — sexual harassment in law offices — is less extensive. But anyone interested should read Judge Pratt's opinion in the disturbing case of Broderick v. Ruder, 685 F. Supp. 1269, 1270 (D.D.C. 1988). Judge Pratt found, as plaintiff claimed, that there was a "sexually hostile work environment" in the Washington Regional Field Office of the Securities and Exchange Commission and that when plaintiff opposed treatment she considered illegal under Title VII of the 1964 Civil Rights Act, her supervisors retaliated against her.

The first of the two dialogues deals with conflicts between family life and work life. The second presents issues when romantic attractions form in hierarchical work situations.

SIMULATED CASE HISTORIES

JANE LORING-KRAFT

I graduated from law school in 1981, clerked for a district judge in Minneapolis (where I'm from) and then came back east where my husband and I each had jobs in New York. We're both associates, though of course at different firms. I chose litigation because I liked to write and I liked evidence and the simulated trial practice course I took. Also it seemed to me that litigators were sort of the last generalists. A lot of different kinds of cases could come along. As it turns out, the cases that have come along are mainly securities and antitrust cases and occasional trademark and breach of contract cases.

In 1982, I had a daughter, Heather, and then a second daughter, Gillian, in 1984. They're 19 months apart and it's hard. We have help, of course — we have to — but it's still hard.

A problem has developed in my firm. The head of the litigation department, Frank Lester, is a hardworking, serious man and a good lawyer. I've learned a lot from him. I wish everyone could have a mentor as competent and concerned as Frank. Frank's a bit gruff and peremptory at times, but we associates know when to lie low and when it's all right to come out of hiding.

The problem that developed is that Frank wants the same sort of time commitment from me, now that I have two children, as he wanted when I first started. In fact, he wants *more*, not more hours but more in the sense that now that I'm a sixth-year associate he says he needs me on the front line — in court, meeting with clients, doing investigations — wherever in the world that front line may happen to be. And at whatever time I may happen to be needed (which means night work). I just can't do it and I shouldn't have to. But my career is, quite suddenly, on the line.

Let me explain what I mean. I'm supposed to bill the New York average (or at least the average for our firm) of 2,100 hours a year. Those are client hours. I'm willing to do it. I'm willing to take work home. I've got a computer there and a hookup. I'm willing to respond to emergencies — real emergencies — when necessary. What I'm not willing to do is not see my children for days at a time. Not now when they're so young. My younger one goes to sleep by 7:30 and I want to spend a little time with her before she does.

I don't know why we can't work this out but it seems that we can't. Frank says I have to be available to work nights on a moment's notice. But my babysitter can't stay on a moment's notice, even if I were willing. And Frank says I have to be available to travel to take depositions, argue motions, and prepare and try cases. Frank's on the road about a third of the year — a few days here, a few days there. Some partners travel more, some a little less. I just can't do that right now. Mike, my husband, is a corporate lawyer and spends a great deal of time in the office too, more than he would like, and while he could cover for me some of the time I'd be away, that isn't the point. I'm a parent and want to spend time with my children too.

A year ago we had a trial in Houston and Frank asked me to go. I knew it was coming. I had been working on the pretrial motions, and the interlocutory appeal, and a lot of the discovery (which fortunately occurred mainly in New York). I hoped the case would settle and expected it would. But it didn't. When it came time to try the case, Frank naturally assumed I would go. It was supposed to be a 10-week trial — it turned out to be a 12-week trial — and I would have had to spend five and a half to six days a week in Houston. Mike could not have handled the kids and his job without even more help. But I didn't want to be away from them that much even if the best help were immediately available. Besides, I don't want a succession of temporary caregivers for my kids. They need me, and they need predictability.

I told Frank I couldn't go. He looked like I had stabbed him in the back. I knew the case better than anyone, he said. I had worked on it for more than a year. I had to go. I was betraying the client. I was betraying him, Frank. How could he explain this to the client? How could he depend on me in the future? But I just refused. I offered to be available on the phone 24 hours a day for conferences on strategy. I offered to do whatever research was needed during the trial and Fax it to Houston. I offered to fully prepare another associate. Frank just said to forget it and walked away.

At first nothing happened. In fact, two months later another litigation partner asked me to work on an international arbitration that would be tried in Zurich. A few years ago, I'd have died for the chance. But I knew the partner had spoken with Frank when he emphasized that the case was almost certain to go to trial and that the trial would require me to spend a month in Zurich. Zurich, of course, is too far to come home from on weekends.

I worried that I might have given up my partnership chances. Now I'm worried that I may have damaged my entire career. Within a few weeks, I stopped getting interesting work. In fact, I wasn't getting enough work to bill the hours expected of me. I'd spend hours reading advance sheets. Naturally I went to Frank and other partners. They gave me some assignments, stuff you'd expect to give a first- or second-year

associate. They said they understood my point, but how could they depend on me? We try cases all over the country (all over the world actually)
and even New York cases sometimes require a good deal of travelling,
which can't always be anticipated. They've got to know, they said, that
they have a team that can do it. I couldn't. And they pointed out that
other women — and men — with kids at home freely took these assignments.

You see, no one was going to fire me. They don't fire people here.
They were going to let me atrophy professionally, just give me the dregs.
I'm not even saying that they were going to do that intentionally or to
punish me. It was just going to happen. I was excluded from significant
work because they stopped thinking about me as an available person.
Third- and fourth-year associates started to give me trivial assignments
on cases, explaining apologetically that the partner in charge had suggested I might be available. I was becoming like a den mother or something. I was being swept to the side.

Lawyers here are said to be very enlightened. It's one of those firms
that gets plaudits around town for having hired women early, for making
women partners, and for all its pro bono work for the homeless. I can tell
you that some of the women partners I've spoken to wonder whether the
sacrifice they've made as mothers has been worth it.

I know what you're thinking. You're thinking it's my fault for not anticipating this and picking another kind of practice or another department — trusts and estates, right? The truth is that before you have kids
you just can't know what it will be like. And my larger point is that even if
I did know, I shouldn't have to make the choice. The firm should bend
and be flexible so I can be a litigator and a mother too. I don't expect all
the compromise to come from the firm, either. I'll compromise too. But
if my situation is representative — and after talking with women at other
firms I believe it is not unusual — the result is pretty clear. Although the
profession has opened to women in name, *in fact* there'll still be male and
female tracks. Or maybe the tracks will be mothers and nonmothers.
Many women with young kids will not get or take certain kinds of jobs.
Some women may just choose not to have kids. Is that the kind of choice
we want to force bright young women to make?

Last week I had lunch with my friend Barry, who was my law school
classmate and works at another large firm in town. Barry and I have
lunch a couple of times a year since we left school. I guess he could see I
was miserable because he asked me what was wrong and I told him the
whole story. He said, "Well, you know, Jane, this is not just a problem for
women. Men want to spend time with their children too." Barry has two
children so I asked him how he solved the dilemma. He thought for a
while and said, "I guess I never really thought I had too little time with
my boys." Right. I don't see any of the young fathers at my firm raising
this issue either. And the partners who are unsympathetic to me all hap-

pen to have kids. Maybe men are naturally more careerist. Maybe there are gender differences after all. That's another debate. I think any parent who wants to be able to spend time with his or her children should be able to do so. I just think mostly it will be women who make that choice. The firm has to recognize that childrearing is valuable to society. Something must be done especially about unpredictable night work.

You know the most painful part of this? Not only don't I get support from men here, but most of the women are unsympathetic. The young ones, just out of law school, think that *they'll* be able to do it all and that it's a personal fault of mine if I can't. They want to be just like the men: tough, on call, ready to go. Little do they know. The older women, who've made the family sacrifice to get into the partnership, are better able to understand my dilemma but figure that's just the way it is. No one helped them. I'll have to choose as they had to choose. Well, they shouldn't have had to choose and neither should I.

FRANK LESTER

Let's say Jane Loring-Kraft wanted to be an airline pilot, worked hard, and got a lot of offers. She chooses Pan Am because it flies all over the world and she wants to go to exotic places. She spends three years doing just that. She has a hell of a time, sows her wild oats or whatever it is people sow these days, and also learns to be a crackerjack pilot. Jane then gets married and has a couple of children. She goes to her boss and says "Boss, I now have two childeren and I want to spend time with them. I no longer want to fly to Japan and Buenos Aires and Rome. I want to fly to Washington and Boston on the shuttle. I want to fly to places where I can be home each night by 6 o'clock."

The boss says: "Jane, a lot of people, men too, want to be home each night. Our business does not allow our pilots to be home each night. Sometimes they have to fly routes that take them away for days or weeks. Someone has to fly those routes. What's more, our people have good reasons other than children to want to be home each night. They have spouses and close friends. They have sick parents. They have other personal obligations. We have only so many shuttle flights and a lot of pilots, with a lot more seniority than you have, who want to fly them.

Jane replies: "You should make special rules for women with young children."

The boss: "First, you have to tell me how we can justify making special rules for women with young children and not anyone else. Then you have to consider what your request would do to our effort to hire more women pilots and navigators. We're an international airline. If women with young children are unable or unwilling to help us fulfill our international obligations, the result will be that we won't hire as many women of childbearing age as pilots. Women have to choose what they'd rather

have: neutral gender rules for employment and promotion in a field traditionally all male. Or special treatment because of their status. I thought
special treatment is what women no longer wanted. I thought the pedes-
tal was the enemy."

Look, I don't want to belabor the analogy. Jane is a lovely person and
an excellent lawyer. I hope we keep her. I looked forward to having her
as a partner one day. But I can't start making assignments based on a person's night or travel availability. Oh, to a limited extent I can. If a spouse
or child or parent is ill, we make allowances. But Jane is looking for a decade of allowances. Today, half of our new hires are women. I can't run a
law firm unless I can depend on the general availability of associates to
stay late and to go where the business takes them. Even if I tried, very
often I can't know what a case will demand when it begins. There can be a
lot of evening emergencies. There can be trips for discovery, to consult
with experts, to get information from the client's far-flung offices. A case
filed in New York can suddenly be transferred to Omaha on a motion to
change venue or because it comes under the jurisdiction of the panel on
multidistrict litigation. You just don't know. And a good number, maybe
a third, of our cases are out of town, including out of the country. Fact is,
that's why Jane chose us to begin with. Now she finds it inconvenient.

We're not freezing her out. No one has malice toward her. What she's
encountering is the effect of a series of small decisions. Every partner
here worries about case staffing. Each is concerned that if he or she takes
Jane on as a senior associate on a matter, Jane won't be there when the
partner needs her. There's no ill will toward Jane in a partner's deciding
not to take that risk. What Jane doesn't realize is that when she says "I
won't go," or "I won't stay tonight," someone else has to, someone who
might also like to be home for whatever reason and, in any event, who
might already have a full load of work.

It all comes down to this: We're a team. Our clients pay us large sums
to give them excellent advice when and where they want it. We're a service operation. We've got to be responsive. Our clients are sophisticated
corporations. They know how to dial the phone numbers of our competitors. They don't even have to dial because our competitors are constantly
wooing our clients (and we woo theirs). Our success depends on keeping
clients satisfied. That case in Houston? The client had formed a close
working relationship with Jane. I had to explain that she wouldn't be
available for the trial. The client didn't understand. The lawyers and
managers I was working with there felt abandoned. It was all I could do
to make excuses. I can't be doing that again and again.

I don't know what will happen to Jane. Maybe she should work in a
government office, where the hours are 9 to 5, no travel. Maybe a smaller
law office that mainly has local work. Our trusts people don't travel and
their hours can be contained. The same with our real estate people,
though to a lesser extent.

I'm sorry Jane is being put to this choice. But we're all put to choices, maybe not the same ones, but choices of one kind or another. You decide whether to marry Sue or Ann, whether to become a lawyer or a poet, whether to live in New York or Seattle, and so on. That's the human condition. I didn't invent it. You learn after a while that life is choice and compromise. If Jane had looked ahead a little, she would have foreseen this dilemma when she interviewed here during her clerkship. She made her choice then and she has to live with the consequences now.

ALEXA JOHNSTON

I am 29 years old, single, and a fourth-year associate in litigation at a large West Coast law firm. It has more than 275 lawyers, about 35 of whom are in litigation. I like my work, I work hard, and I want to be a partner someday.

I specialize in securities litigation. I know the securities laws and I know how to litigate. My cases are factually and legally complex, arise all over the country, and bring me into contact with some powerful and wealthy individuals and companies.

My firm has about 14 litigation partners. A partner named Leonard Newman is the star securities litigator here — indeed he is one of the leading litigators in the state in corporate matters generally. Len is 42, recently divorced, with three children. Because of my interest in securities litigation, I was assigned to work with Len almost from my first month here. We worked together on many cases, with noteworthy success. We have been a good litigation team. I am beginning to develop something of a reputation in the securities litigation world as a result of Len's tutelage and exposure to the important cases that Len handles.

Until recently, I felt I was extremely lucky to have fallen into such an exceptional mentoring relationship. Now it appears that Len was beginning to see it as not a mentoring relationship at all, at least not only that.

About 10 months ago, we were in Chicago on a series of lengthy depositions and had been working hard for three days. We broke early on a Wednesday, I remember, and went to a nice place for dinner. As we were having our coffee, out of the blue, Len invited me back to his room. It was clear it wasn't to work. You know, I didn't know what to say. I was flabbergasted. Len, who is really very courteous, saw it and apologized. I thought that was that and the next day just chalked it up to the fact that we had been working so hard, Len's pressure from his divorce, and the full bottle of wine we had just consumed rather quickly.

A week later, however, Len dropped into my office about eight o'clock one evening and recalled his offer in Chicago. He said he knew it must have shocked me but he believed in being direct and maybe now that I had time to think about it, we could talk. Well, there was no wine to blame it on this time. I was nervous. But look, I've known Len nearly four years. I like him. I told him I was flattered by his attention but that I didn't want an office romance and that I was sure he could understand that. He said yes he could, indeed, and that we would just let it ride for a while. I wasn't sure what "let it ride for a while" meant, but I didn't say anything else and he said good night.

Two weeks later, on a Sunday morning, Len called me at home, not to come down to work, but to ask if he could buy me brunch. This was the first time he ever did that. I tried to walk a thin line between not being rude and not being encouraging. I didn't know how far on either side of the line accepting or rejecting his offer would fall. I gave it the benefit of the doubt and accepted. He offered to pick me up but I prevailed on him to meet me at the restaurant. We had a nice brunch, although it was more informal than I was used to and I kept worrying that he was going to suggest something further. I was practically relieved when all he suggested was a walk in the park, after which I went home. That night I got a delivery of two dozen roses. From Len.

Meanwhile, you have to understand, Len and I were continuing to work together on important cases that would be any fourth-year associate's dream. I was getting a lot of responsibility and learning new things weekly. Everything was perfect except for one thing.

Then, I began to realize that on all of the trips I was taking with Len, we were the only lawyers. In the past, there would often be three or four of us, but now it was just Len and me. In New York, in April, we were walking back to the hotel from dinner, it was windy, and Len put his hand through my arm while we were crossing Fifth Avenue, a perfectly innocent act except for the circumstances of the prior few months. I jumped and Len withdrew his arm.

I realized I had to talk to him. One afternoon when Len was in his office, I knocked and went in and closed the door. I told him I was flattered by his attention but that I simply wasn't interested in a romantic relationship with him. To avoid hurting his pride, I said how hard I realized his divorce must have been and how confused it must have left him. I also said how much I liked working with him and how special a friend he was. But I was very clear that romance was not in our future. Len didn't say anything, just nodded, and I left.

It's several months later now. Len has been unusually distant, even icy. Although I still work with him on a few cases that I had been assigned before all of this arose, I have not received any new matters with Len. I get the feeling he has decided that he'd just as soon not have me around and since there are any number of eager associates interested in working on his cases, he can get his way. It is, in fact, rather obvious that Len has been giving much of his new work, including choice out-of-town cases, to Anita Densen-Shaw, a second-year associate, and in the view of many, not just me, they've become an item. I find that I'm growing increasingly angry. To be blunt, I'm paying a price for not being sexually available and there's nothing I can do about it.

LEONARD NEWMAN

Alexa can't be serious. What does she want to do, ban romance? People who work together often wind up going out together. I can count five marriages between lawyers who met here in the last six or seven years and any number of romances. We're all adults. Many of us are single. Attractions are natural, healthy, and inevitable. Sexual relationships frequently develop in hierarchical contexts. They are a perfectly common, quite satisfying, and in no way harmful form of human behavior. I simply expressed my interest and Alexa declined. Fine. That's how people get to know whether someone else wants to get to know them.

I admit I was a little forward in Chicago. That wasn't the way to begin. We were working hard. We were sitting in this lovely restaurant and had just swallowed a liter of wine in about 20 minutes. I thought I had picked up a signal from Alexa. It seemed she'd be receptive. But it was a little too fast for her and I immediately apologized.

My divorce has nothing to do with it. Alexa is a charming woman and I wanted to get to know her. Are lawyers in the same firm not supposed to date? What about associates? What about partners? What about a fifth-year and a third-year associate? What about a corporate partner and a real estate associate? What if two associates are dating and one becomes a partner? Are they supposed to stop? I don't mean to belabor the obvious, but you see what I mean. This isn't a cloister, a monastery. We work closely all the time and it's natural that attractions will develop, and not only between lawyers.

Sure, I persisted, but gently because sometimes women or men who may initially express no interest will change their minds. For a lot of reasons. You can't blame me for trying.

But look, I'm sensitive to Alexa's position. Technically, I'm her boss. Okay. I don't want to put her on the spot. I've turned my attentions elsewhere. No hard feelings.

Alexa says she hasn't gotten new matters from me. That's true. Given this experience, I don't feel comfortable being around Alexa. I've earned that right. Also, there are other associates here interested in my cases and I want to give them a chance. I don't know if Alexa and I will work together on securities litigation in the future. Right now, I doubt it, but that can change.

And, by the way, not that it matters, but I'm 41, not 42.

Basic Bibliography for Research in Legal Ethics and Professional Responsibility*

The following bibliography was prepared by, and is reprinted with permission of, Professor Vanessa Merton of Pace University School of Law. Professor Merton has also taught professional ethics at New York University School of Law, the City University of New York School of Law, and the College of Physicians and Surgeons of Columbia University. She would like to acknowledge the important contribution of her research assistant, Patricia Bisesto, a third-year student at Pace, to the revision of the bibliography for this third edition.

The bibliography lists sources for research on legal and ethical rules applicable to the practice of law. Its scope is nationwide. However, state and local bar associations also issue ethical opinions based on the particular language of their states' ethical codes. Furthermore, various states have statutes or court rules prohibiting or requiring particular conduct. Professor Merton lists such sources for New York State by way of example. Parallel enactments or provisions should be consulted in the particular jurisdiction in which an ethical problem may arise.

This bibliography does not include books oriented primarily toward law office management or avoidance of malpractice, or historical, sociological, and political analyses of the legal profession.

A. CODES OF ETHICS AND STANDARDS OF CONDUCT

1. American Bar Association*

Canons of Professional Ethics (1908; amended through 1970) and Canons of Judicial Ethics (1924).

> Indexed and annotated version published by the American Bar Association in 1936.

Model Code of Professional Responsibility (1969; amended through 1981). Reprinted in ABA/BNA Lawyers' Manual on Professional Conduct 01:301-01:317.

> Most useful version is the Annotated Code (as amended through 1977) (O. Maru, ed.) (American Bar Foundation, 1979). Also see Code of Professional Responsibility by State (ed. M. Proctor and R. Alexander-Smith) (1980). Compares the Code to the codes of each state.

Model Code of Judicial Conduct (adopted by the ABA House of Delegates in 1972; by the Judicial Conference of the United States in 1974; substantially revised in 1990: new version under consideration by the Judicial Conference). Reprinted in ABA/BNA Lawyers' Manual on Professional Conduct 01:3001-01:3024.

> See L. Milord, Reporter's Notes to Code of Judicial Conduct (1990 Edition) (ABA Center for Professional Responsibility ("ABA Center"), 1991). Some of the commentary on the 1972 version in the Reporter's Notes to Code of Judicial Conduct (E. Wayne Thode, American Bar Association, 1973) may still be useful. Annotations to the 1972 version, along with chapters on sanctions and prevention of judicial misconduct, appear in Ethics for Judges (National Judicial College, 1982).

Model Rules of Professional Conduct (1983; amended through 1990). Reprinted in ABA/BNA Lawyers' Manual on Professional Conduct 01:101-01:175.

> Annotated version available (ABA Center, 1991). For research purposes, it still may be useful to consult the 1981 Final Draft of the Model Rules in both the Blue Book Version (Code of Professional Responsibility format), and the White Book Version (Restatement format) and consider the changes made by the ABA House of Delegates during its deliberations. Another tool for this purpose is the Legislative History of the Model Rules of Professional Conduct: Their Development in the ABA House of Delegates (ABA Center,

*Parenthetical dates refer to date of original approval by the ABA House of Delegates.

1987). Though not officially approved by the House of Delegates or Board of Governors, this appears to be a very complete chronological summary of the discussions in the Commission on Evaluation of Professional Standards and in the six meetings of the House of Delegates. It traces the additions and deletions in the language of the Model Rules from each proposal to final text.

Model Rules for Lawyer Disciplinary Enforcement (1989). Reprinted in ABA/BNA Lawyers' Manual on Professional Conduct 01:601-01:624.

Standards for Imposing Lawyer Sanctions (1986). Reprinted in ABA/BNA Lawyers' Manual on Professional Conduct 01:801-01:851.

Model Federal Rules of Disciplinary Enforcement (1978). Reprinted in ABA/BNA Lawyers' Manual on Professional Conduct 01:701-01:709.

Standards Relating to Judicial Discipline and Disability Retirement (1978). Reprinted in ABA/BNA Lawyers' Manual on Professional Conduct 01:3101-01:3130.

Model Rules for Judicial Discipline and Disability Retirement (not yet adopted by the ABA House of Delegates). Reprinted in ABA/BNA Lawyers' Manual on Professional Conduct 01:3201-01:3209.

Model Rules for Lawyers' Funds for Client Protection (1989). Reprinted in ABA/BNA Lawyers' Manual on Professional Conduct 01:5001-01:5016.
    Supersedes Model Rules for Client Security Funds (1981).

Model Rules for Advisory Opinions on Unauthorized Practice of Law (1984). Reprinted in ABA/BNA Lawyers' Manual on Professional Conduct 01:5401-01:5403.

Model Plan of Specialization (1979). Reprinted in ABA/BNA Lawyers' Manual on Professional Conduct 01:5201-01:5207.

Lawyers' Creed of Professionalism and Lawyers' Pledge of Professionalism (1988). Reprinted in ABA/BNA Lawyers' Manual on Professional Conduct 01:401-01:403).

Standards for Criminal Justice (Little, Brown & Co., 2d ed. 1980) (4 vols.) (hardcover binder) (1988 Supps.).
    A frequently cited and comprehensive set of guidelines for the criminal justice system in the format of black-letter standards and commentary. Cross-referenced to related standards of other organizations such as the NLADA and to case law and treatises. See especially Chapter 3, The Prosecution Function; Chapter 4, The Defense Function; and Chapter 6, Special Functions of the Trial Judge. (The Standards are now available through the American Bar Association, not from Little, Brown.)

Standards for Providers of Civil Legal Services to the Poor (American Bar Association, 1986).

>Standards on the lawyer-client relationship, decision-making, confidentiality, and fees and costs for lawyers representing the indigent.

Standards for Monitoring and Evaluation of Providers of Legal Services to the Poor (American Bar Association, 1991).

2. New York State

The Lawyer's Code of Professional Responsibility (New York State Bar Association, 1970; substantially revised in 1990; adopted by the Appellate Divisions of the New York State Supreme Court in 1990; see Section C.2, infra).

3. Other Standards

Restatement of the Law, Tentative Draft No. 4, The Law Governing Lawyers (American Law Institute, 1991).

California Rules of Professional Conduct (approved by the California Supreme Court 1988; effective 1989).

>Codified at Cal. Bus. & Prof. Code §§6076 et seq. Also available from the Office of Professional Standards of the Division of Competence of the State Bar of California in the California Compendium on Professional Responsibility, a three-volume looseleaf set which includes an index and ethics opinions, and is updated annually.

The American Lawyer's Code of Conduct (Roscoe Pound-American Trial Lawyers Foundation, Revised Draft, May 1982).

Code of Trial Conduct (American College of Trial Lawyers, 1987).*

Code of Professional Responsibility for Prosecutors (National District Attorneys' Association, 1977).* Reprinted in National Prosecution Standards (N.D.A.A., 1991).

Model Code of Judicial Conduct for Federal Administrative Law Judges (ABA Judicial Administration Division, 1989).

---

*These codes are reprinted or excerpted in Codes of Professional Responsibility (ed. R. Gorlin, Bureau of National Affairs, 2d ed. 1990), a useful compilation that also includes the ethical codes of many other professions, a list of organizations and institutions concerned with professional ethics, and a bibliography.

Ethical Considerations for Lawyers in Federal Government Service (Federal Bar Association, 1973).

Standards of Practice for Lawyer Mediators in Family Disputes (American Bar Association, 1984); Standards of Practice for Family and Divorce Mediation (American Academy of Family Mediators, 1983).*

Standards for Dissemination of Disciplinary Information (National Organization of Bar Counsel; ABA Center for Professional Responsibility, 1980).

Code of Ethics (American Association of Law Libraries, 1978).*

Ethical Standards of Professional Conduct in Dispute Resolution (Society of Professionals in Dispute Resolution; adopted 1986, effective 1989);* Code of Ethics for Arbitrators in Commercial Disputes (Joint Committee of the American Arbitration Association and the American Bar Association, 1977);* Code of Professional Responsibility for Arbitrators of Labor-Management Disputes (National Academy of Arbitrators, American Arbitration Association, Federal Mediation and Conciliation Service; adopted 1974, amended 1985).*

Code of Ethics and Professional Responsibility for Legal Assistants (National Association of Legal Assistants, adopted 1975, amended 1988);* Model Standards and Guidelines for Utilization of Legal Assistants (National Association of Legal Assistants, adopted 1984, annotated version 1985);* Affirmation of Professional Responsibility (National Federation of Paralegal Associations, adopted 1981, amended 1987).

> Reprinted in W. Statsky, The Regulation of Paralegals (West Publishing, 1988) at pp. 111-113, 126-129. See Section J, infra.

B. ETHICS OPINIONS

1. American Bar Association Opinions

Beginning with Formal Opinion 323 and Informal Opinion 1127 in 1970, the Opinions interpret the Model Code of Professional Responsibility. Prior to that, they address the Canons of Professional Ethics. Since Formal Opinion 84-349 and Informal Opinion 83-1501, they primarily utilize the Model Rules of Professional Conduct.

---

*These codes are reprinted or excerpted in Codes of Professional Responsibility (ed. R. Gorlin, Bureau of National Affairs, 2d ed. 1990), a useful compilation that also includes the ethical codes of many other professions, a list of organizations and institutions concerned with professional ethics, and a bibliography.

Opinions on Professional Ethics (1967).
> Contains Formal Opinions from their beginning with Opinion 1 (1924) through Opinion 315 (1965). Also includes annotated versions of the original Canons of Professional Ethics and Canons of Judicial Ethics; the Rules of Procedure of the Committee on Professional Ethics; a useful citator to both Formal and Informal Opinions; and an index of Formal Opinions.

Informal Ethics Opinions (1975) (2 vols.) (hardcover).
> Contains the published full-text Informal Opinions from C-230 (a) (1961) through 1284 (1973).

Recent Ethics Opinions (1974-   ) (looseleaf) (updated).
> Contains Formal Opinions from 321 (1969) and Informal Opinions from 1285 (1974) to date. Also includes citators to Model Code of Professional Responsibility, Code of Judicial Conduct, and Informal and Formal Opinions. Opinions indexed by subject-matter. Code amendments.

Formal and Informal Ethics Opinions: Formal Opinions 316-348, Informal Opinions 1285-1495 (1985).
> Contains Formal Opinions from 1967, and Informal Opinions from 1975 through 1982.

Legal Services Office Guide to Special Ethics Opinions (ABA Center, 1991).
> Looseleaf compendium of ABA, state and local ethics opinions especially relevant to legal services office practice.

O. Maru and R. Clough. Digest of Bar Association Ethics Opinions (American Bar Foundation, 1970).
> Indexed summaries of ABA Formal Opinions 1-315 and of ethics opinions of 28 state, and a few local, bar associations through 1966.

O. Maru. 1970 Supplement to Digest of Bar Association Ethics Opinions (American Bar Foundation, 1972).
> Updates summaries as above through 1970.

O. Maru. 1975 Supplement to Digest of Bar Association Ethics Opinions (American Bar Foundation, 1977).
> Includes earlier opinions from jurisdictions not covered in prior volumes as well as 1971-1975 update. Table of Modified and Overruled Opinions.

O. Maru. 1980 Supplement to Digest of Bar Association Ethics Opinions (American Bar Foundation, 1982).
> Includes summarized state and local bar association opinions from 41 jurisdictions through June 1980 and cumulative index for all prior volumes.

2. New York State Opinions

New York State Bar Association Committee on Professional Ethics. Formal Opinions (1964-   ) (looseleaf) (updated).

New York State Office of Court Administration. Selected Opinions (1988-   ) (semi-annual).
> Advisory opinions on judicial conduct.

Opinions: Committee on Professional Ethics (Oceana Publications, 1982) (5 vols.) (looseleaf) (updated).
> Complete set of ethics opinions of the Association of the Bar of the City of New York (1923-   ), the New York State Bar Association (1964-   ), and the New York County Lawyers' Association (1912-   ). Beginning in December 1982, includes opinions of state and local ethics committees from all jurisdictions, published by state with individual state index. Contains current citator tables and subject indices. A little slow to update and more expensive than the alternatives, but convenient. Note that these opinions are also available in summary form in the Maru Digests listed supra. Vol. 1, now outdated, reproduces the Model Rules of Professional Conduct (Proposed Final Draft, May 1981) and the reports of four committees of the Association of the Bar of the City of New York on the original Discussion Draft of the Model Rules.
>
> N.B.: These and other state and local bar associations (e.g., the Nassau County Bar Association) periodically publish ethics opinions in their newsletters or journals, in the New York Law Journal, and in other legal newspapers.

C. RELEVANT STATUTES AND COURT RULES

1. Federal

28 U.S.C. §§144 and 455 (judicial recusal and disqualification).

28 U.S.C. §372 (judicial disability and discipline).

Federal Conflict of Interest Act, 18 U.S.C. §§201-219. (See also 5 C.F.R. Part 735, 28 C.F.R. Parts 45 and 50, and Executive Order 12674 of April 12, 1989.)

Federal Rules of Civil Procedure, Rule 11, 16(f), 26(g), and 37.

Federal Rules of Appellate Procedure, Rule 46.

U.S. Supreme Court Rules, Rules 7 and 8.

2. New York State

New York Judiciary Law §§90, 460-498.

Official Compilation of Codes, Rules and Regulations of the State of New York, Title 22, Subtitle B: Courts (Vol. 22B).

> Rules for every level of the court system with respect to matters such as admission to the bar, court decorum, advertising, fee arrangements, obligations with respect to case files, and various other aspects of practice. See especially Appellate Division Rules, First Department, 22B NYCRR §603.2; Appellate Division Rules, Second Department, 22B NYCRR §691.2; Appellate Division Rules, Third Department, 22B NYCRR §806.2; Appellate Division Rules, Fourth Department, 22B NYCRR §1022.17, which incorporate by reference the New York State Bar Association version of the Model Code of Professional Responsibility as the standard for professional conduct.

D. REPORTER SERVICES, CITATORS, AND DATABASES

ABA/BNA Lawyers' Manual on Professional Conduct (American Bar Association Center for Professional Responsibility and Bureau of National Affairs, 1984-   ) (looseleaf) (updated biweekly).

> The most comprehensive and best-organized reporter service. Topics such as lawyer-client relationships, malpractice, trial conduct, etc., presented in hornbook form, supplemented with caselaw analyses similar to those of the American Law Reports. Full text of A.B.A. Ethics Opinions; state and local opinions summarized. Excellent index to opinions. Current reports issued in standard Law Week format, providing not only case digests but reviews of relevant books, notices of conferences, and reports of disciplinary proceedings, legislative action, and bar association activities. Replaces the Disciplinary Law and Procedure Research System (1977-1983).

> Companion bibliography in a separate volume, ABA/BNA Bibliography (1984). Carefully organized, cross-referenced by topic, collection of cases, articles, and unpublished material, primarily 1979-1983. Somewhat difficult to use. Most useful information: availability of briefs and other documents from the ABA Center for Professional Responsibility.

National Reporter on Legal Ethics and Professional Responsibility (University Publications of America, 1982-   ) (4 vols.) (looseleaf) (updated quarterly).
> State-by-state breakdown of state and local bar association codes, rules of procedure, and ethics opinions; federal and state case law; and survey of literature, legislation and regulatory material. Full text of court opinions published in facsimile, so page number references can be used.

Reporter on the Legal Profession (Legal-Medical Studies, 1969-   ) (looseleaf) (updated annually).
> Broad but shallow coverage and not that current. Does not contain Ethics Opinions. Cases reported sequentially, not organized by topic, although indexed.

Shepard's Professional and Judicial Conduct Citations (Shepard's/McGraw-Hill 1980-   ). Citator of ABA Codes, Rules, and Opinions.

Attorney Sanctions Newsletter (Shepard's/McGraw-Hill, 1989-   ).
> Monthly summaries of judicial opinions on sanctions. Some articles.

Subscription Service to Recent Ethics Opinions (ABA Center).
> All opinions of the ABA Standing Committee on Ethics and Professional Responsibility mailed within month of publication.

LEXIS [Library: ABA; Files: FOPIN (Formal Opinions), INFOP (Informal Opinions), and CODES (Model Code of Professional Responsibility and Code of Judicial Conduct).
> Other files provide Rules and Procedures of the ABA House of Delegates, and descriptions of ongoing ABA research projects and publications.

WESTLAW Databases: LS-ABAEO (ABA Ethics Opinions]); AMBAR (abstracts of ABA documents); JDDD (Judicial Discipline and Disability Digest, consisting of abstracts of post-1960 published and unpublished decisions from state and federal courts and judicial commissions, edited by staff of the American Judicature Society).

E. COMPILATIONS

S. Gillers and R. D. Simon, Jr. Regulation of Lawyers: Statutes and Standards (Little, Brown & Co., 1991).

Contains ABA Model Code, Model Rules, Code of Judicial Conduct, and cross-reference tables for Code, Rules and Canons; sections of the ABA Standards for Criminal Justice; ABA Standards of Practice for Lawyer Mediators in Family Disputes, American Lawyer's Code of Conduct and other specialized ethical codes; extensive selection of federal, New York, and California statutory and ethical materials on confidentiality and privilege, conflict of interest, sanctions, and other issues. ABA Model Rules are annotated with selected state variations, internal cross-references, and legislative history. Leading recent decisions of the U.S. Supreme Court.

T. Morgan & R. Rotunda. Selected Standards on Professional Responsibility (Foundation Press, 1991).

Contains ABA Canons of Professional Ethics, Model Code, Model Rules, and cross-reference tables; ABA and California Codes of Judicial Conduct; sections of the ABA Standards Relating to the Administration of Criminal Justice; relevant federal statutes; California Rules of Professional Conduct and related statutes; and ABA Ethics Committee Rules of Procedure.

Provisions of State Codes of Professional Responsibility Governing Lawyer Advertising and Solicitation (American Bar Association Commission on Advertising, 2d ed. 1990).

Looseleaf format, but not clear whether or how frequently updated. Includes lengthy bibliography of articles about lawyer advertising and solicitation.

N. Redlich. Standards of Professional Conduct for Lawyers and Judges (Little, Brown & Co., 1984).

Includes the ABA Model Code, Model Rules, Code of Judicial Conduct, and Standards for Criminal Justice; California's Rules of Professional Conduct and Code of Judicial Conduct; a sample Multistate Professional Responsibility Examination; and selected federal statutes that affect and regulate the conduct of federal judges and federal officers and employees.

Selected Statutes, Rules and Standards on the Legal Profession (West Publishing, 1990).

Includes the ABA Canons, Model Code, Model Rules, and Code of Judicial Conduct; the ABA Model Rules for Lawyer Disciplinary Enforcement and Standards for Imposing Lawyer Sanctions; sections of the ABA Standards Relating to the Administration of Criminal Justice; ABA Standards of Practice for Lawyer Mediators in Family Disputes; American Lawyer's Code of Conduct; California Rules of Professional Conduct, Code of Judicial Conduct, and related statutes; and selected federal statutes. Compares the Model

Rules with corresponding Model Code provisions, and contains topical indices and a table of cross-references for both.

F. MANUALS, TREATISES, MONOGRAPHS, AND OTHER REFERENCES

R. Abel. American Lawyers (Oxford University Press, 1989).

R. Alexander-Smith. Conflicts of Interest (ABA Center, 1983).

American Bar Association Center for Professional Responsibility. Avoiding Client Grievances: Professional Responsibility and the Lawyer (ABA Center, 1988).
    Booklet of suggestions for proper relations with clients.

American Bar Association Center for Professional Responsibility. Directory of Lawyer Disciplinary Agencies and Lawyers' Funds for Client Protection (ABA Center, annual).

American Bar Association Center for Professional Responsibility and Standing Committee on Professional Discipline. Statistical Report: Sanctions Imposed in Public Discipline of Lawyers (ABA Center, annual).

American Bar Association Center for Professional Responsibility and Standing Committee on Professional Discipline. Survey on Lawyer Discipline Systems (ABA Center, 1987).
    Update of 1984 Survey of Lawyer Disciplinary Procedures in the United States.

American Bar Association Commission on Professionalism. ". . . in the spirit of public service: A Blueprint for the Rekindling of Lawyer Professionalism (American Bar Association, 1986).

American Bar Association Criminal Justice Section. Ethics Resource Manual for Public Defenders (American Bar Association, 1990).

American Bar Association Special Committee on Dispute Resolution. Confidentiality in Mediation: A Practitioner's Guide (American Bar Association, 1985).

American Bar Association Standing Committee on Professional Discipline. The Judicial Response to Lawyer Misconduct (ABA Center, 1989) (looseleaf).
    Useful compendium on judicial role in enforcing ethical standards of lawyers.

American Bar Association Standing Committee on Lawyers' Responsibility for Client Protection. Lawyers On Line: Ethical Perspectives in the Use of Telecomputer Communication (American Bar Association, 1986).

American Bar Association Task Force on Professional Competence. Final Report and Recommendations of the Task Force on Professional Competence (American Bar Association, 1983).

American Corporate Counsel Association. Lawyers' Professional Standards Manual (American Corporate Counsel Association, 2d ed. 1990).

American Law Institute-American Bar Association Committee on Continuing Professional Education. Professional Responsibility (ALI-ABA, 1988).

American Law Institute-American Bar Association Committee on Continuing Professional Education. Professional Ethics and Responsibility: The New Model Rules and a Changing Legal Profession (ALI-ABA, 1991).

L. Andrews. Birth of a Salesman: Lawyer Advertising and Solicitation (American Bar Association, 1980).

R. Aronson & D. Weckstein. Professional Responsibility in a Nutshell (West Publishing, 2d ed. 1991).

Association of American Law Schools. Selected Readings on the Legal Profession (West Publishing, 1962).
    Interesting compendium of historical materials on ethical issues, including sections on the lawyer as counselor, as advocate, as judge, and as scholar.

Association of the Bar of the City of New York. Professional Responsibility of the Lawyer: The Murky Divide Between Right and Wrong (Oceana Publications, 1976).

J. Auerbach. Unequal Justice: Lawyers and Social Change in Modern America (Oxford University Press, 1976).
    Historical account that includes critique of the stratification of bar membership and professional self-regulation.

P. M. Bird. The Law, Practice and Conduct of Solicitors (Pergamon Books, 1989).

L. E. Birdzell. Ethical Problems of Inside Counsel (Matthew Bender, 1984) (looseleaf).

M. T. Bloom. The Trouble with Lawyers (Simon and Schuster, 1968).
    Legal journalist profiles case histories of unscrupulous lawyers.

J. Browning, C. Seitz & C. Clark. Illustrative Rules Governing Complaints of Judicial Misconduct and Disability (Federal Judicial Center, 1986).

J. Burkoff. Criminal Defense Ethics: Law and Liability (Clark Boardman Co., 1986) (looseleaf).

J. Carlin. Lawyers' Ethics: A Survey of the New York City Bar (Russell Sage Foundation, 1966).

Center for Public Resources, Inc. Confidentiality in ADR (Center for Public Resources, 1989).
> Looseleaf collection of articles on obligation of confidentiality in practice of alternative dispute resolution. Sample agreements and table of cases.

M. Comisky & P. Patterson. The Judiciary: Selection, Compensation, Ethics and Discipline (Quorum Books, 1987).

M. Davis & F. Elliston. Ethics and the Legal Profession (Prometheus Books, 1986).
> Collection of essays topically organized with a strong philosophical orientation. Includes several of the classic "standards" by Monroe Freedman, William Simon, Charles Fried, etc. Many hypothetical problems and an extensive bibliography.

J. J. Douglass. Ethical Issues in Prosecution (National College of District Attorneys, 1988).

H. Drinker. Legal Ethics (Columbia University Press, 1953).
> Includes in its appendix summaries of the otherwise unreported and unpublished ABA Informal Ethics Opinions 1-383.

E. Epstein, C. T. Corcoran, J. Keane & R. Spencer. Conflicts of Interest: A Trial Lawyer's Guide (National Law Publishing Corp., 1984).
> Integrates black-letter principles with code and case law references in exhaustive analysis of motions to disqualify and systems for avoiding conflicts. Bibliography.

J. Fischer & D. Lachmann. Unauthorized Practice Handbook (American Bar Foundation, 1972).

S. FitzGibbon. Professional Ethics, Organizing Corporations, and the Ideology of Corporate Articles and By-laws (ABA Center, 1982).

M. H. Freedman. Lawyer's Ethics in an Adversary System (Bobbs-Merrill Co., 1975).

M. H. Freedman. Understanding Lawyers' Ethics (Matthew Bender, 1990).

R. J. Gerber. Lawyers, Courts and Professionalism (Greenwood Press, 1989).

B. Gershman (ed.). Prosecutorial Misconduct (Clark Boardman Co., 1987) (looseleaf).

A. Gerson. Lawyers' Ethics: Contemporary Dilemmas (Transaction Books, 1980).

S. Gillers. The Rights of Lawyers and Clients (ACLU Handbook Series: Avon Books, 1979).

J. Hall. Professional Responsibility of the Criminal Lawyer (Lawyers Co-Operative Publishing Co., 1987 & 1991 supplement).

H. Haynsworth. Expanding Your Law Practice: The Ethical Risks (ABA Section of Economics of Law Practice, 1984).

H. Haynsworth. Marketing and Legal Ethics (ABA Section of Law Practice Management, 1990).

G. Hazard. Ethics in the Practice of Law (Yale University Press, 1978).

G. Hazard & W. Hodes. The Law of Lawyering: A Handbook on the Model Rules of Professional Conduct (Prentice-Hall Law & Business, 2d ed. 1990) (looseleaf).

D. Hermann. Representing the Respondent in Civil Commitment Proceedings (ABA Center, 1985).

R. Jack & D. C. Jack. Moral Vision and Professional Decisions: The Changing Values of Women and Men Lawyers (Cambridge University Press, 1989).

R. J. Jossen & J. J. Lerner. Legal Ethics 1990: What Every Lawyer Needs to Know. (Practising Law Institute, 1990).

K. Kipnis. Legal Ethics (Prentice-Hall, 1986).

J. Lawless. Prosecutorial Misconduct: Law, Procedure, Forms (Kluwer, 1985 & 1987 supplement).

Legal Education Institute, Office of Legal Education, U.S. Department of Justice. Ethics and Professional Conduct for the Federal Attorney (U.S. Department of Justice, 1984).
> Training manual. Contains statutory and regulatory standards governing conduct of federal executive branch employees, concerning, e.g.: outside employment, disclosure of classified information, political activity, whistle-blowing.

J. Lieberman. Crisis at the Bar: Lawyers' Unethical Ethics and What to Do About It (W. W. Norton, 1978).

Critique of professional self-regulation aimed at non-lawyer audience.

D. Luban (ed.). The Good Lawyer: Lawyers' Roles and Lawyers' Ethics (Rowman & Allanheld, 1983).
Collection of essays generated by the Working Group on Legal Ethics of the Center for Philosophy and Public Policy at the University of Maryland.

D. Luban. Lawyers and Justice: An Ethical Study (Princeton University Press, 1988).

S. Lubet. Beyond Reproach: Ethical Restrictions on the Extrajudicial Activities of State and Federal Judges (American Judicature Society, 1984).

F. Marks, with K. Leswing & B. Fortinsky. The Lawyer, The Public and Professional Responsibility (American Bar Foundation, 1972).
Results of an American Bar Foundation study of the private bar's efforts to discharge its pro bono responsibilities.

D. Mellinkoff. The Conscience of a Lawyer (West Publishing, 1977).
Uses an 1841 British homicide case to explore defense counsel ethics.

National Conference on Lawyers' Professional Responsibility. Sixteenth National Conference on Lawyers' Professional Responsibility (ABA Center, 1990).
Most recently published proceedings of the ABA annual workshop for bar counsel. Look for succeeding volumes. Earlier volumes also available from the ABA Center.

National Legal Aid and Defender Association. Testimony to the American Bar Association Standing Committee on Ethics and Professional Responsibility: Ethical Aspects of Restrictions on (Non-Profit) Legal Assistance Offices (National Legal Aid and Defender Association, 1974).

W. Pincus. The Lawyer's Professional Responsibility (Ohio State University College of Law, 1969).

Practical Issues of Professional Responsibility in the Practice of Law (Legal-Medical Studies, Inc., 1984) (looseleaf).
Typewritten caselaw summaries, with some text analysis topically organized (updated annually).

Proceedings: The Airlie House Conference on Ethical Responsibilities of Corporate Lawyers, 33 Business Lawyer 1177 (March 1978).

Professional Ethics & Responsibilities: from the Seventh Annual Immigration Law Conference (Federal Bar Association, 1986).

Professional Responsibility: A Guide for Attorneys (American Bar Association, 1978).
    Collection of essays on specific topics of practice.

Report of the Joint Conference on Professional Responsibility of the Association of American Law Schools and the American Bar Association, 1958 (Council on Education in Professional Responsibility, American Bar Center, 1959).
    An attempt to definitively describe a lawyer's responsibilities in the context of an adversary system of justice.

Review Symposium on Model Rules of Professional Conduct, 1980 American Bar Foundation Research Journal 923 (1980).
    Critical analysis by topic of the original draft of the Proposed Model Rules of Professional Conduct.

L. Raifman & J. Hinlicky. Ethical Issues in Dual Professional Practice: Impact of the Code of Professional Responsibility (ABA Center, 1982).
    Monograph by lawyer-psychologist and physician.

Roscoe Pound-American Trial Lawyers Foundation. Ethics and Advocacy (Roscoe Pound-American Trial Lawyers Foundation, 1978).
    Final report of the 1978 Earl Warren Conference on Advocacy in the United States.

D. Rosenthal. Lawyer and Client: Who's In Charge? (Russell Sage, 1974).
    Empirical study of lawyer-client relations in personal injury practice, with significant analysis of several issues of professional responsibility.

J. Sammons. Lawyer Professionalism (Carolina Academic Press, 1988).

D. Siemer. Understanding Modern Ethical Standards (National Institute for Trial Advocacy, 1985) (see section K, infra).

T. Shaffer. American Lawyers and Their Communities (University of Notre Dame Press, 1991).

T. Shaffer. Faith and the Professions (Brigham Young University Press, 1986).

T. Shaffer. On Being a Christian and a Lawyer (Brigham Young University Press, 1980).
    Some are put off by Shaffer's strong theological orientation, but he engages in searching and sophisticated scrutiny of the lawyer's role and the cultural context of professional standards.

J. M. Shaman, S. Lubet & J. J. Alfini. Judicial Conduct and Ethics (Michie Co., 1990).

T. Smedley. Professional Responsibility Problems in Family Law (National Council on Legal Clinics, 1963).

B. G. Smith. Professional Conduct for Canadian Lawyers (Butterworths, 1989).

R. Thurman. Client Incest and the Lawyer's Duty of Confidentiality (ABA Center, 1985).

R. H. Underwood & W. H. Fortune. Trial Ethics (Little, Brown & Co., 1988).

R. Wheeler & A. L. Levin. Judicial Discipline and Removal in the United States (Federal Judicial Center, 1979).

R. Wise. Legal Ethics (Matthew Bender, 2d ed. 1970) (1973 Supp. on Judicial Ethics).
> A treatise that focuses on the differences between the Model Code of Professional Responsibility and the Canons of Professional Ethics.

B. Wolfman & J. Holden. Ethical Problems in Federal Tax Practice (Michie Co., 2d ed. 1985).

C. Wolfram. Modern Legal Ethics (West Publishing, 1986).
> Hornbook, updated with supplements. Most comprehensive modern treatise.

B. Wunnicke. Ethics Compliance for Business Lawyers (Wiley Law Publications, 1987).
> Treatise on ethical issues relevant to corporate counsel, e.g., audit inquiry (including ABA Guidelines), as well as to securities, insurance, and real estate practice.

R. C. Wydick. Professional Responsibility (Harcourt Brace Jovanovich Legal and Professional Publications, 1982).

G.   SELECTED HISTORICAL REFERENCES

G. Archer. Ethical Obligations of the Lawyer (Fred B. Rothman & Co., 1981; reprint of Little, Brown & Co. 1910 ed.).
> Of historical interest primarily, but one of the few texts to address the professional role of nonpracticing lawyers (in politics and business).

F. Brewster. Rights and Duties of Lawyers (King & Baird, 1861).

G. Brown. The Relation of the Legal Profession to Society (Kelly & Piet, 1868).

W. Butler. Lawyer and Client: Their Relation, Rights, and Duties (D. Appleton & Company, 1871).

J. Dos Passos. The American Lawyer: As He Was, As He Is, As He Can Be (Banks Law Pub. Co., 1907).

H. Jessup. The Professional Ideals of the Lawyer: A Study of Legal Ethics (Fred B. Rothman & Co., 1986 reprint of G. A. Jennings Co. 1925 ed.).
  Unique catechism format.

E. Kinkead. Jurisprudence, Law and Ethics: Professional Ethics (Fred B. Rothman & Co., 1985 reprint of Banks Law Pub. Co. 1905 ed.).
  Collection of law professor's lectures.

G. Sharswood. A Compend of Lectures on the Aims and Duties of the Profession of the Law (T. & J. W. Johnson Co., 1854).
  Always cited as one of the prominent sources of American legal ethics; basis for the ABA canons.

S. Wandell. You Should Not: A Book for Lawyers, Old and Young, Containing the Elements of Legal Ethics (Matthew Bender, 1896).

S. Warren. The Moral, Social and Professional Duties of Attorneys and Solicitors (J. D. Parsons, 1870).

G. Warvelle. Essays in Legal Ethics (Callaghan & Co., 2d ed. 1920).

H. PERIODICALS

Business and Professional Ethics Journal (Rensselaer Polytechnic Institute, 1981-   ).

The Catholic Lawyer (St. Thomas More Institute for Legal Research, St. John's University School of Law, 1955-   ).
  Articles on legal issues with ethical, canonical, or theological implications.

Client Protection Newsletter (ABA Center for Professional Responsibility, 1989-   ).

Criminal Justice Ethics (John Jay College of Criminal Justice, 1982-   ).

The Georgetown Journal of Legal Ethics (Georgetown University Law Center, 1987-   ).

The Journal of the Legal Profession (University of Alabama School of Law, 1976-   ).

Judicial Conduct Reporter (Center for Judicial Conduct Organizations, 1979-   ).

Notre Dame Journal of Law, Ethics and Public Policy (Thomas J. White Center on Law and Government, Notre Dame Law School, 1984-   ).

The Professional Lawyer (ABA Center for Professional Responsibility, 1989-   ).

Social Responsibility: Business, Journalism, Law, Medicine (Washington and Lee University, 1975-1987).

I. LAW SCHOOL CASEBOOKS, TEXTBOOKS, AND THE TEACHING OF PROFESSIONAL RESPONSIBILITY

American Bar Association Center for Professional Responsibility. A Survey on the Teaching of Professional Responsibility (ABA Center, 1986).

American Law Institute-American Bar Association Committee on Continuing Professional Education. Continuing Legal Education for Professional Competence and Responsibility Since Arden House II (American Law Institute, 1984).
> Collection of essays reprinted from ALI-ABA CLE Review 1971-1982. Strong focus on approaches to improving and evaluating lawyer competence.

R. Aronson, J. Devine & W. Fisch. Problems, Cases and Materials on Professional Responsibility (West Publishing, 1985).

G. Bellow & B. Moulton. The Lawyering Process: Ethics and Professional Responsibility (Foundation Press, 1981).

W. Bishin & C. Stone. Law, Language and Ethics: An Introduction to Law and Legal Method (Foundation Press, 1972).

A. J. Bocchino. In re: Cooperman, Professional Responsibility and In re: Masters, Professional Responsibility (National Institute for Trial Advocacy, 1991).
> Two complete case files for conducting simulated disciplinary proceedings based on violations of the Model Rules.

M. T. Bloom (ed.). Lawyers, Clients and Ethics: Using the Law School Clinic for Teaching Professional Responsibility (Council on Legal Education for Professional Responsibility, Inc., 1979).
   Set of case histories of clinical students confronted with ethical dilemmas.

Proceedings of the Asheville Conference of Law School Deans on Education for Professional Responsibility (Council on Education in Professional Responsibility, 1966).

V. Countryman, T. Finman & T. Schneyer. The Lawyer in Modern Society (Little, Brown & Co., 2d ed. 1976).

E. Dvorkin, J. Himmelstein & H. Lesnick. Becoming a Lawyer: A Humanistic Perspective on Legal Education and Professionalism (West Publishing, 1981).

S. Gillers. Regulation of Lawyers: Problems of Law and Ethics (Little, Brown & Co., 3d ed. 1992).

S. Goldberg (ed.). 1977 National Conference on Teaching Professional Responsibility (University of Detroit Law School, 1979).

G. Hazard & D. Rhode. The Legal Profession: Responsibility and Regulation (Foundation Press, 2d ed. 1988).

G. Hazard & S. Koniak. The Law and Ethics of Lawyering (Foundation Press, 1990).

P. Heymann & L. Liebman. The Social Responsibilities of Lawyers: Case Studies (Foundation Press, 1988).

A. Kaufman. Problems in Professional Responsibility (Little, Brown & Co., 3d ed. 1989).

M. Kelly. Legal Ethics and Legal Education (The Hastings Center, 1980).
   Monograph on the state of ethics education in law schools.

D. Mellinkoff. Lawyers and the System of Justice: Cases and Notes on the Profession of Law (West Publishing, 1976).

T. Morgan & R. Rotunda. Professional Responsibility: Problems and Materials (Foundation Press, 5th ed. 1991).

L. R. Patterson & T. B. Metzloff. Legal Ethics: The Law of Professional Responsibility (Analysis and Skills Series: Matthew Bender, 3d ed. 1989).

M. Pirsig & K. Kirwin. Professional Responsibility: Cases and Materials (West Publishing, 4th ed. 1984).

N. Redlich. Professional Responsibility: A Problem Approach (Little, Brown & Co., 2d ed. 1983).

D. Schrader. Ethics and the Practice of Law (Prentice-Hall, 1988).

M. Schwartz. Lawyers and the Legal Profession: Cases and Materials (Michie Co., 2d ed. 1985).

M. Schwartz & R. Wydick. Problems in Legal Ethics (West Publishing, 2d ed. 1988).

T. Shaffer. American Legal Ethics: Text, Readings, and Discussion Topics (Matthew Bender, 1985).

J. Stone. Legal Education and Public Responsibility (Association of American Law Schools, 1959).
> Report of the first Conference on Education of Lawyers for Their Public Responsibilities ("Boulder I").

J. F. Sutton, Jr. & J. S. Dzienkowski. Cases and Materials on the Professional Responsibility of Lawyers (West Publishing, 1989).

D. Weckstein (ed.). Education in the Professional Responsibilities of the Lawyer (University Press of Virginia, 1970).
> Proceedings of "Boulder II," the second national conference on approaches to teaching professional responsibility.

J. PARALEGAL ETHICS

D. Orlik. Ethics for the Legal Assistant (Scott, Foresman & Co., 1986).
> A teaching text, with problem exercises, organized around the Canons of the Model Code of Professional Responsibility. Unfortunately does not mention the Rules of Professional Conduct. Relies almost exclusively on case law for analysis of issues. Appendix summarizes state bar (but not ABA) ethics opinions that discuss conduct of legal assistants and paralegals.

Professional Responsibility Handbook for Legal Assistants and Paralegals (American Bar Association, 1986).

W. Statsky. The Regulation of Paralegals: Ethics, Professional Responsibility, and Other Forms of Control (West Publishing, 1988).
> Thorough treatment, including excerpts from ethics opinions and judicial opinions, summary of both Model Code and Model Rules, forms, and section on legal research of ethical issues. Appendix reprints relevant bar association ethics opinions and charts rules on nonlawyer practice before federal administrative agencies.

C. Todd. Professional Responsibility for the Paralegal (University of Oklahoma Law Center, 1978).

K. AUDIOVISUAL AND VIDEO MATERIALS

American Bar Association. Dilemmas in Legal Ethics (Consortium for Professional Education, 1976).

American Bar Association. Legal Ethics: Applying the Model Rules: Discussion Guides for the ABA VideoLaw Seminar (Consortium for Professional Education, 1984).

American Bar Association Division for Professional Education and ABA Center for Professional Responsibility. Ethical Dilemmas and Professionalism (ABA Center, 1989).
> Series of five videotapes on topics such as associate-partner relations, attorney-client relations, confidentiality, and conflicts.

Center for Computer-Assisted Legal Instruction. Course Materials in Professional Responsibility (CALI, updated regularly).
> Series of computer-based exercises on ethical rules and decisions.

Center on Professionalism, University of Pennsylvania Law School. Professional Responsibilities for Lawyers: A Guided Course (Commerce Clearing House, Inc., 1990 & 1991).
> Case study series of written and videotape materials that raise questions of confidentiality, conflicts of interest, the representation of corporate clients, and the ethics of negotiation, client counseling, and pretrial litigation.

R. Cramton. Audiovisual Materials on Professional Responsibility (ABA Section of Tort and Insurance Practice, 1987).
> Annotated guide to fictional, documentary, and educational film and videotape materials useful for illustrating and teaching issues of professional responsibility.

L. Dubin. Professional Misconduct: Conversations with Victims (Weil Productions, 1977).

L. Dubin. What Went Wrong? Conversations with Disciplined Lawyers (Weil Productions, 1985).

F. Graham. Ethics on Trial (WETA Educational Activities Dept., 1986).

D. Siemer. Understanding Modern Ethical Standards (National Institute for Trial Advocacy, 1985) (companion printed volumes).

Symposium: Applying the Model Rules of Professional Conduct (Practising Law Institute, 1984).

L. BIBLIOGRAPHIES

A Selected Bibliography of Materials on Professional Ethics and Responsibility for Lawyers (P.W.R.W. & G., 1984).

American Bar Association Center for Professional Responsibility. Bibliography on Professional Responsibility, 1970-1983 (ABA Center, 1984).

American Bar Association Standing Committee on Specialization. Lawyer Specialization Bibliography (American Bar Association, 1990).

M. D. Bieber. A Bibliography of Recent Books and Articles on Legal Ethics and Professional Responsibility (Vanderbilt University School of Law Library, Leal Bibliography Project, 1978).

K. Corr & L. Berkson. Literature on Judicial Conduct (American Judicature Society, 1979).

F. Elliston & J. van Schaick. Legal Ethics: An Annotated Bibliography and Resource Guide (Fred B. Rothman & Co., 1984).
>   Monograph intended as reference tool for academics. Organized topically; includes law review articles.

O. Maru. Research on the Legal Profession: A Review of Work Done (American Bar Foundation, 1986).

D. Nagasankara Rao. Legal Ethics, Professional Responsibility: A Selected Bibliography of Articles (Vance Bibliographies, 1985).

J. van Schaick. Selected Literature on Judicial Conduct and Disability (American Judicature Society, 1983).

Table of Cases

877

Table of Code and Rules Provisions

Index